A Textbook of **Social Psychology**

Sixth Edition

J.E. **Alcock**

Glendon College, York University

D.W. **Carment**

McMaster University

S.W. **Sadava**

Brock University

A Textbook of **Social Psychology**

PEARSON

Prentice
Hall

Toronto

National Library of Canada Cataloguing in Publication

Alcock, James E
    A textbook of social psychology / J.E. Alcock, D.W. Carment, S.W. Sadava. — 6th ed.

Includes bibliographical references and index.
ISBN 0-13-121741-0

    1. Social psychology. I. Carment, D. W., 1928– II. Sadava, S. W III. Title.

HM1033.A53 2005   302   C2003-905986-3

Vice President, Editorial Director: Michael J. Young
Acquisitions Editor: Ky Pruesse
Executive Marketing Manager: Judith Allen
Developmental Editor: John Polanszky
Production Editor: Söğüt Y. Güleç
Copy Editor: Bonnie Di Malta
Proofreader: Julie Fletcher
Production Coordinator: Patricia Ciardullo
Page Layout: Jansom
Permissions and Photo Research: Christina Beamish
Art Director: Julia Hall
Cover and Interior Design: David Cheung
Cover Image: Photonica

Statistics Canada information is used with the permission of the Minister of Industry, as Minister responsible for Statistics Canada. Information on the availability of the wide range of data from Statistics Canada can be obtained from Statistics Canada's Regional Offices, its World Wide Web site at http://www.statcan.ca, and its toll-free access number 1-800-263-1136.

8 9   12 11 10

Printed and bound in the USA.

Mary, Vern, Bert
The McMaster Faculty Club Regulars
Kevin Sadava 1970–1998

Brief Contents

Contents

CHAPTER 7

Language and Communication........... **176**

PART FIVE: FRIENDS AND ENEMIES

CHAPTER 8

Interpersonal Attraction and Relationships **208**

CHAPTER 9

Prosocial Behaviour **241**

PART SIX: PEOPLE IN GROUPS

CHAPTER 12

Social Categorization, Groups and Leadership.

CHAPTER 13

Prejudice, Discrimination and Sexism 357

CHAPTER 14

Crowds and Collective Behaviour.

PART SEVEN: SOCIAL PSYCHOLOGY IN ACTION

CHAPTER 15
Social Psychology of Justice and the Law   429

CHAPTER 16
Health and Illness 458

Preface

Welcome to the sixth edition of *A Textbook of Social Psychology,* still the only English-Canadian social psychology textbook written by Canadians, about Canadians, for Canadians. We continue to be delighted by the extent to which this textbook in its various editions has been used from one end of the country to the other. We hope the changes we have made to this edition will continue to make it attractive to students and instructors alike. As in the past, we have benefitted from comments and suggestions from students and instructors, and we welcome your feedback.

As in the earlier editions of *A Textbook of Social Psychology,* we have tried to provide Canadian students of social psychology with an introduction to this exciting field that encourages them to think about the psychology of social behaviour in the context of Canadian society and culture. We have striven to show both the historical roots and the contemporary vitality of this discipline, and in so doing have integrated important classic research with what is happening on the cutting-edge of research today. We have drawn on the best research available, be it from Canada, the United States, Europe or elsewhere in the world. To highlight and illuminate the material, we have provided a wide range of examples drawn, for the most part, from the Canadian social experience.

While we have been careful to cover all the material presented in the typical U.S. social psychology textbook, we also include a chapter on language and communication—including the social psychology of bilingualism—which we consider vital to an understanding of social psychology in Canada. There is also a chapter devoted to collective behaviour, an area that once figured prominently but that is now sadly neglected by most textbooks.

A Textbook of Social Psychology, Sixth Edition, begins with an introduction to the discipline (Part 1) and a discussion of research methods (Part 2). Part 3, Understanding Your Social World, focuses on aspects of social psychology that relate primarily to the individual—how people evaluate themselves and others, and how their attitudes and values relate to their behaviour. In Part 4, Influencing Others, we look at attitude change, conformity, and language and communication.

Part 5, Friends and Enemies, is devoted to social psychological processes associated with relationships among people: Are they attracted to one another? Do they become friends? Do they fall in love? Do they experience conflict? Do they help or hurt one another, and if so, why?

Part 6, People in Groups, concerns social behaviour defined primarily in terms of groups rather than individuals. The nature of groups is explored, as is the subject of large-scale and often seemingly irrational collective behaviour. We have included the discussion of prejudice in this section—rather than in its traditional place alongside attitudes—because it is very much tied up with, and defined in terms of, groups. As unconventional as this may be, it makes sense to us, although we recognize that many instructors may choose to deal with this material subsequent to presenting the chapter on attitudes and values.

Finally, Part 7 is called Social Psychology in Action, and it's an applied social psychology section that includes chapters on justice and health.

To succeed, a textbook must interest students by dealing with matters of importance to them. The boxes throughout the text engage the student by touching on contemporary everyday life. These boxes address topical issues or emerging research interests within the discipline, and are organized by theme: Focus on Research, A Practical Question, A Case in Point, and Critical Thinking. Some topics addressed in these boxes include the following:

- how snapshots of people can be used to understand more about how they see themselves
- how the occupations we choose reflect our self-image
- the role that aging plays in attitude change
- the effects of architectural designs on human relationships
- the emerging phenomenon of intimate relationships that develop through the Internet
- why it is that some people are happy with the prospect of donating organs while others wince at the thought
- the role guns play in homicides and suicides in Canada
- the prevalence of war in the world
- the role alcohol plays in leading people away from the tenets of safe sex

In preparing this sixth edition, we have carefully edited and updated the entire text and carried out minor reorganizations of the material to add to clarity when needed. Much dated material has been removed, and we have integrated a considerable body of new data, research and topics. The following provide a sample of the highlights of this new material:

- We have added to our discussion of self-esteem, and have addressed the benefits of, and the myths about, high self-esteem. We have incorporated new material relating to how we evaluate ourselves, the upwards and downwards social comparisons that we make, and the effects of our efforts towards self-improvement.

- In the discussion of values and attitudes, we give consideration to how the world is responding to the spread of American ideas and customs, and discuss data that show that Canadian and American values are diverging, with Canadians moving towards more liberal values, while people in the U.S. are shifting in a conservative direction.

- We have added a treatment of hypocrisy in the context of cognitive dissonance, we have included a discussion of the attitude-congeniality hypothesis, and we consider the effects of negative political advertising on attitudes towards politicians in the Canadian context.

- We have addressed the incorporation of what were, until relatively recently, taboo words into the language of everyday life.

- We provide an updated and expanded treatment of cyber-relationships—those relationships that develop over the Internet. We also address the effects of investment and commitment on relationships, and we have added a discussion of same-sex relationships.

- We have introduced material regarding gratitude and forgiveness as important factors in prosocial behaviour. We discuss the embarrassment that is forthcoming in some cultures when people are recognized for their generosity, leading to efforts to conceal their kindness.

- Hybrid mediation-arbitration methods of conflict resolution are discussed, as is modern, "post 9/11" terrorism.

- We have updated and expanded our coverage of family violence as well as our exploration of the relationship between gender and aggression.

- There is a new discussion of stereotype activation and stereotype threat. There is also a new section dealing with how victimized groups react to discrimination.

- We provide expanded treatment of emotional contagion, while considering the fact that such contagion did not occur during the SARS epidemic in Toronto. We discuss deindividuation in the context of Internet chat rooms, and explore the Social Identity Model of Deindividuation Effects (SIDE).

- We have updated and expanded our coverage of eyewitness testimony research, distributive and procedural justice and the Just World Hypothesis. We have expanded our discussion of the jury selection process, emphasizing the differences between Canadian and American procedures.

- In the context of the social psychology of health, we have added materials relating to SARS, to the "Mad Cow" problem in Alberta, and to the role that socioeconomic status plays in affecting our health. We introduce a new discussion of theory and research with respect to Terror Management Theory, and we examine the effects of a positive outlook on one's health and recovery from disease.

These are some of the many changes we have made in this sixth edition to reflect what is current and important in social psychology. This list vividly reflects the fact that social psychology is not static—its focus shifts along with the society it studies—and that its subject matter is in a large part the subject matter of our day-to-day existences.

Supplements

TEST ITEM FILE A revised and comprehensive *Test Item File* has been prepared for this edition. Available in Microsoft Word format, the file contains approximately 120 questions per chapter. Answers are referenced to the text by page number.

INSTRUCTOR'S MANUAL An *Instructor's Manual* is available that includes chapter outlines and objectives, chapter overviews (mind map) and lecture suggestions.

POWERPOINT SLIDES A set of PowerPoint slides is available that summarizes a number of key points and concepts from the text. All of the above instructor's supplements are conveniently available online. To access them, please visit: **http://www.pearsoned.ca/instructor**

STUDY GUIDE Features in the *Study Guide* for the Sixth Edition include chapter objectives, chapter overviews (mind map), exercises for key terms and concepts that include questions on the application of the terms, and suggested Internet projects using Web sites included in the text.

Acknowledgments

There are many people for us to thank. First, we want to acknowledge our colleagues, who have prepared the supplemental materials for this edition. Their confidence in our book has been an inspiration to us, and we greatly appreciate their excellent collaboration.

We also wish to convey our thanks to Andrew Winton, Sponsoring Editor, who handled the negotiations for this edition; John Polanszky, Developmental Editor; Söğüt Y. Güleç, Production Editor; Jessica Mosher and Ky Pruesse, Acquisitions Editors; and Bonnie Di Malta, our Copy Editor. We are pleased by the new cover and interior design created by Julia Hall. Finally, we would like to thank Christina Beamish for her photo research. We thank the reviewers who helped us improve this current edition: Valerie Pruegger, University of Calgary; Tara M. Burke, Ryerson University; Steven M. Smith, St. Mary's University; and Darryl Hill, Concordia University.

Finally, of course, we thank once again the instructors and students across the country whose approval has made it possible for yet another edition of *A Textbook of Social Psychology*.

J. E. Alcock
D. W. Carment
S. W. Sadava

Introducing Social Psychology

Tell me what company you keep, and I'll tell you what you are.
Miguel de Cervantes, *Don Quixote de la Mancha*

Imagine yourself alone on a tiny desert island, marooned and with no hope of early rescue. The climate is wonderful, food is abundant, the sea is warm and inviting and there are no wild animals to fear. Ah, paradise … especially if you are experiencing this fantasy in the middle of a Canadian winter!

Or is it really paradise? Can paradise ever be that kind of "table for one"? For almost everyone, being alone, even in such a setting, would soon become an empty, if not outright depressing, existence. However, continue with the fantasy: You are determined that you are going to make the best of what might be a very long stay, and you will not allow yourself to sink into depression. (You may remember the 2000 movie, *Cast Away*, starring Tom Hanks, where he becomes marooned in such a place and becomes friends with a volleyball that he has decorated to look like a human head). Think about how your normal habits might change. Since there is no one around, do you bother

anymore about your appearance? Do you still cover your mouth when you cough? Do you organize your life around three meals a day?

As time goes on and you contemplate your existence, you realize that even though you are alone, a great deal of your activity and thought continues to reflect the society that reared you. You think in words, in your mother tongue, even though language is no longer a means of communication because there is no one with whom to communicate. You brush your teeth with a homemade toothbrush, a habit you feel is worth preserving for the good of your teeth. You fashion a fork to use for eating, for you find it unpleasant to eat certain foods with your fingers. You stand on a hill and sing to the sea, reciting the songs of the culture that spawned you. You come to realize that you cannot escape, and do not want to escape, the social forces that have shaped you; you have internalized them. In other words, the people in your life are still having a great influence on you, and you conform even though they are not there, and you may never see them again.

And then one day, a small raft washes up on the shore, carrying a survivor of a shipwreck. At first, it is wonderful to have the company of another human being. However, you quickly realize that this person's arrival is going to bring some changes to your life. You like to play your makeshift bongos all night long and sleep until midday, while this new arrival wants quiet after the sun goes down. For the first time, you begin to feel embarrassed about your small and cluttered hut, especially as you watch your companion construct a much nicer and more comfortable dwelling. Gradually, you begin to resent the way this newcomer is "taking over," and you cannot help but think that since you were here first, you should have a greater say over what happens on the island. Questions of power and privilege and social comparison start to bother you, just as they did back home. The need for rules, for a primitive social structure, becomes apparent, in order to resolve or stave off conflicts that will make living together on such a small island very unpleasant. It becomes only too apparent that as soon as there are two or more people, the need for social structures, some commonly agreed-upon rules, to coordinate and/or even govern their behaviours become essential to living in harmony. You will have to negotiate with that other person to bring this about.

And so, in every society, everywhere, across all time, rules have been developed to govern social interaction. And every individual in every society, everywhere and across all time, has grown up learning those social rules and generally living by them. Some individuals within a society are born into power and privilege, merely because of the power and privilege of their parents; others work to acquire such power, while still others have to seize it and hold onto it by force. Individuals everywhere and in every era have differentiated themselves into groups on the basis of common characteristics or beliefs or interests—families, circles of friends, gangs, ethnic groups, nations—in order to further and protect their interests. Groups, in turn, have often fallen into conflict with other groups, and such conflict has led to pressures from each group to ensure that its members serve the group interest.

The rules and norms by which we live, the ways that other people influence how we think, feel and act, the effects of group membership, and the pressures amongst groups—these are all part of the fabric of our social lives and what this social psychology textbook is all about.

What Social Psychology Is and Is Not

Social psychology is the discipline that sets out to understand how the thoughts, feelings and behaviours of individuals are influenced by the actual, imagined or implied presence of others (Allport, 1935). What does this definition tell us about social psychology? First, social psychologists study not only actual, observable behaviour, but inferences about people's inner lives: how they feel; their attitudes, opinions and ideologies; how they form impressions and try to make sense of their world. Second, human experience is understood in terms of the influence of other people. Obviously, social influence is not the only kind—we may be affected by our physical health, the weather, what we have learned, our brain and nervous system processes, psychotic and drug states, hormones or what we have eaten. However, social psychologists focus on the vital role of social influences and relationships. Finally, the definition tells us that people are influenced by other people, even those who are not present. We are aware of belonging to certain family, occupational and cultural groups and of liking, loving or feeling responsible towards certain people in our lives. These groups and individuals profoundly influence our thoughts and actions.

To better appreciate the range of phenomena social psychologists study, consider the following examples:

- In a competitive economy, a job interview can be decisive. Social psychologists have studied how *first impressions* are formed and how people act to influence or *"manage" the impression* that others have of them.

- Amnesty International has documented routine torture in many countries. For the most part, torturers are not unusually sadistic by nature, but simply *obedient* to the instructions of authority. A series of important experiments has been conducted on *obedience to authority*.

- A substantial proportion of all marriages in North America will eventually end in divorce. *Social attraction* and the evolution of *intimate relationships* are areas of current, intensive research.

- While Québécois entrepreneurs move into the North American, English-speaking business milieu, English-Canadian parents in unprecedented numbers enrol their children in French immersion programs. There has been extensive research on the social aspects of *bilingualism*.

- Canada's economic policy has shifted dramatically towards deficit reduction and tax relief. Cutbacks in government spending have generated much *conflict*, a subject researched extensively by social psychologists.

- Many trials hinge on the credibility of a key witness. Social psychologists have studied *eyewitness testimony* and other aspects of the legal system.

- Genocide and terrorism continue to erupt in various parts of the world. The ongoing joint Canadian Psychological Association–American Psychological Association *Ethnopolitical Warfare Initiative* is studying why people participate in genocide and terrorist attacks and why some people risk their lives to rescue others from genocide. The project also works to develop interventions to help prevent or de-escalate ethnic conflicts (Suedfeld, 2000).

As you can see, social psychologists study a wide range of social phenomena. Some of their concerns involve practical problems: Why don't patients do what their physicians recommend? What kinds of decisions do groups make and can the decisions be improved? Why do people persist in stereotyping males, females, professors, students and ethnic groups, regardless of the realities? Other equally important questions are

more theoretical: What consistencies and inconsistencies are there between people's attitudes and their behaviour? What biases operate in the perception of cause and effect in interpersonal situations? How can we explain aggression in terms of social learning?

To clarify what social psychology is about, let us compare it with other areas of psychology and other related disciplines. Social psychology shares a focus with other areas of psychology of the individual. In particular, the interests of social psychology overlap the study of personality. However, the study of personality emphasizes individual differences in the way people think, feel or act, and, above all, factors operating within individuals. Social psychology, by contrast, looks at the situational factors that cause people in general to behave in certain ways. Thus, for example, personality psychologists study the *characteristics* of people who tend to behave aggressively; social psychologists investigate *situations* in which people are likely to behave aggressively. Of course, both personal and environmental factors determine behaviour, and students of social psychology must understand both types of variables.

Social psychology also shares many areas of interest with other social sciences, especially sociology (the study of society and social institutions) and anthropology (the study of human culture). Perhaps the major differences are found in each discipline's basic *unit of*

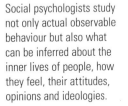

Social psychologists study not only actual observable behaviour but also what can be inferred about the inner lives of people, how they feel, their attitudes, opinions and ideologies.

From Common Sense to Research Hypothesis

There's an old saying: Familiarity breeds contempt. That is, the more familiar we become with people or things, the less attractive they become. Many couples find it difficult or impossible to recapture the magic of their honeymoon stage.

The saying also seems to hold true of objects and places: We often feel an itch to travel for a change of scenery.

But consider the following:

■ Students tend to feel rather uncomfortable in class in the first days of the new school year, particularly if they don't know many other students. As the course goes on, they feel more and more positive about the experience, even though they may not have interacted with many classmates. The people, the professors, the lecture room all seem familiar now. Commuters, immersed in their newspapers or daydreams, grow comfortable with the "familiar strangers" on their bus or train, as Stanley Milgram has called them.

■ When the Eiffel Tower was first built in 1889 for a World Fair, the citizens of Paris so detested it that they felt France had lost its position as a cultural leader in the world (Harrison, 1977). Similar reactions greeted the construction of Toronto's distinctive City Hall. Eventually, residents of both cities developed a strong pride in these monuments as symbols of their civic identity.

■ In recent years, many radio stations have switched from a top-20 format of current music to a play list featuring only familiar and popular music from the recent past.

How can we subject the principle that "familiarity breeds contempt" to experimental test? Zajonc (1968a) conducted a series of controlled experiments in which he varied the number of times different groups of subjects were exposed to certain stimuli. In one such experiment, subjects were shown a series of photographs from a university yearbook and later asked to rate them in terms of their "favourability." Some of the faces were repeatedly shown, as often as 25 times, while others were shown only once or twice. Here are the results:

Frequency of exposure to photograph	Average favourability rating (scale of 1–4)
1 time	2.8
2 times	2.9
5 times	3.0
10 times	3.6
25 times	3.7

As you can see, subjects were considerably more favourable towards the faces seen more frequently. In other experiments by Zajonc, the same was found to be true for other stimuli, including Chinese alphabet characters, foreign words and the frequency with which names of cities, flowers, trees and vegetables occur naturally in speech.

In later chapters, consideration will be given to more of the research on this "mere exposure effect," when and why it occurs, what it means and what other factors influence our like or dislike of someone or something.

analysis and *level of explanation.* The usual focus of study in these other social sciences is the large group, institution or custom (e.g., the school, the family, social norms and social class structure). The *rate* or typical pattern of behaviour in a population is also of concern. Sociologists and anthropologists are not interested in how one individual differs from another, but rather in how one *category* of individual differs from another (Macionis, Clarke & Gerber, 1994), and they seek to explain phenomena in terms of external characteristics such as social class mobility, customs of parental discipline, and the distribution of power in a society. By contrast, social psychology generally focuses on the individual, or at most the small group. Social psychologists generally explain the behaviour of individuals in terms of specific situations as well as psychological processes such as attitudes, emotional states or perception of cause and effect. Psychological social psychologists also are interested in norms and class structure, of course, but the focus is on how they affect the individual, as in the vignette that opens this chapter.

Both psychology and sociology have subdisciplines called "social psychology," which have subject areas in common but which differ in research methods, theories and theoretical orientation. Psychological social psychologists frequently do laboratory experiments, while sociological social psychologists often rely on participant observation, in which the researcher actually joins the institution or group and describes it from the inside. And while most social psychologists in sociology work within the framework of symbolic interactionism (how people come to attach meaning to experience through interaction with others), social psychologists within the field of psychology study the cognitive processes within individuals through which they make sense of the world and how they may or may not act on those impressions and beliefs.

Social Psychology Yesterday and Today

While social psychology is relatively young as a discipline, its roots lie deep in the history of Western thought. Like all of psychology, social psychology emerged from the work of philosophers. Plato was deeply concerned with the nature of leadership and the most desirable form of government, while Aristotle

thought and wrote about the nature of friendship. English empiricist philosophers such as John Stuart Mill and Thomas Hobbes attributed all social behaviour to the search for pleasure and avoidance of pain (hedonism) or to the need for power. The 19th-century French philosopher Gabriel Tarde wrote that "society is imitation." In other words, people have an innate tendency to imitate, which causes them to conform in order to live together. While all these themes continue to be of interest to social psychologists, they have turned from "simple and sovereign theories" that explain social behaviour in terms of a single variable, such as power, pleasure or imitation, to more complex explanations.

Social psychology did not emerge dramatically through the declaration of a doctrine, a scientific breakthrough, or the influence of a personality such as Sigmund Freud. Rather, it evolved over several decades, marked by several key events (see Table 1).

Interest in social psychological theory and research began to grow in the late 19th century. Its roots formed in several quarters: in Germany, as an outgrowth of Wilhelm Wundt's *Völkerpsychologie* ("folk psychology") (Danziger, 1983); in France, through the work of Gabriel Tarde and others (Lubek, 1990); in Great Britain as an extension of evolutionary theory to social interaction (Collier, Minton & Reynolds, 1991); and in the United States, through the research of John Dewey and colleagues at the University of Chicago (Rudmin, 1985). The first known book dedicated to social psychology was Vierkandt's (1896) *Naturvölker und Kulturvölker: Ein Beitrag zur Sozialpsychologie* (Rudmin, 1985). Baldwin's (1897) *Social and Ethical Interpretations of Mental Development: A Study in Social Psychology*, Tarde's (1898) *Études de Psychologie Sociale*, and Ellwood's (1899) *Some Prolegomena to Social Psychology* were also among the earliest social psychology books (Rudmin, 1985).

While psychologists in Western Europe and the United States played fundamental roles in the formation of the new discipline, interest in social psychology was taking root in various countries around the world. For example, a folk psychology focusing primarily on the analysis of language and social habits had been developing in Russia since the mid-19th century, and in 1896, A.M. Bobrishchev-Pushkin published his empirical studies of juries and the psychological factors involved in their decision-making (Strickland, 1991). In 1906, Tokutani's *Social Psychology* brought the basic concepts of this new discipline to Japan (Hotta & Strickland, 1991).

Given this widespread interest in social psychology, it appears somewhat ethnocentric that North American social psychology texts typically credit the beginnings of social psychology to two textbooks published in the United States in 1908: *An Introduction to Social Psychology* by William McDougall, a psychologist and *Social Psychology: An Outline and Sourcebook* by E.A. Ross, a sociologist. That such credit should go to McDougall is especially curious, given that neither he nor those who reviewed his book considered it to be a treatise on social psychology, despite its title; it was actually dedicated to the discussion of instinct theories (Rudmin, 1985).

It was not until 1924 that Floyd Allport published the first textbook based on empirical research. This highly influential book presented a scientific social psychology that was psychological, as opposed to sociological (Parkovnick, 1992), established the individual as the basic unit of analysis and started social psychology on a scientific pathway (Minton, 1992). Allport viewed social psychology as a science of how behaviour is influenced by the presence and reactions of other people, and discussed such topics as conformity and how people recognize emotional states in others.

Research through the decades

There have been several broad trends in the history of social psychology. In the 1920s and 1930s, a dominant concern was the measurement and study of attitudes and related concepts, such as stereotypes. Later, work

---

TABLE 1

Historical timeline in social psychology

A. Vierkandt: first social psychology book (1896)	1890	
Triplett's experiment (1898)		
	1910	World War I (1914–1918)
		Russian Revolution (1917)
F. Allport: textbook (1924)	1920	automobile and radio become part of everyday life (1920s)
Thurstone: attitude measurement (1929)		
		beginning of Great Depression (1929)
LaPiere: attitudes and actions (1934)	1930	Hitler takes power (1932)
Sherif: norms and perception (1935)		
Dollard: frustration and aggression (1939)		
Lewin: leadership and groups (1939)		World War II begins (1939)
research on leadership, morale, propaganda	1940	the Holocaust
		Hiroshima (1945)
		Israeli independence (1948)
		Chinese revolution (1949)
authoritarian personality (1950)	1950	Korean War (1950–1952)
Asch: conformity experiments (1956)		TV age begins (1950s)
Festinger: cognitive dissonance (1957)		Cold War and McCarthyism
Heider: attributions (1958)		
Lambert: bilingualism (1960s)	1960	Cuban revolution
Deutsch and Krauss: conflict resolution (1960)		
Newcomb: attraction (1961)		Kennedy assassinated (1963)
Milgram: obedience (1963)		U.S.–Vietnam war (1965–1974)
Kelley: attribution (1967)		youth counterculture (1966–1973)
Latané and Darley: bystander intervention (1967)		Trudeau elected (1968)
Argyle: nonverbal communication	1970	Quebec October Crisis (1970)
		Watergate (1974)

Gergen: "crisis" in social psychology		
social dilemmas		
psychology of law and justice		
Moscovici, Tajfel: intergroup relations		
social cognition	1980	conflict in Central America
applied social psychology		end of the Berlin Wall
research expands in Europe and Third World		
Berry: cross-cultural social psychology,		
multiculturalism		
Duck: close relationships	1990	collapse of Soviet Union
Eagly and Chaiken: attitudes		Canada endorses NAFTA
		Chrétien takes office
		development of World Wide Web
		Mandela elected President of
		South Africa (1994)
		Quebec referendum (1995)
Psychology references, journals	2000	Y2K crisis
go on-line		beginning of the construction of
		international space station
		destruction of the World Trade
		Center, New York City (2001)
		Columbia explosion (2003)
		massive power failure, Ontario
		and Northeast United States
		hurricane wreaks destruction
		on Halifax
		Invasion of Iraq
		SARS in Toronto
		Mad Cow Disease in Alberta
		devastating forest fires in British
		Columbia (2003)
		Paul Martin succeeds Jean
		Chrétien as prime minister of
		Canada (2003)

began on group-related phenomena—the influence of social norms on perception and action (Sherif), the effects of styles of leadership on group functioning (Lewin) and the effects of frustration on aggression (Dollard, Doob & Miller). The Second World War generated research on topics relating to politics and combat—group morale, leadership and propaganda. By the 1950s, there was a renewed interest in attitudes, evident in research on persuasion by Carl Hovland and colleagues, and on prejudice and personality (Adorno, Frenkel-Brunswick, Levinson & Sanford, 1950). Others studied the relationship between social behav-

iour and individual differences in the need for achievement and social approval and persuasibility.

The 1950s also marked the appearance of two seminal books that are still influential. Leon Festinger's (1957) *A Theory of Cognitive Dissonance* provided an explanation of how people deal with inconsistencies between attitude and behaviour. In the following year, Fritz Heider's (1958) *The Psychology of Interpersonal Relations* outlined a psychology based on how we infer what causes people to act as they do. In the same decade, the laboratory experiment became the predominant research method (Adair, 1980).

In the 1960s, social psychology expanded dramatically in scope. Social psychologists directed their attention to new areas of research—why we sometimes display excessive obedience to authority, how we make judgments about other people's behaviour, how we negotiate and resolve conflicts, how we attract and make friends, and why bystanders often fail to help in emergencies. In Canada, Wallace Lambert, Robert Gardner and others launched groundbreaking research into the social and psychological aspects of bilingualism. In that highly politicized decade, research also continued in areas of social concern, including aggression, prejudice and attitude change.

Several new directions are evident over the past few decades. The first is an interest in social cognition (the study of how we "make sense" of our social world), which has been influenced by fundamental research on cognitive processes such as memory, attention and problem solving. The second is a growing interest in applying social psychology to areas of daily living.

Social psychologists may now be found working in medicine, law, organizational management, the environment and counselling. In the long run, these trends can only enrich social psychology and extend the validity of its theories and findings.

International perspectives

Despite its European roots, throughout most of its history researchers from the U.S. have dominated social psychology. Indeed, one can view the U.S. as the first of three "worlds" in which psychologists carry out research and practice (Moghaddam, 1987, 1990): it is the major producer of psychological knowledge. The second world is made up of the other industrialized nations, including Canada, Great Britain, Australia, France, Germany and Russia. In some ways the second world is as productive as the first world, but its influence is greatest among its own constituents and upon the third world. The third world comprises the developing nations, such as India, China, Nigeria and Cuba. While the first world (U.S.) exports its knowledge to the second and third worlds, it is little influenced by the psychology of the other two worlds. The third world is primarily an importer of psychological knowledge, with limited ability to generate such knowledge.

Psychologists in all three "worlds" are becoming more sensitive to the relevance and appropriateness of first- and second-world psychology for societies of the third world (Moghaddam, 1987). A body of **cross-cultural research** is developing, as a growing number

How do people attract and make friends? Social psychologists began studying this issue in the 1960s.

of collaborative studies involve social psychological experiments carried out in a number of different cultures. A distinctive "second-world" social psychology, with its own areas of expertise, has also developed in Europe. Beginning in the late 1960s, European social psychologists such as Serge Moscovici in France and Henri Tajfel in Great Britain worked to develop a practice not steeped in the individualistic value system of the U.S. (Moghaddam, 1987). European social psychology places much more emphasis on intergroup relations, minority group influence, social control, conformity and the social psychological aspects of political economy and ideology (Taylor & Moghaddam, 1987). Few U.S. social psychologists ever publish in, or read, the leading European English-language journals. This is not the case for Canadian social psychologists, who are really part of the second world (Jaspars, 1980). This textbook offers considerable discussion of European research.

Social psychology in Canada

It is generally accepted that psychology—as an academic discipline—began in Leipzig in 1879 with the establishment of Wilhelm Wundt's laboratory. However, psychology courses had been taught long before that. The first course in psychology taught in a Canadian university was given in 1843 by a philosophy professor at the University of Toronto (Myers, 1965). The first chair of psychology in Canada (actually, the "Chair of Psychology and Metaphysics") was established at Dalhousie University in 1866 (Page & Clark, 1982). The first psychology laboratory in Canada was set up by James Baldwin at the University of Toronto in 1890; he subsequently founded the psychological laboratories at Princeton and Johns Hopkins (Myers, 1965). It was not until 1929, however, that graduate psychology programs were established in Canada, at McGill and the University of Toronto (Wright, 1969).

Psychology followed different paths in francophone and anglophone universities in Canada (Granger, 1996). Anglophone psychology departments began to develop early in the century and, although rooted in British idealistic philosophy and the Wundtian framework (Adair, Pavio & Ritchie, 1996), generally followed the American tradition. Most of the non-Canadian academicians in these departments came from Britain and the U.S. In francophone universities, on the other hand, psychology took root only in the 1940s, and many of the non-Canadian professors came

from France and Belgium, importing the somewhat less experimental and more philosophical form of psychology common in those countries. These two strains of psychology coexisted in Canada for a number of years, but the differences have now disappeared (Granger, 1996).

Not long after psychology began to be recognized as a separate discipline, social psychology took root in Canadian universities, at about the same time as in the U.S. (Gardner & Kalin, 1981). A course in social psychology was introduced at McGill University in 1913 (Ferguson, 1982), at the University of Saskatchewan in 1919 (McMurray, 1982), at the University of Manitoba in 1923 (Wright, 1982), and at the University of Toronto sometime during the 1920s (Wright, 1990). Thus, social psychology in Canada is older than most Canadian universities!

While most Canadian social psychological research is not tied to national character and differs little from research conducted in the U.S. (Rule & Wells, 1981), nonetheless, social psychologists have strived to serve the Canadian context, and research foci in this country reflect particular aspects of our society (Adair, Pavio & Ritchie, 1996). Canadian researchers have become world leaders in the domains of bilingualism, multiculturalism, immigrant acculturation, ethnic identity, prejudice, stereotypes and discrimination.

This book came into being, in part, because of our concern that social psychology, as carried out in the U.S. and discussed in American textbooks, may not accurately describe social behaviour in Canada. For instance, the U.S. has stressed a "melting pot" concept of society, while Canada emphasizes a "cultural mosaic." "Life, liberty and the pursuit of happiness" are promised in the American constitution, while the *British North America Act*, Canada's original constitutional document, offered "peace, order and good government." As you will see later in this book, Canadian and U.S. values have been diverging sharply over the past decade and more, with Canadians becoming more and more socially liberal, while social conservatism has dramatically grown in acceptance in the United States. These and other fundamental differences have important influences on various social psychological phenomena.

Teaching social psychology using textbooks rooted in the social and cultural context of another nation is problematic (Alcock, 1978; Berry, 1978a, 1978b; Kalin & Gardner, 1981; Sadava, 1978a, 1978b). First, what we learn from American texts about such topics as racial prejudice, aggression, and the social psychology of justice and law may be erroneous when applied to the Canadian context. Second, such learning carries the risk of influencing Canadian social behaviour to *become* more American. If people believe that murder rates are going up, for example, they may become more fearful and feel an increased need to arm themselves, bringing about a greater likelihood of lethal aggression. Finally, while American textbooks generally do an excellent job of sensitizing students to social issues in that country, Canadian students may not react in the same way. For example, while prejudice continues to be a problem in Canada, Canadian students using an American book can escape the challenge to their social conscience that their U.S. counterparts must face when reading about racial prejudice in their own country.

This textbook considers that social psychology has both a national and an international flavour. Studying social psychology within the Canadian context and bringing together the best in Canadian, American, European and other research addresses both the culture-specific and universal aspects of social psychology.

Applied Social Psychology

Social psychology involves constant feedback between laboratory-based research and real-life problems. Indeed, from its inception, social psychology has been vitally concerned with the problems of people and society. In its formative years, social psychologists worked to understand such phenomena as the economic depression, labour-management conflicts, racial prejudice and the rise of fascism in the 1930s (Fisher, Bell & Baum, 1984). During the Second World War, social psychologists applied their skills to the war effort: for example, the University of Toronto's David Ketchum employed his social psychological knowledge at the War Information Board in Ottawa (Wright, 1990). Indeed, social psychological research is still employed by the Canadian military—for example, in the study of predictors of leadership (Bradley, Nicol, Charbonneau, & Meyer, 2002). In more recent times, social psychologists in Canada have addressed such important societal concerns as the adaptation and acculturation of immigrants (Dompierre & Lavallée, 1990; Lalonde & Cameron, 1993), the effects of our national multiculturalism policy (Berry & Kalin, 1995), the development of racial identity

among Native children (Corenblum & Annis, 1993), and ways to encourage attitudinal and behavioural change to inhibit the spread of HIV/AIDS (Perlini & Ward, 2000). Canadian social psychologists have also played prominent roles in the study of gender roles and discrimination against women (Marecek, 2001; Pyke, 2001; Stark, 2001).

Social psychological research has been applied to a wide variety of social concerns (see Table 2 for examples). In many cases, theories developed through "pure research" have been applied to social issues; for example, attribution theory has been applied in understanding the experience of being physically ill, marital conflicts and addiction to cigarettes. In other cases, lacking applicable theory, social psychologists begin with the study of a real-life problem, for example, unprotected sex amongst young people in an age of liberal sexual mores and deadly sexually-transmitted diseases.

Recently, the Canadian Space Agency has become interested in psychosocial research and has chosen to fund research in two areas where research by Canadian psychologists has been particularly prominent: the interactions amongst people from various multicultural groups and the effects of isolated and confined environments (Suedfeld, 2003). Both of these subjects will be of considerable importance to the planning of future space missions involving men and women from a variety of cultural, ethnic and linguistic backgrounds living in confined quarters under stressful conditions for long periods of time.

Social psychological knowledge also has considerable application in clinical psychology, since social interaction both influences and is influenced by an individual's mental health (Alcock, 1997). Social psychology can further contribute to the betterment of society through evaluation research—the objective, data-based assessment of social programs or changes.

Can all this research actually have practical benefits for people and societies? Public policy in Canada has been influenced significantly by work in a number of areas (Rule & Adair, 1984). Pioneering research originating with Wallace Lambert's group in Montreal led to an internationally recognized model of bilingual education that combines language training with cultural integration (Gardner & Desrochers, 1981). Research on how northern Native peoples adapted to cultural and economic changes, such as the James Bay hydroelectric project, has provided information that cannot be ignored by governments or by Native groups in future policy decisions (Berry, Wintrob, Sindell & Mawhinney, 1982). Other research has contributed to Canada's multiculturalism policy, which encourages ethnic groups to maintain their cultural heritages while joining the Canadian mainstream (Kalin & Berry, 1979). Recommendations for changes in our legal system by a parliamentary law reform commission drew on research concerning the reliability of eyewitness testimony, the unanimity rule in jury decisions and the assessment of a defendant's fitness for trial. Research on the impact of TV advertising on young children led to a legislated ban on "targeted" advertising in Quebec and some voluntary restraints in the rest of Canada (Goldberg, 1982).

Lewin (1948) has described this type of work as **action research**, in which the researcher obtains data about a problem or organization, feeds these data into the relevant system in order to influence change, measures the change and then repeats the process. Note that this model implies the social psychologist becomes an *agent* of change, a skilled advocate of policies, as well as a theoretician and researcher.

An Overall Perspective

The early history of social psychology was marked by an euphoric optimism. For the first time, the methods of science were to be applied to human problems. Surely, it was believed, the same approach that had yielded spectacular advances in our understanding of medicine, atomic physics, chemistry and geology would help us to understand and eventually solve the problems of violence, crime, poverty and prejudice.

TABLE 2

Some typical topics found in the *Journal of Social Issues*

Topic	Issues
Teenage parenting: Social determinants and consequences	1980, 36(1)
Energy conservation	1981, 37(2)
Sexual harassment on the job	1982, 38(4)
Images of nuclear war	1983, 39(1)
Criminal victimization	1984, 40(1)
Social support	1985, 41(1)
Media violence and antisocial behaviour	1986, 42(3)
Deterrence theory and international conflict	1987, 43(4)
Psychological effects of unemployment	1988, 44(4)
Managing the environment	1989, 45(1)
Moral exclusion and injustice	1990, 46(1)
Perceived control in vulnerable populations	1991, 47(4)
Psychological perspectives on abortion and its alternatives	1992, 48(3)
Gender and close relationships	1993, 49(3)
Constructive conflict management	1994, 50(1)
Religious influence on personal and societal well-being	1995, 51(2)
Social psychological perspective on grassroots organizing	1996, 52(1)
Social science perspectives on tobacco policy	1997, 53(1)
Political development: Youth growing up in a global community	1998, 54(3)
Bilingual education programs: A cross-national perspective	1999, 55(4)
Heterosexism and the study of women's romantic and friend relationships	2000, 56(2)
Gender, ethnicity and power	2001, 57(4)
Understanding the harm of hate crime	2002, 58(2)
Privacy as a social issue and behavioural concept	2003, 59(2)

Surely we could "conquer" war as we had "conquered" infectious diseases, and we could learn to live in harmony as we had learned to fly and to communicate over long distances.

While the discipline has advanced significantly in the succeeding decades, the serious social problems are still with us. Perhaps the fact that war, bigotry and poverty are rooted in culture and in the political, moral and economic realities of the times means that a purely psychological solution is unrealistic. It may also be true that social problems are more complex than biological or physical phenomena and will not be solved so easily. We must also remember that social psychology is a young discipline.

In summary, social psychology is a dynamic field, continually evolving as new ideas, methods, research findings and theories emerge and affect one another: a theory can generate innovative research and controversy; research findings and new ideas can lead to an evolution in the theory; new areas of research can open up as a result of random events (e.g., a widely publicized incident of a murder in the presence of bystanders who failed to intervene stimulated research and theory on the problem). Some areas of research become hot topics almost overnight, generating cutting-edge ideas, while other areas may be slow to build, or even wane, for a while. A textbook can only provide a picture of the discipline at the time of writing—with some idea of where we have been and where we are going.

A Note on the Text

The best way to understand what social psychology is about is to get involved. This involvement begins in the chapter that follows, which introduces the fundamental principles of how research is conducted in social psychology. Then, a series of chapters explores how we come to understand our social world—how we perceive and understand other people and events and how we form values and attitudes. The next set of chapters deals with how people influence one another—how our attitudes change as we interact with others, how social influences lead us to conform, comply with and obey other people and how people communicate through language and non-verbal means. Then,

a series of chapters examines how we interact with other people: what factors determine whether we are attracted to one another, the causes of aggressive and altruistic behaviour and how conflict develops and can be resolved. Next, we look at how the individual functions in a group and larger collectives. Finally, we consider some contemporary areas of practical concern including the law and health.

Summary

1. Social psychology is the study of how the thoughts, feelings and behaviours of individuals are influenced by the actual, imagined or implied presence of others.

2. Although its roots lie deep in philosophical inquiry, social psychology as a separate, research-oriented discipline began to develop around the beginning of the 20th century. Theory and research have been dominated by social psychologists in the U.S. However, as we move into the 21st century, there is a growing interest in an international perspective and in the special benefits and problems presented by cross-cultural research.

3. Social psychologists in Canada have contributed to all aspects of social psychology and have helped focus attention on such areas as bilingualism and multiculturalism.

4. Since its beginnings, social psychology has been concerned with the real-life problems of people and their societies. The application of social psychology to real-world problems has been an area of increasing importance and has contributed significantly to the development of public policy in Canada.

Sources of Information

At the end of each chapter are listed important, recent publications that provide further information on topics discussed in that chapter. The following list of basic reference works will serve as an introduction to most research areas in the field.

Some basic reference works

BERKOWITZ, L. (Ed.). *Advances in experimental social psychology* (Annual Series). New York: Academic Press.

BERRY, J.W., POORTINGA, Y.H. & PANDEY, J. (1997). *Handbook of cross-cultural psychology* (2nd ed.). Boston: Allyn and Bacon.

BICKMAN, L. (Ed.). *Applied social psychology annual* (Annual Series). Beverly Hills, CA: Sage.

GILBERT, D.T., FISKE, S.T. & LINDZEY, G. (Eds.). (1998). *The handbook of social psychology* (4th ed.) (Vols. 1–2). New York: Random House.

ROSENZWEIG, M.R. & PORTER, L.W. (Eds.). *Annual review of psychology* (Annual Series). Palo Alto, CA: Annual Reviews, Inc.

SADAVA, S.W. & McCREARY, D.R. (Eds.). (1997). *Applied social psychology*. Upper Saddle River, NJ: Prentice-Hall.

Journals

Journal articles are also important in keeping abreast of the latest research and findings. A literature search through the Psychological Abstracts or a computerized library database (such as the CD-ROM PsycLIT) will provide specific references. For papers and research of general interest, the following journals are most useful:

British Journal of Social Psychology
Canadian Journal of Behavioural Science
Canadian Psychology
European Journal of Social Psychology
European Psychologist
Journal of Applied Social Psychology
Journal of Experimental Social Psychology
Journal of Personal and Social Relationships
Journal of Personality and Social Psychology
Journal of Social Issues
Journal of Social Psychology
Personality and Social Psychology Bulletin
Psychological Bulletin (literature and methodological reviews in all areas of psychology)
Psychological Review (theory in all areas of psychology)

There are also journals that feature research in one particular area of social psychology:
Aggression and Behaviour
Environment and Behaviour
Health Psychology
Journal of Clinical and Social Psychology
Journal of Conflict Resolution
Journal of Cross-Cultural Psychology
Journal of Language and Social Psychology
Journal of Studies on Alcohol

Further Reading

ADAIR, J.G., PAIVIO, A. & RITCHIE, P. (1996). Psychology in Canada. In J.T. Spence, J.M. Darley & D.J. Foss (Eds.), *Annual review of psychology, 47*, 341–370.

COLLIER, G., MINTON, H.L. & REYNOLDS, G. (1991). *Currents of thought in American social psychology*. New York: Oxford University Press. A study of the people and intellectual currents—including British evolutionary theory, French social theory, and the ideas of Freud and Marx—that spawned social psychology in the United States.

HEWSTONE, M., STROEBE, W. & STEPHENSON, G. (1995). *Introduction to social psychology: A European perspective* (2nd ed.). London: Blackwell. A very good overview of the European approach to social psychology and ongoing European research initiatives.

KALIN, R. & GARDNER, R.C. (1981). The cultural context of social psychology. In R.C. Gardner & R. Kalin (Eds.), *A social psychology of Canadian ethnic relations* (pp. 2–17). Toronto: Methuen. Discussion of how culture influences social psychological research, with particular emphasis on the origins and contemporary state of social psychology in Canada.

LUBEK, I., MINTON, H.L. & APFELBAUM, E. (Eds.). (1992). Social psychology and its history. *Canadian Psychology, 33*(3). Special Issue. Important collection of papers by an international group of authors reflecting on the origins and development of social psychology.

O'NEILL, P. & DUBÉ, L. (Eds.). (1992). The history of psychology in Canada. *Canadian Psychology, 33*(4). Special Section. Collection of papers describing the development of psychology in Canada.

Weblinks

Listed below are a number of useful Web sites. Please keep in mind, however, that Web addresses may change over time.

Compendium of Social Psychology Web Resources
www.msu.edu/user/amcconne/social.html

International Association for Cross-Cultural Psychology
www.fit.edu/CampusLife/clubs-org/iaccp/

National Archives
www.archives.ca/ Public and private records of national significance.

Psyc Site
kenstange.com/psycsite/ Affiliated with the Psychology Department of Nipissing University, this is an excellent starting point for finding information about scientific research in psychology on the World Wide Web.

Psychology of Religion
www.psychwww.com/psyrelig/index.htm

Social and Personality Section, Canadian Psychological Association
www.uwinnipeg.ca/~cpa/

Social Psychology Network
www.socialpsychology.org/ Excellent resource site for social psychologists.

Society for the Psychological Study of Social Issues
www.spssi.org/

Sociology Resource Centre
www.sonic.net/~markbl/socioweb/

Statistics Canada
www.statcan.ca/ Statistical information on all facets of Canada: land, people, economy, and so on.

Chapter 1

Research and Research Methods

We take issue ... with every treatment of psychology that is based on simple self-observation or on philosophical supposition.

William Wundt

Science is built up of facts, as a house is built of stones; but an accumulation of facts is no more a science than a heap of stones is a house.

Henri Poincaré

Chapter Outline

In June 2000, Canada became the first country in the world to require graphic health warning labels on tobacco packaging. Despite the protestations of tobacco manufacturers, the federal government was determined to take this measure in the belief that such fear-inducing labels would lead at least some people to stop smoking. Whether such labels are likely to produce significant attitudinal and behavioural change with regard to smoking is a question that falls directly into the purview of the applied social psychologist, and indeed, it touches on a wealth of laboratory experiments into attitude change that have been carried out over the past several decades (as is discussed in Chapter 5).

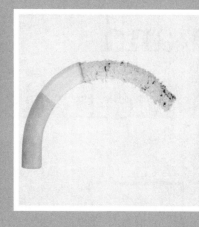

WARNING
TOBACCO USE CAN MAKE YOU IMPOTENT

Cigarettes may cause sexual impotence due to decreased blood flow to the penis. This can prevent you from having an erection.

Health Canada

How can the social psychologist study the effects of such labels on attitudes and behaviour? This is not so easy as it might at first seem. Think for a moment about some of the difficulties involved in trying to determine whether the labels change smoking habits:

- Do we simply look at the sales figures for cigarettes and tobacco across the country? The problem there is that we cannot be sure that, even if there is a decline in tobacco consumption, it had anything to do with the new labels. Maybe people cut down on smoking for unrelated reasons—for example, perhaps unemployment has risen, and unemployed workers have to economize.

- Should we conduct a survey of smokers and ex-smokers and directly ask them how the new labels have affected their smoking habits? We could do so, but do people really know what effect the labels have on their attitudes, and might those who have recently quit smoking attribute their decision to the labels, even if they were on their way to quitting even before the labels appeared?

- Perhaps we could design some sort of laboratory experiment, recruiting smokers as subjects, and then exposing them to fear-arousing stimuli similar but not identical to those found on the tobacco labels. Yet, even if we found that our labels had an effect, how does that compare to the effects of labels that smokers see not just for a short time in a psychology laboratory, but day after day, week after week, on cig-

arette packages? Perhaps it is the novelty of the labels, the initial shock value, that is important, and maybe that effect weakens with further exposure.

The point is, it is difficult to study issues such as this one. Whenever we are confronted with important social issues, there is usually plenty of strong rhetoric and opinion—but little available data. In our everyday lives, we may trust our personal experience to provide the data upon which we base our opinions, but everyday experience is often a poor guide. Forty years ago, everyday experience would have seemed to confirm the then-common view that women could not drive buses or do construction work or serve as front-line police officers. Today, everyday experience leads to a different conclusion. History demonstrates the dangers of making judgments and decisions on the basis of authority, emotion, personal experience or "common sense" alone. We need to look at "data." But data can be accurate or inaccurate, reliable or unreliable. Poor data, like poor common sense or misleading authority, are often worse than no data at all, for they lead us to believe we have a basis for understanding, when, in fact, we do not.

This is why scientific methods are important, for science concerns itself not only with the collection and analysis of data, but also with trying to protect researchers from error in interpreting those data. Of course, scientists make mistakes, but science tends to be self-correcting, and errors are ultimately weeded out, whereas opinions based only on authority or personal experience may never change, even when they are in error. Science is as important in social psychology as it is in physics or chemistry or biology. In this chapter, we shall explore why this is so.

What is "science"? Science is a *method of studying nature*. And it is the method—not scientists, or the equipment used, or the facts proclaimed—that differentiates the scientific approach from other approaches to knowledge. Whether in astronomy, physics or psychology, what is fundamental is generating theory and testing it against observation. **Theory** is essential to guide research, to organize research results into a coherent structure and to provide ideas for testing. Without theory, there is nothing to test. And without testing, there is no way to evaluate which theories are correct. Indeed, as we shall see, the scientific approach is as valuable a tool for studying human social behaviour as for conducting research into chemical reactions and biological processes.

Science is fundamentally a rational process. In its simplest form, the rational model consists of four steps: (1) formulating a theoretical problem, which is then translated into testable **hypotheses**; (2) selecting the appropriate research method, and designing and carrying out the study; (3) analyzing and interpreting the results; and (4) using the results to confirm, deny or modify the theory.

For most people, "science" describes specific fields of study (physics, chemistry, geology, astronomy, biology), impressive laboratory technology and precise measurement. It may seem surprising that a field such as social psychology can be scientific. How can the study of smoking, violence, helping, leadership, bilingual communication, impression formation and attitudes be scientific in the same sense that research into the mysteries of the human cell, the atom and chemical compound reactions is scientific? Yet the scientific method is arguably even more important in a field where data are difficult to quantify, because such areas are most vulnerable to fuzzy and erroneous thinking.

However, it is not nearly as straightforward to apply the scientific method to social behaviour as it is to apply it to inanimate objects or biological processes.

Theory in Social Psychology

Because social psychology is a relatively young discipline, and because human social behaviour is so complex, no single, grand theory has yet emerged.

Moreover, while social psychologists have excelled as experimenters and data collectors, they have tended to ignore the importance of theory development (Kruglanski, 2001). Indeed, much of what we loosely refer to as "theory" in social psychology is not really theory in the sense the term is used in natural sciences. Our theories are more like **models**, usually built upon a loosely related set of assumptions, and the logical deduction process is typically informal in nature.

As we will see in subsequent chapters, various mini-theories or models have been developed to account for specific phenomena, such as leadership, attitude change or aggressive behaviour. While there is considerable variety among these theories, two major theoretical orientations have dominated: the behaviourist and the cognitive perspectives. Both have been adapted from the mainstream of psychological theory and research.

Behaviourism developed through the pioneering work of Ivan Pavlov on conditioned reflexes and of B.F. Skinner on operant conditioning. Its premise is that behaviour is governed by external reinforcement. In the past, "radical behaviourists" such as Skinner argued that reinforcement is all we need to explain and predict behaviour. On the other hand, cognitive psychologists argue that inner psychological processes, such as beliefs, feelings and motives, are influenced by external reinforcement and, in turn, influence behaviour. Most social psychologists prefer the latter approach, in which both external events and psychological states must be studied.

Behaviourist perspective

The behaviourist perspective has led social psychologists to search for environmental or situational factors that influence behaviour. Behaviourism also forms the basis of a number of theories in social psychology, including the following, which are discussed in later chapters:

1. The **reinforcement-affect model of attraction** explains why we come to like someone by associating that person with some positive experience.

2. Researchers have explained the influence of film and television on aggression in terms of **social learning theory**. This theory states that we do not always need to be reinforced in order to learn new behaviours; we can learn simply by watching how other people act and observing the consequences of their actions.

3. **Social exchange theory** explains interactions and relationships in terms of the social reinforcements (e.g., affection, respect, power) that people provide for one another.

Cognitive perspective

Many theorists feel that the behaviourists exaggerated the degree to which we are passive recipients of external influences, arguing that we also act to interpret and change our environment. According to this view, it is also important to look within individuals, particularly at their *cognitive processes*, to understand behaviour. The cognitive perspective gained recognition with the early work on perception by the Gestalt psychologists, and was used early in the development of social psychology by Kurt Lewin (1951) in his field theory. Lewin argued that the "environment" that influences human actions is not a set of physical characteristics and events *per se*, but the "life space" of individuals—the environment in the context of what it means to them. People actively construct or make sense of the situations in which they find themselves. Lewin suggested an example from his own combat experience in the First World War: A physical landscape might consist of hills and valleys, trees, bushes and open spaces. However, this landscape would be a very different environment to soldiers in combat than to friends on a picnic, and would influence their behaviour in different ways.

Many contemporary theories in social psychology have developed within the cognitive perspective, including the following, which are examined in later chapters:

1. **Social comparison theory** explains how we often evaluate ourselves, our beliefs and our actions by comparing ourselves with others: Am I successful? Is my judgment accurate? Did I do a good job?

2. The theory of **cognitive dissonance** explains how we deal with situations in which there is inconsistency between our beliefs and our actions—when, for example, a smoker comes to believe that smoking causes cancer or when someone who has publicly supported a politician begins to doubt the politician's competency.

3. **Attribution theories**—and there are several of them—explain how people make inferences about the causes of another person's actions.

Empirical Research in Social Psychology

In discussing empirical research in social psychology, it is important first to understand what it means to *measure* something. We usually take measurement for granted. We buy a litre of milk or a kilogram of beef; we drive for 100 km; and we know that water boils at 100°C (at sea level). Yet, living in Canada, we are well aware of the arbitrariness of measurement units. For example, we use both pounds and kilograms in stores, and when we cross the border into the United States we must buy gasoline in gallons instead of litres and measure our speed in miles per hour instead of kilometres per hour.

Measurement is as important in social psychology as it is in any other scientific research. However, no psychological attribute can ever be directly observed; it must be inferred on the basis of its presumed manifestation through behaviour. Sometimes this is easy; usually it is difficult. For example, if we study memory, it is easy enough to observe that from a list of 20 paired associates, a research participant correctly recalled 10. Yet it is not nearly as simple to "count" how much conformity there was, or how much aggression occurred, or how altruistically a research participant responded. The fact is that social psychologists deal almost exclusively in *hypothetical constructs*; that is, in variables that we presume exist and that we can use to explain other behaviours or outcomes, but that we cannot directly measure. Thus, if we observe that a particular individual eschews gambling, never buys lottery tickets, abhors alcohol and does not smoke, we might start to presume that this person's attitude structure is of a specific kind and call it "conservative," "traditional" or even "puritanical." And we might predict that he would also be opposed to extramarital sex. However, we are hypothesizing that something called an "attitude" exists and that his "puritanical" attitude accounts for the stability of behaviour across a variety of situations.

If attitudes exist, how do we measure them? How can we measure altruism? Or aggression? To define hypothetical constructs such as these in a quantifiable way, we employ **operational definitions**; that is, we define the construct in terms of the operation we use to measure it. Thus in one experiment, aggression may be defined and measured in terms of how many electrical shocks one research participant believes she is administering to another participant. In another experiment, aggression might be operationally defined in quite a different manner, for example, the number of kicks a child delivers to an inflated doll. The construct as it is operationally defined may or may not correspond to the way we ordinarily view that construct; this will affect the generality of any conclusions we may draw.

What is a good measure? As upper-year psychology students know, whenever we conduct empirical research, we must be concerned with **reliability** (the degree to which a measuring instrument yields the same measurement when used more than once to measure some unchanging object or trait or behaviour) and **validity** (the degree to which a measuring instrument measures what we want it to measure). While it is usually straightforward to establish the reliability of a measuring instrument, it is much more difficult to establish validity. If our measuring instruments lack validity, we measure in vain, only deceiving ourselves.

We also must be concerned about *reactivity*. Measurement can be either *reactive* or *nonreactive*. A **reactive measure** is one that may itself influence the behaviour that we are studying. Administering a questionnaire is a reactive approach because the research participant may answer a formal question differently from the way he answers the same question asked by a friend over a beer. In other words, the questionnaire itself influences the behaviour that it is supposed to measure. A **nonreactive measure**, on the other hand, is one that cannot affect the behaviour being considered. Asking people how much tobacco they smoke is a reactive procedure: they may be less than straightforward in their reply. Counting how many cigarette packages people throw away in their garbage is a nonreactive one—as long as they are unaware that we are spying on their garbage. The measure does not and cannot affect their behaviour.

Simply observing people in a natural setting can provide a great deal of information about behaviour. The difference between casual observation by a layperson and observation by a social psychological researcher is that while the layperson depends on direct experience, the social psychologist relies on *systematic* observation. Usually researchers attempt to control some of the variables that bias casual observation: for example, they follow a standardized scoring system and use observers who are unaware of the researcher's hypothesis.

Suppose, for example, that someone at a New Year's Eve party observes that people seem to be smoking less than at such parties in years past, and concludes that this is because of the apprehension produced by the frightening images on cigarette packages. The social psychologist would not accept such a conclusion out-of-hand, but would want more information. For example, did partygoers really smoke less than in years gone by, or did the observer, sensitized by publicity about the dangers of smoking and of second-hand smoke, watch—really for the first time—how much people were smoking, and then overestimate past consumption? If there really was less smoking, were partygoers smoking less out of consideration for others in light of growing resentment by non-smokers with regard to second-hand smoke, or does this group of partygoers smoke less at home as well? Did the people being observed constitute an adequate sample of the general population, or were they an atypical group particularly concerned about smoking and cancer? Did the decrease in consumption reflect the fact that the people being observed are growing older year by year? Did the people smoke less because each time they went to light a cigarette, they noticed the observer making notes?

How might we go about studying whether people smoke less as a result of the influence of the frightening images on cigarette labels? Before undertaking any formal research, the very first step is to define the research question clearly: Do we want to study changes in smoking patterns from year to year, or are we specifically interested in the impact of the labels? Suppose we decide to focus on the latter. In this case, are we interested only in tobacco consumption, or are we also interested in cognitive and emotional reactions even if people smoke just as much as before? Fear-inducing labels might lead people to become more negative about smoking, and more supportive of public health measures aimed at curbing it, even if they do not reduce their own consumption. Or are we interested only in public smoking behaviour that puts non-smokers at risk?

Once we are clear about what we intend to study, we must choose how we are going to operationally define "tobacco consumption." Should we simply go by industry sales figures, or should we focus on groups of smokers, and measure their blood nicotine levels (not a way to make oneself popular at parties!), or count the number of cigarettes each person smokes? If the latter, how do we deal with the differing number of puffs per cigarette, the differences in terms of how much a person inhales, and the differing amounts of

While most people think of the laboratory when they think of science, much social psychological research is done outside the laboratory.

nicotine in various brands of cigarettes? And what about cigars and pipes? Before we collect any data, we must take care to clearly define our variables and our research design. Only then can we turn to the question of which research method is best for our purposes.

Methods of Empirical Research

Psychological research is overwhelmingly _quantitative_ in nature. That is, we define our variables carefully in terms of how we can measure them, we collect data that is objective rather than subjective (that is, we rely on measurement rather than our feelings or interpretations), and we aggregate the data and rely on statistical analysis to help us draw conclusions (that is, we calculate means, and focus not on individual outcomes but average outcomes for a condition or group).

Because quantitative methods require that we be able to employ objective measures, we may miss out on important information that does not lend itself to ready measurement. How can we quantify grief or patriotism, for example? Further, because we focus on aggregate data, we may miss out on important differences amongst individuals in our groups or conditions.

In recent years, **qualitative methods** have been developing as researchers strive to study social behaviours that are extremely difficult to quantify (Rennie, 2002). Such methods involving case studies, direct observation and interviews (although these methods can be part of quantitative research, when objective measures are applied) are being used more and more, particularly in the study of health psychology. How do we really begin to understand, for example, reactions to a diagnosis of cancer? Through a pencil-and-paper questionnaire, where we ask respondents to rate their anxiety on a scale of one to five? Or through spending considerable time getting to know cancer patients, and gathering qualitative data through in-depth interviews? The latter surely makes sense. One of the thrusts behind qualitative research is to gain more familiarity with the phenomenon one wants to study, rather than starting with hypotheses and then conducting research to test those hypotheses. Consider again the question about the effectiveness of labelling tobacco products with fear-inducing images. We could approach the question by setting up a few hypotheses that seem sensible, and then finding a way to collect data that would help us decide which hypothesis is best supported. However, in order to really understand why tobacco consumption is or is not affected by such labels, it may make more sense to first develop a deeper sense of what is going on through in-depth interviews with people who smoke and people who have stopped.

Qualitative research has its strengths and its limitations. It provides a wealth of descriptive detail from the research participant's own perspective, and this detail helps to place the results of any quantitative data that are gathered into their human context (Trochim, 1999). At the same time, however, there is no control of variables, data are subjective rather than objective, and it is difficult to generalize from such specific data. That is why it makes sense to use both qualitative and quantitative methods together in the study of complex social issues.

Social psychological research methods can be divided into two types: *nonexperimental* and *experimental*. We shall discuss some major examples of each type.

Nonexperimental methods

Nonexperimental methods involve collecting data without manipulating an independent variable. There are a number of different nonexperimental research methods that we might employ, and in the following section, we shall explore the archival approach, the case study, the survey method and the field study. Note that qualitative research is nonexperimental. Correlational research also is nonexperimental, but we shall treat that subject separately, later in this chapter.

The archival approach

We might start our investigation by examining existing data from countries where fear-inducing labels have been used, and comparing their per capita rate of tobacco consumption to our own to see if these rates support the hypothesis that such labels lead to decreased tobacco use. However, in this case, this may not be possible, since Canada is the first country in the world to use such graphic labels.

Using data already collected and tabulated for some other purpose by someone else is referred to as an **archival approach**. The archival approach provides a number of benefits: the exploration of a hypothesis using data from many periods of history and many places; the elimination of the time, cost and effort involved in actually going out and collecting data; and the ability to study events that could not otherwise be studied, such as changes in impaired-driving rates around the world. It also has the advantage of being nonreactive (the researcher cannot interfere with or

influence the behaviour on which the data were based). However, the archival approach has severe limitations. In the example discussed above, we would be limited by whatever data have already been collected and published. Perhaps other countries do not publish data on tobacco consumption, or perhaps some of the data are missing or inconsistent. Moreover, we would have no way of knowing whether other such countries differ in other crucial respects from our own—for example, the general degree of concern about tobacco use. Even if we could forget about such problems, and even if we did discover that the rate of smoking was lower in countries with fear-inducing labels, we could not simply assume that such labels *cause* a reduction in smoking. Perhaps smokers who constantly are exposed to such labelling take whatever opportunity they can to buy their tobacco in neighbouring countries where such labelling does not occur. Or perhaps some third variable is responsible for both the introduction of the labelling laws and the lower tobacco usage. If both are manifestations of a particular attitude towards tobacco in general, then applying fear-inducing labels in a country where tobacco is viewed more positively may not affect tobacco consumption at all.

The case study

The **case study** is an in-depth investigation and analysis of a single instance of a phenomenon of interest. Such a study, which might focus on a single individual, group or specific event, is often the only way of studying a rare phenomenon that cannot be duplicated in the laboratory. For example, in an examination of the effects of graphic labels on tobacco packages, the case study approach might involve in-depth interviews with smokers, examining in detail how the labels have or have not influenced their smoking habits.

The major advantage of the case study approach is that it allows for intensive investigation and lets researchers follow the development of the phenomenon over time. Case studies are often excellent starting points for research, generating hypotheses that can then be explored in more detail by other means.

On the other hand, case studies have several drawbacks:

- The case we study is unlikely to be typical of *all* such cases, and we have no way of knowing how much of the information we gather is idiosyncratic; that is, specific only to that particular instance. Indeed, a researcher may choose to focus on a case that stands out in some way—for example, a prominent politician or film star who has had a long history of heavy smoking—rather than picking a case at random. And the very fact that a case "stands out" makes it less likely that it will tell us much about other cases.

- Another problem is that the respondents' accounts may be inaccurate or distorted, memories may be incomplete or biased, and research participants may deliberately try to put themselves in a good light. Their concern about being evaluated, known as **evaluation apprehension**, may lead them to give responses they consider socially desirable.

- The researcher's own biases can affect both the collection and interpretation of data. The very choice of questions asked may be enough to bias the responses.

- Finally, case study data do not form the basis for **causal inferences**—conclusions about cause and effect.

The survey method

The **survey method** involves going out and asking questions about the phenomenon of interest. For example, to gather more information about the relationship between graphic labels and tobacco consumption, we could ask people whether they have cut down their tobacco consumption as a result of the graphic labels. Or, we might avoid such a direct question and instead ask about smoking habits in various situations, including people's smoking habits when they are in other countries, where tobacco packages do not carry such labels. After collecting the responses, we would then be in a position to see whether those who report lower or higher tobacco consumption when out of the country also react more negatively or are more concerned about the message carried by the graphic labels, possibly indicating a connection between these variables.

The *structured interview* is one of a variety of survey techniques. Using a series of carefully chosen questions, listed in a specific order, the interviewer poses each question to the respondent and records the answer. Another survey technique is the *printed questionnaire*. Respondents who are unwilling to reply orally to potentially embarrassing questions may be willing to give honest answers in response to such a questionnaire. On the other hand, the oral interview is more flexible: the researcher can, when appropriate, seek clarification or greater depth on ambiguous

responses. An advantage of the questionnaire, however, is that it does not require the time and effort that must go into interviews. A large amount of data can be gathered quickly and inexpensively.

Questionnaires can be either *open-ended* (e.g., "How have the graphic labels affected how much you smoke?"), in which case the respondent can provide as detailed an answer as he wishes, or *closed* (e.g., "Do you smoke less as a result of the new graphic labels, yes or no?"), in which case the respondent must choose one of two or more answers available on the questionnaire. While closed questionnaires make scoring and analysis simpler, there is always the danger that the respondents may be forced to choose responses that do not really reflect their position, since none of the alternatives actually apply.

The survey method is especially useful for collecting data from a large number of people and is often the only way of obtaining data about thoughts, feelings and private behaviour not open to direct observation. However, like other methods discussed in this section, it provides only information about interrelationships among variables of interest and cannot directly establish whether one variable *causes* another. If individuals smoked less at parties after the new cigarette labels appeared, that does not necessarily mean that the fear-inducing labels caused them to moderate their smoking.

Survey methods are based on self-reporting, and self-reporting can be unreliable for a number of reasons:

- The questions can either "lead" or confuse the respondent. Suppose an individual believes that physical punishment of children should be used only to teach the child to avoid dangerous acts (e.g., a slap on the hand for putting a nail into an electrical outlet). The question "Do you agree that physical punishment of children is wrong?" might lead this person to answer "yes." How would you answer a question such as "Do you agree that it is irresponsible to smoke on a no-smoking floor of a hotel?" The question cries out for a "yes" and will evoke such a response from just about everyone.

- The order of the questions can have an important influence on how people respond. Imagine that you are first asked to respond to this question: "Should anglophones be given the right to decide Canada's future?" A little later in the same questionnaire, you are asked, "Should francophones be given the right to decide Canada's future?" Your response to this question is likely to be affected by the fact that you have already responded to the earlier one, and you may answer differently than if you had encountered this question first. Indeed, more generally, the interpretation of the meaning of items in a questionnaire can be altered by the content of other items (Marsh & Yeung, 1999).

- The interviewer's bias can easily influence both the course of the interview and the coding or recording of the data. If the interviewer reacts with raised eyebrows or a particular tone of voice to a respondent's answers, or if the interviewer mentally categorizes a respondent in a certain way as a result of an initial impression and does not bother to follow up on certain issues, then the results will be biased. The interviewer's bias can be communicated in many ways: An interviewer who is smoking a cigarette may produce different responses in a survey about smoking than one who is not! In this respect, the questionnaire approach has one advantage: the same questions are always presented in the same manner and in the same order, without any verbal cues.

- The respondents may not accurately report their feelings, thoughts or behaviours. As in case study interviews, they are vulnerable both to faulty memory and to evaluation apprehension. For example, with regard to smoking, because the tide of public opinion is shifting against smoking, people who often want to look good or at least not look bad in the eyes of the researcher may under-report their smoking habits. In order to try to minimize this problem, the researcher may disguise the purpose of the survey by asking questions that do not seem to bear directly on the respondent. Instead of asking about personal attitudes towards smoking, the researcher might ask the respondent to estimate how members of the public would rank a number of offences, including smoking where smoking is prohibited, in order of their relative severity. In this way, even though no information about the respondent's own behaviour is directly elicited, his or her attitude towards smoking can be inferred.

- People tend to respond to questions in "sets" or in a systematically biased manner: some people tend to give answers that are always "middle of the road" while others may lean towards extreme responses. Some even give "yes" responses or "no" responses too frequently, regardless of the questions. (Such people have been referred to as "yea-sayers" and "nay-sayers.") We can minimize this problem by careful design of the question series.

A critical step in using the survey method is choosing a **sample**. Who is going to answer our questionnaire or take part in our interview? If we are simply interested in the responses of a particular classroom of students, there is no problem. But if the goal is to generalize from our sample to a much larger population, then we must be very careful about how representative the sample is of the larger group. Suppose, for example, we were to have our questionnaire printed in a magazine with the request that readers fill it out and mail it to us. We might gather a great many responses this way, but would they allow us a reasonable basis for drawing conclusions? Definitely not. Depending on what magazine is used, we are likely to get a sample representative of only one group of people. The attitudes of the average *Canadian Living* reader may be very different from those of the average reader of *Maclean's*. Moreover, most magazine readers will not bother to fill out and return the questionnaire, which means that those who do might be in some way unrepresentative even of the readership of that magazine. They may be people who are particularly concerned about the issue. Thus, it is extremely important to take great care to select a sample that is likely to be representative of the population in which the researcher is interested.

The field study

The **field study** involves direct observation of the spontaneous behaviour of a group of people in a natural setting (for example, systematic observation of people attending New Year's parties). Data may be recorded by audiotaping or filming, or by manually recording various behaviours by shorthand (and "coding" behaviours of interest). A field study can take one of two forms: the observer may remain aloof and simply observe, or he/she may be a **participant observer**, mixing with the group in as unobtrusive a way as possible. Participant observation is the traditional approach of anthropologists who live among the people they wish to study, usually for periods of a year or more.

However, while the field study can yield penetrating insights matched by no other research method, there are also serious drawbacks to consider:

- One can never be sure just how typical is the situation under study. Can one generalize from it? Maybe, or maybe not. Often one just does not know.

- It is difficult to remain unbiased, working in proximity with the people of interest, often over a considerable period of time. If we are unfamiliar with their ways, we may come to sympathize with them and adopt their point of view, thus losing objectivity.

- The people under observation may change temporarily or permanently, either as a result of knowing they are under study, or as a result of the influence of the participant observer's ideas and personality.

- Again, while one can observe apparent relationships amongst behaviours and events of interest, one cannot determine causal relationships.

Nonexperimental methods are particularly useful for gathering information about what goes on in real-life situations. However, such information, while extremely important for generating hypotheses to guide further research, can offer a distorted picture of reality, owing to the biases of both the researcher and the respondents. The most serious shortcoming of the nonexperimental methods is their inability to demonstrate causal relationships among variables.

Experimental methods

Experimental methods came into being because of the need to draw causal inferences about how variables influence one another. Using the experimental method, the researcher deliberately assigns research participants randomly to two (or more) groups and applies a treatment variable (**independent variable**) to one group (the *experimental group*) and not the other (the *control group*). Then the researcher measures the effect of the treatment by comparing the two groups with regard to some behavioural variable (**dependent variable**), while excluding other factors (**extraneous variables**) that might interfere with the outcome. As an example, a researcher studying smoking behaviour might look at smokers' claims that smoking "calms their nerves" by measuring a physiological measure of relaxation such as finger temperature (dependent variable) and comparing the readings of research participants who were given either a normal cigarette or one which looked, tasted and smelled the same, but from which all active ingredients including nicotine had been removed. (Presence or absence of nicotine is the independent variable.) However, even if those who receive the nicotine are found to be more relaxed, we would of course have to be careful to eliminate other possible explanations for the finding,

such as the research participants' awareness of whether they had ingested nicotine, and whether merely *thinking* that one has been smoking leads one to relax, quite apart from the actual effects of the nicotine itself. The researcher wants to eliminate all such extraneous influences so that any observed differences must be due only to the nicotine.

A note about statistical analysis

Most experimental research—indeed, most empirical research—depends on statistical analysis of the data. Statistical analysis is a powerful tool that helps us make sense of the data. Statistical techniques allow us to calculate, with a specified degree of accuracy, the likelihood that the result we obtained—for example, the difference between an experimental group and a control group with regard to a variable—occurred by chance and was not due to the independent variable. However, we must always be aware of the difference between **statistical significance** and *psychological significance*. We can run an experiment and obtain "highly significant" results according to the criteria we have set, but the effect we observe might be so small that it is of no importance; that is, of no psychological significance. If smoking two cigarettes leads to a 20-percent drop in some measure of stress, that is probably an important finding. If it leads to a 0.5-percent drop, that is most likely totally unimportant, regardless of how statistically significant it is. Unfortunately, we can often be blinded by the statistical significance. We must also take into account the *size* of the effect that the independent variable produced.

Three different types of experimental methods are discussed in the pages that follow: **laboratory experiments**, **field experiments** and **quasi-experiments**.

The laboratory experiment

Most social psychological experiments are conducted in a laboratory setting. Apart from the obvious convenience, there are compelling reasons to bring behaviour into the laboratory for careful scrutiny. First, carrying out experiments in a natural setting is very difficult. The researcher cannot always eliminate extraneous variables; nor can he or she sometimes even foresee the potential sources of such variables. Second, since social behaviour is complex, the researcher must usually reduce it to its component parts, then study each of them in turn to understand how several variables interact to determine behaviour.

However, every method has its strengths and its weaknesses, and the laboratory experiment does have a number of drawbacks. Although the experiment seems straightforward enough, it is actually complex; to avoid being misled by the results, we must take into account a number of important considerations (some of which apply to research in general).

RANDOMIZATION Experimental research, unlike survey research, is not usually concerned with judging the population on the basis of the sample. Rather, **random assignment** is used to generate two or more groups that are presumed to be the same with regard to the characteristic being measured, so that later we can judge whether an independent variable led to changes in a dependent variable. Indeed, the notion that the various samples are undifferentiated prior to the treatment is crucial to the logic of the experiment. Therefore, when we form our groups, we want to be reasonably sure that there is no difference between them with respect to any important variable. Generally, this is done by assigning research participants randomly to conditions. Though random assignment does not allow us to rule out absolutely the possibility of differences among the groups, it makes differences less likely. Furthermore, when we apply statistical analysis to our results, the techniques take into account the possibility that the differences we observed could have arisen by chance at the time we assigned participants to groups.

If we had a great deal of time and a large research participant pool, we might evaluate each research participant on a large number of potentially relevant variables and then assign research participants to groups in such a way that the groups were more or less the same with regard to these variables. This technique is called *matching* and is used only infrequently due to the time, effort and difficulty involved.

EXPERIMENTER EFFECTS The experimenter, knowing the hypothesis under study, can unintentionally influence the research participants to act in a way that confirms his hypothesis (Rosenthal, 1966). Such influences are called **experimenter effects**. Suppose, following the earlier example, we have randomly divided research participants into two groups, and each group is told that they are in a study of group decision-making. For one group, the experimental group, open packages of cigarettes are positioned around the room for their use, while for the control group, the same cigarettes are available, but their packages have been removed. The idea is to see whether or not the manipulation produces differences in cigarette consumption. However, if the experimenter is present, he or she may unconsciously act somewhat differently with the experimental group—for example, smiling when someone in the control group takes a cigarette (for the hypothesis is that more subjects in that group will do so), but not smiling when people in the experimental group take a cigarette. This nondeliberate behaviour

---

FOCUS ON RESEARCH

Importance of Controls

Control groups are essential to the evaluation of causal relationships, as this anecdote about the assessment of surgical procedures, recounted by a physician, makes clear: "One day when I was a junior medical student, a very important Boston surgeon visited the school and delivered a great treatise on a large number of patients who had undergone successful operations for vascular reconstruction. At the end of the lecture, a young student at the back of the room timidly asked, 'Do you have any controls?' Well, the great surgeon drew himself up to his full height, hit the desk and said, 'Do you mean did I not operate on half of the patients?' The hall grew very quiet then. The voice at the back of the room very hesitantly replied, 'Yes, that's what I had in mind.' Then the visitor's fist really came down as he thundered, 'Of course not. That would have doomed half of them to their death.' God, it was quiet then, and one could scarcely hear the small voice ask, 'Which half?'" (Peacock, 1972).

may influence the subjects' behaviour in a manner that supports the hypothesis. Moreover, whether the experimenter also smokes might have an influence on research participants' behaviour.

This is the reason for using blind and double blind techniques. When the research participants are unaware which group they belong to (they are "blind"), they cannot act to support the experimenter's hypothesis, even if they know what it is. When the experimenter who interacts with the research participants is also unaware of the research participants' group (the "double-blind" situation), then she cannot react differently to research participants in the two groups.

RESEARCH PARTICIPANT EFFECTS Research participants can introduce artefact into an experiment in two ways. The first is through guessing or inferring the research hypothesis. The term **demand characteristics** was coined by Martin Orne (1962) to describe characteristics of the experimental situation that seem to cry out for, or "demand," a certain response. A demand characteristic is any cue that gives the research participant an idea, whether correct or incorrect, about the hypothesis under investigation. Consequently, the helpful or compliant research participant, rather than responding spontaneously, may well respond in a manner that supports the perceived hypothesis (Adair, 1973).

A second potential source of artefact is one we first encountered in our earlier discussion of nonexperimental methods—that of evaluation apprehension and social comparison theory. As research participants attempt to "look good" in the eyes of the experimenter, whom they may view as judging them, they may tailor their reactions to the experiment accordingly (Rosenberg, 1969).

It is important to recognize that behaviour in the laboratory is also "real" behaviour. The psychological experiment is a unique social psychological situation, in which people assume the role of research participants being directed by an experimenter. These situations often generate suspicion, since research participants cannot know for certain what is being studied or observed (Adair & Spinner, 1983).

GENERALIZABILITY Much concern has been expressed over the narrowness and lack of realism of many social psychological experiments. Perhaps, the criticism goes, the behaviour observed in the laboratory has little or nothing to do with what occurs in the "real world." The debate about this issue has raged for some time now,

and will no doubt continue. However, in defence of the laboratory experiment, we must be careful to distinguish between experimental realism and mundane realism. **Experimental realism** is defined as the extent to which the experimental situation "grabs" research participants and involves them, so that they react naturally to the situation rather than as they might think appropriate in the laboratory situation (Aronson & Carlsmith, 1968). **Mundane realism** refers to the extent to which the laboratory situation is similar to some situation of interest in the outside world.

While experimental realism is essential, mundane realism is less important than one might think. Even when a situation is "realistic," it does not necessarily follow that the research participants react to it as they would outside the laboratory. After all, they are still aware that they are in an experiment, and are unlikely to become so involved in the situation that they forget this fact (Carlsmith, Ellsworth & Aronson, 1976). What is most important is the *meaning* of what is happening to the research participants, not the external appearances (Berkowitz & Donnerstein, 1982). Thus, in a study of aggressiveness, if a research participant really believes that he is causing pain to another research participant, the results of such a study should generalize to other situations in which research participants have a similar belief, whatever the situation.

Experimental and mundane realism are related in meaning to external validity and internal validity (Campbell & Stanley, 1963). **External validity** refers to the degree to which the behaviour observed in the laboratory corresponds to "real" behaviour in the outside world. **Internal validity**, on the other hand, refers to the degree to which changes in dependent variables have been brought about as a result of changes in independent variables, rather than by some uncontrolled extraneous variable. Obviously, internal validity is absolutely essential, or our results will not be useful. Yet without external validity, we cannot generalize to the "real" world.

The field experiment

One way to increase external validity (as well as mundane realism) is through the **field experiment**—an experiment run not in the laboratory but in the "real world." As in a laboratory experiment, two or more groups of research participants are formed, one a control group, and the experimenter manipulates an independent variable. Research participants in field experiments have no idea that research is being conducted or that their behaviour is being monitored. As a result, the procedure is a nonreactive one, and demand characteristics and evaluation apprehension among the unwitting participants are ruled out. Random assignment occurs automatically in field experiments: the research participants are those who at a given moment happen to be passing a street corner or lining up at an ice cream parlour. In choosing the locale, however, the experimenter must be sensitive to the possibility that only certain types of people frequent the area chosen; thus, the results may not be generally applicable. For example, if we carried out a study in Ottawa's National Arts Centre, it is likely that the research participants would be above average in income and education. A similar study carried out in a pool hall would probably involve people who are less well educated. However, sometimes the experimenter can randomly assign research participants to groups—for example, in a field experiment at a summer camp, one could, with the cooperation of parents and staff, randomly assign children to different "teams."

You might imagine repeating the laboratory experiment described above in the context of a field experiment. Perhaps one could arrange to leave cigarettes either in packages, or with the packaging removed, in various conference rooms at a large convention, and have observers record the number of people in each room and the number of cigarettes consumed. You can also imagine a number of extraneous variables that would have to be dealt with—for example, are the people who go to one particular room in any way different from those who go to another? Perhaps people self-select in some way, on the basis of how close the room is to the washrooms, for example, or on the topic of discussion, if the topics vary from room to room. (Of course, these days, this kind of experiment would be difficult to do because of the plethora of public smoking restrictions.)

A good example of an actual field experiment is provided by Doob and Gross (1968). They wanted to test the notion that frustration leads to aggression (the "frustration-aggression hypothesis") in a natural setting. It occurred to them that traffic jams are a natural source of frustration. However, it is difficult to create a traffic jam for an experiment! Instead, they examined what happened when a driver (a confederate) stalled at a traffic light. They used horn honking as a measure of aggression, and then studied a factor that might influence such aggression—the social status of the driver as reflected by the status (high or low) of the stalled car.

They found, as expected, that there was more honking (i.e., "aggression") aimed at the low-status driver.

Despite the advantages of the field experiment with regard to external validity, it has important shortcomings:

- The field situation makes it more difficult to control or eliminate extraneous variables. In each situation, researchers must carefully evaluate whether the experiment is still worthwhile, in light of the trade-off. What would have happened in the Doob study had a police car cruised by? Such extraneous influences are difficult to control and, indeed, the experimenter may not even be aware of them.

- Accurate measurement of the dependent variable is also more difficult in such real-life situations. Horn honking is easy enough to measure if only one car is honking, but what if several are honking? Should we record the overall decibel level? How would we differentiate between the level caused by the honking and that caused by the background noise? It is not easy to count the number, or to measure the duration, of a number of horn honks occurring simultaneously.

The quasi-experiment: Taking advantage of real life

Sometimes events in the real world provide the opportunity to study the effects of naturally occurring changes in some social psychological variable of interest to the researcher. The researcher has no control over the "independent" variable, but takes advantage of events that happen to be occurring. Such an approach is referred to as a **quasi-experiment**. For example, we might choose research participants at random from each of two border cities at the Canada–U.S.A. border—Windsor and Detroit, for example. Given that the U.S.A. has not introduced graphic tobacco labelling, we could then measure attitudes towards drinking and smoking in the two samples. Such a study is called a **control group post-test design**, since there is a kind of control group. However, each group is only measured once, after the event of interest has taken place (in this case, the introduction of the graphic labels in Canada). Of course, we have no way of knowing whether any observed differences are due to the labels *per se* or due to pre-existing differences between the two groups.

Another quasi-experimental design is the **single group pre-test/post-test design**. In this case, research participants are measured before and after some event that is not under the researcher's control, but is scheduled to occur. Thus, we could measure individuals' tobacco consumption for, say, two months before the introduction of the new labels, and then again for a period of two months afterwards. An actual example is the research carried out by Joy, Kimball and Zabrack (1986) (discussed in detail in Chapter 11), in which the aggressiveness of children was measured before, and two years after, the introduction of television to a small, remote British Columbia logging town. While the results of such a study are inherently interesting, it is difficult to know what has caused the results. Was the introduction of television responsible for any observed changes in aggressiveness? Or did aggressiveness change over the years between the times of measurement for reasons having nothing to do with television? The quasi-experiment provides no answer to these questions.

The correlational approach

Under some research conditions, it is impossible to divide research participants into two groups and compare their scores after exposing one group to a treatment variable. A researcher might wish, for example, to relate various behavioural measures to early childhood experience. In such cases, a **correlational approach** is often necessary.

As researchers of human social behaviour, we are interested in learning what factors determine behaviour. One way of gaining insight is to search for variables that seem to "go together," or, in mathematical terms, are "correlated." Suppose that we want to assess the influence of education campaigns on smoking rates in general, and we choose to compare a number of Canadian cities. We might use the amount of money, per capita, spent on the campaign as a measure of its "vigour." Then, we would also obtain for each city the average rate of tobacco consumption some time after the campaign. Suppose that when we arrange the cities in increasing order with regard to the per capita expenditure on anti-tobacco education, we find that the smoking rate decreases in a more or less regular fashion. We would say that these two variables are *negatively correlated*. If, on the other hand, we find that as the amount of money spent on education increases, so does the smoking rate (an unlikely outcome, one would hope!), we would say that the two variables are *positively correlated*.

Correlation and causality

It is tempting to impute a causal relationship between variables that show a strong correlation. Using our original example, a strong negative correlation between amount of money spent on anti-tobacco education and smoking rates is consistent with the hypothesis that the former causes the latter, that the educational messages lower smoking rates. However, it could also be that the educational campaigns have no effect at all, and that the correlation reflects the influence of a third variable—for example, the general attitude towards smoking in a particular community. It would not be surprising if in those cities where people are most concerned about the dangers of tobacco, people not only want money to be spent on tobacco education, but also smoke less. We should not conclude, even on the basis of a strong correlation, that one of the variables is the cause of variation in the other.

Regression analysis

Regression analysis is an extension of the basic correlational analysis described above, but involves more than two variables and allows the researcher to measure the influence each of several variables has on a particular variable of interest. For example, by measuring the amount a person smokes, along with some numerical representation of the risk the person associates with smoking, his or her general risk-taking propensity, age, and, say, caffeine consumption, and then calculating the correlations among these variables, we could establish a formula that relates tobacco consumption to a weighted sum of the other four variables. This would indicate the relative importance of each of the four variables in terms of the tendency for participants to smoke.

The experimental versus the correlational approach

Given that the experimental approach provides so much more control over situations than the nonexperimental approach and allows us to draw causal inferences, why would we ever choose to use the correlational approach to study human behaviour? The fact is that each approach has its strengths and weaknesses. While the experimental approach allows us to test causal hypotheses, it is tied to the rigid necessity of assigning research participants to groups, manipulating an independent variable and keeping extraneous variables at bay. We may not be able to bend important variables to our control or provide a great enough range within the experiment to illuminate important social questions. By contrast, the correlational approach allows for the study of a large number of variables at the same time. Although the strength of the experimental method in making causal inferences is emphasized in psychology, a caution is in order. Remember the problem of generalizability. Because we infer causal relationships in an experiment, we should not assume that the same relationships exist outside the laboratory. In the real world, many other factors will interact with and possibly change the effects of these variables. Moreover, the experiment by its very nature directs attention to the ways in which behaviour changes as a result of the independent variable, but overlooks the ways in which behaviour stays the *same* (*behavioural stabilities*). Such stabilities are more likely to be detected in **longitudinal correlational studies**—that is, studies in which two or more variables are measured on the same research participants at several different points in time (Bowers, 1973). Moreover, powerful statistical techniques are emerging for the analysis of longitudinal correlational data; these will allow causal inferences to be drawn, though not with the clarity obtained in the experimental setting.

Meta-analysis

In many areas of social psychology, published reports of research findings abound, not all of them consistent. **Meta-analysis** is a statistical technique that can help make sense out of such collections of data. By combining all the relevant studies reported in the literature with respect to a given research hypothesis, and by treating each study outcome as a single observation in a collection of observations, the magnitude of an experimental effect can be estimated.

Going back to our smoking example, suppose a search of the literature revealed 40 studies of smoking that address the hypothesis that men are more likely than women to be influenced to take up smoking when they watch sporting events such as car racing that are sponsored by cigarette companies (something that is no longer allowed in Canada). Suppose that the data in 20 of the studies supported the hypothesis, but that the other 20 studies found no significant difference between men and women. On the face of it, we might think that the studies cancel each other out—half found an effect of gender, half did not.

However, suppose that upon further examination, we find that in 10 of the 20 studies in which no significant effect was found, the nonsignificant difference lay in the direction predicted by the hypothesis. Then, in 30 of the 40 studies, the data lay in the direction predicted by the hypothesis, suggesting a situation quite different from the 20-20 stand-off that first appeared to be the case.

This is a simple form of meta-analysis, a statistical technique devised by Glass, McGaw and Smith (1981) that treats each study of a particular phenomenon as a single observation in a collection of such observations. Although an individual study may not be significant, it is taken to support the hypothesis if its data lie in the direction predicted by the hypothesis. Thus, even a study that seems to have failed to replicate can contribute to a statistical conclusion about the strength and robustness of a phenomenon. Meta-analyses of various social phenomena—such as aggression, prosocial behaviour, and so on—are being used more and more in social psychology to help make sense out of collections of sometimes conflicting findings.

Of course, a meta-analytic conclusion is only as good as the studies upon which it is based. Forty poorly designed studies produce poor or uninterpretable data, whether the studies are considered individually or as a collection. Moreover, a publication bias may seriously distort meta-analyses, in that studies failing to find a significant effect are unlikely to be published. (This is referred to as the **file-drawer problem**, since studies with nonsignificant outcomes are likely to be filed away and never presented publicly.) Thus, if 10 studies find an effect and 20 do not, but all 10 of the former and only a few of the latter are published, a meta-analysis would suggest that a significant effect has been found, when, in fact, most studies found nothing.

Cross-Cultural Research

Most social psychological research has been carried out in North America, primarily in the United States, using undergraduate university students as research participants in laboratory experiments. While this approach is certainly convenient for researchers, it creates a serious problem in that Canadian and American undergraduates are not typical of people in their own societies, let alone of those in the rest of the world (Endler & Speer, 1998).

Research carried out in other cultural settings is very important for a number of reasons. First, of course, the findings of any experiment are much more convincing if they can be **replicated** in diverse populations. Second, culture itself, often ignored in the study of social behaviour, is important for the construction of basic theory in social psychology as well as other areas of psychology (Miller, 1999). One should not assume, however, that culture is strictly defined by geography—that, for example, Swedes are different from Argentines because they live in separate parts of the world (Segall, Lonner & Berry, 1998). In the modern "global village"—and this is especially true in most large urban centres in Canada—people from many different cultural backgrounds mix, mingle, work and share. We all too often use Canadian research participants without paying any attention to the diverse cultural backgrounds from which they come.

Notwithstanding the advantages of doing it, cross-cultural research poses problems (Berry, 1978a). Research methods may be difficult to adapt. Verbal instructions, interviews or questionnaires must be translated into other languages, and the translations must be accurate and equivalent in nuance. It may be troublesome or impossible to find equivalents in several languages of slang, idioms or expressions such as "hassle," "once bitten, twice shy," or "on-line." References to famous personalities or events in one society may be meaningless or, at the very least, not equivalent to students of other societies. For example, a widely used IQ test developed in the United States asks respondents to name the first president of the United States. In adapting this test for Canadians, we cannot assume that Canadians are just as familiar with George Washington, or that if we substitute Sir John A. Macdonald, his name would be as familiar to Canadians as Washington is to Americans.

Situations may also have different meanings in different cultures, confounding the experimental results. To be a research participant in a psychology experiment may, in itself, be a more profound or unusual experience to an Indian or African than to a North American student, because discussion of human relationships has permeated the consciousness of North America more than it has that of some other countries. Experimental manipulations may not represent the same processes in different cultures; for example, being confronted with a group opinion contrary to one's own may be experienced as strong social pres-

sure to conform in one culture but not in another. Similarly, our criteria for measuring a particular behavioural result may not make sense in another culture. For example, our criteria for measuring a leader (e.g., the person who speaks the most, whose ideas are most acceptable, who is selected by a group vote) may not be applicable in an Asian culture.

Research problems may also be defined differently in different cultures. Sampson (1977) has described how the highly individualistic values of U.S. society (a subject that is discussed in more detail in Chapter 4) have shaped much of contemporary psychology. Thus, American social psychologists emphasize research on many problems concerning group influences against people taking individual initiative: why people conform; why they obey authority; why they are persuaded; why people in groups are more likely than individuals to accept wrongdoing and less likely to help in an emergency. Social psychologists in cultures more oriented towards group welfare and communal values might be more interested in why people do *not* conform—perhaps defining the phenomenon as "anti-solidarity behaviour." In short, the researchers who ask the questions and define the problems are inevitably influenced by their own culture.

In the final analysis, our objective is to arrive at an understanding of human behaviour that is universal—valid across time, groups and societies. Reaching this goal involves two different approaches (Berry, 1978a). The first is to seek principles of social behaviour that hold true for all cultures, and attempt to construct a framework that allows for comparison among cultures. For example, "family" is a concept that is universally meaningful and valid, although the details of family life vary considerably from one culture to another. The second approach is to carry out intensive research within one particular culture, using the concepts and worldview of that culture, and not imposing a framework derived from outside that culture. For example, strong in-group identification and pride may be highly valued and encouraged in some multicultural societies, but seen as equivalent to prejudice in others.

Certainly, cooperative research across cultures is valuable, particularly in showing us how far our theories can be generalized. Berry argues for the development of many distinctive, local, social psychologies, each studying problems as defined by that particular culture. Taken collectively, they may furnish the basis

Situations may have different
meaning in different cultures.

for the development of a truly universal social psychology. Over the past 30 years, interest in cross-cultural psychology has grown to the extent that it can now be considered a separate area of psychology.

Ethical Considerations
in Research

As we have seen, the researcher who carries out a psychology experiment is in a position of some authority over the research participant. This authority, especially if age or academic position also confers a difference of status, creates a relationship of trust whereby the research participants assume that the experimenter will not harm or exploit them. Researchers must act ethically and responsibly so participants do not suffer in any way as a result of the research.

Sometimes ethical problems arise not because of what is done to research participants, but because of what is *not* done. This is often most evident in medical research. For example, do researchers have the right to assign disease sufferers to a control group when studying a drug that could halt the progress of a deadly disease such as AIDS? If research proves the drug useful, some of those in the control group, who were denied the treatment, might, in fact, have died as a result. On the other hand, without controlled stud-

ies, how can we determine whether a treatment is effective and without serious risks?

Such dilemmas are rare, but not unknown, in social psychological research. For example, in a study of elderly residents in a nursing home, Langer and Rodin (1976) found that those in the experimental group (who were encouraged to take part in decision-making and thus live somewhat more independently) showed considerable improvement in alertness, activity and general well-being. While 93 percent of those in the experimental group showed overall improvement, 71 percent of the control group were judged to have become more debilitated over the study period. During the 18-month period after the intervention, 15 percent of the research participants in the experimental group died, compared to 30 percent in the control group (Rodin & Langer, 1977). Without the research, the importance of participation in decision-making would not be evident; yet in retrospect, we may regret that those in the control group became more debilitated or even died, when they might have benefited from the intervention.

Society in general and researchers in particular have become much more sensitive to and concerned about ethical issues in research in recent years. Indeed, the three major research granting agencies in Canada (Social Sciences and Humanities Research Council; National Science and Engineering Research Council; Canadian Institutes of Health Research) have recently issued a major joint policy statement ("Tri-Council

Policy Statement: Ethical Conduct for Research Involving Humans") that has been implemented at all Canadian universities. The new policies essentially dictate how ethical concerns will be dealt with in research involving human subjects, whether that research is supported financially by one of those agencies or not (Adair, 2001).

Psychologists have for many years been governed by their own codes of ethics that relate to both the application of psychology (as in clinical psychology), and the use of research participants, both human and animal, in research. These codes reflect concern for the welfare of society, respect for science and psychology, and, of course, the welfare of the research participant or client. The American Psychological Association's Code of Ethics (American Psychological Association, 2002) includes a section that deals with research involving human research participants. The Code of Ethics of the Canadian Psychological Association, which is general enough to apply to research as well as applied practice, is built around four primary ethical principles (Sinclair, Poizner, Gilmour-Barrett & Randall, 1987): respect for the dignity of the person; responsibility to society; integrity in relationships; and responsible caring. Although the fourth principle may be more pertinent to applied psychology, all of them have something to say about how we should treat people who come under our influence, whether as clients, patients or experimental research participants.

Among the ethical concerns with which researchers have to cope, the following have received the most attention: protection from harm; the right to privacy; the practice of deception; the need for informed consent and debriefing; and the social responsibility of researchers.

Protection from harm

Researchers must, obviously, protect research participants from physical harm. For instance, if electrical shocks are being administered, researchers must ensure that the shock apparatus will not harm research participants. However, suppose that the researcher is running a field experiment to observe the influence of the apparent status of a confederate, as indicated by the way she is dressed, on the extent to which pedestrians copy the confederate's action and cross a street against a red light. If a research participant in such a field experiment were to be struck by a car as a result, is the researcher guilty of failing to protect the research

participant from harm? And might not a research participant be put at risk during future jaywalking, which might occur because of such modelling behaviour?

While ethics committees are unlikely to approve research that poses any such physical danger to the research participant, the possibility of emotional harm is often more difficult to assess in advance. Situations that most people would find benign could conceivably be distressing for certain vulnerable individuals. If you participated in an experiment that led you to believe you were in a real emergency situation, and you acted only to save yourself, would this knowledge be emotionally harmful? Some research participants might benefit from the experience, striving in the future to think more about helping others, while others might conceivably suffer long-term loss of self-esteem. As will be discussed later, although appropriate debriefing procedures should prevent any enduring emotional damage, the researcher must still be sensitive to the possibility of such harm, and not simply assume that debriefing will take care of everything.

Right to privacy

We take for granted in our society that except under unusual circumstances sanctioned by some legal or medical authority, other people have no right to pry into our affairs without our knowledge or permission. In case-study research or survey studies, this does not usually pose a problem, since the participants know what information is being solicited. Threats to the right to privacy arise primarily in experiments in which deception is used and research participants do not know what aspect of their behaviour is being studied, and in field studies and field experiments, in which research participants do not even know they are participants. For example, suppose a researcher stealthily goes through garbage cans in your neighbourhood and counts how many empty cigarette packages each contains. This may provide useful data for a study of smoking behaviour, but if done without your knowledge, it provides information about you, and not just about your smoking habits, to some individual unknown to you, but who has your address! Most people would find such research unpalatable and even threatening.

As you become more familiar with social psychological research, you will encounter experiments that have involved invasion of privacy, for example, asking intimate questions or even observing people at urinals. Yet, before concluding that such research should never be undertaken, compare the potential stress, loss of self-esteem and so on that research participants might suffer with the potential benefits; new knowledge about human behaviour that the research may provide. Such evaluations are often difficult to make, and that is why codes of ethics and ethics committees are so important.

Another aspect of the right to privacy issue is *confidentiality*. Whether or not research participants consent to allow their privacy to be invaded, researchers must maintain the confidentiality of research participants' responses, unless explicit permission has been obtained. Yet data records must be stored somewhere, and the ethical researcher needs to ensure that during data analysis, data reporting or data storage, such confidentiality is safeguarded.

Deception

The laboratory experiment has its own special ethical problems brought about by the common use of deception. It is difficult to observe research participants' natural reactions when they are aware of being observed; one of the appeals of field experiments is that research participants act naturally, since they do not know that they are participants. However, if the experimenter is clever, he can often disguise the real aim of the laboratory experiment so that research participants react almost as though they were in a real-life situation (Elms, 1982).

The use of deception was rarely used in social psychology in the 1920s and 1930s, and was not all that common in the 1940s and 1950s either, but its use mushroomed during the 1960s (Adair, Dushenko & Lindsay, 1985; Nicks, Korn & Mainieri, 1997). Between one-half and three-quarters of published social psychological research reports involve some element of deception (Christensen, 1988).

In recent years, many researchers have expressed concern about the ethics of deception (Krupat & Garonzik, 1994; Ortmann & Hertwig, 1997; Wiesenthal, 1989). Clearly, deceit presents a moral problem: to most psychologists concerned with this issue, the term *deception* means "trickery," "deceit" or "lying." It is argued not only that such dishonesty might tarnish the moral authority of professors and experimenters in the eyes of research participants (and lead to a less respectful view of science in general), but also that research participants could experience guilt or lowered self-esteem as a result of learning the true

meaning of an experimental task. What if research participants approach an experiment believing that they are going to be involved in a memory study, and leave having learned that in the face of a contrived emergency they reacted with cowardice? Does the experimenter have the right to foist this truth upon an unsuspecting individual who might otherwise never have confronted that cowardice?

The issue of deception became a major controversy with the publication of Milgram's (1963) study of obedience (see Chapter 6), in which research participants were told they were participating in a study of learning that involved their administration of progressively stronger electric shocks to a "learner." Milgram was heavily criticized (e.g., Baumrind, 1964) for exposing his research participants to potentially disturbing emotional reactions when they learned the true nature of the experiment and, in that context, evaluated their own behaviour. Milgram (1964) countered that the debriefing of the research participants had prevented

What would be the ethical implications of secretly observing and recording the behaviour of this person for research purposes?

any emotional damage, since they learned that no one had actually been hurt and that their behaviour had been reasonable given the circumstances. Psychiatric interviews of the research participants one year after the experiment seemed to indicate that there had been no enduring effects on them.

Certainly, social psychological knowledge is much richer because of the Milgram research; it has brought about an understanding of human compliance with authority that was formerly inconceivable. Yet the ethical dilemma remains: Is it, in principle, ever acceptable to deceive research participants, to decide for them what level of emotional stress is tolerable? If we rule out deception, we make much social psychological research all but impossible. Do we stop our research? In so doing, may we not one day be judged guilty of a greater sin, that of failing to use the powerful methodology of science to understand human social behaviour so that we can learn to reduce aggression, diminish prejudice and enhance quality of life?

On the other hand, perhaps psychologists worry too much about the effects of deception. No one has yet shown any long-term negative consequences resulting from deception in a social psychological experiment (Elms, 1982). Indeed, *most* deception in social psychology experiments is so benign that few would fault it seriously, except on the general principle that we have no right to deceive. After all, if a research participant is led to believe that she is participating in a study of attitudes, but the real aim of the study is to see under what conditions research participants are most likely to help the experimenter pick up a stack of books that is "accidentally" dropped on the floor, how likely is it that research participants will be upset emotionally as a result? Empirical studies of the reactions of participants in experiments using deception indicate that they do not appear to share psychologists' distaste for deception. Rather, they are more likely to view the deception as a necessary withholding of information or a necessary ruse or misrepresentation (Christensen, 1988; Smith, 1983).

Informed consent

Obtaining **informed consent** is one way of safeguarding the rights of research participants. If research participants are told as fully as possible what will happen to them in the experiment (without destroying the effectiveness of the experimental manipulation), they

can freely choose whether to participate. Such informed consent will also help curb resentment towards whatever deception is practised, for if research participants are told that it is impossible to describe the experiment in full detail without influencing their behaviour in it, they are likely to accept the necessity for deception when they eventually learn of it.

Debriefing

Another protection against any long-term harm fostered by deception is the practice of **debriefing**. Most social psychologists go to great lengths to debrief their research participants following an experiment through dehoaxing and desensitization (Holmes, 1976).

Dehoaxing involves informing research participants that they have been deceived and explaining the purpose of the experiment. **Desensitization** is intended to help the research participants accept the new information they have about themselves and put it into context, and to respond to their questions and anxieties. Undoing the effects of the experimental manipulation includes such actions as ensuring that research participants who have been misinformed about real-life events leave the experiment with accurate information. For example, undoing the effects of the manipulation is especially important in pornography research in which research participants are shown pornographic materials, sometimes repeatedly. If, as some researchers indicate, such exposure leads some male research participants to become more accepting of myths about rape (e.g., "rape victims usually enjoy being raped"), particular care must be taken to undo this effect. Some researchers in this area have worked to establish satisfactory ethical procedures to guide the actual practices involved in debriefing, and have even presented evidence suggesting that careful and appropriate debriefing can lead to a lower rate of acceptance of rape myths than existed prior to the experiment (Check & Malamuth, 1984, 1990).

Alternatives to deception

What if we were to try to conduct experiments without using deception at all? Kelman (1967) advocated an approach in which research participants **role-play**. Instead of being deceived about the nature of the research, research participants are given a description of a situation by the experimenter and then asked to behave as they think other people would in such a situation. However, as you can imagine, role-playing studies have not proven very useful to psychologists, for all they tell us is how the research participants *think* others would act in that situation. The researcher's intuition, informed by a thorough knowledge of the scientific literature, would in all likelihood provide a better guide.

A related and somewhat more useful technique is that of **simulation**. Again, no deception is employed. In this case, however, the research participants act and react to each other and to the situation rather than simply playing a role corresponding to how they think others would act. For example, the Stanford Prison study, discussed in Chapter 14, involved putting volunteers into a mock prison for several days. Some were given the role of prisoner, and others the role of guard. Their behaviour was observed as the "guards" and "prisoners" interacted over time. After a short while, the simulation ceased to be make-believe, and the impact on the participants was so strong that the simulation had to be prematurely brought to a close. Although simulations can evoke powerful emotional responses and therefore appear to have both greater experimental and greater mundane realism, they pose several problems. First, although outright deception is not involved, there is another serious ethical question: If the researcher can foresee that the research participants may experience discomfort, is it ethical to expose them to that discomfort even if they are warned in advance? Moreover, what use can be made of the results? Can we be certain that the observed outcome was truly an indication of how people in general would react in such situations, and not merely idiosyncratic? We may be able to generalize from our results less than we think, despite apparent mundane realism.

As you can see, role-playing and simulation cannot eliminate the need for deception in social psychological research. While informed consent and debriefing can help avoid emotional harm, there is no general solution to the problem of deception, except to say that the experimenter must take all reasonable precautions to ensure that risk of harm is minimal, and that even this risk is justified by the importance of what might be learned from the experiment. Canadian universities and granting agencies require that experiments involving human research participants first be cleared by an ethics committee whose task it is to protect research participants from undue exploitation, unnecessary deception or potential harm. Ethics committees, which evaluate the work of peers, are usually more objective in making judgments than individual researchers who are eager to verify an hypothesis.

Social responsibility of researchers

What obligations do researchers have to the society in which they live? While most psychology research is unlikely to harm society or its various subgroups, some research has a great potential for harm: for example, research that is biased because of the influence of racism, sexism or ageism (the tendency to view older people in terms of dismissive stereotypes), which then produces data that feed such prejudices.

Consider this example of potential harm: In January 1989, Philippe Rushton delivered a paper at the annual conference of the American Association for the Advancement of Science entitled "Evolutionary biology and heritable traits (with reference to Oriental-White-Black differences)" (Rushton, 1989). The paper built upon claims made in earlier publications (Rushton, 1988a, 1988b) that Orientals, blacks and whites constitute three distinct races, and that blacks are the least "evolved" while Orientals are the most "evolved." Rushton argued that his review of the empirical literature demonstrated that blacks are not only on average the least intelligent of the three groups, but also least altruistic, most licentious, most criminal, and have the most children but are the least nurturing towards them.

Rushton's claims elicited outrage from other researchers (e.g., Weizmann, Wiener, Wiesenthal & Ziegler, 1990; Zuckerman & Brody, 1988), as well as from politicians and the public. They attacked him for selecting only those data that supported his model, often drawn from sources other scientists viewed as absurd and scientifically inadmissible. He was criticized for distorting the work of biologists by taking their findings out of context and making claims that the original researchers had not made. Furthermore, he had failed to examine or recognize the powerful effects of environment and culture on, among other things, sexual behaviour and fertility. The major problem with his work was an assumption that race characteristics—including sexual behaviour—are primarily genetically determined.

Was Rushton unethical in publishing and publicly stating his findings? Was his university at fault for allowing such research to be carried out? Can we brand research *unethical* on the basis of charges that it is sloppily executed and incorrectly interpreted?

All researchers and scholars place high value on freedom of inquiry and freedom of expression. The principle of academic freedom was developed to protect scholars from the dictates of people who might have a special interest in what can or cannot be researched, and what can or cannot be said. However, those freedoms place special responsibility on researchers to ensure that their data are not misinterpreted or misused to the detriment of others.

Given the gravity of Rushton's claims and the importance his academic stature might impart to them, and given the tremendous, harmful influence they might have on race relations and the treatment of blacks, Rushton had a particular responsibility to be cautious in his selection of data and in the conclusions he reached. While he may claim that he did exercise such caution, it is in these socially sensitive situations that ethics committees are most needed—to ensure that the research is properly conducted, and justifiable, given its potential for harm.

Summary

1. Science is an effective method of gaining knowledge and understanding. It consists of formulating hypotheses, testing them through systematic observation and building theories from these findings.

2. Precise measurement is the basic tool of science. In social psychology it is often difficult to translate a hypothetical construct (such as "attitude") into an operational definition (i.e., a measure). Measurement problems include the following: (a) reliability—does the measure yield consistent readings? (b) validity—does it measure what it is intended to measure? (c) reactivity—does the measure affect the very thing that is being measured? and (d) sampling—are the data obtained representative of a population of interest?

3. In social psychology, both experimental and nonexperimental methods of research are used. All methods have both advantages and disadvantages.

4. Nonexperimental research involves studying the covariation among several characteristics, or variables. Nonexperimental research methods include (a) archival methods; (b) case studies; (c) survey interviews or questionnaires; (d) field studies, in which behaviour is observed systematically in a natural setting; and (e) qualitative research.

5. In experimental research, research participants are assigned randomly to experimental and con-

trol groups so that we assume the groups are identical before the experiment. An independent variable is manipulated so that its effects can be observed by comparison between the two groups. Other confounding variables that may influence results are controlled. Experimental research methods include (a) laboratory experiments; (b) field experiments; and (c) quasi-experiments.

6. The outcomes of both nonexperimental and experimental research can be biased by the expectations and unintentional actions of experimenters, as well as by the actions of subjects who act as they believe the experimenter wants them to act (demand characteristics) or who try to create a "good" impression of themselves (evaluation apprehension).

7. Generalizations drawn from experiments are limited by (a) external validity, i.e., how comparable the experimental situation is to a real-life situation; and (b) internal validity, the extent to which the results were due to manipulation of the independent variable rather than to artefact.

8. Correlational methods, while limited with regard to cause and effect relationships, provide a powerful tool for examining how variables interrelate, and for analyzing both behavioural stability and longitudinal change.

9. Ethical concerns in social psychological research include protection from harm; the right to privacy; the use of deception in experiments; the need for debriefing and informed consent; and the responsibility of researchers to the society in which they live.

Further Reading

AGNEW, N.M. & PYKE, S.W. (1994). *The science game* (6th ed). Englewood Cliffs, NJ: Prentice-Hall. Excellent discussion of the nature of science and its methods, as well as the "culture" of science.

BERRY, J.W., POORTINGA, Y.P., SEGAL, M.H. & DASEN, P.R. (1997). *Cross-cultural psychology: Research and applications* (2nd ed). Boston: Allyn and Bacon. An advanced text written by Canadian and European psychologists that presents an excellent and comprehensive treatment of cross-cultural psychology. The guiding premise of the text is that basic psychological processes are universal, while cultural variables create differences in the way these processes are manifested.

CHERRY, F. (1995). *The stubborn particulars of social psychology*. London: Routledge. This collection of essays examines how social psychological research is affected by its cultural and historical context and poses important challenges to the conventional practice of social psychology.

JUDD, C.M., SMITH, E.R., & KIDDER, L.H. (1991). *Research methods in social relations* (6th ed.). Fort Worth: Holt, Rinehart, and Winston. Well-written treatment of the various research methods used by social psychologists. Includes discussion of research designs, sampling, data analysis, ethics and research report preparation.

KORN, J.H. (1997). *Illusions of reality: A history of deception in social psychology*. Albany, NY: State University of New York Press. The author reviews how deception is used in psychological research to create illusions of reality without revealing the true purpose of the experiment. Controversial experiments are discussed, and the use of deception in research is examined from an ethical perspective.

RENNIE, D. (2002). Qualitative research: History, theory and practice. Special Issue, *Canadian Psychology, 43:3*. Excellent introduction to the uses, and the implications, of qualitative research in psychology.

SHARPE, D., ADAIR, J.G. & ROESE, N.J. (1992). Twenty years of deception research: A decline in subjects' trust? *Personality and Social Psychology Bulletin, 18*, 585–590. A report of research into subjects' views of deception in social psychological experiments, and their general attitudes towards psychological research.

WIESENTHAL, D.L. (1989). Recent developments in social psychology in response to ethical concerns. In D. MacNiven (Ed.), *Moral expertise: Studies in practical and professional ethics*. New York: Routledge. An excellent discussion of ethical issues in social psychological research and how the discipline is changing in response to those concerns.

 # Weblinks

Social Psychology Network (Scott Plaus)
www.socialpsychology.org/ A superb resource; links to pages with social psychology content, graduate programs, people doing research and more.

Social and Personality Section, Canadian Psychological Association
www.uwinnipeg.ca/~cpa/ Home page for Canadian researchers in social psychology.

The Qualitative Report
www.nova.edu/ssss/QR/web.html A good starting point to find out more about qualitative research methodology.

American Psychological Society: Psychological Experiments on the Net
psych.hanover.edu/research/exponnet.html Includes some ongoing social psychological studies being conducted via the Internet.

Canadian Psychological Association Code of Ethics
www.uwinnipeg.ca/~clark/research/cpaethics.html The full text of the CPA's Code of Ethics.

deception

Chapter 2

Social Perception and Cognition

It is perfectly monstrous the way people go about nowadays saying things about one behind one's back that are absolutely and entirely true.

Oscar Wilde

Reality is something the human race doesn't handle very well.

Gore Vidal

Chapter Outline

The Golden Oldie movies are full of glamorous images of smoking: Sherlock Holmes with his pipe, Groucho Marx with his cigar or James Dean and Humphrey Bogart with their cigarettes. Romantic scenes showed lovers gazing at each other through a haze of smoke, and when she asked for a "light," much more was implied. In a less romantic context, the condemned man was offered a cigarette before he faced the firing squad, the professor puffed thoughtfully on his pipe and the big cigar symbolized money and power. Politics was conducted in smoke-filled rooms, and proud new fathers passed out cigars to announce the great event. Smoking represented the sexy sophistication to which we all aspire at some time in our lives.

Times and fashions have changed, and smoking is no longer in style. Indeed, many people now think negatively of someone who smokes. That is, smoking acts as a cue to us in forming a first impression of someone. How do we form impressions of people, and how and why are these impressions affected by such factors as whether the person smokes? How do we come to a conclusion as to why people smoke?

Consider other examples. The juror listens attentively to the witnesses, trying to decide whether they are telling the truth. The student attends the first lecture in social psychology to find out if the professor is interesting or boring, easy or demanding, concerned or distant. While two people converse on a blind date, each wonders, *What is she or he like? Does she or he like me?* Negotiators for labour and management sit down at the bargaining table and immediately begin to size each other up. Winning in games such as poker requires the player not only to discern what the other players have in their hands but also to evaluate their own cards. The personnel manager interviews the applicant to find out whether that person is suitable for the job. The journalist tries to find out what the politician is "really" like and what policies we can expect.

When deciding how to dress this morning, we were influenced not by the objective temperature, but how warm or cold it felt (for instance, a temperature of about 20°C would be comfortable in April, rather cool in August and very warm in January). In other words, we actively construct our reality. Similarly, our impressions of others do not depend directly on what *is* happening but on what we *think* is happening. That is, we respond in terms of our own experience and our own interpretations of people, events and occurrences in our lives. And while we all agree that people are complicated, we tend to arrive at such decisions about them rather quickly and without much conscious thought. Indeed, Fiske and Taylor (1984) describe us as "cognitive misers," expending as little effort as necessary to make judgments about people.

Social psychologists have studied the processes of social perception and cognition, and have made some intriguing discoveries. This chapter begins with a discussion of how we form impressions of people based on traits such as friendliness, honesty, sneakiness or self-discipline. The discussion then turns to the study of **attributions**, how we draw conclusions about why people act as they do. Finally, the chapter outlines more subtle processes of social cognition by which we "construct" our own view of reality and the many shortcuts we take to get there.

Human beings cannot be viewed simply as computers who process information according to the rules of logic. We will examine the extent to which we examine the evidence and then arrive at conclusions about people. In addition, we will highlight our biases as well as our rational thinking. Much of the material in this chapter is fundamental to many areas of social psychology, and will be referred to or elaborated upon in succeeding chapters. For instance, in later chapters we examine how non-verbal communication influences our judgments of others (Chapter 7), how physical attractiveness is a powerful determinant of our impressions of others (Chapter 8), and how we form judgments in the courtroom about the credibility of witnesses (Chapter 15).

Forming Impressions of People

Research on social perception began with investigating how we form initial impressions of other people, how we decide that a person is friendly, arrogant, honest, hot-tempered or interesting. In general, participants were provided with a brief description of a person or a photo of a person, in which one or a small number of traits or actions were varied, and then the participants were asked to rate the target person in terms of a set of characteristics or traits. One of the key findings from these studies concerned the existence of **central traits**, certain characteristics that will affect any other judgments that we make about that person. For instance, when participants were led to believe that a stimulus person was "warm" as opposed to "cold," they tended to make more positive judgments about that individual being popular, wise and imaginative (Asch, 1946; Kelley, 1950). Other kinds of information about a target person can also affect trait judgments. For instance, when informed that the target person was identified as a smoker, that person was rated lower on scales labelled "considerate," "calm," "honest," "healthy," "well-mannered," "happy," less self-controlled, less imaginative or less mature, and was considered to be more likely to use illegal drugs or be an inattentive driver (Dermer & Jacobsen, 1986; Dion, Dion, Coambs & Kozlowski, 1990; Polivy, Hackett & Bycio, 1979).

Of course, we notice many different traits in the same person. We may first notice that a person is attractive, and then, during conversation, discover that this person also appears arrogant. How do we combine these observations about the person to arrive at an overall evaluation? The evidence indicates that we follow a **weighted averaging model** in combining such information about the person (Anderson, 1965, 1978). That is, we keep a rough "running" average of our trait ratings in our heads, as we discover more characteristics

of the person. For example, if we find someone to be highly intelligent (perhaps 8 on a scale of 1 to 10) but only somewhat attractive (4 on a scale of 1 to 10), our overall rating of that person would fall somewhere between high positive (intelligent) and low positive (attractiveness)—around 6 on that 10-point scale. However, if attractiveness were more important to us than intelligence as a basis for judging people, then the overall rating would be weighted more towards the attractiveness scale. That is, while the average of the two ratings (8 and 4) is six, the weighted average would be less than six because attractiveness is more important to us. Of course, we don't consciously think about others in such a mathematical way, but we combine information and impressions about people as if we were doing so.

It is important to understand that people arrive at judgments rather quickly and often with minimal information. Are these first impressions lasting? Intuitively, it would seem that as we get to know someone better over time, our impressions would change and become more accurate. This hypothesis has been tested in a longitudinal study, in which participants met in groups once a week for seven weeks. Before the first meeting, each participant completed self-rating forms, and after weeks 1, 4 and 7, they rated all of the other persons in their group on the same scales. As predicted, over time, their ratings of the other people more closely matched how those other people rated themselves (Paulhus & Bruce, 1992). Thus, first impressions are important but not immutable.

Biases in impression formation

Researchers have noted two interesting biases in how first impressions of people are formed. First, most people tend to form impressions of most others that are positive rather than negative; this is known as a **positivity bias**. Consider, for example, student evaluations of their professors. At one university, students rated 97 percent of their professors as "above average," a mathematical improbability (Sears, 1983). This bias is an example of the *Pollyanna principle* (Matlin & Stang, 1978). Like Voltaire's Candide, we like to believe that we live in the "best of all possible worlds," surrounded by nice people. Of course, a minority of people do not have this bias, and indeed some cynical souls will believe the worst of others until shown otherwise.

Along with the positivity bias, our overall impression of a person will be influenced more by negative than by positive information (Fiske, 1980; Skowronski & Carlston, 1989). Indeed, the **negativity effect** causes us to form a confident and very negative overall impression of a person with one negative trait, regardless of whether the person has other positive, seemingly redeeming, characteristics (Anderson, 1965; Hamilton & Zanna, 1972). For instance, a professor who is seen as distant and "unapproachable" to students will tend to be rated negatively, even if this professor is well-prepared, lectures clearly, is scrupulously fair to students and has interesting insights to offer. Of course, we may be influenced by both the positivity bias and negativity effect at the same time in forming our overall impression (Klein, 1991).

Eye of the beholder

In forming impressions of others, people bring their own personal way of looking at the world. We have our own **implicit personality theories**—a set of unstated assumptions about human nature and people in general (Bruner & Tagiuri, 1954; Anderson & Sedikides, 1990; Sedikides & Anderson, 1994). We may believe people in general are trustworthy or untrustworthy, rational or irrational, altruistic or selfish, and independent or conformist. Implicit personality theories also concern our beliefs about what characteristics go together. For instance, many people believe that friendly people are also people to be trusted. Such assumptions tend to persist, even in the face of contradictory evidence (Anderson, Lepper & Ross, 1980).

There are also cultural differences in implicit personality theories. For instance, we often think in terms of types of people: people who are ambitious, religious or athletic. When people in Western cultures are asked to describe the artistic type of person, they will use adjectives such as creative, temperamental and unconventional. A Chinese person would be mystified by this request, because the "artistic type" is not a concept in that culture. On the other hand, in Chinese culture, people describe a type of person who is worldly, socially skilled and devoted to family (shi gu), one that does not exist as a type in Western cultures (Hoffman, Lau & Johnson, 1986). In later chapters, we will consider how people apply their implicit personality theories about the "criminal type" (Chapter 15) or the type of "persons with AIDS" (Chapter 16).

As we have developed a clearer understanding of how we process information in order to make sense of our world and the people in it, we have come to understand that there is much more to how we form impressions and judgments about people than the attachment of trait adjectives. We turn now to this line of research.

Attributions of Causality

Consider again the case of smoking. You may have a close friend who is intelligent, considerate and interesting, who has shared some important life experiences with you, and who also happens to be a smoker. Disappointed and concerned about health risks to your friend, you want to understand why he or she continues to smoke. There is a wide selection of possible explanations. Perhaps it is caused by a character flaw, perhaps by tenacious addiction, perhaps because of a fear of gaining weight, perhaps by the stress in that person's life, perhaps because of the massive advertising conducted by the cigarette companies (despite government restrictions). These explanations matter. Our conclusions about why a person smokes, pays us a compliment or disagrees with our expressed opinion will determine our reaction to that individual. That is, our interactions with others are rooted in the explanations or attributions we make about what they say and what they do.

Fritz Heider (1958), the pioneer in this area of research, argued that attributions are fundamental to social relations. For instance, when someone compliments you, your response and how you relate to that person will depend on what you believe to have caused the person to make that statement. Remember that nobody has direct access to the mind of the person who compliments you, or someone who smokes. Rather, some cues are noticed, and we apply our own "naive psychology" to try to make sense of the situation. This is the concept of an attribution.

What determines the attributions that people make? Several principles are fundamental. According to the **discounting principle** (Kelley, 1972a), people tend to accept the most likely cause and set aside or "discount" other possibilities. For example, consider the case in which the boss closely supervises a particular worker. The worker is working hard. Since the supervisor has a plausible explanation for that worker's productivity (close supervision), an alternative attribution for that worker's productivity—that she was motivated to do a good job—will be discounted (Strickland, 1958).

The discounting principle can be seen in how people react to politicians. In several studies, it has been shown that politicians are rated as having more integrity and strength when they oppose the position of their own party or when they speak before a hostile, as compared to a friendly, audience (Eagly, Wood & Chaiken, 1978; Pancer, Brown, Gregor & Claxton-Oldfield, 1992). If they follow the party line, we attribute their position to political pressure, and discount the possibility that they really mean it. This causes a dilemma faced by politicians. Of course, they must seek approval and votes from their electorate if they are to accomplish anything. However, when we attribute their behaviour to seeking votes, we also tend to discount any other possible motives for their actions, including a sincere desire to do the right thing. Similarly, when we are told that success in a task indicates that we are competent, we discount other possible explanations, such as being lucky (Braun & Wicklund, 1989). As noted earlier, we are indeed "cognitive misers."

The **covariation principle** applies when two events occur together over a number of instances. For example, suppose a person becomes very angry every time a certain topic of conversation comes up, but rarely on other occasions. We would probably attribute their anger to the topic of conversation, not to that person's temperament. In general, when one event always occurs with another, and does not occur when the other is absent, then people infer that one causes the other.

Finally, in seeking to understand people's behaviour, people use two general categories of attributed causes: *situational* and *dispositional*. Situational causes are those that explain actions in terms of the situation. For instance, the behaviour of students who take notes during lectures can be explained in terms of the demands or social norms of that situation. We attribute their "note-taking behaviour" to the situation. Dispositional causes are those that rest on the characteristics of the person. For instance, if a student were seen taking notes in the cafeteria, in the car, at the movies, in bed and in the mall, then we might attribute their behaviour to a need to take notes.

Attribution theories

Building on the principles of discounting and covariation, several attribution theories explain how people form situational or dispositional attributions. The following discussion focuses on the three theories that have proved most influential: Jones and Davis's model of correspondent inferences; Kelley's covariation model; and Weiner's model of achievement attributions. The first concerns how we make attributions in the context of a single social interaction; the second concerns attributions in a relationship over time; and the third, situations involving success or failure.

Are politicians only motivated by seeking electorate approval and votes? Why do people often discount other possibilities?

Theory of correspondent inferences

A politician promises to solve all your problems—but does she or he really mean it? Does the salesperson that invites you to "Have a good day" really care about your day? When a person tells you how attractive you are, does he or she really mean it? How closely does behaviour (a smile) correspond to a specific disposition (a friendly person)? Can we use someone's behaviour as a guide to what the person is really like, how that person is feeling, or what that person intends, particularly when we have only that one event to guide us?

At first glance, behaviour would seem to be a rich and reliable source of information. After all, "actions speak louder than words." However, at least two important factors complicate the picture. First, a person may seek to mislead others about her true feelings or nature. The poker player with a straight flush, the salesperson who knows the real bottom-line price of an automobile, the daughter who assures her mother that "everything is fine"—all are examples of people being deceptive. Second, actions often stem from situational causes. Politicians are expected to make promises, workers to do their jobs as required, students to take useful notes in lectures, and the salesperson is ordered to gush cheerfully for each customer. Their behaviour is often explained by the situation, not by a personal disposition.

The theory of **correspondent inferences** (Jones & Davis, 1965; Jones, & McGillis, 1976) concerns how we use certain cues to infer the cause of an action (see Figure 2–1). Can we infer what the person intended from their actions? What do we look for? First, we focus upon freely chosen behaviours and ignore those that are required or coerced. We may know that the excessively friendly salesperson is probably following the manager's orders, and a correspondent inference (she or he is sweet and friendly) is unlikely. Second, behaviours that produce uncommon effects—those that seem unique or out of role—are noticed. If your best friend expresses concern that you look tired, you may attribute that behaviour to the role, "That's what friends are for." However, if a real estate agent says the same thing, a dispositional attribution (correspondent inference) is much more likely. We would conclude that the agent really meant it! A third important cue is social desirability. We learn more about a person's taste in clothing if they wear pyjamas to class than if they wear jeans and a t-shirt. As well, if someone has made a choice between two alternatives, we will focus on what is unique or not common in his or her choice.

For instance, when someone decides to live in Vancouver rather than Toronto, both of them large cities, we may attribute their choice of Vancouver for its mountains and ocean location.

These inferences seem to be logical "best guesses" when we don't have much information. There are also two nonlogical biases that arise from our own reactions to an event. People tend to make more confident correspondent inference attributions when the action has a strong consequence for themselves, rather than for someone else (hedonic relevance), and when they believe that the actor *intended* to benefit or harm them (personalism). When you are the target of an insult, you are less likely to make allowance for the person having a bad day than when you see the same person insulting someone else, particularly when it is clear that it is you that he wanted to insult. A series of classic experiments supported the model of correspondent inferences (Jones & Harris, 1976; Jones, Davis & Gergen, 1961).

As we noted, the theory of correspondent inferences concerns a single act, and how we decide whether that act "corresponds" to a disposition. However, we often make attributions about members of our family and friends, people whom we see in various situations. In these cases, the attributions that we make about their behaviour follow somewhat different principles. Our discussion now turns to such cases.

Covariation model

Imagine that you are a reporter for a newspaper, who has been assigned to interview a celebrated musician visiting your city or town. The musician praises you for conducting a great interview. Why did this celebrity go out of his or her way to praise you? Consider a few possibilities. You may decide that this musician is a warm and generous person. That compliment may tell you something about yourself, that you are a skilled interviewer and reporter, and it was your behaviour that caused the person to compliment you. Or you might just explain it in terms of how celebrities and reporters usually behave in an interview situation. In other words, you might attribute the celebrity's behaviour towards you in terms of the "actor" (the person doing the action), the "entity" (the recipient of the action), or the situation in which the action took place.

How would you decide *why* the visiting celebrity paid you that compliment? Kelley (1972a) argues that people behave as "naive scientists" in the sense that we sift through various events and clues, past and present, to arrive at a "best guess" or hypothesis about the "real

FIGURE 2-1

How we decide on a
correspondent inference

Cues	Attribute of a correspondent inference
■ The act was freely chosen. ■ The act produced a non-common effect, not expected of other actions. ■ The act was not considered socially desirable (non-conforming). ■ The act had a direct impact on us (hedonic relevance). ■ The act seemed intended to affect us (personalism).	■ The act reflects some "true" characteristic of the actor (trait, motive, intention, attitude, etc.)

cause" of someone's action. He developed an attributional model of covariation which accounts for how people put together information about the actor (the person performing the behaviour), the entity (the person to whom the behaviour is directed), and the situation (the social context in which the action takes place). Let us consider the example of the reporter and the celebrity. There are three sources of information that we would consider:

DISTINCTIVENESS OF THE ENTITY Is the celebrity generally known for charm and generosity to members of the press? If so, then there is nothing distinctive about you (the entity) as a reporter. On the other hand, if the person's behaviour towards you is distinctive, different from how other members of the press were treated, then it must be something about you that caused him or her to praise you (an entity attribution).

CONSENSUS ACROSS ACTORS Do most of your interview subjects praise you for your interviewing techniques? If so, it says something about you as a reporter (entity). If not, it indicates something about this particular individual (the actor is a nice person) or perhaps about celebrity interviews in general (the situation where the subject always thanks and praises the interviewer).

CONSISTENCY ACROSS SITUATIONS Does the celebrity behave in this way towards you in different situations? When you interviewed her last year at a festival, how did she behave towards you? If consistency is high, we would attribute behaviour to the actor or the entity—either she is a person generous with her praise, or you are a great reporter. However, low consistency would lead to a situational attribution. If she was noncommit-tal or even critical towards you in the past, perhaps you performed unusually well in this situation.

Of course, wherever possible, we would use all three sources of information together. For example, what attribution would you probably make if she praised only you, if she had done so in the past and if other celebrities indicate that they like to be interviewed by you (see Figure 2–2)?

How do people make judgments of "consistency" and "consensus"? How often would a person go out for a run before it was seen as a pattern? Most people would not regard running four times in five years as a consistent pattern of behaviour. However, if someone were to obtain four divorces in five years, this would probably be seen as a steady habit. In short, people use their own experience as a frame of reference. Similarly, consensus judgments will be influenced by the identity of the other people. If members of a political party are observed cheering their own leader, their actions will probably be attributed to loyalty or self-interest, whereas the behaviour of uncommitted voters cheering (also high consensus) might be attributed to the charisma of the leader. It is found that we use consensus information about how others act towards the entity less than expected (Nisbett & Borgida, 1975).

Note the difference between the theories of correspondent inferences and covariation. Kelley has provided us with a useful model of how we use covariation information to make social attributions. However, it presupposes that we have sufficient consensus, consistency and distinctiveness information; that is, we know how a person has acted at other times and how others are acting in the same situation. The theory of correspondent inferences explains how attributions are made when we do not have such informa-tion (Higgins & Bryant, 1982).

Attributions about success and failure

We experience success and failure in many ways. In some cases, it is defined in concrete feedback: a mark on an examination, getting a job or promotion, selling an insurance policy, publishing a research paper, mak-ing a lot of money, winning that tennis match or elec-tion or receiving the Order of Canada. Beyond these

milestones, success and failure can be experienced in more subtle ways: being well-liked at a party, having a child who is admired, being respected by co-workers, being "lucky at love." Many who experience divorce must deal with feelings of having failed in the relation-ship (Weiss, 1975), and attributions regarding success and failure are crucial in dealing with loneliness, as we will see in Chapter 8 (Peplau & Perlman, 1982).

Weiner (1974, 1980) suggests that achievement attributions involve a two-step process. First, we

FIGURE 2-2

How we attribute social behaviour to internal or external causes

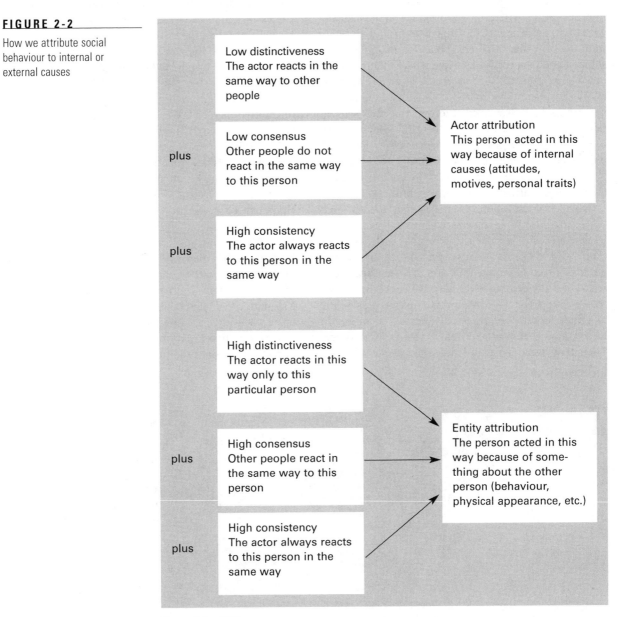

Source: Kelley, 1972

decide whether the success or failure was caused by something about the actor (internal) or something about the situation (external). Then we decide whether the internal or external cause was stable or unstable in nature. In the later (1980) version of the theory, Weiner added a third dimension: whether the occurrence was controllable by the actor. Thus, we can choose among eight types of explanations for success or failure. In Figure 2–3, we outline one example, based on a student's final grade in social psychology.

How do we decide what caused this particular success or failure? In general we attribute an outcome to internal causes when the performance was consistent with past performance by that person and different from the outcome of others. Thus, for example, when someone had succeeded as usual where others usually failed, that person's success was seen as due to great effort or outstanding ability. If someone failed again, but others had also failed, the outcome was seen as due to a very difficult task. Where the outcome was inconsistent with past performance, effort and luck were seen as important in explaining that outcome. Note how cues lead inexorably to an attributional choice, discounting alternative possibilities.

Other research found that males and females tended to attribute male success to internal factors and female success (particularly in a "male task") to luck (Deaux, 1984). As this study was reported two decades ago, we could question whether the same results would be obtained today. However, in a more recent study (Beyer, 1998), students were asked to imagine that they had received either an "A" or an "F" in a course that was required for them to graduate. Then they were asked to rank the various possible causes for their grade. Among those who were to imagine the excellent mark, males tended to attribute their success to their own ability while females emphasized effort, such as studying and paying attention in class. On the other hand, males dealing with failure blamed it on a lack of effort, while females attributed their own failure to a lack of ability. While internal attributions predominated in both cases, gender differences were still evident.

Weiner's model has also been tested with attributional data from the sports pages (Lau & Russell, 1980). Content analyses were performed on reports of games in which causal explanations for winning and losing were recorded. In general, unexpected outcomes ("upsets") generated a greater number of attributions—there seemed to be more to explain or justify. Also a **self-serving bias** (which will be discussed later) was evident. Winning was generally attributed to internal factors ("We all had a great day, everyone gave 150 percent"), and losing to unstable/external factors ("It just wasn't our day"; "The referee made some bad calls"). Other research indicates that winners tend to make attributions to more stable and controllable causes (effort) than do losers (Grove, Hanrahan & McInman, 1991).

When we make attributions about a failure, we may have different purposes. Consider that a student who fails in an exam may attribute the failure to a headache or the unfairness of the instructor, both of them unstable and external (Weiner, Figueroa-Munoz & Kakihara, 1991). Such attributions or excuses serve to protect self-esteem (see Chapter 3), lessen the anger of others (such as parents), and maintain positive expectancies about the future.

FIGURE 2-3

Attributions about achievement: A final grade in social psychology

	Stable		Unstable	
	Internal	External	Internal	External
Controllable	typical effort	professor dislikes student	unusual effort	unusual disruption by other student
Not controllable	lack of ability	task difficulty	mood	luck

Source: Weiner, 1979

Attributional biases

Recall the metaphor of the "naive scientist" who searches systematically for relevant information and uses it logically to explain behaviour. These attribution theories suggest that if people have the information, they will use it in a rational manner. However, research also shows that we often make attributions that are not based on rational thinking. Several attributional biases have been identified. Note that these biases should not be confused with those reviewed earlier about forming impressions of people.

Correspondence bias: Overestimating dispositional causes

Recall that the theory of correspondent inferences explains how we infer that an action corresponds to a disposition, that people smoke because they intend to smoke. We tend to believe that people do what they intend to do, even when logic and evidence suggest otherwise. Thus we find that the salesperson who is friendly to us is a friendly person, discounting what we know about how salespeople are trained and instructed to behave on the job. Similarly we believe that people smoke because they want to, ignoring what we know about the addictive nature of cigarette smoking.

This tendency to exaggerate the importance of dispositional or personal factors and to underestimate the influence of other people and the situation has been called the **fundamental attribution error** (Ross, 1977) because it is so pervasive. For example, a lawyer defending an unpopular client may be seen as sharing the beliefs and even the guilt of that client, even though the job of lawyers is to provide a defence for their clients, regardless of their personal opinions. In experiments, people attributed what someone wrote or said to their "true beliefs" even when they were told that the person had been instructed to argue a certain position (Jones & Harris, 1976).

But what is this fundamental error that we commit in making attributions? Krull (2001) suggests that there are two components to this bias. One is a tendency to believe that a person's actions correspond to a disposition to act in that way: "What you see is what you get." This is the correspondence bias itself. There may also be an underlying belief that Krull refers to as "dispositionalism," in which people act as they do because of their own personal characteristics, and the situation is just not all that important. In fact, it may lead us to

infer that situations are produced solely by personal dispositions. For instance, one might easily explain the unrestrained actions of people at a rock concert by the music and the crowded "party" atmosphere. And yet, a dispositionist bias may lead us to attribute their behaviour to what they are like as people (Sabini, Siepman & Stein, 2001).

The effects of the correspondence bias are strongest where both consensus and distinctiveness are low (Van Overwalle, 1997). That is, when someone says something insulting to you, you will attribute her or his action to the person's true intentions, particularly if others have not insulted you at that time and if that same person was insulting everyone else in the room. This would be a logical conclusion, as predicted by Kelley's model.

THE ACTOR VERSUS OBSERVER BIAS While we are more likely to attribute the actions of others to stable trait dispositions, we make an exception for ourselves. That is, we tend to attribute our own behaviour to situational factors. This is known as the **actor/observer bias**—note that in this sense, the word "actor" refers to the person performing the action, not specifically someone in theatre (Watson, 1982). A good illustration is found in letters to newspaper advice columns. Writers of these letters tend to attribute their own difficulties to the situation (e.g., "We're having marital problems because she refuses to sleep with me"). However, the person giving the advice (the observer), tends to attribute the same marital problems to characteristics of the letter-writer ("You should bathe more often") (Schoeneman & Rubanowitz, 1985; Fischer, Schoeneman & Rubanowitz, 1987).

Several studies illustrate the actor/observer bias. In a simple experiment (Hansen, Kimble & Biers, 2001), participants were randomly assigned to behave in either a friendly or unfriendly way towards a confederate, who had also been instructed to act friendly or unfriendly. That is, both the actor and observer were in the same situation in which their behaviour was constrained by instructions. Participants attributed the unfriendly behaviour of the other person to dispositional reasons ("unfriendliness"), while they attributed their own unfriendly behaviour to the instructions of the experimenter. When asked to explain why students chose their majors and romantic partners, they tended to attribute their own decisions to external reasons (e.g., "I decided to major in psychology because it is interesting"), but their friend's decisions to dispositions (e.g., "He's going out with her because he's insecure") (Nisbett, Caputo, Legant & Maracek, 1973). In a Canadian prison, inmates tended to attribute their actions to situational factors, while their social workers blamed the criminal, even though their professional training stressed the social causes of crime (Saulnier & Perlman, 1981).

Why do the attributions of actors and observers differ? One reason is that they have different perspectives on the same event. The actor's behaviour captures the attention of observers, "engulfing their field of perception" (Heider, 1958). In contrast, as actors, we generally cannot directly observe ourselves, and so are more aware of the situation. Consider that when actors are shown a videotaped replay of themselves in a conversation, they tend to attribute their actions more in terms of their own characteristics rather than the situation (Storms, 1973). Also, as actors and observers, we have access to different information. We know how we have acted in different situations and can remember how these different situations influenced our actions. For instance, we know that we act in a friendlier manner with some people than with others, and when we're at work or at a party, rather than when we are studying or in an intense conversation with someone. Therefore, we attribute our friendly or unfriendly behaviour to the situation. Lacking this information, observers resort to a correspondent inference, that friendly people do friendly things.

LIMITS TO THE CORRESPONDENCE BIAS However, the correspondence bias must not be seen as an invariant effect. Of course, there are times when we know that our behaviour was caused by our own intentions, and the behaviour of someone else was caused by the situation. When external causes for a behaviour are clearly evident, both actor and observer make external attributions (Monson & Hesley, 1982). For example, most of us vividly recall television images of terrified people in the streets of New York after the attacks of September 11, 2001, and we attributed their understandable fear to the situation. Moreover, we are more likely to be able to take on the perspective of a person we know well, both because we have seen them in various situations, and we can empathize with them (Regan & Totten, 1975). While in the earlier stage of a relationship, two people will focus on themselves in defining themselves to their partners. Later on this becomes unnecessary, and the focus shifts outward (Fiedler, Semin, Finkenauer & Berkel, 1995). Research in other cultures suggests that the correspondence bias is more pronounced in Western societies than in India,

Korea or China (Miller, 1984; Morris & Pang, 1994; Choi & Nisbett, 1998), perhaps reflecting the emphasis on individualism, as opposed to collectivism or community (see Chapter 4). Indeed, according to research evidence, East Asians believe, more than those of us in the West, that personal dispositions are more malleable or changeable in response to the situation (Choi, Nisbett & Norenzayan, 1999).

The correspondence bias explains why some of the research reported in this book may seem surprising to the reader. When participants in experiments are shown to conform to the obviously incorrect judgments of others and report that a shorter line is longer, obediently shock an apparent victim despite his protestations of pain, buy something useless to them because it was advertised and decline to help someone in an emergency, one is tempted to attribute such behaviour to the individual's lack of moral character. In doing so, we ignore the power of the situation—a crucial lesson in social psychological inquiry (see Focus On Research—Attributions about Evil and the Correspondence Bias).

One caution about attributing an attributional error: Consider the case of someone such as a banker who dresses very conservatively. Clearly the job requires such attire. But would attributing the clothing to the banker herself be in error? Perhaps banking is a profession chosen by conservative people who feel comfortable in the tailored suit (Gilbert & Malone, 1995). While we are influenced by the situation, we also choose our situations and often can have an influence over them.

Self-serving bias

Protecting their ego and self-esteem is important to people (see Chapter 3). Thus, people tend to attribute their own success to internal factors and their failure to external factors. For example, students receiving good grades in an examination attributed those grades to ability or effort, but those with mediocre grades tended to attribute those results to task difficulty or just bad luck (Bernstein, Stephan & Davis, 1979). Taking credit for success but denying responsibility for failure is most likely when the person has chosen to engage in the activity and is highly involved in the activity, and when the performance and its results are public rather than private (Bradley, 1978). Incidentally, this bias is not limited to Western countries; people in (former) Yugoslavia, Japan and Latin America are also more likely to attribute success rather than failure to their own ability (Chandler, Shama, Wolf & Planchard, 1981).

In most of the research, participants who have succeeded or failed are questioned afterwards about their attributions. In a field experiment by Taylor and Riess (1989), the experience of success or failure was manipulated experimentally in a realistic setting. The participants were competitive skiers who participated in a giant slalom race. Each competitor had two runs, which were timed electronically, and the times were announced after each run. For half the racers, assigned to the "success group," 0.7 seconds were subtracted from their real times before announcement, while in the "failure group," 0.7 seconds were added to their times. Subsequent questioning showed that those in each group perceived their performance as a success or failure as expected, and that none suspected the times had been rigged. Then participants filled out questionnaires that assessed their attributions for their performances. The self-serving bias did not prevail in this

---

FOCUS ON RESEARCH

Attributions about Evil and the Correspondence Bias

In recent years, social psychologists have studied the vexing and challenging problem of evil (Baumeister, 1997; Waller, 2002; Newman & Erber, 2002; Personality and Social Psychology Review 1999, 3(3)). Evil is generally considered as the deliberate harming of human beings by other human beings, usually implying violence that is indiscriminate and often involving extreme cruelty as well. While the Holocaust is generally recognized as the prototype of an evil historical event, subsequent history includes mass murder and other atrocities in the Balkan states, Rwanda, Cambodia and Sudan, terrorism against innocent civilians in many localities and the widespread use of torture by many nations, documented annually by Amnesty International. It also may be invoked to describe certain horrendous crimes, such as those committed against children. In general, we consider actions as evil, rather than simply morally wrong, when they are excessive, incomprehensible, difficult to understand even in terms of the goal or motivation behind the action (Darley, 1992). While people act in morally wrong ways for understandable goals— patriotism, fear, power, money—some actions cannot be explained simply as means to such ends.

How do people explain such actions? Reflecting the correspondence bias, we tend to ignore the situation and attribute evil actions to the perpetrators. That is, we explain evil by assuming that only certain people, unlike the rest of us, could commit such abhorrent acts as torture, the mass murder of help-less people, the victimization of children or the deliberate genocide of a people. In other words, attributions about evil behaviour are entirely internal or dispositional. One simple form of this dispositional explanation is simply that evil is committed by evil people, what Darley refers to as demonization. This, of course, constitutes circular reasoning: Evil acts are caused by evil people, who are evil because of the acts that they commit. It is a circular pseudo-explanation, which may seem genuine since it contains the word "because." It explains nothing.

A more useful dispositional explanation is in terms of personality or psychopathology. The premise is that there is something unique in the personality of people who commit evil acts, perhaps a form of psychiatric disorder. Again, notice the circular reasoning: when we reason, post hoc, that they "must be sick" to do what they did, we explain nothing. Indeed, psychological tests, along with in-depth clinical interviews, were administered to Nazi war criminals, both those in leadership roles who were tried and convicted in the war crimes trials in Nuremburg, and those in rank and file roles as killers. These tests were reanalyzed in terms of more contemporary methods, and compared to test protocols from the general population (Zillmer, Harrower, Ritzler & Archer, 1995). Their findings were that these Nazi mass murderers, on the whole, did not show any consistent pattern of psychopathology. Other research in personality strongly indicates that the capacity for evil cannot be explained by psychopathology.

(continued)

This reasoning is corroborated by historical evidence. Historian Christopher Browning (1992) reported a detailed study of one battalion of German police, assigned to keep order in occupied Poland during World War II. These men were assigned to participate in the infamous "final solution" extermination of Jewish children, women and men. Indeed they are "credited" with the direct murder of 38 000 individuals, and deporting an additional 45 000 to the gas chambers of the Treblinka concentration camp. Browning observed nothing exceptional about these mass murderers. They were "ordinary men," who had been employed as dockworkers, truck drivers, teachers, artisans and salespeople. Nazi physicians in the concentration camps conducted unspeakable "experiments" on prisoners. Some of these physicians had gained international reputations for their legitimate medical research and expertise before the Nazi era (Lifton, 1986).

Social philosopher Hannah Arendt (1963), was assigned by a U.S. magazine to cover the trial in Jerusalem of Adolf Eichmann. Eichmann was a German bureaucrat who was in charge of the logistical planning and execution of the Holocaust, organizing the transport of millions of people to the death camps, their murder and disposal of the corpses. Based on both her own observations and psychological investigations, she described Eichmann as representing the "banality of evil," an ordinary, ambitious civil servant who seized an opportunity for advancement in his career. It is a disturbing insight indeed, that ordinary people are capable of extraordinary evil. Needless to add, ordinary people are also capable of extraordinary kindness, altruism and heroism in certain circumstances, as we will see Chapter 9. What does it imply about how the mass murderers, or all of us, would behave in a different time and place?

If we cannot attribute evil actions solely to the personal characteristics of people who commit them, then we must look to the situation. Baumeister (1997) suggests conditions that may promote evil. These include an idealism in which the end justifies any means in promoting the welfare of one's own group or nation, threatened egotism in which the outgroup or victims are seen as a threat or challenge, and sadistic elements of personality. However, Baumeister argues strongly that sadism is the least important of the roots of evil.

We will see, in succeeding chapters, theories and research concerning prejudice, aggression and violence and blind obedience to an authority who directs a participant to torture another person with electric shock (these famous experiments by Stanley Milgram are discussed fully in Chapter 6). The lesson of this research is clear. We must avoid the correspondence bias, and recognize that evil can be caused or at least promoted by the social situation. However, note that explanation is not justification or excuse. We may explain evil actions, in part, by the situation, but we do not excuse the perpetrators.

case. Participants tended to attribute success to internal facilitating factors (such as strong effort and high ability), but also tended to attribute failure to internal debilitating factors, such as a lack of effort.

An obvious explanation for this effect is that, since success and failure are so important to how we evaluate ourselves, internal attributions for failure would lower our self-esteem and would thus be difficult to accept emotionally. Yet, when people are depressed, they tend to be relatively accurate in judging the extent to which they are personally responsible for their success or failure (Sweeney, Anderson & Bailey, 1986; Alloy & Abramson, 1979). This may be a mixed blessing, in that some degree of self-serving bias, a "positive illusion," may actually contribute to people's comfort and happiness by protecting their self-esteem (Taylor & Brown, 1988).

A second, more subtle, explanation is that self-serving attributions represent strategies of presenting ourselves to others and reflect our concern about our image in the eyes of others. We want people to respect us, to give us credit for success and to excuse our failures. Thus, we may claim that our failures were externally caused, even though we may know better. An interesting exception concerns divorce. People undergoing divorce often attribute the failure of their marriages to themselves, particularly when they are still emotionally attached to their ex-partners (Lussier & Alain, 1986).

Which explanation is correct? Are self-serving attributions used to protect our self-image or the image we

The Overjustification Effect

Imagine that during the past year, you have devoted almost all your spare time to working on environmental issues and campaigning to elect a mayoral candidate committed to these issues. The work has been immensely satisfying, especially because the candidate was elected! Now the newly elected mayor offers you a well-paying job working on the same environmental issues. Nothing could please you more, and you accept the offer. And yet, research suggests, surprisingly, that you will find your well-paying job less satisfying than your former volunteer position.

Why do we sometimes feel strangely dissatisfied in a situation that seems so rewarding? When you were a volunteer, you attributed your behaviour to your commitment, idealism and excitement—to the intrinsic aspects of the work. Now, you are likely to shift at least part of your attributions to an extrinsic factor—money—and so the intrinsic satisfactions become attenuated. This is the overjustification effect, which occurs when extrinsic rewards cause us to discount the importance of intrinsic factors. We then may lose interest in the task itself (Deci, 1971; Lepper, Greene & Nisbett, 1973).

This concept has been applied productively in areas such as sports, suggesting that money can decrease the intrinsic satisfaction that we find in playing (Vallerand & Reid, 1984). When play becomes work, golf may become less satisfying, even to Tiger Woods. How might winning the Stanley Cup compare to winning Olympic gold to professional hockey players?

Now, consider education. Might a school system based on extrinsic rewards (grades, praise, gold stars) and punishment (verbal castigation, detentions, failing grades) cause students to lose interest in school and in learning? To a considerable extent, this is probably true. When teachers use rewards to control classroom behaviour, students' intrinsic motivation is low (Deci, Nezlek & Scheinman, 1981).

However, rewards can be useful as information, to provide people with feedback on how well they are performing. They can be signals of encouragement and acknowledgment of competence. Similarly a disappointing grade need not be taken as a punishment, but as information about how you are doing and where you need to improve to attain your goals. When rewards are interpreted as information, intrinsic motivation is not adversely affected (Deci & Ryan, 1985). Clearly, in using rewards in school, athletics or business, it is important to avoid the competitive and controlling messages usually associated with them. In the end, we don't want people to lose intrinsic satisfaction in what they are doing.

present to others? Riess, Rosenfeld, Melburg and Tedeschi (1981) tested these competing hypotheses in a rather ingenious way. Participants were told that they had succeeded or failed in a test of word associations. They were asked to attribute their success or failure to ability, effort, task difficulty or luck. To measure attributions, half the participants completed the usual questionnaire. The other half were hooked up to electrodes and told that this was a new, improved, extremely powerful lie detector that would indicate how they really felt. Then they were asked to respond to attributional questions in the way that they expected would be shown by the machine.

The experimenters reasoned that if self-serving attributions represented conscious impression-management tactics, then the bias would be greatly reduced. Nobody wants to create an impression of being insincere. However, if the bias were an unconscious, defensive process, then the ruse would have no effect. The results were mixed: participants who believed that the machine would reveal their true feelings showed a self-serving bias, but not as strong a bias as those who completed questionnaires. It appears that both protecting our self-esteem and protecting the image we create for others are important in this attributional bias.

People often have a self-serving bias—taking credit for success but denying responsibility for failure.

Defensive attributions

Other attributions are influenced by a need to feel secure and avoid threatening situations. This is shown in a classic experiment by Walster (1966), in which participants were given a report about an accident. The driver, Lennie, left his car parked at the top of the hill. The parking brake cable came loose; the car rolled down the hill and caused some damage. In one version, the damage was severe and someone was hurt, while in the other, the damage was minimal. Participants were asked to indicate the extent to which they attributed responsibility to Lennie for the accident. Consider that Lennie was held more responsible when there was severe damage and injury than when the damage was minimal, even though there is no logic in making this distinction. Lennie was no more or less negligent in not having his brake checked, whether the consequences were severe, mild or nonexistent. This effect has been found in other studies (Burger, 1981).

Why would severity of consequences affect the attribution of responsibility for the same action? Walster (1966) has suggested that people act in a defensive manner, avoiding the possibility of a threatening event. They often attribute responsibility for a serious crime or accident to the victim, because to interpret it as an outcome of bad luck or an "act of God" would be to admit the possibility that it could happen to them. Of course, this defensiveness would be aroused where the situation might be one that they could be in, or the protagonist is

similar to themselves—they could imagine themselves "in that person's shoes." Students would attribute greater responsibility for a severe-consequences accident when the protagonist is described as a student than a middle-aged business executive (Burger, 1981).

An interesting question to consider is whether attributing responsibility to someone for something is the same as blaming that person. Mantler, Schellenberg and Page (2003) investigated this question with regard to how we perceive people who are seriously ill with HIV/AIDS or lung cancer. Of course, actions such as engaging in unprotected sex or smoking can put us at risk of these illnesses. Participants considered a person with either illness to be "responsible" to some extent, but much less so to be "blameworthy," and therefore we seem to be able to distinguish between the two. Evidently attaching "blame" implies a moral judgment as well as an attribution of responsibility.

Consider, as well, how we attribute responsibility for current or historical events. Research shows that we are more likely to attribute responsibility for a negative event to another group or nation than to our own group or nation. For instance, Jewish participants are more likely to make internal attributions for the Holocaust to Germans, than are German participants to members of their own nation (Doosje & Branscombe, 2003). Similarly, in reporting hate crimes such as a gang murder of a gay person, attributions in the media are represented in ways consistent with more general political orientations. That is, more conservative media who are less sympathetic to gay and lesbian people, often find more situational attributions for such crimes (Quist & Wiegand, 2002).

The illusion of control

Not only do we attribute causes to our actions, but we are also primed to pay attention to the effects of our actions, and to make the connection between our actions and events that follow them (Thompson, Armstrong & Thomas, 1998). Much of what happens in life is beyond our control. Perhaps in response, people cling to an **illusion of control**, an exaggerated belief in their own capacity to determine what happens to them in life (Langer, E., 1975). For instance, people often prefer to select their own lottery ticket, under the illusion that they can increase their chances of winning. In an experimental demonstration (Wortman, 1975), participants were presented with two coloured marbles in a can, each representing a different prize. Some were told which marble represented the desirable prize, while others were not. Then participants either chose a marble without being allowed to see which was which, or were given one. In all cases, the participants had absolutely no control over the outcome. However, they attributed more responsibility to themselves when they picked their marble without looking at it. We will examine some of the implications of this on our health in Chapter 16.

Lerner (1977) has identified an important implication of the illusion of control: an exaggerated **belief in a just world**. Some people simply believe that good outcomes happen to good people and bad outcomes to bad people; you get what you deserve and deserve what you get.

Holding such beliefs has advantages. Believing that we get what we deserve in life will encourage us to invest time and effort in long-term goals (Hafer, 2000). People with strong just world beliefs who suffer negative outcomes, such as poor grades on an exam, are less likely to see such outcomes as unfair than are those with less pronounced just world beliefs (Hafer & Correy, 2000). It also has its costs. Those with strong just world beliefs tend to score higher on measures of depression and stress (Lipkus, Dalbert & Siegler, 1996).

Indeed, people may respond to being victimized with self-blame when they experience traumatic events. Suffering incest, rape or other forms of violence shatters the sense of living in a world that is just, meaningful or predictable. In examining the research on people who have been victimized, Miller and Porter (1983) present the following, rather unexpected, findings: (1) victims often exaggerate their own responsibility for the event and its consequences; and (2) the degree of self-blame is often positively related to how successfully the person will cope. Self-blame may enable the person to maintain the illusion of control in life, which can be channelled into constructive coping strategies. On the other hand, those who have strong just world beliefs tend to see themselves as less vulnerable to serious negative events. If you believe that you get what you deserve in life and you are a deserving person, then why would you be vulnerable to die in a plane crash or from HIV/AIDS? Ironically this may expose them to greater risk. For instance, people with high beliefs in a just world are less likely to use condoms (Hafer, Bogaert & McMullen, 2001).

Self-blame is one way to impose meaning on what appears to be incomprehensible. Victor Frankl (1963), a psychoanalyst and survivor of the Nazi death camps, maintained that a search for meaning in life is an essential component of human experience. The search for satisfactory attributions becomes particularly poignant and significant when suffering and grief are involved. For example, people who have emerged paralyzed from an accident struggle with the question, "Why me?" Their success in finding a satisfactory answer enables them to cope more effectively with their circumstances (Bulman & Wortman, 1977). In some forms of victimization, the search for meaning is more difficult. Silver, Boon and Stones (1983) interviewed 77 adult women in Ontario who had been victimized in childhood by familial incest. Although an average of 20 years had elapsed since the last episode, more than 80 percent were still searching for meaning. In contrast with the accident victims, most of the minority who felt they had made some sense of the event attributed it to specifics such as the psychopathology of the perpetrator, or the troubled marriage of their parents.

Taken to its extreme case, strong beliefs in a "just world" lead one to deny that "victims" exist. If people believe that everyone deserves what they get in life, then people who live in poverty, are attacked on the street at night or become ill are seen as simply experiencing the consequences of their actions and decisions. We will explore the implications of these beliefs on our ideas about justice in Chapter 15.

Society and attributional biases

As noted earlier, the correspondence bias is more strongly evident in the individualistic Western cultures than in the more collectivistic Asian culture. Now consider what causes us to make certain attributional choices—to what do we attribute our attributions? The research reviewed in this chapter points to factors within the person as the causes of attributional choices, such as a need to protect self-esteem or a sense of control, or the attempt by cognitive misers to "minimize effort." This strictly "psychological" orientation to attributions has been challenged by social psychologists, who argue that we have ignored the role of social factors in determining how we make sense of our world (Crittenden, 1983; Hewstone & Jaspars, 1984). For example, in the realm of politics, people tend to be blamed for social problems such as poverty, unemployment or underemployment, delinquency and drug abuse, while the role of the social system is ignored. Terrorism is blamed on an "axis of evil," ignoring other possible causes.

A study by Guimond and Dubé (1989) compared francophone and anglophone attributions for the fact that, even within Quebec at that time, French-speaking Canadians tended to have lower incomes than English-speaking Canadians (Shapiro & Stelcner, 1987). Anglophones attributed the income differences to internal characteristics of francophones, citing lack of initiative or education, while francophones stressed the economic and political situation (e.g., job discrimination, or the economic system in Quebec and in Canada as a whole). In part, this may reflect an actor-observer bias, where French Canadians were more likely to be "actors" in their own disadvantaged economic situation, and English Canadians the observers of the relative poverty of francophones at that time. It may also reflect a self-serving bias, where those afflicted by poverty are reluctant to blame themselves, and those who are doing well are willing to give themselves credit (Guimond, Bégin & Palmer, 1989). Social scientists themselves tend to explain delinquency, alcohol and drug abuse and sexual assault in terms of person factors alone, rather than considering the person and the environment together (Gregg, Preston, Geist & Caplan, 1979).

An evaluation of attribution theories

In the decades following the publication of Heider's (1958) seminal book, attributions became a major focus of attention in social psychology. In any scientific discipline, an idea or trend often brings about its opposite idea or counter-trend. Three critiques have emerged concerning attribution theory: (1) that attribution theory is peculiar to a particular culture and does not describe human nature *per se*; (2) that much of what people do is pretty mindless—they usually do not ask *why* of themselves or others; and (3) that since people are not usually aware of why they behave in a given way, they are forced to come up with some answer when the researcher asks them. Thus, the conclusions from attribution research are based on artefact. Each of these criticisms has some validity.

The cultural critique begins with the premise that both the theorists and the research participants have come almost entirely from the United States. Sampson (1977) characterizes this culture as being based upon the ideal of the self-contained individual, and so the correspondence error would reflect this ideal. Indeed, attribution studies in other cultures reveal differences. For example, Brazilians tend to differ from American participants in their reactions to achievement-related attributions. Participants in these studies were provided with various explanations for successes and failures of hypothetical persons; for example, Juan, the world's greatest tennis player, won without even trying. U.S. participants (and West Germans) tended to reward those with low ability and high effort who succeeded, and to punish those with high ability and low effort who failed (Weiner & Kukla, 1970). However, Brazilians focused on those high in both ability and effort, rewarding them most for success and punishing them most for failure (Rodrigues, 1981). Hindu adults and children in India tend to make situational attributions for both prosocial and deviant behaviour, and do not seem to overestimate dispositional attributions (Miller, 1984).

Even in Western cultures, can it be assumed that people generally are aware of causes, particularly of their own actions? Nisbett and Wilson (1977) reported a series of classic studies that indicate people are often unaware of what has influenced their actions, and often unaware and unconcerned that something is "causing" them to act in a certain way. Some of the experiments are rather ingenious. In one, shoppers were asked to evaluate the quality of four totally identical nightgowns or nylon hose. Participants showed a strong bias towards preferring the article on the right-hand side—although, in later questioning the majority were unaware of this tendency and denied that they were influenced by it. In another experiment, participants were asked to memorize a list of word pairs. Some pairs were designed to influence later responses by association. For example, those who had memorized the pair "ocean–moon" were twice as likely to name Tide when asked for a laundry detergent as were control participants. However, rarely did participants make this connection when asked to explain their choice. Rather, they responded with apparently "top of the head" remarks, attributing their response to the brand their mothers used. Nisbett and Wilson (1977) conclude that people generally do not make attributions in their daily activities unless asked to do so, such as in an experiment.

While people may sometimes think spontaneously about causal explanations for actions (Weiner, 1985), it appears that much of what people do happens in a state of "mindlessness." In an experiment, participants were approached by an experimental stooge, as they were about to use a photocopy machine. Some were asked to let the person use the machine before them, but were given no reason. Others were presented with a similar request along with a meaningful reason: "I'm in a rush." And others were given the same request with a meaningless "placebo" reason: "May I use the machine first because I have to make some copies?" When the delay would be minimal to the participants, they complied when presented with what sounded like a reason, even when it was no reason at all. They simply responded automatically according to a script: when someone asks a small favour and offers a reason or excuse for it, you will usually comply (Langer, Blank & Chanowitz, 1978).

Thus, the question now seems to be, When does attributional thinking occur? What impels us to look for the cause of a behaviour by ourselves or by someone else? The evidence suggests three types of situations in which people tend to ask *why* someone acted as they did: (1) when something unexpected happens, such as when the underdog unexpectedly wins the game, the mark we obtained on an examination is much better or worse than expected, or when a person in obvious distress is not helped by bystanders (Bohner, Bless, Schwarz & Strack, 1988); (2) when an event is personally relevant, when the good mark or the unexpected defeat happens to us rather than to someone else; and (3) when someone feels a desire to find some meaning in an important event, such as a sudden loss of someone close to you, being the victim of major crime, illness or injury. Consider attributions that partners make in marriage. Attributional thinking

occurs most frequently in the early "honeymoon" stages of the relationship and during conflict between the partners (Holtworth-Munroe & Jacobson, 1985). Otherwise, cognitive processes assume a different form, discussed below.

Social Cognition

In assessing what is known about impression formation and attributional processes, two facts stand out. First, people form impressions and make judgments about others quite rapidly, often on limited information. Second, people are active in processing information, often in biased ways. Despite these tendencies to take "cognitive shortcuts," people seem to carry on effectively in their daily lives.

In the past decade, social psychologists have become increasingly interested in these processes, and have linked their work to research in cognitive psychology. There are two basic concepts to learn. First, our information about our world is organized or "coded" in terms of meaningful categories (*schemata*). Second, in making decisions and judgments, we often use cognitive shortcuts or *heuristics*.

Categorical thinking: The schema

Of course, we know that every person is unique, and that no two classes or no two hockey matches are exactly alike. Yet there are similarities among certain types of people or events. If we were to approach every person and every event as totally unique, with no expectations about what they would be like, we would be overwhelmed by uncertainty. Thus, we tend to organize our view of the world in terms of categories. People are generally categorized in terms of easily observable characteristics, such as sex, ethnic group, occupation or age. Similarly, we construct categories of events (parties, classes), activities, objects and even ideas. Then we build a collection of beliefs, assumptions, images and memories around these categories—schemata.

Social schemata

Cognitive schemata (singular **schema**, derived from the Greek word for plan or structure) enable us to organize and simplify information, memories and impressions. These are sets of interconnected beliefs, information, images, memories and examples about social objects: all that we "know" about something. For example, our schema of automobiles might include our knowledge of how they work and how to drive them; our impressions of various brands and models of cars, perhaps memories of cars that we have owned or rented, trips, accidents, repair bills or pleasant events involving cars. Of course, it may also include our images of automobiles, such as the one we drive. Schemata help us to organize and simplify a lot of information that we have received, help us to interpret new information more rapidly, and determine what we will encode and remember.

There are various types of schemata. *Person schemata* refer to specific people such as a famous star, a public figure, your parent, a professor. For example, suppose we have a schema of the current prime minister as being honest, hardworking, decisive, concerned with people in distress, wanting to resolve conflicts between people and regions of the country. If he or she were to appear on TV with an eloquent request that all of us work hard and sacrifice for the good of the nation, we would interpret this speech in terms of our schema. However, if our schema were of a conniving, self-serving politician, we would interpret the same speech quite differently. We also have schemata about types of people, such as people who are "extroverts," "enthusiastic," "outgoing," or "self-assured."

Another interesting type of schema refers to events. For example, we may have an *event schema* referring to a group of friends going to the "good old hockey game." Event schemata include mental images of the arena where the event occurs, which teams participate and what happens during the game—the "script." It begins with purchasing the ticket, presenting it to a ticket-taker and finding our seats. We may buy a program and begin to identify players as they warm up. We recognize the uniforms of the two teams and the referees, and the physical set-up of the rink, with its boards, blue and red lines, circles and goals. We stand for the national anthem, then sit and shout encouragement during the opening face-off. Purchasing snacks and liquid refreshments between periods is usually part of the ritual. We have standard reactions to a goal by our team, a goal by their team, a fight; and we know when and how to express disapproval of actions by the referee or opposition (in much of Europe, they whistle rather than "boo"). All of these events fit as part of what happens to us when we go to a game. Think of other event schemata: a university examination, a date for the movies, supper in a

Chinese restaurant, a trip to the beach, a day at work, a vacation, being on-line. We have learned the script through personal experience and social modelling, and so we experience the events as predictable, understandable and comfortable.

Finally, we have schemata about *social roles*—organized mental structures about people who belong to social categories. We may have role schemata about physicians, rock singers, professors, students, smokers, non-smokers, friends, lovers, insurance salespeople, butchers, mothers and bureaucrats. Role schemata are generally restricted to role-relevant situations, although some such as physicians may often find themselves treated as physicians in a social situation. A role schema may be idealized and unrealistic: few people can live up to a schema of "lover" as being always devoted, understanding, supportive, affectionate, passionate, and never selfish, unreasonable or tired.

Conflict may arise when people in different roles have different schemata of their own and one another's roles. A professor's schema of *student* may include constant interest and attention, while the student feels a need to balance the student role with other roles, demands and problems. Likewise, the student's schema of *professor* may consist entirely of teaching and showing concern for students, while the professor's own schema includes research and publishing, sitting on department and university committees, and consulting in the community. Thus, the professor is exasperated when the student hasn't kept up with assigned reading, while the student is exasperated when the professor is not always available in the office.

Several characteristics are common to these types of schemata. First, schemata tend to be organized hierarchically, from the general to the more specific. For example, we may have a general schema for the concept *party*, and more specific schemata for each of an informal, loud-music bash in someone's basement, a child's birthday party and an art gallery opening. Second, people or groups of people may differ in specific schemata. For example, university students think of "intelligent people" primarily in relation to academic and intellectual matters, while people interviewed in supermarkets tend to see intelligence in terms of practical problem-solving and not "acting foolishly" in social situations (Sternberg, Conway, Ketron & Bernstein, 1981).

Much research has been devoted to the study of the self-schema: the set of images, memories, beliefs and evaluations that people have concerning themselves. We explore this topic further in the next chapter.

Prototypes

Cantor and Mischel (1979) suggest that we often use **prototypes**, mental images of a typical example of that category, as part of a schema. For example, you may picture your own cocker spaniel as a prototype of the category *dog*, with four legs, fur, a tail, characteristic sounds of barking, whining and growling, licking your hand. If you were to see an unfamiliar dog of another breed, you would decide whether it was a dog by comparing the characteristics of that Rottweiler or schnauzer to your prototype. Similarly, you may have a prototype of the elderly, perhaps a grandparent, as the smiling, silver-haired, wrinkled, kindly person often shown on television or in elementary school books.

The extent to which a particular person (or animal) resembles the prototype, and the extent to which you allow for variations, will determine how readily you identify the person with the category. For example, Brewer, Dull and Lui (1981) presented participants with photos and verbal labels of people in certain categories, such as *grandmother*. Then they provided more information about the person. This information was included more frequently in the subject's impression of the person when it was consistent with the prototype (e.g., "kindly" for a grandmother) than when it was not consistent (e.g., "aggressive" for a grandmother).

A **stereotype** refers to a particular kind of shared prototype for members of a social group for which there is a consensus among people of your culture (Taylor, 1981). Since stereotypes are intrinsic to prejudice, we will discuss them fully in that context (see Chapter 13).

Processing social information

Why do we have schemata? We are constantly exposed to a flood of complex, ambiguous information. Schemata enable us to process this information swiftly and efficiently. While we can rarely know everything about everything, schemata help to fill in the gaps by providing us with a "best guess" about what is true. They can help us to be prepared for the future by providing us with expectations. Research over the past few years shows how pervasive and fundamental schemata are in social experience (Fiske & Taylor, 1991). In particular, our schemata guide us, telling us what to pay attention to, and influencing what and how we remember.

Attention

Selective attention is one important effect of schematic thinking. In an environment in which we would be overloaded with sensory information, the schema guides us as to what to notice and process. For instance, at the hockey game, we will attend to the game (particularly where the puck is), and less so to what the spectators are wearing (unless the game is boring).

In one experiment by Swann and Read (1981), participants were asked to rate themselves on the traits of assertiveness and emotionality. They were then told that as part of a "get acquainted" experiment, another person would be asking questions about them. Participants were asked to select from a list the questions they would prefer the other person to ask. The questions were about assertiveness and emotionality, and were phrased or slanted to elicit an answer confirming the presence or absence of a trait. For example, "What makes you think that X would complain in a restaurant?" would be seen as eliciting an answer confirming assertiveness, while "Why do you think X doesn't get angry, even when provoked?" would be perceived as asking for evidence that the person is not highly emotional. Participants showed preference for questions likely to confirm their self-schemata. For example, assertive participants would tend to select the first question, while participants who rated themselves as emotional would tend to avoid the second question.

Memory

Many people assume that memory is akin to a bank or a hard disk; material is deposited (memories) and can be withdrawn later, as needed (Lamal, 1979). Occasionally one of these deposits is lost, and we say that we've "forgotten." If the bank or the hard disk "crashes," we may suffer from amnesia.

To the contrary, current research suggests that memories are encoded as they are stored, in forms dictated by people's assumptions, attention and schemata. For instance, you do not simply store what you read in this textbook, but you interpret what you read in terms of what you have already learned, how it relates to your personal life, what associations you make of the material. It is in this form that your memory of what you read will be encoded into memory. Remembering is much more than retrieval of a file on your hard disk: Rather, it is an active or "constructive" process in which these assumptions and schemata influence the memory that is retrieved.

Think of someone who you would consider to be a "memorable" person. A memory of a person will include both memories of specific things that the person has said or done, and more abstract memories of "what the person is like," such as personality traits, physical characteristics and disposition (Srull & Wyer, 1989). Indeed, we often form clear overall impressions of a person, but cannot explain in any detail why we feel that way. This is explained in <u>terms of the *theory of dual representation* (</u>specific details and general impressions). For example, if we see a person do something very thoughtful for someone else, we will store in memory both the specific behaviour and our evaluation of the person as being thoughtful and kind. Over time, as we get to know the person better and observe many more such actions, we may forget the specific behavioural details. However, these behaviours will have an enduring impact on our overall evaluation. So we have a strong impression of a kind, thoughtful person, though we may be at a loss when someone asks for details.

Schemata may guide our memory of a person, enabling us to remember or ignore specific details about that person. For example, in an experiment (Zuroff, 1989), participants were induced by means of a brief description of a woman to think of her as "traditional" or "liberated" (feminist) in her beliefs and goals. Subsequently they were presented with a long list of adjectives that various people had ostensibly used to describe that woman. Although all participants had the same list, they tended to remember information consistent with the "traditional" or "liberated" schema they had been given. If they had been *primed* to think of her as "traditional," they would be more likely to remember an adjective such as "kind" than "independent." This particular effect of schemata, *priming*, will be explored later in this chapter.

What are your memories about high school? Do you look to your past through "rose-coloured glasses"? If so, you are more likely to remember the good times, and forget about the difficulties. Indeed, we may recall our high school years as happier than they were because we now have a "good old days" schema of that period of our lives (Ross, McFarland, Conway & Zanna, 1983). Many who served in the armed forces during wartime tend to reminisce about happy memories of comradeship and humour, rather than the horrors of combat, although events such as Remembrance Day can evoke such painful memories.

Our memory of past events can also be influenced by our expectation or "theory" about what should

have happened (Ross, 1989). In a study of students enrolled in an extravagantly advertised study skills program, participants first completed an initial questionnaire in which they evaluated their own study skills. Then they were assigned randomly to the program or to a waiting list. After the program, all participants were reinterviewed. A follow-up showed that the program had no significant effect on their grades. However, participants believed that they had improved. When asked to recall how they had rated their skills previously, participants who completed the program recalled "before" as worse than it had seemed to them at the time. They applied the schema of self-improvement to distort their memory of the past in order to feel that they had, indeed, improved (Ross & Conway, 1985).

Thus, our memories of the past can be reconstructed to be consistent with our current thinking. Consider also that people tend to assume characteristics such as memory, activity and other capacities will decline, as they grow older. Older adults remember themselves as having been more capable in these ways earlier in life than a matched group of younger adults. As a result, we may feel our memory has declined because we recall, perhaps in an exaggerated form, our prowess of earlier years (McFarland, Ross & Giltrow, 1992).

Our memories of the past can also be influenced by our mood at the time of recall. In some circumstances, our memories are congruent with our mood states, such as when a sad event evokes memories of when we were unhappy in the past. In other circumstances, our memories may be incongruent with our mood. For instance, when we are mourning the loss of a loved one, we may find consolation in happy memories of that person. A series of studies by McFarland and Buehler (1998) indicate that when people are induced to reflect on their feelings and what they might do to feel better, they tend to remember happy events. On the other hand, when people are simply instructed to ruminate on their feelings, dwelling on how they are feeling without any intention or hope of feeling better, they tend to have unpleasant memories of the past.

We may remember what someone has said in the past. Suppose Simon accuses Jill of having called him an ignoramus. People often do not recall their exact words. So Jill may deny she said that, on the basis of her schema of Simon and her own self-schema: "Do I see Simon as an ignoramus? Would I say such a thing in public?" However, if it is something that she could have said, she may recall having said it. People may remember having said what is familiar to them if it sounds like something they might have said (Buehler & Ross, 1993).

THINKING OF WHAT MIGHT HAVE BEEN In thinking about the past, we often imagine what might have been, how a certain outcome might have been different. This is called **counterfactual thinking**, and some interesting findings have emerged from research on this topic (Roese, 1997). For instance, why might bronze medalists at the Olympics be happier with their outcome than silver medalists? Imagine that you have won a silver medal, which may well stimulate counterfactual thinking about not winning the gold. However, if you were to win a bronze medal it may stimulate thinking about a different outcome, not winning a medal at all. Researchers used video clips in which participants rated the emotional state of competitors at the moment the medal placements were announced. Indeed, bronze medalists were judged to be happier than silver medalists (Medvec, Madley & Gilovich, 1995).

Indeed, counterfactual thinking can lead us to "inaction inertia," an unwillingness to act now because such acting will only lead to second-guessing ourselves, reminding us of missed opportunities. For instance, if you fail to purchase something on sale at 50-percent off, you are no less likely to take the opportunity to purchase that same item at 25-percent off (Tykocinski & Pittman, 1998).

When we reflect on what might have been, we may imagine an outcome that would be better than the reality we face (upward counterfactuals) or worse than what really happened (downward counterfactuals) (Roese & Olson, 1997). For instance, if you receive a "B" in a course, you may imagine that it might have been an "A+" or a "C–." Each kind of counterfactual thinking can serve a different purpose for us. Downward counterfactuals, imagining how it could have been worse, can give us some relief and acceptance of reality. If we have an accident that causes extensive (and expensive) damage to the car, imagining that someone could have been injured can put things into perspective. On the other hand, upward counterfactuals can galvanize us into action to improve the results in the future. Imagining the "A+" that might have been may lead us to making some improvements in the future. However, counterfactual thinking can lead to feelings of regret, even if we were to imagine a worse outcome (Walchli & Landman,

2003). In one study of women with silicone breast implants, counterfactual thinking was related to a poor post-operative adjustment (Parker, Middleton & Kulik, 2002).

Social representations

Where do these schemata come from? While it is reasonable to suggest that schemata are learned, they do not depend entirely on direct experience. For example, people may have schemata about people that they have never met, or life in countries that they have not visited. Certainly much of the learning that shapes our schemata is vicarious in nature, coming from movies, television, books and the experience or imagination of others.

Many of our schemata are both acquired from other people and communicated among people, a process that requires shared meanings and symbols held by members of a culture, community or group. In other words, while cognition is necessarily located in the mind of an individual, the essence of social cognition is that it is shared collectively in a culture. These considerations support the notion of socially constructed schemata, or **social representations** (Moscovici, 1981). Thus, for example, our event schema of a hockey game has evolved in our Canadian culture and is shared by many of its members today. Russians or Swedes might hold a quite different event schema of a hockey game. A schema about a prominent politician shared by many people in the country may change over time as individuals communicate with each other directly and through the mass media. It may also differ in Alberta, Ontario, Quebec or New Brunswick. Reports of behaviour, television images, shared impressions, jokes passed on from person to person, all can contribute to the social representation of that particular politician.

Moscovici (1981) identifies two processes by which social representations emerge and evolve: anchoring and objectification. Anchoring refers to assimilating an unfamiliar event, person or idea into some existing structure of knowledge. Often we classify or categorize the new image or event, imagine it and compare it with what we already know. That is, when we attend a hockey game in a new arena, we can associate what we see with certain images and beliefs that we may hold about hockey arenas, and we can compare that place with other known members of that category. Objectification refers to a process by which an abstract

The Cognitive Attributes of the Entrepreneur

Why do some persons but not others choose to become entrepreneurs, starting their own business or taking an established business in a new direction? Why are some entrepreneurs so much more successful than others? Much of the research constitutes a virtual laundry list of success: vision and drive, ability to raise capital, financial and management skills, ambition, self-efficacy, optimism, self-confidence, willingness to take calculated risks, ability to delay gratification and, of course, the willingness to work hard (VandenBos & Bulatao, 2000). Indeed, one would expect this type of person to succeed in most areas of endeavour.

Social psychology provides some useful insights into entrepreneurship. Baron (1998, 2000) summarizes the set of skills as social competence, the ability to get along with others, to interact effectively and persuasively. Clearly, leadership skills (see Chapter 12) and skills in persuasion (see Chapter 5) are highly important for success in this situation. One interesting study used standardized photographs of 71 female entrepreneurs who had all started their own cosmetics businesses. They found that the physical attractiveness of these persons, as rated by 54 judges, was strongly related to their success: indeed, those rated as most attractive had earned over U.S.$53 000 more than the least attractive group (Baron, 2000). The power of physical attractiveness is discussed fully in Chapter 8.

Do entrepreneurs, particularly the successful ones, think differently than other persons? In order to seize the moment and take advantage of opportunities, the entrepreneur must work in situations that are often novel, unpredictable, complex and under time pressure. Consider as well the intense emotional involvement in making a go of it, and one sees the potential for information overload. In this chapter, we see that people deal with such situations by resorting to cognitive heuristics, enabling rapid decision-making—but with the potential for unfortunate biases. For instance, entrepreneurs tend to be very confident, perhaps overconfident in their own judgment. They also tend to make use of the **representativeness heuristic**—generalizing from small, nonrandom samples (Busenitz & Barney, 1997). Because they tend to be overconfident and optimistic, they are less likely to engage in counterfactual thinking—imagining what might have been (Baron, 2000). Baron (2000) points out that this is a mixed blessing. On one hand, counterfactual thinking generates negative feelings, which may interfere with the ability to focus and function. On the other hand, counterfactual thinking enables one to understand why negative outcomes occurred, and to learn from one's mistakes. It may be that counterfactual thinking does not distinguish entrepreneurs from others, but may be one element in their success.

idea becomes concrete, perceived as part of common-sense experience. For instance, the abstraction of "elections" becomes objectified in our minds through politicians, speeches, advertisements and the reporting of results. Of course, elections in one culture or country may be distinct from those in another. Still, Canadians, Australians, Israelis and Swedes share enough about the experience of elections to be able to understand each other. *Personification* is a common example of objectification (Moscovici & Hewstone, 1983). For example, while most people have some vague ideas about psychoanalysis, they probably know the name Freud and some of the psychological ideas linked to his name. Similarly, while few understand the theory of relativity, most remember the name Einstein and connect it to the mysteries of the atom. Often the policies of a government or a country become personified in terms of the prime minister, premier or president.

Much of the research in this area is descriptive, such as studies of the social representation of mental illness in different historical periods and among people of different age groups (DeRosa, 1986). While Moscovici argues that social representations are the fundamental elements of social psychology, the notion that schemata may be socially constructed does not necessarily exclude the study of how individuals interpret their social world. Indeed, it is individuals who, in the end, interpret and convey the various social representations they share with others.

Rapid reasoning

We must often make complex judgments under conditions where it would be unrealistic to try to think it through. As we have seen, we are "cognitive misers" and tend to avoid expending more energy than seems necessary in making judgments. We will never collect all relevant information about courses, cars or jobs before making our decisions. We have seen how we invoke certain biases in making attributions, and how we invoke a schema to perceive and interpret what we see and hear. Now we turn to how we take other cognitive shortcuts.

We often follow certain unstated "rules" or **heuristics**—assumptions and biases that guide our decisions about uncertain events. One such "rule of thumb" involves medical diagnoses. Physicians are taught to consider the common illness before the rare and exotic disease ("When you hear hoof beats, look for horses before you look for zebras"). In everyday experience, we learn similar rules, without being taught what they are. Recent research has identified a number of these heuristics (Tversky & Kahneman, 1974). (See Table 2–1.)

The representativeness heuristic

Imagine that you are visiting a casino, and you record the outcome of 12 spins of the roulette wheel. Which of the following sequences are you more likely to observe (R = red; B = black)?

1. RBR BRB RBR BRB
2. RRR RRR BBB BBB

Mathematically, both sequences are equally likely to occur. However, most people would choose the first sequence, in which the two colours alternate, because it seems "representative" of what 12 random spins of the wheel should look like (Tversky & Kahneman, 1974).

Now, consider the following description: "Steve is very shy and withdrawn, invariably helpful, but has little interest in people or in the world of reality. A meek and tidy soul, he has a need for order and structure and a passion for detail". Would you guess that Steve is a farmer, a trapeze artist, a librarian or a surgeon?

If you actually had a set of personality test scores of representative samples of people from each profession, you could calculate the probability that Steve is a meek surgeon, a shy trapeze artist, a farmer with a passion

Are these teenagers typical or atypical? Attitudes towards groups tend to be inferred from a particular example—often ignoring other information.

Some heuristics for making judgments in situations of uncertainty

Heuristic	Rule	Example
1. *Representativeness*	Estimate extent to which object is "typical" of category.	Decide that Steve is a librarian because he "acts like one."
2. *Illusory correlation*	Conclude that A and B "belong together."	Since violent crimes are rare and distinctive events, as is seeing members of a small minority group, then violence by them is remembered more, and that group is seen as violent.
3. *Availability*	Assume it's true because it comes to mind readily.	Decide that divorce is very common now because you can think of several couples who recently split up.
4. *Simulation*	Something is more likely if you can imagine it.	Decide that your father will not be angry after you smashed up the family car because you can imagine (from your own experience) how he reacts to a crisis.
5. *False consensus*	Overestimate extent to which others are similar to you.	Assume that most people believe as you do about the abortion issue.

for detail, and so forth. However, this would demand the kind of information that would not be accessible in normal daily social life. The representativeness heuristic provides us with a quick and easy solution: we simply estimate the extent to which Steve is similar to or representative of the typical person (prototype) in each occupation. We would probably conclude that Steve most closely resembles a librarian. Now, imagine that you were told that Steve's name had been drawn from a list of 100 men, only 10 of whom were librarians. Most people would ignore this objective "base rate" information and still assume that Steve was a librarian (Tversky & Kahneman, 1973).

A rather dramatic demonstration of this principle came from a study in which participants saw a videotape of people playing the roles of a psychologist interviewing a prison guard. For half the participants, the guard expressed very hostile attitudes towards prisoners (i.e., They're all "losers" who should be kept locked up). The other half saw a guard expressing more optimistic, humane attitudes towards prisoners and their rehabilitation. Some of each group were told that this guard was quite typical of prison guards, others that the guard was quite atypical, and still others were told neither. Participants then answered a questionnaire about prison guards in general. Those who had viewed an interview with a humane guard expressed significantly more positive attitudes towards guards, regardless of whether the guard was represented as typical or atypical (Hamill, Wilson & Nisbett, 1980).

The availability heuristic

Which is more common, words that begin with the letter *K*, or those that have *K* as the third letter? In fact, in the English language, there are more than twice as many words with *K* as the third letter (e.g., *awkward, like, bake*) as with *K* as the first letter (e.g., *king, know, keep*). However, most people incorrectly estimate that more words begin with the letter "*K*," simply because it is easier to think of such examples (Tversky & Kahneman, 1982). For various reasons, we are accustomed to think of words in terms of their first letter. This is a demonstration of the **availability heuristic**, one of the most important cognitive "rules" discovered

Heuristic Reasoning in Society

Some of the work on cognitive heuristics has extended beyond the lab into some real-life situations, including those related to important social issues. Here are a few examples.

Representativeness

- In genetic counselling, it is found that parents who have had one abnormal child tend to overestimate the probability of their having another (Shiloh, 1994).
- Psychiatrists and clinical psychologists tend to make clinical diagnoses on the basis of prototypes of patients with various disorders, rather than according to established diagnostic criteria (Garb, 1994).
- In sentencing, judges tend to match the defendant before them with prototypical criminals (Lurigio, Carroll & Stalan, 1994).

Availability

- People make judgments about the risk of dying of various causes based on how often that cause is mentioned in the media—which may not correspond to the real risks. For instance, many more people die in automobiles than in airplanes, but most people consider air travel as riskier (Comb & Slovic, 1979).
- Patients often judge illnesses based on a salient symptom (lump in breast = cancer). Physicians

are influenced by cases that they have encountered recently, and arrive at a diagnosis that comes to mind at the time (Schwartz, 1994).

- Teachers use available memories of similar students or siblings in predicting the performance of a current student (Jussim, Madon & Chatman, 1994).

The illusory correlation

- It is commonly assumed that there is a relationship between women's moods and their menstrual cycle. While this may well be true in particular cases, the assumption that all or most women suffer from this syndrome may be illusory. In one study, women kept mood diaries. While the diaries showed that irritability and depression did not increase consistently during the premenstrual or menstrual phases, the same women reported afterward that they had suffered menstrual mood swings during that period (McFarland, Ross & DeCourville, 1989; Nisbett, 1980). That is, people tend to infer about a group from a particular example and to ignore base rate information. We frequently see this dynamic in instances of prejudice. For instance, being treated rudely by one waiter can cause a tourist to condemn an entire nation. It can also lead to a false historical analogy because of some superficial similarities. A dictator in Iraq may be seen as equivalent to Hitler in Europe several decades earlier, ignoring all other relevant information (Spellman & Holyoak, 1992).

by Tversky and Kahneman (1974). It is deceptively simple: If something comes readily to mind, we tend to assume that it's probably true and to use it.

Consider when people are depressed, and tend to see life in negative terms. When asked to anticipate future events in their lives, they would be more likely to imagine negative events happening to them because these events would be more cognitively available to them (Vaughn & Weary, 2002). On the other hand, in

the same situations, optimistic people would have positive future outcomes more available to them.

One instance of the availability heuristic is our tendency to be excessively influenced by extreme examples, again because they come readily to mind. For instance, fame influences our judgments (McKelvie, 2000). When participants heard a list of 42 names (21 famous men and 21 non-famous women or vice versa), and they were subsequently asked to estimate the numbers of men and women in the list, they estimated greater numbers of the gender with the famous names. In a classic study (Rothbart, Fulero, Jensen, Howard & Birrell, 1978), participants read 50 statements about actions by hypothetical strangers. While 40 of the statements described innocuous actions, 10 described crimes. For one group of participants, the crimes were fairly mild and non-violent (e.g., petty vandalism, shoplifting), while for the other, 10 were serious crimes such as murder and rape. When later asked to estimate the frequency of crime in that group, estimates were much higher among those who had read about serious crimes, even though the real proportion was not greater in that group. Since extreme cases bias our inferences about the rate of an event, it is not surprising that television may distort our perception of reality by its focus on crime, scandal, violence and other bad news. How often do we hear about the everyday acts of kindness that people do for each other?

The evidence of an availability heuristic raises interesting questions about the interpretation of ambiguous social events. Are psychiatrists or psychologists more likely to interpret an action as indicating mental illness because these are their working concepts, which are readily available? Do police officers perceive an escalating crime wave when, in fact, one does not exist? Do auto mechanics see problems with their customers' vehicles that do not really need to be repaired? Of course, being an "expert" means having special skills and qualifications to make certain judgments. However, perhaps an availability heuristic bias goes with the territory.

How readily can we imagine or construct various scenarios, to guess what to expect (Kahneman & Tversky, 1982). For example, imagine that Mr. Crane and Mr. Tees were scheduled to leave the same airport at the same time but on different flights. Both are caught in the same traffic jam on the way to the airport and arrive 30 minutes after the scheduled departure of their flights. Mr. Crane is told that his flight left on time, while Mr. Tees is told that his flight had been delayed and left five minutes ago. Who is more upset?

Most people would respond that Mr. Tees is more upset. This is because we cannot imagine that Mr. Crane could have made his flight, while Mr. Tees might well have made it, were it not for that slow traffic light or the illegally parked car or the misunderstanding over the gate number. The **simulation**

heuristic enables us to imagine "if only" conditions, which explains much about our reactions to near misses, second-guessing and other frustrations. Of course, you have correctly associated this principle with our earlier discussion of counterfactual thinking.

The illusory correlation

As noted in our earlier discussion of causal attributions, we tend to look for covarying events in our social world and to assume that they belong together. However, we tend to exaggerate, to inflate the correlations that we assume between things that "go together." This inflation is called the **illusory correlation** and can cause people to make unwarranted inferences or assumptions. For example, in an experiment, participants were shown pairs of words, and later asked to estimate how often each pair had occurred. Although all word pairs were shown the same number of times, participants tended to overestimate the frequency of word pairs that seemed to belong together, such as bacon–eggs and tiger–lion (Chapman & Chapman, 1969).

Participants in another study (Barkowitz & Brigham, 1982) were shown photos of a stranger and later asked to recognize the stranger among a larger group of photos. They were much more successful when the stranger was from their own race (black or white) than from the other race. In a more realistic setting, two experimental accomplices, one black and one white, visited a number of convenience stores in Florida. Each accomplice engaged in at least one activity that was designed to enhance his or her uniqueness (e.g., paying entirely in pennies for a purchase, asking for directions to the airport). About two hours later, the clerks were shown a set of photos of six black people or of six white people and asked to indicate whether any of these people had visited the store recently. While overall accuracy was only 48.6 percent (see discussion on eyewitness testimony in Chapter 15), it was particularly low where the race of the customer differed from the race of the clerk. The implicit assumption that people from an outgroup are "all alike" is a vivid example of the illusory correlation heuristic, and is fundamental to the idea of a stereotype (Hamilton & Gifford, 2000).

Consider the meaning of "masculinity" and "femininity." Findings from contemporary research challenge the notion that masculinity and femininity are opposite ends of one psychological dimension. Thus, associating "male" or "female" with many other traits can be considered an illusory correlation as well as gender stereotypes. Consider that many individuals see themselves as having a mixture of characteristics typically considered masculine (e.g., competitiveness, independence, self-confidence) and those typically seen as feminine (e.g., warmth, kindness, gentleness).

That is, if we consider "masculinity" and "femininity" as separate scales rather than opposite polarities of one scale, some score high in one and low in the other (masculine–feminine sex-typed), some score low in both (undifferentiated), and some score high in both (psychological androgyny). In the latter group, the illusory nature of the correlation is clear: being independent or kind does not represent one gender to the exclusion of the other.

We can consider sex-role self-perception in terms of a particular self-schema: a high–low pattern of sex-role self-typing would be indicative of a schema, while androgynous and undifferentiated individuals would be called *aschematic*; that is, without sex-typed schemata. These two types of individuals were compared in an experiment (Frable & Bem, 1985) in which they listened individually to a taped conversation among six people, while still photographs were shown of each speaker as he or she spoke. For half the participants, the conversation group consisted of three males and three females. For the control participants, the group consisted of three whites and three blacks, all the same sex as the subject. Then, participants were presented with a list of 72 quotes from the conversation and asked to identify the speaker for each one.

The pattern of errors by each group of participants was revealing. In the race-difference condition, no strong pattern was evident. But with the sex-difference group, the sex-typed participants made most of their errors by confusing who said what among the opposite-sex members. That is, a sex-typed self-schema caused participants to see members of the opposite sex as somehow "all alike," a special case of the illusory correlation.

The false consensus effect

In the **false consensus effect**, we tend to see our own behaviour as typical, and thus we tend to assume that other people would hold the same attitudes, make the same decisions and act as we do. This overestimation becomes a useful rule of thumb in social cognition: we simply extrapolate from our own reactions to infer what others' attitudes or behavioural choices would be.

For example, in an experiment (Ross, Greene & House, 1977), students were asked to walk around campus for 30 minutes wearing a large sandwich board carrying a crudely-lettered message, "Eat at Joe's." Some agreed, and some refused, but both groups later estimated that more than two-thirds of the other students on campus would have made the same decision they did. Other studies have shown that participants overestimate the extent to which others have the same smoking habits and hold the same political attitudes they do (Sherman, Chassin, Presson & Agostinelli, 1984; Fields & Schuman, 1976). However, there are limits to this heuristic. We may want to see ourselves as unique on certain very positive attributes, and would thus underestimate the number of people who share those desirable attributes (Campbell, 1986).

Priming and availability

Suppose that we have just watched a particularly tear-jerking episode of a soap opera involving marriage conflict and rampant infidelity. Then we meet the new couple who moved in next door. Are we more likely to notice or interpret signs of tension between them, or to interpret their tension as a marital problem rather than the tensions of fatigue from moving? Research evidence suggests that this is often the case. A schema about marriage problems has been activated or "primed" for us, which we may then use to interpret events. On the other hand, if we had just seen an episode showing passionate married love, we might notice, interpret and remember very different information about our new neighbours.

The activation into availability of certain categories or schemata is called **priming**. In an elaborate experiment (Srull & Wyer, 1980), male and female participants were instructed to construct sentences from four-word sets. Some of the word sets contained hostile content or suggestion (e.g., leg, break, arm, his), while others contained neutral content only (e.g., her, found, know, I). For one group of participants, 15 of the 50 sets suggested hostility, while for the other, 35 of the sets had hostile connotations. The object was to prime a memory category—"hostility"—in the subject group using 35 sets of words conveying hostility.

Then the effects of this priming on the participants' memory of a person were tested. Participants read a paragraph that described the behaviour of a stranger in neutral terms with respect to hostility. Then participants were asked to rate the stranger on a number of characteristics, one of which was hostility. To further explore the effects of priming on person memory, time was also varied. Some participants were given the information about the person immediately after priming, some 24 hours later, and some a week later. The interval between receiving the information and rating the stranger also varied for different participants: No delay, 24 hours or one week. For example, some participants received the information immediately after priming and rated the person 24 hours later, and some received the information 24 hours after priming and rated the stranger one week later.

In short, the experimenters varied the number of word sets with hostile connotations when the information about the target person was given, and then when the ratings were measured. The results confirmed two predictions, and contained a surprise. As expected, the same stranger was perceived as more hostile after participants were primed with 35 items rather than with 15, thus confirming the effect of priming on category availability. Also as expected, the priming effect was greater when the information was received immediately than when there was delay. However, here is the surprise: The effects of priming were greatest when there was a rather long interval between receiving information (the paragraph about the target person) and making judgments about the stranger. Once the category of hostility had been primed and made available, participants formed their initial impression of the person, and then later remembered that person as being even more hostile than he or she had appeared earlier.

Individual differences in social cognition

In discussing the process of social cognition, we have seen the general patterns and biases that characterize how people think. We see that at times, we think things through rationally, and at many other times, we act as cognitive misers, seeking the shortcut to a conclusion. This is the dual-process model of cognition, the idea that our minds function at both a conscious rational level and at a more automatic, thought-less level. However, individuals also differ in their cognitive styles, or dispositions, and these individual distinctions lead to important differences in how people make sense of their social world.

An important difference in cognitive style refers to the **integrative complexity** of the individual's information processing. People high in integrative complexity tend to be open-ended, flexible, able to make free differentiations and multiple integrations: in other

words, they have access to a rich and complex set of social schemata. On the other hand, individuals low in complexity tend to be rather rigid and close-minded, making relatively crude differentiations, and are incapable of integrating different perspectives. For example, the high-complexity person would consider a person in terms of various characteristics and social roles, could see both the favourable and unfavourable characteristics in the same person, might see that the person is an admirable musician and an obnoxious person, and could change her mind about that person. The low-complexity person would tend to see someone simply as good or bad, a friend or an enemy, and would stick doggedly to that conclusion.

Does integrative complexity in thinking reflect competence or performance? That is, do people have low integrative complexity because they are unable to think in more complex ways, or because they prefer to think more simply? In a series of studies, people were encouraged to broaden their thinking about problems such as two quarrelling sons, reconciling one's religious beliefs with the death of a child and whether a thriving company that does not meet environmental standards should be shut down. Suggestions included seeking compromise rather than simply choosing one alternative or the other, looking for alternative approaches to solving a problem and looking for an overall system or philosophy that might underlie different approaches. In general, participants were able to increase the integrative complexity of their thinking when encouraged to do so (Hunsberger, Lea, Pancer, Pratt & McKenzie, 1992). Religious fundamentalism seems to be related to a lack of integrative complexity on existential issues (e.g., reconciling a belief in God with a human tragedy), but this did not generalize to other issues such as jobs versus environment, open Sunday shopping or free trade (Hunsberger, Pratt & Pancer, 1994; Pancer, Jackson, Hunsberger, Pratt & Lea, 1995). Thus, to a considerable extent, integrative complexity appears to represent a choice or a style in thinking.

Suedfeld has explored this dimension of information processing, using nonexperimental evidence in intriguing ways. In one study, the writings of a number of revolutionary leaders were coded for complexity, comparing them before and after the revolution (Suedfeld & Rank, 1976). It was hypothesized that, during a revolutionary struggle, the leader must be relatively categorical and single-minded towards the one goal, whereas after a successful revolution, the leader, in order to govern successfully, must be more complex in both understanding and communicating. The results were striking: leaders who remained powerful after the revolution (e.g., Lenin, Stalin, Castro, Jefferson) showed this shift towards greater complexity after the revolution, while those who lost their influence (e.g., Trotsky, Che Guevara, Hamilton) remained relatively simple in their writings. In another archival study, researchers coded integrative complexity in the speeches of leaders in the U.S. Civil War, World War II and the first Persian Gulf war of 1990. They found that, in all cases, low levels of complexity tended to be related to a decision to go to war (Conway, Suedfeld & Tetlock, 2001). Perhaps looking for alternatives to war demands attention to negotiation and to holding more than one perspective, including understanding the perspectives of the other side. All of this suggests high levels of integrative complexity.

Other archival studies examine integrative complexity of people at different stages of life. In one, the integrative complexity in letters of famous people was studied in relation to significant life events, both positive (e.g., marriage, coronation, major book published, election or appointment) and negative (death of close person, political defeat). In this study, integrative complexity increased, particularly among males, in response to negative life experiences, but not in response to positive events (Suedfeld & Bluck, 1993). In another study, researchers coded the published correspondence of a number of eminent men and women over the last 10 years of their lives (e.g., Lewis Carroll, D.H. Lawrence, Freud, Liszt, Proust, Queen Victoria, Mary W. Shelley). Those who died after a long illness or at a ripe old age showed a gradual decline in integrative complexity over their last four years. However, those who died suddenly and unexpectedly showed a relatively steep decline in integrative complexity in their last year. Suedfeld and Piedrahita (1984) suggest that a decline in integrative complexity, a simplification in schematic processing, may occur naturally over time, particularly as an "intimation of mortality" in the period preceding death. Of course, considerably more direct evidence would be needed to support this intriguing interpretation.

A Final Note

Consider the following paradox. It is important for people to understand and make sense of the people,

events and situations in their lives. Of course, the best way to understand anything is to gather as much information as possible and think about it carefully and logically. However, because there is simply too much information to process and too little time to do it, we rarely act in the optimal manner. We must figure out what is happening, decide what to do, and then act.

While cognitive shortcuts can lead to error, they can in fact be seen as a source of strength and creativity in human functioning (Bargh & Chartrand, 1999; Wegner & Wheatley, 1999). They allow us to go beyond the available information, and to fill in the gaps and make inferences, guesses, hunches. Unlike computers, which are compelled to follow precisely defined rules (algorithms), people make inferential leaps based on incomplete information. Indeed, in the field of artificial intelligence, computers are "taught" to reason by means of the same cognitive shortcuts that characterize human intelligence (Newell & Simon, 1972).

In this chapter, we have seen instances of both algorithms (the attributional search) and heuristics (schemata, prototypes and heuristics); in short, the *dual process model* of cognition. It appears that more often than not, we take the "cognitive shortcut." We quickly form an impression of someone, apply some quick decision rules to arrive at explanations for their actions if we feel the need to do so, apply schemata to filter and interpret information—and then we act. We are subject to an impressive array of biases. And yet, we are sufficiently correct—often enough—to function rather well in our social lives.

Social cognition is currently a very active area of research within the discipline. One emerging trend is social cognitive neuroscience, a field which seeks to bring together our developing understanding of brain mechanisms with what we understand about how we interpret and process the information that we take in. The phenomena that are studied by social psychologists will help us to understand how the mind and brain function, while neuroscience will open new avenues of investigation for social psychologists (see Ochsner & Lieberman, 2001).

Summary

1. In forming an overall impression of a person, we have a bias towards forming positive impressions, and we tend to be influenced more by certain salient characteristics (central traits) than by others,

and more influenced by negative rather than positive information. In addition, we have our own unconscious assumptions about "human nature" (implicit personality theory).

2. In combining information about various traits, we may simply add them together or we may average them to arrive at an overall impression. A weighted averaging model best accounts for most data from research on this topic.

3. Attributions are causal explanations. When more than one explanation seems possible at the time, we tend to be less confident of our attributions (discounting principle). If one event tends to be associated in time and place with another, we tend to infer a cause–effect relationship between them (covariation).

Jones & Davis

4. In making a <u>correspondent inference</u> that an action was caused by a corresponding disposition, we are influenced by whether the act was freely chosen, was not considered socially desirable, led to a non-common outcome, or had a direct effect on us.

Covariation model

5. Kelley suggests that we function as "naive scientists" in making social attributions. We focus on information about consistency across situations, distinctiveness of the entity and, to a lesser extent, consensus among actors in behaviour towards the entity.

6. Weiner's achievement attribution model focuses on whether a result is perceived to have been caused by something internal or external and stable or unstable.

7. Attributions are influenced by certain biases. We overestimate dispositional causes of behaviour (the fundamental attributional error); attribute our own behaviour to situations to a greater extent than we do the actions of others (actor versus observer bias); use self-serving attributions; and attribute greater responsibility to someone after their actions have resulted in severe as opposed to mild consequences.

8. We tend to believe that we control our environment, and that the world is fundamentally "just"; thus we blame victims for their fate. Victims tend to undergo a "search for meaning" through attributions for their misfortune.

9. Attribution theory has been criticized as being peculiar to an individualistic North American cul-ture, and as an artefact of certain experimental procedures. Hence, it may not accurately portray the "mindlessness" of much of our behaviour.

10. Our thinking about our social lives is organized into schemata—complex integration of information and examples of people, roles, events and even ourselves. Schemata may be represented by prototypes, and may assume the rigidity of stereotypes. Schemata influence us in what to attend to or ignore, what to remember and how to interpret new information.

11. We tend to apply certain "rules" (heuristics) as cognitive shortcuts. In making judgments, we often ignore information about base rates, exaggerate the relationships between events (illusory correlation), overestimate the extent to which others believe and act as we do, overemphasize extreme cues and use what readily comes to mind.

12. Social cognition is influenced by individual differences in integrative complexity.

Further Reading

DEVINE, P.G., HAMILTON, D.L. & OSTROM, T.M. (1994). *Social cognition: Impact on social psychology.* New York: Academic Press. A set of scholarly chapters on how social cognition has changed much of social psychology, particularly person perception and attribution, attitudes, influence and intergroup relations. Many of the chapters take a historical approach that shows the evolution of thinking on these topics.

FORGAS, J., WILLIAMS, K.D. & WHEELER, L. (2001). The social mind. *Cognitive and motivational aspects of interpersonal behavior.* New York. Cambridge. An interesting integration of the research on how our strategies in dealing with others are influenced by how we interpret and explain the social world.

GILOIVICH, T., GRIFFIN, D.W. & KAHNEMAN, D. (2002). Heuristics and biases. *The psychology of intuitive judgments.* New York: Cambridge. The definitive review of this topic. It is filled with all kinds of practical implications (note: author Daniel Kahneman won a Nobel prize for his work in this area).

HEATH, L., TINDALE, R.S., EDWARDS, J., POSAVAC, E.J., BRYANT, F.B., HENDERSON-KING, E., SUAREZ-BALCAZAR, Y. & MYERS, J. (Eds.). (1994). *Applications of heuristics and biases to social issues.* New York: Plenum Press. An innovative set of papers that outlines how cognitive heuristics apply to medical decisions, therapist diagnoses, sentencing by judges, choosing a college and policies such as affirmative action and needle exchanges for AIDS prevention.

KAHNEMAN, D., SLOVIC, P. & TVERSKY, A. (Eds.). (1982). *Judgment under uncertainty: Heuristics and biases.* Cambridge: Cambridge University Press. An important and groundbreaking collection of papers on the various heuristics and biases that constitute our cognitive shortcuts.

KUNDA, Z. (1999). *Social cognition: Making sense of people.* Cambridge: MIT Press. A comprehensive review of research and theory, accessible to students. Includes basic processes, applications to problems such as knowing yourself and forming prejudice, along with some cross-cultural perspectives.

MOSKOWITZ, G.B. (2001). Cognitive social psychology. The Princeton symposium on the legacy and future of social cognition. Comprehensive, professional-level volume on how cognition and motivation are related, stereotyping, updates on cognitive dissonance, attribution theory, social identity and self-concept research and heuristics.

PARK, D.C. (1999). Acts of will. *American Psychologist, 54* (7). A set of four challenging integrative papers on the theme of acts of will—how we perceive ourselves to have far more control over our thoughts and actions than we actually do.

ROESE, N.J. & OLSON, J.M. (Eds.). (1997). *What might have been: The social psychology of counterfactual thinking.* Mahwah, NJ: Erlbaum. This book focuses on the nature and effects of thinking about what might have been ... but was not to be, with some interesting applications to various situations.

SPENCER, S.J., FEIN, S., ZANNA, M.P. & OLSON, J.M. (2003). *Motivated social perception. The Ontario Symposium, Vol. 9.* Mahwah, NJ: Erlbaum. Set of advanced papers on how our motives, goals and need to maintain self-esteem impact on how we make sense of our world.

WEINER, B. (1986). *An attributional theory of motivation and emotion.* New York: Springer-Verlag. A classic presentation of Weiner's theory of attribution in achievement situations.

 # Weblinks

Social cognition papers archives
www.psych.purdue.edu/~esmith/scarch.html A recommended set of papers on social cognition research.

Wesleyan University Social Psychology Network
www.wesleyan.edu:80/psyc/psyc260/ A comparative index of social psychological materials.

Chapter 3

The Social Self

The knowledge of thyself will preserve thee from vanity.

Cervantes

One may understand the cosmos but never the ego; the self is more distant than any star.

G.K. Chesterton

Chapter Outline

In his autobiography, Nelson Mandela (1994) traces how he came to an understanding of himself and his identity. Throughout his life, he was pulled by the opposite poles of traditional African society and the dominant white European society. Rolihlahla, his name at birth, literally means "pulling the branch of a tree" in the Xhosa language but has the colloquial meaning of "troublemaker," foreshadowing the many storms in his life. From an aristocratic background in traditional African society, he was sent to a modern, Western school, where he excelled. At the age of sixteen, he underwent a traditional Xhosa initiation into manhood, marked by circumcision rituals. Subsequently he attended a Christian college, run by whites and dedicated to the higher education of an African elite.

In his final year at college, he heard a great Xhosa poet, Krune Mqhayi, whom he describes as a "comet streaking across the night sky." From that experience, he developed an intense pride in his own black South African culture. After completing law school, he began a clerkship at a prominent white law firm in Johannesburg, an unusual opportunity for a black at the time. While his legal training progressed rapidly, he encountered many incidents of racist insults and demeaning treatment. Gradually, his anger evolved into political commitment to the cause of black liberation, even while he worked successfully as a lawyer within the white-dominated system. He describes his life as having run on two separate tracks—his work in the liberation struggle and his livelihood as an attorney.

Ultimately, his political activity led to a dramatic trial, following which he was convicted of treason and imprisoned for more than 27 years. Mandela's commitment did not wane during this long period of imprisonment, and he became an enduring symbol of the liberation movement. Finally, the white leadership of the country, sensing at last the imperatives of history and justice, arranged his release. Mandela and his associates subsequently negotiated a new constitution, which ended the racial "apartheid" system and empowered the black majority of his nation. He  was elected President, advocating not revenge but reconciliation and the building of a new, multiracial cooperative society. In 1999, after serving a full term as president, and overseeing the free election of his successor, Mandela stepped down.

Mandela sacrificed his chosen career, his family life, and 27 years to his commitments. Who is he? He is a member of a prominent Xhosa family, educated in the European traditions, a lawyer, a husband and father, a freedom fighter, a prisoner, a political leader. While all of these roles are part of who he is, circumstances caused some roles to become more salient at various stages of his life. His autobiography is a revealing portrayal of the evolution of self.

In our society, the self has become a preoccupation. Adolescents are said to be consumed by a search for identity. Many people seek to "find themselves" in work, a cause, group therapy, religion—or to "lose themselves" in occult experiences. People are encouraged to disclose themselves ("be open") in their relationships, to not be self-conscious, to avoid self-pity or self-doubt, to develop self-control and to present themselves in a favourable, yet honest manner. A lack of self-esteem is assumed to be the source of many social and personal ills.

The previous chapter addressed how people make sense of their social world—how they form impressions of people, infer why people act as they do (attri-bution) and construct schemata that influence their interactions with others and their memories. This chapter focuses on how similar social cognitive processes are applied to one very important object in our lives: ourselves. While the idea or concept of "self" or **self-concept** is one that we commonly use, it is surprisingly difficult to define. Clearly it includes the body, our beliefs and feelings and our experiences, as well as social identity: our name, memberships in various groups, social roles. It implies something central to us, the core of what makes us unique as individuals. We may express who we are by our relationships with others, what we do and even what we possess (Haggard & Williams, 1992). For example, attending symphony concerts may have as much to do with our self-concept of being cultured as it does with our enjoyment of the music.

Why is it important to study and understand this notion of "self"? This collection of images, beliefs, feelings and memories guides us in our actions and how we interpret experience. That is, self acts as a schema, perhaps the most important of our schemas.

Imagine that someone asked, "Who are you?" How many ways could you complete the sentence "I am _____." Because you are a complicated person living in a complex world, you could answer that question in many ways (try it!). The sum total of your answers would define your own unique self-concept. However, while the specific content of your self-concept is unique, the overall striker or organization of the self-concept is similar for different people. This was evident when Rentsch and Heffner (1994) asked the "Who are you?" question of university students. When the researchers analyzed the responses statistically, they found there were eight groupings or factors—categories by which the participants defined themselves. Some of these categories concerned personal attributes, such as interpersonal characteristics (I am a student, or I date a lot), interests (I'm into psychology or I enjoy ballet), personal beliefs (I am opposed to abortion or I always vote for the Conservative Party), and self-awareness (I am a good person). Others referred to how we are defined in our social environment, such as ascribed characteristics (I am a woman or I am a Chinese Canadian), or social differentiation—how we differ from others (I'm from another country or I am gay).

In this chapter, we will consider several interesting questions. Do we understand ourselves by thinking about ourselves (introspection), or do we discover who we are by our actions and how others react to us? How does our self-image and self-evaluation affect our beliefs, our feelings and our actions? Is it more important to us to be positive about ourselves or to be realistic, even when it hurts? How do we reveal ourselves to others in order to influence their opinions about us? Do we want to be looked at in a positive light by others, or do we want others to understand us as we really are?

All these topics serve to illustrate an apparent paradox in social psychology. Social psychologists, who study how others influence us, have been at the forefront in studying the experience of oneself: the social examines the private (Olson & Hafer, 1990). We will see that the experience of ourselves is not so private after all.

Know Thyself: From Thinking or from Experience?

It is generally believed that awareness of "the self" develops from early experience. Consider that even very young children can easily recognize their own image in a mirror or photograph but that dogs and cats apparently cannot. Indeed, one of the first stages in the development of thinking in the child is the capacity to distinguish between what is "me" and what is "not me." Many readers will recall an object in childhood, perhaps a blanket or stuffed animal, which they cherished, almost as an extension of themselves. As we mature, over time, our concept of ourselves becomes increasingly complex and differentiated.

It is evident that people vary in self-concept clarity, the extent to which their beliefs and understanding of themselves are stable and consistent over time and across situations (Campbell, 1990; Campbell et al., 1996). People who score low on a measure of self-concept clarity tend to be more anxious, tend more to ruminate about what's wrong with themselves. Interestingly, while self-concept clarity is strongly related to self-esteem among Canadian students, this is much less so among Japanese students. This reflects cultural differences that will be explored later in this chapter.

As adults, we are exhorted, "Know thyself." How can we accomplish this? It has long been accepted that we can "discover" our true selves by introspection; that is, by thinking about ourselves, our strengths and weaknesses, what is important to us, what we want out of life as individuals. Philosophers advise us that the unexamined life is not worth living.

Can we be "objective" in how we view ourselves? Recall in the previous chapter that our attributions for success and failure are different when we are involved than when we are judging others. Frequently, people who have failed at a task, or who are going through a divorce, will either avoid accepting any responsibility or will blame themselves excessively. On the other hand, when things go well, we tend to give ourselves credit, perhaps more than we deserve. Canadian scientists Frederick Banting and John Macleod received a Nobel Prize in 1923 for their discovery that insulin could successfully treat people who otherwise would die from diabetes. Afterwards, Banting claimed that Macleod, who was director of the laboratory, was more of a hindrance than a help, and Macleod never mentioned Banting's name in talking about the discovery (Ross, 1981).

Studying the Self through Autophotography

Imagine that as a participant in a research study, you are presented with the following assignment: "We would like you to describe how you see yourself. To do this, we would like you to take, or have someone else take, 12 photos that tell who you are. These photographs can be of anything, just as long as they tell something about who you are. Remember, these photographs are to tell something about you as you see yourself" (Dollinger & Clancy, 1993, p. 1066).

How would you complete this assignment? Would the photos show you dressed in formal attire, in jeans and a T-shirt or in a bathing suit? Would you be alone or with other people? Would you or the other people be smiling, frowning, conversing, showing affection or showing anger? Would some photos portray you working, studying or engaging in a sport or recreation? Would they indicate something of your beliefs and values—how you feel about yourself?

To use such photographs in systematic research, a technique called **content analysis** is employed (see Chapter 1), in which the photos are coded in terms of clearly defined categories. For instance, photos may be coded as portraying self with others, people touching, self with children, self with adults, self in a group, self with a significant other, self alone (Dollinger, Preston, O'Brien & DiLalla, 1996). To establish the reliability of these coding systems, at least two judges code the photos independently, and the agreement between judges is calculated. Other questionnaire or behavioural measures may be related to the content of these photographs.

Some intriguing findings have been reported. People who are shy tend to provide photos that portray themselves in terms of esthetics (art or nature), rather than relationships with others (Ziller & Rorer, 1985). Those who submit photos that show drinking or alcoholic beverages tend to drink more, and more frequently (Dollinger, Rhodes & Corcoran, 1993). Those whose photos contained images of books and school had higher grade-point averages (Combs & Ziller, 1977). Those who are involved in religious practices will portray themselves with religious groups, in churches or synagogues or with sacred objects (Dollinger, 2001).

Perhaps most interesting are studies that contrast people who describe themselves in terms of individual characteristics with those who refer to their social identity—their relationships and social roles. People who portray themselves in a more individualistic manner score higher on questionnaire measures of loneliness and alienation from others (Dollinger, 1999). Women are more likely to provide photos of themselves accompanied by others, while men are more likely to portray themselves alone, involved in physical activities, or accompanied by motor vehicles (Dollinger, Preston, O'Brien & DiLalla, 1996). People judged to have provided a set of photos that revealed material of greater richness and detail tend to stress their individual identity as opposed to their social identity but do not necessarily provide more pictures of themselves alone than with others (Dollinger & Clancy, 1993; Dollinger, Preston, O'Brien & DiLalla, 1996). Physically attractive persons are more likely to appear in photos with other persons (in Chapter 8 we will see how physical attractiveness is a powerful influence on our social relationships) (Dollinger, 2002).

Of course one must be cautious in interpreting these photos. For instance, we are conditioned to smile when the photographer says "cheese!" While a smile generally indicates positive emotions, smiles may also be a way in which we create an impression of ourselves for others. For instance, in a study, participants were asked to imagine themselves applying for a job and the photo was to accompany the applications. They were more likely

(continued)

to smile when the job was relatively lower in status, and women smiled more when the job involved social contacts (Vrugt & Van Eechoud, 2002).

This approach offers several advantages over the conventional self-report measures of self-concept, **self-schema** and self-evaluation. The participants show not only how they see themselves but also what characteristics are important in their self-perception. The approach also invites creativity, which is usually lacking in self-report scales.

Thinking about ourselves can easily lead us to illusions about ourselves. For instance, do we really understand what makes us feel happy or unhappy? Consider studies in which people were asked to record their moods every day for several weeks or months (Stone, Hedges, Neale & Satin, 1985). They were also asked to record other factors believed to affect their emotional state, such as the weather, day of the week and the hours of sleep they had during the previous night. At the end of the study, they were asked to estimate the extent to which each factor had affected their mood. Even though their attention had been drawn every day to their emotional state and to the factors that they recorded, there was little relationship between how accurately the factor predicted their mood and how important the people believed that factor to be. While we believe that our mood is affected by the weather, how much we slept, the days of the week ("blue Monday"), the study found no evidence in support of these assumptions.

Moreover, merely thinking about ourselves may cause changes in how we see ourselves. Suppose, for example, you set out to understand why you love someone. People often find this difficult to verbalize, and therefore may select reasons that simply sound good or that happen to be on their mind at the time (recall the availability heuristic, Chapter 2). Perhaps your partner has just given you a thoughtful gift; you might report generosity as an important reason for your love. Perhaps you think immediately about the physical attractiveness of your partner and state this as a reason. As a result of thinking why you love a person, your reasons might change from what they were before you started to think about it. Your partner's generosity or physical attractiveness may become more important than it had been before (Wilson & Kraft, 1994).

In other words, introspection may well amount to "telling more than we can know" about ourselves (Wilson & Stone, 1985). This was recognized from the onset of scientific study in this area. Cooley (1902) argued that we construct our self-concepts from how we appear to others, which is then reflected back to us—what he called the **looking-glass self**. That is, we do not observe our own generosity; rather, we observe how others respond to us and then come to see ourselves as generous or attractive. People given very brief exposure to photos of someone smiling or scowling subsequently rated themselves lower than control groups; it was as if the people in the photos were smiling or scowling at the experimental participants (Baldwin, Carrell & Lopez, 1990).

There's a catch! Research indicates that our self-concepts generally match what we *believe* others think about us. However, what we think of ourselves often doesn't match what others actually think of us (Kenny & DePaulo, 1993). So, I may see myself as attractive and believe that you see me as attractive—but, in fact, you may actually believe something quite different. What we see in the looking glass may not be reality.

Let us examine several processes by which "reflection" enables us to construct our ideas and impressions of ourselves. These processes include social comparison, self-perception and gender-role socialization.

Comparing ourselves to others

An important source of information about ourselves is social comparison: comparing ourselves to others (Festinger, 1954). Indeed, we often cannot make sense of our own actions and feelings without looking outward to the actions and reactions of others. When we feel any uncertainty about who we are or how well we are doing, we seek comparative information. For example, Mandela, as a black person uncertain as to how he fit into a white-dominated society, was inspired by a nationalistic black poet to seek his identity in his own cultural roots.

Social comparison theory is based on three premises:

1. Humans have a drive to evaluate their opinions, feelings and abilities and want to feel confident that they are accurate.

2. In the absence of objective or nonsocial bases of assessment, individuals will evaluate themselves in comparison with others.

3. People tend to compare themselves with someone similar to them in opinion, background or ability.

For instance, if you consider being generous an important part of who you are, then observing how others behave in similar situations provides feedback as to how generous you really are. Even apparently objective feedback is influenced by social comparison. A grade of 75 percent in algebra may seem like objective information and may support your conception of yourself as mathematically competent. However, if many of your classmates attained marks over 80 percent, that same mark would be a blow to your self-esteem.

Now consider the case in which a close friend has performed better than you did on some task. On one hand, you may feel good about yourself for having such a smart, competent friend. However, your friend's superior performance may, in comparison, lower your own self-evaluation. It depends on how relevant the task performance is to your self-schema. If you identify yourself as a good tennis player, then your friend's championship performance will threaten your self-esteem. However, if tennis performance is not central to your self-schema, you can simply bask in reflected glory and actually feel better about yourself for having such an outstanding player as a friend (Tesser, 1988). Further, social comparison can evoke certain aspects of the self-schema, and these may vary in different situations. For instance, a female chemist may well think of herself primarily in terms of her occupation when in the company of other women who are not chemists but in terms of her gender when in the company of male chemists (McGuire & McGuire, 1988).

As a general rule, we compare ourselves to others who are similar to us on characteristics that are relevant to us (Wood, 1989). For instance, as students, the readers will compare themselves to other students in intelligence. However, at times we engage in *upward or downward comparison*. **Downward comparison**, with someone less able, less attractive or less powerful than ourselves can boost our self-esteem (Wills, 1981). On the other hand, we may at times compare ourselves to someone better than us to inspire us to greater heights. **Upward comparison** will often be ego–deflating but it can actually be ego enhancing (Collins, 1996). If a recreational tennis player plays with a professional and manages to win one of three sets, the recreational player will feel better about himself or herself, even after being defeated. All of these types of social comparison become relevant to prejudice (see Chapter 13).

When does comparing us to someone clearly superior in some way, a "superstar," become inspiring or deflating? For instance, imagine reading an article in your university paper about an outstanding, award-winning student. Lockwood & Kunda (1997, 1999) found that when participants' had been exposed to such a superstar, they tended to feel badly about themselves. If they had first been asked to think of some "peak" experience in school that made them feel proud, then comparing their own day of glory with a genuine "superstar" resulted in their self-esteem taking a nose-dive. However, if they had been asked to think of when they had done something typical of what they were like, then reading about the superstar actually inspired participants to imagine themselves in that position, and their self-evaluations were higher than those not exposed to that newspaper article. In sum, when we focus on ourselves as we are, then upward comparison can generate hope and optimism that we can be better.

Now, imagine that you have been ill and are trying to understand your situation. When the situation is uncertain, as it often may be, then we compare with others. Cancer patients, for example, benefit from both upward and downward comparisons (Wood & VanderZee, 1997; Buunk et al., 1990). They may compare themselves with other patients who are recovering from their illness (upward comparison), who may serve as models for hope and self-improvement. They may also compare themselves with those who are more seriously ill (downward comparison), providing them with a sense that "things could be worse." Through social comparisons, individuals can evaluate how seriously ill they are, how hopeful they can be about the outcome and how they are behaving as patients.

In general, people compare themselves to someone equal when the goal is self-assessment, to someone better when the goal is self-improvement and to someone inferior when the goal is self-enhancement (Wood, 1989). In short, we actively choose to whom we compare ourselves in order to accomplish certain goals. In all cases, social comparison provides us with useful information about ourselves.

Self-knowledge through observing ourselves

As discussed in the previous chapter, people tend to attribute the actions of others to stable dispositions or traits—honest people behave honestly. Bem (1972) suggests that people become aware of their own attitudes, feelings, values and actions in the same way that they form impressions of the characteristics of others —through observation of their own behaviour. If you see someone donating money and time to various good causes, you decide that this is a generous person. Similarly, if you observe yourself acting generously, generosity becomes part of your self-concept.

The notion of self-perception extends back to Schachter's (1964) work on emotion, suggesting that we infer our own emotional state from a sense of internal arousal, coupled with our interpretation of external cues. Thus, for example, you may decide that you found a joke to be funny because you laughed uproariously when the joke was told. However, if you are led to believe that some external factor caused you to laugh (such as the "canned laughter" on television sitcoms), then you decide that you weren't really so amused after all (Olson, 1990). We will see in Chapter 8 how the same reasoning may be applied to understand falling in love.

Of course, illusions may again complicate the picture. Imagine that as a volunteer in an experiment you are looking at pictures of attractive nudes. Electrodes have been attached to record your heart rate, and your heart rate is amplified and played back through a loudspeaker. Not surprisingly, you would tend to conclude that you are more attracted to those nudes for whom your heart rate increased. However, in the actual experiment, the heart rate feedback was false, using previously recorded heart rates that were increasing, decreasing and steady. That is, people who believed their heart rate had increased perceived they were more strongly attracted to that particular nude picture (Valins, 1966). The notion of self-knowledge through self-perception implies that rather than introspecting about what we really believe in, and then acting on those beliefs, we first act and then discover our beliefs and values from our actions. In later chapters, we will pursue this theme of how actions can lead to attitude changes.

Gender and self

In addition to the uniqueness that characterizes each human personality, our self-concept includes our identity in terms of various social categories: age, nationality, ethnicity, occupation, religion, etc. Perhaps most central to your social identity is your gender. Note that while the terms *sex* and *gender* are often used inter-changeably, *sex* generally refers to biological characteristics and *gender* refers to the roles, preferences and behaviours observed or assumed to be typical of men and women. So when psychologists try to explain differences between men and women, they tend to refer to them as gender differences when these explanations have to do with the roles of men and women in society. Beginning in childhood, we learn what *male* and *female* mean and to identify role behaviour appropriate to our own gender identity.

The research consistently indicates that women are more likely to have an interdependent view of themselves, focusing on their relationships, while male self-concepts tend to be constructed around ideas of independence (Cross & Madson, 1997). For instance, recall the "Who Am I?" test described earlier. Women will tend to complete it in terms of roles and relationships (I am a friend) or social characteristics (I am sociable), while men use individual characteristics (I am honest. I am competitive). Similar differences are found between cultures, which are explored later in this chapter, and in Chapter 4 (Watkins, Adair et al., 1998; Watkins, Akande et al., 1998; Kitayama & Marku, 1994).

What images, associations, memories, ideas and beliefs come to mind when you think of the words *man* and *woman*? Clearly, people in our culture (and every culture) have a richly elaborated and complex network of cognitive associations to the concepts of male and female. Indeed, gender may be invoked as a way of categorizing people, even where it is irrelevant to the situation (Bem, 1985). For instance, thinking of physicians as "male" is obsolete in contemporary society. However, the content of gender identity—what it means to identify one's self as male or female—differs markedly from one individual to another. Indeed, having to live up to rigid formulas of "masculinity" or "femininity" can be stressful (McCreary & Sadava, 1995). See Chapter 11 on how notions of "masculinity" may relate to prejudice.

Traditional psychological tests measured masculinity and femininity as polar opposites, in which one selected the "male" or "female" response to each item. Later research has challenged this one-dimensional view (Bem, 1974; Spence, 1985). Rather than forcing participants to choose between "male" and "female" responses, these studies use separate scales measuring "masculinity" and "femininity." Those who score high on one scale and low on the other would be described as traditionally "feminine" or "masculine" while those who endorse items from both scales are described as psychologically androgynous. People characterized by traditional sex-typed thinking tend to think of their social world primarily in terms of "male" and "female," while androgynous men and women tend to view people and events in terms of a greater variety of categories. Androgynous men and women appear to be better liked, more adaptable to situational demands, more satisfied in their relationships and to have higher self-esteem (Rosenzweig & Daley, 1989).

Apart from the obvious biological characteristics, what is called masculinity has been described as instrumentality or **agency**, a concern with achieving goals and being active in the world; while femininity is described as expressiveness or communion, being focused on other people and concerned with interpersonal relationships (Bakan, 1966; McCreary, 1990). Of course, to most people, a satisfying life would include both achieving in the external world and having satisfying close relationships—in other words, having both "masculine" and "feminine" psychological characteristics. Indeed, an excessively strong or unmitigated sense of agency would be destructive to the individual and society, suggesting one who acts regardless of the consequences to others (Spence et al., 1979, p. 1674). Similarly, an individual who is excessively communal, concerned only with the welfare of others, would not be able to function effectively in the external world. Thus, a balance between achievement and caring for others is necessary, avoiding either extreme (McCreary & Korabik, 1994).

Psychological androgyny signifies flexibility—a capacity to act in ways appropriate to the situation without its impinging on one's identity as male or female. Thus, it is important that women be assertive and concerned with achievement where this is appropriate. It is equally important that men be relationship-oriented and caring where the situation calls for this type of behaviour.

One more implication of gender concerns how gender may condition how we evaluate our competence. For instance, women may not consider themselves to be competent in math or science because of their gender. Indeed, in one study (Nosek et al., 2002), women who associated mathematical ability with being male rated themselves lower on mathematical ability, even where they had selected a math-intensive major. In another study, female participants scored as well as males on a test of scientific reasoning (Ehrlinger & Dunning, 2003). However, in self-ratings of various abilities, the women rated their "ability to reason about science" more negatively than the men. Further, when invited to participate in a "science jeopardy" contest with attractive prizes, women were less likely to sign up or express interest in entering. Clearly, we have chronic views about our strengths and weaknesses that may be influenced by gender stereotypes.

Self-Schemata and Their Effects

Schemata, as discussed in Chapter 2, are organized sets of beliefs and feelings about people and events that guide the processing of information. One particularly important schema is about the self. Your schema about yourself includes everything that you know, think or feel about yourself, the images and memories you have of yourself, even the possibilities that you can imagine for yourself in the future. These self-schemata of individuals differ in a number of ways, such as in clarity, complexity and consistency over time (Campbell et al., 1996).

Like other schemata, the self-schema organizes information and impressions. Your self-schema includes both how you might evaluate yourself on various characteristics and which characteristics you consider to be important. For example, John and Joan both consider themselves intelligent and persuasive. For John, intelligence is central, and he describes himself in those terms. When asked, he will also admit to being persuasive, but this is not fundamental to how he defines himself. On the other hand, Joan is a leader, and being persuasive is central to how she defines herself. She seldom mentions intelligence, although if asked she would rate herself highly on this dimension as well. John is schematic with respect to intelligence and aschematic with regard to persuasiveness, while Joan is schematic with respect to persuasiveness and aschematic with regard to intelligence.

What is important to understand is that simply measuring how someone rates themselves on a characteristic is not sufficient. The self-schema acts as a guide, enabling us to process relevant information (Markus, 1977). For instance, you might interpret a mark of 75 percent in social psychology as an achievement or as mediocre, depending on whether you see yourself as a budding psychologist and on how important high grades are to you. People respond differently to information depending on its relevance to the self-schema (Markus, Hamill & Sentis, 1987).

In a study, people were asked to rate themselves along a dimension of independence–dependence, and to indicate how important the trait was to them (Markus, 1977). Several weeks later, participants in the study were shown slides containing various words, and asked to push a button labelled "Me" if it applied to them or "Not Me" if it didn't. Those participants whose self-schema included independence–dependence made decisions more quickly about words related to that dimension (e.g., "conforming") but not about irrelevant words (e.g., "creative"). Thus, self-schemata helped them process information more rapidly. They were also able to think of personal examples of these traits more quickly (e.g., conforming: "I had my ears pierced just because everyone else did"). Similarly, when shown films of men involved in various activities, men whose self-schema stressed masculinity perceived activities such as weightlifting or watching baseball in larger, more meaningful sequences than gender-neutral activities such as eating an apple or playing a record (Markus, Smith & Moreland, 1985).

Self-schemata can also affect memory. This is demonstrated in a study in which people shown 40 adjectives, one at a time (e.g., *shy, ambitious, neat*), were subsequently much more likely to remember words they connected with the question "Does it describe you?" We associate new self-relevant information with a rich store of prior encoded information, and thus our self-schemata provide us with more retrieval cues (Rogers, Kuiper & Kirker, 1977). When older participants were cued to positive stereotypes of aging (e.g., wisdom) rather than negative stereotypes (e.g., incompetence, dementia), they performed better on tests of memory (Levy, 1996). Obviously, when a negative stereotype becomes part of the individual's self-schema, he comes to act as he is expected to act; the stereotype becomes a self-fulfilling prophecy (see Chapter 13).

The **self-reference effect** (Kihlstrom et al., 1988) refers to the fact that individuals remember information better when they can relate it to themselves. For instance, you will remember movie dialogue better if you identify with the character, and you will remember best the sections of a course in social psychology that you can relate to your own experience. The reasoning is that you have an extensive and complex set of knowledge, experience, images and beliefs about yourself, all of which constitute the self-schema, and any of which can be associated with this information. Indeed, people attribute more traits to themselves than they do to other people, and they may even attribute to them-

selves traits that are apparently opposite, such as "serious" and "carefree," or "intense" and "calm" (Sande, 1990). Of course, all of us receive both positive and negative information about ourselves on a daily basis but we differ in how we process it. It appears that chronically lonely people have a negative self-schema that causes them to pay selective attention to negative information consistent with this self-schema, and to remember it (Frankel & Prentice-Dunn, 1990).

Recall from the last chapter that schema effects are observed when a schema is activated, such as by priming. Certain conditions may arouse self-awareness: seeing oneself in a mirror, having one's picture taken or giving a talk in front of an audience (Duval and Wicklund, 1972). This focus on the self leads to self-evaluation, often with unpleasant emotional consequences. People may respond by leaving the situation—looking away from the mirror, avoiding the audience—or may change their behaviour to reduce discomfort over negative self-evaluation (Gibbons & Wicklund, 1983).

In summary, our self-schema influences how we experience our world and our lives. It directs our attention, it guides our interpretation of what we see and hear, and it influences what we remember and how we remember it. While all schemas act in these ways, the self-schema will generally have a more powerful influence.

Self-Evaluation

Feeling positive about oneself has been identified as an important component of effective and happy living. Indeed, low self-esteem has been linked empirically to various maladaptive behaviours. A considerable amount of research has been directed towards identifying the effects of low self-esteem. Much is based on the assumption that low self-esteem leaves people vulnerable to all sorts of personal difficulties and social pressures. While notions of self are derived in large measure from experiences and the reactions of others, some people have relatively secure and consistent self-esteem, while others have self-esteem that fluctuates with the ups and downs of life, depending on the feedback they obtain from others (Baldwin & Sinclair, 1996).

It has been hypothesized that people low in self-esteem are more easily persuaded. However, individuals with low self-esteem tend to have difficulties in receiving and understanding persuasive messages, per-

Do We Choose Occupations That Match Our Self-Image?

It's a familiar script: when we meet someone, the question soon arises, "What do you do?" We usually are not referring to their hobbies, sports or sexual predilections but to their job or occupation or their career aspirations. To a considerable extent, our occupation defines us. It follows that the stereotypes that exist in society about various occupations also become part of our social selves (Vroom, 1964), and reflect our personal values (Rosenberg, 1957).

Men and women try to match their self-images to an image of compatible occupations. If the person's self-image includes being helpful (or communal, associated with femininity, as discussed earlier), then the helping professions such as medicine, social work and teaching would be particularly attractive (Super, 1980). Similarly, a person whose self-image as a man includes being good at solving technical problems will be attracted to more technical occupations. This may explain in part, why, despite some significant progress, gender segregation in occupations remains a fact of life in Canada and other Western nations. That is, men are overrepresented in some occupations, particularly those of a technical nature, while women predominate in clerical and service occupations, perhaps because these choices are consistent with how they view themselves. Indeed, those who enter male-dominated occupations tend to have more "masculine" and less "feminine" self-concepts (Gianakos & Subich, 1988).

Research by Maclean and Kalin (1994) supports this model. First, they set out to establish what the stereotypes were in three traditionally male-dominated occupations (engineering, law, medicine) and three female-dominated occupations (nursing, rehabilitation therapy, teaching). Subjects were asked to rate typical members of each profession on two characteristics: affiliation (wanting to be with others) and dominance (wanting to control others). Engineers and lawyers were rated as high in dominance and low in affiliation, a stereotypically male pattern, while the mirror-image pattern of high affiliation and low dominance characterized ratings of nurses, teachers and rehabilitation therapists.

Subsequently, they recruited students in academic programs leading to these six occupations and found that their self-images were congruent with the stereotypes of their chosen occupation. The self-images of law students, for example, tended to be high in dominance and low in affiliation, while the self-images of student nurses consisted of low dominance and high affiliation.

The interesting exception was medicine. While traditional participation rates are considerably higher for men, the dominance–affiliation profile was closer to that of the "female" professions. Medicine, of course, clearly involves both helping and technical competence, and women have entered the profession in substantial numbers in the past decades.

haps due to anxiety or inability to pay attention (Rhodes & Wood, 1992). Therefore, while high self-esteem individuals have the confidence to resist persuasion, low self-esteem individuals are not easily persuaded when they don't get the message. Those with intermediate scores on measures of self-esteem are more easily persuaded; this is called a curvilinear relationship (see Figure 3–1).

It has been reported that women suffer more from lower self-esteem than do men, and that this difference originates in adolescence. However, recent evidence

does not point to an unusual drop in self-esteem among adolescent women (Kling & Hyde, 1996). Perhaps this difference will disappear in upcoming generations. Indeed, a recent meta-analysis (see Chapter 1) of studies indicates that a statistically significant, but small difference still exists between men and women (Kling, Hyde, Showers & Buswell, 1999). How can we explain why men in our society tend to have only slightly higher self-esteem than women do?

One proposed explanation for the gender difference in self-esteem is that disadvantaged groups such as women are stigmatized as being of less value and therefore evaluate themselves less favourably (Crocker & Major, 1989). Members of such groups, including women, protect their self-concept in several ways: by attributing failure or other unwanted outcomes to prejudice against themselves, by making social comparisons with members of their own group rather than the advantaged group and by placing more value on success in areas where their own group tends to do well. For instance, while women tend to earn less than men in equivalent occupations, they may protect their self-esteem by comparing their earnings to those of other women or to others in occupations where women predominate. Thus, women avoid becoming what the stereotype prescribes—passive victims with low self-esteem.

It is important to understand that the self-concept is not limited to images of the present or memories of the past but may also extend to the future. Imagine yourself in 10 years, 20 years or 40 years. You can imagine yourself as quite different from the way you are now, in both positive and negative ways—what Markus and Nurius (1986) have called "possible selves." We all have visions of the self that we hope to become or dream of becoming, such as being rich, successful or thin. We also have visions of the self that we fear to become, such as being sick, unemployed or lonely.

These possibilities can have powerful effects in the here and now. If you can imagine yourself as successful in business or as a world traveller, you are more likely to act in order to make it happen. On the other hand, if you can imagine yourself as being poor or chronically ill, you may act to prevent this possibility from occurring or you may act fatalistically on the assumption that this *will* happen.

The fact that you can imagine yourself in other possible ways also provides you with a frame of reference for self-evaluation. If you can imagine yourself as being very rich or poor, generous or stingy, happy or sad, then you can evaluate yourself as you are now in relation to these possibilities. **Self-discrepancy theory** provides a formal statement of this idea.

Comparing ourselves to self-guides

What does it mean to have low self-esteem? Self-discrepancy theory is based on the premise that the gaps between actual and possible selves can lead to emotional difficulty (Higgins, 1987). People compare their self-concept—themselves as they are at present—to "self-guides," the standards that they strive to attain. One of these self-guides is the "ideal self" embodying their hopes and aspirations. Another self-guide is the "ought self," the obligations they place on themselves—their own sense of duty and responsibility.

That is, people compare their own conception of themselves with what they would wish for themselves and what they feel they should be. For instance, you might see yourself as a moderately successful student, wish you were at the top of your class (ideal), and feel that you ought to be able to raise all of your marks to at least a *B* level (ought). You might consider yourself generous, which is how you ought to be, but wish you could be even more generous. In other words, the actual self is monitored in comparison with some desired end-state (Higgins, 1996).

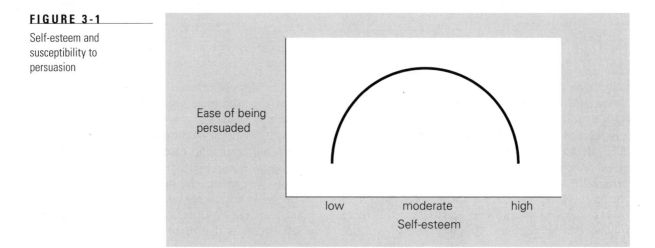

FIGURE 3-1

Self-esteem and susceptibility to persuasion

Ease of being persuaded

low   moderate   high

Self-esteem

Clearly, our self-guides, what we would wish ourselves to be, will usually exceed our concept of ourselves as we are now, and this is all to the good. As the poet Robert Browning wrote, "Ah, but a man's reach should exceed his grasp, or what's a heaven for?" However, if the self-discrepancies are excessive, we may experience emotional distress, and the theory predicts the type of distress for each discrepancy. If we see ourselves as much less than we should be (a discrepancy with the "ought" self), we tend to experience guilt, shame and possibly anxiety. On the other hand, if we see ourselves as much less than we would wish to be (a discrepancy with the ideal), then we experience disappointment, frustration and perhaps debilitating depression. Interestingly, actual self–ideal discrepancies in expectant parents predict increased sadness after the child is born (Alexander & Higgins, 1993). These self-discrepancies tend to be relatively stable over time (Strauman, 1996).

Why would we experience a self-discrepancy? A self-discrepancy may be caused by an excessively low self-evaluation or unrealistically high self-guides. For instance, Jennifer may see herself as a poor tennis player because she doesn't realize her own abilities or because she cannot attain the level of Serena Williams. A large discrepancy between one's self-esteem and unrealistic, perfectionist standards of what one "ought" to be has been related to depression (Flett, Hewitt, Blankenstein & O'Brien, 1991). Does self-discrepancy cause people to become depressed? Perhaps, but it is plausible that depression causes people to evaluate themselves negatively or to adopt unrealistic self-guides.

Another self-guide has been suggested: the feared self. This is the kind of person you worry about becoming and would rather not become (Markus & Nurius, 1986). Imagine yourself in the future, not as you would wish to be but as you would *not* want to be. For instance, if you see yourself as hardworking and ambitious, and imagine yourself as highly successful in the future, can you also imagine yourself as a failure, languishing without having achieved anything? In contrast to the other self-guides, discrepancy from your feared self is much to be desired; the farther you see yourself from this dire possibility, the better you feel. Indeed, research finds a lack of discrepancy to be particularly powerful in arousing feelings of anxiety and guilt (Carver, Lawrence & Scheier, 1999).

Maintaining a positive self-evaluation

Clearly, success enhances one's self-esteem. However, none of us is immune from anxiety and insecurity about our own abilities. Can we do well in school? Can we create the right impression in that job interview? Are we good enough to win that crucial game? Self-doubts can cause people to behave in self-defeating ways. People who are upset are more likely to pursue unrealistic risks: to take wild guesses on exams, or gamble their money, all in the hope of getting out of that blue mood. Usually the risk will not pay off, which gives the person something else to feel bad about and perpetuates a downward cycle (Leith & Baumeister, 1996).

Some people deal with such self-doubt in a way that actually reduces the chances for success. In a strategy called **self-handicapping**, people arrange in advance for impediments to a successful performance. These impediments serve to protect their self-esteem from the aftermath of failure. For example, if Carol is anxious about an upcoming exam, and considers good grades an important aspect of who she is, she may decide to

A large discrepancy between one's self-evaluation and an unrealistically high self-guide can lead to low self-esteem and even depression.

party instead of studying the night before. She can attribute failure to the self-imposed handicap (not studying), rather than to effort or ability. Of course, an unlikely success despite that handicap would enhance self-esteem even more. You can't lose for losing!

Various self-handicapping strategies have been identified. Some involve actual changes in behaviour (e.g., not exerting enough effort), while others involve claims of illness or unfair task demands (Arkin & Baumgardner, 1985). Studies indicate that men tend to self-handicap more than women (Harris, Snyder, Higgins & Schrag, 1986), and that men tend to use alcohol and drugs for this purpose, while women are more likely to claim physical illness or stress (Hirt, Deppe & Gordon, 1991). Note that we're not talking here about finding excuses after the fact but about acting in advance to create an excuse for failure.

Consider drinking. Since alcohol intoxication has been shown to reduce self-awareness (Hull, 1987), it is logical to conclude that people may drink as a self-handicapping strategy (Berglas, 1987). That is, getting drunk (and suffering the inevitable hangover) may protect a person from the consequences of low self-esteem. The heavy drinker no longer feels responsible for acts committed under the influence of alcohol, since the connection between oneself and one's action has been disrupted. Thus, drunken behaviour may become "disinhibited" because one can attribute the act to the alcohol (see also Chapter 16). The opportunity to "blame it on the bottle," whether coping with expected failure or committing antisocial acts, is a powerful incentive to drink excessively for many people.

Culture and the Self

Individualism and collectivism

Nelson Mandela sought to reconcile his sense of who he was as a successful lawyer in the white-dominated society and as a black African from a distinctive culture. The ways in which people perceive and define themselves are influenced by the culture to which they belong. In the Western societies, social norms focus on the individual rather than on the group or community. Indeed, the American ideal is described as the self-contained individual, someone whose identity and sense of self is complete in and of himself or herself (Sampson, 1977). Canadian ideals are fairly similar, leaning towards a lesser degree of individualism (Adams, 2003).

Not all cultures have such **individualistic** concepts (Triandis, 1989). Consider, for example, that we all have two (or more) names, our first name which has been given to us by our parents, uniquely our own, and our family name which we share with those closest to us. What comes first?—what is uniquely us or what we share with the significant others in our lives? In our Western culture, what is uniquely ours is our "first name," but in Chinese culture, the first name is the shared family name, followed by the given name. This suggests that in Chinese culture, what is most valued is one's family connection in one's identity, not the uniqueness of the individual.

That is, in societies such as India, China or Japan, self-concepts are described as more relational or communal or **collectivist** (Markus & Kitayama, 1991; Kitayama & Markus, 1994). In studies of how people describe themselves, Korean respondents describe themselves, first and foremost, in terms of their family, while U.S. respondents describe themselves as individuals with unique characteristics (Maday & Szalay, 1976). Chinese subjects were more likely than U.S. subjects to describe themselves in terms of social roles (e.g., "I am a daughter") and to qualify social roles as friends or partners (Ip & Bond, 1995). These studies reflect how different cultures reconcile independence and interdependence (Markus & Kitayama, 1991). That is, while we all seek to understand ourselves as distinct individuals, we also need to establish meaningful relationships with others. In Western cultures, we define ourselves primarily in terms of internal attributes such as motives, abilities, values and personalities, while in many other cultures, people define themselves primarily in terms of their interdependent relationships with other people, groups and institutions. (Draguns, 1988). It is also interesting to note that, on average, people from Eastern cultures are less clear and consistent in their self-concept than are people in Western cultures such as Canada (Campbell et al., 1996).

However, even in individualist cultures, the self may also be more tied to its social context than people realize. While we stress our uniqueness, we also define ourselves in terms of relevant roles and statuses in society. It has been suggested that men are more likely to see themselves in terms of individual characteristics and activities, whereas women tend to express a "connected self," embedded in a matrix of relationships (Gilligan, 1982). Apart from gender differences, people with a more connected, as opposed to individuated, self-concept tend to have a more sophisticated or complex self-concept (Pratt, Pancer, Hunsberger & Manchester, 1990).

Self-esteem and culture

As noted earlier, self-esteem is widely considered to be essential to happiness, mental health and a productive life. According to this view, it is important not only to have a secure sense of self but also to feel good about it. Indeed, in the United States, a state government adopted programs designed to raise self-esteem in the hope of preventing alcohol and drug abuse, violence, teenage pregnancy and child abuse (California Task Force to Promote Self-Esteem, 1990).

Clearly, the apparent need for high self-esteem that pervades our culture is not a universal need (Heine, Lehman, Markus & Kitayama, 1999). It is interesting that Asian immigrants who have been in Canada for a longer time tend to have higher self-esteem than do those who are more recent immigrants, and that self-esteem increased over seven months among Japanese exchange students at the University of British Columbia (Heine & Lehman, 1995). It is apparent that, in the Japanese and other Eastern cultures, individuals are less concerned with protecting a high self-regard than with self-criticism, seeking to identify and improve what is lacking in themselves. They tend to view themselves habitually as incomplete and feel unsatisfied with their performance. In other words, their reactions are driven by self-guides (ideal, ought), not simply by self-protection.

While this would seem to be distressing to Westerners, such a habit is seen as healthy, leading to self-improvement. The authors cite the example of a

CRITICAL THINKING

Self-Evaluation and Self-Improvement

Clearly there can be advantages to honest self-evaluations. Confronting why we have failed or have been disappointed in some way can lead us to positive changes. However, clarity in evaluating ourselves may be difficult to come by.

One reason is the illusion of control, described in Chapter 2. Recall that we tend to value lottery tickets more highly when we have chosen the numbers, although our objective chances are not affected in the least by this illusory control. An illusion of control may lead us to take unnecessary risks and to blame ourselves excessively for unfavourable outcomes (Thompson, 1999). On the other hand, moderately depressed people seem to be less liable to the illusion of control, having a more fatalistic or realistic sense of their own control over outcomes (Alloy & Abramson, 1979). This suggests that realism may not always be best and that the illusion of control (within limits, of course) leads to positive emotions and motivates us to take on new challenges.

Another bias concerns self-improvement. Why do people persist in attempting to change themselves in some way despite repeated failure and frustration? For instance, we may persist in trying to lose weight despite repeatedly unsuccessful attempts with various diets. This pattern of unrealistic expectations about eventual success after repeated failure is called the **false hope syndrome** (Polivy & Herman, 2000, 2002). Failure leads us to conclude that just a few minor modifications in our strategy will enable us to control our drinking or smoking, lose that weight and keep it off, achieve that "A" average or win a tennis tournament. The pattern repeats itself.

Clearly some kinds of self-change are realistic or at least possible as well as desirable. However, we must learn from experience and distinguish between realistic and unrealistic self-change goals. For instance, we tend to underestimate how long it will take us to complete a task (Buehler, Griffin & Ross, 1995). While hope and optimism are necessary for change, false hope will be a barrier to the kinds of changes that succeed over time.

Membership in a group is an important aspect of self-concept in Eastern societies.

baseball player, who in American society would be assumed to have a certain level of natural ability which practice and concentration can bring to fruition. While the ball player in the West is seen as limited by natural ability, in Japanese culture there is no peak or limit to how well they could perform. Consistent self-criticism is seen as motivating the person, rather than discouraging the person.

In a study by Kitayama et al. (1997), a set of situations was described to participants. Some of the scenarios consisted of successes such as serving an ace in tennis, passing exams, looking good or handsome, while others involved failures such as breaking something valuable due to carelessness, doing unexpectedly poorly on a test or not being invited to a social event. Subjects were asked to indicate the extent to which their own self-esteem would increase or decrease in that situation. American subjects indicated that they would expect strong increases in self-esteem in the success situations and lesser levels or decreases in the failure situations. Conversely, Japanese subjects responded more strongly to the failure situations. Kitayama et al. (1997) attribute their responses to a tendency among the Japanese participants to focus on what can be gained by failure, learning from it.

Recent work by Baumeister and his colleagues challenge the simplistic view that high self-esteem is

necessay and desirable, even in our own culture (Baumeister, Campbell, Krueger & Vohs, 2003). While self-esteem literally refers to how much people value themselves, it does not imply accuracy—we may think more of ourselves than the facts warrant. Indeed, high self-esteem may represent an honest and accurate appraisal of our strengths and weaknesses or it may represent a narcissistic self-absorption (see Critical Thinking—The Perils of Narcissism), a defensive reaction or even conceit or arrogance. Obviously, while realistic self-esteem will help us to perform well, performing well can also boost our self-esteem. Similarly, while a person with high self-esteem may behave in a manner to become a leader, being a leader may also boost self-esteem. Baumeister et al. (2003) review abundant evidence that attempts to boost self-esteem, such as through therapeutic interventions, does not improve performance in school or elsewhere.

It is commonly believed that low self-esteem causes aggression, ranging from juvenile gangs to political terrorism to family violence. Ostensibly, violent acts would permit someone to feel a sense of domination over someone else and thus enhance the individual's self-esteem. Further, people with low self-esteem would feel threatened by insults or disrespect and perhaps react violently. Thus, it is argued that we must raise people's self-esteem in order to reduce violence in society.

The Perils of Narcissism

We live in a culture and an age in which the individual is supreme. The rights and responsibilities of the individual are fundamental to any democracy. The concept of a free market is built on the notion that the individual consumer's choices dictate the success or failure of any enterprise. Indeed, psychology is built on the study of the individual.

Is there a downside to our focus on the individual? Historian Christopher Lasch (published in 1979 but clearly applicable today) observes a malaise in contemporary American society, a loss of confidence in the future. He attributes this malaise to the extremes of competitive individualism, "which, in its decadence, has carried the logic of individualism to the extreme of a war of all against all, the pursuit of happiness to the dead end of a narcissistic preoccupation with the self." **Narcissism** denotes a complete self-absorption, living for you and for the moment, with little concern for the community, the past or the future.

Narcissists depend on others to validate their self-esteem. They need the attention, approval and support of others. "For the narcissist, the world is a mirror" (p. 10). Lasch identifies a number of symptoms or manifestations of this cultural narcissism: excessive concern with self-esteem, the popularity of psychotherapeutic/human potential experiences, withdrawal from political involvement and cynicism about politics and the substitution of "personal development." He observes that "making it" in the corporate environment occurs not by hard work and achievement but by selling oneself and convincing others that you are a "winner." Education, as well, has substituted personal development and raising self-esteem for achievement and skills training. Even sports have become spectacles rather than competition, focusing on the personal lives and contract disputes of celebrities. Consider that one of the most famous persons in hockey is not a superstar player but a commentator, Don Cherry.

Give some attention to advertising as an instructive example. In the past few decades, advertising has shifted in focus from the characteristics of the product to the consumer. The message is that people need a certain product to define themselves as individuals and attain their goals in life—being rich, popular or successful. Researchers refer to the "commodified self-concept," in which one defines oneself in terms of wearing the right clothes, driving the right car, using the right cosmetics (Murphy & Miller, 1997). Consumers choose products not for perceived advantages in quality and price but for what the products represent to themselves and others about themselves.

Lasch does not criticize individualism *per se* but its degradation into narcissism. Baumeister et al.'s (1996) discussion of the "dark side" of self-esteem carries echoes of Lasch's trenchant critique. Indeed, we might consider whether much of psychology conveys a "sanction for selfishness," a message that we should be most concerned about ourselves (Wallach & Wallach, 1983). Keep this issue in mind as you continue to read this textbook.

However, this view is not consistent with what is known about disadvantaged groups and about violent people. Members of groups that tend to be lower in self-esteem, such as women, people suffering from depression and disadvantaged minority groups, do not tend to be more aggressive. On the other hand, perpetrators of violent acts such as murder, rape, spousal and child abuse, political terrorism and genocide are often described as arrogant, confident or narcissistic (Baumeister, Smart & Boden, 1996; Baumeister, Bushman & Campbell, 2002). This is discussed further in Chapter 11.

In other words, there is no consistent evidence that low self-esteem is a cause of violent behaviour or other social ills (Bushman & Baumeister, 2002). Yet, people in Western nations continue to believe that elevating the self-esteem of its members is a panacea for social ills. Perhaps not coincidentally, the society that is most committed to the desirability of raising self-esteem, the United States, is also one of the world's most violent societies. Perhaps some of this commitment should be redirected towards instilling virtues such as modesty, humility and self-improvement (Baumeister, Smart & Boden, 1996).

Thus far, we have discussed how individuals view themselves and how these views influence their behaviour and are influenced by the social environment—the "looking-glass self." People are not, however, simply passive recipients of others' views but also act to influence how others perceive them.

Presenting Ourselves to Others

To be an effective political leader in a heterogeneous nation, Nelson Mandela must have been perceived by others as a leader of his people, as well as one who was highly educated and intellectually sophisticated. Indeed, as an effective leader, Mandela clearly acted in ways to enhance this impression. All of us care what others think of us and thus we seek to create or maintain a positive image of ourselves.

We can compare social interaction to a theatrical performance, in which each of us assumes certain roles or social identities. Indeed, the metaphor of a theatrical performance has become part of our everyday thinking, particularly in the sense of playing a role. Goffman (1959) argues that when circumstances threaten our ability to regulate the impression we create of ourselves, we are compelled to act to save face. We may even use props to help create the right impression; when we dress in a certain style, drive a certain car, serve the right wine or add those personal touches to our home, we are providing information to others about ourselves.

However, Goffman did not claim that creating a favourable image is the only motive underlying social interaction. While we want people to think favourably of us, we also want people to understand and accept us as we are. That is, we want people to like us and to understand us, and so we want both to manage the impression that others have of us and to be open and spontaneous with others. At times, these two motivations are in conflict.

It is also important to understand that self-presentation is not always conscious and deliberate

and indeed may often become automatic (Baumeister, Hutton & Tice, 1989). For example, someone who is usually serious and hardworking on the job may self-present as fun-loving off the job with friends. This does not necessarily imply something artificial in that person's behaviour, only that the person is capable of behaving in ways appropriate to various situations.

Strategies of managing the impression we create

Several **impression management** strategies are available (Jones & Pittman, 1982). One is **ingratiation**, making oneself likable to another, such as by agreeing with the other person, praising the person or doing favours for him or her (see Chapter 8). Of course, a degree of subtlety is necessary—people don't respond warmly if they believe they are being manipulated.

Another strategy is *self-promotion*, an attempt to be seen as competent or outstanding. This is, of course, a necessary goal in situations such as a job interview. An applicant may even admit to a weakness to stress achievement in another, more important area: "I'm not very strong in accounting but I'm great at sales!"

You might present yourself as virtuous, subtly indicating to others how hard you are working or how moral and honest you are. You might supplicate or beg for sympathy. Intimidation is also possible by attempting to convince the person that you are dangerous in some way. Of course, the other party can always call your bluff.

Impression management may seem manipulative and phony. However, it is also appropriate to present those aspects of yourself that best suit your goals in the situation. Your inexhaustible supply of risqué jokes may create a favourable impression at a party but not in a job interview. It is reasonable to want others to be aware of your special qualities and to appreciate them. People can and do develop certain social skills to influence others to like, respect, admire and perhaps even fear them.

Finally, recall our discussion of upward and downward social comparison. How do we present ourselves to others in comparison with others? Feltovich, Harbaugh & To (2002) argue that average people will express these comparisons clearly and in detail, while those who are outstanding or great in some way will say little or nothing to compare themselves to others. They call this phenomenon "countersignalling," playing down the obvious. Thus, for instance, minor bureaucrats will prove their status by displays of their power and authority, while those who are truly powerful will downplay their power, perhaps by showing generosity. Mediocre students may answer the easier questions in class while the best students hold back, embarrassed to prove their knowledge in this way. Acquaintances show their good intentions by ignoring our flaws, while close friends show their intimacy by telling us about our faults, perhaps in a teasing manner. In short, modesty and reticence are ways of self-presentation. When you've "got it," there is no need to flaunt it.

Relative deprivation in self-presentation

Consider how people express resentment or dissatisfaction about lacking something that others may have. This sense of **relative deprivation** stems from social comparison with others. However, the expression of resentment will be governed by the situation as well as the extent of perceived deprivation. For example, unions may exaggerate their dissatisfactions in negotiations to elicit greater generosity from management. On the other hand, people may minimize their statements of dissatisfaction in order to appear reasonable or likable in a marriage or with a colleague at work, for example.

In other words, our expressions of dissatisfaction may be governed by self-presentation motives. Two studies are instructive. In one, subjects role-played an interaction in which they expressed their resentment about a mark in a course. Some were instructed to express their feeling honestly; others were told to act in such a way as to be "taken seriously" by their partner; and a third group was instructed to ingratiate themselves to their partner. Those in the third group, whose goal was simply to be liked, tended to understate their resentment, while those instructed to intimidate their partner (to be "taken seriously") tended to overstate their resentment (Olson, Hafer, Couzens, Kramins & Taylor, 1997).

In a second study, working adults were invited to express their feelings about the lack of day-care facilities, either publicly or privately and anonymously. Before they responded, the experimenter told them that she herself was either satisfied or dissatisfied with day-care availability in that city. When the subjects' answers were public, their reports of how much they resented the lack of day care was influenced by the experimenter's alleged resentment or contentment, while their private responses were unaffected by the experimenter's expressed feelings. Thus, while we may feel the resentment about relative deprivation, how we express it is influenced by how we want others to perceive us (Olson, Hafer, Couzens, Kramins & Taylor, 1997).

Confirming self-concept

As discussed earlier, we want both to create a good impression and to be authentic. Swann (1992) proposes that we present ourselves in ways that will verify or confirm our self-concept. That is, we want to feel that we know ourselves. For example, if you believe that you are not athletic, you may find it disturbing to be praised for playing brilliant tennis because the comment challenges a long-standing aspect of your self-concept. Indeed, in an experiment, subjects with negative self-opinions tended to choose partners who also appraised them unfavourably (Swann, Stein-Seroussi & Giesler, 1992).

Personality and self-presentation

People vary in their need to present themselves in socially desirable ways (Paulhus, 1990). It is important to distinguish between *self-deception,* giving biased self-reports that one honestly believes to be true, and *impression management*—deliberately giving favourable self-descriptions to others (Paulhus & Reid, 1991).

Snyder (1979) has described how individuals vary in **self-monitoring**, adjusting one's self-presentation in response to subtle cues from others. His scale measures people's concern with the appropriateness of their self-presentation, whether they look to others for cues about how to act appropriately and whether they can use these cues to modify their behaviour. As we would expect, high self-monitors tend to be more friendly, conformist, adaptive and less shy. For example, in one study, low self-monitors tended to like an individual acting in an agreeable manner in a video, even if they were told that the person had been paid to be ingratiating. High self-monitors, on the other hand, differentiated between someone paid to be agreeable and someone being agreeable without being paid to do so (Jones & Baumeister, 1976).

High self-monitors have a particularly rich and complex set of social schemata and stereotypes, useful both in categorizing and judging new people or new contexts and in deciding how to respond. Conversely, low self-monitors attend less to others than to themselves, thus developing a more secure and more complex image of who they are, and have more self-schemata available.

A CASE IN POINT

Protecting Ourselves: The Need for Privacy

Altman (1971) argues that in our social lives we must balance and reconcile two opposing needs: the need for intimacy and the need for privacy. In a more general sense, we want to control how much others know about us and how others will interact with us.

Privacy concerns will vary with the situation (Westin, 1970). In solitude, we are secluded physically from intrusions by others, alone in our rooms or in the woods. In the presence of others, we can achieve privacy through anonymity, such as walking in a crowded city street or shopping mall. When we are engaged in interaction with someone, we can maintain privacy through reticence, avoiding self-disclosure. Finally, intimacy allows us to be alone together with a group or person, isolated from others. That is, privacy is not synonymous with being alone.

We can regulate privacy through a number of mechanisms (Altman, 1971). Cultural norms and practices protect us to some extent, for example, by permitting us to drop in on close friends in the early evening but not at 3 a.m. or by not permitting us to eavesdrop on a conversation (at least not too obviously). We can arrange our environment to protect our privacy; for example, we can use doors, drapes or blinds and arrange furniture to create personal zones in shared spaces. Electronically operated locks on the front doors of apartment buildings allow tenants to control access. We can use various nonverbal devices to maintain privacy even when personal space is invaded inadvertently; for example, on a crowded elevator we stand side to side rather than face to face and avoid eye contact. Finally, what we say and how we say it can regulate the degree of intimacy with another person.

In an age of increasingly sophisticated technology and a heightened concern with crime and terrorism, the protection of privacy becomes increasingly difficult. We now have the means of monitoring the movements, speech, e-mails, credit history and buying habits of almost anyone and everyone. Is privacy a thing of the past?

Knowing Yourself, or Feeling Good about Yourself?

Much of the preceding discussion reflects an important controversy in the research concerning the self. Two schools of thought contend self-enhancement and self-verification. The **self-enhancement** position is based on the argument that we seek feedback that increases, or at least maintains, our feelings of self-worth. Recall the discussion in Chapter 2 on the self-serving bias and defensive attributions. Of course, most people *want* to feel good about themselves. In fact, some individuals may go to the point of self-deception, viewing themselves in an unrealistically favourable light. Mild self-deception appears to contribute to a general state of well being, and even good health (Paulhus & Reid, 1991; Taylor, & Brown, 1988). Older people are less likely to engage in self-deception when thinking about the future, not because their expectations are rosier but because they have learned through experience what to expect (Robinson & Ryff, 1999).

Could this self-enhancing bias be peculiar to some cultures but not to others? Research suggests this may be so, particularly when comparing North Americans to people from Eastern cultures such as the Japanese (Markus & Kitayama, 1991). As noted earlier, protecting self-esteem is often less important than a self-critical stance—seeking to learn from experience.

Indeed, using measures of behaviour, studies suggest that the Japanese are not simply saying that they view themselves in a less positive manner—they truly believe it. In a study, students from Ritsumeikan University in Kyoto, Japan, were compared with those from the University of British Columbia (Heine & Lehman, 1999). All participants were asked to rate a series of descriptive adjectives in terms of how well it described them (e.g., I am extremely attractive) and then in describing the type of person they would ideally like to be (e.g., I would ideally like to be extremely attractive). The differences between the two sets of ratings provided a measure of a self-ideal discrepancy as described earlier in this chapter. In comparison with both groups of North Americans, the self-ideal discrepancies were greater among the Japanese students. However, self-ideal discrepancy did not predict higher scores on a commonly used measure of depression among the Japanese as it did among Canadian students. In other words, the Japanese were more dissatisfied with themselves, but these self-critical orientations were less distressful to them. As noted earlier, Japanese tend to be more self-critical so as to promote self-improvement and better fit in with their groups (Kitayama, Markus, Matsumoto & Norasakkunkit, 1997).

Even in our society, people can be realistic about themselves and may have a difficult time accepting unrealistic praise or even unexpected success. We are imbued with the maxim "Know thyself," which implies that accuracy is important. Most weekend tennis players will not feel better among themselves if someone compares them to a Wimbledon champion. Thus, individuals seek **self-verification**—feedback consistent with their actual self-concept.

According to self-verification theory (Swann, 1990), there are two reasons why we might maintain a negative view of ourselves and reject self-enhancing communications. First, if we were to change our opinion of ourselves every time someone told us something different—even if it were more positive—it would be unsettling and confusing, and so we seek to maintain some kind of coherence and consistency in our self-concept. Second, it can be embarrassing when people have unrealistic expectations about us that we cannot hope to fulfill, so we feel we'd better let them know our limitations as soon as possible.

In short, we want to feel good about ourselves *and* to know ourselves. These two competing motives are illustrated in the following classic experiment (Deutsch & Soloman, 1959). Participants worked in four-member teams solving problems. At the end, they received feedback indicating that they had scored the highest (success) or lowest (failure) of their team on this test of "flexible thinking." Following the feedback, subjects received a note, ostensibly from a teammate. In one condition, the note praised the subject's performance and desirability as a teammate; in the other,

the note was very negative. Not surprisingly, those with positive self-evaluations reacted very positively to someone who confirmed their positive self-image and negatively to those who gave unfavourable evaluations. The interesting results came in the condition where the feedback indicated that they had failed. When people were told that they had poor ability in "flexible thinking," they responded favourably to the writer of the positive note but just as favourably to the writer of the rather nasty note. Thus, the study provides some evidence both for a person's need for self-enhancement through creating a positive impression and for self-consistency—confirmation of one's own self-concept.

A Final Note

This chapter does not, by any means, complete our discussion of the self in social psychology. Self-relevant concepts occur in virtually every chapter of this volume. For instance, self-consistency and self-justification will be presented as fundamental to the well-known theory of cognitive dissonance (see Chapter 5). Olson & Hafer (1990) discuss the apparently paradoxical preoccupation with the self within social psychology. We have seen that what is apparently personal and private cannot be understood apart from its cultural context, even in our individualistic culture. The personal is social.

Summary

1. The ways in which people view themselves are derived primarily from social experience rather than private introspection.

2. Social comparison, self-perception and gender-role socialization are some of the processes involved in self-knowledge. Social comparison tends to be with similar others but may be upward or downward in certain conditions.

3. Some people adopt identities that are traditionally masculine or feminine and others manifest features of both (psychological androgyny)—a more flexible orientation.

4. People develop self-schemata, which organize information and impressions about the self, define what is important to the individual's self-concept and guide the processing of self-relevant information.

5. While a positive self-evaluation is important to people, self-esteem may not be as crucial as is commonly assumed.

6. Self-discrepancy theory is based on the proposition that we compare our self-concept to "self guides"— the ideal self and the ought self. Large discrepancies between the self-concept and these "possible selves" are related to emotional difficulties.

7. In the interests of protecting self-esteem, individuals sometimes behave in self-defeating ways and may act to handicap their chance of success.

8. Cultures vary in the extent to which the self-concept is individualist as opposed to collectivist or communitarian. In cultures with the latter orientation, the self is tied more to social roles, relationships and institutions. People in individualist cultures are more likely to see themselves as unique, to derive self-esteem from purely personal accomplishment and to express self-focused emotions.

9. Individuals seek to manage the impression that others have of them, generally without conscious deliberation.

10. Tactics of impression management include ingratiation, self-promotion, supplication (begging) and intimidation.

11. When individuals feel deprived of something relative to others, their expression of resentment will be influenced by impression-management concerns.

12. High self-monitors tend to be more concerned with, and perhaps more adept in, impression management, while low self-monitors tend to have more complex and cognitively available self-schemata.

13. People tend to have competing motives for self-enhancement (maintaining self-esteem through positive feedback from others) and self-verification (self-knowledge through accurate feedback from others).

Further Reading

BAUMEISTER, R.F, CAMPBELL, J.D., KRUEGER, J.I. & VOHS, K.D. (2003). Does high self-esteem cause better performance, interpersonal success, happiness or healthier lifestyles? *Psychological Science in the Public Interest 4*, 1–44. A comprehensive and readable overview of the limitations of high self-esteem.

DECI, E.L. & RYAN, R.M. (Eds.) (2002) *Handbook of self-determination research*. Rochester: U. of Rochester Press. An updated set of papers on intrinsic vs. extrinsic motivation.

JOURNAL OF PERSONALITY AND SOCIAL PSYCHOLOGY (1996). 71 (6). *Special issue: The self and social identity*. A set of papers by some of the leading contributors to the field, considering the self from the perspectives of social cognition, interpersonal relations and individual differences.

MARKUS, H. & KITAYAMA, S. (1994). Culture and the self: Implications for cognition, emotion and motivation. *Psychological Review 98*, 224–253. An important and insightful discussion of the cross-cultural perspective on issues related to the self-concept.

OSBORNE, R.E. (1996). *Self. An eclectic approach*. Needham Heights, MA: Allyn and Bacon. A clearly written, advanced level integration of much of the literature on this vast topic.

Weblink

Society for Personality and Social Psychology
www.spsp.org/ This is the division of APA that pertains to social psychology and personality.

Chapter 4

Values
and Attitudes

As American as apple pie, as Canadian as possible under the circumstances.

Heather Scott

Question: Why does a Canadian chicken cross the road?

Answer: To get to the middle!

Chapter Outline

A few years ago, Sue Rodriguez of Vancouver Island was diagnosed with an incurable disease: amyotrophic lateral sclerosis (Lou Gehrig's disease). The disease gradually destroys muscle function, leaving the afflicted person unable to speak, swallow, breathe or eat without assistance. Not wishing to endure the final stages of the disease process, Ms Rodriguez went to court to obtain the right to a physician-assisted suicide. In Canada it is not an offence to commit suicide, but it is an offence to counsel or assist someone to commit suicide. The court denied her request. Her subsequent appeal to a higher court was dismissed on the basis of a 2–1 split vote. The dissenting judge's opinion was that Ms Rodriguez had the right under the Canadian Charter of Rights and Freedoms, but the other two judges indicated that it would be wrong to grant immunity from liability, in civil or criminal proceedings, to unknown persons for offences not yet committed. In 1995, Sue Rodriguez died by what was alleged to be an assisted suicide. No one was arrested. Assisted suicide remains an important social issue. Only in the Netherlands, under very strict guidelines, are physicians allowed to help patients terminate their lives.

Sue Rodriguez's publicly expressed wishes, her death and the decisions of the courts sparked considerable national debate. Like the question of abortion, the issue of assisted suicide invokes values and attitudes concerning the sanctity of life, religious convictions and even the role of physicians in the treatment of patients. Do people have the right to die? Must every effort be made to prolong life, no matter what the circumstances? The ethical dilemma for physicians and hospitals is fundamental. On the one hand, they are dedicated to preserving life, and on the other, to alleviating suffering. What is the point, for example, of maintaining a patient with irrevocable brain damage on a life-support system? Should quality of life not be taken into consideration?

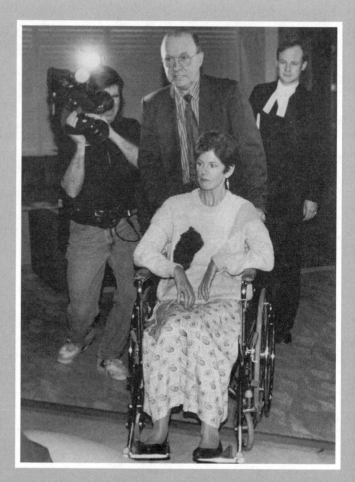

Sue Rodriguez believed it was her life to do with as she wished. Many people object—a cure may be just around the corner; the process may be subject to abuse; it may be reminiscent of what happened in Nazi Germany, where, among other atrocities, healthy people were killed during medical experiments. These are all concerns involving values and attitudes.

Very few examples of human behaviour can be found that are not, in some way, influenced by **attitudes** and **values**. Their effect can range from the mundane, such as food preferences (*chow mein* or *pirogi*, hamburgers or *sushi*), to issues of war and peace and the sublime aspects of religious experience. The form of government we prefer, the candidate we vote for, the type of mate we seek, and even the breed of dog we choose all reflect underlying beliefs and feelings. It is not surprising that the study of attitudes has been at the core of social psychology almost since the beginning.

Indeed, during the 1930s, social psychology and attitude research were almost synonymous.

However, until recently social psychologists did not devote a great deal of attention to the study of values. There is no obvious reason for this neglect, for it certainly cannot be argued that values are any less important than attitudes. Braithwaite and Scott (1991) suggest psychologists may have neglected values because they have seemed so vague and imprecise that adequate measurement and experimentation was impossible. Recently, however, there has been increased interest in values and their relationship to attitudes (Seligman, Olson & Zanna, 1996).

This chapter examines the nature of values and attitudes at both individual and social levels. We then ask why people have attitudes and how values are important in relation to them. We explore how attitudes are structured and, finally, the puzzling problem of why our beliefs often do not match our actions.

Personal and Social Values

Attitudes are associated with specific objects, events or issues, whereas values are global, abstract principles. They are a person's judgments as to what is desirable, what ought to be, and what is ideal or important in life. For example, a person may hold attitudes against racial discrimination and be in favour of equal pay to men and women for work of equal value. Both of these may reflect a value for equality, which is important to that person. Often, when we have intensely felt attitudes about controversial issues, we describe our attitude in terms of a value, such as the so-called pro-life and pro-choice positions on abortion, the ethics of cloning or genetically modifying food. In describing our positions this way, we use the value to define, from our own perspective, what the issue is really all about. Thus, values can be defined as "desirable, trans-situational goals, varying in importance, that serve as guiding principles in people's lives" (Schwartz, 1996, p. 2).

Some social psychologists have attempted to catalogue a set of basic values on which individuals differ. For instance, Allport and Vernon (1931), building on the writings of the German philosopher Spranger, developed a measure for six values: theoretical, economic, social, aesthetic, political and religious. Morris (1956) listed five general value dimensions: social restraint and self-control; enjoyment and progress in action; withdrawal and self-sufficiency; receptivity and sympathetic concern; self-indulgence; and sensuous enjoyment. While it is probably futile to try to establish the exact number of values, it is clear that people have many attitudes and relatively few values.

In later research (Rokeach, 1968, 1979), a distinction is drawn between terminal values and instrumental values. **Terminal values** are preferences for certain end-states in life, such as salvation, a comfortable life, freedom, inner harmony and equality (see Figure 4–1), while **instrumental values** describe people's preferred modes of conduct, such as being ambitious, obedient or imaginative. Subjects are asked to rank a set of 18 terminal and 18 instrumental values in terms of their relative importance. In this way, the value priorities of an individual can be determined. For example, while most people would feel that a comfortable life is a good thing, they would vary tremendously on the issue of its importance.

Using this method, researchers have reported some interesting findings (Rokeach, 1979). Not surprisingly, people who attach high importance to salvation as a value are more likely to attend church regularly, while those who value a world of beauty are likely to be concerned with environmental issues. Habitual cigarette smokers tend to rank the terminal values of an exciting life, freedom, happiness, mature love and pleasure more highly than non-smokers, who value a sense of accomplishment, a world of beauty, family security, salvation and self-respect. Among the instrumental values, smokers feel it is important to be broadminded, capable, imaginative and independent, while non-smokers prefer to be cheerful, obedient, helpful, polite and self-controlled (Weir, Getzlaf & Rokeach, 1984). People who take care of themselves by exercising regularly, using alcohol moderately, eating a balanced diet and wearing a car seat belt, place a high value upon pleasure, an exciting life and happiness.

Health in itself can be considered a value. Rokeach (1973) felt that health would be so important to everybody that there was no point in measuring it. However, Ware and Young (1979) included health in Rokeach's list of terminal values, and found that while the majority rated it first, about one-third of the subjects did not include it among their five highest values. In general, those who value health highly tend to perform health-protective behaviours when they believe that such behaviours will, in fact, improve their own health (Lau, Hartman & Ware, 1986).

Differences in values have been shown to be related to many attitudes and behaviours. These include choice of occupation, cigarette smoking, cheating on exams, political attitudes and voting, as well as choice of friends (Homer & Kahle, 1988). Similarly, Kristiansen and Matheson (1990) found that values predict attitudes towards nuclear weapons.

The values-attitudes-behaviour hierarchy is nicely demonstrated by a study of shopping preferences (Homer & Kahle, 1988). These investigators hypothesized that natural-food shoppers would attach more importance to internal values than people who did not choose natural foods ("non-shoppers"), who would emphasize external values. Examples of internal values are a sense of accomplishment, self-respect

FIGURE 4-1

Rokeach terminal values

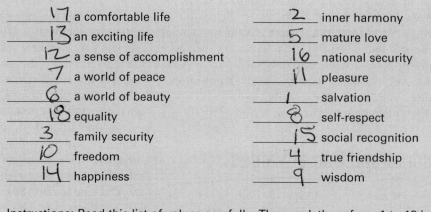

_____ 17 a comfortable life   _____ 2 inner harmony
_____ 13 an exciting life   _____ 5 mature love
_____ 12 a sense of accomplishment   _____ 16 national security
_____ 7 a world of peace   _____ 11 pleasure
_____ 6 a world of beauty   _____ 1 salvation
_____ 18 equality   _____ 8 self-respect
_____ 3 family security   _____ 15 social recognition
_____ 10 freedom   _____ 4 true friendship
_____ 14 happiness   _____ 9 wisdom

Instructions: Read this list of values carefully. Then rank them from 1 to 18 in order of importance to you, as guiding principles in your life.
A sample of Canadian students in 1957 ranked them as follows: 13, 11, 9, 12, 15, 10, 7, 1, 2, 6, 3, 17, 14, 18, 4, 16, 5, 8.

Source: Rokeach, 1973

and enjoyment of life. External values are exemplified by a sense of belonging, being well respected and security. They further hypothesized that these values would be related to attitudes about nutrition. That is, natural-food shoppers would be more concerned than non-shoppers with issues such as additives in meat and the importance of proper nutrition. By means of a statistical method called _structural equation analysis_, researchers were able to show that whether or not people purchased natural foods was based on their attitudes, and that these attitudes in turn were based on whether the participants held internal or external values. These relationships are illustrated in Figure 4–2.

The Rokeach model has been criticized for not having a clear theoretical foundation (Rohan, 2000), as has the validity of the distinction between terminal and instrumental values (Schwartz, 1992). Nevertheless, Rokeach provided an impetus for renewed interest in values and a starting point for much recent research.

For example, Schwartz's (1992, 1996) discomfort with the intuitive approach of Rokeach led him to

FIGURE 4-2

Relationships between values, attitudes and behaviour

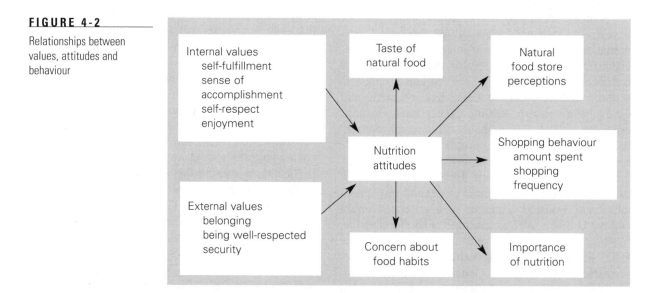

empirically identify two value dimensions. One dimension he named "openness to change versus conservation" and the second "self-enhancement versus self-transcendence." The first dimension underlines the conflict between a desire to take chances and pursue personal interests or to stick with the majority and maintain the status-quo. The second dimension reflects the extent to which a person is concerned with the effects of actions on him or herself rather than the effects on others in a broader social context. Arising out of these dimensions Schwartz (1992, 1996) identified ten "value types." These and examples of representative values can be found in Table 4–1.

Value conflict and change

In certain cases, placing a high priority on one value may cause conflict with another value. For example, it may be difficult to reconcile the values of freedom and equality, when freedom implies the right to earn as much money as you want, while equality implies the duty of the state to tax some of your wealth and redistribute it to people with less wealth. In one study, Rokeach (1968) analyzed the writings of well-known authors representing different political points of view. He found that moderate liberals or social democrats valued both freedom and equality highly, conservatives valued freedom more highly than equality, and an extreme right-wing writer (Hitler) did not consider either freedom or equality to be important. Several other studies of the speeches of U.S. senators and British members of parliament show a similar pattern of values in relation to liberal or conservative ideology (Tetlock, 1986).

Rokeach (1968) also found that while those who were active in U.S. civil rights organizations ranked both freedom and equality quite highly, those who were uninvolved or unsympathetic to that cause ranked freedom as much more important than equality. Rokeach then devised a procedure—value confrontation—in which subjects were made aware of the discrepancies in their rankings of freedom and equality. It was suggested to them that people who consider freedom so much more important than equality may be concerned only with their own freedom, and not that of others. (In a control group, there was no such intervention.) Three months later, all the subjects received a letter from a well-known U.S. civil rights organization, inviting them to join. The rate of favourable responses—joining the organization—was more than twice as high among the group who had been prompted into self-awareness.

To test this procedure with a mass audience, Ball-Rokeach, Rokeach and Grube (1984) produced a television show that featured two well-known actors of the day (Edward Asner and Sandy Hill) talking about freedom versus equality and a world of beauty, as values. Follow-up studies showed that, in comparison with people in a control group who didn't watch the show, those who had were more likely to support or become involved in organizations concerned with sexism, racism and environmental pollution. These studies indicate that even though values are fundamental to humanity, they are susceptible to change through subtle manipulation.

Value pluralism

Tetlock (1986) has investigated how value conflicts are reflected in political attitudes. In one study, subjects were asked to indicate their attitudes about some controversial issues involving conflicting values, such as higher taxes to help the poor (equality versus a comfortable life), whether the U.S. Central Intelligence Agency should be allowed to open the mail of citizens (national security versus individual freedom), and whether physicians should be restrained from setting fees that some people could not afford (equality versus freedom). Then they were asked to write their thoughts about each issue and to rank-order the Rokeach values.

When an issue did not involve a value conflict, subjects responded as expected on the attitude scales. For example, those who ranked equality high and a comfortable life low were quite willing to pay more taxes to assist the poor. However, if both values were ranked high, the conflict in values was shown in their ambivalence about the issue. When subjects were faced with an issue that involved competing values (**value pluralism**), they thought more about the issue and their responses showed higher levels of integrative complexity.

As Tetlock (1996) points out, conflict of this sort is not pleasant. Like cognitive dissonance (see Chapter 5), it creates stress, which people will seek to reduce, often by means of a process termed **trade-off reasoning**, through which one value is chosen over the other. This is not easy. If the wrong choice is made, there can be considerable subsequent regret that the other value was not selected.

When possible, people choose simple solutions to value conflict. If the values are not of equal strength, the easiest route is to choose the stronger one. However, when both values are strong and equally

TABLE 4-1

The values construct

Value Types and Definitions	Representative Values
Power: Social status and prestige, control or dominance over people and resources.	Social power: Control over others, dominance. Authority: The right to lead or command. Wealth: Material possessions, money.
Achievement: Personal success through demonstrating competence according to social standards.	Success: Achieving goals. Capability: Competence, effectiveness, efficiency. Ambition: Hard work, aspirations. Influence: Have an impact on people and events.
Hedonism: Pleasure and sensuous gratification for oneself.	Pleasure: Gratification of desires. Enjoyment in life: Enjoyment of food, sex, leisure and so on.
Stimulation: Excitement, novelty and challenge in life.	Daringness: Adventure-seeking, risktaking. A varied life: Filled with challenge, novelty, change. An exciting life: Stimulating experiences.
Self-Direction: Independent thought and action-choosing, creating, exploring.	Creativity: Uniqueness, imagination. Freedom: Freedom of action and thought. Independence: Self-reliance, self-sufficiency. Curiosity: Interest in everything, exploration. Choose own goals: Select own purposes.
Universalism: Understanding, appreciation, tolerance and protection for the welfare of all people and for nature.	Broad-minded: Tolerant of different ideas and beliefs. Wisdom: A mature understanding of life. Social justice: Correcting injustice, care for the weak. Equality: Equal opportunity for all. A world at peace: Free of war and conflict. A world of beauty: Beauty of nature and the arts. Unity with nature: Fitting into nature. Protecting the environment: Preserving nature.
Benevolence: Preservation and enhancement of the welfare of people with whom one is in frequent personal contact.	Helpful: Working for the welfare of others. Honesty: Genuineness, sincerity. Forgivingness: Willingness to pardon others. Loyalty: Faithful to my friends, group. Responsibility: Dependable, reliable.
Tradition: Respect, commitment and acceptance of the customs and ideas that traditional culture or religion provide the self.	Humility: Modesty, self-effacement. Acceptance of my portion of life: Submission to life's circumstances. Devotion: Hold to religious faith and belief. Respect for tradition: Preservation of time-honored customs. Moderate: Avoiding extremes of feeling or action.
Conformity: Restraint of actions, inclinations and impulses likely to upset or harm others and violate social expectations or norms.	Politeness: Courtesy, good manners. Obedience: Dutiful, meet obligations. Self-discipline: Self-restraint, resistance to temptation. Honour parents and elders: Showing respect.
Security: Safety, harmony and stability of society, of relationships, and of self.	Family security: Safety for loved ones. National security: Protection of my nation from enemies. Social order: Stability of society. Cleanliness: Neatness, tidiness. Reciprocation of favours: Avoidance of indebtedness.

Source: Schwartz, 1992, 1996

important, more complicated strategies are necessary. In these cases, the strategy may require considerable thought. For example, how much old forest should be cut for how much economic growth? Why do other people have differing views? This complex reasoning may extend to include historical and broader social contexts. The various strategies that might be selected and the types of situations that could activate them are illustrated in Figure 4–3.

This model indicates that (1) if the values are not of similar strength, the weaker value will be set aside and the stronger one bolstered. There will be no compromise. One value only will be selected. However, if the values are of roughly equal strength, the question then is (2) whether trade-offs are possible, an approach that is risky. The audience may perceive trade-offs as "selling-out" and thereby compromising

principles. If the person is concerned about this possibility, she may try to conceal the trade-off or to mislead the audience. However, if negative consequences are unlikely, the next question that arises is (3) whether others would be concerned that the person is trying to avoid blame. This may lead to delays and to blaming someone else. If this is not a problem, the next stage (4) takes other characteristics of the audience into consideration. If the audience is apathetic and ill informed, they probably will respond to "demagoguery," which includes tactics such as anger arousal and fomenting agitation. If, however, the audience (5) is more sophisticated and critical, the strategy (6) must be more complex. In this case the person will, for example, make well-thought-out value comparisons such as "How much clear-cut logging am I willing to advocate for how much unemployment?" and

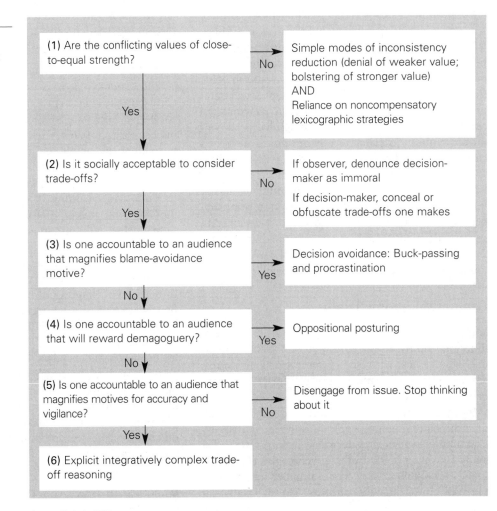

FIGURE 4-3

Possible strategies for dealing with value conflict

(1) Are the conflicting values of close-to-equal strength?

No → Simple modes of inconsistency reduction (denial of weaker value; bolstering of stronger value) AND Reliance on noncompensatory lexicographic strategies

Yes ↓

(2) Is it socially acceptable to consider trade-offs?

No → If observer, denounce decision-maker as immoral

If decision-maker, conceal or obfuscate trade-offs one makes

Yes ↓

(3) Is one accountable to an audience that magnifies blame-avoidance motive?

Yes → Decision avoidance: Buck-passing and procrastination

No ↓

(4) Is one accountable to an audience that will reward demagoguery?

Yes → Oppositional posturing

No ↓

(5) Is one accountable to an audience that magnifies motives for accuracy and vigilance?

No → Disengage from issue. Stop thinking about it

Yes ↓

(6) Explicit integratively complex trade-off reasoning

Source: Tetlock, 1996

try to come to grips with the diversity of values within the audience—why are some people willing to close sawmills and others willing to destroy forests?

Value pluralism has also been studied in relation to political ideologies (Tetlock, 1984). We have already seen that liberal/social democrats, conservatives, fascists and communists differ in their value priorities for equality and freedom. It has also been found that people with liberal/social democratic political attitudes are higher in integrative complexity than others. Many political issues, such as social programs, antidiscrimination laws and government intervention in the economy involve conflicts between freedom and equality. Because liberal/social democrats rank both values highly, they must be able to think flexibly and in more complex ways to resolve the conflicts. On the other hand, people whose political ideologies dictate a clear priority of one value over the other can resolve the issues more easily.

We must be cautious in our conclusions about these studies. It is not possible to infer cause and effect, whether liberals show more integrative complexity because of the equality–freedom conflict, or whether people who think in this way tend as a result to value freedom and equality highly and to adopt social democratic political attitudes. Another issue concerns the culture being studied: Tetlock's research has been conducted entirely in economically developed democracies. Arguably, the realities of poverty, dictatorships and economic underdevelopment in the Third World would make such a trade-off more difficult, if not unrealistic, and could result in a different relationship between values and political ideology. The study of successful revolutionary leaders described in Chapter 2 suggests that more extreme political ideologies are not necessarily lacking in integrative complexity.

Comparing national values

You will recall (Chapter 3) that views of the self can differ depending on the culture in which the individual lives. It is also the case that values, which of course are a fundamental aspect of our self-image, can vary between cultures.

Indeed, it has been demonstrated that we can describe and compare people of different nations by examining their aggregate values. For example, a study of values by a Dutch psychologist (Hofstede, 1983) involved a very large number of subjects (116 000) in 40 different countries. Through statistical analyses of these data, he identified four underlying value dimensions on which inhabitants of various nations could be compared: power distance, avoidance of uncertainty, individualism and masculinity–femininity. Let us examine them, particularly as a way of studying national character.

POWER DISTANCE The dimension of *power distance* refers to differences in the extent to which people can control one another's behaviour. In nations scoring high on this value (e.g., Mexico, India), individuals expect and accept autocratic leaders and employers, and parents expect obedient children. By contrast, in countries low in power distance (e.g., Canada, U.S.), children are trained to be independent, managers tend to consult with subordinates and governments are pluralistic and based on majority votes.

AVOIDANCE OF UNCERTAINTY This refers to the feeling of being threatened by ambiguity and acting to avoid it. In cultures where this value is strong (e.g., Greece), it is reflected in a concern with security, low risk-taking, written rules and the presence of a dominant state religion.

INDIVIDUALISM–COLLECTIVISM This refers to the extent to which people are supposed to look after themselves, rather than expecting certain groups or society to take care of them. Many of the Western nations (e.g., Canada, Australia, U.S.) score high on individualism, while collectivist-oriented cultures included otherwise capitalist nations such as Hong Kong, Taiwan, Singapore, Peru, Venezuela and Chile. In collectivist cultures, there is less occupational mobility but greater group decision-making, while individualist cultures stress achievement, initiative and employees who defend their own interests (Triandis, 1987). This value dimension has occasioned the most research. These investigations have confirmed that societies (and individuals) can be identified as individualist or collectivist.

However, recent research indicates that individualism and collectivism may not be polar opposites; the two factors may be independent. In this case it has been suggested that one dimension consists of individualism opposed by authoritarianism (see Chapter 3) and the other of collectivism opposed by withdrawal from group involvement. In addition, it seems that there are different types of collectivism. For example, Japanese collectivism is probably not the same as the collectivism of the Israeli kibbutz (Gelfand, Triandis & Chan, 1996).

MASCULINITY–FEMININITY The fourth value dimension is called *masculinity–femininity*. It refers to the extent to

The Nature of Attitudes

In the 1930s, Gordon Allport (1935), a pioneer contributor to research on attitudes, defined an attitude as a mental and neural state of readiness, organized through experience, exerting a directive or dynamic influence upon the individual's response to all objects and situations with which it is related. Although opinions differ regarding the adequacy of this definition, it does emphasize certain important characteristics of the construct of attitude. First, an attitude implies an internal state that, given the occurrence of certain stimulus events, will ultimately result in some sort of response or behaviour. The definition also implies that an attitude is learned and that our actions are related to it. This latter characteristic is important because it gives us the basis for deciding whether or not a given attitude exists; that is, whether a label can be attached to an individual (e.g., conservative, separatist, socialist), with some degree of confidence. It is important to note that attitude is a *hypothetical construct* (see Chapter 1). You can never actually observe people's attitudes; you can only infer or guess the existence of an attitude from what people say or do. This is the basis of attitude measurement.

Attitudes probably are best thought of as cognitive structures or internal states that reside in long-term memory (Tourangeau & Rasinski, 1988; Eagly & Chaiken, 1998). These states are activated when a person is presented with a relevant stimulus, such as the question "What do you think about the abortion issue?" Depending on the response, the individual can then be identified as having a pro-abortion or anti-abortion attitude (see Focus on Research—Measuring Attitudes).

Attitude strength

Another feature of attitudes is significant. Not only do we typically describe an attitude a person holds as pro or con (valence), we also estimate the intensity or strength of the attitude from extremely positive to extremely negative. For example, it is one thing for an individual to state, "Government policies leave a lot to be desired," and quite another to claim, "Government policies make me sick!"

Strong attitudes have a number of characteristics. They are *durable*—that is, they do not change over time and they resist persuasion. Strong attitudes also have more effect on people's behaviour. In addition, strong attitudes are more likely to influence information processing and judgments (Krosnick & Petty,

1995; Pomerantz, Chaiken & Tordessillas, 1995; Eagly & Chaiken, 1998).

Models of attitudes

A traditional view has been that attitudes are multidimensional and consist of a relatively enduring organization of three components: a *cognitive component*, an *affective component* and a *behavioural component* (Chaiken & Stangor, 1987; Zanna & Rempel, 1988), as illustrated in Figure 4–5 on page 105. The cognitive component refers to the particular beliefs or ideas held about the object or situation; the *affective* component to the associated emotions; and the *behavioural* component to the associated action or actions. For instance, a person may believe that university students are arrogant (cognitive), may feel uncomfortable in the presence of a university student (affective), and may refuse to pick up a student who is hitch-hiking to classes (behavioural). It is important to add, however, that attitudes are not always directly expressed in action. This issue will be discussed in detail later.

This tripartite model of attitude suggests something about human nature. Many traditional theories and philosophies have grappled with the question of whether the essence of being human lies in thinking (rationality) or in emotions. Indeed, some schools of psychotherapy seek to minimize thinking so that we can get in touch with our real feelings. Former Canadian prime minister Pierre Trudeau, on the other hand, adopted as a family motto "Reason over Passion." However, the concept of attitude implies that our thoughts, feelings and actions are integrated in some way and that we usually think, feel and act in a coordinated fashion.

Nevertheless, it is possible to distinguish among cognition, affect and behaviour. For example, Breckler (1984) was interested in the extent to which these three components gave similar estimates of the direction and strength of attitudes. He used a variety of measures of each component. For example, he monitored changes in heart rate and had subjects rate their mood in the presence of snakes (affective), measured their beliefs about the dangers and benefits of snakes and had them list their thoughts about them (cognitive), had people indicate how they would react to a snake, and observed how closely they were actually willing to approach a snake (behavioural). His analysis showed clearly that beliefs, feelings and behaviour were moderately but not highly interrelated and that each provided distinctive contributions to the hypothetical

Measuring Attitudes

The most common way of measuring attitudes is to ask people a direct question such as, "*What do you think of same-sex marriages?*" This self-report format is the basis for a number of different attitude measurement instruments such as the following:

Likert summated ratings Subjects are presented with a series of statements about the attitudinal object. A 5- or 7-point scale accompanies each statement. For instance, here are two such statements from an instrument questionnaire to measure attitudes towards war:

War brings out the best qualities in people.

strongly   agree   uncertain   disagree   strongly
agree   disagree

I would rather be called a coward than go to war.

strongly   agree   uncertain   disagree   strongly
agree   disagree

A complete questionnaire could contain 20 or more such items.

The subject's choice for each item is assigned a value. The scores for all items are added up (summated) to give a total score that reflects the person's attitude towards war. Note that the assignment of the values for the second item must be reversed because a person who agrees with the first item logically should disagree with the second item. Thus, if "strongly agree" is assigned the value 1 for the first item, it must be assigned the value 5 for the second item.

This is the method most widely used today. It is easy for subjects to understand, it is efficient to administer and yields data that can be analyzed by sophisticated statistical techniques.

Semantic differential (Osgood, Suci & Tannenbaum, 1957). Subjects are asked to rate a concept along a set of bipolar adjective scales. Example: Rate the idea of war by circling one of the numbers for each scale below.

By adding each response, reversing where the negative adjective is at the low end (that is, scoring 7 as 1 and 6 as 2, etc.), we can obtain an evaluation of the overall attitude. Through statistical analysis (e.g., factor analysis), it is possible to determine the groups or sets of items to which people respond in a consistent manner. In this way, we can determine what each group or dimension measures.

Measures such as the semantic differential and the Likert scale are widely used. However, as discussed in Chapter 1, they are subject to a number of biases, particularly the tendency for participants to respond in a socially desirable manner in order to create a favourable impression or to maintain a favourable self-concept. It also is the case that the respondent often can see through the scale and realize what attitude is being measured. Then they may, especially if the attitude is a sensitive one, distort or falsify their responses.

To overcome such problems, a number of indirect attitude measures have been developed in which the connection between what is observed and the attitude is not evident. Some examples are as follows:

- We can infer attitudes from behaviour towards the attitudinal object. For example, Cook and Selltiz (1964) had a confederate present himself as a representative of a publishing company and ask white subjects whether they would be willing to pose for textbook photographs. If so, the sub-

good	1	2	3	4	5	6	7	bad
attractive	1	2	3	4	5	6	7	unattractive
worthless	1	2	3	4	5	6	7	valuable
fair	1	2	3	4	5	6	7	unfair

jects were shown a book of drawings on which the photos would be based, many of which involved blacks in equal, inferior or superior role relationships with the subject-model. Scenes in which the subjects would allow themselves to be photographed constituted a measure of attitudes towards blacks.

- We can infer attitudes from people's performance on an apparently objective test. For example, subjects are presented with a series of multiple-choice questions about some issue that concerns facts, not opinions. The facts might be unknown (e.g., how much soap is used by an average family from a given ethnic group) or have clearly erroneous, even absurd, response alternatives (e.g., since capital punishment was ended in Canada, the murder rate has increased (1000 times? 10 000 times?). Responses would, in fact, directly reflect attitudes, since no subject would have access to the correct information.

- We can infer attitudes from nonreactive measures. For example, what books has one read? People tend to read books that advocate the positions they favour.

construct called "attitude." He argues that we should not assess someone's attitudes *only* by asking about feelings or beliefs, or *only* by observing behaviour.

Other researchers, however, have discarded the behavioural component, and consider attitude to be a two-dimensional construct made up of affect and cognitions (e.g., Zajonc & Markus, 1982). Moreover, some, like Fishbein and Ajzen (1975), maintain a *unitary* view, regarding an attitude as an *affective orientation towards an object*. As yet, there has been no definitive resolution among these competing models and each has earned some experimental support.

Zanna and Rempel (1988) have outlined a model that takes into consideration all these conceptions of attitudes. They begin by defining attitude as a categorization of a stimulus object along an evaluative dimension (for example, abortion: favourable... unfavourable). They then propose that this evaluation can be based on three sources of information: cognitive information, affective information or past-behaviour information. The evaluation can be based on any one source of information or any combination of sources. In other words, an attitude may, for example, be derived from cognitions alone, from cognitions and affect or from cognitions, affect and past behaviour.

This conceptualization of attitudes gives rise to a number of intriguing speculations. For instance, it implies that a person can have more than one attitude towards the same object. Thus, a person's attitude about exercise might be negative when based on affect

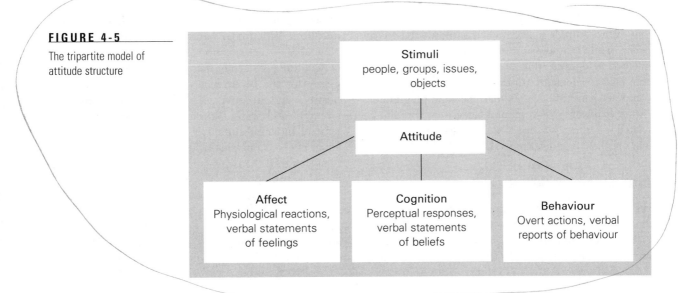

FIGURE 4-5

The tripartite model of attitude structure

Stimuli
people, groups, issues, objects

Attitude

Affect
Physiological reactions, verbal statements of feelings

Cognition
Perceptual responses, verbal statements of beliefs

Behaviour
Overt actions, verbal reports of behaviour

What does it say about Canadian values that we have a police officer for a national symbol? Why were some Canadians upset when uniform changes were made to accommodate women and Sikhs?

(exercise is painful) but positive when based on cognition (it will lower my blood pressure). Depending on the situation (e.g., whether in the gym or the doctor's office), one or the other source might be salient. It is also possible that attitudes based on affect alone may be more resistant to persuasion and that attitudes based on more than one source of information may be better predictors of behaviour.

It also is the case that individuals differ in the likelihood that their attitudes will be based on beliefs or on affect. Haddock and Zanna (2000) showed that subjects who they described as "thinkers" based their attitudes on belief whereas those described as "feelers" were more likely to use emotions. Similarly, Kempf (1999) found that some attitude objects elicit attitudes based on beliefs while attitudes towards other objects are more likely to be derived from affect. For example, he asked subjects to evaluate two different computer programs, a computer game and a grammar checking programme. Attitudes towards the computer game were found to be related to feelings whereas attitudes regarding the grammar checker were determined by beliefs.

Attitude ambivalence

While attitudes have traditionally been viewed as unidimensional—pro or con—the Zanna and Rempel (1988) and Haddock and Zanna (1998) model implies that attitudes can be considerably more complex. For example, MacDonald and Zanna (1998) found that male undergraduates assigned ambivalent ratings to feminists. They rated them positively on "admiration" but negatively on "affection." Then in a simulated job interview, it was shown that the qualities emphasized (depending on whether they were affective or behavioural) influenced the hiring. You can probably think of issues for which you do not absolutely and unequivocally support one side or the other, but have *both* positive and negative cognitions or feelings about the attitude object (Thompson, Zanna & Griffin, 1996). For example, while some people firmly support gun control and others firmly oppose it, many see some merit in both sides of the question. When this happens, the attitude will be "unstable"—that is, ambivalent.

According to current theory, two conditions are necessary for the occurrence of ambivalence. First, the positive and negative elements must be similar in strength; and second, these components must be at least of moderate intensity. Ambivalence will not be experienced if one side of the issue clearly outweighs the other or if the issue is perceived as being relatively trivial or unimportant.

Conflict is a fact of life. Many types of conflict, such as choosing among alternative behaviours and allocating scarce resources, have been extensively investigated. However, the study of attitude ambivalence (conflict), although important, is just beginning.

Attitude complexity

Some attitudes are rather simple and straightforward, while others are complex. For instance, a person may be asked, "What do you think of assisted suicide?" and respond, "I think it's very humane," but if pressed, be unable to present more detail. On the other hand, another person in response to the same query might reply, "I'm generally in favour of it but we have to worry about its possibly being misused." Whether an attitude is simple or complex may be a function of the characteristics of the person or it may be a function of the particular topic. Some issues by their nature do not allow for much mental intricacy. Thus, people's attitudes about brushing teeth after meals would likely be considerably simpler than their attitudes towards the question of the economic or political union of Canada with the U.S.

Attitudes also have more or less complex associations with other attitudes. For example, a person might believe that agricultural cooperatives are economically beneficial and should be fostered, but this attitude may exist in isolation and may not be related to other attitudes concerning, for instance, the NDP, Mennonite communities or socialized medicine. In other cases, very complicated networks of interconnected attitudes may occur. Thus, an individual's attitude towards immigration may be connected with many other attitudes concerning unemployment, multiculturalism, prejudice and city design.

Functions of Attitudes

We have described values as the global abstractions on which we base our attitudes. In other words, values are generalities or basic principles, and attitudes are the more specific instances of those principles. Do attitudes necessarily follow from values? Can we infer people's values from their attitudes towards certain objects or issues? Can we predict people's attitudes towards capital punishment, the welfare state or rock videos if we know their values? The answers are *yes*, *no* and *sometimes*. To understand, we must turn to a more fundamental question: Why do we have attitudes?

In the next chapter, we will focus on how and why attitudes can change. We know that much of what we read and hear (not to mention the entire industry of public relations and advertising) is devoted to changing attitudes. And yet, we know from experience that attitudes are often difficult to change and that people are not easily persuaded. In fact, there is an important reason why people maintain their attitudes: attitudes are functional in the sense that they satisfy important needs. Several functions of attitudes have been identified and studied (Eagly & Chaiken, 1992; Olson & Zanna, 1993).

First, attitudes may serve a utilitarian or **instrumental function**, leading to greater rewards and fewer costs. In particular, holding specific attitudes may help us gain approval and acceptance from others. Indeed (see Chapter 8), people tend to be attracted to other people who apparently hold similar attitudes. Thus, attitudes may enable people to adjust in their society and in their own groups.

Second, attitudes can serve a **knowledge function**, enabling us to make sense of our world, to cope with everyday decisions, and to feel that we do understand (Fazio, Blascovich & Driscoll, 1992). They assist people in selecting, from the myriad objects that enter the visual field, those stimuli that will receive attention (Roskos-Ewoldsen & Fazio, 1992a). That is, attitudes serve as schemata, helping us to avoid the uncomfortable feelings of uncertainty and ambiguity, guiding our reactions and interpretations of events. For example, acts of terrorism are even more terrifying when they seem to be inexplicable—beyond understanding. As a result, we may accept the explanations of politicians that some people are just evil or are agents of some insane leader or evil empire.

Sometimes attitudes enable us to avoid thinking. Fazio and his associates have investigated how quickly subjects respond to various objects by pushing buttons labelled good or bad (Fazio, Sanbonmatsu, Powell & Kardes, 1986). They demonstrate that some attitudes are activated spontaneously or automatically from memory and do not require thinking (e.g., "cockroaches are disgusting"), while other attitudes require more time and thought to be expressed (see peripheral and central routes to persuasion in Chapter 5). Some attitudes are borne with strength and confidence, others with uncertainty. It is argued that strong, automatically activated attitudes free people from the effort required for information-processing and reflective thought and allow them simply to react.

Third, attitudes may also serve an **ego-defensive function**, protecting people from becoming aware of harsh, uncomfortable truths about themselves or their world. People often feel and act in ways that defend them from becoming aware of what may be threatening. As will be discussed in Chapter 13, prejudiced attitudes often serve ego-defensive functions. For instance, the bigot may hate members of some out-group in order to feel more important and powerful than he really is. If people feel bad about themselves, it is comforting and protective to believe that others are worse.

Fourth, attitudes can serve a **value-expressive function**. Value-expressive attitudes demonstrate our uniqueness and what is important to us. They may take an apparently trivial form, as in the case of those who express positive opinions about certain styles in music, clothing and cars that represent certain values, or they may be much more important. For example, members of a religion may adhere to certain salient attitudes that indicate their devotion to their faith.

In this regard, Kristiansen and Zanna (1986, 1988) asked subjects for their terminal value priorities (Rokeach measure) and their attitudes towards two controversial issues: (1) the reinstatement of capital punishment in Canada for certain crimes; and (2) affirmative action in the workplace for women and disadvantaged minorities. On another occasion, the same subjects were asked to rate how action related to these issues helped or hindered them in achieving various goals in their lives, as represented by the 18 values. For example, the subjects were asked to rate how reinstating capital punishment would help or hinder them in achieving freedom, happiness, equality and so on. Attitudes were related to values when the issue was linked, in the subject's mind, to attaining these values. For example, if a subject believed that reinstating capital punishment would help her to achieve freedom (e.g., being free to walk the streets at night) and if freedom was a highly ranked value, then the subject would favour reinstating capital punishment.

It is important to understand that we cannot infer attitudes from values, or values from attitudes. Indeed, people with different attitudes towards the same issue often relate their positions to entirely different values, rather than to differences in the importance of a particular value. For example, both people who favour extensive government involvement in health care and those who oppose it may place high importance on the values of freedom and equality. However, those in favour may base their position on the value of equality and those opposed may refer to the value of freedom. A selective appeal to values may enable them to support and justify their attitudes (Eiser & van der Pligt, 1984; Eiser, 1987).

This **value justification effect** has been demonstrated by Kristiansen and Zanna (1988). Subjects in an experiment were asked to indicate their attitudes towards two controversial issues of the time: abortion on demand and the deployment of nuclear weapons in

Canada. Then they were asked to rank the 18 Rokeach terminal values in terms of how relevant each was to the abortion and nuclear weapons issues. Proponents and opponents of each issue differed significantly in terms of which values were ranked as most relevant. For example, pro-abortion subjects rated freedom, happiness and a comfortable life as more relevant to the issue than did anti-abortion subjects. Interestingly, both sides rated equality, self-respect and inner harmony as equally relevant. On the nuclear weapons issue, national security was more relevant to those in favour, and wisdom and salvation to those opposed. We begin to see why people on opposite sides of some controversies cannot communicate. In terms of fundamental values, neither side understands or agrees with the other.

What can be concluded about the link between values and attitudes? Do people with different value structures arrive at distinctive attitudes that express these values? Or do people with different attitudes relate their opinions to different values? A functionalist theory assumes that we begin with a need to express more fundamental values and then we arrive at attitudes that fulfill that need. Yet, as we saw in Rokeach's work, values can change; in particular, the kind of self-confrontation that occurs when people face intensely controversial issues may give rise to such change.

The Relationship between Attitudes and Behaviour

One of the major reasons for measuring a particular psychological variable is to make some reasonably precise statement about how it affects behaviour. There is no question that attitudes have a powerful influence on how we act, yet attempts to demonstrate that behaviour can be attributed to the underlying attitude have frequently been unsuccessful. In one early study, LaPiere (1934) observed a young Chinese couple as they toured the U.S. In visiting more than 250 hotels and restaurants, they were refused service only once. Later, when LaPiere wrote to the same establishments asking whether they were willing to serve Chinese patrons, a startling 92 percent of those who responded said that they would refuse. The study has been criticized on several grounds: only 50 percent of the establishments responded and there is no way to ascertain whether the person who responded to LaPiere's letter was the same person who had offered service.

A similar study (Kutner, Wilkins & Yarrow, 1952) conducted in the northern U.S., when segregation still existed, revealed that although blacks were served satisfactorily in a number of restaurants, the same restaurants would later refuse to make reservations for a social event including blacks. As with the LaPiere study, different constraints were operating under different conditions. It is much more difficult to discriminate face-to-face than by letter or telephone, and there was no guarantee that the person handling reservations was the same person who originally had served the blacks. Yet despite their flaws, both these studies were important in alerting researchers to the problem of attitude–behaviour discrepancies. More recently, in a simple and better controlled situation, Bickman (1972) found that although 94 percent of 500 individuals questioned said they felt personally responsible for the disposal of litter, only 2 percent actually picked up a piece of litter planted by the experimenter.

It has been argued that these and other such studies fail to show the expected relationships between attitude and behaviour because they rely too much on a single behavioural act (Weigel & Newman, 1976). In an experiment, subjects first filled out a questionnaire that measured their concerns about the environment, including various aspects of pollution and conservation. Then, at different times over the next few months, the subjects were contacted for 14 environment-relevant actions, such as circulating a petition, agreeing to pick up litter, recruiting a friend and recycling bottles and paper. The researchers found that the correlations between attitudes and single behaviours were quite modest (average of 0.29). However, when all 14 behaviours were combined into one index, a strong correlation of 0.62 was obtained (see Table 4–4). Notice that in this study, attitudes were predicting observable behaviour in the real world rather than self-reported behaviour or laboratory behaviour. Thus, there is some compelling evidence that attitudes are linked to actions. But when and why do attitudes predict behaviour?

Variables influencing the attitude–behaviour relationship

A review by Wicker (1969) of the attitude–behaviour problem had a strong influence on the direction of subsequent research. He reviewed extensive evidence, which, in sum, challenged the notion that attitude leads inevitably to action. At the same time, he outlined a set of intervening variables that explain why many studies have been unable to demonstrate a relationship between attitude and action. Characteristics of both the person and the situation can determine whether people will act according to their attitudes.

A number of personal factors can be involved:

- The person may hold other relevant attitudes. For example, people who are or are not willing to demonstrate against nuclear power will be influenced not only by their attitudes towards nuclear power as dangerous but also by their attitudes towards the possible economic benefits of nuclear power.

- The person may be motivated to satisfy other needs. For example, people may have attitudes about the negative environmental effects of extensive logging but also may fear losing their jobs in that industry.

- The person may not see how an action would be relevant to a particular attitude. For example, voters who oppose a certain political party may not realize the party stands for policies that they favour.

It has also been shown that attitudes may be poor predictors if the behaviour is socially proscribed or illegal. Hessing, Elffers and Weigel (1988) interviewed a large number of Dutch taxpayers who were definitely known to be either tax evaders or non-evaders. They asked all subjects whether they had underreported their income or had reported illegal deductions—in other words, whether or not they had cheated on their tax returns. The data indicate that the attitudes and self-reports of these respondents were uncorrelated with their actual behaviour. In other words, many taxpayers who had tried either successfully or unsuccessfully to dupe the tax authorities had attitudes against this sort of behaviour.

Situational factors may also intrude and prevent people from acting in accordance with their attitudes:

- The real or implied presence of others may influence behaviours. For example, a person holding an unpopular attitude may feel too ashamed or pressured to act on it in public.

- Social norms may conflict with certain attitudes. Thus, the prejudiced hotel keeper may feel that it is inappropriate to turn away actual, paying customers of whatever race, creed or national origin.

- People may act in a certain way regardless of attitudes because they have no acceptable alternatives. For example, they may subscribe to a mediocre newspaper with a repugnant editorial policy because it's the only newspaper in town.

- Unforeseen extraneous events can drastically change behaviour, regardless of attitudes. People who are

TABLE 4-4

Correlations between environment attitudes and environment behaviours

Single behaviours	r	Categories of behaviour	r	All behaviours	r
Sign petitions					
offshore oil	0.41	Petitioning	0.50		
nuclear power	0.36				
auto exhaust	0.39				
Circulate petitions	0.27				
Pick up litter				Comprehensive index of behaviours	0.62
yourself	0.34	Litter pick-up	0.36		
recruit friend	0.22				
Recycling program					
week 1	0.34				
2	0.57				
3	0.34	Recycling participation	0.39		
4	0.33				
5	0.12				
6	0.20				
7	0.20				
8	0.34				

r = correlation coefficient

Source: Weigel and Newman, 1976

opposed to welfare may suddenly become unemployed or disabled and thus be compelled to seek public assistance.

In short, behaviour is influenced by more than one specific attitude. Clearly, it is affected by previous experience, habit, social norms and the anticipated consequences of that situation. This latter influence has been shown in a study that took advantage of a referendum on a proposal to raise the minimum drinking age (Sivacek & Crano, 1982). No differences were found in the attitudes expressed by samples from various age groups. However, people who would have been most affected by the change in the law (those under the age of 21) were most willing to work actively to defeat the proposal. Kraus (1995) conducted a meta-analysis of 88 attitude-behaviour studies, and concluded that there is a substantial relationship between attitudes and behaviour. He points out that the correlation is enhanced when factors such as attitude certainty, self-monitoring and the type of attitude measurement are taken into account. Interestingly, he also noted that attitudes predicted behaviour better for non-students than for students.

The MODE model

Fazio and Towles-Schwenn (1990, 1999) have proposed that the inconsistency of the relationship between attitudes and behaviour may be due to the conditions under which the attitude is activated. The important factor may be whether the decision to embark on a particular course of action involves deliberation or whether it is a relatively spontaneous reaction to the immediate situation. Fazio calls this the **MODE model**, which refers to the two processing dimensions: *M*otivation and *O*pportunity as *DE*terminants of which process will occur—reasoned or spontaneous. In other words, deliberation will most likely take place when the behaviour has reasonably serious implications (motivation) and there is no time pressure (opportunity).

For example, Fazio and Towles-Schwenn (1990) report a study in which subjects were asked to evaluate two hypothetical department stores. One, Smith's, was described in generally favourable terms; the other, Brown's, mostly in unfavourable terms. Consequently, the subjects' attitudes would be more positive towards Smith's than towards Brown's. However, the camera departments in the two stores were described in the opposite manner. In other words, Brown's had a better camera department than Smith's. Later the subjects were asked to imagine that they intended to buy a camera and to consider which store they would choose. A choice of Brown's would indicate deliberation because the subject would have to think about all aspects of the store to retrieve the information that the camera department was superior. In contrast, a choice of Smith's would be an automatic strategy whereby the subject's immediate impression of the store precluded any consideration of the merits of the camera department. Two variables were manipulated: fear of invalidity (motivation) and time pressure (opportunity). Some subjects were told that their decision would be compared with the decisions made by others in the study and that they would have to explain their decision (high fear of invalidity). Others were told nothing about having to explain their choice. In each of these conditions, some subjects were given 15 seconds in which to decide. Other subjects had no time pressure. As predicted by the MODE model, subjects with no fear of invalidity but acting under time pressure chose Smith's, while subjects who feared invalidity and who had no time pressure selected Brown's. In one situation, the behaviour was automatic (peripheral) and based on the general attitude towards the store; in the other situation, the specific attributes of the camera department affected the subject's behaviour (central).

It becomes crucial to understand the conditions under which each of these processes may be activated. If we assume that all social behaviour is not deliberate and reasoned, and that much of it is spontaneous in nature, then we must regard attitudes as similar to schemata, which can be activated or primed to influence cognition and behavioural choice. Consider, that of the many attitudes a person holds, only one or a few could possibly be brought into consciousness at one time. Thus, anything that causes an attitude to become more accessible—that is, to be brought readily into consciousness—will lead to behaviours consistent with that attitude.

In a relevant experiment (Jamieson & Zanna, 1988), subjects with varying attitudes towards affirmative action in hiring practices were asked to serve as jurors in a simulated court case of gender discrimination. The instructions emphasized to all subjects that such trials require their most careful consideration of all the evidence and that they were to remain fair and impartial and deliver fair and objective decisions. Thus, all subjects were motivated to process the information in a deliberative fashion. However, some subjects were under time pressure to read the case material and reach a verdict, while others had greater opportunity to study the materials at their own pace. Significantly greater correlations were obtained between attitudes and judgments when the subjects were under time pressure than when they had opportunities for deliberative choices. Thus, lacking sufficient opportunity for cognitive effort, people tend to resort to their spontaneously activated attitudes, perceive the situation in the light of those attitudes and act accordingly.

Behaviour can be predicted to a greater extent when all possible influences are known. Thus, a junior executive who believes unions have some positive aspects but who would support his anti-union boss when the prevailing norm among his colleagues is anti-union would not surprise us: the consequences of stating his views are likely to be negative. Such a multiple-variable approach was followed by Shetz (1974) who was interested in predicting the intentions as well as the actual behaviour of consumers. He took into consideration habits, beliefs, emotions, the general social environment, the anticipated situation and unexpected events. In the end, a multiple correlation of + 0.70 was obtained with the intention of a group of 954 housewives to purchase an instant breakfast product and a correlation of + 0.50 was obtained with the actual frequency of purchases.

Clearly, Shetz was more successful in predicting intentions than actual purchases. The subject of intentions and their relationship to behaviour has dominated much recent attitude research.

Theory of reasoned action

Ajzen and Fishbein (1980) tackled the attitude–behaviour problem directly (see Figure 4–6). They began with the premise that people usually consider the implications of their actions and then act consciously and deliberately. In short, we eventually do what we intend to do and the best single predictor of

Smoking and body building—what attitudes might underlie these apparently discrepant behaviours?

a behaviour is an intention to act in that way. Of course, intentions vary in strength and we may *intend* to do a number of different things. Ana may intend to study tonight unless she is invited to a party—an invitation she intends to accept. Thus, we must specify what determines how strongly Ana intends to study. According to Ajzen and Fishbein, the strength of an intention to act in a certain way is determined by two factors: attitude towards that action and subjective norms. That is, our intention to vote for candidate X is determined by our attitude towards voting in that way (not attitude towards the candidate) and our perception that the action is encouraged or approved by other people. Ajzen and Fishbein suggest the two factors are not necessarily equal in importance and that one may be weighted more than the other by different people and in different situations. For example, while two people may be equally determined to vote for candidate X, one may be influenced primarily by feeling positive about voting in that way (attitudes) and the other by how family and friends intend to vote (subjective norms). In one study of weight loss among women, the subjective norm component (close friends) far outweighed the attitude component in predicting eventual success (Fishbein & Ajzen, 1975).

The Ajzen–Fishbein theory also specifies what determines attitudes and subjective norms. Attitudes towards a given action are (1) determined by beliefs that the action will lead to certain outcomes and (2) weighted by evaluations of these outcomes. For example, you will have a positive attitude towards voting for candidate X if you believe that this action will lead to relatively favourable outcomes (honest government, full employment) and you place a relatively high value on such outcomes. If you believe that voting in this way is unlikely to bring about such outcomes, or you really don't care whether such outcomes occur, your attitude will be less positive. Subjective norms (i.e., perception of social pressure to act) consist of the following: (1) beliefs that certain people or groups expect the action of you; and (2) motivation to comply with these expectancies. Thus, you will feel encouraged or pressured to vote for candidate X if you believe that your friends want you to vote that way and if you want to do what they expect of you.

Putting it all together, behaviour can be predicted by intentions. Intentions to behave in a given way are determined by some combination of attitudes towards acting that way and the subjective norms surrounding the behaviour. Expected consequences and evaluations of those consequences determine attitudes, while subjective norms are determined by beliefs about what others expect and the motives to comply with these expectations. Thus, if you expect to enjoy a certain movie and would really like to enjoy it, and if you perceive that your friends want you to go with them to the movie and you want to please them, you are likely to intend to go.

The Ajzen and Fishbein model has been supported in a series of studies of socially significant behaviours such as family planning, consumer behaviour (buying particular brands), voting in U.S. and British elections, choice

FIGURE 4-6

The Ajzen and Fishbein model of reasoned action

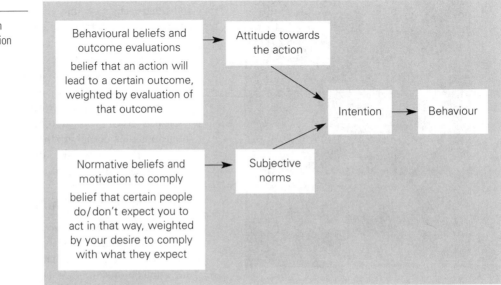

Source: Ajzen and Fishbein, 1980

of occupation, changes in smoking and drinking and losing weight (Ajzen & Fishbein, 1980). While much of the research on attitudes has been criticized for focusing on relatively insignificant, short-term, laboratory-generated attitudes, this model has been tested with real-life behaviours and attitudes. For example, in the Ajzen and Fishbein study, subjects were asked to indicate their intentions to perform various purchasing behaviours with regard to five brand names in each of three classes of products (e.g., intention to buy a Chevrolet/Volkswagen/Mercedes; intention to buy various brands of beer to serve friends at a party). For each behaviour, attitudes were assessed by rating of bipolar adjectives (e.g., buying *X* beer for my own use in the next week would be *wise/foolish*, have *good consequences/bad consequences*). Subjective norms were assessed by having subjects rate the extent to which they believed their families and friends thought that they *should/should not* buy *X* beer, etc. When the attitudes and subjective norms corresponded exactly to the behaviour, these two factors were highly predictive of behavioural intention. In another study, attitudes and subjective norms of married women regarding the use of birth control pills (but not birth control in general) predicted their use of birth control pills two years later (Davidson & Morrison, 1983). The theory of reasoned action has shown some promise in AIDS prevention (Gallois et al., 1994), with research focusing on safe sexual practices, especially the intention to use a condom. In general, these investigations offer considerable support for the theory, setting the stage for advertising and information campaigns.

As we noted earlier, attitudes vary in complexity. Yet the research generated by the Ajzen and Fishbein model usually measures attitudes in terms of simple positive or negative evaluations. As people become more involved and more experienced in an activity, they develop a more complex set of expectancies about various consequences. For example, in a survey of marijuana attitudes among high school students (Schlegel & DiTecco, 1981), a pattern of scores concerning attitudes on various aspects of marijuana use (e.g., the morality of marijuana use, expected pleasant and unpleasant effects, health consequences), predicted the extent of use more accurately than did a single score, pro- or anti-marijuana.

The theory of reasoned action has also been criticized on several other grounds (Liska, 1984). First, according to the model, our attitudes influence our intention to act in a certain way but do not influence our behaviour directly. However, it has been shown in several field studies using sophisticated statistical analysis that attitudes influence behaviour even after accounting for intentions (Bentler & Speckart, 1981). In partially bypassing intentions, the theory of a direct attitude–behaviour link seems to challenge the logic of a sequence of reasoned actions: I am favourable towards doing it, so I decide to do it (intention) and then act.

The theory also seems to confuse normative beliefs (how we expect others to react) and beliefs about behavioural outcomes. The reactions of others are the most significant outcomes of many of our actions. Moreover, the theory neglects a number of other important variables such as other relevant attitudes. Finally, in this theory, attitudes are conceived as a cause and behaviour as the ultimate effect. As the next chapter will show, cause and effect can flow both ways: behaviour is often a cause of subsequent attitude change.

Ajzen (1985, 1987) has pointed out that the predictive utility of the theory can be improved if *volitional control* is also taken into consideration. For example, whether a high school student intends to continue on to university will depend not only on the original factors in the model but also on whether the student perceives that he has the required ability and financial resources—that is, perceived control. This led Ajzen to modify the theory of reasoned action to take this factor into account.

Theory of planned behaviour

Ajzen's modification adds beliefs concerning the resources and opportunities individuals perceive that they possess to the factors in the reasoned action model. *Perceived behavioural control* can influence intention to act as well as directly influence behaviour (see Figure 4–7).

The effect of perceived behavioural control on intentions depends on whether the individual perceives engaging in the behaviour to be easy or difficult. The direct effect on behaviour is based on the extent to which the person perceives the behaviour to be under his control. For example, Madden, Ellen and Ajzen (1992) found that subjects reported less control over getting a good night's sleep than over taking vitamin supplements. If the behaviour is considered to be under high control (e.g., vitamins), then intentions will play the dominant role in predicting action. However, as perceived control decreases, intentions become less influential.

Madden, Ellen and Ajzen (1992) compared the predictive value of the two theories for 10 behaviours that varied as to amount of perceived control. They found that the inclusion of the control factor in the model

FIGURE 4-7

FIGURE 4-7

The theory of planned behaviour

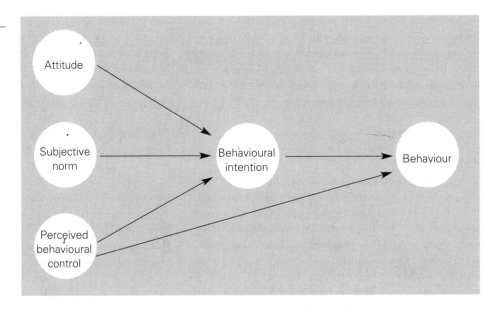

improved prediction. They conclude that while the theory of reasoned action applies when the target behaviour is under volitional control, the theory of planned behaviour is superior when perceived volitional control is reduced. A study of problem drinkers (Schlegel, D'avernas, Zanna, DeCourville & Manske, 1992) provides further support for this differentiation. It was found for non-problem drinkers that perceived control predicted intention to drink but that for problem drinkers, it predicted behaviour (frequency of getting drunk). Presumably problem drinkers perceive less control over their drinking than do non-problem drinkers.

While the Ajzen and Fishbein models have an elegant simplicity and have generated much research, they do not fully account for the complexities of the relationship between attitude and behaviour. Nevertheless, the evidence indicates that the models perform well (Notani, 1998) and an extensive review of the literature revealed that the models predicted intention with an accuracy of between 40 percent and 50 percent and behaviour between 19 percent and 38 percent (Sutton, 1998). Clearly, research will continue and new approaches will emerge, which will contribute to a better understanding of this fascinating and important problem.

A Final Note

From the beginning, the study of attitudes has been at the core of social psychology. Much of the early research was devoted to developing reliable and valid measures of attitudes, largely because it was believed that attitudes are accurate indicators of important social behaviour. However, as the evidence accumulated that attitudes are not as closely linked to behaviour as was expected, social psychologists began to wonder what the fuss was all about. Many turned to other problems and some even predicted that attitude research would soon be a thing of the past.

These prophecies were not fulfilled. Instead, attitude research has progressed through three distinct phases or generations in which different problems have been explored. The first generation asked, "Is attitude related to behaviour?" The second asked when attitudes are related to behaviour. The third generation of research concentrates on how attitudes influence behaviour and, indeed, how behaviour influences attitude. Attitude research has thus become integrated with work on social cognition.

In the next chapter, the influence of social cognition will be evident as the important issue of attitude change is explored. It will become clear that the concept of attitude is alive and flourishing in social psychology.

Summary

1. A value is a higher-order abstraction of what is considered ideal or desirable by a person. Terminal values represent preferences for certain end-states in life—instrumental values, preferences for certain modes of conduct.

2. Value conflicts can lead to changes in values, attitudes and actions. The value pluralism model relates relative priorities of values such as freedom and equality to trade-off reasoning and political ideology.

3. Citizens of various nations show considerable variations in values (national character) related to their culture and history. One study compared nations along value dimensions of power distance, avoidance of uncertainty, individualism–collectivism and masculinity–femininity (i.e., achievement versus interpersonal relations). In particular, individualism–collectivism has been shown to be a reliable and stable factor.

4. An attitude is a predisposition to react in a certain way to an object or experience. It includes cognitive, affective and behavioural components.

5. Attitude ambivalence occurs when both positive and negative cognitions or feelings about an attitude object are present.

6. Attitudes serve a number of functions: instrumental or adaptive, knowledge, ego defensive and expressive. Research has demonstrated the value justification effect, which is a selective appeal to values in order to bolster or justify attitudes.

7. Attitudes are not strongly linked to behaviour. For accurate prediction, specific attitudes and multiple indices of behaviour must be assessed.

8. A variety of personal and situational factors increase or decrease the predictability of behaviour on the basis of attitudes. These include other relevant attitudes, other needs, relevance of the action, the presence of others, social norms, access to alternative behaviours, unforeseen events and personal relevance of the object or issue. Attitudes that are immediately accessible to memory and awareness are more likely to lead to action.

9. The most influential models of the attitude–behaviour relationship are Ajzen and Fishbein's theory of reasoned action, and its extension, Ajzen's theory of planned behaviour. The most immediate determinant of an action is an intention, which is determined by attitudes towards the action (beliefs that it will lead to valued consequences) and perceived norms (beliefs about what others expect of us and our motives to comply). Under some conditions, behavioural control needs to be taken into consideration.

Further Reading

ADAMS, M. (2003). *Fire and ice: The United States, Canada and the myth of converging values.* Toronto: ON: Penguin Canada.

AJZEN, J. (2001). Nature and operation of attitudes. *Annual Review of Psychology.* 52: 27–58.

CHAIKEN, S. & TROPE, Y. (Eds.). (1999). *Dual-process theories in social psychology.* New York, NY: The Guilford Press. A review of all aspects of peripheral and central processing.

EAGLY, A.H. & CHAIKEN, S. (1992). *The psychology of attitudes.* New York: NY: Harcourt Brace Jovanovich. An encyclopedic coverage of attitude theory and research, thorough, analytic and integrative. Certain to become the indispensable resource on the topic.

FRIEDMAN, T.L. (1999). *The Lexus and the olive tree.* New York, NY: Farrar, Straus, Giroux. An interesting anecdotal account of the impact of globalization and the Internet on modern and traditional values.

MAIO, G.R. & OLSON, J.M. (Eds.). (1999). *Why we evaluate: Functions of attitudes.* Mahwah, NJ: Erlbaum.

PETTY, R.E. & KROSNICK, J.A. (Eds.). (1995). *Attitude strength: Antecedents and consequences.* Mahwah, NJ: Erlbaum. This book considers attitude strength from a variety of perspectives.

SELIGMAN, C., OLSON, J.M. & ZANNA, M.P. (Eds.). (1996). *The psychology of values: The Ontario symposium* (Vol. 8). Mahwah, NJ: Erlbaum. A thorough and stimulating review of theory and research on values.

TRIANDIS, H.C. (1995). *Individualism and collectivism.* Boulder, CO: Westview Press. A review of research and antecedents related to this important cultural value dimension.

Weblinks

Implicit Association Test

depts.washington.edu/iat/ This site presents a new method that demonstrates public–private and conscious–unconscious divergences.

"Euthanasia: The Debate Continues" by Robert D. Lane and Richard Dunstan

www.mala.bc.ca/www/ipp/euthanas.htm Essay published by the Institute of Practical Philosophy at Malaspina University-College.

Chapter 5

Changing Attitudes

Advertising may be described as the science of arresting human intelligence long enough to get money from it.

Stephen Leacock

Loyalty to a petrified opinion never yet broke a chain or freed a human soul.

Mark Twain

Chapter Outline

Changes in attitudes can change lives and make history. Consider the following examples:

- In the fall of 1995, the nation held its breath as the referendum on Quebec sovereignty approached. The *Oui* side, favouring independence for Quebec, couldn't win ... or could it? When the leadership of the *Oui* side changed, attitudes shifted significantly in favour of sovereignty. After a massive eleventh-hour pro-Canada rally in Montreal, attitudes shifted again. In the end, *Non* won by a very narrow margin ... and future referenda were promised, until a staunchly federalist government was elected in 2003.

- Three years earlier, a historic agreement on a new constitution was reached among Canada's political leaders. After years of tortuous negotiations, the unanimous agreement, known as the Charlottetown Accord, was presented to the voters in a national referendum on October 26 of that year. At the time of the agreement, public opinion polls indicated that the accord would sweep English Canada and have a good chance of approval in Quebec as well. And yet, 54.2 percent of the electorate rejected the proposed constitutional changes, as did the majorities in six provinces (including Quebec) and the Yukon Territory. What caused voters to turn decisively against a proposal that had been supported by their political leaders? What caused attitudes to change? Those who voted against the agreement did not expect Canada to break up as a result. Rather, they disagreed with any one element of the accord (such as "distinct society" status for Quebec), or they lacked confidence in the prime minister at that time (Ogloff et al., 1993).

- While marijuana was commonly used in the 1920s, it was generally not seen as a social threat or personal hazard (Levinthal, 2002). These attitudes changed in the 1930s when repressive laws were enacted and generally supported by the populace. Dire warnings by politicians and films such as *Reefer Madness* hardened attitudes against marijuana. In the 1960s when marijuana smoking first became common among students, attitudes began to change. While legal reforms were slow in coming, some modest changes relaxing penalties for

possession of small amounts and increasing penalties for cultivation and distribution were proposed in Canada in 2003. An Ipsos-Reid poll at the time (reported in *The Globe and Mail*, May 17, 2003) found that 55 percent of Canadians did not believe that smoking marijuana should be a criminal offence, while 42 percent thought that it should be. Moreover, 63 percent of respondents supported the proposed relaxation of marijuana possession laws.

- In the 1950s, formal religious institutions and practices were highly influential in Canadian society. Indeed, 60 percent of Canadians reported weekly attendance at religious services. By 2002, this figure had declined to about 22 percent. This does not represent a complete detachment from religion; many of those who rarely attend services turn to churches, synagogues and mosques to mark occasions such weddings or funerals, or in raising their children. However, it is clear that attitudes towards religion have not remained stable and consistent over the past decades. Interestingly, while involvement in religious institutions has declined somewhat in Canada, the trend over the past decade or so is dramatically reversed in the United States (Adams, 2003; Bibby, 2002).

Note that attitude change is rapid in some cases and very gradual in others. In everyday life, we encounter attempts to change our attitudes towards beer, toothpaste or taxes. Other attempts are more personal. A friend tries to convince us that her opinion is correct. A professor urges us to keep up with assignments. Some of the messages in advertising, propaganda and person-to-person situations are direct and designed to manipulate us for fun or profit. Since corporations and political parties devote massive resources to advertising in the various media, most recently the SPAM problem on the Internet and text messaging on cell phones, we can conclude that attitude change is a priority in our society.

At the same time, attempts to change attitudes often fail. Opinions on controversial issues such as marijuana decriminalization, gay marriages and immigration policy may shift dramatically or remain consistent over time. Similarly, lavishly financed advertising campaigns may often fail; one such failure with regard to Coca-Cola is documented later in this chapter. While a great deal has been learned about how attitudes change, attitude manipulation is neither foolproof technology nor black magic.

Our study of attitude change is organized around two basic principles: cognitive consistency and external influence. In effect, we will look at how attitudes change "from the inside out" and "from the outside in." The cognitive consistency principle explains why you might vote against a proposal supported by a politician you dislike. It also explains why you may become more committed to your position after you vote than you were beforehand. The study of external influences on attitudes is the study of persuasion and we will examine two very different approaches to this problem.

Cognitive Consistency and Attitude Change

Imagine that you have agreed to take on an important job at your place of work and then you just don't get around to doing it. Or, imagine that you don't like eating mashed potatoes and then find yourself eating them. Or, imagine that you believe that smoking is injurious to your health, and that your friends dislike your smoking habit, and yet you continue to smoke. In all these cases, you may well have feelings of discomfort because we all need to feel that we are consistent in what we believe and how we are acting.

How can this be understood? Originally conceived by Leon Festinger in 1957 and subsequently modified and expanded (Brehm & Cohen, 1962; Aronson, 1968; Wicklund & Brehm, 1976), cognitive dissonance is a disarmingly simple yet provocative theory, which has led to a number of interesting and unexpected predictions.

We will outline the basics of the theory and review some of the research it has generated before considering some criticisms of the original theory and some later developments. The evolution of cognitive dissonance theory is an interesting case history of how theory develops in social psychology.

Basic principles

The theory of **cognitive dissonance** explains how cognitive elements—ideas, beliefs and preferences regarding behaviour—stand in relation to each other. Dissonance is said to exist when one cognitive element is logically opposed to another cognitive element. In other words, cognitive dissonance is a state of psychological tension—the uncomfortable feeling people get when they become aware of inconsistencies in their thoughts. It is important to note that these thoughts can include an awareness of an action that was inconsistent with a belief. Basic is the premise that cognitive dissonance is psychologically uncomfortable and will motivate the person to try to reduce the dissonance.

Of course, not just any inconsistency will cause cognitive dissonance. We all live comfortably with inconsistencies in our lives. You may eat mashed potatoes, if they are served, even though you don't like mashed potatoes, and yet not feel any tension or discomfort at all. Other inconsistencies can, however, cause dissonance and make us very uncomfortable. Two factors determine the overall level of discomfort or cognitive dissonance. The first is the ratio of dissonant cognitions to consonant cognitions. Thus, for example, while smoking may be dissonant with a belief that smoking causes cancer, the overall level of dissonance experienced may be reduced by consonance between smoking and a belief that smoking is relaxing. The second factor in determining dissonance is the relative importance of the various elements to the person involved. While smoking may be consonant with a smoker's various beliefs about pleasure and relaxation, the importance of the health risk to this smoker may outweigh the consonant element. On the other hand, eating mashed potatoes is usually not felt to be inconsistent with anything important to us. We will return later to the subject of when we actually experience cognitive dissonance.

Reducing dissonance

What will a person do to reduce dissonance when it is aroused? A number of solutions are possible, although, depending on the person and the situation, one solution may be preferable to another (see Figure 5–1):

1. The person may modify one of the cognitions to restore a sense of consistency. For example, the smoker may decide to give up smoking in order to achieve consonance with beliefs about the importance of health. As Mark Twain commented, "It's easy to stop smoking, I've done it many times."

2. The person may change the perceived importance of a cognition. For example, the smoker may decide that smoking is not really harmful to health: "It's only statistical and besides, my grandmother smoked and lived to a ripe old age."

3. The person may rationalize that the two cognitions are not really relevant to each other. Thus, smokers may conclude that the health risks of smoking really do not apply to their own smoking.

4. A person may bolster the case for smoking by adding new, consonant cognitions: "Smoking helps me to avoid overeating." One variation is the "worse peril" ploy: "Tobacco smoke may be bad, but air pollution from cars is worse."

Dissonance in action

Now let us turn to when we actually experience cognitive dissonance. Research in cognitive dissonance has concentrated on four areas: the discomfort often experienced after a difficult decision; exposure to new, dissonant information; seeking support from others; and the dissonance experienced after we act in ways contrary to our beliefs.

Post-decision dissonance

Imagine that you are about to purchase a new car and must choose between a Porsche and a Mercedes of equal value. Before the decision, you may experience a state of conflict that produces discomfort. While the conflict is resolved by making a choice, you may still experience discomfort after making the choice because of **post-decision dissonance**, having just rejected the opportunity to buy that Porsche. In other words, you may feel twinges of regret about not having chosen the other car. To reduce this discomfort, your evaluations of the chosen and rejected alternatives will diverge immediately after the decision is made. That is, after the Porsche is chosen, it becomes more attractive and the Mercedes less attractive than before you made the decision. The magnitude of post-decision dissonance will depend on the following: (1) the importance of the decision—for example, choosing a brand of laundry detergent would not be as important to most people as choosing an automobile; (2) the extent to which the choices were equally desirable—for example, if you are a great admirer of both the Porsche and Mercedes, a choice between these two would arouse more dissonance in you than a choice between one of them and a less-desired car; and (3) the extent to which you perceive that you made your choice freely. If you had to choose a Honda Civic rather than a Porsche because your bank account did not give you the freedom to choose, you would not experience cognitive dissonance.

After a difficult decision, people often experience a "regret phase" (Walster, 1964) in which they may undervalue their choice and find the rejected alternative attractive. This phase occurs immediately after the decision and is short-lived. After the regret phase, we tend

FIGURE 5-1

Reducing dissonance

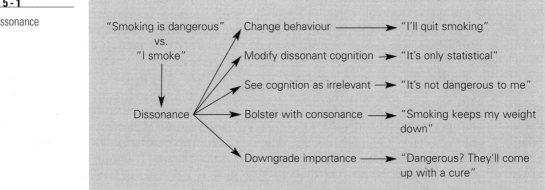

to reduce dissonance by over-valuing the choice that we made. Thus for instance, immediately after writing the cheque for the chosen car, you may have a transitory feeling of panic: "What have I done?" Then you reduce dissonance: "I bought the best car on the market." In time, you can judge your decision more objectively.

Laboratory experiments have usually supported predictions of post-decision dissonance (Festinger, 1964). Furthermore, the phenomenon has been demonstrated outside the laboratory, at a racetrack in British Columbia, where bettors were asked to estimate the chance of their horse winning (Knox & Inkster, 1968). Some of these bettors were interviewed just before they placed their bets, others immediately after they had placed their bets. Those in the second group showed significantly higher confidence that their horse would win the race. In short, placing the bet seemed to create post-decision dissonance, which the bettors then reduced by increasing their confidence in their choice. These results were replicated in a similar study of wagering in a game of chance at the Canadian National Exhibition in Toronto (Younger, Walker & Arrowood, 1977).

The effect of post-decision dissonance extends beyond racetracks to the voting booth. In both a federal and an Ontario provincial election, voters who had just cast their ballots were more inclined to think their candidate was best and would win than were voters just entering the polling station (Frenkel & Doob, 1976). Extensive public opinion polling before and after six presidential elections in the United States showed that voters who supported the winning candidate tended to express greater support for their candidate after the election than before. On the other hand, those who supported the losing candidate tended to express less support for that candidate and more for the winner (Beasley & Joslyn, 2001).

So far, we have seen post-decision dissonance after making a difficult choice between attractive alternatives. But what if we have to choose between two undesirable alternatives—the lesser of evils? Some research indicates that when we choose between attractive alternatives, we reduce dissonance by devaluing the rejected alternative while a choice between undesirable alternatives leads to an increase in positive evaluation of the alternative that we choose (Schultz, Léveillé & Lepper, 1999). That is, choosing between two used cars of dubious quality and ancient lineage will lead you to find the car you chose more attractive after you made your decision.

Two other important factors increase post-decision dissonance. One is the *commitment* to the decision; you will not experience dissonance unless you feel committed to, or bound by, the decision (often by making the decision public) and responsible for its consequences (Kiesler, 1968). The other is *volition* or free choice. If you are instructed or compelled to make a particular decision, you are not likely to feel dissonance (Linder, Cooper & Jones, 1967).

Selective exposure to information

It has long been hypothesized that people seek out, evaluate and remember messages that are "congenial" with their existing attitudes (Eagly, 1996). For example, in judging the results of TV political debates, people tend to judge their own preferred candidate as the winner. After purchasing a new car, you may read only those ads extolling the virtues of that car and avoid those ads which depict other cars you had considered and rejected. Dissonance theory predicts that people will seek out information that decreases dissonance and avoid information that increases it (e.g., Ehrlich, Guttman, Schonbach & Mills, 1957). If new, dissonance-arousing information cannot be avoided, then you might employ other strategies such as discounting or misperceiving the message, denigrating the source or actually changing your attitude. For instance, politicians may attack the opponent personally, rather than arguing the opposing position.

However, the selective exposure effect appears to be unreliable (Eagly, 1996). Some research suggests that people seek out consonant information rather than simply avoiding dissonant information (Frey, 1986). In a revised statement of cognitive dissonance theory, Festinger (1964) argued that dissonant information is not always avoided and may even be preferred in some circumstances. When we perceive that dissonant information can be easily refuted, we may actually seek out such a message in order to bolster our confidence and reduce dissonance. Or, if we believe the information will help us make the right decisions, we may accept some dissonance today to avoid more dissonance tomorrow.

Outside the laboratory, researchers have studied how people respond to new information that disconfirms previously held beliefs (Silverman, 1971; MacDonald & Majunder, 1973; Bishop, 1975). The studies concerned changes in attitudes towards U.S. political figures following highly publicized events such as the resignation of President Richard Nixon over the Watergate scandal. In general, dissonance theory was supported in the studies, although some individuals appeared to tolerate more inconsistency than others in the context of public affairs issues.

One interesting situation concerns information regarding events over which we have no control such as the outcome of an election. We will tend to find an unfavourable result to be more desirable—or, at least, less undesirable—if we had already concluded that this was the likely result. That is, if we expect a candidate other than the one we support is likely to win, we will not experience distress at that outcome. This is particularly the case when we feel a strong sense of personal involvement (Kay, Jimenez & Jost, 2002). Now consider the effects of listening to political pundits and hearing the results of political polls during election campaigns. Dissonance theory offers one explanation for how the outcomes of elections may be influenced by such incessant and incessantly reported polls. We may even change our vote because the likely winner seems more attractive.

Social support

As discussed in the previous chapter, our attitudes are more likely to lead to action if we also perceive that others would support the action. (Recall the theory of reasoned action). Festinger also claimed that dissonance may be aroused by others voicing disagreement with us, especially if the topic is important and the opponents are credible. Again, a number of options are available to reduce dissonance: you might change your mind, get the others to change their opinions or undermine their credibility. If these solutions do not work, you could find other people who support your views or seek to persuade those who are not yet committed.

Festinger, Riecken and Schachter (1956) studied the role of social support among members of a doomsday cult. The members of this cult believed they would escape a worldwide flood by being taken on a spaceship to a distant planet. Eventually, after several false alarms when the spaceship did not show up as predicted by the leader, the members realized that neither the flood nor their rescuers were coming. One would expect that this hitherto secretive group would quietly disband and that members would go about their own lives. Instead of giving up their beliefs, they began to proselytize actively, recruiting others to their cause. It felt more comfortable to claim that they were the cause of the flood being cancelled, thereby avoiding the conclusion that they had been foolish in their actions. While other research failed to replicate this phenome-

non in groups, there are so many variables at work in field settings of this sort that the effect, if it exists, cannot be expected to appear consistently (Hardyck & Braden, 1962; Thompson & Oskamp, 1974).

Counter-attitudinal behaviour and insufficient justification

Perhaps the most important application of cognitive dissonance theory has been to study the relationship between attitude and behaviour. We would suppose that people act on their attitudes—their attitudes come first and their behaviours follow as a consequence. Now, consider the proposition that people may act first and then change their attitudes to be consistent with what they just did. For example, adolescents may smoke along with friends who are smoking, although they believe it to be a bad habit, and then change their attitude towards smoking. This counter-intuitive suggestion—that we may act first and then change an attitude—has generated some interesting and inventive research.

In the pioneering experiment (Festinger & Carlsmith, 1959), participants were brought individually to a laboratory and seated in front of a board containing a large number of pegs. Their task was to turn each peg a one-quarter turn in sequence and to continue turning for 20 minutes. The task was deliberately designed to be tedious and boring. At the end of the "experimental session," the experimenter informed the participants that the experiment was designed to test the effect of prior expectancies on motivation. They were also told that they were in the control group and therefore had not been given any prior instructions. The experimenter then stated that the next participant was waiting and was to be told that the task was interesting and enjoyable. Unfortunately, the assistant who was supposed to pass on this information had not yet shown up. Each individual then was asked to take the assistant's place. Half of the participants were offered $1 for their help; the other half were offered $20—a substantial sum in 1958 dollars (more than U.S. $110 today). The majority of the participants agreed to help whether they were offered $1 or $20 U.S.

The participants then proceeded to tell the waiting "subject" (actually a confederate of the experimenter) that the task, which they knew to be boring, was quite interesting and enjoyable. That is, their actions, what they said, were contrary to their real attitude about the experiment. Then during a post-experimental interview, participants were asked as part of the debriefing to rate how boring or interesting they had found the experimental task. The question was "Would a counter-attitudinal behaviour (lying to the confederate) lead to an attitude change that represented a more positive evaluation of the task?"

Attitude change did occur, but it depended on the magnitude of the incentive to lie. It is important to understand that the two theories predict opposite results. Reinforcement theory would predict that the greater the reward, the more positive people would feel about the experience, including the boring task. On the other hand, dissonance theory would predict that those paid only $1 to lie about the task would show greater attitude change because they would have insufficient external justification (only $1) for their action. They would reduce this discomfort by deciding that the task was "sort of interesting" and that they had not, in fact, lied. Participants paid $20 could justify their actions by this payment, whereas few people would feel comfortable selling out for one paltry dollar.

The results supported dissonance theory. That is, attitude change was greater among those paid $1 than those paid $20. This experiment generated much debate and was followed by a series of other investigations (see Focus on Research—Cognitive Dissonance and a $20 Misunderstanding). In general the principle has been strongly supported: when attitude-discrepant behaviour is not accompanied by circumstances that justify that behaviour to the individual, he or she tends to experience cognitive dissonance and may, subsequently, experience a change in attitude.

Insufficient justification also seems to offer a satisfactory explanation for the outcome of an experiment performed by Aronson and Mills (1959), which was concerned with the relationship between severity of hazing, or initiation into a group and fondness for the group. In this study, female undergraduates were assigned to one of a control condition, a mild initiation condition or a severe initiation condition. The control participants were simply asked by the male experimenter whether they could freely discuss sex. The mild initiation participants were asked the same question and also required to read aloud five sex-connoted but ordinary words (e.g., "screw"). Those undergoing the "severe" initiation, in addition to being asked the question, were required to read aloud 12 obscene words (e.g., "fuck") and two passages containing explicit reference to sexual activity. (Keep in mind that this experiment took place in 1959, when repeating these words aloud would have been experienced as stressful by most women.) All of the partici-

pants then listened to a recording of what appeared to be an earlier, rather tedious, discussion session of the group they were to join. The participants then evaluated the group discussion on a scale.

It was found that those who had experienced the severe initiation made the most favourable evaluations. In their case, enhancing the evaluation of the group could only reduce the dissonance aroused by undergoing a severe initiation into a dull group. In other words, the boring discussion was insufficient justification for enduring the severe initiation, so the participants imagined it to be interesting.

This phenomenon has been replicated in the "forbidden toy" experiments with children (Aronson & Carlsmith, 1963; Freedman, 1965; Lepper, Zanna & Abelson, 1970). We have seen that an activity pursued for insufficient external justification, such as a bribe of

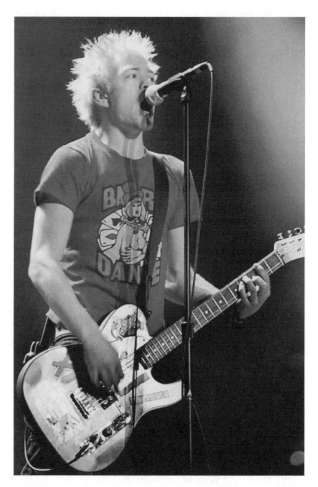

The band Sum 41 helps rally social support during the SARS crisis in 2003.

Cognitive Dissonance and a $20 Misunderstanding

The Festinger and Carlsmith (1959) article generated much debate, discussion and research. Rosenberg (1965) argued from the perspective of reinforcement theory that those receiving a larger incentive for attitude-discrepant behaviour (in this case, lying) would be more likely to change their attitude because of the principle of the *spread of effect*—the good feeling engendered by a larger reward would generalize to anything associated with that reward such as the task. He argued that the results obtained in the $20 condition could be explained as a fatal flaw in how the study was done. The participants were paid an unrealistic $20. This would only arouse *evaluation apprehension*, a suspicion among participants that the experimenters were trying to "buy them off"—so participants would stick to their original position. In his experiment, participants were asked to write an unsigned counter-attitudinal essay, in this case, arguing that an extremely unpopular administrative decision to ban the university football team from an important bowl game was correct. He paid his participants only $5 in the high-incentive condition and, as predicted, obtained more attitude change in the high-incentive condition.

Other studies tested different financial incentives (Elms & Janis, 1965; Janis & Gilmore, 1965) and for a while it appeared that the weight of evidence had swung against cognitive dissonance theory. However, not long thereafter, other experiments (Carlsmith, Collins & Helmreich, 1966; Linder, Cooper & Jones, 1967) provided a solution to the debate. It was pointed out that writing an anonymous essay differs from the face-to-face deception engaged in by the participants in the Festinger and Carlsmith study (Carlsmith, Collins & Helmreich, 1966). Since public commitment was lacking in the counter-attitudinal essay-writing task, it was hypothesized that this factor might be crucial for the occurrence of dissonance. Researchers conducted an experiment in which some participants wrote anonymous essays and others publicly lied for either 50¢, $1.50 or $5. As anticipated, the attitudes of those writing anonymously changed in the direction predicted by reinforcement theory and those of individuals who publicly lied changed in the direction predicted by dissonance theory (see Figure 5–2).

FIGURE 5-2

Attitude after public and private discrepant behaviour

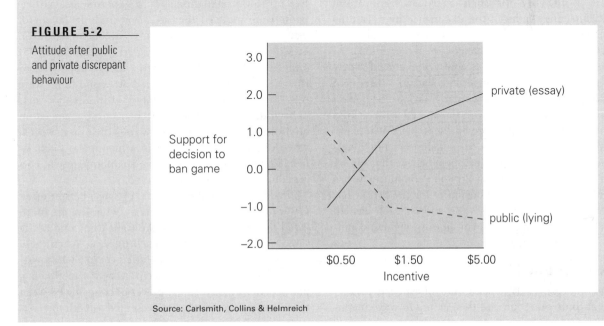

Source: Carlsmith, Collins & Helmreich

only $1, is likely to become more attractive. What would happen if an activity were prohibited for no good reason? Would that activity then become less attractive? In this study, individual young children were at first allowed to play with any of five attractive toys. The experimenter noted each child's order of preference for the toys. He then placed the second most attractive toy on a table and distributed the remainder throughout the room. At this point, the experimenter said that he had to leave for a few minutes, but just before going out the door he told some of the children that he would be "annoyed" if they played with the toy on the table (mild threat condition); for others he substituted "angry" for "annoyed" and also threatened to take all the toys and leave if the child disobeyed (severe threat condition). Other children were assigned to a control condition in which the experimenter did not say anything but took the second-ranked toy with him when he left.

The children were observed for 10 minutes; none played with the forbidden toy. The experimenter then returned, replaced the forbidden toy with the other toys and obtained a second ranking of the toys. It was found that the children in the mild threat condition now ranked the forbidden toy lower than they had previously while none of the other participants decreased the rank of this toy. In fact, those in the severe threat condition actually now ranked it higher. Among those children who received the mild threat, cognitive dissonance was aroused because they could not justify ignoring the toy for such a trivial admonition. Therefore, they reduced the dissonance by devaluing the toy. Another study showed that this devaluation can be a real and lasting change (Freedman, 1965).

In short, behaviour that is contrary to attitudes may arouse cognitive dissonance and lead to subsequent attitude change. This is particularly likely if the person is offered a small reward or threatened with a mild punishment and is therefore unable to justify the act in terms of expected reward or punishment. For dissonance to occur, the individual must believe that the act was freely chosen and that a public commitment has been made in which responsibility for the action has been expressed. Careful analysis and research has led to an understanding of the conditions in which cognitive dissonance occurs.

Dissonance and hypocrisy

Most of us are guilty at some time of espousing a certain attitude or action and then acting in ways incon-

sistent with what we have said. We tell others that wearing a seat belt can be life saving and then we neglect to buckle up on a short trip. We say that we need to exercise and then find excuses to avoid it. We may even tell someone that we like them and then act in a way that betrays our real feelings. When we are aware that our actions are not consistent with our professed attitudes, we experience feelings of hypocrisy.

When these feelings are aroused, they may generate positive changes. In an experiment by Stone et al. (1997), individuals were asked to prepare a videotape in which they advocated the use of condoms to prevent transmission of sexually transmitted diseases. Then they were asked to think about reasons why people in general sometimes fail to use condoms (normative reasons) or why they themselves may have failed to use them (personal reasons). It was reasoned that arousal of hypocrisy would be greatest in the personal reasons condition. Then they were given a choice of purchasing condoms at a reduced price (direct dissonance reduction) or making a donation to a charitable agency (indirect reduction). The results were clear: when they were asked to focus on personal reasons for failing to engage in safe sex, most participants purchased the condoms, while when they focused on people in general, they chose the indirect method of making a donation.

Problems of the environment offer fertile ground for the experience of hypocrisy. We all know that conservation, recycling and not littering are beneficial to all of us and we say so—but our actions may often fail to live up to our stated beliefs. In experiments, participants were induced to state an attitude in favour of water conservation (Dickerson, Thibodeau, Aronson & Miller, 1992) or recycling (Fried & Aronson, 1995) and then made mindful of their wasteful behaviour or their failure to recycle. When both conditions were met (awareness of their stated attitude and their behaviour), their subsequent behaviour changed in environmentally beneficial ways. In other words, when dissonance is aroused in a manner to make us feel like hypocrites and we have an opportunity to correct our actions, we tend to do so.

Finally consider the instance of what Batson et al. (1997) refer to as moral hypocrisy, when we are motivated to appear to be doing the right thing and at the same time acting in our own self-interest. When these two motives are in conflict, we often act in a way to satisfy both of them. For instance in a set of experiments, participants were given the power of choosing between two tasks, one of which was presented as both interesting and with possible financial gain and the other as dull and boring with no rewards. Participants were told that they were to decide between themselves and another person who would do which task. Most participants acted in pure self-interest, choosing the attractive alternative for themselves. What is interesting is that, even where participants were told that there was a fair way to decide such as by flipping a coin, only about half agreed to toss the coin and only 10% assigned the other person to the attractive task. In other words, they did have it both ways: to appear to be fair and to arrange the results to benefit themselves.

The evolution of cognitive dissonance theory

Cognitive dissonance theory was perhaps unique in the history of social psychology as a source of so much research and controversy. The following discussion highlights some of the issues raised in the decades that followed Festinger's (1957) original publication of the theory.

The problem of arousal

It is postulated that cognitive dissonance is an unpleasant state of tension, which the person is motivated to reduce or relieve in some way. Does such a state of tension really exist or is a need to be consistent simply an invention of social psychologists (Kiesler & Pallak, 1976)? What causes people to become aroused in dissonance experiments—actual cognitive dissonance or simply the experience of being a subject in an unusual psychology experiment? Indeed, some studies have shown that negative feelings from dissonance are aroused even where there are no direct personal consequences to the individual (Harmon-Jones, 2000).

Very few of the investigations offered direct evidence of arousal and those that did employed measures of physiological changes. For example, Gerard (1967) created states of dissonance by offering to give some participants one painting chosen from two which they had ranked third and fourth choices in a group of 12 paintings and other participants a choice between a highly desired (third choice) and less desired (eighth choice) painting. Presumably the former participants, facing a more difficult choice, would experience more dissonance than the latter participants would. More significant, blood pressure of participants in that condition was reduced after they made a decision, indi-

cating that their state of arousal or tension was reduced by that decision.

While we can be reasonably confident that arousal does occur under dissonant conditions, is arousal necessary for attitude change to take place? Several studies address this question in ingenious ways (Cooper, Zanna & Taves, 1978; Wright, Rule, Ferguson, McGuire & Wells, 1992; McGregor, Newby-Clark & Zanna, 1999). In some of the experiments, people were to behave in a counter-attitudinal manner and were not given a sufficient justification for their behaviour such as a small incentive or a free choice as to how to behave. While participants might then be expected to feel discomfort, some of them were given another reason to attribute the discomfort that they might feel— they were given a stimulant drug that produces arousal or told that the new lighting arrangements in the room might make them feel nervous and edgy. Participants in these conditions did not show the same attitude change as did those who had no other explanation for their discomfort, which supported the notion that cognitive dissonance is a source of arousal.

Thus if dissonance arousal leads to attitude change, then reducing arousal should lead to no attitude change, even where there is inconsistency. In one study (Steele, Southwick & Critchlow, 1981), participants were asked to write a counter-attitudinal essay. Afterwards, some participants were induced to drink alcohol under the guise of rating the taste of various beverages while others consumed coffee or water. When tested later, those who drank alcohol showed less attitude change. Presumably, the alcohol reduced arousal while the caffeine in the coffee increased it. The results tell us that cognitive dissonance does, indeed, involve arousal.

What is cognitive dissonance?

Now, we return to the question of when we experience cognitive dissonance. Recall that Festinger (1957) described cognitive dissonance as the result of a logical inconsistency in our thinking: B does not follow from A. For example, he suggested that if a person were to observe someone standing in the rain and not getting wet, these two cognitions would be dissonant. However, subsequent research indicates that this is not an example in which the observer would experience cognitive dissonance. People might be amused, amazed, curious or concerned about their own sanity but would not experience the psychological tension or discomfort that leads to attitude change.

Inconsistency is a normal part of life and much of the time does not bother us (Bem, 1970). Indeed, at times, we can accept conflicting, "mixed emotions" such as both happiness and sadness. It is important to distinguish between conflicting evaluations of some attitudinal object such as capital punishment, and the "felt ambivalence," an emotional discomfort about this conflict (Newby-Clark, McGregor & Zanna, 2002). We may believe that capital punishment may have both some benefits and some undesirable consequences, but our emotional reaction to ambivalence may depend, for instance, on how readily these contradictions come to mind. Interestingly, messages which highlight both emotions are more effective with older than younger adults (Williams & Aaker, 2002).

It has also been argued that if people rationalized each decision and each action solely in the service of reducing cognitive dissonance, they would find it difficult to learn from their mistakes (Schultz & Lepper, 1996). In fact, Abelson (1968) suggests that much of our thinking consists of isolated "opinion molecules," consisting of an attitude, a belief and a perception of social support (i.e., a fact, a feeling and a following). For example, "I really like the idea of French immersion programs in schools" (attitude); "I believe that it would help my child become bilingual and get ahead in this world" (a belief); "So do many other people, because most of these programs have waiting lists" (perception of social support). The alert reader will recognize, in this triad, elements of the Ajzen and Fishbein (1980) theory of reasoned action (see Chapter 4). The question now becomes "When and why do certain inconsistencies become uncomfortable to us?"

Is it dissonance or self-justification?

Recall from Chapter 3 that protecting self-esteem is fundamental to much of human behaviour. It has been argued that inconsistency is uncomfortable and motivating only when it threatens our own sense of self-worth (Greenwald & Ronis, 1978; Steele & Liu, 1983). Indeed Aronson (1984), and Thibodeau and Aronson (1992), early pioneers in dissonance research, argue that the effects of cognitive dissonance really amount to *self-justification*. For example, cigarette smokers may be uncomfortable about their behaviour, not because it is inconsistent with their beliefs about smoking and cancer or causing discomfort to non-smokers but because it is inconsistent with their own view of themselves as rational, thoughtful and considerate people—in short, they feel foolish or

guilty about it. Making people aware of their own inconsistencies, particularly those relevant to how they see themselves, is a powerful means of arousing dissonance (McGregor, Newby-Clark & Zanna, 1999).

In several experiments, participants were required to give a speech contradicting their own attitudes, demonstrating the importance of feeling responsible for causing an outcome inconsistent with their self-image. In one (Nel, Helmreich & Aronson, 1969), participants were given high or low incentives to speak in favour of legalizing the use of marijuana. Different participants were led to believe that their audience was in favour of or against this policy or that they were talking to a group of schoolchildren with no position on it. It was in the noncommittal audience condition that participants given low incentives showed more attitude change. Evidently dissonance was aroused when they believed that they were addressing an impressionable audience of children who might be persuaded to use drugs. Another study (Cooper & Worchel, 1970) showed that the dissonance effect occurred when participants were led to believe that they had actually persuaded someone that a boring task was interesting but not if it seemed that the person was unconvinced. In a third experiment, the dissonance effect occurred after participants were induced to lie to someone they liked but not when they lied to someone they disliked (Cooper, Zanna & Goethals, 1974).

Another way to test the hypothesis that cognitive dissonance represents a state in which people feel uncomfortable about themselves is to arouse dissonance in the usual ways and then manipulate the situation so as to enhance the self-esteem of some participants (Steele & Liu, 1983). In one such study (Rodrigues, 1983), some participants were told that the psychological tests administered earlier showed them to be mature and well-adjusted individuals. The dissonance effect (greater attitude change in a low-incentive condition) was not observed among those whose egos had been enhanced but did occur as predicted among those who had not received this treatment. Clearly, a secure sense of self-worth diminishes the need to justify or rationalize our actions.

A revised model of cognitive dissonance

Cooper and Fazio (1984) have outlined a revised model of cognitive dissonance that accounts for the diverse research findings (see Figure 5–3). They reason that when we act contrary to our beliefs, we take note

FIGURE 5-3

"New Look" model of cognitive dissonance

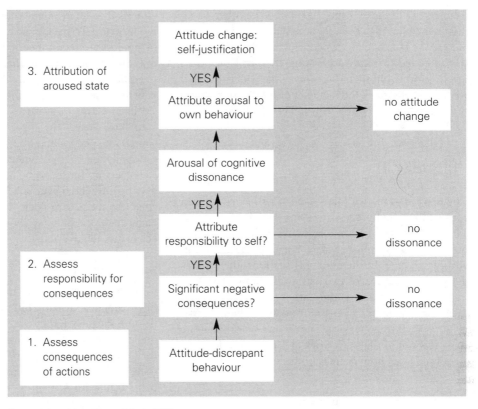

Source: Adapted from Cooper & Fazio, 1984

of the consequences of our actions. If our act is perceived to have actual or potential negative consequences, we search for an explanation. If it is clear that we had a free choice to act and that the consequences could have been foreseen, we attribute responsibility to ourselves. At this point, dissonance is aroused (note that dissonance arousal depends on the belief that one is personally responsible for negative consequences) and we experience psychological discomfort. If we attribute this feeling of discomfort to our reaction to the action rather than to an external source (e.g., a drug or the situation itself), then we are motivated to reduce dissonance. Now our attitude changes and we come to believe that the boring task really was exciting.

Thus, four steps are necessary for cognitive dissonance effects:

1. The attitude-discrepant behaviour produces significant consequences.
2. The person feels personally responsible for these consequences; that is, he or she believes the choice was made freely and the consequences were foreseeable.

3. The person experiences a state of arousal.
4. The person attributes this arousal or discomfort to his or her own behaviour.

Note the many exits from cognitive dissonance that are available along the way. You may decide that no harm was done by your little lie. You may decide that you really had no choice but to lie—the money was too good or the devil made you do it. If you do experience arousal, you may ignore or minimize it, attribute it to the weather, indigestion or nervousness in a psychology experiment. In short, the cognitive dissonance process involves both dissonance arousal and motivation to reduce dissonance, and both processes involve complex sets of attributions.

The Cooper and Fazio model is useful in that it can predict when the insufficient justification effect will occur. Several studies demonstrate, for example, that when people feel personally responsible for what happens as a result of their behaviour then dissonance is aroused as indicated by their subsequent changes in attitudes—even when they have not acted in ways discrepant with their attitudes (Scher & Cooper, 1989;

Johnson, Kelly & LeBlanc, 1995). On the other hand, dissonance has also been demonstrated in the absence of aversive consequences; people who had written that they enjoyed drinking a beverage that, in fact, tasted unpleasant would then throw away the paper they had written on. Perhaps the mere act of lying arouses cognitive dissonance (Harmon-Jones et. al., 1996).

Persuasion

Cognitive dissonance focuses on how behaviour can cause an internal process resulting in attitude change. The study of persuasion, on the other hand, looks at how influences from outside the person may result in attitude change. In the following sections, the topic is discussed in terms of two basic questions. The first question, which drove the earlier research, is what determines whether a person or people in general will be persuaded by a message. The second question—one that grew out of the framework of social cognition (see Chapter 2)—is how persuasion occurs.

What predicts persuasion: Who says what to whom, and how?

The foundation for research on persuasive communication was established in the 1950s by the Yale University Communications Research Program (Hovland, Janis & Kelley, 1953). They consider the following four questions:

- Who presents the message? (source)
- What is the message? (message)
- To whom is the message directed? (audience)
- By what means is the message sent and received, and how is it presented? (channel)

The source of the message

In political campaigns, the credibility or lack of credibility of political leaders is always an important factor. The credibility of a source has been shown to be mainly a function of perceived *expertise* and *trustworthiness*. That is, a communicator is more effective if the audience assumes she is sincere and knows what she is talking about. Trustworthiness is especially enhanced if the audience believes the communicator has nothing personal to gain from his or her

efforts. It is no accident that toothpaste is promoted by individuals in lab coats (expertness) and that detergents are recommended by ordinary people who only want to pass on their experience to others. Credibility is effective only if the audience is aware of it before the message is presented, rather than after (Mills & Harvey, 1972).

In most cases, the topic and the expertise of the source must be compatible. A nuclear physicist is not especially persuasive when talking about nutrition. However, at times high-status or attractive sources may be influential even outside their sphere of knowledge (Aronson & Golden, 1962; Roskos-Ewoldson & Fazio, 1992). Examples abound in the employment of celebrities to advertise various products.

Sleeper effect

Consider the common occurrence in which we somehow recognize a name but can't remember where we heard it (Jacoby, Kelley, Brown & Jasechko, 1989). In one experiment, participants were read a list of names including "Simon Weisdorf," and were informed that none of these people was famous. Afterwards, participants read a list of names, including Simon Weisdorf, some relatively famous people (Roger Bannister, Minnie Pearl) and some who were not famous (Valerie Marsh, Adrian Marr) and were asked to rate the fame of each person on the list. Participants shown the second list immediately after the first did not rate Weisdorf as being famous but those shown the list 24 hours later did. Further investigation revealed that the participants were, in fact, unable to recollect the source of that name.

The implications for persuasion are clear: the effect of the source declines over time, particularly if people cannot remember the source—and the message remains. This has been called the **sleeper effect**. In a pioneering experiment (Hovland, Lumsdaine & Sheffield, 1949), one group of soldiers viewed a propaganda film and another group did not. Attitudes towards the topic of the film were measured five days and then nine weeks later; surprisingly, differences between the two groups were somewhat greater at nine weeks than at five days. The most popular explanation for this effect is the **discounting cue hypothesis**, which states that the source of the film's message (i.e., the U.S. army) was perceived as untrustworthy. This led the soldiers to discount the message, thus reducing its immediate effect. But as time elapsed, the connection between the source and the message was forgotten or weakened and the message itself appeared more prominent.

However, research has indicated that the sleeper effect is reliably produced only when the discounting cue is presented after the message itself. In an experiment (Pratkanis, Greenwald, Leippe & Baumgardner, 1988), participants were presented with a message arguing against a four-day work week and a discounting cue: a note from the editor of the book in which the message was published stating that this conclusion was probably wrong. When participants were given the message only, the initial attitude change was significant, but it dissipated over the following six weeks. When the discounting cue was given before the message, little attitude change was obtained; the participants had been forewarned to expect a wrong conclusion. But when the discounting cue was given after the message, the initial attitude change was less than in the other conditions but greater after six weeks. Apparently, the impact of the message had persisted, but the discounting cue from the editor was long forgotten. Thus, what at first seemed to be a reliable and important phenomenon has proved valid only in a small subset of persuasion situations.

Message factors

Suppose that you are a lawyer about to present your summation to the jury. You must get your message across in the way most likely to persuade your audience. Hovland, Harvey and Sherif (1957) conducted the initial studies on this topic. Among several findings was the discovery that especially with intelligent audiences, it is best to present both the positive and negative sides of the argument and then to refute the negative evidence. However, when the audience has a firm position on an issue (e.g., in the case of a speech to delegates at a political convention), a two-sided presentation is not effective. However if it is probable that the audience will hear the other side from someone else, it is usually more effective for you to present both sides (Karlins & Abelson, 1970).

What about negative political advertising—messages that attack the political record or personal characteristics of the opposing candidate? While the intent is obviously to create negative evaluations of the opposition, the public may react with a "backlash" against the source of the attack or with sympathy towards the victim of the attack. In the Canadian federal election of 1993, two advertisements were aired by the Progressive Conservative Party that played up the facial distortion of Liberal leader (later prime minister) Jean Chrétien. In a quasi-experimental study of attitudes towards the five political party leaders of the time (Haddock & Zanna, 1997), the attitudes of some participants were assessed before and some after the airing of these advertisements (which were quickly withdrawn). Those who were assessed afterward showed significantly more negative feelings towards Conservative leader Kim Campbell and more positive feelings towards Jean Chrétien than those tested before seeing the advertisements. In a debate, insulting the other candidates or their families can result in negative reactions (Roese & Sande, 1993).

Clearly in some cases, negative or "attack" advertising often works and it has become common. However, it does appear that in some cases it can backfire, particularly if seen as unfair.

Primacy–recency

If both sides of an argument are presented, which is likely to have the advantage—the side presented first (primacy) or the side presented last (recency)? Most of the early experiments (e.g., Lund, 1925; Asch, 1946) indicated that the message presented first was more influential: the **primacy effect**. However, Hovland, Harvey & Sherif (1957) and others (Luchins, 1957; Anderson, N.H., 1959) showed that the passage of time is a critical factor. If one set of arguments immediately follows the other, the first set is likely to have the most impact (primacy). However, if a considerable period of time elapses between the presentation of the two arguments, recency becomes more influential (Miller & Campbell, 1959; Insko, 1964; Wilson, W. & Miller, 1968).

If two lawyers, for example, present their cases to the jury on the same day, the one who goes first is likely to have the advantage. However if it is late in the day and the case is adjourned so that the other lawyer will be heard the next morning, the advantage will be with the lawyer heard most recently. In our courts, the prosecution (Crown) presents its case and its final argument to the jury before the defence. This custom is presumably derived from the proposition that a defendant is innocent until proven guilty. However, it may also give the defence the opportunity to take advantage of recency, the last presentation, while the Crown has the advantage of the primacy effect. We can only speculate about which side has the overall advantage in persuading the jury.

Should messages arouse emotions or appeal to reason?

Recall in Chapter 4 that attitudes consist of both affective (emotional) and cognitive (belief) components. Some persuasive messages focus on changing the beliefs of the audience while others attempt to change attitudes by arousing strong emotions in the listeners. Can persuasive messages have a selective effect on attitudes so that emotional messages change feelings but not beliefs while cognitive messages have the opposite effect? Edwards (1990) created positive attitudes towards a fictitious beverage by having some participants taste it (affect) and then read information about its ostensible health benefit while others first read the information then tasted it. Her reasoning was that the message presented first would have the greatest effect (primacy effect). As predicted, she also found cognitive–affective matching effects. Fabrigar and Petty (1999) conducted a pair of similar experiments relevant to the same effect of matching emotion or belief messages. In one, participants again were told that they were in a marketing study and the first product was a new beverage. Some of them read the information about the product while others tasted it. Then the cognitive and affective attitude components were measured. Affect was measured by having participants rate the extent to which 16 different emotions described how the beverage made them feel (e.g., happy, excited, tense, angry). Cognitions or beliefs were measured by having them indicate the extent to which 14 different characteristics described the beverage (e.g., useful, safe, harmful, worthless). Again as predicted, those who had tasted the beverage showed more positive attitudes on the affective measure while those exposed to the informative message were more positive on the beliefs measure.

DO FEAR TACTICS WORK? Suppose you are in charge of public relations for a provincial department of highways and want to encourage citizens to obey mandatory seat belt legislation. What would be your best advertising strategy? For instance, should television ads show the actual gory and fatal aftermath of automobile accidents?

The research on fear messages began with an experiment by Janis and Feshbach (1953) who were interested in finding out how various appeals affected people's dental habits. The researchers created three levels of fear arousal. The most extreme employed colour pictures of diseased mouths, gums and teeth and the least extreme used only X-rays and showed pictures of

healthy mouths. They found that the most threatening appeal had the least effect and that the most change followed the mild appeal. The results seemed to show that the instigation of high fear leads to avoidance and interferes with learning. It is also possible, since the high-fear condition was so unpleasant, that the association decreased the credibility of the source of the message and led to the message being discounted. In some studies (e.g., Higbee, 1969; McGuire, 1969; Leventhal, 1970), attitude change increased as fear increased. However in general, it seems that low to moderate levels of fear will be positively related to attitude change but that at high levels, attitude change becomes less likely (McGuire, 1968) (see Figure 5–4).

Two models have been proposed to explain the effects of fear on persuasion. The *parallel response model* (Leventhal, 1970) states that people respond to such messages to control or avert the danger mentioned in the message and to cope with the unpleasant feelings engendered by the message. Thus, the obese person may respond to messages that stress the dangers of heart disease by following a sensible diet (danger control) or may respond by rationalizing about a 90-year-old obese aunt and ignoring such messages in the future. Messages that arouse fear will probably be ineffective unless accompanied by explicit recommendations about a course of action to avert the danger, such as an effective diet to lose weight, a strategy to stop smoking or information about the location and hours of a clinic to receive tetanus shots (Sutton, 1982). Such recommendations tend to reduce the unpleasant feelings that have been aroused.

When will people respond with "danger control"? According to the **protection motivation model** (Rogers, 1975), motivation to protect oneself from a danger is based on four beliefs: (1) the threat is severe; (2) the person is vulnerable in some way; (3) the person can perform the recommended action; and (4) the recommended action will be effective. Thus in messages designed to protect people from fatal accidents, better driving practices ensue when the person fears an accident, feels personally vulnerable to this possibility, believes that the suggested action is practical and believes that it will work. These beliefs seem to be independent of one another. For instance, people may believe that driving too fast is dangerous and that accidents could happen to them personally, yet not believe that they can change their habits behind the wheel. Unless driving more slowly and cautiously seems plausible and desirable, people tend to respond defensively

FIGURE 5-4

Relationship between fear arousal and persuasion

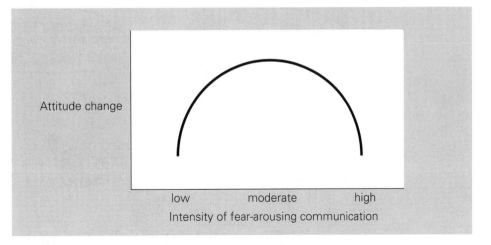

Attitude change

low   moderate   high

Intensity of fear-arousing communication

and change is unlikely (Janis & Feshbach, 1953). (Fear-based communications in health are discussed further in Chapter 16).

The target: Audience factors

Are some people more easily persuaded than others? Much research has been devoted to the question of whether persuasibility is a general trait (Hovland et al., 1953; Janis & Hovland, 1959; Janis & Kelley, 1959). The findings indicate that individual differences in persuasibility, independent of the situation, do exist but that the effect is quite small and easily overwhelmed by other variables. For example, it would appear reasonable to assume that people with low self-esteem are more readily persuaded (recall Chapter 3). However, the research indicates that the effects of self-esteem on persuasibility depend on the message. Uncomplicated messages with poorly supported arguments are more likely to produce attitude change in people with low self-esteem than in people with high self-esteem. On the other hand, intricate, well-supported messages are more effective with people with high self-esteem than with people with low self-esteem (Nisbett & Gordon, 1967).

McGuire (1968) argues that it would inevitably be difficult to show a direct relationship between a personality trait and persuasion because the same trait can affect both the individual's attention to and comprehension of the message (reception) and change her attitude in the direction of the message (yielding). Indeed, any factor that is positively related to reception will be negatively related to yielding. For example, people with high self-esteem tend to be more

receptive or open-minded to a persuasive message. At the same time, however, the likelihood of such individuals succumbing to the persuasive arguments decreases. Indeed, low self-esteem people have difficulty receiving the message, high self-esteem people tend not to yield, but moderate self-esteem people are most readily persuaded (Rhodes & Wood, 1992).

Gender and attitude change

For many years, it was assumed in social psychology that women were more susceptible to influence, were more easily persuaded and conformed more than men. The reasoning behind this assumption was that females in our society have been socialized to be passive and yielding (Middlebrook, 1974). Subsequently, Eagly (1978) thoroughly reviewed the literature dealing with sex differences in persuasibility and concluded that there was little support for this contention. She notes, for example, that some of the reported differences between the sexes resulted from the researchers' use of experimental materials that were biased against the interests and abilities of women. She also suggests that women may indeed have a tendency to comply but that this compliance may indicate a concern for group harmony and a reluctance to disrupt positive group feelings rather than genuine persuasibility.

Age may also be important in considering gender differences. One study examined reactions to image-oriented advertisements for tobacco and alcohol (e.g., personal attractiveness and lifestyle) as opposed to advertisements that focused on the qualities of the products. While female adolescents showed a strong preference for image-oriented advertisements, the

THE MEDICAL POST, AUGUST 5, 1986

same gender difference was not obtained with adults (Covell, Dion & Dion, 1994).

The channel of communicating the message

Does it make any difference whether a persuasive message is presented face-to-face via TV or radio or in a written document? The data on this question are not consistent (Williams, 1975; Worchel, Andreoli & Eason, 1975). Chaiken and Eagly (1976) suggest that these inconsistent findings might be explained if message comprehensibility varied between investigations. There is evidence that complex messages are better understood when written than when presented by video or audiotape (Eagly, 1974).

An experiment that took several factors into account provided participants with two types of persuasive messages: easy or difficult to understand, and either written, audiotaped or videotaped. The difficult messages were more effective when written, while the easy messages were most effective on videotape and least effective in writing. Confronted with the difficult message, the participants rated the written presentation as more pleasant (see Table 5–1 on page 134). The written message in this case seemed to be effective because of its positive tone and because participants retained more information (Chaiken & Eagly, 1976).

What principles of persuasion are embodied in this poster?

How these factors combine

Of course, in real life we cannot hold three of the four sets of variables constant while varying one of them. Source, message, audience and channel effects interact and we must consider them together in various combinations. Several experiments illustrate this problem.

In one experiment (Wiegman, 1985), two interviews were taped with each of two Dutch politicians,

both of them confederates of the experimenter, and representing the main political parties. The issue—whether an airport should be built in a particular location—was one on which neither political party had taken a position. In one interview, the politician advocated the proposal in a cool, sober, rational manner, while in the other, the same politician spoke in a strongly emotional, committed, dynamic manner. One of the four interviews was shown to delegates at meet-

A PRACTICAL QUESTION

Attitude Change and Aging

What is the effect of age on one's openness to attitude change? Two perspectives can be described, both of which assert that people are most open to attitude change when they are young and then become less open to change as they grow older. According to the *impressionable-years hypothesis*, people become socialized into adult roles during adolescence and early adulthood and thus the events and historical environment of that time will have a profound influence on their attitudes for the rest of their lives. For example, people who came of age during the 1960s, a relatively liberal era of political protest, would be expected to remain relatively liberal during their lives, while those who came of age in the more conservative 1980s would remain relatively conservative thereafter. According to the *increasing-persistence hypothesis*, people are relatively flexible and open to change when they are young, but as they age, their flexibility gradually decreases and they become "set in their ways." Perhaps people's capacity for information processing gradually declines with age or perhaps their accumulated store of knowledge and experience causes their attitudes to become more stable as they grow older. Of course, a third possibility is that people remain highly flexible and open to change in opinions throughout their life cycle (Sears, 1983).

In a classic longitudinal study of this issue, a cohort of female students was followed before, during and after their years at Bennington College in

the U.S. (Newcomb, 1943; Newcomb, Koenig, Flacks & Warwick, 1967; Alwin, Cohen & Newcomb, in press). These women, having been raised in socioeconomically advantaged and conservative families, were confronted by a liberal milieu at the college. During their years at the college, the students, particularly those who identified with the college and were involved in its activities, moved gradually towards the liberal end of the political spectrum. When they were re-interviewed 25 years later and again about 40 years after graduation, their liberal attitudes were shown to have remained quite stable despite the important changes in the political climate of the nation during that period. Even given the obvious limits in sampling, these findings document the impact of influences on attitudes during the years at college or university, supporting the impressionable-years hypothesis.

Krosnick and Alwin (1989) examined the data from two longitudinal studies of political attitudes in the U.S. in order to compare the extent to which attitudes change over time in different age groups. In the first study, a national cross-sectional sample of 1132 adults was interviewed at the time of the 1956 presidential elections, again in 1958 (the mid-term elections) and again at the time of the 1960 presidential elections. In the second study, a sample of 769 adults was interviewed on three occasions during the year of the 1980 presidential election campaign—in January, June and September or October. In both studies, the participants were divided into

(continued)

seven age groupings (at the time of the first interview) ranging from age 18–25 for the youngest group, to 66–83 for the oldest. Significantly, both changes during an election campaign and changes between election campaigns followed the same pattern. It showed that attitude changes were greatest in the youngest group, that of early adulthood, and susceptibility to change dropped off afterwards, supporting the impressionable-years hypothesis. Contrary to the increasing-persistence hypothesis, there was no evidence that attitudes became increasingly stable for the groups after the age of 33. Thus, it appears that while young people may be most responsive to shifts in the social and political climate of the times, aging does not inevitably lead to a hardening of the attitudes. In fact, the evidence indicates that commitment to one's attitudes increases during middle adulthood and then declines in late adulthood so that older people are more susceptible to changes (Visser & Krosnick, 1999). Midlife adults may be more resistant to change because they attach more importance to their attitudes, and think more about them (Boninger, Krosnick, Berent & Fabrigar, 1995). It may also be partially the result of a network of friends and associates who support their attitudes. As people move from young adulthood to midlife, they increasingly discuss important issues with a wide range of people outside their immediate families. However, older adults have fewer people with whom they discuss concerns that they share (Marsden, 1987). Therefore, they become more susceptible to changes in attitudes.

ings of the two parties. When attitudes were subsequently measured, the data indicated that a rational presentation resulted in a higher rating for the speaker but not in greater attitude change. Regardless of the content of the message, attitude change was greater when the source and the audience belonged to the same political party.

A second experiment shows how the medium (channel) affects perception of the message (Chaiken & Eagly, 1983). The likability of a speaker as perceived by students was varied by having the speaker praise or derogate the students, faculty and general quality of their institution. Then they were presented with a video, audio or written message from that speaker advocating change to a trimester system. It was found that attitude change was greater when participants liked the speaker if the speaker was seen or heard but that liking was not a factor in the written transcript condition.

A third study shows how a message can be tailored to the audience (Snyder & DeBono, 1985). Participants were presented with advertisements using "hard sell" or "soft sell" techniques. "Hard sell" methods stressed the quality, value and usefulness of the product while "soft sell" techniques stressed the image of the product (colour, texture) or of the consumer (smart, affluent, sexy, discriminating). It was reasoned that certain participants would be more receptive or susceptible to each approach and a measure of *self-monitoring* was administered for this purpose. Since high self-monitors tend to adapt their behaviour to fit the social situation, it was thought that they would be more concerned with how others perceive them and would thus be more sensitive to the "soft sell" emphasis on images. On the other hand, since low self-monitors are guided more by inner feelings, dispositions and beliefs, they would be more receptive to messages

TABLE 5-1

Ratings of message pleasantness on a 5-point scale

Modality	Message difficulty	
	Easy	Difficult
Written	2.94	4.73
Audiotape	3.75	2.32
Videotape	4.78	3.02

Source: Chaiken & Eagly, 1976

about the product itself via the hard sell. In three studies, the data showed these combinations of message and audience characteristics to be most effective in increasing the willingness of subjects to try the product and the amount they would be willing to pay for it.

While the work reviewed thus far provides us with information about the various factors which influence persuasion, it does not explain how people change their attitudes, the process by which attitudes change. Drawing on insights derived from research derived from the study of social cognition (recall Chapter 2), contemporary research on attitude change has shifted its focus to the processes by which our attitudes change. Our discussion now turns to this work.

Persuasion and Cognition

What does it mean to be "persuaded" of something? You may think of persuasion as changing someone's mind. However, while you may respond more favourably to a particular brand of a consumer product, are you really "convinced" that it is better than others? Perhaps you may be convinced when you purchase a car or a house. These are major investments for most people and so you may gather evidence and think about what you want to buy and for how much. But for most purchases, we are influenced by other factors such as the attractiveness of the source, the familiarity of the brand name, an association with pleasant experiences. We may not really be "convinced," but our attitude changes enough for us to buy the product.

The basic question then becomes how we process the information that is contained in a persuasive message. The research has identified two distinct ways in which we deal with the contents of a message. One, known as _systematic or central route persuasion_, involves thinking through the arguments and evidence that is presented. Of course, this way involves time and efforts, and as we have seen in discussing how we form impressions and make judgments about other people, we usually do not expend this time and effort. That is, we usually resort to the second approach called _heuristic or peripheral route_ _persuasion_, because we use mental shortcuts (e.g., trust the experts), and so the factors that cause our attitudes to change are peripheral or tangential to the quality of the arguments. Let us examine this type of persuasion more closely, and then turn to the question of when we actually engage in "central processing"—thinking about arguments and arriving consciously at a conclusion.

Peripheral route persuasion

How does peripheral route persuasion occur? Consider, again, the influence of source characteristics and why they influence us. People will often use simple schemata or heuristic processing (Chaikin, 1980, 1987). For example, they may rely on the rule "Trust the experts" to accept a persuasive argument presented by someone perceived as expert. Similarly, they may respond to an activated rule of thumb that "We agree with people that we like" and thus accept a persuasive communication from a likable source.

Distraction can operate to divert people from thinking about the arguments presented. In an experiment by Norman (1976), female students were asked to read a statement arguing that people should sleep less each night than they customarily do. The communication was presented as either a single statement or as a statement supported by several reasoned arguments. The second communication was expected to elicit more elaboration and to be more convincing. However, the students were presented with a photo and some information about the background of the communicator. Half the participants saw a distracting picture of a young, extremely attractive male and the other half, a photo of an unattractive middle-aged male whose background suggested expertise on the topic. With the unattractive photo, attitude change was greater when several arguments were presented, suggesting that active thinking took place. However with the attractive photo, attitude change was substantial, whether one argument was presented or several, apparently occurring along the peripheral route of pleasant associations.

The effects of distraction will depend on the dominant or usual cognitive reaction to the message. If a communication stimulates counter-arguments, then distraction should lead to more persuasion because it will interfere with the _cognitive elaboration_ necessary to think up counter-arguments. However, if the response to the message is agreement, then distraction should interfere with this rather automatic response and thus lead to less persuasion. In two experiments by Petty, Wells and Brock (1976), distraction was manipulated by having participants record visual stimuli flashed on a screen while they tried to attend to an audio message. The degree of distraction was varied by the frequency with which the visual stimuli were presented while the favourability of the participants' reactions was manipulated by using strong or weak arguments in the audio message. The results were consistent with the **elaboration**

likelihood model (ELM; see Figure 5–5), and the participants' retrospective reports of their thoughts while listening to the communications indicated that the high-distraction condition served to inhibit the number of counter-arguments they could think of when the strong arguments were being presented, and to inhibit the number of favourable thoughts when the weak arguments were presented.

According to **cognitive response analysis** (Petty, Ostrom & Brock, 1981), a contrast is drawn between instances that involve active thought (elaboration), such as weighing the arguments for and against something, and instances in which the person simply invokes a rule of thumb, such as believing an attractive or likable person or trusting an expert, and just does so (Eagly & Chaikin, 1984). Of course, some instances may involve both processes: you might pay attention to a message because it is presented by an attractive person and then think about what the person said. An influential theory dealing with this dual-process model of persuasion is now discussed.

Elaboration likelihood model

"People are motivated to hold correct attitudes but have neither the resources to process carefully every persuasive argument nor the luxury—nor apparently, the inclination—of being able to ignore them all" (Cacioppo, Petty, Kao & Rodriguez, 1988, p. 1032). One would think that the stronger the persuasive message concerning constitutional change in a referendum campaign, the more likely it would persuade the audience. However, people are also influenced by factors not directly relevant to the message such as the source. On the other hand, how a message is worded may stimulate people to think about an issue in a certain way (Eiser & Ross, 1977; Eiser & Pancer, 1979).

Research has identified the conditions under which the arguments themselves will persuade and those in which other, peripheral factors will lead to attitude change. A contemporary dual-process theory of persuasion, the elaboration likelihood model, takes into consideration the fact that people can respond to persuasive messages either by active cognitive scrutiny of the content of the message or by more reactive, less effortful shortcuts to evaluating persuasive message manner (Petty & Cacioppo, 1981, 1986; Petty, Wegener & Fabrigar, 1996).

The term *elaboration likelihood* means the probability that the person will think about a persuasive message rather than react to peripheral cues. The **central route of persuasion** involves cognitive elaboration; that is, making the effort to understand the message and think about the issue. In this case, people are convinced by the quality of the arguments themselves. As discussed above, the **peripheral route** to attitude change involves factors that are not relevant to processing the arguments such as the attractiveness of the source, novelty or humour, a perception that everyone else believes the message or the mood of the individual at the time the message is received.

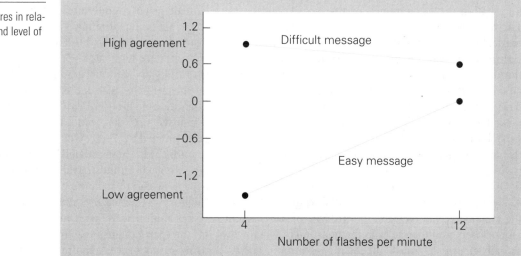

FIGURE 5-5

Mean attitude scores in relation to message and level of distraction

Central route processes tend to lead to relatively enduring and real attitude change and to consistent action. Indeed, we tend to become more committed to our attitudes as we think more about the attitudinal object (Tesser, 1978). While peripheral route changes generally occur more readily because they demand less effort, these changes tend to be rather transitory because we have not really been convinced by the arguments. Thus, attitude change will persist only as long as the relevant cues are salient. For example, we may believe in or accept certain policies only as long as the politician we associate with these policies is popular or attractive to us, and we may purchase a particular brand of beer until a more attractive association with another commercial appears.

Note that the same cue may be relevant to both central and peripheral route change. For example, under conditions of relatively low elaboration likelihood, the attractiveness of the source may act as a strong peripheral cue regardless of the strength of the argument. Under conditions of high elaboration likelihood, source attractiveness becomes less important as a peripheral cue but may be relevant as part of a persuasive argument. For example, does an attractive model with beautiful hair advertising a brand of shampoo serve as an attractive source (peripheral) or as evidence that the shampoo actually works (central)? In other words, concurrent processing by the central and by the peripheral route processes often occurs.

Recall the example of referendum campaigns in which advertisements featured a series of comments by a number of sources (peripheral cues). People are more persuaded by information coming from multiple sources than by the same information presented by only one source (Harkins & Petty, 1987). The ELM explains this multiple-source effect; people must do more elaboration or thinking about the message because each new source cues the person to think about it. If the same source presents the entire message, less effort is expended because this source has already been heard from.

Therefore, variables may affect persuasion in three different ways. First, they may act as arguments, pieces of information or logic that may induce attitude change under conditions of cognitive elaboration. Second, they may serve as peripheral cues affecting attitudes through the peripheral route. Finally, they may influence conditions that promote cognitive elaboration. Let us consider now how people may be influenced to think about the issue at hand.

Conditions under which cognitive elaboration is likely

As noted, we have neither the time nor the energy to think through everything that may be an object of an attitude. Cognitive elaboration, and thus enduring attitude change, is more likely to occur under two conditions: (1) when the person has the opportunity (such as time to think) and (2) when the person is motivated to carefully consider the arguments in the message. For instance, research suggests that a message framed in terms of a self-guide, how you wish you were or feel that you ought to be (recall Chapter 3), tends to stimulate more central processing of the arguments (Evans & Petty, 2003). Motivation is stronger when the issue is novel, unexpected or personally relevant (Zuwerink & Devine, 1996). Personal involvement may be manipulated, for example, by telling student participants that they would be required to pass a comprehensive examination in their major. Some were informed that this would take effect in the coming year (high involvement) or in 10 years (low involvement). Those with high personal involvement should be motivated to examine the arguments carefully while those with low personal involvement should be more likely to rely on peripheral cues such as the expertise of the speaker.

As predicted by the ELM, under high involvement, the strong arguments led to much more attitude change than did the weak arguments. However under low involvement, the source credibility (a peripheral cue) had a stronger effect on persuasion than did the actual arguments. These participants simply invoked a heuristic rule, "Experts know best," to decide on the validity of the arguments (Petty, Cacioppo & Goldman, 1981). Other research has obtained similar results by inducing personal involvement, and thus high motivation through increasing self-awareness (Hutton & Baumeister, 1992). However under high-involvement conditions that reflect people's values or how they define themselves, people are less open to persuasion, perhaps because they are unable to elaborate or think open-mindedly about the message under such conditions (Sherif, & Cantril, 1947; Johnson & Eagly, 1989).

The framing of the message can also have important effects. In a study (Smith & Petty, 1996), messages stressed either the benefits of increased recycling or the costs of not doing it. Strong and weak versions of both arguments were presented to different groups of experimental participants. Negatively framed messages were processed more carefully than positively framed messages in that the strength of the argument in a negatively framed message affected attitude change more. Messages are also processed carefully when the message is framed in an unexpected way. That is if a patient expects dire warnings from the physician and the physician instead extols the benefits of the medicine, the patient is more likely to elaborate on the message, and thus a strong argument would produce more attitude change.

Opportunity to engage in cognitive elaboration has been manipulated by varying time pressure and the comprehensibility of the message. For instance, Hafer, Reynolds and Obertynski (1996) investigated the effect of message difficulty in the legal system. Prior attitude measures indicated that most people were opposed to plea bargaining, the practice of offering a reduced sentence to the accused in return for a plea of guilty. Then participants listened to a speech advocating plea bargaining in which the following conditions were varied: (1) whether the speech was ostensibly given by a high-status or low-status person (a peripheral cue); (2) whether the speech had strong or weak arguments (indicating central processing); (3) whether the speech used complex language (such as jargon, infrequently used words and complex grammatical structure) or simple everyday speech. When the arguments were easily comprehensible, strong arguments produced more favourable attitudes towards plea-bargaining than did weak arguments. However when the message was difficult to comprehend, the strength of the argument did not affect persuasion. In these conditions, persuasion was influenced by the status of the source: an eminent judge or a law student.

Individual differences and elaboration likelihood

Some people are more likely than others to engage in cognitive elaboration. Individuals differ in a "need for cognition," a propensity to analyze the situation, search for clues and work on solving difficult problems. This need can be measured by a scale that includes the following items: "I find satisfaction in deliberating hard and for long hours;" "I like tasks that require little thought once I've learned them;" "I would prefer complex to simple problems;" "Thinking is not my idea of fun." (Of course, some items are worded in the reverse direction.) Note however, that need for cognition is not synonymous with intelligence. While intelligent people may enjoy using their intelligence, they will not neces-

sarily do so. Note as well since people with a high need for cognition tend to seek out information and actively work to bring a clear meaning to the issue, they are unlikely to have ambivalent attitudes (Thompson & Zanna, 1995; Griffin, 1995).

People who are high in a need for cognition will be more resistant to persuasion and more likely to be persuasive in a debate. For instance, Shetowsky, Wegener and Fabrigar (1992) presented participants with a description of a legal case. They were paired up on the basis of scores on need for cognition and asked to discuss the case and come up with a verdict. Those scoring high on need for cognition were more likely than their low-scoring partners to argue their points effectively and to come up with better counter-arguments to their partners' statements. Indeed, they were more likely to convince their partners in this joint decision. In another study, participants viewed a video of an interrogation of a defendant by both police and the defence lawyer. Those with a high need for cognition tended to adopt the perspective of whoever first questioned the suspect (primacy effect) while those with a low need for cognition agreed with whoever had the last word on the subject (recency effect) (Kassin, Reddy & Tulloch, 1990).

People with a high need for cognition are more likely to be influenced by the quality of the arguments while those low on this variable tend to be more influenced by peripheral route factors (Haugtvedt & Petty, 1992). They tend to think more about the arguments, leading to greater acceptance of the position when presented with strong arguments and greater rejection when presented with weak arguments (Cacioppo, Petty, Kao & Rodriguez, 1988). Attitude change among high-need-for-cognition people tends to persist over time (Verplanken, 1991).

While people vary in their need to think things through, they also will differ in the degree of confidence that they have in their own thinking about the issue in the message. We are more likely to be influenced by peripheral cues if the topic seems over our heads. Using both experimental manipulations of confidence and self-reported confidence, Petty, Brinol & Tormala (2002) have shown that, particularly in situations where positive thoughts dominate the message, confidence increases thinking or central processing.

Emotional state

One's mood will also influence the likelihood of elaboration. People in a good mood act the way those low in a need for cognition do, tending to react favourably to weak arguments and to peripheral appeals. Indeed, it has long been known that when people are happy, they are generally more receptive to persuasion (e.g., Biggers & Pryor, 1982). However, several studies indicate that there are different mechanisms for affecting persuasion by mood inductions (such as showing TV comedies or having participants write vivid descriptions of a happy event). Under high elaboration likelihood, positive mood induction affected both the thoughts of the person and the resultant attitudes. However under low elaboration likelihood conditions, a positive mood resulted in attitude change without inducing the person to think actively about the issue; positive mood led directly to positive attitudes without cognitive involvement (Petty et al., 1993).

When people are in a bad mood, they tend to think about arguments and to be more persuaded by the quality of the argument than by peripheral cues (Sinclair & Mark, 1992). In one study (Sinclair, Mark & Clore, 1994), participants answered a survey about university education on days that were either pleasant or unpleasant; some of each cued about weather and mood, the weather had no effect on persuasion; attitudes were affected only by the strength of the argument. On the other hand, when weather was not made salient to participants, argument had an effect on persuasion only when the weather was unpleasant. When the weather was pleasant, people were in a good mood and were willing to agree. However when their good mood was attributed to the weather (rather than to the argument or the source), then the strength of the argument influenced persuasion, suggesting that cognitive elaboration had occurred.

Finally consider the possibility that certain peripheral cues may cause the person to attend more to the message itself. We have seen that certain source characteristics such as the attractiveness or expertise of the source influence persuasion. What if the source is presented as inconsistent, such as unattractive but expert, or very attractive but knowing nothing about the issue? Experiments show that in these cases, the actual content of the message has a greater impact on attitude change (Ziegler, Diehl & Ruther, 2002).

In summary, the ELM suggests real attitude change by means of persuasion is difficult and uncommon. For central route persuasion to occur, the recipient must have both the ability and the motivation to process the information—and, of course, the arguments must be logical or otherwise convincing. As noted in Chapter 2,

we often act as "cognitive misers," taking shortcuts and acting automatically. Thus, in our society of the 20-seconds commercial and the "news bite," it is not surprising that peripheral route change is so common.

As noted earlier, peripheral route processing does not mean that central route cognitive elaboration is impossible; both can occur simultaneously. Indeed, the theory specifies that the two routes form two ends of a continuum bounded at one end by no thought at all about the issue and at the other by complete elaboration of all issue-relevant information and arguments (Petty, Wegener, Fabrigar, Priester & Cacioppo, 1996). Further, even superficial attitude change can lead to immediate behavioural change consistent with it, and bolstering cognitions may then be used to avoid cognitive dissonance. At this point, peripheral becomes central and cognitive processes are set in motion that may lead to enduring attitude change.

Limits to persuasion

It is easy to be impressed by the extensive repertoire of persuasion techniques. Whether on a one-to-one basis or as members of a mass audience, we are subjected to an ever-increasing barrage of persuasive messages. Yet it is important to realize the limits of persuasion. Businesses with lavish advertising budgets, using the latest in expertise, may well fail to sell their product and may even fail to survive. Consider the demise of Eatons, a well-known and respected Canadian institution for generations (see A Case in Point—A Marketing Debacle and the Limits of Persuasion on page 141). Many politicians lose elections, many used cars are not sold and most of us remain unconvinced by a great deal of what we see and hear. It is an enlightening experience to observe the sceptical reactions of young children to many TV commercials so cynically directed at them. In the age of mass communications, people seem to have adapted rather well.

How do people resist persuasion? A number of strategies have been studied (Cameron, Jacks, & O'Brien, 2002).

Forewarning

It is important to distinguish between two types of forewarning although both result in a similar outcome. First, individuals may simply be warned ahead of time of *persuasive intent*, and second, they also may be informed of *message content*. In both instances, the likelihood of persuasion will be

CRITICAL THINKING

Persuasion or Propaganda?

Think about the following words: *persuasion, advertising, selling, education, brainwashing, propaganda.* What are the differences? When do education, persuasion or advertising become propaganda, the systematic propagation of a given doctrine (Pratkanis & Aronson, 1992) and a word that evokes the sinister image of people chanting mindless slogans? Modern politics is rife with "spin doctors" providing the media with their own interpretations of events.

Can propaganda assume more subtle forms that are accepted in our relatively open and democratic societies? Consider the following examples:

■ Some of the present-day religious cults indoctrinate their members under conditions of extreme stress, strong group pressure, endless repetition of messages and deprivation of food or sleep. They may call it "re-education"; we may call it "brainwashing." However, somewhat similar techniques are used to initiate new recruits into some religious orders and into the military (Pfeifer, 1992).

■ Education is also concerned with attitude and behavioural changes usually (or ideally) by providing information and training in intellectual skills and reasoning. Zimbardo, Ebbeson and Maslach (1977) point out that much of the teaching of arithmetic in schools involves problems of buying, renting, selling and calculating interest. Do such examples simply provide practical skills to students or do they serve to legitimate the existing economic system?

■ A study of ubiquitous TV crime shows reveals a consistent pattern: the police solve the crime and the correct culprit is identified, arrested and convicted. Do these programs represent wishful thinking propaganda on behalf of the criminal justice system (Haney & Manzolatti, 1981)?

■ Propaganda may also be achieved by selective reporting—by omission rather than fabrication. Chomsky (1986) studied distortions in how the state of democracy in Central America was presented in U.S. newspapers. In the war against Iraq in 2003, U.S. reporters were "embedded" in units of the United States military, travelling, conversing, eating and drinking with the soldiers in the unit. Can we expect that reporters who have established personal relationships with the soldiers would or could report objectively?

In his terrifying novel, *1984*, George Orwell described a Ministry of Truth, which dispensed outright lies. At times it is difficult to distinguish information from propaganda. When propaganda is subtle, it may be even more effective.

---

reduced. In the second case, it appears that individuals are stimulated by the warning to rehearse their own position and to generate anticipatory counterarguments (McGuire & Papageorgis, 1962). Petty and Cacioppo (1977) provide particularly strong evidence that forewarned participants review their own arguments. Moreover, they have been able to show that unwarned individuals who were asked to record their thoughts and ideas on a given topic were also resistant to a subsequent persuasive appeal.

Of course, people cannot rehearse counterarguments when they are warned simply of intent. The increased resistance observed under this condition is attributed to reactance (Hass & Grady, 1975). In other words, people act to protect their threatened freedom.

Inoculation effect

Usually the more strongly people feel about an issue, the less likely they will be to change their minds about it. Paradoxically, however, cultural truisms—the unquestioned attitudes held by a large majority of the population—are particularly vulnerable to change through persuasion (McGuire & Papageorgis, 1961). Examples include the following: "You should brush after every meal;" "Democracy is the best form of government;" and "Penicillin is a boon to humankind."

McGuire used a medical analogy to account for this finding. He pointed out that an individual is susceptible to infection when the body's defences are weak, and that in order to build up these defences, inoculations are administered. These inoculations or injections of the microbe in weakened form lead the body to build up its defensive system and resist infection. Similarly, cultural truisms are vulnerable to persuasion because the individual has developed no resistance; because the truism is so generally accepted, the individual may never have heard an opposing point of view. He must, therefore, be **inoculated** by being confronted with persuasive arguments against the truism and then having them effectively refuted. The person will then be able to use these counter-arguments to ward off any attempts at persuasion in the future. There is some disagreement about whether the refutation should be passive or active. McGuire felt that active refutation (e.g., writing a counter-attitudinal essay) would not be particularly effective because it would be distracting and because people are not very good at thinking up counter-arguments, especially when dealing with tru-

---

A CASE IN POINT

A Marketing Debacle and the Limits to Persuasion

In 1984, leaders of the mighty Coca-Cola Company were very worried. Their market share was dropping while that of archrival Pepsi was rising. While Coca-Cola was still the leader, a trend that had started two decades earlier seemed to be continuing. Moreover, Pepsi was running a highly successful advertisement—the "Pepsi challenge"—in which, much to their surprise, the majority of regular Coke drinkers preferred Pepsi in blind taste tests. The Coke executives concluded that people wanted a sweeter drink.

Under the cover of strict secrecy, the research and development team set out to develop a new Coke—one that tasted more like the rival beverage. In the development process, market researchers asked Coke drinkers how they would feel if they added a new ingredient to make the drink "smoother." Only 11 percent objected. The reader will notice the wording of the question; researchers did not ask consumers how they would feel if Coca-Cola were to be replaced by a drink that had a different taste. Encouraged, the laboratory folks came up with their new beverage.

The New Coke was launched with a barrage of publicity and a sophisticated, lavishly funded advertisement campaign. Curiosity drove millions to try the new concoction. Overwhelming negative reactions poured in. People called the company to object, wrote to newspapers, spoke out on radio talk shows, even held public ceremonies in which the new Coke was poured down sewers. It became a major news story. After three months, Coke reintroduced the old Coke, now called "Classic Coke," which became a great success while sales of the New Coke were poor. After several years, the New Coke was withdrawn and a Coke once again became a Coke.

What does this story tell us about the social psychology of attitude change? First, if one is to draw valid conclusions from surveys, it is important to ask the right questions. It became apparent that to many consumers, particularly in the United States, Coca-Cola meant more than refreshment. It was part of their culture and way of life, invested with meanings and memories. To tamper with "their" Coca-Cola was to ignore these very intense feelings. The survey researchers clearly asked the wrong questions.

The other lesson is that there are limits to what market researchers, advertisers and social psychologists can persuade us to do. Despite the impressive body of research and knowledge, some of it reviewed in this chapter, individuals can and do resist the most sophisticated attempts to persuade them.

If the reader is interested in learning more about this signal event in the history of market research, see Pendergast (1993) and Rhodes (1997).

isms. He preferred the passive strategy of having the person read a well-reasoned essay on the topic or engage actively in thinking up counter-argument. His data support this contention as do other studies (Bernard, Maio & Olson, 2003).

The attitude congeniality hypothesis

It has been hypothesized that attitudes bias memory in favour of attitudinally agreeable information—that we tend to remember information consistent with our attitudes and forget the information that conflicts with our attitudes (Eagly & Chaiken 1998). In order to defend our attitudes against material that challenges them, we may not attend to that information, distort it or otherwise not store it in memory. Of course this is consistent with a cognitive dissonance interpretation. In a meta-analysis of 70 relevant experiments, Eagly, Chen, Chaiken and Shaw-Barnes (1999) found that the results were inconsistent, sometimes supporting the hypothesis, sometimes not. And so the researchers designed a simple experiment in which attitudes towards some issue were premeasured, and then two weeks later participants were exposed to an audiotape in which a speaker took a pro or con position on the issue. Various versions of the experiment were run concerning attitudes towards abortion, gays in the military or the death penalty and then participants' memory was assessed. The results were clear and consistent: congenial and uncongenial information was remembered equally well, regardless of the issues, regardless of the participants commitment to their attitudes and regardless of whether memory was assessed soon after the message or two weeks later. Indeed, regardless of the message, it was remembered better if the participant was active in some way on that issue, had stronger attitudes and if memory was assessed immediately after. The researchers concluded that participants hearing an uncongenial (or dissonant) message were more likely to process that message centrally and carefully, thinking of counter-arguments, and this enabled them to remember that message. Those receiving a congenial message remembered it as associated with their existing attitudes. In short, central processing overcame defensive dissonant reactions.

CAN WE INSTILL RESISTANCE TO PERSUASION?
Programs have been developed to instill resistance to persuasion, for instance, in assisting adolescents to resist peer group pressure (see Chapter 16). Instilling resistance to persuasion can be successful particularly when they focus on the ulterior motives of the source

and the vulnerability of the target to persuasion (Sagarin, Cialdini, Rice & Serna, 2002). That is, it is important that one dispels the illusion of invulnerability to persuasion: It happens to the best of us. Consider that if we successfully resist a strong attempt to change our attitudes, we subsequently become more confident and committed to our original position (Tormala & Petty, 2002).

Is Attitude Change "Real"?

Most estimates of attitude change depend on an individual's self-report. It is therefore important to consider, first, whether these statements reflect actual changes in the underlying attitude structure and, second, whether persuasion is lasting.

The first question emphasizes the need to distinguish between *compliance* and *attitude change*. Kelman (1958, 1961) defines **compliance** as publicly yielding to a persuasive communication without private acceptance. It usually occurs because the communicator is perceived as having the power to reward and punish. In the absence of power figures (or their agent), the target person would likely revert to the original opinion. Kelman goes on to point out that more basic changes are probable if the recipient identifies with the communicator or is able to internalize the message. Identification enhances persuasion because the individual is attracted to and wishes to be like the communicator. Internalization takes place when the new position is in line with the person's value system and is judged as being useful or valuable. While an attractive source would probably lead to identification, a credible source would more probably lead to internalization (Mills & Harvey, 1972). These characteristics of the communicator are not necessarily exclusive. For example, a parent may be simultaneously powerful, attractive and credible.

During laboratory investigations, attitude change is usually measured only immediately after the administration of the persuasive message. Thus, the permanence of induced change is not known. Investigations into attitude change over time have generally found (as have studies on forgetting) that most of the reversion occurs relatively quickly and then tapers off. For example, McGuire (1969), summarizing the results of a number of experiments, concluded that attitude change has a "half-life" of about six months. In other words, on average, about 50 percent of the initial change is still present six months later. Remember, these data are based on a single administration of a persuasive message. Re-administration of the communication will maintain change.

A Final Note

What, in the end, causes us to change our attitudes or, indeed, to resist attempts to change our attitudes? Wood (2000) identifies three central motives underlying processes of change and resistance. These involve concerns with the self (particularly being consistent with our self-image and self-schemata), concerns with others and how they may reward or punish us and concern with what feels like a valid understanding of the reality of our lives. In some cases, our discomfort with inconsistencies and challenges to our sense of self-worth will cause our attitudes to change even in the absence of persuasion. In other words, our attitudes do not exist in some kind of cognitive vacuum but are embedded in our relationships with others and with our understanding of our world and ourselves.

Summary

1. Attitude change can be viewed in terms of internal processes and external influences.

2. The theory of cognitive dissonance states that when two related cognitions are not consistent, the individual is motivated to reduce discomfort by changing or reducing the importance of a dissonant cognition or adding consonant cognitions (bolstering).

3. Four important areas of study in cognitive dissonance theory are post-decision dissonance, social support, selective information seeking and dissonance after attitude-discrepant behaviour.

4. The magnitude of dissonance experienced after attitude-discrepant behaviour is a function of insufficient external justification for performing that action. This effect occurs when the action involves public commitment and free choice.

5. Cognitive dissonance is a state of arousal, which can be reduced when the arousal itself is reduced or when alternative attributions are made for the resulting uncomfortable state.

6. Dissonance occurs not in response to logical inconsistency but in response to an inconsistency within the self-concept.

7. Cooper and Fazio have developed a "new look" attributional model that explains when cognitive dissonance occurs in response to attitude-discrepant behaviour: significant consequences, personal responsibility, arousal and attributing the arousal to the action's consequences.

8. Factors involved in persuasion include the source, audience, message and channel. Source credibility is generally determined by judging the source's trustworthiness and expertise.

9. Message effectiveness is influenced by the presentation's primacy or recency. Fear arousal up to a moderate level can increase persuasion.

10. The elaboration likelihood model of persuasion differentiates between central routes (understanding the arguments, thinking about the issue) and peripheral routes (focusing on characteristics of the source or distractions in the message, using heuristics). While changes are more likely to occur through the peripheral route, they are less likely to persist in the absence of salient cues; central route changes have more staying power. Central route processing is more likely when the person is motivated, has the opportunity to think and has a strong need for cognition.

11. Whether an audience will be receptive to a message can be determined by certain personality characteristics such as self-esteem. A written communication tends to cause the audience to focus more on the argument than on the source; in oral or visual presentations, the audience focuses more on the source.

12. The effect of persuasion is reduced by forewarning the audience of an attempt to persuade, and by inoculation, confronting the audience with mild counter-arguments.

13. In determining whether an individual has been persuaded, it is necessary to distinguish changes represented by behavioural compliance from changes associated with identification with the source or internalization of the message.

Further Reading

CIALDINI, R.B. (1993). *Influence: Science and practice* (3rd ed.). New York: Random House. An excellent discussion of the variety of means by which people influence people, with many examples from advertising and marketing, public relations, cults, fund-raising and politics. The writing style is clear, non-technical and even witty.

CHAIKEN, S. & TROPE, Y. (1999). *Dual-process theories in social psychology.* New York: Guilford Publications. An excellent set of papers on current thinking in the development of theories such as elaboration likelihood, heuristic-systematic and MODE, as well as social cognition.

EAGLY, A.H. & CHAIKEN, S. (1993). *The psychology of attitudes.* Fort Worth: Harcourt Brace Jovanovich. An encyclopedic coverage of attitude theory and research, thorough, analytical and integrative. It has become an indispensable source on this topic.

EDWARDS, J., TINDALE, R.S., HEATH, L. & POSAVAC, E.J. (Eds.). (1995). *Social influence processes and prevention.* New York: Plenum. A set of papers applying persuasion and other social influence measures to prevention in health and other socially significant areas.

HARMON-JONES, E. & MILLS, J. (1999). *Cognitive dissonance: Perspectives on a pivotal theory in social psychology.* Washington, D.C.: American Psychological Association. More than 40 years after the publication of Festinger's book, cognitive dissonance continues to resonate in social psychology as shown in this set of research and theoretical papers.

HOVLAND, C.I., JANIS, I.L. & KELLEY, H.H. (1955). *Communication and persuasion.* New Haven: Yale University Press. The classic set of studies on persuasion in relation to source, target, message and channel of communication.

PERLOFF, RICHARD M. (2003). *Dynamics of persuasion: Communication and attitudes in the 21st century.* Mahwah, NJ: Erlbaum. A useful and updated overview of what we know about persuasion, looking at both attitude theory and theories about media. Some applied focus on specific attitudes regarding prejudice, politics and health.

PETTY, R.E. & CACIOPPO, J.T. (1986). *Communication and persuasion: Central and peripheral routes to attitude change.* New York: Springer Verlag. A complete presentation of the elaboration likelihood model and the research the model has generated. Some interesting reinterpretations of earlier research are also included.

PRATKANIS, A.A. & ARONSON, E. (1992). *Age of propaganda: The everyday use and abuse of persuasion.* New York: Freeman. The two sides of persuasion in public life: how to induce environmentally friendly behaviour and how to exploit gullible people.

TERRY, D.T. & HOGG, M.A. (1999). *Attitudes, behavior and social context. The role of norms and group memberships.* Mahwah, NJ: Erlbaum. A set of papers linking theories of persuasion and cognitive dissonance to the effects of what others expect; an updated focus on the attitude–behaviour problem.

ZIMBARDO, P. G. & LEIPPE, M.R. (1991). *The psychology of attitude change and social influence.* New York: McGraw-Hill. An engaging, yet remarkably thorough, overview of contemporary thinking and research. Includes good chapters on applications in law and health.

 # Weblinks

Institute for Propaganda Analysis
www.weber.u.washington.edu/~scmuweb/propag/ipa.htm

Social Influence
www.public.asu.edu/~kelton/

American Marketing Association
www.ama.org/resource.htm

Propaganda posters, Canada
www.sfu.ca/history/prop.htm

Chapter 6

Changing Behaviour

The nail that sticks out gets hammered.

Japanese Proverb

Hamlet: Do you see yonder cloud, that's almost in shape of a camel?
Polonius: By the mass, and 'tis like a camel indeed.
Hamlet: Methinks, it is like a weasel.
Polonius: It is backed like a weasel.
Hamlet: Or, like a whale?
Polonius: Very like a whale.

Shakespeare

Chapter Outline

"There's a sucker born every minute." This was the observation of New York banker David Hannum when, in 1869, he realized that people would pay as much as a dollar to view his "fossilized giant" that was actually carved out of stone. Not to be outdone, P.T. Barnum, of circus fame soon discovered another "giant" and claimed Hannum's giant to be a fake! People flocked to see both giants. The financial gains were not trivial. In fact, Barnum offered to buy the rival giant for $50 000, which, at that time, was a very large sum of money. Recorded history is replete with hoaxes, scams, fraud and outrageous promises. In the 1800s Lydia Pinkham claimed that her Vegetable Compound would, among other things, "remove faintness, flatulency, destroy all cravings for stimulants ... it cures bloating, headaches, nervous prostration, general debility, sleeplessness, depression, and indigestion." Mrs. Pinkham's compound is still available. People may be less likely to buy swamps in Florida today, but we haven't stopped succumbing to the many new and creative ways of separating us from our money. The expansion of the Internet has helped. For example, about ten years ago e-mails sent to thousands of recipients began arriving from Nigeria. They all have similar formats such as the following:

Dear Sir,

I have the privilege to request your assistance to transfer the sum of $47 500 000 into your accounts.... The transfer is risk free on both sides ....

Best regards,
Howgal Abul Arhu

Dear Sir,

This letter will definitely come to you as a huge surprise, but I implore you to take the time to go through it carefully as the decision you make will go off a long way to determine the future and continued existence of the entire members of my family.

My name is Dr. (Mrs.) Mariam Abacha, the wife of the late head of state and commander in chief of the armed forces of the federal republic of Nigeria who died on the 8th of June 1998... . My late husband had/has Eighty Million U.S.D. ($80 000 000) specially preserved and well packed in trunk boxes ... yours faithfully,

Mariam Abacha

Interestingly, another message came from the commander in chief's son, Abdul Abacha, who claims the sum is U.S. $155 000 000 kept in a security vault by his mother. He trusts that this will be the beginning of a long lasting business relationship and signs off with "warmest and most honest regards."

It is hard to believe that anyone would be persuaded by messages like this. Yet the RCMP's commercial crime unit reports that people around the world have been bilked of "hundreds of millions" (*The Globe and Mail*, 2003). How does it work? Once a person responds they are led through a series of investments, all aimed at the golden grail. First they are told there are complications which some money will resolve. Then requests for more money for bribes, taxes and multiple other expenses follow. Ultimately, numerous people have become bankrupt, including lawyers and academics. Some have committed suicide (*Hamilton Spectator*, 2003).

It seems that U.S. President Abraham Lincoln was correct when he said, "You can fool some of the people all the time, you can fool all the people some of the time, but you can't fool all the people all the time."

Consider the number of times you have fallen for an offer that was too good to be true or changed your opinion or modified your behaviour so that it becomes more similar to that of another person. Perhaps in an argument you were convinced of the correctness of another point of view; perhaps you simply became aware that you were deviating from common practice. We do not operate in a social vacuum. What others think and how they behave is important to us, and we consistently monitor our thoughts and actions in relation to those of other people in our social environment—friends, classmates, or even the role models depicted in lifestyle advertising. It is no accident that people in a given social group wear similar clothes, vote for the same political party, prefer the same drinks and have similar ideas about how to raise children.

All these situations are examples of social influence, which involve either real or imagined pressures to change one's behaviour, attitudes or beliefs. Sometimes people conform to indirect pressures that change not only their behaviour but also their underlying attitude. At other times, individuals may only comply with requests; that is, they may modify their behaviour but continue to maintain their attitude. In other situations, such as when the pressure involves direct orders from a high-status authority, many people will obey without question.

Of course, we do not always go along with the majority. Sometimes we dig in our heels and maintain our independence in spite of pressures to do otherwise. At other times, in spite of holding a minority view, we are able to swing others to our side.

The Effects of Mere Presence

Social facilitation

Social facilitation, defined as an increment of individual activity resulting from the presence of another individual (Crawford, 1939) was the topic of an article by Triplett in *The American Journal of Psychology* in 1897/98, entitled "The dynamogenic factors in pace making and competition." It is considered to be the first published report of experimental research in social psychology. Triplett, who was apparently interested in bicycle racing, had noticed that cyclists who were paced travelled faster than those who cycled alone (in 1954, the first four-minute mile was achieved by Roger

Bannister while being paced by another runner). This observation led Triplett to ask, "How does the behaviour of a person change when another person is present?" This problem dealt with social influence in its simplest form, in that there was no direct interaction or communication between the individuals involved—only the *presence of another person.*

Rather than pursue his research at the racetrack, Triplett transferred it to the laboratory, using schoolchildren as subjects. The children wound fishing reels both alone and in the presence of a classmate. Triplett then compared the amount of line wound under each of these two conditions. He expected to find that the "together" amount would exceed the "solitary" amount. In fact, 20 subjects were "stimulated positively," 10 subjects were "stimulated adversely," and 10 were unaffected. On the basis of his finding, Triplett concluded that the most probable effect of the presence of another person was to facilitate behaviour. In his words, "From the above facts regarding the laboratory races, we infer that the bodily presence of another contestant participating simultaneously in the race served to liberate latent energy not ordinarily available" (p. 533). Triplett also noted that girls were more likely than boys to be positively influenced by the other person.

Obviously, Triplett's research left many questions unanswered, setting the stage for numerous subsequent studies. These branched in two directions: the study of **audience effects**, resulting from the presence of one or more passive observers, and of **coaction effects**, resulting from participants working simultaneously, but independently, on the same task. Triplett's research also led to extensive research on coaction in species other than human beings, including ants, cockroaches, opossums and armadillos (Zajonc, 1969; Cottrell, 1972; Aillo & Douthill, 2001).

Early studies of audience effects (Meumann, 1904; Travis, 1925) generally found that performance improved in the presence of observers. At about the same time, Allport (1924) carried out an extensive experiment on coaction. Subjects engaged in five different tasks. For each task, they worked half the time alone and half the time in groups of four or five. For four of the five tasks, the results were similar to those obtained in the presence of an audience. The one exception was a task in which subjects read epigrams (e.g., "To err is human, to forgive divine.") and were given five minutes to write as many refutations of the epigram as possible. Subjects did generate more refutations when coacting

Can the mere presence of another person affect behaviour?

than when working alone, but the refutations were of a lower quality. Allport concluded that overt activities such as writing were facilitated by the presence of coworkers while thinking was hampered.

As the research evidence accumulated, it became increasingly clear that audience and coaction situations might either improve or impair individual behaviour (Dashiell, 1935). These seemingly contradictory findings were explained in terms of personality traits or simply as evidence of an unreliable phenomenon. After the flurry of activity in the 1920s and early 1930s, interest in social facilitation waned until it was rekindled by Zajonc (whose name rhymes with *science*) in 1965. Reviewing the research on this topic, he noticed a pattern: People could perform a simple or well-learned task better in the presence of others, but the presence of others interfered with *learning a new or novel response*.

Arousal

Zajonc went on to postulate that the presence of another person increases the level of arousal (defined as a heightened state of physiological activity that enhances the general reactivity of the individual), which can either facilitate or interfere depending on the situation. A person learning a behaviour has not only the correct response but other incorrect responses in her repertoire. Ordinarily these incorrect responses disappear as learning progresses. However according to Zajonc, the arousal induced by the presence of another person has a dual effect: the strength with which the correct response is emitted increases but so does the strength of incorrect responses. This

means that errors will take longer to decline in frequency and learning will be hampered. On the other hand, when only the correct response is available— that is, when the person is performing rather than learning—the increased arousal can only have the effect of facilitating the behaviour in question. Zajonc also proposed that this reaction to the physical presence of others was innate rather than acquired: this question became the focus of many subsequent investigations. Cottrell (1972), for example, argued that the reaction to the presence of others was a *learned drive* based on evaluation apprehension. In other words in order for coaction or audience effects to occur, the subject had to feel that her performance was in some way being evaluated by the others present.

Evaluation apprehension

To test this hypothesis, Cottrell, Wack, Sekerak and Rittle (1968) had subjects perform a task alone, in the presence of two spectators watching from six feet away or in the presence of two people who were blindfolded (ostensibly to prepare for a later experiment). Clearly if mere presence were critical, both types of audience would enhance performance equally; if evaluation apprehension were the key factor, only the observing audience would facilitate task performance.

The results showed no difference between the "alone" and "mere presence" conditions but considerable enhancement when observers were present. The outcome of this and other studies (Paulus & Murdock, 1971) led Cottrell to postulate that the "drive-increasing property of the presence of others is created through social experience." It is not a biological given but "*a learned source of drive*" (Cottrell, 1972, p. 227). For Cottrell, evaluation apprehension meant the anticipation of both rewards and punishments. However, a number of investigations (cf. Geen & Gange, 1977) suggest that only the anticipation of *negative* evaluations increases arousal.

A statistical meta-analysis of 241 studies involving 24 000 subjects (Bond & Titus, 1983) showed that (1) the presence of others heightens physiological arousal only if the individual is performing a complex task; (2) the presence of others increases the speed of simple task performance and decreases the speed of complex task performance; (3) the presence of others impairs the quality of complex performance and slightly facilitates the quality of simple performance; and (4) social facilitation effects are unrelated to the performer's evaluation apprehension.

This should not be taken to mean that evaluation apprehension does not lead to increased arousal and to facilitation of dominant responses. The question is whether evaluation apprehension is *necessary* for social facilitation to occur. An experiment by Schmitt, Gilovich, Goore and Joseph (1986) strongly indicates that mere presence is *sufficient* to produce social facilitation. Subjects believed they were participating in an investigation of sensory deprivation. When they arrived, they were seated at a computer and asked to type in their name (an easy task), then to enter a code name by typing their name backwards, interspersing each letter with ascending digits (a difficult task). The time to complete each task was recorded by the computer. The subjects were assigned to one of three conditions: alone; in the mere presence of a confederate wearing a blindfold and headphones and turned away from the computer (ostensibly being deprived of sensory stimulation); or, in the evaluation apprehension condition, watched closely by the experimenter. As far as the subject was concerned, all this took place *before* the experiment started and the computer was only obtaining background information. As

shown in Table 6–1, mere presence resulted in faster performance of the simple task and slower performance of the difficult task.

These data contradict the contention that evaluation apprehension is necessary for the effects to occur. But it is also evident that evaluation can heighten arousal and facilitate dominant response tendencies. Note that the subjects in the evaluation apprehension condition performed the simple task even more rapidly than did those in the mere presence condition. Arousal has achieved a firm place as the major contributor to the effects observed in these mere presence situations (Platania & Moran, 2001), but the reasons for the aroused state continue to be questioned. Baron and others (Baron, 1986; Sanders, 1983) have developed the *distraction-conflict theory*.

Distraction-conflict theory

In the presence of others, the subject pays attention not only to the task but also to the audience or coactors, producing a state of "attentional conflict." According to **distraction-conflict theory**, this conflict leads to arousal, which in turn facilitates dominant responses (enhancing or impairing performance, depending on the task). A factor in this attentional conflict is the distraction created by social comparison. For example, Sanders, Baron and Moore (1978) had coacting subjects work on either the same or different tasks. Presumably, subjects working on the same task would compare themselves to the other person, providing distraction and social facilitation; social comparison would matter less when the tasks were different and social facilitation would be nonexistent or greatly reduced. As can be seen in Table 6–2 on page 150, this was indeed the outcome.

Non-arousal theories

R.S. Baron (1986) has suggested that the presence of others could lead to "information overload." That is,

TABLE 6-1 Mean time in seconds to complete the easy and difficult tasks	Alone	Mere presence	Evaluation apprehension
Easy task	14.77	9.83	7.07
Difficult task	52.41	72.57	62.52

Source: Schmitt et al., 1986

TABLE 6-2

Mean number of digits copied
correctly and incorrectly

Task difficulty	Alone (n = 20)	Together-different (n = 10)	Together-same (n = 10)
	Digits copied correctly		
Simple	151.65	158.60	179.60
Complex	78.70	81.90	78.00
	Digits copied incorrectly		
Simple	0.25	0.60	0.60
Complex	0.60	0.50	3.90

Source: Sanders et al., 1978

subjects have more sensory input than they can handle efficiently. To bring things under control, they concentrate on the task and shut out distracting cues. Increased attention improves simple task performance, but complex or novel tasks require less focused and intense concentration and suffer accordingly.

Bond (1982) believes that social facilitation arises because the individual is striving to create a good impression—something that is most possible on an easy task where failure is unlikely. On the other hand, the errors that are likely in a complex task cause embarrassment, which leads to task impairment.

Carver and Scheier (1981) argue that the presence of an audience leads to increased "self-attention," which in turn leads to concern about the behaviours that would create a good impression, resulting in enhanced performance. They account for performance decrements with difficult tasks by postulating that self-attention makes subjects periodically interrupt their activity in order to assess their own progress.

It is more difficult to demonstrate the effects of increased arousal in coaction than in audience situations because of the likelihood that competition or rivalry is also present (Carment, 1970). Other studies (Klinger, 1964; Martens & Landers, 1972; Innes, 1972) suggest that knowledge of results and eye contact between the coactors may also be important.

As with many psychological phenomena, culture may play a role. For example, Carment and Hodkin (1973) compared the performance of university students from Canada and India and found that the East Indians were less sensitive than the Canadians both to competitive instructions and to the presence of a coacter. It may be that the East Indian subjects, most of whom lived in extended families under crowded

conditions, were no longer aroused by the presence of others.

To summarize, theoretical approaches to social facilitation derive from three main types of explanation:

1. The presence of others increases drive (distraction/conflict theory (Baron, R.S., 1986); evaluation apprehension (Cottrell, 1972); mere presence (Zajonc, 1980)).

2. The presence of others creates explicit or implicit demands on the person (self-presentation (Bond, 1982); self-awareness (Carver & Scheier, 1981)).

3. The presence of others affects the focus of attention and interferes with information processing (information-processing interpretation of distraction/conflict (Baron, 1986)).

Social loafing: When more is less

We have seen that people tend to work harder in the presence of others than alone. If we were to extend this principle to include people working together towards a common goal, the general principle might become "Many hands make light work." However, if we believe this principle, we might expect lighter work when working with others. Therefore, working collectively where individual efforts cannot be observed might actually reduce the effort of each individual involved. In other words, collective efforts may be less efficient than individual ones. This effect was first observed by Ringelmann (1913) who asked a number of people to pull on a rope and found that as group size increased, the effort of each group member declined (Kravitz & Martin, 1986). Latané, Williams and Harkins (1979)

A CASE IN POINT

Baseball and Social Facilitation

Jackson, Buglione and Glenwick (1988) note that almost all the research on social facilitation has been conducted in the laboratory. So with the assistance of professional shortstop Bobby Mercer, they turned their attention to the real-life situation of baseball. They argue that batting is a complex task that should be adversely affected by high arousal.

Since mid-season trades usually imply that there is something wrong with the player, an impending trade should create considerable stress (arousal) and performance at bat should decline.

However once the player is traded, the arousal should be reduced. The player will perceive himself as wanted by the other team, the likelihood of being traded again will be reduced and the player will be granted a honeymoon period of moderate expectations. The year after the trade, drive (arousal) should reach the same level as before the trade came up.

Jackson et al. (1988) calculated two measures of performance at bat: the batting average and the slugging percentage (the batting average weighted by the number of bases per hit) for 59 major league players. The results of their analysis clearly support their predictions (see Figure 6–1). Since players appear to gain an average of 30 points in their batting average, it would seem wise for managers to engage in mid-season trades.

Of course alternative explanations are possible. For example, a player may improve because owners choose players who are suited to their ballpark. Thus if a ballpark has a close right-field fence, the owner would look for a left-handed power hitter. However, this reasoning could not explain why, in the following year, players' performance declines even though the ballpark conditions remain the same.

Another explanation is that a change in the player's self-esteem—not drive—enhances performance. First, players about to be traded have lowered self-esteem due to poor performance. Then after the trade, self-esteem returns, they become confident and they perform better. While this argument does not conflict with the data, it is more likely that self-esteem changes are the result of performance rather than the cause of it (see Chapter 3.)

FIGURE 6-1

Main effect of drive on baseball performance

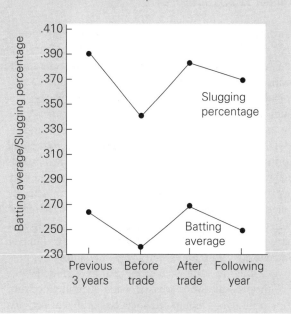

call this phenomenon **social loafing**, defined as a decrease in individual effort due to the presence of others. Figure 6–2 shows Latané and colleagues' findings for two tasks: clapping and cheering.

It is possible that some of these results are due simply to inadequate coordination, a "too many cooks spoil the broth" problem (Steiner, 1972). This proposition was tested by Ingham, Levinger, Graves and Peckhorn (1974) who blindfolded subjects and led each one to believe that others were present although the subjects were actually alone. Subjects pulled at 90 percent of their solitary rate when they *thought* they were with one other person and at 85 percent of this rate when they believed they were assisted by two to

FIGURE 6-2

Intensity of noise as a function of group size and response mode

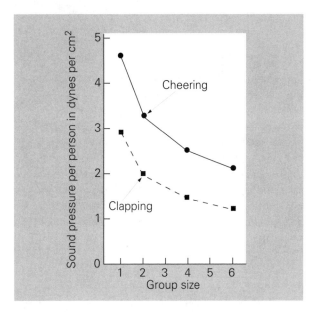

six others. Thus, there does not seem to be any doubt that social loafing accounts for the reduced effort.

The potential for evaluation may account for social loafing as it does for social facilitation. It appears that social loafing occurs only when the participants' outputs cannot be evaluated either by the experimenter or by the participants themselves (Szymanski & Harkins, 1987). Social loafing is eliminated when individual contributions can be identified and when participants believe they are all engaged in the same activity because meaningful comparisons of output can be made. The loafing effect is reduced when participants believe that the overall production of their group will be compared with that of other groups (Harkins & Szymanski, 1989) and when the participants have positive feelings towards each other (Karau & Hart, 1998).

Although caution is advised when generalizing from rope-pulling or clapping to socially significant activity, Latané suggests that social loafing has implications for the efficiency of human organizations such as collective farms in the former U.S.S.R. and *kibbutzim* in Israel. The major question is why the collective farms in the former U.S.S.R. seemed to follow the social loafing principle (the 1 percent of agricultural land worked privately accounted for 27 percent of total Soviet farm output) while the *kibbutzim* did not (22 percent of the egg output is produced with 16 percent of the chick-

ens). Among a number of possible explanations is that individuals usually had a choice about participating in a *kibbutz* but not in a Soviet collective farm.

Many of the tasks used in social loafing research have been relatively simple and physical (e.g., clapping and cheering). Social loafing does, however, occur in the cognitive domain as well. For example, Weldon and Gargano (1988) involved subjects in a complex judgment task and found that subjects working in a group but not held accountable for outcomes, either individually or as a group, produced less complex responses than did those working alone.

Conformity

Imagine yourself in a completely dark room with a pinpoint of light at eye level some distance in front of you. Although the light actually remains stationary, it seems to move and, for some people, it traverses considerable distances. This phenomenon is the well-known **autokinetic effect**. Sherif (1936, 1937) placed groups of subjects in this situation and for a number of trials asked each subject to call out an estimate of how far the light moved. Although the subjects started out with quite different distance estimates, their estimates gradually became more and more similar until there was very little variability among them.

Sherif proposed this as a model of social conformity in which, without any direct pressure, individuals ultimately arrive at a common form of behaviour—a *social norm*, which subsequently exhibits very little variation. In other words, **conformity** is the outcome of interpersonal influence and is accompanied by a reduction in the variability of the behaviour in question. This process is illustrated in Figure 6–3. Over time, the range of output of the workers in this example narrows with both high and low producers coming more into line with the mean. The same pattern shows up in other areas: it is not by chance that many students wear very similar jackets, caps and boots.

In the darkened room, the participants were merely aware of the judgments of the others and the influence was mutual. In a sense, this outcome reflects what happens in the early stages of group formation in which the norms have not yet been clearly defined. However, individuals often join long-standing groups with well-established norms. An early experiment by Asch (1951) illustrates what might then happen, again without any direct pressure on the subject to modify his behaviour.

FIGURE 6-3

Conformity as the outcome of interpersonal influences

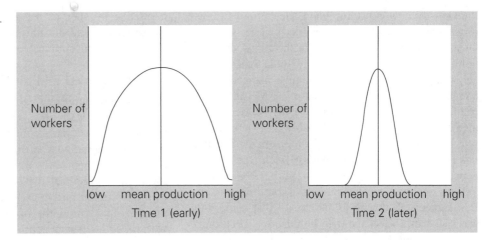

Number of workers

low   mean production   high

Time 1 (early)

Number of workers

low   mean production   high

Time 2 (later)

This study used one real subject along with a number of confederates of the experimenter. Their task was to match the length of a standard line with one of three other unequal lines. (Figure 6–4 shows an example.) The length judgments were easy; on their own, 95 percent of a control group were error-free. However, subjects in the experimental group were placed next to last in a group of confederates who all made the same wrong choice on 12 of the 18 trials. What do you think you would do under these circumstances—trust your eyes or trust the judgments of the others? In the presence of an incorrect majority, 76 percent of the subjects made at least one error by going along with the group.

This type of pressure exists even when the other group members are not physically present. For example, Wiener, Carpenter and Carpenter (1957) first asked subjects to select names for some ambiguous designs, after which they were shown fictitious percentages said to represent the choices of others in their group. On a re-test, the design names given by the subjects shifted in the direction of the popular choices. The assumption that if everybody is doing it, it must be right is sometimes referred to as the *bandwagon effect*. In real life, the bandwagon effect can escalate rapidly once a majority is seen correctly or incorrectly to be acting in a common manner.

Crutchfield (1955) extended the work of Asch by devising a way to work without confederates. Five subjects were simultaneously isolated in booths facing panels with lights ostensibly representing the responses of the other subjects. Since there was no communication between the subjects, the experimenter was free to create any pattern of "other subjects' responses." Crutchfield was able to reproduce Asch's work with a variety of stimuli. For instance, 79 percent of his subjects agreed with an erroneous "group judgment" that one of two (actually identical) circles was larger.

In Asch-type studies, only a few subjects succumb totally to group influence and some resist it completely. However, it is clear that the effect is powerful and that few individuals can maintain complete independence. But would people in other parts of the world respond in the same way as U.S. subjects? Perrin and Spencer (1981) noted that the Asch studies had not been replicated outside the United States. When they placed British students in the same situation, they found that in only one out of 396 critical trials did compliance occur. Asch had asked his American subjects why they went along with the majority; they reported they were afraid of "sticking out like a sore thumb," or having others think "that there was something wrong with them." On the other hand, the British students did not yield because they felt that to conform to an erroneous majority would make them look "weak, ridiculous and stupid."

FIGURE 6-4

Typical comparison lines used in Asch's study of group effects on judgment

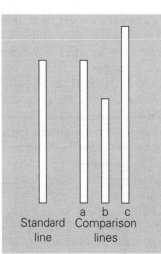

a   b   c
Standard   Comparison
line   lines

Once again, we must not ignore the cultural and historical context in which research takes place. Asch, for instance, carried out his studies in the 1950s when the political and social climate of the United States overtly encouraged conformity (one example being the anticommunist crusade led by Senator Joe McCarthy that resulted in the blacklisting of left-wing politicians and media figures). In the 1970s, Larceny (1974) obtained a rate of conformity in the U.S. about one-half of that reported by Asch. A meta-analysis of Asch-type research between 1952 and 1994 (Bond & Smith, 1996) showed a steady decline over time in levels of conformity among U.S. subjects. The analysis also found that conformity was higher in collectivist than in individualist cultures. Bond and Smith suggest that collectivists conform because they are concerned about how others (especially members of the "in-group") regard them and how others might be affected by their behaviour.

As we noted in Chapter 5, behaviour change does not necessarily imply acceptance. When Asch allowed his subjects to write rather than verbalize their decisions, the number of conforming responses was dramatically reduced. Nevertheless, Flament (1958) found that when he had subjects adjust a measuring device to match a standard line, although it was outside the view of the confederates, the majority opinion still had a marked effect on the accuracy of the subjects' adjustments.

Keep in mind that while conformity (movement towards the source of influence) is common, many people are able to resist the pressures and remain independent. Under some conditions, people may even move in a direction opposite to that advocated (anti-conformity).

Why do people conform?

Most groups do not draw their members at random from the population. Almost all groups are formed for some purpose and the members have in common at least an interest in the group goal. The purpose of the group is also likely to be correlated with certain attitudes and values; therefore, the participants may show other similarities. For instance, the members of a group formed to protect a heritage building will probably share other interests and have similar political and social values. Thus, what appears as conformity may be a matter of acting on the basis of pre-existing common attitudes and values.

When people who come together for some purpose do not have a great deal in common, the pressures to conform will be more evident. Researchers have documented a number of reasons why people conform. These reasons are not mutually exclusive; more than one may operate simultaneously.

Social approval and disapproval

Groups in general are intolerant of heresy in their midst and any individual who contradicts or ignores important social norms may experience unpleasant moments, including the threat of **ostracism**. These pressures by themselves may move a person to conform. Anticipation of the consequences of deviation owing to similar past experiences may serve the same purpose. In addition, the group rewards the conformer with liking and social approval.

It is easy to see why *cohesive groups* (groups in which there is a high degree of interpersonal liking and attachment) exert considerable control over members' behaviour. The individual has more to lose by deviation than she would in less cohesive groups. A striking example came from the Korean conflict (1950–1953). The U.S. government was disturbed to find that 33 percent of U.S. prisoners engaged in some form of collaboration with the enemy. In contrast, none of the Turkish and only a few of the British prisoners collaborated. It has been suggested that the American soldiers broke down because of a lack of group solidarity and morale. Unlike the individualistic Americans, the Turks and the British behaved as a social unit with discipline and order of command remaining intact. As long as the *group* resisted and supported the individual, pressures to deviate were ineffective (Brown, 1963).

Although deviation from group norms is not viewed lightly, high-status group members are allowed more leeway than are low-status members. This may occur (Hollander, 1958; Homans, 1974) because high-status members have earned **idiosyncrasy credits** by contributing more than others to the effectiveness of the group. Each unit of such *good* behaviour is rewarded with an idiosyncrasy credit allowing high-status members, for example, to wear clothes that don't conform to the group's dress code. However once credits have been used in this way, more credits must be earned before further deviation will be allowed. Ostracism for deviant behaviour is, of course, the final threat. If an ostracized individual can tolerate rejection, the group has lost control over that person.

The need for information

Many aspects of our personal worlds, both social and physical, are not clearly defined but are somehow

FIGURE 6-5
What is it?

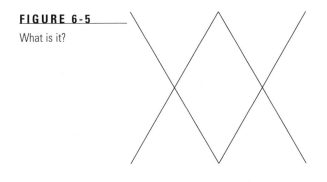

ambiguous. For example, the autokinetic effect arises from an ambiguous situation in which reality has to be almost totally imposed by the observer.

Being wrong can be uncomfortable and being different is often perceived as being wrong. When there is no demonstrably right answer, we often use what Festinger has termed **informational social influence**. Thus although we can determine whether a pound of feathers falls more slowly than a pound of lead, most social questions are not amenable to empirical or objective verification. For answers to these questions, we frequently turn to the judgment of the majority. The result is increased conformity.

Consider the drawing in Figure 6–5. What does it appear to be? Some might say "two Xs," others may insist on a "W sitting on an M," or a "V superimposed on an inverted V," or "a diamond with whiskers." The point is that although the design appears to be simple and straightforward, it can still generate considerable uncertainty. Everyone is similarly confronted with everyday events that are undefined and amenable to a variety of interpretations. In these cases, the group serves to structure, label and identify the situations thus reducing both ambiguity and its accompanying anxiety or discomfort.

Constructive reality is exemplified in an extreme form by the fundamentalist and "cult" religions—the Moonies, Hare Krishna, the Church of Scientology— that provide adherents with "solutions" to all of life's ills. These organizations often go so far as to dictate members' complete daily routines.

Social validation

Dissenters also face the difficulty of questioning their own competence. According to Festinger (1954), we have a basic drive to evaluate our abilities and opinions. The obvious way of doing this is to make comparisons with other people. Students compare test marks; employees compare salaries. Even if your salary is quite adequate, you will probably be dissatisfied if you find that a co-worker with similar skills and seniority is paid more (see Chapter 10).

Any variable affecting a personality trait (e.g., self-confidence) will be associated with a change in dependence on the judgment of others. Research on self-esteem (see Chapter 3) makes this point clear. For instance, people who scored low on a self-esteem test were considerably more likely to conform in a Crutchfield visual judgment situation than were those with high self-esteem (Stang, 1972). (Some sample items from a scale of self-esteem are given in Table 6–3.) It is not difficult to understand why a person who would answer these and similar questions in the affirmative would also be unlikely to maintain an independent position in a conformity situation.

Keep in mind that the group insists on people toeing the line only for those behaviours that are deemed relevant to the group's well being and efficiency. A work group concerned with production would probably tolerate variations in dress; a motorcycle gang would not.

Does the size of the group make a difference?

Among many variations on his basic theme, Asch (1951) tested whether increasing the number of confederates would lead to more conformity. He formed groups of one, two, three, four, eight and 10–15 confederates and found that when only one other person voiced a discrepant judgment, no conformity effects were observed. The effects appeared with two and reached a maximum with three confederates. Larger majorities had no additional impact. Although other investigators have reported an optimum number of confederates of four to six, there is general agreement that the pressure to conform does not simply continue to accumulate as the size of the group increases. Campbell and Fairly (1989) suggest that the importance of group size depends on whether the situation brings *normative* or *informational* mechanisms into play. People trying to decide whether their judgment is correct rely on information obtained from others in the same situation. The first source of information has the most effect and each additional source is less useful because the information is likely to be redundant. However if there is no "correct" answer, the individual may go along with the group to avoid the social penalties of disagreeing with the majority. In this, the normative case, larger majorities should lead to more conformity.

TABLE 6-3

Sample items from self-esteem scale

1. How often do you have the feeling that there is *nothing* you can do well?				
very often	fairly often	sometimes	once in a great while	practically never

2. How often do you worry about whether other people like to be with you?				
very often	fairly often	sometimes	once in a great while	practically never

3. How often do you feel that you dislike yourself?				
very often	fairly often	sometimes	once in a great while	practically never

4. Do you ever feel so discouraged with yourself that you wonder whether anything is worthwhile?				
very often	fairly often	sometimes	once in a great while	practically never

Source: Eagly, 1967

Wilder (1977) pointed out that the effect of group size may be limited because beyond a certain number, the subject does not perceive the individuals as separate entities. That is since all the members express identical judgments, the subject treats them as a single point of view. Thus, information from four individuals would be treated as four separate pieces of information, whereas information from a group of four would be treated as one piece of information. He demonstrated that the judgments of the members of two groups had more effect than the judgments of the members of one group, although the number of people was the same. This outcome implies that candidates for political office should try to get themselves endorsed by individuals with a variety of backgrounds (e.g., physicians, plumbers, professors, housewives) who would be perceived individually by the voters.

Direct influence

In experimental groups, no direct sanctions are applied. Real-life groups, on the other hand, may not be so benign. Schachter (1951) formed groups of university students to discuss the case of Johnny Rocco, an apparently incorrigible delinquent. After reading the case history, each group member voiced his opinion as to how Johnny should be treated. Their opinions could range, on a five-point scale, from extreme kindness to extreme harshness. After group discussion, each participant again publicly voiced an opinion. However three members of the group, confederates of Schachter, had been coached to act in specific ways before and during the discussion. One, the "deviate," took an initial position opposed to the majority and maintained it throughout the session. Another, the "slider," began by acting like a deviate but as the session progressed gradually changed his opinion towards the majority view. A third confederate, the "mode," expressed the majority view from beginning to end. The initial opinions of real subjects are nearly always lenient (i.e., 1, 2 or 3 on the five-point scale) so that the confederates could be reasonably certain beforehand what position they would have to support or oppose.

Schachter observed two processes of interest: (1) the amount of communication directed to each type of confederate; and (2) how each confederate was treated at the end of the discussion session. Figure 6–6 illustrates the direction of communication. Notice that the "mode" received very few communications and that there was only a slight change as the discussion progressed. In other words, there is little merit in preaching to the converted. The group paid almost as much attention to the slider as to the deviate in the early stages of the discussion, but as it became clear that he was modifying his stand, the group diverted more attention to the unchanging deviate in attempts to modify his position.

At the conclusion of each discussion session, Schachter administered two measures of interpersonal attraction. One required the participants to submit nominations for memberships in one of three commit-

FIGURE 6-6

Subjects' communication to the "deviate," the "mode," and the "slider"

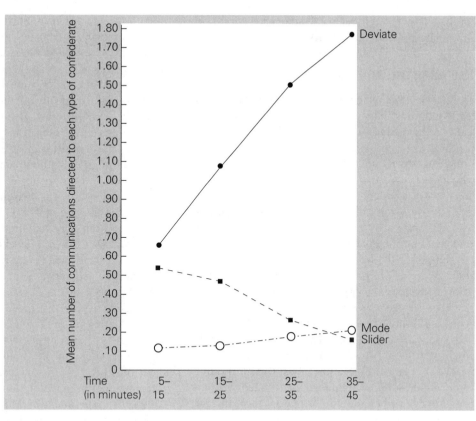

Source: Based on data from Schachter, 1951

tees: executive, steering or correspondence. The deviates were invariably nominated for the least desirable (and least important) job—correspondence. In addition, participants were asked to rank the others on desirability as fellow group members. The instructions emphasized congeniality and compatibility. By now you will not be surprised to learn that the deviate was ranked as a much less desirable group member than either the mode or the slider. Moreover, the slider's case illustrates that the group does not penalize an individual for being different initially as long as he ultimately accepts the group norm.

One final point emerges from Schachter's research. Among those who ultimately rejected the deviate most, communication to the deviate increased as the session progressed. But when it became apparent that the deviate wasn't going to modify his opinion, communication rapidly declined. Not only did these individuals dislike the deviate; they eventually chose to ignore him. This sort of ostracism—or being "sent to Coventry," as it is called in England—is well-documented in industry where work groups pressure fellow workers to conform

to output norms. A "rate buster" who overproduces or a "chiseller" who under produces will be subjected not only to verbal pressure (or abuse) but often to physical harassment. In extreme cases, this treatment is also extended to the worker's family.

For example, a student of one of the authors got a summer job in a factory manufacturing sewer pipes. After a few days, he was surprised and pained to find that the sewer pipes frequently fell onto his legs. At first he attributed these "accidents" to clumsiness and lack of skill because no one else seemed to suffer from the problem. But even after he had learned the necessary techniques, pipes kept falling on him. After some time and numerous bruises, a co-worker casually suggested that it might help if he slowed down a bit. When he did, the pipes no longer fell on him. He had inadvertently been exceeding the output norm; once he got in line, the group pressure stopped.

Obviously, it is not easy to be a deviate. Given the pressures and sanctions the majority bring to bear, it is little wonder that most people simply choose to conform (Levine, 1980). The deviate, however, is not completely without influence. Under some conditions, a minority can affect a majority.

The adamant minority

Asch (1951) discovered that just one other person correctly judging the length of lines was sufficient to radically reduce, and in some cases entirely remove, conforming responses. This observation was later confirmed by Morris and Miller (1975) (see Figure 6–7) who also showed that a supporter (i.e., a person making a correct judgment) who precedes the majority reduces conformity to a greater extent than does one who responds after the majority. There is additional evidence that the quality of the support is not critical; any support is better than none. For example, Allen and Levine (1971) provided some subjects who were being asked to make visual judgments with a supporter who wore glasses so thick as to raise serious doubts about his ability to see anything clearly. Other subjects had a supporter with normal vision. They report that when there was a unanimous majority, subjects conformed 97 percent of the time. With the addition of a "competent" supporter, conformity declined to 36 percent, but even when the supporter was "incompetent," conformity was reduced to 64 percent.

Moscovici and his colleagues (Moscovici, Mugny & Van Auermaet, 1985; Papastamou, 1983) have exam-

ined how a persistent minority can affect the majority. In one of their experiments, groups of six women, two of whom were confederates of the experimenter, were asked to look at slides and report what colour they saw. Actually, all the slides were blue and varied only in terms of light intensity, but the two confederates consistently said they saw green. Moscovici found that about 8 percent of subject responses were "green" and that 32 percent of the subjects said "green" at least once. In a control group without confederates, only 0.25 percent of responses (one subject, twice) were "green." The impact of the minority became even more impressive when subjects were individually given 16 discs ranging in colour from very definitely blue to very definitely green and were asked to label each disc as either green or blue on their own. (They were not allowed to make compromise judgments such as blue-green). Subjects who had been in the experimental group were much more likely to call a disc green than those who had been in the control group. The tendency to say "green" was even observed in subjects who had not said "green" in the group situation. It would seem that the minority had influenced all the subjects even though some of them had not been willing to reveal it publicly.

Another experiment by Moscovici's group showed it is important that the minority be consistent in its view. When the confederates were coached to respond in a more variable and inconsistent manner, the effects out-

FIGURE 6-7

The effect of social support on judgment in a conformity situation

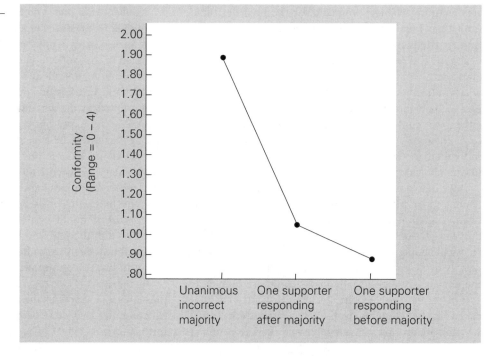

lined above almost entirely disappeared. A consistent minority may be perceived as courageous, thereby fostering respect and thus possibly increasing its influence. Also, confidence gives the impression that there is indeed something to the minority position (Nemeth & Chiles, 1988). However, Papastamou and Mugny (1985) showed that the consistency of the minority is most effective if it is flexible rather than rigid. That is, the consistency should not be carried to extremes. While being consistent on important points, the minority should moderate or negotiate less important issues.

This research indicates that the outcome of majority pressure is usually confined to behaviour, while minorities can produce real changes of attitude (Maass & Clarke, 1984; Moscovici, 1980; Personnaz & Personnaz, 1994). More cognitive work is stimulated by the minority view, whereas the majority view leads to relatively superficial thinking. Although the minority position is often quickly rejected, it can, if stated with consistency and confidence, lead others to consider many alternative and unique viewpoints. This divergent thinking results in decision-making that is therefore more reasoned, complex and stable (Nemeth, C.J., 1986; Nemeth & Kwan, 1987; Martin & Hewstone, 1999).

Justifying conformity

What happens when you submit to the opinion of the majority? One possibility is to simply admit that you have "given in." Another possibility is to decide that the conformity was forced by the facts. Research (Griffin & Buehler, 1993; Buehler & Griffin, 1994) shows that most people take the latter route, rewriting history to justify their acquiescence. This process is automatic and immediate. Those who withstand the majority pressure and dissent engage in the same cognitive process. As Buehler and Griffin (1994) point out, in daily life we often have to decide whether to accept or reject the opinion of one or more others. How we then interpret our decision can have important implications. For example in one study (Buehler & Griffin, 1994), subjects were presented with newspaper, eyewitness and police accounts of an incident in which a black teenager driving a stolen car was shot and killed and a passenger arrested by white police. The reports also included accusations of police wrongdoing and racism. The subjects then answered 10 questions designed to reveal how they construed the situation—whether the victims or the police were responsible for what happened. For example, one item asked, "According to

your image of the situation, what does it mean to say that the vehicle headed directly at both officers?" The choices ranged from "would have hit both officers" (indicating victim responsibility) to " same general direction" (indicating police responsibility).

Subjects then reread the reports and were asked, "Do you agree: The police officers are more than 75-percent responsible for the victim's death." The subjects were in groups of four and while waiting to respond each "inadvertently" learned that the other three had agreed that the police were 75-percent responsible.

This was the conformity manipulation. Subjects could either agree with the majority or dissent. After they had made their choice, they again completed the "construal" scale. Two pieces of information were now available. One, whether a subject agreed or disagreed with the unanimous majority, and two, whether their interpretation of the incident changed pre- and post-decision. The results can be seen in Figure 6–8 on page 160. Not surprisingly, those who agreed with the "group standard" had started out with a more negative view of the role of the police than had those who dissented. However, in all cases, their interpretation of the roles of the victims and the police became more extreme—in the direction that supported their decision to conform or dissent.

Buehler and Griffin (1994) conclude that "when faced with the choice between admitting that one has arbitrarily conformed to a group standard and proving that agreement with the standard was forced by the facts, almost everyone gets busy reconstructing the facts" (p. 993).

Compliance without Pressure

Obviously, people's lives extend beyond their memberships in groups. Frequently, we stand alone, and when we are alone, attempts will be made to gain our **compliance** or influence our behaviour—to get us to buy some product, to vote for a certain politician or to donate to a particular charity. Some of the techniques are sophisticated, employed in a deliberate manner, successful, and undetectable by the individual involved. Five of these procedures are reviewed next.

The foot-in-the-door technique

One process, well known to door-to-door sales representatives, is straightforward: An individual who agrees to carry out a small request is subsequently more likely to agree to carry out a larger request. This

FIGURE 6-8

Pre-decision and post-decision construals by conformity decision

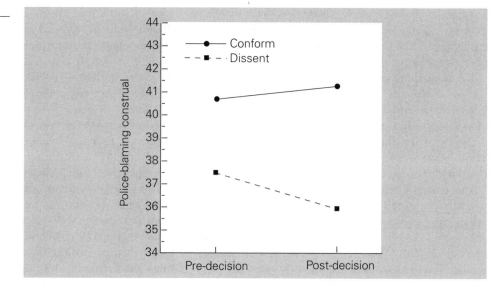

Source: Buehler & Griffin (1994)

means that if you want someone to do something and are not sure whether they will acquiesce, you should first make a request you are reasonably certain will be honoured. Freedman and Fraser (1966) carried out a study of housewives in which the large request was to allow a survey team of five or six men to enter their homes and itemize their household products. In some cases, this was the only request made (one-contact condition); in others, it had been preceded nine days earlier by a telephone call and a request to answer a few questions about their soap brand. Some of these subjects were actually asked the questions (performance condition) while some only agreed to answer the questions (agreement condition).

This allowed the investigators to determine whether acquiescence only was necessary or whether the act actually had to be carried out. To rule out the effects of the initial contact, a fourth control condition was used in which the housewife was told the nature of the survey but was not asked to agree to the product inventory and was not asked any questions (familiarization condition). The results of the study are shown in Table 6–4 on page 162. It is clear from these data that prior compliance considerably increased the likelihood of the larger request being carried out (52.8 percent). Merely agreeing helped a bit (33.3 percent), but the most effective inducement was having the person actually carry out the small request.

Freedman and Fraser (1966) carried out a second experiment that, among other things, showed that the person making the second, larger request does not need

to be the same person who had made the smaller request. In this study the procedure was the same, but the small request was for subjects either to put up a small sign on their lawn or to sign a petition concerning either safe driving or keeping California beautiful. In all cases, the second request was for subjects to allow a large sign that said, "Drive carefully" to be placed on their lawn. The persons who made the first and second request were always different. One result of this experiment can be found in Table 6–5 on page 162. The baseline for comparison here is the one-contact group in which fewer than 20 percent agreed to the large request. Clearly, all the other treatments improved on this outcome, but the most marked improvement occurred when both the issue (safe driving) and the task (putting up a sign) were similar to the large request.

There is some evidence that the timing of the second request may be important. Chartrand, Pinckert and Burger (1999) presented subjects who had already agreed to a small request with a larger request either immediately or two days later and either by the same requester or someone else. Compared to control subjects, the subjects were more likely to agree to the larger request *except* when the same requester made the larger request immediately. In that case, there was *less* agreement to the larger request than in the control condition. As the researchers concluded, this means that the foot-in-the-door can backfire. Similar results have been obtained by Girondola (2002) in a study concerned with agreement to become a potential organ donor.

Conformity in Men and Women

For several decades, social psychologists described women as more susceptible than men to social influences and pressures. This characterization, assumed to be factual and supported by early studies, was consistent with the stereotype of women as meek, submissive and easily swayed by emotion rather than reason. However, careful reviews of the literature and later research punctured this myth (Eagly, 1978; Eagly & Wood, 1985).

The vast majority of persuasion studies, in which subjects are presented with a counter-argument and then asked to indicate their attitudes on a questionnaire (see Chapter 5), show no gender differences. Even conformity situations in which discrepant positions (e.g., an obviously wrong answer) are advanced by a group of people show no significant gender differences.

However, one-third of the published studies show that females are likely to yield to group pressures. Let us consider why. One possible reason is biases in the actual studies. Typically, questions are asked for which there is a "right answer"—lengths of lines, geometric shapes or information on geography, politics or science. It has been argued that men are more familiar with these topics and would therefore be more likely to resist social pressure to conform. A study by Sistrunk and McDavid (1971) set out to correct for this bias. A panel of subjects judged questions as being "typically masculine" (sports cars, mathematics, politics), "typically feminine" (cosmetics, cooking, sewing) or neutral. The questionnaire was then administered to male and female subjects. To induce conformity pressures, subjects were told beside each question how a majority of students had supposedly responded. Results showed that women conformed more on "masculine" items, but men conformed more than women on "feminine" items. Overall, there was no difference in conformity levels of men and women.

There is some evidence that greater female conformity is found when the experiment has been conducted by a male (Eagly & Carli, 1981). There is no reason to believe that male social psychologists are male chauvinists who deliberately set out to prove a female stereotype. However, they may unintentionally design conformity situations in which males feel more comfortable. On the other hand female social psychologists, aware of the stereotype of female submissiveness, may design experiments in which females feel more comfortable and confident. In any case, the conflict reveals the sensitivity of research in social psychology to subtle influences.

It has been argued that women and men are socialized differently in how to respond to social pressures and influence. For example, many traditional tests of sex-role identification link "femininity" with such traits as nurturance, warmth and expressiveness and "masculinity" with dominance, mastery and task-related competence. To the extent that the role-related difference may be a real one, it can be interpreted differently. That is, what may be labelled negatively as "submissive" and "passive" can also be seen as enhancing interdependence rather than independence (Greenglass, 1982) or as reflecting the communal concern of women, a commitment to preserving social harmony and encouraging positive feelings within a group (Eagly & Wood, 1985). In this sense, expressing agreement may be a way of showing concern and support for others, which may be more important in many situations than giving the right answer. Another clue is that men resist conforming only when others are watching in order to convey an image as a nonconformist. Without surveillance, there are no differences in conformity between males and females (Eagly, Wood & Fishbaugh, 1981).

In short, we cannot support a generalization that women are more easily influenced than men. The effect is small, inconsistent and limited to certain situations. It also seems to be tied into another assumption: that women are usually in lower-status positions than men. Indeed, there is evidence that women are expected to conform more because of their low-status positions and that these expectations disappear when we perceive women in a higher-status role (Eagly & Wood, 1982; Conway, Pizzamiglio & Mount, 1996). Stereotypes can become self-fulfilling prophecies and women may conform because of these expectations. As stereotypes change and better opportunities for women emerge in the workplace even this small difference may disappear.

TABLE 6-4

Percentage of subjects complying with large request

Condition	%
Performance	52.8
Agree only	33.3
Familiarization	27.8
One contact	22.2

Source: Freedman & Fraser, 1966

While this experimental paradigm is clear-cut, the reasons for the findings are not as apparent. Freedman and Fraser (1966) and Dejong (1979) have suggested that the "self-perception" of the subjects who agreed to the small request changed. These individuals observed that they had agreed and, from this evidence, came to the conclusion that they were cooperative and helpful people. Then they set out to maintain this image by also agreeing to the second request. This "preference for consistency" has been shown to moderate the foot-in-the-door effect. Individuals who have a strong preference for consistency as measured by a questionnaire (Cialdini, Trost, and Newsom, 1995) are more likely than others with a weaker preference to agree to the second request (Guadagno, Asher, Demaine and Cialdini, 2001).

The door-in-the-face technique

This is a variation of the foot-in-the-door procedure, one that many of us have either deliberately or inadvertently used at one time or another. In this case, the first request made is so extreme that the target is almost certain to refuse. Then the second request is considerably smaller and more reasonable. Cialdini et al. (1975) have shown this strategy to be an effective means of inducing compliance to the second request. For example, they accosted university students on the street and asked them if they would act as unpaid counsellors for two hours a week for two years. Everyone refused the

researchers. Next they asked the students to accompany a group of juvenile delinquents on a trip to the zoo. Fifty percent of the students were then willing to help compared to 16.7 percent from another group who were asked only to go on the zoo trip.

Two explanations have been offered for the effectiveness of this procedure. One is based on the concept of *reciprocal concessions*. When the person making the large request reduces it to a smaller one, the other person then feels obligated to make a matching concession. The second explanation involves *self-presentation*. Most people prefer to present themselves to others in a positive light. By acceding to the second request, the students demonstrated that they were not really as bad as might originally have been implied. For example, Pendleton and Batson (1979) observed that those who refused a moderate request thought that they would be perceived as "less helpful, less friendly and less concerned" than if they had refused an extremely large request.

The low-ball technique

Automobile and other salespeople, to enhance the likelihood of a sale and to maximize the selling price, frequently use the **low-ball technique** (or "bait and switch"). Low-balling is based on the proposition that once an individual has agreed to carry out an act, he will still comply even though the act is made more costly. The process begins typically with the salesperson accept-

TABLE 6-5

Percentage of subjects complying with large request

Issue	Task	
	Similar %	Different %
Similar	76.0	47.8
Different	47.6	47.4
One contact only: 16.7		

Source: Freedman & Fraser, 1966

Salespeople often use the low-ball technique to enhance the likelihood of a sale and to maximize the selling price.

experiment scheduled at 7:00 in the morning. Those in the control condition were told about the study and the time. In the low-ball condition, subjects were first asked whether they would participate and if they agreed, were then told the experiment would take place at 7:00 a.m. Two measures of compliance were obtained—the percentage of subjects in each condition who agreed to participate and the percentage that actually showed up at the scheduled time. The results of the study, shown in Table 6–6, indicate that a much higher percentage of the students who were "low-balled" agreed to participate and actually showed up for the appointment.

In another study, Cialdini, Buchman and Cacioppo (1979) demonstrated the effect under controlled conditions in the field and also showed that low-balling was more effective than the foot-in-the-door procedure. They argue for a commitment interpretation of the low-ball effect: once individuals are committed to a decision, they will be reluctant to change that decision. It also is noted that one means of creating commitment is to get the person to take action—for example, to agree to sign an offer to purchase.

Improving the deal:
The "that's-not-all" technique

This procedure consists of offering a product to a person at a high price, preventing the person from responding for a few seconds, and then enhancing the deal either by adding another product or decreasing the price. For example, Burger (1986) had two experimenters sit at a table in various locations selling cupcakes and cookies. The cupcakes were visible but the cookies were not. Some of those who approached the table were told that the cupcakes were 75 cents each. Just then, the second experimenter tapped the first experimenter on the shoulder. The first experimenter would ask the customer to wait a second. After a brief exchange, the first experimenter turned to the customer and said that the price included two cookies. In the control group, the subjects were told about the

ing an offer of an extremely low price on a car that interests the customer. The intent is to get the customer to make an *active decision* to purchase the automobile. Once this is done and the necessary forms are filled out, the salesperson says that since the price is so low she must check with her supervisor. She then leaves for a few minutes and returns to say that the boss would not allow it because they would be losing money on the deal. (In some cases, it is the generous offer on a trade-in that is negated by the manager). In any case, the purchase price goes up. However, anecdotal evidence indicates that the customer will still enter into the agreement. In spite of the increased cost, the initial decision persists.

Cialdini, Cacioppo, Bassett and Miller (1978) were interested in whether this tactic could be reproduced in the laboratory. They asked students to participate in an

TABLE 6-6		Condition	
		Control %	Low ball %
Made appointment		31	56
Actually appeared		24	53

Percentage of subjects making appointment and complying

Source: Cialdini et al., 1978

The Real World of Compliance

With the exception of a few field experiments, most of the research on compliance has been conducted in the laboratory. This prompted Cialdini (1987) to observe what people who are in the business of influencing people actually do. He got himself hired by a number of sales organizations and at various times took training as a salesman of encyclopedias, photographs, fire alarms, insurance and advertising. He first found that tactics such as the door-in-the-face and foot-in-the-door were used, but not very often.

However, it became clear to Cialdini that although his colleagues in sales might not be able to articulate what they were doing, they did rely on six basic principles, much the same as those we have described. These are as follows:

- People want to appear consistent.
- People want to reciprocate favours.
- People want to do what others are doing.
- People are willing to follow the advice of authorities.
- The perception of scarcity makes commodities more attractive.
- People are more likely to comply with requests of friends than of strangers.

The "four walls technique," often used by encyclopedia salespeople, provides an example of the customer's desire to appear consistent in practice. First, a question is asked that is likely to elicit agreement from the customer. Then, to remain consistent, the customer is also likely to agree with a further question. The technique goes like this:

First wall: "Do you feel that a good general education is important to your children?"

Second wall: "Do you think that a child who does his or her homework well will get a better education?"

Third wall: "Don't you agree that a good set of reference books will help a child do well on homework assignments?"

Fourth wall: "Well, then, it sounds like you'll want to hear about the fine set of encyclopedias I have to offer at an excellent price. May I come in?"

Other methods that also rely on commitment are the *foot-in-the-door, low-ball* and *bait and switch.* Scarcity is implied by time-limited or limited-number offers, and the Tupperware party is a prime example of the use of friendship to increase the likelihood of sales.

---

cookies as soon as they asked the price of the cupcakes. It was found that 73 percent of those in the "that's-not-all" condition bought the cupcakes (and cookies) compared to only 40 percent of those in the control condition. Lowering the price had the same effect. Why does this technique work? Burger suggests two possible explanations: the norm of reciprocity and the effect of different anchoring points in attitudinal judgments.

The norm of reciprocity indicates that people feel under some obligation to reciprocate gifts, favours and concessions. In the case of the "that's-not-all" procedure, the seller improves the offer and the buyer then feels obliged to purchase the product as a reciprocal action.

Attitudinal judgment in this situation would operate as follows: First, customers are likely to have only a vague notion regarding a reasonable price for a cupcake. The salesperson first establishes an anchor

point of $1, allows this to firm up for a few seconds and then reduces the price to 75 cents. Against the anchor point of $1, the 75-cent price looks better than it would if introduced initially and is more likely to fall within the person's latitude of acceptance. Burger (1986) offers a number of studies that support these propositions. Moreover, he also presents data that suggest this technique is more effective than the door-in-the-face method of inducing compliance.

Guilt: "Thus conscience doth make cowards of us all"

Feelings of guilt have been shown to have powerful and pervasive influences on behaviour. Parents, for example, can be experts at creating feelings of guilt in their offspring when some particular action is desired.

"After all I've done for you" is a typical remark. (A mother's "difficult delivery" ploy is also very effective.) In laboratory investigations of guilt, subjects are usually led to transgress in some way; then a request is made of them. For instance, Freedman, Wallington and Bless (1967) induced subjects to lie and then requested their volunteer participation in an additional study. Their data are reproduced in Table 6–7. In comparison with a control group, almost twice as many subjects who had lied complied. Darlington and Macker (1966) used a similar procedure to increase the likelihood of individuals donating blood.

This effect is not confined to helping those against whom the subject transgressed. Regan, Williams and Sparling (1972) had a male confederate ask female shoppers to take a picture with his camera. When they tried, the camera wouldn't work. Some of the subjects were made to feel that it was their fault while others were assured they were not to blame. A second confederate then appeared carrying a torn bag of groceries with the contents falling out. Fifty-five percent of the subjects in the "guilt" condition and only 15 percent in the control condition informed the confederate of the problem. Although in this study there was no direct request for assistance, it does suggest that individuals who have been made to feel guilty are then motivated to expiate the guilt and that the helping act is not necessarily directed at the injured party. In fact, Freedman et al. (1967) found that those made to feel guilty were reluctant to directly contact the injured person and preferred to help a previously uninvolved person. This means that the timing of the request is important. If it does not occur shortly after the guilt manipulation, something else may occur to relieve the transgressor's guilt and remove the incentive to help. Cialdini, Darby and Vincent (1973) refer to this process as *negative-state release*; it may occur through a voluntary altruistic act or as assent to a request.

The target person rarely detects these five procedures although they are often applied deliberately and systematically. In daily life, the most common procedure for inducing compliance is a simple request such as, "Please pick up a case of beer on your way home from work." It is important, however, to distinguish between requests and demands; the latter are also very direct and undisguised. In the case of demands, the option not to comply is considerably reduced. Children should obey their parents, soldiers must obey their officers and students are required to obey their teachers. Why do people set aside their independence of action and do what someone else demands even when they find it distasteful?

Obedience

The attention of social psychologists was drawn to the study of obedience by the controversial research of Milgram (1963, 1965, 1974). Milgram's research arose from his reflections on the Holocaust. During the Holocaust (1933–1945), the Nazis slaughtered millions of innocent people, mostly Jews. He quotes C.P. Snow, who wrote, "The German Officers' Corps were brought up in the most rigorous code of obedience ... in the name of obedience they were party to, and assisted in, the most wicked large scale actions in the history of the world" (1961, p. 24). Was the obedience that led to this horrendous action unique to Germany or could it occur, in certain circumstances, elsewhere? Of course, not all obedience has aggressive action as the outcome, but it was this type of "destructive obedience" that Milgram studied, based on the premise that the individual who is commanded by a legitimate authority usually obeys (Blass, 2002).

His procedure was to record the amount of electric shock a subject would be willing to administer to another person. He devised a fake apparatus, which subjects believed was a "shock machine" with a range of settings from "Slight Shock" to "Danger: Severe Shock" (see Figure 6–9). There were 30 settings in all, from 15 to 450 volts!

In each session in addition to the experimenter, there was one subject and a confederate who, in a rigged selection, were assigned the roles of learner

TABLE 6-7

Number of subjects complying in the "lie" and "non-lie" condition

	Condition	
	Lie %	Non-lie %
Comply	20	11
Not comply	11	20

Source: Freedman, Wallington & Bless, 1967

FIGURE 6-9

The panel of Milgram's shock generator

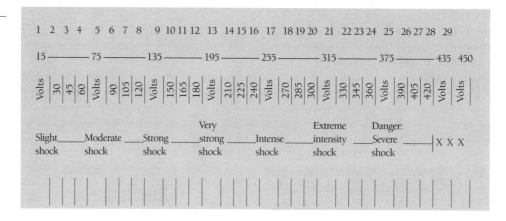

and teacher, ostensibly in a study of the effects of negative outcome on rates of learning. The subject was always designated as teacher and was to teach the learner a list of paired word associates and to administer a shock whenever the learner was unable to recall a correct word. The shock was to be increased one level on each additional trial. The "learner" had been coached to make many errors while other responses presented by means of a tape recorder varied with shock level. For example, at

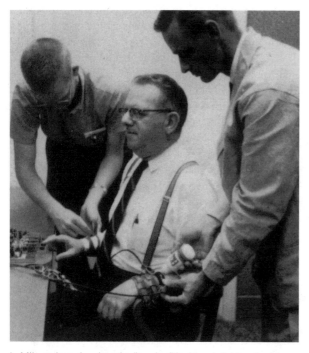

In Milgram's study, when the "teacher" had to administer shock directly to the learner, most subjects refused—but this one continued to obey.

75 volts the learner would grunt and moan, at 150 he demanded to be released, at 180 he cried that he could no longer stand it and at 300 he refused to provide any more answers. The subject was then told to treat silence as a wrong answer. It should be noted that during the introduction, the "learner" deliberately mentioned he had a heart condition.

How far would subjects go? Most of them became agitated and tense and frequently tried to break off the experiment. If a subject showed any sort of hesitation, the experimenter (dressed in a white laboratory coat) told him to proceed and said the experimenter would accept the responsibility if anything happened to the "learner."

Forty psychiatrists predicted that most subjects would not go beyond the tenth shock level (150 volts), that not more than 4 percent would reach the twentieth level (300 volts) and that only about one-tenth of 1 percent would administer the highest shock. However, as Figure 6–10 shows, 62 percent of the subjects completely obeyed the experimenter's commands!

Remember that in this study the victim was hidden from the subject, although they had been introduced at the beginning of the session. Other experiments by Milgram showed that as the victim and the subject became physically closer, the level of obedience was reduced. For example in the closest condition, the subject was required to hold the victim's hand on the shock-plate. In this case, the proportion of subjects who administered the highest level of shock was reduced to 30 percent—still a substantial and disturbing figure. Milgram also found that obedience decreased (to 20.5 percent) when the experimenter was physically absent from the laboratory and gave his orders by phone. These results and others are summarized in Table 6–8 on page 168.

FIGURE 6-10

Predicted and actual behaviour in Milgram's obedience experiment

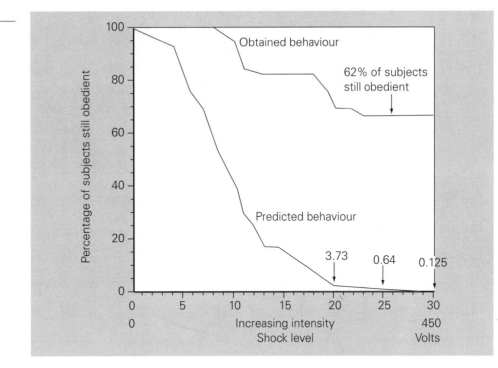

It should be noted that all Milgram's subjects were males; they included university students, postal clerks, high school teachers, salesmen, engineers and labourers. The extent to which women would obey under these conditions has not been thoroughly investigated. However, Hofling, Brodzsman, Dalrymple, Graves and Pierce (1966) reported that 95 percent of the nurses in their experiment were willing to issue an overdose of a certain medicine on the doctor's authority. This figure dropped to 11 percent in another study when the nurses were familiar with the medicine and were given time to consult others (Rank & Jacobson, 1977). Nevertheless, in this setting even an 11-percent rate of obedience could have tragic consequences.

Milgram's research has been repeated many times in various locations in the U.S. and in other countries (Jordan, Spain, Germany, Italy and Australia), with between 50 percent and 85 percent of subjects using the highest shock level overall. Although much attention has been paid to the violent aspects of Milgram's research, obedience is commonplace in many less dramatic situations, as shown in an investigation by Meeus and Raaijmakers (1986). Their study involved a research worker at a university (the experimenter), male and female subjects and an accomplice who was applying for a job. The "applicant" had been invited to the laboratory to take a selection test that, if passed,

would guarantee a job. The subjects were directed to disturb the applicant while he was doing the test by making negative remarks about his test achievement and denigrating remarks about his personality. The remarks were to be made in spite of any objections by the applicant and were scripted to become increasingly strenuous as the time passed. If the subject proceeded, the applicant became unable to cope, failed the test and forfeited the job. The subjects administered the test orally to the applicants whom they knew were currently unemployed. There were a maximum of 15 remarks that the subjects were told they could make; 91.7 percent of the subjects made all 15 remarks, thereby ensuring that the applicant would not get the job. This outcome represents a considerably higher level of obedience than was observed by Milgram and others and suggests that this type of psychological harm is easier to perpetrate than physical violence.

These experiments clearly reveal that destructive obedience, either psychological or physical, is not restricted to any one social or cultural group. Individuals are willing to assign responsibility for their actions to authority figures and carry out their orders even when refusal is relatively easy. In the case of physical harm, obedience is reduced but not eliminated by the proximity of the victim and the absence of the person in authority. The closer the victim and the

TABLE 6-8

Effect of immediacy* on level of shocks administered

Immediacy level	Characterization	Results
7	No feedback at all from victim	M = 450 V; 100% STL
6	Victim pounds on wall at 300 V	M = 405 V; 65% STL
5	Baseline: Audible protests from next room	M = 370 V; 63% STL
4	Like baseline plus victim visible in same room	M = 310 V; 40% STL
3	Teacher forces victim's hand down onto shock plate	M = 265 V; 30% STL
2	Experimenter gives directions by telephone	M = 270V; 20.5% STL
1	No orders from experimenter; teacher has free choice in choosing shock levels	M = 45 V; 2.5% STL

* Immediacy describes how "socially close" the victim appears to the subject. M is the mean maximum shock level for subjects in this group. STL means "shock to limit," and the limit is 450 V.

Source: Brown, 1986

[handwritten in margin: Blass reviewed Milgram's]

more distant the authority the lower the level of obedience. Blass (1999) reviewed the literature that has accumulated in the 35 years since Milgram's studies. He concludes that naive individuals do underestimate actual obedience rates but not to the extent that Milgram reported. He also notes that there are no gender differences and that the rates of obedience have not changed over time.

People are considerably more likely to obey someone who has authority often identified by the trappings of office, symbols such as the white coat of the physician, the chain of office of the mayor or the uniform of the police officer. For example, Bushman (1988) had a female confederate dress either in a uniform (neat attire) or a sloppy outfit. She then stopped pedestrians near the experimenter, who was searching for change next to an expired traffic meter, and ordered, "This fellow is over-parked at the meter and doesn't have any change. Give him a nickel!" When the confederate was wearing a uniform, 72 percent of the pedestrians supplied a nickel whereas in the neat and sloppy conditions about 50 percent obeyed. In addition, no one questioned the confederate when she was in uniform while 23 percent questioned her when she was neatly dressed and 29 percent when she was sloppily dressed.

There is nothing subtle about the manipulation of behaviour in these obedience investigations. However during much of our day-to-day life, we are subjected to unintentional influences that modify our actions. These influences are considered next.

Unintentional Social Influences

Social influence involves direct or indirect pressure exerted by people to encourage or discourage certain actions by others. We may use a wide variety of cues from explicit verbal messages to subtle nonverbal communication to get someone to conform, comply or obey. However, it also is possible to observe other social influences that a person or group may not even be aware of exerting. **Social modelling** is one such process.

Social modelling

From the outset, social psychologists have recognized and been fascinated by imitation. Albert Bandura (1977) has developed a comprehensive analysis (social learning theory) of the process of **observational learning**, which extends beyond the limits of child-like imitation.

In order for modelling to occur, the observer must attend to the model and what the model is doing. The status or attractiveness of the model and the novelty of the behaviour will affect attention. Then the observer must remember what has been observed as an image or in words. As we saw in Chapter 2,

CRITICAL THINKING

Character versus Situational Pressure: What Students Think

If asked, most people underestimate the extent to which the "teacher" will shock the "learner" in Milgram's obedience experiment. However, Safer (1980) discovered that students after viewing a film of Milgram's research and learning about a control study Milgram carried out in which "teachers" could set their own shock levels without being coerced by the experimenter, overestimated how much shock would be delivered when subjects made their own decision. Safer postulated that these students felt the obedience situation—even in the absence of the experimenter—released aggressive reactions that people harbour. In other words, they seemed to believe that people are inherently evil, ordinarily keeping their aggression under control, but displaying it under the right circumstances.

Safer went on to test this hypothesis by asking students who had seen the film and others who had not, how subjects would respond in the Milgram control situation. Students who had *not* seen the film predicted that when subjects had personal responsibility for setting the shock level fewer would choose the maximum shock level and they predicted lower levels of average shock and maximum shock than did students who had seen the film.

Safer points out that the students did not seem to understand how much of behaviour arises from situational pressures rather than the character of the individual. As "naive psychologists," they felt that most people, being evil rather than decent, would harm a stranger.

Many people find it difficult to accept that the situation can have such a profound effect on behaviour. After reading about Milgram's study or after seeing the movie *Obedience* in which Milgram describes his research (Milgram, 1965), they are likely to attribute evil to the subject rather than attribute the obedience to situational influences (see Chapter 2 on the fundamental attribution error).

schemata can strongly influence both attention and memory. In order to duplicate the behaviour that has been observed, the person *must be able to perform it* (i.e., the behaviour itself or a capacity to perform it must be in the observer's repertoire). Although Wayne Gretzky was a compelling model for many young hockey players, few possess his ability to perform.

Finally if modelling is to occur, the observer must be *motivated* to learn and perform what is observed. The observer will be motivated by rewards and punishments already experienced and by her expectations. Bandura points out that reinforcement need not be experienced directly. If you identify with a model on the basis of attractiveness, high status or similarity to yourself and you observe the consequences of the behaviour to the model then you may experience **vicarious reinforcement**. This experience of "feeling what they feel" may influence your behaviour.

This analysis encompasses more than simple imitation. In modelling, we observe what the person does in what situation and with what consequences. For example in the case of television aggression, we see the aggressive act but also observe the situation in which it occurs, the characteristics of the victim and possibly the consequences to the aggressor (see Chapter 11). All these observations provide us with information about what is expected or appropriate in a situation and what is likely to happen.

Modelling may involve the *observational learning of a new behaviour*. Most modelling influences tend to change the probability of a behaviour that already exists (or potentially exists—most of us could fire a gun even if we have never done so). Modelling may have *inhibiting* or *disinhibiting* effects on such behaviour as aggression, sexuality, assertiveness and even suicide. Observing a model may actually reduce the probability of modelling if the model is unattractive or the action has undesirable consequences. On the other hand, modelling may also have **response facilitation** effects, eliciting a behaviour in a specific situation. This may occur because modelling provides information about what is expected or simply because it increases awareness and availability of the act.

The dangers of conformity: Groupthink

Few would deny that some conformity is necessary for the well being of groups and of society in general. A *laissez-faire* system in which individuals made up their own minds about whether to stop at intersections or pay income tax would be highly chaotic. But is conformity counterproductive under some circumstances? Would Bethune have gone to China, Riel mounted a rebellion or Banting and Best discovered insulin if they had been conformists? Those who are willing to take a stand against majority opinion chart progress in many fields. Among these were Freud, whose theory flew in the face of Victorian morality, and the early explorers who, according to common belief, were expected to fall off the edge of a flat world.

Janis (1972, 1982) and Janis and Mann (1977) have coined the term **groupthink** for the tendency for group members, especially elite groups, to assume that the group invariably has the correct answer. It occurs when a group seeks a solution to a problem without fully considering all the possible alternatives (McCauley, 1989). The decision-makers in the group believe that the group cannot fail; there is excessive optimism and risk-taking. Warnings about the preferred solutions are discounted. Group members set aside personal doubts, resulting in an illusion of unanimity. Finally, self-appointed "mind guards" shield the group from external information that might challenge group decisions (Tetlock, Peterson, McGuire, Chang & Field, 1992). In order for groupthink to occur, a number of situational and structural conditions must be present.

The structural conditions include *promotional leadership* whereby the leader reveals a favoured policy alternative early in the proceedings. The group members also tend to have *homogeneous* social backgrounds and ideologies and to be *insulated* from outside information. In addition the group is perceived by its members as more effective than it actually is (Whyte, 1998). The situational conditions include an *external threat*, involving either crisis or time pressure. The problem under consideration will be *complex* and *difficult* and there may have been a recent *group failure*—a poor outcome from a prior decision.

Janis (1972, 1982) developed his ideas about this phenomenon from an analysis of a number of important policy-making committees in the United States. The recommendations of these committees had crucial national implications, but as Janis noted, the members of these groups were more concerned with maintaining group solidarity than with voicing unpopular views that might be correct but were also disruptive. Examples of these decisions—described by Janis (1982) as fiascos—include pursuing the defeated North Korean Army beyond the 38th parallel; launching the Bay of Pigs invasion of Cuba; escalating involvement in the war in Vietnam; and the Watergate cover-up. Other examples include the decision to launch the space shuttle *Challenger*, the Iran-Contra affair (Whyte, 1989) and management decisions which seriously affected British Airways and Marks & Spencer (Eaton, 2001). In Canada, history will judge whether the problems of the Canadian military (especially in Somalia) arose under similar conditions.

To test the hypothesis that type of leadership affects the likelihood of groupthink, Flowers (1977) had groups of college students deal with a crisis. Some of these groups had an open leader and others a closed leader. The open leader in contrast to the closed leader: (1) did not state his or her own solution until all the others had offered their preferred solutions; (2) asked for and encouraged discussion of each suggested course of action; and (3) emphasized that it was important to air all viewpoints to reach a wise decision. In addition, some groups were composed of strangers (low cohesiveness) and others of friends (high cohesiveness).

The groups discussed the problem of a 62-year-old high school teacher who was becoming senile and unable to handle discipline in her classroom. The discussion continued until a solution agreeable to all members was reached. More potential solutions were generated and information was better used under open leadership; it made no difference whether group members were friends.

Tetlock (1979) has pointed out that there are problems with such simulations. For instance, the cohesiveness variable may not be the same among college students as it is among policy-makers. Accordingly, Tetlock (1979) analyzed the content of the statements actually made by important U.S. decision-makers—Harry Truman, John F. Kennedy and Lyndon Johnson—during the crises originally examined by Janis. Tetlock's results strongly support Janis's model. Public statements by policy-makers during a crisis were more simplistic and were more oriented towards their own group. As Janis (1972) indicates, decision-makers believe that the group is invulnerable to external influence. Group members ignore or discount warnings about the validity of their common solution and accept the rightness of the group's policies unquestioningly. Direct pressure is applied to elicit conformity. Self-appointed "mind guards" shield the group from outside counter-attitudinal pressures: individuals such as Robert Kennedy who during the Cuban Missile Crisis (when the U.S. demanded that the U.S.S.R. remove its missiles and blockaded Cuban ports), filtered information from outside so that the group learned little if anything about external, dissenting opinions. It is generally accepted that the groupthink model provides a good basis for understanding these collective decision processes (Esser, 1998; Kramer, 1998). Clearly, conformity under these conditions is both intellectually stultifying and dangerous. There is no room for individualism or innovation. Yet without innovation (and its acceptance), our society would be considerably more primitive than it is. Indeed, Nemeth (1986, p. 31) contends that "robust dissent is not only a manifestation of a democratic principle, but it is the mechanism by which better solutions are found and better decisions are made."

Nonconformity and Innovation

In 1934, the Chrysler Corporation developed a car that was mechanically and stylistically far ahead of its competitors. Yet the Airflow did not sell well and production was soon stopped. Clearly, the Chrysler engineers and stylists had been willing to deviate markedly from the standards of the day, but they misjudged the flexibility of the buying public. Brewers who put "diet beer" on the market in the 1970s made a similar error. It didn't sell. When it was reintroduced later as "light beer," it captured a substantial proportion of beer sales. In the interim, the public had become considerably more health conscious. People have difficulty accepting innovative ideas and products for many reasons. In some cases resistance may be political. The Canadian government, for example, stopped the production of both the world's first commercial jetliner and the Avro Arrow, a jet fighter that would have been by far the best airplane of its type in the world.

Innovation does not simply involve doing something different. Merton (1957), for instance, argues that innovators adhere to group goals while departing from approved means, typically through novel behaviours. Thus, it could be questioned whether the Wright Brothers were true innovators, since they simply improved on available knowledge and techniques. On the other hand, Henry Ford's contribution to modern industry—the assembly line—completely revolutionized the manufacturing process. This ability to break out of the lock-step pattern of conformity is critical. Not only must innovators be able to resist normative pressures, they must also be willing to tolerate the risk of failure as well as potential public ridicule or scorn: recall how Galileo was forced to recant his outlandish view that the Earth was not the centre of the solar system.

Group and individual problem solving

Brainstorming has been advocated as one way to foster innovative ideas. In this group situation, participants must feel no restrictions on the type of ideas they put forth. All notions, no matter how bizarre, are welcome. Such conditions, as Gordon (1961, p. 28) points out, maximize the likelihood of "making the familiar strange"—the essence of innovation. (See A Case in Point—Making the Familiar Strange for an excerpt from Gordon's book on "synectics," the term he prefers.)

Brainstorming is not however a panacea. Individuals working separately generate many more, and more creative, ideas (as rated by judges) than do groups (McGrath, 1984). Yet despite consistent evidence to the contrary, the illusion of group productivity persists. What seems to happen is that group members overestimate the number of ideas that occurred to them during the group session. They also have difficulty in differentiating their own ideas from those of the others in the group and thus take credit for more ideas than they actually produced (Stroebe, Diehl & Abakoumbin, 1992; Paulus, Ozindolet, Poletes & Camacho, 1993). Of course, it is the quality and uniqueness of the ideas expressed that are critical. If these characteristics are not enhanced by the brainstorming procedure, whether group or individual, then quantity alone is likely to be of little value. There is also evidence based on research at Queen's University (Cooper, W.H., Gallupe, Pollard & Cadsby, 1998) that anonymity enhances the process. Participants who communicated anonymously via computers produced more controversial ideas. Groups using this process also produced a greater variety of ideas than did nonanonymous groups.

Making the Familiar Strange

A group was trying to invent a dispenser that could be used with a variety of products and was without a top that had to be removed and replaced.

A: A clam sticks its neck out of its shell ... brings the neck in and closes the shell again.

B: Yeah, but the clam's shell is an exoskeleton. The real part, the real anatomy of the clam is inside.

C: What difference does that make?

A: Well, the neck of the clam doesn't clean itself ... it just drags itself back into the protection of the shell.

D: What other analogies are there to our problem?

E: How about the human mouth?

B: What does it dispense?

E: Spit ... the mouth propels spit whenever it wants ... on, oh. It isn't really self cleaning ... you know, dribbling on the chin.

A: Couldn't there be a mouth, which was trained so that it wouldn't dribble?

E: Maybe, but it would be contrived as hell ... and if the human mouth can't keep itself clean with all the feedback in the human system ...

D: When I was a kid I grew up on a farm. I used to drive a hayrack behind a pair of draft horses. When a horse would take a crap, first his outer ... I guess you call it a kind of mouth, would open. Then the anal sphincter would dilate and a horse ball would come out. Afterwards, everything would close up again. The whole picture would be clean as a whistle.

E: What if the horse had diarrhea?

D: That happened when they got too much grain ... but the horse would kind of wink a couple of times while the anal mouth was drawn back ... the winking would squeeze out the liquid ... then the outer mouth would cover the whole thing up again.

B: You're describing a plastic motion.

D: I guess so ... could we simulate a horse's ass in plastic?

In fact they could and they did (Gordon, 1961, p. 41).

Some people, although intellectually competent, are unable to deviate from standard or expected modes of reasoning because of certain personality traits. One such inhibiting trait is what Rokeach (1960) termed "close-mindedness." Among other things, close-minded individuals have difficulty dealing with problems in new ways. As J.L. Adams (1980) points out, they interpret the problem too narrowly; they fail to consider a variety of viewpoints and they don't use all the information available. For example, a close-minded individual would probably have difficulty with the problem shown in Figure 6–11.

When most people see this problem for the first time, they assume they are not to go outside the boundaries set by the dots themselves—even though that is neither stated nor implied in the puzzle. Once they overcome

that self-imposed constraint, there are a number of possible solutions two of which are given in Figure 6–12.

In the second solution, an additional assumed constraint has been broken. The puzzle said only "Connect the dots"; most people assume that means

FIGURE 6-11

Without lifting your pencil from the paper and using no more than four straight lines, connect these nine dots.

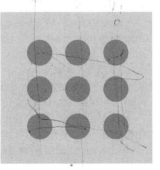

the lines must go through the centre of each dot. Close-minded subjects take longer to solve problems like this and are less able than open-minded individuals to give up an unworkable belief system. Rokeach (1960, p. 256) comments, "[C]losed subjects remain loyal, that is, continue to believe that there is a solution. Conversely, open subjects more frequently find an ingenious creative solution."

The diffusion and acceptance of innovation

Some innovations have no immediate or obvious practical use; others arise in response to real needs and may improve the well being of substantial segments of the human population. We should remember that what is commonplace in one society may be innovative in another. For example, the "Green Revolution" in India and other parts of Asia required farmers to accept a new type of wheat, which had a considerably higher yield than traditional types and which had earned a Nobel Prize for its developer, Norman Borlaug. At the same time, this new wheat had a number of features that could reduce the probability of its acceptance. It did not tolerate drought as well as traditional wheat, which meant that some form of irrigation had to be available in case of a poor monsoon season. Also, the new wheat had a shorter stem than the older varieties and provided less straw for other uses—feeding cattle, for instance. It did not respond well to organic fertilizers so that chemical fertilizers had to be used. Finally, people complained that the new flour made unpleasant-tasting *chapattis* (a type of unleavened bread and a dietary staple throughout Northern India) (Nossiter, 1970). Given these conditions, it is surprising that the hybrid variety did gain acceptance, with ultimately good results.

What happens when an individual is confronted with a new device, seed or manufacturing process that is promoted as a great improvement? Two separate processes are involved: the acquisition of knowledge concerning the innovation and the adoption of that innovation in practice (Bandura, 1986). A considerable body of research has determined some characteristics of the process and of the individuals involved.

You will no doubt have realized that the adoption of innovation involves risk and that some individuals are more willing to tolerate risk than others. It has also been shown that adopters of innovation compared to non-adopters are better off financially, are more modern in their outlook, have had more experience with other innovations and are better able to evaluate abstract and technical information (Weiss, W., 1971; Moulik & Lokhande, 1969).

The rate and likelihood of the adoption of an innovation according to E.M. Rogers and Shoemaker (1971), is a function of five factors:

1. The *relative advantage* of the innovation over the system it supersedes.

2. Its *value compatibility* with the needs and experiences of the receivers.

3. Its *complexity* or the extent to which the innovation is perceived as difficult to understand or use.

4. *Trialability* or the extent to which the innovation can be tested for effectiveness.

5. The *observability* of the outcome, which affects the probability that others will adopt the innovation.

If a person can be persuaded to try an innovation that then proves successful, there is a strong chance that he will continue using it. Obviously this step is the most difficult—although it is actually the *third* step. First, the individual must be made aware of the innovation. Second, the individual must go through an evaluation

FIGURE 6-12

Two possible solutions to Figure 6–11

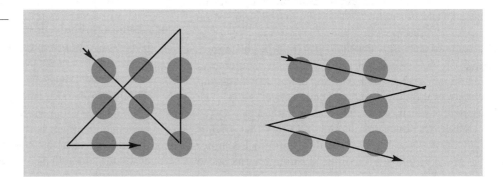

process and decide whether or not to try it out. The role of **opinion leaders** or *key communicators* is important during these preliminary steps. V.P. Singh and Pareek (1970) observed that the best adopters are people with high socioeconomic status and social preference who have greater contact with agents of change; these people can also influence the decisions of other members of their community. Research suggests that *change agents*—e.g., agricultural extension workers, family planning consultants—are most important for inducing awareness while personal contacts—friends and neighbours—are most important at the evaluation, trial and adoption stages (Sawhney, 1967). Clearly if the majority of the members of a community are opposed to the introduction of an innovation, only those who are able to resist the pressures to conform will be willing to give the innovation a try. Among these persons may be those with higher levels of achievement motivation (McClelland, 1961), a motive associated with a greater flexibility in problem solving as well as with more independence of thought and action.

At least three models have been put forward to describe the diffusion process. The *dual-link model* suggests that successful innovations are mainly diffused through social networks of interpersonal contacts via a two-step flow of communication (Katz, 1957). Early adopters tend to be the higher-status members of the community (opinion leaders) who have many contacts over greater geographical distances than do those of lower status (opinion followers). The friends of opinion leaders are usually at similar positions in the social hierarchy and they take the new ideas away to disseminate in their own social context.

The *direct-flow model*, on the other hand, postulates that people are initially influenced directly by the media and consult others only when the activities being advocated involve time, resources and risk. Keep in mind that although people do tend to seek information from as many sources as possible, in some parts of the world very few are available. There may be no television or radio, and written materials are of no use to illiterate people.

A more eclectic view, *multi-pattern diffusion*, argues that the nature of diffusion depends on a number of factors such as the type of innovation, the skills and resources it requires and the social networks that exist as well as social constraints and incentives.

While the dual-link model indicates that friends play an important role in the diffusion process, innovations may actually be diffused through weak social ties (Weenig & Midden, 1991). This is because friends and close acquaintances have much the same views on issues (see Chapter 8) and tend to interact mainly with each other. On the other hand, those who are not involved in such a tight-knit group are likely to move in more diverse company where they can learn and experience different things. People are more likely to come in contact with new ideas and methods from numerous acquaintances than from frequent interaction with a smaller circle of friends.

Overall, the evidence suggests that the diffusion of an innovation will be most successful when four conditions are present (Bandura, 1986; Rogers, 1995):

1. There is an optimal setting for introducing the innovation (e.g., a willingness to try it, at least in the short run).

2. There are the necessary preconditions for change (e.g., increasing awareness and knowledge about the innovation). This would involve disseminating information about the purpose of the innovation, its relative advantages and how adopting the innovation would affect the person's life.

3. An effective program for disseminating information is in place. This should include instruction in the necessary skills (e.g., teaching of rudimentary mechanics so that elementary repairs are possible) and demonstration of the new techniques followed by "guided enactment," which allows the participants to practise the skill using simulation (so that fear of mistakes is reduced). Finally, the innovation can be introduced within the actual situation.

4. Reference can be made to successful examples of adoption to spread usage beyond the initial target area.

Summary

1. The most primitive form of social influence arises from the mere presence of others. Mere presence of an audience or coactors facilitates the performance of simple tasks and impedes performance of complex or novel tasks.

2. Zajonc has postulated that arousal induced by the presence of others is innate. Cottrell has argued that the presence of others leads to arousal due to evaluation apprehension, which is learned.

3. Distraction-conflict theory claims that the arousal is due to conflict, which arises from the need to attend to both the others present and the task.

4. Social loafing refers to the reduction in the effort of individuals in group situations. Conformity is the modification of behaviour or attitudes in order to be consistent with social norms. Compliance is behavioural change that arises in response to requests or demands of others without underlying attitude change. Obedience is a response to a demand or a command of someone who is perceived as having some form of authority.

5. Most conformity and compliance arises in response to majorities, but consistent and confident minorities can affect majorities.

6. Tactics employed to enhance compliance include the following techniques: the foot-in-the-door; the door-in-the-face; low-balling; improving the offer; and guilt inducement.

7. A drawback of conformity is groupthink.

8. Innovation requires open-minded individuals to think in non-normative ways. Innovations are diffused by the media, opinion leaders and modelling.

Further Reading

BASS, T. (Ed.). (2000). *Obedience to authority: Current perspectives on the Milgram paradigm.* Mahwah, NJ: Lawrence Erlbaum Associates. Thirty-five years of research reviewed and integrated. Includes interesting biographical material on Milgram himself.

CIALDINI, R.B. (1998). *Influence: Psychology of persuasion.* New York: William Morrow. Insights and examples of how influence works. Practical as well as theoretical.

DESBARAT, P. (1998). *Somalia cover-up: A commissioner's journal.* Toronto: McClelland and Stewart. Lies, delayed information, tampered documents, conflicting evidence and the investigation into military wrongdoing.

GOLDHAGEN, D.J. (1997). *Hitler's willing executioners: Ordinary Germans and the Holocaust.* Random House. A controversial discussion of whether ordinary Germans supported and participated in the mass destruction of Jews.

JANIS, I.L. (1982). *Groupthink: Psychological studies of policy decisions and fiascos* (2nd ed.). Boston: Houghton-Mifflin. A detailed description of the groupthink phenomenon and the role it has played in U.S. political and military decisions.

MILGRAM, S. (1974). *Obedience to authority.* New York: Harper & Row. The original account of the obedience experiments.

MILLER, A.G., COLLINS, B.E. & BRIEF, D.A. (Eds.). (1995). Perspectives on obedience to authority: The legacy of the Milgram experiments. *Journal of Social Issues* (Vol. 51, No. 3). The history as well as contemporary views of obedient and defiant behaviour in modern societies.

MOSCOVICI, S. (1976). *Social influence and social change.* London: Academic. Social influence from the European perspective.

MOSCOVICI, S., MUCCHI-FAINA, A. & MAASS, A. (Eds.). (1994). *Minority influence.* Chicago: Nelson-Hall. American and European contributors focus on understanding how marginal and unpopular opinions achieve acceptance.

NAYAK, P.R. & KETTERINGHAM, J.M. (1986). *Breakthroughs.* Don Mills: Collier MacMillan Canada. The development of innovations in the real world ranging from Post-it Notes to microwave ovens.

STERNBERG, R.J. & LUBART, T.I. (1995). *Defying the crowd: Cultivating creativity in a culture of conformity.* New York: Free Press. An easy-to-read consideration of problems and solutions associated with excessive conformity.

TUCHMAN, B.W. (1984). *The march of folly: From Troy to Vietnam.* New York: Knopf. The pursuit of fiascos by governments, despite the availability of feasible alternatives, through the ages.

ZANNA, M.P., OLSEN, J.M. & HERMAN, C.P. (Eds.). (1987). *Social influence: The Ontario symposium* (Vol. 5). Hillsdale, NJ: Erlbaum. A series of papers outlining research and theory on persuasion, compliance and conformity.

Weblinks

Social Influence: The Science of Persuasion, Compliance & Propaganda

www.public.asu.edu/~kelton/

Some nice demonstrations, as well as links to other relevant sites

www.piltdown-man.com

www.museumofhoaxes.com

www.historybuff.com/library/refbarnum.html

Chapter 7

Language and Communication

Thanks to words, we have been able to rise above the brutes; and thanks to words, we have often sunk to the level of the demons.

Aldous Huxley

A different language is a different vision of life.

Federico Fellini

Chapter Outline

In the novel *Out of the Silent Planet*, C.S. Lewis describes an English professor, Ransom, who is carried off to Mars. In this strange new environment, Ransom sights a large, black, round-headed animal. Watching cautiously from hiding, Ransom tries to ascertain whether the creature represents danger, when suddenly he hears the creature speak. He cannot see to whom it is speaking and, of course, he doesn't understand what it is saying; but to Ransom, a philologist, the utterance is unmistakably language. That changes everything: if it can speak, Ransom assumes it is a person, no matter what it looks like. Ransom wants to learn its language, to communicate.

This incident from science fiction highlights how central language is to the human experience. Communication is the essence of social interaction. Whether by words, facial expressions or gestures, whether through direct contact, telephone conversations, e-mail or the printed page, humans inform each other of their thoughts and feelings, their wishes and ideals, their intentions and needs. They threaten, command, supplicate, reward, tease, entertain, teach, exchange points of view, coordinate their activities—indeed, it is difficult to imagine being in the presence of another person without continually communicating in one way or another. Even silence can be a form of communication—think of giving someone "the cold shoulder."

While non-verbal communication—communication by means of gestures, facial expressions, body position or vocalizations such as whistles, grunts and groans—provides a powerful channel for conveying information, it is language that distinctly characterizes human communication. It is impossible to do justice to the study of human social activity without examining verbal activity, for virtually every utterance a person makes in the presence of others produces a reaction or demands a response, and that reaction or response reflects aspects of the interaction itself, such as the relative status of speaker and listener or their particular social and emotional relationship. These interactions, in turn, cannot be totally understood without

taking into account the role that language plays in shaping them.

Unfortunately sometimes people *mis*communicate, leading the speakers to believe that they understand each other when, in fact, they do not. Exchanging words is easy; communicating ideas and feelings is not always so. Misunderstanding can lead to serious conflicts among individuals, groups and even nations. As we shall see, dysfunctional communication is more likely to occur when the communicators are of different cultural or linguistic backgrounds, or different gender (Tannen, 1990) or when one of the communicators is in an abnormal mood state such as depression (McCann & Lalonde, 1993).

Given the importance of language in social interaction, it may come as a surprise that until very recently social psychologists have largely neglected the subject. Most social psychology textbooks do not even mention it. However in recent years, interest in the social psychology of language has begun to grow rapidly (Kroger & Wood, 1992); there are now journals (e.g., *The Journal of Language and Social Psychology*) as well as a handbook dedicated to the subject (Giles & Robinson, 1990).

Given the importance of language in our social and political lives, it is not surprising that Canadian researchers have played a leading role in the social psychological study of language and communication.

Reflecting the importance of communication in such a vast and thinly populated land, Canada is also a world leader in research on the social psychology of telecommunications. Electronic communication raises all sorts of important social psychological questions: How do leaders emerge in video conferencing networks? Does using the telephone or e-mail impede or facilitate understanding? Millions of people around the world spend many hours at their computers each day communicating with strangers they will never meet. How does this form of communication, stripped of all nonverbal cues that might provide important information about emotional states, affect the communicators, the development of their understanding and even the relationships between them? As more and more people routinely use the Internet, social psychologists are becoming very interested in how such communication differs from face-to-face communication and how computer networks influence the structure of both work and social groups (e.g., Preece, 1995; Kraut et al., 1998). Some people report "falling in love" with their Internet interlocutors. Does this "make sense"? Is this no different in principle from pen-pal relationships that were so common when letter writing was a vital and highly valued form of communication?

This chapter begins with the examination of non-verbal methods of communication. Next, we discuss language with particular emphasis on its social nature. As we shall see, not only does language play an important role in social interactions between individuals, but it also helps mark group boundaries and define social identities. We shall also examine the social processes involved in bilingual communication.

Non-verbal Communication

Within a given culture or society, virtually everyone understands the meaning of particular facial expressions and gestures, for otherwise, such gestures would be of little use in communication. A raise of the eyebrows, a pucker of the lips or a clenching of the fist can often communicate more about how we feel than could a dozen words. However, no formal training is ever given to teach people how to encode feelings or ideas into gestures or expressions or how to decode (interpret) body language. We study language in school but not **non-verbal communication**. While there may be a biological basis for the facial expres-

sions that correspond to some of the primary emotions, for the most part we learn to use and to react to non-verbal communication through interaction with others just as we initially learn language. As children, we mimic the behaviours and gestures of older people and to one degree or another we grow to be sensitive to various non-verbal cues.

Communication researchers showed little interest in the importance of body movements, gestures and facial expressions until the 1960s. Since that time, however, interest in non-verbal communication has mushroomed, leading to a whole new field of psychological research. Initially the research assumed that non-verbal communication provides a separate communication channel that sometimes works in concert with the verbal system, adding emphasis or subtlety to what is said, and at other times carries information that contradicts the spoken message. Thus, conflicting messages may be sent when a person says one thing but accompanies speech with gestures and expressions that express something else.

However, it is now understood that rather than constituting separate channels, verbal and non-verbal communication are intimately related and generally represent different manifestations of a common process in the brain. While we certainly do use many gestures and facial expressions in a deliberate effort to communicate, a great deal of non-verbal behaviour occurs without our intent or even awareness. Research has shown that when two people in a social interaction cannot see each other, production of non-verbal behaviour continues at almost the same level as when they have visual contact (Rimé, 1983). You have probably seen someone make various spontaneous gestures while using the telephone; obviously the gestures are not intended to communicate. Even speakers who have been blind since birth gesture when talking to listeners who are also blind (Iverson & Goldin-Meadow, 1998). In fact, verbal and non-verbal behaviour are so closely tied that speakers who are prevented from gesturing are more hesitant in their speech (Rauscher, Krauss & Chen, 1996).

The development of gestures and other non-verbal behaviours begins early in life. Before the young child can communicate verbally, there is plenty of communication through body movements and facial expressions. Research indicates that linguistic ability is built on top of this motor activity so that non-verbal behaviour, rather than being an independently generated set of responses, is a fundamental part of the process of translating thoughts into words (Rimé, 1983). Therefore, non-verbal and verbal responses are highly correlated unless we make a deliberate effort to hide what we are thinking or feeling. Indeed, gesturing is done as much to help the speaker, as it is to help the listener. As an example of this, in one study (Goldin-Meadow, Nusbaum, Kelly & Wagner, 2001), adults and children were asked to remember a list of letters and words at the same time that they were explaining how they had solved a mathematics problem. Adults and children alike remembered more of the letters and words when they were permitted to gesture as they talked than when they were not, suggesting that gesturing somehow allows the speaker to devote more cognitive resources to the memory task.

What happens if young children learn two different languages but at different rates? Does gesturing become less frequent in the language that the child knows best? Mayberry and Nicoladis (2000) carried out a longitudinal study of gesture development in French–English bilingual children to see how gesturing changed as a child makes progress in using language. They found that, rather than abandoning gestures as they learned to talk, the children's use of gestures *increased* as language ability increased. Moreover, the use of gestures in each language was tied to the level of development of that language. For example, a child whose French-speaking ability was advanced relative to his or her English-speaking ability used more complex and frequent gestures in French than in English and the opposite was the case for children who were more advanced in speaking English. Again this demonstrates that the use of non-verbal behaviour such as gestures is an integral part of language development rather than something separate from it.

Researching non-verbal communication has proved difficult, for even brief interactions involve many quick and spontaneous exchanges that are difficult to record. The human body is capable of a very large number of physical expressions. It has been estimated that we can produce 700 000 different physical gestures, facial expressions and movements (Pei, 1965), and about 20 000 different facial expressions are possible (Birdwhistle, 1970) as well as 1000 different postures (Hewes, 1957). Research in the past was severely hampered by lack of agreement on how to describe movement, but over time coding systems were developed based on the analysis of changes in a large number of different parts of the body or face over a series of short intervals, a "time-series analysis" (Ekman & Friesen, 1978; Frey, Hirsbrunner, Florin, Daw & Crawford,

1983). By feeding all this information—gathered for the whole body—into a computer, very detailed analyses of movements can be carried out, allowing researchers much greater precision in measuring and quantifying changes in body position or facial expression (see Figures 7–1 and 7–2 in A Practical Question—How Do You Write Down Dance?).

Functions of non-verbal behaviour

As everyone knows, language provides an efficient means of communication. We can communicate the same basic message in many different ways using nuances to finely tune our verbal utterance to the thoughts or feelings being expressed. So why do we not use language for all communication? Why has non-verbal communication persisted as part of our cultural heritage when language has been available to supplant it? There are several possible reasons (Argyle, 1975; Patterson, 1982, 1983):

- In some situations, non-verbal communication is easier to use. For instance, we have a limited vocabulary for shapes; it is easier to show a complex shape with hand movements than to name it. Similarly, it is much easier to point to a flaw in a paint job than to try to verbally describe the precise location. When communicating about shapes or movements, not only do people gesture more, but research has shown that if they are prevented from gesturing, they pause more as if looking for words (Rauscher, Krauss & Chen, 1996). Indeed, it seems that gesturing during spontaneous conversation about spatial subject matter may help us to find the words we want to use.

- In communicating emotion, non-verbal signals are more powerful and subtler than verbal signals. There are many words available to us to describe emotions, but choosing the right one is not always easy. There are more than 2000 adjectives referring to emotions and moods in the English language and researchers are still trying to group them according to the underlying states they describe (Storm & Storm, 1987). For example, what is the relationship between happy and ecstatic? An ecstatic person is presumably happy, but a happy person is not necessarily ecstatic. While adults can teach children to correctly name objects and actions by actually using the label in the presence of the object or action, it is more difficult to teach children what labels to apply to emotional states. An adult can only infer whether

How Do You Write Down Dance?

Music can be written down precisely. So can dialogue at least as far as the words are concerned, although the director of a play decides how the words are said and how the actors move about the stage. But how does one record on paper the many and intricate movements needed for a ballet production? The ballet is all non-verbal behaviour.

Over the years, various attempts have been made to develop a uniform coding system for recording the movements, the earliest being that of Guglielmo Ebreo of Pesaro in 1463. Of many systems in use today, two systems of notation have become predominant. The first, which appeared in 1953, is referred to as *Labanotation*, named after its inventor, Rudolf von Laban. This system (see Figure 7–1) uses three vertical lines and symbols to indicate the dancer's position and movements. It allows for the recording of any human movement (Wilson, 1974). The second system is the *Benesh system*, a simple notational movement copyrighted by Joan Benesh and the Royal Ballet School in 1955. It involves the use of symbols superimposed on a music stave (see Figure 7–2).

FIGURE 7-1

Labanotation, 1953 (opening dance from Balanchine's version of *Swan Lake*)

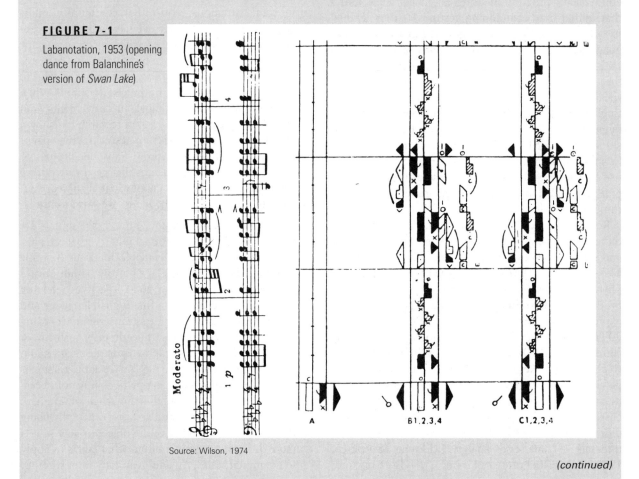

Source: Wilson, 1974

(continued)

FIGURE 7-4

Male/female differences in eye contact under different conditions of expertise

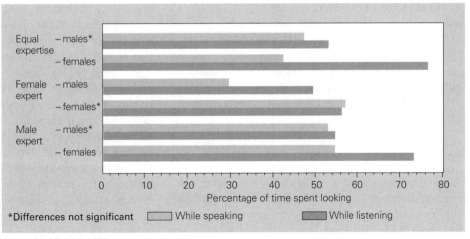

Source: Dovidio et al., 1988

to signal guilt or dishonesty. A Canadian visiting a society where eye contact is avoided may be viewed as showing disrespect and in turn may attribute deceit or "shiftiness" to the people he or she meets.

In general within any given human society, visual behaviour is very important in establishing and maintaining dominance just as it is with primates (Ellyson & Dovidio, 1985). Although we are rarely aware of it, the way we look at others can reflect our perception of our relative social power. For example in a study of pairs of same-sex subjects in the United States, it was found that a subject of high status or power spent as much or more time looking at the other while talking as while listening, while low-power subjects looked at the other significantly more while listening than while speaking (showing that they are "paying attention") (Dovidio & Ellyson, 1985). This effect has been demonstrated with regard to a number of power variables such as educational level, expert power and military rank.

This unconscious manifestation of differences in power is found in male–female interactions as well, for traditional power differences between men and women are to some degree communicated through visual interaction (Berger, Wagner & Zelditch, 1985). In one study (Dovidio, Ellyson, Keating, Heltman & Brown, 1988), male and female subjects were paired and then offered three topics of discussion; the male was expert on one topic, the female on another and they possessed an equal level of expertise with regard to the third. During their discussions, the amount of time each spent looking at the other while talking or listening was recorded. The results (see Figure 7–4)

indicated that when women were in positions of high expertise, they were as likely as men to display their power non-verbally (that is, to look as much or more while speaking as while listening). Most interestingly when there was no difference in expertise, women reacted like women in the low-expertise condition and men reacted like men in the high-expertise condition. These findings not only emphasize the importance of non-verbal cues in communicating social power and dominance but also suggest that a woman may unwittingly signal to males of equal power that she is of low power, thus reinforcing the traditional status difference between males and females.

What would one expect to find when black and white Americans visually interact, given the past low-power status of blacks? Before you conclude that blacks may, as a result of two centuries of slavery, tend to react very much as the low-power people did in the studies discussed above, remember that blacks have historically experienced a degree of low power that has been "off the scale." Indeed, slaves as well as free but "lowly" servants were typically forbidden to make eye contact with their masters or employers—to do so was to show disrespect or even defiance (think of modern "dissing" again). This might suggest that if centuries of degradation have influenced the extent to which black Americans maintain eye contact with whites during conversations, it would be to inhibit looking while the white person is talking. This is, in fact, what has been found in one study (LaFrance & Mayo, 1976). Whites maintained some eye contact while listening while blacks were less likely to do so.

This can lead to misattribution and misunderstanding since whites may assume that someone who doesn't look them in the eye has "something to hide."

Thus while we are usually unaware of how much and why we look at another person during a conversation, our behaviour reflects well-developed norms that involve, among other factors, considerations of relative status and power.

Body language

One need only observe a mime artist to recognize the power of the eyes and face in communicating feelings and thoughts. However, the mime communicates using the whole body. Although less so than the face, the body is a source of non-verbal messages and a number of popular books have promised to teach readers how to understand and exploit "body language." For example, it might be claimed that a woman who sits with her arms crossed while talking to a particular man is unknowingly revealing a protective emotional stance. However, such books rarely back up their claims with empirical evidence and should be approached warily.

Still, there is evidence that others often perceive certain postures as reflecting specific feelings whether or not they actually do so. For example, leaning towards another person or taking a position in close proximity is generally interpreted as a positive stance towards that person. Other examples appear in Figure 7–5.

Gestures, yet another form of body language, also vary from society to society and from culture to culture. Political leaders from French Canada often communicate by means of a simple Gallic shrug, which somehow might seem inappropriate if performed by an anglophone. Some English Canadians, when speaking French, find themselves picking up the practice of hand gesturing! Is it true, as many people seem to think, that French Canadians speaking French typically make many more hand gestures than do English Canadians speaking English? This question was studied at York University's Glendon College by presenting both anglophone and francophone "judges" with videotapes of bilingual people (shown from the neck down) speaking at one time in French and at another time in English. While non-verbal behaviour did *not* vary as a function of the language spoken, it varied substantially according to the native tongue of the speaker. In 71 percent of the cases, the judges successfully identified the speaker's mother tongue on the basis of non-verbal behaviour (Lacroix & Rioux, 1978). Francophone subjects, true

FIGURE 7-5

Body language interpreted

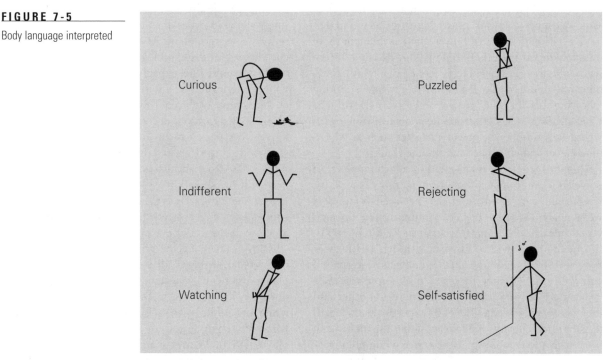

Curious

Puzzled

Indifferent

Rejecting

Watching

Self-satisfied

Source: Argyle, 1975

to the stereotype, gestured more than anglophones regardless of which language they spoke.

We have considerable difficulty in interpreting gestures that are specific to another culture or that are used differently in another culture. For example, the Japanese are surprised when we point to our chest in referring to ourselves; they do so by putting a finger to the nose (DeVos & Hippler, 1969). A sidewise shake of the head means *no* in Canada, but *yes* in much of India; while in Turkey, *no* is signalled by moving the head backwards and rolling the eyes upward (Rubin, 1976). Drawing one's finger across one's throat means "I've had it" in Canada; in Swaziland it means, "I love you." We invite people to approach us by beckoning with an upturned finger. Indians use all four down-turned fingers to do the same thing. These cross-cultural differences in the meaning of some gestures can lead to serious communication difficulty, as when an African chieftain interpreted a female missionary's offer to shake hands as an attempt to throw him to the ground (Argyle, 1975)!

Haptics

Where and when one person touches another serves as a powerful communication agent; the interpretation of the touch reflects both the social context and the relationship between the two individuals. The significance of a man touching a woman differs according to whether that woman is his wife, a stranger, a patient or a casual acquaintance (Argyle, 1975). A slap on the back can vary in meaning too. If a person has just scored a goal in a hockey game, it means one thing, while if a person has just transgressed, it could mean something else. Touches can be organized into a number of different categories. Jones and Yarbrough (1985) analyzed 1500 naturally occurring bodily contacts between people and concluded that touches can be categorized as follows:

- *Positive affect* touches that communicate appreciation, affection, sexual intent or interest, nurturance or reassurance.
- *Playful* touches intended to communicate playfulness and humour.
- *Control* touches used to draw attention or induce compliance.
- *Ritualistic* touches that occur in ritualized situations such as greetings or departures.
- *Task-related* touches associated with the accomplishment of some task as when a nurse takes your pulse or a dance instructor positions your body.

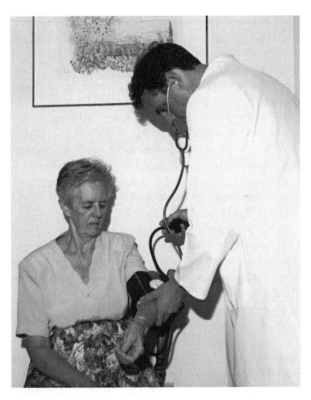

The touching involved in the doctor–patient relationship is task-related.

There are at least two other types of touches, which were not observed in their sampling: *negative affect* and *aggressive* touches (Burgoon, Buller & Woodall, 1989). Gently pushing away someone's annoying hand would be an example of a negative affect touch while any touch intended to hurt—kicks, slaps, shoves, punches—would be an aggressive touch.

The amount of touching behaviour varies considerably from culture to culture. In India, two men who are engaged in conversation often hold hands. To do that in Canada might lead to serious misunderstanding for we have rather strict rules for men about touching men unless they are gay. People in Latin America, Greece, Turkey and the Arab countries tend to touch each other a great deal while relatively little touching occurs among North Americans, Northern Europeans and East Asians (Argyle, 1975). In a study of cross-cultural differences in touching, couples were observed while having coffee in cafés in different countries (Jourard, 1966). The observers recorded the number of times the couples touched each other during a one-hour period. In London, England, there was no touching; in Gainesville, Florida, there were two touches on average; in Paris, 110 touches; and in San Juan, Puerto Rico, 180 touches. Therefore, touching someone in London would probably not have the same effect as touching someone in Paris. Obviously, the potential for misunderstanding is great when people from a "contact" culture visit a "non-contact" culture.

Within a given culture there are also differences with respect to where a person touches another person; the degree of bodily contact in North American society depends very much on the age and relationship of the individuals (Argyle, 1975).

Gender is clearly an important factor in touching. Men have been observed to touch women more often than women touch men and people are much more likely to touch members of the opposite sex than members of their own sex, although this difference is not found in older adults (Henley, 1973; Hall & Veccia, 1990). Men and women also differ with regard to how much pleasure they experience from being touched. Women generally enjoy being touched more than men do, but the circumstances are important. Heslin (1978) asked men and women how much they would enjoy being "squeezed and patted" in various areas of the body either by a close friend or stranger of either the same or the opposite sex. As can be seen from Figure 7–6, both sexes reported touches by someone of the same sex as being more or less unpleasant and touches by an opposite-sex close friend as pleasant. However while men reported that they generally liked being touched by a stranger of the opposite sex, women did not. Henslin also found that men are more likely than women to read sexual connotations into touches. Thus, the woman who uses lots of touching to express herself when talking to a man may inadvertently be taken to be suggesting sexual interest in him (Heslin & Alper, 1983).

Proxemics: Personal space

Would you feel rather uncomfortable if you were sitting at a table in the library and someone came and sat at the same table beside you rather than across from you or at the other end of the table? Suppose you are at a party and someone engages you in conversation; how far from you does he or she stand? When you are on a crowded elevator, have you wondered why people all tend to face the front, usually gazing at the lighted panel indicating which floor they are on, avoiding eye contact and conversation? All these examples suggest

that we have distances at which we feel comfortable in social interaction, depending on whom we are with and what we are doing, and that we react to situations in which these distances between us and others are violated. Sommer (1969) describes the physical space around us as our *personal space*, an area with invisible boundaries. The study of how we use space to regulate our social interactions is called **proxemics**.

Of course, personal space is tied to communication. For example, we can communicate feelings of intimacy by allowing someone to draw physically closer to us as we converse or we can send the opposite message by increasing distance. Hall (1966), an anthropologist, described four distances or "zones" at which people interact (at least in the U.S. where the research was conducted):

- Intimate distance (0 to 46 cm), such as that between close friends in conversation, a couple making love, a mother nursing or comforting her baby
- Personal distance (46 cm to 1.2 m), such as that between friends in casual conversation
- Social distance (1.2 to 2.1 m), the distance for rather formal meetings, seminars or business transactions
- Public distance (2.1 to 7.6 m), as typified by a lecture or speech in which the speakers must raise their voices

About 65 percent of our everyday interpersonal contact while standing occurs between approximately 46 cm and 60 cm. (Altman & Vinsel, 1977). In general, research supports the notion that we use these various distances to signify the type of interaction we are engaging in; for example, friends stand closer than strangers (Ashton, Shaw & Worsham, 1980) and people who are sexually attracted to each other stand even closer (Allegeier & Byrne, 1973).

However, we must be cautious about the estimated distances. Women tend to stand closer together than do men, particularly in same-sex dyads (Horowitz, Duff & Stratton, 1970). Moreover, there are considerable cultural variations. While North Americans, Britons and Swedes stand farthest away, Southern Europeans stand closer and Latin Americans and Arabs stand the closest (Hall, 1966; Sussman & Rosenfeld, 1982). This can lead to serious misunderstandings. For example, an English Canadian and a Latin American in conversation at a party have different spatial preferences; the English Canadian feels most comfortable at about 90–120 cm, while the Latin

American would ordinarily stand much closer. Unaware of the cultural differences the two unconsciously engage in a dance across the room, the Latin advancing and the English Canadian retreating. Then they part, the Latin feeling that the English Canadian was cold and unfriendly and the Canadian feeling that the Latin was pushy and excessively intimate.

Intrusions into one's personal space is generally anxiety-arousing, and bring blood pressure and heart rate changes that are correlated with anxiety (Sawada, 2003). Even "virtual" human beings lead us to maintain a personal space. Participants in three-dimensional virtual rooms maintained a greater distance from virtual humans when approaching them from the front

FIGURE 7-6

Perceived pleasantness of touch from same-sex and opposite-sex strangers and close friends for males and females

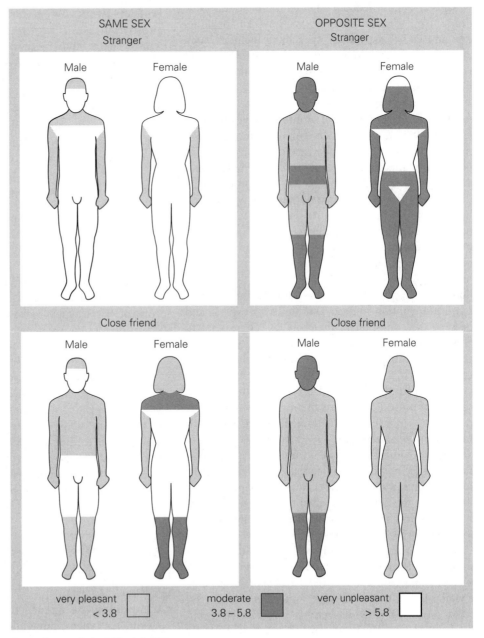

Source: Burgoon, Butler & Woodall, 1989

rather than the back and also maintained a greater distance when the virtual human made eye contact! (Bailenson, Blascovich, Beall & Loomis, 2003).

Paralanguage

We can say exactly the same words in different ways and thereby communicate different messages. The same utterance will be interpreted quite differently if it is said in a light-hearted manner or in a sonorous drone. Paralanguage refers to the "how" of speaking, the non-verbal aspects of speech; it includes such characteristics as volume, stress, pitch, speed, tone of voice, pauses and even non-linguistic sounds such as throat-clearing, grunts and sighs.

Timing, pitch and loudness (the so-called **prosodic features of language** in the terminology of linguists) (Argyle, 1975) are critically important in oral communication for they can confer very different meanings on the same set of words. Saying, "You pig!" to a friend dipping into a box of chocolates can communicate either friendly teasing or admonition, depending on how it is said. Children acquire the ability to use these prosodic elements such as raising the pitch at the end of a sentence to indicate a question early in their language development. Prosodic features of speech are used to give emphasis to certain points, to indicate doubt, to suggest what we are thinking and to communicate emotion. Indeed, our ability to express and perceive the emotional "tone" in speech is vital to communication and a deficit in either ability can have profound consequences for social relationships (Bachorowski, 1999).

Studies of individuals and of cultures suggest that the role of prosodic elements in the expression of emotion is not primarily a learned one for there is very little evidence of variation in this behaviour either among individuals in a given culture or across cultures. Thus, it seems that certain prosodic patterns may communicate specific emotions: aggression or dominance tends to be signalled by a low pitch while happiness and lack of aggressiveness usually involves a higher pitch (Frick, 1985).

Research suggests that often the total impact of a message is determined less by *what* is said than by *how* it is said; and, as we have noted, facial expressions play a vital role in how the message is interpreted by the listener especially when emotion is involved. However, spoken communications are themselves actually double-coded in the sense that meaning is conferred both by the grammar and by the non-verbal structure imposed by prosodic elements (Fonagy, 1971). As a result when spoken words are transcribed into print, punctuation must be added to convey the intended meaning. Even then, some of the message may be lost (Argyle, 1975). People are capable of separating the two communications and interpreting each one individually when the two message elements are inconsistent. For example, in one study (Solomon & Yaeger, 1969) students listened to a teacher talking about a student's work. When the emotion communicated prosodically was at odds with the verbal content of the message, the students tended to interpret the verbal communication as indicative of how the teacher felt about the student's work, and the prosodic information as indicative of how the teacher felt about the student. In fact, research has shown that paralanguage can actually impair one's memory for the specific meaning of utterances (Hertel & Navarez, 1986): in recalling a videotaped conversation, subjects confused *what* was said with *how* it was said. Thus, if someone says something critical, but in a friendly and jocular way, we may later remember the words as having been less harsh than they actually were.

Conversation control

One area in which non-verbal and verbal communication clearly complement each other is **conversation control**. While words make up the content of our conversation, non-verbal signals, especially prosodic cues, regulate its form. Without such regulation—using rules that we have all learned but would have difficulty writing down—conversations would turn into verbal traffic jams. The signals are subtle and not explicit, yet they are there: we seem to know intuitively when to speak and when to listen and we don't require a chairperson to monitor the flow of conversation. In every linguistic group, there are norms covering not only who speaks next but also virtually every aspect of the verbal exchange from beginning to end. Some of the "turn-yielding" signals we use were described by Argyle (1975):

- Coming to the end of a sentence.

- Prolonged intonation—for example, raising or lowering the voice: "Do you like this?"

- **Paralinguistic drawl**—the final syllable is drawn out: "And then I came ho-o-m-me."

- Body motion—if the speaker was using hand gestures, he now ceases; if the speaker's hands have appeared tense, they now relax. The speaker's eyes tend to open wider with the last note of a question, to indicate that the listener can begin to answer; if a question is being asked, the speaker tends to lift his or her head on the final syllable. In television interviews, it has been observed that people tend to look directly at the interviewer only when ready to finish making a point.

- Verbal cues—at the end of phrases: "I was going to go to the movies tonight, but, uh..."

What would happen if someone were to give one or more of these signals but instead of yielding continued to speak? Considerable confusion would be created and the listener would probably interrupt.

Other norms exist as well. For example, North Americans expect other people to respond to their statements right away, while in some cultures, people are taught to leave a gap between responses. As a result, North Americans tend to be uncomfortable if there are periods of silence during a conversation. On the other hand, people in cultures for whom scattered silences are normal may perceive North Americans as overly talkative, even thoughtless or disrespectful.

Sometimes we try to butt in while someone else is speaking. In this case, the speaker who wants to continue puts out **attempt-suppressing signals**: the voice maintains the same pitch; the head remains straight; the eyes remain unchanged; the hands maintain the same gesture; the speaker may speak slightly louder or faster and may keep a hand in mid-gesture at the end of sentences (Argyle, 1975).

How do we signal that we wish to terminate a conversation? When speaking face-to-face, we tend to move slightly away and to look away. (Looking at our watch is also a powerful signal!) When using the telephone, we may allow for a longer interval before responding to the speaker.

During a conversation, the listener regularly signals to the speaker that he or she is still listening and not seeking to interrupt. This is done by means of what is called back-channel communication: the listener nods from time to time, or says "mm-hmm" or "okay." In Japan, **back-channel communication** occurs at a higher rate than in North America (White, 1989). Thus, a Japanese person talking to a Canadian by telephone may frequently ask, "Are you still there?" because the Canadian emits back-channel signals at too slow a pace for the speaker. Back channel communication does more than tell the speaker that we are listening. Bavelas, Coates & Johnson (2000) carried out a study at the University of Victoria that examined the role of listener feedback (back channel communication) when listening to a narrator tell a story. They found that listeners were in a sense co-narrators in that their responses to the narration—in terms of nodding, making verbalizations such as "mhm," wincing and so on, that not only helped illustrate the story but affected the narrator's performance. When listeners were distracted so that they did not provide the same feedback, narrators told their stories less well.

Verbal Communication

It is thought that **language** evolved in primitive humans because of the survival value conferred by the ability to communicate precisely. While non-verbal behaviour may be a better guide to the speaker's feelings and intentions, it does not go very far in helping two people coordinate their attempts to build a bridge or defend a village.

All spoken language is based on a phonetic system in which short, meaningless sounds called **phonemes** are combined into units of meaning called **morphemes**. By using a relatively small number of these sounds (up to 45, depending on the language) and by combining them two, three or more at a time, different human languages have generated as many as 100 000 morphemes (Argyle, 1969). It was quite a step for our ancestors to go from speech to writing and initially a different symbol was used for each word (e.g., a hieroglyphic). Such a system necessitated a very large number of symbols. (Indeed, the Chinese evolved a set of 10 000 characters, each one representing a different word element in the language. These characters are still in use today, a situation that has posed problems with regard to literacy—in order to read a newspaper, it is necessary to know at least several thousand characters). In most languages, a few letters reflecting the spoken phonetic code rather than syllables or words eventually came to be used in place of thousands of symbols.

Language allows a social group to pass its knowledge, beliefs and values from generation to generation. The words of Plato, Shakespeare, Hobbes or Russell can inspire each new generation as much as they did when they were first uttered. Without language, modern culture as we know it could never have developed. Not only does language serve as a vehicle for transmission of ideas, but the form that language takes can itself reflect certain beliefs and values.

Indeed, language is an important aspect of group identity as will be discussed in Chapter 12.

Language and gender

An important aspect of the transmission of values through language is the way the English language has both reflected and reinforced the historical cultural view of masculine superiority and male domination (Smith, 1985). Until recently, we would say "his" instead of "his or her," and we would speak of *mankind, workmen's compensation boards* and so forth, as though women were not all that important. The great majority of agent nouns (e.g., *author, professor, doctor, minister*) evoke the image of a man more readily than that of a woman, while the addition of a diminutive suffix to obtain words such as *authoress* may reflect or lead to a diminution of the importance of the role. Indeed in a recent study (McConnell & Fazio, 1996), subjects rated a target person's personality as more masculine when the target was described as being a "chairman," rather than a "chair." The term *chairperson* led to even lower ratings of masculinity. Words are powerful agents of social perception.

Even the order of words in which the male referent traditionally occurs first—husband and wife, son and daughter, host and hostess—may imply relative importance. Indeed, our use of language has almost implied ownership of females by males: we speak of a woman whose husband has died as "Charley's widow" but are less likely to describe Charley, should his wife predecease him, as "Martha's widower" (Smith, 1985). And ponder this: Why when addressing an audience, do we refer to Ladies and Gentlemen in the introduction? Why is gender invoked at such a time? It makes no more sense, at least in the modern era, than "Good evening, short and tall."

Because of the power of language to not only reflect but also actually shape our cognitions, psychologists have become particularly concerned with the impact of sexist language. The Canadian Psychological Association and the American Psychological Association now both insist on non-sexist language in any manuscripts submitted to their journals. This policy is becoming more common in other areas of Canadian society as a result of growing concern about human rights.

Do women and men speak differently?

Many, if not most, people believe that men and women have typical and distinctive styles of speaking. Women are said to be more polite, more emotional, more positive and supportive in how they evaluate people, more tentative ("It's cold, *isn't it?*"), less assertive and more likely to talk about home and family. On the other hand, men are believed to use more slang and profanity, to argue, criticize, lecture and command more and to be more likely to talk about business, politics and sports. In addition, women are said to be more talkative than men.

Are these simply sex-role stereotypes? The research evidence suggests that there is some reality in these characterizations of male and female speakers, although these differences may be disappearing as social norms change and as women gradually assume levels of power that men have always enjoyed in social relationships. Men tend to use more non-standard forms of speech, such as new terminology (often technical), slang, profanity and puns. Men are more likely to talk about sports, business and politics and women are more likely to talk about family and home. Men are more likely to use words and expressions about time, space and quantity and about hostility and destructiveness while women refer more to emotional states. Men tend to be more direct and assertive in making requests. On the other hand while little girls tend to talk more than little boys, adult women tend to talk less, particularly in the presence of the opposite sex.

Indeed, male–female interactions can sometimes lead to much misunderstanding because of such gender differences. Men are more likely to speak and hear a language of status and independence while women are more likely to speak and hear a language of connection and intimacy (Tannen, 1990). Thus, a woman who tells her male partner that she wishes that he would skip bowling and stay home with her may be seeking emotional closeness while her partner may interpret the request in terms of a threat to his independence and an attempt to control.

Differences in the way that males and females use language have also been observed in the workplace. A study of managers in the business world focused on how male and female career professionals deliver criticism to a colleague. Mulac, Siebold & Farris (2000) found that language use by males and females was so distinctive that it allowed them to accurately determine the gender of the respondent 72 percent of the time, looking at such factors as average sentence length (longer for women), number of judgmental adjectives (more for men) and the number of intensive adverbs (more for women).

Word Power

Ideas, provided that they can be communicated to others, can be much more dangerous than any armament; the pen, so it has been often said, is mightier than the sword. However, words sometimes have power that is almost independent of their meaning. Consider a made-up word, *fac.* One can safely pronounce that monosyllable without fear that anyone will react with any more than a puzzled look, perhaps thinking that one meant to say *fact.* Now change the word slightly to another monosyllable, *fuck.* Seeing the word in print, particularly in a respectable textbook such as this, is enough to arouse considerable negative emotion in many people, and in the not so distant past—a mere 40 or so years ago, would have prevented the book from being published for it was considered a terrible obscenity. While the origin of the word is lost in history (and is not, as some urban legends suggest, connected to acronyms such as that derived from For Undue Carnal Knowledge), that little monosyllable along with some of its sexually related relatives have been taboo words for centuries even though some people, almost always male, used it regularly out of earshot of "decent" women and "respectable" society. The word did not appear in any English language dictionary between 1795 and 1965! Recall (in Chapter 5) that reading a list including words such as "fuck" constituted a "severe" initiation for undergraduate research participants in 1959!

In recent years, *fuck* has come into its own and is now used as a common expletive, or simply to add a bit of emphasis, by both men and women and indeed by boys and girls, teenagers particularly. It is used in all sorts of ways that have nothing to do with its original sexual meaning and it is used in more ways—as a noun, or a verb or in an adjectival form—and to mean more things, many having nothing to do with its original sexual connotation, than almost any other word in the English language (e.g., "You are a stupid fuck," "Fuck what the government says," "All fucked up," "I don't give a fuck," "Why the fuck did you do that?").

According to White (2002), there are in excess of 2.5 million web pages with the word *fuck* indexed, and:

> Fuck is a ubiquitous word, heard everywhere and used in an amazing variety of ways, by young and old alike. From schoolyards to television, street cafes to radio station, its usage is, today, commonplace.

How did such a once-taboo word come to be so commonly used today? And how did such a word originally associated with sex come to take on such an angry edge? What does that reflect about the evolution of our society? However, the power of this word to produce autonomic arousal has not totally diminished despite its common employment. Students may use the word frequently but still feel a sense of shock if a physician or a university lecturer were to refer to *fucking* instead of *intercourse* or *love-making* when discussing sexuality. A recent series of advertisements bore the letters FCUK (acronym for French Connection, United Kingdom, a clothing retailer) with the obvious intention of using the shock value that derives even from a word resembling *fuck.*

Moreover, the use of this word sometimes still elicits a strong reaction from authority and, since it is more likely to be used by people in some sub-cultures than in others, it can lead to discrimination. White (2002) points out that in Australia, aboriginal youth are often the victims of the selective use of Australia's laws against offensive language. He argues that Australian laws dealing with offensive language are a key mechanism in the social control of young indigenous people by the police, and that the application of such laws serves to reinforce popular stereotypes of "indigenous deviancy."

Amongst contemporary youth, *fuck* has become so common that the word is often used without any

(continued)

intent to offend others and without realization of the deep offence that the word is still capable of causing. To the degree that older people do find the word offensive, it serves as a means of social identification and rejection of authority.

Indeed as Drury (2003) has noted, adults, particularly those in positions of authority, typically view adolescents as lacking in communication ability, and the frequent use of swear words reinforces this perception. Adolescents, on the other hand, typically view the problems in communicating with adults as stemming from issues of power and lack of respect for them.

There are also differences between the sexes with respect to the paralinguistic aspects of speech, some of which are based in physiology: so-called feminine speech qualities such as higher pitch, softer volume, more variability and a more relaxed and pleasant tone of voice lead listeners to attribute lower social power, lower intellectual ability and greater interpersonal warmth to the speaker (Montepare & Vega, 1988), reflecting existing stereotypes and differences in power and status.

Both sexes, however, may adapt their speech to the sex of the listener. Women tend to abandon feminine speech and become louder and more dominant when speaking to men perhaps in an effort to reduce a perceived power disadvantage (Hall & Braunwald, 1981). On the other hand, women's voices become more "feminine" when they are talking to an intimate male friend rather than a male acquaintance or stranger (Montepare & Vega, 1988). Interestingly, the pitch of women who are assuming more powerful, traditionally male positions in society is becoming somewhat lower. This is most obvious if one compares the pitch of female newsreaders today with that of the few such women in the field a generation ago.

There are particular conversation styles that, within a given culture, may be taken to indicate that the speaker is high in social power and certain other styles that correspond with powerlessness. Those in a position of dominance or power usually interrupt more. Those lacking in power are more likely to use *intensifiers* such as "very," "really," or "so"; *hedges* such as "kind of," "sort of," and "you know"; *intonations*, which involve a rising pattern in making an ordinary declarative statement; *tag questions* such as, "They did really well, didn't they?"; and *polite forms of address* (Lakoff, 1975; Wiemann & Giles, 1988). Some studies have found that women often tend to address men using a powerless speech style, although this phenomenon is not universal (Wiemann & Giles, 1988). When it does occur, it most likely reflects the fact that even in contemporary society, women are often relegated to less powerful positions than are men. (We shall discuss power further in Chapter 10.) Indeed, one study found that when a woman was in discussion with a man, she was actually more influential when she spoke in a tentative way than when she was assertive, although the opposite was true when she was in discussion with a woman. Conversational style had no effect on how influential men were either with women or with men (Carli, 1990).

Language and Social Interaction

We have seen that language is a central feature in human social interaction. Verbal utterances, like other behaviours, are subject to reinforcement by the reactions of others. According to **speech act theory** (Searle, 1969, 1975), a spoken sentence is more than just a set of symbols linked together; it is a collection of acts. By that we mean there is not always a close correspondence between what is said and what the speaker wants to accomplish by saying it. (Recall how the expression "You pig" can have several different meanings depending on how it is said.) Speech act theory distinguishes between *direct* speech acts in which the meaning of the sentence is consistent with the speaker's meaning and *indirect* speech acts, which lack consistency. The choice of direct or indirect speech acts is often influenced by perceived equality or difference in status between speaker and listener and by the need to maintain "face" (a good public image), among other things.

Through the use of indirect acts, we can avoid direct challenges to authority or to high-status individuals. Suppose you disagree with a pronouncement by your professor. You might start by saying something like "I am not quite sure that I follow you. I don't understand how, if capitalism is related to Protestantism...." The professor, on the other hand, would be more likely to use a direct speech act: " No, you don't understand...." Status difference has a strong influence on the kinds of speech acts chosen.

Indirect speech acts can often spare loss of face (Holtgraves, 1986). For example, if Martha is worried that her co-workers might think her new dress is unbecoming, instead of asking, "Do you like my new dress?" might say, "I bought a new dress!" and point to herself. Instead of commenting that the dress is ugly, which would be a threat to Martha's self-esteem, a co-worker could respond by saying, "Well, it certainly is interesting. Where did you get it?" Face has been spared by the indirect response, but the judgment has also been conveyed. Research has demonstrated that indirect speech acts are indeed more likely than direct ones in face-threatening situations (Holtgraves, 1986). In our daily interactions with others, we continually try to help people save face just as we strive to maintain our own self-esteem.

Every verbal expression demands some degree of response and the degree to which a response is required is actually encoded in the utterance itself (Holtgraves, 1986). When the co-worker asked Martha where she had bought her dress, there was a demand for a response to that question but a clear indication that no response was required to the comment that the dress

was "interesting." Thus Martha was not required to explore exactly what that descriptor meant.

Speech style

The way that people express themselves verbally is "remarkably reliable" across time and situations (Pennebaker & King, 1999). Differences in **speech style** are used as markers of social status helping us to form impressions of others and as indicators of belonging to various social and cultural categories. By listening to a person talk, we can estimate his social class, education and often place of origin (Giles & Powesland, 1975). In Great Britain, especially, some linguists can accurately determine the region of a person's origin—and social class—by listening to her speech. (Recall the words from *My Fair Lady*: "An Englishman's way of speaking absolutely classifies him. The moment he talks he makes some other Englishman despise him.") In the United States, distinctions are also possible: for example, the Brooklyn accent would never be confused with the upper class Boston accent or the Texas drawl!

Canadian English is a blend of U.S. and British English. Geography and accent are much less related in Canada than in the United States or Europe, but even here, there are some distinctive regional variations. For example, francophones from Quebec City and Montreal have different accents (Vinay, Daviault & Alexander, 1962). Anglophones across the country speak in a more or less homogeneous way (Vinay et al., 1962), but Newfoundland and Ottawa Valley accents show some distinctiveness.

Speech style is so important socially that we make inferences not only about people's social class, ethnicity or education but even about their personality and intelligence. We often judge people by their command of language. It is curious, considering the thousands and thousands of words we must learn, that we are often surprised or disappointed when educated people mispronounce a word. It is enough to influence our evaluation of their intellect and "breeding"; yet we accept and even expect mispronunciation from people having little education and it might strike us as odd if we heard a mechanic or a bus driver using "big" words. Vocabulary is more important than grammar in this context; differences in the complexity of vocabulary used by an individual have been found to affect perceptions of competence (Bradac, Davies, Courtright, Desond & Murdock, 1977).

The speech styles of students have been found to affect teachers' judgments of their intelligence as much or more than actual samples of their school work (Seligman, Tucker & Lambert, 1972). In Great Britain, the opportunity for socioeconomic advancement can be seriously affected by accent, and educated people with the "wrong" accent (Cockney, for example) sometimes take elocution lessons to "correct" their speech style. Even in the United States, speech is an important source of information about social status: One study reported a strong correlation between a listener's judgment of a speaker's social status and the speaker's actual social status (Giles & Powesland, 1975). The French are perhaps even more particular in this regard, with native Parisians generally viewing their speech style as superior to all others (see A Case in Point—"I Speak Parisian French").

Standard and non-standard speech styles

Not all varieties of a particular language are treated as equal. Those who speak in a more "refined" manner view some speech styles as being "vulgar" or "low class." Research around the world has demonstrated that from childhood through adulthood, use of the **standard speech style** not only gives an impression of status and competence but elicits cooperation (Wiemann & Giles, 1988; Stewart, Ryan & Giles, 1985).

How is it that one speech style comes to be the "standard" or prestige form against which others are judged? Is standard speech more aesthetically pleasing? If Cockney English or Acadian French sounds less pleasant to some than Oxford English or Parisian French, is it because they actually are less pleasant? Or is it because the listener is reacting to the imposition of a particular accent as the prestige norm? These two possibilities were explored in a study conducted by Giles, Bourhis and Davies (1977), who articulated them in the form of two hypotheses:

THE INHERENT VALUE HYPOTHESIS The standard dialect became the prestige form of the language because it evolved as the aesthetically ideal form of that language.

THE IMPOSED NORM HYPOTHESIS Standard and non-standard dialects are equally aesthetically pleasing, but the non-standard form is viewed negatively because of social norms biased against it.

To test these two hypotheses, researchers had Welsh students who knew no French listen to tape-recordings of the same text spoken by the same person in three different French accents: European ("standard") French, educated Canadian French and working-class Canadian French. Subjects then rated the speech in terms of pleasantness and aesthetic appeal and also rated the speaker in terms of status, intelligence, likability, ambition and toughness. While previous studies had shown that Quebec francophone listeners rated these French accents very differently on each of the ratings (d'Anglejan & Tucker, 1973), no significant differences were noted by the Welsh subjects, supporting the imposed-norm hypothesis. The imposed-norm hypothesis received further validation in a similar study in which British undergraduates who knew no Greek were exposed to both Cretan and the more prestigious Athenian dialects; again, they were unable to pick out the prestige form of the language (Giles, Bourhis, Trudgill & Lewis, 1974).

People learning a second language usually learn the prestige form and thus tend to view other forms as substandard. This affects not just the evaluation of the language but also the evaluation of the person who speaks it. For example, when undergraduate students studying elementary French at McMaster University were asked to rate tape-recorded speakers speaking with either a standard European French accent, a Franco-Ontarian accent, a Québécois accent or an anglophone accent, the standard European French speakers were rated highest in terms of intelligence and linguistic competence while English-accented speakers were rated the least favourably, with the Québécois and Franco-Ontarian accents being rated midway between the two (Hume, Lepicq & Bourhis, 1992).

The prestige associated with the arbitrarily chosen standard dialect is so strong that studies conducted in the early 1970s showed French-speaking Québécois, both workers and students, to have strong preference for European French over their own Quebec French (d'Anglejan & Tucker, 1973)! However, this bias may well have vanished since, given the renewed pride in Québécois culture.

Speech registers

Within a given speech style, there are various **speech registers** or combinations of intonation and pitch, that are employed in different situations. Often different levels of vocabulary are involved as well. We all use different registers in different situations. For example, a professor does not speak to students and colleagues in the same manner—to use the speech register of the

"I Speak Parisian French"

How is it that Parisian French is taken to be the paragon of that language?

Following the French Revolution in 1794, the Parisian bourgeoisie promoted laws to enforce the linguistic and economic unity of France. The use of languages such as Breton in Brittany and Provençal in southern France was banned and the Parisians chose their own "Île de France" variety of French as the national standard of spoken French (Bourhis, 1982). (A more charitable view has been expressed that the revolutionary leaders wanted to ensure that all citizens of France would have the opportunity to rise to the top of society by learning the speech style of those who ruled the country and dominated the universities (Pagès, 1986).) All other varieties of French were vigorously excluded so that the use of non-standard accents and dialects of regional French was banned in schools. To this day, the "Île de France" variety of French is considered the "standard" or "international" style of the French language (Bourhis, 1982).

The French-speaking population of Quebec was not affected because for 200 years following the defeat of Montcalm's army on the Plains of Abraham in 1760, Quebec was virtually cut off from France. During that time, Quebec French and Île de France French evolved quite independently. (Some other francophone groups in Canada such as the Franco-Manitobans trace their ancestry to post-Revolutionary France. It is possible that there are distinctive cultural differences between them and the Québécois as a result.) Even today, the decision by the Parisian bourgeoisie to impose their speech style upon others still leads some people, both anglophone and francophone, to denigrate Quebec French and other non-Parisian French, as "inferior." Modern Quebecers, however, now take justifiable pride in their own speech style that has survived relatively unchanged across several centuries.

classroom situation in a conversation with a colleague or friend would seem quite odd.

The use of certain speech registers reflects a speaker's power relative to the listener. (The speech register used by lecturers provides a familiar example.) In some situations, the choice of speech register can have debilitating effects by reminding listeners of their relative lack of power and independence. For example, one speech register that we all are familiar with is what linguists refer to as **baby talk** or BT. By BT, we are referring not to the way babies speak but to the way adults talk to two- to five-year-olds. It is recognizable by its high pitch and exaggerated intonations (Caporael, Lukaszewski & Culbertson, 1983), and it is a feature of all languages (Ferguson, 1977).

Of more interest to the social psychologist is **secondary baby talk**, which is the use of the BT register in contexts other than talking to babies. Most of us would resent being spoken to in such a manner for we would find it belittling. However, such talk appears to be rather common in institutions for the elderly. Caporael (1981) conducted a field study in a private nursing home in California and found that nearly a quarter of the communications by nurse's aides to elderly patients were in baby talk. While college students who subsequently listened to recordings of the nurse's aides' speech judged the baby talk to be more positive (because of its "nurturant" quality) than non-baby talk, only those elderly people who actually had lower functional ability tended to prefer baby talk. Baby talk to the elderly may promote helplessness and dependency. Indeed in the institutional setting, BT may reflect a process of establishing social control (Ryan, Bartolucci, Giles & Henwood, 1986). In another study (LaTourette & Meeks, 2000), elderly women in a nursing home were spoken to by nurses either in a patronizing style or a non-patronizing style. Those spoken to in a patronizing style were judged by non-residents to be less competent as though these non-residents were in effect "blaming the victim."

Do we use a different speech register to speak to foreigners or to mentally handicapped adults? To answer this question, a study was conducted in which undergraduate women taught a block-design task either to a six-year-old child, a mentally handicapped adult, a peer who spoke English as a second language or a peer who was an unimpaired native speaker of English (DePaulo & Coleman, 1986). It was found that the speech addressed to children was clearer and simpler, used more techniques to maintain attention and included longer pauses. Speech addressed to mentally handicapped adults was similar but even more babyish in some ways (e.g., repetitiveness). On the other hand speech addressed to foreigners, apart from being more repetitive, was not different from that spoken to native speakers.

The way we talk to people tells them a great deal about how we view them. Talking to mentally handicapped people as though they are children may well reinforce feelings of immaturity and helplessness and discourage them from developing to their fullest potential.

Communication accommodation

Do you speak any differently to a person of low education than you would to your lawyer, physician or professor? If you are chatting at a party with a well-educated individual one minute and the next minute find yourself alone with another person whose speech suggests a poor education, does your manner of speech change? People often shift or converge towards the speaking style of the other person although there are times when we are most careful not to converge—we may even on occasion diverge—that is, emphasize the features of our speech style or register that accentuate the difference between "us and them."

Why do people shift their speech style or register in some instances and not in others? According to **communication accommodation theory** (Giles & Wadleigh, 1999), in order to be liked or to fit in, we may modify our speech style so that it is more like the other person's. This process is referred to as *convergence* (Giles, 1973). Convergence may be upward—trying to speak in the style of a speaker from a more

---

Medicine, Language and Power

Most people view physicians as successful, intelligent and high in status and power. Indeed, they exercise a high degree of power in all medical encounters with patients (Watson & Gallois, 2002). When a physician asks someone to undress, the person rarely asks, "Why?" If the physician tells the patient to take two of the little green pills and one of the large red pills each day, few people seek understanding of what the pills really do, what their side effects might be and so forth. They not only trust, they usually dare not ask. Thus, it should come as no surprise that physicians' speech styles reflect power in their interactions with their patients. In summarizing the research from two different studies (Fisher, & Todd, 1983; West, 1984), Wiemann and Giles (1988) found that physicians maintain a very strong position of power in such interactions:

- Physician does most of the talking.
- Physician initiates 99 percent of the utterances.
- Patient poses only 9 percent of the questions asked.
- Physician asks further questions before patient has been able to answer previous one.
- Most interruptions are by physician except when physician is female.
- Physician determines topics of discussion.
- Physician determines when interaction ends.

Such an interaction not only reflects the imbalance in social power but also often leaves the patient feeling as though he or she has not obtained all the information that was desired from a visit to the doctor. Perhaps this contributes to the serious problem of non-compliance with "doctor's orders."

prestigious group—or it may be downward when, for example, an employer from a high-status group tries to be "one of the boys" in interactions with workers. Even one-year-old children show convergence to the pitch patterns of their parents: they lower the basic frequency of their babbling in the presence of the father and raise it in the presence of the mother (Giles & Smith, 1979). However, too much convergence may appear as an attempt at ingratiation or even as mockery. Imagine how British visitors would feel if we tried to mimic their British accent, speech rate and verbal expressions all at once! In each interaction, some optimal level of convergence is needed to gain favourable responses from the listener (Giles & Smith, 1979).

Communication accommodation theory incorporates ideas from four different areas of social psychology: similarity-attraction, social-exchange, intergroup distinctiveness and causal attribution.

- *Similarity-attraction theory* (to be discussed in Chapter 8) suggests that the more similar we are to others in terms of attitudes and beliefs, the more likely it is that we will be attractive to them. Convergence is one way to increase our similarity to other people. Our speech will show a degree of convergence according to how much we want to be liked or approved of (Giles, Taylor & Bourhis, 1973).

- *Social exchange theory* (also to be discussed in Chapter 8) reminds us that convergence may carry with it certain costs as well as rewards. We must evaluate whether we will be perceived as having lost integrity or whether our group identity will be compromised. If the potential costs exceed the rewards, then social exchange theory predicts that convergence would not occur (Giles & Smith, 1979).

- Maintaining *intergroup distinctiveness* (to be discussed in Chapter 12) is an important motivation for groups who feel that their language and culture is threatened. We are likely to see divergence of speech style or register when members of a minority group are interacting with people from a majority group that threatens to assimilate them.

- According *to causal attribution theory* (discussed in Chapter 2), whether or not we react positively to another's convergence would depend upon what we took to be the motives behind it. For example in a study conducted by Simard, Taylor and Giles (1977), French Canadian listeners reacted favourably to an anglophone's convergence to French when they

believed that he was motivated by a desire to break down cultural barriers but not when they were led to believe that he had been forced by circumstances to converge. Conversely, when the anglophone did not converge, the reaction was less negative when the non-convergence was attributed to social circumstances beyond the speaker's control than when it apparently reflected a lack of effort.

Not only does language play an important role in social interactions between individuals, but it also helps groups mark boundaries and define identities. Adolescents' language, while often the bane of their parents, serves first of all to maintain distinctive group boundaries, helping to differentiate themselves from adults and from other groups of adolescents (Ekert, 2003), and secondly to strengthen their individual social identities and promote acceptance within their own group (Fortman, 2003).

Inability to converge to another's speech register can contribute to communication breakdown. An important everyday example is provided by patients who feel unable to communicate with their physicians (recall the Critical Thinking—Medicine, Language and Power). Bourhis, Roth and MacQueen (1989) examined how medical practitioners speak to their patients. The patients and physicians in their study all agreed that it is important for physicians to converge to the patient's speech register rather than vice-versa. Indeed, physicians believed that while they spoke medical language to other health professionals, they converged to the everyday language of their patients when addressing them. However, patients perceived little convergence by physicians, an opinion that squared with the observations of student nurses. Patients reported that they actually tried to converge to medical language when speaking to physicians. Interestingly, similar problems can arise between general practitioners and specialists, the former often being unfamiliar with the terminology spoken by the latter (Barcia, 1985). Physicians enjoy higher status and power than patients, and medical specialists have even more status. It is not surprising to find that the less powerful converge to the speech register of the more powerful.

Communication between bilingual speakers

In response to the growing vigour of the *indépendantiste* movement in Quebec in the 1960s, Canada adopted a policy of official bilingualism. The *Official Languages Act* was passed by Parliament in 1969 declaring that both French and English have equal status as official languages in this country. This policy, which included the provision of bilingual services and schooling where numbers warrant, was intended to demonstrate to francophones that they could be at home not only in Quebec but in the whole of Canada (Bourhis, 1990). Efforts were undertaken to attract more francophones to the federal public service and to teach French to anglophone government workers.

The official bilingualism policy of the federal government improved the provision of French-language services to francophones across Canada and led to an increase in the proportion of francophone civil servants from 21 percent in 1969 to 27 percent in 2002 (Commissioner of Official Languages, 2003).

Nonetheless, despite two decades of effort, a serious imbalance remains in the use of the two official languages in the federal civil service (Bourhis, 1990; Nadon, 1990). All too often, English tends to be used between bilingual anglophones and francophones, depriving the former of the opportunity to practise their French and the latter of the opportunity to work in their own language. Why should this be so? What determines which language is spoken when bilingual individuals of different mother tongues interact? Of course, linguistic skills play an important role. If one person is fluently bilingual while the other has some difficulty in the second language, they will tend to use the language that is easier for both. In some cases, norms governing the particular situation apply. A salesperson, for example, uses the client's language.

Another important factor is **ethnolinguistic vitality**. This term refers to the relative status and strength of a language in a particular social structure (Giles, Bourhis & Taylor, 1977). It reflects the proportion of the population that belongs to the particular language group, their socioeconomic status and the extent of institutional support for the language (such as schools and newspapers). Related to ethnolinguistic vitality is the "linguistic landscape"—the extent to which a language is displayed on public and commercial signs (Landry & Bourhis, 1997). Thus, the ethnolinguistic vitality of French is high in Quebec City but low in Moose Jaw. A bilingual anglophone and a bilingual francophone meeting in Moose Jaw will probably speak English, whereas if they meet in Quebec City, they will probably speak French (Bourhis, 1979). Studies of language switching in bilingual Montreal

and nearly unilingual Quebec City confirm the importance of the relative positions of language groups in the societal structure (Genesee & Bourhis, 1982; 1988). Willingness to communicate in a second language is in part determined by ethnolinguistic vitality (Clément, Baker, & MacIntyre, 2003), and ethnolinguistic vitality has also been identified as important to an understanding of individual behaviour and attitudes as well as intergroup relations in the rapidly changing social structure of South Africa (Bornman & Appelgryn, 1996).

Communication accommodation is also relevant: convergence to English by francophones may reflect not only a desire to communicate efficiently but also a conscious or unconscious effort to socially integrate with a more powerful social group (Bourhis, 1990).

Bourhis (1990) examined the factors that determine choice of language in a bilingual work setting in the federal civil service in New Brunswick, which is the only officially bilingual province. Anglophones in New Brunswick are the dominant, high-status group, so it is not surprising that francophones were more likely to converge to English than vice versa. Although bilingual anglophones were more likely to use French where there were more francophones, the presence of even a minority of unilingual anglophones led to substantially less use of French. This may be due simply to the need to communicate effectively. Language skill was also important. The more skillful an individual was in the second language, the more likely that language was to be used (Bourhis, 1994a).

Lack of linguistic skill can generate anxiety and a non-fluent speaker may misattribute this anxiety to the other person and react negatively to the individual, to the language or to speakers of it in general. Segalowitz (1976) conducted a study in which English-speaking students with medium ability in oral French either listened and spoke to or simply listened to two ostensibly different interlocutors—one speaking in French, the other in English. (Actually, a tape-recorded message of the same speaker speaking in the two languages was used.) For one group within each language condition, the interlocutor spoke in a formal style, while for a second group, he or she used a casual style. The subjects then rated their own levels of anxiety, their ease of communication and the personality of the speaker.

The results showed that the subjects felt more relaxed and thought they were better understood in the formal French condition than in the casual condition, just the opposite of what they felt when speaking English. Even more interesting however is the fact that when French was used, subjects who spoke as well as listened rated the personality of the interlocutor more positively in the formal condition. When English was involved, the casual condition resulted in the most positive personality rating (see Figure 7–7).

When subjects only listened but were not required to talk, the casual style led to the highest personality ratings of both the French and English speakers, but the difference was even more pronounced in ratings of the French speakers. These results support the idea that the discomfort felt by the subjects was misattributed. They felt uncomfortable speaking to the interlocutor and therefore concluded that they didn't like the person. This outcome is in line with Bem's (1972) self-perception theory (see Chapter 3): "I feel uncomfortable talking to him" becomes "He makes me feel uncomfortable," and therefore, "I don't like his personality very much."

Second-language learning

While Canadians continue to wrestle with issues related to bilingualism, it may be surprising to learn that most people in the world are bilingual (Tucker, 1981). Bilingualism is common in many European and Asian nations and is growing as a result of the European Community. The North American Free Trade Agreement is also fostering second-language learning;

the 86 000 000 Spanish speakers in Mexico and the 7 000 000 French speakers in Canada may turn the North American common market into a trilingual marketplace (Bourhis, 1994b).

Since Canada has not followed the "melting pot" strategy of the United States, many descendants of immigrants have learned their parents' tongue as well as they have English or French. Not to be forgotten are the languages of the indigenous peoples of Canada, which are sadly ignored when linguistic policy is discussed. These languages have a long history and are fully adaptable to the complexities of our modern technological society (Darnell, 1971). Yet school children are almost never taught about the diversity of Native languages. There are six distinct languages indigenous to North America and four of them— Algonquin (which includes Cree), Athabascan, Iroquoian and Inuktitut—are widely spoken among Native Canadians. These languages differ from each other more than French differs from English or English from Ukrainian (Darnell, 1971).

Bilingualism is growing across Canada (see A Practical Question—Bilingualism in Canada on page 203). Approximately two-thirds of Canadians report that they speak English at home, while a quarter speak French at home. In 1996, 17 percent of the population indicated that they can carry on a conversation both in English and French, an increase from the 13.4 percent reported in the 1971 census—an increase of one million people (see Figure 7–8) (Statistics Canada, 1997).

FIGURE 7-7

Mean personality rating of interlocutors by speakers and listeners

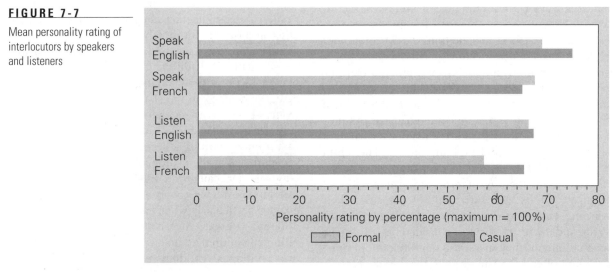

Source: Segalowitz, 1976

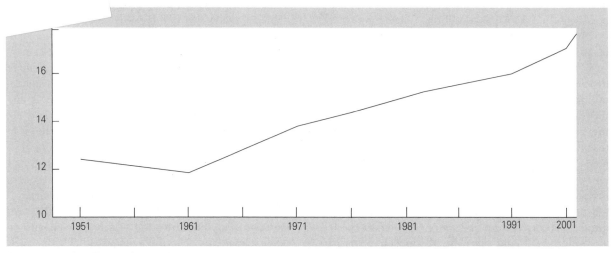

Jian population able to conduct a conversation in both English and
171, 1981, 1991 and 2001

Source: Adapted from Statistics Canada, 2003

Misconceptions about learning a second language

Several popular but erroneous beliefs dissuade people from even attempting to learn a second language, among them the following.

It is very difficult for an adult to learn a second language because the ability to acquire language is strongest in childhood and wanes in the pubertal years. On the contrary, research shows that adults are almost always better at language learning than children, except with regard to pronunciation (MacNamara, 1973; McLaughlin, 1977) and older children usually learn more quickly than younger children (Ervin-Tripp, 1974). We often underestimate the tremendous difficulty a child has in acquiring language, despite the fact that a child learning a first language enjoys a more comprehensive and profound exposure to it than an adult does learning a second language (McLaughlin, 1977). The child must expend a great deal of effort and make many mistakes along the way. In terms of learning a second language, adults with their ability to organize their learning—to use a dictionary, to see regularities in verbs and so forth—have a considerable advantage over children if they invest the same amount of time. Children often invest more time than adults realize; they are busy learning the language when they play with friends. They also are less likely to be inhibited about speaking it.

Children do have an advantage with regard to accent. By the time one reaches adolescence, the neurophysiological mechanisms involved in the production of sounds are generally no longer plastic enough to adapt to the requirements of a new accent.

Learning a second language is quite different from learning a first language and there is considerable "interference" in that a word in one language that is similar to one in another language might have quite a different meaning. Intuitively, we might expect that a person acquiring a second language does so in a way that is qualitatively different from the way in which a person learns a first language, since in the former case, the person can translate from the new language to his or her own. Yet there is no clear evidence to support this view and a number of studies indicate that a child learning a second language follows the same process of acquisition as a native speaker of that language (McLaughlin, 1987). In fact, very little interference seems to occur between the two languages, particularly when each language is used in a different context. And contrary to popular belief, bilingual children do not seem to have any advantage over unilingual children in the learning of a third language (Plastre, 1974).

Bilingualism in Canada

According to the 2001 census (Statistics Canada, 2002), while about 84 percent of Canadians are of English or French mother tongue (58 percent and 23 percent respectively), several other languages are also well represented: Chinese (2.7 percent), Italian (1.5 percent), German (1.4 percent) and Punjabi (0.9 percent) are next in order. Aboriginal languages combined account for 0.6 percent. The two largest Aboriginal language groups are Cree (72 885 people) and Inuktitut (29 010).

The census also reveals the following:

- Canada is becoming more multilingual as a result of immigration from non-English and non-French speaking countries. By 2001, there were almost 5 335 000 allophones (people having a mother tongue other than English or French) in Canada—about one out of every six people. This was an increase of 12.5 percent from 1996, three times the growth rate of 4.0 percent for the population as a whole.
- English–French bilingualism in Canada is increasing: 5 231 500 people reported to the 2001 Census that they were bilingual compared with 4 841 300 five years earlier, an 8.1 percent increase; 43.4 percent of francophones reported that they were bilin-

gual compared with 9.0 percent of anglophones.

- The bilingualism rate increased in every province except Manitoba and Saskatchewan; the decline in those two provinces was related to the decrease in their francophone populations. The francophone population of Ontario was 509 300, up 1.9 percent, while there were 62 250 francophones in Alberta, a 12.6 percent increase.
- Canada-wide, 43.4 percent of francophones were bilingual compared to 9 percent of anglophones. Outside Quebec, 84 percent of francophones were bilingual compared to 7 percent of anglophones, while the rate of bilingualism amongst Quebec anglophones (66.1 percent) was almost double that of francophones (36.6 percent).
- English–French bilingualism is highest in Quebec (going from 28 percent in 1971 to 38 percent in 1996 to 40.8 percent in 2001) followed by New Brunswick (1971: 22 percent; 1996: 32.6 percent; 2001: 34.2 percent) and Ontario (1971: 9 percent; 1991: 11.4 percent; 1996: 11.6 percent; 2001: 11.7 percent).

Source: Statistics Canada, 2003

Immersion programs in schools

Because of growing social and political recognition of both English and French as official languages in Canada, there is increasing interest across the country in fostering bilingualism among children. **Immersion programs** in which the child learns the second language, not as a subject, but through being exposed to it as the language of instruction and interaction, have spread across Canada. In 1978, 237 schools in Canada offered French immersion, with an enrolment of 37 835 students. By 1995, these numbers had grown to 2131 schools and more than 313 000 students (Commissioner of Official Languages, 1995).

Social psychologists in Canada have taken the lead in studying the effectiveness of French immersion.

The St. Lambert project in Montreal, which began in 1965, pioneered immersion schooling and generated a great deal of research into the consequences of receiving one's education in a second language (Lambert & Tucker, 1972). Social psychological theory suggested that young children learning French would be much less affected than older children by ethnic stereotypes, which might interfere with language acquisition. Furthermore, learning French at such an age was expected to produce more tolerant attitudes towards francophones (Genesee, 1984). Children began learning French in kindergarten, and in Grade 1 all subjects were taught only in French. Children were not taught to read in English and their parents were urged not to teach them how at home.

Starting in Grade 2, with a half-hour daily period of instruction in English language arts, the amount of English used increased so that by Grade 7 a little over half of the curriculum was taught in English. The children were not in any way preselected except that their parents desired their enrollment in the program. They were matched with two other groups of students, francophone children instructed in French and anglophone children instructed in English (Lambert & Tucker, 1972).

While the children did not succeed in speaking French as well as native French speakers, they spoke at a level that anglophone students in a French-as-a-second-language program could never achieve. No difference was found in ability to speak and read English between this group and the conventionally educated English students (Lambert, 1974a, 1974b) and the same was true of their ability when tested in English on a subject taught in French such as mathematics. Thus, the children suffered no apparent detrimental effects in terms of their English-language competence or in terms of their general cognitive development. Not only did they attain a high proficiency in French, but they also developed a positive attitude towards francophones while maintaining a healthy attitude towards their own linguistic group.

While there have been fears in the past that immersion schooling might involve some hidden costs such as slower progress in the student's mother tongue or poorer attainment in non-language areas, research indicates that these fears are groundless (Hakuta & Garcia, 1989; Tucker, 1981). However, the same studies have also confirmed that although immersion students achieve very high levels of competence in French, their competence is still not quite that of a native speaker.

Acquiring competence in a second language might well be expected to have important social psychological consequences such as engendering more positive attitudes towards the target language group. Indeed when students have the opportunity both to become bilingual and to mix with members of both linguistic groups, barriers do appear to come down. Guimond and Palmer (1993) examined the attitudes of francophone and anglophone students studying the other language. They found that the greater the degree of bilingualism, the less the favouritism displayed towards the mother-tongue group. Bilinguals appear to see themselves as members of both the anglophone and francophone groups.

Becoming bilingual involves more than just learning a second language; it also requires mastering a new set of social norms. We must learn to recognize when and how the intent of a communication in the second language is different from the meaning of the words spoken. Skill at using a language in a social context is referred to as **sociolinguistic competence** (Holmes & Brown, 1977), something that is difficult to teach formally since often even the native speaker of the language cannot verbalize the rules. When we tell someone to "drop in anytime," how is someone just learning English to know that this is not, in fact, an invitation to drop in anytime? In French, particularly in France, "*Merci*" spoken in response to being offered something usually means "No, thank you," not just "Thank you." In English, "Thanks," means in that context "Yes, thank you."

Bilingual stop signs do more than make people stop. They signal the importance of the two linguistic groups in the society.

Thus, the process of becoming bilingual is more of a socialization process than the student usually expects. Moreover, exposure to speakers of another language in their own language can sometimes produce unexpected social psychological consequences. The learner may become aware of stereotypes held by members of each linguistic group about members of the other. These new insights can even undermine the learner's sense of identity. For example, what happens once you become fluent enough to share jokes or criticisms with speakers of the new language about your own maternal language group? If you laugh at the jokes, you may feel uneasy or even guilty; if you respond defensively, you may be excluded from the group. Within your own language group, you may find yourself defending the other group from criticisms, leading to feelings of estrangement. A person in this situation may become **marginal**—no longer a typical member of his or her own group but never fully one of the new group.

To avoid being placed in this position of psychological inconsistency, some people may withdraw from second-language learning and they may support this attitude with clichés such as "I'm too old to learn a new language," and by avoiding cross-cultural interaction that might remind them of the need to acquire the second language (Lambert, 1981; Taylor & Simard, 1975).

Who succeeds in learning a second language?

Some children are fortunate enough to grow up in a bilingual environment and become proficient in two languages as they grow. For most people, however, learning a second language requires a good deal of formal effort. Why do some people persevere even when their social situation does not demand it? Why do some students go on to become fluently bilingual, while others despite years of instruction, remain essentially unilingual? Several factors that facilitate language learning have been identified (Gardner, 1985; Lalonde & Gardner, 1984):

INTELLIGENCE Intelligence obviously facilitates any kind of learning. Thus, intellectually superior individuals should normally find language learning an easier task than it might be for someone less capable.

SPECIFIC APTITUDE FOR LEARNING LANGUAGE Some people are simply better at learning languages than others; verbal skills that lead to high ability in one's native language are also likely to facilitate learning a second language.

MOTIVATION Someone who wants to become bilingual is more likely to succeed. Motivation has been found repeatedly to be a crucial determinant of second-language success (Gardner, 1984). Individuals whose motivation is primarily instrumental (e.g., improving their chances of a good job) do not do as well as people who are integratively motivated—that is, people who want to become involved in the culture of the other language community: go to plays, see movies, talk to friends, meet members of the opposite sex. This relationship between motivation and achievement has been replicated in other countries and with other languages.

Motivation to learn a second language is greatly dependent upon social context including attitudes in the home and in society in general (Gardner, 1985). A general belief that learning French is very difficult can discourage people from trying to learn or continuing to learn if they encounter difficulty.

Motivation also depends in part on ethnolinguistic vitality. An anglophone living in Quebec City will be more likely to want to learn French than will an anglophone in Moose Jaw (Clément, 1980; 1987). When one of two linguistic groups living side by side is lower in ethnolinguistic vitality (usually the minority group), its members should be motivated to learn the majority language since proficiency brings material and psychological benefits. However if the minority language group fears acculturation, group identity may lead to opposition to learning the majority language (Clément, 1987). Such an opposing motivation has been openly expressed in Quebec by those who fear that francophone language and culture will be swallowed up in the huge North American anglophone milieu. The net motivation to learn the majority language will depend on which of these basic motivations is stronger.

For example, Clément, Gauthier and Noels (1993) found that francophone students in Northern Ontario who reported speaking English predominantly also identified more strongly with the anglophone majority; those who reported speaking French predominantly identified more strongly with the francophone group.

The current discussion relates to what Lambert (1978; Lambert & Taylor, 1984) has termed **additive bilingualism** and **subtractive bilingualism**. When anglophones in South Africa learn Afrikaans, Israelis learn English, or anglophone Canadians learn French, they are not threatening the continued existence of their sociolinguistic group. The individuals have simply acquired another socially useful skill. However when minority groups are struggling to maintain their identity, learning the language of the majority can be considered "subtractive" in that it threatens the continued importance of the native language in that society. Bilingualism is likely to be encouraged, or at worst ignored, when it is additive for a given group. It may be actively discouraged when it is subtractive.

ANXIETY AND SELF-CONFIDENCE When two linguistic groups both possess high ethnolinguistic vitality, then a personal factor, self-confidence in one's ability to use the second language, becomes an important determinant of who does or does not become bilingual (Clément, 1987). Anxiety is a major obstacle in second-language learning (Bailey, Onwuegbuzie, & Daley, 2000) and self-confident individuals will have less anxiety about learning the new language and more success at mastering it (Gardner, 1985; Young & Gardner, 1990).

A Final Note

Most Canadians proudly distinguish their country from the United States by reference to its bilingual character. Burgeoning enrolments in French immersion classes across the country as well as the continuing efforts in some provinces to extend government services in both official languages, reflect a positive attempt by two linguistic groups to coexist and strengthen one another.

Canada is not alone in its official bilingualism. For example, Belgium also has two official languages, Israel and Luxembourg have three, and India has 26. Language unites but language also sometimes divides. How language and other factors promote harmony or division among individuals and groups is the focus of discussion in Chapter 12.

Summary

1. Non-verbal communication is used to provide information about feelings and intentions, to regulate verbal and other interactions, to express intimacy, to promote social control and to facilitate goal attainment.

2. Facial displays of emotion share some universal features although social conditioning modifies whatever biological basis there is for this similarity.

3. Eye contact, "body language" and gestures, along with facial displays, provide powerful non-verbal channels of communication.

4. Paralanguage is the non-verbal component of speech; the prosodic features of paralanguage (timing, pitch and loudness) appear to have a biological component in terms of their involvement in emotional reactions.

5. Differences in speech style are used as markers of social status, as guides for forming impressions of others and as markers of group boundaries.

6. The prestige or standard form of a language develops from the speech style of those who are in a position of power rather than reflecting any aesthetically ideal form of the language.

7. Communication accommodation theory suggests that because people usually want to be liked and approved of by others, they modify their speech style to make it similar to the speech heard around them (convergence). However if group identity is threatened, individuals may accentuate the distinctiveness of their speech style (divergence).

8. Becoming bilingual involves more than learning another language; we must also acquire relevant sociolinguistic skills.

9. Factors involved in successful second-language learning include the following: intelligence, specific language learning ability, motivation and self-confidence. Motivation to master a second language will be influenced by the relative status and ethnolinguistic vitality of the second language compared with the learner's own language.

10. Bilingualism is likely to be encouraged when it provides a socially useful skill without threatening the existence of the speaker's own language, but discouraged when it contributes to assimilation into the majority linguistic group.

Further Reading

BERRY, J.W. & LAPONCE, J.A. (Eds.). (1994). *Ethnicity and culture in Canada: The research landscape.* Toronto: University of Toronto Press. An excellent collection of writings concerning research into bilingualism and multiculturalism in Canada. The editors suggest that ethnicity will be to the 21st century what class has been to the 20th—a major source of social tension and political conflict.

BOURHIS, R.Y. (1994). Introduction and overview of language events in Canada. In Bourhis, R.Y. (Ed.), French–English language issues in Canada. *International Journal of the Sociology of Language, 105–106*, 5–34. This introduction to a special journal issue dealing with French–English language issues in Canada provides a good overview of demographic and political aspects of bilingualism in Canada as well as a comprehensive historical guide to language-related events in Canada.

BURGOON, J.D., BULLER, D.B. & WOODALL, W.G. (1989). *Non-verbal communication: The unspoken dialogue.* New York: Harper & Row. An excellent, in-depth treatment of non-verbal communication from simple facial expressions and gestures to the more complicated signals involved in social influence and impression management.

CUMMINGS, J. (Ed.). (1986). *Heritage language research in Canada.* Ottawa: Secretary of State (Multiculturalism). Heritage language programs in schools provide children of immigrants the opportunity for formal instruction in the language of origin. This publication documents related research.

EKMAN, P. (1992). *Telling lies: Clues to deceit in the marketplace, politics and marriage.* New York: W.W. Norton. Lessons on how non-verbal behaviour can signal attempts to deceive.

EKMAN, P. & ROSENBERG, E.L. (Eds.). (1997). *What the face reveals: Basic and applied studies of spontaneous expression using the facial action coding system (FACS).* New York: Oxford University Press. This book provides a good entry into the fascinating study of facial expression.

GARDNER, R.C. & ESSES, V.M. (1996). Special issue on ethnic relations in a multicultural society. *Canadian Journal of Behavioural Science, 28.* A collection of essays about social psychological aspects of multiculturalism in Canada including cross-cultural communication.

GILES, H., COUPLAND, J. & COUPLAND, N. (Eds.). (1991). *Contexts of accommodation: Developments in applied sociolinguistics.* New York: Cambridge University Press. Collection of papers presenting research relating to communication accommodation theory and how people relate to one another on the basis of their group memberships.

GUERRO, L.L., DEVITO, J.A. et al. (Eds.). (1999). *The non-verbal communication reader: Classic and contemporary reading* (2nd ed.). Prospect Heights, IL: Waveland Press. As the title suggests, this is a comprehensive collection of important research articles about how partners in a communication are affected by non-verbal information of which they are often not even aware.

SMITH, P.M. (1985). *Language, the sexes and society.* Oxford: Basil Blackwell. Examination of the ways in which gender influences language and language influences our treatment of males and females.

 Weblinks

Ethnologue

www.ethnologue.com/web.asp A repository of official languages of the world.

Native Languages of the Americas

www.native-languages.org/index.htm#alpha Information on all of the native languages of North America organized alphabetically.

Office of the Commission of Official Languages, Government of Canada

www.ocol-clo.gc.ca/

Chapter 8

Interpersonal Attraction and Relationships

*I loved you for your beauty
But that doesn't make a fool of me;
you were in it for your beauty too.*

Leonard Cohen

Love conquers all things except poverty and a toothache.

Mae West

Chapter Outline

Jenny and Arnold have been friends for years as well as classmates at university. They are both majoring in psychology. Both of them are generally happy people, busy and ambitious and both have had relationships with others. Recently, Arnold has felt that he has fallen in love with Jenny. However, Jenny does not reciprocate these romantic feelings and in fact is interested in another man. Since she told him, Arnold has felt sad and lonely and being with friends does not seem to help his mood. Jenny is also sad at having lost a friendship with Arnold that she valued, and she misses the fun and the intense discussions that they shared so often in the past. However, she feels that Arnold is not the right man for her. Her sister Sarah with whom she discusses everything agrees, and in fact, has expressed some interest herself in Arnold.

Nothing captures our interest as does close relationships. The tragic tale of Romeo and Juliet endures in the form of Shakespeare's play, periodically renewed on stage and in film, as well as in opera, ballet and music. Innumerable novels, plays, soap operas and songs deal with the theme of human relationships in

general and romantic relationships in particular. The problems of the famous and powerful fascinate millions of ordinary people. In turn, ordinary people are thrust into the temporary limelight of "reality TV" shows.

Why is there so much interest in relationships? Humans are, as Aristotle observed, social animals and so we all seek the company of others, form friendships with a few and seem to find our ultimate states of happiness, tension and despair in our most intimate relationships. It is not surprising that artists, writers, philosophers and religious leaders have long been interested in attraction, friendship and love. However, it is only in recent years that scientific methods have been applied to the study of relationships. Although some are skeptical about applying scientific methods to study these issues, human relationships are too important to be left outside the realm of scientific inquiry.

Attachment and Affiliation

The poet John Donne pointed out that "No man is an island, entire of itself." People need people. This need is expressed in two forms. Even as infants, people show evidence of a need to form special, close relationships, a process called **attachment**. People also need to feel a

sense of belonging, a need to be with other people in general; this is called the *need for affiliation*.

Attachment

Social attachment begins in early infancy when the child learns to distinguish familiar people and to respond in a special way to them. The infant smiles and vocalizes to the attachment figure, shows distress when they leave and is obviously comforted by them. Bowlby (1969) argued that there is a biological basis for attachment. On the other hand, social learning theorists explain attachment behaviours in terms of the child associating caretakers such as their mother with rewards such as food, comfort and physical closeness.

It is generally accepted that the attachments in adulthood are based on early experience. Three types of attachment that have been observed in infancy have also been identified and measured in adulthood (Hazan & Shaver, 1987). These are the following: (1) avoidant, being uncomfortable when too close or intimate with someone; (2) anxious/ambivalent, feeling that others are not as close as one would wish, sometimes clinging to partners to the extent that it drives them away; and (3) secure, finding interpersonal closeness to be relatively easy and comfortable. Bartholomew and Horowitz (1991) propose a four-category model, arguing that there are actually two types of avoidant attachment: fearful avoidant (desire intimacy with others but are afraid of being hurt) and dismissive avoidant (people who feel that they do not need closeness to others). When a romantic relationship ends, people with a fearful avoidant orientation are more upset than those with a dismissive orientation (Sprecher, Felmlee, Metts, Fehr & Vanni, 1998). Those who fear rejection may respond with chronic anxiety (the anxious/ambivalent orientation) or by avoiding intimacy (the fearful avoidant orientation). They tend to be low in self-esteem (Murray, Bellavia, Holmes & Garrett, 2002) and their constant concern with rejection influences how they interact with their partners (Murray, Bellavia, Rose, & Griffin, 2003).

Sensitivity to rejection may be accompanied by a defensive reaction that interferes with our ability to perceive our partners accurately. We may believe that we have communicated romantic interest to someone even though, in reality, our romantic interest was not clearly communicated. We assume that the other person can and will take into account our anxieties and recognize how we really feel: a "signal amplification bias" (Vorauer, Cameron, Holmes & Pearce (2003). Failing to understand that the other person did not get the message, this problem becomes a self-fulfilling prophecy in which this inhibition in communicating that we are attracted to the person leads to rejection by him or her.

Attachment styles are related to various personality characteristics (Shaver & Brennan, 1992). People with secure attachment styles react in a more supportive and trusting way to their partners (Simpson, Rholes & Nelligan, 1992; Keelan, Dion & Dion, 1994). A fearful or preoccupied attachment style may be expressed by anger and is associated in men with spousal abuse (Dutton, Saunders, Starzomski & Bartholomew, 1994).

Recall our discussion of schemas in Chapter 2. Attachment style can be considered as reflecting one's schema about relationships (Baldwin, 1992), which will guide people's actions and reactions in their relationships. In particular, the schema contains interpersonal scripts—cognitive structures representing sequences of actions, thoughts, feelings and motivations. For instance, people with a secure attachment style or schema might want to spend more time with their partners, tell them how deeply they feel about them and

respond to affection in an accepting manner. People with an avoidant orientation might not be able or willing to respond in the same manner (Baldwin, Fehr, Keedian, Seidel & Thomson, 1993). Note, however, that we may invoke different schemas in different situations or different relationships. Indeed, most participants in one study were quite capable of thinking of personal relationships that matched the description of all of the attachment styles: secure in one relationship, anxious in another, avoidant in yet another (Baldwin, Keelan, Fehr, Enns & Koh-Rangarajoo, 1996). Even though your predominant attachment schema is secure, you may well find that an anxious or avoidant mental model or schema has been cued by certain persons.

Attachment can influence our well being and our health (Sadava & Molnar, 2003). A nonsecure attachment style in young adults is related to a greater incidence of health problems. This may be due in part to the fact that a nonsecure attachment orientation is linked to anxiety and depression (Feeney & Ryan, 1994; Sadava & McCreary, 1996).

Affiliation

Social affiliation, being with others, is profoundly important to human beings. Research participants in one study (Csikszentmihalyi & Figurski, 1982) agreed to carry communication devices or "beepers" for several weeks. At random times during their waking hours, research participants were "beeped," a signal to fill out a brief questionnaire on what they were doing at that time. The study showed adults spent 71 percent of their time in situations involving other people (for adolescents, the figure was 74 percent).

Laboratory research has also identified some of the factors that tend to increase or decrease affiliation behaviour. A classic experiment by Schachter (1959) tested the hypothesis that under some conditions, people affiliate to reduce fear. Female research participants were informed by an experimenter—a gentleman dressed in a white lab coat with the rather ominous name of Dr. Gregor Zilstein—either that they would be subjected to electric shocks that would be intense and painful (high fear condition) or that they'd be subjected to shocks that would resemble a tickle or a tingle (low fear condition). Then research participants were allowed to choose to spend a 10-minute waiting period either alone or with other research participants. Those with high fear showed a strong preference to be with others.

The key to understanding this experiment is the process of **social comparison** (as explained in Chapter 3). In an unusual situation, we turn to others as a source of information to compare our feelings with people in the same boat. To demonstrate this finding, another experiment (Schachter, 1959) used different groups of research participants who, after high fear arousal, were given three choices: to wait alone, to be with other experimental research participants or to be with students waiting for interviews with faculty advisors. As social comparison theory predicts, fearful research participants preferred to be with others in the same situation (fearful) rather than with people in a different situation. Misery loves miserable company.

However in a field study (Kulik & Mahler, 1989a), patients about to undergo major surgery (coronary bypass) were interviewed about their preferences for roommates. Contrary to Schachter's hypothesis, the patients expressed a strong preference for a roommate who was already recovering from the surgery. These results suggest that people may prefer to be with someone who can draw on their immediate experience and possibly provide reassurance rather than someone who might be reacting emotionally in a similar way.

Interpersonal Attraction

While all of us need people, we are also selective in our casual and deep friendships and in our love relationships. Much of the research in this area has been devoted to *interpersonal attraction*: the reasons why one person will like another. It has been shown that—

with certain qualifications—we tend to like people who are similar to us, who reward us, who like us, who are nearby, who are physically attractive and who are pleasant, agreeable, competent and otherwise good and desirable people.

Of course, there are many kinds of attraction. You may enjoy a casual conversation with the person beside you on an airplane and leave it at that. You may be attracted to a person as a friend but not a lover, as a tennis partner but not a close friend, as a colleague at work but not a companion. Recall in our opening vignette that while Arnold wanted his friendship to become a romantic relationship, Jenny did not reciprocate and felt sad at the loss of that friendship. What determines liking of a stranger will not necessarily determine attraction in an intimate relationship, as a friend or lover, or whether that relationship will last over time.

Propinquity

Before attraction develops, there has to be an opportunity for the first contact. People are more likely to meet and develop relationships if they are in *geographic proximity* or *propinquity* (the **propinquity effect**). This was shown dramatically in a classic study by Festinger, Schachter and Back (1950), later replicated by Athanasiou and Yashioka (1973). They selected graduate student apartments at Massachusetts Institute of Technology as the site for their investigation. A diagram of a typical apartment building is shown in Figure 8–1.

Notice that the building contains two stories, 10 apartments and a number of stairways. The experimenters asked all the residents to complete a "sociometric test" identifying their three closest friends in the

FIGURE 8-1

Design of a typical apartment building

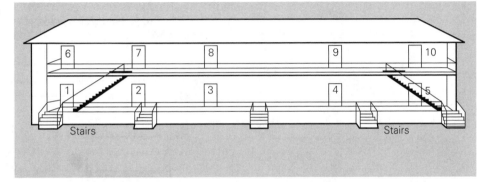

Source: Festinger, Schachter & Back, 1950

Architectural Design and Human Relationships

Architects are concerned with making their design for houses, apartment buildings, shopping centres and universities work for the user in addition to making them technically sound and aesthetically pleasing. Social psychologists focus on how design might contribute to better human interaction and relationships.

Consider for instance, various designs for university residences. In a study (Baum & Valins, 1977; Baum, Aiello & Calesnick, 1978), two basic types of dormitory designs were compared: (1) single and/or double rooms along a single, long corridor with common social areas and bathrooms shared by all on that floor or wing; and (2) suites of several bedrooms located around a smaller common living room and bathroom (see Figure 8–2). While the population density was more or less the same in both designs, the effects on the residents seemed to be quite different.

It was found that students in the suite arrangement tended to be more sociable and friendly. This is not too astonishing since it is much easier to come to know and interact with nine others in close proximity than with 39 others along a large corridor. However, this pattern of social behaviour was also observable in the psychology laboratory. The students who had been recruited for another experiment were taken to a waiting room in which another student, hired by the experimenter, was sitting. Suite residents tended to select a chair closer to the other person than did corridor residents and were much more likely to initiate a conversation.

However, we cannot conclude that the suite design caused differences in social behaviour. Friendly, sociable people may request suites and less sociable people may prefer corridor arrangements. To over-

FIGURE 8-2

Two designs of university residences

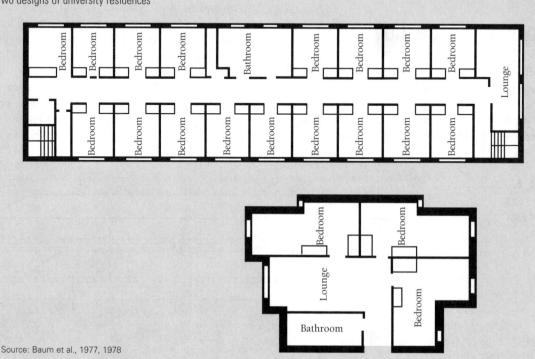

Source: Baum et al., 1977, 1978

come these problems, Baum and Davis (1980) arranged to assign students randomly obtained within the same residence to suites, long corridors or shorter hallways. Students were studied repeatedly over the year.

The findings confirmed the hypothesis that design can influence behaviour. Suite residents perceived their situation as less crowded although they had the same total living area as the others. They were more successful in making friends and they interacted more both in the residence and in the laboratory. Clearly, because of physical propinquity, the suite arrangement is more conducive to the development of friendship. In addition, the smaller living unit increases the residents' sense of personal control over whom they will interact with and therefore they are more comfortable and satisfied.

Another study compared the effects of two different classroom environments (Wollin & Montagne, 1981). The control or "sterile" classroom had white walls, rows of plastic desks and a grey carpet. (Does that describe your classroom?) The experimental or "friendly" classroom was redecorated with brightly painted walls, art posters, large plants, area rugs and colour-coordinated cushions. Two professors teaching sections of the introductory psychology course participated; halfway through the term the classes switched rooms. Research participants were generally more willing to interact with others when they were in attractive surroundings (Russel & Mehrabian, 1978).

Simple design changes can be effective. In the 1950s, a new female geriatric ward in a Saskatchewan hospital had a bright, cheerful, tastefully decorated common room. Yet the patients seemed listless, depressed and withdrawn. Psychological consultants noted that the chairs were lined up neatly, side by side along the walls and facing in the same direction. When the chairs were rearranged in circles around coffee tables, the frequency of conversation doubled within a few weeks (Sommer & Ross, 1958).

Similarly in another study, pairs of research participants asked to evaluate music were seated in chairs that faced each other or were oriented at 9° or 180° angles and were separated by three to nine feet (Mehrabian & Diamond, 1971). Before the music began, conversation was more frequent and positive when the chairs faced each other directly. In another experiment, research participants were required to converse at either a comfortable distance or 11 feet apart. At a greater distance, research participants not only felt ill at ease but also attributed their feelings to an unfriendly partner rather than to the situation (Aiello & Thompson, 1980). (Keep that finding in mind for parties!)

apartment complex. Friends were most likely to be next-door neighbours and the probability of friendship decreased as apartments became more distant. It was also found that people in the central apartments, numbers 3 and 8, were reported as friends more often than were the residents of all the other apartments, probably because they had the advantage of being closest to the most apartments. Those in the end apartments, numbers 1 and 5, received the most friendship choices from the other floor. The reason is obvious from the illustration. The stairs from the upper floor end in front of these two apartments increasing the likelihood of those tenants meeting the upper residents.

Why are people attracted to those near them? First, proximity increases opportunities for interaction thus enabling people to notice their similarities and discover that they like and are rewarding to each other. We generally tend to be pleasant to people we expect to see frequently. However, such explanations do not in themselves seem adequate to account for differences in attraction between neighbours in adjacent apartments and those at the other end of the hall.

The most important factor is the mere exposure effect. Contrary to the old saying "Familiarity breeds contempt," an important body of research (Suedfeld, Rank & Borin, 1975) shows that familiarity with a novel stimulus usually leads to more positive ratings and greater attraction (Zajonc, 1970). In one experiment, research participants shown a photograph of the same person each week for four weeks showed greater liking for that person compared with research participants shown a different photograph each week (Moreland & Zajonc, 1982). In another study, preschoolers who watched *Sesame Street* episodes involving Japanese Canadians and North American Indians were more likely to indicate a desire to play with such children than were children not exposed to these episodes (Goldberg & Gorn, 1979). In general, we tend to prefer people familiar to us and propinquity will obviously be related to a greater probability of increased exposure.

Physical attractiveness

"What a strange illusion it is to suppose that beauty is goodness," observed Tolstoy. Common sense tells us that "beauty is only skin deep" and "you can't judge a book by its cover." And so, people tend to underestimate the impact of attractiveness on how we react to people (Hadjistavropoulos & Genest, 1994). Moreover, it is not enough to say simply that beauty is in the eye of the beholder. Within a given culture and age group, research participants who are asked to make independent ratings of the physical attractiveness of various target persons tend to show high levels of agreement in these ratings (Berscheid & Walster, 1974a). The average ratings of attractiveness by independent judges will predict how much other people will like the target persons (Curran & Lippold, 1975). We also make judgments of attractiveness almost instantaneously. In one experiment, faces were flashed on a screen for 150 ms and the ratings for beauty were identical to those given when participants had a much longer interval to inspect the photograph (Goldstein & Papageorge, 1980).

External conditions can affect our judgment of attractiveness to some extent. For instance, Kenrick and Gutierres (1980) found that men who had just watched an episode of the then popular TV program, *Charlie's Angels*, judged a woman of average attractiveness lower than did other men who had not seen the program. Evidently even an attractive person pales next to a glamorous star, putting most of us at an unfair disadvantage.

While most people might prefer attractive friends and lovers, not everyone can engage such partners. Thus, it is not surprising that pairs of friends and romantic partners tend to be roughly similar in physical attractiveness (Cash & Darlega, 1978; Murstein, 1972; Feingold, 1988). This tendency to choose "matching" partners occurs most strongly among romantic couples, less so among male friends and least of all among female friends (Feingold, 1988).

When someone is highly attractive, others both desire to interact with them and fear rejection (Shanteau & Nagy, 1979). Rather than risk the humiliation of being turned down, many people are satisfied

to form relationships with those they feel similar to in attractiveness and whose attention they feel they deserve. Thus, highly attractive individuals may find themselves admired from a distance (Berscheid & Walster, 1969; Shanteau & Nagy, 1979) while average-looking people may seek out those more in line with their expectations (Kiesler and Baral, 1970; Kalik & Hamilton, 1988).

While men and women are obviously attentive to each other's physical attractiveness, we should keep in mind that this variable is also important to other kinds of relationships. Even children as young as three years old prefer to look at pictures of attractive children (Dion, 1972). Attractive fifth-grade children are more popular among their same-sex peers (Cavior & Dorecki, 1969). In addition, adults treat attractive and unattractive children differently. For example, Clifford and Walster (1973) showed fifth-grade teachers a report card about a hypothetical student that included a photograph of an attractive or unattractive boy or girl. Although the report cards were identical, the attractive child was assessed by the teachers as having a higher IQ and was expected to achieve more in the future.

Together these studies suggest that the power of physical attractiveness cannot be ignored. Indeed, Langlois et al. suggest that this effect may have sociobiological roots. Let us examine this interpretation.

BEAUTY, ATTRACTION AND EVOLUTION In recent years, some social psychologists have focused on sociobiology, a perspective in which attraction and love are linked to evolution, survival of the fittest and maximizing reproductive success (Buss, 1994). The basic premise is rather straightforward: the impulse driving our actions is reproductive success—continuing our genes into the next generation. To do so, we are driven to be attracted to a partner who is reproductively fit.

Since women are limited in how many children they can produce to perpetuate their genes, they are hypothesized to have a greater investment in their children than do men, who can sire many offspring. Sociobiology posits that a woman will seek a mate who can protect and provide for her and their children. Therefore, she will value characteristics such as size and strength as well as financial resources (clearly, lack of money or loss of a job is a strain on many marriages). A man who can continue to provide resources for his family is one who is dependable and stable, intelligent and in good health (unless he is older … but wealthier). Consider that attractive people are perceived to be healthier as well—it is being healthy that is judged as attractive (Kalick, Zebrowitz, Langlois & Johnson, 1996; Hadjistavropoulos, McMurtry & Craig, 1996).

What do men value in women? Again, the driving force is reproductive success. Therefore, they will tend to be attracted to women who are young and attractive, both of which imply reproductive fitness. Note that evolutionary theory differs sharply from mainstream social science in which it is argued that the notion of beauty as a universal standard is largely a "myth" engendered by cultural conditioning and stereotyped associations about the "beautiful people" (Wolf, 1991). Nonetheless, the evidence indicates that standards of beauty are fairly consistent across cultures as predicted by sociobiologicial theory (Ritter, Casey & Langlois, 1991). Men appear to be somewhat more concerned about the physical attractiveness of women than women are about that of men (Miller & Rivenbark, 1970; Krebs & Adinolfi, 1975).

And so attractiveness represents fitness to have or sire children and perpetuate one's own genes. What characteristics are attractive to us? Evidence ranging from Stone Age art to contemporary beauty contests indicates that men are attracted to women whose waists are 30-percent narrower than their hips, a shape associated with fertility (Singh & Young, 1995). Other evidence suggests that both men and women are attracted by symmetry in which facial features, hands, ankles and so forth are equal on the left and right sides (Thornhill & Gangestad, 1993). Sociobiologists argue that this preference for symmetry serves as an indicator of health, which implies reproductive fitness.

In one rather startling study, women sniffed and rated the attractiveness of the scent of 41 T-shirts after each shirt had been worn by the same man over two nights. The extent to which various physical features (ear length, fingers, wrists, ankles, feet) were symmetrical was also measured for each man. The women did not see or know any of the men. Of course, other olfactory cues were controlled such as having the men not wear aftershave, sleep in sheets washed in unscented detergent and not eat foods such as garlic, pepperoni or cabbage. The women preferred the scent of the symmetrical man but only during the times that they were ovulating. At other times of the month, no such preference was observed (Gangestad & Thornhill, 1998). As it is difficult to explain how symmetrical features would be related to scent, this study must be interpreted cautiously.

If you were to describe someone as "average" in physical appearance, it would not seem to be a compliment. However, a set of studies suggests that we are attracted to persons who appear close to the average in terms of facial and physical features (Grammar & Thornhill, 1994). Computers allow us to input thousands of points on the face of each individual. From the photos that result, an image can be generated of a hypothetical person who will be the "average" of all the people whose photos were entered: average size and shape of nose, average mouth, average size and distance between eyes, etc. This composite will be judged as more attractive than photos of individual faces (Langlois & Roggman, 1990). As well, the average is perceived as healthier and more reproductively fit.

Research such as this provides some indirect support for an evolutionary interpretation. However, these findings do not rule out alternative interpretations. Using the same methodology described above, research has found a positive relationship between "averageness" and perceived attractiveness in rating dogs, birds and wristwatches—and we do not evaluate wristwatches in terms of reproductive strategies (Halberstadt & Rhodes, 2000). Clearly, the average represents the prototype, perhaps the familiar that is attractive. Indeed, it is interesting that we continue to seek sexual partners who are healthy and attractive—indicating reproductive fitness—while we take precautions to avoid pregnancy (Etcoff, 1999). While it is difficult to test the theory of evolution as applied to our profound intimate lives, the work in this area represents a challenge to social psychology that cannot be ignored.

Let us turn to an alternative interpretation of the effects of physical attractiveness, one which does not involve biological assumptions.

What is beautiful is good

In fairy tales, the hero is handsome, the heroine beautiful and the villains ugly (e.g., Cinderella and Prince Charming versus the ugly stepsisters). In contemporary movies, television, fashion and popular music, stardom is also linked to physical attractiveness. Thus, it is not surprising that people believe physical attractiveness indicates desirable personality characteristics. Indeed when people are described or presented as physically attractive, they are rated as having more desirable personality characteristics and a higher occupational status; more likely to be happily married and content in their social life and occupation; more intelligent, moral and adjusted; more outgoing; more

FOCUS ON RESEARCH

Maxims or Myths about Beauty

In a thorough review of the extensive literature on physical attractiveness, Langlois et al. (2000) performed a series of meta-analyses to test the validity of several folk sayings about beauty. Think about the following:

1. "Beauty is in the eye of the beholder." If this is the case, then judgments of attractiveness among raters should show little consistency within our own culture and across many cultures. This is not the case. There is strong agreement both within and across cultures on who is beautiful and who is not.

2. "Never judge a book by its cover." This maxim urges us to disregard external appearance and judge others by inner characteristics. If people conform to this maxim, then the physical attractiveness of others should not predict how they evaluate them or how they interact with them. This is not the case: both adults and children are judged and treated differently with those who are more attractive overwhelmingly having the advantage.

3. "Beauty is only skin-deep." According to this maxim, there is in reality no correspondence between external appearance and either the personality or the behaviour of the individual. This again is not the case. Beauty is more than skin-deep: it is related to adjustment and intelligence in children and occupational success, popularity, social competence, extroversion and self-esteem in adults.

pleasant; and of higher status (Dion, Berscheid & Walster, 1972; Adams & Huston, 1975). In short, beauty is assumed to signify goodness in our impressions of people.

A medieval law stated that if two persons fell under suspicion of having committed a crime, the uglier one was to be regarded as more likely guilty. In a more subtle way, the "beautiful is good" assumption may influence judicial decisions today. For example, astute lawyers will usually advise their clients to clean up and dress well. In a mock jury study, research participants were given a description of a case involving cheating in college. The same facts were presented to all research participants along with a photograph of the defendant. Physically attractive defendants were judged less guilty and received less severe punishment than less attractive defendants (Effran, 1974). However in some situations, physical attractiveness may lead to negative outcomes (Sigall & Ostrove, 1975; Izzett & Fishman, 1976). For example, attractive female defendants were more likely to be convicted if they had apparently used their physical assets to accomplish the crime. In addition, those who believe

in a just world—beliefs that people get what they deserve and deserve what they get in life (Chapter 2)—rate physically attractive males as having more socially desirable characteristics than did those without strong just world beliefs. It seems they perceive attractive males as "winners" and thus deserving (Dion & Dion, 1987).

Again, consider that the attractiveness effect is not limited to sexuality. In politics, the physical appearance of candidates is often vital. Effran and Patterson (1974) had judges rate the appearance of 79 candidates in the 1972 Canadian federal election. A comparison then revealed that the unattractive candidates averaged fewer votes than did the attractive ones. Moreover, of the 17 candidates studied who were not affiliated with one of the major parties at the time, only one was rated above the median in attractiveness. In other words, fringe groups such as the Libertarian or Marxist-Leninist parties do not seem to put forward attractive candidates. Why? One possible explanation is the **self-fulfilling prophecy**. An unattractive person may seek out organizations that advocate unpopular policies. Or perhaps those who belong to political movements that do not conform to societal norms are also less concerned with norms of physical attractiveness.

A great deal of research was stimulated by these findings. In a meta-analysis of these studies, Eagly, Ashmore, Makhijani and Longo (1991) found that the effects of physical attractiveness on stereotyping were not as strong as was believed. It appears that we do stereotype attractive people as socially competent (popular, likable, sociable) and, to a lesser extent, intellectually competent. However, physical attractiveness does not affect our judgments of integrity (honesty, faithfulness) or adjustment (high self-esteem, happiness, maturity). Further, people from less individualistic cultures such as the Chinese base their judgments more on group-related attributes such as position in the community or family background, than on individual characteristics such as attractiveness (Dion, Pak & Dion, 1990).

There is also some evidence that because individuals who have everything going for them remind us of our own inadequacies, they may not be liked as much as someone who appears to have at least some human failings. An experiment by Aronson, Willerman and Floyd (1966) dramatically illustrates this phenomenon. On audiotape, some research participants heard a student correctly answer 92 percent of a very difficult series of questions while other research participants heard the same student correctly answer only 30 percent. Half the research participants in each of these conditions then rated how much they liked the person whose voice they heard. The superior student received an average attractiveness rating of 20.8 and the less able student a rating of 17.8. For the remaining research participants, the tape continued and they heard the student exclaim, "Oh, my goodness, I've spilled coffee all over my new suit." Attractiveness rating now averaged 30.2 for the superior student and –2.5 for the less able student. In other words, the competent individual's rating increased after demonstrating at least some inadequacy. Other research has indicated that the "blunder" effect occurs for people of average self-esteem. Both those who are high and low in self-esteem decrease their liking of a person after a blunder, the former because they identify with highly competent people and the latter because they look up to them (Helmreich, Aronson & LeFan, 1970).

Similarity

Do "birds of a feather flock together"? Or do "opposites attract"? One established principle is that we tend to like people similar to ourselves in attitudes, values and interests. In a classic study, transfer students to a U.S. university were offered free housing in exchange for their participation in research (Newcomb, 1961). None of the students knew each other before arriving on campus. At intervals throughout the semester, they were asked to fill out a questionnaire assessing (1) their values and attitudes regarding religion, politics and other matters; (2) their perception of each other's attitudes; and (3) how much they liked each other. The findings showed a strong relationship between friendship and perceived similarity in attitudes and values.

Interestingly, people did not learn about their similarities with others and then become friends. Rather, friendships formed quite rapidly and friends tended to assume from the beginning that they were more similar than they really were. As they came to know each other over time, friendships shifted so that actual attitude similarity was significantly related to attraction in the final weeks of the study. In other words rather than change values and attitudes, the students changed friends (Newcomb, 1961).

In a series of well-controlled experiments, Byrne (1971) applied the similarity-attraction principle in the laboratory. Each subject filled out a brief attitude questionnaire. The experimenter then surreptitiously filled out a questionnaire with views similar or dissimilar, in varying degrees, to the subject's and asked the subject to rate the attractiveness or likability of the person who had made these responses. With factors such as physical appearance, status or personality thus excluded, attraction to the stranger increased as the proportion of similar attitudes increased. This has become known as Byrne's Law: attraction to a stranger is a function of the *proportion of similar attitudes*.

Outside the laboratory, the effect holds up well. Dating partners tend to be similar in age, religion, education and physical attractiveness, even height (Hill, Rubin & Peplau, 1976; Shanteau & Nagy, 1979). Both similarity and physical attractiveness predict satisfaction with one's roommate at university (Carli, Ganley & Pierce-Otay, 1991). It is interesting that in the latter study, similarity predicted satisfaction to a greater extent when the partner was not physically attractive, suggesting that similarity may compensate for a lack of physical beauty.

In one study, males and females were paired on the basis of similar or dissimilar responses to an attitude questionnaire (Byrne, Ervin & Lamberth, 1970). Each couple was introduced and sent away on a brief "Coke date" nearby. (Note: "Coke" referred to the soft drink). When they returned, couples with highly similar attitudes rated each other more favourably, indicated greater attraction and even stood closer to one another.

Limits to the association between similarity and attraction

How do we feel about someone who achieves more than we do? Our reaction depends both upon how important performance is to our sense of self-worth and on our closeness to the other person. If someone outdoes you on a task you perceive as important, then the closer you are to that person, the greater the threat and the worse you will feel. However if the task is not

Would the attractiveness of Sarah McLachlan influence our appreciation of her music?

important to you, you will feel better when the person is close to you, allowing you to bask in reflected glory (Tesser, Millar & Moore, 1988).

It may be the type of similarity that counts. Recall that people scoring high in self-monitoring tend to be guided primarily by cues in the situation, particularly the reactions of others, while those scoring low in self-monitoring tend to be guided primarily by their own feelings and beliefs (Chapter 2). High self-monitors tend to choose romantic partners on the basis of physical attractiveness and friends on the basis of similar recreational preferences. Low self-monitors tend to be guided more by similarities in personality traits and attitudes (Glick, DeMorest & Hotze, 1988; Jamieson, Lydon & Zanna, 1987). Thus, while perceived similarities influence attraction, high and low self-monitors appear to consider different kinds of information in assessing similarity. In a study of adolescent friendship dyads, it was found that best friends tended to be highly similar in attitudes towards drug use and in certain characteristics such as age, school grade and ethnic group. However, best friends did not share similar attitudes towards teachers and parents (Kandel, 1978a, 1978b). Hill and Stull (1981) found that among female roommates at university but not among male roommates, similarity in values was very high among those who chose to room together or to stay together. Finally, a longitudinal study of married couples showed that partners did not become more similar in attitudes and values over 20 years of marriage; rather, their initial similarities remained remarkably constant over that period of time (Caspi, Herbener & Ozer, 1992).

Reasons for the similarity–attraction relationship

Why are attitude similarity and attraction so strongly related? Several explanations are plausible. First, it is *rewarding* to have someone agree with your opinions, for it bolsters your confidence in your own ideas. Similar values and interests provide opportunities for doing things together such as playing tennis, working for a cause or going to a movie (and agreeing on which movie to see). However in certain circumstances, similarity may not be rewarding. In one variation of the Byrne "hypothetical stranger" study (Novak & Lerner, 1968), some research participants were led to believe that the other person had recently suffered a nervous breakdown, had been hospitalized and was still seeing a psychiatrist. In this case, similarity in other characteristics actually decreased liking. Somehow it did not seem rewarding to the participant that an emotionally disturbed person might be otherwise so similar.

Another explanation is derived from the *consistency principle*, which we encountered in relation to changing attitudes (Chapter 5). According to Heider's (1958) model, liking someone while disagreeing with that person about something important is psychologically uncomfortable. Thus if you and your friend hold strong but differing views about abortion, your feelings towards that person may be influenced by her views on the subject. Of course, we rarely agree with our friends about everything and can often tolerate a good deal of inconsistency or imbalance. You and your friend may disagree about a certain band but not see that as an important issue. Indeed, agreement may not always signify liking and balance. If John and Brian agree about the attractiveness of Susan, the result may be bitter competition.

While the balance model predicts change if there is imbalance between orientations towards persons and attitudes, the model cannot predict which of the components will change in order to restore balance. For example if you like baseball and like someone who hates it, will you change your orientation towards the person, your orientation towards baseball or your perception of the other person's attitude? The answer may depend on your needs and emotions, your commitment to the attitude or the relationship and external pressures. If you have already purchased expensive season's tickets, you may be more likely to change your orientation towards the other person. But if you are in love with the other person, you may change your attitude towards baseball or you may decide that baseball is not an important issue between the two of you.

A third interpretation involves our *schema about people we like*. It challenges the proposition that we are attracted to someone as a consequence of perceived similarity. Rather, since being attracted to people who are similar is part of everyday common-sense experience, we expect the people we like to be like us. Indeed Murstein (1972), in a study of engaged couples, asked each to fill out a set of personality scales for themselves and then to predict how their partners would respond to the scales. Research participants tended to expect their partners' responses to be more like their own than they actually were. In fact typically, people assume that others share their attitudes and thus tend to like other people in the absence of contrary information (Byrne, Clore & Smeaton, 1986).

THE REPULSION HYPOTHESIS Finally, it has been argued that similarity itself has no effect on attraction, but people are repelled by those whose attitudes are dissimilar (Rosenbaum, 1986). In one study, research participants were presented with photos of people and were told that the person's attitudes were similar to their own, or dissimilar to their own or were told nothing about the person's attitudes. Consistent with the repulsion hypothesis, attraction did not differ between the similar-attitude and no-information groups but was significantly lower in the dissimilar-attitude condition. But in other studies when the number of dissimilar attitudes was held constant, attraction increased as the number of similar attitudes increased (Smeaton, Byrne & Murnen, 1989). It appears that while attraction is increased by feedback suggesting that the other person has similar attitudes, people may be more affected by dissimilar than by similar attitudes, an example of the negativity effect (see Chapter 2). For some reason, younger children respond more to dissimilarity-rejection and adolescents to similarity-attraction (Tan & Singh, 1995).

Rosenbaum's (1986) repulsion hypothesis led to research that advanced our understanding of the similarity effect. While both similarity and dissimilarity in attitudes influence attraction, the evidence shows that the dissimilarity effect is stronger: we tend to dislike people who are dissimilar to ourselves more than we like people who are similar to ourselves. For instance, in judging politicians, we may claim that we wish that they would be consistent and speak their minds openly, but in fact, we reject those who do not share our views (McCaul, Ployart, Hinsz & McCaul, 1995). It also depends how attraction is being measured. The repulsion effect is particularly strong with regard to being attracted to people's social attributes (e.g. enjoy their company) as opposed to intelligence or general knowledge (Singh & Ho, 2000). In short, while we may find their dissimilar attitudes to be tolerable, we also have a desire to avoid the dissimilar person.

Reinforcement, reciprocity and attraction

People like those who reward them, who say nice things to them and who do good things for them. Indeed, some theorists believe that reinforcement underlies all attraction. Encountering someone with similar attitudes is agreeable, even flattering. It is also rewarding to be with and be seen with an attractive person.

Clearly, we like people who make us feel good in some way. In fact, we evaluate them positively while negative feelings about someone lead to negative evaluations (Dovidio, Gaertner, Ison and Lowrance, 1995). Not surprisingly, we will give more positive evaluations to someone who makes us feel great by a compliment as compared to someone who deflates us with an insult. This will include nonverbal signals— smiling and eye contact will arouse positive emotions in your conversational partner while yawning and avoiding eye contact will arouse negative emotions and lead to negative evaluations. While this may seem obvious at least in our culture, it is important to understand that our evaluation of the performance of a politician, professor or fellow worker can be the result of how we "feel" about that person.

Thus far, we have examined the direct and obvious effects of what a person does that has an impact on how we feel. Now, imagine meeting someone at a pleasant party after a good meal to celebrate success in your exams. The **reinforcement-affect model** predicts that people will be attracted to someone whom they associate with good feelings even if the person was not the cause (Byrne & Clore, 1970). For example, research participants were given false feedback on a personality test they had completed earlier. Half were informed that the test showed many strong, positive characteristics while the other half were told that the test revealed many personal problems and inadequacies. (Of course, research participants were later informed about the deception and reassured). Then the subject met a stranger in the waiting room. Those who received the positive feedback subsequently indicated greater attraction to this person.

Of course, significant attractions can occur in unpleasant circumstances. People who survived the wartime bombardment of London recall the intense relationships that often developed during that time, as did many people in New York during the terrorist attack in 2001. As discussed earlier in this chapter, affiliation with others who share stressful circumstances can bring its own rewards (see also *excitation-transfer theory* in Chapter 11).

Perhaps the most powerful reward that others can give us is to like us (Backman & Secord, 1959). This is the principle of *reciprocity in attraction*—we like people who like us. Indeed, one study by Berscheid & Walster (1978) showed that people liked someone more when they said eight nice things about them than when they said seven nice things and one critical comment. In another study, a female confederate showed liking of male participants by maintaining eye contact, leaning towards them and listening intently to what they said. In this condition, the men expressed great attraction towards her despite the fact that they had been informed that she disagreed with them on some issues that were important to them (Gold, Ryckman & Mosley, 1984). In short, the perception of similarity was trumped by a cue for liking. Finally after being informed in advance that their partner in an experiment disliked them, participants were instructed to have a conversation (Curtis & Miller, 1986). When participants believed that their partners disliked them, they disclosed less about themselves and behaved in a colder and less friendly manner than where they believed that their partner liked them. Thus the reciprocity in liking effect can become a self-fulfilling prophecy.

Limits to the reinforcement-attraction effect

The mere amount of reinforcement may not be sufficient to predict attraction. Aronson and Linder (1965) show that a gain or loss of positive expression, or liking, from another is a more potent source of reward or punishment than is constant praise or criticism. In an experiment involving a complicated series of scenarios, research participants heard themselves being evaluated by a confederate on seven different occasions. In one condition, the confederate was consistently positive about the subject while in another the confederate was consistently negative. In the third condition, the confederate was initially negative but gradually became more positive about the subject ("gain" condition). A fourth group of research participants heard the confederate begin with a positive evaluation and gradually become negative about the subject ("loss" condition). Subsequently, the research participants were asked to indicate their degree of attraction to the confederate.

Needless to say, research participants liked the person who praised them and disliked the person who evaluated them negatively. More important, the confederate was liked more in the gain condition than in the constant positive condition and disliked more in the loss condition than in the constant negative condition. Subsequent research suggests that the **gain effect** tends to be stronger than the **loss effect** (Clore, Wiggins & Itkin, 1975). In part, this outcome may be due to a contrast effect common in perception: positive things said after negative things seem more positive. There may also have been an anxiety reduction in the gain condition that made the later, positive comments even more reinforcing. In any case, we obviously cannot assume that the more liking we receive, the better we feel.

Another limit to the reinforcement effect is represented by the principle of equity, or fairness, in our social relations (Walster, Walster & Berscheid, 1978). While we want rewarding relationships, we also want to feel that we are neither exploiting someone else nor being exploited ourselves. Indeed, people sometimes react quite negatively to generosity from others, particularly if they are unable to reciprocate or if it implies dependency or helplessness on their part (Gergen, Ellsworth, Maslach & Seipel, 1975). This may explain in part why people who receive welfare, and nations that receive aid may not always respond with gratitude and good feelings (see Chapter 9).

So far, we have considered how we might come to like someone with whom we are interacting on a casual, superficial basis. Most of our encounters with people occur in this way and we can accept and enjoy them. However with some people, a more intimate relationship develops. The following section reviews some of the important variables that contribute to the development of intimacy.

Intimacy and Close Relationships

Levinger and Snoek (1972) describe **mutuality** as a stage in which two persons are in an intimate relationship and are now interdependent to an extent and assume some responsibility for the satisfaction and well being of the other. To a considerable degree, the relationship becomes free of external, cultural norms and rules. The individuals have their own understanding, often unspoken, of the "rules" of the relationship, a sense of "we" and "us" as contrasted with "you" and "I." Self-disclosure is fundamental to this kind of a relationship.

Importance of self-disclosure

The development of a relationship involves getting to know the other person, which obviously depends on the willingness of the other person to be known. Although the processes of self-disclosure have been researched extensively, many questions remain. Do we reveal more to people we like or do we come to like people to whom we have disclosed ourselves? Must

self-disclosure be reciprocal or can we accept A knowing more about us than we know about A? Can we reveal too much too soon? We do know that people in general, and especially people of different social classes and cultures, vary in self-disclosure.

It is clear that people will reveal more about themselves to people they like than to people they dislike (Chaiken & Derlega, 1974). But what about the reverse? Will others like us more if we offer them some scintillating personal gossip? The evidence indicates that this may well be the case, but it depends on the stage the interaction has reached. Strangers may be repelled if we are overly intimate. In such cases, intermediate levels of disclosure create a more favourable impression (Cozby, 1973). The research also supports the notion that within certain limits, personal revelations are likely to be reciprocated. Studies by Rubin (1975, 1976) indicate however that if too much is revealed, the other person becomes suspicious and is likely to become less rather than more open. The reciprocity norm is powerful in human affairs: we try to keep the "books balanced," whether in sending Christmas cards or in revealing personal information. However, each of us has a threshold beyond which it would be too costly or too anxiety-provoking to reciprocate (Altman, 1973; Chaiken & Derlega, 1974).

Self-disclosure is also influenced by gender roles (see also Chapter 7). In one study, male and female experimental assistants approached male and female travellers in an airport departure lounge (Rubin, 1974). Half the travellers were asked to participate in a study of handwriting analysis and the other half in a study of self-disclosure. Many refused and the pattern of refusals was interesting. Regardless of the study subject, females were twice as likely to refuse a male as a female assistant. Males were more likely to refuse the disclosure study when asked by a male, but their rate of refusal for the handwriting analysis—whether asked by a man or a woman—was equal to that of females asked by a female assistant. In general as one might expect, self-disclosure tends to be more reserved among males (Dindia, 2000).

Finally, note that verbal self-disclosure and intimate communication are supplemented by nonverbal communication (discussed in Chapter 7). Vocal inflections or dynamics can reveal or conceal our feelings. Facial expressions, interpersonal distance, eye contact and body orientation may all communicate intimacy. The social context or the physical environment may also play a role. The same words in different contexts may be spoken as a profession of love, a description of the weather or a political opinion. Taking a sip of wine may communicate the sipper's feelings about the wine or the companion—depending on the quality and vintage (of the wine and the companion).

Social penetration model

The **social penetration** model describes the process by which we come to know someone well or intimately. According to the model, you can know many aspects of a person or only a few (breadth) and you can know any particular aspect of a person in a more or less personal way (depth). In other words, breadth refers to how many different attributes of a person you know while depth refers to how intimate or personal the information is concerning a particular attribute. For example, several people who work in the same office may take their coffee breaks together and talk about many different topics (breadth) but never at an intensely personal level (low depth). Professional hockey players may come to know everything that there is to know about one another as players but rarely talk about anything else (depth without breadth). Typically, a relationship develops by first talking about a wide variety of topics and later gradually becomes more personal or intimate about a few of the topics. Thus, the process of social penetration is described in terms of a wedge—broad at a superficial level, more narrow as the level of exchange becomes more intimate.

This model also applies to troubled relationships where *social depenetration*, a process of decreasing intimacy, often occurs. Among couples who experience serious marital problems, breadth of communication decreases. As the relationship deteriorates, the partners restrict the number of topics that they are willing to talk about but show a tendency to "bare all" about these topics. Perhaps they are willing to risk more to save the relationship or perhaps they simply feel that they have nothing to lose by being open (Tolstedt & Stokes, 1984).

Of course, relationships tend to fluctuate rather than simply grow in one direction. Even in a successful marriage, the partners feel very close at some times, more distant and casual at others (Altman, Vinsel & Brown, 1981). In an ongoing process, people balance their need for closeness and intimacy with a need to maintain a sense of self and privacy.

Equity and relationships

Equity or fairness is important to any relationship. Even when it entails sacrifice, we are motivated to maintain a sense of fairness between our friends and ourselves. According to the principle of **social exchange**, we try to maximize rewards and minimize costs in our relationships (see Chapter 10). It is most likely to be valid between strangers and casual acquaintances and in the earliest stages of a relationship. As the bonds become more firmly established and mutuality develops, immediate exchange—and even fairness—figures less and less. As intimate partners, we have more to gain and more to give and we become increasingly concerned with building the relationship. Interestingly, while feelings of inequity do not predict later dissatisfaction in a relationship, the reverse is true: when people are dissatisfied, they are more likely over time to feel increasingly underbenefitted in a dating relationship (Sprecher, 2001).

Foa (1971) proposes *six interpersonal resources* that can be exchanged: love, status, information, money, goods and services. When we examine these, we can understand that the value of some resources depends on the person who gives it (**particularism**). For example, money is valuable (subject to the rate of exchange) regardless of who gives it, a supper probably tastes better when cooked by a special person (service) and love is a value that depends almost entirely on who does the loving. On the other hand, resources also vary in concreteness. Goods and services are tangible—things you can see, smell, taste or touch—while status (e.g., praise) and information (e.g., the shortest route from Nelson, B.C., to Corner Brook, Nfld.) are verbal or symbolic, and love and money have both symbolic and concrete value. Generally speaking, we prefer exchanges within the same classes. She helps to repair his car (service) and he responds with flowers (goods), but we rarely exchange money for love.

Social exchange is also complicated by an "egocentric bias": people tend to overestimate their own contributions. In one study of married couples, spouses rated independently how much responsibility they took for 20 relevant activities (e.g., cleaning house, planning recreational activities, childcare). On a 150-point scale, responsibility ratings by husband and wife ought to total 150. For example if he rated himself as 80/150 responsible for childcare, she would rate her responsibility as 70/150. In fact, the average total for

73 percent of the couples came to more than 150 (Ross, & Sicoly, 1979). Generally, more satisfied couples tend to agree about the contribution of each partner to the relationship (Christensen, Sullaway & King, 1983; Sprecher, 2001).

Exchange versus communal relationships

Intimacy involves a transformation from *exchange relationships* to *communal relationships* (Clark & Mills, 1993). **Exchange relationships** are based on an economic model in which people seek to maximize benefits and minimize costs. Equity is established by reciprocity: you do this for me and I do that for you. **Communal relationships** are dramatically different. The goal is not reciprocity but providing a benefit for the other and continuing the relationship. If the relationship is secure and mutually satisfying (i.e., equitable), both participants can forgo immediate reciprocation and will not need to "keep score" of rewards and costs. Indeed, such bookkeeping would seem cold and awkward. Concerns with equity in a relationship are less important when people "include the other in the self," that is, think in terms of "we," the relationship, rather than "you" and "I" (Medvene, Teal & Slavich, 2000). Indeed in longitudinal research, it was found that falling in love was accompanied by increases in both the complexity of the self-concept and feelings of self-worth (Aron, Paris & Aron, 1995).

Not surprisingly, a study of people who were divorced and remarried showed that they expressed a sense of inequity or deprivation in their former marriage but equity in the current marriage. Perhaps more surprisingly, satisfaction for women in the present marriage was strongly associated with feelings of equity whereas satisfaction for men was related to feeling overbenefitted (Buunk & Mutsaers, 1999).

Illusion and reality in close relationships

Common sense and pop psychology both preach the virtues of being realistic. However, Taylor (1989) has made a strong case for the benefits of what she calls "positive illusions," arguing that somewhat unrealistic optimism about oneself, the world and the future is beneficial to mental and physical well-being (see Chapter 16). With regard to intimate relationships, the poets tell us that "love is blind," suggesting that illusions about the partner are part of our schema of romantic love. On the other hand,

we are warned that idealizing one's partner indicates only an infatuation that leaves one vulnerable to disappointment. While love may be blind, we also want the other to "love us as we are."

Research into this dilemma informs us in several ways. First, people tend to be more optimistic about their own relationships than are others who know them. In a longitudinal study of dating couples, actors were asked to indicate their predictions about the future of their relationship as well as their general feelings about romantic love and about their current partners. A same-sex observer, matched to each actor, was presented with all parts of the questionnaire filled out by the actors except for the predictions and was asked to predict the future of that relationship. Although the dating couples had been together less than six months, fully one-third expected to remain together for a lifetime—a level of optimism far above what was shown in the follow-up study. Observers on the other hand were somewhat more pessimistic (Buehler, Griffin & Ross, 1995).

Do people show similar positive illusions about their partners? Participants in a study (Murray, Holmes & Griffin, 1996) who were married or dating, rated themselves and their partners on a number of characteristics (e.g., kind and affectionate, critical and judgmental, distant, emotional, understanding). Then they rated what they would consider to be the "typical partner" and "ideal partner" on the same dimensions. Overall, the results showed evidence that they idealized their partners, rating them as closer to their own ideal than the partners rated themselves. Perhaps more important, those who saw their partners in a positive light—even an illusory positive light—were most satisfied with their relationships. Of course, we cannot infer that idealizing your partner makes you more satisfied or that satisfaction with your relationship leads you to idealize your partner. Seeing your partner in the best possible light may provide a degree of security and may prevent the inevitable irritants and disagreements from becoming major difficulties.

Does this mean that you must avoid reality in order to maintain your most important relationships? Certainly, the Murray et al. study does not suggest an absolute break with reality but rather being positively biased towards your partner and giving your partner the benefit of the doubt. Rusbult (1996) offers another interesting perspective, one that she calls the "Michelangelo phenomenon." The great sculptor did not seek to shape a piece of marble to his specification but rather chipped away at the stone in order to allow an idealized form to emerge. Recall from Chapter 3 that we seek to compare our self-image to an ideal self. Research evidence indicates that this process of changing ourselves depends on the extent to which our partner affirms that ideal (Drigotas, Rusbult, Wieselquist & Whitton, 1999). In the most satisfying relationships, both people act so as to bring out the best in each other, reaching towards some ideal that they implicitly share.

Commitment and investment

Rusbult (1983) adds the important concept of *investment* in a close relationship defined in terms of both tangible things (possessions) and the intangibles, the time and emotional energy spent in sustaining the relationship. She demonstrated that when we are conscious of having invested time, effort and resources, we may remain committed to a relationship although not necessarily satisfied with it. Indeed in a longitudinal study, investment, as measured at one point in time, predicted marital stability or disruption 18 months later, again in addition to relationship satisfaction and even the availability of an attractive alternative. A recent meta-analysis of 52 studies and over 11 000 participants provides impressive support for the importance of this principle (Le & Agnew, 2003).

While investment may intensify commitment, there may still be times when the relationship (friendship or romantic) is in difficulty whether from external circumstances (e.g., financial), disagreements, unfaithfulness, etc. Adversity can indeed bring people together or drive them apart. It depends on two factors: the level of adversity and the level of commitment to the relationship—this is the *commitment calibration hypothesis* (Lydon, 1999; Lydon, Meana, Sepinwall, Richards, & Mayman, 1999; Lydon, Fitzsimons & Naidoo, 2003). If the level of adversity is lower than the level of commitment, the relationship will not be threatened and no action is required. Now consider the case where the level of adversity is significantly greater than commitment. There will be little incentive to persist and try to save the relationship. We act in adversity to save the relationship when adversity and commitment are more-or-less equivalent. In this case, we will act to save a relationship that we are deeply committed to even when there are major difficulties to overcome. Without doubt, acting in these circumstances can in turn increase our commitment (recall Chapter 6 and the discussion of how

behavioural change can arouse cognitive dissonance that can lead to attitude change).

Gender and friendship

Same-sex friendships

Studies within Western cultures consistently show that men's same-sex friendships tend to be less intimate and supportive than female friendships. That is, female friends talk about difficulties and feelings while men engage in activities together (Bank & Hansford, 2000). Several explanations are suggested: that men lack parental models for more intimate friendships, masculine self-identity, perhaps homophobia and a more competitive orientation among men.

Fehr (1996) discusses the confusion that still exists about this topic. One interesting suggestion is that men may only appear less intimate in their friendships because intimacy is defined in a "female" manner. That is, if intimacy is defined in terms of verbal self-disclosure and support and women engage in more of this type of behaviour, then female friends are more intimate. However, if we define intimacy more broadly in terms of an emotional bond, a feeling of closeness or "we-ness," then perhaps this can be attained through self-disclosure (the "female path") or through shared interests, activities and adventures (the male path). Clearly for instance, the intimacy which life partners reach after many years derives at least in part from a wealth of shared experiences, good and bad. Similarly, there is more to friendship than emotionally based self-disclosure (Wellman, 1992). On the other hand, research suggests considerable overlap between male and female patterns, particularly that both men and women specify self-disclosure as part of their definition of intimacy (Monsour, 1992).

Opposite-sex friendships

From an evolutionary perspective, Bleske & Buss (2001) hypothesize that while both men and women may form friendships with the other sex to acquire a possible mate, men also seek (or hope for) sexual access and women seek protection. Questionnaire data from two studies supported these hypotheses. However, the literature on this topic reveals a more complicated picture (Baumgarte, 2002). O'Meara (1989, 1994) suggests a number of challenges to opposite-sex friendships. The two people must define their emotional bond in a way that is comfortable to both of them, such as in how inti-

Cyber-Relationships

Of course the Internet offers people a new and powerful means of communicating with others over great distances. New forms of relationships have emerged with the expansion of the Internet, particularly on chat lines using software such as ICQ and MSN. These relationships can be described as "impersonal intimacy" because the interaction is limited to one channel, which enables each partner to have complete control over the breadth, depth and even accuracy of self-disclosure. They may simply be chat-line partnerships, friendships, even romantic and erotic relationships. The partners do not (or need not) know what the other looks like, eliminating the potent cues of physical attractiveness. They do not hear the voice of the other and thus lack all nonverbal cues. Self-disclosure is limited to what is revealed through this one channel; both the attractions and possible dangers of physical intimacy are absent; and the individuals are, in most cases, completely disconnected from each other's network of family, friends and other relationships. Finally, the cues for detecting deception (Chapter 2) are, for the most part, lacking and so people can present themselves as they wish.

Levine (2000) suggests several ways in which "virtual attraction" is unique in terms of what we understand about social attraction. Self-presentation is more fluid and spontaneous and under personal control (e.g., sending or exchanging sound or picture files). While we may perceive similar interests, it is difficult to confirm. Self-disclosure and intimate communication often takes place more quickly online than in the face-to-face situation perhaps because there is less risk. Indeed, participants sometimes express amazement at the companionship, warmth and intimacy that may develop in these relationships (Lea & Spears, 1995).

Is there any truth to the stereotype that those who are frequent users of the Internet tend to be lonely, unattached people? Several studies bear on this question (Amichai-Hamburger & Ben-Artzi,

2003; Fogel, Albert, Schnabel, Ditkoff & Neugut, 2002; Shaw & Gant, 2002; Leung, 2002; Moody, 2001). It must first be understood that people have different or multiple purposes in using Internet communication: to socialize with relatives and friends over distances, to meet with new virtual partners, and to gain information (Fogel et al., 2002). Some evidence suggests that loneliness is related to frequent Internet use perhaps with the goal of alleviating the loneliness but perhaps increasing the loneliness as the user is isolated from real social interactions. Interestingly, Internet users show decreases in both loneliness and depression during and after Internet use.

Does interpersonal communication over the Internet reduce social involvement as argued by Kraut, Patterson, Lundmark, Kiesler, Mukopadhyay & Scherlis, (1998)? One way of responding to this question is to see how these cyber-relationships develop over time. What happens when an on-line relationship moves from the monitor screen to face-to-face? McKenna & Bargh (2000) found that two people like each other more on meeting each other if their initial encounter was over the Web than if

This picture represents a curious hybrid: a space where people go to be in the physical presence of people while conversing (sometimes intimately) with people who are not there.

(continued)

their initial meeting was face-to-face. Those who can disclose their "true" or inner self to others on-line will be more likely than others to move these friendships to a face-to-face situation (McKenna, 2002).

One can readily understand the allure of such relationships to those who are shy, unattractive or have limited mobility. It is also possible to explore new roles: in one case, an apparently disabled woman turned out to be an able-bodied male psychiatrist who wanted to see what it felt like to be perceived as female and experience the intimacy of female friendships (Van Gelder, 1985). In the absence of the physical cues (age, gender, attractiveness, nonverbal cues) that are so salient in face-to-face interactions, the networks offer a shortcut to intimate self-disclosure and mutual support.

Indeed one longitudinal study of participants before and one to two years after they had become connected to the Internet, reveals that greater use of the Internet was associated with declines in the participants' communication with others in their households and the number of people they socialized with at least once a month. Perhaps more alarmingly, those who spent the most time on-line showed increased levels of loneliness and depression over that time. Thus, Internet relationships may have become an unsatisfactory substitute for genuine strong ties with others (Kraut et al., 1998).

mately they will disclose to each other. Of course, this must include issues of sexuality because sexual attraction may in fact become a source of confusion and tension between them. Since friendship implies equality, then issues of gender equality must be considered. It seems that individuals in cross-gender friendships must deal with societal disapproval (or at least suspicion), having to "explain" their friendship to others. In some occupational settings, gender segregation persists.

The "platonic" friendship

Can former lovers still be friends? Busbook, Collins, Givertz & Levin (2002) interviewed students about their current relationship with former dating partners. Consistent with social exchange theory, those who received more resources from their former lovers (help, support, etc.) were more likely to remain friends. However, involvement in a new romantic relationship and disapproval by friends were barriers to such friendships.

From attraction to intimacy

Clearly, the factors that lead to initial attraction are not those that lead to committed, intimate relationships. After studying factors that predicted the longevity of dating relationships, Kerckhoff and Davis (1962) proposed a sequential filter theory. Individuals first compare themselves on social and demographic characteristics (religion, socioeconomic status). Then they look for what they have in common in attitudes and values. If the relationship survives, long-term commitment will be based on the extent to which their needs are complementary. Consider the common belief that while similarity of factors such as religious and socioeconomic status brings people together, it is the "complementarity" of needs that keeps them together (Winch, 1954, 1958). For example, people who want to be "mothered" or "fathered" are likely to be happy with a partner who needs to take care of someone. However, research evidence does not provide strong support for this apparently sensible idea. In part, this stems from the difficulty in defining needs and in defining which needs will complement others. For instance, a person who has a need to dominate another may not be satisfied by a person with a need to be dominated—it is difficult to feel dominant when one encounters no resistance.

How then can we describe an intimate relationship? A number of criteria for intimacy have been proposed: (1) two people interact with each other more than with others; (2) they seek to restore proximity when they are apart; (3) they engage in self-disclosure; (4) they communicate what is unique about their relationship; and (5) they anticipate the reactions of the other person (Burgess & Huston, 1979). In order to maintain a close and satisfying relationship over time, those involved "mind" their relationship (Harvey & Omarzu, 1997), in a five-step process:

1. Continuing behaviours aimed at understanding one's partner including listening, observing and questioning.

2. Making attributions about both one's partner and about things that happen indicating one cares about the partner and the relationship. (For instance, we may give our partner the benefit of the doubt when things go wrong, expressing the positive illusions described above.)

3. Accepting what one has learned about the partner through self-disclosure and attempting to soothe and neutralize tensions and anger.

4. Reciprocating the thoughts, feelings and actions of the partner.

5. Continuing the process over time. Time allows us not only to know our partner more intimately but also to develop trust, confidence and a sense of investment in the relationship.

Intimacy can be found in relationships among family members and close friends as well as married couples and lovers. Since romantic love is a special form of intimacy, it has received special attention.

Love

While philosophers, poets, songwriters and artists have always been fascinated with the topic of love, it may be considered daring—perhaps presumptuous—for social psychologists to study it scientifically. Indeed, some have argued that science is misplaced in this area and even those public funds for such research are misspent. One of the pioneers in social psychological research on love described her experience as a researcher in this area as analogous to "stepping on land mines" (Berscheid, 2003).

Sternberg and Grajek (1984, p. 312) observe that "people have been known to lie, cheat, steal and even kill in its name, yet no one knows quite what it is." While love would seem to be a universal human experience, about 10 percent of adults believe they have never been in love and a substantial number of others have decided that love is too painful and thus they intend to avoid it in the future (Tennov, 1979). For different people, romantic love may represent a passionate emotional and physical involvement, an interpersonal "game" of manipulation without deep emotional involvement, or a relaxed, down-to-earth friendship. Thompson and Borrello (1992) argue that the predominant characteristic of love is obsessive thought about the loved one. Since we have much to learn about love, perhaps the scientific method, which

has proved so successful elsewhere can be useful here as well (Thompson & Borrello, 1992).

People make a clear and sharp distinction between loving someone and being "in love" with someone (Berscheid & Meyers, 1996). In our culture, we tend to "fall in love" (a revealing expression!) and then marry. But there are many cultures (India, for example) in which the opposite is the rule. The parents arrange marriages and the couple may not even meet until the time of the wedding. In that culture, love is not a motive for marriage but an expected outcome of the union.

A number of theories of love have been specifically developed within social psychology (Hendrick & Hendrick, 2000). Here are some of the most influential of them.

A triangular model of love

Love can assume many forms and varieties, such as the love of one's mate, brother or sister, child, parent or grandparent, friend or country. Further, love can evolve or change over time, such as when the passionate love of the honeymoon becomes companionate love. How can we conceptualize love as a state?

Sternberg (1986) has proposed a **triangular model of love** representing the varieties of love. All love experiences have three components, represented as points on a triangle (see Figure 8–3). These components are as follows.

INTIMACY The closeness or bond between the two people including communication, self-disclosure and a desire to care for the loved one.

PASSION The emotional and physical arousal in the love relationship. While physical attraction and sexuality may be prominent, especially in the early phases of the relationship, other intense feelings may also contribute to the experience of passion. Note that the emotions associated with feeling "madly in love" may be elicited by memories of special times involving the partners or by special songs (Mashek, Aron & Fisher, 2000).

DECISION/COMMITMENT Representing not only the decision to love someone but also the commitment to maintain that loving relationship.

Varieties of love experiences can be described in terms of the relative importance of the three components (indicated by the solid and dotted lines in Figure 8–3). For instance, liking in a friendship involves intimacy and commitment in the absence of passion. Infatuation consists of passion without intimacy or decision/commitment. Romantic love derives from a combination of intimacy and passion without commitment; or liking with the addition of physical arousal and attraction. Companionate love involves intimacy and decision/commitment in which the passion, at least in a physical sense, has subsided. Sternberg also describes the stagnant love relationships ("empty shell") in which commitment persists without intimacy or passion, and the ideal, consummate love represented by an equilateral triangle in which intimacy, passion and commitment are combined in full measure.

An interesting contemporary form of relationship is cohabitation, living together without marriage. Cohabitation offers a way to blend two opposing needs: independence and relatedness. That is, while many people in this period of life are striving for independence and individual validation, they still want and need an intimate, supportive relationship. They seek the relationship of deep intimacy and passion but with limited commitment. Their solution is cohabitation (Newcomb, Huba & Bentler, 1986).

Sternberg's framework pulls together many previous research findings and concepts. For example, Fehr (1993) describes a prototype—what people consider a typical example—of love. Three fundamental features of this prototype have been identified (Aron & Westbay, 1996): passion, intimacy and commitment. Thus, the model corresponds quite closely to how people in general (in Western cultures, at least) understand love. That is, our behaviour and experience in love can be described as schema-driven, the schema of love (Fehr & Russell, 1991).

Another interesting question concerns change over time. For instance, passion is generally recognized as high in the early "honeymoon" phase of a relationship, while intimacy builds more gradually as the relationship is sustained over time. However, does passion change as a consequence of increasing feelings of intimacy or closeness in a relationship? While there is some evidence that passion does increase as people feel more intimacy with each other, further research is needed to establish the conditions under which passion may wax or wane over time (Baumeister & Bratslavsky, 1999).

FIGURE 8-3

Sternberg's triangular model of love

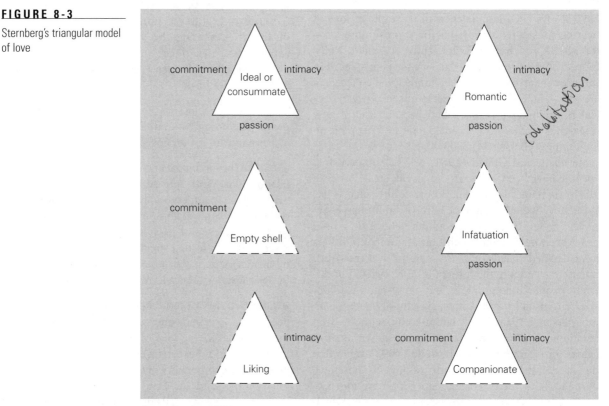

Source: Sternberg, 1986

Liking or Loving: Definition and Measurement

In reviewing the research, Berscheid (1985) suggests several ways in which liking and loving differ:

- Liking is relatively stable over time whereas romantic love tends to be more fragile and volatile.

- Liking is strongly influenced by the actual exchange of rewards whereas romantic love is influenced more by what we anticipate in the future.

- Liking is influenced in a logical way by rewards (we like people more who reward us more) whereas romantic love is often unrelated or even intensified by frustration or rejection.

Of course, romantic love also implies sexuality, and the relationship between love and sex is a topic of enduring interest (Hendrick & Hendrick, 2002). At least three orientations have been identified: love is more important than sex, sex demonstrates one's love and love comes before sex. Note that this research was conducted with U.S. students and differences may be found in other age groups, other societies and other socioeconomic positions in society.

What seems clear is that loving is not simply an extreme form of liking. In order to study how they are interrelated, we must first operationally define both constructs. After reading an assortment of definitions and descriptions of love by novelists, poets, clinicians and scientists, Zick Rubin (1970, 1973) made up a series of statements and asked a number of judges to sort them into "liking" and "loving" categories. He found very high agreement on some items. Through several revisions, he ended up with two nine-item scales, one for liking and the other for loving. The following examples are drawn from both scales:

1. Liking Scale
   a) Evaluation:
      "Most people would react favorably to _____ after a brief acquaintance."
   b) Judgment, Respect:
      "I have great confidence in _____'s good judgment."
   c) Adjustment:
      "In my opinion, _____ is an unusually mature person."
2. Loving Scale
   a) Attachment:
      "If I were lonely, my first thought would be to seek _____ out."
   b) Caring:
      "I would do almost anything for_____."
   c) Intimacy, Absorption:
      "I feel very possessive about _____."

These scales were administered to 182 dating couples. Each person filled them out about his or her partner and best friend. Scores on the liking and loving scales were correlated positively but only moderately so: 0.56 for males liking and loving their girlfriends and only 0.36 for females liking and loving their boyfriends. These results suggest that while the two are related, people, especially females, can like someone very much without loving that person and they can even love someone without liking him or her. The scores of both males and females on the love scale correlated highly with research participants' own reports of being in love and with their estimates of the likelihood that they would eventually marry their partners.

In a laboratory investigation, couples who scored high on the love scale spent more time gazing into each other's eyes during a conversation. In a follow-up six months later, those who had scored high on the love scale reported that their relationship had become more intense. Another study (Dermer & Pyszczynski, 1978) showed that people who have been erotically aroused produced significantly higher love scores (for their partners) but not liking scores. However, Sternberg and Grajek (1984) report that scores on the liking scale were the single most powerful predictor of the long-term success of a love relationship. The research and the arguments about liking and loving continue.

A useful perspective on this question of change is the distinction between passionate love and companionate love (Walster & Walster, 1978). Passionate love is an overwhelming, ecstatic condition, while companionate love is a low-key but deeply felt involvement, commitment and friendship. It would seem reasonable to assume that passionate love characterizes the earlier stages of the relationship and that when the honeymoon ends, passion is inevitably replaced by companionate love. Yet women studied after an average of 33 years of marriage exhibited both companionate love and considerable passion for their mates (Traupmann & Hatfield, 1981). Evidently, these may not be different types of love but phases in a long-term relationship.

While romantic love is a universal experience, prototypes of romantic love are bound to particular cultures. Recall the distinction between individualist and collectivist cultural values (Chapter 3). The prototype outlined above applies to individualist cultures such as those of Canada and the United States. In collectivist societies such as India, China and Japan, romantic love is less likely to be valued as a basis for marriage, and personal fulfillment and intimacy characterizes family relationships as well as romantic dyads (Dion & Dion, 1996). However in this era of the Western-dominated mass media, younger people in societies with collectivist traditions often adopt Western, individualist values, for better or worse.

Gender differences in love

At least in our culture, men and women differ with respect to romantic love (Dion & Dion, 1985; Hendrick & Hendrick, 1986; Peplau & Gordon, 1985). Surprisingly men tend to have a romantic view, believing that true romantic love comes once and lasts forever, conquers all barriers and social customs, is essentially strange and incomprehensible and must be basic to marriage. On the other hand, women tend to be more pragmatic: they believe they can be in love many times, that it may not last, that it inevitably fades into some disillusionment when the honeymoon ends and that economic security and friendship are more important as bases for marriage.

However, women's actual experiences do not always reflect this pragmatism. Men report that they tend to fall in love earlier than do women in a relationship. But women report that they have been in love more frequently and more intensely and are more likely to have had both pleasant and unpleasant experiences such as unrequited love. They tend more to like and even idealize their partners and they more often report

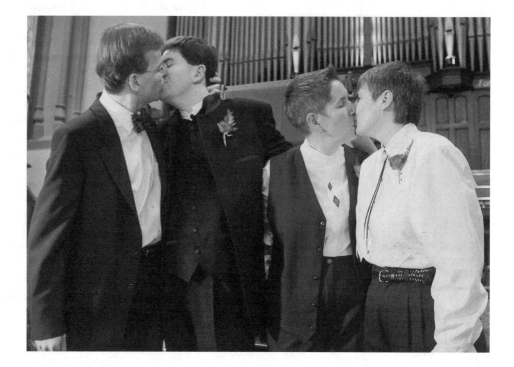

Same-sex marriages necessitate a broader understanding of love and commitment.

emotional experiences and euphoric "symptoms" such as "floating on air" or having trouble concentrating (Brehm, 1985). Perhaps women are more pragmatic in their selection of a love partner and in defining what love means, and yet more able to experience love as an intense emotional experience. Or perhaps women are simply more willing or able than are men to report intimate, intense experiences.

Why have these differences developed in our society in terms of what males and females believe about love and how they experience it? Romantic love enables individuals to adapt to society and maintain social institutions such as marriage, a bond, keeping a couple together (Dion & Dion, 1985). Since women have traditionally contributed less than men to the family income, they would have more to gain by pragmatically linking love and marriage. On the other hand, men are traditionally trained to be economically independent. While

the majority of wives now work, it is still considered less acceptable for husbands to be dependent on the income of their wives than vice versa. It is interesting that men are more likely than women to endorse items such as "Marry whom you love, regardless of social position," while women are more likely to agree that "Economic security should be considered carefully before selecting a marriage partner." Research also suggests that men fall into love more readily and women fall out of love more readily. Evidently, women more than men feel that they cannot waste too much time with the wrong partner (Hill, Rubin & Peplau, 1976).

One fascinating study revealing sex differences was conducted by Dion and Dion (1976). Couples were recruited in the Ontario Science Centre in Toronto. Each was asked to observe the other walking through an Ames room, a perceptual distortion apparatus in which objects look unusually large at one end and

CRITICAL THINKING

Gay and Lesbian Relationships: Are They Different?

Over time, society has come to recognize and accept the reality of same-sex relationships. Recently, this has taken the form of the controversy over same-sex marriages in which society would formally recognize the legitimacy of these committed relationships. In social psychology, the research on intimacy and relationship commitment has been conducted primarily about heterosexual relationships and, to a lesser extent, same sex friendships. While the social psychology of same-sex relationships would be expected to be similar to that of heterosexual relationships concerning intimacy, communication, commitment and love as outlined in this chapter, there are several complicating factors to consider. Among them are the still-controversial societal norms surrounding same-sex relationships; the impact of homophobic prejudices, which may mitigate against their acceptance in some communities; other stressors faced uniquely or more intensely by gay and lesbian people; differences in norms within the subcul-

ture of the gay/lesbian community; perhaps differences in personality among gay and lesbian people; and the role of transgendered and bisexual orientations (Huston & Schwartz, 1995; Herek, 2000; Lewis, Derlega, Berndt, Morris & Rose, 2001). While the social situation is still rapidly evolving, several contemporary research findings are of interest.

Some findings from longitudinal research indicate that the same set of factors predict relationship persistence over time whether same sex or opposite sex (Kurdek, 2000). On the other hand, it cannot be assumed that relationships between lesbian women are similar in all respects to those between gay men. Indeed, Peplau (2003) documents evidence of four important gender differences in sexuality, all of which characterize both heterosexuals and homosexuals: men tend to show greater sexual desire than women; women place greater emphasis than men on committed relationships as the context of a sexual relationship; aggression is more strongly

(continued)

linked to sexuality among men than among women; and women's sexuality tends to be more open to change over time than men's sexuality. Of course, note that these all represent average tendencies and cannot predict the individual behaviours of men and women of same-sex or opposite-sex orientations.

Indeed, recent findings indicate that male homosexuality is predicted by fraternal birth order; that is, with each additional older brother, a male becomes more likely to have a same-sex orientation. This finding suggests that the theories relating male homosexuality to early childhood experience with the mother, siblings or friends are likely not adequate (Bogaert, 2003). No such findings relate birth order to female sexual orientation (Bogaert, 2003).

One finding is that what constitutes a "successful" relationship may differ in same-sex as opposed to opposite-sex relationships. Issues of communication and power, in which we have seen gender differences, become different where power may be defined in male terms as "getting your way" but in female terms as creating consensus and rapport. Male partners tend to be more tolerant than female partners to sexual infidelity, although monogamy is a growing trend due in part to the ever-present threat of HIV/AIDS. Interesting gender differences

are evident here: while gay men more than lesbian women find their partners' emotional infidelity (involvement with another person) as most upsetting (Schrier & Buunk, 2001).

Perhaps with increasing social acceptance, same-sex relationship norms and dynamics will converge with those governing heterosexual relationships. Clearly, "coming out" about one's same-sex orientations and one's sexual partner is a major consideration. This may have implications, for example, about how the individuals are perceived at work and the extent to which they experience stress or support in their job (Griffith & Hebl, 2002). With acceptance, this will cease being a major factor in people's lives.

Of course, one indication of acceptance would be the extension of marriage to include gay couples. In 2003, this was an issue of great controversy in Canada. It is instructive to recall that, historically, marriage between partners of different races or ethnicities was also looked upon unfavourably or even not allowed by law. While marriage has been traditionally seen as a context in which to conceive and raise children, the frequency with which married couples cannot or choose not to have children indicates that these norms are also changing.

unusually small at the other. For males, the distortion effect was evident in observing both their partners and a stranger in the Ames room. However for women, distortion of their partner's appearance was significantly less than that of a stranger. Love seemed to modify women's perception of their partners—in the direction of reality.

Love and cognition

Both men and women believe that a love relationship should be intrinsic, based on concerns about the relationship itself and the partner rather than on external rewards. To study this belief, Seligman, Fazio and Zanna (1980) recruited dating couples and then manipulated their cognitive set by having each subject complete open-ended sentences. Half were sentences containing the phrase "because I," while the others

contained the phrase "in order to" (e.g., I date my boyfriend because I ... or I date my boyfriend in order to ...). Previous research had shown that repeated exposure to the phrase "because I" induced an intrinsic cognitive set while "in order to" led to an extrinsic set, a means to an end. Students given an extrinsic cognitive set then scored only about 50 on Rubin's love scale while both those with the intrinsic set and a control group scored about 61. When the research participants became conscious of possible extrinsic reasons, their feelings of love actually waned. Clearly, we are not supposed to have ulterior motives for love.

The experiment does not suggest that thinking in itself diminishes love. Indeed the more you think about an issue, the more polarized or extreme your attitude will be on that issue (Tesser, 1978). Dating students were asked about their love for their partner and how often they thought about their partner (Tesser &

Paulhus, 1976). The data from two testing sessions two weeks apart showed that loving and thinking did influence each other: the more you love her, the more you think about her, and the more you think about her, the more you love her. Thus, absence may make the heart grow fonder—unless you are too busy or distracted to think about your partner very much.

Can passionate love be a misattribution?

According to an influential attributional model of love, three conditions are necessary for someone to "fall in love," as we understand it (Berscheid and Walster, 1974b). First, the person must be raised in a culture that believes in the idea of romantic love. Second, the person must feel a state of emotional arousal that is interpreted as love, an attribution for their feelings (Chapter 2). Third, an appropriate love object must be present, most often a physically attractive member of the opposite sex. Crucial to this model is how people interpret symptoms of their own physiological arousal such as a faltering voice, faintness, inability to concentrate, blushing, heart palpitations, muscle tremors: An old song aptly advises that "you're not sick, you're just in love."

That is, a person experiences a state of arousal and, in the presence of certain cues, attributes those feelings to romantic love. Of course, sexual attraction may be one source of this arousal and why sexual attraction can lead rapidly to love. What is interesting is that arousal may be elicited by distress and then attributed to romantic sentiments. Many intense relationships occur during the tension and terror of wartime. Seriously ill patients often fall in love with their physicians, nurses or therapists. While we may be quite aware of the initial source of our state of arousal, we may still be vulnerable to romantic involvement because of the intense emotional state and the possibility of reattribution.

Both experimental and field studies have supported the model. In one study, couples were asked to report on aspects of their relationship at two different times, 6 to 10 months apart (Driscoll, Davis & Lipetz, 1972). Examining changes over time, the researchers noted a "Romeo and Juliet effect": among unmarried couples, romantic love increased as parental interference increased. Couples reattributed at least some of their upset towards their parents as love. In another study, men walked across the shaky Capilano suspension bridge, which crosses a deep gorge in North Vancouver (Dutton & Aron, 1974). On the other side, they encountered an attractive female experimental assistant. These men later expressed more sexual imagery in a projective test and that they were more likely to telephone the assistant than were men who had met the same young woman after crossing a solid concrete bridge. Somehow the arousal caused by fear while wobbling in space was subsequently misattributed to attraction to the woman.

This interpretation of the Capilano bridge experiment was challenged. Kenrick and Cialdini (1977) argued that at the moment research participants met the young woman, they were feeling relief at having reached solid ground rather than arousal due to fear. Thus, they associated the woman with this feeling of relief, which constituted negative reinforcement (warning: negative reinforcement is not punishment). However, other research has linked arousal with attraction even when the arousal was caused by exercise (Allen, Kenrick, Linder & McCall, 1989). Given the presence of an appropriate person, a diffuse state of arousal may well be attributed to romantic love.

Relationship Problems

Social psychology has turned recently to the study of relationship problems, an area formerly the preserve of other disciplines. Theories and methods applicable to the study of close relationships can help us understand relationship disruption, loneliness and shyness.

Dissolution of relationships

In 1981, a storybook romance between the long-time bachelor Prince Charles and the elegant and beautiful Lady Diana culminated in a royal wedding. After some years of apparent contentment, the birth of two princes and an increasingly glamorous presence by the new Princess of Wales, tensions between Charles and Diana began to appear in public, amplified by the incessant interest of the tabloids. The marriage finally ended in 1996, 15 years after the storybook wedding, and subsequently Diana died tragically in Paris.

In general, marital failures are explained in terms of the following factors (Kurdek, 1993): (1) social factors such as socioeconomic class differences, differences in religious affiliation or financial difficulties; (2) personality traits that may predispose a person to distort the relationship; (3) an absence of interdependence, perhaps because one or both partners has available alternatives; and (4) large discrepancies between the partners such as incompatible personality traits or conflicts in values, attitudes or interests. However, we still have much to learn.

The antecedents and process of ending a relationship

Can we predict which marriages will survive and which will eventually break up? Several longitudinal studies provide insights. Bentler and Newcomb (1978) compared characteristics of couples who later did and did not separate. Those who later separated were less similar in age, attractiveness, personality and interest in art. The men described themselves as more extroverted and orderly and the women described themselves as less clothes-conscious and less congenial. In another study, it was found that both men and women who remain married are more conventional, less neurotic (over-reactive to stressful events) and less impulsive (Kelly & Conley, 1987).

Gottman and Levenson (1992) describe a "cascading" effect in which couples at risk of subsequent separation communicate in an "unregulated" manner, characterized by more conflict, anger, withdrawal and whining and less affection and interest in their partner. These couples also experience less marital satisfaction (not surprisingly) and poorer health, all of which lead to more stubbornness and withdrawal from interaction and to active consideration of separation. Interestingly, while couples tend to act directly to terminate the relationship, friends are more likely to use more passive strategies such as avoidance or withdrawal, simply letting the friendship "fade away" over time (Fehr, 1996).

To understand the process of ending an intimate relationship, Hill, Rubin and Peplau (1976) compared 103 dating couples who had broken up with 117 who were still together. Women initiated the majority of the break-ups and dissatisfied women were more likely than dissatisfied men to make the decision to leave the relationship. Similarity played a role; couples who broke up tended to be less similar in age, future educational plans, intelligence and physical attractiveness than couples who remained together. However, they were not less similar than intact couples in romanticism, sex-role attitudes or religious beliefs. Whether the couples had engaged in sexual relations early or late in the relationship or abstained from sexual involvement altogether did not predict whether the couple remained

together or broke up. A longitudinal study of dating couples found that, among those who broke up, the quality of the relationships was lower and an alternative partner was often available (Simpson, 1987). In addition among those who had broken up, emotional distress was related to how close they still felt towards the former partner. Finally, an interview study of dating couples by Felmlee (1995) found that, in some cases, the same qualities that first attracted one to the other such as being "unusual," "exciting," "unpredictable" were then cited as reasons for the breakup.

Why do people remain in unsatisfying relationships?

Levinger (1979) argues that in deciding to remain in or leave a marriage, people consider both the rewards and costs of staying and the rewards and costs of leaving. Rewards such as an alternative relationship or the freedom of being single again will tend to lead the person to dissolve the relationship, while anything that makes separation more costly will tend to maintain the relationship. A person may stay in an unsatisfactory marriage because of a concern about the children, a fear that friendships and social networks will be disrupted or a realization that a break-up will entail major financial sacrifices. This is the "empty shell marriage," where the marriage itself is unsatisfactory but formidable barriers to leaving remain. As noted earlier, when people feel that they have invested a great deal of time and effort in a relationship, they tend to persist in seeking improvement (Rusbult, 1983). Longitudinal research shows that couples who will break up tend to be less dependent on the marriage and on each other and also that one partner is less dependent than the other on the relationship (Drigotas & Rusbult, 1992; Kurdek, 1993). A balanced dependence is critical to a successful relationship.

Why do people who have been physically abused by their partners sometimes choose to stay in the relationship? While some have tried to explain such behaviour in terms of personal dispositions such as low self-esteem or masochism, such explanations ignore the crucial role of the *situation*. Rusbult and Martz (1995) interviewed women at a shelter, reporting that their commitment to remaining in the relationship was determined by three important variables: (1) satisfaction with the relationship despite the abuse (which was often attributed to external circumstances rather than to the abuser); (2) the quality of available alternatives such as another relationship or other living arrangements, education and employment opportunities; and (3) the woman's investment in the relationship, including the duration of the marriage, shared material possessions and children. This **investment model** (discussed earlier in the chapter) has been successful in predicting the course of various types of close relationships and it is striking indeed to find that abusive relationships follow similar patterns (Truman-Schram, Cann, Calhoun & Vanwallendael, 2000).

The impact of dissolving a relationship

There is abundant research evidence linking marital separation to a wide variety of stress-related disorders (Bloom, Asher & White, 1978; Burman & Margolin, 1992). In comparison with both now-married and never-married persons, separated and divorced persons are more prone to automobile accidents, psychiatric disorders, alcoholism, suicide, and death from tuberculosis, cirrhosis of the liver and certain forms of cancer and coronary diseases. More recent research has shown that people who are unhappily married tend to be less healthy than those who are no longer married. Obviously, stressful factors in divorce—financial difficulties, sexual problems, feelings of shame, guilt or failure, problems with children and sheer loneliness—play a role. Compounding these burdens may be a profound feeling of conflict or ambivalence, and each partner can have both intense negative and positive feelings towards the other. Weiss (1975) observes that a strong attachment often persists after love has disappeared.

Some evidence also suggests that men suffer more adverse effects of divorce than women (Chiriboga, Roberts & Stein, 1978). Perhaps a partial explanation may be found in evidence discussed earlier concerning gender differences in friendships. Wright (1982) describes friendships between females as "face-to-face" and those between males as "side-by-side." In our culture, males are generally reluctant to be intimate with other males (Rand & Levinger, 1979) and tend to be more dependent on marital relationships than are women.

Fischer and Phillips (1982) found that when a man marries, he tends to give up friendships (often including nonphysical friendships with women) but to keep in touch with casual acquaintances including people at work. Women tend to do the opposite. Their circle of casual acquaintances diminishes, but access to intimate friends is not affected. Thus even with a greater social network, the male who loses the romantic relationship may be emotionally isolated. This may explain why divorced women report that the most stressful period was before the separation while divorced men consider the period after the separation to have been the most difficult (Hagestad & Smyer, 1982).

Jealousy

Shakespeare's, *Othello*, is but one of many familiar characters destroyed by a tragic susceptibility to "the green-eyed monster" of **jealousy**. Salovey and Rodin (1984) argue that people distinguish between social relations jealousy (or possessiveness, the desire for exclusivity in a relationship) and social comparison jealousy (or envy, the desire to feel better than or at least as good as someone else).

Envy, or resentment at someone else's achievements or possessions can even lead to satisfaction at others' misfortune or suffering (Smith et al., 1996). In a clever study by Salovey & Rodin (1984), research participants working separately in same-sex pairs believed they were being tested for suitable personality for various career choices. Then they were given bogus scores that were either surprisingly high or surprisingly low on a dimension that was either relevant or irrelevant to their career choice (e.g., artistic sensitivity, business acumen). They then saw the bogus test results of their partner along with a self-descriptive essay ostensibly written by the partner. All research participants received the same essay but received different test results indicating the partner's success or failure.

Each subject was then asked to evaluate his or her partner on a questionnaire just before meeting that partner. The group of interest consisted of those in whom social comparison jealousy had been aroused: research participants who had just received negative, relevant self-feedback (e.g., those who wanted to go into medicine and scored poorly on that scale) and who believed that their partners had scored very well on the career-relevant scale. They tended to disparage their partners and rated them lower on a number of socially desirable characteristics but nevertheless expressed interest in a possible friendship. They also scored higher in measures of anxious and depressed mood states. Other research shows that people tend to disparage a rival on those characteristics believed to be most important to their partners although they may admire the rival on less salient characteristics (Schmitt, 1988).

To experience jealousy in a relationship, individuals must evaluate both the possible threat to the relationship and the behaviour of the partner (White,

1981a). That is, they first appraise whether there is a threat to the relationship that exceeds their tolerance level. Characteristics of the potential rival make a difference. In fact, greater jealousy is experienced when the attainments of the rival are in a domain important to self-definition. For instance if earning a good income is an important aspect of Bob's self-concept, he will feel more jealous of a partner who earns a higher salary than of one who is more popular or a better tennis player (DeStefano & Salovey, 1996).

Studies by Puente & Cohen (2003) indicate that people are generally ambivalent in how they view jealousy, seeing it as both a sign of insecurity and a sign of love. More disturbing, both male and female participants who equate jealousy with love are more accepting of violence by one partner against the other over a jealousy-related matter. Of course, this carries over into the courtroom where domestic violence in response to real or perceived infidelity may be treated more lightly.

The individual will then try to understand the situation by reviewing evidence about the threat (Was he really interested in Katherine?), alternative possibilities (She really was working late that night) and evidence that the relationship really isn't in danger (We're getting along so well together lately). While this thinking can be rational, the arousal of feelings of threat may lead to "catastrophic thinking" (She wasn't working that night or other nights either, she's cheating on me, making a fool of me, everyone probably knows, she'll leave and I'll be alone and miserable for the rest of my life) (Pines & Aronson, 1983; White, 1981b). When we feel jealous, we must deal with both the threat to the relationship and the threat to our self-esteem (Sharpsteen, 1995).

Recall our earlier discussion of attachment. Attachment style also relates to jealousy and how it is expressed. While securely attached persons express anger when jealousy is aroused, they tend to maintain the relationship. Those who show the fearful-avoidant style often blame others rather than their partner and the anxious preoccupied individuals express strong negative emotions in response to jealousy. On the other hand, dismissive-avoidant individuals experience little emotional response in such circumstances (Sharpsteen & Kirkpatrick, 1997).

Do research findings about gender differences correspond to stereotypes of clinging wives and insanely jealous husbands? There does not seem to be any global difference between males and females in self-reported levels of jealousy (White, 1981b), but there are differences in how jealousy seems to be experienced and expressed. Males tend to react to jealousy either by denial or in an angry, competitive way. Females tend to acknowledge their jealousy, blame themselves, become depressed and exhibit increasingly dependent behaviour. Interestingly, males seem to be more concerned with the rival than with their partner, a reaction that has been called the "rooster effect" (Thompson & Richardson, 1983).

How can we best cope with jealousy? Brehm (1985) suggests that we must first "de-romanticize" jealousy as representing "true love." Indeed more than 300 years ago, LaRochefoucauld remarked, "In jealousy there is more self-love than love." Then we must distinguish between rational and irrational reactions to this threat.

Loneliness

Most people have experienced situations in which they feel lonely—visiting a new country or location, being temporarily separated from a loved one. However, some people suffer from chronic or **dispositional loneliness**. During their first year of university, 75 percent of students questioned experienced some degree of loneliness (Cutrona, 1982). By the end of the year, only 25 percent were still lonely. These individuals tend to be more self-focused, asking fewer questions and making fewer statements about the other person. They also tend to be inappropriate in their style of self-disclosure (Solano, Batten & Parish, 1982). Either they pour their hearts out to a total stranger or they are unusually closed, revealing little of themselves even to someone they know well. Chronically lonely persons also tend to be less effective in nonverbal communication such as expressing and judging emotions (Gerson & Perlman, 1979). They are also more anxious about their perceived deficiencies in social skills (Solano & Koester, 1989).

What is loneliness? Perlman and Peplau (1981) identify three characteristics:

- It results from the individual's perception of deficiencies in the person's relationships.
- It is distressing and unpleasant.
- It is subjective rather than objective—we can feel intensely lonely in a crowd and not at all lonely when alone. (It is said that in order to portray loneliness, an artist must portray a person with others.)

Peplau, Russell and Heim (1979) outline an attributional model of loneliness based upon Weiner's (1974)

Shyness

Can social psychology offer understanding and help to people who hang back, withdraw, are unwilling to take social risks? This is the problem of shyness in which people excessively restrain their social interactions. Philip Zimbardo (1977) describes shyness in terms of being afraid of people, particularly those who may be emotionally threatening: friends who may not like you, members of the opposite sex who may reject you, authorities who may disapprove of you, strangers who are unpredictable. Many people are shy in some situations but not in others. For example, a student may be terrified of speaking in class but totally comfortable at a party—or vice versa. Some people in the performing arts are at ease on stage but quite shy in one-to-one encounters. Other people are painfully shy in most types of social encounters and suffer intensely because of it.

Zimbardo and his colleagues developed a number of techniques through a shyness clinic at a U.S. university. One involves a cognitive "restructuring" of social encounters that arouse anxiety. For example, shy people may enter an interaction with their own agenda such as getting to know as much as possible about another person in a conversation. Concentrating on such a goal may distract them from their own anxiety and give them a sense of control.

Another technique involved assigning shy people to a particular social role such as an interviewer in a survey. Here their role is sanctioned by the situation and a script is provided—the participants are just doing what they are trained to do. Thus "their egos are completely off the hook" (Zimbardo, p. 224). For each of about 100 interviews, the shy person was required to make the initial telephone contact, meet the stranger and carry out the interview

for up to two hours. Often they invited the respondents for coffee afterwards.

Shyness can also be treated through social skills training in which clients may observe models who interact comfortably, practise through role-playing, observe videotape replays of their social behaviour and carry out assignments involving social situations. Thus, they may learn how to speak comfortably on the telephone, carry on a conversation, give and receive compliments and express opinions. They may also learn how to interpret the reactions of others. Because they expect and fear rejection or disapproval, shy people may tend to misinterpret how others respond to them—giving them more to fear and more reason to be shy.

Finally, it may be important to look at how shy people interpret themselves (Brodt & Zimbardo, 1983). Usually, the shy person experiences physiological symptoms in an encounter such as increased heart rate, slight hand (or knee) tremors, and a dry mouth. According to attribution theory, the person attributes these responses to shyness, thus feeling more uncomfortable than ever ("There I go again... "). Shy female students were told they were participants in an experiment on the effects of noise and that they would probably feel effects such as increased heart rate, which would persist for some time after the noise ended. Just after being bombarded with the unpleasant noise, the students met an attractive male confederate. The shy females behaved in a more outgoing way to this person and afterwards reported having felt less shy. Because they were able to reattribute their physical symptoms to the noise rather than their own shyness, they were able to overcome the problem in that situation.

---

model of achievement attributions (see Chapter 2). Weiner observes that we explain our successes and failures in terms of internal or external causes and stable or unstable causes. Thus, I may attribute a victory in a tennis match to my inherent talent (stable inter-

nal), my effort on this occasion (unstable internal), the lack of talent of my opponent (stable external) or sheer good luck (unstable external). Peplau et al. argue that the experience of loneliness depends on how we explain the time or circumstance in which we find ourselves alone or relatively isolated. Our response to loneliness may also depend on it.

Not surprisingly, married people in general are less lonely particularly in comparison with the divorced or widowed (Perlman & Peplau, 1981). Among people who are separated, divorced, widowed or who have never married, men tend to experience greater loneliness than women (Peplau, Bikson, Rook & Goodchilds, 1982; Rubenstein & Shaver, 1982). However, surprising levels of loneliness are found in those who have been recently married (Sadava & Matejcic, 1987). In this study, loneliness was higher among husbands who felt less intimacy towards their wives and had greater worries about communicating with them and among wives who felt less love towards their husbands and did not self-disclose to them. That is loneliness reflected the quality of the relationship rather than simply its presence or absence. Since the research participants were recently married, some of them may have been chronically lonely persons who chose mates unwisely or who lacked the social skills to make the marriages function more satisfactorily. A comparative study of Chinese, Anglo and Italian Canadians showed that loneliness was more highly related to lower satisfaction with life in the latter group, perhaps reflecting the social cohesion in Chinese culture (Goodwin, Cook & Yung, 2001). In the late stages of life, con-

trary to stereotyped expectations, loneliness is not normative; it is reported in about 5–15 percent of older adults (Pinquart & Soerensen, 2001). Being female, of lower socioeconomic status, lower social competence and living in nursing homes all increase the risk of loneliness according to this meta-analysis.

Weiss (1973) distinguished between **social loneliness** or a lack of a network of friends, acquaintances and colleagues and **emotional loneliness**, a lack of intimate relationships. People may feel lonely because they lack romantic involvement, friendships, family bonds or ties in the larger community (Sermat, 1978). The research suggests that a lack in one area does not necessarily mean a lack in other areas; nor can one kind of relationship compensate for deficiencies in another.

There also seems to be a generalized underlying disposition or trait called loneliness and several scales have been developed to measure it (see Table 8–1) (Rubenstein & Shaver, 1982; Russell, Peplau & Cutrona, 1980). People who score high on global measures of loneliness tend to manifest introversion, self-consciousness, a lack of assertiveness, low self-esteem, anxiety, depression (Peplau & Perlman, 1982) and shyness. There is also some evidence that lonely people, particularly males, are more likely to be hostile or aggressive especially towards women (Check, Perlman & Malamuth, 1985) and that lonely people who drink are more vulnerable to alcohol problems

TABLE 8-1

Sample items from loneliness scale

1. I feel in tune with people around me.				
	never	rarely	sometimes	often
2. There is no one I can turn to.				
	never	rarely	sometimes	often
3. I feel part of a group of friends.				
	never	rarely	sometimes	often
4. I feel isolated from others.				
	never	rarely	sometimes	often
5. There are people who really understand me.				
	never	rarely	sometimes	often
6. People are around me but not with me.				
	never	rarely	sometimes	often

Source: Russell, Peplau and Cutrona, 1980

(Sadava & Thompson, 1986). Of course, any of these personal characteristics may be both a cause and a consequence of loneliness. For example, hostile or depressed people may experience failures in relationships thereby increasing their loneliness and their anger or depression.

A Final Note

The vast majority of the earlier studies consisted of laboratory experiments exploring initial attraction to a stranger. Such research has proven to be useful in establishing and refining our understanding of the importance of such variables as attitude similarity, physical proximity, physical attractiveness, reinforcement, reciprocated liking, communication patterns and arousal. The study of real-life relationships such as marriage and friendship has in the past been left largely to other social sciences and clinical disciplines. However, contemporary research has focused increasingly on the study of relationships over time and how they are established, maintained and terminated. Such research is helping to understand how interpersonal relationships evolve and is laying the groundwork for more effective approaches in helping couples in distress (Holmes & Boon, 1990).

Summary

1. The need to affiliate with others begins at the stage of infant attachment and persists throughout life. Certain factors such as intense fear or stress increase affiliative needs while others such as social anxiety, decrease affiliation.

2. We tend to be attracted to people in close physical proximity and to those who are physically attractive. To an extent, we are influenced by a stereotype that equates attractiveness with goodness and we are motivated to choose others who are roughly equal to ourselves in attractiveness.

3. When people are first getting to know each other (surface contact), attraction is related to the perception that people are similar and that the interaction is rewarding. We are attracted to people with similar attitudes because it is rewarding to be

with them, because we seek consistency in our attitudes and relationships and because we expect people we like to be similar to us.

4. If we have no choice about interacting in a situation, our liking of neutral or even negative persons may be enhanced.

5. Mutuality involves the perception of interdependence and intimacy. Reciprocity in self-disclosure is crucial to intimacy. According to the social penetration model, self-disclosure increases in depth and breadth as intimacy increases but is limited by a need to preserve privacy and by the use of nonverbal as well as verbal communication.

6. Equity is important to social relations including exchange in love, status, information, money, goods and services. In intimate relationships, exchange becomes more particularistic, more flexible and less egocentric.

7. In intimate relationships, the principle of complementarity becomes more important. The sequential filter model suggests that similar values are more important in the earlier stage of a relationship and that complementarity needs assume more prominence at a later stage.

8. Romantic love consists of varying degrees of passion, commitment and intimacy. It is perceived as depending on intrinsic, not extrinsic, reasons. An attributional model suggests that if a culture propagates the notion of romantic love, a state of arousal may, in the presence of certain cognitive cues, lead to an attribution of "being in love."

9. According to the evolutionary perspective, we are attracted to a potential partner by their "reproductive fitness," which may be represented by their beauty.

10. The dissolution of a relationship may depend on the anticipated costs and rewards of leaving it and on the anticipated costs and rewards of staying within it.

11. Research distinguishes between social relations jealousy (the need for exclusivity in a relationship) and social comparison jealousy (the need to feel as good as somebody else).

12. Loneliness arises from a perception of deficiencies in one's relationships. It may be social or emotional in nature and may have nothing to do with being alone.

Further Reading

BREHM, S. (1995). *Intimate relationships*. New York: Random House. A well-written, readable and comprehensive overview of contemporary social psychological research and thinking.

ETCOFF, N. (1999). *Survival of the prettiest: The science of beauty*. New York: Doubleday. A fascinating discussion of the effects of physical attractiveness, based on research, which takes a decidedly evolutionary perspective. Based on voluminous research but written in an engaging and nontechnical manner.

FEHR, B. (1996). *Friendship processes*. Thousand Oaks, CA: Sage Publications. An excellent review of theory and research into how friendships are formed, maintained and alas dissolved. One of a fine series of volumes on various aspects of close relationships.

HARVEY, J. (1995). *Odyssey of the heart: The search for closeness, intimacy and love*. New York: Freeman. A review of what social psychologists and other have learned, written in a nontechnical manner and with interesting case studies.

HENDRICK, C. & HENDRICK, S.S. (Eds.). (2002). *Close relationships: A sourcebook*. Thousand Oaks, CA: Sage Publications. A useful set of updated reviews of theoretical thinking and research in this rapidly-expanding area of social psychology.

RHODES, G. & ZEBROWITZ, L. A. (Eds.). (2002). *Facial attractiveness: Evolutionary, cognitive and social perspectives. Advances in visual cognition*, Vol. 1. Westport, CT.: Ablex Publishing. What's in a pretty face? A set of papers look at facial attractiveness from the perspectives of biological and evolutionary theory, social status and cross-cultural research. The notion that beauty is simply in the eye of the beholder is challenged.

SIMPSON, J.A. & RHOLES, W.S. (Eds.). (1998). *Attachment theory and close relationships*. New York: Guilford Press. A very useful set of papers on the theoretical foundations of adult attachment orientation and its measurement and the implications of attachment style for emotional self-regulation, close relationships and clinical applications.

Weblinks

International Society for the Study of Personal Relationships

www.uwinnipeg.ca/~isspr/ An organization of researchers who focus on friendships and love relationships. Includes reviews of recent journal articles, links to researchers, contents of recent conventions.

Personal relationships from a cognitive perspective

www.artsci.wustl.edu/~msahrend/SC.html A page of references for articles about applying social cognition to the study of close relationships.

Chapter 9

Prosocial Behaviour

Any man's death diminishes me, because I am involved in mankind; and therefore never send to know for whom the bell tolls; it tolls for thee.

John Donne

"It is a far, far better thing that I do, than I have ever done; it is a far, far better rest that I go to, than I have ever known."

Sydney Carton, upon taking the place of his friend at the guillotine

A Tale of Two Cities by Charles Dickens

Chapter Outline

Norman Bethune (1890–1939), son of a Gravenhurst, Ontario, evangelical minister, became one of North America's leading thoracic surgeons, inventing some of his own surgical instruments while working in Montreal's Royal Victoria Hospital. However, he eschewed a life of fame and luxury in order to pursue causes he thought were in the interests of the downtrodden masses. Having witnessed Franco's massacre of defenceless civilians on the streets of Madrid at the outbreak of the Spanish Civil War—a war supplied on Franco's side with tanks, planes and backup soldiers, courtesy of Hitler and Mussolini—Bethune went to work as a battlefield physician for the Loyalist forces who opposed Franco.

He founded the Canadian Blood Transfusion Service, the world's first mobile blood bank, which saved the lives of hundreds of Spaniards. After attempting unsuccessfully to rouse Canadian public opinion against the Nazi threat in Spain, his disillusionment with democracy led him to become a Communist. When the Loyalist side was all but beaten in Spain, Bethune went to China to help in the fight against the Japanese invasion. He soon became chief medical officer to Mao Zedong's armies, training uneducated peasants to be field physicians and taking his mobile field hospital wherever it was most needed. He died on November 12, 1939 after contracting an infection from a wound sustained during emergency

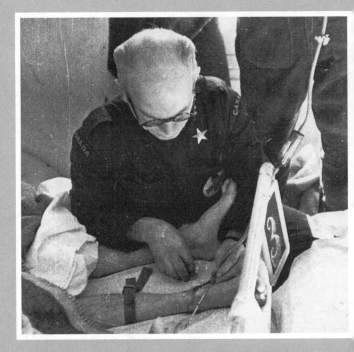

surgery. Although recognition was slow to come in his native Canada because of his Communist affiliation, he is revered as a legendary hero—"Comrade Beth"—in China to this day.

Norman Bethune is just one example of selfless service to others. Mother Teresa is another. A Roman Catholic nun, she chose to dedicate her life to the orphaned, the sick and the poor in the slums of Calcutta where she worked until her death in 1997. She was awarded the 1979 Nobel Peace Prize in recognition of her work.

People such as Bethune and Mother Teresa are testimony to the willingness of some individuals to sacrifice their comfort and security to help other less fortunate people. Sadly, the human story has its darker side: most people not only do not live up to these models of selflessness, but they sometimes fail to assist people in urgent need of help even when doing so might simply involve telephoning for an ambulance or the police. For example in 1999, two Winnipeg men on their way to a Halloween party encountered two teenage girls engaged in a fight at a street corner. One of the men went to intervene and was attacked and

stabbed in the chest 20 times. The second man picked up his bleeding friend but was unable to persuade several other passers-by to help him and finally had to seek out a pay telephone to call 9-1-1 (*Globe and Mail*, November 1, 1999).

This chapter examines the factors that influence individuals to help others and to intervene in crises and the reasons why bystanders sometimes fail to help someone in distress even in situations that involve minimal risk to the helper.

Helping Others

Prosocial behaviour and *altruism* are synonyms often used interchangeably to describe actions that are voluntarily carried out for the sole purpose of helping others without expectation of reward from external sources. The term **prosocial behaviour** is a neologism invented by social psychologists to avoid some of the connotations historically associated with **altruism**. Theologians and philosophers have traditionally defined altruism as behaviour intended to help others, not only without anticipation of external reward but without anticipation of *self*-reward as well. Self-reward could be in the form of enhancement of self-esteem or avoidance of guilt or shame (possible effects of not helping). From a philosophical point of view then, it could be argued that an act that brings pleasure, satisfaction or relief (internal self-rewards) to the actor is no different in principle from one that brings praise or profit or escape from punishment (external rewards).

There have been debates across the centuries about whether any act can ever be "truly" altruistic in that sense. However from the point of view of the social psychologist, it is difficult, if not impossible, to ascertain whether a person acted a certain way without anticipated self-reward. Moreover, to people who need help and perhaps even to society as a whole, it makes little difference whether people help because it makes them feel good or solely to benefit others. Thus, social psychologists focus on prosocial behaviour—helping behaviour without expectation of external reward—and do not generally concern themselves with whether it is "altruistic" in the pure philosophical sense or not.

How do we decide that someone has acted prosocially? Attributions play a major role in evaluating prosocial behaviour for we must decide what motivates an individual's actions. Of course, motives are often difficult or impossible to assess, and as well, we sometimes make faulty attributions. A campaigning politician who helps an elderly person across a busy street may not be seen as acting prosocially if we attribute that behaviour to the desire to "look good" to win votes, but can we be sure that he or she was simply trying to look good? A policewoman helping a lost child is unlikely to be viewed as acting prosocially for she is only doing her job. But what if she risks her life to plunge into a raging river to save a child? During the 2003 SARS crisis, health-care workers in Toronto literally risked their lives, and two nurses died, as they struggled to care for victims of this new and frightening disease; only a handful of them chose not to report to work. Were they acting prosocially or just doing their jobs? And what about Richard Gatling (1818–1903), inventor of the machine gun (which was tested in battle in the suppression of the

Northwest Rebellion at Batoche, Saskatchewan, in 1885)? Was he a "merchant of death"? Or was he actually acting prosocially as he claimed? He had studied medicine and was deeply disturbed by the carnage of war. He believed that by inventing a weapon that would do the work of 10 guns, only one-tenth as many soldiers would be needed in battle and therefore lives would be saved on the battlefield. An erroneous assumption of course—but should we consider his actions to have been prosocial because of his motivation, or antisocial because of the outcome?

Prosocial behaviour can take many forms: direct help to others, intervention in emergencies, volunteer work, cooperating with others, working to save the environment (Kollmuss & Agyeman, 2002), employee "whistle-blowing" (Gundlach, Douglas & Martinko, 2003), political activities aimed at bringing about positive social change and helping others develop skills or standing up for others (Bergin, Talley & Hamer, 2003).

The Bases of Prosocial Behaviour

Suppose we stopped people in the street and asked them why people such as Norman Bethune and Mother Teresa and others act as they do. Among the answers might be the following:

- Some people just seem to be born saints, always putting other people first.

- Physicians and nuns are supposed to act unselfishly: it's what's expected of them.

- A good upbringing—they were obviously brought up to be helpful to others.

- First you have to feel at peace with yourself, feel good about yourself; only then can you take on other people's problems.

- If you can put yourself in other people's shoes, if you can feel their suffering, then you've just got to help.

Each of these common-sense explanations touches on a body of social psychological theory and evidence bearing on the subject of prosocial behaviour.

"Born saints": Prosocial behaviour as an inborn tendency

Some theorists argue that natural selection favours the genetic transmission of factors that predispose an organism to act prosocially towards other members of its species. This was suggested by Darwin (1871) himself in his *Descent of Man*:

As man is a social animal it is almost certain that he would form an inherited tendency to be willing to defend, in concert with others, his fellow men; and be ready to aid them in any way which did not too greatly interfere with his own welfare or his own strong desires (Latané and Rodin, 1969, p. 189).

Some researchers (Buck, 2002) go even further than Darwin and argue that empirical evidence exists showing that genes can provide the basis not only for prosocial behaviour, but for genuine altruism and even "true love." A modern evolutionary approach to prosocial behaviour is embodied in the controversial theory known as **sociobiology**, which was introduced in Chapter 8. Sociobiology (Crawford & Krebs, 1998; Wilson, 1978) assumes that there are biological bases to at least some social and moral behaviours and that, consequently, these behaviours are subject to the same evolutionary processes that affect physical characteristics. According to this view, each organism is engaged in a struggle to send as many of its genes as possible into the next generation; any behaviour promoting this end is itself likely to be "selected" and reproduced from generation to generation.

Sociobiology posits a **kin selection** principle. Since we share some of the same genes with our close relatives, we improve the chance that our own genes will be well-represented in the gene pool of the next generation by helping relatives to survive at least long enough to reproduce. Therefore, a pattern of behaviour may be "selected" by the processes of evolution, even if it is not directly beneficial to the individual or to the individual's ability to reproduce, provided it benefits other closely related individuals.

As well as predicting more prosocial behaviour towards relatives than towards strangers, sociobiology has spawned a number of other hypotheses. For example, since males are much more capable of reproducing their genes than are females (because a male can have many more children), mothers should be more protective and prosocial than fathers towards each child for they have limited opportunities to get their genes into the next gene pool. The same reasoning would suggest that parents should be more prosocial towards male children than towards female children because males carry a greater potential for transporting each parent's genes into the next generation.

As fascinating as such hypotheses may be, sociobiology continues to engender considerable controversy within social psychology, and it is wise to view its claims with caution. The theory is difficult to test, and support for it comes largely from archival data and examples from the animal kingdom. Moreover, its failure to give much importance to learning and social influences is a particular shortcoming.

In conclusion, the contention that prosocial behaviour has a genetic basis has not been empirically verified. However, more general aspects of personality such as anxiety-proneness appear to be influenced by heredity and they might, in turn, combine with the learning history of the individual to make prosocial behaviour more or less likely.

"It's what's expected": Prosocial behaviour and norms

As we saw in Chapter 6, social norms exert considerable and often unrecognized control over behaviour. Essentially, they refer to what acts are not to be done and what acts should be done. We should not blow our noses on our sleeve; we should say "thank you" when someone serves us coffee. There are also more specific norms associated with particular roles, although behaviour carried out in the discharge of role responsibilities is not usually considered to be prosocial. The crossing guard is expected to show more helpfulness to children who wish to cross the street than to other pedestrians. Physicians and nuns are expected to help others, though only in a narrowly defined context. It's their job.

Several norms are relevant to prosocial behaviour. The **norm of reciprocity**, which operates in all cultures (Gouldner, 1960), requires us to help people who have helped us in the past; in other words, we reciprocate their assistance. On the other hand, the **norm of social responsibility** requires that we help people who are in need regardless of what they have done for us in the past or might do for us in the future (Berkowitz & Daniels, 1963). It is difficult to separate the effects of these two norms in any given situation— that is, to determine whether a person helps because of the obligation to help others in need or because of anticipated repayment.

A third norm, the **norm of equity**, specifies that fairness should serve as a criterion for the way we treat others (Walster, Walster & Berscheid, 1978). If we perceive that another person has tried as hard as we have, whether at some specific task or at life in general but has not been as fortunate, this norm would push us to share some of our good fortune with that individual: "It is only fair." If however, we perceive that the individual caused his or her misfortune then, according to this norm, we need not help. Thus, equity considerations would motivate us to help an individual who has "lost everything" in a fire but not an individual who "lost everything" in a gambling game. (See the discussion of distributive justice in Chapter 15).

We must be careful when trying to explain behaviour in terms of social norms. The research literature indicates generally that people's behaviour often departs from what is prescribed by these norms and that a large number of situational variables influence whether normative behaviour will be performed (Krebs & Miller, 1985). Norms are often vague in that they do not generally specify what behaviour is required (e.g., "We should help those less fortunate than ourselves") and moreover they can conflict with one another (e.g., we are taught to "keep our nose out of other people's affairs" and also to help others when they need help). While social norms may appear useful after the fact for describing behaviour, they may actually mislead or confuse us when we must choose what to do.

"A good upbringing": Prosocial behaviour and learning

Norman Bethune was the son of a clergyman and grew up in an atmosphere that stressed caring for others. The socialization process—perhaps involving reinforcement for prosocial behaviour and the acquisition of parental values that encouraged selflessness—may have played a critical role in shaping his character.

Many studies have demonstrated that at least in the context of North America and Western Europe, prosocial behaviour increases steadily with age up to about the age of 10 (Bar-Tal, 1976) and children as they grow become less self-centred and more willing to share (Benenson, Markovits, Roy & Denko, 2003). What accounts for the development of such behaviour? According to the cognitive-developmental perspective, prosocial behaviour is the consequence of attitudes and values (a "personal morality") shaped by the developing child's experience in the social environment. The social learning view, on the other hand, emphasizes the importance of reinforcement and modelling.

Cognitive-developmental perspective

According to this perspective, people help other people because of a personal set of values and attitudes that obligate them to provide assistance in certain situations. Failure to do so brings about feelings of guilt, which are aversive to the individual. This personal morality is said to develop gradually as the growing child moves from a view that adult rules are sacrosanct and unchangeable to a view that rules are made by human beings and are therefore somewhat arbitrary (Piaget, 1932). Building on Piaget's work, Kohlberg (1964) described a six-stage typology of **moral development**, which he also argued represented an invariant and universal developmental sequence, each stage occurring one after the other and always in the same order. In the first stage, the child is only concerned with the physical consequences of his actions and behaves properly only to avoid punishment. Later in the third and fourth stages, the child's conduct is governed by the desire to appear to be a good person in the eyes of other people through adherence to society's rules. Finally in the sixth stage, not always attained, the individual's behaviour is guided by reference to self-chosen, abstract, ethical principles that encompass a sense of responsibility towards other persons. Thus, a young child may help another child in order to avoid chastisement and an older child may provide assistance to others in order to "look good," but the "mature" person will do so on the basis of personal principles.

Although it has many critics, Kohlberg's theory continues to stimulate research and provoke controversy (Arnold, 2000; Dawson, 2002). One major source of criticism, as with Piaget's theory, is the claim for a universal sequence of stages in the acquisition of morality. Another serious limitation of Kohlberg's theory is that it presupposes a Western conception of the individual as an autonomous being who is free to make choices and determine his or her future (Dien, 1982). It assumes that morality develops as the individual makes personal decisions when faced with pressure to act contrary to ethical principles. However, it is not clear whether this applies in Eastern societies where group harmony and collective decision-making are stressed rather than individual responsibility.

Social learning approach

Unlike the cognitive-developmental approach that ties prosocial behaviour to moral values and attitudes, the social learning approach views prosocial behaviour as learned behaviour and takes for granted that such

Why Do Some People Donate Organs While Others Refuse?

More than 1800 transplants of kidneys, hearts, lungs or livers are carried out in Canada each year (London Health Sciences Centre, 2003). Yet in 2000, more than 3700 Canadians were awaiting transplants of these organs, and in that same year, 147 people died before suitable donors could be found. Indeed, Canada has one of the lowest rates of organ donation amongst industrialized nations, with fewer than 14 donors per million people as compared for example with more than 31 in Spain (Health Canada, 2001).

Canadians are urged to sign organ donor cards, which are attached to drivers' licenses in many provinces. Yet, according to an Environics poll conducted for Health Canada in 2001, while more than 90 percent of Canadians approve of organ and tissue donations, less than half have signed organ donor cards (Health Canada, 2002). The decision to donate was found to be higher than average among women, middle-aged Canadians and those with higher levels of education and income. Curiously, 19 percent of the respondents reported a fear that potential donors might be prematurely declared dead in order to get their organs and tissues!

The reluctance to sign an organ donor card appears to be related to some extent to personality variables as well as attitudes about life and death (Sanner, 1994). In one study (Lefcourt & Shepherd, 1995), subjects who were averse to signing organ donor cards were also reluctant to visit a dying friend or to attend a funeral. They appeared unwilling to deal with issues or situations related to dying. A study of Canadian university students found reluctance to donate organs to be significantly associated with high anxiety, low self-esteem and low internal locus of control (Campbell and deMan, 2000). Individuals with low self-esteem and high-trait anxiety apparently view organ donation as more threatening, for it makes them think about death, and they avoid the threat by not signing donor cards.

What about living organ donors—people who voluntarily give up a kidney or donate bone marrow while still young and healthy? In 2003, 40-year-old Sheryl Wymenga of Welland, Ontario, flew to Fargo, North Dakota, to donate a kidney to a total stranger after having advertised her willingness to donate a kidney on a website that invites people to become living donors (*The Globe and Mail*, May 26, 2003). What accounts for such behaviour? In a large British study of people who donated bone marrow to strangers, many donors, even when interviewed a year later, felt that their donation reflected a trait of generosity that was central to their characters (Simmons, Schimmel & Butterworth, 1993). In many cases, this trait could be traced to a strong emphasis in their families of origin on helping others.

behaviour is learned in the same way that any other behaviour is learned: through reinforcement, self-attributions and modelling. Parental discipline is assumed to play a key role.

REINFORCEMENT Prosocial behaviour is acquired and maintained, at least in part, through consequences deriving from the behaviour. As you will recall from Chapter 1, social learning theorists have pointed out that a rigid view of reinforcement suggesting that humans are automatons responding on the basis of external reinforcement is misleading; in part, people regulate their actions by *self*-produced consequences (Bandura, 1974). Thus, a child may learn to share toys or to help a sibling because he or she anticipates reward in the form of parental praise—praise that has been given for similar behaviour in the past. Both material and social reinforcement (such as praise) have been found to induce prosocial behaviour in children.

As children develop, so does the capacity for internal self-reward (i.e., feeling good about oneself in some way). In other words, the child learns to help others because he or she anticipates either gain through self-reward or, if no action is taken, punishment through guilt.

SELF-ATTRIBUTIONS Self-reward involves making attributions about ourselves: "I helped because I am a good person." Such self-attributions help define a standard for our behaviour, which we strive to maintain to avoid negative feelings about ourselves. If you see an elderly person struggling to pick up a dropped bag of groceries, it is hard to walk by without admitting to yourself that you are unhelpful and even callous. If such a statement contradicts your self-image as a helpful person, you will no doubt experience some discomfort. Fostering the development of positive self-attributions encourages prosocial behaviour.

Children are more likely to behave well if they attribute their behaviour to internal causes (their own personal morality) rather than to external causes such as threats of punishment or hopes of reward (Walters & Grusec, 1977). For example, a child who is tempted to steal and who attributes feelings of anxiety to moral self-judgment is more likely to avoid antisocial behaviour than a child who interprets anxiety as fear of the teacher coming back into the room. And a child who attributes his acts of charity to a personal concern with the welfare of others may be more likely to repeat such prosocial behaviour than the child who interprets her own generosity as the result of pressure from a parent.

In a classic study (Grusec & Redler, 1980), children who had won some marbles in a game had the choice of sharing these marbles with a child who had none. Children in one condition were praised when they gave away some of their marbles while children in another condition were helped to make positive self-attributions by being told that their donations reflected their inherent helpfulness. Children in a third condition were given neither praise nor help with their attributions. Children in the first and second groups gave about the same number of marbles, which was considerably more than the control group. However when the children were observed in a different context by different adults two weeks later, the children who had received the attributional statements were the most generous both in their efforts to be of help and in their willingness to make donations. Children who had been given reinforcement (praise) were the next most generous while the children in the control condition showed considerably less generosity.

MODELLING Several studies have demonstrated that children's responses to charitable models are durable and can be generalized. For example, seeing an adult donate to a charity positively influenced the children's own donations 10 days later even when the donations were elicited in a different setting by a different experimenter (Midlarsky & Bryan, 1972).

When models, like many parents, say one thing and do another, children's actions are influenced by the model's actions while children's words are influenced by the model's words (Radke-Yarrow & Zahn-Waxler, 1984). Hence, the child imitates the inconsistency of the model. This has been confirmed empirically (Grusec & Skubiski, 1970): third- and fifth-grade children were more likely to make a donation after seeing a model donate than after simply hearing the model say that people *should* donate. Yet, more recent research indicates that direct suggestions and instructions by themselves may nonetheless have a much more immediate influence on children's prosocial behaviour than was earlier believed and with enduring long-term results (Eisenberg & Mussen, 1997).

Although research often focuses on TV violence, psychologists have also naturally been interested in whether prosocial models on TV elicit imitative prosocial behaviour. In one study (Sprafkin, Liebert & Poulos, 1975), 30 first-grade children watched one of three half-hour programs popular with children in the 1970s: an episode from the *Brady Bunch* (a situation comedy), an episode from *Lassie* in which a boy risks his life by hanging over the edge of a mining shaft to rescue a trapped puppy, and an episode from *Lassie* that did not portray helping behaviour. The children then played a game in which each child at some point had to choose between continuing to play the game (which led to prizes for points accumulated) and helping a puppy in distress. Those who had seen the *Lassie* program with the helping scene helped significantly more than did the children from the other two groups (see Figure 9–1).

Other studies have produced similar findings. Whether what is used is a five-minute film clip presented only once, or a series of one-hour programs spread over several weeks, the effect on children's free-play behaviour is the same: watching prosocial behaviour on television produces prosocial behaviour in children (Hearold, 1986; Liebert & Sprafkin, 1988). Whether adults are similarly influenced has not yet been established.

On the other hand, prosocial behaviour may suffer as a result of violent video games. A meta-analysis of research into the effects of violent video games on

Duration of children's helping behaviour in Sprafkin, Liebert & Poulos (1975) study

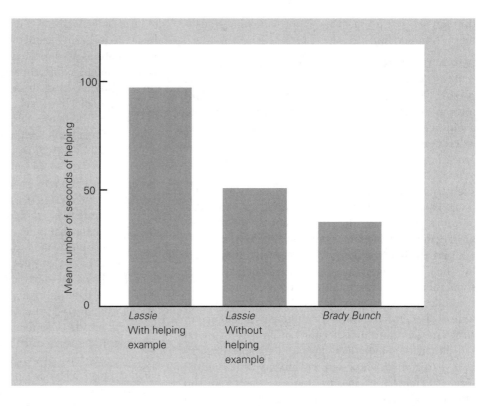

children and young adults found that playing violent video games is associated with decreases in prosocial behaviour (Anderson & Bushman, 2001).

PARENTAL DISCIPLINE One of the most important determinants of the development of prosocial behaviour is the emotional atmosphere of the home and the degree to which the parent displays a nurturing, affectionate attitude towards the child (Eisenberg, 2002). In a meta-analysis of five studies, two carried out in British Columbia and the other three in Ontario, involving a total of 150 families with young children, children's prosocial behaviours were found to be positively related to the extent to which parents responded to the child's own emotional distress in a tolerant and non-punishing manner (Roberts, 1999). By being guided and controlled through affectionate means, the child is likely to develop an internalized code of conduct involving a positive regard for others and a sensitivity to other people's needs and feelings.

Does the prosocial disposition developed in childhood endure? Apparently so. A longitudinal study examined the relationship between prosocial behaviour in childhood (as documented by reports and observations of prosocial behaviour in preschool) with proso-

cial characteristics when the participants were in their twenties (as reported by the participants themselves and by their friends). It was found that prosocial dispositions in adulthood were related both to demonstrations of empathy/sympathy and to prosocial behavior in early childhood (Eisenberg, Guthrie, Cumberland, Murphy, Shepard, Zhou, & Carlo, 2002).

What sort of discipline promotes the development of prosocial behaviour? Most discipline techniques involve both an arousal component (often synonymous with power-assertion, e.g., raising one's voice) and an inductive component through which the child is alerted to the consequences of his behaviour (e.g., "How do you think mommy feels when she sees ink all over her new carpet?"). If there is too little arousal, the child may ignore the parent but too much arousal can produce anxiety or anger, which will interfere with the assimilation of the inductive message.

The frequent use of induction leads to a moral orientation characterized both by a high capacity for guilt and by independence from external sanctions. In other words, the individual has a strongly internalized moral code and deviations from it lead to guilt. The frequent use of power-assertive techniques, on the other hand, tends to produce a moral orientation based on fear of

Socialization in the East and in the West

Child-rearing practices in the East differ in many ways from those of Western societies. For example, Japanese children are brought up to have a keen ability to participate vicariously in the experiences and feelings of their family members. Greater importance is attached to "skinship," prolonged body contact between family members through breastfeeding practices that encourage skin-to-skin contact well beyond the feeding itself, bathing in groups and sharing the bed with the mother (and even other members of the family as the child grows older). Such activities, it is argued, push the child to develop a close alignment with other people. Japanese parents emphasize disciplinary methods that promote empathy such as teaching the child how her behaviour will hurt other people's feelings (Weisz,

Rothbaum & Blackburn, 1984). Similarly, a recent study of children in Hong Kong found that harmonious family life was key to the development of a prosocial outlook: high levels of prosocial behaviour were associated with cohesiveness in family life and low family conflict (Ma & Leung, 1995).

In collectivist cultures such as Japan and China where cooperation and harmony are stressed, moral development is linked to conformity to group norms (see Chapter 4). In contrast, child training techniques in the United States focus on encouraging autonomy and individualism, goals reflected in Kohlberg's theory, which states that the ideal condition is one in which an individual relies on personally constructed principle (Weisz, Rothbaum & Blackburn, 1984).

---

external detection and punishment. The individual worries more about being caught than about whether a behaviour is morally correct. However, the occasional use of power-assertive techniques to communicate to the child that the parent has particularly strong feelings about a particular behaviour or value or to control an openly defiant child contributes positively to moral internalization (Hoffman, 1984).

"Feeling good about yourself": Prosocial behaviour and mood

Do people such as Norman Bethune and Mother Teresa help others because they already feel good? There is evidence that positive mood facilitates individual acts of charity or helping, while bad moods impede such behaviour (Forgas, 1998). For example when children in one study were asked to reminisce about happy experiences, they gave more to charity than did children asked to reminisce about sad experiences or children who were not asked to reminisce at all (Rosenhan, 1972). In another study, subjects who had just viewed sad movies donated less money to charity than other subjects who watched neutral movies (Underwood et al., 1977).

Several explanations have been offered for the relationship between mood and helping behaviour.

The warm glow of success

If success produces a good mood, then prosocial behaviour should be more evident following success than following failure. This was demonstrated in a study (Isen, 1970) in which subjects were given false feedback about their achievement in a series of tasks. Some subjects were told that they had scored well above the norm while others were told that they had scored well below the norm. Control subjects were exposed to the same tasks but did not do them. Then, when the experimenter was out of the room, the subjects (who waited one at a time) were observed to see whether or not they would help another person. A confederate, laden down with books, passed in front of the subject and "accidentally" dropped a book. Subjects who had experienced success were more often helpful than subjects in either the failure or the control conditions. In a related study, it was found that "success" led to larger contributions to a charity than did failure. Isen (1970) interpreted these results in terms of a positive mood engendered by success—the

warm glow of success, which predisposes people towards events that will engender more good feelings.

Image repair

Although the "failure" subjects in Isen's study were not especially helpful, other studies have found that making a mistake or committing a *faux pas* in public actually influences people to help others. A person who is embarrassed by her behaviour may take advantage of a situation in which helping others may help to improve or repair a damaged image. In one study (Bégin, 1976), subjects who experienced failure in a motor task subsequently helped the experimenter more than did either subjects who had experienced success or subjects who were in a control condition—especially when the potential beneficiary knew about the previous failure. In a related study, subjects were assigned to either success or failure conditions on the basis of their actual scores obtained on a real exam. As they were leaving the teaching assistant's room after learning their score on the exam, subjects were asked individually to contribute to a worthy cause. The helpfulness of the "success" subjects was not influenced by whether the canvasser knew their marks. Yet when the canvasser knew the marks of the "failure" subjects, those who had been told their grades were below the class mean contributed considerably more than did "success" subjects. When the canvasser did not know their marks, subjects contributed significantly less than did the "success" subjects.

These findings lend support to the **image-repair hypothesis**. While the warm glow of success leads successful people to act prosocially, those who have failed are likely to help only those who know of their failure. It is a form of impression management (see Chapter 3). In a related vein, other experiments have shown that a person who has harmed or hindered another often resorts to **reparative altruism**, trying to compensate for the harm done, although these efforts are not always directed at the person who was harmed. For example, subjects who administered shocks in a Milgram-type obedience experiment (see Chapter 6) were more likely to volunteer to help in a humanitarian project than were those who did not give shocks (Carlsmith & Gross, 1969). In this case, it can be argued that subjects are trying to expiate guilt by helping others.

Need for approval

It has also been found that subjects who have more need for approval are more generous in their donations, particularly when the donations are made publicly (Deutsch & Lamberti, 1986). This makes intuitive sense; by being publicly charitable, they can court the approval and admiration of others.

"Other people's shoes": Prosocial behaviour and empathy

Bethune was distressed at the sight of helpless civilians being massacred in the streets of Madrid during the Spanish Civil War. Is this why he later returned to Spain to help the Loyalist forces? No one knows for sure, but empathy with the suffering of others is a major factor in eliciting prosocial behaviour (Eisenberg & Miller, 1987, Grusec, 1991; Litvack-Miller, McDougall & Romney, 1997). Empathic arousal appears to be a universal human response, which is present to a degree even in one- and two-day-old infants, although it is modified by experience (Hoffman, 1981).

Yet, the exact nature of empathy is uncertain and it may well be that more than a single concept is involved. Empathy is not just sympathy. While **sympathy** refers to a heightened awareness of another person's suffering and a desire to eliminate it, **empathy** is usually defined as a vicarious emotional response (a feeling) elicited by and congruent with the perceived emotional state of another person. Empathy has also been defined in cognitive terms as the ability to detect accurately what another person is feeling (Levenson & Ruef, 1992) and to "see things from the other person's point of view" (Goldstein, Davis & Hermon, 1975).

Probably both cognitive and affective processes are involved, with cognitive appraisal preceding emotional arousal. First, we must evaluate the distress produced by another person's plight by putting ourselves in the other person's situation. This leads to an empathic emotional response, which motivates us to reduce the other person's distress. For example, if we see a legless man sitting on the sidewalk asking for money, we may sidestep him with some annoyance unless we ask ourselves (cognitive evaluation) how the man must feel being reduced to the status of beggar. Then we may feel an empathic response of sadness that will lead us to make a donation. Not only are empathic individuals more likely to be sensitive to the needs of other people, they are also more likely to be sensitive to the consequences of their intervention for the recipient (Sibicky, Schroeder & Dovidio, 1995). The empathic person, for example, may hesitate to offer money to a needy friend for fear of embarrassing the friend.

Will this person's situation arouse empathy in the people who observe it? Does it involve impression management?

Empathy has *not*, however, been shown to be a necessary condition for prosocial behaviour. For example, donations to charities are generally impersonal and it is hard to imagine an empathic response to any of the potential recipients; rather, donations may be seen as "the right thing to do" (norm of social responsibility).

Research into the role of empathy in prosocial behaviour has rekindled the debate about whether true selfless altruism exists. Batson and others (e.g., Batson, 1990; Batson & Powell, 2003) have presented data in support of the **empathy–altruism hypothesis**, which posits that pure altruism is elicited as a result of empathy induced by witnessing a person in distress. This brings us full circle to the philosophical debates of old, mentioned at the beginning of this chapter. Batson and colleagues have run numerous experiments that they argue support this hypothesis, while critics point out that they have failed to eliminate other (self-serving) factors that can explain their data. For example, observed helping might be the result of one of these factors:

1. *Negative state relief*—The observer's empathic response to a sufferer's distress produces personal distress and the individual acts to help the sufferer because of the egoistic motivation to relieve his or her own negative emotional state (Schaller & Cialdini, 1988).

2. *Self-reward or self-punishment*—Empathy may lead to prosocial behaviour because the individual seeks specific self-rewards such as pride or satisfaction, or wants to avoid self-punishment in the form of guilt.

3. *Self–other overlap*—It has been argued that the experimental conditions used by Batson and his colleagues produce feelings of **self–other overlap** (defined as the extent to which the potential helper feels a sense of "oneness" with the other and would use the term "we" to describe his or her relationship with the person) (Cialdini, Brown, Lewis, Luce & Neuberg, 1997). As an example of self–other overlap, if you see a friend or relative in need of help, you will be motivated to provide assistance because when that person suffers, you suffer too in some way because of the feeling of "we-ness." This sense of we-ness is not the same as empathic distress for it reflects *self-interest*. If your sister drowns, you suffer a serious personal loss quite apart from whatever empathy is elicited for her. Such we-ness can develop even with strangers in some circumstances. Reanalysis of Batson's data suggest that self–other overlap

accounts for the association between empathy and helping (Neuberg, Cialdini, Brown, Luce, Sagarin & Lewis, 1997).

All in all then, the evidence for the empathy–altruism hypothesis is not very persuasive and the hypothesis itself is not really very relevant to the understanding of helping behaviour. In any case, we should not assume that empathy-induced altruism, were it to exist, would always be benevolent. Indeed, it could pose as much of a threat to the common good as pure self-interest. As Batson et al. (1999, p. 14) conclude, "It can lead me to narrow my focus of concern to those for whom I especially care—the needing friend—and in so doing lose sight of the bleeding crowd."

Other Factors Influencing Prosocial Behaviour

Cultural differences

When and how concern is shown for others varies greatly among the many cultures of the world. In individualist societies, prosocial motivation may be expressed differently than in collectivist societies (see Chapter 4). Unfortunately, perhaps because of the inherent methodological difficulties, few psychological studies of prosocial behaviour have been conducted cross-culturally—although they have produced interesting findings. In research comparing children in India, Kenya, Mexico, the Philippines, Japan and the United States, children in the United States were least likely to offer assistance or advice to others in distress (Whiting & Whiting, 1975). The authors of that study concluded that prosocial behaviour is most evident among children whose culture requires it—for example, where families are large and children help care for siblings and manage the household. Another example: Canadian university students showed more sympathy and were more willing to provide financial assistance to victims of international disasters than were Dutch university students (den Ouden, & Russell, 1997). Such individual studies can only whet our appetite for a wider study of cultural similarities and differences.

Personality variables

As with any other behaviour, even individuals within the same cultural environment differ in the degree to which they exhibit prosocial behaviour. Naturally, social psychologists have attempted to find personality correlates of prosocial behaviour, but studies have not been conclusive. For example, subjects who help have been found to be more socially oriented and more "internal" in terms of locus-of-control than subjects who do not help (Ubbink & Sadava, 1974).

Although some researchers feel it is futile to seek general personality predictors of helping behaviour (Gergen, Gergen & Meter, 1972), Rushton (1980, 1984) argues that there is an "altruistic personality" associated with higher internalized standards of justice and responsibility and with greater empathy, self-control and integrity. However, much more evidence is required to demonstrate the existence of such a personality pattern. In any case, the way in which a particular personality trait is manifested is likely to vary with the situational context (Carlo, Eisenberg, Troyer, Switzer & Speer, 1991) so that an individual who acts prosocially in some situations (e.g., making donations to the United Appeal) may not do so in others (e.g., helping a drunk across a busy street).

Gender differences in empathy

As we have seen, empathy may play an important role in prosocial behaviour. There are, of course, individual differences in empathy just as there are differences in the extent to which various situations elicit empathy (Archer, Diaz-Loving, Gollwitzer, Davis & Foushee, 1981). There may also be differences in empathy resulting from gender roles. Since women have been found to experience more vicarious affective responses than men, perhaps because men have traditionally been trained to suppress emotional displays (Hoffman, 1977), we might expect women to be more empathic. Yet, it is not clear whether genuine gender differences in empathy exist; females do describe themselves as being more empathic than do males but this may reflect more the image that is expected of them than some predisposition (Eisenberg & Lenin, 1983). Nor is there clear evidence about gender differences in the willingness to help others, although women appear to be more willing to help highly dependent people while men appear more helpful to those who are not so dependent (Scholar & Batten, 1965). This could reflect the "caring" role that many females are brought up to assume. (Recall from A Practical Question—Why Do Some People Donate Organs While Others Refuse? that more women than men are willing to donate their organs).

Batson et al. (1996) found that prior experience affected male and female empathic responses somewhat differently. When subjects observed other same-sex subjects who had been assigned the role of learner in a teacher–learner shock paradigm, males and females did not differ in terms of the empathy they expressed. However, if the observing subjects were first given a taste of the distress that the learner subjects might be expected to suffer, women showed *more* empathy as a result of this experience while men actually expressed *less* empathy. It is not clear how such gender differences come about. One might speculate that since traditional child-rearing has allowed and encouraged females to be sensitive to distress, they recognize their own anxiety or distress and therefore are more touched by the plight of others in a similar situation. Males, who have been discouraged from such sensitivity, may try to deny or minimize personal anxiety and therefore downplay its effects when they witness others undergoing it.

Males and females are also subject to somewhat different norms regarding helping (Eagly & Crowley, 1986; Eagly, 1987). Men are expected both to rescue others who are in difficulty and to demonstrate courtesy and protectiveness towards subordinates both in close relationships and among strangers. Women, on the other hand, are expected to help through caring and nurturing other people, especially those within a close relationship. Women in the past have been discouraged from associating with strangers; this prohibition most likely also discourages women from giving help to strangers.

Overall, the research suggests that men help more often than women do, although the findings are inconsistent. Moreover, social psychological research has typically focused on short-term interactions with strangers and has therefore largely ignored the very behaviours prescribed for the female gender role—behaviours manifested primarily in close, long-term relationships (Eagly & Crowley, 1986). The "masculine" roles and the skills that are acquired in them may better prepare men to assist others in distress. As women begin to assume traditional male roles, the differences in helping between the two sexes, even in the short-term interactions of the laboratory, may begin to disappear.

Effects of religion

How does religion affect helpfulness? After all, Christianity, Judaism, Islam, Hinduism and Buddhism all promote prosocial behaviour to some degree and view selflessness as a virtue. Yet there may be differences from religion to religion in the way that helping is seen as an obligation (Jha, Yadav & Kumari, 1997; Kanekar, 2001).

Research suggests that, while individuals who believe that helping others is a religious duty are more likely to volunteer help (Sappington & Baker, 1995), simply being "religious" in itself does not correlate well with helping behaviour or compassion for those in need (Batson & Gray, 1981). Perhaps *how* one is religious is more important. For example, some religious people (sometimes referred to as *intrinsically oriented*) view religion as an end in itself; that is, they see their whole duty in life as ultimately to serve God. Others (*extrinsically oriented*) view being religious as a means of obtaining other goals such as power and influence in the community. Still other religious people view their religion as an open-ended quest for meaning and understanding and ultimate values (Batson & Ventis, 1982).

One study (Batson & Gray, 1981) examined the willingness of religious people to help a woman either in a situation where she expressed a desire for such help or in a situation where she expressly indicated that she did not want help. Intrinsically oriented religious people offered help whether or not the woman in need desired it, while individuals who viewed their religiousness as a quest for meaning offered help only when it was wanted. Other studies (e.g., Batson et al., 1989; Chau et al., 1990) have also shown that an intrinsic but not an extrinsic religious orientation is linked to prosocial behaviour. Intrinsically oriented religious people then may see providing help to others either as a duty or as a way of helping themselves achieve grace or a reward in an afterlife. Thus, the focus may be more on their own needs than even they realize.

Rural–urban differences

Is a person from the country generally more inclined than a person from the city to help others? We must begin with the common-sense notion that we are more likely to help or become involved with people we know or relate to, and city-dwellers encounter many more strangers than do residents of small towns. Some studies indicate, for example, that people in large cities are less likely to mail a lost letter that was stamped and addressed (Korte & Kerr, 1975) or to assist someone who reached them by dialing a wrong number

(Milgram, 1970). Certainly, specific aspects of the social climate of cities, such as a concern with crime would inhibit helping (House & Wolf, 1978). As well, the highly stimulating environment of the city may lead to overload with the result that city-dwellers may be less likely to notice that their help is needed. None of this is to suggest that urbanites are necessarily more self-centred, less caring or more alienated in comparison with their small-town compatriots.

In one field study, requests for help (e.g., "I wonder if you could tell me what time it is") were made in downtown Toronto, in a Toronto suburb and in a small town just outside Toronto (Rushton, 1978). People were asked for the time, for directions and for change. They were also asked, "What is your name?" as a control question that involved personal intrusion and no need for help. The response rates along with comparable data collected in New York City (Latané & Darley, 1970) are shown in Table 9–1. For every type of request, the percentage of people giving help dropped, moving from the small town to the suburbs to downtown. There was little difference between the results in downtown Toronto and New York City. Further evidence of significant rural–urban differences in helping comes from a review of 67 pertinent empirical studies. Steblay (1987) found that people in rural areas do, indeed, show significantly more willingness than do city-dwellers to help others in distress.

Are city people themselves different from rural people or is it the situation? Milgram (1970) argued that it is the latter—that people in the city, surrounded as they are by so many other people, out of necessity limit their social relationships. The urban person cannot afford to help every person who is in need and must be selective to survive in the urban culture. In addition, while rural people are considerably affected by rare emergencies such as fires, the city-dweller becomes blasé about them, assuming that authorities will deal with the situation. Furthermore, the city-dweller who sees an emergency is more likely to be in the company of other witnesses or to assume that there are other witnesses (Latané & Darley, 1969). Moreover, since the city person must compete for service (taxis, etc.), norms develop (privacy, aloofness, etc.) to protect people from constant interaction with others. It has been suggested that the intensity of urban stimuli (noise, pollution) may also decrease prosocial behaviour. People living in cities have been found to be less trusting than people living in towns (Merrens, 1973; Milgram, 1970). Fischer (1976) suggests another reason why the city environment may discourage prosocial behaviour: a large city usually provides a great diversity of people; thus, there is a greater chance that the stranger in need of assistance will appear to be a member of an unfamiliar group, producing fear in the onlooker and resulting in less willingness for the onlooker to "get involved."

An Australian study (Amato, 1983) also found that small population size was a strong and consistent predictor of helping. However, the results also suggested that urban lack of helpfulness was primarily limited to individuals suddenly faced with the need to provide help to a stranger, a situation that may be perceived as

TABLE 9-1

Rural–urban differences in helping behaviour

Type of request	Population Density							
	Low		Medium		High		High	
	Small Town		*Toronto Suburbs*		*Toronto Inner City*		*New York City**	
	% Helping	N	% Helping	N	% Helping	N	% Helping	N
Time	97	92	95	150	91	272	85	92
Directions	97	85	90	150	88	276	85	90
Change	84	100	73	150	70	279	73	90
Name	51	65	39	150	26	246	29	277

*Based on data from Latané & Darley, 1970
Source: Rushton, 1978

being more potentially dangerous by the city-dweller than by the rural inhabitant.

Likewise in a study of 36 U.S. cities, Levine, Martinez, Brase & Soreson (1994) examined six different kinds of helping behaviour (including giving change for a quarter, helping a person pick up dropped objects, helping a blind person cross the street, helping a person in a leg brace pick up a pile of dropped magazines). They found a high negative correlation between population density and overall helping behaviour as well as a negative correlation between population size and helping behaviour. Yet, the propensity to help a blind person cross the street was almost unaffected by population density. Presumably, city-dwellers may learn to be wary of requests for help, but remain willing to assist those they assume to pose no threat.

Volunteerism

In 1998, almost 8 000 000 Canadians—one in three adults—did volunteer work with a charitable group. This work is the equivalent of 578 000 full-time jobs and would involve payment of more than $16 000 000 000, if it were not volunteer work. Further, almost 17 000 000 million Canadians worked informally as volunteers helping others (*Globe and Mail,* November 1, 1999).

Omato and Snyder (1995) have developed a model to explain **volunteerism**: the "volunteer process model." According to this model, (1) it is dispositional factors such as personal motives, social needs and current circumstances that influence the initial decision to volunteer; (2) whether an individual continues to serve as a volunteer or volunteers again depends on whether one develops a positive evaluation of the volunteer setting and the experience. When Omato and Snyder tested this model by studying volunteers helping AIDS victims, they found that satisfaction with and positive feelings about the organization were directly related to the length of time that the volunteers served. Personal motivations were also involved to some degree, but it was self-centred motives rather than prosocial motives that correlated with length of service. However, a subsequent study of AIDS volunteers (Penner & Finkelstein, 1998) found that the only motive associated with length of service was a prosocial one. Obviously, much more research is needed to understand the various influences on volunteerism.

Not Helping Others: The Bystander Effect

Consider this: In March 1999, a 55-year-old man sitting at the front of a Toronto bus was beaten by two drunk, white, heavily built assailants in their twenties, who punched him in the head a dozen times, smashing his glasses into his eye socket and severely damaging his eye. No one—not even the bus driver who could have radioed the police—intervened. Why not?

Of all the forms of prosocial behaviour, the most dramatic is intervention—or its absence. Intervention is the act of an individual voluntarily giving assistance in an emergency, often at personal risk. Emergencies share several elements that make them somewhat unique (Darley & Latané, 1970):

1. They typically involve threat or harm to a victim. The person who intervenes can at best prevent further damage or possibly return the situation to the way it was before the emergency occurred.

2. Since recipients of such aid are rarely better off following an emergency than before it, the rewards for positive action are often nonexistent. Yet the possible costs including legal action or even death or injury are high.

3. They are rare, so few people have experience in dealing with them.

4. They are unpredictable, occurring suddenly and without warning, and immediate action is required. Thus people usually cannot plan for emergencies or consult with others about how to respond. The urgency of the situation is in itself stressful.

5. They vary widely in their form and in terms of what response is appropriate, making it impossible to prepare people by teaching them a short list of rules on dealing with emergencies.

There are all too many real-life examples in which people have stood by and observed an individual suffering harm while doing nothing to help. This is the **bystander effect**: people witness an emergency but, inhibited by the presence of others, stand by passively. Not everyone will necessarily be passive, but the probability of any particular person helping decreases with the number of other people present. The first well-researched example of bystander inaction was the "Kitty" Genovese murder (see A Case in Point—The

Bystander Effect). When asked later why they had not called the police, most of the witnesses said they had been afraid to get involved but seemed unable to furnish a basis for this fear. Various social scientists proposed a variety of *ad hoc* explanations for their inaction (Latané & Darley, 1970): alienation and apathy resulting from "depersonalization"; confusion of fantasy and reality brought about by a steady diet of television violence; even the vicarious gratification of sadistic impulses.

However, the witnesses were not apathetic. They did not turn away and ignore what was going on in the street below:

> Caught, fascinated, distressed, unwilling to act but unable to turn away, their behaviour was neither helpful nor heroic; but it was not indifferent or apathetic…(Darley & Latané, 1970).

Almost 15 years after the Genovese murder, a number of these witnesses reported that they still felt responsible for Genovese's death (Walster, Walster & Berscheid, 1978).

The behaviour of these witnesses was very similar to that of any crowd that gathers around an accident victim, each waiting for someone else to take charge, to indicate what behaviour is appropriate. Sometimes people act; sometimes they do not. Yet in any case, they are likely to experience distress. Several studies have found that when people witness another person being harmed, they show marked signs of emotional upheaval such as gasping, running aimlessly around, having sweating or trembling hands, chain-smoking and experiencing an increase in galvanic skin response (Walster, Walster & Berscheid, 1978). Think back to the man on the Toronto bus mentioned earlier: Had you been a passenger on that bus, what would you have been thinking or feeling?

What accounts for the bystander effect, the inhibitory effect of the presence of others? If people are not apathetic, if their behaviour is not callous, what is it that holds them back from helping a person in distress? There are several possible answers to these questions.

Norms and the bystander effect

The failure of people to help others is sometimes taken to suggest an alarming breakdown in the power of

A CASE IN POINT

The Bystander Effect

In March of 1964 in New York City, a man attacked Catherine ("Kitty") Genovese with a knife as she was walking home at night. Her screams brought her neighbours to their windows and the sudden glow of their bedroom lights and the sounds of their voices drove the attacker away temporarily. However when he saw that no one responded to her cries for help, he attacked her again. She managed to get away from her attacker a second time, but again, despite her shouts for help, no one responded. The man returned to attack her yet again—this time killing her. Half an hour had elapsed between the first attack and the killing. Even though at least 38 people watched from the windows of their apartments and houses as he attacked and repeatedly stabbed the young woman, no one even telephoned the police.

Before dismissing this as an example of New York incivility, consider this incident:

In September 1973, a man dragged a struggling, screaming 18-year-old girl 300 yards down a Scarborough, Ontario, street while cars swerved to avoid them but did not stop. She was taken to a grassy area opposite an apartment building, forced at knifepoint to undress, and then raped. Despite the fact that several people were sitting on apartment balconies opposite her as she cried for assistance, no one helped—even though an anonymous phone call to the police would have posed no risk to any of them. (Ironically enough, at some later time, the assailant was himself the victim of bystander inaction. He was beaten by three toughs on a busy thoroughfare while pleading in vain with the occupants of a stopped bus and taxi to call the police (Silverman, 1974).)

social norms to regulate social behaviour. However we saw earlier that while there are social norms involved in prosocial behaviour, their role is limited. In an emergency, norms are not very useful guides, partly because they are too vague about what to do and partly because they are conflicting (Darley & Latané, 1970). Suppose that you are walking down Lovers' Lane on a wintry night and you see a couple sitting motionless in a parked car with the engine running. One norm tells you to try to help others who need your help: if they are dying of carbon monoxide, you should do something. Yet another norm teaches you to respect people's privacy. After all, they are in Lovers' Lane: if they are just making out or communing with nature, you should not butt in. Thus, the bystander effect does not seem to reflect a breakdown of social norms—only the inadequacy of such norms.

The inhibiting presence of others: The lady in distress

It might seem reasonable to assume that the sort of person who is likely to help someone in an emergency would be even more likely to do so if there were other people about, for these other people might lend at least moral support. Yet, recall the discussion on social facilitation in Chapter 6: the presence of others facilitates simple or well-learned tasks but interferes with complex or novel tasks. A helping response to an emergency is generally both complex and novel.

The influence of the presence of others was evident in one of the earliest experimental studies of the bystander effect (Latané & Rodin, 1969). Subjects who thought they were participating in a market research study heard a woman who had just left them to go into an adjoining room, climb up on a chair to get something and then fall down and cry for help. (In fact, both the climb and fall were on tape.) Subjects could go directly into her office (the two rooms were separated only by a curtain), could go out into the hallway to seek help or could call to her to find out what they could do to help.

In one condition, each subject was alone. In a second condition, each subject was with a confederate who had been instructed to be as passive as possible, responding to any queries from the real subject in a natural but neutral way. At the sound of the crash the confederate looked up, stared for a moment at the curtain, then shrugged his shoulders and went back to work. In a third condition, two real subjects who were strangers to

each other were tested together while a fourth condition involved two subjects who were friends.

When assistance was offered, it was always direct, either going into the room (75 percent of the intervening subjects) or calling out to the woman to see if she wanted help (24 percent). The most notable finding was that while 70 percent of the subjects who were alone offered help, the presence of another person strongly reduced the frequency of intervention: only 7 percent of subjects paired with a passive confederate intervened while only 40 percent of those in the "two strangers" condition offered help. The effect was reduced when friends were paired: in 70 percent of the pairs of friends, at least one person offered help. (However, it can be shown mathematically that if 70 percent of individuals who are alone are likely to intervene, then pairs of such individuals should contain at least one intervener 91 percent of the time. So even with friends, the presence of another person is inhibitory.)

It seems strange at first that the presence of others inhibits rather than promotes helping. However in post-experimental interviews, 59 percent of non-intervening subjects indicated that they were unsure about what had happened while another 46 percent said they had thought that nothing serious had occurred. Perhaps people hesitate to help because the emergency situation seems ambiguous to them.

Ambiguity of the situation: The smoke-filled room

Many emergencies are ambiguous and it is often surprisingly difficult to decide whether an emergency is occurring. If new neighbours in your apartment building seem to be having a squabble and you hear screams through the walls, do you intervene directly or call the police? It is difficult to decide whether someone is in trouble in such a situation and usually people (especially men) do not want to look foolish by intervening if there is no emergency (Siem & Spence, 1986).

Although hearing a woman fall off a chair may not seem particularly ambiguous, remember that the "accident" occurred out of sight of the subjects and the sounds of climbing and falling and the calls for help were played over a tape recorder. It is possible that the reproduction did not sound totally real, thus producing some ambiguity. In fact when the Lady in Distress study was repeated using live rather than taped noise, there was a high frequency of intervention (Staub, 1974).

This outcome might suggest that the presence of others contributes to the ambiguity of the situation and that non-responding others lead an individual to wonder whether his feeling that intervention is required is in error. Of course if all those present feel the same way, then all may hold back.

The following experiment explored whether the presence of others could inhibit even when there was little ambiguity about the physical situation itself. Imagine yourself writing an examination. The examiner leaves the room; a few minutes later the room begins to fill up with smoke. What would you do? Would you leave the room (particularly if other examinees are not reacting)? We would not expect such a situation, which carries some potential for personal harm, to give rise to a bystander effect. Latané and Darley (1968) created such a situation. Subjects who were engaged in filling out a questionnaire worked either alone, with two "passive" confederates or with two other naive subjects. Several minutes after the person in charge left the room, smoke was introduced into the room via a small wall vent. By the end of four minutes, the room was filled with acrid smoke to the extent that it obscured vision.

Only 75 percent of the subjects in the alone condition left the room to report the smoke to someone. The others toughed it out, working on their questionnaires despite the cloud of smoke! This is very surprising, and when a subject was in the company of two passive confederates, only one of 10 subjects reported the smoke. The others coughed, rubbed their eyes and even opened the window but did not leave the room. When three naive subjects worked together, in only 38 percent of the groups did someone intervene. In fact, naive subjects working together did not intervene significantly more often than a single naive subject working with two passive confederates.

These results support the interpretation that the passivity of others contributes to the ambiguity of the situation. In other words, we use the reactions of others to help decide whether there is an emergency and what action is appropriate. However, it might also be that the hesitancy to act is due to a fear of looking foolish by doing "the wrong thing."

To differentiate between inhibition brought about on one hand by the ambiguity produced by the inaction of others and on the other hand by the fear of looking foolish, Ross and Braband (1973) carried out a study that used either a blind or a sighted confederate in each of two emergency conditions. In the "inter-nal" emergency condition, the subject and the blind confederate worked in a room that filled with odourless smoke; since the blind man could not see the smoke, he could not serve as a source of information about what reaction would be appropriate. In the "external" condition, the emergency was signalled by a scream from outside the room; in this case, the blind man would be aware of the emergency and his reaction could serve as a guide to appropriate behaviour.

In fact, the subjects in the internal condition responded to the emergency just as quickly as did subjects in a control condition who worked alone. It could be argued, however, that these subjects were not concerned about acting inappropriately since the blind man could not see them. Yet this explanation is not tenable, for in the external condition in which the blind man's reaction could be used as a guide, the subjects were inhibited to the same extent as when they were with a sighted confederate.

This experiment lends strong support to the notion that non-responding others inhibit a person's response because their inaction helps to define the situation as a non-emergency and thus makes intervention seem inappropriate.

Diffusion of responsibility: The epileptic seizure

If non-intervention is largely caused by misinterpreting other people's reactions and believing that they know there is no cause for alarm, it follows that not knowing people's reactions should result in the subject not being misled. Therefore, will people who know that others are aware of the possible emergency, but who cannot observe their reactions, be just as likely to intervene as people in an "alone" condition? This was the question addressed by the next experiment (Darley & Latané, 1968). Each subject sat in a separate room and was told that he or she would take part in a discussion of personal problems associated with college life. The discussion was to be conducted by means of an intercom system, ostensibly in order to protect the subjects' identities and spare them any embarrassment. Subjects had been told that the experimenter would not be listening to the initial discussion and that a mechanical switching device would automatically give each subject in turn about two minutes to talk while all other microphones were switched off.

There was actually only one real subject at any one time. The other subjects, all confederates, had prerecorded their comments. From the point of view of the real subject who believed that all the other speakers were actually present in the discussion, the following occurred. The first person to speak discussed his adjustment difficulties and the fact that he was prone to epileptic seizures, especially when under stress. The next time it was his turn to speak, he became increasingly loud and incoherent and in a stuttering voice asked for help. Amid choking sounds, he stammered that he was going to die, called once more for help and then was silent. When the seizure occurred, the real subject believed that all subjects could hear the seizure but that only the microphone of the seizure victim was switched on.

The major independent variable in this study was the apparent size of the group of participants, while the dependent variable was the time it took the subject to go and report the emergency to the experimenter. Comments made during the staged seizure and in later self-reports indicated that virtually all subjects believed the emergency was real. Yet the belief that other people were listening had a strong effect on both the rate and the speed of subjects' intervention (see Table 9–2). The larger the group, the less likely it was that the subject would respond and the longer it took those who did.

Thus, it appears that a person is less likely to offer help if others are present or presumed to be present even in the absence of ambiguity produced by the passivity of others. Subjects in this study who did not report the emergency did not show signs of apathy or indifference. In fact, when the experimenter finally entered the room to end the study, they appeared to be considerably emotionally upset and concerned for the victim. They found themselves in a conflict situation, worried about the victim and about the guilt they would feel if he was not helped, yet concerned about looking foolish, overreacting or ruining the experiment by leaving the room. When only the subject and the victim were involved, the victim's need could be met only by the subject while when others seemed to be present (even in this case, via intercom), the subject had less responsibility in the matter. In other words, a **diffusion of responsibility** occurred: "Other people are listening and so it is not up to me to take action; someone has probably already done something about it."

The Latané–Darley intervention model

Three factors have emerged from the discussion so far. The bystander effect is the result of the following: (1) misperception of the emergency situation based on the observation that others are not responding; (2) fear of doing the wrong thing and looking foolish; and (3) diffusion of responsibility. The social inhibition of helping is a remarkably consistent phenomenon and, in general, a victim stands a greater chance of being helped when only a single person witnesses the emergency (Latané & Nida, 1981). Many other studies and demonstrations have found results similar to those obtained by Latané and Darley. For example, the bystander effect has been demonstrated on the streets of downtown Toronto (Ross, 1978). In one demonstration, which was filmed by a hidden camera, a confederate collapsed on busy Yonge Street. Many people walked by, stepping around the man before someone finally stopped to offer help. In another demonstration, a confederate grabbed another confederate's purse in front of City Hall in full view of a lunchtime crowd. The victim called for people to stop him as she ran after him. No help was forthcoming. It had been expected that for each demonstration, several trials would have to be made before such blatant non-intervention could be observed and filmed. In fact in each case, only one trial was necessary. (What do you think about the ethical implication of such demonstrations?)

TABLE 9-2

Effects of group size on likelihood and speed of response

Group size	N	% responding by end of seizure	Total % responding within six minutes	Average time in seconds
2 (subject and victim)	13	85	100	52
3 (subject, victim and one other)	26	62	85	93
6 (subject, victim and 4 others)	13	31	62	166

Source: Latané & Darley, 1970

TABLE 9-3

The Latané–Darley model of bystander intervention

1. The bystander must notice that something is happening.
2. The bystander must interpret the situation as an emergency.
3. The bystander must decide whether or not he or she has a responsibility to intervene.
4. The bystander must decide in what way he or she can best be of assistance.
5. The bystander must choose how best to carry out this course of action.

Latané and Darley (1970) summarize the effects of ambiguity, fear of looking foolish and diffusion of responsibility in a five-step, decision-making model of the intervention process (see Table 9–3).

First, we must notice that something is happening and then decide whether it is an emergency. If it is, the next step is to select an appropriate action: Do we personally try to do something? Do we call the police?

After contemplating the alternatives, particularly if they involve personal risk, we might go back a step to the definition stage and decide that it really is not an emergency after all. The more ambiguous the situation, the greater the likelihood that this backtracking will occur. (In the Lovers' Lane scenario for example, the bystander might think, "If they're really being gassed, I don't know what to do. I'll get them out of the car, I guess, but how do I give them artificial respiration? What if they die? Mind you, they're probably OK—just making out quietly. Boy, will I look stupid when I pound on their window and they turn out to be in no danger. Yeah, there's no problem here—after all, this is Lovers' Lane.") So we might decide not to do anything, risking some guilt if it turns out there really was an emergency. If others are standing around doing nothing, we risk even more embarrassment if we intervene when help is not needed—and the inactivity of others may add to the ambiguity of the situation.

Rewards and costs of helping

Not all research has found a bystander effect. A classic field experiment carried out in New York—a city with no outstanding reputation for altruism—found no bystander effect when a confederate of the experimenter collapsed on a moving subway car. The experiment examined the effects of certain characteristics of a victim (whether he appeared drunk or ill, whether he was black or white) on the amount of help given. It was expected that the "drunk" confederate (who carried a bottle in a paper bag and who smelled of alcohol) would elicit less aid than an ill one (carrying a cane) since it was assumed people·might anticipate the

drunk becoming disgusting, embarrassing or violent. The most surprising outcome was that there was a generally high rate of help giving in all conditions. In fact, the "ill" person received help on 95 percent of the trials and even the "drunk" was helped on half the trials. Moreover on 60 percent of those occasions when help was given, more than one person helped. Since the ill person was not thought to be ill by choice while the drunk was clearly in need of help as a result of his own actions, people may have been less willing to help the drunk because he "deserved" his suffering (Piliavin, Rodin & Piliavin, 1969). (Note however that in this study, unlike in the case of the Toronto bus incident mentioned earlier, there was no apparent risk of becoming a victim oneself.)

Why was so much inaction observed in the Darley and Latané laboratory research but not in the Piliavin field experiment? Why was there less diffusion of responsibility on the subway? There were important differences between the two sets of studies. First, the victim was in full view in the Piliavin study; thus the need for help was less ambiguous. Second, the natural groups were considerably larger than the laboratory groups. Thus, any diffusion of responsibility that might have occurred may have been more than offset by the increased probability of someone actually helping in a large group. In other words, the larger number of bystanders in the subway study may have increased the probability of getting a prosocial response from someone (Piliavin et al., 1972). Moreover, it was much more difficult for the subjects in the Piliavin study to leave the area than it was for participants in the Latané and Darley studies to avoid the victim. This difference bears more examination.

Whether a person helps another may depend on how easily he or she can avoid the helping situation. In an experiment designed to examine this hypothesis (Staub, 1974), a confederate collapsed, holding either his chest or his knees (to vary the apparent seriousness of his condition), either in the pathway of a pedestrian (difficult escape) or across the street (easy escape). As can be seen in Table 9–4, many more people helped

Consider two field studies carried out on the campus of the University of Waterloo (Holmes, Miller & Lerner, 2002). In the first study, university students donated more to a charity when offered a product in return for their donation, even though they had little interest in the product. Moreover, the size of their donations was more in line with the apparent need of the victim group when offered a product in exchange for their donation, supporting the hypothesis that this exchange provided a kind of psychological cover for their prosocial behaviour. In the second study, participants were more willing to purchase a product from a charitable organization when offered a better bargain, but this occurred only when the victim's need was high, again suggesting that the true motivation was not to obtain the product.

Why should this be? Why might people be reluctant to demonstrate their generosity? Holmes et al. (2002) suggest that straightforward generosity may threaten the individual's peace of mind in that it would remind him or her of the needs of many other groups and raise awkward questions about why one is not also helping them. It may also risk setting up some sort of ongoing relationship with the recipient of a donation so that further demands might be made in future. The "fiction" of an economic exchange allows the individual to feel good by acting on the impulse to give help without making any future commitments and without raising questions about the need to help others in general. This may, as Holmes et al. (2002) suggest, wittingly or unwittingly underlie the practice of many charitable groups to offer something—greeting cards, address stickers or the like—in return for a donation.

Heroism

Consider the following examples:

- In June 1944, Pilot Officer Andrew Charles Mynarski of Winnipeg was flying an RCAF Lancaster bomber in an attack on German positions when the airplane was hit and set afire. The crew parachuted to safety except for the tail-gunner, Pat Brophy, who was trapped in his tiny rear compartment by a damaged door, and Mynarski, who lurched back through the flames to attempt to free him. Covered with blazing hydraulic fluid, he worked barehanded to try to get the door open. Finally, driven back by the fire, he stood and saluted Brophy before bailing out. He had no chance of survival: his parachute was on fire. He

was posthumously awarded the Victoria Cross on the evidence of the tail-gunner who ironically survived the crash of the bomb-laden airplane when he was thrown free upon impact (Franklin, 1977).

- On February 18, 1995, Blair Claybourne and Stephen Moran of Calgary rescued an elderly man from his burning home. Trying to enter by the front door, they were driven back by smoke but then managed to crawl into the burning house. They found the man on the floor of his kitchen and managed to get him out to safety. He was treated for smoke inhalation and minor burns. The rescuers were awarded Carnegie Medals of Heroism in 1996.

- On November 20, 1989, Karen Ridd of Winnipeg was arrested in El Salvador while working in a church that was providing sanctuary to hundreds of Salvadoreans fleeing from persecution and civil war. She was blindfolded, handcuffed and occasionally slugged by the police who led her to believe that she would be taken to an area well known as a dumping spot for people killed by the "death squads." Following four hours of interrogation during which she could hear the screams of torture victims, she was finally released into the custody of Canadian diplomatic officials. However rather than take advantage of her freedom, she refused to leave without her colleague, a Colombian woman who was being even more roughly interrogated in the room next door. She was again blindfolded and taken back inside the prison where she was berated and threatened by the police. Finally, they capitulated and let both women go (*Globe and Mail*, November 24, 1989).

These three stories of heroic action demonstrate the finest prosocial behaviour: individuals risking their own lives to try to save others. Such **heroism** is greatly admired in all societies. In 1972, three decorations were created by the Canadian government to honour those who perform such selfless acts of courage—the Cross of Valour, the Star of Courage and the Medal of Bravery.

What is the stuff of heroism? While heroism is difficult to define because it is based on perception and attribution, most acts that are considered heroic involve intervention in the face of extraordinary personal risk.

Heroism and gender

The Carnegie Hero Fund Commission was founded in the United States in 1904 to award medals for "outstanding acts of selfless heroism performed in the United States and Canada." Since 1904, it has recog-

Canada recognizes its heroes: courage, bravery, valour.

nized close to 8732 people (Carnegie Hero Fund Commission, 2003). Almost all the recipients have been men and almost all acted alone. In an analysis of recipients of Metropolitan Toronto Police Civilian Citations, awarded to people who have spontaneously come to the aid of the police, it was also found that males were more likely than females to directly intervene and again they generally acted alone (Lay, Allen & Kassirer, 1974).

Given the literature on bystander intervention, it is not surprising that these heroes acted alone. Why are men so much more often recognized for heroic acts than are women? Of course, women may be deterred by a relatively greater physical risk given that men are generally larger and stronger. Yet, it is not that women are not given to heroism but rather that the concept of heroism is defined (by men, of course) in stereotypically male terms (Polster, 1992). Indeed, the Carnegie Hero Commission excludes from consideration people who rescue family members except if the rescuer dies or is severely injured. Thus, women (who according to the female gender role should be particularly concerned with the welfare of their children) are not considered heroic if they risk their lives in saving their own children! As society becomes more egalitarian and as male and female gender roles become less differentiated and less rigid, the tendency to view women as less heroic will no doubt change.

The Scarlet Pimpernel phenomenon

The Scarlet Pimpernel is the name of a book and a fictional character created by Baroness Orczy. Set during the French Revolution, the book concerns a British nobleman who could have followed the goings-on from the comfort and safety of his own homeland. Instead, he risked his life to smuggle French aristocrats out of Paris and out of the country, saving them from the certain fate of the guillotine.

This fictional tale of heroism was replayed again and again during the days of the Third Reich when an estimated 50 000 to 500 000 individuals repeatedly risked their lives and often those of their families to help Jews escape from the Nazis (Oliner & Oliner, 1988; 1992). Many of them perished as a result of their efforts; the vast majority have never been identified. Only a very few became famous for their courage—for example, Raoul Wallenberg, a wealthy Swedish diplomat who was able to save tens of thousands of Jews by issuing them false Swedish documents (Henry, 1985, 1986).

It was during the trial of Adolph Eichmann in 1960 that interest began to focus on such rescue efforts. Eichmann was charged with crimes against the Jewish people and against humanity arising from his zealous implementation of the Nazi genocidal policy. During the trial, reference was made to Christians who had rescued Jews from concentration camps. Subsequently, social psychologists began to track down as many of these rescuers as possible to determine whether there were any common factors in their personalities or family backgrounds.

An early study, which had to be terminated because of a lack of funds, located 27 rescuers and 42 rescued people (London, 1970). In a subsequent and much more extensive study, known as the Altruistic Personality Project, Oliner and Oliner (1988) interviewed 406 rescuers whose actions had been documented by Yad Vashem (an Israeli institution set up as a memorial to the victims of the Holocaust, which has now identified some 6000 rescuers) as well as 150 rescued survivors. The rescuers were compared with 126 non-rescuers—people who had been in situations in which they *could* have become rescuers but had chosen not to do so.

Motivation of the rescuers

No single motive for the behaviour of these individuals has been identified. Some had deliberately chosen to rescue Jews. Others got involved without thinking about it or even by mistake: one person reluctantly agreed to let his secretary's Jewish husband stay in his office over the weekend to hide from the Nazis. Once involved however, he was drawn in more deeply and developed considerable compassion for those he helped, eventually rescuing about 200 people at great personal risk and cost. Some of the rescuers were very religious while others were atheist and some were even anti-Semitic!

There seem to have been at least three different motivations for the actions of the rescuers (Oliner & Oliner, 1988): (1) Some rescuers were motivated by empathy for the suffering of the Jews. In some cases this empathy was based primarily on emotional attachment to specific victims, which led to a sense of responsibility and caring; (2) Others were motivated by the social norms (e.g., "Do good unto others") of groups to which they were strongly attached such as church congregations; and (3) For a small minority, it was dedication to a moral code based in justice and social responsibility that motivated them to risk their lives. Morally motivated rescuers rescued people whether they liked the victims or disliked them and whether or not they had known the victims previously (Fogelman & Weiner, 1985; Fogelman, 1994).

Characteristics of the rescuers

What personal characteristics did the rescuers share? In his early study, London (1970), while cautioning about the possible non-representativeness of

his sample, found three common characteristics. First, rescuers showed a fondness for adventure and excitement, which was crucial to the initiation of the rescue work. Second, the rescuers tended to be socially deviant and their social marginality provided the impetus and endurance necessary to carry out this rescue work. Third, and most important, the rescuers showed a strong identification with a very moralistic parent who had definite opinions on moral questions and who provided a model for moral conduct.

The importance of the moralistic parental influence was apparent in the much larger sample studied by Oliner and Oliner (1988). The rescuers they studied were distinguished from non-rescuers by their capacity to feel responsible for the welfare of others including people outside their circle of family and friends: this sense of moral responsibility was directly attributable to

Doing unto others. . . . Does assisting others help us feel good about ourselves?

their upbringing. Many rescuers reported that their parents had stressed—both in words and by behaviour—the importance of helping others and the importance of accepting that differences in group, race or culture do not make a person superior or inferior. The typical rescuer in their study was raised in a close family relationship in which parents acted in a loving manner towards the children and communicated caring values. The parents set high standards with respect to caring for other people, and children were encouraged to develop qualities such as dependability, self-reliance and responsibility: qualities associated with caring. Parental discipline experienced by rescuers rarely involved physical punishment and there was almost never any gratuitous aggression. Discipline involved a great deal of reasoning with efforts made to explain to the children why some behaviours are inappropriate and what their consequences are for other people (see for comparison, the discussion of child rearing and aggression in Chapter 11).

Incidentally, not all rescuers had such strong moral values. For example, Oskar Schindler (whose story was chronicled in the film *Schindler's List*) apparently acted at first out of narcissistic self-interest (Rappoport & Kren, 1993) but became more prosocially motivated as time went on.

These studies of rescuers recall our earlier discussion of the effects of models and upbringing on prosocial behaviour in general. Identification with a prosocially oriented parent, a parent who both teaches and practises the importance of caring for and helping others, appears to be of outstanding importance in inculcating selflessness in individuals. Most of those brave people who rescued Jews from the Nazis had been reared by their parents to believe in justice that applies to all and not merely to members of one's own group or class or nation (Reykowski, 2002). Strong identification with a moralistic parent was also found to be an important characteristic of "fully committed" American civil rights workers in the late 1950s and early 1960s. These activists had been taught by their parents not only to believe in certain principles but to act upon them (Rosenhan, 1970).

Summary

1. Some theorists propose that altruism is genetically transmitted, a position not held by most psychologists.

2. Norms of reciprocity, social responsibility and equity can influence prosocial behaviour, but their role is usually a minor one.

3. Cognitive developmental theory proposes that moral thinking matures from a state of concern with pure self-interest to responsiveness to the reactions of others, and then to being guided by abstract principles.

4. Social learning theory emphasizes the acquisition of prosocial motivation and behaviour through processes of reinforcement, self-attribution, modelling and parental discipline.

5. Prosocial behaviour may be influenced by various emotional states and may involve attempts to repair self-image.

6. Empathy is not a necessary condition for prosocial behaviour but may enhance the probability of such behaviour.

7. The manifestation of prosocial behaviour varies from one culture to another, between males and females and between people in cities and rural areas.

8. Emergency situations involve threat or harm to the victim, are rare and unpredictable, vary widely in form and appropriate response and may involve risk or costs to the benefactor.

9. People are less likely to help in an emergency when other bystanders are present (the "bystander effect").

10. The bystander effect occurs when each bystander feels that he or she is less responsible for the victim's welfare because there are other people present who could take action ("diffusion of responsibility") and because the inaction of others makes the situation more ambiguous to each bystander with regard to whether help is needed and what response is appropriate.

11. Bystander behaviour is also influenced by the anticipated rewards and costs of helping.

12. Bystander intervention could be encouraged by increasing public awareness of the bystander effect, by teaching children to "break the rules" of social convention when necessary, by training children to take responsibility for helping others and by encouraging leadership roles.

13. People are less likely to receive help if they are perceived as being overly dependent or if their need for help appears to be controllable or brought on by their own actions.

14. Recipients of help who cannot reciprocate sometimes react with resentment.

15. People who repeatedly act heroically to assist others have been typically raised in close-knit, loving families where discipline was not physical in nature and where parents taught the importance of caring for others.

Further Reading

EISENBERG, N. & MUSSEN, P. (1989). *The roots of prosocial behavior in children*. New York: Cambridge University Press. A review of research into the various factors that influence the development of prosocial behaviour in children.

FOGELMAN, E. (1994). *Conscience and courage: Rescuers of Jews during the Holocaust*. New York: Doubleday. Based on 300 rescuers, this is a fascinating description of the motivations and behaviour of individuals including Oskar Schindler and Raoul Wallenberg.

GRUSEC, J., DAVIDOV, M. & LUNDELL, L. (2002). Prosocial and helping behavior. In P.K. Smith & C.H. Hart (Eds.), *Blackwell handbook of childhood social Development*. (pp. 457–474). Malden, MA: Blackwell Publishers. A review of the biological, developmental and social influences on prosocial behaviour

OLINER, S.P. & OLINER, P.M. (1992). *The altruistic personality: Rescuers of Jews in Nazi Europe*. New York: Free Press. A detailed report of the findings of the Altruistic Personality Project, which studied the psychological make-up of rescuers.

SCHROEDER, D.A., PENNER, J.F., DOVIDIO, J.F. & PILIAVIN, J.K. (1995). *The social psychology of helping and altruism: Problems and puzzles*. New York: McGraw-Hill. A textbook that focuses on why some people help in some situations while others do not.

STEIN, A. (1988). *Quiet heroes: True stories of the rescue of Jews by Christians in Nazi-occupied Holland*. Toronto: Lester & Orpen Dennys. Another interesting examination of the characters of heroic rescuers.

STAUB, ERVIN. (2002). Preventing terrorism: Raising "inclusively" caring children in the complex world of the twenty-first century. In Chris E. Stout (Ed.). *The psychology of terrorism: Programs and practices in response and prevention, Vol. IV. Psychological dimensions to war and peace*. (pp. 119–129). Westport, CT: Praeger Publishers/ Greenwood Publishing Group, Inc. The author discusses the socialization practices of becoming caring, helpful and altruistic human beings and the experiences that children require to achieve this.

 # Weblinks

Volunteerism

www.volunteer.ca Information on volunteerism in Canada

Amnesty International

www.amnesty.org Information on the activities of this Nobel Prize-winning organization.

Chapter 10

Cooperation and Conflict

War doesn't determine who is right—only who is left.

Bertrand Russell

When I see the falling bombs / Then I see defended homes. / Men above and men below / Die to save the good they know.

Frank R. Scott (1945 "Conflict")

Chapter Outline

FIGURE 10-1

Social exchange theory: The CL and the CLalt

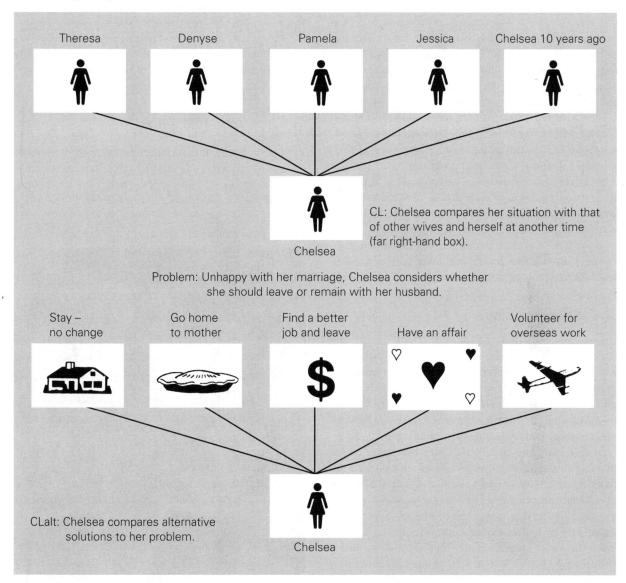

Theresa · Denyse · Pamela · Jessica · Chelsea 10 years ago

Chelsea

CL: Chelsea compares her situation with that of other wives and herself at another time (far right-hand box).

Problem: Unhappy with her marriage, Chelsea considers whether she should leave or remain with her husband.

Stay – no change · Go home to mother · Find a better job and leave · Have an affair · Volunteer for overseas work

CLalt: Chelsea compares alternative solutions to her problem.

Chelsea

lead to strategists actually making war more likely as they analyze what actions are most likely to produce what effects or how many citizens their side could "afford" to lose in an international atomic showdown (Rapoport, 1968).

A "game" in its broadest sense is virtually any kind of situation in which two or more interdependent parties (or "players") make decisions that affect one another according to rules. The outcomes of these decisions depend on the joint actions of the players.

There are two major classes of games. In **zero-sum games**, one party's gain is exactly matched by the opponent's loss—gains and losses always add up to zero and no cooperation is possible (e.g., a two-handed poker game). In **non-zero-sum games**, some of the outcomes are mutually preferable to some of the others. While the mathematical analysis of such games treats the players as rational (maximizing gains and minimizing losses), such rationality is not always—or even usually—present in real-life conflicts.

Sometimes it is difficult to assess the magnitude of gains and losses for the parties, for money or other resources may have different value or importance for different people. A dollar means much more to a pauper than it does to a millionaire. Game theory requires that *utilities* rather than objective measures of value be used. **Utility** refers to the importance or value that a given outcome has for an individual. It is assumed that people can rank a number of different possible outcomes with regard to utility. For example, a new CD player probably has more utility than a glass of water—unless you are in the middle of a desert. Rational players act to obtain the greatest possible utility.

However, this fundamental assumption of rationality does not mean that purely selfish ends always motivate people; it is the utility and not the objective value of an outcome that is involved. If an adult plays a game of cards with a child and wants the child to win, then the maximum utility for the adult would be associated with the adult's loss, not his or her win.

The zero-sum game

In any game situation, the range of possible outcomes and the interdependence of the players is most simply represented in the form of a *payoff matrix*. In most laboratory studies using experimental games, each of two players must choose between two possibilities in order to obtain one of four possible outcomes. As an example, consider the zero-sum matrix in Figure 10–2.

In this case, the matrix indicates that each of the players, *A* and *B*, has a choice between two alternatives. *A* can choose action a_1 or a_2 and *B* can choose b_1 or b_2. The various cells of the matrix indicate the joint outcome of their choices. Since this is a zero-sum game, Player *A* receives the amount indicated while *B* loses the same amount. Thus if *A* chooses a_1 and *B* chooses b_1, then *A* will win 10 (points, dollars, etc.) and *B* will lose 10. However if *A* chooses a_1 and *B* chooses b_2, *A* will lose 10 and *B* will gain 10. This situation represents pure competition. What one person wins, the other must lose. No cooperation is possible and communication would not help in any way, since if players informed each other of their choices, their opponents could take advantage of the information.

Since zero-sum games allow for no cooperation, from the standpoint of reducing conflict, it is important to alter the perception of protagonists who think they are involved in a zero-sum game. For example, the historic reluctance of Israel and the Palestine Liberation Organization to enter into negotiations may have been due to the zero-sum perception that gains by one side would necessarily jeopardize the national existence of the other. Yet, the fact that they did eventually negotiate shows that perceptions can change, even though at least some, and possibly many, Israelis and Palestinians continue to view the conflict as zero-sum and are convinced that their opponents do as well.

The non-zero-sum game

Zero-sum games fail to capture the most important feature of most real-life conflict situations: even while two people may compete, they may also have some cooperative motivation. For example, while the Allies

In social psychology terms, most competitive games are zero-sum games: you win or you lose.

FIGURE 10-2

Payoff matrix for zero-sum game

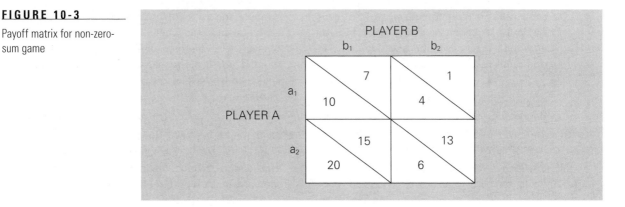

and the Germans were engaged in a life-and-death struggle in the First World War, they still managed to cooperate by mutually banning the use of poison gas after it was used against Canadian soldiers at Ypres. The gas was never used in the Second World War because both sides considered it too dangerous. (Similarly, germ warfare has never been used.) Such agreements or rules regarding how conflicts should be regulated have a long history (see A Case in Point—The Duel of Honour).

Non-zero-sum games are also called **mixed-motive games** because more than pure competition is involved. As well as competition, there is also a motivation to cooperate to a degree. Consider the example of the two-person payoff matrix shown in Figure 10–3. The number in the lower left half of each quadrant represents the payoff to player *A* for each combination of choices and the upper right-hand number, the payoff to player *B*. No longer is it the case (as it was in the zero-sum game) that one player's gains are always matched by the other's losses. Thus, it is no longer a pure conflict situation; cooperation is also possible as players attempt to avoid mutually undesirable outcomes. In this particular matrix, *A* is clearly at an advantage since for three of the possible outcomes *A* will gain more than *B*. But what outcome is likely if the two players simultaneously choose one of their two possible responses? *A*, if rational, will recognize that a_2 is a better choice than a_1 since more will be gained (20 instead of 10, or 6 instead of 4) regardless of whether *B* chooses b_1 or b_2. Similarly, *B* stands to be better off regardless of *A*'s choice by choosing b_1 (7 instead of 1 if *A* chooses a_2, 15 instead of 13 if *A* chooses a_1). So we should expect that the players would choose the lower left-hand quadrant. Even if the game were repeated several times, there would be no reason for the players to change their choice provided they are only interested in their own gains. However, such individualistic orientation is not the only motive that affects real (as opposed to theoretically rational) players.

FIGURE 10-3

Payoff matrix for non-zero-sum game

The Duel of Honour

In 15th-century Europe, assaulting someone as a means of redressing actual or imagined slights and insults became so frequent that rules were developed to ensure that a fight between two adversaries would be fair. Ultimately, these rules governed every aspect of the duel of honour, such as what constituted a legitimate cause for quarrelling, the form of the challenge, the choice of weapons and, of course, the fight itself.

One of the most detailed of these regulations was the *Irish Code Duello* adopted at the Clonmel Summer Assizes in 1777 for the "government of duelists by the gentlemen of Tipperary, Galway, Mayo, Sligo and Roscommon and prescribed for general adoption throughout Ireland." Similar codes were enforced in England and on the continent.

The *Code Duello* contained 26 rules among which, in the original wording, were:

III. If a doubt exists who gave the first offence, the decision rests with the seconds. If they will not decide or cannot agree, the matter must proceed to two shots, or to a hit if the challenger requires it.

IV. When the lie direct is the first offence, the aggressor must either beg pardon in express terms, exchange two shots previous to apology, or three shots followed by explanation, or fire on till a severe hit be received by one party or the other.

IX. All imputations of cheating at play, races, etc., to be considered equivalent to a blow, but may be reconciled after one shot, on admitting their falsehood and begging pardon publicly.

X. Any insult to a lady under a gentleman's care or protection to be considered as by one degree a greater offence than if given to the gentleman personally, and to be regarded accordingly.

XIV. Challenges are never to be delivered at night, unless the party to be challenged intends leaving the place of offence before morning; for it is desirable to avoid all hotheaded proceedings.

XV. The challenged has the right to choose his own weapons unless the challenger gives his honour he is no swordsman, after which, however, he cannot decline any second species of weapon proposed by the challenged.

XVI. The challenged chooses his ground, the challenger chooses his distance, and the seconds fix the time and terms of firing.

XXI. Any wound sufficient to agitate the nerves and necessarily make the hand shake must end the business of the day.

XXIV. When the seconds disagree and resolve to exchange shots themselves, it must be at the same time and at right angles with their principals. If with swords, side by side, with five paces interval.

In addition to such rules, there were firm expectations regarding how a "gentleman" should act if hit. For example:

If, upon discharge, his adversary's ball has taken effect, he must not be alarmed or confused, but quietly submit the part to the examination of his surgeon, who should close around him, with his second, the moment the discharge has taken place.

I cannot impress upon an individual too strongly the propriety of remaining perfectly calm and collected when hit; he must not allow himself to be alarmed or confused; but summoning up all his resolution, treat the matter coolly; and, if he dies, go off with as good grace as possible.

Duelling was formally prohibited in Britain in 1888 but continued in France into the early 1900s and in Germany until the 1940s.

In a similar fashion, nations have entered into agreements governing the etiquette of war. Among other matters, these rules regulate how civilians and prisoners are to be treated. For example, at one time captured soldiers were executed or sold into slavery and those of high rank were held for ransom. The Hague conventions of 1899 and 1907 and the Geneva conventions of 1864, 1899, 1907 and 1929 all contained clauses concerning the treatment of prisoners of war who are protected from coercion or torture and are required to give only their name, rank, service number and date of birth. The most recent Geneva Convention was formulated in 1949 and has been signed by 154 countries and territories. While most nations claim that they adhere to the rules, agreements of this sort often are ignored especially in desperate moments. Numerous breaches of the rules occurred in Vietnam and more recently poison gas was used by Iraq's Saddam Hussein in the Iran–Iraq conflict. (However, the latter did *not* use poison gas or other weapons of mass destruction when the United States and its allies invaded Iraq in 2003).

That said, let's come back to the Mi'kmaq and the Tsawassen and the non-aboriginal fishers. Clearly, at least at the height of the dispute, the latter saw the conflict as a zero-sum game—whatever lobsters or salmon were taken by the Mi'kmaq and Tsawassen were not there to be taken by the non-aboriginals. Worse, if the conservation rules are not applied to Aboriginals as well, non-aboriginals feared that everyone would suffer from the depleted breeding stock. A negotiator's job is to try to find a way to turn such a situation into a *non*-zero-sum game so that there are some mutually desirable outcomes perceived to be available and requiring cooperation to attain. To achieve this is often difficult and may involve bringing more resources—for example, financial compensation from government—into play.

The prisoner's dilemma

Some conflicts are very difficult to resolve because actions that are rational on an individual level can lead to collectively irrational or mutually destructive outcomes. The prototype of this problem is the so-called Prisoner's Dilemma Game (PDG), which continues to be used in laboratory studies of conflict (Chaudhuri, Sopher, & Strand, 2002; Wildschut, Insko & Gaertner, 2002). It is a special type of non-zero-sum game and it takes its name from the following dilemma:

Two suspects are apprehended following the murder of a wealthy man. The police are quite certain that the two are guilty but lack the necessary evidence to convict them. A clever Crown prosecutor decides to suggest a little plea-bargaining and visits both suspects separately. She tells each suspect that she cannot hope to convict either of them on the murder charge without a confession but promises that if the suspect confesses, she will agree to ask the court for clemency for him. The murder conviction of the other suspect will carry a sentence of 30 years while the confessor will get off with only a one-year sentence. However if both confess, they will each get 20 years in prison and if neither confesses, she will see to it that they are charged with breaking and entering, which will lead to a two-year sentence. She then leaves each suspect to think about her offer by himself.

As it turns out, each of the suspects possesses some knowledge of game theory and scratches out a matrix (see Figure 10–4 on page 280) on the wall of his police cell. A half-hour later each suspect confesses. The Crown prosecutor has succeeded.

Why, you might ask, would the two prisoners choose to confess when by keeping silent each would have received only two years in prison? Was each prisoner so eager to get off with only a one-year sentence that friendship ceased to matter?

Before condemning the two as victims of their own selfishness, we must more carefully examine their choices. Since they could not communicate, each had to anticipate what the other would do. *A* may have said to himself, "Whatever he does, I am better off by confessing. If he confesses, by confessing, I'll get 20 years instead of 30. If he doesn't confess, I'll get one year instead of two. So to confess is my best strategy. But it's also *B*'s best strategy for the same reason. Now even if I put my self-interest aside and choose not to confess, how can I be sure that he will not confess? After all for him not to confess, he must not only be prepared to accept two years instead of one, but he must also trust that I won't confess, or he will end up with 30 years." Thus held *incommunicado*, each prisoner has little choice but to confess. Yet the product

FIGURE 10-4

Prisoner's dilemma

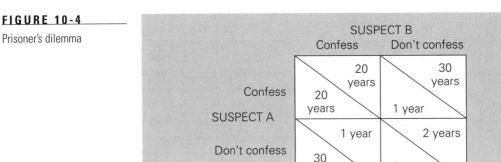

of their individually rational choices is collectively irrational since they each receive sentences of 20 years instead of two. That is the nature of the dilemma. Neither person, *regardless of what the other person does*, can improve his or her outcome by remaining silent. Yet by both being "rational," they each end up with 20 years in prison.

Because such factors as trust and suspicion are important in this game, the Prisoner's Dilemma captured the interest of experimental social psychologists. How would people behave in this kind of situation? Research using a matrix equivalent to the dilemma (where outcomes were points or money instead of prison terms) and that involved pairs of players playing the same game many times in succession demonstrated that real players do not play cooperatively. The percentage of mutually cooperative responses is typically quite low (around 30 to 40 percent) and tends to decrease as the game progresses. However if enough trials are played, there is usually some increase in mutual cooperation, up to about 65 percent (Rapoport 1963; Rapoport & Chammah, 1965).

You may find the "normative" (i.e., theoretical) outcome of the Prisoner's Dilemma Game (mutual confession) a little unsatisfying. Surely, you might ask, two people would not act collectively in such an irrational way. This has bothered a great many researchers even though laboratory studies using the PDG indicate that people do just that. However, one factor that has to be considered is the actual value of the outcomes to the players.

Consider the Prisoner's Dilemma story again, but this time suppose that the suspects are a pair of lovers, Henry and Marie. For these two, the prospect of one going free after one year while the other languishes in jail for another 29 years is much more unpleasant than it would

be for two ordinary criminals. Furthermore, each lover "knows" (i.e., trusts) that the other feels likewise. For these players, the only two outcomes worth thinking about are both players confessing and both players not confessing. Being free when the other is in prison has little utility for either one. Furthermore, each no doubt strongly believes that the other will react the same way and the only thing to do is to not confess. Neither confesses and they go free after two years in prison.

Thus, the utility of the possible outcomes for each person is not based solely on that person's preference. In addition, both Henry and Marie assume (or "trust") that the other person has the same utility preferences. Judging the other person's ordering of utility is obviously crucial since if one party misjudges (e.g., if Marie assumes that Henry values personal liberty above anything else), then that person's predictions of the other's behaviour will reflect that misjudgment. In negotiation situations, people often try to misrepresent their real utility preferences as well as to modify the other person's utility (e.g., "I am really very attached to this car, so unless I get a very good offer, I won't sell it" or "This suit really makes you look very dashing").

Now, suppose the Crown prosecutor has persuaded both Henry and Marie that the other is emotionally involved with a third person. In such a case, they would presumably modify their judgment of the other's utility structure and would also likely modify their own.

However if they really trust one another, they will not believe the allegations about the third party. There is no doubt that trust promotes cooperation in all types of conflict situations. Trust reduces fear of exploitation and increases perceptions of fairness (De Cramer, 1999).

One constraint placed on the behaviour observed in the Prisoner's Dilemma Game (PDG) is the absence of communication. Although communication channels by themselves do not always lead to more cooperation, in a situation as simple as the PDG, the opportunity to communicate would at least allow the parties a chance to inform each other of their real intentions. After all, the non-cooperative response in the PDG might be a defensive rather than an offensive move. In fact when players in a PDG have been allowed to communicate, it has usually had a positive effect on the level of cooperation. However as in real life, communication is sometimes used only to try to manipulate the other party rather than to aid in resolving the dilemma.

Dangerous games

In 1963, the Soviet Union was intent on shipping nuclear missiles to Cuba, and the United States was determined to stop them. The Americans put up a naval blockade around Cuba and threatened to sink any Soviet ship carrying missiles to Cuba. Nevertheless the Soviets sent out ships, one of which was eventually spotted and appeared to be heading directly into the blockade. However while the world held its breath, the ship eventually stopped and turned back ending the tense confrontation. Then United States secretary of state Dean Rusk told a reporter, "Remember when you report this … that eyeball to eyeball, they blinked first." Someone had to back down or mutual disaster would result. Such a conflict is a **dangerous game** in the language of game theory, in that if neither side backs down, both may suffer catastrophic loss.

There are two important characteristics of the prototypical dangerous game:

1. It is non-negotiable. There can be only one winner; the other must lose—although both can lose disastrously. There is no way that cooperation can help and any conciliatory move by one player will only encourage the other to press on.

2. The dangerous aspect is that the goal-directed behaviour and the threat behaviour are identical: the closer a person gets to the goal, the greater the likelihood of attaining it and the greater the probability of a mutual loss (Swingle, 1970).

Why do people or nations play such games? Insofar as nations are concerned, it is often appealing to force the opponent to back down by appearing to be more ready to accept mutual loss than one actually is (i.e., to deceive the other about one's utility structure). For example, during the Cold War, the leaders of the Soviet Union sought to put the United States at a disadvantage by claiming that they were quite prepared to accept the loss of 60 percent of their people in an all-out nuclear war. If the leaders of a government can appear hardened or demented enough not to care about such losses, they can presumably "pre-empt" the confrontation, forcing the other side to back down. Some game theorists (e.g., Schelling as reported by Roddy, 2003) have interpreted the 2003 invasion of Iraq as the pursuit of a "chicken" strategy by the United States, one in which the steering wheel has been thrown out the driver's window.

Collective dilemmas

A **collective dilemma** is an expanded form of the Prisoner's Dilemma. It involves many participants, more closely reflects many real-life conflict situations and occurs whenever the individually rational actions of a number of interacting parties produce an outcome that is collectively undesirable. In other words, people must decide whether to behave selfishly (maximize their own outcomes) or cooperatively (maximize group outcomes). If all those involved act selfishly, everyone will be worse off than if the group interests had been maximized. Collective dilemmas, also referred to as *social dilemmas* (Dawes, 1980), have been receiving more attention from researchers in the past few years (Komorita & Parks, 1995, 1999), no doubt because they occur repeatedly in everyday life.

For example if two-cycle or even four-cycle engines significantly increase pollution, everyone should be willing to switch to an alternative form of power such as electricity, propane or hydrogen. However, closer analysis reveals that the "rational" choice, at least for the short term, is to adopt the selfish alternative; in other words, do nothing. If the majority of people opt for such means of propulsion, the air will be better even if you do not act. If only a few people are willing to accept alternative sources of energy, your investment will be a waste of time since the air quality will not improve anyway (see Figure 10–6 on page 283). Population growth and resource depletion represent the same sort of dilemma. Why, even in the face of catastrophic overpopulation, should a peasant in India limit his family to two children? He will receive no old age pension so he will need to depend on his children to support him. The more children he has, the better off he will be even though his society may ultimately suffer. Even in an overpopulated world, he would be at

The Game of "Chicken"

The prototypical dangerous game is the game of "chicken," which was played by teenagers in the 1950s. In the words of Bertrand Russell (1959):

> This sport is called chicken! It is played by choosing a long straight road with a white line down the middle and starting two very fast cars towards each other from opposite ends. As they approach each other mutual destruction becomes more and more imminent. If one of them swerves from the white line before the other, as he passes, he shouts chicken!, and the one who has swerved becomes an object of contempt.

In a later variation, teenagers would stand on airport runways at night daring each other to remain in the path of an approaching airplane (Swingle, 1970). The game of chicken is not restricted to teenagers. In one way or another, many games of chicken are played out in politics, in labour-management negotiations and in international disputes.

This game can be translated into a laboratory form by using a matrix such as that shown in Figure 10–5. If one "does not swerve" and the other does, one gains prestige (indicated by +100) while the other loses face (–100). If both decide not to swerve, they lose more than face (–1000) while if both swerve, there is a draw, with a slight loss of prestige

(e.g., –10). It is obviously a high-risk game, each player being forced to risk substantial loss in order to threaten the other into yielding. If one player can make it clear that he is committed to not swerving, the other must either back down or face almost certain heavy loss. As long as one person believes that the other will back down, he will continue. H. Kahn (1962) suggests that getting into the car dead drunk, wearing very dark glasses and throwing the steering wheel out of the window as soon as the car is travelling at maximum speed will put considerable pressure on your opponent to back down. You have reduced or eliminated your freedom to act: The opponent, who can act, is now in a weaker position and must back down or face suicide. You have pre-empted control of the game.

"Brinkmanship," pushing each other to the brink of war, describes the game of chicken as played at the international level. It is the "deliberate creation of a recognizable risk of war, a risk that one does not completely control" (Schelling, 1960, p. 200). The effectiveness of brinkmanship depends on how much the other nation believes you. If one country believes that another is committed to attack it if it invades some third country, it will hesitate. If the country does not believe that, but it is in fact true, both sides will end up in a mutually destructive war.

FIGURE 10-5

Chicken

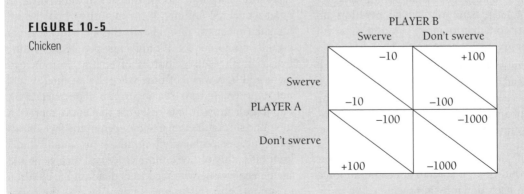

a disadvantage in his old age if he had fewer children than his neighbours.

Collective dilemmas take two forms: the *resource dilemma* and the *provision of public goods dilemma:*

1. The **resource dilemma** (or *commons problem*, as it is also called): This involves a collective good that already exists, and the group members can use it at will. Individuals have to decide how much of the public resource each should take for personal use, and overuse leads to a loss for all. Thus, the individual who acts in personal interest and ignores the common good is guilty of a "sin of commission." The historical example comes from Hardin's (1968) description of the "tragedy of the commons." In the 1800s in England, all farmers set public pastures aside for common use. However, as individual farmers expanded the size of their cattle herds, the commons were so overgrazed that the herds were threatened, leading to an enclosure movement that eventually led to fencing off the commons into individual pastures. The heart of the problem was this: for each herdsman, the positive utility associated with enlarging his herd was much greater than the negative utility derived from the overgrazing. The short-term gains were more enticing than the possibility of losses in the long term. Thus, each enlarged his herd to the point where everyone suffered.

Note that the resource dilemma has an important temporal component, and is essentially a dilemma with delayed consequences. For example, the Canadian fishery gradually increased its take to a point where over-fishing threatened the continued existence of cod on the East Coast and salmon on the West Coast. However, the collective dilemma evolved gradually, beginning long before there was any obvious danger to the commons. The Mi'kmaq lobster dispute and the Tsawwassen salmon dispute were in part—but only in part for reasons discussed earlier— resource dilemmas.

2. **Public goods dilemma** (also referred to as the *free rider problem*): While the resource dilemma involves people drawing individually from a common resource, the public goods dilemma is related to the contributions by individuals to the collective or public good (for example, public television or installing pollution controls) that benefit everyone—contributors and non-contributors alike. As long as most people act in line with the common good (e.g., install pollution controls, donate blood), the individual who does not contribute benefits as much from the efforts of the majority as does the majority. Since an individual does not have to contribute in order to benefit, the "rational" action is to not contribute. Yet if everyone does this, there will be no public good. For example, there would be no need to collect tickets on a train if everyone were honest about paying the fare. Such a system would most likely break down because **free riders** (literally) would exploit the situation. Think back as well to the discussion of social loafing in Chapter 6 that is another instance of the public goods dilemma.

Both dilemmas are identical in terms of the decision facing the individual. He or she must decide whether

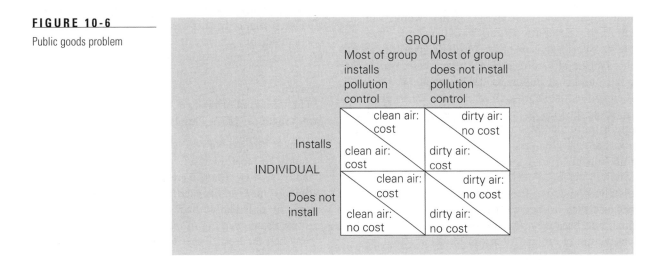

FIGURE 10-6

Public goods problem

to act according to individual self-interest and risk suffering in the long run if most others do the same, or to act according to the collective interest at some personal cost. The problem in each dilemma arises when each individual's behaviour has a relatively minor influence on the group outcome while the overall group behaviour has a strong effect on each individual's outcome.

Three separate motives are involved in both the resource dilemma and the public goods problem: self-interest, conformity to group norms and the wish to act responsibly (Samuelson & Messick, 1986). Ideally, each individual wants to profit as much as possible while acting in a socially responsible manner and staying within the limits of group norms.

Unfortunately, it is not always obvious to people just what social responsibility involves and sometimes no relevant norms exist. Is it or is it not socially responsible: (1) to use herbicides that kill dandelions but leave toxins in the soil?; (2) to develop genetically modified foods that are more disease resistant, tastier and better in appearance?; (3) to drive cars, which produce emissions that contribute to acid rain? Like our predecessors who overused the commons in England, we damage our environment partly because we cannot easily foresee all the consequences of our actions.

How should people deal with collective dilemmas? The philosopher Immanuel Kant suggested this imperative: "Act only according to that maxim which you can at the same time will to be a universal law" (Joad, 1957, p. 393). Thus, you should keep using weedkillers in your garden only if you are content to have everyone do likewise. If everyone acted according to the Kantian imperative, we would be acting in the common interest and collective dilemmas would vanish, although we might continue to damage our environment over disagreement or misunderstanding about the dangers of various actions. In any case, people do not, by and large, follow Kant's dictum and it is against their individual short-term interests to do so. In reality, some people do see collective dilemmas as an opportunity to exploit others while others see them as occasions in which they should try to solicit cooperation from their co-actors (e.g., Brann & Foddy, 1987; Moore, Shaffer, Pollak & Taylor, 1987). In some instances, people may hesitate to cooperate, not because they do not want to contribute to the group goal but because they suspect or misinterpret the motivation of others (Alcock & Mansell, 1977).

The effects of group size

Game theory predicts that individualism will predominate when a group is large enough that no individual's contribution makes a significant difference to the group as a whole; individuals will attempt to maximize their own payoffs. It may seem natural that more cooperation should exist in a small group than in a large group—after all, in a small group, an individual receives a large proportion of the beneficial effects of her action while at the same time her action has a much more significant effect on the group outcome. But what would happen if we compared the behaviour of people in two groups, one a small group and the other a large group, in which the reward magnitude for the individual was exactly the same? In other words if only the size of the group but not the actual reward, varies, will people still be more cooperative in smaller groups? This is, indeed, what has been observed in laboratory experiments. Hamburger, Guyer and Fox (1975) developed a game structure in which the size of the reward for an individual was the same whether a three-person or seven-person group was involved. The three-person groups were more cooperative.

Even when the temptation to be non-cooperative (i.e., the amount by which non-cooperation brings greater reward than cooperation) and the gain to the group brought about by one's cooperation are held constant, cooperation decreases with increasing group size (Messick & McClelland, 1983). It is possible, of course, that this is due to the greater likelihood of having one or more "non-cooperators" in a larger group, but anonymity may play a role: the larger the group, the more anonymous the actions of each participant. Yet, in a study in which subjects in a five-person group either (1) were anonymous to each other and were informed after each trial only of the total number of people who cooperated, or (2) were told how each of the people identified by name responded, no difference was found in the degree of cooperation (Mansell & Alcock, 1978). Anonymity *per se* is not the explanation.

The explanation appears to lie with the size of the group itself. In 1833, Lloyd discussed this very point:

Suppose the case of two persons agreeing to labour jointly, and that the result of their labour to be common property. Then, were either of them, at any time, to increase his exertions beyond the previous amount, only half of the resulting benefit would fall to his share; were he to relax them, he would bear only half the loss. If, therefore, we may estimate the motives of exertion by the magnitude of the personal consequences expected by each individual, these motives would in this case have only half the force which they would have were each labouring separately for his own individual benefit. Similarly, in the case of three partners, they would have only one-third of the force—in the case of four, only one-fourth—and in a multitude, no force whatsoever. For beyond a certain point of minuteness, the interest would be so small as to elude perception, and would obtain no hold whatever on the human mind (p. 8).

This brings us back to the same conclusion: when a group is large enough that the actions of a given individual have little effect and when the immediate outcome is about the same whether one invests time or energy or resources to cooperate or whether one does not, non-cooperation becomes the typical response.

Enhancing cooperation in a collective dilemma

One way to foster **cooperation** or behaviour based on the collective good is to make the identity of the group more salient. For example in one set of laboratory studies, individuals were found to be more likely to act in line with the collective good when the identity of the group as a whole was emphasized rather than the identities of subgroups (Croson & Marks, 1998).

Another way to foster collectively oriented behaviour is through coercion. Indeed, Hardin (1968) suggested that mutual coercion, mutually agreed upon, is the only way out of the commons dilemma: we all agree to pay taxes and to punish those who do not. It may well be that only similar laws can regulate problems such as pollution or overpopulation. Sometimes, coercion in the form of normative pressure is enough to prevent individuals from acting only from self-interest and ignoring the common good (Samuelson, Messick, Rutte & Wilke, 1984; Allison & Messick, 1985).

Both group identity and mutually agreed upon coercion were found to be relevant when Tyler and Degoey (1995) examined the willingness of citizens in California to restrict their use of water during a serious drought in 1991. They found that restraint was related to the extent to which individuals identified with their community *and* believed that the civic authorities were acting fairly in the imposition of penalties for high consumption.

Oftentimes, the people immediately involved best solve resource dilemmas. Berkes, Feeny, McCoy and Acheson (1989) identified a number of cases in where resources have been protected from overexploitation by the members of the group immediately concerned. These include control over hunting in the James Bay area of Canada, the protection of lobster stocks in Maine and the safeguarding of forests in Thailand and Nepal. In each case, controls were not imposed by the state and the right to govern the local resource was

"It started with one of their pigeons pecking one of ours."

assigned to those parties most likely to be affected by misuse. In contrast in the Maritimes, the federal government unilaterally imposed a ban on cod fishing accompanied by severe legal penalties. Then the Supreme Court decision seemed to imply that the Mi'kmaq could catch lobster out of season. Such interventions often generate considerable hostility and resentment, especially where the relationship between the authorities and the public has deteriorated.

Factors Affecting the Course of Conflict

Analogues of these two game structures—the dilemma and the dangerous game—appear over and over in real life. However, real-life situations are much more complex than any matrix game. Whether or not protagonists in a conflict will seek to resolve matters peacefully or by force depends on three classes of variables: (1) *Structural* variables, which are directly related to the nature of the conflict situation (e.g., whether the situation is purely cooperative or if cooperation is also possible; whether promises or threats can be made; whether communication is possible; whether the protagonists have equal power); (2) *strategic* variables (e.g., whether one or more of the protagonists adopts a conciliatory stance); and (3) *predispositional* variables, which refer to characteristics such as cultural background, the protaganists' personalities, their ages and gender, their beliefs about each other and their prior history of interaction.

Structural variables

The situation

Some situations are more likely to encourage cooperation than others. Two strangers both on the verge of drowning in icy water and trying to climb onto a piece of flotsam only large enough for one are much less likely to avoid competition than if the flotsam can easily accommodate them both. The situation in which a man finds that his wife has eaten up the entire box of chocolates that she gave him for his birthday is much easier to resolve than one in which a spouse catches the partner in bed with someone else. Thus, not all situations are equally amenable to constructive conflict resolution. However, it is rare that destructive conflict resolution is the only course available. Even the drowning strangers may be able to take turns on the flotsam.

Promises and threats

Sometimes, promises are made in the attempt to resolve a conflict. Consider the conflict involving a father who wants a child to clean her room and a child who wants to play instead. The father may try to influence the outcome of this basic conflict of interest by making a "promise"—"If you clean up your room, we will go to play in the park," or more generally, "If you do *A*, I will bring about *B* (some desirable consequence)." If father has generally carried out his promises in the past, the child is likely to believe that *B* will be done if *A* is done.

A **threat** is like a **promise** except that the outcome, *B*, is undesirable. For example, "If you do *A* (fail to clean your room), I will bring about *B* (you will not be able to watch your favourite show on TV tonight)."

As with a promise, for a promise or threat to be successful, it must first be credible. Credibility depends on three factors:

1. *Past record*—If the party making the promise or threat has in the past failed to carry it out, credibility will be low. Credibility can be increased if the person making the promise or threat can show that he or she has little choice but adhere to it. If someone promises money to you if you carry out a certain action and gives it to a neutral third party to hold, the promise is more credible; if a union leader threatens a walkout and persuades management that the union council will replace him if he backs down on the threat, the threat is more credible.

2. *Reasonableness*—The threat or promise must be within the realm of reason. The promise by a parent to a child that he will not have to go to school ever again as long as he cleans his room is unlikely to be believed. As for a threat, it must not carry too high a cost to *either* party or it is likely to suffer in terms of credibility. Loving parents who threaten to send their child to an orphanage if the child misbehaves are unlikely to be believed; both parents and child would suffer too much if the threat were carried out.

3. *Contingency*—There must be reason to believe that the promised or threatened *B* is actually contingent on *A*. If parents promise a trip to Canada's Wonderland if a child obtains good grades and if the child has overheard her parents saying that the whole family is going to Canada's Wonderland, the

promise is unlikely to be effective. With regard to threat, the threatened action must have negative consequences for the person making the threat to assure the threatened party that the threat will not be carried out anyway even if compliance is forthcoming. If a father tells a child hiding under the bed that he will spank him if he does not come out right away, the threat will be ineffective if the child believes that he will be spanked in any case. The child needs to believe that the father does not enjoy delivering a spanking. Thus while promises achieve their goal only if they bring about a behaviour that warrants that they be carried out, threats serve their purpose only if they *do not* have to be carried out. A parent who threatens a child with a spanking does not actually want to give the spanking; otherwise, he would just get on with it rather than wasting words.

Unlike promises (unless they are not carried out when they should be), threats by their very mention have negative effects on the process of conflict resolution, often turning what might be a constructive process into a destructive one. The introduction of threat typically changes a conflict about scarce resources into a contest that only one can win, a zero-sum game.

Deutsch and Krauss (1960) carried out a classic study of threat. They devised a "trucking game" to study the effects of a number of variables including threat and communication on the outcome of a mixed-motive situation. Two subjects were each given the role of manager of a trucking company; their task was to move their "trucks" from their factories to the markets. Several trials were run; for each completed trip, the subject received 60¢, less the "operating costs" calculated at the rate of one cent for each second taken to make the trip. The two players, labelled ACME and BOLT, operated electronic boxes to move the simulated trucks over the roadways shown in Figure 10–7 on page 288.

As you see in the figure, part of the roadway for each player was a common single-lane road, which meant only one truck could pass through at a time. If the trucks met in this stretch of the road, either one had to back up while the other advanced, both could back up or they could sit there facing each other. The clock, however, kept moving. Thus, the person whose truck backed up would lose more money than the person who passed directly through. Each subject also had an alternative route, considerably longer than the main route, and subjects were told that they could expect to

incur a net loss each time they used that route. Since each pair of players played several trials, the cooperative strategy would be for the players to alternate across trials in their use of the common section of road; that is, for one player to pass over the common roadway first on one trial and for the other player to do so on the subsequent trial.

There were several experimental conditions. In one condition, no threat capability was present but in another condition, one of the players was given a "gate" (unilateral threat) and in a third condition, each player controlled a gate (bilateral threat). The gates were at the ends of the single-lane road. By closing the gate, a player implicitly threatened that it would remain closed and each would have to use the unprofitable alternative routes.

While subjects in the no-threat condition did learn to alternate cooperatively, the presence of either or both gates impeded such cooperation. While the player with the gate in the unilateral condition lost less money than did the other player (but also lost more than either player in the no-threat condition), the presence of two gates led to even greater losses for both players. (This outcome suggests that if your opponent has a weapon, you may suffer more by having a similar weapon than if you cannot retaliate)! The effects of allowing the players in such a game to communicate will be discussed later in this chapter.

Why does threat often lead to increased conflict? It seems that the presence of a threat capability inevitably leads to its use as an individual tries to resolve the conflict. As indicated above, once the threat is used, the nature of the conflict changes and the material payoffs are no longer the only payoffs involved. In our culture as in many others, yielding to threats or coercion leads to a loss of face (Goffman, 1955) or self-esteem. Face-saving is important, not only in terms of self-esteem but in terms of future interaction as well, for yielding now may encourage more threats in the future. For example if a government gives in to terrorists' demands, other terrorists may be encouraged to make demands.

So once a threat has been made, the preservation of face becomes a primary goal for each player, thus leading to increased determination to "hold one's ground" and to respond with a counter-threat. For example, a couple disagrees on something benign such as where to go on an evening out. Then one of them makes a threat ("Maybe I should just stay home") and the other responds with a counter-threat ("Fine—I'll have a good

FIGURE 10-7

The trucking game

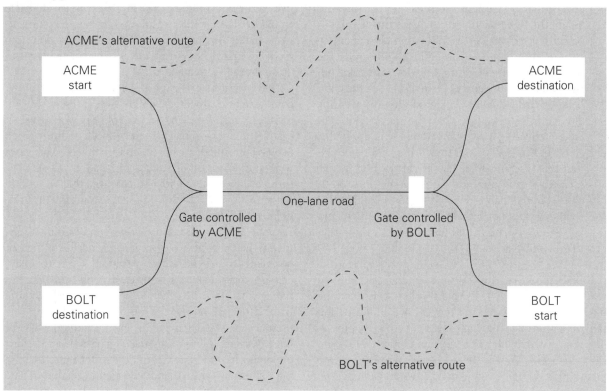

Communication

In real-life conflict, it is rare to have no communication between protagonists. Yet as in the example above, communication can take the form of a threat–counter-threat spiral, in which case it is of little help in resolving the conflict. It is interesting to note that in the trucking game, Deutsch (1958) found that cooperation was fostered by communication only when the subjects were given an "individualistic" orientation; that is, they were instructed to try to make as many points for themselves as they could with no concern for the other person's gains or losses. The mere existence of channels of communication was found to be no guarantee that communication would, in fact, take place and the greater the competitive orientation of the parties, the less likely it was that such channels would be used. Even compulsory communication did not improve cooperation in the bilateral threat conditions of the trucking game: subjects used the communication channel only to insult each other.

time without you"). Now the dispute is not about where to spend the evening but over who is going to win and who is going to back down. Often there is a series of escalating threats, a _threat–counter-threat spiral_ (or more simply, a _conflict spiral_): each disputant responds to the other's threats by more severe threats. The threats about just staying home are replaced by threats to end the marriage and on and on—parry, thrust; thrust, parry—the dispute builds. It becomes very difficult to cool it down because now the real issues have been lost in the struggle to win the face-saving battle. Such escalation tends to be self-sustaining: if a threat is successful, a person is likely to resort to it again and if it fails (i.e., leads to counter-escalation), it is likely to result in a hardening of resolve and another round of escalation.

An arms race involves a threat–counter-threat spiral. Nation _A_ interprets Nation _B_'s actions as a threat to its security and expands its armaments. This very action is, however, perceived as a threat by Nation _B_, which then adds to its arsenal, confirming Nation _A_'s impression that Nation _B_ was, indeed, preparing for war. The arms race can thus escalate rapidly.

Why is communication beneficial in some situations and not in others? It seems most likely that communication can help by improving each person's perception of the other's intentions. In situations such as that posed by the trucking game, however, the presence of a threat option eliminated this advantage. Players attempted to shortcut the negotiation process by means of threat and coercion, thus changing the game into a situation in which not backing down became of greatest importance. If the only outcomes are now "win" or "lose," there can be no compromise and communication cannot help. However, communication can be beneficial when face-saving is not an important factor or when no clear competitive motivation exists. Another important feature of communication is that it gives participants the opportunity to make promises (Orbell, Van-de-Kragt & Dawes, 1989). As long as the promises are kept, cooperation will be fostered.

Of course even when communication does occur, there is no guarantee that it will be understood. This can have serious implications especially if the conflict is in the sphere of international relations. The war between Britain and Argentina in 1982 over the Falkland Islands (Malvinas) is one example. Naturally, the two countries perceived the situation from their own perspectives. As far as Argentina was concerned, the Malvinas were part of its territory that had been occupied by a foreign power since 1833. Moreover, recent history had revealed that Britain was quite willing, even eager, to give up its colonies. There seemed little reason to believe that Britain would not release the Falklands as well. However, the British had quite a different point of view. They did not consider the Falklands to be a colony. It was populated by British citizens who wanted to remain part of Britain. Thus, the Argentine attack was not considered one of liberation but one of pure aggression. Argentina did not believe Britain would defend the Falklands, but Britain thought no other course of action was possible, leading to tragic consequences for both sides (Jervis, Lebow & Stein, 1985).

Power

Power, the ability to influence what happens to another individual, is discussed in some detail later (see Chapter 12). We now examine how different degrees of power among protagonists can influence the course of conflict. Of course, power is essential in carrying out a threat. A parent who threatens to spank a 17-year-old high school boxing champion probably lacks the power to carry out the threat.

Sitting Down to Negotiate

In real-life situations, even the physical set-up for negotiations is important, or at least is believed by negotiators to be important. For example, the seating order is often a matter of dispute, since where people sit may reflect either their status or their perceived relationship to each other (Lott & Sommer, 1967).

In 1848, it took six months of discussion before delegates to the Peace of Westphalia could agree on the order in which they should enter and be seated (Durant & Durant, 1961), and at the 1945 Potsdam conference, Truman, Churchill and Stalin insisted on entering the room by emerging simultaneously from three separate doors (Kelman, 1965).

In the Paris peace talks dealing with the war in Vietnam, considerable debate raged prior to the talks about the seating plan and the table shape. North Vietnam wanted a seating plan and table shape that would suggest that the National Liberation Front had status as an independent political entity, while the United States and South Vietnam were opposed to this (Kitchens, 1974). Similarly, the participants in the 1993 Middle East peace talks sat at a T-shaped table and none of the Arab delegation directly faced Israel's representatives. Whether the seating plan actually influences the course of the negotiations is unimportant as long as the participants believe that it has an effect. Pre-negotiation may be as important as, if not more important than, negotiation (Rubin, 1989).

There is evidence (Pruitt, 1976) that parties involved in a conflict may be more likely to use coercion when they have a moderate rather than great or small amount of power. This may at first appear counter-intuitive, but it becomes clearer when one realizes that little power is often viewed as ineffective while great power risks mutual destruction. If you are guarding the cookie jar and if your only coercive response is to say, "Bad, bad" when the child takes a cookie without permission, the measure may have no effect on the child—so why bother to use it? Similarly if your only coercive power is a pistol, you are unlikely to use it to protect the cookie jar from marauding toddlers.

Strategy

Whether at chess or at war, or at the car dealer's or at the bargaining table, many people try to work out in advance a plan or "strategy." A formal strategy is simply a plan that contains instructions about what to do in every imaginable contingency. In theory, any "game" can be reduced to a series of choices. For example in a game of tic-tac-toe, you could plan the following: "If she chooses a corner on the first move, I'll choose the centre. If she chooses another corner on the second move but not the corner directly opposite, I'll choose the middle position between the two corners. However, if she instead chooses …." This interior monologue could continue until the game ends. There are many different possible strategies, but once you have chosen one, there is nothing left to decide. In a game of chess, there are such a large number of possible strategies available that one could never hope to specify them all. However in a 2×2 matrix game, it is relatively easy to construct strategies because of the limited number of possible response patterns.

In experimental studies, the effects of a given strategy are examined either by having a confederate follow a pre-selected strategy or (where subjects communicate via computer terminals) presenting a computer-generated response as the "other player." Many strategic factors can be studied. For example, does an opponent who cooperates 10 percent of the time (choosing these occasions at random) have more or less influence on the subject than one who cooperates 90 percent of the time? In fact, such fixed strategies have been found to have very little success in influencing subjects (Vinacke, 1969). Unconditionally cooperative or unconditionally "tough" strategies fail to produce cooperative responses from the opposition (Solomon, 1960).

More effective are dynamic strategies responsive to the other subject's behaviours. One of these is the so-called "tit-for-tat" (or "delayed matching") strategy whereby the confederate begins with a cooperative response and then makes the same response on trial $n + 1$ as the subject made on trial n. (In other words in a series of interactions, each time one person is cooperative, the other cooperates the next time.) This strategy responds in a positive way to the other person's cooperativeness but does not reinforce hostile moves by the other player. There is a wealth of empirical evidence that shows that this approach is the best way to induce cooperative responding in others (Wing-Tung & Komorita, 2002).

According to the research of Axelrod and Dion (1988), three essential properties of the tit-for-tat strategy lead to stable cooperation: (1) *niceness*—interaction must begin with a cooperative move; (2) *provocability*—at the first non-cooperative move by the other player, there must be retaliation; and (3) *forgiveness*—after appropriate retaliation, it is necessary to go back to cooperation and not punish past defection forever. In other words, the tit-for-tat strategy leads to the perception that the other person is "fair but firm" (Komorita, Hilty & Parks, 1991; Van-Lange & Visser, 1999).

Strategy studies have also used a buyer–seller type game in which two players negotiate over the sale of some item. Generally, a tough strategy (extreme opening offer and infrequent concessions) has been the most successful in terms of obtaining the larger share of the joint payoff (Chertkoff & Conley, 1967). Pacifist strategies, on the other hand, typically result in exploitation.

Overall, the bulk of the evidence indicates that in a conflict or bargaining situation, neither an overly generous nor an overly tough position is effective in bringing about mutual cooperation. The most effective strategy is one of firm resistance to exploitation coupled with reciprocation of the other's cooperative behaviour.

Predispositional Variables

Would the course of the Second World War have been different had Hitler, Churchill, Stalin and Roosevelt been replaced by others? Would the 1995 Quebec referendum have had different results if Kim Campbell had been prime minister—or if Lucien Bouchard, then leader of the Bloc Québécois, had switched places with Premier Jacques Parizeau? The study of predispositional variables focuses on the effects of personal characteristics of the individual protagonists—cultural variables, age and gender, personality beliefs about each other—on the course of conflicts.

Culture

Cultural differences have been found in studies comparing the behaviour of subjects from various countries. For example, Carment (1973) compared the behaviour of students in Canada and India in a mixed-motive game in which one player (the "benefactor") could, by means of choosing one alternative, allow the other player (the "beneficiary") to choose an outcome that led either to equal point-gain or to a large point-gain for the benefactor. While East Indians were more generous than Canadians at the outset, their response did not last long. More importantly, the East Indian subjects, unlike the Canadians, avoided taking advantage of the other player's generosity. When the players later switched roles (something they did not anticipate), the new East Indian beneficiary continued to be reluctant to accept the other's generosity, while the Canadians were even more eager to accept it. However in another study involving a different game, when East Indian subjects were led to believe that the opponent had an advantage over them, they became very submissive while, when they thought they were at an advantage, they became very competitive—exactly the opposite of what was observed with Canadian males (Alcock, 1975). Many other similar cross-cultural comparisons have been made. Canadian Blackfoot Indian children have been found to be more cooperative in a game situation than urban Canadian children and, in fact, are even more predisposed towards cooperative behaviour than are children from the Israeli *kibbutzim* where cooperation and sharing are explicitly encouraged (Miller & Thomas, 1972).

Age and gender

Both age and gender appear to influence the course of conflict. It seems that competitiveness increases with age (McClintock & Nuttin, 1969; Leventhal & Lane, 1970), especially among males. Vinacke and Gullickson (1964) compared subjects of ages 7 and 8, 12 to 14 and university age and found that while females were similarly accommodating at all three age

levels, males became steadily more exploitative with age. Such gender differences are not always found, although, in general, studies consistently indicate that females are more responsive to cues to cooperate than are males. It is likely that while boys are traditionally raised to be independent and aggressive, girls are trained to be sensitive to methods of reducing conflict. This conclusion is supported by a study by Stockard, Van-de-Kragt and Dodge (1988), which found that while women were slightly more cooperative than men in a social dilemma simulation, whether a woman had cooperated or not, she was more likely than a man to say that her motivation was altruistic and that she was interested in fostering harmonious group relations.

Personality

It also seems that some people are more predisposed towards cooperation than others, quite apart from gender, cultural or age considerations, but such people are still likely to act competitively when dealing with other competitive people (Alcock & Mansell, 1977; Kelley & Stahelski, 1970). A competitive person, on the other hand, seems to act competitively regardless of the behaviour of others. For such a person, everyone else will seem to be competitive since even cooperators will act competitively against such a person. Cooperators are more likely, as a result of their experience, to develop the view that some people are cooperative while some others are not and to adjust their behaviour according to the behaviour of the other party. It also appears that cooperators believe that cooperation reflects intelligence and is the proper way to act, whereas non-cooperators see cooperation as a sign of weakness, and competition as a sign of strength (Komorita & Parks, 1995).

As important as these predispositional effects may be, the evidence from game studies suggests that they are generally overridden by the effects of the structure of the situation. This overriding influence of structural variables may explain why correlations between personality variables and cooperative behaviour are repeatedly found to be low.

Beliefs about each other

How can we account for enduring conflicts steeped in hatred and violence that transcend years, decades or even centuries? Intergroup violence based on ethnic, religious or national group identity continues to bedevil the modern world every bit as much as it has bedevilled our ancestors. Consider the awful violence associated with modern events such as the Protestant–Catholic conflict in Northern Ireland, the Arab–Israeli conflict, the break-up of Yugoslavia, the civil strife in Rwanda, the events of September 11, 2001, the Iraq–Iran war and the 2003 war in Iraq. There is much more to this destructiveness than the failure to solve conflicts about resources. Often, the roots of such conflicts are all but lost in history.

- Every Irish schoolchild learns about the importance of the year 1690. The Protestant King William III, head of the Dutch Royal House of Orange, had been invited by powerful Protestant political figures in England to seize the throne from King James II, a devout convert to Roman Catholicism and, incidentally, his father-in-law! James had fled to France but later, with the help of Irish soldiers, began an attempt to retake the throne. The decisive battle occurred on the banks of the Boyne River in Ireland. Irish Catholics have never forgotten their defeat at the *Battle of the Boyne*. Irish Protestants have not forgotten either and every year members of the Protestant Orange Order in Northern Ireland lead a ceremonial march on July 12 to honour that historic Protestant victory, a practice which raises the ire of the Roman Catholics, especially since the Protestants insist on marching through Catholic neighbourhooods.

- The "ethnic cleansing" carried out by Christian Serbs in 1999 against their Muslim compatriots in Kosovo, resulting in the deaths of at least 6000 of the latter, has its roots in the terrible *Battle of Kosovo Polje* fought on June 28, 1389 between some 80 000 Serbian knights—defenders of the Christian faith—and an army of invading Muslim warriors from the Ottoman Empire. The Serbs were defeated and surrendered their land, and by the late 20th century, ethnic Albanian Muslims made up 90 percent of Kosovo's population. However, Serbs never forgot the Battle of Kosovo Polje. For example on the 600th anniversary of the Battle of Kosovo Polje on June 28, 1989, over one million Serbs (about ten percent of the Serbian population) made a pilgrimage to the battle site to honour their Serbian heroes who fell so long ago.

Such terrible conflicts that transcend the centuries, while sometimes fed by contemporary resource disparities, have much more to do with the strong and enduring intergroup enmity and the beliefs that accompany it. The "we versus they" orientation, the intergroup bias that grows from remembering such history, is the breeding ground for destructive conflict resolution (Hewstone, Rubin and Willis, 2002).

Eidelson and Eidelson (2003) have identified five types of core collective beliefs that are particularly important in such intergroup conflicts and that can even serve to define the groups for their members:

- *Superiority*—This is a belief that members of one's group are in some way superior to members of the other group. Sometimes this sense is theologically driven in the sense that one's own religion is viewed as the only true religion and that all others are pagan or even diabolical. At other times—as in Nazi Germany with its concept of the Aryan master race—ethnic origin may be the distinguishing factor. Sometimes both sides hold identical, mirror-image views of one another, each seeing the other as inferior for the same reasons.

- *Injustice*—This is a belief that another group has significantly wronged one's group and that there has been an injustice that needs avenging. Certainly, the enmity between the Serbs and the Muslims of Kosovo reflect such a belief on the part of the Serbs.

- *Vulnerability*—This is the belief that one's group is very vulnerable to harm from the opposing group. Both Israelis and Palestinians feel themselves to be particularly vulnerable to harm from each other, leading to a situation where disputes over resources and territory are viewed as issues of basic survival.

- *Distrust*—The belief that leaders and members of the opposing group are untrustworthy and out to deceive, often held by both sides, make constructive conflict resolution extremely difficult to achieve.

- *Helplessness*—A belief in collective helplessness can keep a group from defending itself against an oppressor. Black South Africans shared such a belief under apartheid, which served to dampen the enthusiasm for any movement aimed at rebelling against the white masters. This belief, while promoting the status quo, also militates against any action that will resolve the underlying conflict between the subjugators and the subjugated.

Bearing this in mind, it helps us to understand the seeming intractability of conflicts such as those in the

about. Yet, some insights derived from psychological studies of conflict have been applied to the resolution of international negotiations.

There are two existing and contradictory schemata regarding conflict and how it can lead to war: the deterrence schema and the conflict spiral schema (Tetlock, 1983, 1987):

- The **deterrence schema** begins with the image of two protagonists, the "aggressor" and the "status quo" power. The aggressor power may doubt the ability of the status quo power to resist encroachment even in issues or areas unimportant to its vital interests. If this doubt arises, the aggressor makes increasingly ambitious claims, with each concession from the other side leading to a greater demand. Finally, a situation occurs in which the status quo power must resist, but the aggressor cannot believe it—and war results. Thus Hitler, despite clear and repeated warnings, did not believe that Poland was the end of the line because earlier concessions had allowed Germany to take the Rhineland, Austria, the Sudetenland and the remainder of Czechoslovakia. Ironically, war can only be prevented by having a war-making capacity and a willingness to use it: a balance through mutual fear.

- In a war, the nation that acts first is most likely to come out best (if it can successfully cripple the opponent's machinery for retaliation). Thus, each side strives to protect its counter-strike capability in order

to deter the other from the temptation of striking first. If each side can assure the other that it will always be able to destroy the other even if the other strikes first, the other will not be tempted to strike. This is referred to by U.S. military strategists as MAD: **Mutually Assured Destruction**. The development of anti-missile missiles, nuclear missile-carrying submarines and the housing of missiles in underground concrete silos were all designed to deter others from giving in to the "first strike" temptation.

- The **conflict spiral schema** begins with the notion of competition between protagonists. In this schema, the defensive and deterrent actions of each side are interpreted as threatening by the other, who must respond with greater levels of counter-threat. Interests and goals are seen as incompatible and the mutual fear itself causes an escalation (e.g., an arms race) and intensified competition at all levels. (As we saw in Sherif's (1958) Robbers' Cave experiment, a relationship defined in purely competitive terms leads to outgroup stereotyping and generalized mistrust.)

As of the year 2003, the United States was determined to develop an anti-missile shield to protect the U.S. (and Canada) from missile attacks. However, the development of such a capability, while seen as purely defensive by the United States, will undoubtedly be seen as offensive by some other nations and is likely to rekindle the arms race. Think of two children with water guns who have agreed not to shoot at each other.

United Nations peacekeeping forces attempt to prevent continuing war while nations attempt to resolve conflict.

Then one puts on a plastic rain garment. What is the other child to think? Is the rain gear a defensive measure or is it preparation for an attack, since that child is now relatively invulnerable?

Both the deterrence and the conflict spiral schemata have elements of historical and contemporary validity and it is important to understand that they underlie the decision-making process, particularly at an international level. Both are concerned with the possibility that misunderstanding and misperception can cause an unintended war. Deterrence types worry that "they" will underestimate "our" resolve to defend our interests, while conflict spiralists worry that "they" will overestimate our hostility (and vice versa). Perhaps by making the two schemata explicit and available for critical examination, an "unfreezing" in the thinking of international politicians and geopolitical strategists is possible.

Ever since the destruction of the World Trade Center in New York, the problem of international terrorism has taken on new urgency and the world's only remaining superpower, the United States, has been quick to react. U.S. President Bush has declared a War on Terrorism, and invited other countries to join the battle. The invasions of Afghanistan in 2001 and Iraq in 2003 were part of a new U.S. policy of pre-emptive strikes against countries considered to be supporting terrorism and/or harbouring weapons of mass destruction that might be used by terrorists. Only time will tell whether this strategy succeeds in deterring future terrorism or generates a conflict spiral of more frequent and more destructive terrorism pitted against more frequent and more destructive military intervention. In the long run however, it will be humankind's ability to understand the roots of conflict and to find ways to resolve conflicts that are fair and acceptable to all sides that will determine whether terrorism continues to escalate around the world or eventually dies away (Moghaddam & Marsella, 2004). Terrorism is both a product of unresolved conflict and an extreme method for attempting to force resolution. It is all the more difficult to counter, regardless of whatever realistic conflict might be involved, when it is associated with an ideology that makes heroes of and promises heavenly rewards to those who kill members of the "enemy group" even while committing suicide themselves. Meeting terrorism with a modern militaristic ideology that can rain down missiles anywhere with impunity only adds to the spiral of intergroup hatred and destruction.

Summary

1. Realistic conflict refers to situations in which there is a real basis for dispute, such as competition for scarce resources, incompatible goals or incompatible principles.

2. There are six types of conflict: veridical, contingent, displaced, misattributed, latent and conflict based on false premises.

3. Social exchange theory concerns the perception by each person of the relative value of rewards and costs in a relationship evaluated in terms of the comparison level (CL) of others in that situation and the comparison level for alternatives to that relationship (CLalt).

4. A "game" refers to a situation in which two or more interdependent parties make decisions that affect each other according to rules. The two types of games are zero-sum, in which one party's gains match the opponent's losses, and non-zero-sum (mixed motive), in which some outcomes are mutually preferable to others.

5. Games such as the Prisoner's Dilemma are based on the assumption that people act rationally to maximize utility. They may be motivated by individualistic, competitive or cooperative concerns.

6. A collective dilemma occurs when rational behaviour by individuals produces an outcome that is collectively undesirable (e.g., the commons problem and the provision of public goods problem).

7. A game that is non-negotiable (only one winner) in which the goal-directed behaviour is threatening and in which both players can lose disastrously is called a dangerous game.

8. A threat is more credible when the threatener has behaved consistently in the past, the threatened action has negative consequences for the threatener as well as the party threatened and the threatened consequences are not excessive in the situation.

9. Threat often intensifies conflict because of people's need to "save face"; a spiralling series of threats and counter-threats can develop.

10. Communication sometimes reduces conflict by clarifying the intentions of either side, but it is unlikely to be helpful in a "win or lose" situation or when face-saving is important.

11. The most effective strategy in bargaining combines firm resistance to exploitation with reciprocation of the other party's cooperative behaviour.

12. Mediation and arbitration are third-party interventions designed to reduce conflict.

13. Conflict reduction may be accomplished through the graduated reciprocation of tension-reducing acts (GRIT) and the introduction of superordinate goals.

14. Deterrence and conflict-spiral models are two opposing schemata of conflict at the international level.

Further Reading

BUDESCU, D.V. & EREV, I. (Eds.). (1999). *Games and human behavior: Essays in honor of Amnon Rapaport.* Mahwah, NJ: Lawrence Erlbaum Associates.

FISHER R.J. (1990). *The social psychology of intergroup and international conflict resolution.* New York: Springer-Verlag. A critical appraisal of new and traditional methods of resolving conflicts between groups.

GOULD, R.V. (2003). *Collision of wills: how ambiguity about social rank breeds conflict.* Chicago: University of Chicago Press. This sociological analysis of conflict argues that conflict is more likely to occur in symmetrical relationships—among friends or social equals—than in hierarchical ones and that striving for dominance is a major motivator for destructive conflict resolution. Vendettas, revolutions and everyday disagreements are examined from this perspective.

JERVIS, R., LEBOW, R.N. & STEIN, J.G. (1985). *Psychology and deterrence.* Baltimore, MD: Johns Hopkins University Press. An analysis, with examples, of the psychological aspects of international conflict.

KEEGAN, J.S. (1999). *The first world war.* Toronto, ON: Key Porter Books. How the "war to end all wars" was started, conducted and won and how it had a lasting effect on the political structures of the world. A must for anyone who wants to go beyond mere description or who has time to read only one book on the subject.

MOGHADDAM, F.M. & MARSELLA, A.J. (Eds). (2004). *Understanding terrorism: Psychosocial roots, consequences, and interventions.* Washington, DC: American Psychological Association. This book provides a social psychological and cross-cultural examination of the complex cultural and historical roots of modern terrorism and suggests strategies for social change that will eliminate the conditions that give rise to it.

RUBIN, J.Z., PRUITT, D.G. & KIM, S.H. (1994). *Social conflict: escalation, stalemate, and settlement* (2nd ed.). New York: McGraw-Hill. Easy-to-read coverage of conflict from sources to solutions with experimental and practical examples.

WHITE, H.C. (Ed.). (1986). *Psychology and the prevention of nuclear war.* New York: New York University Press. A variety of views on the role played by psychological factors in easing tensions surrounding the nuclear arms race.

WORCHEL, S. & SIMPSON. J.A. (Eds.). (1993). *Conflict between people and groups: causes, processes, and resolutions.* Chicago: Nelson-Hall. An encyclopedic compendium of research, ideas and applications related to interpersonal, intergroup and international conflict.

Weblinks

Amnesty International
www.uib.no/isf/people/amnesty/whatis.htm

Nuclear Age Peace Foundation
www.napf.org   Research and analysis on critical issues of peace and global survival.

Worldwatch
www.worldwatch.org   The site of a group dedicated to fostering the evolution of an environmentally sustainable society.

Chapter 11

Aggression and Violence

> Movie violence is like eating salt. The more you eat, the more you need to eat to taste it. People are becoming immune to its effects. That's why death counts have quadrupled and blast power is increasing by the megaton.
>
> *Alan J. Pakula, film director*

> It shall be prohibited unnecessarily to torture or brutally to ill-treat an animal …. To ill-treat an animal means to cause it pain. Ill-treatment is deemed brutal when it is inspired by lack of feeling.
>
> *Animal Protection Act of the Third Reich*
> *Drafted by Goering, signed by Hitler*

Chapter Outline

■ In June 1983, Rebecca Guno disappeared from Vancouver's downtown eastside, a squalid ten-block area of dilapidated shops and hotels that is home to legions of drug dealers and prostitutes, and has the the highest HIV infection rate in North America. It is one of the poorest neighbourhoods in all of Canada. She was herself a drug addict and a prostitute; she was never seen again. Rebecca Guno's disappearance passed almost without notice at the time; she was the first of over 60 women who disappeared without a trace from that same area of Vancouver over the next 19 years. Public interest in the mystery of the missing women was slow to develop—could this have anything to do with the fact that many of the women were prostitutes and drug addicts and a half or more were aboriginals?

In response to charges that the police had been slow to react, a Missing Women's Task Force was eventually set up and in 2002, it began to investigate a pig farm in a Vancouver suburb, digging up the soil for possible traces of the missing women. Based on DNA evidence uncovered in that search, 53-year-old Robert William Pickton was charged with the murder of 15 of the missing women. While Pickton's trial would not begin until 2004, the Task Force continued to scour his farm for further forensic evidence and in 2003 51 additional anthropologists were hired to assist the 52 who were already hard at work sifting through the soil looking for traces of the missing women in what was being dubbed Canada's largest serial murder.

■ On June 23, 1985, Air India flight 182 from Montreal to London, carrying luggage that originated in Vancouver, blew up as it neared the Irish coast over the North Atlantic, killing all 329 passengers and crew, most of them Canadians. Eighteen years later in 2003, three suspects finally went to trial in a Vancouver courtroom, accused of having placed a bomb in some

of that Vancouver luggage, in what was expected to be the longest trial in Canadian history.

■ On December 6, 1989, 25-year-old Marc Lepine took a semi-automatic hunting rifle to the École Polytechnique, an engineering school affiliated with the Université de Montréal, entered a classroom, fired a shot into the air and ordered the men to leave the room. He was heard to say in French, "I want the women" and "You're all a bunch of feminists. I hate feminists." A few moments later, he opened fire on the group of women, killing six. Then for the next 20 minutes, he prowled the corridors hunting for other victims. In the worst massacre in Canadian history, he killed 14 women and injured 13 other people, almost all women, before killing himself. On his body was found a three-page letter that violently condemned "feminists" and that included a "hit list" of 15 women, some of them well-known public figures.

These particular acts of violence are well known to Canadians because of the extensive media coverage they received. So too are the actions of terrorists, be they those of the Front de libération du Québec in the late 1960s that culminated in the murder of Pierre Laporte and the imposition of the War Measures Act in 1970, or the long history of violence on the part of the Irish Republican Army and the Ulster Defence League, or the suicide bombers in the Middle East or the horrific destruction of the World Trade Center in New York on September 11, 2001. Yet there is much more violence, with many more victims, that does not make it to the national news—sexual assaults, spousal and child abuse, "road rage," aggression by schoolyard

Some parts of the world are beset by a cycle of violence. How can the cycle be broken?

bullies—in other words, the violence of everyday life. And some of this violence is lethal: Every year in Canada, between 500 and 700 people—including 50 to 60 children—are murdered. Between 1974 and 2002, almost 2600 Canadians have died as the result of spousal violence, the majority of them women (although the good news is that the rate of spousal homicide has dropped over that period by 62% for women and 50% for men) (Statistics Canada, 2002). In 2000, Canadian police reports listed 116 202 victims of physical assault (almost a quarter of the victims were less than 18 years old), and another 12 243 victims of sexual assault (with almost two-thirds of the victims being less than 18 years old).

According to the World Health Organization (WHO) (2002), more than 1.6 *million* people are killed by violence around the world every year: On an average day, 1424 people are killed in acts of homicide—almost one person every minute. Roughly one person commits suicide every 40 seconds. About 35 people are killed every hour as a direct result of armed conflict. In the 20th century, an estimated 191 000 000 people lost their lives directly or indirectly as a result of conflict, and well over half of them were civilians (WHO press release, Geneva, October 3, 2002).

Why are human beings so prone to aggression? Are we, as Freud suggested, innately violent, or are we more like Rousseau's "noble savage," born good and gentle but corrupted over time? Is aggressiveness in our genes or is it something that, along with the ability to read the alphabet or ride a bicycle, we acquire?

Social psychologists are interested in such questions because aggression by its very nature is social behaviour: the aggressor uses aggressive acts to harm, punish or control others or to communicate feelings of anger. Therefore, it seems likely that social learning, social norms and cultural values all play a role in aggression, as they do in any other social behaviour.

What Is Aggression?

While it may seem at first that it should be easy to identify aggressive acts, a moment's reflection shows that this is not so, for the term is applied to a variety of behaviours that vary greatly in terms of action and accompanying emotion. A neighbourhood bully who "accidentally" bumps into someone on the sidewalk; a hockey player who delivers a body check to an adversary; a mother who yells at her children; a child who hits another child in order to retrieve a favourite toy; an Air Force bombardier who drops tons of bombs on unseen targets miles below; a rapist who overpowers a woman on her way home from work—all of these people could be described as acting aggressively, even though their actions, emotions and motivations may have little in common.

Indeed, aggression is essentially in the eye of the beholder; it is a concept more than it is an action or a thing. A particular behaviour can be viewed as either aggressive or nonaggressive depending on the social context in which it occurs. Is punching someone in the abdomen aggressive? That depends on whether the punch was intended to hurt an adversary or to dislodge food from the throat of a choking dinner companion.

What then are the defining features of aggression? It has to involve more than simply a deliberate action that produces pain or distress, for otherwise a physician who administers a painful injection to a struggling, protesting child would be considered aggressive. Thus, the intention to hurt or harm is surely central to the concept of aggression—but is it necessary that someone actually be hurt or is the *attempt* to do harm sufficient? Is emotional involvement (anger) necessary? What about verbal attacks, poison pen letters or giving someone the cold shoulder? Must aggression be directed towards people, or is kicking the wall or the cat included as well?

Taking these considerations into account, social psychologists typically define **aggression** as behaviour that is intended to harm or destroy another person. Thus, someone who fires a gun intending to hit another person would be considered to have committed an aggressive act even if the shot misses its mark.

Aggression is not easy to study, given the need to assess the intent of a person who hurts someone else, and cognitive biases can influence the attribution of such intent. Indeed, research shows that observers tend to be overly influenced by both the severity of harm that a given act produces (the more severe the harm, the more likely that the actor will be judged as having intended to harm) and the extent to which the actor could have avoided harming the victim (Lysak, Rule & Dobbs, 1989). Avoidability is often the major basis people use for attributing blame. If the actor could not have foreseen the harmful outcome, then the harm is considered to be accidental. Even when an act is judged to be aggressive, observers will assess the moral justification for the aggression on the basis of the perceived motive (Reeder, Kumar, Hesson-McInnis & Trafimow, 2002). When the aggression appears to have been self-serving, it will be judged more harshly than if it appears to have been motivated by self-defence or even in some cases by "justifiable" revenge.

Aggressive behaviour is often accompanied by both aggressive cognitions and aggressive affect (anger) (Buss & Perry, 1992) and differences in cognitions and affect lead to qualitative differences in aggressive acts. Such differences have led some psychologists to distinguish between **instrumental aggression**, which is a premeditated means to some desired end (e.g., the aggression of a bully who forcibly takes someone's candy) and **hostile aggression**, which is motivated by anger and which appears to have as its end the infliction of harm upon someone else (Anderson & Bushman, 2002; Berkowitz, 1984, 1989).

How can aggression be studied? This is not so easy at it might first appear. We cannot rely on simple observation, for the presence of the observer produces serious methodological and ethical problems, and it is also difficult to be in the right place at the right time in order to observe aggression. However, Pepler and Craig (1995) have developed a new approach to the study of aggression in children that overcomes many of the limitations of naturalistic observations. They used unobtrusive video cameras and wireless microphones to observe school children's interactions remotely wherever they were at play on the school ground, without their being aware that they were under constant observation.

What about studying aggression in the laboratory? Although aggression is defined in terms of intention to harm, it is so difficult to measure intention that most laboratory studies study behaviours that appear to be aggressive instead (Tedeschi, Smith & Brown, 1974). For example, many research studies have operationally defined *aggression* in terms of the number and intensity of shocks delivered in a Milgram teacher–learner paradigm (see Chapter 6).

However even in that situation, there is some ambiguity about the nature of the response. Could subjects sometimes administer shock in the belief that they are helping rather than hurting? Apparently so, as Rule and Nesdale (1974) found when they compared the behaviour of subjects who were told that increasing the shock intensity would help the learner learn ("prosocial" condition) with that of other subjects who were told that it would hinder the learner ("hostile" condition). In addition, half the subjects in each group were insulted by the learner during the learning sequence. As Figure 11–1 illustrates, when subjects were insulted in the prosocial condition, less intense shocks were given than when no insults occurred. Yet more intense shocks were given in the

FIGURE 11-1

Mean intensities of shock as a function of the confederate's insult and the value of the response

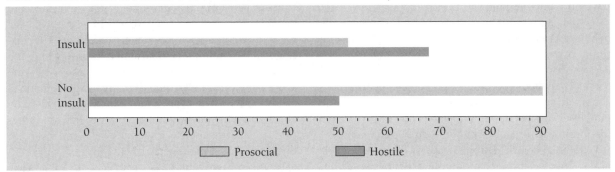

Source: Rule & Nesdale, 1974

hostile condition than when no insult had been made. Thus, if the subject believed the shock to be helpful and if he or she was not negatively disposed towards the other subject, more intense shock was given not as an outburst of "aggression" but apparently as an incentive to learn. Even though subjects believed that they were causing pain to another person, they believed that the victim's own interests justified the pain. This kind of reasoning is used by parents and teachers who physically punish children: the line between what is benevolent and what is malevolent can be fuzzy. Thus, bear in mind that it is not always easy to ascertain whether behaviour that appears to be aggressive was actually intended to harm or destroy.

Causes of Aggression

We shall use the tragic Lepine massacre, whose victims are commemorated by a national day of remembrance each December 6, as a framework for approaching the study of aggression and violence. To begin, how can such an outburst of violence be explained? Had we interviewed people at the time, we might have obtained responses such as these:

- Sometimes the pressure builds up inside a person and you just have to get it out of your system, so you end up hurting or killing somebody.
- Could be he had a brain tumour or something.
- He must have been brought up that way, to see violence as the way to deal with problems.
- He's just a tough character who lost control of himself.
- It's our society; it encourages violence.

- What with all the violence on TV, it's a wonder that this sort of thing doesn't happen more often.
- It's just too easy; any nut can buy a gun in this country.
- This was an expression of men's deep-seated hostility towards women.

These hypotheses can apply to most violence and we will explore each of them. A note of caution however: Following any outburst of violence, the media are usually filled with emotional pronouncements about the possible causes. While we can discover influences that promote aggressive behaviour, it is extremely difficult to determine the cause of a particular act of "senseless" violence. How could we ever test the hypothesis that Lepine's actions represented an undercurrent of male hostility towards women? What evidence would we need to persuade us that violent films had influenced Lepine's actions?

Remember too that most violence does not make the headlines. Some of it is impulsive, involving sudden deadly outbursts, but some is calculated and cold-blooded and some, especially that which occurs in the home, goes on day after day without ever being reported. Our larger focus is on understanding aggression in general and not just the stuff of headlines.

"You just have to get it out of your system": Aggression as instinct or drive

In the face of irrational violence, it is often tempting to view such behaviour as the product of biological forces that in turn produce an uncontrollable outburst of aggression. This idea goes back to Freud and even beyond. Freud believed that all behaviour is driven by two basic **instincts**: the life instinct, **Eros**, and the death instinct, **Thanatos**. Thanatos works towards returning the organism to its original inanimate state through self-destruction. When blocked by Eros, Thanatos "displaces" some of its aggressive energy outward onto other human beings (Freud, 1933). Thus according to this view, aggression in some form or another is inevitable and we need to try to channel and control it.

Could Marc Lepine have been driven by some sort of death instinct, by Thanatos? Such speculation is not helpful for understanding aggression, for as fascinating as Freud's ideas may be, his theorizing about aggression has held up poorly in the face of empirical evidence. There is simply no evidence of either an aggressive instinct or aggressive "energy" in humans.

Catharsis

Instinct theories of aggression assume the build-up of energy, held in check by various inhibiting forces, but which eventually must be discharged through aggression or activities that are somehow related to aggression (e.g., contact sports). Freud referred to such discharge as **catharsis**. According to this point of view, the simple witnessing of aggression will lead to some degree of catharsis.

Even if the instinct approach is misguided, could it be that aggressive impulses are reduced following some kind of cathartic release? Aristotle believed that people's feelings of sorrow would diminish through watching dramatic tragedy and identifying with a hero. His predecessor, Plato, on the other hand believed that witnessing emotional discharges *increased* emotional feelings. A difference of opinion regarding the effects of witnessing emotional outbursts continues to this day.

Research indicates that watching aggression or participating in aggression enhances rather than reduces the likelihood of further emotional arousal or aggressive behaviour. For example, Doob and Kirshenbaum (1973a) studied the arousal effects of film violence by monitoring the blood pressure of university students who watched either a seven-minute clip in which 150 people were shot and killed, or a neutral film. In addition, the subjects were either in a "frustrated" condition (having been interfered with by the experimenter during an earlier task) or were not frustrated. They found that the effects on arousal of both frustration and the violent film were additive. Subjects who had

witnessed the violence and had been frustrated exhibited the most arousal. This finding is one of many that contradicts the idea that watching violence is tension-reducing for either frustrated or non-frustrated people. Other studies have shown that blood pressure and feelings of hostility decrease more rapidly when insulted or irritated subjects are left by themselves rather than when they have the opportunity to face their antagonist and verbalize their annoyance (Kahn, 1966; Vantress & Williams, 1972). Evidence against the catharsis hypothesis is rather compelling: watching film violence, directing violence towards objects, watching or participating in aggressive sports and lashing out verbally at other people are not effective means of reducing hostile arousal and may well promote further aggression (Baron, 1983a; Bushman, Baumeister & Stack, 1999). Plato, it now appears, was right; Aristotle was wrong.

The frustration–aggression hypothesis

While rejecting the idea of innate aggressive energy, some theorists have speculated that there may be an inborn tendency to aggress following frustration of some kind. This **frustration–aggression hypothesis** was originally proposed by Dollard, Doob, Miller, Maurer & Sears (1939) who suggested that every instance of frustration, defined as interference with behaviour directed towards a goal, produces some tendency towards aggression and that every instance of aggression is preceded by some sort of frustration. It was assumed that both learning and environmental cues would determine the particular form that aggressiveness would take and what its target would be. However research has shown that this view, like Freud's, is also untenable and that while frustration may lead to aggression, it may lead to other behaviours as well (e.g., passive withdrawal). Moreover, aggression is not always preceded by frustration.

Cognitive neo-associationist model

Most people know that when they are in pain or distress, they are more irritable and perhaps more ready to lash out at others with little provocation. Taking this into account, Berkowitz (1983, 1989, 1990, 1993) revised the frustration–aggression hypothesis through his **cognitive neo-associationist model** (which simply means a new—"neo"—form of an associationist model, based on "associations" between two stimuli that draws heavily on cognitive theory). Rather than starting with frustration, his model begins with an aversive stimulus (pain, excessive heat, frustration, frightening news, etc.) that produces arousal in the autonomic nervous system (the so-called "fight or flight response"), which in turn produces both the tendency to escape and the tendency to attack (see Figure 11–2). The negative emotion will also stimulate various thoughts and memories that have been associated with that emotion or situation in the past. If these thoughts are themselves related to anger ("No one does this to me and gets away with it"), then the individual is likely to react with aggression. However, if the thoughts are related to fear ("I'm going to suffocate"), then the response is likely to be flight. Imagine that you are in your car, in busy traffic and someone suddenly cuts in front of you. You take evasive action, but your heart pounds and you feel a rush of adrenaline. In other words, you are experiencing autonomic arousal. What do you do next? Some people, in this era of growing road rage, will interpret the situation as an affront and think angry thoughts ("You jerk! Get out of my way!"), making aggression more likely. Others, because of their upbringing and background of experience, may react more with fearful thoughts ("I could have been killed! I've got to get off this highway!"), which is unlikely to result in aggressive behaviour. Still others may react simply by calming themselves down.

This same model suggests that cues associated with aggression can promote aggression from an individual in a state of autonomic arousal—aggression that would not have occurred without the cue. Berkowitz suggests that people sometimes react violently in certain situations of negative affect, not because they anticipate a positive outcome, nor because they are less inhibited about aggression, but because a situational cue (e.g., the presence of a gun) actually elicits an aggressive response due to a classically conditioned association with violence through movies and television (**stimulus pairing**). That is, suppose in the situation described above you are a hunter and you happen to have a shotgun beside you in your car. This model suggests that simply seeing the gun will make it more likely that you will react aggressively to having been cut off in traffic This is the so-called **weapons effect** (Berkowitz & LePage, 1967).

Berkowitz (1994) adds that other thoughts may prevent any aggression from occurring ("If I do anything violent, I could be arrested" or "I have to stay calm—it's not worth getting upset over"), but if the arousal is too high, people can react in a blind rage before there has been enough time for cognitive influences to have any effect. The aggressor may subsequently claim with sincerity, "I didn't mean to hurt anybody." Thus, according to this model, aggressive behaviour can occur without any deliberation or decision-making and people can act aggressively without any awareness of *why* they are doing so.

FIGURE 11-2

Berkowitz's model of impulsive aggression

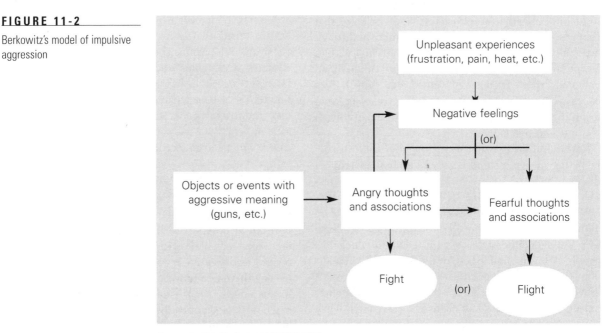

Source: Kenrick, Neuberg and Cialdini, 2002

The Berkowitz model states that excessive heat is one of the negative conditions that can lead to aggression, and because of the interest in factors affecting violence in inner cities in the United States—violence that seems more prevalent during long, hot summers—a number of social psychological studies have examined the correlation between temperature and aggression. The results have been somewhat inconsistent. For example, some studies report that as temperature increases, so does aggression (linear relationship), and it is assumed that the increased aggression is because of increased hostility and aggressive cognitions brought about by the discomfort caused by the heat. Such findings have even led to a warning that global warming may provoke increased rates of violent crime (Anderson, 2001)! Yet, other research (Rotton & Cohn, 2000) that has correlated temperature to police reports of aggravated assaults has found that during the daylight hours in the spring months, there is *less* aggression reported to the police when the temperature is either very high or very low, while at other times, aggression increases as temperature increases. This messiness in the data suggests that we should be very careful not to assume that there is a direct relationship between temperature and violence.

Not just those data, but data in general are insufficient at this time to justify Berkowitz's argument about an inborn predisposition to react aggressively when experiencing negative affect. Moreover, social learning theorists see no need to speculate about inborn mechanisms. They argue that the evidence shows aggressive behaviours (including hostile and instrumental aggression) are *learned*, not inborn.

Sociobiology

An evolutionary approach to aggression is provided by the controversial theory of **sociobiology** (already discussed in Chapters 8 and 9). It assumes that there are biological bases to at least some social behaviours, making them subject to the same evolutionary processes that apply to physical characteristics. Sociobiologists expect animals and humans to be aggressive towards others of their species but only when such aggression will improve their reproductive success or that of close relatives sharing many of the same genes. Thus, sociobiology predicts that conflicts are likely to be more perilous if the individuals involved are distantly—rather than closely—related (Daly & Wilson, 1988). Homicide, for example, will more often occur between unrelated men than between related men because unre-

lated men do not lose any reproductive advantage for their genes by killing someone who does not share many of them. In fact, they increase the reproductive advantage of their genes by killing those who might otherwise be in competition for women who will furnish the means for reproduction.

The same criticisms made in the last chapter with regard to the sociobiological view of prosocial behaviour apply to the sociobiological view of aggression (see Chapter 9).

"Could be he had a brain tumour, or something": Physiological influences on aggression

There have been various attempts to demonstrate that aggressiveness is genetically transmitted or that aggressiveness is best understood in terms of hormones (an idea discussed later in this chapter) or in terms of areas of the brain that either promote or inhibit aggressive behaviour (see A Case in Point—Aggression and Reptile Brains). Of course, our behaviour is never completely free of the influence of physiology and it is clear that many factors—neural, hormonal and genetic—influence it. However, any effect of such factors on human aggressiveness is most likely indirect; there is no gene or set of genes responsible for aggression and there is no "aggression centre" in the brain (Montague, 1973; Nelson, 1974, 1975; Valenstein, 1975).

As was discussed earlier, as a result of increased emotionality, pain, irritability or frustration—whether brought about by a brain tumour, a back injury or unrequited love—some people may become physically aggressive and strike out. But the evidence does not support the view that we *must* strike out. Although neurophysiological mechanisms are involved in the expression of aggressive behaviours, the use of these mechanisms is not automatic but subject to cognitive control. In fact, attributions are usually involved even in the case of hostile aggression, which is often viewed as uncontrollable and irrational (Ferguson & Rule, 1983). For example, a comment that is interpreted as an insult will lead to activity in the hypothalamus while the same comment interpreted as an innocent remark will have no such effect (Bandura, 1983).

Although the biological approach to aggression is quite appropriate when dealing with animals, the powerful influence of learning upon human behaviour and

Aggression and Reptile Brains

In January 1985, 17-year-old Andrew Leyshon-Hughes went to visit his close friend Nancy Eaton, a great-great-granddaughter of the founder of what was once Canada's largest chain of department stores, Eatons, in her Toronto home. She was a steady companion who had often helped him during difficult times in the past. Leyshon-Hughes had a history of periodic outbursts of explosive violence for which he had been treated in the past and for which he had sought treatment earlier that month. Nancy Eaton let Leyshon-Hughes spend the night on her living room sofa. The next morning he took a kitchen knife, went to her bedroom and stabbed her repeatedly. He left the apartment and returned several hours later to rape her corpse.

In the fall of 1986, Leyshon-Hughes was found not guilty of murder by reason of insanity, which was said to be the result of congenital brain damage. Testifying at the trial, psychiatrist Frank Ervin of McGill University stated that at the time of the murder the boy was essentially a "crocodile man,"

using only that primitive part of the brain that humans have in common with reptiles.

Can a "crocodile brain" be responsible for such obviously acquired behaviour as stabbing with a knife? Leyshon-Hughes's behaviour did not reflect total loss of reasoning: he went to the kitchen, took a knife, walked to the bedroom and stabbed the sleeping woman. His actions following the murder were carried out in a cool and deliberate manner.

While the legal defence of insanity might be justified, is such insanity to be blamed on the brain? Or did a disorder in his personality or a history of unfortunate experiences produce feelings of hostility leading to fantasies of murder and destruction that, at a certain point, became so attractive that they were acted out? Leyshon-Hughes's brain disorder may have produced pain and frustration: it may have increased his anger at life and the world. But the disorder was not necessarily responsible for the violence, which ultimately involved the powers of reason.

the complexity of human social interaction compels a shift from a biological to a social-cultural perspective (Tedeschi, 1983). There is no doubt that our reaction, whether to fight or to withdraw, depends on how we have learned to react in similar situations in the past and on how our society encourages us to respond.

"He must have been brought up that way": Social-developmental influences

Various factors influence whether or not we learn "aggression" as a response. We can be reinforced for aggression or we can imitate others. Moreover, the physical constitution of an individual interacts with the environment to produce a particular set of experiences, which may help or hinder the learning of aggressiveness. The boy who is small for his age is not likely to be successful at throwing his weight around, while a larger child may soon learn that aggression is

useful in achieving certain goals. (One such goal may be simply the attention that aggression brings.) On the other hand, the small individual may tire of having sand kicked in his face and take measures to become more powerful, gradually adopting the role of bully; the larger child may be left alone, never developing the need to learn aggression-related physical skills.

Children learn not only how to aggress but also when to aggress and against whom to aggress (Bandura, 1973). Most research has shown that the early period of life is a particularly critical time for learning about aggression (Olweus, 1972). According to the social learning theory, both fear-withdrawal and rage-attack behaviours develop out of a single, undifferentiated response, which corresponds to the "fight or flight" response discussed earlier in this chapter. The learning process probably proceeds in the following manner (Sawrey & Telford, 1975): the newborn infant responds to a limited range of stimuli—a loud noise, a sensation of falling, a cold draft,

Do water guns ignite aggression or do they just get kids wet?

a hampering of body movement—with a single, diffuse emotional response pattern that might be labelled "excitement" or "fright." Through classical conditioning, other stimuli can come to evoke the same response. The "startle" reaction in infants is accompanied by internal physiological changes as well as behavioural changes. There is first a stiffening of the body followed by tantrum-like behaviour involving squirming, uncoordinated thrashing about of the arms and legs and crying. It is through reducing this discomfort that the infant learns to "aggress" or "withdraw" when frightened. If the child's outbursts are effective in removing the aversive stimulus, the diffuse outburst may be perpetuated. However, it is more likely that certain features of this reaction pattern are more effective in specific situations than others. Waving the arms, for example, may stop the advances of an overly friendly cat, but crying may be totally ineffective.

Eventually, language gains some control over behaviour. While pushing or hitting may reduce or eliminate pain or frustration, the child also learns that in certain situations, aggression is met with counter-aggression. Overt aggression may then be replaced by verbal or symbolic aggression. Moreover, the child who communicates through language learns to use verbal means (e.g., flattery and persuasion) to obtain goals that were previously obtained through the use of force. What young children learn about aggression and how acceptable it is exerts a very strong influence on their social behaviour as they grow up (Huesmann & Guerra, 1997).

Modelling

Although reinforcement is important in the development and maintenance of aggressive behaviour, children are capable of acquiring aggressive behaviour simply by watching someone else do it. Whether the behaviour is actually imitated depends on a number of factors including the child's emotional state (for example, frustrated or not), the observed consequences to the model and who the model is (the child will not imitate just anyone).

What happens to the model helps inform the observer about the reinforcement contingencies that are in effect. If the model is rewarded or at least not punished, children may imitate such behaviour when they find themselves in a similar situation. Bandura and his colleagues (Bandura, Ross & Ross, 1963a, 1963b) have performed a series of classic experiments that demonstrate this. For example, children were shown a television film of a boy who refused to share his toys with a second boy. The second child then began to beat the boy and throw darts at his toy cars. In one version of the film, the aggressor ended up with all the toys and the film finished by showing him taking them all away. The second version ended differently with the aggressor being subjected to a punishing counter-attack by the first boy. While most of the children said they disapproved of the aggression, those who saw the unopposed-aggression ending were subsequently observed to behave more aggressively in a play situation than those who saw the other ending or those who saw no film at all (1963a). Other similar experiments found that filmed models are as effective as live ones (Ross, 1963b).

These findings are supported by a naturalistic study carried out in an urban daycare centre. Goldstein, Arnold, Rosenberg, Stowe and Ortiz (2001) found that children were more likely to behave aggressively if one child's aggressive act resulted in a positive outcome for that child than if it resulted in an aversive outcome.

It is not just children of course who model aggressive behaviour. Adults too can be led to imitate a model's aggression, particularly if the model is rewarded or at least not punished. A model may facilitate behaviour already in the repertoire of the individual; a spectator at a football game who observes others throwing beer cans at the referee may be prompted to throw things as well. Moreover, a model's aggressive behaviour can heighten emotional arousal, which in turn can facilitate an aggressive response, given the appropriate situational cues. For instance, watching an individual savagely fight against an opponent may increase emotional arousal: If one of the protagonists takes a swipe at you, you may react more vigorously as a result of that arousal.

Child rearing

Parents play at least four different roles in the raising of children (Klama, 1988). One, they are usually the child's first partner in social interaction and teach the child how to interpret the social environment. Two, they are managers of the child's behaviour, enforcing rules and setting standards of conduct both within and outside the home. Three, they provide models for the children to imitate. Finally, they serve as teachers, directly supplying knowledge, imparting values and encouraging particular attitudes and manners.

Therefore from the social learning perspective, the behaviour of parents—who largely control the young child's world—will play a critical role in determining whether a child grows up to be aggressive. It is not easy to study empirically the relationship between parents' characters, their child-rearing style and the subsequent aggressiveness of their children since the researcher cannot manipulate independent variables or exclude all extraneous variables. Because experimentation is inappropriate, the typical study examines the correlation between aspects of the parenting style and aspects of the child's behaviour or personality.

Such correlational studies present their own problems of course. Suppose it were found that "aggressive" children had punitive parents. We could not be sure that the punitiveness caused the aggression; it could be that the children's aggressiveness brought about the punitive behaviour. And except for expensive and time-consuming longitudinal studies, we cannot be sure whether a particular behaviour exhibited by a child will be exhibited in the future or whether the behaviour is only temporary. Neither can we detect whether there are certain periods ("critical periods") in the child's development during which she is particularly sensitive or responsive to parental influence. However despite these difficulties, a body of reliable research relating to the effects of parent characteristics and parenting styles on children's aggression has gradually emerged (Coie & Dodge, 1997).

If we think about the effects that a punitive disciplinary style is likely to produce in children, it should not be surprising that parents who frequently use power-assertive techniques (e.g., physical punishment or threats) tend to have highly aggressive children:

- Such parents provide aggressive models for their children to imitate, indirectly teaching them that aggression is effective and acceptable if one is in a position of power. Physical punishment also may produce resentment and anger in a child, sentiments that may contribute to subsequent aggression.

- If aggression is used as a method of problem solving in the family ("Shut your mouth. If I hear another peep out of you, you're going to get slapped."), the child will learn to use this approach as a means of conflict resolution as well as a method for gaining control over others (Sarles, 1976). This also deprives the child of the opportunity to learn non-violent problem-solving strategies, which may add to the risk that such children will use violence in later life (Moore, Pepler, Mae & Kates, 1989).

- Punitive discipline also influences the moral development of children. Rather than coming to act morally and responsibly because of an internalized set of moral principles, the children of power-assertive parents often learn to behave morally only in order to avoid punishment by others (Hoffmann, 1984).

A CASE IN POINT

Bully for You

In Victoria, B.C., on November 14, 1997, 14-year-old Reena Virk, an "overweight teen who didn't fit in," was severely beaten and then drowned. Six teenage girls and one boy were subsequently charged with causing her death. While most bullying does not end in such tragic circumstances, many children's lives are significantly affected by bullying, and research indicates that not only the children who are bullied but the bullies as well are at greater risk of suffering from depression, and anxiety and even at greater risk for suicide. Forty-five percent of boys and 32 percent of girls sampled in a World Health Organization (WHO) study of Canadian schoolchildren reported they had bullied another student at least once during the school term. Consistent with those figures, 42 percent of boys and 35 percent of girls reported having been the targets of bullying in school during the term. "Bullying" was defined as verbal or physical behaviour designed to disturb someone less powerful. These figures were in the mid-range relative to other countries in the 11-nation survey. The WHO study reported a reduction of bullying by between 30 and 50 percent as a result of intervention programs in England and Norway.

Bullying has generally been ignored by society at large, but governments are finally beginning to take notice. As part of the Government of Canada's National Crime Prevention Strategy, York University's LaMarsh Centre for Research on Violence and Conflict Resolution was awarded a grant of $600 000 in 2003 in order to create a national strategy to deal with bullying.

Bullying has many roots. Some become bullies because they are more aggressive in general. For example, a Swedish study (Olweus, 1978) found that schoolyard bullies have both weak controls regarding aggression and a positive attitude towards violence, leading them to react aggressively in many different situations. Others may bully because they seek affirmation of their strength and social status from others. Still others bully to be accepted as part of a group of bullying friends. And bullying does not necessarily end when school is over. Bullies often go on to have other problems in their social interactions as they grow up, and what was considered bullying in the school context may become relationship violence later in life (Pepler, Craig, Connolly, & Henderson, 2002).

While bullies' lives may be marked by aggressivity, if no successful intervention occurs, it is the bullied who are likely to suffer the most serious consequences, both short-term and long-term. Bullies harass those who are least likely to be able to defend themselves, and thus children with developmental difficulties may be especially vulnerable for being singled out for bullying (Zopito, Fairbairn & Zuber, 2001). Similarly, boys who do not seem "masculine" enough may be bullied. A British study of 11- to 14-year-old boys in 12 London schools (Phoenix, Frosh & Pattman, 2003) reported that a common feeling amongst these boys was that they had to present themselves as properly masculine to avoid being bullied by other boys and labelled as "gay."

Once accepted as "part of growing up," leading parents to encourage their children—boys in particular—to stand up for themselves, bullying is now coming to be recognized as a pervasive form of violence that brings misery to the lives of many children at a time in their development when they lack the resources to respond appropriately.

- Parents who use physical punishment are more likely to condone aggression in situations of conflict and may directly or indirectly reinforce the child's aggression in disputes with other children ("If he ever tries to take your sandwich again, kick him. Don't let him push you around.").

- Parents who rely on physical punishment for discipline are often emotionally cold and rejecting as well. Some of these parents closely control or restrict their children's activities while others are permissive, taking little interest in what their children do as long as they are not causing problems.

Cold but permissive parents often rear highly aggressive children while children of cold but restrictive parents typically learn to hide their feelings, developing strong covert aggressive tendencies and resentment, but little overt hostility (Becker, 1964). On the other hand, parents who discipline their children through techniques such as praise and reasoning usually have children whose incidence of aggression is low regardless of the degree of permissiveness or restrictiveness.

It may not be parental punitiveness *per se* that promotes aggression. In fact, physically punitive parents are not always bent on teaching their children how to behave nor is their punishment always effective. Patterson (1982) examined the family interactions of boys who had been labelled aggressive and "out of control" by their families, schools, or the courts, and compared them with those of a control group of non-problem boys of the same age and socioeconomic background. Observers went to the homes of these children and coded the behaviour of each family member every five seconds during the course of the observations. While the parents of the problem boys were the most punitive, their punishment was often ineffective and actually led to more, rather than less, subsequent antisocial behaviour. On the other hand, the parents of the non-problem boys were more tolerant of undesirable behaviour ("permissive"), but when they did react, they were effective in stopping the behaviour. Patterson argued that the parents of the aggressive boys were punitive but essentially uninvolved; they responded to the boys' aversive behaviours as though they were children themselves. They did not attempt to explain their actions to their sons and made no effort to teach problem-solving skills. Indeed, members of the problem families tended to avoid each other in general rather than talking over their problems. Thus, lack of parental involvement and the failure to teach children how to resolve interpersonal difficulties, even in the absence of punitive parental discipline, is a breeding ground for aggression.

Although child abuse (to be discussed next) is a major social problem, it is important to keep in mind that child neglect is more common than physical abuse (Éthier, Palacio-Quintin & Jourdan-Ionescu, 1992) and neglected children may actually show higher rates of violence in adulthood than do children who have been physically abused (Widom, 1989).

Family violence and child abuse

Punitive discipline sometimes takes the form of physical abuse, and physical abuse by fathers and mothers is a significant predictor of aggressive behaviour both for boys and girls (Muller & Diamond, 1999). This certainly is borne out in the example of Marc Lepine. His parents separated when Marc was only seven, and in her divorce petition, Marc's mother described his father, Rachid Gharbi, as a brutal man who regularly lost control. He beat his wife, Marc and Marc's sister for so little a provocation as failing to say "good morning" to him. Did such treatment of Marc later lead him to react with such horrific violence towards others? In recent years, considerable attention has been directed to the problem of family violence including child abuse. The latter is distinguished from the "physical punitiveness" discussed in the previous section. This distinction is based in part on the severity of the physical attack and whether it was intended as punishment or was simply the result of uncontrolled anger, but also on what a given society views as appropriate discipline. For example, spanking a child is considered to be abusive in Sweden although it is generally accepted among Canadians as appropriate punishment in some circumstances. Child abuse is rare in societies where physical discipline is rarely used (Durrant, 1993).

Domestic violence is a worldwide problem (Walker, 1999) and Canada is no exception. While spousal abuse is examined later in this chapter, much domestic violence is directed at children, and statistics on child abuse are startling. It is infants under the age of one year who face the greatest danger. In 1998, according to Statistics Canada, 23 babies *under one year of age* were murdered. In the decade 1974–1983, 150 infants under one year of age were killed, and in more than half the cases, the killer was the child's mother (Daly & Wilson, 1988). Although most child abuse does not lead to death, abused children are at risk for problems of psychological and behavioural adjustment and there is reason to suspect that even witnessing family violence (e.g., children who watch their mothers being battered) may produce as much destructiveness in the children as abuse of the children themselves (Jaffe, Wolfe, Wilson & Zak, 1986). Sadly, many children are regularly exposed to scenes of spousal violence. Studies of children as young as 12 months of age have shown that children that are exposed to anger, even when it is not directed at them, react in a distressed manner that sometimes includes aggressive behaviours (Emery, 1989). The long-term consequences of experiencing or observing violence on a regular basis may place children at risk to perpetuate violence and abuse in adulthood (Moore, Pepler, Mae & Kates, 1989). In addition, long-term exposure to insults and other verbal abuse, especially on the part of mothers and especially in the context of family violence, has very destructive effects on children's emotional well-being and overall adjustment (Moore & Pepler, 2004).

Longitudinal research has also shown that aggression tends to perpetuate itself within the family with each new generation of parents repeating the same child-rearing techniques they experienced (Sarles, 1976). Children from aggressive families are more likely to marry aggressive individuals and their children in turn are more likely to be aggressive (Huesmann, Eron, Lefkowitz & Walder, 1984). This effect has been observed across three generations (Huesmann, Eron & Yarmel, 1987). Yet, we must be careful not to assume that every abused child will become a violent adult and a child abuser, for the link between child abuse and adult violence is not straight-forward and a careful examination of the empirical evidence reveals that the generality of this "cycle of violence" has been somewhat exaggerated (Kaufman & Zigler, 1987; Widom, 1989). Although there is a greater likelihood of child abuse if the parents were abused as children, most child abusers were never themselves abused. Furthermore, most delinquents were not abused as children and most abused children do not turn into delinquents (Widom, 1989).

Child abuse often produces depression, withdrawal and even self-destruction rather than interpersonal violence. Although the reasons are not yet understood, some abused or neglected children become more aggressive, others become depressed, while still others appear to be relatively unaffected by abuse or neglect. Some children simply seem to be more resilient than others. Various psychological characteristics of the child, as well as aspects of family life apart from violence, all play some role in determining the impact of violence on the child; the child's appraisal and cognitive processing of the violence in the home is most likely an important factor (Rutter, 1987; Werner, 1989). Some children may be able to distance themselves emotionally from family violence, and may be less apt to blame the situation on some shortcoming in themselves (Moore & Pepler, 1989). The presence of one adult who plays a significant role in the child's life and who provides a warm and secure relationship may, for some children, be a very important component.

Although more research is needed to understand fully why some children are resilient while others are not, it is important to remember that not all children born into violent or neglectful families grow into violent adults. Nor do aggressive children necessarily grow to be aggressive adults. In a 15-year longitudinal study of more than 1000 boys in Montreal, it was found that only one in eight boys who were particularly aggressive in kindergarten maintained their aggressiveness into the high school years (Nagin & Tremblay, 1999).

"He's just a tough character who lost control": Aggression as a personality trait

Marc Lepine's personality was no doubt marked by the poor relationship he had with his father. Following the parents' separation, his father deserted him and at age 14, he insisted on changing his surname to that of his mother. He was described by teachers as being a loner, keeping to himself even when he was at school. When he applied to join the Canadian Forces, he was rejected as having an unsuitable personality for a military career.

Our personalities are influenced both by learning and by genetic factors (for example, newborns differ in the degree to which they emotionally react to loud noises). Inborn reaction tendencies interact with the environment to produce response patterns in the child. Some personality theorists view personality as a collection of such response patterns or traits. Is there a trait of aggressiveness? Can we characterize people as being more or less aggressive? Was there aggressiveness lurking beneath Lepine's quiet exterior?

The problem is that there is no single cluster of traits that describe the aggressive person. The same behaviour may be judged as aggressive or nonaggressive, depending on such variables as age or sex. Moreover, research shows that situational factors generally have more impact on aggression than do personality factors. For example, automobile drivers are more likely to experience aggressiveness and stress when driving in highly congested traffic conditions than when there is little congestion (Hennessy & Wiesenthal, 1999; 2002). However, while there is no good basis for talking about a trait of aggressiveness *per se*, there are a number of individual characteristics that have a bearing on aggressiveness:

Intelligence

In a 22-year longitudinal study of intellectual competence and its relationship to aggression (Eron et al.,

1987), it was found that aggressiveness of most toddlers decreases as they grow and learn other coping strategies, many of them verbal. However, the lower the child's IQ, the more difficult it may be to learn coping and conflict resolution skills. In fact, success at any endeavour may be more difficult for children of lower intelligence, leading to increased frustration and more aggression. In turn, aggressive children may be avoided by teachers and peers, thereby limiting their learning opportunities.

Self-esteem and narcissism

As was discussed in Chapter 3, self-esteem is a central personality variable. Until recently, it has been assumed that poor self-esteem is a major factor in aggressive behaviour and that threats to self-esteem such as criticism or insults often produce anger and aggression (daGloria, 1984; Rule & Nesdale, 1974). We are all familiar with the bully who throws his or her weight around; such people may be insecure and actually trying to bolster their image by being tough. However, more recent evidence suggests that aggressive individuals often possess *inflated* self-esteem and are more likely to view the feedback they receive from the world around them as very inadequate given their perceived self-importance; they then react with aggression because of the apparent injustice (Baumeister, Smart & Boden, 1996). Indeed, accumulating evidence indicates that it is not so much low self-esteem but rather a type of *high* self-esteem associated with narcissism, which produces aggression. People with inflated but unstable self-esteem (narcissists) are more prone to react with anger and aggression to events that challenge and threaten their high self-image (Baumeister et al. 1996; Bushman & Baumeister 1998; Kernis et al. 1989).

Social rejection, real or imagined, threatens or challenges one's self-image, and narcissists have been found to be more likely to react to it with anger and aggression. Twenge and Campbell (2003) first asked participants to complete a measure of narcissism (the Narcissistic Personality Inventory) and then randomly assigned them to one of two conditions, a "social acceptance" or a "social rejection" condition. Participants first interacted socially as a group, and then participants were taken to separate rooms where each was asked to fill out a rating scale indicating the two other participants with whom he or she would like to have further social interaction. Participants were then given false feedback: In the social rejection condition, each was informed that no one had chosen to have any further interaction with him or her, whilst in the social accept-

ance condition, each was told that he or she had been chosen by everyone. Then after filling out questionnaires designed to measure anger, each participant was then asked to play a computer video game, ostensibly against one other person. Each player was told that he or she could set in advance the noise level of a sound that would be played into the earphones of the other player each time that player lost on a trial in the game. The higher the level, the more unpleasant it would be for the other player and thus the noise level was the operational definition of aggression. Subsequently, narcissism scores were correlated with the noise levels and the results showed that those who were high in narcissism were more aggressive after they had experienced social rejection, but there was no such effect following social acceptance. Similarly, a measure of anger was correlated with narcissism, but only in the social rejection condition; narcissists were not angrier following social acceptance. The study was repeated but this time the participants believed that they were playing against someone who was not a participant, in other words, an innocent third party. Yet, very similar results were obtained with aggression being produced towards an innocent third party when narcissists had experienced social rejection. The researchers concluded that while self-esteem on its own plays a small role in predicting response to rejection, narcissism combined with social rejection is a powerful predictor of aggression (see Figures 11–3 and 11–4).

Authoritarianism

Authoritarianism is a personality syndrome characterized by cognitive rigidity, prejudice and an excessive concern for power (see Chapter 8). Higher authoritarianism in males is also associated with a higher likelihood of sexual harassment (Begany & Milburn, 2002). Authoritarianism may be accompanied by authoritarian aggression—a general aggressiveness directed at various individuals and perceived as sanctioned by authority figures (Altmeyer, 1988).

Self-control

The ability to control aggressive impulses varies from person to person. Weak controls lead to obvious problems of aggressiveness. The individual angers quickly and responds to frustration or provocation with physical aggression.

While under-control of aggression is obvious, over-control sometimes poses the larger hazard (Megargee, 1966). Such a person operates under rigid inhibitions

FIGURE 11-3

Anger following social
acceptance or rejection

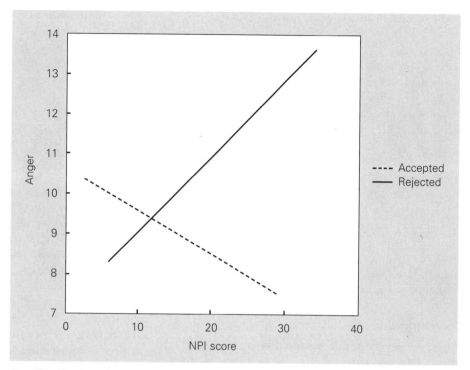

Note: NPI = Narcissistic Personality Inventory
Source: Twenge & Campbell, 2003

FIGURE 11-4

Aggression towards an innocent
third party following social
acceptance or rejection

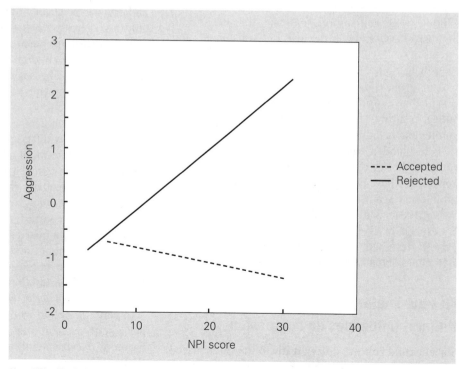

Note: NPI = Narcissistic Personality Inventory
Source: Twenge & Campbell, 2003

and, even when frustrated or provoked, keeps the lid on anger. The extremely aggressive offender, such as Marc Lepine, who has been a rather passive person with no previous history of aggression but who suddenly explodes in savage aggression, is almost certain to fall into this category. Such extreme aggression requires careful study and cannot be explained by extrapolation from studies of mild aggression.

"Road rage" has become more and more a part of our vocabulary in recent years. It was pointed out above that situational variables such as traffic congestion play the major role in producing stress and anger. There is also empirical evidence that some people—those with over-controlled personalities—are more prone to erupt in anger. This is because people with such personalities experience more pressure and more challenge to their self-esteem in stressful situations (Neighbors, Vietor & Knee, 2002).

Psychopathy

The term **psychopathic personality** (or the synonymous *antisocial personality* or *sociopath*) refers to a particular cluster of personality traits that has a strong connection with antisocial behaviour. Psychopaths typically lack empathy, remorse or guilt, have little concern for the feelings and well-being of others, exhibit weak self-control, extreme selfishness and impulsiveness, show little fear of punishment and often fail to learn from the negative consequences of their behaviour. They receive more convictions for violent crimes and behave more violently while in prison than do other prisoners (Hare & McPherson, 1984). A study of convicted murderers in Canadian penitentiaries found psychopaths' crimes to be typically "cold-blooded" and lacking in understandable motivation, although revenge was sometimes a factor. They appeared to have poorly developed emotions and weak inhibitions against aggression (Williamson, Hare & Wong, 1987). Sadly, not only are psychopathic offenders especially likely to be violent but treatment programs designed to reduce their dangerousness sometimes actually serve to increase it (Rice, 1997).

"It's our society": Cultural influences on aggression

Societies and cultures differ greatly in the value placed on aggression. Some encourage it but there are many in which violence of any kind is actively discouraged. For example, the Pygmies of the Congo, the Zuni

Indians of the southwest United States, the Lepchas of Sikkim, and in Canada the Blackfoot, the Saulteaux and the Inuit have historically been peace-loving groups. While the influence of Western culture is modifying the values of many societies, the fact that such groups can still be found who prefer and practise a non-aggressive existence illustrates that violence is not an inevitable aspect of social life.

Peaceful societies share several characteristics (Gorer, 1968). They are generally small and technologically backward and live in remote or inaccessible areas, making it unnecessary to have a warrior class for self-defence. Typically, even though they are hunting societies, they do not idealize bravery or aggression as particularly masculine traits. Indeed, they make little distinction between masculine and feminine traits. They lack aggressive deities and enjoy eating, drinking and sex without guilt. Typically, they base their world views on cooperation and discourage competition; children do not play competitive games and achievement is devalued because of its association with competition and aggression (Bonta, 1997).

However, people do not have to live in remote regions and possess gentle deities in order to live peaceful lives. Even within contemporary society, the Mennonites, the Amish and the Hutterites renounce all kinds of force, and crime is practically unknown among them. In such cultures, aggressive behaviour goes unrewarded or discouraged while pacifism is stressed as a lifestyle. And even though the children experience severe pressure in the course of being socialized (which should lead to frustration), they are virtually free of interpersonal aggression (Bandura & Walters, 1963).

Thus while conflicts will always occur from time to time among individuals and groups, our culture plays a large role in determining how we deal with conflict, whether by negotiation, a flurry of fists or a knife in the side. While Canadian children often are taught the importance of winning, and aggression is often a means to that end, by contrast, children in Japan are actively discouraged from quarrelling. They learn that yielding is more honourable and more desirable than being assertive in the quest for personal goals. Japanese mothers tell their children when they start to argue or fight, "*Makeru ga kachi*," which means literally, "To lose is to win." The child who gives in, who contains his or her assertiveness in order to promote group peace and harmony, receives reinforcement from the mother and is viewed as more mature (Azuma, 1984).

Canadians often like to believe that their history has proved them more peaceful and less aggressive than other nationalities, especially their neighbours to the south, and in many ways this is true.

The homicide rate (1.83 per 100 000 in 1998, the lowest it has been in 30 years) is only a quarter of that of the United States. Our cities still seem relatively safe: Compared to a murder rate of 78 per 100 000 in Washington, D.C., and 28 per 100 000 in Los Angeles, the rate per 100 000 is 3.6 in Saskatoon (the highest metropolitan rate in Canada in 1997), 3 in Edmonton and Halifax, 1.7 in Toronto, 1.0 in Calgary and 0 in Chicoutimi–Jonquière. Violent crime rates in general, including those for robbery and sexual assault, have seen steady declines over the past several years. However, Canadians should not be complacent. The problem of violence in this country is very serious: Homicide rates are higher than those of most Western countries; abuse of children and women is frequent (most homicides in this country occur in domestic settings); and levels of police and prison violence are disturbing (Gurr, 1995).

"What with all the violence on TV … ": Media and aggression

Traditional members of the Cree community of Norway House on Lake Winnipeg refer to television by the Cree word *koosapachigan*, which means "shaking tent," a place where the shamans of the past conjured up spirits of the living and spirits of the dead. Some of these spirits were not very friendly. Indeed, much of what is shown on television is not very friendly and many Canadians are expressing increasing concern about it. In November 1992, 21 cartons filled with petitions calling for legislation to control and ultimately eliminate violence from Canadian television and signed by more than a million Canadians were carried into the office of the Communications Minister in Ottawa. Virginie Larivière, a 14-year-old Quebec girl, had organized the campaign following the rape and murder of her younger sister. She and her family laboured for seven months to gather the signatures, which came in from across Canada

Does television violence promote violent behaviour? Children, adolescents and adults spend a considerable proportion of their leisure time in front of the television set and many children play video games that often involve very violent themes. Moreover, concern is growing about the influence of the Internet as more and more children and adults use the net regularly, with the opportunity to access thematically violent materials from around the world.

As published in The Calgary Herald, Oct. 11, 1984. Reprinted by permission of the artist.

In 1983, the U.S.-based National Coalition on Television Violence presented the results of its study of 30 television networks around the world to the United Nations Educational, Scientific and Cultural Organization (UNESCO). It concluded that Canada's CTV was the most violent of the 30, which included American, German, British, Japanese and Australian networks. Sixty-five percent of CTV programming was found to be in the "high violence" category, with an average of 11.1 violent acts occurring per hour. Almost all this violent programming was imported from the United States. Little has changed over the intervening years. Living next door to the United States in an era of satellite television dishes makes it very difficult to pursue an independent course with regard to television broadcasting, even though Canadian regulators still attempt to do so.

It is not just television that often seems addicted to violence. Modern youth-oriented music often has violent themes. In the 1980s, rock videos became popular, and some incorporated violent and sexually aggressive themes, mostly at the expense of women. The 1990s saw the rise of violent songs and videos directed at women, racial minorities and unpopular authority figures such as the police.

Currently, violent video games are becoming more and more popular especially with young males, and again, there is growing concern that such games lead their players to deal with real-life conflicts by means of physical aggression. Anderson and Bushman (2001b) conducted a meta-analysis of 35 studies of the effects of violent video games and concluded that playing violent video games is definitely associated with heightened aggressive behaviour. By way of comparison, they reported that the strength of the relationship between playing violent video games and aggression is just as strong as the relationship between condom use and lowered risk of HIV infection! Of course, it makes sense that there should be a causal link between condom use and lowered HIV transmission, whereas it is still not clear just what the causal link, if it exists, might be between violent video games and aggression. However, one possibility is suggested by another study by Bushaman and Anderson (2002). Participants played either a violent or a non-violent video game and then read ambiguous introductions to stories involving potential interpersonal conflicts. They were then asked to guess at what the main character would do or say or think as the story goes on. Those who had played the violent games suggested that the main character would feel angrier, have more aggressive thoughts and act more aggressively than those who played the non-violent games. The authors concluded that the violent games produced a "hostile expectation bias," the tendency to expect others to react aggressively to conflicts.

Effects of television and film violence

In 1995, a 14-year-old boy in La Ronge, Saskatchewan, with the help of his seven-year-old accomplice, stabbed, bludgeoned and suffocated to death a seven-year-old neighbour boy. Later, he returned to the crime scene and peeled skin from the child's body in apparent imitation of a scene in *Warlock*, a movie that he had watched 10 times. Tried in adult court, he was later found not guilty by reason of insanity. However since he himself suggested to police that the movie had been a strong influence on the murder, this grisly crime produced a wave of public concern about media violence.

Marc Lepine was also described as having been obsessed with film violence, especially war videos such as *Rambo*. Was that because of a penchant for violence, or did watching violent films contribute to his aggressiveness? Of course, isolated cases like these do not prove that film violence brings about real violence. Perhaps Lepine had a penchant for violence that made violent films more attractive to him. Defenders of vio-

lent programming sometimes even argue that viewers become *less* aggressive as a result of watching violence because it has a cathartic effect. Setting aside the catharsis theory (which we have already examined and rejected), what are the effects of media violence? Does it lead to increased violence on an individual and societal level? What are the consequences for the developing child who is exposed to violent television fare every day for several years?

Historically, the research evidence has been somewhat mixed with regard to the effects of viewing violence, but because of the social importance of the issue, several inquiries have been carried out. Such inquiries have generally concluded that viewing film or television violence leads to an increase in aggressive behaviour by the viewer (Goranson, 1977; Hearold, 1986). The Ontario Royal Commission on Violence in the Communications Industry came to this conclusion in 1976, as did the U.S. Surgeon General's Report in 1972 and the U.S. National Institute of Mental Health Report on Television and Behaviour (Pearl, Bouthilet & Lazar, 1982). The American Psychological Association (1985) also spoke out about the causal effect of media violence on childhood and adolescent aggression. In recent years, more and more evidence is accumulating that supports a significant positive link between television violence and real-life aggression by those who watch it (Bushman and Anderson, 2001).

However as we shall see, it is not easy to assess the role that media violence plays in fostering or discouraging real-life aggression. Most studies of the effects of media violence have been carried out with children. One reason for this is that children are assumed to be more vulnerable than adults since their beliefs, values and attitudes are actively developing. Aside from the issue of which population to study, there are many pitfalls to avoid in this type of research. For example, we must be certain that any increase in aggressiveness is not due simply to the excitement created by the film (rather than the aggressive content of the film). Likewise, we must be careful to distinguish between a real decrement in aggressiveness and increased inhibition, for watching a weakling who attacks a powerful bully get beaten to a pulp hardly motivates a viewer to risk attacking a powerful bully (Howitt & Cumberbatch, 1975).

Social psychological studies of the effects of watching violent television have taken several forms, primarily the following:

LABORATORY STUDIES Subjects are exposed to either a violent or a non-violent film and then observed when presented with the opportunity to aggress.

Story-Hour Violence

According to Geoffrey Handler-Taylor who carried out an informal survey of nursery rhymes in 1952, "The average collection of 200 traditional nursery rhymes contains approximately 100 rhymes which personify all that is glorious and ideal for the child. Unfortunately, the remaining 100 rhymes harbour unsavoury elements. The incidents listed below occur in the average collection and may be accepted as a reasonably conservative estimate based on a general survey of this type of literature:

8 allusions to murder (unclassified)

2 cases of choking to death

1 case of death by devouring

1 case of cutting a human being in half

1 case of decapitation

1 case of death by squeezing

1 case of death by shrivelling

1 case of death by starvation

1 case of boiling to death

1 case of death by drowning

4 cases of killing domestic animals

1 case of body-snatching

21 cases of death (unclassified)

7 cases relating to the severing of limbs

1 allusion to a bleeding heart

1 case of devouring human flesh

5 threats of death

1 case of kidnapping

12 cases of torment and cruelty to human beings and animals

8 cases of whipping and lashing

3 allusions to blood

14 cases of stealing and general dishonesty

15 allusions to maimed human beings and animals

1 allusion to undertakers

2 allusions to graves

23 cases of physical violence (unclassified)

1 case of lunacy

16 allusions to misery and sorrow

1 case of drunkenness

4 cases of cursing

1 allusion to marriage as a form of death

1 case of scorning the blind

1 case of scorning prayer

9 cases of children being lost or abandoned

2 cases of house burning

9 allusions to poverty and want

5 allusions to quarrelling

2 cases of unlawful imprisonment

2 cases of racial discrimination

Expressions of fear, weeping, moans of anguish, biting, pain and evidence of supreme selfishness may be found in almost every other page." (Report of the Ontario Royal Commission on Violence in the Communications Industry, 1977)

FIELD STUDIES Children in natural (usually residential) settings are randomly assigned to a television diet either high or low in violence then observed and measured for aggressiveness.

CORRELATIONAL STUDIES In these studies, some of them longitudinal, measures of the amount of violent television watched are correlated with measures of aggressiveness.

While laboratory studies have clearly demonstrated that the viewing of television or film violence in the laboratory leads to increased aggression, we must hesitate to apply these results elsewhere (Freedman, 1984). It is not clear, for instance, that the measures of aggression in the laboratory (e.g., pushing a button to deliver shock to another person) have much to do with real-life aggression. More importantly, the demand characteristics of the laboratory situation would suggest that the experimenter approves of or permits the aggressive behaviours the subject is subsequently given the choice to perform. It is also important to note that in reality no one is exposed to a single violent film; television violence is more likely to be viewed on a regular basis over a period of years. Furthermore, the violence will be interrupted with a good deal of non-violent programming changing the net effect.

Many field studies have been carried out. For example, Parke, Berkowitz, Leyens, West and Sebastian (1977) investigated the impact of movie violence on the behaviour of juvenile delinquents living in an institution. Initially, the behaviour of each of the boys was observed for a two-hour period on each of three successive days. During the following five days, all boys saw a film each evening. Boys in one group watched violent movies while boys in the other group saw neutral, non-violent films. Records were kept of the boys' behaviour before, during and after the films. On the day following the final film, the boys participated in a laboratory study in which they were given the opportunity to shock a confederate. Some of the boys were "angered" and some "non-angered." Then during a three-week follow-up period, the boys' behaviour was observed on three consecutive evenings each week. The results showed that exposure to film violence led to an increase in both physical and verbal aggression. Boys who were initially more aggressive were most influenced by the violent films, suggesting that the effects of media violence may differ depending on the aggressiveness of the viewer.

Longitudinal studies generally find a positive correlation between watching violent television and aggressiveness. In one such study, children's aggression and television-viewing habits were measured in Grade 3 then again a decade later (Eron, Huesmann, Lefkowitz & Walder, 1972). The authors of the study concluded that the viewing of television violence over an extended period is a probable and long-lasting cause of violence in children.

Yet could it be that rather than violent television causing aggression, a tendency towards aggressiveness leads aggressive people to choose violent television? In an attempt to examine this possibility, Eron et al. (1972) used what is called a **cross-lagged procedure**. They examined the relationship between the viewing of violence by boys at age eight and their level of aggression at age 18, and the relationship between aggression at age eight and violence viewing at age 18. It was found that violence viewing at age eight predicted aggression at 18 but that aggression at eight did not predict violence viewing at 18. A 22-year longitudinal study supports these observations. Subjects, first studied when they were eight, were contacted again at age 30. It was found that those who had watched more TV as children and had preferred violent programs were later more likely to have been convicted of serious criminal acts (Huesmann, 1986).

Even though this evidence suggests that viewing television violence is linked to violent behaviour, it is likely that not all children are affected in the same way. It is likely that the vast majority of students reading this book have watched television or movie violence and yet have not grown up to be aggressive individuals. How then do we account for the differential effects of media violence? Personality differences likely influence an individual's cognitive and emotional responses to portrayals of violence (Bushman & Geen, 1990) and individuals already prone to aggression may be most affected by violent films. Such people are more likely to choose to watch violent films, to report feeling angry after watching a violent film and to act in an aggressive manner subsequently (Bushman, 1995).

Moreover, what is seen on television may not be as important as the home in which it is viewed. Children are exposed to both aggressive and non-aggressive models on television and it is likely that the more the child identifies with and is similar to the television character, the more modelling will occur (Eron, 1980). The child who is raised in a peaceful and loving family may well be less affected by TV violence than one raised in a violent family. A study by Heath, Kruttschnitt and Ward (1986) supports this view. They examined the self-reported TV-viewing habits during childhood and adolescence of a group of male inmates incarcerated for violent crimes and a control group of non-violent, non-incarcerated males matched on age, race and neighbourhood of residence during adolescence. They found that amount of TV watching by itself did not differentiate the members of the two groups, but large amounts of TV watching combined with exposure to parental abuse was related to violent criminal behaviour.

Indirect effects of television and film violence

There are a number of indirect ways in which television violence can lead to negative social consequences:

STIMULUS PAIRING Recall Berkowitz's (1984) cognitive neo-associationist model. One of its implications is that

FOCUS ON RESEARCH

Life before and after Television

A quasi-experimental study carried out in a small British Columbia logging town—one of the last communities in North America to get television—compared the aggressiveness of children before the introduction of TV and two years later when 90 percent of the homes had TV sets (Joy, Kimball & Zabrack, 1977, 1986). The behaviour of children in this town ("Notel") was compared with that of children in a similar town ("Unitel") that received only one TV channel (CBC) and that of children in another similar town ("Multitel") where CBC and three American channels were available. The children, all primary school students, were each observed at free play during 21 one-minute intervals over a period of seven to ten days. In addition, teacher and peer ratings of aggressiveness were noted. While there were no differences among the three samples of children at the time of the initial measurement, by the time the children were measured again two years after the introduction of CBC-TV service to

Notel, the Notel children showed a significantly greater increase in aggression both verbal and physical than the children in the other two towns (see Figure 11–5).

These results were not based simply on the fact that the children were two years older; the children were compared with children who were two grades behind them and there were no differences in aggressiveness. It is important to note that this increase in aggressiveness occurred regardless of whether the children were initially low or high in aggressiveness. No changes in the kinds of aggressive acts were observed. The findings suggest a kind of ceiling effect; violence on television may lead to increased aggressiveness up to a certain point beyond which no change will occur. As well, the fact that their aggressiveness increased to a level beyond that of children in the other two towns suggests a "novelty" effect: an initial surge in aggression following exposure to aggressive models.

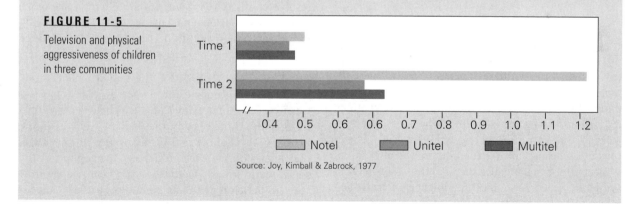

FIGURE 11-5

Television and physical aggressiveness of children in three communities

Source: Joy, Kimball & Zabrock, 1977

watching violence on television that is repeatedly associated with weapons ("stimulus pairing") may give weapons the power to prime aggressive thoughts and elicit aggressive behaviour in situations of anger or fear. In a seminal study more than 30 years ago, Berkowitz and LePage (1967) demonstrated that the mere presence of a weapon produced a greater level of retaliatory

aggression in a laboratory experiment than did the presence of badminton rackets. This "weapons effect" has been successfully replicated in different contexts by a number of different researchers and the weapon itself is not necessary: Use of a picture of a weapon or even the name of a weapon produced a similar effect (Anderson, Benjamin & Bartholow, 1998).

However while the importance of aggression-related cues has been amply demonstrated (Carlson, Marcus-Newhall & Miller, 1990), the effects of such cues may depend on the extent to which an individual has characteristically used violence in the past. Josephson (1987) carried out a study of cue-elicited aggression with nearly 400 second- and third-grade Winnipeg schoolboys. Prior to the experiment, the teacher first rated each boy in terms of characteristic level of aggressiveness. Half the children watched a television clip in which a neutral object, a walkie-talkie, was employed just before an act of major violence. The other children watched an exciting but non-violent clip. Shortly afterward, the children played a game of floor hockey. When a walkie-talkie was in clear view on the sidelines, there was more aggressiveness in the hockey game—but this effect occurred primarily with boys who had been rated at the outset as highly aggressive.

DESENSITIZATION Media violence may lead to increased **desensitization**. Watching someone being beaten, it is argued, may be less upsetting if similar incidents have been seen on television. For example, one study (Drabsman & Thomas, 1975) found that children aged eight to eleven who had just watched a violent television episode were markedly slower in breaking up a squabble than those who had just watched a film of a baseball game. This was interpreted in terms of the children being temporarily desensitized to violence.

Is such desensitization enduring or transient? In an experiment conducted by Mullin and Linz (1995), male university students were shown a series of violent films, with two days separating each film. Self-reported emotional response and physiological arousal diminished over the series of films. Moreover, three days after viewing the last film in the series, the subjects showed considerably less sympathy towards victims of domestic violence than did a control group of subjects. Yet five days after the final film, their level of sympathy towards domestic violence victims had returned to the same level as that of the control group. This study demonstrates that people whose sensitivity to violence is diminished as a result of watching violence films can rather quickly resensitize. But what happens if a viewer chooses a steady diet of such violent films? Perhaps such resensitization will become less and less pronounced.

IMITATION AND CONTAGION We have seen how children can learn to imitate aggressive models even in a vicari-

ous way (recall the account of the La Ronge murder mentioned earlier in this chapter). An equally important issue is the imitative repetition by adults of spectacular crimes of violence recounted in newspaper headlines. Such "contagion" is common; even in the 19th century, the news of Jack the Ripper's exploits provoked a series of female mutilations in the English countryside (Berkowitz, 1971). Other examples of contagion abound. A flurry of assassination attempts around the world followed U.S. President Kennedy's assassination in 1963 (Weisz & Taylor, 1969) and both that assassination and other well-publicized murders have been followed by an unusual increase in violent crimes in the United States (Berkowitz & Macaulay, 1971).

EFFECTS ON VALUES AND ATTITUDES It is not difficult to manipulate the emotions of viewers so that they welcome violence in a film even if they do not normally enjoy watching violence. Scripts that lead us to sympathize with victimized individuals or groups, eventually forced to "stand up and fight" for their rights and vanquishing their tormentors in the process, can produce positive feelings even when violence and lawbreaking are the means used. An analysis of violent television programming suggests that, at least in the television world, violence is generally a successful means of obtaining personal goals: it is usually not punished and law enforcement agencies whose job is to reduce violence often use violence to resolve conflicts (Gerbner, 1969). There is also concern that television and cinema may encourage the idea that women want to be victimized (Malamuth & Briere, 1986).

INCREASED APPREHENSION The rate of violent crime in Canada continues to drop year by year (Statistics Canada, 1999). Yet many Canadians believe, as do citizens of the United States, that violent crime is on the increase. M. Gerbner and his associates (1980) argue that television violence cultivates a perception of the social world as a dangerous place where people must constantly be on guard. Television perpetuates stereotypes about criminals and their crimes that have little to do with reality. For example while most murders in television dramas are committed by strangers to the victim, more than 80 percent of murders in Canada are carried out by people who know the victim (Gartner, 1995).

"SCHOOL FOR SCANDAL" Television and cinema dramas—especially those that have been carefully researched and present criminal activities with considerable attention to detail—may actually teach people how to commit crimes.

NOTORIETY Often, the media appear to promote the imitation of social aggression by showering attention on perpetrators of violence: bombers, hijackers and murderers. As a result, some attention-seekers may try to emulate the violence described in order to acquire celebrity status.

Thus, there are many ways that television violence can affect viewers negatively. However, it is important to understand that there continues to be controversy not only about the strength of these effects but even about their very existence. For example, Freedman (2002) reviewed the extant research literature and concluded that the data do *not* support the conclusion that media violence contributes to real-life violence. This debate has raged for several decades now and it will no doubt continue to rage for years to come.

"Any nut can buy a gun": Firearms and homicide

The .223-calibre Sturm Ruger Carbine is a lightweight, accurate and devastating semiautomatic weapon used by the military, police assault teams and hunters. It is sold in Canadian gun stores to any consumer with a licence to purchase a gun. It is one of the most popular hunting rifles in Canada; about 2000 are sold annually in this country. It is the rifle that Marc Lepine used to kill his victims. Marc Lepine did not have a history of violent behaviour. Even if he had been violent before, in the absence of confrontation with the law, it would not have been on record. He obtained a Firearms Acquisition Certificate (see A Case in Point—Guns Kill) without difficulty.

There is little doubt that gun controls do reduce the rate of homicide by firearms; the stricter the controls, the smaller the proportion of murders committed with guns (Lester, 1984; Lester & Murrell, 1986). The use of handguns to commit murder is a growing problem in the United States, where gun control is virtually non-existent. In 1997, the rate of handgun use in homicides in the United States was 10 times that in Canada. Sloan et al. (1988) analyzed crime rates, assault rates and homicide rates in Vancouver, British Columbia, and Seattle, Washington, for the interval 1980–1986. While the crime rates for the two cities were similar, there were seven times as many assaults involving guns in Seattle as in Vancouver. The chances of being murdered by a handgun were nearly five times higher in Seattle

than in Vancouver. The use of guns in homicides and firearm suicides continues to drop in Canada and there is no indication that this leads to increases in other methods of murder or suicide (Carrington & Moyer, 1994; Sproule & Kennett, 1988, 1989). In 1996, the federal Department of Justice published an evaluation of the impact of the 1977 firearms control legislation, which concluded that the legislation has contributed to as much as a 20-percent reduction in the homicide rate over the past two decades. Indeed, fewer homicides involve guns: In 1974, 47 percent of homicides involved firearms compared to only 33 percent in 1997 (Canadian Centre for Criminal Justice Statistics, 1998).

Remember that most murderers do not stalk anonymous victims the way Marc Lepine did. Eighty percent of murders involve victims who are known to their killers and people involved in a close relationship with the victim commit about 20 percent of murders. Having a gun in the home may in itself be a dangerous situation, for when emotions are running high, guns may come into play all too easily.

"Men's deep-seated hostility": Aggression, gender and relationships

Marc Lepine's violence was a deliberate act against women. According to his mother, Marc's father regularly expressed the view that women are servants to men. Marc Lepine had wanted to study engineering at the École Polytechnique. He apparently had applied but had been turned down. Is this why he decided to kill women at that institution? When a wounded young woman pleaded with him, he said, "Why should women be engineers and not men?"

Many across the nation saw Lepine's actions as symptomatic of a current trend in Canadian society that teaches, condones and excuses violence towards women. That such violence and fear of violence exists, there is no doubt. Fifty-six percent of urban Canadian women as compared with only 18 percent of men report that they are fearful about going out at night in their own neighbourhoods (MacLeod, 1989). Although 90 percent of murderers are male, one-third of homicide victims are female (Statistics Canada, 1989). However, it is also important to remember that only a minority of men ever commits violent crimes and that the majority of victims of violence are men.

Why is violence such a male behaviour? Why is masculinity so often tied up with aggressiveness? It has been men not women who have marched off to

Guns Kill

Consider these Canadian statistics (Canadian Centre for Criminal Justice Statistics, 1998; Statistics Canada, 2003):

- In 1997, one-third of all homicides were committed with a firearm, half of them handguns (which have been restricted for some years now).

- In 1996, 78 percent of firearms deaths were suicides.

- The rate of robberies in which a firearm was used dropped in 2002 to 11.05 (per hundred thousand Canadians) from 12.27 in 2002 and from 30.79 in 1992!

- A home with a gun is three times more likely to suffer a homicide and five times more likely to suffer a suicide than a home without a gun. A 2000 study found that 17 percent of Canadian households possessed at least one firearm compared to almost 24 percent ten years earlier.

- One woman is shot dead in Canada every six days. Most women are killed by a current or former male partner.

- Gunshot wounds are 2 to 15 times more lethal than knife wounds.

There are approximately 7 000 000 firearms in Canada—rifles and shotguns for the most part. The vast majority of guns are used for hunting or target shooting and only a small percentage are described as being owned for "protection." Handguns and fully automatic rifles have long been restricted weapons in Canada and may be possessed only by special permit. Permits to carry a loaded and concealed handgun are very, very rare: for example, only 20 people in all Ontario, almost all of them current or former police officers who have received death threats, have been granted such permits, and each permit must be reviewed each year.

Following the Lepine murders, many Canadians called for stricter gun control legislation. As of January 1993, gun control regulations were toughened and 60 types of assault pistols and other military-type weapons were banned in Canada. As well, the minimum age for gun ownership was raised from 16 to 18 years and henceforth guns were to be stored separately from ammunition and in a locked room or with a vital part removed. The new legislation also provided for more careful screening of applications to acquire a gun and applicants had to wait 28 days before an acquisition certificate would be issued. Further legislation passed in 1996 made gun laws tougher still. Under federal gun control legislation enacted in 1977, all persons who wish to buy a rifle or shotgun must apply for a Firearms Acquisition Certificate. Anyone with a history of violent behaviour is not to be issued such a certificate. Each year, about 170 000 certificates are issued. In 1998, a new and controversial *Firearms Act* came into effect requiring that all firearms be registered, and for the first time, a licence is required for the purchase of ammunition. The use of firearms in the commission of a crime now leads to a mandatory minimum sentence of four years in prison and a lifetime prohibition against owning restricted firearms.

battle; men not women who duelled to the death to avenge wounded pride; men not women who smash away as savagely as possible at each other to see who can remain standing longer in a boxing match. The difference shows up early in development: studies of nursery-school children have found boys to be twice as aggressive as girls, both physically and verbally (Hutt, 1974). And when asked how they would have responded to hypothetical interpersonal conflict situations in adolescence, male university students selected physical aggression significantly more often than did women (Reinisch & Sanders, 1986). Why is this so? Does this situation reflect a basic difference between male and female physiologies or does it reflect differences in rearing?

In most parts of the world, males are often concerned with being "properly" masculine. In North America, the concept of masculinity is associated with qualities of courage, loyalty, aggressiveness, dominance, independence, risk-taking, assertiveness and competitiveness (Weinstein, Smith & Wiesenthal, 1995; Garbarino, 1999). As a result, boys are often strongly discouraged from showing emotional "weakness." However, while it may be considered a weakness to show fear, sadness and so on, anger is one emotion that can be expressed without fear of appearing to be a sissy.

Being masculine or "macho" is often associated with being a "jock," and, indeed, organized sports may implicitly teach boys that masculinity and aggressiveness go hand in hand. More than 450 000 Canadian boys play hockey (Gruneau & Whitson, 1993) and thus hockey might be expected to play an important role in their socialization. In a study of players in Bantam and Junior A teams, Weinstein, Smith and Wiesenthal (1995) found a positive correlation between masculinity and violence on the ice, especially at the older and more skilled Junior A level. Indeed, the perception of competence by both teammates and coaches was influenced more by the amount of violence than by playing or skating skills.

As long as we teach young boys that aggressiveness is desirable and masculine, we should not be surprised if they later respond aggressively in the face of threats to their masculinity. Even relatively small differences in cultural background can influence the link between masculinity and aggressiveness in particular social contexts. For example, U.S. male university students reared in the northern states were found to be much less bothered than their counterparts who grew up in the south when they were "accidentally" bumped into and then called an "asshole." Students from the south were more likely to take the insult as a threat, and they exhibited greater physiological arousal (levels of both cortisol—a stress hormone associated with anger—and testosterone went up) and were more likely to think in aggressive terms and respond with aggressive behaviours (Cohen, Nisbett, Bowdle & Schwartz, 1996). This difference was seen to reflect a "code of honour" that exists in southern U.S. society that promotes aggression in response to a perceived insult.

What about female aggression?

Laboratory research does *not* show a strong gender effect with regard to aggressiveness: While some studies have reported greater physical aggression by males, the differences are relatively small (Eagly & Steffen, 1986; Loeber & Hay, 1997) and are greatly diminished if one takes provocation into account (Bettencourt & Miller, 1996). When provoked, females are as likely as males to respond with aggressive behaviour.

Yet real-life experience would seem to suggest that men are much more aggressive than women. In Canada in 1991, males accounted for almost 90 percent of all persons charged with violent crimes (Statistics Canada, 1992a). In the United States, at age 18, ten times as many males as females are arrested for murder (Cairns & Cairns, 1985). Why this difference between laboratory findings and crime statistics? It could be that laboratory research situations are not representative of real life; such research typically focuses on the behaviour of university students who are strangers to each other and who interact in one of a small number of situations over a short period of time (Krebs & Miller, 1985). To some extent, crime statistics may be misleading too, for men and women may be treated somewhat differently by the justice system. There is evidence that (at least in the past) a "chivalry factor" has protected women: women who did commit crimes were less likely than men to be reported to the police, less likely to be charged and less likely to be found guilty (Reckless & Kay, 1967). This situation is likely to change as more and more women become active participants in law enforcement and jurisprudence. Another important consideration is that males and females appear to differ in the kind of aggression they use, with females tending to be more indirect and verbally aggressive while males tend to be more physically aggressive (Loeber & Stouthamer-Loeber, 1998).

In recent years, not only has it become clearer that females are also quite capable of acting aggressively but this tendency appears to be on the rise. Violence amongst adolescent girls is the only area consistently showing an increase in reported rates of violent offending in Canada and yet, relative to male adolescent violence, the rate remains low (Leschied, Cummings, Van Brunschot, Cunningham, & Saunders, 2001).

Hilton, Harris and Rice (2000) used a survey technique to question 1452 Ontario high school students about aggression, both in terms of acting aggressively and being victims. They concluded that male to male aggression is more prevalent than male to female aggression, but while male to male aggression more often than not was directed towards strangers, male to female aggression was more often directed at girlfriends than at strangers. On the other hand, boys were significantly more likely to report that they had been the victims of female aggression, which includes severe aggression in some cases. Their findings were in line with other studies that suggest that women are as likely as men to use both violent and non-physical forms of aggression (e.g., ridicule, threats).

Our culture, like almost all cultures, has long associated masculinity with aggressiveness. Research clearly shows that aggression is more strongly linked to the concept of sexuality for men than it is for women (Peplau, 2003). Anderson, Cyranowski and Espindle (1999) examined the dimensions that heterosexual individuals use to characterize their own sexuality. Males and females both evaluated themselves in terms of being romantic, but unlike those of women, men's sexual self-concepts also were characterized by a dimension of aggression—the degree to which they saw themselves as aggressive and powerful and domineering in sexual interactions.

As was discussed earlier, for men to "back down" in the face of a threat has traditionally been considered "sissyish" or "effeminate." Men (but not women) may proudly wear the scars of warfare—or water polo. Parents often openly encourage their sons to grow up to "be a man," while girls traditionally have been encouraged to be non-aggressive and more concerned with maintaining interpersonal harmony. Perhaps as a result, women typically experience more guilt and anxiety as a result of aggression and are more concerned with the harm that comes to victims and with the danger that might come to them if they are aggressive (Eagly, 1987).

What about sex hormones?

Research has shown that within many species there are substantial sex differences in aggressiveness: the males fight readily while the females do not, except in defence of their young (Archer, 1976). Such differences do not seem to be the result of learning and have often been attributed to the so-called sex hormones: the "male" **androgens** and the "female" **estrogens**. Stallions, bulls and other animals are castrated to render them more docile. Such animals rarely fight. Castration eliminates one of the androgens—testosterone—and since the administration of testosterone will restore "normal" aggressiveness, testosterone would appear to play an important role in animal aggression.

Castration seems to reduce aggressiveness in human males (Johnson, 1972). And when testosterone is administered to normal adult human females, their physical activity and their general aggressiveness often increase to a level typical of males (Bardwick, 1971). However, while androgens are related to male aggres-

sion, it should not be assumed that the relationship is directly causal. For example, androgens enhance musculature and increase available energy (Zillman, 1984). This muscle building and energizing is why testosterone is, as one sports' official put it, the "granddaddy" of all the steroids illicitly used by some athletes. How that physique and energy are employed depends on socialization: in our society, the male role accepts, even demands aggressiveness while the female role discourages it (Eagly & Steffen, 1986; Lubek, 1979).

Spousal abuse

"Let's say I committed this crime [the murder of ex-wife Nicole Brown Simpson]. Even if I did do this, it would have to be because I loved her very much, right?"

O.J. Simpson, famous U.S. football player accused and later acquitted of murdering his wife (Puente & Cohen, 2003).

Domestic violence is the most common form of violence in North America (Widom, 1989) and women in Canada are seven times more likely to be assaulted by the man they love than by a stranger (Jaffe, 1990). According to Statistics Canada's national survey of violence against women (Canadian Centre for Criminal Justice Statistics, 1994), 29 percent of women who have been married to or have lived with a man have been assaulted by him and almost half of these assaults resulted in physical injury. A fifth of these assaults occurred during pregnancy. There is growing evidence that violence occurs frequently in dating relationships as well as at the teenage level, and such violence is very similar in pattern to spousal abuse (Pedersen & Thomas, 1992; Princz, 1992).

It is difficult to come up with good data but in U.S. studies about 11 percent of husbands actually report having used violence against their wives. Although no similar national studies have been carried out in Canada, research in Alberta reported an almost identical figure (Kennedy & Dutton, 1989). Although it goes against the conventional wisdom that suggests men are much more likely than women to be the aggressors in relationship violence, a follow-up report indicated that men and women in Alberta were actually very similar in terms of their reported rates of both perpetration of violence and of victimization and that a substantial proportion of women's violence could not be explained in terms of self-defence (Kwong, Bartholomew & Dutton, 1999).

Females are just as likely to be aggressive towards their heterosexual partners as are males in the context of a relationship, while males are clearly much more likely than females to behave aggressively when relationship aggression is excluded (Archer, 2000b). However, women of college age and education are at least as likely as males— perhaps more so—to engage in aggressive acts of all forms in the context of dating relationships, and these female acts are perceived as no less severe than the male acts (Jenkins & Aubé, 2002).

Archer (2000a) carried out a meta-analysis of studies of sex differences in physical aggression directed at heterosexual partners. He found that women were slightly more likely to be physically aggressive than men were, although men were more likely to inflict a significant injury, and of those who were injured by a partner, 62 percent were women. They were careful to point out that cultural values play an important role in aggression towards intimate partners and that these data come from the United States where patriarchal power has less impact and where a norm of disapproval of physical aggression towards women by men has greater impact. They found that most of the studies in which frequent female physical aggression was found were carried out in circumstances where "modern secular liberal values together with economic and familial emancipation of women" had occurred. In cultures where women are subject to the control of their husbands and their husbands' families, where they are dependent on men economically and lack the support of female allies, then aggression, both sexual and physical, towards women is much more common. It is increased further when there are pronounced inequalities amongst men so that a few powerful men can exert control over women and their sexual lives.

Because society is slow to accept that women also commit violence against their spouses—although they may be less capable of inflicting serious damage because of relative size—almost all research into spousal violence has focused on male perpetrators and on the question "Why do men violently abuse the people they presumably love?" The root of men's violence against women is generally the misuse of power: Some men are socialized to believe that they are justified in controlling the women in their lives even if they use violence to do so (Walker, 1989) and the risk of violence increases if the woman is perceived as pulling out of the relationship (Buss & Shackelford, 1997). A number of factors increase a man's risk for spousal assault (Dutton, 1984):

- a strong need to dominate or control others
- poor verbal skills by which to obtain such control

- witnessing violence as a mode of conflict resolution while growing up
- ongoing marital conflict
- job stress or unemployment
- lack of close friends who could help reduce this stress
- living in a culture that relegates women to subordinate roles, condones the use of violence for obtaining goal satisfaction and promotes "non-interference" in family matters
- growing independence of his partner whether through employment or the development of new friendships

Based on a review of 15 earlier batterer typologies, Holtzworth-Munroe (2000) predicted that there are three different types of batterers and then tested the prediction by studying a group of 102 men who had been physically aggressive towards their wives. Their wives were also involved in the study, and for comparison, two other groups of non-violent couples were studied—couples who were experiencing marital distress and couples who were not. The three predicted subgroups were found:

- "family-only"—violence only towards wives and family members; least violent; little or no psychopathology
- dysphoric-borderline—moderate to severe violence, confined primarily to the wife; most psychologically distressed—most symptoms of depression and anxiety and borderline personality characteristics (fear of rejection, intense, unstable relationships, extreme emotional lability)
- generally violent antisocial—most violent subtype—violence directed martially but also the highest levels of extra-familial violence—most likely to have antisocial personality disorder characteristics

Jealousy (discussed in detail in Chapter 8) is one of the major triggers of domestic violence (Puente and Cohen, 2003) and to some degree society has accepted jealousy-based violence. In a study by Peunte and Cohen (2003), it was found that indeed, violence in the context of a non-jealousy related argument is viewed quite negatively, but when jealousy is a factor, the level of this negativity is much reduced.

Sexual arousal and aggression

Every year in Canada between 25 000 and 30 000 sexual assaults are reported to police and this probably reflects only a fraction of the actual number. A survey of a large national sample of male and female post-secondary students in the United States found that considerably more women and men (as perpetrators) in this normal sample reported incidents of rape, attempted rape and sexual coercion than are represented by the usual crime statistics (Koss, Gidycz & Wisnieski, 1987). The rape victimization rate among the females of this group was 10 to 15 times greater than the reported crime data and the admission by men of committing rape, two to three times greater.

Sexual aggressors appear to be characterized by two sets of traits (Malamuth, Linz, Heavey, Barnes & Acker, 1995):

- **hostile masculinity**, which involves an insecure, distrustful, defensive and hypersensitive orientation towards others, especially women, as well as gratification from dominating and controlling women;

- proclivity to **promiscuous-impersonal sex**; that is, a tendency to avoid commitment and to be unfaithful in sexual relationships. Such an inclination may promote distress in relationships—which in turn leads to conflict and possible violence—as well as making it less likely that the partner's feelings or well-being will be considered to be of much importance, thus removing a barrier to sexual aggressiveness.

Excitation transfer theory

Sexual arousal and aggressive arousal along with other kinds of arousal reflect the same underlying sympathetic nervous system activation. The excitation brought about by conflict or physical pain is no different from the excitation that underlies sexual desire and activity, and an individual cannot differentiate excitation as "sexual" or "aggressive" on the basis of nervous system activity alone (Zillmann, 1984).

According to Zillmann's (1984) **excitation transfer theory**, emotion involves a dispositional component, an excitatory component and an experiential component. The *dispositional component* refers to skeletal-motor behaviour that is largely under the control of stimuli and reinforcements (i.e., someone insults you and you raise your fist because you have learned to do so in such situations in the past). The *excitatory component* is a response-energizing mechanism that prepares the organism for vigorous action. It corresponds physiologically to heightened sympathetic nervous system arousal and it may be innate, as in the case of a response to pain or to genital stimulation, or learned,

as in the case of a response to stimuli that signal *forth-coming* pain or pleasure. The *experiential component* is the conscious experience of emotion and it may operate to alter substantially the unfolding emotional behaviour. You experience the insult as anger-inducing, but you realize that a child made it, so you consciously work to reduce or change your emotional reaction.

According to this model, excitation transfer can occur; it is assumed that the excitatory component does not disappear immediately when the stimuli that elicited it have disappeared. Residues of the excitation from one emotional reaction can add to and intensify a subsequent emotional state brought about by a new stimulus. Thus, following sexual arousal, residues of this excitation can intensify subsequent emotional states, such as those associated with aggression, just as residues following aggression can intensify subsequent sexual reactions. This was the theme of David Cronenberg's 1996 film *Crash*, in which people amplified their feelings of sexual excitement through the physiological arousal produced by being involved in car crashes.

In a demonstration (Zillmann, 1971) of how sexual arousal can facilitate aggression, subjects who had previously been provoked by a confederate of the experimenter watched either a sexually arousing film, an aggressive film or a neutral film. Next, they were given the opportunity to administer electric shocks to the confederate; in addition, researchers took measures of subjects' physiological arousal. Physiological arousal was greatest in the sexual film condition and the aggressive film condition was next. Aggressive behaviour followed this same pattern: subjects who watched the sexual film were *more* aggressive than those who watched the aggressive film, who were in turn *more* aggressive than those who saw the neutral film. It would appear that the arousal, whatever its cause, translated to aggressiveness when the situational context made aggression relevant.

The attribution the individual makes for the arousal is critical, and if arousal from erotica is interpreted as sexual, it may actually reduce aggression possibly because of its distracting features (Donnerstein, Donnerstein & Evans, 1975).

Aggressive stimuli can also elicit sexual reactions and there is evidence that aggression-generated sexual arousal is related to violence against women, not only in the laboratory but also in the context of dating (Malamuth, 1986). It has also been reported that there is a high positive correlation among rapists between arousal from non-sexual aggression and arousal from rape (Abel, Barlow, Blanchard & Guild, 1977). And it has been suggested that serial murderers—people who kill many times, sometimes over a period of years—often experience sexual arousal from aggressive activities (Leyton, 1986). Furthermore, there are reports that some wife beaters (about 15 percent) experience sexual arousal from non-sexual assaults on their wives (Davidson, 1978).

Indeed, aggression may be sexually stimulating for a substantial minority of the general male population. In one study (Malamuth, Check & Briere, 1986), male subjects listened to a tape-recorded story that reflected one of four orientations: sexual/aggressive, sexual/non-aggressive, non-sexual/aggressive and non-sexual/non-aggressive. Sexual arousal was measured both by self-report and through penile tumescence monitored with a special strain gauge. Both measures indicated that sexual arousal in about 70 percent of the subjects was inhibited by aggressive activity in the story. However for the remaining 30 percent, sexual arousal was enhanced by the presence of aggression. The authors of that study speculate that the relationship between aggression and arousal is based on experience: during adolescence, teenagers who believe that women need to be coerced into sexual behaviour may behave or fantasize in an aggressive way while experiencing actual sexual pleasure. Through classical conditioning, depictions of sexual aggression or actually behaving aggressively may elicit sexual arousal.

The effects of pornography

The admixture of sexuality and aggression in some readily available pornography provides a perfect seedbed for excitation transfer and for an emotional confluence of aggressive and sexual responses. Psychologists have been concerned with the possibility that pornography may encourage antisocial attitudes and behaviours especially towards women, since almost all pornography is directed to the titillation of men. Several effects have been attributed to the consumption of pornography.

GENDER SCHEMATIZATION As discussed in Chapter 2, schematic processing is involved in much of our thinking about and perception of others. Schemata based on gender greatly influence the way males view and act towards females and vice versa. There are a number of subschemata associated with gender and one of them is a **heterosexuality subschema**, which leads individuals, when it is primed, to view interactions with people of the opposite sex in sexual terms.

This subschema is most pronounced among **gender-schematic** individuals, those who tend generally to view males and females in terms of sex-typed dimensions ("men are strong, women are weak" and so on).

A study using male introductory psychology students at the University of Waterloo found that exposure to pornography can prime this subschema: gender-schematic males who watched a non-violent pornographic film were more likely, subsequently, to treat a female research assistant as a sexual object than were those who watched a neutral film (McKenzie-Mohr & Zanna, 1990).

Pornographic films probably do more than prime such a subschema; they may greatly contribute to the form that such a subschema takes, for many adolescent males learn about female sexuality from such films.

INCREASED SEXUAL CALLOUSNESS If non-violent pornography can lead men to view women as sexual objects, what is the effect of violent pornography upon a male viewer? Studies have shown that male viewers of violent pornography differ from non-viewers in their attitude towards rape (Malamuth, 1984); they view rape as less horrible and the victim as more desirous of being violated. This is not surprising since most violent pornography implies that women secretly want to be assaulted and will derive pleasure from the assault.

Check (1985) distinguishes between *erotica* (sexually explicit materials emphasizing sharing of sexual pleasure rather than satisfaction of male needs and fantasies), *nonviolent dehumanizing pornography* (which portrays women as the playthings of men, enjoying sexual degradation) and *violent pornography* (in which women are forced into painful or dangerous sexual acts). Non-violent dehumanizing pornography can also lead to sexual callousness towards women and decreased concern about the effects of rape (Check & Guloien, 1989).

HABITUATION Research has shown that repeated exposure to pornography leads to excitatory **habituation**: that is, as individuals watch more and more pornography, there is a gradual decrease in the physiological arousal produced by it leading to diminishing pleasurable reactions and even disappointment and boredom (Zillmann & Bryant, 1984). This physiological habituation effect, measured in terms of sympathetic nervous activity, penile tumescence and other variables, has been demonstrated to endure for at least eight weeks (Zillmann, 1989).

Such habituation might seem to suggest that people will eventually become bored by pornography. However, other research has shown that habituation to one form of pornography increases interest in more extreme and even violent forms (Zillmann & Bryant, 1986).

Increased tendency to act violently towards women

What about the influence of violent pornography on actual aggression? In some studies, subjects have been offered the opportunity to aggress after exposure to pornography (in a non-sexual manner, using the usual procedures of aggression studies). Violent pornography that depicts women as willing victims who enjoy their plight has been shown to increase subsequent male-to-female aggression but not male-to-male aggression (Donnerstein, Linz & Penrod, 1987; Linz, Donnerstein & Penrod, 1988).

Presenting women as enjoying their victimization is crucial to the production of heightened aggression towards women. Moreover, the viewer may well come to believe that women "need to be forced" but will ultimately come to enjoy it (Check & Malamuth, 1986). Such a belief plays a critical role in linking violent pornography to actual sexual violence. While most men find non-coercive sexual scenes more arousing than sexual violence, some men are just as aroused or even more aroused by watching violent sex such as rape. Whether this particular group is more likely to carry out such sexually violent acts depends largely on their attitudes about the acceptability of violence towards women (Malamuth, 1986, 1988).

How should society handle these problems with pornography? Politicians and the public sometimes react by calling for the suppression or ban of pornography and sometimes such action is based on overgeneralizations from the psychological literature (Linz, Donnerstein & Penrod, 1987). The Fraser Committee, set up to examine problems associated with pornography as well as prostitution, recommended that while pornography that involves neither violence nor exploitation of children should be allowed for adult consumption, films that depict or promote sexual exploitation of minors or sexually violent behaviour should be subject to criminal sanctions (Ministry of Supply and Services Canada, 1985). Indeed, pornography is becoming accepted by mainstream Canadian society, as is indicated by regular showings of "hardcore" (but non-violent) pornography on cable and satellite networks and, for a fee, in even the best hotels in the country. Thus, the threat that even non-violent pornography once seemed to pose may prove to be much less serious than anticipated.

Perhaps the most reasonable response to whatever problems pornography poses is to develop programs to educate males, especially teenage males, about the reactions of women to coercive sex and to counter the development of potential harmful attitudes towards women (Donnerstein, Linz & Penrod, 1987). Even a little information can go a long way: Sinclair, Lee and Johnson (1995) examined the effect of a single "social comparison cue" on reactions of male University of Alberta students to erotic films, violent sexual films and violent non-sexual films. The cue consisted of a male confederate saying aloud, just before the film clip ended, "This is really disgusting. It's incredibly degrading towards women." This cue was enough to lead the male subjects to evaluate the portrayal of women as being more negative in both the erotic and the non-violent sexual film clips. Further when these subjects participated in an ostensibly unrelated subsequent experiment in which they had the opportunity to deliver electric shocks to a female confederate in a Milgram-type learning paradigm, they delivered shocks of lower intensity in all film conditions, although this effect seemed to decay in the violent sexual film condition. This suggests that the presentation of appropriate social-comparison information to men might lead to a reduction in male violence towards women although it is not clear just how one might make such social-comparison cues available and relevant.

The Reduction of Aggression

It is unlikely that aggression can be eliminated entirely from our society. For one thing, violence is often a symptom of social inequality and injustice. When some groups are disadvantaged economically and socially relative to others, violence will often appear to be the surest and quickest way to force the majority group to recognize minority needs and to correct the injustice. Television with its display of lifestyles far beyond the reach of the average person, let alone the socially disadvantaged, may raise expectations and increase feelings of powerlessness, possibly leading to violent responses (Lore & Schultz, 1993).

However, some suggestions about how to reduce violence flow from the social psychological literature.

Reduce and de-glorify media violence

Reducing violence in the media would focus less attention on violent events in general. As long as violence is presented as an efficient masculine manner of solving problems and obtaining justice, it will continue to be used, and in many contexts to be viewed in a positive light. Some moves are already being made in this direction. In 1994, the Canadian Association of Broadcasters revised its *Voluntary Code on Violence in Television Programming* with the goal of reducing gratuitous and glamourized violence on television. In 1996 in response to public pressure, U.S. President Clinton signed into law a bill requiring that by 2000 all new television sets sold in the United States be equipped with a V-chip (the "V" stands for "violence"). The V-chip is a Canadian invention that allows parents to decide whether their television sets can receive programs rated as violent or sexual. V-chips screen out programs that are identified by an electronic coding rating system as containing sex, violence or crude language. While such a coding system is already in place in the U.S., the Canadian Radio-television and Telecommunications Commission (CRTC) has not mandated the classification and coding of television programs that would allow the V-chip to be used in this country. Whether the use of such a device has any positive effect on violence in society remains to be determined.

Educate parent*s*

Parent education is crucial to the effort of reducing aggression and violence. Many parents are unprepared for the extremely difficult task of training, educating and socializing their children and do not think about or know about child-rearing styles that reduce aggressiveness. As has been discussed, child-rearing practices such as excessive use of punishment and an emphasis on traditional masculine/feminine role behaviour are likely to encourage aggressive behaviour. Parents also differ in their mediating styles when reacting to children's anger or aggression. Most often the reaction is "Stop it!" While an aggressive incident does need to be stopped quickly, discussion and explanation are also needed to effectively change future behaviour especially over the long term (Singer & Singer, 1986). Increasing sensitivity to the products of violence—the suffering, the increased hostility—has been shown to reduce anger and aggression.

People most sensitive to the risks of media violence and people most receptive to education about parenting styles are likely to be those whose children are brought up to be relatively non-aggressive in any case. Those whom society may really need to reach are likely to be the least interested.

Societies around the world and indeed the world community as a whole have so far failed to put much of a damper on interpersonal and intergroup aggression. However, we should not be discouraged, for it takes a long time to change values, to teach people to teach their children peaceful methods of conflict resolution and to correct social injustices. As we come to better understand the roots of aggression, the better equipped we will be to work towards its reduction.

Summary

1. Aggression is defined as behaviour that is intended to harm or destroy.

2. Aggression can be instrumental—used to achieve a desired goal; or hostile—instigated by anger and directed at harming another person.

3. Instinct theories such as Freud's lack empirical support. Such theories assume that aggressive energy held in check must eventually be released either directly or indirectly (catharsis). However, research evidence does not support catharsis as a means of reducing aggressive behaviour.

4. The frustration–aggression hypothesis does not hold up empirically although aggression may be due to frustration under certain circumstances. Sometimes aggression is a result of pain or other aversive states.

5. Attempts to isolate specific biological systems directly associated with aggression in humans have not been successful. Neural, hormonal and genetic influences are indirect and are overlaid by learned behaviour.

6. Social learning is concerned with the way children learn how to aggress, when to aggress and against whom to aggress. Learning about aggression can occur by means of reinforcement and punishment or by observation of others.

7. Certain child-rearing practices may enhance the aggressiveness of children. Emotionally cold, punitive parents often have highly aggressive children, especially sons. The socialization factor most strongly related to aggression is the use of

physical punishment, especially within a rejecting atmosphere.

8. The long-term consequences of experiencing or observing violence in the home on a recurrent basis may place a child at risk to perpetuate violence or child abuse in adulthood.

9. Certain personality types are likely to be aggressive. These include "right-wing authoritarians" and individuals who are "under-controlled." Although personality traits play some role in aggression, the effects are generally outweighed by situational factors.

10. The prevalence of aggressive behaviour varies considerably among cultures. In some, aggression is actively encouraged while in others violence of any sort is frowned upon and rarely occurs.

11. There has been considerable research on the effects, especially on children, of violence in the media. The consensus is that viewing violence and aggressive behaviour does increase the likelihood of violence in children and has long-lasting effects. However, not all children react in the same way and characteristics of the family setting play an important moderating role.

12. Media aggression has other potentially harmful consequences. The pairing of stimuli (e.g., guns and aggression) may increase the likelihood of guns being used when an individual is angry. Media violence may also desensitize viewers or lead to imitative real-life aggressive acts.

13. Stricter gun control has been followed by a decrease in the use of firearms in homicides in Canada without any corresponding increase in the use of other methods.

14. The relationship between gender and aggression is not straightforward. Women are as aggressive as men in some circumstances. Learned gender roles, which encourage aggressiveness in males and discourage it in females, are an important factor.

15. Through excitation transfer and classical conditioning, sexual stimulation can elicit heightened aggressiveness and vice versa.

16. Pornography whether violent or non-violent may teach males negative attitudes towards women and may mislead them into believing that women enjoy coercive sex even when they resist it.

17. Violence in society can be reduced by reducing media violence and by teaching parents how to socialize their children using appropriate forms of discipline and de-emphasizing the traditional male/female roles.

Further Reading

CICCHETTI, D. & CARLSON, V.K. (Eds.). (1989). *Child maltreatment*. New York: Cambridge University Press. Presents recent research findings about the impact of neglect and abuse on children's cognitive, linguistic, social and emotional development.

DUTTON, D.G. (1995). *The domestic assault of women: Psychological and criminal justice perspectives*. Vancouver: University of British Columbia Press. An in-depth exploration of the social psychology of the wife assaulter, how such men differ from other men, the effects of such abuse on the victim and how wife abuse is dealt with by the criminal justice system.

FREEDMAN, J.L. (2002). *Media violence and its effect on aggression*. Toronto: University of Toronto Press. This book presents a comprehensive review of research into the effects of media violence and aggression, and concludes that the research evidence does not support the hypothesis that exposure to media violence causes aggression or criminal behaviour.

HUESMANN, L.R. & MALAMUTH, N.M. (Eds.). (1986). Media violence and antisocial behavior. *Journal of Social Issues, 42* (3). The entire issue of this journal is devoted to the connection between depictions of violence in the media and real-life aggression.

LIEBERT, R.M. & SPRAFKIN, J. (1988). *The early window,* 3rd ed. New York: Pergamon Press. Comprehensive review of research into the effects of televised violence on the development of aggressive behaviours.

LOEBER, R. & HAY, D. (1997). Key issues in the development of aggression and violence from childhood to early adulthood. *Annual Review of Psychology, 48,* 371–410. Up-to-date review of personality, cognitive and social factors related to the development of aggressive behaviour.

MILLER, A.G. (1999). Special issue: Perspectives on evil and violence. *Personality and Social Psychology Review, 3* (3). This special issue deals with harm-doing and evil from a variety of conceptual and empirical perspectives.

PEPLER, D., CRAIG, W.M. & O'CONNELL, P. (1999). Understanding bullying from a dynamic systems perspective. In A. Slater, D. Muir et al. (Eds.), *The Blackwell reader in development psychology*. Malden, MA: Blackwell. A discussion of various causes of bullying and how it is promoted and maintained by the social situation.

ROSS, J.I. (Ed.). (1995). *Violence in Canada*. Don Mills, ON: Oxford University Press. A fascinating and highly informative collection of articles, written primarily from a sociological perspective, examining interpersonal violence in Canada. Topics include labour violence, male violence against women, violence in the Aboriginal community, violence both by and against children and terrorism.

SMITH, P.K., MORITA, Y., JUNGER-TAS, J., OLWEUS, D, CATALANO, R.F. & SLEE, P. (Eds.). (1999). *The nature of school bullying: A cross-national perspective*. Florence, KY: Taylor and Francis/Routledge. This book provides a unique global perspective of the current state of knowledge and of how bullying is dealt with in 21 countries, including Canada, and includes definitions of bullying, the nature and types of school bullying, descriptive statistics about bullying and initiatives and interventions.

STAUB, E. (1989). *The roots of evil: The psychological and cultural origins of genocide and other forms of group violence*. New York: Cambridge University Press. An examination of the roots of group aggression and genocide.

ZILLMAN, D. & BRYANT, J. (Eds.). (1989). *Pornography: Research advances and policy considerations*. Hillsdale, NJ: Erlbaum. A compendium of research findings regarding the social effects of pornography.

 # Weblinks

Family violence in Canada

http://www.hc-sc.gc.ca/hppb/familyviolence/

Health Canada'a National Clearinghouse on Family Violence

World Health Organization *First World Report on Violence and Health*

http://www5.who.int/violence_injury_prevention/main.cfm

Chapter 12

Social Categorization, Groups and Leadership

We still think of a powerful man as a born leader and a powerful woman as an anomaly.

Margaret Atwood

Who built the seven gates of Thebes? In the books are listed the names of kings. Did the kings heave up the building blocks?

Bertolt Brecht

Chapter Outline

In the 1960s, "Trudeaumania" swept a political neophyte—Pierre Elliott Trudeau—into the leadership of the Liberal Party and eventually into the position of prime minister of Canada. For the next 16 years, Trudeau amazed, amused, astounded and angered his fellow citizens depending on their political views and their willingness to accept the idiosyncratic aspects of his behaviour. Whether wearing sandals and an open shirt into the House of Commons, doing a pirouette behind Queen Elizabeth at an official event, being adored by the world press or asking farmers, "Why should we sell your wheat?"—Trudeau had a powerful effect on everyone he encountered. Even in early 2000 when he was briefly hospitalized with pneumonia, newspapers across the country paid careful attention to the state of his health and recalled the heady and tumultuous days when he was the country's leader. When he died later in 2000, a few weeks short of his 81st birthday, virtually the entire nation mourned the loss of such a rare, stimulating and thought-provoking public figure.

Leaders are defined in large part by the groups or societies that they lead. The notion of a leader without followers does not make much sense and, on the other hand, it is difficult to imagine a group without at least some semblance of leadership, formal or otherwise. Thus in order to study and understand leaders, we must first come to understand groups.

Groups are a fundamental aspect of human society. We live our lives in groups and spend most of our waking hours in one group context or another—our families, our circles of friends, the people we work with or with whom we go to school. We define ourselves in terms of groups: "I am a Canadian," "I am a U Vic student," "I am Québécois." Many of the most important changes in our lives—for example, leaving home to go to university or to get a job—involve becoming a part of new groups and lessening our participation in old ones. Membership in new groups often leads to changes in our attitudes and values.

As shall be discussed later, the term "group" has a specialized meaning in social psychology, which can easily lead to confusion because of the way the word is used in everyday discourse—for example, "See that group of teenagers leaning against the wall over there." To a social psychologist, the mere fact that several teenagers are together does not necessarily mean that they constitute a group. It is also important to distinguish between *social categories* and groups. For example, as you walk along the street, you may categorize people into "drivers" and "pedestrians." You would be unlikely to think of these categories as distinct groups: there is little or no interaction among members of "the drivers" or "the pedestrians." They probably do not know one another and the categorization is temporary for drivers become pedestrians the moment they get out of their cars.

This chapter deals with how social categories and group membership affect individuals, how groups function, how they interrelate to other groups, how social power plays a role in group dynamics and how people achieve and maintain positions of leadership.

Social Categorization

It would be difficult to interact with other people if we could not view them as part of some organized pattern. We tend automatically to put people into categories or schemata (see Chapter 2) that we already know something about (e.g., "male, teenager, school drop-out"). This quick categorization allows us to act "appropriately" and to know roughly what to expect from that person according to the social norms and stereotypes we have learned. Each of us belongs to many different social categories, probably many more categories than we realize. We are male or female, Canadian, American, black, white, tinker, tailor, soldier and so on. We also belong to categories based on religion, age group, ethnic group, geographical origin and marital status. Although such categories may not always mean much to us, under certain circumstances they can become very important.

Although individuals interact directly with other individuals, they often do not deal with each other as individuals *per se* but rather as members of particular social categories. At any given time, our interpersonal behaviour falls somewhere along a continuum. At one extreme is pure interpersonal behaviour in which the interaction between two or more people is determined solely by their individual characteristics. For example, consider two deeply infatuated lovers. Initially at least, they may ignore social categories and focus on each other as individuals. At the other extreme is pure intergroup behaviour in which the interaction between two or more people is determined by their membership in social categories. For example, when armies confront one another on the field of battle, each soldier treats enemy soldiers as though they were all the same, without any individuality. Most of the time, however, behaviour in a social context depends both on our characteristics as individuals and on the social categories describing ourselves and the people with whom we interact.

Since we each belong to many social categories, our behaviour at any given time will be influenced by whatever category is salient at that moment. If you are the only female engineer at a meeting of engineers and someone starts telling jokes that denigrate women, being a woman will suddenly become very important to you (and perhaps to the men at the meeting too). If you then go to a women's rights group and someone now denigrates the fact that because you are an engineer, it differentiates you from the other women present, this will likely also strongly influence your reaction.

Often without being aware of it, we organize the social world in such a way that various social categories have some relationship to one another. Some people are viewed as superior and others as relatively inferior as a result of the social categories to which they appear to belong. Thus, we may act with deference towards

someone we assume to be older and better educated than ourselves and with condescension towards someone younger. Perhaps the most important element of this "subjective" social order that we all construct for ourselves is the division into **in-groups** (categories to which we belong) and **out-groups** (categories to which we do not belong) (i.e., into "we" and "they").

The emphasis placed on in-group versus out-group—the *we* versus *they* division in our society—often produces a competitive relationship between the members of different social categories. We want "our" team, our age group, our sex, our neighbourhood, our province or our country to win, whether it is a spelling prize in elementary school or an Olympic medal. If Calgary football fans watch a Western Conference final between Calgary and Edmonton, they will want Calgary to win and will view the Eskimos as the enemy. Yet if Edmonton wins and goes to the Grey Cup game, those same Calgary fans will probably

Rejection by peers is particularly aversive to teenagers, who are still forming their social identities.

cheer for the Eskimos because they are "Westerners" and want the West to win.

Teams can become an extension of our own identity. Back in 1972, Canadians were in an uproar when it appeared the hockey team representing Canada, a team made up for the first time of professional players from the NHL, came close to losing to the Soviet Union's team. Why did people care so much about whether Team Canada won or lost? The competition focused attention on a "we–they" contest that went far beyond the hockey game. It was as though the hockey series involved the whole Canadian citizenry against the population of the Soviet Union: The ultimate Canadian victory engendered feelings of well-being and superiority (at least in terms of hockey). The same feelings were aroused when both the Canadian women's and the men's hockey teams won gold medals by defeating the American teams in the 2002 winter Olympics. Yet these feelings of success, a sort of "basking in reflected glory," were based on the efforts of strangers—hockey players whom they had never even met—but strangers who shared the category of being *Canadian*.

A generic norm

Repeated exposure to in-groups and out-groups, many of which involve some degree of resentment towards the out-group (e.g., Asians are buying all the best property in Vancouver; Ontario has no interest in the economic plight of Western beef producers; Westerners don't care about the impact of the SARS epidemic on the Ontario economy), leads to what has been called a **generic norm of out-group discrimination** (Tajfel, 1970). We are prepared to act in a similarly discriminatory, competitive or rejecting way toward all out-groups regardless of the out-group and regardless of the context of the interaction. Discrimination against an out-group occurs even when such discrimination in no way contributes to self-interest; and such discrimination may occur even in the absence of pre-existing hostility toward the out-group and it may manifest itself in discriminatory behaviour even before any hostility or prejudice has formed. This was clearly demonstrated in a number of experiments carried out by Tajfel and colleagues that showed how arbitrary or even random assignments of individuals to artificial "minimal" groups (i.e., groups with no structure, no pre-existing norms, no history) leads to discrimination favouring the in-group.

In one such study (Tajfel, 1970), students were arbitrarily divided into artificial groups on the supposed basis of whether they had been "over-estimators" or "under-estimators" in a previously administered visual perception task. Participants actually worked alone and did not know the identities of the other group members. Each participant participated in several trials in which it was necessary to select one of several different ways to assign a number of points to two other people. These points were later to be exchanged for money and so something of real value was involved. On some trials, the participants had to divide a number of points between two members of their own group, while on other trials the assignment was to be made to two members of the other group. On still other trials, the participants were to assign points to one member of the in-group and one member of the out-group.

When a participant had the opportunity to assign points to two members of either the in-group or the out-group, each person was given about an equal number of points. However when points were assigned to both a member of the in-group and a member of the out-group, a large majority of participants awarded more points to members of their own group than to members of the other group. They thus discriminated in favour of their own group (1) even though they did not know who was in their group and who was in the other group; (2) even though the division into groups was based on a trivial criterion; and (3) even though they would in no way benefit personally as a result of their choices. This discrimination occurred with no conflict of interest or pre-existing antagonism and even without any social interaction.

Why did the participants act in this manner? It is possible that they were discriminating because of social desirability: they simply wanted to look good in the experimenter's eyes. Yet even if that were the case, it would be revealing that they believed it "looks good" to favour their own group over an out-group (Tajfel & Turner, 1979; Lemyre & Smith, 1985, Hewstone, Robin & Willis, 2002).

It appears then that as a result of years of experience in which in-group/out-group discrimination has been subtly and not so subtly encouraged, people are prepared to discriminate more or less automatically against out-groups and to favour their in-group.

Social identity and social comparison

If someone were to ask, "Who are you?" how would you respond? You might give your name but if the interlocutor continued with "Yes, but who are you?"

what would you say? Depending on the circumstances, you might describe yourself as a student, a man or a woman, a psychology student, a resident of Victoria or Fredericton, a Canadian, a North American or even a member of a certain club. Thus we not only categorize other people, but we also categorize ourselves. Indeed, our self-esteem and how we perceive ourselves in relation to other people is tied up with such identification: "She wouldn't want to go out with me. I'm just in first year and she's in third."

Social identification is the process whereby individuals define themselves with respect to other people, and *social identity* refers to those aspects of self-image of persons that depend upon the social categories and groups to which they belong (Tajfel & Turner, 1979). Once an individual identifies with a particular category, the typical norms, attitudes and behaviours that distinguish the groups will determine his or her behaviour to a large degree as a result of conformity (Turner, 1982, 1985).

Social groups distinguish themselves from one another through members' striving to evaluate their own in-group positively, relative to out-groups (Tajfel and Turner, 1979). Since the aim of social identification is to provide a positive comparison with regard to some other relevant group, such identification is basically competitive (Gagnon & Bourhis, 1996). When people's social identities cease to be satisfactory, they either strive to improve their in-group relative to various out-groups or they will eventually leave the in-group and join some other group.

Categorical differentiation

In the psychology of perception and cognition, there is the well-known phenomenon of assimilation and contrast: we tend to exaggerate the similarities among objects from the same category and the differences among objects from different categories. The same phenomenon occurs with social groups. When we compare people from two different social groups, we may perceive the members of a group as more similar than they really are and the differences between the members of each group as greater than they really are. This tendency is referred to as **social differentiation** (Lemaine, Kastersztein & Personnaz, 1978). For example, if we know little about motorcycle clubs, all motorcyclists may seem very similar to us in terms of style of dress, attitudes and so on. And if we were to compare three motorcycle club members with three

members of a baseball team, we might perceive the two sets of people as being more different than they actually are. Indeed whatever the out-group, we tend to view them as though they are all cut from the same cloth, while we recognize that there is a great deal of variation amongst the members of our own in-group. This **out-group homogeneity effect** occurs because we are more likely to relate to our colleagues as individuals and to know more about each one; lacking such knowledge of out-group members, we see them as all more or less alike.

To demonstrate social differentiation, Doise, Deschamps and Meyer (1978) conducted several experiments. In one, schoolchildren were assigned to one of two conditions. Participants in the "no-anticipation" condition were told only that they would be required to describe members of their own social category. Participants in the "anticipation" condition were informed that they would be describing both members of their own category and members of another category.

An equal number of boys and girls were assigned to each condition. They were shown three photographs of girls and three photographs of boys, all unknown to them, and asked which of 24 adjectives applied to each child. Participants in the no-anticipation group were first shown only the three same-sex photographs; the other three photographs were presented later. Participants in the anticipation group were given all six photographs at once although they were to begin by rating the three photos of the children the same sex as themselves. When the children knew that they would be rating both boys and girls, inter-category (boy–girl) differences were greater but intra-category differences (differences within each gender group) were smaller. Gender had become a salient variable leading the participants to differentiate the two categories. Similar results were obtained in an experiment using language rather than gender as the salient dimension.

Cross-categorization

Depending on the context in which you meet someone, some social features of that person may be much more important to you than others. In fact, the importance of each feature or dimension may change as the interaction continues. Suppose that you are a young woman and a classical pianist. You consider male football players to be "macho jerks." Such a belief may be based on past experience or it may not. You are inclined not to like the man you've just met at a party when you learn he's a fullback with the university football team. Suppose, however, that he sits down at the piano and plays a touching rendition of Beethoven's "Moonlight Sonata." How will you react after this? Now this man falls into two categories, one to which you respond negatively and the other to which you attach value.

This dilemma is applicable whenever we encounter someone who shares one category with us but is part of an out-group with regard to another. Since we all belong to many overlapping groups, this situation, called **cross-categorization**, is likely to occur often (Hewstone, Islam & Judd, 1993).

In another experiment, Deschamps and Doise (1978) asked teenage students in a "simple" condition to describe, by means of an adjective checklist, females, males, young people and adults. Students in a "mixed" condition were asked to describe "crossed" categories: young females, young males, female adults and male adults (Figure 12–1).

The crossing of the categories led to a decrease in the social differentiation. For example, participants in the simple condition saw that there was much more difference between males and females than participants in the mixed condition saw between young males and young females. While each participant belonged to either the male or female category, all par-

ticipants belonged to the "young" category. When rating adult males and females, the perceived differences were also smaller than when rating males and females. When the participants characterized groups of people similar to themselves with respect to one criterion but different with respect to another, the perceived differences were smaller than when comparisons were made on the basis of a single feature.

In another experiment (Deschamps & Doise, 1978), it was observed that while a simple division of people into in-group and out-group could produce a positive bias towards the participants' own group, the introduction of a second, neutral characteristic (i.e., producing no bias of itself) could eliminate the original discrimination in favour of the in-group. The participants were nine- and ten-year-old boys and girls. Half the participants were in the simple category (male versus female) condition. The rest were in the crossed category condition: half the boys and half the girls were assigned to a "red" category and the remainder to a "blue" category. The children worked individually on a series of pencil and paper games. Later, they were asked to estimate the number of games that each of the other children had correctly completed.

Participants in the simple category condition rated the probable success of the other participants of their

FIGURE 12-1

Design of categorization experiment

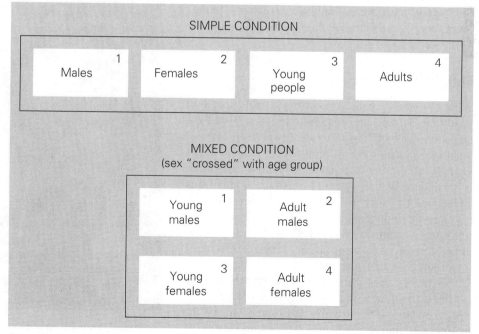

Source: Deschamps & Doise, 1978.

sex as significantly higher than that of opposite-sex participants. However, no such distinction was made in the crossed-category condition (e.g., red male versus red female), even though the red–blue split did not by itself produce any difference. Thus, adding a meaningless variable and crossing it with the gender variable eliminated gender discrimination. Similar findings have been observed in experiments aimed at fostering cooperation in social dilemmas (Wit and Kerr, 2002).

Coser (1967) anticipated all this when he wrote that conflict serves to bind the elements of society together. A society is composed of many categories, and subcategories often in conflict with each other. Yet since individuals belong to many different categories, it is highly unlikely that a given set of people will be on the same side in every conflict. Thus, a woman may oppose a man on the women's rights issue but agree with him on a conservation issue and so on. Hence, society is knit together. It is easy to see how this binding process applies to the Canadian nation: French Canadians and English Canadians, or natives and immigrants, or Easterners and Westerners may find themselves in conflict each with the other. However, as long as they are not divided on every major issue along linguistic or ethnic or geographic lines but instead find these categories "crossed" with other categories (e.g., males versus females, capitalists versus socialists, environmentalists versus "exploiters"), the fabric of the whole society will be held together.

Redefinition of the social field

What do we do when, in comparison with people in another social category, we come off second best? How do people deal with threats to identity and self-esteem? Members of the "inferior" group may attempt to be assimilated into the more favourable group when that is possible or they may try to avoid such comparisons altogether. However, there is also another common reaction: the individual often tries to distinguish herself from the comparison group in such a way that the dimension of comparison is no longer relevant or important (Lemaine, Kastersztein & Personnaz, 1978).

This process was demonstrated in a series of field studies carried out with children (Jamous & Lemaine, 1962; Lemaine, 1966; Lemaine & Kastersztein, 1972). In one experiment (Lemaine, 1974), two groups of boys competed for a prize, although they did not

directly interact. Each group had to build a hut in the forest. One group—picked by the toss of a coin—was allowed to use string; the other was not. The "handicapped" group was less efficient in organizing tasks; they were preoccupied with their disadvantage and considered withdrawing from the competition. They wasted a lot of time watching the other group before they buckled down to work themselves and then only after "closing their frontiers" and not allowing members of the advantaged group to observe what they were doing. They then set about to compensate for their handicap by doing things differently from the other group. While the goal was to build a hut, the disadvantaged group redefined the situation by arguing that building a hut also involved making a garden, a table and a fireplace, items they had built and the other group had not.

Similarly, Lalonde (1992) studied how the players on a last-place hockey team reacted to their inability to win. After each of eight games, he asked the players to rate how they perceived their team, the opposing team and themselves. Lalonde found that the inferior team was quite realistic concerning their lack of skill, but they chose to distinguish themselves in a positive

The Famous People Players demonstrate cross-categorization: the mentally and physically challenged and a successful theatre troupe.

Language and Group Identity: Two Solitudes in Quebec

Language and group identity are deeply intertwined, and a threat to one is a threat to both. Nowhere in Canada has the power of language to define groups been more clearly shown than in Quebec. Francophones in the province long feared assimilation, and this fear of loss of language and group identity, as well as enduring feelings of having been dominated by anglophones in the past, have fed the fires of a sovereignty campaign.

In 1977, the government of Quebec passed Bill 101, a law intended once and for all to make French the language of the workplace and the sole official language of Quebec. At least four factors prompted the Quebec government to adopt the Bill 101 language law (d'Anglejan, 1984): (1) the decline of the French Canadian population outside Quebec; (2) the decline of the French Canadian birth rate in Quebec from the highest to the lowest of the 10 Canadian provinces; (3) the tendency of immigrants to become integrated with Quebec's English-speaking minority by sending their children to English schools; (4) the domination of English in Quebec business.

Bill 101 reduced fears among Quebec francophones (for a while at least) that they would one day be linguistically assimilated among the 240 000 000 English speakers in Canada and the U.S. While Bill 101 received overwhelming support from Quebec francophones, the anglophone minority (about 20 percent of the Quebec population) saw it as a threat (Bourhis, 1984a). The greatest symbolic threat was the insistence that public signs be in French only. (Subsequent amendments allowed bilingual signs inside but not outside stores.)

This bill, combined with the 1976 victory of the Parti Québécois government, catalyzed the exodus of 15 percent of the Quebec anglophone population to other parts of Canada and to the U.S. Many large corporations also moved their headquarters from Montreal to Toronto (Caldwell, 1984). By the mid-1980s, however, as anglophones who stayed behind became proficient in French and the heartbeat of Quebec nationalism faded to a barely perceptible murmur, anglophones began to reassert themselves and their children began to stay at home rather than move to Ontario.

Yet as we know from the politics of the '80s and the '90s, fears about assimilation into the English majority were still deeply felt by many francophones, driving the sovereignty movement and a new exodus of anglophones. However, this may well have changed. The defeat of the Parti Québécois and the election of a Liberal government in 2003 may reflect a new confidence in the enduring sustainability of French language and culture within a united Canada.

manner from the other team by claiming that their opponents played more "dirty."

As people try to maintain their self-esteem in a situation that gives another party an advantage, they will look for some new point of comparison. For example, in a study conducted some years ago, it was found that while East Indians in South Africa considered themselves inferior to whites in the context of science and the economy, they saw themselves as superior in spiritual and social matters (Mann, 1963). Canadians may react to a perceived economic and technological superiority of the United States by defining ourselves more

in terms of our social programs and multicultural mosaic, and downplaying the value of economic or technological superiority.

Language and identity

Speech style, dialect and even language, among other characteristics, differentiate in-groups and out-groups. In-group speech can serve as a symbol of ethnic identity or cultural solidarity (Bourhis, 1979). Language reminds the group of its cultural heritage, transmits group feeling, excludes members of out-groups and emphasizes in-group feelings under conditions of ethnic threat. In Canada, language of origin has served as the central force to unite immigrants into ethnic groups. Yet groups such as Germans, Italians and Ukrainians are no longer being replenished by large-scale immigration and are not likely to survive as distinct linguistic entities (Berry, Kalin & Taylor, 1977). Without a unique language, ethnic survival is very difficult. Native Canadians are particularly aware of this problem. In other countries, concerns about the association of language and group identity have led people both to revive languages (for example, modern Hebrew) in order to foster group identity, and to invent a common language for all peoples (for example, Esperanto) to reduce the effects of group identification and foster world peace and understanding.

Recall the discussion of speech accommodation in Chapter 7. A wealth of evidence demonstrates that when group membership is an important issue, divergence rather than convergence is used. Giles, Bourhis and Taylor (1977) view strategies of convergence/divergence in terms of Tajfel's (1970) theory of intergroup distinctiveness. When members of a subordinate group accept their low status as appropriate, they may try to merge with the higher-status group and may converge to its speech style. On the other hand, if they view their inferior status as unjust, they may attempt to redefine their group attributes more positively and accentuate their distinctiveness by speech divergence. Thus the argument might go, English Canadians who accept Canada's apparently inferior status may adopt U.S. usage and, in writing to Americans, use U.S. spellings (e.g., *color*). However, those who reject a subordinate position for Canada may accentuate language differences by using Canadian spellings (e.g., *colour*), as we do in this book.

Groups

So far, the discussion has focused on general categories or loosely defined groups of people, even though it has been difficult to avoid the use of the word "group" from time to time. A group in social psychological terms is more than just a collection of people or a social category. If you are part of a crowd milling about the baggage carousel at an airport while waiting for your luggage, it is unlikely you would think that you had just joined a group. What about spectators at a hockey game? Or a classroom of students? Where is the line to be drawn between "groups" of people and

simple clusters of individuals who happen to be sharing the same physical space?

Social psychologists define a group in the following manner:

MUTUAL AWARENESS AND INFLUENCE First, there must be two or more people involved in an interaction in which they both (a) are aware of and (b) influence each other. Without mutual influence, there is no group. In a family, for example, each individual has some influence on every other individual.

ENDURING RELATIONSHIP Mutual awareness and influence alone, however, do not define a group. Consider a driver who splashes a pedestrian. The driver's actions certainly influence the pedestrian and the pedestrian's reactions are likely to have some influence on the driver. But the two do not constitute a group because their interaction lacks continuity. The driver and the pedestrian may never encounter each other again—at least not as driver and pedestrian. Groups involve enduring relationships within a relatively stable framework. A family, a poker club and a local organization all involve continuing relationships, stability of members' roles and stability of the unwritten rules, or norms, that govern the members' interactions.

COMMON PURPOSE This developing description of what constitutes a group is still incomplete, however. A prisoner and a guard in a penitentiary, for example, mutually influence each other and they certainly may have an enduring relationship within a very stable framework, but we would hardly view them as belonging to the same group. They stand in opposition to one another, while group members typically share a sense of purpose, a common goal—whether to accomplish something tangible or simply to have fun.

FEELING OF BELONGING But still something is missing. Suppose that every morning you share a bus shelter with the same set of people. There is likely to be at least some mutual influence, and the relationship, minimal as it is, endures over time in a relatively stable way. Moreover, all of the individuals share a common goal—to get on the bus. Yet they are not likely to consider themselves part of a "group." In the final analysis, a crucial characteristic of a group is the belief held by the individual members that they *belong to the group,* they are part of a specific entity (Tajfel, 1978, 1982).

To summarize: A group involves two or more people who are aware of each other, who both influence and are influenced by one another, who are engaged in an ongoing and relatively stable relationship, who share common goals and who view themselves as belonging to a group.

There are, of course, various kinds of groups. Some are formal with a clearly specified structure and clearly delineated roles for members. Others are informal, such as a group of friends who go to the pub every Friday. Some groups begin informally but gradually grow into more formal organizations (e.g., the Parti Québécois or Greenpeace, see Chapter 14). Groups can also be differentiated on the basis of whether they are task-oriented—formed to accomplish some specific job—or social-oriented, focusing on pleasure and social interaction.

Attraction to the group: Cohesiveness

While children cannot decide what family to join and people called for jury duty cannot choose their fellow jurors, many groups involve voluntary membership. Why does an individual become involved in one group and not in another? There are two major reasons. Sometimes we join groups as a means to a goal. If you want to improve your photography, learn how to sail or stop acid rain, you may join a camera club, a sailing club or an environmental group.

A second reason is the company the group provides—especially with social groups but also, for some people, with task-oriented groups. People with a high need for affiliation may find membership in almost any group rewarding.

All the factors that contribute to members' desires to belong to a particular group are referred to collectively as **cohesiveness**. Cohesiveness is a difficult concept to define (and measure), but in general terms, a cohesive group sticks together and displays feelings of harmony and solidarity. The members are committed to the group and to the group task (Cota, Evans, Dion & Longman, 1995). The more factors keeping individuals in the group and the fewer factors tempting them to leave, the more cohesive the group. Factors that contribute to cohesiveness include personal attraction among members, congruity between group goals and individual goals and uniqueness in being able to satisfy individual needs. For example, if you belong to a poker group, love playing poker and know no poker players outside the group, leaving the group would involve considerable cost. On the other hand, if various groups were constantly trying to get

you to play poker with them, your allegiance to your current group would be based on other factors, such as your attraction to the individual members or the quality of play. Cohesiveness within groups usually increases when the group becomes more important to its members—for instance, when it is in competition with other groups or when there is some kind of external threat.

Cohesiveness can both help and hinder the productivity of task-oriented groups. Members of highly cohesive groups are usually somewhat more influenced by group norms since group membership is very important to them (Berkowitz, 1954; Schachter, Ellertson, McBride & Gregory, 1951). Thus if the group norm calls for high productivity, cohesiveness will foster productivity, while if the norm calls for low productivity (as might be the case in some industrial settings), cohesiveness will promote lower output (Mullen & Copper, 1994). Members of highly cohesive groups can also lose productivity if their attraction to one another leads them to spend too much time in social interaction or to become so absorbed by the social interaction as to lose sight of the group goal (Langfred, 1998).

Finally, cohesiveness typically leads to greater participation by each member in the group's activities as well as more cooperation and greater communication (Lott & Lott, 1961). As a result, members experience greater satisfaction.

Group beliefs

When a group of people are aware that they have similar beliefs and see their beliefs as defining the group, we refer to them as *group beliefs*. Individuals in a particular religious group, for instance, hold personal beliefs about a variety of issues but probably share beliefs about such things as morality, life after death and the authority of the Pope or the need to eat kosher food. These shared beliefs are central to how the members of the group see themselves and are seen by others, and distinguish them from nonmembers. Group beliefs often serve to draw the line between in-groups and out-groups, showing how other people are different from "us" and even encouraging members to feel and act superior to others (recall as well the discussion of group beliefs in Chapter 10 that beliefs can make conflict resolution extremely difficult). Group beliefs also serve as a filter through which members can interpret new information (Bar-Tal, 1986).

Differentiation within the group: Roles and status

In most groups, and especially in task-oriented groups, different members have different duties to perform. Roles may be informal and evolve gradually (such as "keeper of the chips," the person who looks after the poker chips between games in a poker club) or they may be organizational with titles such as "secretary" or "chairperson." Two important informal roles that are found in most task-oriented groups are the "task specialist" and the "social-emotional specialist." The person perceived as most competent to direct the group to its objective generally fills the first role. However, such a person may not be suited to the task of guiding the group through all the emotional upsets that arise as the group is being pushed towards its goal. That task is left to the social-emotional specialist.

Within any group, there tends to be a kind of "pecking order." High-status members tend to dominate group discussions, play a more important part in decision-making and have a greater influence on low-status members than low-status members have on them. High-status members are naturally more likely to assume leadership roles and will be discussed in a later section. High status can derive from a number of factors: helping the group achieve its goals, personal popularity or a recognized role within the group (e.g., social convenor).

Regulation by the group: Norms

As you will recall, norms are shared beliefs about what behaviours are and are not acceptable for group members. They usually involve a certain amount of judgment on the part of group members. For example, if one of the norms of a poker club is that members should be available to play the third Wednesday of each month, no one may actually be able to specify how many times a player can miss before being considered to be letting down the group. A silent judgment is involved since there is no explicit rule. Similarly, if you are part of a factory work group, there is unlikely to be any rule about productivity, but if you produce more than your fellow workers, you may be ostracized (see Chapter 6). Sometimes, of course, groups try to codify their norms into rules. However, it is impossible to anticipate all situations, and rigid rules may prove detrimental by discouraging judgment and innovation (see Chapter 6) when it is most needed.

When norms are not observed and if the transgression is considered serious, group members will usually take measures to draw the deviant member back into line. The ultimate threat, of course, is rejection from the group. To the extent that membership in a particular group is important, such a threat can push the member to conform to the norms. Recall the group rejection that occurred in Schachter's (1951) discussion groups when the "deviate" was ultimately excluded from the group discussion (see Chapter 6).

Group decision-making

Groups are often faced with decisions involving choosing among actions that carry varying degrees of risk. Near the end of the 1960s, group risk-taking became a major research area in North American social psychology. Studies generally examined hypothetical situations. Typically, a group of participants (usually four) would begin by individually filling out questionnaires. Each item describes a person forced to decide between pursuing an attractive but risky outcome or a less attractive but more certain outcome (see Table 12–1). The participant was to indicate the minimum probability of success required before she would recommend the riskier choice. The participants then discussed the situation and were instructed to reach a unanimous group decision (consensus). Individual participants then filled out a new copy of the same questionnaire. The measures of interest were as follows: (1) the differences between individuals' initial choices and the consensus position of the group; and (2) the differences between individuals' initial and final choices.

Numerous experiments demonstrated that both the group decision and the average of the individuals' final decisions were more "risky" than the individuals' initial decisions. The **risky shift effect** was found not only with participants in Canada and the United States but also with participants in several European countries and New Zealand. Even when the experimental situations involved real monetary gain or loss for the participants or when the participants were risking painful shocks, the "risky shift" was still observed (Bem, Wallach & Kogan, 1965).

Both group discussion and the necessity of consensus play critical roles in the risky shift phenomenon. Kogan and Wallach (1964) found that groups only showed the risky shift when they were required to reach consensus through discussion. The shift did not occur among groups that discussed the situation but were not required to reach consensus before restating their individual decisions or among groups that voted with no discussion. Initial divergence of opinion among group members is also necessary for the shift to occur (Moscovici & Zavolloni, 1969).

Various explanations have been offered for the risky shift. Diffusion of responsibility (recall Chapter 9) has been suggested: in a group, each member may feel less personally responsible for the decision (Kogan & Wallach, 1967). It has also been suggested that since risk-taking is valued in Western society, discussion will produce more arguments favouring risk than favouring prudence. Not wanting to look stodgy and conservative, members will opt for the riskier proposals (Brown, 1965).

However, the shift towards risk is only a specific example of a much more general phenomenon: **group-induced attitude polarization**. In a wide variety of situations, group decisions are found to be more extreme than the initial decisions of the individuals involved and in the direction of the views of the majority. Risky groups shift towards risk and cautious groups shift towards caution (Turner, Wetherell & Hogg, 1989). The group polarization effect is also evident in such situations as group aggression, in which individual tendencies towards aggressiveness are magnified by the group and bystander intervention when helping is inhibited in group situations because individuals want to avoid looking foolish.

The sources of polarization

What accounts for group polarization? Why does the group shift away from the *average* attitude in the group? Research has focused on three possible explanations.

SOCIAL COMPARISON The social comparison interpretation of the polarization effect assumes that individuals try to see themselves and present themselves to others in as favourable a light as possible; this is called a **self-enhancement bias** (Krueger, 1998). To that end, they carefully observe how others act or express themselves and tend to shift in the direction in which the group is perceived to be leaning.

PERSUASIVE ARGUMENTATION Group discussion has been suggested as the source of the polarization effect. Individuals in a group discussion are exposed to arguments for and against a particular position and, according to this view, a group shift will occur only if members present persuasive arguments new to the other individuals. The direction of any group shift will depend upon the preponderance of persuasive and novel argumentation in one direction or the other (Isenberg, 1986).

SOCIAL IDENTIFICATION As discussed earlier, social identification is a process whereby individuals define themselves with respect to other people and conform to the norms and stereotypes associated with their

TABLE 12-1

Sample item from the Choice Dilemmas Questionnaire

Mr. E is the president of a light metals corporation in the United States. The corporation is quite prosperous and has strongly considered the possibilities of business expansion by building an additional plant in a new location. The choice is between building another plant in the U.S., where there would be a moderate return on initial investment, or building a plant in a foreign country. Lower labour costs and easy access to raw materials in that country would mean a much higher return on the initial investment. On the other hand, there is a history of political instability and revolution in the foreign country under consideration. In fact, the leader of a small minority party is committed to nationalizing—that is, taking over—all foreign investments.

Imagine that you are advising Mr. E. Listed below are several probabilities or odds of continued political stability in the foreign country under consideration.

Please check the lowest probability that you would consider acceptable for Mr. E's corporation to build a plant in that country.

___ The chances are 1 in 10 that the foreign country will remain politically stable.
___ The chances are 3 in 10 that the foreign country will remain politically stable.
___ The chances are 5 in 10 that the foreign country will remain politically stable.
___ The chances are 7 in 10 that the foreign country will remain politically stable.
___ The chances are 9 in 10 that the foreign country will remain politically stable.
___ Place a check here if you think Mr. E's corporation should not build a plant in the foreign country, no matter what the probabilities.

Source: Kogan & Wallach, 1964

group. Thus, someone in a decision-making group may reason as follows: "I am a police officer, I am part of a group and I don't want to lose status in it or be rejected by departing too far from the others; the others will take a risky stance because police are brave and take many risks all the time." According to this explanation, individuals hold a stereotype of their group as more extreme than it actually is and are motivated to conform to the perceived extreme group norm.

There has been empirical support for all three explanations (Isenberg, 1986; Mackie, 1986). Which explanation is most accurate probably depends on the particular situation and on the personalities of the individuals. For example, the persuasive argumentation view applies when rational evaluation of input is likely. However, persuasion will be less effective if members are emotionally involved with the issue, since they may already have examined most possible arguments.

Social Power

Within any group, especially a task-oriented group, some members enjoy much more power than others. Similarly, some groups have more power than others. Power refers to a person's or group's capacity to influence another person or group in a direction desired by the first (Pruitt, 1976). In its most primitive form, as exhibited, for example, by the bully in a school, power derives from physical might.

Power has always interested and intrigued social scientists and philosophers and some of them have even argued that it should be the primary focus of the social sciences. To quote the English philosopher Bertrand Russell (1962): "I shall be concerned to prove that the fundamental concept in social science is Power, in the same sense in which Energy is the fundamental concept in physics" (Pollard et al., 1972, p. 9).

While power has not so far attained such an important position in social psychological theory, various theories of social power have been developed. Six major sources or "types" of power have been discussed in the literature (Stahelski & Frost, 1989; Hinkin & Shriesheim, 1989; Raven, Schwarzwald & Koslowsky, 1998).

REWARD POWER One person can reward another (via money, approval, love, etc.) for complying. A mother can lead her son to clean up his room by promising him some chocolate cake as a reward. If the boy wants

the cake and has no other way of obtaining it, he will probably do what his mother has asked.

COERCIVE POWER One can punish another for noncompliance. The same mother can threaten her child with a spanking if he does not clean up his room. Since she is bigger than he is, she can carry through on the threat.

LEGITIMATE POWER Legitimate authorities (teachers, police) exercise their duties. Individuals comply with the demands of such people by accepting their authority. While such power is ultimately backed up by coercive power, if the individual has internalized the respect for designated authorities, no coercion is necessary.

EXPERT POWER Individuals who have important and special knowledge offer guidance. We follow the orders of a physician not because of coercion but because we believe that the physician knows more than we do about how to maintain our health.

INFORMATIONAL POWER "People in the know" (newspaper editors, governmental press secretaries, university professors) provide or withhold information (Pruitt, 1976).

REFERENT POWER Individuals exact obedience from followers who want to be like them. If you are a member of a political party and you admire and respect the party leader, you will probably do as the leader says because you assume it is appropriate and because you want to act as the leader does.

These forms of power are not mutually exclusive; they can reside in the same individual. More research still needs to be done to substantiate this classification of sources of power and the list is not necessarily exhaustive. For example, Pruitt (1976) adds _reciprocal power_ to the list: the influence one person has over another as a result of having helped the person in the past. The norm of reciprocity often leads to an obligation to return the favour. Various studies have shown that the strength of this norm varies not only from person to person but as a function of the situation. For example, a politician may help other politicians (possibly by supporting their cause in a debate) with the goal of gaining "political IOUs" to call in when he needs support.

Stahelski and Frost (1989) measured how often the various forms of power were used in three different organizations. They found that in all the organizations, referent and expert power were employed significantly more often than were legitimate, reward and coercive power. However, they also noted that as the number of employees supervised increased, the use of coercive power increased.

Despite the real power many of us wield in our relationships, only a few people rise to positions of power within an institution (e.g., a company or a government). Power in the institutional setting can be vast. Henry Kissinger once referred to power as "the greatest aphrodisiac," while others have viewed power as having a corrupting influence: in the words of Lord Acton, "Power tends to corrupt, and absolute power corrupts absolutely." We often both admire those who have such power and regard them with some suspicion.

It is sometimes disappointing to see the changes that power can bring to an individual's personality. Being surrounded by flatterers and sycophants can easily lead the individual to magnify his or her own abilities. In addition, power often demands a changed perspective. While an employee may be very considerate of others, if she becomes a manager, it may be necessary to step on some people's toes in order to carry out the job of managing the department. A prime minister who is unwilling to be firm and decisive in dealing with incompetent subordinates will be accused of weakness. It is also easier to influence others by maintaining a psychological distance from them and avoiding emotional involvement ("the loneliness of command"). This may lead to the perception by subordinates that the person who has assumed power has changed and lost interest in them. Moreover, the power holder may begin to take more and more credit for the accomplishments of the "underlings," thereby devaluing their efforts and abilities. Gradually, harmonious interpersonal relationships may become more and more difficult to maintain.

The effects of power on the relationship between the power holder and those subject to that power were demonstrated in an experiment carried out by Kipnis (1972). Participants were individually given the role of a "manager" who was in charge of some "workers" said to be in another room. In fact, there were no workers. The manager could speak to the "workers" but was told that the workers would not be able to respond. The manager's task was to maximize the workers' "output."

Every three minutes, pre-programmed "output records" were brought from the (nonexistent) worker to the manager. In one condition, managers were given "power" to give rewards (extra pay) or punishments (deduction from pay) or to transfer the worker to a more boring job. In a second condition, no such power was available.

As predicted, researchers found the following:

- Participants with power made more attempts to influence the workers than did those without it. Very few participants (16 percent) relied solely on persuasion: most used the power at their disposal. The presence of power seemed to bring about its use.
- Participants with power devalued the worth of their workers more than did participants without power, and they were more likely to attribute the workers' efforts to a desire to obtain pay. Only 28 percent of those with power versus 72 percent of those without it viewed the workers' performance as a self-motivated effort to do a good job.
- Psychological distance, as measured by the stated willingness to meet with the workers after the study, was greater among those with power. Seventy-nine percent of those without power but only 35 percent of those with power expressed a desire to meet socially with the workers.

These findings support the view that power over others, at least in an institutionalized setting, leads both to devaluation of the efforts of those subject to the power and to increased psychological distance from them. However, remember that in this study there was no resistance by the "workers." Possibly when the influence of the power holder is actively resisted, devaluation does not occur so readily.

For historical reasons, women have had difficulty achieving positions of power (see Chapter 13). Moreover, gender-role stereotypes that associate power with men and not with women may lead to women not being given the opportunity to wield power and to their being perceived as having less power than they actually have (Ragins & Sundstrom, 1989). (Read again Margaret Atwood's statement at the beginning of this chapter). It also appears that men are more likely than women are to use expert and **legitimate power**, whereas women are more likely to use referent power, no doubt reflecting the historic power imbalance between men and women. This means that women develop different strategies than men to influence others. If they try to use reward or coercive methods, which are not expected from women, such methods may not be effective (Carli, 1999). Some women may also feel that power is incompatible with femininity and thus avoid situations and positions that involve the use of power. Such behaviour, of course, will only prolong the life of the stereotype.

Leadership

We began the chapter by referring to leadership, and now the focus shifts back to that subject. Power and influence in a group are usually distributed across the membership, sometimes uniformly, especially in social groups. Yet there is often one person who is more influential than the others. This person, designated or not, is the **leader**. The difference between leader and follower in terms of influence may, however, only be one of degree. Indeed, a group may have more than one leader at the same time. One group member having the most knowledge about how to achieve the group goal may serve as the task leader, while another member may be more influential in getting members to coordinate their efforts. Another member may play the key role of maintaining cohesiveness by helping sort out emotional situations that arise (Hamblin, 1958).

Moreover, the person chosen to be the formal "head" of a group may not be the actual leader. Heads are usually imposed from outside while leaders emerge from within. If you are a soldier under the command of a weak sergeant who is laughed at by others in your unit, it may happen that someone else whose competence is more respected—a corporal, for example—becomes your real leader. The sergeant may have legitimate power, but the corporal's referent power will be much more effective in managing the unit. Gradually, the sergeant may come to recognize this and actually yield to the implicit power of the corporal.

Rush and Russell (1988) have shown that individuals in varying situations have similar prototypes regarding how a leader should (or should not) act. When asked to describe their ideas of an effective and an ineffective leader, participants consistently emphasized four dimensions of leader behaviour: (1) *initiating structure* (letting followers know what is expected); (2) *consideration* (concern for the comfort and well-being of followers); (3) *role assumption* (the active exercise of the leadership role); and (4) *production emphasis* (pressure for productive output).

Exactly how a person comes to be a leader is a question that social psychologists have been studying for many years without finding a totally satisfying answer.

A related question concerns whether a person who becomes a leader in one set of circumstances is likely to become a leader in another.

Characteristics of the leader

Great leaders have shaped history, it has often been said. Indeed, we often think of historical eras in terms of their leading figures: Genghis Khan, Charlemagne, Joan of Arc, Napoleon, Catherine the Great, Churchill, Nehru, Mao to name but a few. What is it that made such leaders so remarkable? Was it their character that led to their rise to greatness or was it their situation—did they just happen to be in the right place at the right time? These possibilities, referred to in the literature as the *great person* (or *trait*) *approach* and the *situational approach*, have been explored in considerable detail by social psychologists. A more recent view, the *interactionist approach*, holds that both traits and situation are important.

The great person approach

In the 19th century, Francis Galton investigated the hereditary background of "great men" and attempted to explain leadership on the basis of inherited capability (Stogdill, 1974). Good leaders, he assumed, were born and not made. Can hereditary influences on personal characteristics determine leadership capability?

Although this question has been studied in detail, there has been little empirical evidence to support the great person view of leadership. Yet, a study (Albright & Forziati, 1995) showed that leaders in one task were

Successful leadership demands good communication skills.

also likely to lead in other, different tasks and, in addition, that an individual who was a leader in one group also was likely to become a leader in other groups made up of different people. This suggests that there may be a set of traits associated with leadership. Indeed, a number of traits are correlated with becoming a leader:

- *Intelligence* seems to have the strongest relationship with leadership. This is not surprising since leadership is achieved at least partly on the basis of the leader's ability to provide followers with something they cannot provide for themselves. Yet, if the gap in intelligence between the leader and followers is too great, the followers may become dissatisfied since they cannot identify with the leader and may have difficulty following his or her reasoning (Gibb, 1969).

- There is also evidence of modest positive correlations between leadership and *physical size*, *health* and *physical attractiveness*. Are these correlations due to the visual impact of such traits on followers? Or do they have an early and indirect effect on personality by influencing the reactions of other people? A tall person, for example, may develop greater self-confidence as a result of being given more respect for physical prowess. Steadily maturing self-confidence, rather than height itself, might then be responsible for the leadership capacity. Indeed, leaders generally rate higher than followers in terms of self-confidence (Gibb, 1969).

- Another leadership characteristic that has been confirmed consistently is *talkativeness*. The group member who talks the most is most likely to be chosen as leader (Mullen, Salas & Driskell, 1989), a phenomenon that has been observed in India as well as in the United States (Janowski & Malloy, 1992; Ruback & Dabbs, 1988). Why should talkativeness be associated with leadership? Perhaps participation rate is perceived as a measure of how motivated the person is to be a member of the group and to assist the group in achieving its goals. Participation also allows individuals to demonstrate their relevant expertise and leadership characteristics. Perhaps this salience leads people to identify the high participator as the leader. Conversely, people who are shy and thus have a low rate of participation may not be perceived to have leadership qualities or may be thought to be lower in intelligence.

- Individuals who are *high in the need and willingness to dominate others* have also been found to be more likely to emerge as leaders in small groups (Nyquist & Spence, 1986).

The quest for a relationship between personality and leadership continues. One study followed Canadian Forces officer candidates over a four-year period (Bradley, Nicole, Charbonneau & Meyer, 2002). At the end of six to nine months it was found that ratings of leadership were predicted by *internal locus of control*, *dominance* and *energy level*. Overall, dominance was the most significant predictor of who would be identified as a leader.

Even though these traits discussed above have shown some correlation with the emergence of leadership, their overall influence is not great and the trait approach has not succeeded in providing a satisfactory explanation as to why some people emerge as leaders and others do not.

The situational approach

Another approach to leadership is based on the idea that different situations call for different kinds of leaders and that the person who happens to have those traits and abilities needed at a particular time will emerge as leader. For example, Churchill was a great wartime leader but lost the election following the war. Postwar Britain, it seems, wanted a different kind of leader to rebuild the country. Leaders have more influence when a group is facing a crisis; however, the group is likely to look for a new leader if the old one cannot deal with the crisis (Hamblin, 1958).

The situational approach in contrast to the trait approach does not assume that a person who is a good leader in one situation will be a good leader in other situations. Not only do leaders influence followers, but followers also influence leaders and to be a successful leader an individual must be in tune with the expectations and needs of the followers (Hollander, 1992; Sims & Manz, 1984). Thus, successful leadership is a combination of "right leader" and "right situation"—in other words, an interaction between the characteristics of the leader and the characteristics of the situation.

The interactionist approach

So far, we have assumed that it is possible to evaluate whether a leader is an effective leader. But how should effectiveness be measured? Stogdill (1974) speaks of

Leadership and the Perception of Height

People tend to overestimate the height of people in high-status positions (Keyes, 1980). During the Trudeau era in Canadian politics, for example, most people believed that Trudeau was rather tall and certainly taller than then opposition leader Joe Clark. Students at the University of New Brunswick, when asked to estimate the heights of Trudeau and Clark, gave average estimates of 180 cm (six feet) for Trudeau and 172.7 cm (five feet eight inches) for Clark (Gillis, 1983). In reality, the opposite is the case.

Napoleon, whom the British referred to as the "little corporal," was not so little for the times. In fact, he was the same height as Nelson, 172.7 cm or five foot eight, which was the average height of a Frenchman in those days. Calling him "little" was a British putdown.

The height of adults is fairly stable, although we may shrink a little as we get older. However, a study (Higham & Carment, 1992) has shown that people adjust their estimates of tallness according to changes in the target's status and prestige.

People were asked to judge how tall Brian Mulroney, John Turner and Ed Broadbent were before and after the 1988 Canadian federal elec-

tion. Before the election, Turner was judged taller than Mulroney, and Broadbent was seen as the shortest. However after winning the election, Mulroney grew taller while Turner shrank, now giving Mulroney the edge over Turner. Broadbent, the other loser, was judged to be shorter still. Moreover, the taller the candidate, the more votes he obtained. According to their offices in Ottawa, Mulroney is 185 cm, Turner is 181.7 cm and Broadbent is 180 cm, the exact order of the election results. Similarly, it has been shown that U.S. presidents from 1905 to 1980 have been significantly taller than the runners-up.

More recent research has found that in the United States, taller people earn more money, at the rate of about U.S. $1500 per inch (Landsburg, 2003). Also, the benefits of height appear early according to Persico and Postlewaite (2002), who found that men shorter than their peers as adolescents earned less as adults even though they had subsequently grown taller.

Research involving the perception of height of women in high-status positions has never been done but would undoubtedly yield interesting results.

effectiveness in terms of the output of the group, the morale of the group and the degree to which the members are satisfied. In a task-oriented group, output may be the most important of these (Fiedler, 1967).

Early studies of leadership effectiveness focused on democratic and autocratic leadership styles. Democratic leadership, which involves group members in decision-making rather than emphasizing clear-cut orders, produces greater satisfaction among followers (Shaw, 1981). But does it lead to greater productivity? Some research has indicated that it does (Kahn & Katz, 1953); other researchers have reported that autocratic leadership is more effective in this regard (Hare, 1962). Further research has found that the situation itself is a key factor. Autocratic leadership

leads to greater productivity in stressful situations, while democratic leadership produces greater productivity in non-stressful circumstances (Rosenbaum & Rosenbaum, 1971). Thus, no one leadership style is likely to be effective in all situations.

Fiedler (1967, 1971, 1981) proposed a theory of leadership called **contingency theory**, based on the ideas that there are two basic styles of leadership (task-oriented and socio-emotional) and that the leader's effectiveness is contingent upon appropriate matching of the leadership style to the situation. The task-oriented leader will not be overly concerned with the feelings and personal needs of the followers. The socio-emotional leader may strive for good interpersonal relationships even at the cost of efficiency in attaining group goals. Style of leadership according to Fiedler reflects the basic drive of the individual and is very resistant to modification.

Contingency theory proposes that the best way to measure leadership orientation is to assess the leader's attitude towards the "least preferred co-worker" (LPC) in the group. The LPC is determined by asking the leader to indicate who, out of all the people he or she has ever encountered at work, was the most difficult to work with. Then the leader rates that person on a set of 18 pairs of bipolar adjectives (see Table 12–2), such as "boring–interesting," using an eight-point scale. If the leader rates the LPC in a negative way, he is a low-LPC leader; if the leader rates the LPC in a positive manner, he is a high-LPC leader. The high-LPC leader is assumed to be more people-oriented while the low-LPC leader is assumed to be more task-oriented.

In Fiedler's model, style of leadership interacts with *situational control*, the amount of control the leader can exert over the members of the group. This depends on a combination of three factors: (1) the affective relationship between leader and followers; (2) how highly structured the group's task is; and (3) the leader's power to reward or punish. Power is the least important of the three. The theory suggests that both the productivity and the morale of members will be increased when the leadership style matches the situational control (Chemers, 1983).

Task-oriented leadership should be most successful in situations that are either very favourable or very unfavourable for the leader. Under unfavourable leadership conditions (ambiguous task, poor leader–follower relations, low leader power), the group may be more receptive to a leader who can get them moving towards their goal; a person-oriented leader may spend too much time on trying to promote interpersonal harmony and not enough time on the group goal. When conditions are highly favourable (structured task, good leader–follower relations, high leader power), the task-oriented leader, content that the group is moving towards its goal, may become more attentive to the "people" concerns. On the other hand, a people-oriented leader in a situation already characterized by interpersonal harmony may now try to demonstrate that she is *really* a leader by pursuing self-aggrandizing activities. In so doing, the leader may actually lose some esteem while not being concerned enough with the task (Fiedler, 1971).

In intermediate conditions, friction between group members may become more serious and the person-oriented leader can do more to cope with the group's needs (see Figure 12–2).

The contingency model has received support from a large number of different studies (Strube & Garcia, 1981) and, despite continuing controversy, has been viewed as the most useful approach for ascertaining the effectiveness of leadership (Peters, Hartke & Pohlmann, 1985).

Transformational leadership

Pierre Trudeau was a *transformational leader* and his political life was distinguished by *charisma*. People admired him or detested him or both, but few were indifferent. Many of those who jumped on the Trudeau bandwagon in the days of Trudeaumania later grew disappointed with his performance. They had had a vision of a new leader who would uplift them, who would breathe new life and purpose into their nation—perhaps an impossible task for any person.

Weber (1947) coined the term "charismatic leader" (also referred to as a transformational leader). He described **charisma** (which is Greek for "divine gift") as an exceptional quality in a person, enabling him or her to gather a large number of disciples as a

TABLE 12-2 Sample LPC items	Leaders are asked to select the person whom they least liked as a co-worker in their whole careers and then to evaluate that person on a series of scales such as the following:								
	Friendly	8	7	6	5	4	3	2	1	Unfriendly
	Agreeable	8	7	6	5	4	3	2	1	Disagreeable
	Pleasant	8	7	6	5	4	3	2	1	Unpleasant
	Cooperative	8	7	6	5	4	3	2	1	Uncooperative
	Helpful	8	7	6	5	4	3.	2	1	Frustrating

By adding up the scale values, a total LPC score is derived. Rating the LPC in a negative way yields a low score; an individual producing such a rating is a *low-LPC leader*, while an individual who produces a high score is referred to as a *high-LPC leader*.

FIGURE 12-2

Contingency model of leadership and group performance

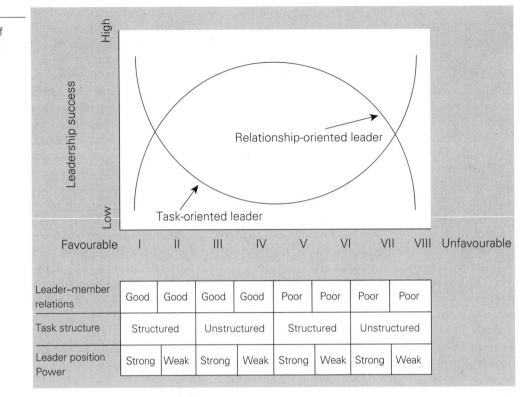

Leader–member relations	Good	Good	Good	Good	Poor	Poor	Poor	Poor
Task structure	Structured		Unstructured		Structured		Unstructured	
Leader position Power	Strong	Weak	Strong	Weak	Strong	Weak	Strong	Weak

result of appearing to possess supernatural, providential or extraordinary powers. Charismatic leadership is characterized by an intensely personal relationship between the leader and followers. The follower is inspired to unquestioned obedience, loyalty, commitment and devotion (Howell & Frost, 1989). In return, these leaders affect their followers in specific ways (Bass, 1990; Conger & Kanungo, 1998; Conger, Kanungo & Menon, 2000). They push their followers into acting in ways that go beyond personal self-interest and current needs, and inspire a vision of a better future, providing "transcendent" goals, often expressed in moral rhetoric. Because the leader has high expectations of the followers as well as confidence in them, the self-esteem of the followers is enhanced and they are motivated to achieve goals. (Of course, charisma is not always directed towards the good of followers; many cult leaders have been highly charismatic, using their powerful influence to indoctrinate followers into a highly authoritarian social structure that they control (Raubolt, 2003).)

Frequently, the phrases that embody the charismatic leader's vision enter the language. Consider Trudeau's speeches about a "Just Society"; Martin Luther King's civil rights utterances ("I have a dream …"); Churchill's depiction of the British as invincible ("We shall never surrender …"); Hitler's appeal to past and future German glory ("Germany awake!"); Gandhi's vision of an India free of British rule ("Quit India"); and John Kennedy's call to patriotism ("Ask not what your country can do for you …").

How do leaders come to wield such power over their followers? How are they capable of appealing to their followers on a raw emotional level? House (1977) argues that the charismatic leader is typified by a specific set of characteristics:

1. An extremely high level of self-confidence.

2. An extremely high level of dominance. Such leaders seem to have a strong need to influence others, which drives them to acquire the persuasive skills they need to do so.

3. An apparently strong conviction in the moral righteousness of their beliefs. However, House suggests that it is at least possible that some charismatic leaders believe neither in themselves nor in their beliefs but are capable of acting as

though they do. Certainly, there have been charismatic religious leaders who were later shown to be manipulators using their charismatic abilities for their own ends.

To these can be added a fourth point:

4. Personal characteristics such as charm, originality and speech fluency (Sashkin, 1977).

The charismatic leader often provides a role model and a value system for the followers that are effective even after the leader's death. Even today, Gandhi is respected and admired and his teachings are followed by millions of East Indians and non-East Indians.

Yet, charisma may not reside solely in the leader but depend on the relationship between a leader who possesses charismatic qualities, a follower who is receptive to charisma and a situation that is conducive to charisma (Klein & House, 1998). The charismatic leader often emerges in a time of stress, and he or she most often epitomizes the deeply held feelings of the followers. As the situation changes, the charismatic leader may lose his or her appeal. Once the stress is lifted, the public can quickly throw off its fascination for the leader.

Gender and leadership

Traditionally, leadership has been the prerogative of males. Research indicates that even now, despite some advances in the quest for the elimination of sexual discrimination, males do predominate in leadership roles. Indeed, men and women alike are inclined to look towards males rather than females for leadership (Eagly & Karau, 1991). This is not surprising given that children grow up in a patriarchal society where the father is traditionally invested with ultimate authority in the family.

Women continue to face a number of obstacles to becoming leaders in mixed-sex groups. There is perhaps, above all else, the expectation held by many men and women that women are not "suited" to leadership. Sexual stereotypes describe men as capable of being tough, assertive, brave and commanding respect, while stereotypes of women emphasize not only their gentleness but weakness, fickleness and submissiveness. Not only is it more difficult for women to assume leadership positions in mixed-sex groups, but when they do, they are scrutinized more carefully. Ironically, female subordinates of female leaders in mixed-sex groups have been found to be more negative towards these leaders than are male subordinates of the same

leaders (Eagly & Karau, 1991). In other words, the successful woman has to struggle against the negative attitudes of both sexes.

These sexual stereotypes combined with the socially inferior position of women result in even more trouble for female leaders: they are not likely to receive the same treatment as male leaders from other people (both male and female) of equal or greater stature in the power hierarchy. Their viewpoints are less likely to be given attention in meetings and they are more likely to be interrupted when speaking, even by other women. This negative evaluation is especially likely to occur if a woman employs a masculine leadership style (tough, decisive, aggressive) (Eagly, Makhijani & Klonsky, 1992). Moreover, since the leadership role has traditionally been defined in terms of this masculine stereotype, women who do succeed in leadership positions may experience a conflict between that role and their "femininity," a conflict not experienced by men.

Yet despite the history of discrimination, women are moving more and more into leadership roles in government and industry and are becoming an increasingly significant force at the highest levels of world leadership (Adler, 1999a). Indeed, globalization of industry and communication networks may require leadership that differs significantly from other forms of leadership. Rather than leading a single group or society, the global leader has to deal with the differing goals, expectations and cultural values of many groups and societies. It has been argued that the "feminine" qualities often associated with female leaders such as greater interpersonal sensitivity and concern and a desire to compromise rather than dominate are needed to meet many of the challenges posed by positions of global leadership (Adler, 1999b).

Do men and women actually lead differently? After many years of research into the relationship of gender to leadership, all that safely can be concluded is that the appearance of gender differences in leadership is determined by the situation in which the leadership occurs (Butterfield & Grinnell, 1999). For example, in one study (Gardiner & Tiggemann, 1999), women more often than men adopted an interpersonally oriented leadership style when working in a female-dominated industry, while no such differences between men and women were found in male-dominated industries. Nonetheless, in male-dominated industries, women who adopted an interpersonal leadership style reported greater stress and poorer mental health than did those who did not, whereas in those same male-dominated industries, men who chose an interpersonal style actually reported better mental health than did males who did not. Thus, the effects of gender on leadership style and the ultimate consequences for the leader depend on situational variables—not just on gender. As a result, men are more effective in positions defined in masculine terms (for example, in the armed services) and women are more effective in situations that require a less autocratic, more participative style (for example, in education and social service organizations) (Eagly, Karau, & Makhijani, 1995).

In the future, we shall no doubt see many more female leaders. It was only in 1957 that Ellen Fairclough became Canada's first female cabinet minister; now having (a few) women in the cabinet is relatively commonplace. Subsequently, Rita Johnson became the first female premier of a province (British Columbia, 1980); Catherine Callbeck the first elected female premier (P.E.I., 1993); Audrey McLaughlin the first female to lead a national party (NDP, 1989); Kim Campbell the first female prime minister (1993); and Jeanne Sauvé the first female Governor General (1994). In 2000, Governor General Adrienne Clarkson swore into office the first ever female Chief Justice of Canada, the Right Honourable Justice Beverley McLachlin.

Yet at least in politics, progress is slow, as the data in Table 12–3 attest. These are partial results of a 2003 survey of the percentage of women in 181 national bodies of government. Canada ranks thirty-sixth. Only in nine countries do women hold more than one-third of the parliamentary seats. The report also points out that, overall, women hold only 15.4 percent of parliamentary seats, not much higher than the 14.6 percent in 1988, and about the same as in the 1970s (Inter-Parliamentary Union, 2003).

A Final Note

Originally, social psychologists pursued twin interests in the area of groups: group processes as they influenced the *individual* in the group (the "individualistic" approach), and how groups interrelate and mutually influence each other (the "systems" approach). However, beginning in the 1960s and continuing to the present, the dominant approach in North America, almost to the total exclusion of the systems approach,

TABLE 12-3

The percentage of women in national parliaments

Rank	Country	Total Seats	Women	Percentage
1	Sweden	349	158	45.3
2	Denmark	179	68	38.0
3	Finland	200	75	37.5
5	Norway	165	60	36.4
6	Cuba	609	219	36.0
10	Germany	603	194	32.2
24	Australia	150	38	25.3
26	Switzerland	200	46	23.0
31	China	2979	650	21.8
36	Canada	301	62	20.6
49	United Kingdom	659	118	17.9
59	United States	435	62	14.3
65	France	574	70	12.2
98	Japan	480	35	7.3
125	Yemen	301	1	0.3
126	Saudi Arabia	120	0	0.0

Source: Inter-Parliamentary Union, 2003

has been individualistic. In many ways this reflects the predominant ideology of the United States (Sampson, 1977), in which group relations are considered an extension of the psychology of interpersonal relations. Systems concerns, such as those associated with international conflict, have mainly been left to sociologists and political scientists (Brewer & Kramer, 1985). North American social psychologists, more so than Europeans and Asians, continue to be preoccupied with the reactions of individuals to events that occur in the group context.

Summary

1. In any society, individuals define themselves largely in terms of groups and social categories.

2. We construct our social world in terms of social categories and govern our behaviour according to the salient category in a particular situation.

3. One basic construct is the distinction we make between the in-group and the out-group. A "generic norm" of discrimination against an out-group leads to discrimination even in the absence of self-interest or pre-existing hostility towards the out-group.

4. Individuals tend to see members of one category as more similar than they really are and the differences between members of different categories as greater than they really are (social differentiation).

5. Since individuals belong to different categories simultaneously, some being in-groups and others being out-groups, this leads to categories that reduce discrimination.

6. When we are at a disadvantage relative to people of another category, we tend to minimize that disadvantage by either assimilating into that group or differentiating ourselves from them in terms of other criteria.

7. Mutual interaction and influence, ongoing and relatively stable relationships, shared goals and the perception of belonging to a group are the defining characteristics of groups.

8. People join groups to accomplish goals and to satisfy needs for affiliation. These factors contribute to group cohesiveness.

9. Within a group, members may assume various roles, and norms regulate their behaviour.

10. Group decisions tend to be more polarized than do individual decisions. Three explanations have been suggested: social comparison, persuasive argumentation and social identification.

11. Leadership has been explained in terms of the traits of the leader, characteristics of the situation, and the interaction of leader and group characteristics.

12. Fiedler's contingency model of leadership effectiveness relates the characteristics of the group to task-oriented and relationship-oriented leadership styles.

13. Leaders described as transformational or "charismatic" tend to be self-confident and dominant with strong convictions; they provide their followers with transcendent goals and a model for values.

Further Reading

BASS, B.M. (1981). *Stogdill's handbook of leadership*. New York: Free Press. A broad-based review of all aspects of leadership, theoretical and empirical.

CONGER, J.A. & KANUNGO, R.N. (1998). *Charismatic leadership in organizations*. Thousand Oaks, CA: Sage Publications. Comparisons, with supporting evidence, of a number of theories of charismatic leadership. Includes examples of charismatic leaders.

MUGNY, G. & PEREZ, J.A. (1991). *The social psychology of minority influence*. New York: Cambridge University Press. A European perspective on minority influences on social processes.

PAULUS, P.B. (1989). *Psychology of group influence* (2nd ed.). Hillsdale, NJ: Erlbaum. A thorough analysis of all aspects of group life.

POWELL, G.N. et al. (Eds.). (1999). *Handbook of gender and work*. Thousand Oaks, CA: Sage Publications. An extensive review of the literature on many aspects of the relationship between gender and work. Both practical and theoretical.

SANDYS, C. & LITTMAN, J. (2003). *We shall not fail: The inspirational leadership of Winston Churchill*. East Rutherford, NJ: Penguin U.S.A. An insightful and interesting account of Churchill's very deliberate approach to leadership and the lessons he learned. Co-authored by his granddaughter.

TAJFEL, H. (Ed.). (1978). *Differentiation between social groups: Studies in the social psychology of intergroup relations*. London: Academic Press. The European perspective on social categorization.

WORCHEL, S. & AUSTIN, W.G. (Eds.). (1986). *Psychology of intergroup relations*. Chicago: Nelson-Hall. A discussion of theory and research related to the structure and resolution of intergroup and intragroup conflict.

 Weblinks

Group Dynamics Resource Page
www.vcu.edu/hasweb/group/gdynamic.htm

Center for Leadership Studies
cls.binghamton.edu

Chapter 13

Prejudice, Discrimination and Sexism

There are, in every age, new errors to be rectified and new prejudices to be opposed.

Samuel Johnson (1709–1784)

Prejudice is opinion without judgment.

Voltaire (1694–1778)

Whatever women do they must do twice as well as men to be
thought half as good. Luckily this is not difficult.

Charlotte Whitton (former mayor of Ottawa)

Chapter Outline

The Nature of Prejudice

The cognitive component: Stereotypes
Are stereotypes accurate?
Illusory correlation and stereotypes
The activation of stereotypes
The affective component of prejudice
Discrimination: The behavioural
    component of prejudice
Reverse discrimination
Relationships among the three
    components

Acquisition of Prejudice

Innate or acquired?
Conflict between groups
Learning
Teachers and schools
The media
Peer groups

The Reduction of Prejudice

Intergroup contact
Acculturation and multiculturalism
Education

The Victims of Prejudice

Sexism

Summary

On January 4, 1998, 65-year-old Nirmal Singh Gill, the caretaker at the Guru Nanak Sikh temple in Surrey, B.C., was found bleeding in the temple parking lot; he died in hospital a few hours later. He had been brutally beaten by five young men who had chosen to attack him simply because he was a member of a non-white minority. His killers belonged to a local neo-Nazi/skinhead/white supremacist group. Taped conversations later obtained by undercover officers revealed that one of the men was "proud" of what he had done; another said he had done it for pleasure; another commented that he had done his "good" for his lifetime. Nirmal Singh Gill was killed not because of anything he had said or done; his assailants did not even know him. He died because of his assailants' anger and loathing for people whose skin is not white.

Racist groups are found throughout the world; they go by various names: skinheads, Aryan Nations, al Qaeda, white supremacists, Ku Klux Klan, Church of the Creator. Dedicated to spreading prejudice and hatred against racial minorities, they have linked up with similar groups in other countries and now exploit the Internet to disseminate their prejudice. The white supremacist Heritage Front, which calls itself "Canada's largest racialist group," has several chapters across Canada along with a telephone hotline, a Web site and a magazine with about 1000 subscribers. Their meetings in Toronto regularly attract audiences of 200 or more. Such activity has moved the government of Canada to add a new clause to the *Criminal Code* that allows judges to hand down more severe sentences for crimes motivated by racial hatred.

While Canada is a relatively tolerant society, it is not free of prejudice. Mosques and synagogues are subjected to threats and vandalism. Women are subjected to physical threat and demeaning actions. People who are poor or homeless are often subjected to ridicule and insensitivity. Gays and lesbians are subjected to discrimination, contempt and occasional physical attacks. Immigrants who speak an accented English or French may be subjected to rejection and mockery.

Prejudice is defined as a positive or negative attitude based on information or knowledge that is either illogical, unrelated to reality or a distortion of fact, and that is unjustifiably generalized to all the members of a group. Although prejudice can be either favourable or unfavourable, psychologists use the term almost exclusively in the negative sense.

To be prejudiced then means to prejudge a person based on which group he or she is seen to belong to and what characteristics one associates with that group. Prejudices about individuals or groups are usually developed on the basis of perceived differences of one or more characteristics or traits. These differences need not be only about race. There is prejudice against people based on their national origin, language or accent, social status, age or sexual orientation. In other words, any characteristic that in some way sets a person or persons apart from others is potentially the basis for a categorization that may ultimately lead to prejudice. Once persons have identified themselves as belonging to one group (the *in-group*) and others as belonging to another group (the *out-group*) regardless of the original reasons for this *social categorization*, they will expect to find *intergroup* differences and will go so far as to create them if necessary (Tajfel & Turner, 1979). Moreover, they will probably overestimate *intragroup* similarity (see Chapter 12).

The Nature of Prejudice

As with other attitudes, prejudice can be thought of as comprising the following components: cognitive, affective and behavioural.

The cognitive component: Stereotypes

The beliefs that make up the *cognitive* component of prejudice are called **stereotypes** (see Chapter 2). The term is usually attributed to the United States journalist Walter Lippman (1922), who borrowed it from the lexicon of the printing industry to describe "pictures in the head" about members of a group. However, Rudmin (1989) points out that the English author James Morier was the first to use the word stereotype to describe human behaviour, in his book *The Adventures of Hajji Baba* (1824).

Stereotypes are cognitions concerning the members of a particular group. These cognitions are usually simple, often over-generalized and frequently inaccurate, although not *necessarily* incorrect or illogical (Taylor & Lalonde, 1987). In one sense, stereotypes serve a useful purpose in that they help us deal more efficiently with our environment. They can be thought of as cognitive "energy-saving devices" (Macrae, Milne & Bodenhausen, 1994). For example, consider how complicated it would be if every new person you met would have to be considered as a separate entity instead of being included in some general category such as teenager, nun, construction worker or professor. By invoking your stereotype—placing the newcomer into some category—you can begin the interaction as though you already know quite a bit about the person. If we know that a person comes from Mexico or Chile, we can be quite certain that the person will speak Spanish.

In the context of prejudice, stereotypes are generally negative: Stereotypes can refer to any characteristics of individuals including appearance ("Homosexuals are effeminate"), aptitude ("Blacks are good dancers"), personality ("Italians are gregarious") and attitude ("The French are anti-Semitic"), none of which are generally correct.

Key characteristics (real or imagined) used to differentiate among groups are called *diagnostic attributes*. For example, identifying Scots as intelligent would not be very useful in terms of distinguishing Scots from others since many ethnic or national groups such as the English, Americans and Canadians are stereotyped in this manner. However, people may seize on what they perceive as different about a group, whether accurate or not, such as the Scots being parsimonious. This would be more useful because it sets the Scots apart from the English, Americans and Canadians (Ford & Stangor, 1992). Stereotypes are more than abstractions about group categories. They can act as "cognitive filters" through which we select what information to use, what to ignore and how to interpret it. Bodenhausen (1988) and Macrae et al. (1998) have found that people paid more attention to and were better able to recall information that was consistent with their stereotypes than inconsistent information, which was neglected. In addition to stereotypes about specific attributes of the members of a group, we may also have more abstract, **symbolic beliefs**—beliefs which imply that a group threatens (or upholds) social values and norms (Esses, Haddock & Zanna, 1993; Donakowski & Esses, 1996).

Three important aspects of stereotypes are as follows: pervasiveness, persistence and accuracy.

Pervasiveness

Do the residents of Newfoundland, Saskatchewan and British Columbia maintain similar beliefs about the members of particular out-groups? Unfortunately, there is little information on this question, but it would be unwise to assume, for example, that stereotypes about Ukrainian Canadians in Manitoba, where they reside in large numbers, would be the same as the stereotypes in Cape Breton, where many locals have probably never met a Ukrainian. A classic study conducted in the United States (Allport & Kramer, 1946) found that attitudes about blacks and Jews in a part of South Dakota where almost no blacks and Jews lived were more negative than attitudes in one of the eastern states. Berry and Kalin (1993, 1995) asked respondents in Montreal, Toronto and Vancouver how comfortable they would feel being around individuals from a number of groups, first, if these individuals were immigrants to Canada, and second, if these individuals had been born and raised in Canada. The results, based on a scale of 1 to 7, are presented in Figures 13–1 and 13–2. "Comfort levels"—and by inference, attitudes—vary considerably among the three cities, with Montreal being the least positive.

Persistence

How stable are stereotypes? Do they change readily or do they last over long periods of time? As with attitudes in general, stereotypes are often modified over time. Obvious examples can be found in the characterization of the Japanese or Germans during the Second World War, and today, Arabs when terrorist incidents may occur. As might be expected, stereotypes about the outgroup become more negative in the face of overt conflict such as war, but other less aggressive forms of conflict—economic and social—can have similar effects.

Not surprisingly, governments facing increasing unemployment usually curtail immigration. Canadians generally are tolerant towards immigration. However, if there is a perceived competition for resources such as jobs, attitudes towards immigration and immigrants may become more negative (Berry, Kalin & Taylor, 1977; Esses, Jackson & Armstrong, 1998). This relationship

is clearly indicated in Figure 13–3 on page 362. (See also Table 13–1.) Palmer (1996) notes that surveys do not support the proposition that all opposition to immigration is based on racism. Indeed, the strongest opposition comes from younger people concerned with jobs and careers, although they are more tolerant as a group than older people.

In three classic U.S. studies (Katz & Braly, 1933; Gilbert, 1951; Karlins, Coffman & Walters, 1969)—often referred to as the "Princeton trilogy studies" because they were carried out at Princeton University using a common procedure but across a span of 36 years—subjects were asked to select from an extensive list of traits those that best described the members of each of 10 ethnic groups: Americans, Chinese, English, Germans, Irish, Italians, Japanese, Jews, Turks and blacks. The traits most frequently assigned to blacks by Katz and Braly's subjects in 1933 were "superstitious," "lazy," "happy-go-lucky," "ignorant" and "musical." As shown in Table 13–2 on page 362, over the years fewer people endorsed "superstitious" and "lazy," while more endorsed "musical."

Does this mean that stereotypes of blacks in the United States have lost their impact? Not necessarily.

FIGURE 13-1

Ratings for members of ethnic groups who were born in Canada

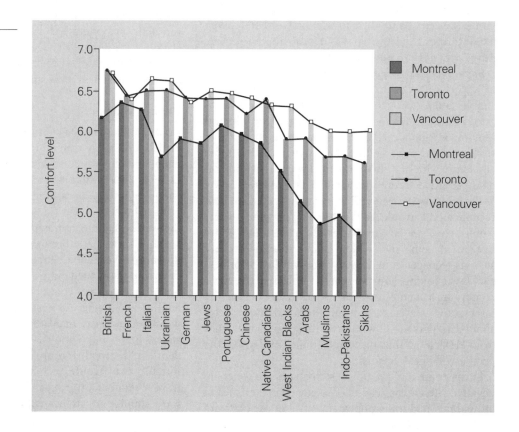

FIGURE 13-2

Ratings for members of ethnic groups who had immigrated to Canada

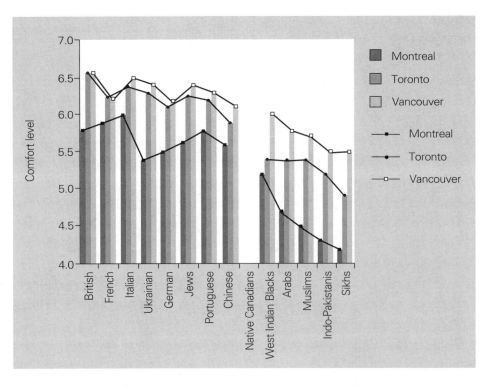

First, these data were obtained from university students who do not necessarily represent the general population. Second, we do not know whether other equally derogatory characteristics have taken the place of the old ones. Third, social desirability bias may have had some effect (see Chapter 1). Do the responses reflect the person's true feelings or were they responding as expected? To test this possibility, Sigall and Page (1971) replicated the Karlins et al. study but used a procedure—they hooked up subjects to a bogus lie detector—that led half the subjects to believe any lies they told would be detected. Subjects who believed that lies would be detected gave considerably more negative evaluations.

A study by Devine and Elliot (1995) also suggests that certain stereotypes have not faded. They repeated the Princeton trilogy study with Caucasian undergradu-

TABLE 13-1

Public opinion on immigration into Canada

Do you agree strongly, agree somewhat, disagree somewhat or disagree strongly that overall there is too much immigration into Canada?

	Total %	Atlantic %	Quebec %	Ontario %	West %	18–29 %	Over 60 %	University educated %	Professionals/ administrators %	Skilled/ semi- skilled workers %
Agree strongly	39	40	41	35	42	37	43	13	15	49
Agree somewhat	26	24	26	25	29	30	27	22	22	25
Disagree somewhat	23	22	22	25	21	20	22	40	40	14
Disagree strongly	9	9	10	11	5	10	6	23	20	9
No opinion	3	5	1	3	3	3	3	3	3	3

Source: Environics Research Group, 1987

FIGURE 13-3

Unemployment and opposition to immigration in Gallup surveys between 1975 and 1995

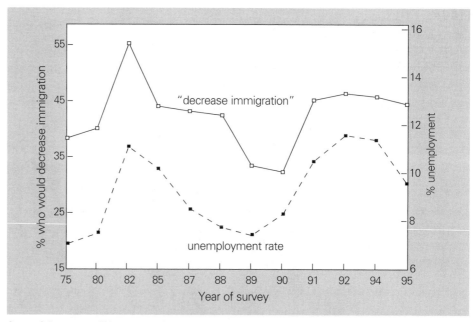

Source: Gallup surveys, "If it were your job to plan an immigration policy for Canada at this time, would you be inclined to increase immigration, decrease immigration or keep the number of immigrants at about the same level?"

ates from the University of Wisconsin, adding an experimental condition. They asked participants not only to list the adjectives that "make up the cultural stereotype of blacks" but also to list "those adjectives you personally believe characterize blacks." Their data led them to conclude that there continues to be a consistent and negative stereotype of blacks and that the Princeton trilogy studies in fact measured subjects' personal beliefs rather than their knowledge of the stereotype. Knowledge of the stereotype was the same among both high- and low-prejudiced individuals, but they differed greatly in their acceptance of the stereotype. There's an interesting footnote to this study: While all the participants were willing to complete the stereotype task, 21 percent refused to do the personal beliefs component.

For a variety of reasons such as social desirability or workplace harmony, negative stereotypes are frequent-

ly suppressed. On the face of it, this would seem to be a good thing. But we are left with an interesting question: Why do such negative stereotypes persist when they are inconsistent with many people's personal beliefs? It is clear that most people, the tolerant as well as the prejudiced, know the prevailing stereotypes.

Are stereotypes accurate?

It has been argued that because stereotypes seem both persistent and pervasive, they must, at least to some extent, be true (the **kernel-of-truth hypothesis**). However, there are a number of grounds on which this notion often can be refuted:

■ the simultaneous existence of incompatible stereotypes concerning the same group of people ("Jews are pushy"; "Jews keep to themselves")

TABLE 13-2

Percentage of respondents assigning traits to blacks

Trait	Katz & Braly (1933)	Gilbert (1951)	Karlins, Coffman & Walters (1969)
Superstitious	84	41	13
Lazy	75	31	26
Happy-go-lucky	38	17	27
Ignorant	38	17	27
Musical	26	33	47

- the labelling of the same behaviour in positive or negative terms, depending on which group exhibits it ("The Dutch are frugal and careful about their finances"; "Scots are miserly and penny-pinching")

- changes in the stereotype not accompanied by any change in the target group ("Immigrants are energetic, reliable workers"; "Immigrants work excessively and take jobs away from Canadians")

- the application of the stereotype to all members of the group without consideration of individual differences ("The Welsh are good singers"—no doubt some are mediocre singers).

Nevertheless in some instances, it seems possible to verify the accuracy of stereotypes. It is true, for example, that Native Canadians often score below the national average on standardized intelligence tests and that many blacks excel at sports and music. However, this does not mean that Native Canadians are innately unintelligent and that blacks have a built-in sense of rhythm. What the prejudiced person usually ignores is the situational pressure that prejudice creates to make stereotypes come true.

For instance if it is believed that Native Canadians are genetically inferior, there will be little effort to satisfying their educational needs, and the attempts made may be thwarted by cultural bias. Moreover, the measure itself is likely to be inaccurate since typical intelligence tests are standardized on middle-class U.S. whites. Similarly, sports and entertainment are occupational fields in which blacks have had a reasonable opportunity for success, so it has been a rational step for them to enter these professions. While they have had great success as players, they have been underrepresented as coaches and managers at the professional level.

An additional factor that validates stereotypes is the **self-fulfilling prophecy**. Members of minorities may hear the stereotypes so often that they come to believe them and so behave accordingly. For example, because females are often stereotyped as inadequate at mathematics, they may be less motivated to learn mathematics and even avoid related careers.

One of the difficulties in testing the accuracy of stereotypes is to find a reliable measure of the characteristic in question. For example, can a reasonably precise estimate be obtained of the extent to which a group is "happy-go-lucky," or "stingy" or "smart"? Ashton and Esses (1999) at the University of Western Ontario tackled this problem by using academic performance as the target characteristic and having undergraduates estimate the academic performance of Toronto high school students from nine ethnic groups. Since these were actual students, their marks were available for comparison with the estimates. The results indicated that the estimates were on average actually quite accurate and that none of the ethnic groups was substantially over- or underestimated. It also was noted that individual subjects who overestimated the degree of difference in academic performance among the groups tended to be themselves of lower intelligence, while those who underestimated the between-group variability tended to score lower on a measure of authoritarianism. This study suggests that stereotypes *can* be relatively accurate. Note however that "academic performance" may not elicit as powerful a stereotype as might some more emotion-laden terms that have long been associated with racism.

Illusory correlation and stereotypes

It has been suggested (Hamilton & Sherman, 1989) that many instances of stereotyping arise and are maintained through the operation of **illusory correlation**, an information-processing bias whereby the association between characteristics or events is overestimated (see Chapter 2). Hamilton and Gifford (1976) postulated that one basis for illusory correlation is that observers tend to overestimate the frequency of co-occurrence of infrequent but distinctive events. An example of this might be a nurse noting on a couple of occasions that the maternity ward is particularly busy and that there also happens to be a full moon—leading to the common but incorrect belief that this is a reliable association.

When one group of persons "occurs" less frequently than another—that is, it is a minority—and when one type of behaviour occurs infrequently, then researchers argue that observers are likely to overestimate the frequency of that type of behaviour being performed by members of that group. And so if we see a member of a minority group behaves in an obnoxious manner, we tend to generalize and stereotype as typical of that group. Once such an association has been made, subsequent judgments will be biased in the same direction. Disconfirmations of the stereotype are learned more slowly or are forgotten more quickly than neutral or confirming information (Hamilton & Rose, 1980; Hilton & Von Hippel, 1996). In other words, "Believing is seeing."

Stereotypes and prejudice

Will prejudice inevitably follow because of the existence of stereotypes? Not necessarily. The inevitability argument ignores the distinction between *knowledge* and *acceptance*. There is no good evidence that knowing a stereotype goes hand in hand with prejudice (Devine, 1989; Taylor & Lalonde, 1987). Studies show that while both high- and low-prejudice individuals know the cultural stereotype (e.g., women are not mechanically minded), their personal beliefs about the target group (e.g., more women should enter engineering) are different. Recall the results of the Devine and Elliot (1995) study discussed earlier in the context of persistence of stereotypes. Thus, the beliefs and stereotypes of a prejudiced person overlap, while the beliefs and stereotypes of a tolerant person conflict. Tolerant individuals will not use a stereotype as a personal schema but will instead activate their beliefs to judge others. Studies by Esses and colleagues (Esses, Haddock & Zanna, 1993) confirm that the relationship between individual stereotypes and attitudes, while significant in some instances, is nonetheless weak.

To further complicate things, individuals may hold ambivalent beliefs about a group. Katz and Hass (1988) point out that U.S. whites often perceive blacks as both deviant *and* disadvantaged. This duality leads to feelings of both aversion and sympathy derived from the opposing values of humanitarianism/egalitarianism and the protestant work ethic (individualism). Blacks may be perceived as deserving help but at the same time as not doing enough to help themselves.

The activation of stereotypes

While we are all aware of culturally shared negative stereotypes, they may not affect how we judge an individual from that group. This often happens for example in work situations or in team sports where we may react favourably to a colleague even if she or he is from a certain stereotyped group. However if a member of that group happens to act in an obnoxious manner, this may cause people to revert to the stereotype—he acted in that way because he belongs to that group, not because he happened to be in a bad mood. One racist comment by someone may activate the stereotype that white people hold about black people and this comment may lead them to evaluate a black person's performance negatively (Greenberg & Pyszczynski, 1995).

Devine (1989) suggests that, under certain conditions, a stereotype may just pop into our mind, such as

one that homosexual men are all effeminate. Usually, we can consciously suppress this stereotype perhaps by simply reminding ourselves that generalizing in this way about people is not fair, or by recalling the gay men that we know who do not act in an effeminate way. However, people who are highly prejudiced will act on this stereotype regardless of whether they are conscious of it or not. Indeed, Fazio, Jackson, Dunton & Williams (1995) suggest that there are three types of people: unprejudiced people who do not have an automatic negative stereotype towards an out-group; those who have this negative stereotype but consciously try to suppress this reaction; and those who have no qualms about expressing and acting on the negative stereotype.

Whether we may bring a stereotype to mind (activate it) or suppress our awareness of it may depend on motives such as self-enhancement (Sinclair & Kunda, 1999; Kunda & Spencer 2003). When a stereotyped reaction to another person will make an individual feel better about himself or herself or when it enables us to understand and make sense of a situation, the stereotype will more readily come to mind and be used. Recall from Chapter 2 that stereotypes are cognitive structures and that they can be useful to us for self-enhancement or comprehension (Wheeler & Petty, 2001).

In one experiment, white male students answered a series of questions designed ostensibly to assess their interpersonal skills and then received a video feedback from a white or black "manager." Half the participants in each group received positive feedback and the other half received a negative evaluation. Sinclair & Kunda (1999) predicted that those who received positive feedback from the black manager would suppress the negative stereotype about blacks, while that stereotype would be activated among those who had received a negative evaluation from a black confederate.

Their assessment of stereotype activation was rather ingenious. After this "management evaluation" procedure, the participants were asked to participate in a supposedly unrelated study. They were presented with word fragments and asked to complete the word. In some cases, the word fragment could be seen as representing a racial word (e.g., _ _ ACK may be completed as "black" or "stack" or "shack") or a word suggesting a negative stereotype about blacks (e.g., CR _ _ _ may be completed as "crime" or "crisp" or "cream"). The results were as predicted. Those who had been praised by the black manager completed fewer racial/stereotypic words than even those in the control group who had been evaluated by a white confederate, indicating that the stereotype had been suppressed. On the other hand, those who had been poorly evaluated by the black manager completed more racially tinged words than any other participants, indicating that the stereotype had been activated.

In other work, Sinclair & Kunda (2000) found similar reactions in stereotypes about women. Male participants evaluated female instructors as less competent than their male instructors only when they had received a low grade in that course. When they had received a high grade, no differences were observed. Indeed their evaluations of male instructors were not influenced by their grades. This work shows that we can push the stereotype out of mind or we can use it to salvage our self-esteem when it is threatened.

One additional factor that may activate a stereotype is our belief that members of the other group hold a stereotype about us. For instance, Vorauer, Main & O'Connell (1998) found that white students at the University of Manitoba believed that Native Canadians perceive whites as prejudiced, selfish, arrogant and materialistic. Not surprisingly, those who most strongly hold these "meta-stereotypes" are more likely to anticipate an unpleasant interaction with members of this group and to express more prejudice.

The affective component of prejudice

Stereotypes are accompanied by *emotions,* which are usually expressed in terms that can be distributed along a continuum ranging from the intensely negative (e.g., contempt, disgust, hate) to the very positive (e.g., admiration, liking, identification). Feelings may be accompanied by arousal of the sympathetic nervous system, and the increased physiological activity can be measured by galvanic skin response (GSR). Such responses can be used, at least for research purposes, to determine emotional reaction even when the subject is unable or unwilling to overtly express it. In this way, Porier and Lott (1967) demonstrated that individuals who scored high on **ethnocentrism** (belief in the superiority of one's own ethnic or cultural group) showed a greater GSR in the presence of black compared with white research assistants than did those who scored low on the scale.

A study in the Netherlands (Dijker, 1987) illustrates the relationship between emotions and attitudes, in this case, towards immigrants from Suriname (a former Dutch colony) and Turks and Moroccans. Analyses of the data showed that for all groups the emotions expressed fell into four categories: positive (e.g., admiration), irritation (e.g., annoyance), anxiety (e.g., fear), and concern (e.g., worry). Positive emotions were more predictive of attitudes towards Surinamers who were generally perceived favourably by the Dutch, whereas attitudes towards those from Turkey and Morocco, who were not well received, were better predicted by the negative categories of irritation and concern.

Mood can affect the application of stereotypes. In particular, studies by Esses and Zanna (1995) found that individuals in a negative mood were more likely to assign unfavourable stereotypes to out-groups (especially Native Canadians, Pakistanis and Arabs) than were individuals in a neutral or positive mood.

Discrimination: The behavioural component of prejudice

While prejudice is an attitude, **discrimination** refers to negative *behaviour* towards members of out-groups. At one time, black members of the Hamilton Tiger Cats (football team) were refused haircuts in a major Hamilton hotel, blacks in Dresden, Ontario, were refused service in local restaurants and some medical schools restricted the admission of Jewish students. Considerable opposition was voiced in 1989 when the RCMP agreed to allow Sikh officers to wear a turban rather the traditional Stetson. In reaction to the RCMP decision, some posts of the Canadian Legion would not allow Sikhs on their premises unless they removed their turbans. In 1999, a Canadian amateur boxer was prevented from taking part in a tournament because in line with his Sikh religion he would not cut his hair or shave. (Beards were outlawed in amateur boxing, both at the Canadian and world levels, on the grounds that they could somehow increase the likelihood of injuries). And in 2003, a female student was expelled from a private school in Montreal because, in accordance with Islamic custom, she was unwilling to adhere to the student dress code and remove her hijab.

Fortunately, the frequency of such acts of overt discrimination has decreased, in part perhaps because of safeguards, such as the *Canadian Charter of Rights and Freedoms,* and more active prosecution. Halifax restaurants no longer have signs reading (as they did during the Second World War) "Sailors and dogs not admitted." In fact not all that long ago, a Nova Scotia Human Rights Board ordered that souvenir buttons proclaiming "I'm a big mouth Cape Bretoner—so kiss

Do Laws against Inciting Hate Reduce or Increase Hate?

In Canada, there are penalties for inciting hatred against members of a minority group. Such laws are controversial, for some argue that they infringe upon free speech, while others counter that free speech does not give anyone the right to cry "Fire!" in a crowded room. In 2003, a law was proposed in Parliament to extend these laws to include the incitement of hatred against people because of their sexual orientation. But do such laws reduce or increase prejudice in a society? Some have argued that prejudice should be reduced because society has clearly defined it as wrong. Others are concerned that bigots are granted a public forum for their views, which seems to make those views a matter for legitimate debate.

In 1985, Toronto publisher Ernst Zundel was tried and convicted of transgressing section 177 of the *Criminal Code* of Canada by willfully publishing " ... a statement, tale or news that is known to be false and that causes or is likely to cause injury or mischief to a public interest." Zundel's press and Web site churned out material that portrayed Zionism as a racist and manipulative creed and claimed that the Holocaust was a hoax perpetrated by Jews to extort money from West Germany and garner political support around the world. One passage spoke of "vicious, greedy and militant people who call themselves Jews ... as God's Chosen People."

At that time, a study revealed some interesting shifts in public sentiment (Weimann & Winn, 1986). Only about half of Canadians knew why Zundel had been convicted, casting some doubt on the proposition that the trial was an effective publicity stunt for him. Moreover, those who were most sympathetic to his position were least aware of the trial. When asked whether their attitudes towards Jews had changed as a result of the trial, 24 percent said

they had become more sympathetic and only 2 percent said they were less sympathetic (the others were unchanged or uncertain). The vast majority of people continued to believe that six million Jews had died in the Nazi Holocaust and that the Jews were blameless. Thus, the trial did not incite anti-Semitism, although the data reveal that such prejudice persists among a minority of Canadians.

And yet a "climate of doubt" appeared. Respondents were asked whether they believed the trial affected the attitudes of other Canadians. Those who were aware of the trial were twice as likely as others to believe others doubted the historical record of the Holocaust. That is, while the trial increased sympathy for Jews and knowledge of this terrible and tragic crime, it also led people to believe that their friends and neighbours had changed in the opposite direction. In the long run, such an outcome may create the impression that prejudice has considerable social support and could conceivably become a self-fulfilling prophecy.

In 1987, Zundel appealed his conviction, which led in 1988 to a second trial on a false-news charge. Zundel was again convicted but again appealed. In 1990, the Ontario Court of Appeal upheld the conviction. However, the case was then taken to the Supreme Court of Canada, which struck down the conviction by a four-to-three majority. The decision found that the law prohibiting the spreading of false news is unconstitutional because it is an unjustifiable limit on the right to freedom of expression contained in the *Charter of Rights and Freedoms*. With the advent of the Internet, control over the dissemination of hate literature has become considerably more difficult. Many white supremacist organizations and individuals have Web sites.

me" be destroyed on the grounds that the message was offensive to a group of Maritimers (Hunter, 1987). More recently, legislation has been enacted in many provinces requiring employers to move towards equitable hiring of women, the handicapped and members of minority groups.

Does this mean that prejudice in Canada is declining or is it simply that because of "political correctness," its outlets have become more subtle and indirect? Certainly discrimination is difficult to eradicate. Many foreign students (especially the "visible minorities") have trouble locating accommodation, even when there is no shortage of rooms or apartments. It is not always obvious when an apartment that the landlord says has already been rented out is actually still available but is being denied to a potential tenant because of his or her race.

Discrimination may occur at the level of interaction between individuals, as in these examples, or it may be institutionalized and supported by either implicit or explicit regulations. For instance, apartheid in South Africa was a case of discrimination required by law. Examples of groups falling victim to state-sanctioned discrimination are also all too numerous in Canadian history: the Hutterites of Alberta were legally restricted in their purchase of land; Canadians of Japanese origin during the Second World War had all their possessions taken from them; until 1954, schools in Nova Scotia were racially segregated. The treatment of First Nations and Inuit peoples has varied from condescending paternalism to outright racism (Backhouse, 1999).

Until the abolition of capital punishment in Canada, even the likelihood of being executed for murder in Canada was affected by prejudice—leading to deadly discrimination. Avio (1987) reviewed 440 capital murder cases (1926–1957) and discovered that Canadians of English descent were significantly less likely than Natives, Ukrainians and French Canadians to be executed. In other words, English Canadians were more likely than others to have had their sentence commuted by the federal cabinet. Those at the greatest risk were Native Canadians who, according to Avio, were the subject of memoranda from the Ministry of Indian Affairs emphasizing that they needed "special deterrence." In the United States and in South Africa, the race of the victim is also a factor in establishing the defendant's guilt and penalty. Hooker (1988) reported that in Florida, 47 percent of black defendants, as opposed to 24 percent of white defendants, were sentenced to death if they were arrested for murdering a white. In South Africa during apartheid, black defendants who killed whites were 19 times more likely to receive the death penalty than were blacks that killed blacks.

It has been argued that the language, educational and sign laws enacted in Quebec in the 1970s constitute legal support for discrimination (see Bourhis (1994b) for a review of ethnic and language attitudes in Quebec). Of course, many of us have forgotten that the Manitoba government passed a law in 1890 abolishing French as an official language and prohibiting education in that language, a law struck down in modern times by the Supreme Court of Canada.

Aside from the problems encountered by its minorities, Canada faces another problem: discrimination against Canadians by Canadians who believe that Canada is second-rate. For example, Canadian entertainers, artists and writers are often not taken seriously unless they "make it" in the U.S. This became such a serious problem that government imposed Canadian-content rules for television and radio. Because Canadians encountered similar problems in getting jobs in their own universities, foreign applications for academic positions may now be considered only if no qualified Canadian candidates are available.

Clearly, discrimination can take many forms and can be disguised in many ways. The expulsion of the Japanese Canadians from the West Coast during the Second World War, mentioned on the previous page, is a case in point. Because they were considered a security risk, these citizens were rounded up on short notice; their homes and goods, including their fishing boats were seized; and they were relocated in often-secluded areas of British Columbia, Alberta and Ontario. The comments of one Japanese victim express the resentment many must have felt:

> Don't think the authorities weren't waiting for us when Pearl Harbor came. Within two hours things began to happen…. I got a call from Navy Headquarters to report at 9 o'clock next morning. The Commander was very frank. He said, "Mr. Suzubi, we were caught with our pants down," and he said that all fishing vessels would have to be turned over to the authorities right then. To this day I don't know what they thought about those fishing boats…. They were small boats, made of wood. We had no radar, no radio, no echo sounder…. But try and convince these people that we were not spies, we were just ordinary fishermen. As far back as the late 1890s they had determined that one day they would kick the damn Japs off the river. There was one common statement you could hear along the river: "There's only one damn good Jap and that's a dead Jap" (Broadfoot, 1977).

Yet there was not a single instance of a breach of security on which to base this action. There was however a history in British Columbia of hostility towards Asians and it is of interest that the most active agitators for the removal of the Japanese were rival Canadian fishermen to whom the government eventually sold the Japanese boats and equipment at giveaway prices. The

It can even happen here: Thousands of innocent Japanese-Canadians were herded into camps and had their property taken from them during the World War II.

CANADA
DEPARTMENT OF THE SECRETARY OF STATE
OFFICE OF THE CUSTODIAN
———
JAPANESE EVACUATION SECTION

PHONE PACIFIC 6131
PLEASE REFER TO
FILE No. 4610

508 ROYAL BANK BLDG.
HASTINGS AND GRANVILLE
VANCOUVER, B.C.

January 29, 1946.

REGISTERED

Mr. Kyusuke YASUI,
Registration No. 06514,
Popoff Farms,
SLOCAN, B. C.

Dear Sir:

This is to inform you that your account with this office shows a credit balance of $14.59 at the present time. This money represents the net proceeds from the saleable parts of your Buick Sedan, which were sold by this office.

A trunk and a valise, identified as your property, are in storage at Custodian warehouse in Vancouver.

On October 29, 1942, we sent you statements in regard to your contracts with the Cameron Logging Company and the Royston Lumber Company, which showed that a balance of $684.64 was payable to you after all adjustments had been made. Cheque for this sum was received from P. S. Ross & Sons and was credited to your account. The sum of $300.00 was paid to Mr. Matsutaro IWASA in settlement of his claim against you, and the balance of $384.64 was remitted to you in January 1943.

You were informed on January 20, 1943, of the sale of your Packard Sedan.

It would appear that we have accounted for all the property of every kind left by you in the protected area which vested in the Custodian, and, in order that you may confirm this, we enclose a stamped, addressed envelope for your convenience in replying.

Yours truly,

F. Matheson,
Protection Department.

Enclosures (1)

Japanese Canadians have never been fully compensated for the government's action (Adachi, 1976; Broadfoot, 1977). However in 1988, the government finally apologized and agreed to a form of redress, the terms of which included payment of $21 000 to those affected who were still living; granting of citizenship to persons of Japanese ancestry who had been expelled from Canada or had had their citizenship revoked; and clearing of the names of persons of Japanese ancestry who were convicted under the *War Measures Act,* the *National Emergency Transitional Powers Act* or other related legislation. There were 12 000 surviving Japanese in Canada for whom the $21 000 was compensation for their enforced isolation and for the loss of homes, businesses and fishing boats.

Nor should we forget the experience of those Chinese who helped to build the Canadian Pacific Railway. Some 15 000 Chinese worked on the transcontinental line and 600 of them died on the job, yet in 1922 the government imposed a head tax of $500 on each Chinese and in 1923 passed the *Chinese Exclusion Act* (reducing Chinese immigration to fewer than 50 people in the 24-year period!), which was not repealed until 1947 (*Maclean's*, 1999).

Does history repeat itself? After the terrorist attacks on the World Trade Center in New York and the Pentagon in Washington, several thousand people, most of them young Muslim men, were apprehended by the United States forces in other countries. These men were held in detention on a U.S. base in Cuba, without any rights whatsoever, not even the rights accorded to prisoners-of-war under the Geneva convention.

Too often, discrimination is based on the belief that certain races are genetically inferior to others—with disturbing consequences. The so-called "medical experiments" conducted by the Nazis on concentration camp inmates were rationalized in this manner and it is probably no accident that the first human trials of the contraceptive pill were carried out on women in Puerto Rico. More recently, an experiment has been brought to light in which the United States Public Health Service allowed 200 men to go untreated for syphilis in order to study the disease and its side effects. All the men were black. Similarly, the flawed research of Philippe Rushton (1989, 2000) (Chapter 1 and Wiesenthal & Ziegler, et al., 1996), which tries to show that members of certain races are intellectually superior or inferior, could be used to support discriminatory actions. This situation actually developed in the United States in the early part of the century when intelligence tests were first administered to immigrants. Not unexpectedly, many immigrants coming as they did from other cultures were shown to be "intellectually deficient." On this basis, it was argued that certain ethnic groups were "genetically inferior," and restrictive immigration quotas were applied for many years (Kamin, 1974).

Keep in mind that in 1928 a sterilization law was enacted in Alberta (see A Case in Point—Eugenics in Canada) that was not repealed until 1972, and that British Columbia had a similar law from 1933 to 1973. It was to Alberta that the Nazi government of Germany turned for specific advice on eugenics practices in a western "Aryan" jurisdiction. In Germany, 400 000 people were sterilized because they were judged unfit to reproduce.

Reverse discrimination

As society becomes more sensitive to racial issues, many people will resist expressing prejudicial attitudes. In fact, some may go so far as to behave in a manner that implies they are more tolerant than they really are. This process called **reverse discrimination** (or "modern racism") has been demonstrated in a number of studies by Dutton and colleagues (Dutton, 1971, 1973; Dutton & Lake, 1973; Dutton & Lennox, 1974). In the first experiment, either black or white couples entered a restaurant in Vancouver or Toronto. In each case, the man was wearing a turtleneck sweater, in violation of

the restaurant's dress code requiring ties for men. Only 30 percent of the white couples were seated compared to 75 percent of the black couples. It is evident that the persons in charge went out of their way to appear nondiscriminatory. Accordingly, Dutton (1973) hypothesized that minority groups perceived by the public as being most discriminated against would experience the most reverse discrimination. A survey had indicated that middle-class whites in Vancouver felt that blacks and Native peoples were the focus of considerable discrimination but that Asians were not. Dutton then asked Natives, blacks and Asians to solicit donations for a charity and found, as hypothesized, that more money was given to the Natives and blacks than to the Asians.

It should be noted that this effect appears to be most common among educated middle- and upper middle-class whites who are especially concerned not to appear intolerant. Dutton and Lake (1973) selected 80 students who had been identified as having a low degree of anti-black prejudice and who valued equality. Through means of false feedback, half the students were made to feel that they might be prejudiced; the rest of the students acted as controls. After the laboratory session, either a white or a black panhandler approached all the participants. Those subjects who had been led to doubt their tolerance towards blacks gave significantly more money to the black panhandler. The experimental manipulation had no effect on the amounts given to the white panhandler.

The behaviour described in these studies is relatively trivial. But a person who has demonstrated tolerance by such a token act may be less likely to exhibit reverse discrimination the next time. In a study by Dutton and Lennox (1974), three groups of students were made to doubt their tolerance towards blacks. Subsequently, one group was approached by a black panhandler, the second by a white panhandler, while the third was not panhandled. The next day they were all asked to give some of their time for an "interracial brotherhood campaign." Students who had been panhandled by the black volunteered less of their time than did those in the other two groups. Reverse discrimination may be restricted to relatively unimportant behaviours and may have the counterproductive effect of discouraging real and long-lasting tolerance.

Relationships among the three components

As we noted in Chapter 4, the various components that make up an attitude may be incongruent—that is,

A CASE IN POINT

Eugenics in Canada

Alberta's *Sexual Sterilization Act* led to the sterilization of approximately 3000 citizens labelled "mentally defective." Although consent was required, it is not clear whether these people were aware of what they were agreeing to or whether compliance was obtained by coercion. In 1996, the plight of these victims was brought to light by Leilani Muir who at the age of 14 was sterilized without her consent while having an appendectomy. She was classified as a "moron" and placed in the province's School for Mental Defectives. Intelligence tests administered later in her life placed her IQ in the normal range. Ms. Muir sued the Government of Alberta and in January 1996 was awarded $740 000. The judgment

read, in part: "The circumstances of Ms. Muir's sterilization were so highhanded and so contemptuous of the statutory authority to effect sterilization and were undertaken in an atmosphere that so little respected human dignity that the Community, and the Court's sense of decency is offended" (*Globe and Mail,* March 12, 1996). This and the other sterilizations were supported by many as a way of protecting the community from the possibility that people deemed unfit would procreate and pass on their deficient genes to future generations. In 1999, the Government of Alberta settled with the 247 remaining victims of forced sterilization for $82 000 000.

not in agreement. Prejudice is no exception. A crucial factor in prejudice appears to be the affective component (Esses, Haddock & Zanna, 1993). Thus, an individual may intellectually accept that Native people are not inherently less capable or lazier than whites but may nevertheless avoid them because of an emotional reaction. However, attitude components are more likely to be highly correlated in extreme bigots. This type of person will not only have strong negative feelings but will usually have an extensive set of negative stereotypes some of which may be quite bizarre. For instance, a man charged with assaulting a Sikh in Toronto expressed the view that "Pakis" worshipped a number of animal gods and ritually slaughter goats in their living room "gardens" during their religious festivals. Their living rooms, he claimed, were filled with earth and posed a danger to the structure of the buildings they lived in (Pittman, 1977).

Acquisition of Prejudice

Innate or acquired?

Hebb and Thompson (1968) have described incidents that suggested to them that the higher animals—chimpanzees and human beings—have an inherent fear of

the unfamiliar and unusual. If Hebb was correct, it would be reasonable to argue that this tendency could form the basis for the development of prejudice, which is directed towards people perceived as being in some way different. It is generally agreed that people are anxious or fearful in situations that they do not understand. Perhaps the negative emotions directed at the members of an out-group have their roots in the spontaneous arousal generated by a novel stimulus. Infants as young as three months of age are able to distinguish between the face of their mother and that of a stranger. Although at this age their reactions to the unfamiliar stimulus do not show signs of avoidance or fear, by about the age of nine months, aversive reactions often do appear, frequently to the mother's embarrassment (when, for instance, the unfamiliar stimulus is the child's grandmother).

It is also possible that a finding first reported by Zajonc (1968a) can be used to support Hebb's view (Chapter 8). Zajonc demonstrated that frequent exposure to a stimulus makes it more attractive. Initially, it was thought that this "mere exposure" effect happened regardless of the subject's initial attitude, but later research (Perlman & Oskamp, 1971) indicates that only positive or neutral stimuli are enhanced. Evaluation of initially disliked stimuli are unlikely to improve and may deteriorate further.

Conflict between groups

Clearly when groups are in conflict, prejudice and discrimination tend to increase. Indeed in some cases, conflict can be related to "mirror image" stereotypes where for instance each group sees the other as threatening or as inferior in some way. Of course, the question then become one of causality—is prejudice the cause or the result of conflict?

According *to realistic conflict theory,* in cases where there are limited resources, groups may find themselves in conflict and prejudice can increase. Recall Sherif's Robbers Cave experiments (Chapter 10) where the conflict induced between the two groups of boys led to name-calling and prejudiced statements about the other group. Consider also the situation of limited fish stocks on both the east and west coasts of Canada, leading to fishing limits set by the federal government, which has led to conflict between Native and non-Native fishers and expressions of resentment and prejudice in some cases.

Similarly when unemployment is high and few jobs are available, negative attitudes towards immigration and immigrants increase (Palmer, 1996). Esses, Jackson & Armstrong (1998) set out to establish evidence on whether scarcity of jobs caused negative attitudes towards immigrants or whether these negative attitudes might cause the perception that they were in conflict over scarce jobs. Participants read one of two statements about immigration in Canada. In one version, the statement focused on scarce jobs and the tendency of immigrants to take those jobs while the other did not mention employment problems. Then the participants read about a new group of immigrants who were arriving in Canada. This fictitious group, the Sandirians, were described in positive terms as ambitious, hardworking, smart, family-oriented and religious. However when the participants had first been primed to think about immigration in terms of "realistic conflict" over jobs, they construed these characteristics in a negative manner. For instance, being "family-oriented" was interpreted as being non-accepting of others. These participants also expressed more opposition than the control group to allowing immigration in general and by this group in particular.

Learning

Whether inherent predispositions form the rudiments of prejudice remains to be confirmed. There is however little doubt of the importance of learning in the development of prejudice.

Role of the parents

Parents have a powerful influence not only because they play a role in what the child learns from day to day but also because this learning forms the foundation for all subsequent experience. For prejudicial attitudes to be acquired, children must first become "racially aware." That is, they must be able to distinguish themselves from others who are in some way different. Children are aware of different ethnic groups by the age of four or five (Aboud, 1988). Racial awareness has been shown to be present in children as young as three years of age and one study found that 25 percent of the four-year-old children observed were already expressing strong race-related values (Goodman, 1964).

Aboud (1988) argues for a three-stage process of prejudice acquisition. In the early years, she says ethnic attitudes are based on emotions and needs. The child then moves on to a second stage in which perception is dominant. At this stage, perception of the child's own appearance and another's appearance and behaviour may influence attitudes. The child reaches the third stage, the cognitive stage, by the age of seven or eight. At this point, three important ethnic beliefs are established:

- Members of an ethnic group have psychological as well as physical and behavioural characteristics.

- There may be variations in skin colour or clothing among members of the same ethnic group (cognitive constancy).

- Different attributes can exist in two people who are ethnically the same, and the same attribute can exist in two people who are ethnically different (cognitive flexibility).

A number of the steps in this sequence occur before the child's horizons have expanded much beyond the home. In these early years, the parents have control over the child's rewards and punishments. It should be noted that in increasing number, children are being placed in daycare facilities. They may spend as much or even more time with an employee of the daycare centre as with their parents. These employees also may have a significant influence on attitude development.

Social learning can occur in a number of ways and under a variety of conditions. Three types of learning that are usually distinguished are instrumental conditioning, classical conditioning and modelling. Each has different implications for the acquisition of prejudice.

Instrumental conditioning

One of the basic principles of instrumental (or operant) learning is that any behaviour or response that is followed by a reinforcement will be more likely to be repeated. Most of the reinforcements associated with the acquisition of prejudice are likely to be verbal or non-verbal indications of approval. For example if a child says, "Those people are dirty" and the mother smiles and nods, then the child is likely to repeat this remark, make it part of her belief system and generalize it to other similar-looking people.

Classical conditioning

Since Pavlov's first experiments with his salivating dogs, the classical conditioning paradigm has become part of almost everyone's psychological repertoire. In the original situation, an unconditioned stimulus (UCS), food, was used to elicit salivation in a dog. This UCS was then paired for a number of trials with the sound of a bell, the conditioned stimulus (CS). Subsequently, it was found that the CS in the absence of the UCS elicited salivation. This process is illustrated in Figure 13–4.

A similar process may account for at least some portion of the emotional or evaluative aspect of prejudice. For example, suppose a white child is playing with a West Indian child and that the white child's mother, noticing this interaction, rushes out, yells at her child to stop, slaps her and drags her into the house. This treatment is the unconditioned stimulus that arouses hostility, fear and anxiety in the child. The conditioned stimulus is the West Indian child. If this situation is sufficiently traumatic and is repeated either with the same child or with other out-group children, ultimately the sight or presence of such a conditioned stimulus will be sufficient to elicit at least some portion of the negative feelings that were aroused in the original situation. This process is illustrated in Figure 13–5.

Modelling

Not all learning involves the active intervention of a rewarding or punishing agent. Children often copy behaviour they have observed. Models—usually individuals with whom the child identifies, such as parents or teachers—have been shown to be highly effective in teaching attitudes and prejudice (Bandura, 1965). The process is both subtle and insidious because the child is not a direct participant in the event and the model may be aware neither of the information being transmitted nor its effect. It also should be kept in mind that what the model does not do may be just as important as what the model does. Thus, avoiding an Asian cashier in a supermarket or commenting that "you should always count your change after those people wait on you" may each communicate similar information to the observing child.

The prejudiced personality

Parents who have authoritarian traits typically use harsh punishment, do not tolerate any hostility or aggression by the child towards them, act in a cold and impersonal manner and withdraw love in order to maintain "proper" behaviour. Thus, the children are forced to submit without question to their superiors and to suppress the hostility aroused naturally under

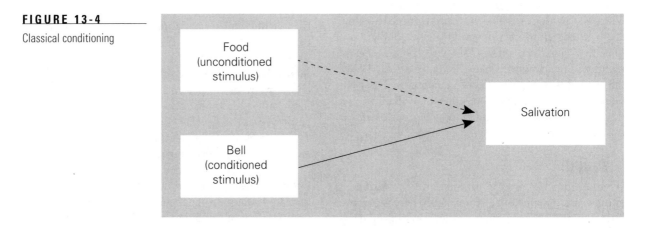

FIGURE 13-4

Classical conditioning

these frustrating conditions. At the same time by defining what is different as "inferior," the parents give their children an acceptable outlet for pent-up feelings: out-groups. They also teach their children that the world is a dangerous place, thereby setting the stage for fear based on feelings of vulnerability (Altemeyer, 1988).

Those who are identified as having an authoritarian personality also are likely to be prejudiced and ethnocentric. In this case, prejudice is incorporated in a belief and value system that forms a personality pattern first identified by Adorno, Frenkel-Brunswick, Levinson and Sanford (1950). Adorno and his colleagues were initially interested in anti-Semitism but later broadened their perspective to include attitudes towards ethnic groups in general. As part of their study, they constructed a number of scales to measure anti-Semitic attitudes, ethnocentrism and authoritarianism. However, the concept of the authoritarian personality attracted the most attention and stimulated further research (Christie & Jahoda, 1954; Cherry & Byrne, 1977). It was found that individuals who can be characterized as authoritarian have rigid and punitive views towards authority. They are likely to be prejudiced and to have a rigid personality, perceiving the world in categorical black/white, superior/inferior, us/them terms. Moreover, these individuals are usually highly conventional and cynical.

Much of the research on *right-wing authoritarianism* (RWA) has been carried out by Altemeyer (1981, 1988) who has constructed a scale to measure this characteristic. Some of the items from his scale are as follows:

- The way things are going in this country, it's going to take a lot of "strong medicine" to straighten out the troublemakers, criminals and perverts.

- It would be best for everyone if the proper authorities censored magazines and movies to keep trashy material away from the youths.

- The real keys to the "good life" are obedience, discipline and sticking to the straight and narrow.

An authoritarian would agree with the items above and disagree with items such as the following:

- There is nothing wrong with premarital intercourse.

- "Free speech" means that people should even be allowed to make speeches and write books urging the overthrow of the government.

- There is absolutely nothing wrong with nudist camps.

In addition to confirming that authoritarians are conventional, highly submissive to authority and aggressive towards those they believe to be inferior or "different," Altemeyer (1988) found that they also feel themselves to be morally superior. Esses, Haddock and Zanna (1993) report that English Canadians who were identified by Altemeyer's scale as high authoritarians had more negative attitudes towards French Canadians, Native peoples, Pakistanis and homosexuals (especially the latter two) than did low authoritarians. An Australian study corroborates the link between RWA and prejudice towards Asians and Australian Aboriginals (Heaven & St. Quintin, 2003).

One other manifestation of authoritarian aggression may be **scapegoating**, which occurs when individuals are frustrated by conditions or situations they cannot directly control or change such as crime, the economic situation or the government. When the source of the frustration is vague and difficult to locate, tension and

FIGURE 13-5

Classical conditioning in the development of prejudice

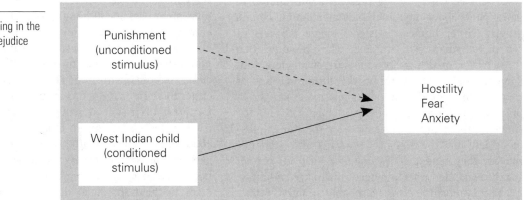

hostility may be aroused and displaced onto a convenient out-group. This out-group is then blamed for the discomfort and difficulties being experienced. Much of the treatment of the Jews during the Nazi regime in Germany may have been an example of scapegoating. Jews were blamed for all the economic woes that the Germans experienced after the First World War and into the 1930s. A more recent example may be the frequently heard claim that immigrants are taking jobs away from Canadians. Extreme authoritarians form a small proportion of the population but make up for it by their vociferousness. Among them are people who belong to neo-Nazi and white-supremacist movements, distribute hate literature, publish newsletters warning us that psychiatry is a communist plot, claim that immigration is swamping the country and insist that J.D. Salinger's *Catcher in the Rye,* or Margaret Laurence's *The Diviners,* be removed from school curricula and libraries.

Among the aspects of authoritarianism and prejudice that have been investigated is their association with religious fundamentalism, such as the Moral Majority in the United States and various forms of Islam in the Middle East and Afghanistan. The fact that many of the greatest crimes in history have been committed in the name of religion (e.g., the Inquisition, the Salem witch trials, the conflict in the former Yugoslavia, terrorism in the name of fundamentalist Islam) does not seem to have affected the general perception that religion is associated with tolerance and goodwill. Yet the evidence indicates that prejudice and religion, specifically fundamentalism, are positively correlated (Hunsberger, 1995). Indeed, fundamentalists of all persuasions—Christian, Muslim, Hindu or Jewish—are likely to be authoritarian (Altemeyer and Hunsberger, 1992; Hunsberger, 1996).

Jackson & Esses (1997) presented information to participants about high unemployment among certain groups, either homosexuals and single mothers or Native Canadians and students. They reasoned that those who scored high in a measure of religious fundamentalism would perceive the former groups as immoral and would then judge them more harshly. As predicted, the fundamentalist participants blamed the single mothers and homosexuals for their unemployment but not the Native Canadians and students. Indeed, they tended to recommend that the former groups be denied unemployment insurance benefits.

The relationship seems reasonably straightforward. These fundamentalists, like authoritarians more generally, are self-righteous and fear a dangerous world with people who are "different." In addition, they don't question authority and are closed-minded. As Altemeyer and Hunsberger (1993, p. 127) point out, "It is easy to see why persons trained in such thinking would tend to accept uncritically the stereotypes about minorities that abound in our culture and would be relatively willing to do whatever the authorities said had to be done to such a minority." Of course, regimes identified as atheist have also committed atrocities, such as the Khmer Rouge in Cambodia or Stalin in the former USSR. It may not be religion as such, but it is how religion or any ideology is interpreted and practiced by some that causes the problems.

The work on authoritarianism and prejudice has been important and enduring. However, there are several ways in which we can interpret their findings. Adorno et al. (1950) argued that the children of authoritarian parents identify with those parents, becoming authoritarian themselves, and displace their anger on to minority group scapegoats. However when we consider that those same authoritarian parents will usually show high levels of prejudice themselves, then it is plausible to conclude that the children simply learn their prejudice from them.

Parents, for better or worse, eventually give up their central role in children's lives. As children grow older, their world increases in size. They interact with peers, enter school and begin to read and watch TV. All these situations may contribute to the formation or reinforcement of prejudice.

Teachers and schools

While parents are the child's first authority figures, other people—teachers for instance—also exert considerable influence. Like everyone else, teachers have their prejudices and although they may try to be as tolerant as possible, there are many opportunities in the classroom for less-than-desirable attitudes to be communicated. For example, how will children in multiracial classrooms be treated? How will children who are either the butt or the source of racial slurs be handled? Certain courses such as geography and history give the teacher the opportunity to impart correct information about ethnic, racial or other groups but there are dangers here as well. Does the teacher give equal time to both sides of an issue? Can attitudes towards communism be held in check during a discussion about Cuban, Russian or Chinese history? And if not all topics can be covered in the time allotted, what material is omitted? In some fortunately rare instances, teachers have deliberately taught prejudice and bigotry. For example in the 1980s in Eckville, Alberta, James Keegstra taught history for over 10 years, based on anti-Semitism. He claimed that the Nazi Holocaust was a hoax and that the Jews were responsible for the French Revolution, the American Civil War, the Bolshevik Revolution in Russia and the First World War. He was finally removed from his position, charged and convicted of willfully promoting hatred and sentenced to a one-year suspended jail sentence, another year of probation and 200 hours of community service. Parents were aware of his teachings and few objected.

Until recently when some of the worst examples started to be eliminated, many textbooks contained biased and inaccurate information about ethnic and other groups. For example, First Nations peoples were frequently depicted as alcohol-addicted, primitive "savages" with only a rudimentary social organization (or conversely, the depiction was highly sentimental). Texts also typically relegated males and females to traditional roles. Bias has also been evident in the context in which material is presented to the student. For instance, what message do students get when arithmetic problems involve only white-collar business applications? Why is it that union officials or plumbers never do any calculations?

The media

Textbooks are only a step away from the mass media: magazines, newspapers, radio, television and films. North American children spend a lot of time watching TV. In fact, Lambert and Klineberg (1967) reported that by the age of 10, children obtain most of their information from TV and school rather than from their parents. Attitudes can be influenced by the media through selective or biased reporting in newspapers or by the repetition of stereotypes in television shows. Henry (1999) analyzed more than 2000 crime stories that appeared in the *Globe and Mail*, the *Toronto Star* and the *Toronto Sun* between 1994 and 1997. She found a number of subtle indicators of racism. For example, "black" was mentioned twice as often as "white." Very few of the articles mentioned anything positive about blacks. A similar analysis by Wortley (1999) showed that black victims of crimes received less coverage than did white victims and that more attention was given to "black-on-white" crime than to

"white-on-black" crime. Visible minorities and women are still underrepresented in television commercials and magazine advertising in Canada.

Peer groups

Peers exercise more influence over attitudes as the child matures and by adolescence, peers are likely to be more influential in many respects than a child's parents. In the early years, parents exercise considerable control over children's relationships and since playmates are likely to come from similar socioeconomic backgrounds, attitudes that are encountered in the home are likely to be reinforced and strengthened outside the home. But as children grow older, their contacts become more diverse and they are less apt to be influenced by parental standards. Like parents, the members of peer groups are effective in influencing attitudes and behaviour because they offer information, reward conformity and punish nonconformity. This pressure to conform, which continues throughout a person's life is powerful and difficult to resist. Thus, expressing ideas and beliefs that the group considers as being correct are just as important as wearing clothes that the group considers appropriate. Indeed Pettigrew (1961) argued that in the United States, most prejudice is based on conformity. One welcome aspect of this theory is that, unlike prejudice associated with deep-seated personality patterns, prejudice based on conformity may be more flexible. If the group norm changes or if individuals join new groups with different views, then their attitudes are likely to shift in the same direction.

The Reduction of Prejudice

Although discrimination is a behaviour and can be controlled by laws, prejudice obviously cannot be dealt with in the same way. Is it possible to reduce prejudice and make individuals more tolerant?

Intergroup contact

It is often assumed that increased interaction between the members of various groups will enhance mutual understanding and goodwill. However the nature of the contact is as important as frequency. A substantial body of research indicates that a number of conditions must be met for prejudice to be decreased through interethnic contact (Amir, 1976; Pettigrew, 1998):

1. The members of each group must be of equal status (e.g., same income group or similar occupations) or the members of the minority group should be of a higher status than the majority of group members.

2. There must be a favourable climate for intergroup contact and the contact must be of an intimate rather than a casual nature as well as rewarding and pleasant. Indeed, situations which will induce members of one group to take the perspective of the others, to see things as they see them, will contribute to the reduction of prejudice (Vescio, Sechrist & Paolucci, 2003).

3. The two groups should have a mutual goal that requires interdependent and cooperative action. Recall Sherif's Robber's Cave experiments described in Chapter 10 (Sherif et al., 1961).

Can learning to appreciate the art of other cultures reduce prejudice?

Rarely are all these conditions likely to be present in actual interethnic situations. Tourism, for example, has been advocated as a means of improving national as well as international understanding, but experienced at its worst and most typically from the windows of a bus or a souvenir shop, it will meet none of these conditions.

Ideally, intergroup contact should disconfirm the negative stereotypes associated with the out-group. However as Rothbart and John (1985) suggest, this will not always happen because the susceptibility of a stereotype to disconfirmation (or confirmation) is a function of three factors as illustrated in Figure 13–6. Suppose, for instance, you endorsed a stereotype for a member of some group as being "stingy" or "cheap." What contact experience might lead to change?

CLARITY OF THE POTENTIALLY DISCONFIRMING BEHAVIOUR Some traits ascribed to out-groups such as "messy" or "talkative" are associated with clearly observable behaviours and can therefore be easily confirmed or disconfirmed. We can easily see instances of generosity in making a donation or picking up the cheque in a restaurant. However, the behaviours that would confirm or disconfirm stereotypes such as "devious" are more difficult to specify and to observe and therefore those kinds of stereotypes are more resistant to change.

NUMBER OF RELEVANT OBSERVATIONS Observing one person from a stereotyped group behaving in a counter-stereotypical way (making a generous donation), can easily be explained away as an exception to the rule. Indeed, Rothbart and John (1985) report that the more unfavourable a trait, the greater the number of instances are required for disconfirmation of the stereotype. Thus, it takes a good deal of intergroup contact to change negative stereotypes.

FREQUENCY OF INTERGROUP CONTACT Obviously there must be an occasion during which confirming or disconfirming actions can occur, but the situation will also determine what type of behaviour is likely to be expressed. In most social situations, friendly behaviour is likely to be evident but if the stereotype includes characteristics such as "devious" or "cowardly," a situation may never arise in which these traits can be confirmed or disconfirmed. Indeed, we may never have the opportunity to see members of the out-group behaving generously. Therefore, contact in various different situations will often be necessary to lead to positive change.

FIGURE 13-6

Factors influencing the susceptibility of stereotype traits to disconfirmation

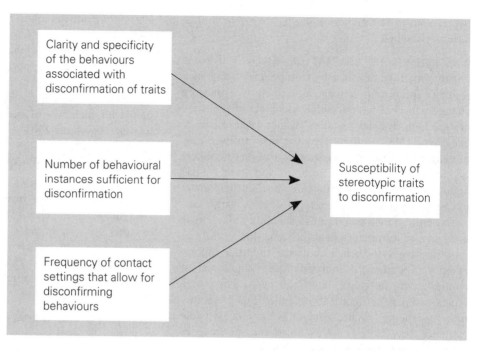

Clarity and specificity of the behaviours associated with disconfirmation of traits

Number of behavioural instances sufficient for disconfirmation

Frequency of contact settings that allow for disconfirming behaviours

Susceptibility of stereotypic traits to disconfirmation

RESEARCH To test the contact hypothesis in a Canadian setting, Clement, Gardner and Smythe (1977) studied 379 anglophone Grade 8 students from London, Ontario. About half the students (181) went on an excursion to Quebec City while the control group (198) remained at home. All the students completed a battery of tests before and after the trip. Those who visited Quebec were subsequently divided into two groups on the basis of the amount of interaction they reported having had with francophones while in the city. The high-contact group had more favourable attitudes than did either the low contact or control groups towards French Canadians and towards learning French as a second language. In fact, the low-contact group had a less favourable attitude towards learning French after the trip than before. However, those students who reported more frequent contact had more favourable attitudes before the trip. Clement et al. concluded that with unstructured excursions perhaps intergroup contact reduces prejudice only in those who are favourable beforehand.

In a study of contact between German and Turkish students in Germany, only leisure-time contact was related to reduced prejudice and then only for the German students. The Turkish students were unaffected by contact whether it happened in the neighbourhood, the school or during leisure time (Wagner, Hewstone & Machleit, 1989).

A study by Henderson-King and Nisbett (1996) suggests that even a small amount of negative behaviour by a member of a minority group can have a significant impact. They found that the negative behaviour of one black person led white participants in their research to stereotype blacks more and subsequently to avoid a black person whom they encountered. In fact, simply overhearing a conversation in which a black person was alleged to have committed a crime was sufficient to increase negative stereotypes and in-group favouritism. Equally subtle and similarly powerful effects can arise from the labels used to identify groups. For example, Donakowski and Esses (1996) identified a group as either Aboriginal peoples, First Nations peoples, Native Canadians, Native Indians or Native peoples. They found that the attitudes of subjects were more negative when the labels "Native Canadians" and "First Nations peoples" were used. Donakowski and Esses suggest that this outcome may arise because the labels elicit symbolic beliefs of a political nature. The label "First Nations people" may make individuals think about the political activism of groups such as the Assembly of First Nations. Their work towards Native autonomy and increased political power may make non-Natives feel threatened. It should be noted that this study was done in Ontario and the effect might be different in other parts of Canada. For example, the label "Indian" is preferred in Saskatchewan but has negative connotations elsewhere.

WILL INTERGROUP CONTACT GENERALIZE? If some positive modification of a stereotype does occur as a result of intergroup contact, how likely is it that the change will generalize to other members of the same group? Unfortunately, studies (Cook, 1984; Esses & Seligman, 1996) indicate that the new attitude may not extend beyond the situation or to other members of the group. This is so, Rothbart and John (1985) argue, because the individuals involved in the contact may not be perceived as "exemplars" of the larger category. Thus, a man could praise the ability of a female colleague or teammate and at the same time reveal traditional stereotypic beliefs about the supposed incompetence of women. If confronted with this apparent contradiction, he would likely say, "Well, she isn't a typical woman!" Allport (1954) called this phenomenon "re-fencing." When categories conflict with the evidence, special cases are excluded and the category is kept intact (Kunda & Oleson, 1995).

The "dilution effect" (Nisbett, Zukier & Lemley, 1981), which occurs when varying amounts of information are provided about a given member of a group (the exemplar), is also of concern. It has been shown that when more information is provided, it is less likely that the person will be perceived as a typical group member. Thus, the effect of the information on the perception of the group in general will be diluted or lost. This is especially evident if the information is "individualized" (Denhaerinck, Leyens & Yzerbt, 1989). The researchers used the example of a stereotype that most engineers fix their own cars. Then according to the dilution effect, an "engineer with blue eyes and four children" is less likely to fix his car himself because the information about the blue eyes and children dilutes the prototypicality of the stereotype.

In the final analysis, the prescription for stereotype-disconfirming information, however difficult it may be to fill, is that it should be (1) linked to typical out-group exemplars; (2) presented to highly motivated perceivers; and (3) provided under conditions that do not induce intergroup anxiety (Hewstone, 1989). It also is evident that even when the opportunity for contact exists, many people will not take advantage of it (see Table 13–4). In your own university, there are substantial numbers of international students from various nations and ethnic groups but many Canadian-born students have little or no contact with them. The importance of close relationships is emphasized by Pettigrew

(1997, 1998) and his colleagues who conducted surveys in four European countries. They found that respondents who reported they had out-group friends were more tolerant and had more positive feelings towards out-groups generally. While intergroup contact is generally effective, particularly in reducing anxiety about being with members of the other group, it is not a panacea (Hewstone, 2003).

Contact and intergroup anxiety

One reason for the lack of contact between members of in- and out-groups is **intergroup anxiety** (Stephan & Stephan, 1985). That is, anxiety about being with the other group may cause people to avoid them and may also be a consequence of a lack of contact, fear of the unknown (Plant & Devine, 2003). This anxiety could result in one or more of four types of negative consequences:

NEGATIVE PSYCHOLOGICAL CONSEQUENCES FOR THE SELF People often know very little about the values, norms, non-verbal behaviours and expectations of the members of other groups. This ignorance about the "subjective culture" of the other group (Triandis, 1972) may lead to fear of embarrassment or of being made to appear incompetent in intergroup interactions. These fears can be quite realistic. For example if an orthodox Hindu is present at a meal, can beef be served to the other guests? Or when introduced to someone from Japan, should one bow and, if so, how low? Such concerns lead to anticipation of discomfort and awkwardness in these types of interactions. One solution is not to get involved.

NEGATIVE BEHAVIOURAL CONSEQUENCES FOR THE SELF In-group members may also believe that they will be taken advantage of or exploited especially when they harbour stereotypes about the out-group as devious and dishonest. In extreme cases, they may fear that they will be physically abused.

NEGATIVE EVALUATIONS BY IN-GROUP MEMBERS Members of the in-group may be afraid that if they interact with the out-groups, their own group will reject them.

NEGATIVE EVALUATIONS BY OUT-GROUP MEMBERS Another possibility is fear of rejection, ridicule or disapproval by the out-group if contact is attempted. Wilder and Shapiro (1989) point out that the anxiety generated by the anticipation of an encounter with an out-group member may decrease the impact of any positive behaviour by that out-group member. The anxiety interferes with information processing and thus reduces the effect that any positive actions might have.

Obviously there must be an opportunity for contact to occur. Such opportunities will be related to the number of members of a particular ethnic group who reside in a given location. This observation is confirmed by Kalin and Berry (1982) and Kalin (1996) who found that attitudes were more negative where the concentration of an ethnic group was low. (Once again, think back to the Hamilton and Gifford (1976) study of illusory correlation.)

We do not know from these data to what extent tolerance results from the actual contact itself. It may be that individuals who are tolerant are more willing to interact with out-group members. However since the prejudiced avoid associating with the members of other groups, opportunities for effective contact simply do not occur for them. This is a problem that interferes with any attempt, deliberate or otherwise, to modify the attitudes of people; we are often preaching only to the converted.

It is likely that if we could somehow, without using force, propel prejudiced individuals into the appropriate social milieu, some positive change might occur. Cook (1970) carried out extensive laboratory research in the United States that supports this contention. He employed a simulation game in which black and white women interacted over a one-month period. All the black women and half the white women were confederates of the experimenter. The real subjects, all white, initially had very negative attitudes towards blacks. (Their attitudes had been measured in a different context so that there would be no connection with the study.) The game required the participants to cooperate and to be in close contact in an equal-status situation. If they won, they shared the rewards. There were also breaks during each two-hour session so that the participants had the opportunity for more social and personal contact "off the job," during which the black

confederate led the conversation to race-related issues. She also interjected personal comments that emphasized her individuality and distinguished her from the stereotype. In comparing the subjects' attitudes before and after this experience, it was found that about 40 percent of these white women compared with only 12 percent of those in the control group became more tolerant towards blacks. Obviously, this sort of contact is effective—even though a majority of the white women didn't change and, inexplicably, a small number became more prejudiced.

While it would be expensive and difficult to mount a project of this sort to reduce prejudice among the public, it would be quite feasible to create similar situations in schools where many opportunities exist for students to work together on cooperative educational projects. Weigel, Wiser and Cook (1975) and DeVries and Edwards (1974) tried this approach and found that students who worked together in small, interdependent, interethnic groups were more likely later to engage in cross-ethnic helping behaviour and to have greater respect for each other than were those students from racially homogeneous groups.

Some support for this outcome emerges from a classic study conducted by Reich and Purbhoo (1975) in Toronto. They measured the attitudes of children attending an ethnically heterogeneous school and a more homogeneous school and found that the former were considerably more tolerant of ethnic diversity. Because they lived in the neighbourhood and had no choice about which school they attended, pre-selection bias is not likely to have seriously influenced this outcome. This observation has been supported experimentally in Toronto by Ziegler (1981) who assigned Grade 6 children either to cooperative teams or to conventional individual teaching methods. The cooperative teams were set up in such a way as to ensure heterogeneity of ethnicity (Anglo, Italian, Chinese, Greek and West Indian Canadian children). The students worked together for eight weeks, three class

TABLE 13-4 Prejudice and social contact: How subjects described themselves		Little or no contact (%)	Close or very close contact (%)
	Very prejudiced	82	18
	Somewhat prejudiced	64.7	35.3
	Somewhat tolerant	48.3	51.7
	Very tolerant	43.5	56.4

Source: Henry, 1978

periods per week. Measures obtained at the end of the procedure showed that in the cooperative teams, both casual and close cross-ethnic friendship had increased significantly compared to that in the control teams.

We should be aware that competition often leads to interpersonal hostility and teachers frequently use competition as a means of enhancing the motivation of their students. Maybe this is a dangerous tactic: recall how Sherif and his colleagues (1961) created intergroup hostility at a summer camp through competition (Chapter 10).

In this context, Aboud and Doyle (1996) examined how children's racial attitudes are affected by talking about race. They gave white Grade 3 and 4 children a test to measure prejudice and then paired a low-prejudice child with a high-prejudice child and asked them to discuss their racial evaluations. Low-prejudice children tended to say more negative things about whites and to refer more to cross-race similarities; high-prejudice children were more likely to show post-discussion increases in tolerant attitudes. Aboud and Doyle comment that one way of increasing tolerance may be to get tolerant children to talk with their prejudiced peers.

Acculturation and multiculturalism

When a country has many ethnic groups as Canada does, intergroup contact is very likely. The amount of contact and the desire to interact should influence the extent of change that may occur in the values, attitudes and behaviour of each group. This is the process of **acculturation**, which takes place when "two groups come into continuous firsthand contact with subsequent changes in the original culture pattern of either or both groups" (Redfield, 1955, p. 149).

As Berry (1986, 1992) points out, in plural societies there are two important intergroup issues: the strength of the desire to maintain one's cultural distinctiveness and the strength of the propensity for interethnic contact. These two orientations are not really compatible and Berry (1984, 1999) has constructed a framework (see Figure 13–7) that distinguishes the potential outcomes of the four possible combinations of the two motives. These are as follows: assimilation, integration, separation (or segregation) and marginalization. *Assimilation* occurs when a group surrenders its cultural identity and is absorbed into the larger society (the "melting pot" concept). *Integration* is the result when the group maintains its culture but also interacts

with other groups. In cases where intergroup contact is unwelcome and cultural integrity is maintained, the outcome will be either *segregation* (if the group is a weak minority) or *separation* (if the group is more powerful). The final possibility, *marginalization,* results when the traditional culture is lost and there is little contact with the larger society. Marginalization is usually accompanied by confusion, anxiety, hostility and feelings of alienation, a syndrome that has been termed *acculturative stress* (Berry, 1987).

This model can be applied to individuals as well as groups and does not describe an all-or-nothing process. Positions can be taken between the two extremes of cultural distinctiveness and interethnic contact.

Berry, Kalin and Taylor (1977) found that in many instances, ethnicity interacts with other factors to determine interaction. In particular, the status of the individual and the type of relationship entered into appear to be important to people. In their study, respondents were asked to indicate on a scale from 1 to 7 the extent to which they would be willing to interact with immigrants in both a business relationship and a friendship relationship. In addition, the immigrants were classified as representing four occupations: two of high status (dentist and teacher) and two of low status (shoemaker and plumber). Not surprisingly, the results indicated that in friendship relationships, individuals of high status would be preferred over those of low status, and that French and English Canadians would be preferred over immigrants as friends. However, the data concerning business relationships were more complicated. It was found that the respondents were willing to do business with English and French Canadians regardless of their status, but they expressed much greater willingness to seek the services of a low-status immigrant (shoemaker, plumber) than of a high-status immigrant (teacher, dentist). This result implies that while Canadians are happy to admit well-educated, high-status immigrants into the country, they may be reluctant to use their professional services.

One factor that may contribute to in-group identity is the number of members of the group in a given location. Kalin and Berry (1979) observe that a very high concentration of a given group may be detrimental to national unity by leading to cultural encapsulation of that group and, therefore, to greater ethnocentrism. If this is so, increased ethnocentrism should challenge the multicultural philosophy of the Canadian social system. The **multiculturalism hypothesis** states that

FIGURE 13-7

FIGURE 13-7

Types of in-group and
out-group relationships

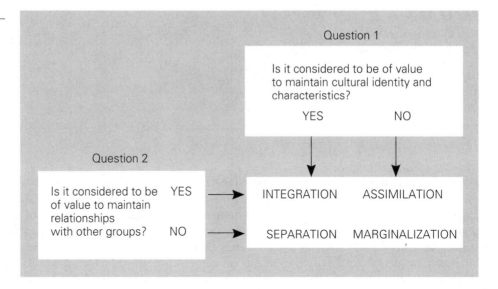

positive feelings towards members of other groups will be related to how secure and comfortable a person feels with his own cultural identity and background.

This proposition was tested by Lambert, Mermigis and Taylor (1986) using Greek Canadians in Montreal as subjects. They measured attitudes towards their own group, other ethnic groups, cultural assimilation and cultural maintenance. Data also were obtained on the degree of ethnocentrism, religiosity and amount of formal education. It was found that the respondents took a strong stand on the need to maintain Greek culture and language and, compared with a number of other ethnic groups (English Canadians, French Canadians, Jewish Canadians, Black Canadians, Italian Canadians and Portuguese Canadians), rated their own group most positively. In addition, social contacts with members of their own group were preferred over contacts with members of the other groups. The other groups were rated most favourably by Greek Canadians who were the most culturally secure and who were the most ethnocentric. However, these same individuals were less willing to interact with members of those groups. The Greek Canadians who were least ethnocentric and better educated were most willing to associate with members of the other groups.

These results do not fully support the multiculturalism hypothesis. Cultural security and well being, although correlated with a positive evaluation of other groups, was not associated with a willingness to socialize with them. Lambert et al. suggest that further research may reveal education as the critical factor in

decreasing ethnocentrism while maintaining security and increasing the likelihood of social interaction between groups.

Education

Many studies have examined the relationship between level of education and prejudice. The outcome has been generally consistent in showing that as education increases, prejudice decreases (see Table 13–5). However, you will recall from our discussion of correlations in Chapter 1 that we cannot conclude from these data that education necessarily *produces* tolerance. Other factors associated with school attendance might account for the relationship. For example, individuals with more education are on average more intelligent, are more flexible thinkers and come from higher socioeconomic levels of society. Also, extracurricular activities that offer the potential for social conformity—clubs, sports, discussions—rather than the formal education experience, may be the critical factor.

Research that could delineate clearly the variables in the education process affecting prejudice is difficult to do and few, if any, experiments dealing with this question are completely satisfactory. For example, it is not sufficient to demonstrate, as some studies have done, that first-year university students are more prejudiced than those in their final year. Final-year students are three years older, more highly selected and have had three years' more extracurricular experience than new students. As a matter of fact, the effect may simply be

TABLE 13-5

Level of education and prejudice: How subjects described themselves

	Education attained		
	Primary (%)	Secondary (%)	University (%)
Very prejudiced	17.4	17.9	3.5
Somewhat prejudiced	53.7	33.6	19.8
Somewhat tolerant	23.6	36.4	37.9
Very tolerant	5.3	12.11	38.8

Source: Henry, 1978

due to a higher failure or dropout rate among the less tolerant. Better investigations take a longitudinal approach and follow the same individuals from one point in their educational career to a later one. These studies also reveal an increase in tolerance over time but again are unable to specify the precise variables that account for the change. Nevertheless, we can state in a general way that education in or out of the classroom increases tolerance.

An extensive project conducted by Six (1989) emphasizes the importance of using more than one educational approach to modify prejudice. The purpose of the study was to reduce prejudice of German students towards Turkish students. To this end, two TV films were produced that showed both the positive and negative aspects of life for a Turkish girl and boy living in Germany. In addition, a teaching program was developed with similar goals to those of the films—that is, to present new information, to teach different ways of social categorization, to inform about prejudice in general and to create positive emotional involvement. Students between the ages of 10 and 15 were assigned to five conditions: (1) films only; (2) soundtrack only; (3) teaching program only; (4) a shorter teaching program and the films; or (5) a no-treatment control group. Measures of prejudice were obtained over a 10-week period, beginning one week prior to treatment and then continuing immediately after treatment and three, six and nine weeks later. All treatments caused short-term changes but long-term change was significant only with the combined teaching and film program. In addition the more prejudiced a student had been, the less the prejudice was reduced. In fact, the television conditions (video or audio only) had no effect on highly prejudiced students. It appears that pre-existing prejudice causes information to be devalued, distorted and misinterpreted. The teaching program that prepared the students for the films reduced the negative influence of the pre-existing prejudice and so the films became more effective.

In Canada, the relationship of second-language learning to attitudes has also received attention as an educational issue. Much of the research has been carried out by Lambert and his associates at McGill (Lambert et al., 1963; Gardner & Lambert, 1972). The social-psychological effects of bilingualism are discussed in detail in Chapter 7, but it should be mentioned here that individuals who have acquired a second language seem to have more positive attitudes towards other cultural groups than do monolinguals, if their initial orientation was integrative (an interest in the culture) rather than instrumental (such as to improve job prospects). It has also been shown that anglophone parents with an integrative orientation have positive attitudes towards francophones even though they may not know any (Gardner & Lambert, 1959).

The relationship of such attitudes and integrative motivation to competence in another language has been found to hold in locations as diverse as Maine, Louisiana, Connecticut and the Philippines (Gardner, Gliksman & Smythe, 1978).

The Victims of Prejudice

While much has been written on how prejudice develops and is maintained, less attention has been devoted to the victims of prejudice and discrimination. How do minority group members respond and how do they defend themselves? Over 40 years ago, Gordon Allport (1954) identified more than 15 possible consequences of being victimized. Among these are withdrawal and passivity, clowning, militancy, aggression against own-group and self-hate. In some cases, minority group members will be hostile to their own group, whereas others will be loyal to their own group and aggressive towards other groups. Extending Allport's approach, Tajfel and Turner (1979) postulate three types of responses. The victimized can simply accept their situation with passivity and resignation—although not without resentment; they can try as individuals to break free and "make it" in society; or they can attempt collective action and improve the status of the group itself. Subsequent research has enhanced our understanding of the variety of individual and collective reactions to prejudice. See Critical Thinking—How Groups May React to Deal with Discrimination, which outlines stages through which victimized groups deal with prejudice and discrimination.

The experience of prejudice and discrimination

The members of different ethnic groups report experiencing varying amounts of prejudice and discrimination. Dion (1989) and Dion & Kawakami (1996) compared the experiences of six ethnic groups in Toronto: Chinese, East Indian, Italian, Jewish, Portuguese and blacks. The visible minorities perceived greater discrimination towards their group than did white minorities, with blacks reporting the highest levels of discrimination both against the group and against themselves in particular. The white minority members perceived lower levels of group and individual discrimination except for the Jewish respondents, who perceived greater group discrimination with regard to joining clubs. In spite of this, the Jewish respondents, unlike the blacks and East Indians, were satisfied with their life in Toronto.

Dion points out that it is common for people to report more discrimination against their group than against themselves as individuals. For example in one survey of university women, respondents consistently reported that they believed there was more discrimination directed at women in general than they had personally experienced (Taylor, Wright & Porter, 1994). Why would individual members of disadvantaged groups (such as women) minimize personal discrimination? One argument is that minority group members are reluctant to admit that their failures are due to discrimination because this would indicate that what happens to them is controlled by others. By believing that they are responsible for their own successes and failures, they are able to maintain their self-esteem. An unfortunate implication is that if individuals attribute failures to their own shortcomings, they are less likely to try to improve their status or that of their group such as through protest or legal action. It is also important to consider the situations in which discrimination might occur. For example, Dion and Kawakami (1996) found that visible minorities reported most discrimination was in the areas of jobs, pay and promotions.

Reactions to prejudice and discrimination

When people encounter frustration because of the barriers of discrimination, they may attribute their failure to that discrimination, they may blame the failures of their own group or they might well blame themselves for failure in order to avoid blaming other members of the group. In research by Ruggiero and colleagues (Ruggiero & Taylor, 1995, 1997), self-blame has been the focus of studies. For instance in one study, female students completed a test ostensibly measuring their future career success and were told that a high mark made them eligible for a $50 prize. They were told that a panel of male students would then evaluate them and that 100 percent, 75 percent, 50 percent, 25 percent or none of them were known to discriminate against women. Then all participants were told that they had failed the test. When asked to explain why they felt they had performed so poorly, those who had been told that they would be evaluated by a panel of male chauvinists attributed their failure to discrimination as one would expect. However, the female participants in other groups tended to blame themselves—indeed those who were told that there was a 75 percent chance that they had been the victims of discrimination blamed themselves as much as those told that there was only a 25 percent chance. That is, where there is any room for doubt, they tended to deny that they were the target of sexist discrimination. However in another study, participants attributed their failure to discrimination only in the 100 percent condition. It seems that people can often see their group as being the target of discrimination but will deny any personal experience (Foster & Matheson, 1999).

Dion and his colleagues (1975, 1986) have demonstrated experimentally other reactions when minority group members perceive that they have been the targets of prejudice. In these studies, a situation was created in which members of an out-group (e.g., Jews, Chinese and women) were asked to complete a task on which their success or failure depended on the action of in-group members (e.g., Christians and men). It was found that perceived prejudice led both Jews and women to strengthen their positive stereotypes of themselves. However, the Chinese subjects reacted more defensively, denying the negative stereotypes

How Groups May React to Deal with Discrimination

Over time and history, victimized groups evolve in how they react to their disadvantaged situation. A five-stage model has been outlined showing how groups deal with prejudice and social disadvantage in various societies (Taylor & McKirnon, 1984; Louis & Taylor 1999). Notice that the model is attributional, explaining how the victimized may both interpret and respond to their situation.

CLEARLY STRATIFIED GROUP RELATIONS This is a historical situation of deeply entrenched relationships of power and subordination between groups where everyone "knows their place." The power difference is so clear and absolute as to be essentially unchallenged. In some cases, the subordinate group members react with self-hate (Allport, 1954), downgrading themselves as members of the "inferior" group and attributing their own inferior status to their belonging to that group. Thus in another era, women may have attributed restrictions in their lives to their "natural inability" to compete with men.

EMERGENCE OF AN INDIVIDUALISTIC IDEOLOGY An industrialized economy places great value on education, skills and achievement. In this "meritocracy," it becomes increasingly awkward to discriminate against whole groups and more focus is placed on the individual *per se*. How can such societies explain the persistence of status differences between groups? Attributions also shift from group membership in and of itself to the ability, effectiveness and responsibility of individuals. Thus if women do not succeed in engineering, it may not be because of their inherent characteristics as women, but their lack of ability or interest.

INDIVIDUAL SOCIAL MOBILITY Certain group members try to be accepted into the society of the dominant group on the terms of the society. Where possible, they may change their names, language, culture or religion in order to penetrate the dominant group. Or they may accommodate the dominant norms in every way possible, though unable to shed the recognizable characteristics of race or sex.

Success or failure has now become seen as almost entirely a matter of personal characteristics, particularly among the exceptional members of the disadvantaged group who have some chance of success.

CONSCIOUSNESS RAISING Of course, the dominant group needs a few successes from the out-group to support its ideology of individual responsibility and the myth of equal opportunity. Thus, some succeed through tokenism or extraordinary talent or effort, but many more fail and the disadvantaged status of the group remains unchanged. Over time, attributions within this group shift again as the majority of those who cannot be accepted and successful in society realize that the fault does not lie in their inherent characteristics as individuals or as group members. It now becomes apparent that their disadvantaged status in society is an injustice, has been determined collectively and can only change through collective action. Attribution for failure is attached to a group again, but now the in-group rather than the out-group is blamed.

COMPETITIVE INTERGROUP RELATIONS Collective action by the disadvantaged group to improve their position can succeed only at a cost in power and privilege to the dominant group. Thus, it will be resisted in some way and a competitive relationship will endure until some sort of rough equality is obtained. However once significant numbers of the disadvantaged group succeed, individuals in the group may revert to individualistic striving: "If I made it, so can you." Notice an interesting divergence between attributions about the past and the future: "our" disadvantaged position was due primarily to "them," but "our" future success must depend on "us."

The theorists argue that groups proceed through these stages in sequence, coming ultimately to the point at which self-blame is futile but collective action is necessary. In terms of attributions, the implications of prejudice are particularly crucial. Recall the self-serving bias in which individuals attribute their own successes to themselves and their failures to external factors. Because our identity as individuals is influenced so powerfully by our identity as members of groups—religious, ethnic, national, sexual—we can also conceive of a group-serving bias in which we attribute successes to positive group characteristics and failures to external factors such as discrimination. In some cases, attributing failure and frustration to being a victim of prejudice can protect people from feeling depressed about the rejection (Major, Kaiser & McCoy, 2003).

associated with that group. Dion, Earn & Yee (1986) suggest that the "visibility" of the minority group may account for these different reactions. The members of visible minorities focus on the negative stereotypes (*defensive self-presentation*). On the other hand, members of groups that are not so easily identified emphasize the positive stereotypes.

Other factors observed by Dion included self-esteem and amount of stress. Contrary to expectation, it was found that the experience of prejudice resulted in enhanced self-esteem for the members of the three groups—Jews, women and Chinese. Crocker and her colleagues (Crocker, 1999; Crocker & Lawrence, 1999; Crocker & Quinn, 1998) suggest that many individuals who are stigmatized, whether by ethnic membership or physical characteristics such as obesity, do not have low self-esteem, because self-esteem arises from different sources of information. Thus, African Americans who do not have low self-esteem are less likely to internalize devaluation and discrimination. In other words, they attribute these experiences to prejudice rather than to their own shortcomings. On the other hand, surprisingly perhaps, Asian Americans have significantly lower self-esteem than do other groups. Crocker argues that this is because they base their self-esteem, as do whites, on the approval of others. Thus, prejudice and discrimination are assumed to reflect actual personal defects.

Not surprisingly, however, the targets in these studies also experienced some degree of stress. For example in the face of anti-Semitism, Jewish subjects reported feeling aggressive, sad and anxious. Clearly, discrimination is perceived as threatening and under some circumstances those discriminated against may act overtly against the dominant group. For example when prejudice and discrimination lead to deprivation and inequality in the distribution of employment or educational opportunities, militancy and violence may result. Caplan and Paige (1968) have reported that blacks who took part in the U.S. race riots in the 1960s were more sensitive to perceived discrimination, reported that they more frequently experienced discrimination and were less willing to accept the stereotype of black inferiority than were blacks who remained inactive.

Indeed, being the victim of prejudice can have severe consequences on one's physical and mental health. For instance, the stigma, prejudice, discrimination and even the threat of violence experienced by many gay, lesbian and bisexual persons creates a social environment of chronic stress. Whether they react by internalizing homophobic attitudes or concealing their sexual orientation, or live with expectations of hostility and rejection by others, the evidence suggests a relatively high prevalence of psychiatric disorders among them, all related to stress reactions (Meyer, 2003).

Consider how stereotypes can become self-fulfilling prophecies. If some immigrant or aboriginal groups come to believe the stereotype that they are academically inferior, or if women come to accept the stereotype that they are unable to succeed in mathematics or hard sciences, then they come to "disidentify" with these areas of achievement and avoid them. Steele (1997) points out that when members of a stereotyped group are placed in a situation involving performance, they are at a disadvantage, having to struggle with the stereotype that they may have internalized and that they feel others will have accepted. The resultant apprehension and anxiety will undermine their performance. This is known as the **stereotype threat** effect (Steele, 1997). Thus for instance if women are stereotyped as less competent in mathematics, they may be at a disadvantage in writing a mathematics examination because of the stereotype threat effect, particularly when the stereotype has been cognitively activated.

Why do disadvantaged groups sometime not respond to the injustices that they experience? Dion (2001) adds that individuals who are deprived of their expected social status or economic rewards may experience anger and a determination to gain their just rewards in life.

However, the anger that they experience will depend on "relative deprivation," which comes from social comparison with others. Those who belong to disadvantaged stereotyped groups may compare themselves to others of their own group rather than the larger society and consequently not feel so deprived. This may explain the paradox of apparent acceptance of discrimination and prejudice by its victims.

Finally, it is quite possible that individuals will not accept and internalize the stereotype imposed on their group. For instance, stereotypes about aging people may include positive attributes such as wisdom and experience, but also may include being slow, rigid even cognitively incapable. However, many resist the stereotype by not identifying themselves as "old" or "elderly," finding positive information about themselves and developing compensatory behaviour that staves off the self-fulfilling prophecy of the stereotype (Zebrowitz, 2003). However, the stereotype, when activated, can still influence the behaviour of others towards aging individuals.

Sexism

Among the many groups experiencing prejudice and discrimination, the largest by far comprises women. In Canada, women have struggled long and hard to achieve the far from satisfactory status they have today. In many other parts of the world, progress has been minimal or nonexistent and women continue to be relegated to the inferior roles they have occupied throughout history (see Figure 13–8). Prejudice and discrimination towards women are often subtle and rarely accompanied by the overt hostility that is frequently directed at other out-groups.

In a majority of the societies of the world, to be female means to be perceived as less competent and to have lower status than men (see A Case in Point—Gender and Culture on page 388) for an extreme example and also consider the status of women in countries such as Saudi Arabia). Canada is no exception. Among the many social stereotypes that are maintained about women (by both men and women) are those pertaining to *role assignments*. Certain occupations, such as nursing, secretarial positions and truck driving are sex-typed (see Table 13–6) and those of the other sex who enter nontraditional occupations such as engineering or nursing may be viewed as aberrant. Similarly, levels within occupations are often available to men and women on an unequal basis. We find relatively few women in positions of power in industry or commerce, even though women may be equally represented or over represented in the lower ranks. For instance, 73 percent of Canadian bank employees are women. However, these women, like their counterparts in many other sectors of Canadian business soon hit the "glass ceiling." They can see the prospects that are available, but because of biased attitudes, they can't achieve them. Subsequent to the tragedy at the École Polytechnique in Montreal in 1989, where 14 female engineering students were murdered, considerable attention has been focused on women in engineering. More than a decade later, relatively few women enter engineering at university and few of those who graduate achieve senior positions (see Figure 13–9 and Table 13–7 on page 389).

Broverman, Vogel, Broverman, Clarkson & Rosenkrantz (1972) define the sex-role stereotype of women as including the perception that women are less competent, less independent, less objective and less logical than men. On the other hand, men in comparison with women are perceived as lacking interpersonal sensitivity, warmth and expressiveness. The researchers also point out that masculine traits are often perceived as more desirable than feminine traits. If these perceptions become incorporated into the self-image of women, it is not surprising that many women have a negative self-concept and low self-esteem, making them more vulnerable to "the self-fulfilling prophecy" syndrome. For instance, they may reduce their aspiration levels and remain satisfied with positions much below their real ability and competence.

Even when women do well, they may not receive appropriate credit. For example, Deaux and Emswiller (1974) had subjects observe males and females successfully complete either a "male" or a "female" task. They then scored the performance on a scale indicating the extent to which the outcome was due to luck or ability. The observers did not discriminate between males and females on the feminine task but both male and female observers attributed male success on the male task to *ability* and female success on the same task to *luck*.

There is no doubt that the situation is changing although more slowly than is desirable. Some evidence that attitudes towards women—and out-groups in general—may not have changed as much as expected has been presented by Bechtold, Naccarato and Zanna (1986). They suggest that although overt discrimina-

FIGURE 13-8

Ethiopian emporer Haile Selassie's edict of 1935 issued during the Italian invasion

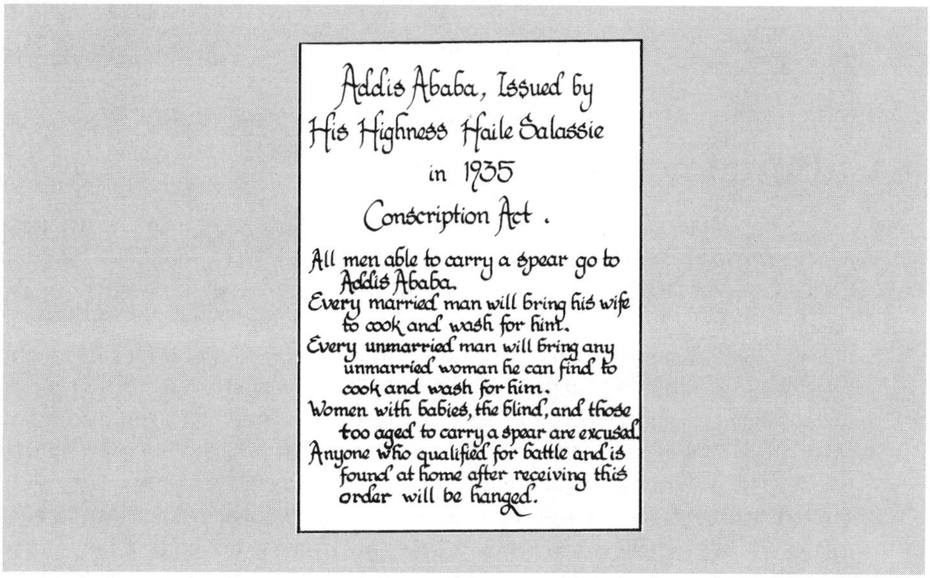

> Addis Ababa, Issued by
> His Highness Haile Salassie
> in 1935
> Conscription Act.
>
> All men able to carry a spear go to Addis Ababa.
> Every married man will bring his wife to cook and wash for him.
> Every unmarried man will bring any unmarried woman he can find to cook and wash for him.
> Women with babies, the blind, and those too aged to carry a spear are excused.
> Anyone who qualified for battle and is found at home after receiving this order will be hanged.

Source: Espy, 1975

tion has declined in Canada, it has not been accompanied by a parallel decline in underlying prejudice.

Current social norms are such that tolerance and goodwill are expected, but under certain conditions, prejudicial attitudes may surface. To test this proposition, Bechtold et al. (1986) asked male and female subjects to act as personnel officers and make hiring decisions based on the résumés of either male or female applicants for a marketing position. Some of the subjects were allowed ample time to arrive at a decision while others were placed under considerable time pressure. It was found that subjects under time pressure discriminated more against female applicants than did subjects who had no time constraints. In addition, the men discriminated against female applicants more than the women did. Another analysis showed that "traditional" female subjects compared with "modern" female subjects discriminated against the female applicants in the same way the male subjects had done.

The purpose of personnel selection is to select the best possible applicant for the job. Therefore, rigid stereotyping on the basis of sex (or age, or ethnic origin or any other category) is not only an injustice to the job applicant but also a detriment to the employer. Research using the concepts and methods of social perception and cognition has shed light on the problem.

TABLE 13-6

Top ten occupations in Canada by sex

Rank	Males	Females
1	Truck driver	Retail salesclerk
2	Retail salesclerk	Office secretary
3	Janitor/caretaker	Cashier
4	Retail manager	Registered nurse
5	Farmer	Accounting clerk
6	Sales rep	Elementary/kindergarten teacher
7	Vehicle mechanic	Waitress
8	Material handler	Office clerk
9	Carpenter	Baby-sitter
10	Construction labourer	Receptionist

Source: Statistics Canada, Census 1986, Special Tabulations

Culture and Gender

Every census conducted in India has recorded more males than females. In most Western societies, the sex ratio at birth is about 105 males to 100 females. However in India, this ratio is 112 males per 100 females. What accounts for this disparity? The answer lies in a bias at all levels of Indian society that discriminates against women. In India, sons are desired because they stay at or near home after marriage and continue to contribute to the welfare of the family. Daughters not only leave home after marriage but also require expensive dowries in order to be married. In addition, sons are obligated to take care of their parents and play an important role in funeral ceremonies.

With the availability of tests to identify the sex of the fetus, selective abortions are common. One study found that of 8000 abortions in Mumbai (formerly known as Bombay), 7999 were female fetuses (Freed & Freed, 1989). In addition, at the All India Institute of Medical Sciences, of all the surgeries carried out on children, 70 percent are on boys and only 30 percent on girls. It is also the case that girls are not brought to hospital until their illness is advanced and even then parents are often willing to forgo treatment. One father who was asked to donate blood for his daughter said, "She is to go away after marriage. Why should I harm my health for her?" The girl died a few days later. Less traumatic but important evidence of this discrimination lies in the fact that female infants are breastfed less frequently or for less time than boys and that older girls receive less food especially leafy vegetables, fruit and calcium than boys. Finally, females, except in the state of Kerala, receive less education and have a much lower level of literacy than males. In 1991, the literacy rates were 64 percent for males and 39 percent for females. Although laws have been passed abolishing dowries and prenatal sex determination, they have had little effect. All the statistics have remained distressingly stable (based on reports in the *Times of India,* January 16, 2000).

The cultural stereotype used to state that "women are not strong enough to handle all that heavy camera equipment."

Arvey (1979) argues that many jobs are sex-typed as being more appropriate to one sex than to the other and that employment decisions are influenced by the congruency between the sex of the applicant and the sex-typing of the job. It is clear that there is still a distinct pattern of occupational segregation in Canada. Women make up the overwhelming majority of restaurant servers, telephone operators, secretaries, nurses, baby-sitters, dental hygienists, librarians, physiotherapists and elementary and kindergarten teachers, while most of the lawyers, dentists, truck drivers, accountants, secondary school teachers, janitors and industrial engineers are men (Statistics Canada, 1998; Greenglass, 1982).

Kalin and Hodgins (1984) note that sex-role congruence tends to be important only in the abstract situation where no other information is available. However in reality, the decision-maker has considerable information from interviews, letters and résumé about the appli-

FIGURE 13-9

Equal opportunity?

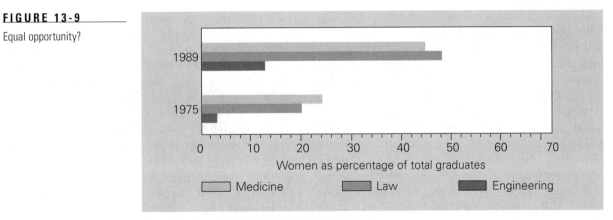

Source: *Report on Business Magazine*, September 1992

cant's background and personal characteristics. They outline a social cognition model of occupational suitability judgments in which the person begins with applicant–job schemata including the following: (1) associations between social categories such as sex and occupation (e.g., "bank teller" is associated with a female and "construction worker" with a male); (2) associations between social categories (sex, occupation) and personal characteristics (these are the stereotypes held by people about men, women, insurance agents, truck drivers, professors of psychology and so forth); and (3) associations among various personal characteristics (e.g., "friendly" is associated with "trustworthy" (implicit personality theory)). Thus using information about social categories and personal characteristics, we base evaluations on patterns of associations among them. When we know only the categories, we may use a simple congruency rule between sex and occupation (e.g., "A suitable truck driver is male"). However when we have information about personal characteristics, we rely more on these impressions and match them with

occupational stereotypes. If the occupation is strongly sex-typed, then the occupational stereotype will include "masculine" or "feminine" characteristics. While far from ideal, occupational stereotyping is an improvement over simple sex stereotyping and sex–job matching in that it does not exclude men or women from the job.

Hodgins and Kalin (1985) tested this model in two experiments in which the subjects (university students) were asked to play the role of guidance counsellors. They were given brief descriptions of three male and three female high-school students and were asked to rate the students' suitability for each of four male-typed occupations (commercial traveller, surveyor, engineering technician, sales manager) and four female-typed occupations (social worker, nurse, librarian, occupational therapist). In this minimal information situation, subjects showed a strong tendency to match sex of person with sex-type of the job. However in a second experiment, subjects were also provided with brief descriptions of personality consisting of traits previously rated by other subjects as "masculine"

TABLE 13-7

Women need not apply

Very few women have secured management positions in engineering, or full-time engineering faculty appointments at Canadian universities

Job Responsibility	Number of Women Employed	Women as Percentage of Total
Senior Supervisor	100	3
Senior Manager	66	2
Executive	41	1
Full-time Professor	54	2

Source: *Report on Business Magazine*, September 1992

(self-confident, strong, assertive, opportunistic), "feminine" (affectionate, warm, sensitive, charming) or neutral (formal, calm, determined). In this case, subjects matched the sex-type of personality characteristics with the sex-type of the job regardless of whether the actual client was male or female.

In this study, the occupations selected as female-typed and male-typed were those that previous research has shown to be equivalent in status. However in the real world of contemporary Canada, although women have gained access to some of the high-status "male" occupations, most still work in "female" jobs, which tend to be lower in both status and pay (Greenglass, 1982). Indeed, Statistics Canada reports that over a 10-year period, female full-time, full-year employed workers earned an average of 71.8 percent of their male counterparts in 1992 and 71.6 percent in 2001, representing no progress at all.

Along similar lines, it has been found (Conway, Pizzamiglio & Mount, 1996) that individuals perceived as being of lower status male *or* female are also perceived as more communal (a stereotypic female trait) and less agentic (a stereotypic male trait) than individuals of higher status. Similarly, men in low-status jobs are less assertive and less dominant (less agentic) than men in high-status jobs and women in high-status jobs are less sensitive and more leadership-oriented (less communal) than women in low-status jobs. It seems that gender not only assigns status to occupations, but conversely, the status of an occupation assigns male or female characteristics to those in the occupation irrespective of their gender. Fortunately in addition to removing barriers to occupational choice and abolishing inequities in pay for the same occupation, our society is becoming aware of inequities based on the sex typing of occupations. Such awareness is manifest in the slogan "Equal pay for work of equal value."

Glick, Zion and Nelson (1988) point out that while an employer's stereotypes may be responsible for that employer hiring a male or female in the first place, once an occupation has been labelled as "male" or "female" even if stereotypes change, discrimination is likely to continue. Krefting, Berger and Wallace (1978) found that the best prediction of the sex-type of job was the percentage of men and women in the various occupations and that the actual job content—that is, what the person was required to do—was not significant. This implies that the reduction or elimination of sex stereotypes may not have a large effect on employment practices at least in the short run.

Discrimination against women is not confined to the workplace. For example, more than 20 years ago in a well publicized study (Goldberg, 1968), identical essays were submitted to judges to be assigned a grade. In half the cases, the "author" was identified as male; in the other half, as female. Essays ostensibly written by males received higher grades.

This straightforward and uncomplicated result spawned numerous replications and variations and obtained considerable space in textbooks. However, some of these studies do not completely support Goldberg's (1968) contention that females are generally perceived as less competent than males (Pheterson, Kiesler and Goldberg, 1971). Swim, Borgida and Maruyama (1989) reviewed 123 of these studies and concluded that there was little evidence to support Goldberg's original conclusion. However in a later review of 58 controlled experiments conducted over a period of 20 years, Swim & Sanna (1996) found results that were remarkably consistent: when a man was successful on a task, observers attributed his success to ability but the success of a woman on a similar task tended to be attributed to hard work. Failure on a similar task was attributed by observers to bad luck or a lack of effort when the protagonist was male but to lesser ability when the protagonist was female.

Clearly, gender stereotypes persist in our society (Martin, 1986). For example, Simpson, McCarrey and Edwards (1987) studied supervisors in a large organization and found that those with traditional attitudes towards women judged the women they supervised as less able than men to do the following: (1) autonomously direct their subordinates; (2) assist in the career development of subordinates; and (3) effectively monitor the day-to-day performance of their subordinates. Moreover, these supervisors were unwilling to assign technical, high profile projects to women. Along the same lines, Dion (1987) and Dion and Schuller (1991) found that women who used the title Ms. were stereotyped as being more achievement-oriented, socially assertive and dynamic than women who used Mrs. or Miss—but also as less warm. And the stereotypes associated with the Ms. label included those of a successful middle manager whereas those associated with the traditionally labelled person did not.

While overt instances of old-fashioned sexism are decreasing in frequency, sex discrimination is far from dead. Tougas and her colleagues (Tougas, Brown, Beaton & Joly, 1995) refer to a new form of gender attitudes as **neosexism** defined as a "manifestation of a conflict between egalitarian values and residual negative feelings towards women." It is similar to modern racism. In this case, the public expression of gender-related beliefs is inhibited, but some underlying prejudice remains, which may be manifest in disguised forms of discrimination. Traditional sexism was characterized by the support of traditional gender roles, differential treatment of men and women and stereotypes about lesser female competence. Modern sexism denies that discrimination continues. Those who maintain these attitudes are antagonistic towards women's demands and do not support policies such as job equity designed to assist women.

Summary

1. Prejudice is a positive or negative attitude towards perceived differences or characteristics that are unjustly generalized to all the members of a group. Like other attitudes, it has three components: cognitive, affective and behavioural.

2. Stereotypes are cognitions or beliefs about the members of other groups. They are usually overgeneralizations and are often inaccurate.

3. Stereotypes can change depending on changes in social conditions and changes in the relationships between members of different groups.

4. Those stereotypes that have some validity may arise from the operation of the "self-fulfilling prophecy" and the situational pressure created by prejudice.

5. The behavioural component of prejudice is called discrimination, and in its more extreme form, racism. While laws have been enacted making discrimination illegal, many subtle forms, such as biased hiring practices, still exist.

6. Innate fear of the unusual or the unfamiliar may be a primitive basis for prejudice. The acquisition of prejudice begins in the home when the child is about three years of age. Parents, teachers, peers and the media all contribute at various times to this process.

7. Some individuals who have been raised in a certain way are called authoritarian personalities. They are likely to be prejudiced and ethnocentric and may be hostile.

8. One manifestation of pent-up hostility is called scapegoating and results in the individual blaming out-groups for the frustration he or she experiences.

9. Under the appropriate circumstances, prejudice can be reduced by intergroup contact. Unfortunately, intergroup anxiety often prevents people from interacting with the members of other groups.

10. Acculturation refers to the changes in values, attitudes and behaviour that occur when groups come into direct contact.

11. A higher level of education is associated with increased tolerance.

12. The victims of prejudice may react with aggression, changes in self-esteem, changes in group allegiance or modification of the strength of positive or negative stereotypes held about their own group.

13. The stereotype threat can impair performance by members of stereotyped groups.

14. Sexism is usually directed at women and results, among other things, in differential treatment in employment.

Further Reading

ABOUD, F. (1988). *Children and prejudice.* Oxford: Basil Blackwell. An account of the developmental aspects of intolerance that culminates in a new social-cognitive theory of prejudice.

ALLPORT, G.W. (1954). *The nature of prejudice.* Reading: Addison-Wesley. This classic account of the development and maintenance of prejudice is still relevant today.

ALTEMEYER, B. (1988). *Enemies of freedom: Understanding right-wing authoritarianism.* San Francisco: Jossey-Bass. This very readable, award-winning book outlines the results of a long-term research program and discusses the role of parents, religion and education in the development of authoritarian attitudes.

BACKHOUSE, C. (1999). *Colour-coded: A legal history of racism in Canada, 1900–1950.* Toronto: The Osgoode Society for Canadian Legal History. A disturbing examination of the effects of direct and indirect racism on the framing of laws and the administration of justice in Canada.

BERRY, J.W. & LAPONCE, J. (Eds.). (1994). *Ethnicity and culture in Canada: The research landscape.* Toronto: University of Toronto Press. A review of multiculturalism and ethnicity in Canada from the perspectives of a variety of disciplines including history, literature, education and demography.

EBERHARDT, J.L. & FISKE, S.T. (Eds.). (1998). *Confronting Racism: The problem and the response.* Thousand Oaks, CA: Sage Publications Inc. A wide-ranging set of articles on the intrapersonal, interpersonal and intergroup processes that lead to racism.

ESSES, V.M. & GARDNER, R.C. (Eds.). (1996). Multiculturalism in Canada: Context and current status. *Canadian Journal of Behavioural Science,* Vol. 28, No. 3. This special issue is devoted to multiculturalism from a variety of perspectives including immigration, ethnicity, communication and discrimination.

FISKE, S. (1998). Prejudice, stereotyping and discrimination. In D.Gilbert, S. Fiske & G. Lindzey (Eds.). *Handbook of social psychology* (4th ed.). Vol.1. New York: McGraw-Hill. An excellent overview on the topic, particularly the discussion of stereotyping.

OSKAMP, S. & CONSTANZO, E. (Eds.). *Gender issues in contemporary society.* Newbury Park, CA: Sage Publications Inc. A comprehensive discussion of various aspects of gender, with excellent treatment of gender discrimination and stereotypes.

SWIM, J.K. & STANGOR, C. (Eds.). (1998). *Prejudice: The target's perspective.* San Diego, CA: Academic Press. A summary of research focusing on the victims of prejudice.

TAYLOR, D.M. & MOGHADDEM, F.M. (1987). *Theories of intergroup relations: International social psychological perspectives.* New York: Praeger. Survey of contributions by social psychologists to our understanding of phenomena such as race riots, labour disputes, sexism, religious intolerance and social prejudice.

ZANNA, M.P. & OLSON, J.M. (Eds.). 1993. *The psychology of prejudice: The Ontario symposium.* Vol. 7. Hillsdale, NJ: Erlbaum. Expert reviews of current research, theories and directions.

Weblinks

Anti-defamation League of B'nai B'rith

www.adl.org Founded in 1913, this American organization is the premier civil rights/human relations agency fighting anti-Semitism, prejudice and bigotry.

Anti-racism

www.nizkor.almanac.bc.ca A list of sites related to anti-racism.

Chapter 14

Crowds and Collective Behaviour

Only individuals think; gangs merely throb.

Robertson Davies

Fashions, after all, are only induced epidemics.

George Bernard Shaw, The Doctor's Dilemma

Chapter Outline

In May 2001 New Delhi was gripped by reports of people being attacked in their sleep by a hairy "Monkey Man." He was four feet tall, had a dark face, large eyes and metal claws and was equipped with super powers including being able to jump to a height of six metres and the ability to become invisible. The Monkey Man had been blamed for injuries to 100 people and 50 such attacks were reported on one night alone. The police commissioner was quoted as saying, "*People are in a state of terror. This creature attacks people who sleep in rooftops or out in the open. It strikes when there is a power cut in the area.*" An additional 1000 police officers were deployed to patrol the streets of New Delhi at night. People began sleeping in groups for greater protection and some were injured—one man was killed—as a result of jumping from the rooftops to avoid the attacker. According to one woman interviewed by the police, "*It has three buttons on its chest. One makes it turn into a monkey, the second gives it extra strength and the third makes it invisible. It touches a lock and it breaks. But he is afraid of the light.*" (*The Globe and Mail*, 16 May 2001).

The wave of reports soon died away following the report of a committee of experts that analyzed the personality, socioeconomic and psychological profiles of the victims and concluded that the reports were the result of "mass hysteria and rumour mongering."

- On the night of May 7, 1945, tens of thousands of sailors streamed into the streets of Halifax to celebrate Germany's surrender. They broke into and emptied a liquor store and then set a streetcar ablaze. The next day, a parade of soldiers, sailors and airmen marched to the centre of the city in official celebration of VE-Day (Victory in Europe), a parade authorities believed would bring an end to the disorderly behaviour that had begun the night before. Instead, the festivities turned into a riot fuelled by alcohol looted from government liquor stores. Uniformed servicemen aided and abetted by a large number of civilians looted and demolished hundreds of stores, burned a police vehicle and turned into a "solid wall of drunken humanity," with some couples making love on Citadel Hill in broad daylight. When the melee ended two nights later, two people had been killed and damage

to property totalled $5 million. It was a celebration gone wild (*Maclean's*, May 1, 1995).

- In October 1990, a rumour spread throughout Lagos, Nigeria, that organ robbers were stealing men's penises. This supposedly occurred magically while the organ robber made some sort of physical contact with the victim, often through a handshake as the victim was approached and asked for directions. It was believed that the penis would magically reappear on the body of someone else who had paid a great deal of money for it. The fear became so rampant and the emotion ran so high that some suspects were beaten and even lynched by irate mobs. In November, riots broke out in city streets resulting in several deaths. Despite assurances from hospitals and police that examinations of supposed victims showed their genitals to be normal, the rumours and fear continued over a period of many months. It became common for men walking through crowded markets to check their genitals following any bodily contact with a passerby.

395 Chapter Fourteen **Crowds and Collective Behaviour** 395

You will recall (from Chapter 6) the effects of the mere presence of others on the behaviour of a person (social facilitation) as well as the pressures those individuals, groups and organizations can exert (producing conformity, compliance and obedience). The situations described above, however, cannot be readily understood in terms of these interpersonal or group processes. There was no leader or system demanding obedience, nor did pre-existing group norms generate pressures to conform. Each of these examples involved collections of people who for the most part were strangers to one another. But in each case, the early actions of a few people stimulated the later actions of a great many people. Once some people reported having been attacked by the Monkey Man, once the drunken Halifax celebration turned destructive, and once it became common belief that penis-thieves were about, the stage was set for imitation by many others. Somehow such behaviours depend on the presence of other people who are acting or are prepared to act similarly and who have a mutual influence on each other. It would have been more difficult and unreasonable, indeed even bizarre, to have been the only one to talk about a super-powered Monkey Man, to make love publicly on Citadel Hill or to worry about penis theft.

What Is Collective Behaviour?

The foregoing examples illustrate three defining characteristics of **collective behaviour**:

1. It is a relatively rare phenomenon that emerges spontaneously in a collectivity of people (e.g., a crowd or an entire society).

2. It is unplanned, relatively unorganized and not governed by a pre-existing set of norms. Because it is unplanned, its course is difficult to predict. Because it reflects an absence of normal social convention, such behaviour is most likely to arise in situations where people are strangers, leaving them without the support and the normative framework of their usual groups.

   Since collective behaviour is never institutionalized behaviour, the label does not apply to large-scale behaviour governed by existing social norms such as the activities of a large group of strangers on New Year's Eve (Brown, 1965). People at a New Year's Eve party may appear to be out of control as they suddenly rush around kissing each other.

However, this activity is controlled by a norm that allows it to occur at midnight of that particular day and not at other times or on other days. But if on one New Year's Eve, all the party participants rush out into the street and begin to roll around wildly in the snow or go on a rampage smashing store windows, they are then engaging in collective behaviour.

3. It is the product of interstimulation among the participants—that is, individuals are influenced by the actions of others and their reactions, in turn, influence the very people who have affected them (Milgram & Toch, 1969). Sometimes collective behaviour involves an intensification of *anticipated* reactions. For example, while teenagers may go to a rock concert expecting to be excited, interaction among audience members can create a collective experience more powerful than anticipated and more intense than anything the individual would experience alone or in a small group. The interstimulation of members of the collectivity is also reinforcing to some extent; otherwise the behaviour would quickly die out. If a spectator at a football game throws a pop can onto the field and no applause or encouragement is forthcoming, others are unlikely to act similarly. However, if the crowd cheers, then a second person may also throw something onto the field and the behaviour may spread throughout the audience.

The study of collective behaviour is an important part of social psychology, not only in its own right, but because there is hardly any aspect of social behaviour that does not occasionally find extreme expression in some type of collective behaviour episode (Milgram & Toch, 1969). For example, prejudice is sometimes expressed through mob behaviour, which can in turn involve aggression, and both attitude change and impression management are evident in fads and fashions.

It is all but impossible to study most kinds of collective behaviour in the laboratory both for practical and ethical reasons. We would have no idea how to generate a laboratory experiment equivalent to a rock concert or a mob. However, sporadic attempts have been made to do so. In one such study, subjects were successfully convinced that a terrible crime had been committed. The researchers' confederate then attempted to generate and lead a mob to seek out the perpetrators. Only about 12 percent of the subjects were inclined to join the mob (Meier, Mennenga & Stoltz, 1941). In another study, French (1944) tried to simulate a panic by locking groups of subjects in a room, then sounding a fire alarm while forcing smoke under the door and into the room. However, ethics aside, the study was a failure: One group of subjects calmly discussed the possibility that they were being observed for their psychological reactions, while in a second group, the first person to notice the smoke kicked the door open, knocking over the smoke machine. There have been reports that Nazi researchers studied panic by using prisoners in real-life panic situations (Farago, 1942).

It is also difficult to study actual collective behaviour because, in most instances, the behaviour is under way before we have time to prepare to study it. Furthermore, it is difficult to isolate and measure the relevant variables; even the participants are unlikely to be aware of all the important influences upon them. This no doubt explains why, despite the fact that the earliest social psychology texts gave considerable discussion to collective behaviour, relatively little has been done by psychologists to advance our understanding of the subject over the intervening years.

Crowds and Crowding

Crowds can be joyous; crowds can be frightening. And crowds sometimes seem to have a mind of their own, an idea that was the focus of the seminal book *Psychologie des Foules* (*Psychology of the Crowd*) published by the French sociologist Gustave Le Bon in 1895. Although Le Bon's approach, which treats crowds as phenomena that can be examined independently of the social context in which they occur, is viewed as highly flawed by modern theorists, his ideas have had significant impact. Le Bon's book not only stimulated modern psychological interest in collective behaviour, his crowd psychology was credited by leaders such as Mussolini and Hitler as providing the basis for their techniques of mass manipulation (Reicher, 1996).

What is a crowd? A crowd is a relatively large collection of people who are physically close enough to influence each other's behaviour although there is no particular relationship among these individuals. A crowd *is unorganized, anonymous, casual* and *temporary* (Milgram & Toch, 1969). Such a collectivity of people is ideal for the development of collective behaviour, which depends on a lack of group structure and appropriate norms.

Most of the time crowds do not act inappropriately or irrationally. People live together, sometimes in very crowded circumstances, but their behaviour is generally governed by social norms that ensure orderly conduct and general harmony. Sometimes, people deliberately seek out crowds—such as when they congregate in large numbers at various festivals. Other times, it can be unpleasant to be caught up in a large collection of people. What is "crowded" to one person at a particular time may not seem crowded to another person or even that first person at a different time. The feeling of being crowded depends on several factors including the important influence of culture.

Density and crowding

Population density is not the same as **crowding**—the subjective feeling of discomfort when the individual perceives there to be "too many people." For example, we might enjoy being in a high-density situation at a concert or hockey game, but we might dislike it intensely in a library or on a bus at rush hour. And as we all know, there are situations in which "three is a crowd" even though there is, objectively, very low density.

Much of the earlier research equated sheer population density with high rates of crime and mental illness: the **density–social pathology hypothesis**. Proponents of this hypothesis point to animal research such as Calhoun's (1962) "behavioural sink" study in which a colony of 48 rats was allowed to increase its population to 80 within the same space. Although they were provided with sufficient food and water, these rats became aggressive and exhibited much abnormal behaviour in nest-building, courtship, mating and treating offspring. In general, social disorganization was apparent. Autopsies revealed signs of severe stress such as enlarged adrenal glands. Clearly these rats were reacting to crowding. Of course, in nature the animals would have expanded their area and reduced density in order to obtain adequate food and water and to satisfy territorial needs.

Cities have been blamed for many social ills. Indeed, controlled studies reveal a modest but significant correlation ($r = 0.35$) between crime and population density if *only* those two variables are considered (Freedman, Heshka & Levy, 1975). However, the most densely populated cities or neighbourhoods tend to be the poorest, and poverty is invariably related to crime and other social problems. When we control statistically for income levels, quality of housing and representation of disadvantaged minority groups, the relationship between density

FIGURE 14-1B

Psychological distress as a function of residential density and cultural group.

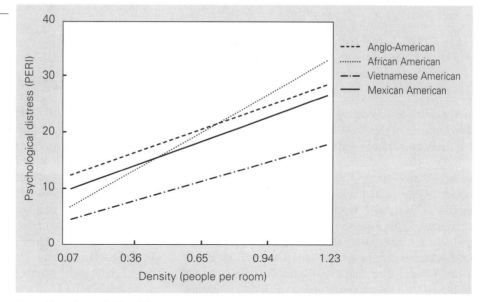

Source: Evans, Lepore & Allen, 2000

button with which to signal the experimenter that they "wanted out," high density had considerably less effect on their performance or subjective experience (Sherrod, 1974). Just because they knew that they were free to leave, the effects of high density were less stressful. Thus, we do not feel crowded at a game or party because we had expected to find a lot of people, we chose to be there and we know that we are free to leave.

Attibution theory and crowding

Independent of cultural background, different individuals may react quite differently to a particular situation with a particular population density. To account for this phenomenon, a model of crowding has been developed based on attribution theory (Worchel & Teddlie, 1976; Schmidt & Keating, 1979). It postulates that people feel crowded when they have been aroused by circumstances such as a violation of personal space or other stressors and then attribute this arousal to the density of people around them. Thus, crowding will not result if people do not feel aroused or if they do not attribute their arousal to violations of their personal space. Indeed, many high-density situations are experienced as enjoyable because the people involved do not feel that their space is invaded or because they attribute their arousal to the excitement of the occasion. Note that this is an alternative to the density–intensity interpretation of the positive and negative experiences engendered by crowding.

These four different perspectives, each applying to somewhat different aspects of crowding, together provide considerable insight into the ways in which crowding influences individuals and their social behaviour.

We have reviewed four theories of crowding: sensory overload, density–intensity, loss of control and attribution theory. Each attempts to explain why a given level of crowding sometimes is pleasant and sometimes unpleasant. However, there is much more to emotion in a crowd than one's pleasure or displeasure in being there—for example, how can the bizarre and apparently irrational crowd behaviour discussed earlier in this chapter be explained? We now turn to that fascinating subject.

Contagion

Contagion in social psychology refers to the rapid spreading of emotionality, beliefs and behaviour throughout a crowd or population, somewhat analogous to the way that diseases spread as one individual infects another. The concept of contagion goes back to Le Bon, who believed that in some situations a crowd can develop a "collective mind" that is inherently irrational:

Under certain given circumstances, and only under those circumstances, an agglomeration of people presents new characteristics very different from those of the individuals composing it. The sentiments and ideas of all the persons in the gathering take one and the same direction and their conscious personality vanishes. A collective mind is formed, doubtless transitory but presenting clearly defined characteristics. The gathering has become what … I will call an organized crowd … or a psychological crowd (Le Bon, 1895/1960, pp. 23–24).

According to Le Bon, several factors contribute to the development of this "collective mind." First, he argued, the sheer number of people in the collectivity produces a feeling of overwhelming power accompanied by a sense of anonymity and a reduction in individual responsibility (anticipating Darley & Latané's (1968) model of bystander nonintervention as reviewed in Chapter 9). This leads to the liberation of "savage, animalistic instincts" that are normally suppressed, he said. Members of the crowd imitate the behaviours of others around them and in turn stimulate others to act similarly. He saw suggestibility as the most important factor producing a vulnerability to contagion, which he considered to be a kind of hypnotic process that leads people to set their own judgment aside.

This early psychology of the crowd put forward by Le Bon can be viewed as a reaction to the threat that the "masses" seemed to pose to the existing social structure of the time. He and his contemporaries devalued crowd behaviour by characterizing it as pathological and focusing on its apparent mindlessness and hysteria rather than on the relationships of crowd members to each other or their reasons for acting together as a crowd (Apfelbaum & McGuire, 1986).

However, even though the notion of a hysterical collective mind and hypnotic influence has not borne up under careful scrutiny, the metaphor of contagion in a crowd is appealing. Modern contagion theory is similar to Le Bon's conception except that the basis for the crowd's behaviour is attributed to the observable inter-stimulation of crowd members by one another rather than some hypnotic influence or the development of a mystical group mind (Wright, 1978).

While the contagion approach to collective behaviour continues to be prominent, it has several drawbacks (Turner, 1964). First, it is extremely difficult to submit it to an empirical test. How might we measure how people stimulate emotional states in each other, for example? Another difficulty is that the theory tells us nothing about the development of leadership and other roles within the collectivity. Moreover, its defenders tend to cite uncommon and dramatic events, which they have not observed directly but have gleaned from the notoriously unreliable eyewitness testimony of laypeople. Further, such events are hardly typical of collective behaviour in general and care must be taken in generalizing from them.

Emotional contagion

Certainly we are all familiar with the notion that people's emotions are influenced by the emotions of others around them. We might expect that if someone is caught up in an angry crowd protesting some change in campus parking regulations, that person's mood might well become more hostile as a result. Or you might expect that when you are in a cinema, a movie gag would produce a more humorous response from you if the audience around you were laughing uproariously. That is, of course, the reason that so many television comedies carry laugh tracks in the background.

There is accumulating evidence that emotional contagion is a genuine phenomenon. For example, Neumann and Fritz (2000) carried out a study in which participants who had been led to believe that they were in a study involving text comprehension listened to the text being read either in a slightly sad or in a happy voice. They then measured the participants' moods by means of a questionnaire and concluded that the happy or sad voice did indeed induce a congruent mood state in the listeners. Of course, this should not be surprising for we know just how readily our moods can be changed by watching good actors emote even though we know they are acting. (Think back to the discussion of empathy in Chapter 9.)

While the above research focused on how individuals react to the mood of another person, other recent research has studied small groups of workers in their natural setting. For example, in one study, 65 community nurses in 13 teams recorded daily their moods and hassles for three weeks. It was found that there was a significant correlation between their moods and those of their team members and this correlation was not due to sharing the same hassles (Totterdall, Teuchman & Briner, 1998). If not due to shared circumstances that create similar moods in people who work together, what could account for this phenomenon? There is research evidence that suggests that the induction of a shared mood comes about in a nonconscious manner through what has been called *primitive emotional contagion*. This refers to the notion that without realizing it, people automatically mimic the expressive displays of people around them including

Deindividuation and the Internet

Consider how the proliferation of e-mail communication and Internet chat rooms allows for varying levels of anonymity in social interaction amongst people from all over the world. This provides a natural testing ground for ideas about "deindividuated" behaviour and already a number of studies have used actual computer-based communications in this way. As one example, Taylor and MacDonald (2002) manipulated the degree of personal anonymity and strength of group identity in e-mail discussion groups and then examined the content of communications for the emergence of "uninhibited" commentary—that is, commentary which departed from the social norms of the larger society. How much more are correspondents willing to communicate unpopular information when anonymity prevails? They found no support for the deindividuation hypothesis but did find some support for the SIDE perspective.

Indeed, Postmes, Spears & Lea (2002) conclude, on the basis of their study of international participants, that the individual anonymity offered by computer-mediated communication may actually increase and accentuate differences between groups rather than reduce barriers between groups. This can come about because e-mail addresses may be chosen to convey a degree of anonymity (e.g., checkers@sympatico.ca) and yet offer group-salient information. Imagine a discussion of United States military policy carried on over the Internet through e-mail. The "ca" at the end of the sender's address is a strong clue to others that the sender is a Canadian rather than an American, and this may lead to more importance being given to the apparent national origin of the communicator than might otherwise be the case.

---

crowd or society appears trapped in a collective delusion (Klapp, 1972). They typically rise up slowly and then, as more and more people become involved, rise rapidly to a peak, after which most then die down quickly—although unlike typical crowd behaviour, they often last for days or weeks and sometimes even for months and years.

The contagion of emotion and behaviour has typically been categorized in terms of the predominant emotion or goal. Thus, the literature speaks of contagions of expression, enthusiasm, anxiety, fear and hostility. We shall consider each of these in turn.

Contagions of expression

Expressive contagions have no particular goal other than emotional release, whether they be motivated by joy, sorrow, frustration or guilt (Klapp, 1972). Although such behaviour may affect an entire society, it is often most apparent in crowd settings. An expressive crowd may gather to pay homage to a new pope or cheer the return of a Stanley Cup champion hockey team. The emotionality that seems to spread though

throngs of gasping teenagers that flock around a rock star provides another example. Such contagions are propelled in part by their own success: as the contagion grows, more people are drawn to see the Pope or cheer the team or surround the rock star, which lends increasing importance to the event, in turn drawing more people to join the crowd.

Contagions of enthusiasm

Tulips were introduced into Western Europe from Turkey in the middle of the 16th century. Over the next 100 years, they became objects of such admiration, especially in Holland, that any man of substance without a decent collection of bulbs was held in some contempt. In the period 1634–1636, the Great Tulip Mania swept Holland, England and France. The cost of bulbs soared so high that tracts of land and even small fortunes were sometimes traded for a single bulb. Special arrangements were made for the sale of rare tulip bulbs on the Amsterdam and Rotterdam stock exchanges. So greedy were the speculators, so anxious were rich and poor alike to profit from the rising

The Stanford Prison Study

At times, the contrived situation of the psychological laboratory can become startlingly real. Researchers in one study (Haney et al., 1973; Zimbardo et al., 1982) set out to simulate the deindividuating conditions of a real social institution by setting up a mock prison in the basement of the Stanford University psychology department. Voluntary subjects were randomly assigned the roles of guards and prisoners. Those designated as "guards" were given identical khaki uniforms, reflecting sunglasses, billy clubs, handcuffs, whistles and sets of keys. The "prisoners" were picked up on the first day at their homes by police cars, taken to the police station where they were "processed" and then taken blindfolded to the "prison." They were assigned numbers as identification and wore identical hospital-type gowns and stocking caps. The guards were instructed to maintain "law and order" and events were allowed to unfold.

While subjects initially approached their role-playing in a light-hearted fashion, the situation soon began to deteriorate. The guards became increasingly abusive and punitive towards the prisoners while the prisoners became passive, helpless and showed symptoms of stress such as crying, agitation, confusion and depression. Even the principal researcher, Zimbardo, found himself preoccupied with rumours of a "prison break," forgetting his responsibilities as a scientist. At this point, after six days, an experiment planned to last two weeks was terminated. The roles had become reality to the participants.

The experiment has been criticized on several grounds (Banuazizi & Movahedi, 1975; Thayer & Saarni, 1975). Subjects had signed consent forms in which they agreed to be paid to participate in a study in which some of their rights would be waived. Thus,

they might have felt a moral or legal obligation to continue and might have exaggerated their symptoms of distress in order to get out of their obligation. The "guards" might have been acting according to their stereotypes of prison guards in order to succeed as "good participants" because it was expected of them in order to make the study more realistic. (This would be in line with the SIDE model.) There were also some individual differences; some of the prisoners did not become apathetic or distressed and some of the guards were not abusive.

Nonetheless, the study shows the power of the situation particularly in total institutions such as prisons. In a group of normal young people participating in a simulation experiment, loss of personal identity can cause dramatic changes in behaviour over a short period of time. We can readily extrapolate from this to the profound impact of long-term exposure in institutions such as prisons, hospitals and the military.

Thus, although the deindividuation concept is intriguing, perhaps articulating a collective fear of the "madness of crowds," more evidence is required to demonstrate its existence as a psychological state. Moreover, the concept of the "irrationality of crowds" is probably incorrect. Owing to its spontaneous formation, a crowd has little means by which to plan rational actions and no pre-existing norms for behaviour. Yet the behaviour of people in a crowd, which might be coupled in the heat of the moment with a spurious sense of belonging to—and identifying with—a group, may be better described as "non-rational" rather than irrational (Klapp, 1972); that is, people in a crowd may set aside their critical judgment. However, even in a crowd, norms may rapidly develop to govern behaviour.

market in bulbs that normal industry in Holland fell into serious neglect: the nation had gone tulip-mad. Finally, the market for bulbs, held artificially high by speculators, collapsed and many people suddenly realized they had given up most of what they owned for a collection of tulip bulbs that no one wanted anymore.

The Great Tulip Mania is an example of a contagion of enthusiasm. Such contagions embody an extraordinary hope or delusion, usually about becoming wealthy. Thus the Cariboo Gold Rush, which began in 1858, attracted many tens of thousands of people to British Columbia (at a time when the normal population of

B.C. was only 7000), almost all of whom dreamed of striking it rich. Forty years later "Klondike Fever," spiked by rumours of massive deposits of readily obtainable gold, led tens of thousands of people, most of whom had never mined before and knew nothing about survival in the north, to the Yukon gold fields. Few made their fortune (see Pierre Berton's *Klondike* (1972) for an excellent description of this contagion). As with other contagions, the bubble finally burst.

Contagions of anxiety

Contagions of anxiety (often referred to as **hysterical contagions**) involve the rapid dissemination of exaggerated fears and often evoke unrestrained emotionalism.

The great Windshield Pitting Epidemic provides a good example. In the spring of 1954, Canadian newspapers were filled with reports of the American H-bomb tests at Eniwetok in the South Pacific. The power of the bomb seemed almost incomprehensible: a whole island disappeared as a result of one blast. One of the blasts was described as a "runaway," an out-of-control explosion that produced effects far beyond what was expected. The Russians were thought at that time to be very close to the development of their own H-bomb and many newspaper stories dealt with politicians' and scientists' preoccupation with the imminent danger of nuclear war. Canadians looked into building bomb shelters.

Radioactivity had been detected in snow in Manitoba and Saskatchewan, presumably a result of the H-bomb tests. Paranoia was rampant on the international stage. Western countries feared communism as much as they feared war, and in the United States the McCarthy "witch hunts" were persecuting thousands of Americans on the slimmest evidence of political disloyalty. It was claimed—out of fear—that there were 500 communist organizations in the Toronto area alone.

It was in the context of this combined fear of atomic war and communist subversion that the great Windshield Pitting Epidemic began. It started in Seattle, Washington, where it was reported that hundreds of people had found small pockmarks in the windshields of their cars. The windshields also bore small blobs of a metallic substance which, although not radioactive, was quickly assumed to be atomic fallout. While initial reports of damage were attributed to vandals using BB guns, the news emphasis gradually changed to one of mystery. Seattle's mayor finally declared that windshield damage was no longer a

In 2003, hundreds of thousands of people gathered to hear The Rolling Stones and to show the world that despite SARS, it was safe to come to Toronto.

police matter, referred to the recent H-bomb test as a possible cause and made an appeal to the governor and the president for emergency aid. The stage was set.

While physical scientists from the University of Washington had all emphasized road damage, hysteria and air pollution as the causes, engineers from Boeing Aircraft suggested physical causes for the pitting, including supercharged particles from the H-bomb explosion and a shifting in the earth's magnetic field. By April 19, 1954, the citizens of Vancouver were reporting the same kind of windshield damage and even those who were initially skeptical changed their tune when they found that their cars too had been affected. A Victoria used-car dealer discovered that the marks suddenly appeared in the windshields of the cars on his lot.

The reports quickly became front-page news and the incidents spread from B.C. to the prairies to Ontario. During the approximately two weeks that the "epidemic" lasted, the windshield-pitting delusion spread across Canada, although in the U.S. it was confined to the Seattle area. Newspapers reported that scientists and police officers were desperately searching for the cause. Some car dealers covered the windshields of their cars to protect them. Yet a short time later, the interest suddenly vanished as quickly as it had materialized. It was noted that although used-car dealers were reporting that their cars had been damaged by the mysterious pittings, dealers of new cars could not find any damage to their windshields. The greater the car's mileage, the more likely it was that the windshield would be pitted. Once this began to sink in, it was realized that the pitting was the result of normal damage caused by pebbles thrown up from the roadway. People had not paid much attention to such pitting before. Once the publicity struck, however, people took a good look at their windshields for the first time. The newspapers then dropped their coverage and the epidemic died.

Two researchers (Medalia & Larsen, 1958) interviewed 1000 randomly selected Seattle residents. About 93 percent of the respondents knew of the windshield pitting: about half of those had learned of it from the newspapers, a quarter from radio and TV, about one-fifth from talking to others and the rest (6 percent) from direct experience. Some 50 percent of the respondents accepted the "unusual physical agent" explanation, while only 21 percent believed the "ordinary road damage" explanation.

The anxiety generated by the fear of after-effects from the H-bomb explosion apparently was relieved by focusing attention on automobile windshields. "Something is bound to happen to us as a result of the H-bomb tests—windshields became pitted—it's happened—now that threat is over" (Medalia & Larsen, 1958, p. 25). In other words, the waning of interest was not brought about simply by a more reasonable interpretation of the events and the subsequent lack of media interest but by the diffusion of the anxiety responsible for the original reports.

Sometimes more than anxiety is involved; there may be symptoms of physical illness or a belief that one's body has been damaged or altered in some way. The term **mass psychogenic illness** is sometimes used to describe such a phenomenon (Colligan, Pennebaker & Murphy, 1982). For example, in the 15th century, a nun in Germany developed a compulsion to bite other nuns who, in turn, began compulsively to bite others. Gradually, this bizarre mania spread to convents throughout Italy, Holland and Germany. In the 18th century, there was an epidemic of nuns meowing like cats (Singer, Baum, Baum & Thew, 1982) and between the 10th and 14th centuries, episodes of dancing

mania periodically spread through parts of Europe; victims would experience an uncontrollable impulse to dance in a frenzied manner. In one such epidemic in Italy, entire populations of people danced convulsively in the belief that this behaviour was the result of having been bitten by a tarantula. The tunes to which they danced are still popular today and the dance is known as the *Tarantella*.

The modern era is no stranger to such episodes, although the resulting behaviours are not usually so dramatic. For example, in 1986, two brief power failures affected the operation of visual display terminals in the Manitoba Telephone System. Over the next two weeks, 55 operators complained of numbness and tingling in the limbs, head or face as well as lightheadedness and fatigue. Despite the failure of a panel of physicians and engineers to find an objective basis for the symptoms, rumours of "permanent nerve damage" began to circulate, leading to a walkout and eventual shutdown of the workplace. Repeated outbreaks of such symptoms continued for more than 18 months. Only when the union and management combined their efforts to set up a stress-reduction program did symptoms dwindle away. A similar outbreak occurred among telephone operators in St. Catharines, Ontario (Yassi, Weeks, Samson & Raber, 1989).

In 1983, 900 people in the Israeli-occupied West Bank, most of them Arab schoolgirls, complained of headaches, stomach aches, blue discolouration of the arms and legs and even blindness. Initially, Arab leaders charged that Israelis spreading toxins deliberately caused the malady, while Israeli leaders claimed the symptoms were being deliberately faked. However, the list of victims grew to include some Israeli military and police personnel. Ten days later, poisoning was ruled out and authorities concluded that the symptoms were due to hysterical contagion (Hefez, 1985).

In 1984–85 and again in 1987, two epidemics of the rare *koro* disorder swept through Guangdong, China, affecting thousands of men (Tseng et al., 1988). *Koro* is a hysterical disorder characterized by complaints of shrinkage of the penis and an overwhelming fear of impending death. In April 1993, a wave of swooning swept through Egyptian schools, afflicting more than a thousand schoolgirls and leading to school closings and political debates. Physicians could find no physical basis for the fainting spells and nausea.

A pilot study carried out in Quebec schools in 1973 estimated that there is one hysterical contagion for every 1000 school settings each year (Sirois, 1982). One factory in the U.S. experienced 20 outbreaks of mass psychogenic illness in 18 months, while in 1976, the American Footwear Manufacturers' Association reported that half their member companies had experienced such incidents (Hopson, 1981). Thus, it seems that contagions of hysteria occur with surprising frequency.

Such hysterical outbursts occur when generalized and diffuse anxiety builds up in a group of people and when some precipitating event allows the anxiety to be attached to some external threat. Psychological stress may produce discomfort, sweating, palpitations, nausea, vomiting, terror and even fainting. Without an apparent explanation, these symptoms may be more extreme and embarrassing than if people can point to a supposed "logical" cause (a disease or a poisoning). Personality factors may also play a role in susceptibility to such hysteria. Insecure people or those who are on the fringes of the social structure and thus less constrained by group norms may be more vulnerable. Cultural factors are also important. Outbreaks in traditional societies are much more likely to involve physical acting out, as can be seen in some of the above examples (Bartholomew & Sirois, 1996). It is now suspected that many cases of apparent illness following combat duty (such as Gulf War Syndrome, for example), the symptoms of which are similar to those typically seen in mass psychogenic illness, are indeed manifestations of the latter rather than an actual illness (Pastel, 2001).

Note that neither mass psychogenic illness nor panic occurred following the destruction of the World Trade Center in New York City in September 2001 nor did any such thing occur during the extremely serious outbreak of Severe Acute Respiratory Syndrome (SARS) in Toronto in 2003. This is because in each case, facts about the actual crisis and risks to the population were discussed in great detail by the media. People thus had a reality-based fear, which was limited in terms of personal risk.

Contagions of fear: Panic

While anxiety refers to a generalized feeling of unease, which often cannot be attributed to any specific cause, fear always has some identifiable source and always involves the perception of danger. Sometimes fear of impending doom, provided the threat is not immediate, leads to resignation. However, when a crowd is frightened and in danger, it is not surprising that people in the crowd will try to escape the danger. When a panic occurs in a building (as in the case of a fire), most people cannot even see the exit but assume that the movement of the crowd is directed towards one. Often, there is a **front-to-rear communications**

Even during epidemics, most people stay calm as long as the outbreak appears to be under control.

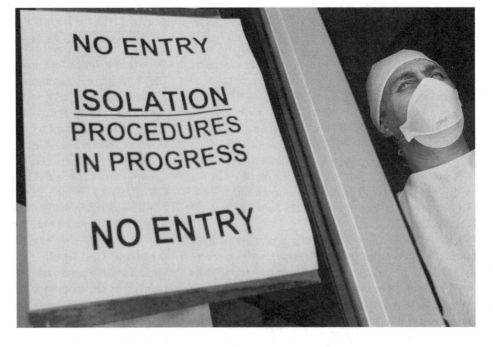

failure (Janis, Chapman, Gillin & Spiegel, 1964), with those at the back unaware that people at the front are unable to move more quickly, causing those at the front to be trampled. Consider this example.

On the afternoon of January 9, 1927, children flocked to the Laurier Palace theatre in Montreal's east end to see a comedy called, ironically, "Gets 'Em Young." Most of the children, contrary to the law of the time, were admitted to the theatre unaccompanied by adults. During the film, a child in the balcony dropped a lighted cigarette, starting a small fire. When someone in the balcony cried "Fire!" the theatre ushers were able to hush the resultant anxiety and begin an orderly evacuation. Smoke began to appear in larger and larger quantities. The ground-floor spectators were evacuated without incident while the children in the balcony moved quickly to two exit stairways and clambered downstairs towards the sidewalk:

> Five steps from the sidewalk, five steps from safety, the tragedy was born. Boys and girls at the front of the stampeding mob, pressed suddenly from the rear, stumbled and fell. Instant panic grasped those at the rear ... a minute or two was enough for the stairway to be a solid, suffocating, groaning, shrieking and dying mass (*Globe*, January 10, 1927).

Seventy-eight children died: 60 from asphyxiation, 11 from compression and five from both asphyxiation and burns. No one need have died at all. The fire was a minor one and there was enough time for an orderly exit. They died, so it was said, because they panicked.

What is the nature of panic? The term is used very loosely in ordinary parlance: "I panicked when I realized I'd lost my wallet." Yet panic is more than anxiety or fear or terror, although some earlier conceptualizations emphasized the emotional state of the individual (Cantril, 1940). In the context of collective behaviour, panic involves fear, flight and an avenue of escape (Quarantelli, 1954; Schultz, 1964). Yet not all flight is panic. In a panic, flight is "non-social and non-rational" (Quarantelli, 1954): the individual thinks of his or her own physical survival and pays no attention to how this action may be detrimental to the collective welfare of the group.

Panic usually occurs in crowds where individuals mutually reinforce each other's fears. However, sometimes there is only an implied crowd—individuals interpret events around them to suggest that others are reacting as they are. Consider this example (Cantril, 1940): in 1939, Orson Welles's Mercury Theatre radio program carried a dramatization of H.G. Wells's, *The War of the Worlds*. Of an estimated 6 000 000 listeners, about 1 000 000, many of whom had tuned in after the program had begun, ignored cues to the fictional nature of the broadcast and reacted with panic, "heading for the hills" or looking for a place to hide. Police switchboards were jammed with calls and traffic snarls occurred as people tried to flee the "invasion." This was the first demonstration that mass panic can be triggered without the involvement of either rumours or crowds (Klapp, 1972). Most of those who were so affected had shown little critical ability and had made no attempt to check by switching to other radio stations or calling friends.

How could so many people react in this way to a radio drama? Faced with what appeared to be a genuine news report, many telephoned the police. Unable to get through because other people were making the same call, they were persuaded that the Martians had already knocked out telephone lines. Once begun, the panic reaction was hard to slow down. As people began to flee, it would have been easy for them to assume others who were going about their normal business were just unaware of the emergency while the sight of anyone else hurrying to get somewhere would confirm the need to escape.

When a truly catastrophic event occurs, its impact alone may be great enough to trigger panic flight (Foreman, 1953). This is what happened on the morning of December 6, 1917, at the height of the First World War, when a Belgian ship collided with a French munitions carrier in Halifax harbour. Fifteen minutes later, the munitions ship exploded, producing the greatest human-made explosion in the history of the world until the atomic bombing of Hiroshima. Almost one-third of the population of Halifax was killed and many thousands were seriously injured. Some 1600 buildings were totally destroyed. Just as occurred in the aftermath of the atomic bombings of Hiroshima and Nagasaki, people who were not killed outright or incapacitated fled in panic.

The impact of such life-threatening events may be even greater psychologically if the events have been defined in the past as unmanageable. People may run in terror simply after hearing a powerful term such as the alarm "Gas!" in the First World War. Yet even in such cases, the panic states do not usually last for more than a very short time and non-adaptive behaviour can generally be dealt with if effective leadership and appropriate information is provided (Janis et al., 1964).

Panic as a collective dilemma

While it is both socially responsible and individually practical for you to await your turn during the orderly exit from a burning building, once there has been a departure from this orderliness, being cooperative is no longer individually profitable. Once again, we encounter the collective dilemma (see Chapter 10). Each individual is faced essentially with two choices of action: remain calm and proceed in turn or run and push towards the exit. If everyone exits in a calm and orderly manner, then perhaps all will escape. If others run and you remain calm, you may not escape. If everyone runs, then there is likely to be crowding at the door and many may die. But running and pushing may improve your chances. Even smelling smoke in a crowded building may be enough to lead people to act non-cooperatively, since they have been taught the danger of people panicking in a burning building! They expect others to run, so they do so first.

Simulating panic

The classic simulation of panic is one provided by Mintz (1951), who observed subjects in groups of 15 to 20 persons whose task it was to remove aluminum cones from a narrow-necked bottle by means of a string attached to the cones (Figure 14–2).

After the cones were placed in the bottle, each subject was given a piece of fishing line attached to only one of the cones. Only one cone could pass through

the neck of the bottle at a time. At the signal to start, water began flowing into the bottom of the bottle. Subjects were instructed to try to get their cones out without getting them wet. No "traffic jams" at the bottle's neck occurred when no rewards were given for success. However in a second condition, subjects were told that they could win 25 cents by getting a cone out completely dry. If a third or less of the cone was wet, there would be no reward, and if more than a third was wet, there would be a fine. In this case, more than half the groups had "traffic jams"—whether or not the subjects were allowed to communicate. Mintz concluded that intense fear is not necessary to cause non-adaptive behaviour similar to panic behaviour.

Organized groups such as military units are rarely subject to panic. Because of their training, the individuals respond to the orders of the leader. Only when the leadership structure breaks down is there a danger of panic.

Social inhibition of escape behaviour

Sometimes a crowd can actually inhibit escape from a dangerous situation by its refusal to become aroused. There have been several instances of fires in nightclubs and theatres in which patrons warned of a fire have refused to leave. In 1977, the Beverly Hills nightclub in Kentucky caught fire and although a busboy ran to the stage and announced that there was a fire, the audience assumed he was part of the act. Most people ignored his warning; 165 lives were lost. A fire broke

FIGURE 14-2

Mintz's apparatus

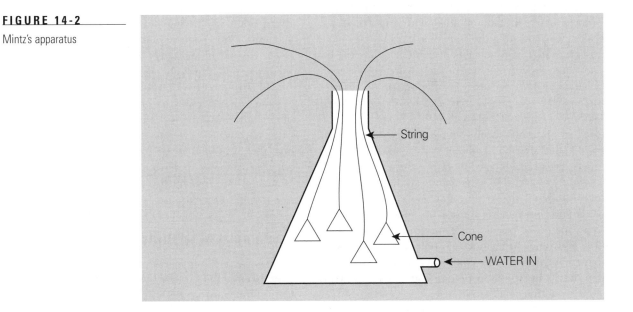

out during a New Year's Eve party in a social club in Chapais, Quebec, in the early hours of January 1, 1980. Most of the 44 people who died could have escaped. As in so many other similar circumstances, the victims apparently underestimated the danger. They carried on dancing or stood in a semicircle watching a pile of dry pine branches that had ignited blaze away. The euphoria of the crowd, the loud music, the alcohol and the wish to avoid looking foolish or cowardly—all these combined to inhibit escape behaviour.

Rational behaviour in disasters

The popular press and even some agencies whose job it is to deal with disasters typically describe people caught up in a disaster as disorganized, irrational and hysterical. Authorities sometimes hesitate to give the alarm for fear of causing panic. (For example, the alarm bells on the *Andrea Doria*, which sunk in a collision at sea in 1956, were not rung, even though collision with an approaching ship was unavoidable.) In recent times, there has been great worry that if so-called weapons of mass destruction are used, they will cause panic and chaos in addition to death and destruction. Yet careful analysis of actual disasters in several different cultures shows that disorganized flight, "mass panic," is rare (Pastel, 2001). Most people manage to maintain a rational approach. For example, people reacted relatively calmly and rationally following the destruction of the World Trade Center in New York City in September 2001. The same thing happened during a major earthquake in San Francisco in the fall of 1989, when a baseball stadium filled with frightened and shaken fans awaiting the start of a World Series game was evacuated with no signs of panic. However, it has also been shown that when people are supposed to evacuate an area because of some oncoming disaster, the majority of people may not leave (Quarantelli, 1960). For example, during the 1997 "flood of the century" in Manitoba, many people wanted to stay with their homes despite imminent danger, and evacuation orders had to be enforced by police and the military.

Again, researchers who have studied disastrous high-rise hotel fires report that most people do not panic and that most of those who miss opportunities to escape do so because of errors in judgment rather than irrational behaviour (Keating & Loftus, 1981). Remember, though, that panic is a collective behaviour that occurs in crowds; people in high-rises are usually alone or with a small group.

Another common perception is that once the immediate danger has passed, people sit around dazed and unable to cope. Yet in actual observations, only a minority of disaster victims succumb to apathy and shock and only for a short time. In general, people react immediately and logically to their situation. Looting in such situations is actually very rare, also contrary to popular belief. The myth of "disaster syndrome" may have arisen because people *seem* to run about aimlessly while in fact they are desperately looking for missing friends and relatives (Killian, 1952). That is precisely what occurred on June 30, 1912, when the worst storm in the history of Western Canada struck Regina, killing 36 people, toppling houses and moving one grain elevator 50 feet. There was no panic and once the storm abated, the populace rallied to locate survivors and care for the injured and homeless. (The same scene was played out 75 years later in Edmonton, when a tornado killed 25 people and injured at least 250 others.)

When panic does occur, several elements are generally present: a dangerous situation, a possibility both of being trapped and of escape, and limited avenues of escape (Foreman, 1953; Fritz & Marks, 1954). Trapped coal miners do not panic (Lucas, 1968) for no way of escape is open to them. Consider the difference between the passengers of CP's *Empress of Ireland*, which went down in 1914, and those of the *Noronic*, a cruise ship that burned in Toronto harbour in 1949. In the former case, people had no avenue of escape. Bound for Liverpool with 1500 persons aboard, the *Empress* was rammed in heavy fog in the St. Lawrence River. Only 337 people survived. According to news accounts, "no panic prevailed." On the other hand, panic ensued immediately aboard the *Noronic* when fire broke out, although help was close at hand and the fire department arrived quickly: 121 lives were lost.

Panic can be viewed as the consequence of a process of attributional appraisal. First, something occurs that causes arousal. If the context is perceived as dangerous, that arousal is labelled as *fear*. Whether a person engages in panic behaviour, then, depends on the behaviour of others in the vicinity whose actions serve as a model to increase or decrease the arousal level.

Contagions of hostility

We have seen how anxiety can sometimes lead to mass psychogenic illness—the hysterical contagion of medical symptoms. In other circumstances, people do not seek out a physical cause for a psychophysiological anxiety but react with irrational hostility and violence towards scapegoats—individuals who provide safe and easy targets. (The word *scapegoat* comes from the Biblical account of the Hebrews ridding themselves of evil by loading their sins onto a goat that was allowed to escape into the wilderness while a companion goat was sacrificed to God. Today, scapegoats do not escape; they are the objects of hostility and violence; see Chapter 13.)

In the Middle Ages, commonplace events—a poor crop, hail, a stillbirth—were attributed to the actions of witches. Between 500 000 and 700 000 people were convicted of witchcraft and burned at the stake in Europe between the 15th and 17th centuries (Harris, 1974). In 1692 in Salem, Massachusetts, a witch mania occurred on a much smaller scale. Some young girls who had dabbled in black magic developed hysterical illness, which involved convulsive behaviour. They blamed witches for their problems and readily pointed out the "guilty" adults. The mania spread beyond Salem to Boston. Twenty people, including a minister, as well as two dogs, were executed as witches.

Aggressive crowds provide localized and short-lived instances of contagions of hostility. Whether the aggressive crowd takes the form of a mob (the aggression is directed against a relatively powerless individual or a small group of individuals) or a riot (the aggression is expressed against another group having similar or greater power), the behaviour of the participants reflects the lifting of normal social restraints.

It is impossible to predict when an aggressive crowd is likely to form. In June 1972, 2500 angry fans who could not get into a sold-out Rolling Stones concert in Vancouver rioted and hurled bottles, rocks and even Molotov cocktails at the more than 200 police who fought to keep them out of the Pacific Coliseum. In Montreal in 1971, a riot broke out at Blue Bonnets Raceway after angry spectators reacted against what they thought was an exceptionally low quinella payoff. Soccer games have often been marred by rioting, and on a number of occasions in 1985, violence by British soccer fans spilled out into the streets, resulting in pitched battles with police. While some of these incidents appeared to reflect racial tensions, others did not. In 1984, rowdiness by British soccer fans during a game played by a British team against an Italian team in Belgium turned into violence and resulted in the deaths of 38 Italian spectators.

When the Montreal Canadiens won the 1993 Stanley Cup at the Forum, the post-game celebrating produced a mob of several thousand people that moved down Ste. Catherine Street, causing more than $10 000 000 damage. More than 100 stores were ransacked; 15 city buses and 47 police cars were destroyed; and 168 people, including 49 police, were injured. Such spectator violence is not new. In Constantinople, fans at the chariot races burned down the Coliseum in 491 AD and again in 498 and 507. In 532 AD, 30 000 people died in riots at those chariot races and once again the Coliseum was burned down. The Roman Senate imposed a 10-year ban on gladiator contests in Pompeii following a rash of violence between fans of differing allegiances in 59 AD (Horn, 1985).

Rumours, Fads and Fashions

As we have seen, collective behaviour often occurs in crowds but crowds are not necessary for its appearance. It can occur as readily within a collectivity of people who are not in physical proximity. Indeed, some of the most dramatic instances of collective behaviour, such as rumour transmission (which creates a collective belief or apprehension), fads and fashions usually occur in the absence of crowds.

Rumours

A **rumour** is "a specific … proposition or belief, passed along from person to person, usually by word of mouth, without secure standards of evidence being present" (Allport & Postman, 1947, p. ix). It is an important part of many collective behaviour episodes and, in the view of emergent norm theorists, is the mechanism by which a collective perception of a situation is formed within a crowd (Wright, 1978).

We are all familiar with rumours—rumours that the prime minister is going to resign, that a leading public figure is having an affair, that the company we work for or the university we go to may be going broke. Some rumours have a basis in fact, but often they simply reflect uninformed fear or consist of bits of speculation and gossip woven into a coherent story.

To be the subject of a rumour can be an extremely trying experience, for rumours, once begun, are very difficult to stop. Denying the allegations carried in a rumour often makes the rumour even more believable to many, for one would *expect* the guilty to protest. Rumours in the marketplace can also have a devastating effect not only on sales but even on company survival. Would you ignore a rumour that a new candy product has been implicated in the deaths of several children, especially if you are a parent? Could you overlook the rumour that a huge international fast-food chain is owned by the Church of Satan? Or that a major brand of bubble gum contains spider eggs? These are examples of actual rumours that have flourished and then died away (Koenig, 1985).

Sometimes rumours in the business world have been deliberately generated in an attempt to harm a competitor. For example, in 1934, sales of Chesterfield cigarettes in the United States were adversely affected by the rumour that a person suffering from leprosy had been found working in the cigarette factory. Allegedly, a rival firm started the rumour. Two-person teams would enter a crowded commuter train or subway car from opposite ends, move towards each other and then have a conversation about the leper while other passengers stood between them (Shibutani, 1966). (See A Case in Point—Satan on a Soap Box for a more recent corporate rumour.) Rumours based on fact may also cause damage—as the war posters had it, "Loose lips sink ships."

Why do rumours form? Why are they often repeated so uncritically? Four variables influence the development and transmission of rumours (Rosnow (1991): general uncertainty, outcome-relevant involvement, personal anxiety and credibility.

General uncertainty

The term **general uncertainty** refers to widely held doubt and apprehension within a collectivity of people—uncertainty about the identity of a stranger who has been "hanging around town"; uncertainty about whether the fish plant will be closed and everyone laid off; uncertainty about why the mayor suddenly resigned.

The importance of uncertainty can be seen in a study in which a rumour was planted in a girls' school (Schachter & Burdeck, 1955). Six classes were used, with two classes assigned to each of the three experimental conditions: (1) the cognitive ambiguity condition in which a situation of ambiguity (uncertainty) was created; (2) the rumour condition in which a rumour was planted; and (3) the combined cognitive ambiguity—rumour condition. To create the cognitive ambiguity, the school principal went to the four classrooms for conditions (1) and (3) and did something unprecedented: she pointed to one of the girls and instructed her to take her hat, coat and books and accompany her out of the room. Presumably, the students would seek an explanation for this curious event. Then a rumour was planted in the classes in conditions (2) and (3): a teacher asked two girls in each of the pertinent classes, "Do you know anything about some exams that were taken from the office?" Teachers were instructed to record all questions directed

Although many stock exchanges are now electronic, they are still influenced by collective behaviour. The stock market can be swamped by buy or sell orders in response to rumours about a company.

Satan on a Soap Box

Even a large corporation can be the target of rumours. Around the beginning of 1980, malicious (and it seems deliberately inspired) rumours began to circulate in the United States and Canada that Procter & Gamble was linked to devil worship and that it regularly turned over some of its profits to Satanic cults. The basis for the rumour was the company's 135-year-old logo (see illustration), which portrays the Man in the Moon, a popular figure of the 1800s, and 13 stars (representing the original 13 colonies). To some people, the pattern of stars forms two *6*s and these augmented by another *6* half hidden in the man's beard constitute the "mark of the Beast"—the number *666*, which the Biblical book of Revelation associates with Satan. Derivative rumours claimed that Procter & Gamble was owned by the Unification Church (the "Moonies") and that the head of Procter & Gamble had appeared on television and admitted the Satanist connections.

A leaflet campaign in English and in French that called for a boycott of Procter & Gamble products helped spread the rumours far and wide and despite police investigations, the source of the leaflets was never uncovered. It seemed that many different individuals, alarmed by the charges, made photocopies of the leaflets and distributed them on their own.

Procter & Gamble took many steps to fight the rumours. The company obtained testaments of faith from prominent religious leaders including high-ranking members of the Roman Catholic Church and several evangelical groups, which they disseminated to local clergy wherever the rumours were current. They set up telephone hotlines to deal with consumers' concerns about the subject and by early 1982 were receiving about 15 000 calls per month from people wanting to find out if the rumours were true. Procter & Gamble's Canadian headquarters in Toronto received thousands of inquiries from concerned individuals and church groups across Canada requesting clarification of the company's position with regard to Satanism. The rumours died off for a while following an extensive information campaign by the company but then emerged again in 1985.

On April 24, 1985, the company announced that it would eliminate the Man in the Moon trademark from its packages, although the logo still appears on all corporate communication. In 1991, the logo was redesigned to eliminate the possibility of perceiving a 6 in the curly hairs of the man's beard.

The basis for the rumour: Procter & Gamble's company logo

---

to them by the students and this information plus that gathered from individual interviews of all the students at the end of the day provided the basic data. As it turned out, practically every girl had heard the planted rumour and made inquiries to one or more teachers. Almost all the questions were of the form "What happened to *K*?" or "Why did the principal take *K* out of class?" And in classes in which the cognitive ambiguity had been generated, the rumour had the greatest impact. The girls in those classes reported having spent twice as much time discussing the rumour as did girls from the classes given the rumour without the ambiguity manipulation.

Rumour spreading was by no means confined to the planted rumour. The students generated a number of new rumours of their own. Figure 14–3 shows both the numbers of new rumours reported in each condition and the percentage of subjects who reported hearing these new rumours.

New rumours were most prevalent in the conditions involving cognitive ambiguity where there was presumably a greater need to make sense out of the ambiguity of the situation. Note in Figure 14–3 that cognitive ambiguity alone led to almost as many new rumours as did cognitive ambiguity combined with a planted rumour.

Outcome-relevant involvement

We are likely to be interested in and to repeat to others information about something relevant to us. If the fish plant is not relevant to us, we are not likely to pass on the rumour of its closing. However, the involvement does not have to be direct. We may become involved in rumours about a particular actor's marital problems or Madonna's latest sexual preferences if we are interested in those people or enjoy being titillated by or titillating others with such gossipy tidbits.

Personal anxiety

In this context, personal anxiety refers to anxiety—acute or chronic—produced by apprehension about an imminent and disappointing outcome (Rosnow, 1991). If you work for the fish plant and production is down, you may be legitimately worried about your job and anxious to find out what is going on, making you more susceptible to rumours. Anxiety may in turn diminish the ability to tolerate uncertainty (Rosnow & Fine, 1976). Cognitive dissonance theory suggests that when people are anxious but without good reason, they will strive to find a reason in order to reduce the dissonance between the cognitions "I am anxious" and "I have no reason to be anxious." Rumour may reduce this dissonance (e.g., "I am anxious because civil war is imminent"). In a similar vein, hostility towards some group can be justified via the rumour "I don't like the neighbours because they may be communist spies."

Only a little research has been carried out to examine the role of anxiety in rumour transmission. In one such study, students were assigned to either high or low chronic anxiety groups on the basis of their scores on a measure of anxiety (Anthony, 1973). Telling a few students from each group that certain extracurricular activities were going to be reduced for budgetary reasons began a rumour. The results (see Figure 14–4) showed predictably that there was considerably more rumour transmission in the groups who scored high in chronic anxiety.

In a more recent experiment (Walker & Beckerle, 1987), subjects were asked to retake orally an examination that they had previously written ostensibly to help the professor assess the validity of the test. Half the subjects were assigned to a "high-anxiety" condition: while waiting their turn, they witnessed a confederate of the experimenter fail the exam. The other subjects were assigned to a "low-anxiety" condition: they were not exposed to the failing confederate but instead simply reviewed easy sample questions. The confederate also planted a rumour relating to the "real" reason for having the subject redo the examination. Again, it was found that high-anxiety subjects

FIGURE 14-3

The number of new rumours and the percentage of students reporting new rumours in the Schachter & Burdeck study

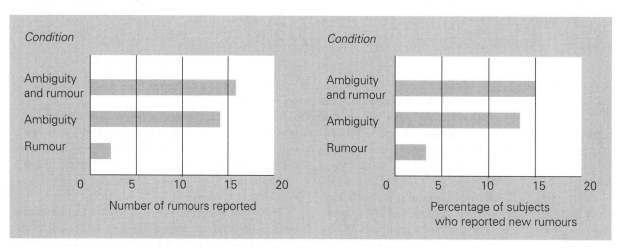

Source: Rosnow & Fine, 1976

make differential personality inferences about others—including inferences about friendliness and popularity—on the basis of the brand of jeans worn (Calvin Klein, Levi Strauss or Sears) (Solomon, 1986).

Women are faced with a special problem as they compete with men for career positions: to "dress for success," they must avoid traditionally feminine styles. In one study, business executives gave higher evaluations to female job applicants who wore plainly tailored clothes, little makeup and shorter hair than to women who adopted more traditionally feminine styles (Solomon, 1986). A survey of readers of a magazine for female executives found that most indicated little interest in fashion but were highly conscious of the tactical importance of clothing (Solomon, 1986).

Banality

Novelty appears to be a primary reinforcer of human behaviour (Berlyne, 1960); the same is true of many animals ("Curiosity killed the cat"). We seem to be predisposed to be curious and attracted to new stimuli. Thus if everyone wears a grey flannel suit and white shirt, one person may wear a blue shirt to be "a little different." If all cars were grey, many people would prefer a red one or a yellow one. Thus, changing fashion, whether clothing or cars, may be an attempt to alleviate boredom and to assert our individuality.

How do fashions spread? While an element of contagion is involved, there is reason to believe that most people hesitate before risking ridicule or rejection by adopting some new fashion. It seems that there is a "two-step flow of communication" (Katz & Lazerfield, 1955; Rogers, 1962): Local opinion leaders who are most knowledgeable about fashion trends are the first to don the new garb and their action indicates to others that such fashion is acceptable (see also the discussion of acceptance of innovation in Chapter 6).

Fashion plays an important role in self-definition and in interpersonal relationships, a role social psychologists are only now beginning to study.

Social Movements

The contagions described thus far arise relatively quickly in crowds and are generally short-lived. Social movements, on the other hand, are a form of collective behaviour that usually begins very slowly but then spreads and eventually produces a formal group oriented towards bringing about social change. Such groups can endure for years, decades or longer. A **social movement** is "a spontaneous large group constituted in support of a set of purposes that are shared by the members" (Milgram & Toch, 1969). Although unlike any behaviour examined so far in this chapter, social movements are considered to be a type of collective behaviour since they are spontaneous and involve large collectivities. Generally, a social movement is aimed at either promoting or resisting change in society. It attracts people who feel that a problem exists, believe that something can be done about it and *want* to do something about it (Toch, 1965).

Social movements are more likely to arise in a society undergoing rapid social change than in a stable one (Lang & Lang, 1961) because changing aspirations and needs cannot be satisfied by the existing social norms. For example, following changes in the Quebec educational system during the Quiet Revolution of the 1960s, a large number of French-speaking students pursued studies in areas previously left to the English: business administration, commerce and marketing. But when these students graduated, they found that proficiency in English was a prerequisite for a good job in the business world. Social change was obviously needed.

Canada has given birth to many social movements, reflecting the high degree of social fragmentation and lack of consensus that has been prevalent from time to time in this country (Grayson & Grayson, 1975). Various groups—farmers, women, French-speaking Canadians, gays and lesbians, people with disabilities—have at one time or another felt estranged from the mainstream of society. As a result, movements such as the Farmers' Union, the Cooperative Commonwealth Federation, Social Credit, the National Action Committee for the Status of Women and the Parti Québécois have evolved. Sometimes, however, such movements can take on an ugly form and express the dark side of human nature.

The Depression of the 1930s, coupled with the prairie drought, was a natural crucible for the birth of social movements. Communists appealed to the hungry unemployed to throw off their capitalist masters and assume control of their nation.

Fascism also made an appearance. The first Canadian Fascist group was the Ordre Patriotique des Goglus, founded in 1929. By 1930, it claimed 50 000 members, although this is probably a gross exaggeration. The leader, Adrien Arcand, edited a weekly newspaper that praised Hitler (even before he came to power) and urged the expulsion of Jews. He won support from some businessmen by attacking communism and socialism and appealed to the anti-Semitism prevalent in Canada at the time (Abella & Troper, 1983). Once Hitler came to power, rising interest in fascism led to competition between Arcand's group, who wore blue shirts, and other groups such as the brown-shirted Canadian Nationalist Party headed by William Whittaker, an ex-British soldier.

It became almost chic for young people to sport swastikas. (Jean-Louis Roux resigned soon after his appointment as Lieutenant-Governor of Quebec in 1996 when it was revealed that, as a university student in the early 1940s, he had briefly worn a swastika on his lab coat.) In Ontario, "swastika clubs" sprang up comprising gangs of youths who wore swastika insignia and who harassed Jews on public beaches or in parks. In 1939, a National Fascist convention held in Massey Hall in Toronto drew about 2000.

The movement gathered momentum until the Nazis invaded Western Europe. When war was declared, Fascist leaders were arrested and the movement died down—though neo-Nazi and anti-Semitic activities have resurfaced repeatedly on a smaller scale (see Chapter 13).

Types of social movements

The goals of social movements vary from very general (e.g., to gain equality for women or to fight for better working conditions in developing countries) to very specific (e.g., to prevent clear-cutting in B.C. forests or to oppose the World Trade Organization). **Reform movements** accept the basic structure of society but seek to modify part of it (Blumer, 1969), while **revolutionary movements** seek to overthrow the existing social order. As a result, revolutionary movements are often driven underground while reform movements appear respectable and attempt to gain support through discussion and persuasion. Reform movements try to win the support of the middle class, while revolutionary movements typically appeal to those in the oppressed or distressed group. The Front de libération du Québec (FLQ), which never achieved the status of a social movement, was nevertheless typical of a revolutionary movement, trying to alter the social order radically by force. The Parti Québécois, on the other hand, provides a good example of a reform movement that began as an unorganized collectivity and grew into an institution. While the Parti Québécois spoke to the genuine injustices that have been suffered by French Canadians, the FLQ went far beyond that and advocated militant socialism, a stance not very likely to win support from the Québécois middle-class. The Reform Party attempted to become a force in Canada partly by presenting itself as a social movement aimed at reform of the Canadian political scene.

While many social movements are nationalistic in nature, others are of a religious nature (Blumer, 1951). The Moral Majority in the U.S. is an example of a religiously oriented social movement; in this case, there has been a genuine attempt to win political power to change the social order. (Religious social movements are discussed in more detail in the section on cults.)

Some social movements evolve into mainline political forces, as was the case with the Parti Québécois. The Social Credit Party as well as the CCF party, which evolved into the New Democratic Party, grew out of social unease on the Prairies and the feeling that existing political parties did not serve Prairie interests and needs. Their aim was to achieve political and social change.

The life of a social movement

A social movement often develops through a series of four stages (Blumer, 1969).

Social unrest stage

At its inception, a social movement often reflects no more than a restless dissatisfaction with contemporary society, coupled with a dream about a new kind of society. At this stage, there are no definite goals, and agitators are likely to play an important role as they try to make people aware of the shortcomings of contemporary society. Such "consciousness raising" is important, for unless others become aware of the problems they apparently endure, they are unlikely to show interest in the movement. The suffragist movement, the women's liberation movement and the gay liberation movement all began when various individuals expressed their dissatisfaction with their role in society.

The poverty and hunger of the 1930s formed a natural breeding ground for social movements as people struggled to change a system that seemed to be keeping them down. Communism and socialism had a natural appeal to the unemployed and to the drought-ridden farmers since the blame for economic depression could be placed on the capitalistic system of ownership in the country.

Poverty and hunger give rise to many social movements in many underdeveloped and developing coun-

A Women's Social Movement

Dr. Emily Stowe, Canada's first female physician, had to study medicine in the U.S. because no Canadian medical school would take a woman. In 1876, she founded the Toronto Women's Literary Club, a reform organization whose name was changed in 1888 to the Toronto Women's Suffrage Association. This group was composed primarily of business and professional women and the wives of wealthy men. In other parts of Canada, other women, most notably Thérèse Casgrain in Quebec and Nellie McClung on the Prairies, joined the quest for suffrage. They sought the right to vote not simply to obtain personal equality with men but also to influence governments to work towards the elimination of serious social problems.

Canadian women working for suffrage preferred to be referred to as "suffragists" rather than "suffragettes" as their British counterparts called them-selves. They did not want to be seen as sharing the sometimes-radical political views associated with the suffragette movement.

The vote for women was first won on the Prairies where women received widespread support from various farmers' organizations. Manitoba extended suffrage to women in 1916, followed by Saskatchewan and Alberta in the same year. In 1917, British Columbia and Ontario did the same. Nova Scotia followed in 1918, New Brunswick in 1919, Prince Edward Island in 1922, Newfoundland (then not yet a part of Canada) in 1925 and Quebec in 1940. Women were given the right to vote at the federal level in 1918, but it was only in 1929 that the Supreme Court reversed an earlier ruling and determined that women were indeed "persons" within the meaning of the *British North America Act*.

---

tries today. Some of these actually lead to the overthrow of governments. Castro's 26th of July Movement evolved from a social movement to the controlling political force in Cuba. There are many other examples.

Popular excitement stage

More definite ideas about the causes of the problems and about the goals emerge. More and more individuals are drawn into the movement, some because they identify with the cause and others because the perceived potential benefits outweigh the costs (Simon et al., 1998). Challenges to the contemporary social order become more frequent and powerful. For example, during the 1930s in Canada, organizers recruited workers, and many demonstrations were held demanding more help for the unemployed and changes in the economic order. The federal government tried to intimidate the organizers, many of them admitted Communists, by arresting them under a provision of the *Criminal Code* passed during the Winnipeg General Strike of 1919, which made it unlawful to belong to any party that advocated political change by means of force or violence. Agitators who were not Canadian citizens were deported. Between 1930 and 1934, 22 968 people suffered this fate!

Formalization stage

As a social movement gathers impetus, it gradually takes on organizational form with formal leaders, division of duties and an agenda (Blumer, 1951). Policies are formalized and a leader, likely to be a kind of statesperson, is chosen. An ideology or a collection of beliefs, myths and doctrines develops along with it. The ideology defines and defends the goals of the group, condemns the existing social order, outlines the policies and tactics and contains the myths of the group. The intelligentsia of the group generally provides a highly respectable formal ideology that can be defended to certain of the intelligentsia outside the movement. However, the ideology also takes on a popular form for the masses, composed of emotional symbols, stereotypes and so on. In the 1930s, the CCF Party emerged as a formal manifestation of the social movement started by workers and farmers.

Institutionalization

As social movements gather momentum, participants are often led to believe that their continued survival depends on being acceptable to outsiders; thus they may gradually drop their most radical ideas (Milgram & Toch, 1969). For example, the Social Credit dropped its plan for radical changes to the banking system. This leads to an institutionalization of the movement whereby it evolves into a fixed organization with a formal structure and specific division of duties and becomes a part of regular society. As a result, it may cease to appeal to those who are most discontented. Forced to look elsewhere, these people often try to start another movement. In the case of the Parti Québécois, "separatism" became "sovereignty association" and steps were taken to appease large industries that felt threatened by the party's policies. However, to increase its support among the public at large, such a movement has to moderate its policies and water down its goals, thereby alienating those members who want radical social change. Only after the Parti Québécois lost power as a result of an erosion in its popular support, did it once again, in the late 1980s, return to a platform of outright separatism. Subsequently in the 1990s, the premier of Quebec, Lucien Bouchard, had to grapple vigorously with the problem of trying to increase general public support through policies that alienated core supporters, and ultimately gave up and left office. His successor also downplayed separatism in order to try to maintain public support, but his party lost the 2003 election to the federalist Liberals. The "social movement" had been a success; it led to a Quebec where French is the predominant language and French culture is flourishing. Having achieved some of its goals even while failing in its aspirations for an independent state, the social movement seemed to many Quebecers to be no longer needed. Having begun as a highly focused and ideological social movement, the Parti Québécois had reached the end of the cycle of social movements and had become just another institutionalized political party.

Social movements are an important engine of change in a society that forces the society to respond to long-overlooked or changing needs. As yesterday's social movements become today's institutions, new movements, some large, some relatively small, grow up. Even in societies dominated by rigidity and totalitarianism, social movements sometimes take root despite powerful efforts to prevent them. Nelson Mandela, discussed in Chapter 3, spent many years in a South African prison, finally to emerge and become the president of the nation! Not all leaders are so fortunate; many perish at the hands of dictatorial governments. However, as long as important needs in the society go unmet, the unrest will continue and sooner or later it is likely that a social movement of one kind or another—reform or revolutionary—will make its presence felt.

Why do social movements emerge in some circumstances and not in others? It cannot simply be hunger and privation, for these conditions have reigned in many parts of the world for centuries with no particular signs of the social unrest that could give birth to a social movement. Indeed, it is not the actual degree but the *relative* degree of privation that is important. (Recall the discussion of social comparison in Chapter 10.) When people compare themselves to other appropriate groups and find that the others are better off, it leads to frustration and discontent and becomes the basis for the social unrest that underlies the growth of social movements. Of course, people only begin to agitate for change when they feel that there is some chance that change will occur. In totalitarian states, demands for change can produce massive reprisals and so dissent is stifled, as, for example, in Tiananmen Square.

Relative deprivation occurs at both the interpersonal and intergroup levels. Poor individuals in British Columbia or Newfoundland may be frustrated when they compare themselves to a neighbour with a better house and income, but if they do not see themselves as being part of a deprived group—that is, the comparison stays at the interpersonal level—collective action is unlikely to emerge. If, however, a number of poor people have richer neighbours all of whom belong to some other group, then this intergroup comparison may lead to collective action. Aboriginal groups may compare themselves to whites, francophones may compare themselves to anglophones, workers may compare themselves to industrialists. If the comparison leads to the belief that the other group is exploiting them in some way, a social movement may emerge.

This intergroup comparison need not be in terms of housing or food or material wealth; it may reflect perceived differences in power or status within the larger society (see Chapter 13 with regard to how people deal with being the focus of prejudice). For example, Guimond and Dubé-Simard (1983) asked francophones in Quebec to compare their level of satisfaction over their personal situation with (1) other francophones (interpersonal comparison) and (2) anglophones (intergroup comparison) (see also Chapter 2). They found no relation between interpersonal relative deprivation and sociopolitical attitudes, but a strong relationship between perceived intergroup relative deprivation and

Chapter 15

Social Psychology of Justice and the Law

Many that live deserve death. And some die that deserve life. Can you give it to them? Then be not too eager to deal out death in the name of justice, fearing for your own safety. Even the wise cannot see all ends.

J. R. R. Tolkien (1892–1973), The Lord of the Rings, *Book Four*

A jury consists of twelve persons chosen to decide who has the better lawyer.

Robert Frost (1874–1963)

Brutus: Remember March, the ides of March remember: Did not great Julius bleed for justice' sake? What villain touch'd his body, that did stab, And not for justice?

W. Shakespeare, Julius Caesar

Chapter Outline

In July 2003, Romeo Phillion was released on bail from prison after serving 31 years. He had been convicted in 1972 for the murder of Ottawa firefighter Leopold Roy. Phillion came from a background of family strife and, after committing a string of juvenile offences, was one of a number who suffered abuse at training schools. At the time of the crime, Phillion had established a criminal record. A witness to the crime enabled police to draw a composite sketch of the killer, and on this basis, Phillion was arrested. When the victim's wife was unable to identify him from a police lineup, he was released. Indeed, according to a police investigation report, he had been in Trenton, Ontario, 237 km from Ottawa at the time of the crime, and a report was filed. Four years later, Phillion attempted an armed robbery on a taxi driver. Arrested along with his partner, Phillion was induced to sign a confession to the earlier murder ostensibly as a joke so his partner could collect the reward. Hours later, he retracted the confession. However, he was charged and convicted of the murder of the firefighter. Defence lawyer Arthur Cogan learned of the police report that absolved his client, reported only years later, although court procedures clearly prescribe that the defence has the right to examine all relevant evidence. This alibi report was buried in police files for years until a copy mysteriously appeared in Phillion's penitentiary files where it was discovered. Phillion consistently claimed his innocence and adamantly refused parole. He became the object of a campaign that ultimately met with success.

This case of wrongful conviction hinged on the apparent suppression by police of evidence. It also raises questions of interest to social psychologists. Why was the wife unable to identify Phillion in a lineup and why was she not believed? Why was his "confession" accepted but not his recanting of the confession soon afterwards? Indeed, why did Phillion confess to a crime that he did not commit and for which he had earlier been absolved?

Other cases of wrongful conviction have emerged. Some of them have been based on later evidence that included DNA evidence. In 1971, Donald Marshall, an 18-year-old Mi'kmaq Indian was convicted in a Nova Scotia court of second-degree murder following the stabbing death of Sandy Seale, a 17-year-old acquaintance. After serving 11 years in a penitentiary, new evidence was uncovered, Marshall was absolved on appeal and another man was subsequently convicted of manslaughter in the killing. In recent years, two other Canadians, Guy Paul Morin and David Milgaard, who were convicted of murder, were subsequently absolved on the basis of new evidence. In the United States, over 100 cases have been documented in which a convicted person who spent time in prison was subsequently exonerated by DNA evidence (Turtle, Lindsay & Wells, 2003). In response, one state governor suspended capital punishment because of the frequency of wrongful conviction. Clearly, our system of law and justice, while admirable, is fallible.

Cases involving law and justice often attract wide public and media attention. An eminent jurist, Louise Arbour, now on our Supreme Court, led investigations of war crimes committed in the former Yugoslavia that culminated in a trial of the former president of Serbia and others. In Canada, the notorious case of Paul Bernardo and Karla Homolka, convicted of the sexual assault, torture and murder of teenage girls in St. Catharines, Ontario, continues to resonate years later, particularly as the latter was refused parole in 2001 and must serve her full sentence which ends in July, 2005. In 2003 in British Columbia, a man was tried for the serial murders of countless women, and a father was tried for the killing of his six children after the breakup of his marriage. Few events in contemporary life have the compelling drama of the criminal trial. Countless novels, movies and popular television programs have been built around this familiar sequence of legal events. The intensely competitive atmosphere, the consequences for the accused, victim, families and lawyers, the clash of different interpretations of the same evidence all contribute to a fascinating arena in which to observe human social behaviour.

Thus, it is not surprising that psychologists have been interested in the legal system since the early days of the discipline (Munsterberg, 1908). Events in the courtroom constitute a social world in miniature in which everyday social psychological processes are magnified because the stakes are so high (Pennington & Hastie, 1990). Consider these questions:

- The police take reports of eyewitnesses. Do the eyewitnesses remember and report accurately?

- On the basis of eyewitness and other evidence, the police develop a hypothesis about the crime. How does this influence their investigation and their interpretation of evidence?

- A suspect is apprehended and identified from a police lineup. Could the witness have been subtly pressured by the police to make an identification or could the lineup itself have biased this identification?

- The suspect is charged and given an opportunity to confess. Can people be subtly coerced or tricked into a false confession?

- The case goes to trial. How do the persuasive abilities of the Crown and defence lawyers influence the jury? How could biases amongst the jurors influence the verdict? How might the instructions of the judge influence the verdict?

How jurors are selected; how witnesses recall and recount events; how the characteristics of the defendant, lawyer, witness and judge affect the verdicts of juries; how juries, as groups, arrive at decisions; how judges determine sentences—these are some of the questions posed by social psychologists. Social scientific evidence has gained increasing acceptance in courts in demonstrating, for example, the impact of racial or sexual discrimination (Tomkins & Pfeifer, 1991). Research has illuminated such topics as understanding criminal behaviour, conducting criminal investigations and the treatment and rehabilitation of the convicted criminal.

In this chapter, we explore some social psychological research on these issues. One caution is in order:

most of the research has been conducted in the U.S. While the two countries have similar judicial systems, important differences between Canadian and U.S. practices must be taken into account.

The Defendant

Ideally, verdicts should be based only on relevant facts. The appearance, status and attitude of the defendant should be disregarded. However jurors, like other people, are subject to such psychological effects as the similarity-attraction rule, the "beautiful is good" stereotype and schemata about types of people.

For instance in some places, law enforcement officers tend to suspect criminality when the suspect is black and of a lower socioeconomic level (Ruby & Brigham, 1996). While gender may be important in certain crimes and attractive defendants are often treated more leniently, no consistent evidence has been found that social class makes a difference (Dane & Wrightsman, 1982). Other research clearly shows a bias in favour of one's own group. When whites evaluate black defendants and English Canadians judge French and Native Canadian defendants, they perceive them as more guilty and recommend more severe punishments (Pfeifer & Ogloff, 1988; 1989; Pfeifer & Bernstein, 1993). However, Pfeifer (1990) makes the important point that while prejudice will often exist among jurors, the actual decisions of juries are not necessarily discriminatory, particularly when the jurors are instructed in their role and responsibilities.

What's in a face? In an experiment, participants rated a series of photos for characteristics including honesty and aggressiveness (Macrae & Shepherd, 1989). These rated photos were then shown in pairs to other participants who were asked to select which person was responsible for a specific crime. Even after accounting for physical attractiveness, research participants tended to choose photos of those with facial features stereotypically linked to the crimes such as "aggressive-looking," with violent crimes. Indeed, there is evidence jurors will be influenced by whether the defendant "looks like a criminal" (Shoemaker, South & Lowe, 1973). Conversely, adults with "baby faces," large eyes, short noses and low placement of facial features are less likely to be convicted (Berry & Zebrowitz-McArthur, 1988).

In Canada, someone convicted of a series of crimes can be designated a "dangerous offender" and given an indeterminate sentence. Unattractive defendants or those with some physical abnormality, such as a facial scar, tend to be perceived as more "dangerous-looking" (Wormith & Ruhl, 1986; Webster, Dickens & Addario, 1985; Esses & Webster, 1988).

The Witness

While physical evidence such as a fingerprint, a document or a weapon may be available, the most convincing and decisive evidence is often the testimony of an eyewitness, someone who can identify the perpetrator and describe what happened. Indeed in cases where a person later shown to be innocent has been convicted, eyewitness testimony was often the most important reason for the conviction (Loftus, 1974, 1979; Lindsay, Wells & O'Connor, 1989).

Even if the eyewitness is honestly attempting to be truthful and accurate, there are two related issues to consider: (1) Is the testimony of an eyewitness usually accurate?; (2) Will the judge or jurors believe the testimony? Let us consider these questions in the light of research evidence.

Eyewitness accuracy

Can we depend on the accuracy of eyewitnesses? Consider the following experiments in which a crime was staged (Buckhout, 1980). Television viewers in New York City were shown a 127-second tape of an incident in which a mugger stole a woman's purse and then ran directly towards the camera. Viewers were then shown a six-person lineup that included the actual criminal and were invited to identify that person. Of the 2145 viewers who called the station, only 15.3 percent correctly identified the mugger, which is close to what would be expected by pure chance. In fact, 33 percent identified the white assailant as being black or Hispanic and a few were even convinced that the same actor had also victimized them. In other similar experiments, research participants later showed large variations in their estimates of the perpetrator's height (average error of 20 cm), hair colour (83 percent in error) and age (average error of eight years) (Loftus, 1979).

Since witnesses can be inaccurate, it is important to know when their testimony can be trusted. The U.S. Supreme Court in 1972 suggested five criteria for evaluating an eyewitness:

1. the opportunity of the witness to view the criminal clearly at the time and place of the crime;
2. the extent to which the witness was paying attention to the incident;
3. the accuracy of the witness's description of the criminal before seeing the accused;
4. the extent to which the witness is confident of what he or she saw;
5. the time elapsed between the crime and the identification.

Most people, as potential jurors, would accept these assumptions (Kassin & Barndollar, 1992), but the research does not give us reasons for confidence in any of them (Wells & Murray, 1983).

In one study (Yarmey, 1986a), research participants were asked to imagine that they were in a park and had witnessed a crime in which a man assaulted a woman. They were shown a sequence of 60 colour slides depicting the crime in which the level of illumination was varied to simulate broad daylight, early or late twilight or night. Participants, as expected, recalled with greater accuracy in daylight or early twilight conditions that were consistent with the first criterion—the opportunity of the witness to view the criminal at the time of the crime. However, there was no relationship between the witnesses' accuracy in recalling the event and their later identification of the assailant. In addition, research participants who expressed a high degree of certainty in their choice were no more accurate than those who were less certain (criterion # 4) were. While police officers consider themselves to be capable and credible witnesses, defence lawyers and the public are somewhat more skeptical (Yarmey, 1986b). Indeed, the evidence indicates that trained officers are no more accurate than others as eyewitnesses (Yarmey, 1979).

Now, consider this experiment by Wells & Olson (2002) in which participants were shown a video of what appeared to be a terrorist planting a bomb. At one point, the camera zoomed in to focus clearly on the perpetrator's face. Participants were then shown a photo lineup of six people who looked similar to the bomber, but none of the photos were actually of the bomber. Nonetheless all participants identified one of the pictures as the perpetrator. Having made a choice, participants were then randomly assigned to several conditions. Some were told of evidence that corroborated their identification, others of evidence that exonerated the accused perpetrator and still others were given no feedback. In some cases, the feedback was given immediately after their identification and in others, 48 hours later in a second session. Participants were then asked a series of questions such as about how confident they were in their choice, how good a view they had and how much attention they had paid to the perpetrator. As expected, those immediately told that the evidence confirmed their decision were more confident than those who were not. Perhaps of more concern, exactly the same thing happened when the confirmation was given 48 hours later. Of course, the trial occurs months or even years after the incident and so the delayed condition is more representative of the actual situation and much more difficult to control.

Other factors influence our ability to remember a criminal incident accurately. For example, we are usually more able to identify people of our own race than those of other races (Brigham & Malpass, 1985; Luce, 1974; Shepherd, Deregowski & Ellis, 1974). In general, people tend to perceive people of other races as more similar to each other than they really are or "they all look alike." Thus errors are more likely to occur (Barkowitz & Brigham, 1982).

Memory distortion

Often the capacity to remember a face is crucial. In an analysis of 128 relevant experiments involving 16 950 research participants, Shapiro and Penrod (1986) found that a number of variables influenced accuracy in facial recognition. These included whether research participants made inferences about psychological traits or looked for distinctive features of the face; whether identification was tested in the same context in which the target had been observed; whether the target was seen as distinctive or unusual; whether the target's face had been changed in some way between the time of observation and identification (glasses, pose, hairstyle or expression); and whether the target's face was associated at the time with descriptive adjectives.

People who witness an event may later be exposed to new, often misleading information about that event on TV or in newspapers or through "leading questions" by investigating officers, lawyers or even therapists. As a result, recollections of the event may become distorted (Loftus, 1992). In one study, research participants saw a simulated traffic accident. Then they received a written report about the accident, which, in some cases, provided incorrect information. For example, a stop sign was referred to as a yield sign. Research participants given this misinformation tended to report that they had seen a yield sign; that is, witnesses will incorporate misleading information into their memories. This is particularly true when they believe that the questioner was well informed, or when the leading question has been repeated (Zaragoza & Mitchell, 1996).

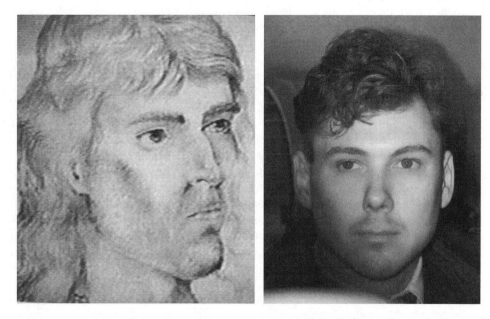

A composite of the murderer of teenage girls in southern Ontario, published while the case was still under investigation, illustrates stereotypes of what a dangerous criminal looks like (left). The reality, a deceptively angelic-looking Paul Bernardo (right) is somehow more chilling.

Witnessing actual or threatened violence can be stressful even when the violence has not been directed at that witness, and this stress may distort their memory of the event (Yarmey & Jones, 1983a). There is also research showing that people tend to fix their gaze on unusual or significant objects such as a gun or other weapon or an injured person (see Yarmey & Jones, 1983b; Christianson & Loftus, 1991). Thus, their attention may be distracted from the face and other characteristics of the person committing the crime. As witnesses are often not aware of how distracted they were at the time, their testimony may be well-intended but unreliable, especially if the event was traumatic. Research on the relationship between emotional stress and memory shows that eyewitnesses tend to be relatively accurate under these conditions in remembering central details but relatively inaccurate in remembering peripheral details (Christianson, 1992). However in another experiment (Porter, Spencer & Birt, 2003), participants viewed a series of photographs which had been previously shown to arouse positive emotions, or negative, disturbing emotions (e.g., a graphic fatal accident) or to be neutral with regard to emotional arousal. Half of each group was then exposed to misleading questions such as the suggestion of a large animal in the picture. Later, all participants were asked to recall the scene and asked a series of questions including some about the large but nonexistent animal. As expected, having been exposed earlier to the misleading questions increased false memories about the picture. This was particularly the case where strong negative feelings had been aroused. Clearly, our memories of past events are reconstructed rather than simply recorded (recall Chapter 2) and we can all be "blinded by emotion."

Loftus and Burns (1982) compared the recall of research participants who had viewed a movie of a bank robbery in which a boy was shot in the face with the recall of a control group who saw the robbery but not the shooting. Research participants who had viewed the violent episode were much less likely to remember what they had witnessed prior to the shooting such as the number on the boy's sweater. Other studies suggest that repeated recall trials may assist the person in remembering accurately. In one such experiment by Scrivner and Safer (1988), research participants first viewed a two-minute excerpt from a police training film in which a burglar breaks into a house, shoots several people and then escapes. Expert viewers had identified 45 important details about the crime and the suspect. Immediately afterwards, research participants were given a few minutes to write down important details from the videotape on an answer sheet containing the numbers 1 through 47. The research participants were instructed to "replay the videotape" as though they had a VCR in their heads. Recall was then re-tested and then re-tested again 48 hours later. Research participants recalled more details on each successive recall trial.

The police lineup

In the standard police identification lineup, the suspect stands among a group of five to nine persons and the witness attempts to identify the guilty party. The procedure was devised to overcome the effects of bias that would arise if the witness were asked directly whether a particular person did it. Indeed, witnesses are more likely to select someone from a lineup as the perpetrator than to positively identify a person presented as a single suspect (Gonzalez, Ellsworth & Pembroke, 1993). Why? It is argued that a show-up of a single suspect requires an absolute judgment ("This is [or is not] the person that I saw") while a lineup leads to a relative judgment as to which of the persons most resemble the witness's memory of the perpetrator.

It would seem to be self-evident that when witnesses express confidence, they are more likely to be accurate. When people have chosen someone from the lineup, those who are highly confident in their choice are more likely to be correct in their choice. However with witnesses who have rejected the entire lineup as not matching the perpetrator, confidence does not predict whether they are correct in that judgment (Sporer, Penrod, Read & Cutler, 1995) (see also Table 15–1 on page 436).

Think of a lineup procedure as similar to the design of research itself (Yarmey, 1979; Wells & Luus, 1990; see Chapter 1). Lineups are conducted by police officers to test their "hypothesis" regarding a suspect and can be subject to "experimenter biases" such as asking leading questions of the witness. Sometimes the suspect is placed among a group of police officers (out of uniform) who tend to turn their eyes slightly towards the accused (Gilligan, 1977). In other cases, the lineup consists entirely of suspects in the case, which tends to increase the probability of misidentification perhaps because all of them show signs of nervousness (Wells & Turtle, 1986). Varying instructions such as whether the subject is told that the perpetrator is in the lineup can influence responses (Kohnken & Maass, 1988).

Eyewitnesses, like participants in an experiment, generally want to be helpful and may react to subtle

Eyewitness Recall in Real Life

On a spring afternoon in Burnaby, B.C., a thief entered a gun shop, tied up the proprietor and took some money and guns. After the thief left the store, the owner freed himself, grabbed a revolver and rushed outside to record the licence plate number of the thief. However, the thief had not yet entered his car. In a face-to-face encounter separated by less than two metres, the two men engaged in a gunfight in which the thief was killed and the owner was seriously wounded. The incident occurred on a busy street and was witnessed by people from adjacent buildings and passing automobiles. The police interviewed 21 witnesses in the aftermath of the event.

About five months later, researchers interviewed 13 of the witnesses (Yuille & Cutshall, 1986). In general, they found that the witnesses were remarkably accurate when their responses were compared with the composite report of the police. While witnesses varied in some details such the colour of clothing or people's height, weight and age, their memories of

the sequence of events and the actions of various people were largely free of errors. Moreover, they were not misled by biased or leading questions (e.g., asking whether they recalled seeing a broken headlight when there was, in fact, no such broken headlight). Research participants who reported feeling intense anxiety at the time of the incident did not recall the accident with greater or less accuracy than did the other witnesses.

Of course, this study lacks the controls of a laboratory experiment. Some witnesses were directly involved in the event and others observed at a distance; and witnesses varied in what they had been able to see before, during and after the shooting. Nonetheless, the findings are not consistent with the essentially negative view of the eyewitness that emerges from laboratory research. More similar field studies should provide us with a real-world database from which the laboratory experiments can be interpreted.

demand characteristics. For example, they may feel compelled to identify someone although none of the persons in the lineup may be guilty. Stereotypes regarding dress, race, age, hairstyle and other physical features may lead to response biases particularly if the officers conducting the inquiry share these stereotypes. Even lighting and noise levels in the room may influence judgments, particularly if these conditions differ from those at the scene of the crime.

Another study was based on an actual case, Regina vs. Shatford (Doob & Kirshenbaum, 1973b). Shatford had allegedly taken part in a holdup in which the cashier could later recall only that the robbers were very neatly dressed, rather good-looking and they looked enough alike to be brothers. In spite of this vague description, she was able to pick Shatford out of a 12-person lineup nine days later. Further inquiry revealed that she had simply selected the best-looking person in the lineup. If the lineup had included other attractive people, she might have identified one of them instead.

The critical feature of a lineup is not the absolute number of people but the functional number from which the witness may identify the culprit. For example, if the suspect is known to have been fat and there is only one other fat person in the lineup, the total number of people in that lineup may be nine but the functional number is only two and there is a 50-percent probability of one being identified by pure chance.

After people have witnessed a crime, they are often asked by the police to view a series of "mugshot" photographs of possible suspects. Brigham and Cairns (1988) have shown how this practice may bias later identification of the suspect in a lineup. After viewing a videotape of a staged assault, some research participants were asked to identify the assailant from a set of 18 photos; others were asked (as an experimental control) to rate each of the same photos for attractiveness; and still others were not exposed to the photos. The actual assailant was not among the photos. Two days later, each subject attempted to identify the assailant from among six suspects. Research participants who had viewed the mugshots, particularly those who had incorrectly named one of the photos as that of the assailant, were much less likely to make the correct choice in the later lineup.

Research suggests a number of changes in the procedures of lineups in order to enhance accuracy (Brigham & Pfeifer, 1994; Wells, Small, Penrod, Malpass, Fulero & Brimacombe, 1998). First, the lineup must be large enough that the probability of selecting the wrong person by chance is relatively low. In cases of multiple suspects, a mixed lineup might include both the suspects and "foils" that are not suspected of having committed that crime (Wells & Turtle, 1986). Further, a "preceding blank lineup" consisting entirely of non-suspects could be used to identify eyewitnesses who are particularly prone to making false identifications (Wells, 1984). Yarmey (1979) argues that lineup identification procedures should be standardized more carefully and that the lineup procedure should be conducted by an officer not involved in the case. Even better would be a *double-blind procedure* similar to that used in drug research in which neither the experimenter nor the participant knows whether the drug or a placebo has been administered. In this case, the procedure would be that neither the individual conducting the inquiry nor the others in the lineup would know who is suspected. Social scientists working with professionals in the law could develop standards for lineups that would be scientifically defensible and consistent with the goals of justice.

Estimator and system variables

How can eyewitness testimony be made more accurate (Wells, 1978)? We must distinguish in the first instance between two types of factors affecting accuracy: estimator variables and system variables (Wells, 1978; Wells & Olson, 2003). Estimator variables refer to characteristics of the witness, the event and how the testimony is presented (e.g., confidence). System variables are factors under the control of the justice system: the interval between the event and testimony, the biasing effect of mugshot identification, the structure of the lineup and the types of questions asked. Clearly, the research indicates that some of these procedures can be improved.

Estimator variables are beyond control of the system, such as the seriousness and complexity of the criminal event; the amount of time that the witness has been exposed to the event or the accused; the race, sex, age and physical attractiveness of the defendant;

TABLE 15-1

Eyewitness testimony: What we know

How would you respond to the following statements?

(1) Eyewitness testimony about an event can be affected by how the questions put to the witness are worded.

(2) Police instructions can affect an eyewitness's willingness to make an identification and/or the likelihood that she or he will identify a particular person.

(3) Eyewitness testimony about an event often reflects not only what was actually seen but information obtained later on.

(4) Eyewitness confidence is not a good predictor of identification accuracy.

(5) An eyewitness's perception and memory of an event may be affected by his or her attitudes and expectations.

(6) The less time an eyewitness has to observe an event, the less well he or she will remember it.

(7) An eyewitness sometimes identifies someone previously seen in another situation or context as a culprit.

(8) The use of a one-person show-up instead of a full lineup increases the risk of misidentification.

(9) The rate of memory for an event is greatest right after an event and then levels off over time.

Kassin, Ellsworth & Smith (1989) submitted these and other items to 63 experts on eyewitness testimony, all of whom had published significant research on this topic. At least 80 percent of them agreed that the data concerning these items are reliable enough to present in court. Research evidence accumulated since the publication of this report has strengthened the case.

Protecting the Jurors from Bias

In order to ensure a fair trial, members of the jury must not bring biases into their deliberations. One point of view is that juries must be selected to minimize biases and that jurors must be protected in some way from information or opinion external to what happens in the courtroom. Another is that juries must be selected to minimize potential biases. For instance, if research showed that young men in a certain area who hold certain beliefs about other matters tend also to have biases against homosexual men, then such jurors would be excluded. Indeed, psychologists sometimes act as consultants in jury selection.

It is important to understand that in the Canadian system jury selection follows strict procedures, which would make deliberate selection of jurors more difficult. Jurors are selected at random from a panel of eligible adults. Potential jurors may be excused by the trial judge for specific reasons such as having a personal interest in the matter to be tried, a relationship with any participant in the trial, personal hardship such as family or unavoidable work responsibilities. In some circumstances, one of the lawyers may challenge a potential juror for cause such as a conflict of interest, having been convicted of an offence for which a sentence of more than 12 months was imposed or unable to speak the language of the trial. If the challenge is on grounds of non-impartiality, then only questions specific to that challenge may be asked after being screened by the trial judge. Two jurors previously selected act as "triers" and must decide unanimously if the juror is acceptable or unacceptable (if two jurors have not been selected, then two potential jurors selected randomly act as triers). Finally a trial lawyer may exclude the potential juror on peremptory challenges, which are limited in number: 20 for murder or treason, 12 for a charge with a potential sentence of more than five years, and four in other cases. In short, the lawyers on both sides are more restricted in jury selection than is the case in U.S. trials or the trials as dramatized in American television or movies.

Two highly publicized trials involved concerns of juror bias from exposure to massive media coverage. In the mid-1990s, Karla Homolka and Paul Bernardo were tried separately for the sexual abuse and murder of two teenage girls in St. Catharines, Ontario. The judge in the first trial, Homolka's, ordered a publication ban until her husband was tried, on the grounds that publicizing the evidence presented in the first case would likely bias jurors in the second case.

O.J. Simpson was tried in Los Angeles for the murders of his ex-wife and a friend. While the system in that country did not allow for the temporary suppression of publicizing details surrounding the case, the jurors were sequestered for the nine months of the trials, away from their families, work and incessant media reports of the trial. Many jurors who have been sequestered for extended periods find the experience highly stressful. Reported reactions include depression, feelings of hopelessness and helplessness, difficulty in concentration and memory, reduced self-confidence and loneliness: a "sequestered juror syndrome" (Chopra, Dahl & Wrightsman, 1996). Do such conditions increase objectivity or merely decrease the jurors' alertness and judgment skills? Is it necessary to keep them uninformed?

Another opinion is that jurors, placed as they are in a role with strong norms, will act conscientiously and impartially. In this volume, we have seen how the demands of the role can sometimes have a powerful influence on behaviour whether as a "guard" in a mock prison or a teacher in a "learning" experiment. Some of the mock jurors in an experiment (Burke & Freedman, 1996) were exposed to newspaper articles describing the crime and providing damaging information against the defendant. Other mock jurors were not exposed to this information. Neither group showed evidence of bias when asked to deliberate in groups after presentation of the relevant trial.

Perhaps the jury system works better than legal experts have suspected!

even given the honest attempt by most to perform their role fairly and competently. For instance, one mock juror experiment indicates that jurors asked to evaluate a case involving homicide or child abuse are more likely to convict if satanic cult involvement was alleged, even without evidence or admission (Pfeifer, 1999).

To what extent can we predict how individual jurors will vote? Jurors who are older, less educated and of lower socioeconomic levels are more likely to vote to convict (see Nemeth, 1981). Male and female jurors show different patterns only in rape cases where women are more likely to convict and to favour harsh sentences (Nemeth, 1981). Another predictor is the extent of similarity between jurors and the defendant. For example, a French-speaking female carpenter is more likely to receive a lenient judgment from jurors who also have one or more of these characteristics (see Chapter 8).

One characteristic that has been studied extensively is authoritarianism, the pattern in which individuals display rigid thinking, political conservatism and social conventionality, submissiveness to authority and a hostile, punitive orientation towards those who deviate in any way from social norms (Adorno, Frenkel-Brunswick, Levinson & Sanford, 1950; see Chapter 13). Authoritarians are more apt to convict and to recommend severe sentences particularly if the defendant is not similar to themselves (Mitchell & Byrne, 1973). However, authoritarians are less likely to convict if the defendant is a police officer. Apparently, authoritarians and non-authoritarians have different schemata and use different kinds of information in arriving at their decisions. When mock-jury research participants were contacted one week after an experiment, high authoritarians recalled more about the defendant's character but less about the evidence (Berg & Vidmar, 1975).

Overt prejudice may be relatively easy to detect in questioning potential jurors. However, more subtle forms of prejudice may influence their decisions. In a study (Pfeifer, 1989), research participants acting as jurors viewed an audiovisual presentation of a trial. The prosecuting lawyer played by a male or female was vigorously engaged in questioning a submissive male defendant. Male but not female research participants rated the defendant as less likely to be guilty when the prosecutor was female. Interestingly, the male jurors also rated the female prosecutor as more effective than did female jurors. Thus, the research participants expressed their sexism in an indirect or "symbolic" manner, not by downgrading the female prosecutor who acted against stereotypic expectations but by voting "not guilty."

The Verdict: Processes of Judgment

What cognitive processes do jurors go through in arriving at a verdict? Pennington and Hastie (1992) observe that jurors construct a story, a narrative of what happened based on information presented at the trial. Causal relationships between events and intentions of the actors are crucial to the decision. Of course, the credibility of the witnesses and the arguments of lawyers will have a bearing on how the jurors put together pieces of information to construct a narrative that makes sense to them.

Consider an actual case in which an application for child support was accompanied by evidence from a blood test showing it to be 99.8 percent probable that the man being sued was the father of the child. The application was dismissed ("99.8% probability" 1986). Indeed, jurors and judges alike tend to dismiss purely statistical evidence and rely more on eyewitness accounts, which we know to be error-prone (Wells, 1992). If rather than giving a finding in terms of probability, the expert in the paternity case had stated, "I conclude, based on this evidence, that the defendant is the father," the plaintiff might well have won the case.

Detecting deception

To determine that the accused is guilty, the judge and jurors must make judgments regarding who is telling the truth and who is not and must make an attribution that the person not only acted in a certain way but is responsible for the consequences of that action. But how do people detect deception and attribute responsibility? Some interesting research has addressed this problem (DePaulo, 2003).

It has been found that, in general, people can distinguish truth from lies at slightly above a chance level (Miller & Burgoon, 1982; Zuckerman, DePaulo & Rosenthal, 1981). Surprisingly, those with training and experience do not seem to be more effective. For instance in one study, law enforcement officers and students viewed videotapes of individuals interviewed about their attitudes. The trained officers did no better than the students at distinguishing truthful from untruthful responses although the officers expressed increasing confidence over the series of trials (DePaulo & Pfeifer, 1986). In another, mock customs inspections were conducted with real airline passengers, some of whom were smuggling various kinds of contraband.

On viewing the videotapes, the trained customs officers did not perform better than a sample of laypeople (Kraut & Poe, 1980). However, another study found that research participants were less successful at hiding facts when they thought the target person was an expert (Fugita, Hogrebe & Wexley, 1980).

What are these cues? In general when people are lying, their speech has a higher pitch, they are more nervous and less fluent and they give less plausible and shorter answers with longer hesitations prior to responding. The long pause seems to be particularly powerful in alerting observers to the possibility that deception is taking place (Kraut, 1978). While individuals make some effort to control facial expression when trying to deceive someone, they are less aware of the "language" of the rest of the body (Ekman & Friesen, 1974). While observers are more accurate in detecting disguised emotions when viewing the body rather than the face, when factual material is involved, judgments based on the face are more accurate (Littlepage & Pineault, 1979).

Cues to deception can be classified as **deception clues**, behaviour that suggests the speaker is lying, and **leakage** in which the truth is mistakenly revealed (Ekman & Friesen, 1969). For example, a patient who wrings her hands while assuring the doctor that she feels fine provides a deception clue that she may feel ill. Of course, such cues are ambiguous; the patient

---

Lie Detection and the Polygraph

It is obvious that we cannot have justice in a criminal justice system unless we can determine the truth. In medieval Britain, an accused was required to swallow a "trial slice" of bread and cheese. It was reasoned that an inability to swallow it would indicate a dry mouth, which might indicate lying. The high-tech descendant of this technique is the polygraph, a controversial device.

The polygraph measures physiological changes particularly skin conductance (which indicates perspiration) and often blood pressure and respiratory rate. In general, the polygraph can indicate changes in the level of physiological arousal as the person responds to various questions. However, we cannot conclude that a person is lying if he or she shows increased arousal to critical questions ("Did you murder your wife?") but not to neutral questions ("Did you eat ice cream in the past week?"). There are many possible reasons for arousal: grief over the murder, fear of being falsely accused, shame at being suspected by the police.

Thus, more sophisticated techniques are used. For example, reactions are compared while the person responds to critical, neutral and control questions. It is reasoned that while the person may show increased arousal to any questions concerning an emotionally upsetting situation, a greater level of arousal would be shown if upset is combined with lying. Hence, reactions might be compared while the person responds to a general, control question ("Did someone murder your wife?") and then to a specific question ("Did you murder your wife?"). Another technique is to ask about details that only the perpetrator and police would know. For example if the victim was wearing a green sweater, one can ask a series of yes/no questions: Was the victim wearing a white sweater? a blue ski jacket? a green sweater? a grey parka? If the accused answers, "I don't know" to all the questions but shows arousal only to the green sweater then we may be on to something.

The research indicates accuracy from 70 to 90 percent of the time, which is impressive but not foolproof or beyond a reasonable doubt (Lykken, 1974; Yarmey, 1979; Horvath, 1977, 1984).

There is evidence that certain types of people or those who have been coached beforehand can "beat the machine" by using such techniques as mentally distracting themselves during critical questions or biting their tongues during neutral questions (Honts, Hodes & Raskin, 1985). There are also important ethical and legal issues such as invasion of privacy and self-incrimination. Perhaps, in the end, there is no substitute for competent and professional police work.

may be angry at the doctor or fearful about the future. A slip of the tongue or a nonverbal response to a specific question may provide leakage. For instance, a patient who has just claimed that back injury curtails his mobility may bend over easily to tie his shoes. People who are skillful at detecting one of these types of clues are not necessarily also skillful in detecting the other. Moreover, they may be too dependent on certain cues particularly when dealing with an experienced liar (Alcock, 1996).

In an interesting study (De Paulo & Rosenthal, 1979), male and female students were videotaped while they described several acquaintances that they liked, felt ambivalent about or disliked. They were then instructed to lie by pretending they liked some of the people they disliked and vice versa. Research participants watched excerpts from both sets of videotapes and attempted to identify cases of deception. They were good at identifying the occurrence of deception but not at identifying the real underlying feelings. Those research participants who were especially good at recognizing the leakage of favourable attitudes were not necessarily good at recognizing the leakage of unfavourable attitudes. In a similar vein, people who know when women are lying do not necessarily know when men are lying. In fact, there is some suggestion that women and men may behave in different ways when lying (Mehrabian, 1971; McClintock & Hunt, 1975). However with practice, it is possible to improve one's skill at detecting deception (Zuckerman, Koestner & Alton, 1984). Indeed, other studies indicate that some professional law enforcement officers and clinical psychologists can dramatically increase their accuracy in detecting who is lying by taking specialized training workshops. These workshops consist of providing videotapes and discussion about the cues that generally indicate lying (Ekman, O'Sullivan & Frank, 1999).

Attribution of responsibility

The concept of responsibility in law is crucial. The older and simpler view is that when laws are broken, the causal agent must be identified in order to rectify the situation and maintain the social order: an eye for an eye, a tooth for a tooth, or amputation of the hand of a thief. Viewed in this manner, an attribution of responsibility is not affected by motives, intentions or consequences of the action. You are simply responsible for your own actions regardless of the circumstance.

The more modern conception of responsibility is based on the intentions of the actor not just the act: an

attribution (recall Chapter 2). Convicting someone of a crime such as murder implies not only that an action occurred but that the person intended to cause a consequence. For example, the murderer shot with the purpose of killing the victim rather than in self-defence or because the person accidentally confused the victim with a nearby moose.

Of course, the law also considers the consequences of the act. The only difference between murder and attempted murder might be inaccurate shooting, yet we attribute more responsibility when there is a dead victim. Recall the study cited in Chapter 2 in which the driver of a car with a failed parking brake was deemed more responsible when the runaway car hurt someone than when it caused minimal damage.

The law also accepts the attribution of diminished responsibility. In 1843, a young man named Daniel M'Naghten, while attempting to kill British prime minister Sir Robert Peel, killed the prime minister's private secretary instead. M'Naghten's lawyer presented a novel defence that M'Naghten could not be held legally responsible for his actions because he was under the insane delusion that he was being hounded by the prime minister and many other enemies. In the judge's historic judgment known as the **M'Naghten Rule**, the defendant was acquitted because "he did not know the nature and quality of the act he was doing or if he did know it, he did not know he was doing wrong." With various modifications, this rule still applies in most jurisdictions. For example, in 1982 a man who shot and wounded U.S. president Reagan was not convicted of the attempted murder because he was acting under the obsession of winning the heart and mind of the movie star Jodie Foster. It has been found in a simulation study that individuals described as highly anxious or paranoid are assigned less responsibility. However, a protagonist described as an alcoholic was assigned more blame even though the alcoholic was also rated as highest in mental illness (Sadava, Angus & Forsyth, 1980).

The principle of legal insanity is still controversial. People are often reluctant to see an accused "get off" from a heinous crime on these grounds. In some nations, diagnoses of psychiatric disorders have been abused to suppress political dissent (Stover & Nightingale, 1985).

A related ground for diminished responsibility is intoxication. The Supreme Court of Canada as well as courts in other countries have wrestled with the drunkenness defence. Can a person be too drunk to form intent? Should people be held responsible, legally or morally, for their actions while they are intoxicated?

How Do We Attribute Responsibility to Corporations?

- A large brokerage firm was found to have been involved in a "cheque-kiting operation," a scheme in which cheques were systematically shuffled between banks, several of which recorded deposit of the same cheque in order to produce as much as $10 000 000 000 in overdrafts. The corporation was merely fined.

- A Canadian firm involved in recycling batteries was convicted of violating environmental and work safety standards and causing serious illnesses in workers. The firm was fined $25 000.

- The Ford Motor Company was acquitted of charges of reckless homicide in relation to the explosion of a Pinto gas tank.

- Tobacco companies have been sued successfully by individuals and governments for having contributed to the addictions, illnesses and deaths of their clients. Some large financial settlements have been awarded in the United States.

- Many corporations have recently declared bankruptcy under suspicious circumstances where the employees and stockholders lost a lot of money but where some high executives gained wealth. Some of the cases have been moving slowly through the legal system.

Many argue that if individuals rather than corporations had been tried and convicted of these offences, the penalties might have been more severe. Others argue that corporations are often treated more harshly by the legal system. For example, juries tend to award larger sums to plaintiffs suing for personal injury when the defendant is a corporation or government than if the plaintiff is an individual: this is known as the "deep pockets effect."

In an experiment by Hans and Ermann (1989), research participants read of a case in which five workers were hired to clear a newly purchased lot of debris. After two weeks, four of the workers complained of dizziness to the employer who told them to continue working but to notify him again if they felt worse. By the third week, three of the workers were hospitalized with severe respiratory problems and subsequent tests revealed permanent lung damage in all five employees caused by a highly toxic chemical on the site. The workers sued the employer, identified as either Mr. Jones or The Jones Corporation, for medical expenses and for pain and suffering. Research participants awarded greater amounts to the workers (an average of $96 000 more) from a corporate as opposed to an individual defendant. Research participants judged the corporation to have been more reckless and morally wrong in its actions: more than the "deep pockets effect" was involved.

In some jurisdictions, the chief executive officers of corporations are held personally liable for transgressions of environmental protection laws, and executives may actually be jailed. To what extent can or should corporations be held responsible for selling hazardous products to those who use them or may even be addicted to them?

When we see people act stupidly or out of character when they are drunk, we tend to excuse their behaviour. This notion of "time out" from the usual social norms and personal responsibilities is found in many cultures (MacAndrew & Egerton, 1969). Recall the discussion in Chapter 3 of how people protect their own self-esteem by drinking and then attributing a failure to alcohol rather than to their own inadequacies.

In a study (Critchlow, 1985), research participants considered short scenarios in which a person interrupted a conversation, ate too much or committed crimes such as vandalism or forgery. In general, less responsibility and blame for the act was attributed to intoxicated actors particularly with criminal behaviour. It seems that, especially in more unusual criminal acts, we are impelled to search for a cause. When alcohol is present, we will discount other possible explanations (recall Chapter 2).

It is commonly believed that alcohol is the cause of violence and inappropriate sexual behaviour. While alcohol as a drug may play a role, careful experiments reveal that even drinking a placebo lowers inhibitions against sexual or aggressive behaviour (Marlatt & Rohsenow, 1980; Hull and Bond, 1986). Many people apparently believe that drinking grants "time out" from the usual restraints of society.

Addiction in itself is an attribution. For example, why do people continue to smoke in the face of the dire risks to their health, which are believed by smokers and non-smokers alike (Loken, 1982)? Smokers may attribute their actions to situational factors (pleasure, difficulty quitting, presence of others) and non-smokers to the dispositional weakness of smokers (Eiser, 1982). However, perhaps as a result of changes in social norms, many smokers are unwilling to endorse any reason for smoking other than as a persistent habit (Sadava & Wiethe, 1985).

The Judge

Instructions of the judge

Even in a jury trial, the judge can exert enormous influence. The judge must interpret the law to the jury explaining the notions of presumption of innocence, burden of proof and the phrase "beyond a reasonable doubt." The judge must rule on motions by the lawyers on both sides concerning procedural matters including the admissibility of evidence. After all evidence has been presented and all arguments made, the judge instructs the jury on the meaning of the charges, the alternative decisions open to them (e.g., first- or second-degree murder, manslaughter, self-defence) and even on the evidence and the credibility of key witnesses (Cavoukian & Doob, 1980). However, some judges' instructions are so lengthy and technical that the jurors fail to understand them (Elwork, Sales & Alfini, 1982; Hafer, Reynolds & Obertynski, 1996). Using plain English would help!

Judges may also have to explain a difficult legal concept. Consider for example, the case in which the accused has sold illegal drugs to an undercover police officer. If a judge or jury considers that a typical person might well have been induced by the officer to commit the crime, then the crime has been in effect created by that officer and thus the accused is not guilty by reason of entrapment. Two different arguments are used in such cases. One concerns inducements used by the officer; if the promise of large profits, appeals to sympathy or badgering were such as

to tempt the normal, law-abiding person, then the accused person would not be guilty even if he or she seems likely to have committed the act. On the other hand if the individual seems to have been predisposed to commit the act and if the defendant had the drugs already packaged for sale, then the person would be judged to be legally responsible regardless of the behaviour of the undercover officer. The judge must instruct the jury on which argument is applicable in the particular case. In general, jurors tend to find the argument about the imputed motives or dispositions of the accused easier to understand and special efforts must be made to present the inducement argument in comprehensible, nontechnical terms (Morier, Borgida & Park, 1996).

Judges may instruct juries to disregard a piece of evidence, such as the prior record of the accused person, as unreliable or as irrelevant. Jurors do not always heed these instructions (Doob & Kirschenbaum, 1972). Indeed, one experiment (Wolf & Montgomery, 1977) found that when judges gave strong instructions—"It must play no role in your consideration of the case. You have no choice but to disregard it"—the disallowed testimony had even greater impact on jurors than it did in the absence of any instructions. Even judges may be influenced subtly by the defendant's prior record. A study of actual trials reveals that when judges were aware of the prior record of the defendant, the final instructions tended to lack tolerance and verdicts were more likely to be guilty (Goleman, 1986).

A realistic experiment was conducted by Tanford and Penrod (1984) in which experienced jurors watched videotaped reenactments of trials involving a defendant charged with either a single offence or that same offence plus two others. Jurors judging the offence by itself were less likely to vote guilty than were those judging the offence in combination with the two other charges (24 percent as opposed to 39 percent). Elaborate and pointed instructions from the judges to ignore the fact that there were three charges did not affect the decisions of jurors.

On the basis of evidence from both experimental studies and trial records, Tanford (1990) argues that admonitions to the jury are ineffective and even counterproductive. However, other studies show that these judicial instructions can have an effect. Jurors who scored high on a measure of *dogmatism* (a generalized form of authoritarianism) tended to be more influenced by the judges' instructions (Kerwin & Shaffer, 1991). In another experiment (Carretta & Moreland, 1983), research participants served as jurors in a trial in which the defendant was accused of murdering a storekeeper. Some crucial evidence was obtained by wiretapping, a procedure under strict legal limitations, in which the accused admitted that he had a lot of extra money (an admission presumably favouring the prosecution). In one experimental condition, a judge told juries that the evidence was inadmissible while in the other condition, juries were told that the evidence was admissible. A guilty verdict was more likely when the wiretapped conversation was ruled admissible.

In another experiment (Stephan & Stephan, 1986), subject jurors read summaries of an assault case and then heard the testimony of the defendant who spoke either English or another language (Spanish, Thai) translated by an interpreter. Research participants were more likely to find a non-English-speaking defendant guilty. However, the language bias was offset among research participants who had been instructed by the judge to ignore the fact that the testimony had been translated. Perhaps in multicultural nations such as Canada instructions of this nature should be standard procedure.

Sentencing practices

The moment finally arrives when the jury is finished with its deliberations, brings in a decision to convict and the judge must now decide on a sentence. The law sets lower and upper limits on sentences and may also provide latitude in alternatives such as prison, fines or restitutional public service. The judge must examine the severity of the crime, the prior record of the defendant and other factors about the defendant that may suggest possibilities of recidivism or rehabilitation. One archival study of the sentencing decisions in 400 cases in San Diego, California, revealed three important factors: sentences tended to be harsher when the offence was severe, the defendant had a number of previous convictions and the defendant was attending the trial from prison (Konecni & Ebbeson, 1979). Another study found great variability in sentences imposed for the same offence; this variability related to the characteristics of the case and the defendant, the orientation of the judge and the geographical region in which the trial took place (Clancy, Bartholomew, Richardson & Wellford, 1981).

What leads us to conclude whether people "deserve" a sentence? According to Feather's (1999) model, we first judge the extent to which the accused was responsible and the seriousness of the offence. These two factors together lead us to conclude that

the individual deserves a penalty and how harsh that sentence would be. However, other factors can bias this judgment. The reader will recall the concept of authoritarianism, a belief in submission to authority that is linked to prejudice (see Chapter 13). As one might expect, people with authoritarian attitudes tend to make recommendations for harsh punishment in hypothetical case descriptions unless the offender is identified as a police officer. Judgments about sentencing may also be influenced by characteristics of the defendant. One study recorded the fines or bail amounts set by male and female judges for more than 2000 male and female defendants. Attractiveness of each defendant was rated by police officers. Attractive defendants tend to be treated somewhat more leniently in misdemeanour cases but not in the more serious felony cases (Downs & Lyons, 1991).

The values or philosophies of judges may differ even at the level of the U.S. Supreme Court (Tetlock, Bernzweig & Gallant, 1985). Some may be biased towards the victim or see crime as a moral problem and thus impose harsher sentences while others may favour rehabilitation of the offender (note that our prison system is defined as a system for corrections, that is, changing behaviour). Still others may be influenced by the deterrent effect of severe sentences, particularly with crimes of particular concern to society at that time. Moreover, sentencing decisions are influenced by factors peculiar to each case such as the criminal's apparent remorsefulness, his or her employment and family responsibilities and the victim's suffering (Dane & Wrightsman, 1982).

In a telling study (Roberts & Edwards, 1989), research participants first read a news story of a crime of low seriousness (petty theft), medium seriousness (assault) or high seriousness (homicide). Later, they were asked to react to another description of an unrelated crime and perpetrator, which also varied in seriousness. Research participants who had first read the story of the homicide rated the unrelated crime and criminal more negatively and were more punitive in their recommended sentences. Note that this effect held even when the preceding offence (homicide) was very different from the crime being rated (theft). Apparently, the anchoring effect of the news stories on serious crimes (and we encounter very little reporting of less serious crimes) generalizes to a more punitive orientation towards all crimes. Even judges are not likely to be immune from such effects (Padawer-Singer & Barton, 1975).

Attitudes towards crime and punishment

Many Canadians believe that the sentences imposed by our courts are generally too lenient (Doob & Roberts, 1984). However, this impression of leniency by the courts is largely an illusion. After one particular case, which had been given extensive and critical newspaper coverage, 63 percent of research participants rated the sentence as too lenient. However when given a summary of the information actually presented in court, only 19 percent rated the sentence as too lenient and 52 percent as too harsh. Similarly while public attitudes towards parole in general may be negative, early release is generally accepted when people are informed of the circumstances in specific cases (Cumberland & Zamble, 1992). Evidently, we are influenced by the availability heuristic (see Chapter 2) in which we use the few, sensationalized cases that we can remember to arrive at a generalized judgment about the courts.

The most controversial and persistent issue is capital punishment. Proponents of capital punishment support their position for both retributive justice and utilitarian reasons (Vidmar, 1974; Honeyman & Ogoloff, 1996). That is, many argue that for a crime such as murder, the death penalty is the only punishment that "fits," and that justice is retribution in kind. They also argue that capital punishment can fulfill utilitarian functions for society such as deterring others from committing such crimes, ensuring that the criminal will never do it again or saving taxpayers' money. Opponents to capital punishment argue in terms of the sacredness of human life and the possibility of a mistake (see the beginning of this chapter for important examples). They also dispute the assumption that capital punishment deters violent crime.

Retribution is the most important reason cited by proponents (Vidmar, 1974) and the majority of them would still favour the death penalty if provided with information showing that there was no deterrent effect (Sarat & Vidmar, 1976). Those who favour capital punishment also tended to score higher on measures of authoritarianism, prejudice towards various outgroups and acceptance of military "crimes of obedience" (Hamilton, 1976) and are more likely to vote to convict a defendant than are those opposed to the death penalty (Bersoff, 1987).

It may also be true that many jurors would be more reluctant to convict murderers if the death penalty were a possible outcome. Unlike the U.S., in Canada, it is not permitted to contact and question jurors after a trial. Freedman (1990) arranged for special permission to interview Canadian jurors after verdicts had been rendered in murder cases. Fully 30 percent of them reported that they would have been less likely to convict if the death penalty had been in effect. On the other hand, where the death penalty exists, jurors are usually dismissed if they oppose capital punishment. These individuals also tend to be less authoritarian and thus, the remaining, more authoritarian jurors are more likely to convict (Pennington & Hastie, 1990). Note also that jurors who oppose capital punishment can be convinced to recommend the death penalty while those in favour of the death penalty are less likely to recommend life imprisonment when given arguments against the death penalty (Honeyman & Ogoloff, 1996).

The evidence does not support the hypothesis that capital punishment deters murder. In Canada, while 66.5 percent of Canadians believe that more murders have been committed in the years since the abolition of capital punishment in 1976, the facts show a decrease in that period (Doob & Roberts, 1984). A study conducted in the U.S. also shows that in the last century 343 people are known to have been wrongfully convicted of murder and 25 have actually been executed (*Globe and Mail*, November 15, 1985). In view of the evidence of bias and error in our judicial procedures, we can assume a similar injustice in Canada. After a study of how the death penalty is applied across the world, Amnesty International has adopted a position opposing the practice for all prisoners without reservation. In 1987, the Canadian parliament voted to continue abolition of capital punishment, consistent with the practice in most Western democracies except for some states in the United States.

Justice

Social scientists have been concerned with the concept of justice in social behaviour (Homans, 1961, 1974, 1982; Lerner, 1977; Walster, Walster & Berscheid, 1978). One concern of these theorists and researchers has been **distributive justice**, the conditions under which the allocation of a resource or the outcome of an event would be judged as just or unjust. Other researchers have been concerned with procedural justice, the process of arriving at a decision. In other words, social psychologists are concerned with both what has been decided and how it has been decided.

Prior Record of the Victim: The Case of Rape

What is the effect of evidence regarding the previous behaviour of the victim on judgments of the accused? Consider the crime of sexual assault (formerly called "rape"). To perceive someone as a victim, we must assume that she or he did not wish the act to occur. This is reasonable; what is not reasonable is a bias towards blaming the victim such as by making allegations about the sexual behaviour of the victim in order to cast doubt on her intentions.

In one revealing study (Coates, Wortman & Abbey, 1979), male and female research participants listened to a tape-recorded interview with a rape victim. Following a description of the event, the interviewer asked the victim a number of questions including "Do you feel in any way responsible for what happened?" In one version, the victim attributed the event to pure bad luck and in another version she said the rape was largely her own fault. In general, research participants were more favourable to the victim when she accepted responsibility and when she seemed to have regained her emotional balance than when she denied personal responsibility and was still suffering consequences. Paradoxically while women empathized more with the victim, they also expressed more derogatory feelings towards the victim. We reject the victim precisely when she seems to be most victimized (echoes of the *just-world hypothesis*).

Borgida and White (1978) manipulated two factors in a mock jury study of a rape case: the likelihood that the victim consented, and the introduction of evidence on the victim's prior sexual history. Interestingly, jurors were less likely to convict the accused rapist when evidence about the victim's prior history was introduced even when it showed the victim in a favourable light. Perhaps more understandable is the tendency of juries to find the complainant less credible if there were a previous history of sexual involvement between the complainant and the defendant (Schuller & Hasting, 2002). Another study showed that irrelevant characteristics of the victim including her marital status (especially if divorced), her sexual experience and her profession influenced judgments about the case (Feldman-Summers & Lindner, 1976). It also seems that rape victims who do not express visible emotional distress are viewed as less believable (Calhoun, Selby & King, 1976). Finally if the couple had sex a number of times previously, people are more reluctant to label an act of forced intercourse as rape (Shotland & Goodstein, 1992).

Clearly, there are a number of reasons why many crimes including rape are not reported to the authorities: fear of reprisal, feelings of helplessness and the conviction that the police are powerless to arrest and punish (Kidd & Chayet, 1984). Indeed, many cases of sexual assault in which the victims seek help but do not press changes consist of women assaulted in the context of pursuing normal heterosexual activities (Yurchesyn, Keith & Renner, 1992). Perhaps most disturbing is the fear of being further victimized by the authorities. Interviews with 140 rape victims in the U.S. revealed that the primary reason the victim often did not press charges was her belief that she would be held up for judgment and that she would be traumatized in court (Holstrom & Burgess, 1978). In recent court practice, evidence about the personality or sexual history of the victim is usually not permitted.

However, conceptions of justice differ between cultures. For example, consider the following two situation: (1) For selfish reasons, someone takes another person's train tickets from a coat pocket without permission; the other person has enough money to buy another ticket; (2) For selfish reasons, a person does not deliver the wedding rings to his best friend's wedding. The first involves an undesirable breach of justice (violating someone's rights) while the latter involves violating interpersonal responsibilities or expectations. In a comparative study of children and adults in India and the U.S., it was found that the research participants in the U.S. gave priority to justice concerns while East Indians tended to see interpersonal responsibilities as moral issues and at times to give them precedence over matters of justice (Miller & Bersoff, 1992).

Finally the condition of both the accused and the complainant may be involved. Recall our earlier discussion of legal insanity and responsibility. When participants were given a description of a sexual assault case, the description included whether either or both or neither party was intoxicated. Harsher judgments were rendered when the defendant was intoxicated particularly when the complainant was sober. Apparently an intoxicated female complainant was seen as more sexually disinhibited and thus less the victim (Wall & Schuller, 2000).

Distributive justice

We arrive at justice decisions on the basis of distribution rules or norms that are an integral part of our value system. It appears that these rules are universal although how and why they are applied will vary from one culture to another. Three major rules of distributive justice have been identified: equity, equality and need (Austin, 1979).

Equity

Aristotle argued that distributive justice requires an equality of proportions: we measure our gains against what we view as our contributions and our worthiness and we compare this ratio with the ratio for other people in similar or dissimilar situations. Thus for instance, the notion of "pay equity" implies not that everyone be paid the same amount but that pay reflects the amount of responsibility, training and effort required to perform a job and that people doing work that is equally demanding should be paid the same amount. This concept has been developed as equity theory (Adams, 1965; Austin, 1979; Walster, Walster &

Berscheid, 1978; see also Chapter 9). Equity theory is related to the theory of cognitive dissonance in the sense that fairness can be restored by changing behaviour or by changing perceptions. It proposes that a relationship between parties is a just one when the ratio of perceived outcomes to perceived inputs (assets and liabilities that lead to a deserved outcome) are equal (Austin, 1979). In a job situation, the inputs and corresponding outcomes might look like Table 15–3.

Gender may be considered an input by a "traditional" male who feels that he should be compensated at a better rate than women. The existence of the "equal pay for work of equal value" movement emphasizes that this problem has yet to be satisfactorily resolved. Some individuals may also consider other unexpected factors as inputs. For example, at one time, Parisian bank workers felt that they should receive more pay than coworkers who had come from the provinces (Homans, 1961).

All other things being equal, the individual who works hardest on a job (has the largest input) should reasonably expect to receive the most pay; otherwise, the exchange will be perceived as being unfair or inequitable. It is important to remember that perceptions are crucial here. For example, an employee may feel that she is working too hard and the exchange is inequitable while the employer views the output as appropriate and the exchange as equitable.

People who feel they receive too little reward become angry, hostile and frustrated. An attempt to correct the situation may follow, such as asking for a raise or filing a grievance. If this doesn't work, the person might put less effort into the work, take more days off sick, seek other employment or even resort to sabotage.

An exchange is also inequitable if the outcomes are perceived as excessive relative to the inputs, leading to feelings of guilt and embarrassment. Not surprisingly, people are slow to conclude they receive too many rewards and can tolerate the situation quite well.

TABLE 15-3 Inputs and outcomes in a job situation	Inputs	Outcomes
	effort	salary
	training	fringe benefits
	experience	company car
	seniority	interesting job
	gender	opportunity for promotion

However in extreme cases, people may attempt to restore equity, for example, by working harder or donating some of their salary to charity.

Equality

Sometimes resources are distributed equally rather than equitably even though the participants have not made equal contributions. When group stability and *esprit de corps* are of primary concern, it may be disruptive to allocate outcomes differentially to group members (Sampson, 1975). Research has shown that allocations are likely to be equal if the participants expect to meet again and that females have a preference for equality while males prefer equity (Major & Deaux, 1982). These different orientations based on gender have been shown to be present in children as young as seven years of age (Vinacke & Gullickson, 1964). It has been suggested (Benton, 1971; Weinstein, DeVaughan & Wiley, 1969) that females are more concerned than males with the interpersonal aspects of the situation, exhibit less desire to create status differentials and avoid actions that could disrupt the harmony of the group.

Need

Another rule of distributive justice is that those who need the most should get the most. Need is closely associated with the norm of social responsibility and, not surprisingly, affects such activities as charitable donations (see Chapter 9): you perceive a need so your sense of social responsibility motivates you to respond to that need. Need also is taken into consideration at the interpersonal level in groups. For instance, an individual who has few resources (Leventhal, Weiss & Long, 1969) or who lacks ability may be over-rewarded in a work situation (Taynor & Deaux, 1973) but only if the person is not considered responsible for his own misfortune.

Distributive justice and trials

Our system offers equality under the law. However in some situations, equity is more appropriate. For instance, different defendants who have committed the same offence may be given very different sentences depending on factors such as criminal record, family, employment status and evidence of remorse. Many Canadians were outraged when Karla Homolka received a relatively light sentence for her part in the murders as part of a plea bargain with the Crown.

Procedural justice

In law, an appeal of a court decision is generally based on the contention that errors were made in procedures that led to the decision such as the admissibility of evidence. The interest of social psychologists in procedural justice (e.g., Thibaut & Walker, 1975; Tyler & Lind, 2001) focuses on the relationship between the methods used to arrive at a decision and the perception that the decision was just. For example, research participants' ratings of politicians and teachers are strongly influenced by the perceived fairness of how they make their decisions; that is, how the teachers grade papers or how the politicians arrive at voting decisions independent of their actual decisions about grades or votes (Tyler & Caine, 1981).

In one study by LaTour, Houlden, Walker and Thibaut (1976), research participants were presented with a description of a dispute over money and asked how they would like to see the dispute resolved. The available procedures were as follows: (1) autocratic, in which a third party controlled the presentation of evidence and the final decision; (2) arbitration, in which disputants presented their own case to a third party, whose decision was final; (3) a procedure in which the two disputants and a third party shared the decision; (4) mediation in which a third party would assist the two sides in arriving at their own settlement; and (5) bargaining in which the two sides would seek a solution without a third party. The five procedures were then evaluated in relation to three criteria: how likely it was that the dispute would be resolved, the fairness of the resolution and whether the decision would be explained to the research participants. It is interesting to observe that arbitration was the preferred choice and that bargaining was the least-preferred alternative because it was seen as unlikely to result in a resolution.

As one would expect, the outcome can have a bearing on whether people feel that justice has been served. In experiments in which research participants played the role of criminal lawyers, those who had a strong case to present were more favourable to the prompt decision guaranteed by having a third party impose a binding decision (Heuer & Penrod, 1986; Conlon, Lind & Lissak, 1989). That is, if people feel that they will win, they are less sensitive to issues of procedural justice. It can also be the case that unfair procedures may provide us with a credible explanation for unfavourable outcomes and indeed we may look for such unfairness when the outcome is not what we would have wished (van den Bos, Bruins, Wilke &

Dronkert, 1999). For instance, students are certainly more likely to question the fairness of marking when their own mark was lower than they expected.

When we are compelled to do something such as pay taxes, our sense of procedural justice may be violated (Tyler, Rasinski & McGraw, 1985). In a study by Gordon and Fryxell (1989), workers in a number of involuntary (closed shop) and voluntary (open shop) unions were surveyed about their satisfaction with the fairness of grievance procedures (procedural justice) and their satisfaction with both their union and management. Involuntary members' satisfaction was strongly related to their sense of procedural justice. Because they were compelled to join the group, perhaps they needed assurance of predictability and control from procedures they viewed as fair.

Concern with procedural justice also depends on whether individuals emphasize equity or equality (Rasinski, 1987). In general, equity tends to be the dominant concern when the group values economic considerations such as productivity, while equality becomes paramount when the group values solidarity and harmonious relations, and need is preferred when values such as personal growth or welfare are important (Deutsch, 1985). In a second study (Azzi, 1992), research participants (from both the U.S. and South Africa) participating in a simulation study of human relations were more likely to divide political power equally between two groups rather than to apportion more power to the majority when they were induced to identify with the minority. When people think of justice, they tend to think simultaneously of procedural and distributive justice.

The experience of injustice

Imagine that as a participant in a classic experiment you watch whom you believe to be another volunteer receive what seem to be painful and severe electric shocks. After ten minutes of this ordeal, you are given a break before the next session of observing the shocking treatment of another person. You may have been told that you can stop the shocks yourself before the second session begins or you may be told that you'll just have to observe the second shock session and there is nothing that you can do about it. Now you are asked to rate the victim along with other ratings. In the actual experiment, those who thought that they could control the shocks rated the victim in a much more positive manner than those who would have no

influence. Indeed, only a minority of the later group placed any blame on the experimenter. They blamed the victim. Lerner & Simmons (1966) reasoned that those who believed that the suffering was inevitable denigrated the victim so as to justify what they had seen and what they were helpless to prevent. Similarly in Milgram's obedience experiments (1977) as described in Chapter 6, many of the participants who had apparently delivered the escalating series of shocks to the "learner" blamed the victim for not giving the right answers to the word pairs or even for volunteering for the experiment.

Recall the discussion of the just world hypothesis in Chapter 2. To a greater or lesser extent, people consider the world to be a just place and believe that "you get out of it what you deserve." The good prosper and the wicked suffer. One of the interesting consequences of this belief is the tendency of people to "derogate the victim."

In other words, we often assume that a person who is being harmed deserves to suffer even though she is perfectly innocent. Indeed, the situations in which people are confronted with an innocent victim threaten their beliefs that the world is just and that people get what they deserve. In experiments involving a perceptual task in which participants identify words, those previously exposed to someone becoming an innocent victim performed poorly when the words connoted justice and tended to derogate the victim (Hafer, 2000). Thus it seems that responses to a threat to just-world beliefs, when we see someone who clearly is an innocent victim, may be considered as ego-defensive, responding in a way to protect those beliefs (recall chapter 4). Interestingly, some evidence indicates that some people may see the world as just or fair to others but not to themselves. For instance, those who believe that the world is just for others tend to stigmatize those who are poor, and advocate more severe sentences for criminals. But these attitudes are not related to how we believe that the world is just towards ourselves (Begue & Bastounis, 2003).

It also is the case that people who strongly believe in a just world tend to react less strongly to situations that do not seem to be fair even to themselves. For instance in two experiments, Hafer and Olson (1989) found that believers in a just world who had received feedback that they had failed in a task did not feel as aggrieved as those who did not believe in a just world. This occurred even if they had been denied a choice of tasks that had been granted to others or denied the opportunity to practise beforehand. Women with strong just-world beliefs also express less dissatisfaction with the job situations of women, and are less likely to act on employment problems either by advocating better opportunities for women as a group or by self-improvement (Hafer & Olson, 1993). A set of studies indicate that, indeed, believers in a just world do not feel the same sense of injustice, anger and resentment as do those with weaker just-world beliefs, both in a laboratory experiment and among working women faced with various types of job dissatisfactions (Hafer & Olson, 1996).

In a comparative study of both children and university students, scores on a scale of just-world beliefs were higher among white South Africans (during the era of apartheid) than among white British participants (Furnham, 1985). In the extreme case, just-world beliefs allow us to be indifferent to evil because we see no evil (Waller, 2002). Some have even argued that the six million Jewish victims of the Holocaust were responsible for their own fate, ignoring both the overwhelming and brutal force directed against them and the heroic revolts that did occur in ghettos and concentration camps (Davidowicz, 1975). One recent discussion considers the question of whether social psychological explanations of evil behaviour, which stress the situation, exonerate the perpetrators of these atrocities (Miller, Buddie & Kretschmar, 2002). These authors argue that such explanations do not replace moral culpability and indeed show that these actions are within the capability of normal human beings (see earlier discussion in Chapter 2 on evil and the demonization of perpetrators).

When do people experience a sense of unfairness or injustice? Three factors have been identified (Mikula, 1994): (1) violation of entitlement, the extent to which people perceived that they have been deprived of what they had come to expect; (2) causation, the extent to which people attribute this violation of entitlement to some external agent (another person, the government, the court) rather than themselves; and (3) lack of justification for the decision or action. Thus for example in court decisions, people on the losing side would feel a sense of injustice if they realistically expected to win the case, attributed the decision to the unfairness of the judge or jury, felt that the judge or jury deliberately wanted to deprive them of what was deserved and felt that there was no justification for the decision.

Feelings of injustice may not be predictable from the objective outcome. A professional athlete receiv-

ing what to most people would be an impressive seven-figure salary may feel that it is unjust in comparison with that received by certain other players. Satisfaction or a sense of injustice often pertains to relative deprivation, a perceived discrepancy between one's own outcome and some point of reference (Olson & Hafer, 1996). As discussed in Chapter 13, people often report more deprivation for their group than for themselves (Taylor, Wright, Mogghaddam & Lalonde, 1990). People may be reluctant to point to a perpetrator or to justify having done nothing about it (Taylor, Wright & Porter, 1994). Or they may exaggerate the injustice to which their group has been subjected to validate claims for more benefits (Olson & Hafer, 2001; see also Chapter 3).

While people are generally motivated in part by a concern for justice, we must also consider the individual's **scope of justice**, the boundaries within which justice is perceived to be relevant (Hafer & Olson, 2003). There will be situations in which our judgments are not influenced by motivations to be just or fair even where harm is done. For instance, most people are willing to kill certain species of animals (e.g., mosquitoes) and we differ on whether doing harm to animals, which provide food or which serve in laboratory experiments, is within our scope of justice. Genocide or slavery may be seen as resulting from the exclusion of entire groups of people from the scope of justice (Waller, 2002). This may result from the belief that certain targets deserve certain consequences, for instance, in considering categories of people as less than fully human. During the Second World War, the Nazis justified the extermination of millions of Jews by referring to the supposedly harmful effects of Jews on society. An alternative explanation may be in terms of "different rules." For instance, we may justify the extermination of millions of insects for the protection of agricultural fields from infestation, implying that our food supply is more important than doing justice to the insects. Indeed we may also feel that we endorse different rules of justice for people who are close to us than for people whom we do not know.

Individual attitudes may also play a role in perceptions involving justice. Consider for example, the issue of affirmative action policies, ones that many support and many others oppose with equal vehemence. In addition to the rhetoric of injustice, those who oppose affirmative action programs tend to endorse "neosexist" attitudes, those that are expressed with somewhat more subtlety (e.g., "Women's requests in terms of equality are simply exaggerated"; "It is difficult to work for a female boss") (Tougas, Crosby, Joly & Pelchat, 1995). That is, justice and injustice may be to a great extent in the eye of the beholder.

Adversarial and inquisitional models

Subsequent research has focused on two contrasting models, the adversary procedure and the inquisitional procedure. In the **adversary procedure** derived from the British model and used in Canadian and U.S. courts, the case is developed, argued and defended by the parties to the dispute or their lawyers. In the **inquisitional procedure** as used in France, a judge is assigned a role in supervising the collection of evidence and occasionally questioning witnesses rather than simply listening to the two sides in the dispute. Not surprisingly, Americans prefer the adversary system familiar to them and judge it to be fairer than the inquisitional system (Houlden, Latour, Walker & Thibaut,

1978; Lind, Kurtz, Musante, Walker & Thibaut, 1980). Interestingly however, in France, people also prefer the adversary procedure (Lind, Erickson, Friedland & Dickenberger, 1978). The crucial psychological differences between the adversarial and inquisitional trial procedures involves who controls the process of the trial (Houlden, Latour, Walker & Tibaut, 1978). In the adversarial system, the two parties control the gathering of evidence, the calling of witnesses and the presentation of arguments, while in the inquisitional system the judge, at least in part, directs the gathering and presentation of evidence. Maximizing the sense of process control by the participants will tend to increase the perception of fairness; participants feel more confident that all important aspects of their case will be presented. In the inquisitional system, people may feel that something important was omitted or misinterpreted (Thibaut & Walker, 1975). It may also be argued that the intrinsically dramatic and competitive environment of the courtroom as portrayed in so many

---

A CASE IN POINT

Euthanasia: A Case of Ambivalence

Tracey Latimer, who was 12 years old, had a severe form of cerebral palsy and could not walk, talk or feed herself. She had undergone several painful operations to keep her alive, and faced more. So in 1993 her father, Robert Latimer, a Saskatchewan farmer, carried her to the cab of his pickup truck and ran a hose from the exhaust to the window. He sat on a tire nearby until Tracey died of carbon monoxide poisoning. Once she was dead, he carried the body back to the house and then reported that she had died in bed. However, when it was determined that Tracey had died of carbon monoxide poisoning, he confessed to having killed his daughter. At his trial, his defence was that the killing was a "loving act" done to relieve Tracey's unending suffering, which medicine was apparently unable to do. He was convicted of second-degree murder, and while the conviction was overturned on appeal because of improper questioning of jurors (a matter of procedural justice), Latimer was convicted again in the retrial.

This case brought into sharp focus the issue of euthanasia, an action by an individual to encourage the death of another who is suffering from a terminal condition (Brigham & Pfeifer, 1996). We have already encountered this issue in terms of the values surrounding the case of Sue Rodriguez (see Chapter 4). It is an issue with a long history. The ancient Greeks and Romans freely allowed for euthanasia to relieve suffering. However, both Judaism and Christianity discouraged the practice on the grounds that the right to decide on life and death belongs to God, not to human beings. While these early positions were diametrically opposed, current secular attitudes have become more complex and confusing. While death in earlier times was usually relatively quick from acute diseases, today's medical technology makes it possible to keep people alive much longer, extending life but also often extending pain and suffering to the patient and to the family.

We must look closely at how euthanasia may be done. In some cases, the act may be active such as in the Latimer case or when a physician prescribes a deliberate overdose of medication. Indeed, at about the same time, Dr. Nancy Morrison of Halifax was charged with murder in the drug overdose of a terminal cancer patient. While the legal charges were subsequently dropped, Dr. Morrison was reprimanded by the provincial College of Physicians and Surgeons. In other cases, the euthanasia is passive such as in orders not to resuscitate when the patient stops breathing or to discontinue treatment. Public attitudes are much more accepting of the passive euthanasia (Ho & Penney, 1992). We must also distinguish between cases in which the individual expresses a wish to die and others in which the individual may be comatose and unable to respond.

Euthanasia may be performed by the physician or by someone else. Recall that the case of Sue Rodriguez centred on her demand for physician-assisted suicide (see Chapter 4). Indeed, a physician in the U.S. gained considerable notoriety for setting up an apparatus to enable seriously ill people to kill themselves. The public is more accepting of euthanasia when performed by a physician than when performed by others (Albright & Hazler, 1995). Attitudes towards euthanasia and acceptance of a "right to die" are also influenced by factors such as whether effective relief of pain and suffering is made available, concern that such an irrevocable decision may be made when an individual is seriously depressed, and the possibility that an individual may accept euthanasia to relieve the stress on others (Soifer, 1996).

In an interesting study, Pfeifer, Brigham and Robinson (1996) constructed a set of alternative scenarios surrounding a homicide case involving a 52-year-old man who ended the life of his terminally ill 49-year-old wife. Three conditions were varied in the videotaped presentations: (1) whether death was caused by unplugging a respirator or by gunshots to the head; (2) whether the accused showed a state of sadness or lack of emotional arousal; and (3) whether the instructions to the jury allowed for "jury nullification," a principle of law in which juries are free to disregard both the judge's instructions and the law itself if they see fit. (Note that while the jury has the right to decide as it sees fit, judges rarely inform the jury of this right.) Participants were then less likely to indicate a decision to convict when they were aware of the possibility of jury nullification. Jurors were also more accepting of euthanasia when the respirator was disconnected, representing a more passive form than gunshots to the head. Interestingly, the wishes of the patient will not always carry the day in public attitudes. In another study, only about half the participants recommended euthanasia even when the individual was in intractable pain and had requested death, although they would not resuscitate such a patient whose heart and lungs had failed (Darley, Loeb & Hunter, 1996).

Clearly, acts of commission such as assisted suicide are generally seen as unacceptable, while acts of omission, terminating treatment or intravenous feeding are more acceptable (Wellman & Sugarman, 1996). In the first case, the breach of justice is in violating someone's rights, while in the second case, it is in failing to carry out the duties that one as a physician has taken on. As medical technology develops and the population ages, the issue of euthanasia becomes increasingly salient.

novels, plays, films and TV shows is more familiar and attractive to many people.

Individual values affect preferences for various procedures. For example, mediation (recall Chapter 10) is preferred by Japanese (Peterson & Skimada, 1978) and Chinese Americans (Doo, 1973) and Mexicans (Nader, 1969). Chinese and Mexicans value collectivism and also prefer inquisitorial or mediating procedures (Leung & Lind, 1986). Note that collectivism is associated with an emphasis on interpersonal harmony and group solidarity while individualism stresses personal goals and interests and values self-sufficiency.

Bennett and Feldman (1980) suggest that in the adversary system, the side that tells the most coherent story, regardless of its actual truth, tends to win the case. In an experiment, they found that research participants tended to believe people who told coherent but false stories about themselves (that is, where everything "fit") more than they did people who told truthful but less coherent stories. If two competing interpretations of evidence are presented, even where both interpretations are favourable to the same side, that side will likely lose the verdict (Holstein, 1985). This outcome suggests the power of "apparent coherence": two different stories in favour of innocence cannot both be right; and therefore, one must be wrong. Thus, the emphasis in the adversarial system of finding apparent contradictions in the evidence may bias jury decisions sometimes at the cost of truth.

A Final Note

Social psychology has found fertile ground in the study of legal processes. Aside from increasing our understanding of judicial processes, the research has contributed a great deal to an understanding of basic psychological processes such as how we perceive and remember persons and events, how groups make important decisions, and the influence of authority. We have been able to touch upon only some of the research and a few of the problems under study. Research is also under way concerning the child as a witness, police investigation, biases in civil law (virtually all of the research has concerned criminal law) as well as the influence of law and the justice system outside the courtroom. The research, despite obvious limitations and difficulties, can inform the system.

Indeed, Monohan and Walker (1988) suggest three areas in which such research may have a bearing on the law. Research may contribute to the making or changing of laws; for example in the U.S. in 1954, psychologists presented research-based testimony indicating that black children in segregated schools suffered from low self-esteem and poor motivation for learning, leading to the conclusion of the U.S. Supreme Court that such schools were inherently unequal and that laws that mandated racially segregated schools were unconstitutional. A second use of psychological and other social science research is in assisting the courts to decide on questions of fact in a case. For example if obscenity laws refer to violations of community standards, then research evidence can assist the courts in deciding whether a particular movie actually violates those standards. The third area of concern is where research provides a social framework to evaluate evidence and determine factual issues; for example, research on eyewitness testimony has been used to evaluate the reliability of a particular witness.

Acceptance of such research is far from universal within the domain of the law; there is still some skepticism and misunderstanding about the scientific method, sampling and simulation research. As research advances and methods become more sophisticated, we can expect the effects on the legal process to expand accordingly.

Summary

1. Defendants who are attractive or baby-faced tend to be treated better by judges and juries. Jurors tend to be more lenient towards defendants who belong to their own racial group and whose attitudes are similar to their own.

2. The reliability of eyewitnesses is questionable in a number of circumstances. Important factors include police lineup procedures, stress, time elapsed between incident and recall, the nature of the protagonist—but not the confidence of the eyewitness.

3. Testimony can be influenced and biased by the phrasing of questions.

4. Witness credibility is affected by the capacity of the witness to recall trivial detail, the credibility of the attorney and whether the witness identifies or does not identify the defendant.

5. Findings from simulated jury studies indicate bias in the selection of jurors and biases among jurors particularly related to authoritarianism.

6. Juries are sometimes not influenced by the instructions of the judges.

7. Deception may occur by commission (telling a lie) or omission (concealing or omitting something). Individuals vary in their capacity to use verbal and non-verbal cues to detect deception.

8. Attributions of responsibility are influenced by the severity of consequences of the act.

9. Inconsistencies in sentencing are related to the characteristics of the defendant and the crime, prior record, the values and legal philosophy of the judge and social climate regarding crime.

10. The perception of justice concerns both what is fair (distributive justice) and how such decisions are arrived at (procedural justice).

11. How we make judgments about people and situations will depend on factors such as whether we believe in a "just world" and whether the target

or situation fall within our scope of where justice is relevant.

12. Distributive justice follows the rules of equity (a fair ratio of inputs to outputs in comparison with other people), equality (a uniform distribution of resources) and need (distribution of resources according to need).

13. Procedural justice may be arrived at through the adversary system in which both sides present evidence and argue their side of the case before a judge and perhaps a jury, and the inquisitional system in which a decision-maker such as a judge supervises the collection and presentation of arguments and evidence for both sides of the case.

Further Reading

ANDERSON, P.R. & WINFREE, L.T. (Eds.). (1987). *Expert witnesses*. New York: New York University Press. Chapters deal with the practical, ethical and scholarly issues involved in the use of social scientists as experts in trials.

EKMAN, P. (1985). *Telling lies: Clues to deceit in the marketplace, politics and marriage*. New York: Norton. A fascinating nontechnical discussion of the practice and uses of deception in society. Based on solid research; includes examination of historical and ethical issues. See also Ekman, P. (2003). *Emotions revealed: Recognizing faces and feelings to improve communication and emotional life*. New York: Times Books/Henry Holt.

HASTIE, R., PENROD, S.D. & PENNINGTON, N. (1983). *Inside the jury*. Cambridge: Harvard University Press. Report on a comprehensive program of research on juries including an examination of the unanimity rule.

OGLOFF, J. & SCHULLER, R. (Eds.) (2001). *Introduction to psychology and law: Canadian perspectives*. Toronto: University of Toronto Press. An excellent textbook expanding on material of this chapter and well beyond and with a Canadian focus.

PFEIFER, J.E. (1997). Social psychology in the courtroom. In S.W. Sadava & D.R. McCreary (Eds.), *Applied social psychology* (pp. 157–184). Upper Saddle River, NJ: Prentice-Hall. Concise and up-to-date review of research and thinking on juries, evidence and judicial instructions.

ROSS, M. & MILLER, D.T. (Eds.). (2002). *The justice motive in everyday life*. New York: Cambridge University Press. Why are people generally committed to acting in a fair way towards others and seeing that others are treated fairly? This book includes a series of thoughtful chapters by major figures in this area of inquiry.

SANDERS, J. & HAMILTON, V.L. (Eds). (2001). *Handbook of justice research in law*. Dordrecht, Netherlands: Kluwer Academic Publishers. A set of professional-level papers on justice research in applied areas.

YARMEY, A.D. (1990). *Understanding police and police work. Psychosocial issues*. Irvington, NY: Columbia University Press. An excellent review of issues such as personality characteristics of police officers, leadership and stress in police roles, the decision-making process, interrogation and eyewitness testimony, aggression and criminal victimization and stereotypes.

Weblinks

Psychology and the law

www.users.cts.com/king/h/hflowe/ Links about eyewitness testimony, jury deliberations, theories on crime and more.

Access to Justice

www.acjnet.org Very useful links to legislation, organizations, databases and discussions.

Chapter 16

Health and Illness

It is much more important to know what sort of patient has the disease than what sort of disease the patient has.

Sir William Osler

I enjoy convalescence. It's the part that makes illness worthwhile.

George Bernard Shaw

Chapter Outline

A IDS. SARS. Mad cow disease. West Nile. Lyme disease. In the first years of the new century, our attention was focused on a series of infectious diseases known by their nicknames or acronyms. The diseases may be novel but the outbreaks are not. Human history is marked by periodic outbreaks of infectious diseases, and the behavioural reactions to them are remarkably consistent.

For instance in 1885, a patient was admitted to Montreal's Hôtel-Dieu hospital with smallpox. At first, the disease seemed a mild threat, usually consisting of mild fever, chills, a cough and red spots. Many of those afflicted survived although they ended up visibly scarred. However when the highly contagious disease spread rapidly through the hospital, the medical staff in panic discharged 80 percent of their patients—a monumental mistake. The disease now began to spread throughout the community in an epidemic that raged into the next year. Out of a population of 167 000 in Montreal at that time, almost 3000, the majority of them children lost their lives to the disease (Bliss, 1991). Notice the contrast with the SARS outbreak in Toronto in 2003; again, the disease was concentrated in hospitals, but this time careful identification of cases and social contacts and widespread quarantine controlled the outbreak.

Public health policy in 1885 was at best, reactive. Everyone agreed on the need for cleanliness, but public health officials had neither the power nor the resources to enforce standards. While an effective vaccine existed, smallpox had become relatively rare, people were complacent and some argued that the vaccine was dangerous. Since it was derived from the lymph glands of cattle, many believed that it could cause "minotaurization," the development of cattle-like features in humans.

Thus for several years, Montrealers lived in fear of the disease. French–English relations were strained. Some anglophones blamed the epidemic on the high birth rate

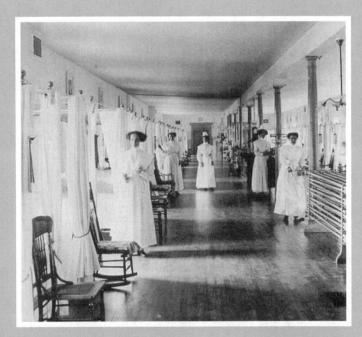

among francophones and falsely accused Roman Catholic priests of refusing to cooperate with vaccination programs. A columnist in a French-language newspaper claimed that the English were fomenting a smallpox panic so that they could boycott and starve the French. A compulsory vaccination law was passed which led to street riots (see Chapter 10, A Case in Point—A Conflict over False Premises on page 273). To a limited extent, the parallels with the SARS outbreak are instructive. Some stereotyping of ethnic groups was evident. Because the diseases appeared to have begun in China, many people in Toronto avoided Chinese restaurants. Nurses and other health-care workers worked under unusual disruption and stress and were, in some regrettable cases, ostracized out of an exaggerated fear of contagion.

By the mid-20th century, the threat of smallpox had been virtually eliminated in Europe and North America. Indeed, although infectious diseases, including AIDS, SARS, West Nile and other new strains of viruses and bacteria pose threats to health, the major causes of death in industrialized nations are the chronic diseases (coronary and circulatory, respiratory, cancers) and accidents. Recall our discussion in Chapter 2 of the availability heuristic. In making decisions and judgments, we tend to use what is on our minds at that time. Because of the massive media attention to these infectious illnesses, we feel more concern, even fear, about them than we do about the conditions that will kill most of us: heart disease, cerebrovascular disease, cancer and accidents.

Health care is a priority for Canadians and its future has been a major political issue in recent elections. However, health policies that focus almost exclusively on the treatment of illness fail to address some major problems of public health. Federal health policy has identified three important goals or "national challenges" which have guided policy for almost two decades (Health and Welfare Canada, 1989):

- to reduce the inequities in income and opportunity that adversely affect health;

- to increase the efforts to prevent injuries, diseases and chronic disabilities by means such as immunizing school children against a wider range of diseases; reducing drunk driving, smoking, poor dietary choices; and promoting prenatal and neonatal care;

- to enhance people's capacity to cope with chronic conditions, disabilities and mental health problems such as depression, respiratory ailments, hypertension and arthritis as well as to assist seniors who are partially incapacitated to live as freely and independently as possible.

Accomplishing these goals would involve community participation and effective coordination of policies in many areas. In the case of the Montreal smallpox epidemic, the tragedy was exacerbated by an absence of public health policy and by public mistrust of the available vaccine. Today, public health measures are recognized as both useful and cost effective, having a substantial impact on killer diseases and accidents. This of course becomes evident when problems arise in the sanitary practices of restaurants and the safety of our food and our water (recall the tragedy of infected water in Walkerton, Ontario, in 2000).

Similarly, public health can contribute to the control of many life-threatening illnesses (heart and circulatory diseases, cancer, respiratory diseases). All of them are caused in part by voluntary behaviour such as smoking, excessive drinking, overeating, dietary choices, leading a sedentary lifestyle and engaging in unprotected sex, as well as the stress and environmental pollution that marks our way of life. An understanding of why people choose to act in ways that enhance or undermine their health, such as how their values influence their health, can lead to more effective public health measures (Kristiansen, 1986). Thus, our efforts to reduce illness and mortality must focus on individual behaviour as well as societal factors.

Social psychologists have conducted research in two areas of inquiry: prevention and treatment. The first section of this chapter focuses on what determines whether and how people will take care of their own health and what psychosocial factors make them vulnerable to illness. In the second, the focus shifts to the health care system, what it means to be sick and how patients relate to their physicians.

Health Risks: Taking Care of Yourself

Taking care of yourself: Is it a pattern?

Consider all of the behaviours that may affect our health: our dietary choices, smoking, excessive drinking and other substance use, exercise, how we deal with stress, using seatbelts and other driving habits, using sunscreen and insect repellant, avoiding violence and abuse, our sexual practices, getting adequate and restorative sleep, brushing and flossing our teeth, taking medication as prescribed and following other instructions from our physicians. Are we consistent across these behaviours in the sense of generally taking care of ourselves? Jessor and colleagues (Jessor & Jessor, 1977; Jessor, 1993) argue that, among adolescents, the use of alcohol and other drugs is part of a more general pattern of behaviour that includes the use of marijuana and other drugs, deviant or delinquent acts such as lying and stealing and precocious sexual involvement along with less participation in school and church activities. The model has been supported by the results of a longitudinal study of high school and university students who have been followed into their fourth decade of life (Donovan, Jessor & Jessor, 1983), by the results of several other major longitudinal studies that used a national U.S. sample (Jessor, Donovan & Widmer, 1980) and samples of Canadian high school and university students (Schlegel, Manske & D'Avernas, 1985; DiTecco & Schlegel, 1982; Sadava & Forsyth, 1977a, 1977b).

However, the assumption of a pattern or "syndrome" of problem or health-risk behaviours has received only mixed support (Willoughby et al., 2003). One interesting finding is that people are generally not consistent in taking care of themselves. That is, while some people may exercise regularly, they will not necessarily eat well, drive carefully or take medications as prescribed and they may well smoke (Sadava, DeCourville & McCreary, 1996; Donovan, Jessor & Costa, 1993; Norman, 1985). Sexual activity; smoking, using alcohol and illicit substances; and exercise appear to be relatively independent of each other at least among adolescents (Kulbok & Cox, 2002).

Social Status, Money and Health

According to the Romanow report on health care (2002), living in poverty is identified as a major risk to health. Economically disadvantaged groups have relatively lower life expectancies, poorer health and are more likely to become disabled (Townsend & Davidson, 1982). It is important to note that the effects of poverty on health are observed both in societies with publicly funded health care such as Canada and Europe and those with private insurance and personal funds such as the United States. Clearly nutrition, sanitation, pollution, crime, characteristics of the neighbourhood and access to other resources all play a role.

However, we cannot explain these socioeconomic effects on health as only a result of living in poverty. As we move up the ladder of socioeconomic status, health improves, life expectancy increases and the incidence of many chronic and infectious diseases decreases. That is, those at the highest socioeconomic levels tend to be healthier than those who are somewhat less advantaged, who in turn are healthier than those still less advantaged. This is known as the socioeconomic gradient effect on health. While living in poverty has obvious risks to health as described above, poverty cannot fully explain why the socioeconomic "gradient" affects health between groups at different economic levels, none of whom are living in poverty.

Research is trying to unravel this mystery (Adler et al., 1994; Marmot, Ryff, Bumpass, Shipley & Marks, 1997). One hypothesis is selection: those who are healthier may have greater economic success in life as a result. Another is the nature of the work: while job stresses can be found in occupations at all levels of the ladder, the work becomes more rewarding and fulfilling at the higher levels. Young adults who see themselves as being underemployed tend to report less favourable health even after accounting for the effects on health of income and lifestyle (Sadava, O'Connor & McCreary, 2000). It may also be the case that individuals at the higher socioeconomic levels take better care of themselves in terms of diet, exercise, smoking and substance abuse.

Gottfredson (2003) suggests that the socioeconomic gradient effect may be explained by differences in general intelligence. Higher intelligence would be expected to contribute to economic success, and represents the ability to function well in a society that offers more choices and greater complexity than ever. She suggests that more intelligent people are more capable of understanding how to be healthy, and make more informed choices concerning their health. This argument must be examined with caution. Clearly, there is more that determines our economic status in life than just intelligence, such as ethnic and gender discrimination, parental values and sheer luck. The argument is based on data from the United States, and may not apply equally in other societies.

In part, this is because people are often motivated by reasons other than their own health. For example, dieting and exercising may have more to do with being attractive than with being healthy, while substance use or non-use may reflect cultural or religious values. We may avoid violence for moral reasons, we may or may not smoke because of social pressures and we may diet and exercise to look attractive. While good health is a consequence common to them, it is not always the reason behind them.

Another complicating factor is that even where the behaviour may be a statistical risk to health, that risk may be quite variable from one person to another. For instance, driving 20 km over the speed limit on the highway represents an increased risk of accidents but will be more of a risk to inexperienced or impulsive drivers. The risk of heavy drinking cannot be predicted accurately if we know only how much alcohol is consumed (Sadava, 1985; DeCourville & Sadava, 1997). Consider, for example, that women who drink

Are people driven to exercise by a desire to improve their overall health, or by concerns about their personal appearance and attractiveness?

heavily are more vulnerable to adverse consequences than are heavily drinking men (Wilsnack, 1982) perhaps for physiological differences and perhaps because of different gender role expectations. Some heavy drinkers are more likely than others to suffer adverse consequences from their drinking if they also are highly lonely or under stressful life circumstances (Sadava & Thompson, 1986; McCreary & Sadava, 1999).

Modelling influences

It has been shown (see Chapter 6) that social influence may often be unintentional and that our actions are often modelled after others (Bandura, 1977). Recall that modelling may influence behaviour in three ways: (1) in the acquisition or learning of a new behaviour; (2) in the inhibition or disinhibition of a behaviour in certain situations; and (3) in direct, immediate imitation at a given time (response facilitation). Peer groups influence adolescents to smoke not necessarily through direct pressure but in these subtler but powerful ways. It has also been demonstrated through longitudinal research that when adolescents have parents who drink heavily, they tend to seek out friends who drink heavily and then begin to drink in the same manner (Huba, Dent & Bentler, 1980).

In a laboratory experiment (Caudill & Marlatt, 1975), subjects were asked to taste several wines and to rate each on flavour, aroma and other characteris-

tics. The task involved allowing subjects to take any amount—from one small sip to an entire beaker if they wished—of each wine. A confederate drank either a lot or a little of each wine. Subjects who participated with a heavy-drinking model consumed significantly more than those with a light drinker or those without a partner.

The experiment was repeated in a bar (Reid, 1978). A male and a female observer sat at a corner table acting as an affectionate couple to avert intrusion by waiters, waitresses or other patrons. Other confederates of the experimenter who were trained to behave in a friendly or cold way to single patrons at the bar consumed either one or five drinks during a one-hour period. (Models were all selected for having a relatively high tolerance for alcohol). As you will recall (Chapter 5), models may inhibit or disinhibit behaviour depending on factors such as whether the person likes or dislikes the model. In this study, a warm model strongly influenced subjects' drinking but a cold, unlikable model did not.

Modelling influences on drinking behaviour have also been shown in studies such as one that observed drinkers in four Vancouver taverns (Cutler & Storm, 1975). Do people who are drinking together actually influence each other's drinking or do they simply spend a longer period of time together? It was reported that patrons tended to drink at a relatively constant rate of almost three drinks per hour regardless of the size of the group or the time spent in the tavern. However, larger groups tended to stay longer in the tavern (ordering rounds); thus individuals actually consumed more. This study has been replicated with larger samples in the U.S. (Hennessy & Saltz, 1993). Since this rate of drinking is above the rate at which alcohol can be metabolized, the blood alcohol levels of people in larger drinking groups eventually reached higher levels and intoxication was therefore more frequent, particularly when the group consisted largely of young males (Sykes, Rowley & Schaeffer, 1993).

Modelling effects have also been shown on our eating behaviour. For instance, binge eating is more common in some university residences than in others (Crandall, 1988). By the end of the academic year, a person's binge eating could be predicted from the binge eating of her friends, and as friendships became more cohesive over time, a young woman's eating behaviour became increasingly similar to that of her closest friends. Thus while binge eating may in part reflect psychological disturbances, it can also be seen as an acquired pattern of behaviour, learned and altered through social modelling.

Thus far, we have seen that social psychological variables can influence the extent to which people act to protect or endanger their health. Apart from choices in behaviour, individuals also differ greatly in how vulnerable they are to certain illnesses. Let us examine some of the evidence.

While the concept of life-change stress has been widely applied in research, it has also been criticized. The weightings for each event were derived from a particular sample at a particular time and place and so the impact of the same event may differ considerably for other times, places and types of people. Some obviously stressful events such as the death of a child are not even mentioned. In addition, the weightings do not account for the quality of the event. For example, they would predict that a person who divorces (weight of 73) and subsequently remarries (weight of 50) would experience more stress than the person who divorces but remains single, while common sense would suggest otherwise. Indeed, another study in which subjects completed daily diaries over a period of time showed that conflicts in intimate relationships are, by far, the most important sources of stress in daily life (Bolger, DeLongis, Kessler & Schilling, 1989).

Richard Lazarus and colleagues (Kanner, Coyne, Schaefer & Lazarus, 1981) argue that most of us can cope with most crises in time, but the daily hassles of life take their toll. The annoyances of commuting to work on a crowded bus or freeway; the delivery that does not show up; a missing and desperately needed book in the library; the repair job that must be done

Modelling influences on drinking behaviour have been shown in a number of studies, but do people who are drinking together actually influence each other's drinking, or do they simply drink more because they spend more time at the bar when they are together?

Measuring Stress: Major Trauma and Minor Hassles

From the pioneering research by Hans Selye (1956) at the Université de Montréal, it has become commonly accepted that our state of health and sense of well-being can be adversely affected by stress (Cohen & Williamson, 1988; Watson & Pennebaker, 1989). For instance, stress tends to elicit the release of stress hormones (e.g., adrenaline) that have negative effects on the immune system and thus leave the person more vulnerable to illness (Johansson, Collins & Collins, 1983; McClelland, Alexander & Marks, 1982). Indeed, one study measured stress and negative affect, exposed volunteers to the common cold virus, quarantined them and then monitored them for illness. Those who had recently experienced stressful events in their lives were more likely to become ill particularly if they had reacted badly to the stress (Cohen, Tyrrell & Smith, 1993). Thus, it is important to define and measure stress accurately.

Stress has been defined in various ways. One is a diagnostic category, post-traumatic stress disorder (PTSD), defined as a reaction to unusual events such as war, a major accident or abuse. It includes repeated disturbing memories or images of the event or events, avoidance or psychological "numbing" of emotions and hyperarousal or sensitivity of situations that may evoke painful memories. Peacekeeping soldiers from Canada and other nations under the United Nations have often experienced traumatic events in places such as the Middle East, Bosnia and Rwanda and these reactions may have an impact on both physical health and mental health (e.g., depression) (Asmundson, Stein & McCreary, 2002).

Holmes and Rahe (1967) propose that stress is the outcome of the major changes in our personal lives. They developed a "social readjustment scale" that measures the impact of such changes. The following are examples (the numbers refer to "life change units" or the relative amount of disruption or readjustment caused):

Death of spouse	100
Divorce	73
Jail term	63
Personal illness/injury	53
Marriage	50
Fired at work	47
Retirement	45
Pregnancy	40
Sexual difficulties	39
Mortgage or major loan	31
Trouble with boss	23
Change in social activities	18
Vacation	13

over; the car that won't start on a January morning; the mouthy teenager or whining child; an upcoming examination in a course where the requirements are not clear; minor arguments with friends—these are examples of daily hassles that infect our lives. Kanner et al. (1981) found the following to be the top 10 daily hassles, at least in their samples in the U.S.: concern about weight; health of family member; increased price of common goods; home maintenance; too many things to do; misplacing or losing things; yard or outside home maintenance; property investment and taxes; crime; physical appearance, including weight.

These and several other studies suggest significant linkages of stress with physical and emotional health (Stone & Neale, 1982; DeLongis, Coyne, Kakof, Folkman & Lazarus, 1982). It is also suggested that positive everyday experiences ("daily uplifts") may contribute to our health. Commonly endorsed examples of daily uplifts include relating well to spouse or lover and to friends (74.4 percent), completing a task, getting enough sleep and eating out—although surely the last example would be dependent on the restaurant. Exercise has also been shown to protect people from the negative impact of stressful events on their health (Brown & Siegel, 1988).

Terror and Its Management

Probably unique among species, we are aware that we are mortal, that our lives will all inevitably end. Of course in day-to-day existence, we function largely by denial, by pushing our own demise into the indefinite future and out of consciousness (Pyszczynski, Greenberg & Solomon, 1999). A group of researchers theorizes that we have developed ways of protecting ourselves from this fear of our own death (Greenberg, Solomon & Pyszczynski, 1997). In fact, they see this as fundamental to other human motivations.

Terror management theory (TMT) suggests ways in which we cope with the "terror" of our own eventual nonexistence. One is by a worldview that is derived from our own culture. This consists of a set of social norms and values which provide us with some sense of meaning and permanence, something of us that will transcend our own mortality. A sense of self-esteem, living up to the values and norms of our culture (recall Chapter 3), also enables us to "manage terror." Thus, we need both a sense of belonging to something larger than ourselves, our culture, and a sense of self-worth to function in the face of our own mortality. Of course, we may also gain a sense of transcendence through our children, religious involvement and our own work and accomplishments, but these also occur in the context of the society and culture to which we belong.

From this basic theory, several interesting hypotheses have been generated. According to the *mortality salience hypothesis*, conditions which cue an awareness of death will cause people to react more favourably to people and ideas that validate their own cultural world view and negatively to people and ideas that challenge their culture. For instance, participants in various studies were asked open-ended questions about their own death, shown gory footage of an accident or simply participated in the experiment in proximity to a funeral home (Greenberg et al., 1994; Nelson et al., 1997). Then compared to control groups in which these cues were absent, attitudes of cued participants

revealed greater faith in their own country, culture and its values and greater rejection of other cultural worldviews. Consider that other studies aroused anxiety or other negative emotions such as by eliciting thoughts of intense physical pain or performing poorly on a supposed intelligence test, and the same results were not obtained. Thus, it is the salience of death imagery that seems to produce these effects on ethnocentrism.

The theory is controversial and not without challenges (Baron, 1997; Lerner, 1997; Muraven & Baumeister, 1997; Paulhus & Trapnell, 1997; Snyder, 1997). Some critics question the premise that managing the terror of our own deaths is a basic or fundamental motive. In fact, Vallacher (1997) points out that most people just do not experience much concern about death in their daily lives. Baron (1997) suggests that the ultimate "terror" for human beings is to be socially disconnected and unable to bridge the gap, and Snyder (1997) argues that terror management is part of our larger concern with a sense of control over our lives (Chapter 2). While the experiments are intriguing and consistent with terror management theory, they are open to other interpretations. And yet, this work merits attention as it highlights the neglected role that personal death plays in human behaviour and experience.

It is important for us not to confuse the "terror" which may underlie being conscious of our own mortality and the "terrorism" that afflicts the world today. Consider what this may mean in the context of September 11, which made terrorism a salient threat to Americans and to other countries in the West (see Levant, 2002). Clearly, the repeated media exposure to the death-related imagery as results of terrorist acts, particularly in graphic and horrifying detail, is stressful to the viewers (Silver et al., 2002; Pyszczynski, Solomon, & Greenberg, 2003). Specific cognitive consequences have been reported. For instance, Suedfeld and Leighton (2002) scored the speeches of prominent world leaders in the period

(continued)

immediately before and immediately after the September 11 attack. They found that integrative complexity (Chapter 2), the degree to which the speaker perceives several dimensions and points of view relevant to the topic (differentiation) and the degree to which such characteristics are seen as related to each other (integration) decreased during that period. Research has shown that in stressful circumstances, integrative complexity tends to diminish as we look to simple solutions.

Clearly such incidents within our own culture will increase mortality salience and cause people to react with anxiety, such as by curtailing travel plans. Similarly, other images of death such as in epidemics (SARS, AIDS, Mad Cow disease, West Nile, etc.) and graphic images of war will increase mortality salience. Therefore if terror management theory is correct, then media cues of terrorism and violence may also fuel allegiance to one's own society and culture perhaps increasing nationalism, ethnocentrism and intolerance of dissent. Recall that values reflecting this cultural rigidity have indeed increased in recent years in the United States but not in Canada (Adams, 2003).

Vulnerability to illness

Research has shown that people with certain personal characteristics and in certain stressful social circumstances are more vulnerable to a range of diseases and disabilities and are less likely to recover successfully. Let us look briefly at research pertaining to three important sources of vulnerability: social support, perceived control and the notion of an illness-prone personality.

Lack of social support

In 1951, Janis conducted a study of how soldiers coped with the conditions of combat. He found that those who belonged to a cohesive combat unit were able and willing to endure such severe stress. Those who did not belong to such a close-knit group often experienced psychological breakdown. Subsequent research shows that people who lack supportive bonds with others are more likely to suffer illnesses and are less likely to recover quickly (Gottlieb, 1985; Cohen & Herbert, 1996). Some of these people have not been able to establish intimate relationships while others are separated or widowed (Bloom, Asher & White, 1978; Stroebe & Stroebe, 1983; Burman & Margolin, 1992). While **social support** may be found through involvement and participation with community groups and institutions, the experience of intimacy, feeling close to certain others, is particularly important to well-being (Wills, 1991).

Social support is also important to recovery from illness. For example, many clinical and survey studies show relationships between an absence of social supports and heart disease (Lynch, 1977). Cardiac patients who receive strong support suffer less from the effects of their heart attack and experience fewer symptoms of angina (Fontana, Kerns, Rosenberg & Colonese, 1989). Another study showed that after major surgery, married patients who received support from their spouses while they were in hospital subsequently took less medication and recovered more quickly than their less-supported fellow patients (Kulik & Mahler, 1989b). A longitudinal study that followed patients who had coronary bypass surgery found that esteem support, which involves feedback that the person is valued and respected by others, was most consistently related to feelings of well-being as well as a lessening of uncomfortable physical symptoms (King, Reis, Porter & Norsen, 1993).

Although most cancer patients report relatively high levels of support, some report that those closest to them don't understand or are unwilling to talk openly about the illness. Consequently, some join self-help groups of cancer patients through which they can seek support from others in a similar situation (Taylor, Falke, Shoptaw & Lichtman, 1986). One study found that, in comparison with a control group, patients with later-stage breast cancer who participated in support groups survived an average of 18 months longer (Spiegel, Bloom, Kraemer & Gottheil, 1989). This effect is equally true for health care workers. Nurses who report having a friend to confide in report fewer stress-related health problems (Walters, Lenton, French, Eyles, Mayr, & Nrebold, 1996).

Another longitudinal study followed groups of teenage mothers through their pregnancies and after the birth of their babies. Social support from their families, friends, neighbours and the fathers contributed to the mothers' adjustment, life satisfaction and effectiveness as parents. Social support was also correlated with the birth weight and the subsequent health and development of the child. These findings inspired programs in which experienced, older women acted as "resource mothers" (Unger & Wandersman, 1985). The presence of the father in the delivery room can be a source of social support for the mother particularly with the first child (Keinan & Hobfoll, 1989).

Why is social support related to health (Cohen, 1988)? According to one hypothesis, social support "buffers" or protects the person against stress. Indeed, people are clearly better able to avoid illness when under stress and to recover from any illness that might develop if they interact with others rather than remaining isolated (Roy, Steptoe & Kirschbaum, 1998; Scrimshaw, 2002). Similar findings are reported in coping with other sources of stress including peacekeeping and other military duty (Britt & Bliese, 2003; Langholtz, (Ed.), 1998; Lamercon & Kelloway, 1996) and other occupational stress (Bellman, Forster, Still & Cooper, 2003; Bradley & Cartwright, 2002). In another interesting demonstration, Cohen, Tyrell and Smith (1993) actually exposed volunteers to the cold virus. They found that while those exposed to the virus were more likely to develop cold symptoms, people who had recently experienced stressful life events were equally likely to develop symptoms even if they had not been exposed experimentally to the virus.

Another reason for the effect of social support on health is that a lack of social support itself may be a stressor. That is, the person who is alienated from others or who loses support through death or separation may be at greater risk of disease. Evidence indicates that some men show a detectable mobilization of components of the immune system during marital conflict (Miller, Dopp, Myers, Stevens & Fahey, 1999). Being absent from one's significant relationships may amount to more than an absence of support in that it may become a source of stress as well. For instance, Canadian peacekeeping soldiers experience stress because of their concerns with the welfare of their families (McCreary, Thompson & Pasto, 2003). Loneliness, a pervasive feeling of distress arising from the sense that one's relationships are inadequate (Chapter 8), has been identified as a health risk. Indeed, chronically lonely individuals tend to have poor quality of sleep and some indications of higher blood pressure (Cacioppo et al., 2002) as well as less effective immune system functioning (Dixon et al., 2001).

Social support may also contribute to health indirectly. For instance, being able to count on the support of others may enhance a person's self-esteem and thereby contribute to good health (see Chapter 3). Finally, an individual with support from others may be more likely to comply with treatment, quit smoking or otherwise take better care of themselves.

Note, however, that social support may not always be beneficial. Family and friends, with the best of intentions, may reinforce maladaptive behaviours by protecting individuals from the consequences of their drinking, overeating or sedentary ways. Also, overprotecting elderly people—denying them the normal privileges of adults to care for themselves and make their own decisions—can be profoundly debilitating to them (Langer & Rodin, 1976).

Nevertheless the research shows that in most cases, social support can protect the individual from stress and provide her with a sense of self-worth and stability in life (Cohen & McKay, 1984). In societies such as our own where people move frequently and divorce almost as frequently, a lack of social support is increasingly apparent. In these circumstances, community services such as rape crisis centres, family services, support groups, child-care, hostels or services for senior citizens are vital (Pilisuk & Minkler, 1985).

Perceived lack of control

As we saw earlier (Chapter 3) when people feel that they are not in control of their lives, there can be adverse consequences for health. This has been shown in much research. For instance as noted earlier, socioeconomic differences have a demonstrable impact on health, but we are not clear as to why this happens. One study found that lower income individuals who have a high sense of control show levels of health comparable to those of higher income groups. A lower status in society tends to be reflected in a lower sense of control and this may partly explain why they are at risk (Lachman & Weaver, 1998). People with an internal sense of control (Rotter, 1966) tend to know more about their illnesses, are more likely to take care of themselves (Strickland, 1978) and, if given appropriate information, tend to cope with illness somewhat better.

Although they have spent a lifetime making their own decisions, institutionalized elderly persons live in a situation where all decisions are made for them. In short, they are often treated as children and even spoken to in that way. In a classic field experiment previously mentioned in Chapter 1, Langer and Rodin (1976) investigated the consequences of such treatment in a residential nursing home for seniors. The

The Loss Effect:
Bereavement, Psychology and Immunology

Inevitably, we must all cope with the death of a family member, spouse or lover or close friend. Beyond the painful period of mourning and the permanent sense of loss, there is evidence that such a death can threaten the health of the survivors. Careful analyses of data from Britain, Japan, the U.S. and West Germany show that in the year following the death of a spouse, the survivor is more likely to die than are people of the same age group overall. After accounting for the possibility of suicide and of death from the same illness or accident, there is still a significantly higher mortality rate: the *loss effect* (Stroebe, Stroebe, Gergen & Gergen, 1982).

How can this be explained? Certainly, it is related to stress. Most people rate the loss of a spouse as one of the most stressful of all conceivable life changes (Holmes & Rahe, 1967). Of course, the sur-

viving spouse has lost the social and emotional support of intimacy. One study indicates that such a loss is followed by lowered self-esteem and greater emotional loneliness in the surviving partner; such loneliness is not entirely alleviated by the presence of supportive other people (van Baarsen, 2002).

In addition, he or she now must assume sole responsibility for matters that were formerly shared—finances, running the home, parenting, to name a few. Interestingly, males seem to be more adversely affected by the loss effect than are females (Kiecolt-Glaser & Newton, 2001). Perhaps women are more able to seek and obtain social support from family and friends. Recall as well (Chapter 8) that those female friendships tend to be more supportive particularly in an emotional sense than male friendships.

---

residents and staff were divided into two groups. Residents of one floor were told that they would be well cared for and that staff would assume all decisions and responsibilities, which is the usual situation in such institutions. The members of the other group were given messages, which stressed that they were responsible. For example, they, rather than the staff, would select and care for the plants in the rooms, select movies and decide on activities and the arrangement of furniture.

Three weeks later, those who had assumed more control over their daily lives were found to be feeling happier and healthier and were rated by nurses as being more active and having a more positive outlook. Eighteen months later, the differences were even more dramatic (Rodin & Langer, 1977). Nurses rated these residents as more active, sociable and vigorous and physicians reported that they were in better health. In addition, 30 percent of the control group had died during this period while only 15 percent of the personally responsible group had died. In another study, geriatric patients who participated actively in their treatment

program had better relationships with the nurses (who were trained in this type of program), had a greater sense of involvement in their care and adjusted more effectively to their situation (Stirling & Reid, 1992).

However, it should not be assumed that such is the case for all medical patients. Indeed, patients differ in the extent to which they want to be actively involved in their treatment and rehabilitation. One study of coronary bypass patients after surgery showed that those who desired a high level of involvement tended to experience more emotional problems (Mahler & Kulik, 1991). Other research shows the importance of matching the treatment to the individual (Cromwell, Butterfield, Brayfield & Curry, 1977). Participants in this study were classified as either "internals" or "externals" and then some of them were given lots of information and discussion of their treatment and recovery (high participation) while others were provided with good care but no discussion (low participation). Of the 229 patients in the study, 12 were re-admitted to hospital and five died within three months of discharge. All of these were in incongruent conditions: internals with low participation and externals with high participation. In general, all the externals showed more undesirable physical symptoms (such as higher sedimentation rates) while the internals were more cooperative in treatment and were discharged earlier from hospital.

Personality and health

An issue of some controversy concerns the relationship between personality and illness (Scheier & Bridges, 1995; Angell, 1985; Friedman & Booth-Kewly, 1987). A review of the literature has shown personality to be related to risk in the case of five diseases: asthma, chronic headaches, peptic ulcers, arthritis, and circulatory and heart disease. The three most consistently identified personality variables include anxiety, depression or pessimism, and anger or hostility. Indeed, depression has been linked to allergies and to deficiencies in the immune system (Herbert & Cohen, 1993). Cancer patients characterized by helplessness, hopelessness and repression tend to have poorer prognoses (Levy & Heiden, 1990).

One example is the well-known **Type-A personality**. Even after controlling for risk factors such as family history, serum cholesterol levels, cigarette smoking and hypertension, patients who suffer heart attacks are frequently competitive, achievement-oriented, rather impatient and somewhat hostile (Rosenman, Brand, Jenkins, Friedman, Straus & Wurm, 1975; Nielson & Neufeld, 1986). However, other studies have failed to confirm the linkage with this global syndrome (Ragland & Brand, 1988; Thoreson & Powell, 1992; Tett et al., 1992).

The inconsistencies in this research may be because only one or two components of the Type A syndrome really represent risk (Booth-Kewley & Friedman, 1987). Some studies suggest that an unexpressed "cynical hostility," in which people tend to expect the worst of others, is the specific predictor of chronic high blood pressure (Raikkonen et al., 1999) and coronary illness (Matthews, Glass, Rosenman & Bortner, 1977; Check & Dyck, 1986; Weidner, Istvan & McKnight, 1989). Of course, such people would have more difficulty in obtaining social support. In a laboratory experiment (Carver & Glass, 1978), subjects were put to work solving puzzles. In one condition, a confederate of the experimenter made derogatory remarks and wisecracks about the subjects while they worked whereas in the control condition, the confederate made no such remarks. When subjects were given the opportunity to administer what they believed to be electric shocks to the confederate (in the guise of a "teacher–learner" procedure often used in experiments on aggression), Type A's responded to the provocation with much higher levels of aggression. It also has been found that when Type A's express anger, angiographic measures show evidence of more stress on the heart than is found in other people (Krantz & Glass, 1984).

It is ironic that the people most at risk through their Type-A personality are those who are rewarded with success in our competitive, individualistic society (Thoreson & Powell, 1992). Perhaps for this reason, it is difficult for Type-A people to modify their pattern of living (Burke & Weir, 1980). Programs have been devised to help Type A's cope with stress. However, although the Type-A behaviours may change as a result, corresponding changes in physiological reactions do not necessarily follow (Roskies et al., 1986).

Decisions and actions about health

Understanding how people make decisions about their health is vital for promoting health-enhancing behaviour. Consider this question: why do people persist in acting in ways harmful to themselves even when they are aware of the risks? Part of the answer appears to be that they are concerned with protecting their sense of self-worth by avoiding failure (Sherman & Cohen, 2002). The key seems to be that they must be given an alternative, a way out of this dilemma. Keep this in mind as we examine two decision-making models.

Health beliefs model

What will lead us to change our behaviour in a way that is beneficial to our health? We can reason that there are two stages to this process of change. First, we must decide that we must "do something" to help our health; lose some weight, get more exercise, stop smoking. Then we must decide what to do how to achieve that goal of losing weight, getting exercise and quitting smoking. The **health beliefs model** represents such a two-stage process (Becker, 1974).

Let's take the example of Bob who works in an office and has a sedentary lifestyle. His physician has recommended some form of exercise (jogging, swimming, cycling and aerobics classes) to promote cardiovascular fitness and to reduce the risk of heart attack.

The process begins with a person's readiness to act, to "do something" in order to become more physically fit (A). Bob comes to believe that he is susceptible

Positive Psychology and Health

Recently, a group of research psychologists have questioned the focus of much of contemporary psychology on the negative, the pathological, the social problems (e.g., Seligman & Csikszentmihalyi, 2000). Even in this textbook, we ask why people conform and obey excessively, take cognitive shortcuts, accept prejudice and sexism, behave aggressively but not altruistically, make poor decisions in groups and larger collectivities and fail to resolve conflicts in a rational manner. They have argued for a more balanced approach, considering as well the positive strengths, virtues and the resilience of people. We present a few brief examples of this burgeoning field of research and theory that have implications for health.

- Positive emotions are associated with good health. It would seem reasonable that the more we experience joy, happiness, satisfaction, pride, love and pleasure, the less we experience anger, depression, anxiety, hate and the other negative emotional states related to poor health. While positive emotions enable us to undo lingering negative feelings and even to attend more comfortably to uncomfortable information, positive emotional states also enable us to broaden our repertoire of reactions to various situations and to build the kinds of personal resources (including the support of other people) that enhance our health (Frederickson, 2001).

- Optimism has also been shown to be associated with good health. Indeed, Taylor, Kemeney, Reed, Bower & Grunewald (2000) present evidence that positive illusions, optimism and hope, even in the face of rather negative prospects, can help in the recovery from cancer and in slowing the progress of AIDS. Note, however, that we distinguish between genuine optimism and acting in an optimistic manner as a "good patient." This will be discussed later in the chapter.

- A recent body of research shows that some kind of religious or spiritual experience in one's life has a positive effect on health (McCullough, Hoyt, Larson, Koenig & Thoreson, 2000; Miller & Thoresen, 2003) including blood pressure and immune system functioning (Seeman, Dubin & Seeman, 2003). It is not clear what this kind of experience may or may not include. For instance, earlier studies linking health to attendance at religious services was confounded by the obvious fact that serious illness may prevent one from attending those services. However the later studies, some of them longitudinal, show a robust effect of religious involvement defined in different studies in terms of religious attendance and involvement, membership in religious institutions or simply finding strength and comfort in religious beliefs and practices. The social support of fellow members of the congregation may play a role as will the religious practices that encourage a healthy lifestyle and discourage many of the health-risk behaviours. These, however, do not fully explain the effect.

- Resilience is a concept borrowed from metallurgy and means the capacity of a metallic structure to bend but not break under physical stress. Kobasa (1979) studied middle-level executives, all experiencing high stress levels. He found that the healthier executives, those showing resilience in the face of constant stress, responded differently to stress, interpreting it as a challenge rather than a threat. People who score high on a measure of "hardiness" show less of an increase in diastolic blood pressure while attempting a difficult task, indicating that these people are less responsive physically to stress (Contrada, 1989). Indeed, people characterized by hardiness do not experience fewer stressful events in their lives but may interpret the same events as less stressful (Roth, Wiebe, Fillingim & Shay, 1989). The hardy personality style includes a strong sense of self, a belief in an internal **locus of control** and a sense of life as being personally meaningful.

Other areas of inquiry within the positive psychology framework include hope, creativity, social solidarity, forgiveness, and of course, love. We must be cautious about inferring causality or the mechanisms by which these variables may be associated with health.

to a health problem: he could have an early heart attack unless he acts. For example, being middle-aged, Bob senses that life is finite and he is more concerned with health risks than when he was young. Bob has seen TV spots and newspaper campaigns for fitness, his doctor has urged him to exercise, his friend Jacques is in hospital after a heart attack and Bob has been noticing that his heart races when he has to run for his commuter train.

If the perceived threat of possible illness is accompanied by *cues to action*, then he decides to "do something." Now he must decide what to do. The choice of action will depend upon the relative costs and benefits perceived for various alternatives. Bob has been "sold" aerobic exercise as an effective preventive action and also likes the prospect of losing weight and looking and feeling better. He considers joining his sister's health club. But perceived barriers include the time required, the inconvenience, the cost of designer clothing and running shoes, membership fees and the shin splints that his sister complains of. Note, of course, that he must weigh the long-term benefits against the costs, which are immediate and tangible. Still, Bob decides it's worth it and so he is likely to begin—and continue—aerobic exercise. In short, he believes that coronary disease is a real and personal threat and perceives exercise as an effective way to reduce that threat without excessive personal sacrifice.

In general, the model has been helpful in showing how beliefs about health become translated into action (Janz & Becker, 1984; Harrison, Mullen & Green, 1992; Strecher, Champion & Rosenstock, 1997). For instance, it predicts wearing protective helmets by cyclists (Quine, Rutter & Arnold, 2000), and AIDS-related sexual behaviours such as having multiple partners or being intoxicated while having a sexual encounter, although it was not a strong predictor of condom use (Lollis, Johnson & Antoni, 1997). The model also predicts adherence to a medical regimen

for insulin-dependent diabetes among adolescents (Bond, Aiken & Somerville, 1992) and breast self-examination as a means of detecting early-stage breast cancer among women (Savage & Clarke, 1996).

All of this begins with the general becoming the personal: "It could happen to me." Now consider that people often are unrealistically optimistic about their own health (Weinstein, 1984). A study of sexually active female students showed that they tended to be accurate in rating their own risk of pregnancy but overestimated the risk to others. Those who were using relatively unreliable methods of contraception tended to overestimate the effectiveness of these methods (Whitlet & Hern, 1991). Much of the effort on health promotion is directed towards the perceived threat component of this model. Another theory focuses on the threat.

Protection motivation theory

This theory was outlined in Chapter 5 in relation to the effects of fear-arousing persuasive messages (Rogers, 1975, 1983). Briefly, **protection motivation theory** states that individuals engage in a health behaviour to the extent that they are motivated to protect themselves from a threat. It involves two processes of judgment or appraisal: threat appraisal and coping appraisal. Individuals first evaluate the threat—is it a severe threat? Are they personally susceptible to it? Then they appraise the suggested behavioural response to the threat—would the behaviour be effective? What are the obstacles to the behaviour? Note that the four appraisals—threat severity, personal vulnerability, behavioural effectiveness and obstacles—are similar to those suggested in the health beliefs model.

However, these factors would not be sufficient to lead to action. The person must also believe that he has the ability and self-discipline to perform the recommended action consistently. Indeed self-efficacy beliefs, a fifth component of the model, strongly predict actions such as exercising daily, quitting smoking or using condoms (Wulfert & Wan, 1993). This model predicts a response to a persuasive message indicating willingness to participate in early detection of breast cancer by means of mammography screening (Seydel, Taal & Wiegman, 1990). Other research shows the importance of self-efficacy beliefs in predicting whether manufacturing workers were likely to use hearing protection devices when they were exposed to harmful noise levels (Melamed, Rabinowitz, Feiner, Weisberg & Ribak, 1996). In another study, reactions to messages concerning the danger of cancer from smoking were predicted by elements of the theory (Sturges & Rogers, 1996). Interestingly, the perception of this danger led to change only when the subjects felt personally capable of not smoking; otherwise, higher levels of perceived threat resulted in more smoking.

Of course, the effects of fear depend on the issue under consideration. Studies in which fear concerning smoking has been aroused (Best et al., 1984; Evans, Raines & Hanselka, 1984) indicate that in some cases, fear of adverse consequences may be irrelevant and the most effective component of the anti-smoking program was its discussion of how to resist the social pressures to smoke. Indeed, it is likely that the decreasing social acceptability of public smoking has had significant benefits for the health of smokers and non-smokers alike. Many people who adopt healthier habits do so for reasons other than health, such as to conform, to save money or to look more attractive (Health and Welfare Canada, 1987).

Other studies have found that fear-arousing messages affect attitudes and intentions but have little effect on actual behaviour. Leventhal (1970) reports that although he could get people to agree that tetanus inoculations were worthwhile and that they should have one, the only way he could get them to actually show up at the clinic was to explicitly indicate its location and how to get there and to set up an appointment at a specific time.

Consider, however, that suggesting a threat to a person's health will often arouse anxiety. In studies by Conway and Dubé (2002), the threats to health consisted of melanoma (skin cancer) and AIDS and, of course, the recommended actions were using sunscreen and condoms respectively. Two messages were devised—one using humour and the other without humour—investigating the premise that humour might attenuate the excessive threat that distracts from the message. Indeed, persuasion as measured by the intent to use the recommended course of action was greater in the humour condition—but only for those male and female participants who scored high on a measure of traditional masculinity (recall Chapter 3). It appears that those scoring high on such measures are particularly averse to experiencing emotional distress and thus would be amenable to the distracting effect of a health-threat message that includes humour. Once again, in persuasion involving health, one size does not fit all.

Framing the message

In the field of public health, a distinction is drawn between primary and secondary prevention. **Primary prevention** refers to reducing the rate of occurrence of the disease or health problem while **secondary prevention** refers to the earliest possible detection and treatment of the problem in order to minimize the risk to health. Examples of primary prevention include exercise, moderation in alcohol consumption, not driving after drinking, use of seat belts and child restraints in cars, not smoking, a moderate and balanced diet, inoculation against various infectious diseases and proper care and precautions during pregnancy. Secondary prevention measures include the Pap smear for early detection of cervical cancer, early detection and intervention in problem drinking, dental check-ups, periodic stress-electrocardiograms in higher-risk persons, early diagnosis and treatment of hypertension, dietary restrictions to control diabetes and self-examination for early signs of various cancers (Matarazzo, Weiss, Herd, Miller & Weiss, 1984; Lichtenstein & Glasgow, 1992; Velicer, Prochaska, Rossi & Snow, 1992).

In communicating health messages for both stages of prevention, an important concern is in how to frame the message. Should the message be framed in a negative way, stressing loss, emphasizing what can happen to one's health unless…? For instance, consider the messages mandated by the Government of Canada on cigarette packages, warning of cancer, birth defects and heart disease. Or should the message be framed in a positive way, stressing gain, emphasizing what benefits can occur when the message is heeded? For instance, some messages regarding smoking portray the freedom from addiction that occurs when you quit, along with the improvement in how your clothes smell and the money you will save.

The research literature suggests that it all depends on what you are trying to accomplish by your message. If you want to promote the idea of detecting a prob-

strophize about the pain report significantly more negative pain-related thoughts, greater emotional distress and greater pain intensity than non-catastrophizers. The tendency to catastrophize during pain contributes to more intense pain experiences and increased emotional distress (Sullivan et al., 2001).

The experience of pain itself is related to social psychological factors (Alcock, 1986). We have all learned to identify and label pain particularly in accidents. The child falls down and cries and the parent immediately asks, "Where does it hurt?" even though the child may be crying because of fear or surprise rather than pain itself. Once we learn how to identify pain, we must learn to express it appropriately (Craig, 1978). And we learn that while pain is unpleasant at best, it may also have its rewards. We need and want the sympathy and attention of others and to be excused from usual responsibilities. If we suffer from low back pain and complain about it but walk and sit normally with little observable suffering, our complaints may not be taken seriously. Thus, behaving in a disabled manner "showing our pain" may become habitual. The disabling effects of pain from rheumatoid arthritis, for example, are similarly increased when people perceive that they lack any personal control over the level of pain that they experience (Tennen et al., 1992).

These problems become magnified when the pain is chronic, and may become an issue in the relationship between patient and physician. Conflicting attributions may be made: the patient attributes this persisting condition to the inability of the physician to "cure" it while the physician attributes it to malingering or neurotic exaggeration by the patient. A breakdown in the patient–physician relationship may result, adding to the patient's stress.

Illness and stigma

In some circumstances illness can become a stigma, a cause for rejection. For example, 94 adult epileptics in London, England, were interviewed (Scambler, 1984). When first diagnosed, most of them reacted with shock to the very word *epilepsy* and immediately recognized that this label could distance them from other people and cause them to be rejected. Therefore, they tended to conceal their condition and live in constant fear that their secret would become known. In some cases, people with cancer are stigmatized particularly when there has been obvious physical deterioration or disfiguration.

Being mentally ill is also frequently a difficult and stigmatized role. This is shown clearly in a classic experiment (Fariña & Ring, 1965) in which voluntary participants worked in pairs on a cooperative task. Before beginning the task, participants in separate booths were asked to write out and exchange brief descriptions of themselves to "get to know each other." Participants actually received "self-descriptions" prepared by the experimenter. In one case, the person described herself as a relatively normal student, fairly popular, engaged, with no real problems. In the other, the person wrote that he had experienced problems since high school, kept to himself with no close friends and twice suffered a "nervous breakdown" in the past. Self-description was not related to performance in the cooperative task. After successful completion of the task, subjects who believed their partner to be mentally ill blamed that partner for an inadequate job (a false assertion), described him as less helpful and said they would prefer to work alone in the future. In other words, when someone is perceived by others as mentally ill, whether now or in the past, even that person's successes are perceived as failures.

This experiment was reported about 40 years ago. Has the situation for people with serious psychiatric illnesses changed?

People suffering from AIDS often find themselves isolated and deprived of social support (Triplet & Sugarman, 1987). Those identified as AIDS patients have been evicted by landlords, fired from a wide variety of jobs by employers and refused baptism by church elders. Parents have even tried to bar children who have contracted AIDS from public schools. In short, people with AIDS often suffer from being stigmatized, defined as flawed, incapable, morally degenerate or generally undesirable (Crawford, 1996).

The interesting question is why people with AIDS are socially rejected and stigmatized. Clearly, one factor is homophobia, an unreasonable fear of and rejection of homosexuals (Triplet & Sugarman, 1987). People who have an unrealistic fear of contracting AIDS from casual contact sources (dishes, sharing a bar of soap, sneezes) and who favour compulsory quarantine for AIDS victims also hold negative attitudes towards homosexuals (Winslow, Rumbaut & Hwang, 1989). Other studies show stigmatization of AIDS victims as related to negative attitudes towards homosexuality (Pryor, Reeder & McManus, 1991; Triplet & Sugarman, 1987). Research shows that as well as being homophobic, people who are more fearful of

AIDS also tend to have conservative political and religious attitudes (Bouton et al., 1989; Temoshok, Sweet & Zich, 1987) and to score high on the F-scale, a measure of authoritarianism (Witt, 1989; see also Chapter 13). Many such reactions are related to public misconceptions about how HIV infection is contagious (Pryor, Reeder & Vianacco, 1989).

In contrast, female students were told they were to interview another person who was described as having AIDS, as having cancer, as being homosexual or who was described only as another student. They were asked to set up two chairs in a manner that would enable them to conduct a comfortable interview. These subjects set the chairs for interview with the person who had AIDS farther away than they did in the other three cases. Thus in this situation and with regard to females, the stigma and accompanying social distance was specific to AIDS not to homosexuality (Cohn & Swift, 1992).

In summary, there are several reasons why AIDS can be considered a stigma (Herek & Glunt, 1988). First because it is incurable and transmissible, AIDS victims are often erroneously perceived as placing others at risk. Second, people with AIDS are often blamed for having caused their illness through high-risk, avoidable behaviour. Further, people with advanced AIDS may be considered "repulsive" if they have visible, disfiguring symptoms. Finally, AIDS victims are associated with intravenous drug users and homosexuals, whether or not they belong to those stigmatized groups. Indeed while homosexuals and needle-drug abusers are high-risk groups in North America, many people still consider AIDS to be a disease only of stigmatized groups and not a risk to themselves—a misconception that may prove fatal.

Communication between physicians and patients

The relationship between physician and patient has long been recognized as crucial to effective treatment and recovery. As in any interpersonal relationship, communication is fundamental. Consider that the average appointment with a family physician lasts less that 20 minutes (Nelson & McLemore, 1988). During that time, the physician would want to establish or renew feelings of trust and cooperation with the patient, gain information about medical history and current complaints, conduct the appropriate physical examination, order appropriate tests and procedures

and discuss alternatives for further diagnosis and treatment. Clearly, communication skills are necessary to effective medical practice. Indeed, social psychologists have developed programs in medical schools designed to train physicians in more effective communication with their patients (Roter & Hall, 1992).

Communication and being a "good patient"

Self-disclosure by a patient is dependent to a large degree on the nature of the relationship with the physician. Patients may be reluctant to disclose information that seems trivial; they want to be "good patients" and may feel intimidated by the physician (Taylor, 1979). Indeed, being a "good patient" may be good for the staff but not for the patient. Most people try to be cooperative, unquestioning of medical authority or hospital rules, passive, and as cheerful (or at least, uncomplaining) as they can manage in the circumstances. Physicians like their patients more when they are in better physical and emotional health, and when patients are more satisfied with their care (Hall, Epstein, Deciantis & McNeil, 1993).

While these patients are well liked by staff, they pay a price.

- *Depersonalization,* a loss of personal identity; they now assume identity as a medical insurance number or become the "hernia repair in 214A."

- *Loss of control,* a sense that they must sacrifice the freedom normally expected by adults to a set of institutional rules and professional decisions.

- *Ignorance* of matters about which a normal adult would feel a right to know. In some cases, the patient may sink into a state of passive helplessness, which has been linked to depression and to a further erosion of health (Abramson, Seligman & Teasdale, 1978).

Is it better to be a "bad patient?" Taylor (1979) suggests that being a "bad patient" is a state of psychological reactance, acting in ways to counteract feeling uninformed and helpless. The patient may demand information and treatment as an individual. Often, reactant behaviour becomes excessive, resulting in frequent complaints, demands and attention-seeking ploys. It may also involve minor acts of mutiny such as smoking where prohibited, making passes at nurses (or physicians) or refusing to follow a prescribed diet. Of course, patients and staff often dislike "bad patients," which is inevitably distressing. Their complaints may not be taken seriously, and accurate diagnosis becomes more difficult.

As we discussed earlier (see Chapter 7), much of interpersonal communication is non-verbal. Friedman (1982) suggests that non-verbal cues play a vital role both in the diagnostic process and in communicating concern and empathy for the patient. For example, eye contact may be encouraging to a patient during a difficult time, but either excessive staring or avoiding eye contact may make the person feel like a "bad patient" or an object of curiosity. In an experiment, physicians were instructed to act in differing ways to different patients such as folding their arms or not, leaning towards the patient or not and so forth. The same physicians were evaluated most favourably by the patients when they leaned forward without folding their arms and nodded their heads in response to patients' comments (Harrigan & Rosenthal, 1983).

A careful observational study of communication between patients and their physicians revealed that the gender of the physician could be important (Hall et al., 1993). Specifically, female physicians conducted longer visits, asked more questions, made more back-channel non-verbal responses and smiled more at their patients. Perhaps more important, patients regardless of whether they were male or female revealed more medical information to them. It was also found that male patients were liked more than females and that female physicians liked their patients more than did male physicians.

FOCUS ON RESEARCH

Principles of Physician–Patient Communication

As a result of considerable research, Roter and Hall (1992) suggest the following as basic to physician–patient interaction and to a more effective manner of practising medicine:

1. Allow patients to tell the "story" of their illness or symptoms in their own words. Of course, this will take time and often must allow for a "by the way, doctor …" revelation that may be extremely important.

2. While the physician has the medical expertise, patients also have "expertise" in day-to-day living with symptoms. Indeed, simply asking people to "rate your health at the present time" will predict subsequent illness and survival after accounting for the effects of patients' current symptoms, family history, medical history, diagnoses and lab test results. There is something that people can detect in their health that eludes the medical sciences (Idler & Binyamini, 1997).

3. Understand both the physical and mental state of the patient; these are indivisible. Indeed, note the emotional context of the situation. Patients may be nervous about seeing the doctor and need reassurance that the doctor cares about them. Non-verbal cues can be very important (see Chapter 7).

4. Maximize the expertise of the physician. Patients want information that is clear and relevant to them. In accord with speech accommodation theory (Chapter 7), the physician must be able to communicate complicated matters in understandable, nontechnical language—not an easy task.

5. Communication should be reciprocal and overcome stereotyped roles. While the relationship is one-sided (physicians don't usually tell patients about *their* symptoms and problems), the physician can be courteous and a good listener.

Some medical school curricula have been revised to include training in interpersonal skills. Of course, all of this demands not only the physician's interpersonal communication skills but also his or her time. Consider that while we all want our physician to spend as much time with us as we feel we need, we also want to be seen at the appointed time and we resent being late. Consider also that most physicians are paid on a fee-for-service basis that demands time efficiency and does not reward patience.

Nonverbal communication is particularly important between physician and patient—often providing important cues about the illness and its prognosis.

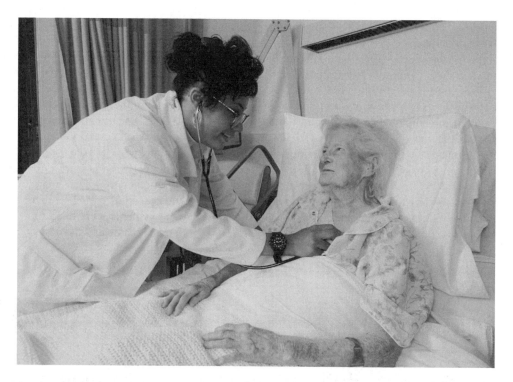

Non-verbal communication is particularly important to the patient for several reasons. Patients looking for information may find important non-verbal cues from their physician about their disease and its prognosis. Because physicians are in positions of considerable social power relative to their patients, the patients may be reluctant to ask questions and may thus be compelled to rely on non-verbal cues if the physician does not volunteer the information. Finally, certain medical procedures make conversations difficult and awkward, if not impossible, and so the non-verbal channel becomes the only practical channel of communication.

In one study of 25 family-practice physicians, a self-report measure of non-verbal expressiveness was administered. Over the subsequent six months, the more emotionally expressive physicians had more patients, and were more in demand (Friedman, Prince, Riggio & DiMatteo, 1980). Such physicians also may be more effective, for example, by helping the patient to believe in the treatment. The most obvious example of this is the well-known placebo effect in which an inert or non-effective substance (e.g., a sugar pill) can have a powerful effect. If the physician and the patient expect the placebo to work, then it will tend to have a beneficial effect in at least some cases (recall the discussion in Chapter 2).

What to tell the patient

How much should the physician tell the patient particularly about a life-threatening illness or a painful medical procedure? The question is troublesome from both sides of the relationship. On one hand, becoming a patient need not imply that a person sacrifices the right to decide about his body and health—or the right to receive the information needed to make such decisions. On the other hand, the physician bears the legal and ethical responsibility for the patient and may honestly believe that full disclosure would damage the patient's health. Being human, physicians do not like to deliver bad news (Saul & Kass, 1969) and patients who are seriously ill may honestly prefer to cling to illusions and hopes (Miller & Mangan, 1983) even if most say that they want to be informed (Blumenfeld, Levy & Kaufman, 1979). Consequently, perception may not accord with reality in communication between physicians and patients.

In one study, the interactions of more than 300 physicians and their patients were recorded (Waitzkin, 1984). In visits that lasted about 20 minutes, the physician spent only about one minute on average actually giving information to the patient. However, the physicians *estimated* that up to 50 percent of the visit had been spent giving information. When asked to estimate their patients' desire for more information, more than 65 percent of the physicians underestimated how much information the patients actually said they wanted. Moreover, physicians sometimes rely excessively on medical terminology or "medspeak" (Christy, 1979; see also Chapter 7).

What if the physician must relay unpleasant news? The reluctance of people to transmit bad news has been labelled the **MUM effect** (Tesser & Rosen, 1975). A study by Shapiro, Boggs, Melamed and Graham-Pole (1992) focused on women at risk for breast cancer. These participants viewed a videotape of a physician presenting results of a mammogram to a patient. The results were ambiguous and more testing was necessary. In one version, the physician acted tense and anxious indicating that he was worried; in the other, he acted calm and reassuring while presenting the same results. Subjects were asked to imagine that they were the patients. Those viewing the "worried" version perceived the situation as more severe and showed greater anxiety. Most interesting, they recalled less of the information presented. This suggests that patients may have difficulty in remembering what they were told, not because they lack information but because of their anxiety (see Chapter 5 on fear-arousing communication and persuasion).

Physicians may fear that bad news will upset their patients, but pioneering field research by Janis (1958) indicates that such upset is not necessarily detrimental. When people must face major surgery, those who are moderately anxious about it actually fare best in post-operative recovery. These people tend to seek out information and to prepare themselves mentally for what is ahead—the "work of worrying." Low-anxiety patients do not think about it until they discover unexpectedly how terrible they feel, while highly anxious people avoid the topic. The key here is that accurate information allows the patient to prepare for and cope with the future event.

In a field experiment (Johnson & Leventhal, 1974), patients were given information about an upcoming endoscopic examination, an unpleasant procedure in which a tube is slowly snaked down the patient's throat to view the gastrointestinal system from the inside. Two messages were given. One provided information about the uncomfortable sensory aspects of the experience such as gagging and the feeling of fullness when air was pumped into the stomach. The other consisted of behavioural information such as guidance in how to reduce gagging and ease insertion of the

tube. Patients were divided into four groups—those who received both messages, one of the two messages or very minimal information and instruction. The results showed that gagging was significantly reduced and ease of insertion of the tube was significantly enhanced among those patients who received both messages. The sensory information was most effective in reducing signs of emotionality while the behavioural instructions most effectively reduced fear.

Outside influence

There is an implicit hypothesis that the physician–patient relationship must be independent of outside influence to be effective. Some physicians and medical organizations have attributed an apparent erosion of the physician–patient relationship to control over the financial aspects of medical practice by governments or insurance companies. Most of the research on physician–patient interaction has been conducted in the U.S. where the patient usually pays for services directly or through private insurance companies. In Canada, provincial governments administer fee-for-services health insurance and in many Western European nations, physicians are paid a salary by the government. Still other countries have a combination of public and private medicine. Given the importance of maintaining optimal relationships between physicians and their patients and the urgency of preserving adequate medical care in times of economic difficulty, research in this area should have an impact on policy.

Patient noncompliance

Typically, a visit to the doctor's office concludes with one or more recommendations: follow a restricted diet, begin physiotherapy, have your child inoculated for polio or diphtheria or make another appointment. However, research shows that overall noncompliance with medical advice is around 50 percent (Haynes, McKibbon & Kanani, 1996). Of course this will be higher where a change in long-standing habits is recommended (e.g., changing the diet), when there are unpleasant side effects (e.g., medications, withdrawal from cigarette addiction) or when the recommendations are complex ("Take the blue pill once a day, the red pill every eight hours …") and when the treatment or change is long-lasting. Despite their best efforts, physicians are remarkably ineffectual in influencing patients to exercise more, drink less, smoke less and eat sensibly.

Non-compliance is also a common problem when the original symptoms are no longer evident. If the patient feels better after a few days, she may stop taking the prescribed antibiotic prematurely, often leading to a recurrence of the illness. However if a therapeutic measure continues to relieve severe pain or is seen as potentially life saving (e.g., chemotherapy for cancer), the patient will usually comply. Thousands of patients quit smoking, lose weight and exercise diligently—after their first heart attack.

One good example occurs in the treatment of **hypertension** (high blood pressure). Easily diagnosed and present in 17 to 25 percent of adults, it can lead to strokes, heart failure, renal failure, blindness and coronary disease (Herd & Weiss, 1984). The patient is rarely able to detect symptoms of hypertension. However, many believe mistakenly that they can tell when their blood pressure is high, relying on unreliable cues such as an elevated pulse rate, warm hands and feet or "stress" (Leventhal, Meyer & Nerenz, 1980). High blood pressure can be treated effectively, primarily by medication (beta-blockers and diuretics), weight control, a sodium-restricted diet or biofeedback relaxation techniques. Yet between 70 and 90 percent of patients diagnosed as hypertensive fail to take their medication regularly or to comply with other recommendations (Leventhal & Hirschman, 1982).

It is misleading to attribute noncompliance simply to the personality characteristics of patients. Rather, the health professional's approach must be examined. Research shows that patients comply when they perceive their physician as friendly, caring and interested in them as well as having sound knowledge and technical ability (DiNicola & DiMatteo, 1984). Warmth in an interpersonal relationship can be communicated non-verbally by eye contact, physical posture and movement.

Rodin and Janis (1979) also suggest that physicians can enhance the therapeutic relationship by encouraging self-disclosure by the patient, giving positive feedback of acceptance and understanding, asking whether the patient understands and accepts the recommendations and implying that the patient has the ultimate control and responsibility in the situation. Patients are also more likely to comply with physicians who are satisfied in their profession, who are specialists in the relevant area, who have busier practices (more patients seen per week) and who make definite follow-up appointments with their patients to track progress (DiMatteo et al., 1993).

However, the research evaluating attempts to increase compliance is rather discouraging. The effects are fairly weak and not lasting (Roter et al., 1998; Haynes, McKibbon & Kanani, 1996). Perhaps this reflects the role defined for the physician as expert and healer, and neglecting the responsibility of the patient.

Maintenance or relapse

While many people have begun exercise programs and have shown significant improvements in fitness, less than 30 percent of them continue to be active beyond a period of 3.5 years (Oldridge, 1982). While a calorie-restricted diet may help, North Americans collectively lose tons of fat each year but few can keep it off beyond one year (Wilson, 1984). While many alcoholics, heroin addicts and smokers successfully complete treatment programs or quit by themselves, about two-thirds relapse within three months after withdrawal from the addictive substance (Hunt, Barnett & Branch, 1971).

Almost inevitably, the individual will deviate from the prescribed pattern: a person forgets to take the antibiotic one night, the weight-watcher gives in to the lure of a Thanksgiving feast, the ex-smoker accepts an offered cigarette. Why does a "slip" become a relapse? The evidence shows that it is not some internal mechanism triggered by the slip that causes the person to lose control. For example in an experimental situation in which subjects were asked to rate the taste and quality of various alcoholic beverages, even diagnosed alcoholics did not lose control over how much they drank (Marlatt, Demming & Reid, 1973).

To understand why people lose control after a lapse, it is important to understand how people interpret the slip, a phenomenon called the *abstinence violation effect* (Marlatt & Gordon, 1979). The person experiences cognitive dissonance between the slip as a behaviour and their self-image as an ex-smoker, dieter or recovering alcoholic. Further, the person will tend to make a dispositional attribution explaining the slip in terms of personal weakness and inadequacy rather than blaming the situation or viewing it as a momentary lapse in judgment.

Thus, people see themselves differently and are emotionally upset about it. The person is now in a poor state in which to regain self-control and the slip becomes a full-blown relapse. Learning to have a "blow-out" once in a while and revert to good behaviour the next morning without drowning in self-recrimination is one of the keys to regaining control.

Alcohol Myopia and Safe Sex

Why do people engage in unsafe or unhealthy behaviours when they are drunk? Many assumptions exist regarding the effects of alcohol such as alcohol reduces tension or alcohol disinhibits behaviour. An alternative has been proposed by Steele and Josephs (1990): that alcohol induces a social and behavioural nearsightedness or "myopia." It is based on two premises, both of which are supported by empirical evidence. The first is that alcohol impairs the capacity to process the kind of information that requires close attention. The second is that alcohol narrows attention to the most immediate and obvious internal and external cues, inducing people to devote their limited attention to the here-and-now and less to long-term consequences.

Thus for example, people deciding whether to drive home after drinking must consider both the possibility of accidents or arrest and the inconvenience and expense in getting home. While the sober person can weigh both sets of concerns, the attention-impaired drunken person will focus myopically on the immediate cues (inconvenience) and drive home (MacDonald, Zanna & Fong, 1995).

Because intoxicated drinkers are unable to attend to anything beyond the immediate situation, alcohol may "disinhibit" social behaviour if the inhibiting cues are not obvious and immediate to the individual. Drinking in our culture also signals to the drinker that they can be granted "time out," a kind of lessening of moral and normative restraints that lets them get away with otherwise frowned-upon behaviours.

Of course, alcohol has also been linked to sexuality. A set of studies shows that alcohol decreases the likelihood of using condoms during casual sex (MacDonald, Zanna & Fong, 1996). Survey data indicate that male students who had been intoxicat-ed when they last had intercourse were less likely to have used condoms than those who had been sober. In subsequent experiments, male subjects consumed three drinks, placebo drinks or nothing. Subjects were then shown a video vignette simulating a situation in which individuals were tempted to engage in unprotected sex. It concerns a couple on their first date, enjoying each other dancing at a campus pub, proceeding to her apartment where they begin to make out, and discovering that they are without condoms. Subjects were asked whether, in the man's situation, they would have intercourse without a condom. The intoxicated subjects were more likely than those in the other groups to say they would.

Given that this problem could not be studied directly by experimental manipulation and observation of actual sexual behaviour, the procedure is rather ingenious and the results consistent with the notion that intentions are the most powerful predictor of actions (recall Chapter 4, theory of reasoned action). It is also consistent with the hypothesis of alcohol-induced myopia, in which people are governed almost exclusively by the immediate cues, in this case an attractive and willing partner.

The implications are clear: changing health-risk behaviour must involve more than changing attitudes and intentions. Virtually everybody believes that driving while intoxicated and having unprotected casual sex are not good ideas. This research suggests that the salience of restraining cues must somehow be increased particularly in drinking situations. It also suggests that people should be warned that under the influence of alcohol they are at risk of acting in ways that, if sober, they would not want to act.

To maintain healthier behaviour patterns, people must develop expectations of self-efficacy (Bandura, 1977), the conviction that they can cope with high-risk situations even allowing for temporary transgression. Most cigarette smokers who quit successfully do so after several relapses (Schachter, 1982). Social support from others is important both in bolstering the motivation to resist temptation and in buffering against stressful situations. For example, one study found that ex-smokers who did not relapse felt that they had more support at work both from co-workers and supervisors than did those who relapsed (Caplan, Cobb & French, 1975).

Several other tactics also may be useful. For example, the health practitioner may first recommend the most beneficial regimen and then retreat to a less demanding but still adequate regimen (see Chapter 5). Patients might be invited to write down their own health goals on the premise that behaviour discrepant with a public, self-selected commitment would arouse more cognitive dissonance (Sensenig & Cialdini, 1984). Ideally of course, the new behaviour should become an internalized response rather than external compliance. In this context, the physician becomes a source of expertise rather than an authority figure. Social support from significant others can be vital in this regard as well. For example, people with hypertension are more likely to continue taking their medication if encouraged by their spouses (Caplan, Robinson, French, Caldwell & Shinn, 1976).

A Final Note

This chapter represents the beginning of an outline of a rapidly expanding field within social psychology and much could not be included or only mentioned. For instance, the process of education and socializing of physicians in medical school, the relationships and patterns of communication within institutions such as hospitals, the ways in which illness and symptoms are constructed cognitively, social psychological factors in what has become known as psychoneuroimmunology, the impact of acute and chronic illnesses on marital and other close relationships, the social psychology of reproductive health and sexuality and the impact of both positive and negative emotional states on health are all topics of intensive research.

This chapter began with the assumption that people want to be healthy and can be motivated to act accordingly. However, the research evidence does not show that people act in a consistent manner relevant to their health. Clearly, health promotion must be seen in a much broader context than simply encouraging people to take care of themselves and follow the doctor's orders. Most people do not need to be convinced that their health is important to them. The gap in time between behaviour and its health consequences, the gap between attitudes and behaviour and the inconsistencies among health-relevant behaviours all present

unusual challenges to social psychology, the health professions and society itself.

Summary

1. Behaviour is highly relevant to health, particularly in our society.

2. **Problem behaviour theory** regards adolescent health-risk behaviour such as drug abuse as part of a syndrome of non-conventional personal characteristics (expectations, values, controls), social environment (peer groups, parent behaviour) and behaviours (sexuality, deviance, absence of school and church involvement).

3. Social modelling influences health-risk behaviours by promoting the onset of the behaviour and eliciting it more frequently.

4. Vulnerability to illness is increased by an absence of social support, a perception that life cannot be controlled and by characteristics of the Type-A personality, particularly hostility.

5. According to the health beliefs model, people become ready to do something to promote health if they believe they are personally susceptible to a serious illness or problem. Their actions are determined by the perceived benefits and costs and modified by characteristics of the person and by environmental cues.

6. Protection motivation theory indicates that individuals react to protect themselves from a threat to their health if it is perceived as severe and personally relevant, if the behaviour seems effective and if they feel a sense of personal efficacy.

7. Both models have been criticized as assuming that a purely rational decision-making process underlies health-relevant behaviour.

8. Being ill involves a social role in which we see ourselves differently and others treat us differently.

9. Patients often fail to comply with medical recommendations. Patient compliance and accurate diagnosis are strongly influenced by the relationship and communication between patients and physicians.

10. In general, conveying accurate information to patients contributes to their recovery even when it provokes anxiety.

Further Reading

CONNER, M. & NORMAN, P. (1996). *Predicting health behaviour.* Buckingham, UK: Open University Press. Useful review of basic models including health beliefs, protection motivation, theory of planned behaviour and social cognition.

CUTRONA, C.E. (1996). *Social support in couples.* Thousand Oaks, CA.: Gage. A detailed examination of what social support means in the context of marriage and how this is relevant to the health of both partners.

EVANS, R.G., BARER, M.L. & MARMOR, T.R. (1994). *Why are some people healthy and others not? Determinants of population health.* New York: Aldine de Gruyter. A very useful set of papers relating research to questions of public health developed through the Canadian Institute for Advanced Research.

HORNICK, R.C. (Ed.). (2002). *Public health communication. Evidence of behavior change.* Mahwah, NJ: Erlbaum. This book brings together the results of 16 large-scale programs on preventing smoking, heart disease, childhood illnesses, highway safety, HIV/AIDS as well as family planning— what works and why?

KIECOLT-GLASRE, J.K. & NEWTON, T.L. (2001). Marriage and health: His and hers. *Psychological Bulletin 127,* 472–503. An excellent review of research on the advantage to health of marriage, as well as how and why the protective effects appear to be greater for men than for women.

POOLE, G., MATHESON, D.H. & COX, D.N. (2001). *The psychology of health and health care. A Canadian perspective.* Toronto: Prentice-Hall. An excellent general textbook of health psychology, ranging from epidemiology to psychoneuroimmunology and health care and including the social psychological aspects.

PLANTE, T.G. & SHERMAN, A.C. (2001). *Faith and health.* New York: Guilford. Focus on the psychological aspects underlying the linkages between religious experience and health both in health maintenance and in recovery from illnesses.

PRYOR, J.B. & REEDER, G.D. (Eds.). (1993). *The social psychology of HIV infection.* Hillsdale, NJ: Erlbaum. An excellent set of review papers on basic social psychology applied to coping with the threat and the illness, prevention and stigma.

RADLEY, A. (1994). *Making sense of illness: The social psychology of health and disease.* London: Sage. A well-written analysis from the perspectives of social cognition on the experience of being ill.

ROTER, D.L. & HALL, J.A. (1992). *Doctors talking with patients/Patients talking with doctors.* Westport: Auburn House. A groundbreaking review of studies about what actually happens in encounters between patients and physicians, with some recommendations for improvement.

TAYLOR, S.E., REPETTI, R.L. & SEEMAN, T. (1997). Health psychology: What is an unhealthy environment and how does it get under the skin? *Annual Review of Psychology 48,* 411–447. An integration of a substantial body of research that traces how environmental factors, such as those related to socioeconomic class and racial differences, have an impact on health through stress, safety and health habits.

Weblinks

Health Psychology (American Psychological Association Journal)
www.apa.org/journals/hea.htm/

Health psychology links
www.swix.ch/clan/ks/CPSP24.htm#Health A good set of links to health topics, some with social psychology content.

Health psychology contents page
www.soton.ac.uk/~er194/ Reviews of research, graduate programs and relevant links.

The Body
www.thebody.com/cgi-bin/body.cgi A set of links concerning HIV and AIDS, some of them dealing with social psychology issues such as stigmas.

European Health Psychology Society
www.fub46.zedat.fu-berlin.de:8080/~ahahn/ehp/ ehps.htm

Stress and Anxiety Research Society
www.uib.no/STAR/

Healthy Weight
www.healthyweight.com/ This site includes a feature that allows you to assess your own weight.

Glossary

abstinence violation effect (16) People recovering from substance abuse may experience this if they slip backwards, attribute the slip to themselves, and experience the slip as dissonant. They are then likely to relapse.

acculturation (13) The process that occurs when groups come into contact with one another, resulting in changes in the original cultural patterns.

action research (Introduction) Studies in which the data are fed back into a system in order to influence change.

actor/observer bias (2) The tendency to attribute our own behaviour to situations and the behaviour of others to dispositions.

additive bilingualism (7) Bilingualism of members of a majority language group for whom bilingualism represents the acquisition of a socially useful skill.

adversary procedure (15) A trial system in which both sides are responsible for gathering their own evidence and presenting their own case to a neutral judge and/or jury.

agency (3) A concern with achieving goals and being active in the world.

aggression (11) Behaviour that is intended to harm.

altruism (9) Actions that are carried out voluntarily to help someone without expectations of reward from external sources. Sometimes used to mean such behaviour without expectation of internal self-reward either (see *prosocial behaviour*).

androgens (11) Male sex hormones.

arbitration (10) A process by which the intervener in a conflict reaches a decision about what is a fair resolution to the conflict and the decision is usually binding.

archival approach (1) Approach in which the researcher uses data that have already been collected and tabulated for some other purpose by someone else.

attachment (8) A state of intense emotional dependence on someone.

attempt-suppressing signals (7) Non-verbal cues used by a speaker in a conversation to prevent interruption.

attitude (4) A relatively stable pattern of beliefs, feelings and behavioural tendencies towards some object.

attribution theory (1, 2) An inference of the reason for or cause of a person's behaviour.

audience effects (6) The effect of passive observers on performance.

authoritarianism (11) A personality syndrome characterized by cognitive rigidity, prejudice and an excessive concern with power.

autokinetic effect (6) An illusion in which a stationary spot of light in a dark environment appears to be moving.

availability heuristic (2) A strategy of making judgments in terms of information that readily comes to mind.

averaging model (2) The hypothesis that our overall impression of someone is the sum of our evaluations of the person with regard to various traits, divided by the number of traits evaluated.

baby talk (7) The manner in which adults talk to two- to five-year-olds.

back-channel communication (7) Non-verbal signals from listeners indicating attention and interest in a conversation.

behaviourism (1) A psychological theory based on the premise that behaviour is governed by external reinforcement.

belief in a just world (2) The belief that good outcomes only happen to good people and bad outcomes only happen to bad people.

blind (1) (of an experimental subject) Unaware of which experimental group one is in—e.g., unaware of whether one is receiving an intervention or a placebo.

brainstorming (6) The uncritical and uninhibited expression of ideas, usually in a group setting.

bystander effect (9) A phenomenon in which the presence of others inhibits helping in an emergency.

case study (1) An in-depth investigation and analysis of a single instance of a phenomenon of interest.

catharsis (11) Reduction in arousal, e.g., anger, as a result of acting out or observing the actions of someone else.

causal inference (1) A conclusion about cause and effect.

central route of persuasion (5) Attitude change that follows logical argumentation and thought about the issue.

central trait (2) A characteristic of people that determines how we evaluate them on other characteristics.

charisma (12) Exceptional personal qualities in some leaders that enable them to attract many committed followers.

coaction effects (6) A situation in which people work or perform in a similar way at the same time and place without interacting.

cognitive dissonance (1, 5) A state of uncomfortable arousal that occurs when one cognition is logically opposed to another.

cognitive neo-associationist model (11) This model is a revision of the frustration–aggression hypothesis in which an aversive stimulus triggers a fight or flight response depending on whether the thoughts triggered are related to anger or fear.

cognitive response analysis (5) A contrast is drawn between instances that involve thought (elaboration) and instances that do not involve thought (invoking a rule of thumb).

cohesiveness (12) Extent to which members are attracted to a group.

collective behaviour (14) Relatively unorganized and unplanned actions that emerge spontaneously among a collectivity of people as a result of inter-stimulation among them. These actions are not governed by social norms.

collective dilemma (10) A situation in which the individually rational actions of a number of people produce an outcome that is undesirable for all involved.

collectivist culture (3) A set of norms and values that stress the group or community rather than the individual.

communal relationships (8) Relationships built not on maximizing one's own rewards, but on providing a benefit for the other and continuing the relationship.

communication accommodation theory (7) The modification of personal speech style to a speech style that is like the person being spoken to.

competition (10) A form of social exchange in which individuals act to maximize their gains in relation to others.

compliance (5, 6) Acquiescent behaviour in response to a direct request.

conflict (10) Discord between two or more parties.

conflict spiral schema (10) A series of escalating threats and counter-threats.

conformity (6) Behaviour that adheres to group norms and yields to perceived group pressures.

conspiracy theory (14) An irrational set of beliefs, or a "theory" about a supposed group of conspirators. These beliefs are held in common by a group of people, and then applied with a very rational and stubborn logic.

constructive reality (6) A view of the world, especially of its ambiguities, that is provided by the group.

contact hypothesis (13) The notion that if members of different groups can get together under certain circumstances, prejudice will be reduced.

contagion (14) The rapid spreading of emotions, attitudes and behaviour throughout a crowd or population.

content analysis (3, 13) The systematic study of verbal or written materials to determine underlying trends.

contingency theory (12) A theory attributing leadership effectiveness to a good match between leadership style and aspects of the group situation.

control group post-test design (1) A type of quasi-experiment in which samples from two different groups are measured only once, after the event of interest has taken place.

conversation control (7) Use of non-verbal communication to regulate the form and pace of a conversation.

cooperation (10) A form of social exchange in which two or more parties act together to achieve a shared goal.

correlational approach (1) An approach to the study of social behaviour based on trying to find which variables "go together."

correspondent inference (2) Attribution of an act to a stable disposition.

counterfactual thinking (2) Thoughts about the past in which it is imagined how the outcome of events might have been different.

covariation principle (2) A principle stating that if two events are perceived as occurring together and never separately, one will be interpreted as the cause of the other.

cross-categorization (12) A situation in which a person is similar to others on one dimension but different from them on another.

cross-cultural research (Introduction) Studies in which subjects from more than one society or ethnic group are compared.

cross-lagged procedure (11) Method of comparing correlations between two variables over two points in time in order to infer which is more likely to be a cause of the other.

crowding (14) A subjective state of discomfort arising from the perception that there are too many people present.

dangerous game (10) A mixed-motive conflict in which if neither side backs down, both may suffer catastrophic losses.

debriefing (1) Following an experiment, discussing with the subjects the true nature of the experiment and exposing any deception.

deception clues (15) Behaviour that suggests an individual is lying.

dehoaxing (1) As part of debriefing, informing subjects that they have been deceived and explaining the purpose of the experiment.

deindividuation (14) A complex process in which individuals come to see themselves more as members of a group than as individuals, leading to a lowered threshold for normally restrained behaviour.

demand characteristics (1) Characteristics of an experimental situation that seem to cry out for a certain response, thus biasing results.

density–intensity hypothesis (14) The hypothesis that high-density situations magnify our usual reactions so that they tend to seem either extremely unpleasant, or quite pleasant and exciting.

density–social pathology hypothesis (14) The hypothesis that population density itself produces or is in some way related to high rates of crime and mental illness.

dependent variable (1) A variable that is being measured and that is hypothesized to relate to some other variable (the independent variable).

desensitization (1) Part of debriefing; intended to help the subjects accept the new information they have about themselves, put it into context and respond to questions and anxieties that might arise.

desensitization (11) Decrease in reactivity to violence as a result of having witnessed violence on television or elsewhere.

deterrence schema (10) The assumption that a realistic threat can prevent war or other hostile acts.

diffusion of responsibility (9) A tendency for the individual to feel less of a sense of personal duty to act in a prosocial manner when others are present.

discounting cue hypothesis (5) An hypothesis stating that when the source of a communication is not trusted, the message tends to be disregarded.

discounting principle (2) In attributions, the principle that the role of one factor is perceived as less important if other plausible causes are present.

discrimination (13) Negative actions directed to members of a specific group.

dispositional loneliness (8) Unpleasant emotional state arising out of perceived deficiencies in relationships due to the perceiver's innate disposition.

distraction-conflict theory (6) The theory that when people are in the presence of others, they may experience arousal caused by a conflict over whether to attend to the task or the audience.

distributive justice (15) Fairness of outcomes provided for various parties involved.

double-blind (1) A control in research whereby neither the subject nor the experimenter who interacts with the subject knows which condition the subject has been assigned to.

downward comparison (3) A tendency to evaluate ourselves with reference to people who are lower in status or advantage.

ego-defensive functions (4) The ability of certain attitudes to protect or enhance the self-esteem of the person who holds them.

elaboration likelihood model (5) A theory that central and peripheral routes of attitude change are differentiated by the amount of cognitive activity involved.

emergent norm theory (14) Crowds are initially heterogeneous with regard to goals, feelings and behaviour, but a shared perception of the situation develops, and norms emerge.

emotional loneliness (8) Loneliness due to a lack of intimate relationships.

empathy (9) A vicarious emotional response (a feeling) elicited by and congruent with the perceived emotional state of another person.

empathy–altruism hypothesis (9) The hypothesis that pure altruism is elicited as a result of empathy induced by witnessing a person in distress.

ethnocentrism (13) A belief in the superiority of one's own ethnic or cultural groups.

ethnolinguistic vitality (7) The relative status and strength of a language in a particular social structure, reflecting the proportion of the population that speaks the language.

Eros (11) The life instinct, according to Freud.

estrogens (11) Female sex hormones.

exchange relationships (8) Relationships built on an economic model, in which people seek to maximize benefits and minimize costs.

evaluation apprehension (1) A concern about the evaluation of one's behaviour.

excitation transfer theory (11) Intensification of an emotional reaction to a new stimulus brought about by residues of nervous system arousal from an earlier emotional reaction.

experimental method (1) A research approach in which subjects are randomly assigned to two or more groups and an independent variable is varied, in order to assess its effect on a dependent variable.

experimental realism (1) The extent to which the experimental situation "grabs" subjects and involves them so that they react naturally to the situation rather than as they might think appropriate to the laboratory situation.

experimenter effects (1) Biases in an experiment due to the influence of the experimenter, who, knowing the hypothesis under study, can unintentionally influence the subjects to act in a way that confirms the hypothesis.

external validity (1) The degree to which the behaviour observed in the laboratory corresponds to "real" behaviour in the outside world.

extraneous variable (1) A variable that might interfere with the outcome of the research.

facial feedback hypothesis (14) Emotional experience is directly affected by the feedback our brains receive about our facial expressions.

fad (14) A short-lived, extreme and frivolous collective behaviour.

false consensus effect (2) The tendency to overestimate the extent to which others act or think as we do.

false hope syndrome (3) A pattern of unrealistic expectations about eventual success after repeated failures.

fashion (14) A widespread collective preference that is relatively short-lived.

field experiment (1) The use of the experimental method in a natural setting, in which the subjects are not aware that they are subjects.

field study (1) Direct observation of people in a natural setting.

file-drawer problem (1) A study with non-significant findings that is never presented to the public.

forgiveness (9) A prosocial response in which the recipient of malice or harm forgives the transgressor.

free rider (10) Someone who benefits from a public good without contributing.

front-to-rear communications failure (14) A situation in which people at the front of a crowd trying to escape from danger are trampled because those at the back, unaware that people at the front are unable to move more quickly, continue to push ahead.

frustration–aggression hypothesis (11) The hypothesis that aggression follows frustration and frustration precedes aggression.

fundamental attribution error (2) Tendency of people to exaggerate the importance of personal dispositions as the causes of behaviour.

gain effect (8) In a social interaction, the tendency for a person to be more attracted to someone who expresses increasing liking or praise for him or her than to someone who expresses constant liking or praise.

game theory (10) A model of social conflict in which people are assumed to act rationally in order to maximize their gains and minimize their losses.

gender schematic (11) A characteristic of individuals who tend generally to view males and females in terms of sex-typed dimensions.

general uncertainty (14) Widely held doubt and apprehension within a collectivity of people that is likely to give rise to rumours.

generic norm of out-group discrimination (12) Disposition to reject or discriminate against members of all out-groups, regardless of the group or context.

gratitude (9) A prosocial response in which the recipient of others' good deeds is grateful.

GRIT (Graduated and Reciprocated Initiatives in Tension reduction) (10) A possible method of reversing a conflict spiral by making credible but non-damaging concessions.

group (12) A collection of people distinguished by common goals and stable relationships rather than superficial similarities.

group-induced attitude polarization (12) Group decisions are typically more extreme—more risky or more cautious—than the average of the individual members' positions.

groupthink (6) Tendency of a highly cohesive and elitist group to achieve a rapid consensus without dissent or outside influences.

habituation to pornography (11) The effect by which, as individuals watch more and more pornography, there is a gradual decrease in the physiological arousal produced by it, leading to diminishing pleasurable reactions, and even disappointment and boredom.

haptics (7) The use of touch as communication.

health beliefs model (16) A theory that accounts for health-related behaviour in terms of recognizing a personally relevant threat and a choice of actions.

heroism (9) Altruistic act in the face of extraordinary risk.

heterosexuality subschema (11) A schema that, when primed, leads to viewing interactions with people of the opposite sex in sexual terms.

heuristics (2) Assumptions and biases that guide our decisions about uncertain events.

hostile aggression (11) Aggression that expresses anger or some other negative emotion (contrast with *instrumental aggression*).

hostile masculinity (11) An insecure, distrustful, defensive and hypersensitive orientation towards others, especially women, as well as gratification from dominating and controlling women.

hypertension (16) High blood pressure.

hypothesis (1) A testable proposition derived from theory.

hysterical contagion (14) The spread of a strong emotional reaction, sometimes accompanied by apparent physical symptoms that in reality have no physical cause.

idiosyncrasy credit (6) Tolerance for nonconformity to group norms from a high-status member who is perceived to have contributed much to the group.

illusion of control (2) A commonly held and exaggerated belief that people can determine their lives and the events around them.

illusory correlation (2, 13) Perception that two variables are related to one another when they are not.

image-repair hypothesis (9) The idea that a person who is embarrassed by his or her behaviour may help others in order to improve a damaged image.

immersion program (7) A form of second-language education in which the second language is used for instruction and interaction rather than being treated as a separate subject.

implicit personality theory (2) The assumptions of people about which traits go together and about human nature.

impression management (3) Actions taken by individuals to control or influence how others evaluate them.

in-group (12) A social category to which a person belongs.

independent variable (1) The variable manipulated (varied) by the experimenter in a psychological experiment.

individualistic bias (15) A North American ideal of the self-contained person, which has influenced the definition of concepts and problems in social psychology.

individualistic culture (3) A set of norms and values that stress the individual rather than the group or community.

informational social influence (6) The matching of our own ideas to the group in order to determine whether they are "correct."

informed consent (1) Agreement of subjects to participate in an experiment after being told what will happen to them.

ingratiation (3) Strategies of enhancing our attractiveness to others in order to create a positive impression.

inoculation effect (5) An effect by which exposure to relatively weak arguments against our own position strengthens our later resistance to persuasion.

inquisitional procedure (15) A courtroom approach in some countries in which the judge is assigned a role in collecting evidence and questioning witnesses.

instinct (11) Supposed inborn behavioural tendencies that motivate certain actions.

instrumental aggression (11) Behaviour intended to harm as a means to some desired end (contrast to *hostile aggression*).

instrumental function (4) A function served by an attitude that brings rewards or lessens costs.

instrumental values (4) Preferred modes of conduct, such as honesty or thrift.

integrative complexity (2) Extent to which people can use several schemata and standards in a flexible way when processing information.

intergroup anxiety (13) Negative feelings regarding anticipated adverse consequences of contact between groups.

internal validity (1) Degree to which changes in behaviour were brought about by experimental manipulations rather than extraneous factors.

investment model (8) A model of intimate relationships that considers commitment to a relationship in terms of the investment put into the relationship.

jealousy (8) An unpleasant reaction to a perceived rival, arising out of social comparison or a desire for exclusivity.

kernel-of-truth hypothesis (13) The idea that social stereotypes are necessarily based on some supportable evidence.

kinesics (7) All bodily movements except those that involve contact with someone else; the "body language" of popular literature.

kin selection (9) A putative process in which helping relatives survive long enough to reproduce improves the chances of being able to pass our genes on to the next generation.

knowledge function (4) A function served by an attitude that helps one make sense of the world.

laboratory experiment (1) The use of the experimental method in a laboratory setting.

language (7) A system of vocal sounds, writing or formal gestures embodying symbols that have meaning in communication.

leader (12) An individual in a group who has the greatest influence over other members.

leakage (15) Behaviour that unintentionally reveals the truth when a person is lying.

legitimate power (12) Our capacity to influence others based on their acceptance of our authority.

locus of control (16) The extent to which people believe that the events in their lives are caused by their own actions (internal), or by luck, higher forces, or other powerful people (external).

loneliness (8) Unpleasant emotional state arising out of perceived deficiencies in relationships.

longitudinal study (1) Research in which two or more variables are studied in the same subjects at several different points over a span of time.

looking-glass self (3) A self-concept constructed from the way we appear to others, which is then reflected back to us.

loss effect (8) In a social interaction, the tendency for a person to be less attracted to someone who expresses decreasing liking or praise than to someone who expresses constant dislike or criticism.

loss of control (14) A sense of not being in control in a high-density situation, leading to feelings of helplessness and vulnerability.

low-ball technique (6) A means of inducing someone to carry out a requested act by first requesting him or her to carry out the act, and only then increasing the cost of fulfilling the request.

marginality (7) A feeling experienced by immigrants or people learning a new language of being estranged from their own group, yet not part of the new group.

mass psychogenic illness (14) Symptoms of physical illness, without any physical basis, that spread through a collectivity of people.

mediation (10) Third-party intervention in a conflict that assists in the negotiation process but does not impose solutions.

meta-analysis (1) A method of statistically combining the results of many different studies on the same topic in order to identify consistent patterns in these results.

mixed motive game (10) A conflict in which there are rewards for both competition and cooperation.

M'Naghten rule (15) A principle of law in which a person is not held legally responsible for an action if he or she did not know the nature and quality of the act or did not know that the action was wrong.

MODE model (4) Motivation and Opportunity as DEterminants of whether deliberate or spontaneous actions are taken between attitudes and behaviour.

model (1) A mini-theory, or set of propositions and assumptions, about a specific phenomenon.

moral development (9) The process by which the capacity for moral judgments matures throughout childhood.

morpheme (7) Unit of meaning in language.

multiculturalism hypothesis (13) The contention that positive feelings towards members of other groups vary with how secure and comfortable people feel about their own cultural identity and background.

MUM effect (16) Reluctance of someone, e.g., a physician, to communicate bad news.

mundane realism (1) Extent to which a situation encountered in an experiment is perceived as naturalistic or corresponding to some real-life situation.

mutuality (8) A relationship characterized by some degree of involvement, commitment and intimacy between two people.

mutually assured destruction (10) A situation in which each of two protagonists has the ability to destroy the other, even if the other strikes first. Thus, neither is tempted to attack the other.

narcissism (3) Complete self-absorption, living for yourself and for the moment, with no concern for the community, the past or the future.

negative-state relief hypothesis (9) The hypothesis that an observer's empathic response to a sufferer's distress produces personal sadness, and that the individual acts to help the sufferer because of the egoistic motivation to relieve his or her own sadness (negative-state).

negativity effect (2) Tendency for overall impressions of people to be more influenced by negative than by positive traits.

neosexism (13) A form of gender attitudes defined as a manifestation of a conflict between egalitarian values and residual negative feelings towards women.

non-reactive measure (1) A measurement that cannot influence the behaviour being considered.

non-verbal communication (7) The sending of information to another person (or persons) without the use of words.

non-zero-sum game (10, 12) A conflict situation in which some outcomes are mutually preferable—a mixed-motive game.

norm of equity (9) The generally shared belief that fairness should serve as a criterion for the way that we treat others.

norm of reciprocity (9) The generally shared belief that people should help those who have helped them.

norm of social responsibility (9) The generally shared belief that people should help those who need help.

obedience (6) Acquiescent behaviour in response to a direct order.

observational learning (6) The experience of modelling influence through which a novel behaviour is acquired.

operational definition (1) A definition of a construct in terms of how it is measured.

opinion leaders (6) Highly influential people who transmit new attitudes to many others.

ostracism (6) Rejection by the group.

out-group (12) A social category to which an individual does not belong.

out-group homogeneity effect (12) The effect by which members of another group are perceived to be more similar to one another than are the members of one's own group to each other.

paralanguage (7) Non-verbal aspects of speech that convey information.

paralinguistic drawl (7) The practice of speaking the final syllable in an utterance in a slow, drawn-out fashion.

participant observer (1) A researcher who participates in the group being studied.

particularism (8) In social exchange, the extent to which the value of a resource is influenced by the person who provides it.

perceived norm (4) An expectation of how significant other people would react to a particular action by a person.

peripheral route of persuasion (5) Attitude change not accompanying deliberate thought about the issue, usually occurring in association with distractors.

personal anxiety (14) Anxiety produced by apprehension about an imminent and disappointing outcome; contributes to development of rumours.

personal space (7) The comfortable physical distance that we maintain between ourselves and others.

phonemes (7) The system of short, meaningless sounds.

positivity bias (2) A tendency to perceive others in a favourable light.

post-decision dissonance (5) A state of psychological discomfort that occurs after a difficult choice has been made.

prejudice (13) Illogical, inaccurate and unjustifiable attitudes about members of a group.

primacy effect (5) Tendency for information presented early in a sequence to have a greater impact than information presented later.

primary prevention (16) Measures taken to reduce the incidence of a disease or other health problems.

priming (2) Activation of a particular category or schema by a specific cue.

problem behaviour theory (16) A model of adolescent behaviour based on a syndrome of personal, environmental and behavioural nonconventionality linked with consequences.

promiscuous-impersonal sex (11) A tendency to avoid commitment and to be unfaithful in sexual relationships.

promise (10) A communication that the other person or group will experience positive consequences if a demand is complied with.

propinquity effect (8) The principle that when people are in close physical proximity, the probability of interaction and attraction increases.

prosocial behaviour (9) Actions voluntarily carried out for the sole purpose of helping others, without expectation of reward from external sources.

(Synonym for *altruism* intended to eliminate questions about internal self-reward.)

prosodic features of language (7) Non-verbal aspects of speech, such as timing, pitch and loudness.

protection motivation model (5, 16) A model of fear-arousing communication that states that people respond to danger if they believe the danger to be severe and personally relevant.

protection motivation theory (16) Individuals engage in a health behaviour to the extent that they are motivated to protect themselves from a threat.

prototype (2) A typical example of a category.

proxemics (7, 15) The study of how we use space to regulate our social interactions.

psychopathic personality (11) A particular cluster of personality traits that has a strong connection with antisocial behaviour (synonymous with *antisocial personality* or *sociopathy*).

public goods dilemma (10) A collective dilemma in which individuals must decide how much to contribute to a public good, knowing that their own contribution will have little or no effect on what they receive in return.

qualitative method (1) A method of studying behaviours that cannot be quantified.

quasi-experiment (1) A research method, using a pre-post comparison or a comparison of two groups, that examines the effects of some real-life event or change over which the experimenter has no control.

random assignment (1) Assigning subjects by chance to generate two or more groups that are presumed to be the same with regard to the characteristic being measured, so that the researcher can later judge whether an independent variable led to changes in a dependent variable.

reactive measure (1) A measurement that may influence the behaviour being considered.

reform movement (14) A social movement that accepts the basic structure of a society but seeks to modify a part of it.

regression analysis (1) An extension of basic co-relational analysis that involves more than two variables and allows the researcher to measure the influence of each of several variables on a particular variable of interest.

reinforcement-affect model of attraction (1, 8) The idea that through a process of conditioning, people become attracted to others with whom they associate stimuli or events that arouse positive feelings.

relative deprivation (3, 14) When people compare themselves to other appropriate groups and find that the others are better off, this leads to frustration and discontent, and becomes the basis for the social unrest.

reliability (1) The degree to which a measure yields the same results when used more than once to measure some unchanging object, trait or behaviour.

reparative altruism (9) Helping or other prosocial acts performed by someone after having done something harmful in order to compensate for the harm done (not necessarily to the person harmed).

replication (1) Reproducing the results of a scientific study.

representativeness heuristic (2) A cognitive shortcut for making judgments in conditions of uncertainty, whereby we estimate the likelihood that a person or object belongs to a particular category on the basis of how much resemblance there is to members of that category.

resource dilemma (10) A decision faced by individuals about how much of a public resource they should take for their own good, in circumstances where the rational individual choices produce an irrational collective outcome (also known as the "problem of the commons").

response facilitation (6) Increase in the likelihood that a behaviour will occur in a given situation as a result of modelling influence.

reverse discrimination (13) Excessively positive actions towards members of a specific group, which may not reflect positive attitudes.

revolutionary movement (14) Social movement that seeks to overthrow the existing social order and replace it with something else.

risky shift effect (12) Tendency for some group decisions to involve higher levels of risk than the average individual decision (see *polarization effect*).

role play (1) A method in which subjects are given a description of a situation by the experimenter and then asked to behave as they think other people would in such a situation.

rumour (14) Information, often distorted, which is transmitted through a collectivity.

sample (1) A relatively small group of subjects taken to be representative of a larger, defined population of interest.

scapegoating (13) A response to frustration whereby the individual displaces aggression onto a socially disapproved out-group.

schema (2) An organized system of cognitions about something such as an event, a role, a type of person or ourselves.

scope of justice (15) The range of situations in which an individual takes into account issues of right and wrong or fairness.

secondary baby talk (7) Speech register similar to that used to talk to babies but used to speak to certain categories of adults, such as the elderly and infirm.

secondary prevention (16) Measures taken to detect and treat an illness at the earliest possible stage.

self-concept (3) The sum of feelings, beliefs and impressions that individuals have of themselves.

self-discrepancy theory (3) A theory based on the premise that the gaps between actual and possible selves can lead to emotional difficulty.

self-enhancement bias (3, 12) The extent to which individuals seek to maintain or improve their evaluation of themselves.

self-fulfilling prophecy (8, 13) A phenomenon whereby people's expectations lead them to behave in a way that causes the expectations to come true.

self-handicapping (3) Acting in a way that will interfere with the successful performance of a subsequent task in order to protect one's self-esteem from the effects of failure.

self-monitors (3) People who are unusually sensitive to the subtle responses of others in evaluating their own behaviour.

self–other overlap (9) The extent to which a potential helper feels a sense of oneness with the person to be helped.

self-presentation (3) Acting in ways that create or maintain a positive image of ourselves.

self-reference effect (3) People's tendency to remember information better when they can relate it to themselves.

self-schema (3) An organized set of cognitions, impressions and memories about ourselves.

self-serving bias (2) Attributions motivated by a desire to protect or enhance our own self-esteem.

self-verification (3) Seeking feedback from others that is consistent with our actual self-concept.

semantic differential (4) The rating of a concept along a set of polar adjective scales.

sensory overload (14) The hypothesis that when people are exposed to too much stimulation, sensory inputs are received too fast to be processed. People react by screening out much of the stimulation, paying attention only to what seems important or unusual.

simulation (1) A study using an artificially created situation made to resemble a real-life situation, in which subjects are observed as they act and react to each other and to the situation.

simulation heuristic (2) A cognitive shortcut by which we estimate the likelihood of an event by the ease with which we can imagine it occurring.

single group pre-test/post-test design (1) Quasi-experiment in which subjects are measured before and after some event.

sleeper effect (5) Tendency for a communication to increase in persuasiveness over time when emanating from a low-credibility source.

social comparison theory (1, 3, 8) A tendency for people to evaluate themselves in relation to other people, especially when a situation is ambiguous or uncertain.

social differentiation (12) Tendency to overestimate the similarities among members of the same category and to overestimate the differences among members of different categories.

social exchange theory (1, 8, 10) A view of social interaction based on the rewards and costs that people provide for each other.

social facilitation (6) An increment in performance resulting from the presence of one or more other individuals.

social identification (12) The process whereby individuals define themselves with respect to other people.

social identity model of individuation (14) Conformity to the norms associated with the specific group or social identity rather than the general norms of the larger society.

social learning theory (1) A learning experience through the observation of others' actions and the consequences of those actions.

social loafing (6) A decrease in individual effort when coacting with others.

social loneliness (8) Loneliness reflecting a lack of a network of friends.

social modelling (6) Social influence experienced as a result of observing the behaviour of someone else.

social movement (14) A spontaneous, large collectivity constituted in support of a set of purposes shared by the members.

social penetration process (8) As a relationship develops over time, self-disclosure increases in both breadth (range of topics discussed) and depth (intimacy).

social psychology (Introduction) The discipline that sets out to understand how the thoughts, feelings and behaviours of individuals are influenced by the actual, imagined or implied presence of others.

social representation (2) A schema about persons, roles and events not based solely on personal experience but developed by a group or society and communicated or taught to its members.

social support (16) Relationships with others that provide encouragement, acceptance and assistance.

sociobiology (9) An evolutionary theory which states that behaviours are subject to the same evolutionary processes that affect physical characteristics.

sociolinguistic competence (7) Skill at using a language in a social context.

speech act theory (7) The study of correspondence (or lack thereof) between what the speaker says and what is intended (i.e., direct versus indirect speech acts).

speech register (7) Combination of intonation and pitch within a given speech style that is used in speaking to a particular type of person or in a particular situation.

speech style (7) Manner of speaking a language that is particular to a specific geographic location, social class or educational level.

standard speech style (7) A style of speaking defined socially as desirable or preferable.

statistical significance (1) Refers to results that are unlikely to have occurred by chance.

status marking (14) Actions taken by people to distinguish themselves from people of a different social status.

stereotype (2, 13) A rigid set of cognitions about a group that are applied indiscriminately to all members of the group.

stereotype threat (13) Stereotyped individuals are at a disadvantage in a performance situation if they have internalized the stereotype.

stimulus pairing (11) An effect whereby a situational cue (e.g., a gun) elicits an aggressive response because of its past classically conditioned association with violence.

subtractive bilingualism (7) Bilingualism of members of a minority language group for whom bilingualism is a threat to the continued importance or existence of their first language in that society.

superordinate goal (10) An outcome desired and shared by parties who must cooperate in order to achieve it.

survey method (1) A research technique involving going out and asking questions about the phenomenon of interest, usually using a structured interview or a questionnaire.

symbolic beliefs (13) Beliefs that a particular group threatens or supports social values and norms.

sympathy (9) A heightened awareness of another person's suffering and a desire to eliminate it.

terminal values (4) Preferences for certain end-states of life, such as freedom or equality.

Thanatos (11) According to Freud, a death instinct that at an unconscious level promotes a return to an inanimate state.

theory (1) A set of statements and assumptions that link concepts and hypotheses to observations.

threat (10) A communication that the other person or group will suffer negative consequences unless a demand is complied with.

trade-off reasoning (4) In conditions of value pluralism, a flexible way of thinking in which all sides of an issue are considered, leading to the selection of one value over another.

triangular model of love (8) A model that defines love in terms of intimacy, passion and commitment.

Type-A personality (16) A pattern of competitiveness, impatience and unexpressed anger.

upward comparison (3) A tendency to evaluate ourselves with reference to people who are higher in status or advantage.

utility (10) The importance or value of an outcome to the recipient.

validity (1) Extent to which a measure corresponds to the characteristic that it is intended to measure.

value (4) Central, higher-order set of preferences for goals in life and ways of living that are felt to be ideal and important.

value pluralism (4) Competing values associated with a particular issue.

value-expressive function (4) An aspect of an attitude that serves to demonstrate a uniqueness and that reflects one's values.

value justification effect (4) Justifying a particular attitude by relating it to a specific value.

vicarious reinforcement (6) A positive feeling of reward in response to observing someone else being rewarded.

volunteerism (9) Use of volunteers to perform charitable or educational work.

warm glow of success (9) An increased tendency to engage in prosocial behaviour under the influence of a good mood induced by success.

weapons effect (11) Cues associated with aggression can promote aggression from an individual in a state of autonomic arousal.

weighted averaging model (2) A model of impression formation in which our overall evaluation of a person consists of the average of how we rate a person on various characteristics, influenced more by those characteristics judged to be more important.

zero-sum game (10) A conflict situation in which one party's gains match exactly the losses of the other.

Bibliography

ABEL, G.G., BARLOW, D.H., BLANCHARD, E., & GUILD, D. (1977). The components of rapists' sexual arousal. *Archives of General Psychiatry, 34,* 895–903.

ABELLA, I., & TROPER, H. (1983). *None is too many.* Toronto: Lester & Orpen Dennys.

ABELSON, R.P. (1968). Psychological implication. In R.P. Abelson, E. Aronson, W.J. McGuire, T.M. Newcomb, M.J. Rosenberg & P.H. Tannenbaum (Eds.), *Theories of cognitive consistency: A sourcebook.* Chicago: Rand McNally.

ABOUD, F. (1988). *Children and prejudice.* Oxford: Basil Blackwell.

ABOUD, F.E., & DOYLE, A.B. (1996). Does talk of race foster prejudice or tolerance in children? *Canadian Journal of Behavioural Science, 28,* 161–170.

ABRAMSON, L.Y., SELIGMAN, M.E.P., & TEASDALE, J.D. (1978). Learned helplessness in humans: Critique and reformulation. *Journal of Abnormal and Social Psychology, 87,* 49–74.

ADACHI, K. (1976). *The enemy that never was: A history of the Japanese Canadians.* Toronto: McClelland and Stewart.

ADAIR, J.G. (1973). *The human subject.* Boston: Little, Brown.

ADAIR, J.G. (1980). Psychology at the turn of the century: Crises, challenges, promises. *Canadian Psychologist, 21,* 165–178.

ADAIR, J.G. (2001). Ethics of psychological research: New policies; continuing issues; new concerns. *Canadian Psychology, 42,* 25–37.

ADAIR, J.G., & SPINNER, B. (1983). Task perceptions and behavioural expectations: A process-oriented approach to subject behaviour in experiments. *Canadian Journal of Behavioural Science, 15,* 130–141.

ADAIR, J.G., DUSHENKO, T.W., & LINDSAY, R.C.L. (1985). Ethical regulations and their impact on research practice. *American Psychologist, 40,* 59–72.

ADAIR, J.G., PAVIO, A., & RITCHIE, P. (1996). Psychology in Canada. *Annual Review of Psychology, 47,* 341–370.

ADAMS, G., & HUSTON, T. (1975). Social perception of middle-aged persons varying in physical attractiveness. *Developmental Psychology, 11,* 657–658.

ADAMS, J.L. (1980). *Conceptual blockbusting: A guide to better ideas* (2nd ed.). New York: Norton.

ADAMS, J.S. (1965). Inequity in social exchange. In L. Berkowitz (Ed.), *Advances in experimental social psychology* (Vol. 2). (pp. 267–295). New York: Academic Press.

ADAMS, M. (2003). Fire and ice. The United States, Canada and the myth of converging values. Toronto: Penguin Books.

ADLER, N.E., BOYCE, T., CHESNEY, M.A., COHEN, S., FOLKMAN, S., KAHN, R.L., & SYME, S.L. (1994). Socioeconomic status and health: The challenge of the gradient. *American Psychologist, 49,* 15–24.

ADLER, N.J. (1999a). Global leaders: Women of influence. In G.N. Powell (Ed.), *Handbook of gender and work* (pp. 239–261). Thousand Oaks, CA: Sage Publications.

ADLER, N.J. (1999b). Global leadership: Women leaders. In W.H. Mobley (Ed), *Advances in global leadership* (Vol. 1). (pp. 49–73). Stamford, CT: Jai Press, Inc.

ADORNO, T.W., FRENKEL-BRUNSWICK, E., LEVINSON, D.J., & SANFORD, R.N. (1950). *The authoritarian personality.* New York: Harper.

Advances in experimental social psychology (Vol. 7). (pp. 152–215). New York: Academic Press.

AGUIRRE, B.E., QUARANTELLI, E.L., & MENDOZA, J.L. (1988). The collective behaviour of fads: The characteristics, effects and career of streaking. *American Sociological Review, 535,* 569–584.

AIELLO, J.R., & THOMPSON, D.E. (1980). Personal space, crowding and spatial behavior in a cultural context. In I. Altman, J.F. Wohlwill, & A. Rapaport (Eds.), *Human behavior and environment: Vol. 4. Environment and culture.* New York: Plenum Press.

AJZEN, I. (1985). From intentions to actions: A theory of planned behavior. In J. Kuhl & J. Beckmann (Eds.), *Action-control: From cognition to behavior* (pp. 11–39). Heidelberg: Springer.

AJZEN, I. (1987). Attitudes, traits and actions: Dispositional prediction of behaviour in personality and social psychology. In L. Berkowitz (Ed.), *Advances in experimental social psychology* (Vol. 20). (pp. 1–63). New York: Academic Press.

AJZEN, I., & FISHBEIN, M. (1980). *Understanding attitudes and predicting social behavior.* Englewood Cliffs, NJ: Prentice-Hall.

ALBARRACIN, D., MCNATT, P.S., KLEIN, C., HO, R.M., MITCHELL, A.L., & KUMKALE, G.T. (2003). Persuasive communications to change actions; An analysis of behavioral and cognitive impact in HIV prevention. *Health Psychology 22,* 166–177.

ALBRIGHT, D.E., & HAZLER, R.J. (1995). A right to die? Ethical dilemmas of euthanasia. *Counselling and Values, 39,* 177–189.

ALBRIGHT, L., & FORZIATI, C. (1995). Cross-situational consistency and perceptual accuracy in leadership. *Personality and Social Psychology Bulletin, 21,* 1269–1276.

ALCOCK, J.E. (1975). Motivation in an asymmetric bargaining situation: A cross-cultural study. *International Journal of Psychology, 10,* 69–81.

ALCOCK, J.E. (1978, June). Social psychology and the importation of values. Annual Conference of the Canadian Psychological Association, Ottawa.

ALCOCK, J.E. (1986). Chronic pain and the injured worker. *Canadian Psychology, 27,* 196–203.

ALCOCK, J.E. (1996). Training, experience and the detection of lying. *Legal Medical Quarterly, 20,* 20–23.

ALCOCK, J.E. (1997). Social psychology and mental health. In S.W. Sadava & D.R. McCreary (Eds.), *Applied Social Psychology* (pp. 113–135). Upper Saddle River, NJ: Prentice-Hall.

ALCOCK, J.E., & MANSELL, D. (1977). Predisposition and behaviour in a collective dilemma. *Journal of Conflict Resolution, 21,* 443–458.

ALEXANDER, B.K., & HADAWAY, P.F. (1982). Opiate addiction: The case for an adaptive orientation. *Psychological Bulletin, 92,* 367–381.

ALEXANDER, M.J., & HIGGINS, E.T. (1993). Emotional trade-off of becoming a parent: How social roles influence self-discrepancy effects. *Journal of Personality and Social Psychology, 65,* 1259–1269.

ALLEGEIER, E.R., & BYRNE, D. (1973). Attraction toward the opposite sex as a determinant of physical proximity. *Journal of Social Psychology, 90,* 213–219.

ALLEN, J.B., KENRICK, D.T., LINDER, D.E., & MCCALL, M.A. (1989). Arousal and attraction: A response-facilitation alternative to misattribution and negative-reinforcement models. *Journal of Personality and Social Psychology, 57,* 261–270.

ALLEN, V.L., & LEVINE, J.M. (1971). Social support and conformity: The role of independent assessment of reality. *Journal of Experimental and Social Psychology, 7,* 48–58.

ALLISON, S.T., & MESSICK, D.M. (1985). Effects of experience on performance in a replenishable resource trap. *Journal of Personality and Social Psychology, 49*, 943–948.

ALLOY, L.B., & ABRAMSON, L.Y. (1979). Judgements of contingency in depressed and non-depressed students: Sadder but wiser. *Journal of Experimental Psychology: General, 108*, 441–485.

ALLPORT, F.H. (1924). *Social psychology*. Boston: Houghton-Mifflin.

ALLPORT, G.W. (1935). Attitudes. In C.M. Murchison (Ed.), *Handbook of Social Psychology* (pp. 798–844). Worchester, MA: Clark University Press.

ALLPORT, G.W. (1954). *The nature of prejudice*. Reading, MA: Addison-Wesley.

ALLPORT, G.W., & KRAMER, B.M. (1946). Some roots of prejudice. *Journal of Psychology, 22*, 9–39.

ALLPORT, G.W., & POSTMAN, L.J. (1947). *The psychology of rumour*. New York: Holt, Rinehart & Winston.

ALLPORT, G.W., & VERNON, P.E. (1931). *A study of values*. Boston: Houghton-Mifflin.

ALTEMEYER, B. (1981). *Right-wing authoritarianism*. Winnipeg: University of Manitoba Press.

ALTEMEYER, B. (1988). *Enemies of freedom*. San Francisco: Jossey-Bass.

ALTEMEYER, B., & HUNSBERGER, B. (1992). Authoritarianism, religious fundamentalism, quest, and prejudice. *The International Journal for the Psychology of Religion, 2*, 113–133.

ALTEMEYER, B., & HUNSBERGER, B. (1993). Religion and prejudice: Lessons not learned from the past: Reply to Gorsuch. *International Journal for the Psychology of Religion, 3*, 33–37.

ALTMAN, I. (1973). Reciprocity of interpersonal exchange. *Journal of the Theory of Social Behavior, 3*, 249–261.

ALTMAN, I. (1975). *The environment and social behavior: Privacy, personal space, territory, crowding*. Monterey, CA: Brooks/Cole.

ALTMAN, I. (1976). Privacy: A conceptual analysis. *Environment and Behavior, 8*, 7–29.

ALTMAN, I., & TAYLOR, D.A. (1973). *Social penetration: The development of interpersonal relationships*. New York: Holt, Rinehart & Winston.

ALTMAN, I., & VINSEL, A.M. (1977). Personal space: An analysis of E. T. Hall's proxemics framework. In I. Altman & J.F. Wohlwill (Eds.), *Human behavior and environment: Advances in theory and research* (pp. 181–259). New York: Plenum.

ALTMAN, I., VINSEL, A., & BROWN, B.A. (1981). Dialectic conceptions in social psychology: An application to social penetration and privacy regulation. In L. Berkowitz (Ed.), *Advances in experimental social psychology* (Vol. 14). (pp. 107–160). New York: Academic Press.

AMATO, P.R. (1983). Helping behavior in urban and rural settings: Field studies based on a taxonomic organization of helping episodes. *Journal of Personality and Social Psychology, 45*, 571–586.

AMERICAN PSYCHOLOGICAL ASSOCIATION. (1985). *Violence on TV. A social issue release from the Board of Social and Ethical Responsibility for Psychology*. Washington, DC: Author.

AMERICAN PSYCHOLOGICAL ASSOCIATION (2002). Ethical principles of psychologists and code of conduct. *American Psychologist, 57*, 1060–1073.

AMICHAI-HAMBURGER, Y., & BEN-ARTZI, E. (2003). Loneliness and Internet use. *Computers in Human Behavior, 19*, 71–80.

AMIR, Y. (1976). The role of intergroup contact in change of prejudice and ethnic relations. In P.A. Katz (Ed.), *Towards the elimination of racism* (pp. 245–308). Elmsford, NY: Pergamon Press.

ANDERSON, B.L., CYRANOWSKI, J.M., & ESPINDLE, D. (1999). Men's sexual self-schema. *JPSP, 76*, 645–661.

ANDERSON, C.A. (2001). Heat and violence. *Current Directions in Psychological Science, 10*, 33–38.

ANDERSON, C.A., BENJAMIN, A.J. JR., & BARTHOLOW, B.D. (1998). Does the gun pull the trigger? Automatic priming effects of weapon pictures and weapon names. *Psychological Science, 9*, 308–314.

ANDERSON, C.A., & BUSHMAN, B.J. (2001). Effects of violent video games on aggressive behavior, aggressive cognition, aggressive affect, physiological arousal, and prosocial behavior: A meta-analytic review of the scientific literature. *Psychological Science, 12*, 353–359.

ANDERSON, C.A., & BUSHMAN, B.J. (2002). Human aggression. *Annual Review of Psychology, 53*, 27–51.

ANDERSON, C.A., & SEDIKIDES, C. (1990). Thinking about people. Contributions of a typological alternative to associationistic and dimensional models of person perception. *Journal of Personality and Social Psychology, 60*, 203–217.

ANDERSON, C.A., LEPPER, M.R., & ROSS, L. (1980). Perseverance of social theories: The role of explanation in the persistence of discredited information. *Journal of Personality and Social Psychology, 39*, 1037–1049.

ANDERSON, N.H. (1959). Test of a model of opinion change. *Journal of Abnormal and Social Psychology, 59*, 371–381.

ANDERSON, N.H. (1965). Adding versus averaging as a stimulus combination rule in impression formation. *Journal of Experimental Psychology, 70*, 394–400.

ANDERSON, N.H. (1978). Cognitive algebra: Integration theory applied to social attribution. In L. Berkowitz (Ed.), *Cognitive theories in social psychology*. New York: Academic Press.

ANDERSON, N.H., & HUBERT, S. (1963). Effects of concomitant verbal recall on order effects in personality impression formation. *Journal of Verbal Learning and Verbal Behavior, 2*, 379–391.

ANDREAS, C.R. (1969). "To receive from kings..." An examination of government-to-government aid and its unintended consequences. *Journal of Social Issues, 25*, 167–180.

ANGELL, M. (1985). Disease as a reflection of the psyche. *New England Journal of Medicine, 312*, 1570–1572.

ANTHONY, S. (1973). Anxiety and rumor. *Journal of Social Psychology, 89*, 91–98.

APFELBAUM, E., & LUBEK, I. (1976). Resolution vs. revolution? The theory of conflicts in question. In L. Strickland, F. Aboud, & E. Gergen (Eds.), *Social psychology in transition* (pp. 71–94). New York: Plenum.

APFELBAUM, E., & MCGUIRE, G.R. (1986). Models of suggestive influence and the disqualification of the social crowd. In C.F. Graumann & S. Moscovici (Eds.), *Changing conceptions of crowd mind and behavior* (pp. 27–50). New York: Springer-Verlag.

ARANOFF, C. (1974). Old age in prime time. *Journal of Communication, 24*, 86–87.

ARCHER, J. (1976). Biological explanations of psychological sex differences. In B. Lloyd & J. Archer (Eds.), *Exploring sex differences* (pp. 241–266). New York: Academic Press.

ARCHER, J. (2000a). Sex differences in aggression between heterosexual partners. *Psychological Bulletin, 126*, 651–680.

ARCHER, J. (2000b). Sex differences in physical aggression to partners: A reply to Frieze (2000), Leaery (2000), and White, Smith, Koss and Figueredo (2000). *Psychological Bulletin, 126*, 697–702.

ARCHER, R.L., DIAZ-LOVING, R., GOLLWITZER, P.M., DAVIS, M.H., & FOUSHEE, H.C. (1981). The role of dispositional empathy and social evaluation in the empathic mediation of helping. *Journal of Personality and Social Psychology, 40*, 786–796.

ARGYLE, M. (1969). *Social interaction*. London: Tavistock.

ARGYLE, M. (1971). *The psychology of interpersonal behaviour.* Harmondsworth: Penguin Books.

ARGYLE, M. (1975). *Bodily communication.* London: Methuen & Co.

ARGYLE, M., & DEAN, J. (1965). Eye-contact, distance and affiliation. *Sociometry, 28,* 289–304.

ARKIN, R.M., & BAUMGARDNER, A.H. (1985). Self-handicapping. In J.H. Harvey & G. Weary (Eds.), *Attributions: Basic issues and applications* (pp. 169–202). New York: Academic Press.

ARMSTRONG. E.G. (1992). The rhetoric of violence in rap and country music. *Sociological Inquiry, 63,* 64–83.

ARNOLD, M.L. (2000). Stage, sequence, and sequels: Changing conceptions of morality, post-Kohlberg. *Educational Psychology Review, 12,* 365–383.

ARON, A., & WESTBAY, L. (1996). Dimensions of the prototype of love. *Journal of Personality and Social Psychology, 70,* 535–551.

ARON, A., PARIS, M., & ARON, E.N. (1995). Falling in love: Prospective studies of self-concept change. *Journal of Personality and Social Psychology, 69,* 1102–1112.

ARONSON, E. (1968). Dissonance theory: Progress and problems. In R.P. Abelson, E. Aronson, W.J. McGuire, T.M. Newcomb, M.J. Rosenberg, & P.H. Tannenbaum (Eds.), *Theories of cognitive consistency: A sourcebook* (pp. 5–27). Chicago: Rand-McNally.

ARONSON, E. (1984). *The social animal* (4th ed.). New York: W.H. Freeman.

ARONSON, E., & CARLSMITH, J.M. (1963). Effect of the severity of threat on the devaluation of forbidden behavior. *Journal of Abnormal and Social Psychology, 66,* 584–588.

ARONSON, E., & CARLSMITH, J.M. (1968). Experimentation in social psychology. In G. Lindzey, & E. Aronson, (Eds.), *Handbook of social psychology* (2nd ed.). (Vol. 2). (pp. 1–79). Reading, MA: Addison-Wesley.

ARONSON, E., & GOLDEN, B.W. (1962). The effect of relevant and irrelevant aspects of communicator credibility on attitude change. *Journal of Personality, 30,* 135–146.

ARONSON, E., & LINDER, D. (1965). Gain and loss of esteem as determinants of interpersonal attractiveness. *Journal of Experimental Social Psychology, 1,* 156–171.

ARONSON, E., & MILLS, J. (1959). The effect of severity of initiation on liking for a group. *Journal of Abnormal and Social Psychology, 59,* 177–181.

ARONSON, E., WILLERMAN, B., & FLOYD, J. (1966). The effect of a pratfall on increasing personal attractiveness. *Psychonomic Science, 4,* 157–158.

ARVEY, R.D. (1979). Unfair discrimination in the employment interview: Legal and psychological aspects. *Psychological Bulletin, 86,* 736–765.

ASCH, S.E. (1946). Forming impressions of personality. *Journal of Abnormal and Social Psychology, 41,* 258–290.

ASCH, S.E. (1951). Effects of group pressure upon the modification and distortion of judgements. In H. Guetzkow (Ed.), *Groups, leadership and men* (pp. 177–190). Pittsburgh: Carnegie Press.

ASHTON, M.C., & ESSES, V.M. (1999). Stereotype accuracy: Estimating the academic performance of ethnic groups. *Personality and Social Psychology Bulletin, 25,* 225–236.

ASHTON, N.L., SHAW, M.E., & WORSHAM, A.P. (1980). Affective reactions to interpersonal distances by friends and strangers. *Bulletin of the Psychonomic Society, 15,* 306–308.

ASMUNDSON, G.J.G., STEIN, M.B., & MCCREARY, D.R. (2002). Post-traumatic stress disorder symptoms influence health status of deployed peacekeepers and nondeployed military personnel. *Journal of Nervous and Mental Disease, 190,* 807–815.

ATHANASIOU, R., & YASHIOKA, G. (1973). The spatial character of friendship formation. *Environmental Behavior, 5,* 43–65.

ATKINSON, M.L. (1986). The perception of social categories: Implications for social comparison process. In J.M. Olson, C.P. Herman, & M.P. Zanna (Eds.), *Relative deprivation and social comparison: The Ontario symposium* (Vol. 4). (pp. 177–134). Hillsdale, NJ: Erlbaum.

ATWOOD, M. (1972). *Survival.* Toronto: House of Anansi.

AUSTIN, W. (1979). Justice, freedom, and self-interest in intergroup conflict. In W.G. Austin, & S. Worchel (Eds.), *The social psychology of intergroup relations* (pp. 121–144). Monterey, CA: Brooks/Cole.

AVIO, K.L. (1987). *The quality of mercy: Exercise of the Royal Prerogative in Canada.* Unpublished manuscript, Department of Economics, University of Victoria.

AXELROD, R., & DION, D. (1988). The further evolution of cooperation. *Science, 242,* 1385–1390.

AZUMA, H. (1984). Secondary control as a heterogeneous category. *American Psychologist, 9,* 970–971.

AZZI, A.E. (1992). Procedural justice and the allocation of power in intergroup relations: Studies in the United States and South Africa. *Personality and Social Psychology Bulletin, 18,* 736–747.

BACKHOUSE, C. (1999). *Colour-coded: A legal history of racism in Canada, 1900–1950.* Toronto: The Osgoode Society for Legal Canadian History.

BACKMAN, C.W., & SECORD, P.F. (1959). The effect of perceived liking on interpersonal attraction. *Human Relations, 12,* 379–384.

BAER, D.E., & CURTIS, J.E. (1984). French-Canadian/English-Canadian differences in values: National survey findings. *Canadian Journal of Sociology, 9,* 405–427.

BAILENSON, J.N., BLASCOVICH, J., BEALL, A.C., & LOOMIS, J.M. (2003). Interpersonal distance in immersive virtual environments. *Personality and Social Psychology Bulletin, 29,* 819–833.

BAILEY, P., ONWUEGBUZIE, A.J., & DALEY, C.E. (2000). Correlates of anxiety at three stages of the foreign language learning process. *Journal of Language and Social Psychology, 19,* 474–490.

BAKAN, D. (1966). *The duality of human existence.* Chicago: Rand McNally.

BALDWIN, M.W. (1992). Relational schemas and the processing of social information. *Psychological Bulletin, 112,* 461–468.

BALDWIN, M.W., & SINCLAIR, L. (1996). Self-esteem and "if … then" contingencies of interpersonal acceptance. *Journal of Personality and Social Psychology, 71,* 1130–1141.

BALDWIN, M.W., FEHR, B., KEEDIAN, E., SEIDEL, M., & THOMSON, D.W. (1993). An exploration of the relational schemata underlying attachment styles: Self-report and lexical decision approaches. *Personality and Social Psychology Bulletin, 19,* 746–754.

BALL-ROKEACH, S.J., ROKEACH, M., & GRUBE, J.W. (1984). *The great American values test. Influencing behavior and belief through television.* New York: The Free Press.

BANDURA, A. (1965). Influence of a model's reinforcement contingencies on the acquisition of imitative responses. *Journal of Personality and Social Psychology, 1,* 589–595.

BANDURA, A. (1973). *Aggression: A social learning analysis.* Englewood Cliffs, NJ: Prentice-Hall.

BANDURA, A. (1974). Behavior theories and the models of man. *American Psychologist, 29,* 859–869.

BANDURA, A. (1977). *Social learning theory.* Englewood Cliffs, NJ: Prentice-Hall.

BANDURA, A. (1983). Psychological mechanisms of aggression. In R.G. Geen, & E.I. Donnerstein, (Eds.), *Aggression: Theoretical and empirical reviews* (Vol. 1). (pp. 1–40). New York: Academic Press.

BANDURA, A. (1986). *Social foundations of thought and action: A social cognitive theory*. Englewood Cliffs NJ: Prentice Hall.

BANDURA, A., & WALTERS, R. (1963). *Social learning and personality development*. New York: Holt, Rinehart & Winston.

BANDURA, A., ROSS, D., & ROSS, S.A. (1963a). Vicarious reinforcement and imitative learning. *Journal of Abnormal and Social Psychology, 67*, 601–607.

BANDURA, A., ROSS, D., & ROSS, S.A. (1963b). A comparative test of the status envy, social power, and secondary reinforcement theories of identificatory learning. *Journal of Abnormal and Social Psychology, 67*, 527–534.

BANK, B.J., & HANSFORD, S.L. (2000). Gender and friendship: Why are men's same-sex friendships less intimate and supportive? *Personal Relationships, 7*, 63–78.

BANUAZIZI, A., & MOVAHEDI, S. (1975). Interpersonal dynamics in a simulated prison: A methodological analysis. *American Psychologist, 30*, 152–160.

BARBER, T.X. (1976). *Hypnosis: A scientific approach*. New York: Psychological Dimensions.

BARCIA, D. (1985). Communication between psychiatrists and general practitioners. *Actas Luso-Espanolas Neurol. Psiquiat. Cienc. Afines, 13*, 259. Cited by Bourhis, Roth, & MacQueen, 1989.

BARDWICK, J.M. (1971). *Psychology of women: A study of bio-cultural conflicts*. New York: Harper & Row.

BARGH, J.A., & CERNY, R. (1983). *Automatic and conscious processes in impression formation*. Unpublished manuscript, New York University.

BARGH, J.A., & CHARTRAND, T.L. (1999). The unbearable automaticity of being. *American Psychologist, 54*, 462–479.

BARKOWITZ, P.B., & BRIGHAM, J.C. (1982). Recognition of faces: Own-race bias, incentive and time delay. *Journal of Applied Social Psychology, 12*, 255–268.

BARON, R.A. (1983). The control of human aggression: An optimistic perspective. *Journal of Social and Clinical Psychology, 1*, 97–119.

BARON, R.A. (1998). Cognitive mechanisms in entrepreneurship: Why and when entrepreneurs think differently than other people. *Journal of Business Venturing, 13*, 275–294.

BARON, R.A. (2000). Psychological perspectives on entrepreneurship: Cognitive and social factors in entrepreneurs; success. *Current Directions on Psychological Science, 9*, 15–18.

BARON, R.A. (in press). Counterfactual thinking and venture formation: The potential effects of thinking about "what might have been." *Journal of Business Venturing, 15*, 79–92.

BARON, R.M. (1997). On making terror management theory less motivational and more social. *Psychological Inquiry, 8*, 21–22.

BARON, R.M., & RODIN, J. (1978). Perceived control and crowding stress: Processes mediating the impact of spatial and social density. In A. Baum, & Y. Epstein (Eds.), *Human response to crowding*. Hillsdale, NJ: Erlbaum Associates.

BARON, R.S. (1986). Distraction—conflict theory: Progress and problems. In L. Berkowitz (Ed.), *Advances in experimental social psychology* (Vol. 19). (pp. 1–40). New York: Academic Press.

BAR-TAL, D. (1976). *Prosocial behavior*. Washington, DC: Hemisphere.

BAR-TAL, D. (1986, June). Group political beliefs. Annual Meeting, International Association of Political Psychology, Amsterdam.

BARTHOLOMEW, K., & HOROWITZ, L.M. (1991). Attachment style among young adults: A test of a model. *Journal of Personality and Social Psychology, 61*, 226–244.

BARTHOLOMEW, R.E., & SIROIS, F. (1996). Epidemic hysteria in schools: An international and historical overview. *Educational Studies, 22*, 285–311.

BASS, B.M. (1990). From transactional to transformational leadership: Learning to share the vision. *Organizational Dynamics, 18*, 19–31.

BATSON, C.D. (1987). Prosocial behavior: Is it ever truly altruistic? In L. Berkowitz (Ed.), *Advances in experimental social psychology* (Vol. 20). (pp. 65–162). Cambridge: Cambridge University Press.

BATSON, C.D. (1990). How social an animal? The human capacity for caring. *American Psychologist, 45*, 336–346.

BATSON, C.D., & GRAY, R.A. (1981). Religious orientation and helping behaviour: Responding to one's own or the victim's needs? *Journal of Personality and Social Psychology, 40*, 511–520.

BATSON, C.D., & VENTIS, W.L. (1982). *The religious experience: A social psychological perspective*. New York: Oxford University Press.

BATSON, C.D., AHMAD, N., YIN, J., BEDELL, S.J., JOHNSON, J.W., TEMPLIN, C.M., & WHITESIDE, A. (1999). Two threats to the common good: Self-interested egoism and empathy-induced altruism. *Personality and Social Psychology Bulletin, 25*, 3–16.

BATSON, C.D., BATSON, J.G., GRIFFITT, C.A., BARRIENTOS, S., BRANDT, J.R., SPRENGELMEYER, P., & BAYLY, M.J. (1989). Negative-state relief and the empathy-altruism hypothesis. *Journal of Personality and Social Psychology, 56*, 922–933.

BATSON, C.D., DUNCAN, B., ACKERMAN, P., BUCKLEY, T., & BIRCH, K. (1981). Is empathic emotion a source of altruistic motivation? *Journal of Personality and Social Psychology, 40*, 290–302.

BATSON, C.D., DYCK, J.L., BRANDT, J.R., BATSON, J.G., POWELL, A.L., MCMASTER, M.R., & GRIFFITT, C. (1988). Five studies testing two new egoistic alternatives to the empathy-altruism hypothesis. *Journal of Personality and Social Psychology, 55*, 52–77.

BATSON, C.D., KOBRYNOWICS, D., DINNERSTEIN, J.L., KAMPF, H.C., & WILSON, A.D. (1997). In a very different voice: Unmasking moral hypocrisy. *Journal of Personality and Social Psychology, 72*, 1335–1348.

BATSON, C.D., OLESON, K.C., WEEKS, J.L., HEALY, S.P., REEVES, P.J., JENNINGS, P., & BROWN, T. (1989). Religious prosocial motivation: Is it altruistic or egoistic? *Journal of Personality and Social Psychology, 57*, 873–884.

BATSON, C.D., SAGER, K., GARST, E., KANG, M., RUBCHINSKY, K., & DAWSON, K. (1997). Is empathy-induced helping due to self-other merging? *Journal of Personality and Social Psychology, 73*, 495–509.

BATSON, C.D., SYMPSON, S.C., HINDMAN, J.L., DECRUZ, P., TODD, R.M., WEEKS, J.L., JENNINGS, G., & BURRIS, C.T. (1996). "I've been there, too": Effect on empathy of a prior experience with a need. *Personality and Social Psychology Bulletin, 22*, 474–482.

BATSON, D.C., & POWELL, A.A. (2003). Altruism and prosocial behaviour. In T. Millon & M. Lerner (Eds.), *Handbook of psychology: Personality and social psychology* (Vol. 5) (pp. 463–484). New York: John Wiley & Sons, Inc.

BAUM, A., & DAVIS, G.E. (1980). Reducing the stress of high-density living: An architectural intervention. *Journal of Personality and Social Psychology, 38*, 417.

BAUM, A., & VALINS, S. (1977). Architecture and social behavior. *Psychological studies and social density*. Hillsdale, NJ: Erlbaum.

BAUM, A., AIELLO, J.R., & CALESNICK, L.E. (1978). Crowding and personal control: Social density and the development of learned helplessness. *Journal of Personality and Social Psychology, 36*, 1000–1011.

BAUMEISTER, R., HUTTON, D., & TICE, D. (1989). Cognitive processing during deliberate self-presentation: How selfpresenters alter and misinterpret the behavior of interaction partners. *Journal of Experimental Social Psychology, 25*, 59–78.

BAUMEISTER, R.F. (1987). How the self became a problem: A psychological review of historical research. *Journal of Personality and Social Psychology, 52*, 163–176.

BAUMEISTER, R.F. (1997). Evil. *Inside human cruelty and violence*. New York: W.H. Freeman and Company.

BAUMEISTER, R.F., & BRATSLAVSKY, E. (1999). Passion, intimacy and time: Passionate love as a function of change in intimacy. *Personality and Social Psychology Bulletin, 3*, 49–67.

BAUMEISTER, R.F., CAMPBELL, J.D., KRUEGER, J.I., & VOHS, K.D. (2003). Does high self-esteem cause better performance, interpersonal success, happiness or healthier lifestyles? *Psychological Science in the Public Interest, 4*, 1–44.

BAUMEISTER, R.F., CHESNER, S.P., SENDERS, P.S., & TICE, D.M. (1988). Who's in charge here? Group leaders do lend help in emergencies. *Personality and Social Psychology Bulletin, 14*, 17–22.

BAUMEISTER, R.F., SMART, L., & BODEN, J.M. (1996). Relation of threatened egoism to violence and aggression: The dark side of high self-esteem. *Psychological Review, 103*, 5–33.

BAUMGARTE, R. (2002). Cross-gender friendships: The troublesome relationship. In R. Goodwin (Ed.), *Inappropriate relationships: The unconventional, the disapproved and the forbidden. LEA series on personal relationships* (pp. 103–125). Manwah, NJ: Erlbaum.

BAUMRIND, D. (1964). Some thoughts on ethics of research: After reading Milgram's "Behavioral study of obedience." *American Psychologist, 19*, 421–423.

BAVELAS, J.B., COATES, L., & JOHNSON, T. (2000). Listeners as co-narrators. *Journal of Personality and Social Psychology, 79*, 941–952.

BEASLEY, R.K., & JOSLYN, M.R. (2001). Cognitive dissonance and post-decision attitude change in six presidential elections. *Political Psychology, 22*, 521–540.

BECHTOLD, A., NACCARATO, M.E., & ZANNA, M.P. (1986, June 19). Need for structure and the prejudice-discrimination link. Annual Meeting of the Canadian Psychological Association, Toronto.

BECKER, M.H. (Ed.). (1974). The health belief model and personal health behavior. *Health Education Monographs, 2* (whole no. 4).

BECKER, W.C. (1964). Consequences of different kinds of parental discipline. In M.L. Hoffman, & L.W. Hoffman (Eds.), *Review of child development research* (Vol. 1). New York: Russell Sage.

BEGANY, J.J., & MILBURN, M.A. (2002). Psychological predictors of sexual harassment: Authoritarianism, hostile sexism and rape myths. *Psychology of Men & Masculinity, 3*, 119–126.

BÉGIN, G. (1976). *The effects of success and failure on helping behaviour*. Unpublished doctoral thesis, McMaster University, Hamilton.

BELL, B.E., & LOFTUS, E.F. (1989). Trivial persuasion in the courtroom: The power of (a few) minor details. *Journal of Personality and Social Psychology, 56*, 669–679.

BELLMAN, S., FORSTER, N., STILL, L., & COOPER, C.L. (2003). Gender differences in the use of social support as a moderator of occupational stress. *Stress & Health, 19*, 45–58.

BEM, D.J. (1970). *Beliefs, attitudes and human affairs*. Belmont, CA: Brooks/Cole.

BEM, D.J. (1972). Self-perception theory. In L. Berkowitz (Ed.), *Advances in experimental social psychology* (Vol. 6). (pp. 1–62). New York: Academic Press.

BEM, D.J., WALLACH, M.A., & KOGAN, N. (1965). Group decision making under risk of aversive consequences. *Journal of Personality and Social Psychology, 1*, 453–560.

BEM, S.L. (1974). The measurement of psychological androgyny. *Journal of Consulting and Clinical Psychology, 42*, 155–162.

BEM, S.L. (1985). Androgyny and gender schema theory: A conceptual and empirical integration. In T. B. Sonderegger (Ed.), *Nebraska symposium on motivation: Psychology and gender* (pp. 179–226). Lincoln, NE: University of Nebraska Press.

BENENSON, J.F., MARKOVITS, H., ROY, R., & DENKO, P. (2003). Behavioural rules underlying learning to share: Effects of development and context. *International Journal of Behavioral Development, 27*, 116–121.

BENNETT, W.C., & FELDMAN, M.S. (1980). *Reconstructing reality in the courtroom: Justice and judgement in American culture*. New Brunswick, NJ: Rutgers University Press.

BENTLER, P.M., & NEWCOMB, M.D. (1978). Longitudinal study of marital success and failure. *Journal of Consulting and Clinical Psychology, 40*, 1053–1070.

BENTLER, P.M., & SPECKART, G. (1981). Attitudes "cause" behavior: A structural equation analysis. *Journal of Personality and Social Psychology, 40*, 226–238.

BENTON, A.A. (1971). Productivity, distributive justice, and bargaining among children. *Journal of Personality and Social Psychology, 18*, 68–78.

BENTON, A.A., KELLEY, H.H., & LIEBLING, B. (1972). Effects of extremity of offers and concession rate on the outcomes of bargaining. *Journal of Personality and Social Psychology, 24*, 73–83.

BERG, K.O., & VIDMAR, N. (1975). Authoritarianism and recall of evidence about criminal behavior. *Journal of Research in Personality, 9*, 147–157.

BERGER, J., WAGNER, D.G., & ZELDITCH, M., JR. (1985). Introduction: Expectation states theory. In J. Berger, & M. Zelditch, Jr. (Eds.), *Status, rewards, and influence* (pp. 1–72). San Francisco: Jossey-Bass.

BERGIN, L., TALLEY, S., & HAMER, L. (2003). Prosocial behaviors of young adolescents: A focus group study. *Journal of Adolescence, 26*, 13–32.

BERGLAS, S. (1987). The self-handicapping model of alcohol abuse. In H.T. Blane, & K.E. Leonard (Eds.), *Psychological theories of drinking and alcoholism* (pp. 305–345). New York: Guilford Press.

BERKES, F., FEENY, D., MCCAY, B.J., & ACHESON, J.M. (1989). The benefits of the Commons. *Nature, 34*, 91–93.

BERKOWITZ, L. (1954). Group standards, cohesiveness, and productivity. *Human Relations, 7*, 509–519.

BERKOWITZ, L. (1971). The contagion of violence: An S-R mediational analysis of some effects of observed aggression. *Nebraska Symposium on Motivation 1970*. Lincoln: University of Nebraska Press.

BERKOWITZ, L. (1973). Reactance and the unwillingness to help others. *Psychological Bulletin, 79*, 310–317.

BERKOWITZ, L. (1983). Aversively stimulated aggression: Some parallels and differences in research with animals and humans. *American Psychologist, 38*, 1135–1144.

BERKOWITZ, L. (1984). Some effects of thoughts of anti- and prosocial influences of media events: A cognitive-neoassociation analysis. *Psychological Bulletin, 95*, 410–427.

BERKOWITZ, L. (1989). Frustration-aggression hypothesis: Examination and reformulation. *Psychological Bulletin, 106*, 59–73.

BERKOWITZ, L. (1990). On the formation and regulation of anger and aggression. *American Psychologist, 45*, 494–503.

BERKOWITZ, L. (1993). Pain and aggression: some findings and implications. *Motivation and Emotion, 17*, 277–93.

BERKOWITZ, L. (1994). Is something missing? Some observations prompted by the cognitive-neoassociationist view of anger and emotional aggression. In L.R. Huesmann (Ed.), *Aggressive behavior: Current perspectives* (pp. 35–57). New York: Plenum Press.

BERKOWITZ, L., & DANIELS, L.R. (1963). Responsibility and dependency. *Journal of Abnormal and Social Psychology, 66*, 664–669.

BERKOWITZ, L., & DONNERSTEIN, E. (1982). External validity is more than skin deep: Some answers to criticism of laboratory experiments. *American Psychologist, 37,* 245–257.

BERKOWITZ, L., & LEPAGE, A. (1967). Weapons as aggression-eliciting stimuli. *Journal of Personality and Social Psychology, 7,* 202–207.

BERKOWITZ, L., & MACAULAY, J. (1971). The contagion of criminal violence. *Sociometry, 34,* 238–260.

BERLYNE, D.E. (1960). *Conflict, arousal and curiosity.* New York: McGraw-Hill.

BERNARD, M.M., MAIO, G.R., & OLSON, J.M. (2003). The vulnerability of values to attacks: Inoculation of values and value-relevant attitudes. *Personality and Social Psychology Bulletin, 29,* 63–75.

BERNSTEIN, W.M., STEPHAN, W.G., & DAVIS, M.H. (1979). Explaining attributions for achievement. A path analytic approach. *Journal of Personality and Social Psychology, 37,* 1810–1821.

BERRY, D.S., & ZEBROWITZ-MCARTHUR, L.Z. (1988). What's in a face? Facial maturity and attribution of legal responsibility. *Personality and Social Psychology Bulletin, 14,* 23–33.

BERRY, J.W. (1978a). Social psychology: Comparative, societal and universal. *Canadian Psychological Review, 19,* 93–104.

BERRY, J.W. (1978b, June). Teaching social psychology IN and OF Canada. Annual Conference of the Canadian Psychological Association, Ottawa.

BERRY, J.W. (1984). Multicultural policy in Canada: A social psychological analysis. *Canadian Journal of Behavioural Science, 16,* 353–370.

BERRY, J.W. (1986). Ethnic minorities and immigrants in a cross-cultural perspective. In L.H. Ekland (Ed.), *Selected papers from the regional IACCP conference: Ethnic minority and immigrant research.* Lisse: Swets and Zeitlinger.

BERRY, J.W. (1987). Finding identity: Separation, integration, assimilation, or marginality. In L. Driedger (Ed.), *Ethnic Canada: Identities and inequalities.* Toronto: Copp-Clark-Pitman.

BERRY, J.W. (1992). Acculturation and adaptation in a new society. *International Migration, 30,* 69–85.

BERRY, J.W. (1999). Intercultural relations in plural societies. *Canadian Psychology, 40,* 12–21.

BERRY, J.W., & KALIN, R. (1993, May). *Multicultural and ethnic attitudes in Canada: An overview of the 1991 national survey.* Canadian Psychological Association annual meeting, Montreal.

BERRY, J.W., & KALIN, R. (1995). Multicultural and ethnic attitudes in Canada: An overview of the 1991 national survey. *Canadian Journal of Behavioural Science, 27,* 301–320.

BERRY, J.W., KALIN, R., & TAYLOR, D. (1977). *Multiculturalism and ethnic attitudes in Canada.* Ottawa: Supply and Services Canada.

BERRY, J.W., WINTROB, R.M., SINDELL, P.S., & MAWHINNEY, T.A. (1982). Psychological adaptations to cultural change among the James Bay Cree. *Naturaliste Canadien, 109,* 965–975.

BERSCHEID, E. (1985). Interpersonal attraction. In G. Lindzey, & E. Aronson (Eds.), *The handbook of social psychology* (3rd ed.). New York: Random House.

BERSCHEID, E. (2003). On stepping on land mines. In R.J. Sternberg (Ed.), *Psychologists defying the crowd: Stories of those who battled the establishment and won* (pp. 33–44). Washington, DC: American Psychological Association.

BERSCHEID, E., & WALSTER, E. (1974a). Physical attractiveness. In L. Berkowitz (Ed.), *Advances in experimental social psychology* (Vol. 7), pp. 152–215. New York Academic Press.

BERSCHEID, E., & WALSTER, E. (1974b). A little bit about love. In T.L. Huston (Ed.), *Foundations of interpersonal attraction.* (pp. 356–382). New York: Academic Press.

BERSCHEID, E., & WALSTER, E. (1978). Interpersonal attraction. Reading, MA: Addison-Wesley.

BERSOFF, D. (1987). Social science data and the Supreme Court: Lockhart as a case in point. *American Psychologist, 42,* 52–58.

BERTON, P. (1972). *Klondike: The last great gold rush, 1896–1899.* Toronto: McClelland & Stewart.

BEST, J.A., FLAG, B.R., TOWSON, S.M.J., RYAN, K.B., PERRY, C.L., BROWN, K.S., KERSELL, K.W., & D'AVERNAS, J.R. (1984). Smoking prevention and the concept of risk. *Journal of Applied Social Psychology, 14,* 257–273.

BETTENCOURT, B.A., & MILLER, N. (1996). Gender differences in aggression as a function of provocation: A meta-analysis. *Psychological Bulletin, 119,* 422–447.

BIBBY, R. (2002). *Restless gods: The renaissance of religion in Canada.* Toronto: Stoddart.

BICKMAN, L. (1972). Environmental attitudes and actions. *Journal of Social Psychology, 87,* 323–324.

BIGGERS, T., & PRYOR, B. (1982). Attitude change as a function of the emotion-eliciting qualities of the environment. *Personality and Social Psychology Bulletin, 8,* 203–214.

BIRDWHISTLE, R. (1970). *Kinesics and context: Essays on body movement communication.* Philadelphia: University of Pennsylvania Press.

BISHOP, G.F. (1975). Resolution and tolerance of cognitive inconsistency in a field situation: Change in attitude and beliefs following the Watergate affair. *Psychological Reports, 36,* 747–753.

BLASS, T. (1999). The Milgram pardigm after 35 years: Some things we now know about obedience to authority. *Journal of Applied Social Psychology, 29,* 955–978.

BLAXTER, M. (1990). *Health and lifestyles.* London: Tavistock/Routledge.

BLESKE-RECHECK, A.L., & BUSS, D.M. (2001). Opposite sex friendship: Sex differences and similarities in initiation, selection and dissolution. *Personality and Social Psychology Bulletin, 27,* 1310–1323.

BLISS, M. (1991). *Plague. A story of smallpox in Montréal.* Toronto: HarperCollins.

BLOOM, B., ASHER, S.J., & WHITE, S.W. (1978). Marital disruption as a stressor: A review and analysis. *Psychological Bulletin, 85,* 867–894.

BLUMENFELD, M., LEVY, N.B., & KAUFMAN, D. (1979). The wish to be informed of a fatal illness. *Omega, 9,* 323–326.

BLUMER, H. (1951). Social movements. In A.M. Lee (Ed.), *New outline of the principles of sociology* (2nd ed.). (pp. 199–220). New York: Barnes & Noble.

BLUMER, H. (1969). *Symbolic interactionism.* Englewood Cliffs, NJ: Prentice-Hall.

BODENHAUSEN, G.V. (1988). Stereotype biases in social decision making and memory: Testing process models of stereotype use. *Journal of Personality and Social Psychology, 55,* 726–737.

BOHNER, G., BLESS, H., SCHWARZ, N., & STRACK, F. (1988). What triggers causal attributions? The impact of valence and subjective probability. *European Journal of Social Psychology, 18,* 335–345.

BOLGER, N., DELONGIS, A., KESSLER, R.C., & SCHILLING, E.A. (1989). Effects of daily stress on negative mood. *Journal of Personality and Social Psychology, 57,* 808–818.

BONACICH, P., SHURE, G.H., KAHAN, J.P., & MERKER, R.J. (1976). Cooperation and group size in the N-person Prisoner's Dilemma. *Journal of Conflict Resolution, 20,* 687–706.

BOND, C.F., JR. (1982). Social facilitation: A self-presentational view. *Journal of Personality and Social Psychology, 42,* 1042–1050.

BOND, C.F., JR., & TITUS, L.J. (1983). Social facilitation: A meta-analysis of 241 studies. *Psychological Bulletin, 94,* 265–292.

BOND, G.G., AIKEN, L.S., & SOMERVILLE, S.C. (1992). The health beliefs model and adolescents with insulin-dependent diabetes mellitus. *Health Psychology, 11,* 190–198.

BOND, M.H. (1988). Finding universal dimensions of individual variation in multicultural studies of values: The Rokeach and Chinese value surveys. *Journal of Personality and Social Psychology, 55,* 1009–1015.

BOND, R., & SMITH, P.B. (1996). Culture and conformity: a meta-analysis of studies using Asch's line judgement task. *Psychological Bulletin, 119,* 111–137.

BONINGER, D.S., KROSNICK, J.A., BERENT, M.K., & FABRIGAR, L.R. (1995). The causes and consequence of attitude importance. In R.E. Petty, & J.A. Krosnick (Eds.), *Attitude strength: Antecedents and consequences* (pp. 159–189). Mahwah, NJ: Erlbaum.

BONTA, B.D. (1997). Cooperation and competition in peaceful societies. *American Psychologist, 121,* 299–320.

BOOTH-KEWLEY, S., & FRIEDMAN, H.S. (1987). Psychological predictors of heart disease: A quantitative review. *Psychological Bulletin, 101,* 343–362.

BORGIDA, E., & WHITE, P. (1978). Social perception of rape victims: The impact of legal reforms. *Law and Human Behavior, 2,* 339–351.

BORNMAN, E., & APPELGRYN, A.E.S. (1996). *Ethnolinguistic vitality under a new political dispensation in South Africa.* Unpublished manuscript, Human Sciences Research Council, South Africa.

BORNSTEIN, G., RAPOPORT, A., KERPEL, L., & KATZ, T. (1989). Within-and-between-group communication in intergroup competition for public goods. *Journal of Experimental Social Psychology, 25,* 422–436.

BOUCHER, J.D. (1974). Display rules and facial affective behavior: A theoretical discussion and suggestions for research. *Topics in Culture Learning, 2,* 87–102.

BOULDING, K.E. (1980). Science: Our common heritage. *Science, 207,* 831–836.

BOURHIS, R.Y. (1979). Language in ethnic interaction: A social psychological approach. In H. Giles, & B. Saint-Jacques (Eds.), *Language and ethnic relations.* Oxford: Pergamon.

BOURHIS, R.Y. (1982). Language policies and language attitudes: Le monde de la francophonie. In E.R. Ryan, & H. Giles (Eds.), *Attitudes towards language variation* (pp. 34–62). London: Edward Arnold.

BOURHIS, R.Y. (1984a). The charter of French language and cross-cultural communication in Montréal. In R.Y. Bourhis (Ed.), *Conflict and language planning in Québec.* Clevedon, England: Multilingual Matters.

BOURHIS, R.Y. (1990). Organizational communication in bilingual settings: The linguistic work environment survey. In H. Giles, N. Coupland, & J. Coupland (Eds.), *Contexts of accommodation: Developments in applied psycholinguistics.* Cambridge: Cambridge University Press.

BOURHIS, R.Y. (1994a). Langage et ethnicité: Communication interculterelle à Montréal, 1977–1991. *Canadian Ethnic Studies, XXVI,* 86–107.

BOURHIS, R.Y. (1994b). Ethnic and language attitudes in Quebec. In J.W. Berry, & J.A. La Ponce (Eds), *Ethnicity and culture in Canada: The research landscape* (pp. 322–360). Toronto: University of Toronto Press.

BOURHIS, R.Y., ROTH, S., & MACQUEEN, G. (1989). Communication in the hospital setting: A survey of medical and everyday language use amongst patients, nurses and doctors. *Social Science and Medicine, 28,* 339–346.

BOUTON, R.A., GALLAHER, P.E., GARLINGHOUSE, P.A., LEAL, T., ROSENSTEIN, L.D., & YOUNG, R.K. (1989). Demographic variables associated with fear of AIDS and homophobia. *Journal of Applied Social Psychology, 19,* 885–901.

BOWERS, K.S. (1973). Situationism in psychology: An analysis and critique. *Psychological Review, 80,* 307–336.

BOWLBY, J. (1969). *Attachment and loss: Vol. 1 Attachment.* New York: Basic Books.

BOYD, J.R., COVINGTON, T.R., STANASZEK, W.F., & COUSSONS, R.T. (1974). Drug defaulting: II Analysis of noncompliance patterns. *American Journal of Hospital Pharmacy, 31,* 485–491.

BRADAC, J.J., DAVIES, R.A., COURTRIGHT, J.A., DESMOND, R.J., & MURDOCK, J.I. (1977). Richness of vocabulary: An attributional analysis. *Psychological Reports, 41,* 1131–1134.

BRADLEY, G.W. (1978). Self-serving bias in the attribution process: A re-examination of the fact-or-fiction question. *Journal of Personality and Social Psychology, 36,* 56–71.

BRADLEY, J.P., NICOL, A.A.M., CHARBONNEAU, D., & MEYER, J.P. (2002). Personality correlates of leadership development in Canadian Forces officer candidates. *Canadian Journal of Behavioural Science, 34,* 92–103.

BRADLEY, J.R., & CARTWRIGHT, S. (2002). Social support, job stress, health and job satisfaction among nurses in the United Kingdom. *International Journal of Stress Management, 9,* 163–182.

BRAITHWAITE, V.A., & SCOTT, W.A. (1991). Values. In J.P. Robinson, P.R. Shaver, & L.S. Wrightsman (Eds.), *Measures of personality and social psychological attitudes.* New York: Academic Press.

BRANDON, R., & DAVIES, C. (1973). *Wrongful imprisonment.* London: Allen and Unwin.

BRANDT, A.M. (1988). AIDS in historical perspective: Four lessons from the history of sexually transmitted diseases. *American Journal of Public Health, 78,* 367–371.

BRANN, P., & FODDY, M. (1987). Trust and the consumption of a deteriorating common resource. *Journal of Conflict Resolution, 31,* 615–630.

BRAUN, O.L., & WICKLUND, R.A. (1989). When discounting fails. *Journal of Experimental Social Psychology, 25,* 450–461.

BRAY, R.M., & KERR, N.L. (1982). Methodological considerations in the study of the psychology of the courtroom. In N.L. Kerr, & R.M. Bray (Eds.), *The psychology of the courtroom* (pp. 287–323). Orlando, FL: Academic Press.

BRECKLER, S.J. (1984). Empirical validation of affect, behavior and cognition as distinct components of attitude. *Journal of Personality and Social Psychology, 47,* 1191–1205.

BREHM, J.W., & COHEN A.R. (1962). *Explorations in cognitive dissonance.* New York: Wiley.

BREHM, S.S. (1985). *Intimate relationships.* New York: Random House.

BREWER, M.B., & KRAMER, R.M. (1985). The psychology of intergroup attitudes and behavior. *Annual Review of Psychology, 36,* 219–243.

BREWER, M.B., & KRAMER, R.M. (1986). Choice behavior in social dilemmas: Effects of social identity, group size, and decision framing. *Journal of Personality and Social Psychology, 50,* 543–549.

BREWER, M.B., DULL, V., & LUI, L. (1981). Perception of the elderly: Stereotypes as prototypes. *Journal of Personality and Social Psychology, 41,* 656–670.

BRICKMAN, P. (1974). Rule structures and conflict relationships. In P. Brickman (Ed.), *Social conflict* (pp. 1–33). Lexington, MA: D.C. Heath.

BRIGHAM, J.C., & CAIRNS, D.L. (1988). The effect of mugshot inspections on eyewitness identification accuracy. *Journal of Applied Social Psychology, 18,* 1394–1410.

BRIGHAM, J.C., & MALPASS, R.S. (1985). The role of experience and contact in the recognition of faces of own- and other-race persons. *Journal of Social Issues, 41,* 139–156.

BRIGHAM, J.C., & PFEIFER, J.E. (1994). Evaluating the fairness of lineups. In D.F. Ross, & M.P. Toglia (Eds.), *Adult eyewitness testimony: Current trends and developments* (pp. 201–222). New York: Cambridge University Press.

BRIGHAM, J.C., & PFEIFER, J.E. (1996). Euthenasia: An introduction. *Journal of Social Issues, 52* (2), 1–11.

BRITT, T.W., & BLIESE, P.D. (2003). Testing the stress-buffering effects of self-engagement among soldiers on a military operation. *Journal of Personality, 71,* 245–265.

BROADFOOT, B. (1977). *Years of sorrow, years of shame.* Toronto: Doubleday Canada.

BROADSTOCK, M., BORLAND, R., & GASON, R. (1992). Effects of suntan on judgements of healthfulness and attractiveness by adolescents. *Journal of Applied Social Psychology, 22,* 157–172.

BROOKS-GUNN, J., BOYER, C.B., & HEIN, K. (1988). Preventing HIV infection and AIDS in children and adolescents. *American Psychologist, 43,* 958–964.

BROVERMAN., I.K., VOGEL, S.R., BROVERMAN, D.M., CLARKSON, F.E., & ROSENKRANTZ, P.S. (1972). Sexual stereotypes: A current appraisal. *Journal of Social Issues, 28,* 59–78.

BROWN, J., & SIEGEL, J.M. (1988). Exercise as a buffer of life stress: A prospective study of adolescent health. *Health Psychology, 7,* 341–353.

BROWN, J.A.C. (1963). *Techniques of persuasion: From propaganda to brainwashing.* London, Penguin Books.

BROWN, R. (1965). *Social psychology.* New York: Free Press.

BROWN, R. (1986). *Social Psychology* (2nd ed.). London: Collier MacMillan.

BROWNING, C.R. (1992). *Ordinary man. Reserve Police Battalion 101 and the Final Solution in Poland.* New York: HarperCollins.

BROWNMILLER, S. (1984). *Femininity.* New York: Simon & Schuster.

BRUNER, J.S., & TAGIURI, R. (1954). The perception of people. In G. Lindzey (Ed.), *Handbook of Social Psychology* (pp. 634–654). Reading, MA: Addison-Wesley.

BRUNVAND, J.H. (1981). *The vanishing hitchhiker: American urban legends and their meanings.* New York: Norton.

BRUNVAND, J.H. (1986). *The choking Doberman.* New York: Norton.

BRYAN, J.H., & WALBECK, N. (1970). The impact of words and deeds concerning altruism upon children. *Child Development, 41,* 747–757.

BUCK, R. (2002), The genetics and biology of true love: Prosocial biological affects and the left hemisphere. *Psychological Review, 109,* 739–744.

BUCKHOUT, R. (1980). Nearly 2000 witnesses can be wrong. *Bulletin of the Psychonomic Society, 16,* 307–310.

BUEHLER, D., & GRIFFIN, D. (1994). Change of meaning effects in conformity and dissent: Observing construal process over time. *Journal of Personality and Social Psychology, 67,* 984–996.

BUEHLER, R., & ROSS, M. (1993). How do individuals remember their past statements? *Journal of Personality and Social Psychology, 64,* 538–551.

BUEHLER, R., GRIFFIN, D., & ROSS, M. (1995). It's about time: Optimistic predictions in work and love. In W. Stroebe, & M. Hewson (Eds.), *European Review of Social Psychology,* (Vol. 6). (pp. 1–32). London: Wiley.

BUGENTAL, D.E., KASWAN, J.E., & LOVE, L.R. (1970). Perception of contradictory meanings conveyed by verbal and nonverbal channels. *Journal of Personality and Social Psychology, 16,* 647–655.

BULMAN, R.J., & WORTMAN, C.B. (1977). Attributions of blame and coping in the "real world": Severe accident victims react to their lot. *Journal of Personality and Social Psychology, 35,* 351–363.

BURGER, J.M. (1981). Motivational biases in the attribution of responsibility for an accident: A meta-analysis of the defensive attribution hypothesis. *Psychological Bulletin, 90,* 496–513.

BURGER, J.M. (1986). Increasing compliance by improving the deal: The that's-not-all technique. *Journal of Personality and Social Psychology, 51,* 277–283.

BURGESS, E.W., & HUSTON, T.L. (Eds.). (1979). *Social exchange in developing relationships.* New York: Academic Press.

BURKE, R.J., & WEIR, T. (1980). The Type A experience: Occupational and life demands, satisfaction and well-being. *Journal of Human Stress, 6,* 28–38.

BURKE, T.M., & FREEDMAN, J.L. (1996, August). *The effects of pretrial publicity on jurors' verdicts.* 104th Convention of the American Psychological Association, Toronto.

BURMAN, B., & MARGOLIN, G. (1992). Analysis of the association between marital relationships and health problems: An interactional perspective. *Psychological Bulletin, 112,* 39–63.

BURNSTEIN, E., CRANDALL, C., & KITAYAMA, S. (1994). Some neo-Darwinian decision rules for altruism: Weighing cues for inclusive fitness as a function of the biological importance of the decision. *Journal of Personality and Social Psychology, 67,* 773–789.

BUSBOOM, A.L., COLLINS, D.N., GIVERTZ, M.D., & LEVIN, L.A. (2002). Can't we still be friends? Resources and barriers to friendship quality after romantic relationship dissolution. *Personal Relationships, 9,* 215–223.

BUSENITZ, L.W., & BARNEY, J.B. (1997). Differences between entrepreneurs and managers in large organizational biases and heuristics in strategic decision-making. *Journal of Business Venturing, 12,* 9–31.

BUSHMAN, B.J. (1988). The effects of apparel on compliance: A field experiment with a female authority figure. *Personality and Social Psychology Bulletin, 14,* 459–467.

BUSHMAN, B.J. (1995). Moderating role of trait aggressiveness in the effects of violent media on aggression. *Journal of Personality and Social Psychology, 69,* 950–960.

BUSHMAN, B.J., & ANDERSON, C.A. (2001). Media violence and the American public: Scientific facts versus media misinformation. *American Psychologist, 36,* 477–498.

BUSHMAN, B.J., & ANDERSON, C.A. (2002). Violent video games and hostile expectations: A test of the General Aggression Model. *Personality and Social Psychology Bulletin, 28,* 1679–1686.

BUSHMAN, B.J., & BAUMEISTER, R.F. (2002). Does self-love or self-hate lead to violence? *Journal of Research in Personality, 36,* 543–545.

BUSHMAN, B.J., & GEEN, R.G. (1990). Role of cognitive-emotional mediators and individual differences in the effects of media violence on aggression. *Journal of Personality and Social Psychology, 58,* 156–163.

BUSHMAN, B.J., BAUMEISTER, R.F., & STACK, A.D. (1999). Catharsis, aggression, and persuasive influence: Self-fulfilling or self-defeating prophecies? *Journal of Personality and Social Psychology, 76,* 367–376.

BUSS, A.H., & PERRY, M. (1992). The aggression questionnaire. *Journal of Personality and Social Psychology, 63,* 452–459.

BUSS, D.M. (1994). *The evolution of desire: Strategies of human mating.* New York: Basic Books.

BUSS, D.M., & SHACKELFORD, T.K. (1997). From vigilance to violence: Retention tactics in married couples. *Journal of Personality and Social Psychology, 72,* 346–361.

BUTTERFIELD, D.A., & GRINNELL, J.P. (1999). Reviewing gender, leadership, and managerial behavior: Do three decades of research tell us anything? In G.N. Powell (Ed.), *Handbook of gender and work* (pp. 223–238). Thousand Oaks, CA: Sage Publications.

BUUNK, B.P., & MUTSAERS, W. (1999). Equity perceptions and marital satisfaction in former and current marriage: A study among the remarried. *Journal of Social and Personal Relationships, 16,* 123–132.

BUUNK, B.P., COLLINS, R.L., TAYLOR, S.E., VAN YPEREN, N.W., & DAKOF, G.A. (1990). The affective consequences of social comparison: Either direction has its ups and downs. *Journal of Personality and Social Psychology, 59,* 1238–1249.

BYRNE, D. (1971). *The attraction paradigm.* New York: Academic Press.

BYRNE, D., & CLORE, G.L. (1970). A reinforcement model of evaluative responses. *Personality: An International Journal, 1,* 103–128.

BYRNE, D., CLORE, G.L., & SMEATON, G. (1986). The attraction hypothesis. Do similar attitudes affect anything? *Journal of Personality and Social Psychology, 51,* 1167–1170.

BYRNE, D., ERVIN, C., & LAMBERTH, J. (1970). Continuity between the experimental study of attraction and real-life computer dating. *Journal of Personality and Social Psychology, 51,* 157–165.

CACIOPPO, J., HAWKLEY, L.C., CRAWFORD, E., ERNST, J.M., BERLESON, M.H., KOWALEWSKI, R.B., MALARKEY, W.B., VAN CAUTER, E., & BERNTSON, G.G. (2002). Loneliness and health: Potential mechanisms. *Psychosomatic Medicine, 64,* 407–417.

CACIOPPO, J.T., & PETTY, R.E. (1981). Electromyograms as measures of extent and affectivity of information processing. *American Psychologist, 36,* 441–456.

CAIRNS, R., & CAIRNS, B. (1985). The developmental-interactional view of social behavior: Four issues in adolescent aggression. In D. Olweus, J. Block, & M. Radke-Yarrow (Eds.), *Development of anti-social and prosocial behavior: Theories, research and issues* (pp. 315–342). New York: Academic Press.

CALDWELL, G. (1984). Anglo-Québec: Demographic realities and options for the future. In R.Y. Bourhis (Ed.), *Conflict and language planning in Québec.* Clevedon: Multilingual Matters.

CALDWELL, J.R., & SHINN, M. (1976). *Adherence to medical regimens.* Ann Arbor: Institute for Social Research.

CALHOUN, J.B. (1962). Population density and social pathology. *Scientific American, 206,* 139–148.

CALHOUN, L.G., SELBY, J.W., & KING, H.E. (1976). *Dealing with crisis.* Englewood Cliffs, NJ: Prentice-Hall.

CALL, K.T., FINCH, M.A., HUCK, S.M., & KANE, R.A. (1999). Caregiver burden from a social exchange perspective: Caring for older people after hospital discharge. *Journal of Marriage and the Family, 61,* 688–699.

CALLWOOD, J. (1987, March 18). Sanitized textbooks reflect a pious paradise that never was. *The Globe and Mail.*

CAMERON, K.A., JACKS, J.Z., & O'BRIEN, M.E. (2002). An experimental examination of strategies for resisting persuasion. *Current Research in Social Psychology, 7,* 205–224.

CAMPBELL, D.T., CONVERSE, P.E., & RODGERS, W.L. (1976). *The quality of American life.* New York: Russell Sage Foundation.

CAMPBELL, J.B., & FAIRLY, P.J. (1989). Informational and normative routes to conformity: The effect of faction size as function of norm extremity and attention to the stimulus. *Journal of Personality and Social Psychology, 57,* 457–468.

CAMPBELL, J.D. (1986). Similarity and uniqueness: The effects of attribute type, relevance, and individual differences in self-esteem and depression. *Journal of Personality and Social Psychology, 50,* 281–293.

CAMPBELL, J.D. (1990). Self-esteem and clarity of the self-concept. *Journal of Personality and Social Psychology, 59,* 538–549.

CAMPBELL, J.D., TRAPNELL, P.D., HEINE, S.J., KATZ, I.M., LAVALLEE, L.F., & LEHMAN, D.R. (1996). Self-concept clarity: Measurement, personality correlates and cultural boundaries: Correction. *Journal of Personality and Social Psychology, 70,* 141–156.

CAMPBELL, J.D., TRAPNESS, P.D., HEINE, S.J., KATZ, I.M., LAVALEE, L.F., CAMPBELL, K., & DEMAN, A.F. (2000). Threat perception and reluctance to donate organs. *North American Journal of Psychology, 2,* 21–26.

CAMPBELL, K., & DEMAN, A.F. (2000). Threat perception and reluctance to donate organs. *North American Journal of Psychology, 2,* 21–26.

CANADIAN CENTRE FOR CRIMINAL JUSTICE STATISTICS (1994). Wife assault, the findings of a national survey. *Juristat, 14*(9).

CANNING, H., & MAYER, J. (1966). Obesity: Its possible effect on college acceptance. *New England Journal of Medicine, 275,* 1172–1174.

CANTOR, N., & MISCHEL, W. (1979). Prototypes in person perception. In L. Berkowitz (Ed.), *Advances in experimental social psychology, 3–52* (Vol. 12). New York: Academic Press.

CANTRIL, H. (1940). *The invasion from Mars.* Princeton, NJ: Princeton University Press.

CAPLAN, N.S., & PAIGE, J.M. (1968). A study of ghetto rioters. *Scientific American, 219,* 15–21.

CAPLAN, R.D., COBB, S., & FRENCH, J.R.P. (1975). Relation of cessation of smoking with job stress, personality and social support. *Journal of Applied Psychology, 60,* 211–219.

CAPLAN, R.D., ROBINSON, E., FRENCH, J.R.P., JR., CALDWELL, J.R., & SHINN, M. (1976). *Adherence to medical regimens.* Ann Arbor: Institute for Social Research.

CAPORAEL, L.R. (1981). The paralanguage of care-giving: Baby talk to the institutionalized aged. *Journal of Personality and Social Psychology, 40,* 876–884.

CAPORAEL, L.R., LUKASZEWSKI, M.P., & CULBERTSON, G.H. (1983). Secondary baby talk: Judgments by institutionalized elderly and their caregivers. *Journal of Personality and Social Psychology, 44,* 746–754.

CARLI, L.L. (1990). Gender, language, and influence. *Journal of Personality and Social Psychology, 59,* 941–951.

CARLI, L.L. (1999). Gender, interpersonal power and social influence. *Journal of Social Issues, 55,* 81–99.

CARLI, L.L., GANLEY, R., & PIERCE-OTAY, A. (1991). Similarity and satisfaction in roommate relationships. *Personality and Social Psychology Bulletin, 17,* 419–426.

CARLO, G., EISENBERG, N., TROYER, D., SWITZER, G., & SPEER, A.L. (1991). The altruistic personality: In what context is it apparent? *Journal of Personality and Social Psychology, 61,* 450–458.

CARLSMITH, J.M., & GROSS, A.E. (1969). Some effects of guilt on compliance. *Journal of Personality and Social Psychology, 11,* 232–239.

CARLSMITH, J.M., COLLINS, B.E., & HELMREICH, R.L. (1966). Studies on forced compliance: I. The effect of pressure for compliance on attitude change produced by face-to-face role-playing and anonymous essay writing. *Journal of Personality and Social Psychology, 4,* 1–13.

CARLSMITH, J.M., ELLSWORTH, R.C., & ARONSON, E. (1976). *Methods of research in social psychology.* Reading, MA: Addison-Wesley.

CARLSON, M., MARCUS-NEWHALL, A., & MILLER, N. (1990). Effects of situational aggressive cues: A quantitative review. *Journal of Personality and Social Psychology, 58,* 622–633.

CARMENT, D.W. (1970). Rate of simple motor responding as a function of coaction, competition, and sex of the participants. *Psychonomic Science, 19,* 342–343.

CARMENT, D.W. (1973). *Giving and receiving in Canada and India* (Technical Report #53). Hamilton: McMaster University.

CARMENT, D.W., & HODKIN, B. (1973). Coaction and competition in India and Canada. *Journal of Cross-Cultural Psychology, 4,* 459–469.

CARNEGIE HERO FUND COMMISSION (2003). Downloaded on July 15, 2003, from http://www.carnegiehero.org/Awardee.shtml.

CARNEVALE, P.J. (1986). Strategic choice in negotiation. *Negotiation Journal, 2,* 41–56.

CARNEVALE, P.J., & HENRY, R.A. (1989). Determinants of mediator behavior: A test of the strategic choice. *Journal of Applied Social Psychology, 19,* 481–498.

CARNEVALE, P.J., & PRUITT, D.G. (1992). Negotiation and mediation. *Annual Review of Psychology, 43,* 531–582.

CARRETTA, D.K., & MORELAND, R.L. (1983). The direct and indirect effects of inadmissible evidence. *Journal of Applied Social Psychology, 13,* 291–309.

CARRINGTON, P.J., & MOYER, S. (1994). Gun control and suicide in Ontario. *American Journal of Psychiatry, 151,* 606–608.

CARROLL, J.M., & RUSSELL, J.A. (1997). Facial characteristics in Hollywood's portrayal of emotion. *Journal of Personality and Social Psychology, 72,* 164–176.

CARROLL, J.S. (1978). The effect of imagining an event on expectations for the event: An interpretation in terms of the availability heuristic. *Journal of Experimental Social Psychology, 14,* 88–96.

CARVER, G.S., & GLASS, D.C. (1978). Coronary-prone behavior pattern and interpersonal aggression. *Journal of Personality and Social Psychology, 36,* 361–366.

CARVER, G.S., & SCHEIER, M.F. (1981). The self-attention-induced feedback loop and social facilitation. *Journal of Experimental Social Psychology, 17,* 545–568.

CARVER, G.S., LAWRENCE, J.W., & SCHEIER, M.F. (1999). Self-discrepancies and affect: incorporating the role of feared selves. *Personality and Social Psychology Bulletin, 25,* 783–792.

CASH, T.F., & DERLEGA, V.J. (1978). The matching hypothesis: Physical attractiveness among same-sexed friends. *Personality and Social Psychology Bulletin, 4,* 240–243.

CASPI, A., HERBENER, E.S., & OZER, D.J. (1992). Shared experience and the similarity of personalities: A longitudinal study of married couples. *Journal of Personality and Social Psychology, 62,* 281–291.

CAUDILL, B.D., & MARLATT, G.A. (1975). Modeling influences in social drinking: An experimental analogue. *Journal of Consulting and Clinical Psychology, 43,* 405–415.

CAVIOR, N., & DORECKI, P.R. (1969, April). Physical attractiveness and popularity among fifth grade boys. Meetings of the Southwestern Psychology Association, Austin, TX.

CAVOUKIAN, A., & DOOB, A.N. (1980). The effects of a judge's charge and subsequent recharge on judgements of guilt. *Basic and Applied Social Psychology, 1,* 103–116.

CHAIKEN, A.L., & DERLEGA, V.J. (1974). *Self-disclosure.* Morristown, NJ: General Learning.

CHAIKEN, S. (1980). Heuristic versus systematic information processing and the use of source versus message cues. *Journal of Personality and Social Psychology, 39,* 752–766.

CHAIKEN, S. (1987). The heuristic model of persuasion. In C.P. Herman, M.P. Zanna, & E.T. Higgins (Eds.), *Social Influence: The Ontario Symposium* (pp. 3–39). Hillsdale, NJ: Erlbaum.

CHAIKEN, S., & EAGLY, A.H. (1976). Communication modality as a determinant of message persuasiveness and message comprehensibility. *Journal of Personality and Social Psychology, 34,* 605–614.

CHAIKEN, S., & EAGLY, A.H. (1983). Communication modality as a determinant of persuasion: The role of communicator salience. *Journal of Personality and Social Psychology, 45,* 241–256.

CHAIKEN, S., & STANGOR, C. (1987). Attitude and attitude change. *Annual Review of Psychology, 38,* 575–630.

CHANDLER, T.A., SHAMA, D.D., WOLF, F.M., & PLANCHARD, S.K. (1981). Misattributional causality: A five cross-national samples study. *Journal of Cross-Cultural Psychology, 12,* 207–221.

CHAPMAN, L.J., & CHAPMAN, J.P. (1969). Illusory correlations as an obstacle to the use of valid psychodiagnostic signs. *Journal of Abnormal and Social Psychology, 74,* 271–280.

CHARTRAND, T., PINCKERT, S., & BURGER, J.M. (1999). When manipulation backfires: The effects of time delay and requester on the foot-in-the-door technique. *Journal of Applied Social Psychology, 29,* 211–221.

CHAU, L.L, JOHNSON, R.C., BOWERS, J.K., & DARVILL, T.J. (1990). Intrinsic and extrinsic religiosity as related to conscience, adjustment, and altruism. *Personality and Individual Differences, 11,* 397–400.

CHAUDHURI, A., SOPHER, B., & STRAND, P. (2002).Cooperation in social dilemmas, trust and reciprocity. *Journal of Economic Psychology, 23,* 231–250.

CHECK, J.V.P. (1985). *The effects of violent and nonviolent pornography.* Ottawa: Department of Justice.

CHECK, J.V.P., & DYCK, D.G. (1986). Hostile aggression and Type A behavior. *Personality and Individual Differences, 7,* 819–827.

CHECK, J.V.P., & GULOIEN, T.H. (1989). Reported proclivity for coercive sex following repeated exposure to sexually violent pornography, nonviolent dehumanizing pornography, and erotica. In D. Zillmann, & J. Bryant (Eds.), *Pornography: Research advances and policy considerations* (pp. 159–184). Hillsdale, NJ: Erlbaum.

CHECK, J.V.P., & MALAMUTH, N.M. (1984). Can there be positive effects of participation in pornography experiments? *The Journal of Sex Research, 20,* 14–31.

CHECK, J.V.P., & MALAMUTH, N.M. (1986). Pornography and sexual aggression: A social learning theory analysis. *Communication Yearbook, 9,* 187–213.

CHECK, J.V.P., & MALAMUTH, N.M. (1990). Ethical considerations in sex and aggression research. In D. MacNiven (Ed.), *Moral expertise: Studies in practical and professional ethics.* London: Routledge.

CHECK, J.V.P., PERLMAN, D., & MALAMUTH, N.M. (1985). Loneliness and aggressive behavior. *Journal of Social and Personal Relationships, 2,* 243–252.

CHEMERS, M.M. (1983). Leadership theory and research: A systems-process integration. In P.B. Paulus (Ed.), *Basic group processes.* New York: Springer-Verlag.

CHERRY, F. (1995). *The "stubborn particulars" of social psychology.* London: Routledge.

CHERRY, F., & BYRNE, D. (1977). Authoritarianism. In T. Blass (Ed.), *Personality variables in social behavior.* Hillsdale, NJ: Erlbaum.

CHERTKOFF, J.M., & CONLEY, M. (1967). Opening offer and frequency of concession as bargaining strategies. *Journal of Personality and Social Psychology, 7,* 181–185.

CHIRIBOGA, D., ROBERTS, J., & STEIN, J.A. (1978). Psychological well-being during marital separation. *Journal of Divorce, 2,* 21–36.

CHOI, I., & NISBETT, R.E. (1998). Situational salience and cultural differences in the correspondence bias and actor-observer bias. *Personality and Social Psychology Bulletin, 24,* 949–960.

CHOI, I., NISBETT, R.E., & NORENZAYAN, A. (1999). Causal attribution across culture: Variation and universality. *Psychological Bulletin, 125,* 47–63.

CHOMSKY, N. (1986). *Turning the tide: The U.S. and Latin America.* Montreal: Black Rose Books.

CHOPRA, S.R., DAHL, L.M., & WRIGHTSMAN, L.S. (1996, August 9–13). *The sequestered juror syndrome.* 104th convention of the American Psychological Association, Toronto.

CHRISTENSEN, L. (1988). Deception in psychological research: When is its use justified? *Personality and Social Psychology Bulletin, 14,* 664–675.

CHRISTIANSEN, A., SULLAWAY, M., & KING, C. (1983). Systematic error in behavioral reports of dyadic interaction: Egocentric bias and contrast effects. *Behavioral Assessment, 5,* 131–142.

CHRISTIANSON, S. (1992). Emotional stress and eyewitness memory: A critical review. *Psychological Bulletin, 112,* 284–309.

CHRISTIANSON, S., & LOFTUS, E.F. (1991). Remembering emotional events: The fate of detailed information. *Cognition and Emotion, 5,* 81–108.

CHRISTIE, R., & JAHODA, M. (Eds.). (1954). *Studies in the scope and method of "The Authoritarian Personality."* New York: Free Press.

CHRISTY, N.P. (1979). English is our second language. *New England Journal of Medicine, 300,* 979–981.

CIALDINI, R.B. (1987). Compliance principles of compliance professionals: Psychologists of necessity. In M.P. Zanna, J.M. Olson, & C.R. Herman (Eds), *Social influence. The Ontario Symposium* (Vol. 5). (pp. 165–184). Hillsdale, NJ: Erlbaum.

CIALDINI, R.B., BROWN, S.L., LEWIS, B.P., LUCE, C., & NEUBERG, S.L. (1997). Reinterpreting the empathy-altruism relationship: When one into one equals oneness. *Journal of Personality and Social Psychology, 73,* 481–494.

CIALDINI, R.B., BUCKMAN, L., & CACIOPPO, J.T. (1979). An example of consumeristic social psychology: Bargaining tough in the new car showroom. *Journal of Applied Social Psychology, 9,* 115–126.

CIALDINI, R.B., CACIOPPO, J.T., BASSETT, R., & MILLER, J.A. (1978). Low-ball procedure for producing compliance: Commitment then cost. *Journal of Personality and Social Psychology, 36,* 463–476.

CIALDINI, R.B., DARBY, B.L., & VINCENT, J.E. (1973). Transgression and altruism: A case for hedonism. *Journal of Experimental Social Psychology, 9,* 502–516.

CIALDINI, R.B., SCHALLER, M., HOULIHAN, D., ARPS, K., & FULTZ, J. (1987). *Journal of Personality and Social Psychology, 52,* 749–758.

CIALDINI, R.B., VINCENT, J.E., LEWIS, S.K., CATALON, J., WHEELER, D., & DARBY, B.L. (1975). Reciprocal concessions procedure for inducing compliance: The door-in-the-face technique. *Journal of Personality and Social Psychology, 31,* 206–215.

CLANCY, K., BARTOLOMEW, J., RICHARDSON, D., & WELLFORD, C. (1981). Sentence decision making: The logic of sentence decisions and the extent and sources of sentence disparity. *Journal of Criminal Law and Criminology, 72,* 524–554.

CLARK, H.H. (1985). Language use and language users. In G. Lindzey & E. Aronson (Eds.), *Handbook of social psychology,* (3rd ed.). (Vol. 2). (pp. 179–232). New York: Random House.

CLARK, M., & MILLS, J. (1993). The difference between communal and exchange relationships. What it is and is not. *Personality and Social Psychology Bulletin, 19,* 684–691.

CLÉMENT, R. (1980). Ethnicity, contact and communication competence in a second language. In H. Giles, W.P. Robinson, & P.M. Smith (Eds.), *Language: Social psychological perspectives* (pp. 147–154). Oxford: Pergamon.

CLÉMENT, R. (1987). Second language proficiency and acculturation: An investigation of the effects of language status and individual characteristics. *Journal of Language and Social Psychology, 5,* 271–290.

CLÉMENT, R., BAKER, S.C., & MACINTYRE, P.D. (2003). Willingness to communicate in a second language: The effects of context, norms, and vitality. *Journal of Language and Social Psychology, 22,* 190–209.

CLÉMENT, R., GARDNER, R.C., & SMYTHE, P.C. (1977). Inter-ethnic contact: Attitudinal consequences. *Canadian Journal of Behavioural Science, 9,* 205–215.

CLÉMENT, R., GAUTHIER, R., & NOELS, K. (1993). Choix langagiers en milieu minoritaire: Attitudes et identité concomitantes. *Revue Canadienne des Sciences du Comportement, 25,* 149–164.

CLIFFORD, M., & WALSTER, E. (1973). The effects of physical attraction on teacher expectation. *Sociology of Education, 46,* 248.

CLORE, G.L., WIGGINS, N.H., & ITKIN, G. (1975). Gain and loss in attraction: Attributions from non-verbal behavior. *Journal of Personality and Social Psychology, 31,* 706–712.

COATES, D., WORTMAN, C.B., & ABBEY, A. (1979). Reactions to victims. In I.H. Frieze, D. Bar-Tal, & J.S. Carroll (Eds.), *New approaches to social problems* (pp. 21–52). San Francisco: Jossey-Bass.

COHEN, D., NISBETT, R.E., BOWDLE, B.F., & SCHWARZ, N. (1996). Insult, aggression, and the Southern culture of Honor: An "experimental ethnography." *Journal of Personality and Social Psychology, 70,* 945–960.

COHEN, S. (1988). Psychosocial models of the role of social support in the etiology of physical disease. *Health Psychology, 7,* 269–297.

COHEN, S., & HERBERT, T.B. (1996). Health psychology: Psychological factors and physical disease from the perspective of human psychoimmunology. *Annual Review of Psychology, 47,* 113–142.

COHEN, S., & MCKAY, G. (1984). Social support, stress and the buffering hypothesis: A theoretical analysis. In A. Baum, J.E. Singer, & S.E. Taylor (Eds.), *Handbook of psychology and health* (Vol. 4). (pp. 253–267). Hillsdale, NJ: Erlbaum.

COHEN, S., & WILLIAMSON, G.M. (1988). Perceived stress in a probability sample of the United States. In S. Spacapan, & S. Oskamp (Eds.), *The social psychology of health* (pp. 31–67). Beverly Hills, CA: Sage Publications.

COHEN, S., TYRRELL, D.A.J., & SMITH, A.P. (1993). Negative life events, perceived stress, negative affect and susceptibility to the common cold. *Journal of Personality and Social Psychology, 64,* 131–140.

COHN, E.S., & SWIFT, M.B. (1992). Physical distance and AIDS: Too close for comfort? *Journal of Applied Social Psychology, 22,* 1442–1452.

COIE, J.D., & DODGE, K.A. (1997). Aggression and antisocial behavior. In W. Damon, & N. Eisenberg (Eds.), *Handbook of child psychology: Vol. 3 Social, emotional and personality development* (5th ed).

COKE, J.S., BATSON, C.D., & MCDAVIS, K. (1978). Empathic mediation of helping: A two-stage model. *Journal of Personality and Social Psychology, 36,* 752–766.

COLLIER, G., MINTON, H.L., & REYNOLDS, G. (1991). *Currents of thought in American social psychology.* New York: Oxford.

COLLIGAN, M.J., PENNEBAKER, J.W., & MURPHY, L.R. (1982). *Mass psychogenic illness.* Hillsdale, NJ: Erlbaum.

COLLINS, R.L. (1996). For better or worse: The impact of upward social comparison on self-evaluations. *Psychological Bulletin, 119,* 51–69.

COLMAN, A.M. (1991). Crowd psychology in South African murder trials. *American Psychologist, 46,* 1071–1079.

COMBS, J., & ZILLER, R.C. (1977). The photographic self-concepts of counselees. *Journal of Counseling Psychology, 24,* 452–455.

COMMISSIONER OF OFFICIAL LANGUAGES (2003). *Annual Report, 2001–2002.* Ottawa.

CONGER, J.A., & KANUNGO, R.N. (1998). *Charismatic leadership in organizations.* Thousand Oaks, CA: Sage Publications.

CONLON, D.E., MOON, H., & NG, K.Y. (2002). Putting the cart before the horse: The benefits of arbitrating before mediating. *Journal of Applied Psychology, 87*, 978–984.

CONLON, S.E., LIND, E.A., & LISSAK, R.I. (1989). Nonlinear and non-monotonic effects of outcome on procedural and distributive fairness judgements. *Journal of Applied Social Psychology, 19*, 1085–1099.

CONTRADA, R.J. (1989). Type A behavior, personality hardiness and cardiovascular responses to stress. *Journal of Personality and Social Psychology, 57*, 895–903.

CONWAY, L.G., SUEDFELD, P., & TETLOCK, P.E. (2001). Integrative complexity and political decisions that lead to war or peace. In D.J. Christie, & R.V. Wegner (Eds.), *Peace, conflict and violence: Peace psychology for the 21st century* (pp. 66–75). Upper Saddle River, NJ: Prentice-Hall.

CONWAY, M., & DUBE, L (2002). Humour in persuasion on threatening topics: Effectiveness is a function of audience sex role orientation. *Personality and Social Psychology Bulletin, 28*, 863–873.

CONWAY, M., & ROSS, M. (1984). Getting what you want by revising what you had. *Journal of Personality and Social Psychology, 47*, 738–748.

CONWAY, M., PIZZAMIGLIO, M.T., & MOUNT, L. (1996). Status, communality, and agency: Implications for stereotypes of gender and other groups. *Journal of Personality and Social Psychology, 71*, 25–38.

COOK, S.W. (1970). Motives in a conceptual analysis of attitude-related behavior. In W.J. Arnold, & D. Levine (Eds.), *Nebraska symposium on motivation, 1969* (pp. 179–235). Lincoln, NE: University of Nebraska Press.

COOK, S.W. (1984). *Experimenting on social issues: The case of school desegregation.* 92nd Annual Convention of the American Psychological Association, Toronto.

COOK, S.W., & SELLTIZ, C. (1964). A multiple-indicator approach to attitude measurement. *Psychological Bulletin, 62*, 36–55.

COOLEY, C.H. (1902). *Human nature and the social order.* New York: Scribner.

COOPER, J., & FAZIO, R.H. (1984). A new look at dissonance theory. In L. Berkowitz (Ed.), *Advances in experimental social psychology* (Vol. 17). (pp. 229–266). New York: Academic Press.

COOPER, J., & WORCHEL, S. (1970). Role of undesired consequences in arousing cognitive dissonance. *Journal of Personality and Social Psychology, 16*, 199–206.

COOPER J., ZANNA, M.P., & GOETHALS, G.R. (1971). Mistreatment of an esteemed other as a consequence affecting dissonance reduction. *Journal of Experimental Social Psychology, 10*, 224–233.

COOPER, J., ZANNA, M.P., & TAVES, P.A. (1978). Arousal as a necessary condition for attitude change following induced compliance. *Journal of Personality and Social Psychology, 36*, 1101–1106.

COOPER, M.L., AGOCHA, V.B., & POWERS, A.M. (1999). Motivations for condom use: Do pregnancy prevention goals undermine disease prevention among heterosexual young adults? *Health Psychology, 18*, 464–474.

COOPER, W.H., GALLUPE, R.B., POLLARD, S., & CADSBY, J. (1998). Some liberating effects of anonymous electronic brainstorming. *Small Group Research, 29*, 147–178.

COPPER, C., & MULLEN, B. (1994). The relation between group cohesiveness and performance: An integration. *Psychological Bulletin, 115*, 210–227.

CORENBLUM, B., & ANNIS, R.C. (1993). Development of racial identity in minority and majority children: An effect discrepancy model. *Canadian Journal of Behavioural Science, 25*, 499–521.

CORNWELL, D., & HOBBS, S. (1992). Rumour and legend: Interactions between social psychology and folkloristics. *Canadian Psychology, 33*, 609–613.

COSER, L.A. (1956). *The functions of social conflict.* New York: Free Press.

COSER, L.A. (1967). *Continuities in the study of social conflict.* New York: Free Press.

COTA, A.A., EVANS, C.R., DION, K.L., & LONGMAN, R.S. (1995). The structure of group cohesion. *Personality and Social Psychology Bulletin, 21*, 572–580.

COTTRELL, N.B. (1972). Social facilitation. In C.G. McClintock (Ed.), *Experimental social psychology.* New York: Holt, Rinehart & Winston.

COTTRELL, N.B., WACK, D.L., SEKERAK, G.J., & RITTLE, R.H. (1968). Social facilitation of dominant responses by the presence of an audience and the mere presence of others. *Journal of Personality and Social Psychology, 9*, 245–250.

COVELL, K., DION, K.L., & DION, K.K. (1994). Gender differences. In evaluations of tobacco and alcohol advertisements. *Canadian Journal of Behavioural Science, 26*, 404–420.

COZBY, P.C. (1973). Self-disclosure: A literature review. *Psychological Bulletin, 79*, 73–91.

CRAIG, K.D. (1978). Social modeling influences on pain. In R.A. Sternbach (Ed.), *The psychology of pain* (pp. 73–110). New York: Raven Press.

CRANDALL, C.S. (1988). Social contagion of binge eating. *Journal of Personality and Social Psychology, 55*, 588–598.

CRANDALL, C.S. (1991). Do heavy-weight students have more difficulty paying for college? *Personality and Social Psychology Bulletin, 17*, 606–611.

CRAWFORD, A.M. (1996). Stigma associated with AIDS: A meta-analysis. *Journal of Applied Social Psychology, 26*, 398–416.

CRAWFORD, C., & KREBS, D. (Eds.). (1998). *Handbook of evolutionary psychology: Ideas, issues, and applications.* Mahwah, NJ: Lawrence Erlbaum Associates.

CRAWFORD, M.P. (1939). The social psychology of the vertebrates. *Psychological Bulletin, 36*, 407–466.

CRITCHLOW, B. (1985). The blame in the bottle: Attributions about drunken behavior. *Personality and Social Psychology Bulletin, 11*, 258–274.

CRITTENDEN, K.S. (1983). Sociological aspects of attribution. *Annual Review of Sociology, 9*, 425–446.

CROCKER, J. (1981). Judgement of covariation by social perceivers. *Psychological Bulletin, 90*, 272–292.

CROCKER, J. (1999). Social stigma and self-esteem: situational construction of worth. *Journal of Experimental Social Psychology, 35*, 89–107.

CROCKER, J., & LAWRENCE, J.S. (1999). Social stigma and self-esteem: The role of contingencies of worth. In Prentice, D.A., & Miller, D.T. (Eds.), *Cultural divides: Understanding and overcoming group conflict* (pp. 364–392). New York: Russell Sage Foundation.

CROCKER, J., & MAJOR, B. (1989). Social stigma and self-esteem: The self-protective properties of stigma. *Psychological Review, 96*, 608–630.

CROCKER, J., & QUINN, D. (1998). Racism and self-esteem. In J.L. Eberhardt, & S.T. Fiske (Eds.), *Confronting racism: The problem and the response.* Thousand Oaks, CA: Sage Publications, Inc.

CROMWELL, R.L., BUTTERFIELD, E.C., BRAYFIELD, F.M., & CURRY, J.L. (1977). *Acute myocardial infarction: Reaction and recovery.* St. Louis, MO: Mosby.

CROSON, R., & MARKS, M. (1998). Identifiability of individual contributions in a threshold public goods experiment. *Journal of Mathematical Psychology, 42*, 167–190.

CROSS, S.E., & MADSON, L. (1997). Models of the self: Self-construals and gender. *Psychological Bulletin, 122*, 5–37.

CRUTCHFIELD, R.A. (1955). Conformity and character. *American Psychologist, 10,* 191–198.

CSIKSZENTMIHALYI, M., & FIGURSKI T.J. (1982). Self-awareness and overside experience in everyday life. *Journal of Personality, 50,* 15–28.

CUMBERLAND, J., & ZAMBLE, E. (1992). General and specific measures of attitudes towards early release of criminal offenders. *Canadian Journal of Behavioural Science, 24,* 442–455.

CURRAN, J.P., & LIPPOLD, S. (1975). The effects of physical attraction and attitude similarity on attraction in dating dyads. *Journal of Personality, 43,* 528–538.

CURTIS, R.C., & MILLER, K. (1986). Believing another likes or dislikes you; Behavior makes the beliefs come true. *Journal of Personality and Social Psychology, 51,* 284–290.

CUTLER, R.E., & STORM, T. (1975). Observational study of alcohol consumption in natural settings. *Journal of Studies on Alcohol, 36,* 1173–1183.

CUTRONA, C.E. (1982). Transition to college: Loneliness and the process of social adjustment. In L.A. Peplau, & D. Perlman (Eds.), *Loneliness: A sourcebook of current theory, research and therapy* (pp. 291–309). New York: Wiley.

D'ANGLEJAN, A. (1984). Language planning in Québec: An historical overview and future trends. In R.Y. Bourhis (Ed.), *Conflict and language planning in Québec* (pp. 1–27). Clevedon: Multilingual Matters.

D'ANGLEJAN, A., & TUCKER, G.R. (1973). Sociolinguistic correlates of speech style in Québec. In R.W. Shuy, & R.W. Fasold (Eds.), *Language attitudes: Current trends and prospects* (pp. 1–27). Washington: Georgetown University Press.

DA GLORIA, J. (1984). Frustration, aggression and the sense of justice. In A. Mummendey (Ed.), *Social psychology of aggression: From individual behavior to social interaction* (pp. 127–142). New York: Springer-Verlag.

DALY, M., & WILSON, M. (1988). *Homicide.* New York: Aldine De Gruyter.

DANE, F., & WRIGHTSMAN, L. (1982). Effects of defendant's and victim's characteristics on jurors' verdicts. In N.L. Kerr, & R.M. Bray (Eds.), *The psychology of the courtroom* (pp. 83–115). New York: Academic Press.

DANZIGER, K. (1983). Origins and basic principles of Wundt's Volkerpsychologie. *British Journal of Social Psychology, 22,* 303–313.

DARLEY, J.M., & LATANÉ, B. (1968). Bystander intervention in emergencies: Diffusion of responsibility. *Journal of Personality and Social Psychology, 8,* 377–383.

DARLEY, J.M., & LATANÉ, B. (1970). Norms and normative behavior: Field studies of social interdependence. In J. Macaulay, & L. Berkowitz (Eds.), *Altruism and helping behavior* (pp. 83–101). New York: Academic Press.

DARLEY, J.M., & SHULTZ, T.R. (1990). Moral rules: Their content and acquisition. *Annual Review of Psychology, 41,* 525–556.

DARLEY, J.M., LOEB, I., & HUNTER, J. (1996). Community attitudes on the family of issues surrounding the death of terminal patients. *Journal of Social Issues, 52,* 85–104.

DARLINGTON, R.B., & MACKER, D.F. (1966). Displacement of guilt-produced altruistic behavior. *Journal of Personality and Social Psychology, 4,* 442–443.

DARNELL, R. (1971). Sociolinguistic perspectives on linguistic diversity. In R. Darnell (Ed.), *Linguistic diversity in Canadian society.* Edmonton: Linguistic Research.

DARWIN, C. (1871). *The descent of men and selection in relation to sex.* New York: Appleton.

DASHIELL, J.F. (1935). Experimental studies of the influence of social situations on the behavior of individual human adults. In C. Murchison (Ed.), *Handbook of social psychology* (pp. 1097–1158). Worcester, MA: Clark University.

DAVIDOWICZ, L.C. (1975). *The war against the Jews, 1933–1945.* Holt, Rinehart & Winston: New York.

DAVIDSON, A.R., & MORRISON, D.M. (1983). Predicting contraceptive behavior from attitudes: A comparison of within- versus across-subjects procedures. *Journal of Personality and Social Psychology, 45,* 997–1009.

DAVIDSON, T. (1978). *Conjugal crime.* New York: Ballantine Books.

DAWES, R.M. (1980). Social dilemmas. *Annual Review of Psychology, 31,* 169–193.

DAWSON, T.H. (2002). New tools, new insights: Kohlberg's moral judgement stages revisited. *International Journal of Behavioral Development, 26,* 154–166.

DE CREMER, D. (1999) Trust and fear of exploitation in a public goods dilemma. *Current Psychology, 18,* 153–163.

DE VILLIERS, M. (2003). *Water.* Toronto: McClelland and Stewart.

DEAUX, K. (1984). From individual differences to social categories. *American Psychologist, 39,* 105–116.

DEAUX, K., & EMSWILLER, T. (1974). Explanations of successful performance on sex-linked tasks: What is skill for the male is luck for the female. *Journal of Personality and Social Psychology, 29,* 80–85.

DECI, E.L. (1971). Effects of externally mediated rewards on intrinsic motivation. *Journal of Personality and Social Psychology, 15,* 105–115.

DECI, E.L., & RYAN, R.M. (1985). *Intrinsic motivation and self-determination on human behavior.* New York: Plenum.

DECI, E.L., NEZLEK J., & SHEINMAN, L. (1981). Characteristics of the rewarder and intrinsics of the motivation of the rewardee. *Journal of Personality and Social Psychology, 40,* 1–10.

DECOURVILLE, N., & SADAVA, S.W. (1997). The structure of problem drinking in adulthood: A confirmatory approach. *Journal of Studies on Alcohol, 58,* 146–154.

DEJONG, W. (1979). An examination of self-perception mediation of the foot-in-the-door effect. *Journal of Personality and Social Psychology, 37,* 2221–2239.

DELONGIS, A., COYNE, J.C., KAKOF, G., FOLKMAN, S., & LAZARUS, R.S. (1982). Relationship of daily hassles, uplifts and major life events to health status. *Health Psychology, 1,* 119–136.

DEN OUDEN, M.D., & RUSSELL, G.W. (1997). Sympathy and altruism in response to disasters: A Dutch and Canadian comparison. *Social Behavior and Personality, 25,* 241–248.

DENHAERINCK, P., LEYENS, J.P., & YZERBT, V. (1989). The dilution effect and group membership: An instance of the pervasive impact of outgroup homogeneity. *European Journal of Social Psychology, 19,* 243–250.

DEPAULO, B.M., & PFEIFER, R.L. (1986). On-the-job experience and skill at detecting deception. *Journal of Applied Social Psychology, 16,* 249–267.

DEPAULO, B.M., & COLEMAN, L.M. (1986). Talking to children, foreigners, and retarded adults. *Journal of Personality and Social Psychology, 51,* 945–959.

DEPAULO, B.M., & ROSENTHAL, R. (1979). Telling lies. *Journal of Personality and Social Psychology, 37,* 1713–1722.

DERMER, M., & PYSZCZYNSKI, T.A. (1978). Effects of erotica upon men's loving and liking responses for women they love. *Journal of Personality and Social Psychology, 36,* 1302–1309.

DERMER, M.L., & JACOBSEN, E. (1986). Some potential negative social consequences of cigarette smoking: Marketing research in reverse. *Journal of Applied Social Psychology, 16,* 702–725.

DEROSA, A.S. (1986). The social representation of mental illness in children and adults. In W. Doise, & S. Moscovici (Eds.), *Current issues in European social psychology* (pp. 47–138). New York: Cambridge.

DESCHAMPS, J.C., & DOISE, W. (1978). Crossed category memberships in intergroup relations. In H. Tajfel (Ed.), *Differentiation between social groups: Studies in the social psychology of inter-group relations* (pp. 141–158). London: Academic Press.

DESTEFANO, D.A., & SALOVEY, P. (1996). Jealousy and the characteristics of one's rival: A self-evaluation maintenance perspective. *Personality and Social Psychology Bulletin, 22,* 921–932.

DEUTSCH, F.M., & LAMBERTI, D.M. (1986). Does social approval improve helping? *Personality and Social Psychology Bulletin, 12,* 149–158.

DEUTSCH, M. (1958). Trust and suspicion. *Journal of Conflict Resolution, 2,* 265–279.

DEUTSCH, M. (1973). *The resolution of conflict: Constructive and destructive processes.* New Haven: Yale University Press.

DEUTSCH, M. (1985). *Distributive justice.* New Haven: Yale University Press.

DEUTSCH, M., & KRAUSS, R.M. (1960). The effect of threat on interpersonal bargaining. *Journal of Abnormal and Social Psychology, 61,* 181–189.

DEUTSCH, M., & SOLOMON, L. (1959). Reactions to evaluations by others as influenced by self-evaluations. *Sociometry, 22,* 92–113.

DEVINE, P.G. (1989). Stereotypes and prejudice: Their automatic and controlled components. *Journal of Personality and Social Psychology, 56,* 5–18.

DEVINE, P.G., & ELLIOT, A.J. (1995) Are racial stereotypes really fading? The Princeton trilogy revisited. *Personality and Social Psychology Bulletin, 21,* 1139–1150.

DEVOS, G.A., & HIPPLER, A.E. (1969). Cultural psychology: Comparative studies of human behavior. In G. Lindzey, & E. Aronson (Eds.), *The handbook of social psychology* (2nd ed.). (Vol. 4). (pp. 322–417). Reading, MA: Addison-Wesley.

DEVRIES, D.L., & EDWARDS, K.J. (1974). Student teams and learning games: Their effects on cross-race and cross-sex interaction. *Journal of Educational Psychology, 66,* 741–749.

DICKENBERGER, M. (1978). Reactions to procedural models for adjudicative conflict resolution. *Journal of Conflict Resolution, 22,* 318–341.

DICKERSON, C., THIBODEAU, R., ARONSON, E., & MILLER, D. (1992). Using cognitive dissonance to encourage water conservation. *Journal of Applied Social Psychology, 22,* 841–854.

DIEN, D. (1982). A Chinese perspective on Kohlberg's theory of moral development. *Developmental Review, 2,* 331–341.

DIENER, E. (1977). Deindividuation: Causes and Consequences. *Social Behavior and Personality, 5,* 143–155.

DIJKER, A.J.M. (1987). Emotional reactions to ethnic minorities. *European Journal of Social Psychology, 17,* 305–325.

DIMATTEO, M.R., SHERBOURNE, C.D., HAYS, R.D., ORDWAY, L., KRAVITZ, R.L., MCGLYNN, E.A., KAPLAN, S., & ROGERS, W.H. (1993). Physicians' characteristics influence patients' adherence to medical treatment: Results from the medical outcomes study. *Health Psychology, 12,* 93–102.

DINDIA, K. (2000). Sex differences in self-disclosure, reciprocity of self-disclosure and self-disclosure and liking: Three meta-analyses reviewed. In S. Petronio (Ed.), *Balancing the secrets of private disclosure. LEA communication series* (pp. 21–35). Manwah, NJ: Erlbaum.

DINICOLA, D.D., & DiMATTEO, M.R. (1984). Practitioners, patients and compliance with medical regimes: A social psychological perspective. In A. Baum, S.E. Taylor, & J.E. Singer (Eds.), *Handbook of psychology and health* (Vol. 4). (pp. 55–64). Hillsdale, NJ: Erlbaum.

DION, K.K. (1972). Physical attractiveness and evaluations of children's transgressions. *Journal of Personality and Social Psychology, 24,* 207–213.

DION, K.K. (1992). *Relative deprivation, perceived discrimination and militancy.* Paper presented at the meeting of the International Congress of Psychology, Brussels. In R.Y. Bourhis, & J-P. Levy (Eds.), *Stéréotypes, discrimination, et relations intergroupes.* Liège: Mardaga.

DION, K.K., & DION, K.L. (1985). Personality, gender and the phenomenology of romantic love. *Review of Personality and Social Psychology, 6,* 209–20.

DION, K.K., & DION, K.L. (1996). Cultural perspectives on Romantic love. *Personal Relationships, 3,* 5–17.

DION, K.K., BERSCHEID, E., & WALSTER, E. (1972). What is beautiful is good. *Journal of Personality and Social Psychology, 24,* 285–290.

DION, K.K., PAK, A.W., & DION, K.L. (1990). Stereotyping physical attractiveness: A perspective. *Journal of Cross-Cultural Psychology, 21,* 378–398.

DION, K.L. (1987). What's in a title? The Ms. stereotype and images of women's titles of address. *Psychology of Women Quarterly, 11,* 21–36.

DION, K.L. (1989). *Ethnicity and perceived discrimination: A comparative survey of six ethnic groups in Toronto.* 10th Annual Conference of the Canadian Ethnic Studies Association, Calgary.

DION, K.L. (2002). The social psychology of perceiver prejudice and discrimination. *Canadian Psychology, 43,* 1–10.

DION, K.L., & DION, K.K. (1976). The Ames phenomenon revisited: Factors underlying the resistance to perceptual distortion of one's partner. *Journal of Personality and Social Psychology, 33,* 170–177.

DION, K.L., & DION, K.K. (1987). Belief in a just world and physical attractiveness stereotyping. *Journal of Personality and Social Psychology, 52,* 775–780.

DION, K.L., & EARN, B.M. (1975). The phenomenology of being a target of prejudice. *Journal of Personality and Social Psychology, 32,* 944–940.

DION, K.L., & KAWAKAMI, K. (1996). Ethnicity and perceived discrimination in Toronto: Another look at the personal/group discrimination discrepancy. *Canadian Journal of Behavioural Science, 28,* 203–213.

DION, K.L., & SCHULLER, R.A. (1991). The Ms. Stereotype: Its generality and its relation to managerial and marital status stereotypes. *Canadian Journal of Behaviour Science, 23,* 25–40.

DION, K.L., DION, K.K., COAMBS, R., & KOZLOWSKI, L. (1990, June). *Smokers and drinkers: A tale of two stereotypes.* Annual Convention of the Canadian Psychological Association, Ottawa.

DION, K.L., EARN, B.M., & YEE, P.H.N. (1986). The experience of being a victim of prejudice: An experimental approach. In B. Earn, & S. Towson (Eds.), *Readings in social psychology: Classic and Canadian contributions.* Peterborough: Broadview Press.

DIPBOYE, R.L. (1977). Alternative approaches to deindividuation. *Psychological Bulletin, 84,* 1057–1075.

DITECCO, D., & SCHLEGEL, R.P. (1982). Alcohol use among young males: An application of problem-behavior theory. In J.R. Eiser (Ed.), *Social psychology and behavioral medicine.* (pp. 199–233). Chichester: J.R. Wiley.

DITTO, P.H., & HILTON, J.L. (1990). Expectancy processes in the health care interaction sequence. *Journal of Social Issues, 46* (2), 97–124.

DIXON, D., CRUESS, S., KILBOURNE, K., KLIMAS, N., FLETCHER, M., IRONSON, G., BAUM, A., SCHNEIDERMAN, N., & ANTONI, M.H. (2001). Social support mediates loneliness and human herpesvirus Type 6 (HHV-6) antibody titers. *Journal of Applied Social Psychology, 31,* 1111–1132.

DOAN, B.D., & GRAY, R.E. (1992). The heroic cancer patient: A critical analysis of the relationship between illusion and mental health. *Canadian Journal of Behavioural Science, 24,* 253–266.

DOISE, W., & DANN, H-D. (1976). New theoretical perspectives in the study of intergroup relations. *Italian Journal of Psychology, 3,* 285–304.

DOISE, W., DESCHAMPS, J-C., & MEYER, G. (1978). The accentuation of intra-category similarities. In H. Tajfel (Ed.), *Differentiation between social groups: Studies in the social psychology of intergroup relations* (pp. 159–168). London: Academic Press.

DOLLARD, J., DOOB, L.W., MILLER, N.E., MOWRER, O.H., & SEARS, R.R. (1939). *Frustration and aggression.* New Haven: Yale University Press.

DOLLINGER, S.J. (1999). Correlates of autophotographic individuality: Therapy experiences and loneliness. *Journal of Social and Clinical Psychology, 18,* 325–340.

DOLLINGER, S.J. (2001). Religious identity: An autophotographic study. *International Journal for the Psychology of Religion, 11,* 71–92.

DOLLINGER, S.J. (2002). Physical attractiveness, social connectedness and individuality: An autophotographic study. *Journal of Social Psychology, 142,* 25–32.

DOLLINGER, S.J., & CLANCY, S.M. (1993). Identity, self and personality: II. Glimpses through the autophotographic eye. *Journal of Personality and Social Psychology, 64,* 1064–1071.

DOLLINGER, S.J., PRESTON, L.A., O'BRIEN, S.P., & DILALLA, D.L. (1996). Individuality and relatedness of the self: An autophotographic study. *Journal of Personality and Social Psychology, 71,* 1268–1278.

DOLLINGER, S.J., RHODES, K.A., & CORCORAN, K.J. (1993). Photographically portrayed identities, alcohol expectancies and excessive drinking. *Journal of Personality Assessment, 60,* 522–531.

DOMPIERRE, S., & LAVELLÉE, M. (1990). Degré de contact et stress acculturatif dans le procéssus d'adaptation des refugiés africains. *International Journal of Psychology, 25,* 417–437.

DONAKOWSKI, D.W., & ESSES, V.M. (1996). Native Canadians, First Nations, or aboriginals: The effect of labels on attitudes toward native peoples. *Canadian Journal of Behavioural Science, 28,* 86–91.

DONNERSTEIN, E., DONNERSTEIN, M., & EVANS, R. (1975). Erotic stimuli and aggression: Facilitation or inhibition. *Journal of Personality and Social Psychology, 32,* 237–244.

DONNERSTEIN, E., LINZ, D., & PENROD, S. (1987). *The question of pornography.* New York: Free Press.

DONOVAN, J.E., JESSOR, R., & COSTA, F.M. (1993). Structure of health-enhancing behaviors in adolescence: A latent-variable approach. *Journal of Health and Social Behavior, 34,* 346–362.

DONOVAN, J.E., JESSOR, R., & JESSOR, L. (1983). Problem drinking in adolescence and young adulthood. A follow-up study. *Journal of Studies on Alcohol, 44,* 109–137.

DOO, L. (1973). Dispute settlement in Chinese-American communities. *American Journal of Comparative Law, 21,* 627–663.

DOOB, A.N., & GROSS, A.E. (1968). States of frustration as an inhibitor of horn-honking responses. *Journal of Social Psychology, 76,* 213–218.

DOOB, A.N., & KIRSHENBAUM, H.M. (1972). Some empirical evidence on the effect of S. 12 of the Canada Evidence Act on an accused. *Criminal Law Quarterly, 15,* 88–96.

DOOB, A.N., & KIRSHENBAUM, H.M. (1973a). The effects on arousal of frustration and aggression films. *Journal of Experimental Social Psychology, 9,* 57–64.

DOOB, A.N., & KIRSHENBAUM, H.M. (1973b). Bias in police lineups—Partial remembering. *Journal of Police Science and Administration, 1,* 287–293.

DOOB, A.N., & ROBERTS, J.V. (1984). Social psychology, social attitudes and attitudes toward sentencing. *Canadian Journal of Behavioural Science, 16,* 269–280.

DOUGLAS, K. M., & MCGARTY, C. (2002). Internet identifiability and beyond: A model of the effects of identifiability on communicative behavior. *Group-Dynamics. 6,* 17–26.

DOVIDIO, J.F., & ELLYSON, S.L. (1985). Patterns of visual dominance behavior in humans. In S.L. Ellyson, & J.F. Dovidio (Eds.), *Power, dominance, and noverbal behavior* (pp. 129–149). New York: Springer-Verlag.

DOVIDIO, J.F., & MORRIS, W.N. (1975). Effects of stress and commonality of fate on helping behavior. *Journal of Personality and Social Psychology, 31,* 145–149.

DOVIDIO, J.F., ALLEN, J.L., & SCHROEDER, D.A. (1990). Specificity of empathy-induced helping: Evidence for altruistic motivation. *Journal of Personality and Social Psychology, 59,* 249–260.

DOVIDIO, J.F., ELLYSON, S.L., KEATING, C.J., HELTMAN, K., & BROWN, C.E. (1988). The relationship of social power to visual displays of dominance between men and women. *Journal of Personality and Social Psychology, 54,* 233–242.

DOVIDIO, J.F., GAERTNER, S.L., ISEN, A.M., & LOWRANCE, R.M (1995). Group representations and intergroup bias: Positive affect, similarity and group size. *Personality and Social Psychology Bulletin, 28,* 856–865.

DOWNS, A.C., & LYONS, P.M. (1991). Natural observations of the links between attractiveness and initial legal judgements. *Personality and Social Psychology Bulletin, 17,* 541–547.

DRABSMAN, R.S., & THOMAS, M.H. (1975). Does TV violence breed indifference? *Journal of Communications, 25,* 86–89.

DRAGUNS, J.G. (1988). Personality and culture: Are they relevant for the enhancement of quality of mental life? In P.R. Dasen, J.W. Berry, & N. Sartorius (Eds.), *Health and Cross-cultural Psychology: Towards applications.* Newbury Park, CA: Sage.

DRIGOTAS, S.M., & RUSBULT, C.E. (1992). Should I stay or should I go? A dependence model of breakups. *Journal of Personality and Social Psychology, 62,* 62–87.

DRIGOTAS, S.M., RUSBULT, C.E., WIESELQUIST, J., & WHITTON, S.W. (1999). Close partner as sculptor of the ideal self: Behavioral affirmation and the Michelangelo phenomenon. *Journal of Personality and Social Psychology, 77,* 293–323.

DRISCOLL, R., DAVIS, K.W., & LIPETZ, M.E. (1972). Parental interference and romantic love. *Journal of Personality and Social Psychology, 24,* 1–10.

DRURY, J. (2003). Adolescent communication with adults in authority. *Journal of Language and Social Psychology, 22,* 66–73.

DUNKEL-SCHETTER, C., & WORTMAN, C.B. (1982). The interpersonal dynamics of cancer: Problems in social relationships and their impact on the patient. In H.S. Friedman, & M.R. DiMatteo (Eds.), *Interpersonal issues in health care* (pp. 69–100). New York: Academic.

DUNKEL-SCHETTER, C., FEINSTEIN, L.G., TAYLOR, S.E., & FALKE, R.L. (1992). Patterns of coping with cancer. *Health Psychology, 11,* 79–87.

DURANT, J.E. (1993). Spare the rod and spoil the child? The physical discipline of children and child abuse. *Institute for Social Research Newsletter, 8,* 2.

DURANT, W., & DURANT, A. (1961). *The story of civilization: Part VII. The age of reason begins.* New York: Simon and Schuster.

DUTTON, D.G. (1971). Reactions of restaurateurs to blacks and whites violating restaurant dress requirements. *Canadian Journal of Behavioural Science, 3,* 298–331.

DUTTON, D.G. (1973). The relationship of amount of perceived discrimination toward a minority group on behaviour of majority group members. *Canadian Journal of Behavioural Science, 5,* 34–45.

DUTTON, D.G. (1984). Interventions into the problem of wife assault: Therapeutic, policy and research implications. *Canadian Journal of Behavioural Science, 16,* 281–297.

DUTTON, D.G., & ARON, A.P. (1974). Some evidence for heightened sexual attraction under conditions of high anxiety. *Journal of Personality and Social Psychology, 30,* 510–517.

DUTTON, D.G., & LAKE, R. (1973). Threat of own prejudice and reverse discrimination in interracial situations. *Journal of Personality and Social Psychology, 28,* 94–100.

DUTTON, D.G., & LENNOX, V.I. (1974). The effect of prior "token" compliance on subsequent interracial behaviour. *Journal of Personality and Social Psychology, 29,* 65–71.

DUTTON, D.G., SAUNDERS, K., STARZOMSKI, A., & BARTHOLOMEW, K. (1994). Intimacy—Anger and insecure attachment as precursors of abuse in intimate relationships. *Journal of Applied Social Psychology, 24,* 1367–1386.

DUVAL, S., & WICKLUND, R.A. (1972). *A theory of objective self-awareness.* New York: Academic Press.

EAGLY, A.H. (1974). Comprehensibility of persuasive arguments as a determinant of opinion change. *Journal of Personality and Social Psychology, 29,* 758–773.

EAGLY, A.H. (1978). Sex differences in influenceability. *Psychological Bulletin, 85,* 85–116.

EAGLY, A.H. (1987). *Sex differences in social behavior: A social-role analysis.* Hillsdale, NJ: Erlbaum.

EAGLY, A.H. (1996, August 16–21). *Attitudes and the processing of attitude-relevant information.* XXVI International Congress of Psychology, Montréal.

EAGLY, A.H., & CARLI, L.L. (1981). Sex of researcher and sex-typed communications as determinants of sex differences in influenceability: A meta-analysis of social influence studies. *Psychological Bulletin, 90,* 1–20.

EAGLY, A.H., & CHAIKEN, E. (1998). Attitude structure and function. In D.T. Gilbert, S.T. Fiske, & G. Lindzey (Eds.). *Handbook of social psychology* (4th ed.) (Vol. 1). (pp. 269–322). New York: McGraw-Hill.

EAGLY, A.H., & CHAIKEN, S. (1984). Cognitive theories of persuasion. In L. Berkowitz (Ed.), *Advances in experimental social psychology* (Vol. 17). (pp. 267–359). New York: Academic Press.

EAGLY, A.H., & CHAIKEN, S. (1992). *The psychology of attitudes.* Fort Worth, TX: Harcourt Brace Jovanovich.

EAGLY, A.H., & CHAIKEN, S. (1998). Attitude structure and function. In D.T. Gilbert, & S.T. Fiske (Eds.), *The handbook of social psychology* (pp. 269–322). Boston, MA: McGraw-Hill.

EAGLY, A.H., & CROWLEY, M. (1986). Gender and helping behavior: A meta-analytic review of the social psychological literature. *Psychological Bulletin, 100,* 283–308.

EAGLY, A.H., & KARAU, S.J. (1991). Gender and the emergence of leaders: A meta-analysis. *Journal of Personality and Social Psychology, 60,* 685–710.

EAGLY, A.H., & STEFFEN, V.J. (1986). Gender and aggressive behavior: A meta-analytic review of the social psychological literature. *Psychological Bulletin, 100,* 309–330.

EAGLY, A.H., & WOOD, W. (1982). Inferred sex differences in status as a determinant of gender stereotypes about social influence. *Journal of Personality and Social Psychology, 43,* 915–928.

EAGLY, A.H., & WOOD, W. (1985). Gender and influenceability: Stereotype versus behavior. In V.E. O'Leary, R.K. Unger, & B.S. Wallston (Eds.), *Women, gender and social psychology* (pp. 225–256). Hillsdale, NJ: Erlbaum.

EAGLY, A.H., ASHMORE, R.D., MAKHIJANI, M.G., & LONGO, L.C. (1991). What is beautiful is good but... A meta-analytic review of research on the physical attractiveness stereotype. *Psychological Bulletin, 110,* 109–128.

EAGLY, A.H., CHEN, S., CHAIKEN, S., & SHAW-BARNES, K. (1999). The impact of attitudes on memory: An affair to remember. *Psychological Bulletin, 125,* 64–89.

EAGLY, A.H., KARAU, S.J., & MAKHIJANI, M.G. (1995). Gender and the effectiveness of leaders: A meta-analysis. *Psychological Bulletin, 17,* 125–145.

EAGLY, A.H., KULESA, P., BRANNON, L.A., SHAW, K., & HUTSON-COMEAUX, S. (2000). Why counterattitudinal messages are as memorable as proattitudinal message: The importance of active defense against attack. *Personality and Social Psychology Bulletin, 26,* 1392–1408.

EAGLY, A.H., MAKHIJANI, M.G., & KLONSKY, B.G. (1992). Gender and the evaluation of leaders: A meta-analysis. *Psychological Bulletin, 111,* 3–22.

EAGLY, A.H., WOOD, W., & CHAIKEN, S. (1978). Causal inferences about communicators and their effects on opinion change. *Journal of Personality and Social Psychology, 36,* 424–435.

EAGLY, A.H., WOOD, W., & FISHBAUGH, L. (1981). Sex differences in conformity: Surveillance by the group as a determinant of male non-conformity. *Journal of Personality and Social Psychology, 40,* 384–394.

EASTERBROOK, J.A. (1959). The effect of emotion on cue utilization and the organization of behavior. *Psychological Review, 66,* 183–201.

ECKERT, P. (2003). Language and adolescent peer groups. *Journal of Language and Social Psychology, 22,* 112–118.

EDWARDS, K. (1990). The interplay of affect and cognition in attitude formation and change. *Journal of Personality and Social Psychology 59,* 202–216.

EDWARDS, W. (1954). The theory of decision-making. *Psychological Bulletin, 51,* 380–417.

EFFRAN, M.G. (1974). The effect of physical appearance on the judgment of guilt, interpersonal attraction, and severity of recommended punishment in a simulated jury task. *Journal of Research in Personality, 8,* 45–54.

EFFRAN, M.G., & PATTERSON, E.W.J. (1974). Voters vote beautiful: The effect of physical appearance on a national election. *Canadian Journal of Behavioural Science, 6,* 352–356.

EHRLICH, D., GUTTMAN, I., SCHONBACH, P., & MILLS, J. (1957). Post-decision exposure to relevant information. *Journal of Personality and Social Psychology, 54,* 98–102.

EHRLINGER, J., & DUNNING, D. (2003). How chronic self-views influence (and potentially mislead) estimates of performance. *Journal of Personality and Social Psychology, 84,* 5–17.

EIDELSON, R.J., & EIDELSON, J.I. (2003). Dangerous ideas. Five beliefs that propel groups toward conflict. *American Psychologist, 58,* 182–192.

EISENBERG, N. (2002). Empathy-related emotional responses, altruism, and their socialization. In R.J. Davidson, and A. Harrington (Eds). *Visions of compassion: Western scientists and Tibetan Buddhists examine human nature* (pp. 131–164). London, Oxford University Press.

EISENBERG, N., & LENNON, R. (1983). Sex differences in empathy and related capacities. *Psychological Bulletin, 94,* 100–131.

EISENBERG, N., & MILLER, P.A. (1987). The relation of empathy to pro-social and related behaviors. *Psychological Bulletin, 101,* 91–119.

EISENBERG, N., GUTHRIE, I. K., CUMBERLAND, A., MURPHY, B. C., SHEPARD, S.A., ZHOU, Q., & CARLO, G. (2002) Prosocial development in early adulthood: A longitudinal study. *Journal of Personality and Social Psychology, 82,* 993–1006.

EISER, J.R. (1987). *The expression of attitude.* New York: Springer-Verlag.

EISER, J.R., & PANCER, S.M. (1979). Attitudinal effects of the use of evaluatively biased language. *European Journal of Social Psychology, 9,* 39–47.

EISER, J.R., & ROSS, M. (1977). Partisan language, immediacy and attitude change. *European Journal of Social Psychology, 7,* 477–489.

EISER, J.R., & VAN DER PLIGT, J. (1984). Attitudes and social factors in adolescent smoking: In search of peer group influences. *Journal of Applied Social Psychology, 14,* 348–363.

EKMAN, P. (1982). *Emotion in the human face.* New York: Cambridge.

EKMAN, P. (1994). Strong evidence for universals in facial expressions: A reply to Russell's mistaken critique. *Psychological Bulletin, 115,* 268–287.

EKMAN, P., & FRIESEN, W.V. (1969). Nonverbal leakage and clues to deception. *Psychiatry, 32,* 88–106.

EKMAN, P., & FRIESEN, W.V. (1974). Detecting deception from the body or face. *Journal of Personality and Social Psychology, 29,* 188–198.

EKMAN, P., & FRIESEN, W.V. (1978). *Facial action coding system.* Palo Alto, CA: Consulting Psychologists Press.

EKMAN, P., FRIESEN, W.V., O'SULLIVAN, M., CHAN, A., DIACOYAN-NI-TARLATZIS, I., HEIDER, K., KRAUSE, R., LECOMPTE, W.A., PITCAIRN, T., RICCI-BITTI, P.E., SCHERER, K., TOMITA, M., & TZAVARAS, A. (1987). Universals and cultural differences in the judgments of facial expressions of emotion. *Journal of Personality and Social Psychology, 53,* 712–717.

EKMAN, P., O'SULLIVAN, M., & FRANK, M.G. (1999). A few can catch a liar. *Psychological Science, 10,* 263–266.

ELLYSON, S.L., & DOVIDIO, J.F. (Eds.). (1985). *Power, dominance, and nonverbal behavior.* New York: Springer-Verlag.

ELMS, A.C. (1982). Keeping deception honest: Justifying conditions for social scientific research strategies. In T.L. Beauchamp, & R. Faden (Eds.), *Ethical issues in social science research.* Baltimore: Johns Hopkins University Press.

ELMS, A.C., & JANIS, I.L. (1965). Counter-norm attitudes induced by consonant versus dissonant conditions of role-playing. *Journal of Experimental Research in Personality, 1,* 50–60.

ELWORK, A., SALES, B.D., & ALFINI, J.J. (1982). *Making jury instructions intelligible.* Charlotteville, VA: Michie Press.

EMERY, R.E. (1989). Family abuse. *American Psychologist, 44,* 321–328.

ENDLER, N., & SPEER, R.L. (1998). Personality psychology: Research trends for 1993–1995. *Journal of Personality, 66,* 621–669.

ERON, L.D. (1980). Prescription for reduction of aggression. *American Psychologist, 35,* 244–252.

ERON, L.D., HUESMANN, L.R., DUBOW, E., ROMANOFF, R., & YARMEL, P.W. (1987). Aggression and its correlates over 22 years. In N.H. Crowell, R.J. Blanchard, I. Evans, & C.R. O'Donnel (Eds.), *Childhood aggression and violence: Sources of influence, prevention and control.* New York: Academic Press.

ERON, L.D., HUESMANN, L.R., LEFKOWITZ, M.M., & WALDER, L.O. (1972). Does television violence cause aggression? *American Psychologist, 27,* 253–263.

ERVIN-TRIPP, S.M. (1974). Is second-language learning really like the first? *TESOL Quarterly, 8,* 111–127.

ESPY, W.R., (1975). *An almanac of words at play.* New York: Clarkson N. Potter.

ESSER, J.K. (1998). Alive and well after 25 years: A review of groupthink research. *Organizational Behavior and Human Decision Processes, 73,* 116–141.

ESSES, V.M., & SELIGMAN, C. (1996). The individual-group distinction in assessments of strategies to reduce prejudice and discrimination: The case of affirmative action. In R.M. Sorrentino, & E.T. Higgins (Eds.), *Handbook of motivation and cognition: (Vol. 3) The interpersonal context.* New York: Guilford Press.

ESSES, V.M., & WEBSTER, C.D. (1988). Physical attractiveness, dangerousness and the Canadian Criminal Code. *Journal of Applied Social Psychology, 18,* 1017–1031.

ESSES, V.M., HADDOCK, G., & ZANNA, M.P. (1993). Values, stereotypes, and emotions as determinants of intergroup attitudes. In D.M. Mackie, & D.C. Hamilton (Eds.), *Affect, cognition and stereotyping: Interactive processes in group perception* (pp. 137–166). New York: Academic Press.

ESSES, V.M., JACKSON, L.M., & ARMSTRONG, T.L. (1998). Intergroup competition and attitudes towards immigrants and immigration. *Journal of Social Issues, 54,* 699–724.

ETCOFF, N. (1999). *Survival of the prettiest: The science of beauty.* New York: Doubleday.

ÉTHIER, L.S., PALACIO-QUINTIN, E., & JOURDAN-IONESCU, C. (1992). Abuse and neglect: Two distinct forms of maltreatment? *Canada's Mental Health, 40,* 13–18.

EVANS, G.W., LEPORE, S.J., & ALLEN, K.M. (2000). Cross-cultural differences in tolerance for crowding: Fact or fiction? *Journal of Personality and Social Psychology, 79,* 204–210.

EVANS, L.M. & PETTY, R.E. (2003). Self-guide framing and persuasion: Responsibility increasing message processing to ideal levels. *Personality and Social Psychology Bulletin, 29,* 313–324.

EVANS, R.I., RAINES, B.E., & HANSELKA, L. (1984). Developing data-based communication in social psychological research: Adolescent smoking prevention. *Journal of Applied Social Psychology, 14,* 289–295.

FABRIGAR, L.R., & PETTY, R.E. (1999). The role of the affective and cognitive bases of attitudes in susceptibility to affectively and cognitively based persuasion. *Personality and Social Psychology Bulletin, 25,* 363–381.

FABRIGAR, L.R., SMITH, S.M., & BRANNON, L.A. (1999). Applications of social cognition: Attitudes as cognitive structures. In Durso, F.T. (Ed.), *Handbook of applied cognition* (pp. 173–206). New York: Wiley.

FARAGO, L. (1942). *German psychological warfare.* New York: G.P. Putnam's Sons.

FARINA, A., & RING, K. (1965). The influence of perceived mental illness on interpersonal relations. *Journal of Abnormal Psychology, 70,* 47–51.

FAZIO, R.H. (1990). Multiple processes by which attitudes guide behavior: The MODE model as an integrated framework. In M.P. Zanna (Ed.), *Advances in experimental social psychology* (pp. 75–109). New York: Academic Press.

FAZIO, R.H., BLASCOVICH, J., & DRISCOLL, D.M. (1992). On the functional value of attitudes: The influence of accessible attitudes on the ease and quality of decision making. *Personality and Social Psychology Bulletin, 18,* 388–401.

FAZIO, R.H., JACKSON, J., DUNTON, B.C., & WILLIAMS, C.J. (1995). Variability in automatic activation as an unobtrusive measure of racial attitudes: A bona fide pipeline. *Journal of Personality and Social Psychology, 69,* 1013–1027.

FAZIO, R.H., SANBONMATSU, D.M., POWELL, M.C., & KARDES, F.R. (1986). On the automatic activation of attitudes. *Journal of Personality and Social Psychology, 50,* 229–238.

FEARN, G.F.N. (1973). *Canadian social organization.* Toronto: Holt, Rinehart & Winston.

FEENEY, J.A., & RYAN, S.M.F. (1994). Attachment style and affect regulation: Relationship with health behavior and family experiences of illness in a student sample. *Health Psychology, 13,* 334–345.

FEHR, B. (1993). How do I love thee? Let me consult my prototype. In S. Duck (Ed.), *Individuals in relationships* (Vol. 1). (pp. 87–120). Newbury Park, CA: Sage.

FEHR, B. (1996). *Friendship processes.* Thousand Oaks, CA: Sage.

FEHR, B., & RUSSELL, J.A. (1991). The concept of love viewed from a prototype perspective. *Journal of Personality and Social Psychology, 60,* 425–438.

FEINGOLD, A. (1988). Matching for attractiveness in romantic partners and same-sex friends: A meta-analysis and theoretical critique. *Psychological Bulletin, 104,* 226–235.

FELDMAN-SUMMERS, S., & LINDNER, K. (1976). Perceptions of victims and defendants in criminal assault cases. *Criminal Justice Behavior, 3,* 135–149.

FERGUSON, C.A. (1977). Baby talk as a simplified register. In C.E. Snow, & C.A. Ferguson (Eds.), *Talking to children: Language input and acquisition.* New York: Cambridge University Press.

FERGUSON, G. (1982). Psychology at McGill. In M.J. Wright, & C.R. Myers (Eds.), *History of academic psychology in Canada* (pp. 33–67). Toronto: Hogrefe.

FERGUSON, T.J., & RULE, B.G. (1983). An attributional perspective on anger and aggression. In R.G. Geen, & E.I. Donnerstein (Eds.), *Aggression: Theoretical and empirical reviews* (Vol. 1). (pp. 41–74). New York: Academic Press.

FESTINGER, L. (1954). A theory of social comparison processes. *Human Relations, 7,* 117–140.

FESTINGER, L. (1957). *A theory of cognitive dissonance.* Stanford, CA: Stanford University Press.

FESTINGER, L. (1964). *Conflict, decision and dissonance.* Stanford, CA: Stanford University Press.

FESTINGER, L., & CARLSMITH, J.M. (1959). Cognitive consequences of forced compliance. *Journal of Abnormal and Social Psychology, 58,* 203–210

FESTINGER, L., PEPITONE, A., & NEWCOMB, T. (1952). Some consequences of deindividuation in a group. *Journal of Personality and Social Psychology, 47,* 382–389.

FESTINGER, L., RIECKEN, H.W., & SCHACHTER, S. (1956). *When prophecy fails: A social and psychological study of a modern group that predicted the destruction of the world.* New York: Harper.

FESTINGER, L., SCHACHTER, S., & BACK, K.W. (1950). *Social pressures in informal groups: A study of human factors in housing.* New York: Harper & Brothers.

FIEDLER, F.E. (1967). *A theory of leadership effectiveness.* New York: McGraw-Hill.

FIEDLER, F.E. (1971). *Leadership.* Morristown, NJ: General Learning Press.

FIEDLER, F.E. (1981). Leadership effectiveness. *American Behavioral Scientist, 24,* 619–632.

FIEDLER, K., SEMIN, G.R., FINKENAUER, C., & BERKEL, I. (1995). Actor–observer bias in close relationships: The role of self-knowledge and self-related language. *Personality and Social Psychology Bulletin, 21,* 525–538.

FIELDS, J.M., & SCHUMAN, H. (1976). Public beliefs about beliefs of the public. *Public Opinion Quarterly, 40,* 427–448.

FISCHER, C.S. (1976). *The urban experience.* New York: Harcourt, Brace, Jovanovich.

FISCHER, C.S., & PHILLIPS, S.L. (1982). Who is alone? Social characteristics of people with small networks. In L.A. Peplau, & D. Perlman (Eds.), *Loneliness: A sourcebook of current theory, research and therapy* (pp. 21–39). New York: Wiley Interscience.

FISCHER, K., SCHOENEMAN, T.J., & RUBANOWITZ, D.E. (1987). Attributions in the advice columns: II. The dimensionality of actors' and observers' explanations for interpersonal problems. *Personality and Social Psychology Bulletin, 13,* 458–466.

FISHBEIN, M., & AJZEN, I. (1975). *Belief, attitude, intention and behavior: An introduction to theory and research.* Reading, MA: Addison-Wesley.

FISHER, J.D. (1988). Possible effects of reference-group-based social influence on AIDS-risk behavior and AIDS prevention. *American Psychologist, 43,* 914–920.

FISHER, J.D., & FISHER, W. A. (1992). Changing AIDS-risk behavior. *Psychological Bulletin, 111,* 455–474.

FISHER, J.D., BELL, P.A., & BAUM, A. (1984). *Environmental psychology* (2nd ed.). New York: Holt, Rinehart & Winston.

FISHER, J.D., NADLER, A., & DEPAULO, B.M. (1983). *New directions in helping.* (Vol. 1). New York: Academic Press.

FISHER, J.D., NADLER, A., & WHITCHER-ALAGNA, S. (1982). Recipient reactions to aid. *Psychological Bulletin, 91,* 27–54.

FISHER, R.J. (1982). *Social psychology: An applied approach.* New York: St. Martin's.

FISHER, R.J. (1983). Third Party Consultation as a method of intergroup conflict resolution. *Journal of Conflict Resolution, 27,* 301–334.

FISHER, R.J. (1989). *The social psychology of inter-group conflict resolution.* New York: Springer-Verlag.

FISHER, R.J. (1998). Applying group processes to international conflict analysis and resolution. In R.S. Tindale, & L. Heath (Eds.), *Theory and research on small groups: Social psychological applications to social issues* (Vol. 4). (pp. 107–126). New York: Plenum Press.

FISHER, S., & TODD, A.D. (Eds.). (1983). *The social organization of doctor-patient communication.* Washington: Center for Applied Linguistics.

FISHER, W.A., FISHER, J.D., & RYE, B.J. (1995). Understanding and promoting AIDS-preventive behavior: Insights from the theory of reasoned action. *Health Psychology, 14,* 255–264.

FISKE, S.T. (1980). Attention and weight on person perception. *Journal of Personality and Social Psychology, 38,* 889–906.

FISKE, S.T., & TAYLOR, S.E. (1991). *Social cognition* (2nd ed.). Reading, MA: Addison-Wesley.

FLAMENT, C. (1958). Influence sociale et perception. *Année psychologique, 58,* 378–400.

FLEMING, I., BAUM, A., & WEISS, L. (1987). Social density and perceived control as mediators of crowding stress in a high-density residential neighbourhood. *Journal of Personality and Social Psychology, 52,* 899–906.

FLETT, G.L., HEWITT, P.L., BLANKENSTEIN, K.R., & O'BRIEN, S. (1991). Perfectionism and learned resourcefulness in depression and self-esteem. *Personality and Individual Differences, 12,* 61–68.

FLOWERS, M.L. (1977). A laboratory test of some implications of Janis's groupthink hypothesis. *Journal of Personality and Social Psychology, 35,* 888–896.

FOA, U.G. (1971). Interpersonal and economic resources. *Science, 171,* 345–351.

FOGEL, J., ALBERT, S.M., SCHNABEL, F., DITKOFF, B., & NEUGUT, A.I. (2002). Internet use and social support in women with breast cancer. *Health Psychology, 21,* 398–404.

FOGELMAN, E. (1994). *Conscience and courage: Rescuers of Jews during the Holocaust.* New York: Doubleday.

FOGELMAN, E., & WIENER, V.L. (1985). The few, the brave, the noble. *Psychology Today, 19,* 61–65.

FONAGY, I. (1971). Double coding in speech. *Semiotica, 3,* 189–222.

FONTANA, A.F., KERNS, R.D., ROSENBERG, R.L., & COLONESE, K.L. (1989). Support, stress and recovery from coronary heart disease: A longitudinal causal model. *Health Psychology, 8,* 175–193.

FORD, T.E., & STANGOR, C. (1992). The role of diagnosticity in stereotype formation: Perceiving group means and variances. *Journal of Personality and Social Psychology, 63,* 356–367.

FOREMAN, P.B. (1953). Panic theory. *Sociology and Social Research, 37,* 295–304.

FORGAS, J.P. (1998). Asking nicely? The effects on mood of responding to more or less polite requests. *Personality and Social Psychology Bulletin, 24,* 173–185.

FORTMAN, J. (2003). Adolescent language and communication from an intergroup perspective. *Journal of Language and Social Psychology, 22,* 104–111.

FOSTER, M., & MATHESON, K. (1999). Perceiving and responding to the person-group discrimination discrepancy. *Personality and Social Psychology Bulletin, 25,* 1319–1329.

FRABLE, D.E.S., & BEM, S.L. (1985). If you are gender schematic, all members of the opposite sex look alike. *Journal of Personality and Social Psychology, 49,* 459–468.

FRANKEL, A., & PRENTICE-DUNN, S. (1990). Loneliness and the processing of self-relevant information. *Journal of Social and Clinical Psychology, 9,* 303–315.

FRANKL, V. (1963). *Man's search for meaning.* New York: Washington Square Press.

FRANKLIN, S. (1977). *A time of heroes 1940/1950.* Toronto: Natural Science of Canada Ltd.

FREDERICKSON, B.L. (2001). The role of positive emotions in positive psychology. *American Psychologist, 56,* 218–226.

FREED, R.S., & FREED, S.A. (1989). Beliefs and practices resulting in female deaths and fewer females than males in India. *Population and Environment, 10,* 144–161.

FREEDMAN, J.J., BIRSKY, J., & CAVOUKIAN, A. (1980). Environmental determinants of behavioral contagion: Density and number. *Basic and Applied Social Psychology, 1,* 155–161.

FREEDMAN, J.L. (1965). Long–term behavioral effects of cognitive dissonance. *Journal of Experimental Social Psychology, 1,* 145–155.

FREEDMAN, J.L. (1975). *Crowding and behavior.* New York: Viking Press.

FREEDMAN, J.L. (1982). Theories of contagion as they relate to mass psychogenic illness. In M.J. Colligan, J.W. Pennebaker, & L.R. Murphy (Eds.), *Mass psychogenic illness* (pp. 171–182). Hillsdale, NJ: Erlbaum.

FREEDMAN, J.L. (1984). Effects of television violence on aggressiveness. *Psychological Bulletin, 96,* 227–246.

FREEDMAN, J.L. (1990). The effects of capital punishment on jurors' willingness to convict. *Journal of Applied Social Psychology, 20,* 465–477.

FREEDMAN, J.L., & FRASER, S.C. (1966). Compliance without pressure: The foot-in-the-door technique. *Journal of Personality and Social Psychology, 4,* 195–202.

FREEDMAN, J.L., HESHKA, S., & LEVY, A. (1975). Population density and pathology: Is there a relationship? *Journal of Experimental Social Psychology, 11,* 539–552.

FREEDMAN, J.L., WALLINGTON, S.A., & BLESS, E. (1967). Compliance without pressure: The effect of guilt. *Journal of Personality and Social Psychology, 7,* 117–124.

FRENCH, J.R.P. (1944). Organized and unorganized groups under fear and frustration. *University of Iowa Studies of Child Welfare, 20,* 231–308.

FRENKEL, O.J., & DOOB, A.N. (1976). Post-decision dissonance at the polling booth. Canadian *Journal of Behavioural Science, 8,* 347–350.

FREUD, S. (1968). Why war? In J. Rickman (Ed.), *Civilization, war and death: Selections from five works by Sigmund Freud* (pp. 82–97). London: Hogarth.

FREY, D. (1986). Recent research on selective exposure to information. In L. Berkowitz (Ed.), *Advances in experimental social psychology* (Vol. 19). (pp. 41–80). New York: Academic Press.

FREY, S., HIRSBRUNNER, H.P., FLORIN, A., DAW, W., & CRAWFORD, R. (1983). A unified approach to the investigation of nonverbal and verbal behavior in communication research. In W. Doise, & S. Moscovici (Eds.), *Current issues in European social psychology* (Vol. 1). (pp. 143–199). Cambridge: Cambridge University Press.

FRICK, R.W. (1985). Communicating emotion: The role of prosodic features. *Psychological Bulletin, 97,* 412–429.

FRIED, C., & ARONSON, E. (1995). Hypocrisy, misattribution and dissonance reduction: A demonstration of dissonance in the absence of aversive consequences. *Personality and Social Psychology Bulletin, 21,* 925–933.

FRIEDMAN, H.S. (1982). Nonverbal communication in medical interaction. In H.S. Friedman & M.R. DiMatteo (Eds.), *Interpersonal issues in health care* (pp. 51–68). New York: Academic Press.

FRIEDMAN, H.S., PRINCE, L., RIGGIO, R., & DiMATTEO, M. (1980). Understanding and assessing nonverbal expressiveness. *Journal of Personality and Social Psychology, 14,* 351–364.

FRIEDMAN, M., & BOOTH-KEWLEY, S. (1987). The "disease-prone personality": A meta-analytic view of the concept. *American Psychologist, 42,* 539–555.

FRIEZE, I., & WEINER, B. (1971). Cue utilization and attributional judgments for success and failure. *Journal of Personality, 39,* 591–605.

FRITZ, C.E., & MARKS, E.F. (1954). The NORC studies of human behavior in disaster. *Journal of Social Issues, 10,* 26–41.

FROHLICH, N., & OPPENHEIMER, J. (1970). I get by with a little help from my friends. *World Politics, 23,* 104–120.

FU, G., LEE, K., CAMERON, C-A., & XU, F. (2001). Chinese and Canadian adults' categorization and evaluation of lie- and truth-telling about prosocial and antisocial behaviors. *Journal of Cross-Cultural Psychology, 32,* 720–727.

FUGITA, S.S., HOGREBE, M.C., & WEXLEY, K.N. (1980). Perception of deception: Perceived expertise in detecting deception, successfulness of deception and nonverbal cues. *Personality and Social Psychology Bulletin, 6,* 637–643.

FURNHAM, A. (1985). Just world beliefs in an unjust society: A cross-cultural comparison. *European Journal of Social Psychology, 15,* 363–366.

GAGNON, A., & BOURHIS, R.Y. (1996). Discrimination in the minimal group paradigm: Social identity or self-interest? *Personality and Social Psychology Bulletin, 22,* 1289–1301.

GANGESTAD, S.W., & THORNHILL, R. (1998). Menstrual cycle variation in women's preferences for the scent of symmetrical men. *Proceedings of the Royal Society of London, 265,* 927–933.

GARB, H.N. (1994). Cognitive heuristics and biases in personality assessment. In L. Heath, R.S. Tindale, J. Edwards, E.J. Posavac, F.B. Bryant, E. Henderson-King, Y. Suarez-Balcazar, & J. Myers (Eds.), *Applications of heuristics and biases to social issues* (pp. 73–90). New York: Plenum Press.

GARBARINO, J. (1999). *Lost boys: Why our sons turn violent and how we can save them.* New York: The Free Press.

GARDINER, M., & TIGGEMANN, M. (1999). Gender differences in leadership style, job stress and mental health in male- and female-dominated industries. *Journal of Occupational and Organizational Psychology, 72,* 301–315.

GARDNER, R.C. (1984). *Social psychological aspects of second language learning.* London: Edward Arnold.

GARDNER, R.C. (1985). *Social psychology and second language learning.* London: Edward Arnold.

GARDNER, R.C., & DESROCHERS, A. (1981). Second language acquisition and bilingualism: Research in Canada (1970–1980). *Canadian Psychology, 22,* 146–162.

GARDNER, R.C., & KALIN, R. (Eds.). (1981). *A social psychology of Canadian ethnic relations.* Toronto: Metheun.

GARDNER, R.C., & LAMBERT, W.E. (1959). Motivational variables in second language acquisition. *Canadian Journal of Psychology, 13,* 266–272.

GARDNER, R.C., GLIKSMAN, L., & SMYTHE, P.C. (1978). Attitude and behaviour in second language acquisition: A social psychological interpretation. *Canadian Psychological Review, 19,* 173–186.

GARNER, D.M., GARFINKEL, P.E., SCHWARTZ, D., & THOMPSON, M. (1980). Cultural expectations of thinness in women. *Psychological Reports, 47,* 483–491.

GARTNER, R. (1995). Homicide in Canada. In J.I. Ross (Ed.), *Violence in Canada* (pp. 186–222). Don Mills: Oxford University Press.

GEEN, R.G., & GANGE, J.J. (1977). Drive theory of social facilitation: Twelve years of theory and research. *Psychological Bulletin, 84,* 1267–1288.

GENESEE, F. (1984). Beyond bilingualism: Social psychological studies of French immersion programs in Canada. *Canadian Journal of Behavioural Science, 16,* 338–352.

GENESEE, F., & BOURHIS, R.Y. (1982). The social psychological significance of code switching in cross-cultural communication. *Journal of Language and Social Psychology, 1,* 1–27.

GENESEE, F., & BOURHIS, R.Y. (1988). Evaluative reactions to language choice strategies: The role of sociostructural factors. *Language and Communication, 8,* 229–250.

GERARD, H. (1967). Choice difficulty, dissonance, and the decision sequence. *Journal of Personality, 35,* 91–108.

GERBNER, G. (1969). The television world of violence. In R.K. Baker, & S.J. Ball (Eds.), *Mass media and violence: A staff report to the National Commission on the causes and prevention of violence.* Washington, DC: U.S. Government Printing Office.

GERBNER, G., GROSS, L., MORGAN, M., & SIGNORIELLI, N. (1980). The mainstreaming of America: Violence profile No. 11. *Journal of Communication, 30,* 10–29.

GERGEN, K.J., ELLSWORTH, P., MASLACH, P., & SEIPEL, M. (1975). Obligation, donor resources, and the reactions to aid in three nations. *Journal of Personality and Social Psychology, 31,* 390–400.

GERGEN, K.J., GERGEN, M.M., & METER, K. (1972). Individual orientations to prosocial behavior. *Journal of Social Issues, 28,* 105–130.

GERSON, A.C., & PERLMAN, D. (1979). Loneliness and expressive communication. *Journal of Abnormal Psychology, 88,* 258–261.

GIANAKOS, I., & SUBICH, L. (1988). Student sex and sex role in relation to college major choice. *The Career Development Quarterly, 36,* 259–268.

GIBB, C.A. (1969). Leadership. In G. Lindzey, & E. Aronson (Eds.), *Handbook of social psychology* (2nd ed.). (Vol. 4). Reading, MA: Addison-Wesley.

GIBBINS, K., & CONEY, J.R. (1981). Meaning of physical dimensions of women's clothes. *Perceptual and Motor Skills, 53,* 720–722.

GILBERT, D., & MALONE, P.D. (1995). The correspondence bias. *Psychological Bulletin, 117,* 21–38.

GILBERT, G.M. (1951). Stereotype persistence and change among college students. *Journal of Abnormal and Social Psychology, 46,* 245–254.

GILES, H. (1973). Accent mobility: A model and some data. *Anthropological Linguistics, 15,* 87–105.

GILES, H. (Ed.). (1998). Applied research in language and intergenerational communication. Special Issue of *Journal of Applied Communication Research, 26* (1).

GILES, H., & POWESLAND, P. (1975). *Speech style and social evaluation.* London: Academic Press.

GILES, H., & ROBINSON, W.P. (Eds.). (1990). *Handbook of language and social psychology.* New York: Wiley.

GILES, H., & SMITH, P.M. (1979). Accommodation theory: Optimal levels of convergence. In H. Giles, & R. St. Clair (Eds.), *Language and social psychology.* Oxford: Basil Blackwell.

GILES, H., & WADLEIGH, P.M. (1999). Accommodating nonverbally. In H. Giles, P. M. Wadleigh, K. Floyd, A. Ramirez Jr., J.K. Burgoon, J.N. Cappella, P.A. Andersen, N. Miczo, & L. Allspach (Eds.), *The nonverbal communication reader: Classic and contemporary readings* (2nd ed.). Prospect Heights, IL: Waveland Press.

GILES, H., BOURHIS, R.Y., & DAVIES, A. (1977). Prestige speech styles: The imposed norm and inherent value hypotheses. In W.C. McCormack, & S. Wurm (Eds.), *Language and society: Anthropological issues.* The Hague: Mouton.

GILES, H., BOURHIS, R.Y., & TAYLOR, D.M. (1977). Towards a theory of language in ethnic group relations. In H. Giles (Ed.), *Language, ethnicity and intergroup relations* (pp. 307–348). London: Academic Press.

GILES, H., BOURHIS, R.Y., TRUDGILL, P., & LEWIS, A. (1974). The imposed norm hypothesis: A validation. *The Quarterly Journal of Speech, 60,* 405–410.

GILES, H., TAYLOR, D.M., & BOURHIS, R.Y. (1973). Toward a theory of interpersonal accommodation through speech: Some Canadian data. *Language in Society, 2,* 177–192.

GILLIGAN, C. (1982). *In a different voice: Psychological theory and women's development.* Cambridge, MA: Harvard University Press.

GILLIGAN, F. (1977). Comments: Eyewitness identification. *Military Law Review, 58,* 183–207.

GILLIS, J.S. (1983). *Too tall too small.* Montreal: Book Centre.

GLADUE, B.A., & DELANEY, H.J. (1990). Gender difference in the perception of attractiveness of men and women in bars. *Personality and Social Psychology Bulletin, 16,* 378–391.

GLICK, P., DEMOREST, J.A., & HOTZE, C.A. (1988). Self-monitoring and beliefs about partner compatiblity in romantic relationships. *Personality and Social Psychology Bulletin, 14,* 485–494.

GLOBE AND MAIL. (2003, May 17). No law ban possession of marijuana, court rules.

GOFFMAN, E. (1955). On face-work: An analysis of ritual elements in social interaction. *Psychiatry, 18,* 213–231.

GOFFMAN, E. (1959). *The presentation of self in everyday life.* New York: Doubleday.

GOLD, J.A., RYCKMAN, R.M., & MOSLEY, N.R. (1984). Romantic mood induction and attraction to a dissimilar other: Is love blind? *Personality and Social Psychology Bulletin, 10,* 358–368.

GOLDBERG, M.E. (1982). TV advertising directed at children: Inherently unfair or simply in need of regulation? In S.J. Shapiro, & L. Heslop (Eds.), *Marketplace Canada: Some controversial dimensions.* Toronto: McGraw-Hill Ryerson.

GOLDBERG, M.E., & GORN, G.J. (1979). Television's impact on preferences for non-white playmates: Canadian Sesame Street inserts. *Journal of Broadcasting, 23,* 27–32.

GOLDBERG, P. (1968). Are some women prejudiced against women? *Trans-Action, 5,* 28–30.

GOLDIN-MEADOW, S., NUSBAUM, H., KELLY, S.D., & WAGNER, S. (2001). Explaining math: Gesturing lightens the load. *Psychological Science, 12,* 516–522.

GOLDSTEIN, A.G., & PAPAGEORGE, J. (1980). Judgments of facial attractiveness in the absence of eye movements. *Bulletin of the Psychonomic Society, 15,* 269–270.

GOLDSTEIN, J.H., DAVIS, R.W., & HERMON, D. (1975). Escalation of aggression: Experimental studies. *Journal of Personality and Social Psychology, 35,* 162–170.

GOLDSTEIN, N.E., ARNOLD, D.H., ROSENBERG, J.L., STOWE, R.M., & ORTIZ, C. (2001). Contagion of aggression in day care classrooms as a function of peer and teacher responses. *Journal of Educational Psychology, 93,* 708–719.

GOLEMAN, D. (1986, April 8). Studies point to power of nonverbal signals. *New York Times,* C1–C6.

GONZALES, R., ELLSWORTH, P.C., & PEMBROKE, M. (1993). Response biases in lineups and showups. *Journal of Personality and Social Psychology, 64,* 525–537.

GOODMAN, M. (1964). *Race awareness in young children* (2nd ed.). New York: Crowell-Collier.

GOODWIN, R., COOK, O., & YUNG, Y. (2001). Loneliness and life satisfaction among three cultural groups. *Personal Relationships, 8,* 225–230.

GORANSON, R.E. (1977). Television violence effects: Issues and evidence. *Report of the Royal Commission on Violence in the Communications Industry* (Vol. 5). (pp. 1–31). Toronto: Publication Centre, Government of Ontario.

GORDON, M.E., & FRYXELL, G.E. (1989). Voluntariness of association as a moderator of the importance of procedural and distributive justice. *Journal of Applied Social Psychology, 19,* 993–1009.

GORDON, W.J.J. (1961). *Synectics: The development of creative capacity.* New York: Harper & Row.

GORER, G. (1968). Man has no "killer" instinct. In M.F.A. Montagu (Ed.), *Man and aggression* (pp. 27–36). New York: Oxford University Press.

GOTTFREDSON, L. (2003). Intelligence: Is it the epidemiologists' elusive "fundamental cause" of social class inequities in health? *Journal of Personality and Social Psychology,* in press.

GOTTLIEB, B.H. (1985). Social networks and social support: An overview of research, practice and policy implications. *Health Education Quarterly, 12,* 221–238.

GOTTMAN, J.M., & LEVENSON, R.W. (1992). Marital processes predictive of later dissolution: Behavior, physiology and health. *Journal of Personality and Social Psychology, 63,* 221–233.

GOULDNER, A.W. (1960). The norm of reciprocity: A preliminary statement. *American Sociological Review, 25,* 161–179.

GRAMMAR, K., & THORNHILL, R. (1994). Human (Homo sapiens) facial attractiveness and sexual selection: The role of symmetry and averageness. *Journal of Comparative Psychology 108,* 233–242.

GRANGER, L. (1996, August). *Francophone and anglophone psychology in Canada: siblings or strangers?* XXVI International Congress of Psychology, Montreal.

GRANT, P.R. (1978). *Attribution of an ethnic stereotype.* Unpublished masters thesis, University of Waterloo.

GRAUMANN, C.F., & MOSCOVICI, S. (Eds.). (1987). *Changing conceptions of conspiracy.* New York: Springer-Verlag.

GRAYSON, J.P., & GRAYSON, L. (1975). Social movements and social change in contemporary Canada. *Quarterly of Canadian Studies, 4,* 50–57.

GREENBERG, J., & PRSZCZYNSKI, T. (1985). The effect of an overheard slur on evaluation of a target. *Journal of Experimental Social Psychology, 21,* 61–72.

GREENBERG, J., PRSZCZYNSKI, T., & SOLOMAN, S. (1994). Role of consciousness and accessibility of death-related thoughts in mortality salience effects. *Journal of Personality and Social Psychology, 67,* 627–637.

GREENBERG, J., SOLOMAN, S., & PRSZCZYNSKI, T. (1997). Terror management theory of self-esteem and cultural worldviews: Empirical assessments and conceptual refinements. In M. Zanna (Ed.), *Advances in experimental social psychology* (Vol. 29). (pp. 61–139). San Diego, CA: Academic Press.

GREENGLASS, E.R. (1982). *A world of difference: Gender roles in perspective.* Toronto: Wiley.

GREENWALD, A.G., & RONIS, D.L. (1978). Twenty years of cognitive dissonance: A case study of the evaluation of a theory. *Psychological Review, 85,* 53–57.

GRIFFIN, D., & BUEHLER, R. (1993). Role of construal processes in conformity and dissent. *Journal of Personality and Social Psychology, 65,* 657–669.

GROH, D. (1987). The temptation of conspiracy theory, or: Why do bad things happen to good people. Part I: Preliminary draft.

GROSS, A.E., & FLEMING, J. (1982). Twenty years of deception in social psychology. *Personality and Social Psychology Bulletin, 8,* 402–408.

GROVE, J.R., HANRAHAN, S.J., & MCINMAN, A. (1991). Success/failure bias in attributions across involvement categories in sport. *Personality and Social Psychology Bulletin, 17,* 93–97.

GRUBE, J.W., WEIR, I.L., GETZALF, S., & ROKEACH, M. (1984). Own value system, value images, and cigarette smoking. *Personality and Social Psychology Bulletin, 10,* 306–313.

GRUDER, C.L. (1974). Cost and dependency as determinants of helping and exploitation. *Journal of Conflict Resolution, 18,* 473–485.

GRUNEAU, R., & WHITSON, D. (1993). *Hockey night in Canada.* Toronto: Garamond Press.

GRUSEC, J.E. (1991). The socialization of altruism. In M.S. Clark (Ed.), *Prosocial behavior* (pp. 9–33). Newbury Park, CA: Sage.

GRUSEC, J.E., & REDLER, E. (1980). Attribution, reinforcement and altruism: A developmental analysis. *Developmental Psychology, 16,* 525–534.

GRUSEC, J.E., & SKUBISKI, S.L. (1970). Model nurturance, demand characteristics of the modelling experiment, and altruism. *Journal of Personality and Social Psychology, 14,* 352–359.

GUIMOND, S., & DUBÉ, L. (1989). La représentation des causes de l'infériorité économique des québecois francophones. *Revue Canadienne des Sciences du comportement, 21,* 28–39.

GUIMOND, S., & DUBÉ-SIMARD, L. (1983). Relative deprivation theory and the Québec nationalist movement: The cognitive– emotion distinction and the personal–group deprivation issue. *Journal of Personality and Social Psychology, 44,* 526–535.

GUIMOND, S., & PALMER, D.L. (1993). Developmental changes in ingroup favouritism among bilingual and unilingual francophone and anglophone students. *Journal of Language and Social Psychology, 12,* 318–351.

GUIMOND, S., BÉGIN, G., & PALMER, D. L. (1989). Education and causal attributons: The development of "person-blame" and "system-blame" ideology. *Social Psychology Quarterly, 52,* 126–140.

GUNDLACH, M.J., DOUGLAS, S.C., & MARTINKO, M.J. (2003). The decision to blow the whistle: A social information processing framework. *Academy-of-Management-Review, 28,* 107–123.

GUREVICH, M. (2001). W(h)ither psychology of women? Current trends and future directions for the section on women and psychology. *Canadian Psychology, 42,* 301–312.

GURR, T.R. (1995). Forward. In J.I. Ross (Ed.), *Violence in Canada* (pp. VIII–XVII). Don Mills, ON: Oxford University Press.

HAAS, A. (1979). Male and female spoken language differences: Stereotypes and evidence. *Psychological Bulletin, 86,* 616–626.

HADDOCK, G., & ZANNA, M.P. (1997). Impact of negative advertising on evaluation of political candidates: The 1993 Canadian Federal elections. *Basic and Applied Social Psychology, 19,* 205–223.

HADDOCK, G., & ZANNA, M.P. (1998). Assessing the impact of affective and cognitive information in predicting attitudes toward capital punishment. *Law and Human Behavior, 22,* 325–339.

HADJISTAVROPOULOS, T., & GENEST, M. (1994). The underestimation of the role of physical attractiveness in dating preferences: Ignorance or taboo? *Canadian Journal of Behavioural Science, 26,* 298–318.

HADJISTAVROPOULOS, T., MCMURTRY, B., & CRAIG, K.D. (1996). Beautiful faces in pain: biases and accuracy in the perception of pain. *Psychology and Health, 11,* 411–420.

HAFER, C.L. (2002). Why we reject innocent victims. In M. Ross, & D.T. Miller (Eds.), *The justice motive in everyday life* (pp. 109–126). New York: Cambridge University Press.

HAFER, C.L. (in press). Investment in long-term goals and commitment to just means drive the need to believe in a just world. *Personality and Social Bulletin.*

HAFER, C.L., & CORREY, B.L. (in press). Mediators of the relation between beliefs in a just world and emotional responses to negative outcomes. *Social Justice Research.*

HAFER, C.L., & OLSON, J.M. (1989). Beliefs in a just world and reactions to personal deprivation. *Journal of Personality, 57,* 799–823.

HAFER, C.L., & OLSON, J.M. (1993). Beliefs in a just world, discontent and assertive actions by working women. *Personality and Social Psychology Bulletin, 19,* 30–38.

HAFER, C.L. & OLSON, J.M. (2003). Analysis of empirical research on the scope of justice. *Personality and Social Psychology Review, 7,* 311–323.

HAFER, C.L., BOGAERT, A.F., & MCMULLEN, S. (2001). Belief in a just world and condom use in a sample of gay and bisexual men. *Journal of Applied Social Psychology, 31,* 1–20.

HAFER, C.L., REYNOLDS, K.L., & OBERTYNSKI, M.A. (1996). Message comprehensibility and persuasion: Effects of complex language in counterattitudinal appeals to laypersons. *Social Cognition, 14,* 317–337.

HAGESTAD, G.O., & SMYER, M.A. (1982). Dissolving long-term relationships: Patterns of divorcing in middle-age. In S. Duck (Ed.), *Personal relationships, 4: Dissolving relationships* (pp. 211–235). New York: Academic Press.

HAGGARD, L.M., & WILLIAMS, D.R. (1992). Identity affirmation through leisure activities: Leisure symbols of the self. *Journal of Leisure Research, 24,* 1–18.

HAKUTA, K., & GARCIA, E.E. (1989). Bilingualism and education. *American Psychologist, 44,* 374–379.

HALBERSTADT, J., & RHODES, G. (2000). The attractiveness of nonface averages: Implications for an evolutionary explanation of the attractiveness of average faces. *Psychological Science, 11,* 285–289.

HALL, E.T. (1966). *The hidden dimension.* New York: Doubleday.

HALL, J.A., & BRAUNWALD, K.G. (1981). Gender cues in conversations. *Journal of Personality and Social Psychology, 40,* 99–110.

HALL, J.A., & VECCIA, E.M. (1990). More "touching" observations: New insights on men, women and interpersonal touching. *Journal of Personality and Social Psychology, 59,* 1159–1162.

HALL, J.A., EPSTEIN, A.M., DECIANTIS, M.L., & MCNEIL, B.J. (1993). Physicians' liking for their patients: More evidence for the role of affect in medical care. *Health Psychology, 12,* 140–146.

HAMBLIN, R.L. (1958). Leadership and crises. *Sociometry, 21,* 322–335.

HAMBURGER, H., GUYER, M., & FOX, J. (1975). Group size and cooperation. *Journal of Conflict Resolution, 19,* 503–531.

HAMILL, R., WILSON, T.D., & NISBETT, R.E. (1980). Insensitivity to sample bias: Generalizing from atypical cases. *Journal of Personality and Social Psychology, 39,* 578–589.

HAMILTON, D.L. (1976). Individual differences in ascriptions of responsibility, guilt and appropriate judgement. In G. Berman, C. Nemeth, & N. Vidmar (Eds.), *Psychology and the law* (pp. 239–264). Lexington, MA: Heath.

HAMILTON, D.L., & GIFFORD, R.K. (2000). Illusory correlation in interpersonal perception: A cognitive basis of stereotypic judgments. In C. Stangor (Ed.), *Stereotypes and prejudice: Essential readings. Key readings in social psychology* (pp. 161–171). Philadelphia, PA: Psychology Press.

HAMILTON, D.L., & ROSE, T.L. (1980). Illusory correlation and the maintenance of stereotypes. *Journal of Personality and Social Psychology, 39,* 832–845.

HAMILTON, D.L., & SHERMAN, S.J. (1989). Illusory correlations: Implications for stereotype theory and research. In D. Bar-Tal, C.F. Graumann, A.W. Kruglanski, & W. Stroebe (Eds.), *Stereotyping and prejudice: Changing conceptions* (pp. 59–82). New York: Springer-Verlag.

HAMILTON, D.L., & ZANNA, M.P. (1972). Differential weighting of favorable and unfavorable attributes in impressions of personality. *Journal of Experimental Research in Personality, 6,* 204–212.

HANEY, C., & MANZOLATTI, J. (1981). Television criminology: Network illusions of criminal justice reality. In E. Aronson (Ed.), *Readings about the social animal* (3rd ed.). (pp. 125–136). San Francisco: W.H. Freeman.

HANEY, C., BANKS, C., & ZIMBARDO, P. (1973). Interpersonal dynamics in a simulated prison. *International Journal of Criminology, 1,* 69–97.

HANS, V.P., & ERMANN, M.D. (1989). Responses to corporate versus individual wrongdoing. *Law and Human Behavior, 13,* 151–166.

HANSEN, E.M., KIMBLE, C.E., & BIERS, D.W. (2001). Actors and observers; Divergent attributions of constrained unfriendly behavior. *Social Behavior and Personality, 29,* 87–104.

HARBAUGH, R., & TO, T. (2002). Too cool for school. Signalling and countersignalling. *RAND Journal of Economics, 33,* 630–649.

HARDIE, E.A. (1997). Prevalence and predictors of cyclic and noncyclic affective change. *Psychology of Women Quarterly, 21,* 299–314.

HARDIN, G. (1968). The tragedy of the commons. *Science, 162,* 1243–1248.

HARDYCK, J.A., & BRADEN, M. (1962). When prophecy fails again: A report of a failure to replicate. *Journal of Abnormal and Social Psychology, 65,* 136–141.

HARE, A.P. (1962). *Handbook of small group research.* Glencoe, NY: Free Press.

HARE, R.D., & MCPHERSON, L.M. (1984). Violent and aggressive behavior by criminal psychopaths. *International Journal of Law and Psychiatry, 7,* 35–50.

HARKINS, S.G., & PETTY, R.E. (1987). Information utility and the multiple sources effect. *Journal of Personality and Social Psychology, 52,* 260–268.

HARKINS, S.G., & SZYMANSKI, K. (1989). Social loafing and group evaluation. *Journal of Personality and Social Psychology, 56,* 934–941.

HARMON-JONES, E. (2000). Cognitive dissonance and experienced negative affect: Evidence that dissonance increases negative affect even in the absence of aversive consequences. *Personality and Social Psychology Bulletin, 26,* 1490–1501.

HARMON-JONES, E., BREHM, J.W., GREENBERG, J., SIMON, L., & NELSON, D.E. (1996). Evidence that the production of aversive consequences is not necessary to produce cognitive dissonance. *Journal of Personality and Social Psychology, 70,* 5–16.

HARRIGAN, J.A., & ROSENTHAL, R. (1983). Physicians' head and body positions as determinants of perceived rapport. *Journal of Applied Social Psychology, 13,* 496–509.

HARRIS, M. (1974). *Cows, pigs, wars and witches: The riddles of cultures.* New York: Random House.

HARRIS, R.N., SNYDER, C.R., HIGGINS, R.L., & SCHRAG, J.L. (1986). Enhancing the predictability of self-handicapping. *Journal of Personality and Social Psychology, 51,* 1191–1199.

HARRISON, A.A. (1977). Mere exposure. In L. Berkowitz (Ed.), *Advances in experimental social psychology* (Vol. 1). (pp. 39–83). New York: Academic Press.

HARRISON, J.A., MULLEN, P.D., & GREEN, L.W. (1992). A meta-analysis of studies of the health beliefs model with adults. *Health Education Research, 7,* 107–116.

HARVEY, J.H., & OMARZU, J. (1997). Minding the close relationship. *Personality and Social Psychology Review, 1,* 224–240.

HASS, R.G., & GRADY, K. (1975). Temporal delay, type of forewarning, and resistance to influence. *Journal of Experimental Social Psychology, 11,* 459–469.

HATFIELD, E., CACIOPPO, J., & RAPSON, R. (1994). *Emotional contagion.* New York: Cambridge Press.

HAUGTVEDT, C.P., & PETTY, R.E. (1992). Personality and persuasion: Need for cognition moderates the persistence and resistance of attitude changes. *Journal of Personality and Social Psychology, 63,* 308–319.

HAYNES, S.G., MCGIBBON, K.A., & KANANI, R. (1996). Systematic review of randomized trials of intervention to assist patients to follow prescriptions for medications. *Lancet, 348,* 336–348.

HAZAN, C., & SHAVER, P.R. (1987). Romantic love conceptualized as an attachment process. *Journal of Personality and Social Psychology, 59,* 270–280.

HEALTH & WELFARE CANADA (1987). *The active health report: Perspectives on Canada's health promotion survey, 1985.* Catalogue No. H–39–106/1987E. Ottawa: Supply and Services Canada.

HEALTH CANADA (2001). Organ donation in Canada. Downloaded on July 11, 2003 from http://www.hc-sc.gc.ca/english/media/releases/2001/2001_36ebk1.htm.

HEALTH CANADA (2002). Highlights from public opinion research on organ and tissue donation. Downloaded on July 11, 2003 from http://www.hc-sc.gc.ca/english/media/releases/2002/2002_28bk2.htm

HEAROLD, S. (1986). A synthesis of 1043 effects of television on social behavior. In G. Comstock (Ed.), *Public communications and behavior* (Vol. I). (pp. 65–133). New York: Academic Press.

HEAVEN, P., & ST. QUINTIN, D. (2003). Personality factors predict racial prejudice. *Personality and Individual Differences, 34,* 625–634.

HEBB, D.O. (1971). Comment on altruism: The comparative evidence. *Psychological Bulletin, 76,* 409–410.

HEBB, D.O., & THOMPSON, W.R. (1968). The social significance of animal studies. In G. Lindzey, & E. Aronson (Eds.), *The handbook of social psychology* (2nd ed.). (Vol. 1). (pp. 729–774). Reading, MA: Addison-Wesley.

HEFEZ, A. (1985). The role of the press and the medical community in the epidemic of "mysterious gas poisoning" in the Jordan West Bank. *American Journal of Psychiatry, 142,* 833–837.

HEIDER, F. (1958). *The psychology of interpersonal relations.* New York: Wiley.

HEINE, S.J., & LEHMAN, D.R. (1995). Cultural variation in unrealistic optimism: Does the West feel more invulnerable than the East? *Journal of Personality and Social Psychology, 68,* 595–607.

HEINE, S.J., & LEHMAN, D.R. (1999). Culture, self-discrepancies and self-satisfaction. *Personality and Social Psychology Bulletin 25,* 915–925.

HEINE, S.J., LEHMAN, D.R., MARKUS, H.R., & KITAYAMA, S. (1999). If there a universal need for positive self-regard? *Psychological Review, 106,* 766–794.

HEJMADI, A., DAVIDSON, R.J., & ROZIN, P. (2000). Exploring Hindu Indian emotional expressions: Evidence for accurate recognition by Americans and Indians. *Psychological Science, 11,* 183–187.

HELMREICH, R., ARONSON, E., & LeFAN, J. (1970). To err is humanizing sometimes: Effects of self-esteem, competence, and a pratfall on interpersonal attraction. *Journal of Personality and Social Psychology, 16,* 259–264.

HENDERSON-KING, E.I., & NISBETT, R.E. (1996) Anti-black prejudice as a function of exposure to the negative behaviour of a single black person. *Journal of Personality and Social Psychology, 71,* 654–664.

HENDRICK, C., & HENDRICK, S.S. (1986). A theory and a method of love. *Journal of Personality and Social Psychology, 50,* 392–402.

HENDRICK, S.C., & HENDRICK, C. (2000). Romantic love. In C. Hendrick & Susan Hendrick (Eds.), *Close relationships: A sourcebook* (pp. 203–215). Thousand Oaks, CA: Sage Publications.

HENDRICK, S.C., & HENDRICK, C. (2002). Linking romantic love with sex: Development of the perceptions of Love and Sex scale. *Journal of Social and Personal Relationships, 19,* 361–378.

HENLEY, M. (1973). Status and sex: Some touching observations. *Bulletin of the Psychonomic Society, 2,* 21–27.

HENNESSY, D.A., & WIESENTHAL, D.L. (1999). Traffic congestion, driver stress, and driver aggression. *Aggressive Behavior, 25,* 409–423.

HENNESSY, D.A., & WIESENTHAL, D.L. (2002). Aggression, violence, and vengeance among male and female drivers. *Transportation Quarterly, 56,* 65–75.

HENNESSY, M., & SALTZ, R.F. (1993). Modeling social influences on public drinking. *Journal of Studies on Alcohol, 54,* 139–145.

HENRY, F. (1985/86). Heroes and helpers in Nazi Germany: Who aided Jews? *Humboldt Journal of Social Relations, 13,* 306–319.

HENRY, F. (1999, August 31). *Globe and Mail.*

HERBERT, T.B., & COHEN, S. (1993). Depression and immunity: A meta-analytical review. *Psychological Bulletin 113,* 472–486.

HERD, J.A., & WEISS, S.M. (1984). Overview of hypertension: Its treatment and prevention. In J.D. Matarazzo, S.M. Weiss, J.A. Herd, N.E. Miller, & S.M. Weiss (Eds.), *Behavioral health* (pp. 789–804). New York: Wiley.

HEREDIA, R.R., & ALTARRIBA, J. (2001). Bilingual language mixing: Why do bilinguals code switch? *Current Directions in Psychological Science, 10,* 164–168.

HEREK, G.M., & GLUNT, E.K. (1988). An epidemic of stigma: Public reactions to AIDS. *American Psychologist, 43,* 886–891.

HERMAN, C.P., & POLIVY, J. (1975). Anxiety, restraint and eating behavior. *Journal of Abnormal Psychology, 84,* 666–672.

HERTEL, P.T., & NAVAREZ, A. (1986). Confusing memories for verbal and nonverbal communication. *Journal of Personality and Social Psychology, 50,* 474–481.

HESLIN, R., & ALPER, T. (1983). Touch: A bonding gesture. In J.M. Wiemann, & R.P. Harrison (Eds.), *Nonverbal interaction* (pp. 47–75). Beverly Hills, CA: Sage.

HESSING, D.J., ELFFERS, H., & WEIGEL, R. (1988). Exploring the limits of self-reports and reasoned action: An investigation of the psychology of tax-evasion behavior. *Journal of Personality and Social Psychology, 54,* 405–413.

HEUER, L., & PENROD, S. (1986). Procedural preference as a function of conflict intensity. *Journal of Personality and Social Psychology, 51,* 700–710.

HEWES, G.W. (1957). The anthropology of posture. *Scientific American, 196,* 123–132.

HEWSTONE, M. (1989). Changing stereotypes with disconfirming information. In D. Bar-Tal, C.F. Graumann, A.W. Kruglanski, & W. Straube (Eds.), *Stereotyping and prejudice: Changing conceptions.* New York: Springer-Verlag.

HEWSTONE, M. (2003). Intergroup contact. Panacea for prejudice? *The Psychologist, 16,* 352–355.

HEWSTONE, M., & JASPARS, M.F. (1984). Social dimensions of attribution. In H.Tajfel (Ed.), *The social dimension* (pp. 379–404). Cambridge: Cambridge University Press.

HEWSTONE, M., ISLAM, M.R., & JUDD, C.M. (1993). Models of cross-categorization and intergroup relations. *Journal of Personality and Social Psychology, 64,* 779–793.

HEWSTONE, M., RUBIN, M., & WILLIS, H. (2002). Intergoup bias. *Annual Review of Psychology, 53,* 575–604.

HICKS, R.D. (1990a). Police pursuit of satanic crime. *Skeptical Inquirer, 14,* 276–286.

HICKS, R.D. (1990b). The satanic conspiracy and urban legends. *Skeptical Inquirer, 14,* 378–389.

HIGBEE, K.L. (1969). Fifteen years of fear arousal: Research on threat appeals: 1953–1968. *Psychological Bulletin, 72,* 426–444.

HIGGINS, E.T. (1987). Self-discrepancy: A theory relating self and affect. *Psychological Review, 94,* 319–340.

HIGGINS, E.T. (1996). The "self digest": Self-knowledge serving self-regulatory functions. *Journal of Personality and Social Psychology, 71,* 1062–1083.

HIGGINS, E.T., & BRYANT, S.L. (1982). Consensus information and the fundamental attribution error: The role of development and in-group versus out-group knowledge. *Journal of Personality and Social Psychology, 43,* 889–900.

HIGHAM, P.A., & CARMENT, D.W. (1992). The rise and fall of politicians: The judged heights of Broadbent, Mulroney and Turner before and after the 1988 Canadian federal election. *Canadian Journal of Behavioural Science, 24,* 404–409.

HILGARD, E.R. (1978). Hypnosis and consciousness. *Human Nature, 1,* 2–49.

HILL, C.T., & STULL, D.E. (1981). Sex differences in the effects of social and value similarity in same-sex friendships. *Journal of Personality and Social Psychology, 41,* 488–502.

HILL, C.T., RUBIN, Z., & PEPLAU, L.A. (1976). Breakups before marriage: The end of 103 affairs. *Journal of Social Issues, 32,* 147–168.

HILTON, J.L., & VON HIPPEL, W. (1996). Stereotypes. *Annual Review of Psychology, 47,* 237–271.

HILTON, N.Z., HARRIS, G.T., & RICE, M.E. (2000). The function of aggression by male teenagers. *Journal of Personality and Social Psychology, 79,* 988–994.

HINKIN, T.R., & SCHRIESHEIM, C.A. (1989). Development and application of new scales to measure the French and Raven (1959) bases of social power. *Journal of Applied Social Psychology, 74,* 561–567.

HIRT, E.R., DEPPE, R.K., & GORDON, L.J. (1991). Self-reported versus behavioral self-handicapping: Empirical evidence for a theoretical distinction. *Journal of Personality and Social Psychology, 61,* 981–991.

HO, R., & PENNEY, R.K. (1992). Euthenasia and abortion: Personality correlates for the decision to terminate life. *Journal of Social Psychology 132,* 77–86.

HODGINS, D.C., & KALIN, R. (1985). Reducing sex bias in judgements of occupational suitability by provision of sex-typed personality information. *Canadian Journal of Behavioural Science, 17,* 346–358.

HOFFMAN, C., LAU, I., & JOHNSON, D.R. (1986). The linguistic relativity of person cognition. An English-Chinese comparison. *Journal of Personality and Social Psychology, 51,* 1097–1105.

HOFFMAN, M.L. (1984). Parent discipline, moral internalization, and development of prosocial motivation. In E. Staub, D. Bar-Tal, J. Karylowski, & J. Reykowski (Eds.), *Development and maintenance of prosocial behavior* (pp. 117–137). New York: Plenum.

HOFFMANN, M.L. (1977). Sex differences in empathy and related behaviors. *Psychological Bulletin, 84,* 712–722.

HOFFMANN, M.L. (1981). Is altruism a part of human nature? *Journal of Personality and Social Psychology, 40,* 121–137.

HOFLING, C.K., BRODZSMAN, E., DALRYMPLE, S., GRAVES, N., & PIERCE, C.M. (1966). An experimental study in nurse physician relationships. *The Journal of Nervous and Mental Disease, 143,* 171–180.

HOFSTEDE, G. (1983). Dimensions of national cultures in fifty countries and three regions. In J.B. Deregowski, S. Dziurawiec, & R.C. Annis (Eds.), *Explications in cross-cultural psychology* (pp. 335–355). Lisse: Swets & Zeitlinger B.V.

HOLLANDER, E.P. (1958). Conformity, status, and idiosyncrasy credit. *Psychological Review, 65,* 117–127.

HOLLANDER, E.P. (1992). The essential interdependence of leadership and followership. *Current Directions in Psychological Science, 1,* 71–75.

HOLMES, D.S. (1976). Debriefing after psychological experiments: II. Effectiveness of post-experimental desensitizing. *American Psychologist, 31,* 868–876.

HOLMES, J.G., & BOON, S.D. (1990). Developments in the field of close relationships: Creating foundations for intervention strategies. *Personality and Social Psychology Bulletin, 16,* 23–41.

HOLMES, J.G., MILLER, D.T., & LERNER, M. (2002). Committing altruism under the cloak of self-interest: The exchange fiction. *Journal of Experimental Social Psychology, 38,* 144–151.

HOLMES, T.H., & RAHE, R.H. (1967). The social readjustment rating scale. *Journal of Psychosomatic Research, 11,* 213–218.

HOLSTEIN, J. (1985). Jurors' interpretations and jury decision-making. *Law and Human Behavior, 9,* 83–100.

HOLSTROM, L., & BURGESS, A. (1978). *The victims of rape: Institutional reactions.* New York: Wiley.

HOLTGRAVES, T. (1986). Language structure in social interaction: Perceptions of direct and indirect speech acts and interactants who use them. *Journal of Personality and Social Psychology, 51,* 305–314.

HOLTGRAVES, T. (1997). Styles of language use: Individual and cultural variability in conversational indirectness. *Journal of Personality and Social Psychology 73,* 624–637.

HOLTSWORTH-MUNROE, A., & JACOBSON, N.S. (1985). Causal attributions of married couples: When do they search for causes? What do they conclude when they do? *Journal of Personality and Social Psychology, 48,* 1398–1412.

HOLTSWORTH-MUNROE, A., & STUART, G.L. (1994). Typologies of male batterers, three subtypes and the differences among them. *Journal of Personality and Social Psychology, 116,* 476–497.

HOLTZWORTH-MONROE, A. (2000). A typology of men who are violent toward their female partners: Making sense of heterogeneity in husband violence. *Current Directions in Psychological Science, 9,* 140–143.

HOMANS, G.C. (1958). Social behavior and exchange. *American Journal of Sociology, 63,* 597–606.

HOMANS, G.C. (1961). *Social behavior: Its elementary forms.* New York: Harcourt, Brace and World.

HOMANS G.C. (1974). *Social behavior: Its elementary forms* (Revised ed.). New York: Harcourt Brace Jovanovich.

HOMER, P.M., & KAHLE, L. (1988). A structural equation test of the value-attitude-behavior hierarchy. *Journal of Personality and Social Psychology, 54,* 638–646.

HONEYMAN, J.C., & OGLOFF, J.R.P. (1996). Capital punishment: Arguments for life and death. *Canadian Journal of Behavioural Science, 28,* 27–35.

HONTS, C.R., HODES, R.L., & RASKIN, D.C. (1985). Effects of physical counter measures on the physiological detection of deception. *Journal of Applied Psychology, 70,* 177–187.

HOOKER, S. (1988, May 9). It's still a question of black and white. *The Globe and Mail.*

HOPSON, J. (1981, October). Evil spirits in the factory. *Science Digest, 58,* 114.

HORN, J.C. (1985). Fan violence: Fighting the injustice of it all. *Psychology Today, 19* (10), 30–31.

HORN, M.J. (1975). *The second skin: An interdisciplinary study of clothing.* Boston: Houghton-Mifflin.

HOROWITZ, M.J., DUFF, D.F., & STRATTON, C.O. (1970). Personal space and the body buffer zone. In H. Proshansky, W. Ittelson, & L. Rivlin (Eds.), *Environmental psychology: Man and his physical setting* (pp. 244–272). New York: Holt, Rinehart and Winston.

HORVATH, F. (1977). Effect of selected variables on interpretation of polygraph records. *Journal of Applied Psychology, 62,* 127–136.

HORVATH, F. (1984). Detecting deception in eyewitness cases: Problems and prospects in the use of the polygraph. In G.L. Wells, & E.F. Loftus (Eds.), *Eyewitness testimony: Psychological perspectives* (pp. 214–255). Cambridge: Cambridge University Press.

HOTTA, M., & STRICKLAND, L.H. (1991). Social psychology in Japan. *Canadian Psychology, 32,* 596–611.

HOULDEN, P., LATOUR, S., WALKER, L., & THIBAUT, J. (1978). Preference for modes of dispute resolution as a function of process and decision control. *Journal of Experimental Social Psychology, 14,* 13–30.

HOUSE, J.S., & WOFD, S. (1978). Effects of urban residence on interpersonal trust and helping behavior. *Journal of Personality and Social Psychology, 36,* 1029–1043.

HOUSE, R. (1977). A 1976 theory of charismatic leadership. In J.G. Hunt, & L. Larson (Eds.), *Leadership: The cutting edge* (pp. 189–207). Carbondale: Southern Illinois University Press.

HOVLAND, C.I., HARVEY, O.J., & SHERIF, M. (1957). Assimilation and contrast effects in reactions to communications and attitude change. *Journal of Abnormal and Social Psychology, 55,* 244–252.

HOVLAND, C.I., JANIS, I., & KELLEY, H.H. (1953). *Communication and persuasion.* New Haven: Yale University Press.

HOVLAND, C.I., LUMSDAINE, A.A., & SHEFFIELD, F.D. (1949). *Experiments on mass communication.* Princeton, NJ: Princeton University Press.

HOWELL, J.M., & FROST, P.J. (1989). A laboratory study of charismatic leadership. *Organization Behavior and Human Decision Processes, 43,* 243–269.

HOWITT, D., & CUMBERBATCH, G. (1975). *Mass media violence and society.* London: Paul Elek.

HUBA, G.J., DENT, C., & BENTLER, P.M. (1980, September). *Causal models of peer-adult support and youthful alcohol use.* American Psychological Association, Montréal.

HUESMANN, L.R. (1986). Psychological processes promoting the relation between exposure to media violence and aggressive behavior by the receiver. *Journal of Social Issues, 42,* 125–139.

HUESMANN, L.R., & GUERRA, N.G. (1997). Children's normative beliefs about aggression and aggressive behavior. *Journal of Personality and Social Psychology, 72,* 408–419.

HUESMANN, L.R., ERON, L.D., & YARMEL, P.W. (1987). Intellectual functioning and aggression. *Journal of Personality and Social Psychology, 52,* 232–240.

HUESMANN, L.R., ERON, L.D., LEFKOWITZ, M.M., & WALDER, L.O. (1984). Stability of aggression over time and generations. *Developmental Psychology, 20,* 1120–1134.

HULL, J.G. (1987). Self-awareness model. In H.T. Blane, & K.E. Leonard (Eds.), *Psychological theories of drinking and alcoholism* (pp. 272–303). New York: Guilford.

HULL, J.G., & BOND, C.F. (1986). Social and behavioral consequences of alcohol consumption and expectancy: A meta-analysis. *Psychological Bulletin, 99,* 347–360.

HUME, E., LEPICQ, D., & BOURHIS, R.Y. (1992). Attitudes des étudiants canadiens anglais face aux accents des professeurs de français en Ontario. *La revue canadienne des langues vivantes, 49,* 210–235.

HUNSBERGER, B. (1995). Religion and prejudice: The role of religious fundamentalism, quest, and right-wing authoritarianism. *Journal of Social Issues, 51,* 113–129.

HUNSBERGER, B. (1996). Religious fundamentalism, right-wing authoritarianism, and hostility toward homosexuals in non-Christian religious groups. *International Journal for the Psychology of Religion, 6,* 39–49.

HUNSBERGER, B., LEA, J., PANCER, S.M., PRATT, M., & MCKENZIE, B. (1992). Making life complicated: Prompting the use of integratively complex thinking. *Journal of Personality, 60,* 95–114.

HUNSBERGER, B., PRATT, M., & PANCER, S.M. (1994). Religious fundamentalitsm and integrative complexity of thought: A relationship for existential content only? *Journal for the Scientific Study of Religion, 33,* 335–346.

HUNT, W.A., BARNETT, L.W., & BRANCH, L.G. (1971). Relapse rate in addiction programs. *Journal of Clinical Psychology, 27,* 455–456.

HUNTER, I. (1987). Human rights: Liberty can't be legislated. In R. Jackson, D. Jackson, & N. Baxter-Moore (Eds.), *Contemporary Canadian politics: Readings and notes* (pp. 61–64). Scarborough: Prentice-Hall.

HURT, W., SCHNURR, P.P., SEVERINO, S.K., FREEMAN, E.W., GISE, L.H., RIVERA-TOVAR, A., & STEEGE, J.E. (1992). Late-luteal phase dysphoric disorders in 670 women evaluated for premenstrual complaints. *American Journal of Psychiatry 149,* 525–530.

HUTT, C. (1974). Sex: What's the difference? *New Scientist, 62,* 405–407.

IDLER, E. L., & BINYAMINI, Y. (1997). Self-rated health and mortality: A review of 27 community studies. *Journal of Health and Social Behavior, 38,* 21–37.

IMPETT, E.A., BEALS, K.P., & PEPLAU, L.A. (2002). Testing the investment model of relationship commitment and stability in a longitudinal study of married couples. *Current Psychology: Developmental, Learning, Personality, Social, 20,* 312–326.

INGHAM, A.G., LEVINGER, G., GRAVES, J., & PECKHORN, V. (1974). The Ringelmann effect: Studies of group size and group performance. *Journal of Experimental Social Psychology, 10,* 371–384.

INGLEHART, R. (1987). Extremist political positions and perceptions of conspiracy: Even paranoids have real enemies. In C.F. Graumann, & S. Moscovici (Eds.), *Changing conceptions of conspiracy* (pp. 231–244). New York: Springer-Verlag.

INKELES, A., & SMITH, D.H. (1974). *Becoming modern: Individual change in six developing countries.* Cambridge, MA: Harvard University Press.

INNES, J.M. (1972). The effect of presence of co-workers and evaluative feedback on performance of a simple reaction time task. *European Journal of Social Psychology, 2,* 466–470.

INSKO, C.A. (1964). Primacy versus recency in persuasion as a function of the timing of arguments and measures. *Journal of Abnormal and Social Psychology, 69,* 381–391.

IP, G.W., & BOND, M.H. (1995). Culture, values and the spontaneous self-concept. *Asian Journal of Psychology, 1,* 29–35.

ISEN, A.M. (1970). Success, failure, attention and reaction to others. *Journal of Personality and Social Psychology, 15,* 294–301.

ISENBERG, D.J. (1986). Group polarization: A critical review and meta-analysis. *Journal of Personality and Social Psychology, 50,* 1141–1151.

IVERSON, J.M., & GOLDIN-MEADOW, S. (1998). Why people gesture as they speak. *Nature, 396,* 228.

IZZETT, R., & FISHMAN, L. (1976). Defendant sentences as a function of attractiveness and justification for actions. *Journal of Social Psychology, 100,* 285–290.

JACKSON, J.M., BUGLIONE, S.A., & GLENWICK, D.S. (1988). Major league baseball performance as a function of being traded: A drive and theory analysis. *Personality and Social Psychology Bulletin, 14,* 46–56.

JACKSON, L.M., & ESSES, V. (1997). Of scriptures and ascriptions; The relation between religious fundamentalism and intergroup helping. *Personality and Social Psychology Bulletin, 23,* 893–906.

JACOBY, L.L., KELLEY, C., BROWN, J., & JASECHKO, J. (1989). Becoming famous overnight: Limits on the ability to avoid unconscious influences of the past. *Journal of Personality and Social Psychology, 56,* 326–338.

JAFFE, P. (1990, June). *Hidden victims: The effects of witnessing violence.* Annual Conference of the Canadian Psychological Association, Ottawa.

JAFFE, P., WOLFE, D., WILSON, S., & ZAK, L. (1986). Similarities in behavioural and social adjustment among child victims and witnesses to family violence. *American Journal of Orthopsychiatry, 56,* 142–146.

JAFFEE, S., & HYDE, J.S. (2000). Gender differences in moral orientation: A meta-analysis. *Psychological Bulletin, 126,* 703–726.

JAIN, H.C., NORMAND, J., & KANUNGO, R.N. (1979). Job motivation of Canadian anglophone and francophone hospital employees. *Canadian Journal of Behavioural Science, 11,* 160–163.

JAMIESON, D.W., & ZANNA, M.P. (1988). Need for structure in attitude formation and expression. In A.R. Pratkanis, S.J. Breckler, & A.G. Greenwald (Eds.), *Attitude structure and function.* Hillsdale, NJ: Erlbaum.

JAMIESON, D.W., LYDON, J.E., & ZANNA, M.P. (1987). Attitude and activity preference similarity: Differential bases of interpersonal attraction for low and high self-monitors. *Journal of Personality and Social Psychology, 53,* 1052–1060.

JAMOUS, H., & LEMAINE, W. (1962). Compétition entre groupes d'inégales resources. Expérience dans un cadre naturel. *Psychologie française, 7,* 216–222.

JANIS, I.L. (1958). *Psychological stress.* New York: Wiley.

JANIS, I.L. (1972). *Victims of groupthink.* Boston: Houghton Mifflin.

JANIS, I.L. (1982). *Groupthink* (2nd ed.). Boston: Houghton Mifflin.

JANIS, I.L., & FESHBACH, S. (1953). Effects of fear-arousing communications. *Journal of Abnormal and Social Psychology, 48,* 78–92.

JANIS, I.L., & GILMORE, J.B. (1965). The influence of incentive conditions on the sources of role playing in modifying attitudes. *Journal of Personality and Social Psychology, 1,* 17–27.

JANIS, I.L., & HOVLAND, C.I. (1959). An overview of persuasibility research. In C.I. Hovland, & I.L. Janis (Eds.), *Personality and persuasibility* (pp. 1–28). New Haven, CT: Yale University Press.

JANIS, I.L., & MANN, L. (1977). *Decision making.* New York: Free Press.

JANIS, I.L., CHAPMAN, D.W., GILLIN, J.P., & SPIEGEL, J.P. (1964). The problem of panic. In D.P. Schultz (Ed.), *Panic behavior* (118–127). New York: Random House.

JANOWSKI, C.L., & MALLOY, T.E. (1992). Perceptions and misperceptions of leadership: Components, accuracy and dispositional correlates. *Personality and Social Psychology Bulletin, 18,* 700–708.

JANZ, N.K., & BECKER, M.H. (1984). The health belief model: A decade later. *Health Education Quarterly, 11,* 1–47.

JASPARS, J. (1980). The coming of age of social psychology in Europe. *European Journal of Social Psychology, 10,* 421–428.

JENKINS, S.S., & AUBÉ, J. (2002). Gender differences and gender-related constructs in dating aggression. *PSPB, 28,* 1106–1118.

JERVIS, R., LEBOW, R.N., & STEIN, J.G. (1985). *Psychology of deterrence.* Baltimore: Johns Hopkins University Press.

JESSOR, R. (1993). Successful adolescent development among youth in high-risk settings. *American Psychologist, 48,* 117–126.

JESSOR, R., & JESSOR, S.L. (1977). *Problem behavior and psychosocial development: A longitudinal study of youth.* New York: Academic Press.

JESSOR, R., DONOVAN, J.E., & WIDMER, K. (1980). Psychosocial factors in adolescent alcohol and drug use: The 1978 national sample study and the 1974–78 panel study. Boulder, CO: Institute of Behavioral Science, University of Colorado. 1–161 (unpublished report).

JHA, P.K., YADAV, K.P., & KUMARI, U. (1997). Gender difference and religio-cultural variation in altruistic behaviour. *Indian Journal of Psychometry and Education, 28,* 105–108.

JOAD, C.E.M. (1957). *Guide to philosophy.* New York: Dover.

JOHANSSON, G., COLLINS, A., & COLLINS, V.P. (1983). Male and female psychoneuroendocrine response to examination stress: A case report. *Motivation and Emotion, 7,* 1–9.

JOHNSON, B.T., & EAGLY, A.H. (1989). Effects of involvement on persuasion: A meta-analysis. *Psychological Bulletin, 106,* 290–314.

JOHNSON, J.E., & LEVENTHAL, H. (1974). Effects of accurate expectations and behavioral instructions on reactions during a noxious medical examination. *Journal of Personality and Social Psychology, 29,* 710–718.

JOHNSON, R.D., & DOWNING, L.L. (1979). Deindividuation and valence of cues: Effects on prosocial and antisocial behavior. *Journal of Personality and Social Psychology, 37,* 1532–1538.

JOHNSON, R.N. (1972). *Aggression in man and animals.* Philadelphia: Saunders.

JOHNSON, R.W., KELLY, R.J., & LEBLANC, B.A. (1995). Motivational basis of dissonance: Aversive consequences or inconsistency? *Personality and Social Psychology Bulletin, 21,* 850–855.

JOHNSTON, I.F., & STRICKLAND, L.H. (1985). Communication mode, affect and recall. *Canadian Journal of Behavioural Science, 17,* 226–231.

JONES, E.E. (1964). *Ingratiation: A social psychological analysis.* New York: Appleton-Century-Crofts.

JONES, E.E., & BAUMEISTER, R. (1976). The self-monitor looks at the ingratiator. *Journal of Personality, 44,* 654–674.

JONES, E.E., & DAVIS, K.E. (1965). From acts to dispositions: The attribution process in person perception. In L. Berkowitz (Ed.), *Advances in experimental social psychology* (Vol. 2). (pp. 220–266). New York: Academic Press.

JONES, E.E., & HARRIS, V.A. (1976). The attribution of attitude. *Journal of Experimental Psychology, 3,* 1–24.

JONES, E.E., & MCGILLIS, D. (1976). Correspondent inferences and the attribution cube: A comparative reappraisal. In H.H. Harvey, W.J. Ickes, & R.F. Kidd (Eds.), *New directions in attribution research* (Vol. 1). (pp. 389–420). Hillsdale, NJ: Erlbaum.

JONES, E.E., & PITTMAN, T.S. (1982). Towards a general theory of strategic self-presentation. In J. Suls (Ed.), *Psychological perspectives on the self* (pp. 231–262). Hillsdale, NJ: Erlbaum.

JONES, E.E., DAVIS, K.E., & GERGEN, K. (1961). Role playing variations and their informational value for person perception. *Journal of Abnormal and Social Psychology, 63,* 302–310.

JONES, R.A. (1990). Expectations and delay in seeking medical care. *Journal of Social Issues, 46* (2), 81–95.

JONES, S.E., & YARBROUGH, A.E. (1985). A naturalistic study of the meanings of touch. *Communication Monographs, 52,* 19–56.

JOSEPHSON, W.L. (1987). Television violence and children's aggression: Testing the priming, social script, and disinhibition predictions. *Journal of Personality and Social Psychology, 53,* 882–890.

JOURARD, S.M. (1966). An exploratory study of body-accessibility. *British Journal of Social and Clinical Psychology, 5,* 221–231.

JOY, L.A., KIMBALL, M.M., & ZABRACK, M.L. (1977). *Television exposure and children's aggressive behaviours.* Canadian Psychological Association Annual Conference, Vancouver.

JOY, L.A., KIMBALL, M.M., & ZABRACK, M.L. (1986). Television and children's aggressive behavior. In T.M. Williams (Ed.), *The impact of television: A natural experiment in three communities* (pp. 303–360). New York: Academic Press.

JUSSIM, L., MADON, S., & CHAPMAN, C. (1994). Teacher expectations and student achievement: Self-fulfilling prophecies, biases and accuracy. In L. Heath, R.S., Tindale, J. Edwards, E. Posovac, F.B. Bryant, E. Henderson-King, Y. Suarez-Balcazar, & J. Myers (Eds.), *Applications of heuristics and biases to social issues* (pp. 303–333). New York: Plenum Press.

KAHN, G.R., & KATZ, D. (1953). Leadership practices in relation to productivity and morale. In D. Cartwright, & A. Zander (Eds.), *Group dynamics: Research and theory* (pp. 612–628). Evanston, IL: Row, Peterson.

KAHN, H. (1962). *Thinking about the unthinkable.* New York: Avon.

KAHN, M. (1966). The physiology of catharsis. *Journal of Personality and Social Psychology, 3,* 278–286.

KAHNEMAN, D., & TVERSKY, A. (1982). The simulation heuristic. In D. Kahneman, P. Slovic, & A. Tversky (Eds.), *Judgements under uncertainty: Heuristics and biases.* New York: Cambridge University Press.

KAKUTA, K., BIALYSTOK, E., & WILEY, E. (2003). Critical evidence: A test of the critical-period hypothesis for second-language acquisition. *Psychological Science, 14,* 31–38.

KALICK, S.M., ZEBROWITZ, L.A., LANGLOIS, J.H., & JOHNSON, R.M. (1996, August 9–13). *Does attractiveness advertise health or are we blinded by beauty?* American Psychological Association, Toronto.

KALIK, S.M., & HAMILTON, T.E. (1988). A closer look at a matching simulation. *Journal of Personality and Social Psychology, 54,* 447–452.

KALIN, R. (1996). Ethnic attitudes as a function of ethnic presence. *Canadian Journal of Behavioural Science, 28,* 171–179.

KALIN, R., & BERRY, J.W. (1979). *Ethnic attitudes and identity in the context of national unity.* Final report to Multiculturalism Directorate, Secretary of State, Government of Canada.

KALIN, R., & BERRY, J.W. (1982). The social ecology of ethnic attitudes in Canada. *Canadian Journal of Behavioural Science, 14,* 97–109.

KALIN, R., & GARDNER R.C. (1981). The cultural context of social psychology. In R.C. Gardner, & R. Kalin (Eds.), *A social psychology of Canadian ethnic relations* (pp. 2–17). Toronto: Methuen.

KALIN, R., & HODGINS, D.C. (1984). Sex bias in judgements of occupational suitability. *Canadian Journal of Behavioural Science, 16,* 311–325.

KAMIN, L.J. (1974). *The science and politics of I.Q.* New York: Halsted Press.

KANDEL, D.B. (1978a). Convergences in prospective longitudinal surveys of drug use in normal populations. In D.B. Kandel (Ed.), *Longitudinal research on drug use: Empirical findings and methodological issues.* Washington, DC: Hemisphere.

KANDEL, D.B. (1978b). Similarity in real-life adolescent friendship pairs. *Journal of Personality and Social Psychology, 36,* 306–312.

KANEKAR, S. (2001). Helping norms in relation to religious affiliation. *Journal of Social Psychology, 141,* 617–626.

KANNER, A.D., COYNE, J.C., SCHAEFER, C., & LAZARUS, R.S. (1981). Comparison of two models of stress measurement: Daily hassles and uplifts versus major life events. *Journal of Behavioral Medicine, 4,* 1–29.

KANUNGO, R.N., GORN, G.J., & DAUDERIS, H.J. (1976). Motivational orientation of Canadian anglophone and francophone managers. *Canadian Journal of Behavioural Science, 8,* 107–121.

KARAU, S.J., & HART, J.W. (1998). Group cohesiveness and social loafing: Effects of a social interaction manipulation on individual motivation within groups. *Group Dynamics, 2,* 185–191.

KARLINS, M., & ABELSON, H.I. (1970). *How opinions and attitudes are changed* (2nd ed.). New York: Springer.

KARLINS, M., COFFMAN, T.L., & WALTERS, G. (1969). On the fading of social stereotypes: Studies in three generations of college students. *Journal of Personality and Social Psychology, 13,* 1–16.

KASSIN, S.M., & BARNDOLLAR, K.A. (1992). The psychology of eyewitness testimony: A comparison of experts and prospective jurors. *Journal of Applied Social Psychology, 22,* 1241–1249.

KASSIN, S.M., ELLSWORTH, P.C., & SMITH, V.L. (1989). The "general acceptance" of psychological research on eyewitness testimony. *American Psychologist, 44,* 1089–1098.

KASSIN, S.M., REDDY, M.E., & TULLOCH, W.F. (1990). Juror interpretation of ambiguous evidence: The need for cognition, presentation order and persuasion. *Law and Human Behavior, 14*, 43–55.

KATZ, D., & BRALY, K. (1933). Racial stereotypes of one hundred college students. *Journal of Abnormal and Social Psychology, 28*, 280–290.

KATZ, E. (1957). The two-step flow of communication: An up-to-date report on a hypothesis. *Public Opinion Quarterly, 21*, 61–78.

KATZ, E., & LAZERFIELD, P.F. (1955). *Personal influence: The part played by people in the flow of mass communication.* Glencoe, IL: Free Press.

KATZEV, R., BLAKE, G., & MESSER, B. (1993). Determinants of participation in multi-family recycling programs. *Journal of Applied Psychology, 23*, 374–385.

KAUFMAN, J., & ZIGLER, E. (1987). Do abused children become abusive parents? *American Journal of Orthopsychiatry, 57*, 186–192.

KAWAKAMI, K., & DION, K.L. (1993). The impact of salient self-identities on relative deprivation and action intentions. *European Journal of Social Psychology, 23*, 525–540.

KAWASHIMA, R., SUGIURA, M., KATO, T., NAKAMURA, A., HATANO, K., ITO, K., FUKUDA, H., KOJIMA, S., & NAKAMURA, K. (1999). The human amygdala lays an important role in gaze monitoring: A PET study. *Brain, 122*, 779–783. Cited by Mcrae et al. (2002).

KAY, A.C., JIMENEZ, M., & JOST, J.T. (2002). Sour grapes, sweet lemons and the anticipatory rationalization of the status quo. *Personality and Social Psychology Bulletin, 28*, 1300–1312.

KEASHLY, L., & FISHER, R.J. (1996). A contingency perspective on conflict interventions: Theoretical and practical considerations. In J. Bercovitch (Ed.), *Resolving international conflicts: The theory and practice of mediation* (pp. 235–261). Boulder, CO: Lynne Rienner Publishers.

KEASHLY, L., FISHER, R.J., & GRANT, P.R. (1993). The comparative utility of third party consultation and mediation within a complex simulation of intergroup conflict. *Human Relations, 46*, 371–391.

KEATING, J.P., & LOFTUS, E.F. (1981). The logic of fire escape. *Psychology Today, 15* (6), 14–18.

KEEFE, J.M. & FANCEY, P.J. (2002). Work and eldercare: Reciprocity between older mothers and their employed daughters. *Canadian Journal on Aging, 21*, 229–241.

KEELAN, J.P.R., DION, K.L., & DION, K.K. (1994). Attachment style and heterosexual relationships among young adults: A short-term panel study. *Journal of Personal and Social Relationships, 11*, 201–214.

KEINAN, G., & HOBFOLL, S.E. (1989). Stress, dependency and social support: Who benefits from the husband's presence in delivery? *Journal of Social and Clinical Psychology, 8*, 32–44.

KEINAN, G., SADEH, A., & ROSEN, S. (2003). Attitudes and reactions to media coverage of terrorist acts. *Journal of Community Psychology, 31*, 149–165.

KELLEY, H.H. (1950). The warm-cold variable in first impressions of persons. *Journal of Personality, 18*, 431–439.

KELLEY, H.H. (1972a). Attribution in social interaction. In E.E. Jones, D.E. Kanouse, H.H. Kelley, R.E. Nisbett, S. Valins, & B. Weiner (Eds.), *Attribution: Perceiving the causes of behavior* (pp. 1–26). Morristown, NJ: General Learning Press.

KELLEY, H.H., & STAHELSKI, A.J. (1970). The social interaction basis of cooperators' and competitors' beliefs about others. *Journal of Personality and Social Psychology, 16*, 66–91.

KELLEY, H.H., HOVLAND, C.I., SCHWARTZ, M., & ABELSON, R.P. (1955). The influence of judges' attitudes in three methods of scaling. *Journal of Sociological Psychology, 42*, 147–158.

KELLY, J.R., & BARSADE, S.G. (in press). Mood and emotions in small groups and work teams. *Organizational Behavior in Small Groups and Work Teams.*

KELLY, L.E., & CONLEY, J.J. (1987). Personality and compatibility: A prospective analysis of marital stability and marital satisfaction. *Journal of Personality and Social Psychology, 52*, 27–40.

KELMAN, H.C. (1958). Compliance, identification, and internalization: Three processes of attitude change. *Journal of Conflict Resolution, 2*, 51–60.

KELMAN, H.C. (1961). Processes of opinion change. *Public Opinion Quarterly, 25*, 57–78.

KELMAN, H.C. (1965). Social-psychological approaches to the study of international relations: The question of relevance. In H.C. Kelman (Ed.), *International behavior: A social-psychological analysis.* New York: Holt, Rinehart and Winston.

KELMAN, H.C. (1967). Human use of human subjects: The problem of deception in social psychological experiments. *Psychological Bulletin, 67*, 1–11.

KENNEDY, L.W., & DUTTON, D.G. (1989). The incidence of wife assault in Alberta. *Canadian Journal of Behavioural Science, 21*, 40–54.

KENNEDY, T.D., & HAYGOOD, R.C. (1992). The discrediting effect in eyewitness testimony. *Journal of Applied Social Psychology, 22*, 70–82.

KENRICK, D.T., & CIALDINI, R.B. (1977). Romantic attraction: Misattribution versus reinforcement explanations. *Journal of Personality and Social Psychology, 35*, 381–391.

KENRICK, D.T., & GUSTIERRES, S.E. (1980). Contrast effects and judgements of physical attractiveness: When beauty becomes a social problem. *Journal of Personality and Social Psychology, 38*, 131–140.

KERCKHOFF, A.C., & DAVIS, K.E. (1962). Value consensus and need complementarity in mate selection. *American Sociological Review, 27*, 295–303.

KERWIN, J., & SHAFFER, D.R. (1991). The effects of jury dogmatism on reactions to jury nullification instructions. *Personality and Social Psychology Bulletin, 17*, 140–146.

KEYES, R. (1980). *The height of your life.* Boston: Little, Brown.

KIDD, R.F., & CHAYET, E.F. (1984). Why do victims fail to report? The psychology of criminal victimization. *Journal of Social Issues, 40*, 39–50.

KIECOLT-GLASER, & NEWTON. (2001). Marriage and health: his and hers. *Psychological Bulletin, 127*, 472–503.

KIESLER, C.A. (1968). Commitment. In R.P. Abelson, E. Aronson, W.J. McGuire, T.H. Newcomb, M.J. Rosenberg, & P.H. Tannenbaum (Eds.), *Theories of cognitive consistency: A sourcebook* (pp. 448–455). Skokie, IL: Rand-McNally.

KIESLER, C.A., & PALLAK, M.S. (1976). Arousal properties of dissonance manipulations. *Psychological Bulletin, 83*, 1014–1025.

KIHLSTROM, J.F., CANTOR, N., ALBRIGHT, J.S., CHEW, B.R., KLEIN, S.B., & NIEDENTHAL, P.M. (1988). Information processing and the study of the self. In L. Berkowitz (Ed.), *Advances in experimental social psychology* (Vol. 21). (pp. 145–178). New York: Academic Press.

KILLIAN, L.M. (1952). The significance of multiple-group membership in a disaster. *American Journal of Sociology, 57*, 309–314.

KING, K.B., REIS, H.T., PORTER, L.A., & NORSEN, L.H. (1993). Social support and long-term recovery from coronary artery surgery: Effects on patients and spouses. *Health Psychology, 12*, 56–63.

KIPNIS, D. (1972). Does power corrupt? *Journal of Personality and Social Psychology, 24*, 33–41.

KITAYAMA, S. & MARKUS, H.R. (1994). Culture and the self: How culture influences how we view ourselves. In D. Matsumoto (Ed.), *People: Psychology from a cultural perspective* (pp. 17–37). Pacific Grove, CA: Brooks/Cole.

KITAYAMA, S., MARKUS, H.R., MATSUMOTO, H., & NORASAKKUNKIT, V. (1997). Individual and collective processes of self-esteem management: Self-enhancement in the United States and self-depreciation in Japan. *Journal of Personality and Social Psychology, 72*, 1245–1267.

KITCHENS, A. (1974). Shape-of-the-table negotiations at the Paris peace talks on Vietnam. In C.M. Loo (Ed.), *Crowding and behavior* (pp. 224–245). New York: MFS Information Company.

KLAMA, J. (1988). *Aggression.* Burnt Hill: Longman.

KLAPP, O.E. (1972). *Currents of unrest.* New York: Holt, Rinehart & Winston.

KLEIN, J.G. (1991). Negative effects in impression formation: A test in the political arena. *Personality and Social Psychology Bulletin, 17*, 412–418.

KLEIN, K.J., & HOUSE, R.J. (1998). On fire: Charismatic leadership and levels of analysis. In F. Dansereau, & F.J. Yammarino (Eds.), *Leadership: The multiple-level approaches: Contemporary and alternative. Monographs in organizational behavior and industrial relations, 24*, Part B. (pp. 3–52). Stamford, CT: Jai Press, Inc.

KLING, K.C., HYDE, J.S., SHOWERS, C.J., & BUSWELL, B.N. (1999). Gender differences in self-esteem: A meta-analysis. *Psychological Bulletin, 125*, 470–500.

KLINGER, E. (1964). Feedback effects and social facilitation of vigilance performance: Mere coaction versus potential evaluation. *Psychonomic Science, 14*, 161–162.

KLOHN, L.S., & ROGERS, R.W. (1991). Dimensions of the severity of a health threat: The persuasive effects of visibility, time of onset and rate of onset on young women's intentions to prevent osteoporosis. *Health Psychology, 10*, 323–329.

KNOX, R.E., & INKSTER, J.A. (1968). Post-decision dissonance at post time. *Journal of Personality and Social Psychology, 8*, 319–323.

KOBASA, S.C. (1979). Stressful life events, personality and health: An inquiry into hardiness. *Journal of Personality and Social Psychology, 37*, 1–11.

KOENIG, K. (1985). *Rumor in the marketplace.* Dover, MA: Auburn House.

KOGAN, N., & WALLACH, M.A. (1964). *Risk taking.* New York: Holt, Rinehart and Winston.

KOGAN, N., & WALLACH, M.A. (1967). Risk taking as a function of the situation, the person, and the group. In G. Mandler, P. Mussen, N. Kogan, & M.A. Wallach (Eds.), *New directions in psychology III.* New York: Holt, Rinehart and Winston.

KOHLBERG, L. (1964). Development of moral character and moral ideology. In M. Hoffman, & L. Hoffman (Eds.), *Review of child development research.* New York: Russell Sage Foundation.

KOHNKEN, G., & MAASS, A. (1988). Eyewitness testimony: False alarms on biased instructions? *Journal of Applied Psychology, 73*, 363–370.

KOLLMUSS, A. & AGYEMAN, J. (2002). Mind the gap: Why do people act environmentally and what are the barriers to pro-environmental behavior? *Environmental Education Research, 8*, 239–260.

KOMORITA S.S., & PARKS, C.D. (1995). Interpersonal relations: Mixed-motive interaction. *Annual Review of Psychology, 46*, 183–207.

KOMORITA, S.S., & PARKS, C.D. (1999). Reciprocity and cooperation in social dilemmas: Review and future directions. In D.V. Budescu, & I. Erev, (Eds.), *Games and human behavior: Essays in honor of Amnon Rapoport* (pp. 315–330). Mahwah, NJ: Lawrence Erlbaum Associates.

KOMORITA, S.S., HILTY, J.A., & PARKS, C.D. (1991). Reciprocity and cooperation in social dilemmas. *Journal of Conflict Resolution, 35*, 494–518.

KONECNI, V.J., & EBBESON, E.B. (1979). External validity of research in legal psychology. *Law and Human Behavior, 3*, 39–70.

KOSS, M.P., GIDYCZ, C.A., & WISNIESKI, N. (1987). The scope of rape: Incidence and prevalence of sexual aggression and victimization in a national sample of higher education students. *Journal of Consulting and Clinical Psychology, 55*, 162–170.

KRAMER, R.M. (1998). Revisiting the Bay of Pigs and Vietnam decisions 25 years later: How well has the groupthink hypothesis stood the test of time? *Organizational Behavior and Human Decision Processes, 73*, 236–271.

KRAMER, R.M., & BREWER, M.B. (1984). Effects of group identity on resource use in a simulated commons dilemma. *Journal of Personality and Social Psychology, 46*, 1044–1057.

KRANTZ, D.S., & GLASS, D.C. (1984). Personality behavior patterns and physical illness: Conceptual and methodological issues. In W.D. Gentry (Ed.), *Handbook of behavioral medicine* (pp. 38–86). New York: Guilford Press.

KRANTZ, M.J., & JOHNSON, L. (1978). Family members' perceptions of communications in late stage cancer. *International Journal of Psychiatry in Medicine, 8*, 203–216.

KRAUS, S.J. (1995). Attitudes and the prediction of behavior: A meta-analysis of the empirical literature. *Personality and Social Psychology Bulletin, 21*, 58–75.

KRAUT, R., PATTERSON, M., LUNDMARK, V., KIESLER, S., MUKOPADHYAY, T., & SCHERLIS, W. (1998). Internet paradox: A social technology that reduces social involvement and psychological well-being. *American Psychologist, 53*, 1017–1031.

KRAUT, R.E. (1978). Verbal and non-verbal cues in the detection of lying. *Journal of Personality and Social Psychology, 36*, 380–391.

KRAUT, R.E., & POE, D. (1980). Behavioral roots of person perceptions: The deception judgements of the customs inspectors and laymen. *Journal of Personality and Social Psychology, 39*, 784–798.

KRAVITZ, D.A., & MARTIN B. (1986). Ringelmann rediscovered: The original article. *Journal of Personality and Social Psychology, 50*, 936–941.

KREBS, D.L. (1970). Altruism: An examination of the concept and a review of the literature. *Psychological Bulletin, 73*, 258–302.

KREBS, D.L., & ADINOLFI, A.H. (1975). Physical attractiveness, social relations and personality style. *Journal of Personality and Social Psychology, 31*, 245–253.

KREBS, D.L., & MILLER, D.T. (1985). Altruism and aggression. In G. Lindzey, & E. Aronson (Eds.), *Handbook of social psychology* (3rd ed.). (Vol. 2). (pp. 1–71). New York: Random House.

KREBS, D.L., & VAN HESTEREN, F. (1994). The development of altruism: Towards an integrative model. *Developmental Review, 14*, 103–158.

KREFTING, L.A., BERGER, P.K., & WALLACE, M.J. (1978). The contribution of sex distribution, job content, and occupational classification to job sex-typing: Two studies. *Journal of Vocational Behavior, 13*, 181–191.

KREMER, J., GALLAGHER, A., & SOMMERVILLE, P. (1988). Social categorization and behavior in mixed-motive games: A Northern Ireland study. *Social Behavior, 3*, 229–236.

KRISTIANSEN, C.M. (1986). A two-value model of preventive health behavior. *Basic and Applied Social Psychology, 7*, 173–183.

KRISTIANSEN, C.M., & MATHESON, K. (1990). Value conflict, value justification, and attitudes toward nuclear weapons. *Journal of Social Psychology, 130*, 665–675.

KRISTIANSEN, C.M., & ZANNA, M.P. (1986, June). When do attitudes express values? Annual Meeting of the Canadian Psychological Association, Toronto.

KRISTIANSEN, C.M., & ZANNA, M.P. (1988). Justifying attitudes by appealing to values: A functional perspective. *British Journal of Social Psychology, 27*, 247–256.

KROGER, R.O., & WOOD, L.A. (1992). Whatever happened to language in social psychology? *Canadian Psychology, 33*, 584–594.

KROSNICK, J.A., & ALWIN, D.F. (1989). Aging and susceptibility to attitude change. *Journal of Personality and Social Psychology, 57*, 416–425.

KROSNICK, J.A., & PETTY, R.E. (1995) Attitude strength: An overview. In R.E. Petty, & J.A. Krosnick (Eds.), *Attitude strength: Antecedents and consequences; Ohio State University series on attitudes and persuasion* (Vol. 4). (pp. 1–24). Mahwah, NJ: Lawrence Erlbaum Associates.

KRUEGER, J. (1998) Enhancement bias in descriptions of self and others. *Personality and Social Psychology Bulletin, 24*, 505–516.

KRUGLANSKI, A.W. (1987). Blame-placing schemata and attribution research. In C.F. Graumann, & S. Moscovici (Eds.), *Changing conceptions of conspiracy* (pp. 191–202). New York: Springer-Verlag.

KRUGLANSKI, A.W. (2001). That "vision thing": The state of theory in social and personality psychology at the edge of the new millennium. *Journal of Personality and Social Psychology, 80*, 871–875.

KRULL, D.S. (2001). On partitioning the fundamental attribution error: Dispositionism and the correspondence bias. In G.B. Moscowitz (Ed.), *Cognitive social psychology. The Princeton Symposium on the Legacy and Future of Social Cognition* (pp. 211–227). Manwah, NJ: Erlbaum.

KRUPAT, E., & GARONZIK, R. (1994). Subjects' expectations and the search for alternatives to deception in social psychology. *British Journal of Social Psychology, 33*, 211–222.

KUGIHARA, N. (2001). Effects of aggressive behaviour and group size on collective escape in an emergency: A test between a social identity model and deindividuation theory. *British Journal of Social Psychology, 40*, 575–598.

KUIJER, R.G., BUUNK, B.P., & YBEMA, J.F. (2001). Are equity concerns important in the intimate relationship when one partner of a couple has cancer? *Social Psychology Quarterly, 64*, 267–282.

KUIJER, R.G., BUUNK, B.P., YBEMA, J.F., & WOBBES, T. (2002). The relation between perceived inequity, marital satisfaction and emotions among couples facing cancer. *British Journal of Social Psychology, 41*, 39–56.

KULBOK, P.A., & COX, C.L. (2002). Dimensions of adolescent health behavior. *Journal of Adolescent Health, 31*, 394–400.

KULIK, J.A., & MAHLER, H.I.M. (1989a). Stress and affiliation in a hospital setting: Preoperative roommate preferences. *Personality and Social Psychology Bulletin, 15*, 183–193.

KULIK, J.A., & MAHLER, H.I.M. (1989b). Social support and recovery from surgery. *Health Psychology, 8*, 221–238.

KUNDA, Z., & OLESON, K.C. (1995). Maintaining stereotypes in the face of disconfirmation: Constructing grounds for subtyping deviants. *Journal of Personality and Social Psychology, 65*, 657–669.

KUNDA, Z., & SPENCER, S.J. (2003). When do stereotypes come to mind and when do they colour judgment? A goal-based theoretical framework for stereotype activation and application. *Psychological Bulletin, 129*, 522–544.

KURDEK, L.A. (1993). Predicting marital dissolution: A five-year prospective longitudinal study of newlywed couples. *Journal of Personality and Social Psychology, 64*, 221–242.

KUTNER, B., WILKINS, C., & YARROW, P.R. (1952). Verbal attitudes and overt behavior involving social prejudice. *Journal of Abnormal and Social Psychology, 47*, 649–652.

KWONG, M.J., BARTHOLOMEW, K, & DUTTON, D.G. (1999). Gender differences in patterns of relationship violence in Alberta. *Canadian Journal of Behavioural Science, 31*, 150–160.

LACHMAN, M.E., & WEAVER, S.L. (1998). The sense of control as a moderator of social class differences in health and well-being. *Journal of Personality and Social Psychology, 74*, 763–773.

LACROIX, J.M., & RIOUX, Y. (1978). La communication non-verbale chez les bilingues. *Canadian Journal of Behavioural Science, 10*, 130–140.

LAFRANCE, M., & MAYO, C. (1976). Racial differences in gaze behavior during conversation: Two systematic observational studies. *Journal of Personality and Social Psychology, 33*, 547–552.

LAI, J., & LINDEN, W. (1993). The smile of Asia: Acculturation effects on symptoms reporting. *Canadian Journal of Behavioural Science, 25*, 303–313.

LAKOFF, R. (1975). *Language and the woman's place.* New York: Harper & Row.

LALONDE, M. (1974). *A new perspective on the health of Canadians.* Ottawa: Ministry of Supply and Services Canada, Catalogue No. H31–1374.

LALONDE, R.N. (1992). The dynamics of group differentiation in the face of defeat. *Personality and Social Psychology Bulletin, 18*, 336–342.

LALONDE, R.N., & CAMERON, J.E. (1993). An intergroup perspective on immigrant acculturation with a focus on collective strategies. *International Journal of Psychology, 28*, 57–74.

LALONDE, R.N., & GARDNER, R.C. (1984). Investigating a causal model of second language acquisition: Where does personality fit? *Canadian Journal of Behavioural Science, 16*, 224–237.

LAMAL, P.A. (1979). College student common beliefs about psychology. *Teaching of Psychology, 6*, 336–342.

LAMBERT, W.E. (1974a). The St. Lambert project. In S.T. Carey (Ed.), *Bilingualism, biculturalism and education* (pp. 231–247). Edmonton: University of Alberta.

LAMBERT, W.E. (1974b). Culture and language as factors in learning and education. In F.E. Aboud, & R.D. Meade (Eds.), *The fifth western symposium on learning and education.* Washington: Bellingham.

LAMBERT, W.E. (1978). Some cognitive and sociocultural aspects of being bilingual. In J.P. Alatis (Ed.), *International dimensions of bilingual education.* Washington, DC: Georgetown University Press.

LAMBERT, W.E. (1981). Bilingualism and language acquisition. *Annals of the New York Academy of Sciences, 379*, 9–22.

LAMBERT, W.E., & KLINEBERG, O. (1967). *Children's views of foreign people: A cross-national study.* New York: Appleton.

LAMBERT, W.E., & TAYLOR, D. (1984). Language and the education of ethnic minority children in Canada. In R.J. Samuda, J.W. Berry, & M. Laferriere (Eds.), *Multiculturalism in Canada.* Toronto: Allyn & Bacon.

LAMBERT, W.E., & TUCKER, G.R. (1972). *Bilingual education in children: The St. Lambert experiment.* Rowley, MA: Newbury House.

LAMBERT, W.E., GARDNER, R.C., BARIK, H.C., & TUNSTALL, K. (1963). Attitudinal and cognitive aspects of intensive study of a second language. *Journal of Abnormal and Social Psychology, 66*, 358–368.

LAMBERT, W.E., MERMIGIS, L., & TAYLOR, D.M. (1986). Greek Canadians' attitudes toward own group and other Canadian ethnic groups: A test of the multiculturalism hypothesis. *Canadian Journal of Behavioural Science, 18,* 35–51.

LAMERSON, C.D., & KELLOWAY, E.K. (1996). Towards a model of peacekeeping stress: Traumatic and contextual influences. *Canadian Psychology, 37,* 195–204.

LANDRY, R., & BOURHIS, R.Y. (1997). Linguistic landscape and ethno-linguistic vitality: An empirical study. *Journal of Language and Social Psychology, 16,* 23–49.

LANG, K., & LANG, G.L. (1961). *Collective dynamics.* New York: Crowell.

LANGER, E.J. (1975). The illusion of control. *Journal of Personality and Social Psychology, 32,* 311–328.

LANGER, E.J., & RODIN, J. (1976). The effects of choice and enhanced personal responsibility for the aged: A field experiment in an institutional setting. *Journal of Personality and Social Psychology, 34,* 191–198.

LANGER, E.J., BLANK, A., & CHANOWITZ, B. (1978). The mindlessness of ostensibly thoughtful action: The role of "placebic" information in interpersonal interaction. *Journal of Personality and Social Psychology, 36,* 635–642.

LANGFRED, C.L. (1998) Is group cohesiveness a double-edged sword? An investigation of the effects of cohesiveness on performance. *Small Groups Research, 29,* 124–143.

LANGHINRICHSEN-ROHLING, J., PALAREA, R.E., COHEN, J., & ROHLING, M.L. (2000). Breaking up is hard to do: Unwanted pursuit behaviors following the dissolution of a romantic relationship. *Violence and Victims. Special issue: Stalking and obsessive behaviors in everyday life, 15,* 73–90.

LANGHOLTZ, H.J. (Ed.) *The psychology of peacekeeping.* Westport, CT: Praeger.

LANGLOIS, J.H., & ROGGMAN, L.A. (1990). Attractive faces are only average. *Psychological Science 1,* 115–121.

LANGLOIS, J.H., KALAKANIS, L., RUBENSTEIN, A.J., LARSON, A., HALLAM, M., & SMOOT, M. (in press). Maxims or myths of beauty: A meta-analytic and theoretical review. *Psychological Bulletin.*

LAPIERE, R.T. (1934). Attitudes vs. actions. *Social Forces, 13,* 230–237.

LARSEN, K. (1974). Conformity in the Asch experiment. *Journal of Social Psychology, 94,* 303–304.

LASCH, C. (1979). *The culture of narcissism: American life in an age of diminishing expectations.* New York: Norton.

LATANÉ, B., & DARLEY, J.M. (1968). Group inhibition of bystander intervention. *Journal of Personality and Social Psychology, 10,* 215–221.

LATANÉ, B., & DARLEY, J.M. (1969). Bystander "apathy." *American Scientist, 57,* 244–268.

LATANÉ, B., & DARLEY, J.M. (1970). *The unresponsive bystander: Why doesn't he help?* New York: Appleton-Century-Crofts.

LATANÉ, B., & NIDA, S. (1981). Ten years of research on group size and helping. *Psychological Bulletin, 89,* 308–324.

LATANÉ, B., & RODIN, J. (1969). A lady in distress: Inhibiting effects of friends and strangers on bystander intervention. *Journal of Experimental Social Psychology, 5,* 187–202.

LATANÉ, B., WILLIAMS, K., & HARKINS, S. (1979). Many hands make light the work: The causes and consequences of social loafing. *Journal of Personality and Social Psychology, 37,* 822–832.

LATOUR, S., HOULDEN, P., WALKER, L., & THIBAUT, J.W. (1976). Some determinants of preferences for modes of conflict reduction. *Journal of Conflict Resolution, 20,* 319–356.

LATOURETTE, T.R., & MEEKS, S. (2000). Perceptions of patronizing speech by older women in nursing homes and in the community: Impact of cognitive ability and place of residence. *Journal of Language and Social Psychology, 19,* 463–473.

LAU, R.R., & RUSSELL, D. (1980). Attribution in sports pages. *Journal of Personality and Social Psychology, 39,* 28–38.

LAU, R.R., HARTMAN, K.A., & WARE, J.E. (1986). Health as a value: Methodological and theoretical considerations. *Health Psychology, 5,* 25–43.

LAURSEN, B., & JENSEN-CAMPBELL, L.A. (1999). The nature and functions of social exchange in adolescent romantic relationships. In W. Furman, B.B. Brown et al. (Eds.), *The development of romantic relationships in adolescence: Cambridge studies in social and emotional development* (pp. 50–74). New York: Cambridge University Press.

LAVER, J. (1964, July 13). Laver's law. *Women's Wear Daily.* Cited by Horn (1975).

LAVERY, J.J., & FOLEY, P.J. (1963). Altruism or arousal in the rat? *Science, 140,* 172–173.

LE, B., & AGNEW, C.R. (2003). Commitment and its theorized determinants: A meta-analysis of the investment model. *Personal Relationships, 10,* 37–57.

LEA, M., & SPEARS, R. (1995). Love at first byte? Building personal relationships over computer networks. In J.T. Wood, & S. Duck (Eds.), *Under-studied relationships: Off the beaten track* (pp. 197–233). Thousand Oaks, CA: Sage.

LEBON, G. (1895/1960). *The crowd: A study of the popular mind.* London: Ernest Benn.

LEE, B. (1988). Prosocial content on prime-time television. Special issue: Televison as a social issue. *Applied Social Psychology Annual, 8,* 238–246.

LEE, K. (2001). Taiwan and Mainland Chinese and Canadian children's categorization and evaluation of lie- and truth-telling: A modesty effect. *British Journal of Developmental Psychology, 19,* 525–542.

LEE, K., XU, F., FU, G., CAMERON, C-A., & CHEN, S. (2001). Taiwan and Mainland Chinese and Canadian children's categorization and evaluation of lie- and truth-telling: A modesty effect. *British Journal of Developmental Psychology, 19,* 525–542.

LEFCOURT, H.M., & SHEPHERD, R.S. (1995). Organ donation, authoritarianism, and perspective-taking humor. *Journal of Research in Personality, 29,* 121–138.

LEHMAN, D.R. (1996). Self-concept clarity: Measurement, personality correlates and cultural boundaries. *Journal of Personality and Social Psychology, 70,* 141–156.

LEIPPE, M.R., MANION, A.P., & ROMANCZYK, A. (1992). Eyewitness persuasion: How and how well do fact finders judge the accuracy of adults' and children's memory reports? *Journal of Personality and Social Psychology, 63,* 181–197.

LEITH, K.P., & BAUMEISTER, R.F. (1996). Why do bad moods increase self-defeating behavior? Emotion, risk-taking and self-regulation. *Journal of Personality and Social Psychology, 71,* 1250–1267.

LEMAINE, G. (1966). Inégalité, comparaison et incomparabilité: Esquisse d'une théorie de l'originalité sociale. *Bulletin de Psychologie, 20,* 24–32.

LEMAINE, G. (1974). Social differentiation and social originality. *European Journal of Social Psychology, 4,* 17–52.

LEMAINE, G., & KASTERSZTEIN, J. (1972). Recherches sur l'originalité sociale, la différentiation et l'incomparabilité. *Bulletin de Psychologie, 25,* 673–693.

LEMAINE, G., KASTERSZTEIN, J., & PERSONNAZ, B. (1978). Social differentiation. In H. Tajfel (Ed.), *Differentiation between social groups: Studies in the social psychology of intergroup relations* (pp. 269–300). London: Academic Press.

LEMYRE, L., & SMITH, P.B. (1985). Intergroup discrimination and self-esteem in the minimal group paradigm. *Journal of Personality and Social Psychology, 49,* 660–670.

LEPPER, M.R., GREENE, D., & NISBETT, R.E. (1973). Undermining children's intrinsic interest with extrinsic reward: A test for the over-justification hypothesis. *Journal of Personality and Social Psychology, 28,* 129–137.

LEPPER, M.R., ZANNA, M.P., & ABELSON, R.P. (1970). Cognitive irreversibility in a dissonance reduction situation. *Journal of Personality and Social Psychology, 16,* 191–198.

LERNER, M.J. (1974b). Social psychology of justice and interpersonal attraction. In T. Huston (Ed.), *Foundations of interpersonal attraction.* New York: Academic Press.

LERNER, M.J. (1977). The justice motive: Some hypotheses as to its origins and forms. *Journal of Personality, 45,* 1–52.

LERNER, M.J. (1997). What does the belief in a just world protect us from? The dread of death or the fear of undeserved suffering. *Psychological Inquiry, 8,* 29–32.

LESCHIED, A.W., CUMMINGS, A.L., VAN BRUNSCHOT, CUNNING-HAM, A., & SAUNDERS, A. (2001). Aggression in adolescent girls: Implications for policy, prevention, and treatment. *Canadian Psychology, 42,* 200–215.

LESTER, D. (1984). The murder of police officers in American cities. *Criminal Justice and Behavior, 11,* 101–113.

LESTER, D., & MURRELL, M.E. (1986). The influence of gun control on personal violence. *Journal of Community Psychology, 14,* 315–318.

LEUNG, K., & LIND, E.A. (1986). Procedural justice and culture: Effects of culture, gender, and investigator status on procedural preference. *Journal of Personality and Social Psychology, 50,* 1134–1140.

LEUNG, K., BOND, M.H., CARMENT, D.W., KRISHNAN, L., & LIEBRAND, W.B.G. (1990). Effects of cultural feminity on preference for methods of conflict processing: A cross-cultural study. *Journal of Experimental Social Psychology, 26,* 373–388.

LEUNG, L. (2002). Loneliness, self-disclosure and ICQ ("I seek you") use. *CyberPsychology and Behavior, 5,* 241–251.

LEVANT, R.F. (2002). Psychology responds to terrorism. *Professional Psychology: Research and Practice, 33,* 507–509.

LEVENSON, R.W., & RUEF, A.M. (1992). *Journal of Personality and Social Psychology, 63,* 234–246.

LEVENTHAL, G.S. (1970). Findings and theory in the study of fear communications. In L. Berkowitz (Ed.), *Advances in experimental social psychology* (Vol. 5). (pp. 119–186). New York: Academic Press.

LEVENTHAL, G.S., & LANE, D.W. (1970). Sex, age, and equity behavior. *Journal of Personality and Social Psychology, 15,* 312–316.

LEVENTHAL, G.S., WEISS, T., & LONG, G. (1969). Equity, reciprocity, and reallocating the rewards in the dyad. *Journal of Personality and Social Psychology, 13,* 300–315.

LEVENTHAL, H., & HIRSCHMAN, R.S. (1982). Social psychology and prevention. In G.S. Sanders, & J. Suls (Eds.), *Social psychology of health and illness* (pp. 387–401). Hillsdale, NJ: Erlbaum.

LEVENTHAL, H., MEYER, D.C., & NERENZ, D. (1980). The common sense representation of illness danger. In S. Rachman (Ed.), *Medical psychology* (Vol. 2). (pp. 184–211). New York: Pergamon.

LEVINE, D. (2000). Virtual attraction: what rocks your boat. *CyberPsychology and Behavior, 3,* 565–573.

LEVINE, J.M. (1989). Reaction to opinion deviance in small groups. In P.B. Paulus (Ed.), *Psychology of Group Influence* (pp. 326–337). Hillsdale, NJ: Lawrence Erlbaum Associates.

LEVINE, R.V., MARTINEZ, T.S., BRASE, G., & SORENSON, K. (1994). *Journal of Personality and Social Psychology, 67,* 69–82.

LEVINE, S., & SALTER, N.E. (1976). Youth and contemporary religious movements: Psychosocial findings. *Canadian Psychiatric Association Journal, 21,* 411–420.

LEVINGER, G.A. (1979). A social psychological perspective on marital dissolution. In G.A. Levinger, & O.C. Moles (Eds.), *Divorce and separation.* New York: Basic Books.

LEVINGER, G.A., & SNOEK, J.D. (1972). *Attraction in relationships: A new look at interpersonal attraction.* Morristown, NJ: General Learning.

LEVINTHAL, C.F. (2002). *Drugs, behavior and modern society.* (3rd ed.). Boston; Allyn & Bacon.

LEVY, B. (1996). Improving memory in old age through implicit self-stereotypes. *Journal of Personality and Social Psychology, 71,* 1092–1107.

LEVY, S.M., & HEIDEN, L.A. (1990). Personality and social factors in cancer outcome. In H.S. Friedman (Ed.), *Personality and disease* (pp. 254–279). New York: Wiley.

LEWIN, K. (1948). *Resolving social conflicts.* New York: Harper & Row.

LEWIN, K. (1951). *Field theory in social science.* New York: Harper.

LEYTON, E. (1986). *Hunting humans: The rise of the modern multiple murderer.* Toronto: McClelland & Stewart.

LICHTENSTEIN, E., & GLASGOW, R.E. (1992). Smoking cessation: What have we learned over the past decade? *Journal of Consulting and Clinical Psychology, 60,* 518–527.

LIEBERT, R.M., & SPRAFKIN, J. (1988). *The early window* (3rd ed.). New York: Pergamon Press.

LIFTON, R.J. (1986). *The Nazi doctors: Medical killing and the psychology of genocide.* New York: Basic Books.

LIND, E.A., ERICKSON, B.E., FRIEDLAND, N., & DICKENBERGER, M. (1978). Reactions to procedural models for adjudicative conflict resolution. *Journal of Conflict Resolution, 22,* 318–341.

LIND, E.A., KURTZ, S., MUSANTE, L., WALKER, L., & THIBAUT, J. (1980). Procedure and outcome effects on reactions to adjudicated resolution of conflicts of interest. *Journal of Personality and Social Psychology, 39,* 643–653.

LINDER, D.E., COOPER, J., & JONES, E.E. (1967). Decision freedom as a determinant of the role of incentive magnitude in attitude change. *Journal of Personality and Social Psychology, 6,* 245–254.

LINDSKOLD, S., HAN, G., & BETZ, B. (1986). The essential elements of communication in the GRIT strategy. *Personality and Social Psychology Bulletin, 12,* 179–186.

LINDSKOLD, S., WALTERS, P.S., & KOUTSOURIS, H. (1983). Cooperators, competitors, and response to GRIT. *Journal of Conflict Resolution, 27,* 521–532.

LINZ, D., DONNERSTEIN, E., & PENROD, S. (1987). The findings and recommendations of the Attorney General's Commission on Pornography: Do the psychological "facts" fit the political fury? *American Psychologist, 42,* 946–953.

LINZ, D., DONNERSTEIN, E., & PENROD, S. (1988). Effects of long-term exposure to violent and sexually degrading depictions of women. *Journal of Personality and Social Psychology, 55,* 758–768.

LIPKUS, I.M., DALBERT, C., & SIEGLER, I.C. (1996). The importance of distinguishing the belief in a just world for self versus others: Implications for psychological well-being. *Personality and Social Psychology Bulletin, 22,* 666–677.

LIPSET, S.M. (1989). Voluntary activities: More Canadian comparisons—a reply. *Canadian Journal of Sociology, 14,* 377–382.

LIPTON, J.A., & MARBACH, J.J. (1984). Ethnicity and the pain experience. *Social Science & Medicine, 19,* 1279–1288.

LISKA, A.E. (1984). A critical examination of the causal structure of the Fishbein/Ajzen attitude-behavior model. *Social Psychology Quarterly, 47,* 61–74.

LITTLEPAGE, G.E., & PINEAULT, M.A. (1979). Detection of deceptive factual statements from the body and the face. *Personality and Social Psychology Bulletin, 5,* 325–328.

LITVACK-MILLER, W., MCDOUGALL, D., & ROMNEY, D.M. (1997). The structure of empathy during middle childhood and its relationship to prosocial behavior. *Genetic, Social, and General Psychology Monographs, 123,* 303–324.

LLOYD, W.F. (1833). On checks to the population. Reprinted in G. Hardin, & J. Baden (Eds.). (1976). *Managing the commons* (pp. 8–15). San Francisco: W.H. Freeman.

LOCKWOOD, P., & KUNDA, Z. (1997). Superstars and me. Predicting the impact of role models on the self. *Journal of Personality and Social Psychology, 73,* 91–103.

LOCKWOOD, P., & KUNDA, Z. (1999). Increasing salience of one's best selves can undermine inspiration by outstanding role models. *Journal of Personality and Social Psychology, 76,* 214–228.

LOEBER, R., & HAY, D.F. (1997). Key issues in the development of aggression and violence from childhood to early adulthood. *Annual Review of Psychology, 48,* 371–410.

LOEBER, R., & STOUTHAMER-LOEBER, M. (1998). Development of juvenile aggression and violence. *American Psychologist, 53,* 242–259.

LOFTUS, E.F. (1974). Reconstructing memory: The incredible eyewitness. *Psychology Today, 8,* 116–119.

LOFTUS, E.F. (1979). *Eyewitness testimony.* Cambridge, MA: Harvard University Press.

LOFTUS, E.F. (1983). Silence is not golden. *American Psychologist, 38,* 504–572.

LOFTUS, E.F. (1992). When a lie becomes memory's truth: Memory distortion after exposure to misinformation. *Current Directions in Psychological Science, 1,* 121–123.

LOFTUS, E.F., & BURNS, T.E. (1982). Mental shock can produce retrograde amnesia. *Memory and Cognition, 1,* 318–323.

LOLLIS, C.C., JOHNSON, E.H., & ANTONI, M.H. (1997). The efficacy of the health beliefs model for predicting condom use and risky sexual practices in university students. *AIDS Education and Prevention, 9,* 551–563.

LONDON, P. (1970). The rescuers: Motivational hypotheses about Christians who saved Jews from the Nazis. In J. Macaulay, & L. Berkowitz (Eds.), *Altruism and helping behavior* (pp. 241–250). New York: Academic Press.

LONDON HEALTH SCIENCES CENTRE (2003). Multi-organ Transplant Program. Downloaded on July 11, 2003 from http://www.lhsc.on.ca/transplant/stats.htm#ratecanada

LORE, R.K., & SCHULTZ, L.A. (1993). Control of human aggression. *American Psychologist, 48,* 16–25.

LOTT, A.J., & LOTT, B.E. (1961). Group cohesiveness, communication level, and conformity. *Journal of Abnormal and Social Psychology, 62,* 408–412.

LOTT, D.F., & SOMMER, R. (1967). Seating arrangements and status. *Journal of Personality and Social Psychology, 7,* 90–94.

LOUIS, W.R., & TAYLOR, D.M. (1999). From passive acceptance to social disruption: Towards an understanding of behavioural responses to discrimination. *Canadian Journal of Behavioural Science, 31,* 19–28.

LOWERY, C.R., DENNEY, D.R., & STORMS, M.D. (1979). Insomnia: A comparison of the effects of pill attribution and non-pejorative self-attributions. *Cognitive Therapy Research, 3,* 161–164.

LUBEK, I. (1979). A brief social psychological analysis of research on aggression in social psychology. In A.R. Buss (Ed.), *Psychology in social context* (pp. 259–306). New York: Irvington.

LUBEK, I. (1990). Interactionist theory and disciplinary interactions: Psychology, sociology and social psychology in France. In W. Baker, R. Hezeuijk, B. Hyland, & S. Terwee (Eds.), *Recent trends in theoretical psychology, 2* (pp. 347–350). New York: Springer-Verlag.

LUCAS, R.A. (1968). Social implications of the immediacy of death. *The Canadian Review of Sociology and Anthropology, 5,* 1–16.

LUCE, T.S. (1974). *The role of experience in inter-racial recognition.* Annual meeting of the American Psychological Association, New Orleans.

LUCHINS, A.S. (1957). Experimental attempts to minimize the impact of first impressions. In C.I. Hovland et al. (Eds.), *The order of presentation in persuasion* (pp. 62–75). New Haven: Yale University Press.

LUND, F.H. (1925). The psychology of belief: IV. The law of primacy in persuasion. *Journal of Abnormal and Social Psychology, 20,* 183–191.

LURIGIO, A.J., CARROLL, J.S., & STALANS, L.J. (1994). Understanding judge's sentencing decisions: Attributions of responsibility and story construction. In L. Heath, R.S. Tindale, J. Edwards, E. Posovac, F.B. Bryant, E. Henderson-King, Y. Suarez-Balcazar, & J. Myers (Eds.), *Applications of heuristics and biases to social issues* (pp. 91–116). New York: Plenum Press.

LUSSIER, Y., & ALAIN, M. (1986). Attribution et vécu émotionnel post-divorce. *Canadian Journal of Behavioural Science, 18,* 248–256.

LYDON, J.E. (1999). Commitment and adversity: A reciprocal relation. In A. Jeffrey & J. Warren (Eds.). *Handbook of interpersonal commitment and relationship stability* (pp. 193–203). New York: Plenum Press.

LYDON, J.E., FITZSIMONS, G.M., & NAIDOO, L. (2003). Devaluation versus enhancement of attractive alternatives: A critical test using the calibration paradigm. *Personality & Social Psychology Bulletin, 29,* 349–359.

LYDON, J.E., MEANA, M., SEPINWALL, D., RICHARDS, N., & MAYMAN, S. (1999). The commitment calibration hypothesis: When do people devalue attractive partners? *Personality and Social Psychology Bulletin, 25,* 152–161.

LYKKEN, D. (1974). Psychology and the lie detector industry. *American Psychologist, 29,* 725–739.

LYNCH, J. (1977). *The broken heart: The medical consequences of loneliness.* New York: Basic Books.

LYSAK, H., RULE, B., & DOBBS, A.R. (1989). Conceptions of aggression: Prototype or defining features? *Personality and Social Psychology Bulletin, 15,* 233–243.

MA, H.W., & LEUNG, M.C. (1995). The relation of altruistic orientation to family social environment in Chinese children. *Psychologia: An International Journal of Psychology in the Orient, 38,* 109–115.

MAASS, A., & CLARKE, R.D. III. (1984). Hidden impact of minorities: Fifteen years of minority influence research. *Psychological Bulletin, 95,* 428–450.

MAASS, A., BRIGHAM, J.C., & WEST, S.G. (1985). Testifying on eyewitness reliability: Expert advice is not always persuasive. *Journal of Applied Social Psychology, 15,* 207–229.

MACANDREW, C., & EGERTON, R.B. (1969). *Drunken comportment: A social explanation.* Chicago: Aldine.

MACCOUN, R.J., & KERR, N.L. (1988). Asymmetric influence in mock jury deliberation: Juror's bias for leniency. *Journal of Personality and Social Psychology, 54,* 21–33.

MACDONALD, D., Jr., & MAJUNDER, R.K. (1973). On the resolution and tolerance of cognitive inconsistency in another naturally occurring event: Attitudes and beliefs following the Senator Eagleton incident. *Journal of Applied Social Psychology, 3,* 132–143.

MACDONALD, T.K., ZANNA, M.P., & FONG, G.T. (1995). Decision making in altered states: Effects of alcohol on attitudes toward drinking and driving. *Journal of Personality and Social Psychology, 68,* 973–985.

MACDONALD, T.K., ZANNA, M.P., & FONG, G.T. (1996). Why common sense goes out the window: Effects of alcohol on intentions to use condoms. *Personality and Social Psychology Bulletin, 22,* 763–775.

MACIONIS, J.J., CLARKE, J.M., & GERBER, L.M. (1994). *Sociology.* Scarborough: Prentice Hall Canada.

MACKIE, D.M. (1986). Social identification effects in group polarization. *Journal of Personality and Social Psychology, 50,* 720–728.

MACLEAN, H., & KALIN, R. (1994). Congruence between self-image and occupational stereotypes in students entering gender-dominated occupations. *Canadian Journal of Behavioural Science, 26,* 142–162.

MACLEAN, P.D. (1993). Cerebral evolution of emotion. In M. Lewis, & J. Haviland (Eds.), *Handbook of emotions* (pp. 67–83). New York: Guilford Press.

MACLEAN'S (1992). Referendum file: A Maclean's/Decima poll on why Canadians voted. *Maclean's,* 12–24.

MACLEAN'S (1999, July 1). How Canada tried to bar "the yellow peril." *Maclean's,* 31.

MACLEOD, L. (1989, October). The city for women: No safe place. First European and North American Conference on Urban Safety and Crime Prevention, Toronto.

MACNAMARA, J. (1973). Nurseries, streets and classrooms. *Modern Language Journal, 57,* 250–254.

MACRAE, C.N., & SHEPHERD, J.W. (1989). Do criminal stereotypes mediate juridic judgements? *British Journal of Social Psychology, 28,* 189–191.

MACRAE, C.N., MILNE, A.B., & BODENHAUSEN, G.V. (1994). Stereotypes as energy-saving devices: A peek inside the cognitive toolbox. *Journal of Personality and Social Psychology, 66,* 37–47.

MADAY, B.C., & SZALAY, L.B. (1976). Psychological correlates of family socialization in the United States and Korea. In T. Williams (Ed.), *Psychological anthropology* (pp. 276–324). The Hague: Mouton.

MADDEN, T.J., ELLEN, P.S., & AJZEN, I. (1992). A comparison of the theory of planned behavior and the theory of reasoned action. *Personality and Social Psychology Bulletin, 18,* 3–9.

MAHLER, H.I.M., & KULIK, J.A. (1991). Health care involvement preferences and social-emotional recovery of male coronary-artery bypass patients. *Health Psychology, 10,* 399–408.

MAJOR, B., & DEAUX, K. (1982). Individual differences in justice behavior. In J. Greenberg, & R. Cohen (Eds.), *Equity and justice in social behavior* (pp. 43–76). New York: Academic Press.

MAJOR, B., KAISER, C.R., & MCCOY, S.K. (2003). It's not my fault; When and why attributions to prejudice protect self-esteem. *Personality and Social Psychology Bulletin, 29,* 772–281.

MALAMUTH, N.M. (1984). Aggression against women: Cultural and individual causes. In N.M. Malamuth, & E. Donnerstein (Eds.), *Pornography and sexual aggression* (pp. 19–52). Orlando, FL: Academic Press.

MALAMUTH, N.M. (1986). Predictors of naturalistic sexual aggression. *Journal of Personality and Social Psychology, 50,* 953–962.

MALAMUTH, N.M. (1988). Predicting laboratory aggression against female and male targets: Implications for sexual aggression. *Journal for Research in Personality, 22,* 474–495.

MALAMUTH, N.M., & BRIERE, J. (1986). Sexual violence in the media: Indirect effects on aggression against women. *Journal of Social Issues, 42* (3), 75–92.

MALAMUTH, N.M., CHECK, J.V.P., & BRIERE, J. (1986). Sexual arousal in response to aggression: Ideological, aggressive, and sexual correlates. *Journal of Personality and Social Psychology, 50,* 330–340.

MALAMUTH, N.M., LINZ, D., HEAVEY, C.L., BARNES, G., & ACKER, M. (1995). Using the confluence model of sexual aggressiveness to predict men's conflict with women: A 10–year follow-up study. *Journal of Personality and Social Psychology, 69,* 353–369.

MANN, J.W. (1963). Rivals of different rank. *Journal of Social Psychology, 61,* 11–27.

MANN, L., NEWTON, J.W., & INNES, J.M. (1982). A test between deindividuation and emergent norm theories of crowd aggression. *Journal of Personality and Social Psychology, 42,* 260–272.

MANSELL, D., & ALCOCK, J.E. (1978). Communication and deindividuation in a collective dilemma. Paper presented at the Annual Meeting of the Canadian Psychological Association, Ottawa.

MARECEK, J. (2001). After the facts: Psychology and the study of gender. *Canadian Psychology, 42,* 254–267.

MARKS, M.M., MUTRIE, N., BROOKS, D.R., & HARRIS, D. V. (1984). Causal attributions of winners and losers in individual competitive sports: Toward a reformulation of the self-serving bias. *Journal of Sport Psychology, 6,* 184–196.

MARKUS, H. (1977). Self-schemata and processing information about the self. *Journal of Personality and Social Psychology, 35,* 63–78.

MARKUS, H., & KITAYAMA, S. (1991). Culture and the self: Implications for cognition, emotion and motivation. *Psychological Review, 98,* 224–253.

MARKUS, H., & NURIUS, P. (1986). Possible selves. *American Psychologist, 41,* 63–78.

MARKUS, H., HAMILL, R., & SENTIS, K. (1987). Thinking fat: Self-schemas for body weight and processing of weight-relevant information. *Journal of Applied Social Psychology, 17,* 50–71.

MARKUS, H., SMITH, J., & MORELAND, R. (1985). Role of the self-concept in the perception of others. *Journal of Personality and Social Psychology, 49,* 1494–1512.

MARLATT, G.A., & GORDON, J.R. (1979). Determinants of relapse: Implications for the maintenance of behavior change. In P. Davidson (Ed.), *Behavioral medicines: Changing health lifestyles* (pp. 410–452). New York: Brunner/Mazel.

MARLATT, G.A., & ROHSENOW, D. (1980). Cognitive processes in alcohol use: Expectancy and the balanced placebo design. In N. Mello (Ed.), *Advances in substance abuse: Behavioral and biological research* (pp. 159–199). Greenwich, CT: JAI Press.

MARLATT, G.A., DEMMING, B., & REID, J.B. (1973). Loss of control of drinking in alcoholics: An experimental analogue. *Journal of Abnormal Psychology, 81,* 233–241.

MARMOT, M., RYFF, C.D., BUMPASS, L.L., SHIPLEY, M., & MARKS, N.F. (1997). Social inequalities: Nest questions and converging evidence. *Social Science and Medicine, 44,* 901–910.

MARQUIS, K.H., MARSHALL, J., & OSKAMP, S. (1972). Testimony validity as a function of question form, atmosphere and item difficulty. *Journal of Applied Social Psychology, 2,* 167–186.

MARSDEN, P.V. (1987). Core discussion networks of Americans. *American Sociological Review, 52,* 122–131.

MARSH, H.W., & YEUNG, A.S. (1999). The liability of psychological ratings: The chameleon effect in global self-esteem. *Personality and Social Psychology Bulletin, 25,* 49–64.

MARTENS, R., & LANDERS, D.M. (1972). Evaluation potential as a determinant of coaction effect. *Journal of Experimental Social Psychology, 8,* 347–359.

MARTIN, C.L. (1986). A ratio measure of sex stereotyping. *Journal of Personality and Social Psychology, 52,* 489–499.

MASHEK, D., ARON, A., & FISHER, H. (2000). Identifying, evoking and measuring intense feelings of romantic love. *Representative Research in Social Psychology, 24,* 48–55.

MATARAZZO, J.D., WEISS, S.M., HERD, J.A., MILLER, N.E., & WEISS, S.M. (Eds.) (1984). *Behavioral health: A handbook of health enhancement and disease prevention.* Toronto: Wiley.

MATLIN, M., & STANG, D. (1978). *The Pollyanna principle: Selectivity of language, memory and thought.* Cambridge, MA: Schenkman.

MATTHEWS, K.A., GLASS, D.C., ROSENMAN, R.H., & BORTNER, R.W. (1977). Competitive drive, Pattern A and coronary heart disease: A further analysis of some data from the Western Collaborative Study. *Journal of Chronic Disease, 30,* 489–498.

MAYBERRY, R.I., & NICOLADIS, E. (2000). Gesture reflects language development: Evidence form bilingual children. *Current Directions in Psychological Science, 9,* 192–196.

MCALLISTER, H.A., & BREGMAN, N.J. (1989). Juror underutilization of eyewitness nonidentification: A test of the disconfirmed expectancy explanation. *Journal of Applied Social Psychology, 19,* 20–29.

MCCANN, C.D., & LALONDE, R.N. (1993). Dysfunctional communication and depression. *American Behavioral Scientist, 36,* 271–287.

MCCARRY, M. (1988). Work and personal values of Canadian anglophones and francophones: Implications for organizational behavior. *Canadian Psychology, 29,* 69–83.

MCCAUL, K.D., PLOYART, R.E., HINSZ, V.B., & MCCAUL, H.S. (1995). Appraisal of a consistent versus a similar politician: Voter preferences and intuitive judgments. *Journal of Personality and Social Psychology, 68,* 292–299.

MCCAULEY, C. (1989). The nature of social influence in group-think: Compliance and internalization. *Journal of Personality and Social Psychology, 57,* 250–260.

MCCLELLAND, D.C. (1961). *The achieving society.* Princeton, NJ: D. Van Nostrand.

MCCLELLAND, D.C., ALEXANDER, C., & MARKS, E. (1982). The need for power, stress, immune function and illness among male prisoners. *Journal of Abnormal Psychology, 91,* 61–70.

MCCLINTOCK, C.G., & HUNT, R.G. (1975). Nonverbal indicators of affect and deception in an interview setting. *Journal of Applied Social Psychology, 5,* 54–67.

MCCLINTOCK, C.G., & NUTTIN, J.M., Jr. (1969). Development of competitive game behavior in children across two cultures. *Journal of Experimental Social Psychology, 5,* 203–218.

MCCLOSKEY, M., & EGETH, H.E. (1983). Eyewitness identification: What can a psychologist tell a jury? *American Psychologist, 38,* 550–563.

MCCONNELL, A.R., & FAZIO, R.H. (1996). Women and men as people: Effects of gender-marked language. *Personality and Social Psychology Bulletin, 22,* 1004–1013.

MCCREARY, D.R. (1990). Multidimensionality and the measurement of gender role attributes: A comment on Archer. *British Journal of Social Psychology, 29,* 265–272.

MCCREARY, D.R., & KORABIK, K. (1994). Examining the relationship between socially desirable and undesirable aspects of agency and communion. *Sex Roles, 31,* 637–651.

MCCREARY, D.R., & SADAVA, S.W. (1995). Mediating the relationship between masculine gender role stress and work satisfaction: The influence of coping strategies. *Journal of Men's Studies, 4,* 141–152.

MCCREARY, D.R., & SADAVA, S.W. (2000). Stress, alcohol use and alcohol problems: The mediating role of negative and positive affect in two cohorts of young adults. *Journal of Studies on Alcohol, 61,* 466–474.

MCCULLOUGH, M.E. (2001). Forgiveness: Who does it and how do they do it? *Current Directions in Psychological Science, 10,* 194–197.

MCCULLOUGH, M.E., EMMONS, R.A., & TSANG, J. (2002) The grateful disposition: A conceptual and empirical topography. *Journal of Personality and Social Psychology, 82,* 112–127.

MCCULLOUGH, M.E., HOYT, W.T., LARSON, D.B., KOENIG, H.G., & THORESEN, C. (2000). Religious involvement and mortality: A meta-analytic review. *Health Psychology, 19,* 211–222.

MCCULLOUGH, M.E., KILPATRICK, S.D., EMMONS, R.A., & LARSON, D.B. (2001). Is gratitude a moral affect? *Psychological Bulletin, 127,* 249–266.

MCDOUGALL, W. (1908). *An introduction to social psychology.* London: Methuen & Co.

MCFARLAND, C., & BUEHLER, R. (1998). The impact of negative affect on autobiographical memory: The role of self-focused attention to moods. *Journal of Personality and Social Psychology, 75,* 1424–1440.

MCFARLAND, C., ROSS, M., & DECOURVILLE, N. (1989). Women's theories of menstruation and biases in recall of menstrual symptoms. *Journal of Personality and Social Psychology, 57,* 522–531.

MCFARLAND, C., ROSS, M., & GILTROW, M. (1992). Biased recall of older adults: The role of implicit theories in aging. *Journal of Personality and Social Psychology, 62,* 837–850.

MCGILL CONSORTIUM FOR ETHNICITY AND STRATEGIC SOCIAL PLANNING (1997). *Diversity, mobility and change: The dynamics of black communities in Canada.*

MCGRATH, J. (1984). *Groups: Interaction and performance.* Englewood Cliffs, NJ: Prentice-Hall.

MCGREGOR, I., NEWBY-CLARK, I.R., & ZANNA, M.P. (1998). Epistemic discomforts as moderated by simultaneous accessibility of inconsistent elements. In E. Harmon-Jones, & J. Mills (Eds.), *Cognitive dissonance theory 40 years later: A revival with revisions and controversies* (pp. 166–192). Washington, DC: American Psychological Association.

MCGUIRE, W.J. (1968). Personality and susceptibility to social influence. In E.F. Borgatta, & W.W. Lambert (Eds.), *Handbook of personality: Theory and research* (pp. 1130–1187). Chicago: Rand-McNally.

MCGUIRE, W.J. (1969). The nature of attitudes and attitude change. In G. Lindzey, & E. Aronson (Eds.), *The handbook of social psychology* (2nd ed.). (Vol. 3). (pp. 136–314). New York: Addison-Wesley.

MCGUIRE, W.J., & MCGUIRE, C.V. (1988). Content and process in the experience of self. In L. Berkowitz (Ed.), *Advances in experimental social psychology* (Vol. 21). (pp. 97–144). New York: Academic Press.

MCGUIRE, W.J., & PAPAGEORGIS, D. (1961). The relative efficacy of various types of prior belief-defense in producing immunity against persuasion. *Journal of Abnormal & Social Psychology, 62,* 327–337.

MCGUIRE, W.J., & PAPAGEORGIS, D. (1962). Effectiveness of forewarning in developing resistance to persuasion. *Public Opinion Quarterly, 26,* 24–32.

MCKAY, S., & PITTAM, J. (Eds.) (2002). Language and the meaning of illness. Special Issue of the *Journal of Language and Social Psychology.*

MCKENNA, K.Y.A. (2002). Relationship formation on the Internet. What's the big attraction? *Journal of Social Issues, 58* (1), 9–31.

MCKENNA, K.Y.A., & BARGH, J.A (2000). Plan 9 from cyberspace: The implications of the Internet for personality and social psychology. *Personality and Social Psychology Review, 4,* 57–75.

MCKENZIE-MOHR, D., & ZANNA, M.P. (1990). Treating women as sexual objects: Look to the (gender schematic) male who has viewed pornography. *Personality and Social Psychology Bulletin, 16,* 296–308.

MCLAUGHLIN, B. (1977). Second-language learning in children. *Psychological Bulletin, 84*, 438–459.

MCLAUGHLIN, B. (1987). *Theories of second-language learning.* London: Arnold.

MCMURRAY, G.A. (1982). Psychology at Saskatchewan. In M.J. Wright, & C.R. Myers (Eds.), *History of academic psychology in Canada* (pp. 178–191). Toronto: Hogrefe.

MCRAE, C.N., HOOD, B.M., MILNE, A.B., ROWE, A.C., & MASON, M.F. (2002). Are you looking at me? Eye gaze and person perception. *Psychological Science, 13*, 460–464.

MEDALIA, N.Z., & LARSEN, D.N. (1958). Diffusion and belief in a collective dilemma: The Seattle windshield pitting epidemic. *American Sociological Review, 23*, 222–232.

MEDVENE, L.J., TEAL, C.R., & SLAVICH, S. (2000). Including the other in the self: Implications for judgments of equity and satisfaction in close relationships. *Journal of Social and Personal Relationships, 19*, 396–419.

MEEKER, R.J., & SHURE, G.H. (1969). Pacifist bargaining tactics: Some "outsider" influences. *Journal of Conflict Resolution, 13*, 487–493.

MEEUS, W., & RAAIJSMAKERS, Q. (1986). Administrative obedience as a social phenomenon. In W. Doise, & S. Moscovici (Eds.), *Current issues in European social psychology* (Vol. 2). (pp. 19–52). Cambridge: Cambridge University Press.

MEGARGEE, E.I. (1966). Undercontrolled and overcontrolled personality types in extreme antisocial aggression. *Psychological Monographs, 80*, whole issue.

MEHRABIAN, A. (1968). Communication without words. *Psychology Today, 2 (September)*, 53–55.

MEHRABIAN, A. (1971). Nonverbal betrayal of feeling. *Journal of Experimental Research in Personality, 5*, 64–73.

MEHRABIAN, A., & DIAMOND, S. (1971). Seating arrangement and conversation. *Sociometry, 34*, 281–289.

MEIER, N.C., MENNENGA, G.H., & STOLTZ, H.J. (1941). An experimental approach to the study of mob behavior. *Journal of Abnormal Psychology, 36*, 506–524.

MELAMED, S., RABINOWITZ, S., FEINER, M., WEISBERG, E., & RIBAK, J. (1996). Usefulness of the protection motivation theory in explaining hearing protection device use among male industrial workers. *Health Psychology, 15*, 209–215.

MERRENS, M.R. (1973). Nonemergency helping behavior in various sized communities. *Journal of Social Psychology, 90*, 327–328.

MERTON, R.K. (1957). *Social theory and social structure* (revised ed.). Glencoe, IL: Free Press.

MESSICK, D.M., & BREWER, M.B. (1983). Solving social dilemmas: A review. *Review of Personality and Social Psychology, 4*, 11–44.

MESSICK, D.M., & MACKIE, D.M. (1989). Intergroup relations. In M.R. Rosenzweig, & L.W. Porter (Eds.), *Annual Review of Psychology* (Vol. 40). (pp. 45–81).

MESSICK, D.M., & MCCLELLAND, C.L. (1983). Social traps and temporal traps. *Personality and Social Psychology Bulletin, 9*, 105–110.

MESSMAN, S.J., CANARY, D.J., & HAUSE, K.S. (2000). Motives to remain platonic, equity and he use of maintenance strategies in opposites-sex friendships. *Journal of Social and Personal Relationships, 17*, 67–94.

MEUMANN, E. (1904). Haus-und schularbeit: Experimente an kindern der volksschule. *Die Deutsche Schule, 8*, 278–303, 337–359, 416–431.

MEYER, I.H. (2003). Prejudice, social stress and mental health in lesbian, gay and bisexual populations: Conceptual issues and research evidence. *Psychological Bulletin, 129*, 674–697.

MIDDLEBROOK, P.N. (1974). *Social psychology and modern life.* New York: Alfred A. Knopf.

MIDLARSKY, E., & BRYAN, J.H. (1972). Affect expressions and children's imitative altruism. *Journal of Experimental Research in Personality, 6*, 195–203.

MIKULA, G. (1994). Perspective-related differences in interpretations of injustice by victims and victimizers: A test with close relationships. In M.J. Lerner, & G. Mikula (Eds), *Entitlement and the affectional bond: Justice in close relationships. Critical issues in social justice* (pp. 175–203). New York: Plenum Press.

MILGRAM, S. (1963). Behavioral study of obedience. *Journal of Applied Social Psychology, 67*, 371–378.

MILGRAM, S. (1964). Issues in the study of obedience: A reply to Baumrind. *American Psychologist, 19*, 848–852.

MILGRAM, S. (1965). Some conditions of obedience and disobedience to authority. *Human Relations, 18*, 57–76.

MILGRAM, S. (1970). The experience of living in cities. *Science, 167*, 1461–1468.

MILGRAM, S. (1974). *Obedience to authority.* New York: Harper & Row.

MILGRAM, S., & TOCH, H. (1969). Collective behavior: Crowds and social movements. In G. Lindzey, & E. Aronson (Eds.), *The handbook of social psychology* (2nd ed.). (Vol. 4). (pp. 507–610). Reading, MA: Addison-Wesley.

MILLER, A.G., & THOMAS, R. (1972). Cooperation and competition among Blackfoot Indian and rural Canadian children. *Child Development, 34*, 1104–1110.

MILLER, A.G., BUDDIE, A.M., & KRETSCHMAR, J. (2002). Explaining the Holocaust. Does social psychology exonerate the perpetrators? In L.S. Newman & R. Erber (Eds.) *Understanding genocide: The social psychology of the Holocaust* (pp. 302–324). New York; Oxford University Press.

MILLER, D.T., & PORTER, C.A. (1983). Self-blame in victims of violence. *Journal of Social Issues, 39*, 139–152.

MILLER, G.E., DOPP, J.M., MYERS, H.F., STEVENS, S.Y., & FAHEY, J.L. (1999). Psychosocial predictors of natural killer cell mobilization during marital conflict. *Health Psychology, 18*, 262–271.

MILLER, G.R., & BURGOON, J.K. (1982). Factors affecting assessments of witness credibility. In N. Kerr, & R. Bray (Eds.), *The psychology of the courtroom* (pp. 169–194). New York: Academic Press.

MILLER, J.G. (1984). Culture and the development of everyday social explanation. *Journal of Personality and Social Psychology, 46*, 961–978.

MILLER, J.G. (1999). Cultural psychology: Implications for basic theory and practice. *Psychological Science, 10*, 85–91.

MILLER, J.G., & BERSOFF, D.N. (1992). Culture and moral judgment: How are conflicts between justice and interpersonal responsibilities resolved? *Journal of Personality and Social Psychology, 62*, 541–554.

MILLER, N., & CAMPBELL, D.T. (1959). Recency and primacy in persuasion as a function of the timing of speeches and measurement. *Journal of Abnormal and Social Psychology, 59*, 1–9.

MILLER, R.M., & RIVENBARK, W. (1970). Sexual differences in physical attractiveness as a determinant of heterosexual liking. *Psychological Reports, 27*, 701–702.

MILLER, S.M., & MANGAN, C.E. (1983). Interacting effects of information and coping style in adapting to gynecologic stress. Should the doctor tell all? *Journal of Personality and Social Psychology, 45*, 223–236.

MILLER, W.R., & THORESEN, C.E. (2003). Spirituality, religion and health. An emerging research field. *American Psychologist, 58*, 24–35.

MILLS, J., & HARVEY, J. (1972). Opinion change as a function of when information about the communicator is received and whether he is attractive or expert. *Journal of Personality and Social Psychology, 21*, 52–55.

MINISTRY OF SUPPLY & SERVICES CANADA. (1985). *Pornography and prostitution in Canada: Report of the Special Committee on Pornography and Prostitution.* Ottawa: Author.

MINTON, H.L. (1992). Root metaphors and the evolution of American social psychology. *Canadian Psychology, 33,* 547–553.

MINTZ, A. (1951). Non-adaptive group behavior. *Journal of Abnormal and Social Psychology, 46,* 150–159.

MITCHELL, H.E., & BYRNE, D. (1973). The defendant's dilemma: Effects of juror's attitudes and authoritarianism on judicial decisions. *Journal of Personality and Social Psychology, 25,* 123–129.

MOGHADDAM, F.M. (1987). Psychology in the three worlds, as reflected by the crisis in social psychology and the move toward indigenous third-world psychology. *American Psychologist, 42,* 912–920.

MOGHADDAM, F.M. (1990). Modulative and generative orientations in psychology: Implications for psychology in the three worlds. *Journal of Social Issues, 46,* 21–41.

MOGHADDAM, F.M. & MARSELLA, A.J. (Eds). (2004). *Understanding terrorism: Psychosocial roots, consequences, and interventions.* Washington, DC: American Psychological Association.

MOGY, R.B., & PRUITT, D.G. (1974). Effects of threatener's enforcement costs on threat credibility and compliance. *Journal of Personality and Social Psychology, 29,* 173–180.

MONGRAIN, M., & VETTESE, L.C. (2003). Conflict over emotional expression: Implications for interpersonal communication. *Personality and Social Psychology Bulletin, 29,* 545–555.

MONOHAN, J., & WALKER, L. (1988). Social science research in law: A new paradigm. *American Psychologist, 43,* 465–472.

MONSON, T.C., & HESLEY, J.W. (1982). Causal attributions for behaviors consistent or inconsistent with an actor's personality traits: Differences between those offered by actors and observers. *Journal of Personality and Social Psychology, 18,* 416–432.

MONSOUR, M. (1992). Meanings of intimacy in cross- and same-sex friendships. *Journal of Social and Personal Relationships, 9,* 277–295.

MONTAGUE, A. (1973). *Man and aggression* (2nd ed.). London: Oxford University Press.

MONTEPARE, J.M., & VEGA, C. (1988). Women's vocal reactions to intimate and casual male friends. *Personality and Social Psychology Bulletin, 14,* 103–113.

MOODY, E.J. (2001). Internet use and its relationship to loneliness. *CyberPsychology and Behavior, 4,* 393–401.

MOORE, S.F., SHAFFER, L.S., & POLLACK, E.L. (1987). The effects of interpersonal trust and prior commons problem experience on commons management. *Journal of Social Psychology, 127,* 19–29.

MOORE, T.E., & PEPLER, D. (1989, August 11–15). *Domestic violence and children's adjustment: Exploring the linkage.* American Psychological Association Annual Meeting, New Orleans.

MOORE, T.E., PEPLER, D., MAE, R., & KATES, M. (1989). Child witnesses to family violence: New directions for research and intervention. In B. Pressman, G. Cameron, & M. Rothery (Eds.), *Intervening with assaulted women: Current theory, research, and practice* (pp. 75–91). Hillsdale, NJ: Lawrence Erlbaum Assoc.

MOOS, R.H. (1982). Coping with acute health crises. In T. Millon, C. Green, & R. Meagher (Eds.), *Handbook of clinical health psychology* (pp. 129–151). New York: Plenum.

MORELAND, R.L., & ZAJONC, R.B (1982). Exposure effects in person perception: Familiarity, similarity and attraction. *Journal of Experimental Social Psychology, 18,* 395–415.

MORIER, D., BORGIDA, E., & PARK, R.C. (1996). Improving juror comprehension of judicial instructions on the entrapment defence. *Journal of Applied Social Psychology, 26,* 1838–1866.

MORRIS, C. (1956). *Varieties of human value.* Chicago: University of Chicago Press.

MORRIS, M.W., & PANG, K. (1994). Culture and cause: American and Chinese attributions for social and physical events. *Journal of Personality and Social Psychology 67,* 949–971.

MORRIS, W.N., & MILLER, R.S. (1975). The effects of consensus-breaking and consensus preempting partners on reduction of conformity. *Journal of Experimental Social Psychology, 11,* 215–223.

MOSCOVICI, S. (1980). Toward a theory of conversion behavior. In L. Berkowitz (Ed.), *Advances in experimental social psychology* (Vol. 13). (pp. 202–239). New York: Academic Press.

MOSCOVICI, S. (1981). On social representations. In J.P. Forgas (Ed.), *Social cognition: Perspectives on everyday understanding* (pp. 211–254). London: Academic Press.

MOSCOVICI, S., & HEWSTONE, M. (1983). Social representation and social explanation: From the naive to the amateur scientist. In M. Hewstone (Ed.), *Attribution theory: Social and functional explanations* (pp. 145–189). Oxford: Basil Blackwell.

MOSCOVICI, S., & ZAVOLLONI, M. (1969). The group as a polarizer of attitudes. *Journal of Personality and Social Psychology, 12,* 125–135.

MOSCOVICI, S., MUGNY, G., & VAN AVERMAET, E. (1985) (Eds.). *Perspectives on minority influence.* Cambridge: Cambridge University Press.

MOULIK, T.K., & LOKHANDE, M.R. (1969). Value orientation of North Indian farmers and its relation to adoption of farm practices. *Rural Sociology, 34,* 375–382.

MULAC, A., SIEBOLD, D.R., & FARRIS, J.L (2000). Female and male managers' and professionals' criticism-giving: Differences in language use and effects. *Journal of Language and Social Psychology, 19,* 389–415.

MULLEN, B., & COPPER, C. (1994). The relation between group cohesiveness and performance: An integration. *Psychological Bulletin, 115,* 210–227.

MULLEN, B., SALAS, E., & DRISKELL, J.E. (1989). Salience, motivation, and artifact as contributions to the relation between participation rate and leadership. *Journal of Experimental Social Psychology, 25,* 545–559.

MULLET, R.T., & DIAMOND, T. (1999). Father and mother physical abuse and child aggressive behaviour in two generations. *Canadian Journal of Behavioural Science, 31,* 221–228.

MULLIN, C.R., & LINZ, D. (1995). Desensitization and resensitization to violence against women: Effects of exposure to sexually violent films on judgments of domestic violence victims. *Journal of Personality and Social Psychology, 69,* 449–459.

MUNSTERBERG, H. (1908). *On the witness stand: Essays on psychology and crime.* New York: Doubleday Page.

MURAVEN, M., & BAUMEISTER, R.F. (1997). Suicide, sex, terror, paralysis and other pitfalls of reductionist self-preservation theory. *Psychological Inquiry, 8,* 36–40.

MURPHY, P.L., & MILLER, C.T. (1997). Post-decisional dissonance and the commodified self-concept: A cross-cultural examination. *Personality and Social Psychology Bulletin, 23,* 50–62.

MURRAY, S.L., BELLAVIA, G.M., ROSE, P., & GRIFFIN, D.W. (2003). Once hurt, twice hurtful. How perceived regard regulates daily marital interactions. *Journal of Personality and Social Psychology, 84,* 126–147.

MURRAY, S.L., HOLMES, J.G., & GRIFFIN, D.W. (1996). The benefits of positive illusions: Idealization and the construction of satisfaction in close relationships. *Journal of Personality and Social Psychology, 70,* 79–98.

MURRAY, S.L., ROSE, P., BELLAVIA, G., HOLMES, J.G., & GARRETT, A. (2002). When rejection stings: How self-esteem constrains relationship enhancement processes. *Journal of Personality and Social Psychology, 83,* 556–573.

MURSTEIN, B.I. (1972). Physical attractiveness and marital choice. *Journal of Personality and Social Psychology, 22,* 8–12.

MYERS, C.R. (1965). Notes on the history of psychology in Canada. *Canadian Psychologist, 6,* 4–19.

NADER, L. (1969). Styles of court procedure: To make the balance. In L. Nader (Ed.), *Law in Culture and Society* (pp. 69–91). Chicago: Aldine.

NADLER, A., & FISHER, J.D. (1984). Effects of donor-recipient relationship on recipient's reactions to aid. In E. Staub, D. Bar-Tal, J. Karylowski, & J. Reykowski (Eds.), *Development and maintenance of prosocial behavior* (pp. 397–418). New York: Plenum Press.

NADON, J.C. (1990). Towards a new social contract: Public servants' language of work. *Language and Society, 31,* 24–26.

NAGIN, D., & TREMBLAY, R.E. (1999). Trajectories of boys' physical aggression, opposition, and hyperactivity on the path to physically violent and non-violent juvenile delinquency. *Child Development, 70,* 1181–1196.

NEIGHBORS, C., VIETOR, N.A., & KNEE, C.R. (2002). A motivational model of driving anger and aggression. *PSPB, 28,* 324–335.

NEL, E., HELMREICH, R., & ARONSON, E. (1969). Opinion change in the advocate as a function of the persuasibility of his audience. *Journal of Personality and Social Psychology, 12,* 117–124.

NELSON, C., & MCLEMORE, T. (1988). *National Centre for Health Statistics. The National Ambulatory Medical Care survey: U.S. 1975–1981 and 1985 trends.* Vital and Health Statistics, series 13, no. 93, DHHS pub. no. (PHS) 88–1754. Washington, DC: U.S. Government Printing Office.

NELSON, S.D. (1974). Nature/nurture revisited I: A review of the biological bases of conflict. *Journal of Conflict Resolution, 18,* 285–335.

NELSON, S.D. (1975). Nature/nurture revisited II: Social, political, and technological implications of biological approaches to human conflict. *Journal of Conflict Resolution, 19,* 734–761.

NEMETH, C. (1981). Jury trials: Psychology and law. *Advances in Experimental Social Psychology, 14,* 309–367.

NEMETH, C. (1986). Differential contributions of majority and minority influence. *Psychological Review, 93,* 23–32.

NEMETH, C.J., & CHILES, C. (1988). Modelling courage: The role of dissent in fostering independence. *European Journal of Social Psychology, 18,* 275–280.

NEMETH, C.J., & KWAN, J.L. (1987). Minority influence, divergent thinking and detection of correct solutions. *Journal of Applied Psychology, 17,* 788–799.

NEUBERG, S.L., CIALDINI, R.B., BROWN, S.L., LUCE, C., SAGARIN, B.D., & LEWIS, B.P. (1997). Does empathy lead to anything more than superficial helping? Comment on Batson et al. (1997). *Journal of Personality & Social Psychology, 73,* 510–516.

NEUMANN, R., & STRACK, F. (2000). "Mood contagion": The automatic transfer of mood between persons. *Journal of Personality and Social Psychology, 79,* 211–223.

NEWBY-CLARK, I.R., MCGREGOR, I., & ZANNA, M.P. (2002). Thinking and caring about cognitive inconsistency: When and for whom does attitudinal ambivalence feel uncomfortable? *Journal of Personality and Social Psychology, 82,* 157–166.

NEWCOMB, M.D., & BENTLER, E.M. (1980). Cohabitation before marriage: A comparison of married couples who did and did not cohabit. *Alternative Life Styles, 3,* 65–85.

NEWCOMB, M.D., HUBA, G.J., & BENTLER, E.M. (1986). Determinants of sexual and dating behavior among adolescents. *Journal of Personality and Social Psychology, 50,* 428–438.

NEWCOMB, T.M. (1943). *Personality and social change: Attitude formation in a student community.* New York: Dryden.

NEWCOMB, T.M. (1961). *The acquaintance process.* New York: Holt, Rinehart & Winston.

NEWCOMB, T.M., KOENIG, L.E., FLACKS, R., & WARWICK, D.P. (1967). *Persistence and change: Bennington College and its students after twenty-five years.* New York: Wiley.

NEWELL, A., & SIMON, H.A. (1972). *Human problem solving.* Englewood Cliffs, NJ: Prentice-Hall.

NEWMAN, L.S., & ERBER, R. (Eds.) (2002). *Understanding genocide. The social psychology of the Holocaust.* New York: Oxford University Press.

NICKS, S.D., KORN, J.H., & MAINIERI, T. (1997). The rise and fall of deception in social psychology and personality research, 1921 to 1994. *Ethics and Behavior, 7,* 69–77.

NIDA, S.A., & KOON, J. (1983). They get better looking at closing time around here, too. *Psychological Reports, 52,* 657–658.

NIELSON, W.R., & NEUFELD, R.W.J. (1986). Utility of the uncontrollability construct in relation to the Type A behaviour pattern: A multidimensional investigation. *Canadian Journal of Behavioural Science, 18,* 224–237.

NISBETT, R.E., & BORGIDA, E. (1975). Attribution and the psychology of prediction. *Journal of Personality and Social Psychology, 32,* 932–943.

NISBETT, R.E., & GORDON, A. (1967). Self-esteem and susceptibility to social influence. *Journal of Personality and Social Psychology, 5,* 268–276.

NISBETT, R.E., & WILSON, T.D. (1977). Telling more than we can know: Verbal reports on mental processes. *Psychological Review, 84,* 231–259.

NISBETT, R.E., CAPUTO, C., LEGANT, P., & MARACEK, J. (1973). Behavior as seen by the actor and as seen by the observer. *Journal of Personality and Social Psychology, 27,* 154–164.

NISBETT, R.E., ZUCKIER, H., & LEMLEY, R.E. (1981). The dilution effect: Nondiagnostic information weakens the implications of diagnostic information. *Cognitive Psychology, 13,* 248–277.

NORMAN, R. (1976). When what is said is important: A comparison of expert and attractive sources. *Journal of Experimental Social Psychology, 12,* 294–300.

NORMAN, R.N.G. (1985). *The nature and correlates of health behaviour.* Ottawa: Health Promotion Directorate.

NOSEK, B., BANAJI, M.R., GREENWALD, A.G. (2002). Math = male, me = female, therefore math not = me. *Journal of Personality & Social Psychology, 83,* 44–59.

NOSSITER, B.D. (1970). *The soft state.* New York: Harper & Row.

NOTANI, A.S. (1998). Moderators of perceived behavioral control's predictiveness in the theory of planned behavior: A meta-analysis. *Journal of Consumer Psychology, 7,* 247–271.

NOTZ, W.W., & STARKE, F.A. (1987). Arbitration and distributive justice: Equity or equality? *Journal of Applied Psychology, 72,* 359–365.

NOVAK, D., & LERNER, M.J. (1968). Rejection as a consequence of perceived similarity. *Journal of Personality and Social Psychology, 9,* 147–152.

NYQUIST, L.V., & SPENCE, J.T. (1986). Effects of dispositional dominance and sex role expectations on leadership behaviors. *Journal of Personality and Social Psychology, 50,* 87–93.

O'MEARA, J.D. (1989). Cross-sex friendship; four basic challenges of an ignored relationship. *Sex Roles, 21,* 525–543.

O'MEARA, J.D. (1994). Cross-sex friendships opportunity challenge: Uncharted terrain for exploration. *Personal Relationships Issues, 2,* 4–7.

OCHSNER, K.N., & LIEBERMAN, M.D. (2001). The emergence of social cognitive neuroscience. *American Psychologist, 56,* 717–734.

OGLOFF, J.R.P., ACHILLE, M., BROWN, L., OLLEY, M.C., SALEKIN, R., & WHITTEMORE, K.E. (1993, May). Why Canadians said No: People's attitudes towards and knowledge of the Charlottetown Accord. Annual meeting of the Canadian Psychological Association, Montréal.

OLINER, S.P., & OLINER, P. (1992) *The altruistic personality: Rescuers of Jews in Nazi Europe.* San Francisco: Free Press.

OLSON, J.M. (1990). Self-inference processes in emotion. In J.M. Olson, & M.P. Zanna (Eds.), *Self-inference processes: The Ontario symposium* (Vol. 6). (pp. 17–42). Hillsdale, NJ: Erlbaum.

OLSON, J.M., & HAFER, C.L. (1996). Affect, motivation and cognition in relative deprivation research. In R.M. Sorrentino, & E.T. Higgins (Eds.), *Handbook of motivation and cognition* (pp. 85–117). New York: Guilford.

OLSON, J.M., & ZANNA, M.P. (1993). Attitude and attitude change. *Annual Review of Psychology, 44,* 117–154.

OLSON, J.M., HAFER, C.L., COUZENS, A., KRAMINS, I., & TAYLOR, L. (1997). *Resentment about deprivation: A self-presentation perspective.* Unpublished manuscript, University of Western Ontario.

OLWEUS, D. (1972). *Personality and aggression. In Nebraska symposium on motivation, 1972* (pp. 261–323). Lincoln, NB: University of Nebraska Press.

OLWEUS, D. (1978). *Aggression in the schools: Bullies and whipping boys.* Washington: Hemisphere Publishing.

OMATO, A., & SNYDER, M. (1995). Sustained helping without obligation: Motivation, longevity of service, and perceived attitude change among AIDS volunteers. *Journal or Personality and Social Psychology, 68,* 671–687.

ONTARIO ROYAL COMMISSION ON VIOLENCE IN THE COMMUNICATIONS INDUSTRY. (1977). *Report* (Vols. 1–7). Toronto: Government of Ontario.

ORBELL, J.M., VAN-DE-KRAGT, A.J., & DAVIES, R.M. (1989). Explaining discussion-induced cooperation. *Journal of Personality and Social Psychology, 54,* 811–819.

ORNE, M.T. (1962). On the social psychology of the psychology experiment: With particular reference to demand characteristics and their implications. *American Psychologist, 17,* 776–783.

ORTMANN, A. & HERTWIG, R. (1997) Is deception acceptable? *American Psychologist, 52,* 746–747.

OSGOOD, C.E. (1962). *An alternative to war or surrender.* Urbana: University of Illinois Press.

OSGOOD, C.E., SUCI, D.J., & TANNENBAUM, P.H. (1957). *The measurement of meaning.* Urbana, IL: University of Illinois Press.

OSKAMP, S. (1971). Effects of programmed strategies on cooperation in the prisoner's dilemma and other mixed-motive games. *Journal of Conflict Resolution, 15,* 225–229.

PADAWER-SINGER, A., & BARTON, A.H. (1975). Free press, fair trial. In R. Simon (Ed.), *The jury system: A critical analysis* (pp. 123–139). Beverly Hills, CA: Sage.

PAGE, F.H., & CLARK, J.W. (1982). Psychology at Dalhousie. In M.J. Wright, & C.R. Myers (Eds.), *History of academic psychology in Canada* (pp. 20–32). Toronto: Hogrefe.

PAGÈS, R. (1986). Personal communication.

PALER, D.L. (1996). Determinants of Canadian attitudes toward immigration. More than just racism. *Canadian Journal of Behavioural Science, 28,* 180–192.

PALMER, D.L. (1996). Determinants of Canadian attitudes toward immigration: More than just racism. *Canadian Journal of Behavioural Science, 28,* 180–192.

PANCER, S.M., BROWN, S.D., GREGOR, P., & CLAXTON-OLDFIELD, S.P. (1992). Causal attributions and the perception of political figures. *Canadian Journal of Behavioural Science, 24,* 371–381.

PANCER, S.M., JACKSON, L.M., HUNSBERGER, B., PRATT, M.W., & LEA, J. (1995). Religious orthodoxy and the complexity of thought about religious and nonreligious issues. *Journal of Personality, 63,* 213–232.

PAPASTAMOU, S. (1983). Strategies of minority and majority influence. In W. Doise, & S. Moscovici (Eds.). *Current Issues in European Social Psychology* (Vol. 1). (pp. 33–83). Cambridge: Cambridge University Press.

PAPASTAMOU, S., & MUGNY, G. (1985). Rigidity and minority influence: The influence of the social in social influence. In S. Moscovici, G. Mugny, & E. Van Avermaet (Eds.). *Perspectives on minority influence* (pp. 113–136). Cambridge: Cambridge University Press.

PARKE, R.D., BERKOWITZ, L., LEYENS, J.P., WEST, S.G., & SEBASTIAN, R.J. (1977). Some effects of violent and non-violent movies on the behavior of juvenile delinquents. In L. Berkowitz (Ed.), *Advances in experimental social psychology* (Vol. 10). (pp. 135–172). New York: Academic Press.

PARKER, P.A., MIDDLETON, M.S., & KULIK, J.A. (2002). Counterfactual thinking and quality of life among women with silicone breast implants. *Journal of Behavioral Medicine, 25,* 317–335.

PARKOVNICK, S. (1992). The implications of social influence research for a conceptual framework for psychological social psychology. *Canadian Psychology, 33,* 619–622.

PASTEL, R.H. (2001). Collective behaviors: Mass panic and outbreaks of multiple unexplained symptoms. *Military Medicine, 166,* 44–46.

PATTERSON, G.R. (1982). *Coercive family processes.* Eugene, OR: Castilia Press.

PATTERSON, M.L. (1982). A sequential functional model of nonverbal exchange. *Psychological Review, 89,* 231–249.

PATTERSON, M.L. (1983). *Nonverbal behaviour: A functional perspective.* New York: Springer.

PAULHUS, D.L. (1990). Measurement and control of response bias. In J.P. Robinson, P.R. Shaver, & L. Wrightsman (Eds.), *Measures of personality and social-psychological attitudes* (pp. 17–59). New York: Academic Press.

PAULHUS, D.L., & BRUCE, M.N. (1992). The effects of acquaintanceship on the validity of personality impressions: A longitudinal study. *Journal of Personality and Social Psychology, 63,* 816–824.

PAULHUS, D.L., & MORGAN, K.L. (1997). Perceptions of intelligence in leaderless groups: Effects of shyness and acquaintance. *Journal of Personality and Social Psychology, 72,* 581–591.

PAULHUS, D.L., & REID, D.B. (1991). Enhancement and denial in socially desirable responding. *Journal of Personality and Social Psychology, 60,* 307–317.

PAULHUS, D.L., & TRAPNELL, P.D. (1997). Terror management theory: Extended or overextended. *Psychological Inquiry, 8,* 40–43.

PAULUS, P.B. (1988). *Prison crowding: A psychological perspective.* New York: Springer-Verlag.

PAULUS, P.B., & MURDOCK, P. (1971). Anticipated evaluation and audience presence in the enhancement of dominant responses. *Journal of Experimental Social Psychology, 7,* 280–291.

PAULUS, P.B., OZINDOLET, M.T., POLETES, G., & CAMACHO, L.M. (1993). Perception of performance in group brainstorming: The illusion of group productivity. *Personality and Social Psychology Bulletin, 19*, 78–89.

PEARL, D., BOUTHILET, L., & LAZAR, J.B. (Eds.). (1982). *Television and behavior: Ten years of scientific progress and implications for the 80's* (Vols. 1–2). Washington, DC: U.S. Government Printing Office.

PEDERSEN, P., & THOMAS, C.D. (1992). Prevalence and correlates of dating violence in a Canadian university sample. *Canadian Journal of Behavioural Science, 24*, 490–501.

PEER, B. (2001). 'Monkey man' does not exist: Delhi police. http://www.rediff.com/news/2001/jun/20monk.htm.

PEI, M. (1965). *The story of language* (2nd ed.). Philadelphia: Lippincott.

PENDERGAST, M. (1993). *For God, country and Coca-Cola: The unauthorized history of the great American soft drink and the company that makes it.* New York: Charles Scribner.

PENDLETON, M.G., & BATSON, C.D. (1979). Self-presentation and the door-in-the-face technique for inducing compliance. *Journal of Personality and Social Psychology, 5*, 77–81.

PENNEBAKER, J.W., & KING, L.A. (1999). Linguistic styles: Language use as an individual difference. *Journal of Personality and Social Psychology, 77*, 1296–1312.

PENNEBAKER, J.W., DYER, M.A., CAULKINS, R.S., LITOWITZ, D.L., ACKERMAN, P.L., ANDERSON, D.B., & MCGRAW, K.M. (1979). Don't the girls get prettier at closing time?: A country and western application to psychology. *Personality and Social Psychology Bulletin, 5*, 122–125.

PENNER, L.A., & FINKELSTEIN, M.A. (1998). Dispositional and structural determinants of volunteerism. *Journal or Personality and Social Psychology, 74*, 525–537.

PENNINGTON, N., & HASTIE, R. (1981). Juror decision-making models: The generalization gap. *Psychological Bulletin, 89*, 246–287.

PENNINGTON, N., & HASTIE, R. (1990). Practical implications of psychological research on jurors and jury decision-making. *Personality and Social Psychology Bulletin, 16*, 90–105.

PENNINGTON, N., & HASTIE, R. (1992). Explaining the evidence: Tests of the story model for juror decision making. *Journal of Personality and Social Psychology, 62*, 189–206.

PEPLAU, L.A. (2003). Human sexuality: How do men and women differ? *Current Directions in Psychological Science, 12*, 37–40.

PEPLAU, L.A., & GORDON, S.L. (1985). Women and men in love: Gender differences in close heterosexual relationships. In V.E. O'Leary, R.K. Unger, & B.S. Wallston (Eds.), *Women, gender, and social psychology* (pp. 257–291). Hillsdale, NJ: Erlbaum.

PEPLAU, L.A., & PERLMAN, D. (1982). Perspectives on loneliness. In L.A. Peplau, & D. Perlman (Eds.), *Loneliness: A sourcebook of current theory, research and therapy* (pp. 1–20). New York: Wiley.

PEPLAU, L.A., BIKSON, F.K., ROOK, K.S., & GOODCHILDS, J.D. (1982). Being old and living alone. In L.A. Peplau, & D. Perlman (Eds.), *Loneliness: A sourcebook of current theory, research, and therapy* (pp. 327–349). New York: Wiley Interscience.

PEPLAU, L.A., RUSSELL, D., & HEIM, M. (1979). The experience of loneliness. In I.H. Frieze, D. Bar-Tal, & J.S. Carroll (Eds.), *New approaches to social problems: Applications of attribution theory.* San Francisco: Jossey-Bass.

PEPLER, D.J., CRAIG, W-M., CONNOLLY, J., & HENDERSON, K. (2002). Bullying, sexual harassment, dating violence, and substance use among adolescents. In C. Wekerle, & A-M. Wall (Eds.), *The violence and addiction equation: Theoretical and clinical issues in substance abuse and relationship violence* (pp. 153–168). New York: Brunner-Routledge.

PERLINI, A.H., & WARD, C. (2000). HIV prevention interventions: The effects of role-play and behavioural commitment on knowledge and attitudes. *Canadian Journal of Behavioural Science, 32*, 133–143.

PERLMAN, D., & OSKAMP, S. (1971). The effects of picture content and exposure frequency on evaluations of Negroes and Whites. *Journal of Experimental Social Psychology, 7, 503–514.*

PERLMAN, D., & PEPLAU, L.A. (1981). Toward a social psychology of loneliness. In S. Duck, & R. Gilmour (Eds.), *Personal relationships 3: Personal relationships in disorder.* London: Academic Press.

PERRIN, S., & SPENCER, C. (1981). Independence or conformity in the Asch experiment as a reflection of cultural and situational factors. *British Journal of Social Psychology, 20*, 205–209.

PERSONNAZ, M., & PERSONNAZ, B. (1994). Perception and conversion. In S. Moscovici, F. Mucchi, & A. Maass, (Eds.), *Minority influence* (pp. 165–183). Chicago: Nelson-Hall.

PETERS, L.H., HARTKE, D.D., & POHLMAN, J.T. (1985). Fiedler's contingency theory of leadership: An application of the meta-analytic procedure of Schmidt and Hunter. *Psychological Bulletin, 97*, 274–285.

PETERSON, R.B., & SKIMADA, J.Y. (1978). Sources of management problems in Japanese-American joint ventures. *Academy of Management Review, 3*, 796–804.

PETTIGREW, T.F. (1961). Social psychology and desegregation research. *American Psychologist, 16*, 105–112.

PETTIGREW, T.F. (1997). Generalized intergroup contact effects on prejudice. *Personality and Social Psychology Bulletin, 23*, 173–185.

PETTIGREW, T.F. (1998). Intergroup contact theory. *Annual Review of Psychology, 49*, 65–85.

PETTY, R.E., & CACIOPPO, J.T. (1977). Forewarning, cognitive responding, and resistance to persuasion. *Journal of Personality and Social Psychology, 35*, 645–655.

PETTY, R.E., & CACIOPPO, J.T. (1981). *Attitude and persuasion: Classic and contemporary approaches.* Dubuque, IO: W.C. Brown.

PETTY, R.E., BRINOL, P., & TORMALA, Z.L. (2002). Thought confidence as a determinant of persuasion: The self-validation hypothesis. *Journal of Personality and Social Psychology, 82*, 722–741.

PETTY, R.E., CACIOPPO, J.T., & GOLDMAN, R. (1981). Personal involvement as a determinant of argument-based persuasion. *Journal of Personality and Social Psychology, 41*, 847–855.

PETTY, R.E., OSTROM, T.M., & BROCK, T.C. (1981). *Cognitive responses in persuasive communication: A text in attitude change.* Hillsdale, NJ: Erlbaum.

PETTY, R.E., SCHUMANN, D.W., RICHMAN, S.A., & STRATHMAN, A.J. (1993). Positive mood and persuasion—different roles for affect under high- and low-elaboration conditions. *Journal of Personality and Social Psychology, 64*, 5–20.

PETTY, R.E., WELLS, G.L., & BROCK, T.C. (1976). Distraction can enhance or reduce yielding to propaganda: Thought disruption versus effort justification. *Journal of Personality and Social Psychology, 34*, 874–884.

PFEIFER, J.E. (1989). Courtroom prejudice: An application of symbolic sexism. *Contemporary Social Psychology, 13*, 1–8.

PFEIFER, J.E. (1990). Reviewing the empirical evidence on jury racism: Findings of discrimination or discriminatory findings? *Nebraska Law Review, 69* (1), 230–250.

PFEIFER, J.E. (1992). The psychological framing of cults: Schematic representations and cult evaluations. *Journal of Applied Social Psychology, 22*, 531–544.

PFEIFER, J.E., & BERNSTEIN, D. (1993). *Mock juror decision making and modern racism: Examining the role of task and target specificity on judgemental evaluations.* Unpublished manuscript.

PFEIFER, J.E., & OGLOFF, J.R.P. (1988). *Prejudicial sentencing trends of simulated jurors in Canada.* 49th annual meeting of the Canadian Psychological Association, Montreal.

PFEIFER, J.E., BRIGHAM, J.C., & ROBINSON, T. (1996). Euthanasia on trial: Examining public attitudes towards nonphysician-assisted death. *Journal of Social Issues, 52* (2), 119–129.

PFUNGST, A. (1911). *Clever Hans (the horse of Mr. von Osten): A contribution to experimental, animal and human psychology.* (C. Rahn, Trans.). New York: Holt.

PHETERSON, G.I., KIESLER, S.B., & GOLDBERG, P.A. (1971). Evaluation of the performance of women as a function of their success, achievements, and personal history. *Journal of Personality and Social Psychology, 19,* 114–118.

PHOENIX, A., FROSH, S., & PATTMAN, R. (2003). Producing contradictory masculine subject positions: Narratives of threat, homophobia and bullying in 11–14 year old boys. *Journal of Social Issues, 9,* 179–195.

PIAGET, J. (1932). *The moral development of the child.* London: Routledge & Kegan Paul.

PILIAVIN, I.M., & PILIAVIN, J.A. (1972). The effect of blood on reactions to a victim. *Journal of Personality and Social Psychology, 23,* 253–261.

PILIAVIN, I.M., RODIN, J., & PILIAVIN, J.A. (1969). Good Samaritanism: An underground phenomenon? *Journal of Personality and Social Psychology, 13,* 289–299.

PILIAVIN, J.A., DOVIDIO, J.F., GAERTNER, S.L., & CLARK, R.D. (1981). *Emergency intervention.* New York: Academic Press.

PILISUK, M., & MINKLER, M. (1985). Supportive ties: A political economy perspective. *Health Education Quarterly, 12,* 93–106.

PINES, A., & ARONSON, E. (1983). Antecedents, correlates and consequences of romantic jealousy. *Journal of Personality, 51,* 108–136.

PINQUART, M., & SORENSEN, S. (2001). Influences on loneliness in older adults: A meta-analysis. *Basic and Applied Social Psychology, 23,* 245–266.

PITTMAN, W. (1977). *Now is not too late.* Toronto: Metropolitan Council Task Force.

PLANT, E., & DEVINE, P.G. (2003). The antecedents and implications of interracial anxiety. *Personality and Social Psychology Bulletin, 29,* 780–792.

PLASTRE, G. (1974). Bilinguisme d'enfance et apprentissage ultérieur d'une langue vivante. In S.T. Carey (Ed.), *Bilingualism, biculturalism and education* (pp. 59–74). Edmonton: University of Alberta.

POLIVY, J., & HERMAN, C.P. (2000). The false-hope syndrome: Unfulfilled expectations of self-change. *Current Directions in Psychological Science, 9,* 128–131.

POLIVY, J., & HERMAN, C.P. (2002). If at first you don't succeed. False hopes of self-change. *American Psychologist, 57,* 677–689.

POLIVY, J., & HERMAN, P. (1983). *Breaking the diet habit.* New York: Basic Books.

POLIVY, J., HACKETT, R., & BYCIO, P. (1979). The effect of perceived smoking status on attractiveness. *Personality and Social Psychology Bulletin, 5,* 401–404.

POLLARD, W.E., & MITCHELL, T.R. (1972). Decision theory analysis of social power. *Psychological Bulletin, 78,* 433–446.

POLSTER, M.F. (1992). *Eve's daughters: The forbidden heroism of women.* New York: Jossey-Bass.

POMERANTZ, E.M., CHAIKEN, S., & TORDESILLAS, R.S. (1995) Attitude strength and resistance processes. *Journal of Personality and Social Psychology, 69,* 408–419.

PORIER, G.W., & LOTT, A.J. (1967). Galvanic skin responses and prejudice. *Journal of Personality and Social Psychology, 5,* 253–259.

POSTMES, T., & SPEARS, R. (1998). Deindividuation and antinormative behavior: A meta-analysis. *Psychological Bulletin, 123,* 238–259.

POSTMES, T., SPEARS, R., & LEA, M. (2002). Intergroup differentiation in computer-mediated communication: Effects of depersonalization. *Group Dynamics. 6,* 3–16.

PRATKANIS, A.R., GREENWALD, A.G., LEIPPE, M.R., & BAUMGARDNER, M.H. (1988). In search of reliable persuasion effects. III. The sleeper effect is dead. Long live the sleeper effect. *Journal of Personality and Social Psychology, 54,* 203–218.

PRATT, M.W., PANCER, M., HUNSBERGER, B., & MANCHESTER, J. (1990). Reasoning about the self and relationships in maturity: An integrative complexity analysis of individual differences. *Journal of Personality and Social Psychology, 59,* 575–581.

PREECE, D.A. (1995). *Organizations and technical change: Strategy, objectives, and involvement.* London: Routledge.

PRENTICE-DUNN, S., & ROGERS, R.W. (1982). Effects of public and private self-awareness on deindividuation and aggression. *Journal of Personality and Social Psychology, 43,* 505–513.

PRINCZ, M. (1992). Dating violence: Not an isolated phenomenon. *Vis-à-vis, 9,* 1–4.

PRSZCZYNSKI, T., GREENBERG, J., & SOLOMAN, S. (1999). A dual-process model of defense against conscious and unconscious death-related thoughts. An extension of terror-management theory. *Psychological Review, 106,* 835–845.

PRSZCZYNSKI, T., SOLOMON, S., & GREENBERG, J. (Eds.). (2003). *In the wake of 9/11: The psychology of terror.* Washington: American Psychological Association.

PRUITT, D.G. (1976). Power and bargaining. In B. Seidenberg, & A. Snadowsky (Eds.), *Social psychology: An introduction* (pp. 343–376). New York: Free Press.

PRUITT, D.G., & KIMMEL, M.J. (1977). Twenty years of experimental gaming: Critique, synthesis, and suggestions for the future. *Annual Review of Psychology, 28,* 363–392.

PRUITT, D.G., & RUBIN, J.Z. (1986). *Social conflict: Escalation, stalemate, and settlement.* New York: Random House.

PRYOR, J.B., REEDER, G.D., & MCMANUS, J.A. (1991). Fear and loathing in the workplace: Reactions to AIDS-infected co-workers. *Personality and Social Psychology Bulletin, 17,* 133–139.

PRYOR, J.B., REEDER, G.D., & VINACCO, R. (1989). The instrumental and symbolic functions of attitudes towards persons with AIDS. *Journal of Applied Social Psychology, 19,* 377–404.

PUENTE, S., & COHEN, D. (2003). Jealousy and the meaning (or non-meaning) of violence. *Personality and Social Psychology Bulletin, 29,* 449–460.

PYKE, S. (2001). Feminist psychology in Canada: Early days. *Canadian Psychology, 42,* 268–275.

QUARANTELLI, E. (1954). The behavior of panic participants. *Sociology and Social Research, 41,* 187–194.

QUARANTELLI, E.L. (1960). Images of withdrawal behavior in disasters: Some basic misconceptions. *Social Problems, 8,* 1968–1978.

QUINE, L., RUTTER, D.R., & ARNOLD, L. (2000). Comparing the Theory of Planned Behavior and the Health Beliefs Model: The example of helmet use among schoolboy cyclists. In P. Norman, & C. Abraham (Eds.), *Understanding and changing health behavior:*

From health beliefs to self-regulation (pp. 73–98). Amsterdam: Harwood Academic Publishers.

RADKE-YARROW, M., & ZAHN-WAXLER, C. (1984). Roots, motives, and patterns in children's prosocial behavior. In E. Staub, D. Bar-Tal, J. Karylowski, & J. Reykowski (Eds.), *Development and maintenance of prosocial behavior* (pp. 81–99). New York: Plenum Press.

RAGINS, B.R., & SUNDSTROM, E. (1989). Gender and power in organizations: A longitudinal perspective. *Psychological Bulletin, 105,* 51–88.

RAGLAND, D.R., & BRAND, R.J. (1988). Type A behavior and mortality from coronary heart disease. *New England Journal of Medicine, 318,* 65–69.

RAIKKONEN, K., MATTHEWS, K.A., FLORY, J.D., & OWENS, J.F. (1999). Effects of hostility on ambulatory blood pressure and mood during daily living in healthy adults. *Health Psychology 18,* 44–53.

RAND, M., & LEVINGER, G. (1979). Implicit theories of relationships: An intergenerational study. *Journal of Personality and Social Psychology, 37,* 645–661.

RANK, S.G., & JACOBSON, C.K. (1977). Hospital nurses' compliance with medication overdose orders: A failure to replicate. *Journal of Health and Social Behavior, 18,* 1888–1993.

RAPOPORT, A. (1963). Mathematical models of social interaction. In R.D. Luce, R.R. Bush, & E. Galanter (Eds.), *Handbook of mathematical psychology* (pp. 493–579). New York: Wiley.

RAPOPORT, A. (1968). Prospects for experimental games. *Journal of Conflict Resolution, 12,* 461–470.

RAPOPORT, A., & CHAMMAH, A.M. (1965). *Prisoner's dilemma: A study in conflict and cooperation.* Ann Arbor: University of Michigan Press.

RAPPOPORT, L., & KREN, G. (1993). Amoral rescuers: The ambiguities of altruism. *Creativity Research Journal, 6,* 129–136.

RASINSKI, K.A. (1987). What's fair is fair—or is it? Value differences underlying public views about social justice. *Journal of Personality and Social Psychology, 53,* 201–211.

RAUBOLT, R.R. (2003). Attack on the self and authoritarian group supervision. *Group, 27,* 65–77.

RAUSCHER, F.H., KRAUSS, R.M., & CHEN, Y. (1996). Gesture, speech, and lexical access: The role of lexical movements in speech production. *Psychological Science, 7,* 226–231.

RAVEN, B.H., SCHWARZWALD, J., & KOSLOWSKY, M. (1998). Conceptualizing and measuring a power/interaction model of interpersonal influence. *Journal of Applied Social Psychology, 28,* 307–332.

RAYKO, D.S. (1977). Does knowledge matter? Psychological information and bystander helping. *Canadian Journal of Behavioural Science, 9,* 295–304.

RECKLESS, W.C., & KAY, B.A. (1967). The female offenders. President's Commission on Law Enforcement and the Administration of Justice 1967. Cited by Simon, R.J. (1975). *Women and crime.* Lexington, MA: Heath.

REDFIELD, R. (1955). *The little community.* Chicago: University of Chicago Press.

REEDER, H.M. (2000). I like you as a friend: The role of attraction in cross-sex friendships. *Journal of Social and Personal Relationships, 17,* 329–348.

REGAN, D.T., & TOTTEN, J. (1975). Empathy and attribution: Turning observers into actors. *Journal of Personality and Social Psychology, 32,* 850–856.

REGAN, D.T., WILLIAMS, M., & SPARLING, S. (1972). Voluntary expiation of guilt: A field experiment. *Journal of Personality and Social Psychology, 24,* 42–45.

REICH, C., & PURBHOO, M. (1975). The effect of cross-cultural contact. *Canadian Journal of Behavioural Science, 7,* 313–327.

REICHER, S. (1996). "The crowd" century: Reconciling practical success with theoretical failure. *British Journal of Social Psychology, 35,* 535–553.

REICHER, S., SPEARS, R., & POSTMES, T. (1995). A social identity model of deindividuation phenomena. In W. Stroebe, & M. Hewstone (Eds.), *European review of social psychology* (Vol. 6) (pp. 161–198). Chichester: Wiley.

REID, J.B. (1978). Study of drinking in natural settings. In G.A. Marlatt, & P. Nathan (Eds.), *Behavioral approaches to alcoholism* (pp. 58–75). New Brunswick, NJ: Rutgers Center of Alcohol Studies.

REINISCH, J.M., & SANDERS, S.A. (1986). A test of sex differences in aggressive response to hypothetical conflict situations. *Journal of Personality and Social Psychology, 50,* 1045–1049.

REISENZEIN, R. (1986). A structural equation analysis of Weiner's attribution-affect model of helping behavior. *Journal of Personality and Social Psychology, 50,* 1123–1133.

RENNIE, D. (2002). Qualitative research: History, theory and practice. Special Issue, *Canadian Psychology, 43* (3).

RENTSCH, J.R., & HEFFNER, T.S. (1994). Assessing self-concept: Analysis of Gordon's coding scheme using "Who am I?" responses. *Journal of Social Behavior and Personality, 9,* 283–300.

REYKOWSKI, J. (2002). The justice motive and altruistic helping: Rescuers of Jews in Nazi-occupied Europe. In M. Ross, & D.T. Miller (Eds.), *The justice motive in everyday life* (pp. 251–270). New York: Cambridge University Press.

RHODES, N. (1997). Consumer behavior. In S.W. Sadava, & D.R. McCreary (Eds.). *Applied social psychology* (pp. 185–208). Upper Saddle River, NJ: Prentice-Hall.

RHODES, N., & WOOD, N. (1992). Self-esteem and intelligence affect influencibility: The mediating role of message reception. *Psychological Bulletin, 111,* 156–171.

RICE, G.E., & GAINER, P. (1962). "Altruism" in the albino rat. *Journal of Comparative and Physiological Psychology, 55,* 123–125.

RICE, M.E. (1997). Violent offender research and implications for the criminal justice system. *American Psychologist, 52,* 414–423.

RIESS, M., ROSENFELD, R., MELBURG, V., & TEDESCHI, J.T. (1981). Self-serving attributions: Biased private perceptions and distorted public descriptions. *Journal of Personality and Social Psychology, 41,* 224–231.

RIMÉ, B. (1983). Nonverbal communication or nonverbal behavior? In W. Doise, & S. Moscovici (Eds.), *Current issues in European social psychology* (Vol. 1). (pp. 85–141). Cambridge: Cambridge University Press.

RINGELMANN, M. (1913). Recherches sur les moteurs animés: Travail de l'homme. *Annales de l'Institut National Agronomique, 2e Série-tome XII,* 1–40.

RITTER, J.M., CASEY, R.J., & LANGLOIS, J.H. (1991). Adults' responses to infants varying in appearance of age and attractiveness. *Child Development, 62,* 68–82.

ROACH, M.E., & EICHER, J.B. (1965). *Dress, adornment, and the social order.* New York: Wiley.

ROBERTS, J.V., & EDWARDS, D. (1989). Contextual effects in judgements of crimes, criminals and for purposes of sentencing. *Journal of Applied Social Psychology, 19,* 902–917.

ROBERTS, W.L. (1999). The socialization of emotional expression: Relations with prosocial behaviour and competence in five samples. *Canadian Journal of Behavioural Science, 31,* 72–85.

ROBINSON, M.D., & RYFF, C.D. (1999). The role of self-deception in perceptions of past, present and future happiness. *Personality and Social Psychology Bulletin, 25,* 595–606.

ROBINSON, R.J., KELTNER, D., WARD, A., & ROSS, L. (1995). Actual versus assumed differences in construal: Naive realism in intergroup perception and conflict. *Journal of Personality and Social Psychology, 68,* 404–417.

RODDY, D.B. (2003, March 16). Bush is playing 'chicken' not only with Saddam, but with the U.N. and allies, as well *Pittsburg Post-Gazette.* Downloaded on September 24, 2003 from http://www.post-gazette.com/nation/20030316brinkmanship0316p3.asp.

RODIN, J. (1992). The social construction of premenstrual syndrome. *Social Science and Medicine 35,* 49–56.

RODIN, J., & JANIS, I.L. (1979). The social power of health care practitioners as agents of change. *Journal of Social Issues, 35,* 60–81.

RODIN, J., & LANGER, E.J. (1977). Long-term effects of a control-relevant intervention with the institutionalized aged. *Journal of Personality and Social Psychology, 35,* 897–902.

RODIN, J., SILBERSTEIN, L., & STRIEGEL-MOORE, R. (1985). Women and weight: A normative discontent. In T.B. Sanderegger (Ed.), *Psychology and gender: Nebraska Symposium on Motivation, 1984* (pp. 267–308). Lincoln: University of Nebraska Press.

RODRIGUES, A. (1981). Latin-American social psychology: A review. *Spanish-Language Psychology, 1,* 39–60.

RODRIGUES, A. (1983). Replication: A neglected type of research in social psychology. *Interamerican Journal of Psychology, 16,* 91–109.

ROESE N.J., & SANDE, G.N. (1993). Backlash effects in attack politics. *Journal of Applied Social Psychology, 23,* 632–653.

ROESE, N.J. (1997). Counterfactual thinking. *Psychological Bulletin, 121,* 133–148.

ROGERS, J.K., BULLER, D.B., & WOODALL, W.G. (1989). *Nonverbal communication: The unspoken dialogue.* New York: Harper & Row.

ROGERS, E.M. (1962). *The diffusion of innovations.* New York: Free Press.

ROGERS, E.M., & SHOEMAKER, F. (1971). *Communication of innovations: A cross-cultural approach.* New York: Free Press.

ROGERS, R.W. (1975). A protection motivation theory of fear appeals and attitude change. *Journal of Psychology, 91,* 93–114.

ROGERS, R.W. (1983). Cognitive and physiological processes in fear appeals and attitude change: A revised theory of protection motivation. In J.T. Cacioppo, & R.E. Petty (Eds.), *Social psychophysiology: A sourcebook* (pp. 153–176). New York: Guilford.

ROGERS, T.B., KUIPER, N.A., & KIRKER, W.S. (1977). Self-reference and the encoding of personal information. *Journal of Personality and Social Psychology, 35,* 677–688.

ROKEACH, M. (1960). *The open and closed mind.* New York: Basic Books.

ROKEACH, M. (1968). *Beliefs, attitudes, and values.* San Francisco: Jossey-Bass.

ROKEACH, M. (1973). *The nature of human values.* New York: Free Press.

ROKEACH, M. (1979). *Understanding human values: Individual and societal.* New York: Free Press.

ROKEACH, M., & BALL-ROKEACH, S.J. (1989). Stability and change in American value priorities. *American Psychologist, 44,* 775–784.

ROLLINS, B. (1976). *First you cry.* Philadelphia: Lippincott.

RONIS, D.L. (1992). Conditional health threats: Health beliefs, decisions and behaviors among adults. *Health Psychology, 11,* 127–134.

ROSEN, S., TOMARELLI, M.M., KIDDA, M.L., Jr., & MEDVIN, N. (1986). Effects of motive for helping recipient's inability to reciprocate, and sex on devaluation of the recipient's competence. *Journal of Personality and Social Psychology, 50,* 729–736.

ROSENBAUM, L.L., & ROSENBAUM, W.B. (1971). Morale and productivity consequences of group leadership style, stress and type of task. *Journal of Applied Psychology, 55,* 343–348.

ROSENBAUM, M.E. (1986). The repulsion hypothesis: On the nondevelopment of relationships. *Journal of Personality and Social Psychology, 51,* 1156–1166.

ROSENBERG, M. (1957). *Occupations and values.* Glencoe, IL: Free Press.

ROSENBERG, M.J. (1965). When dissonance fails: On eliminating evaluation apprehension from attitude measurement. *Journal of Personality and Social Psychology, 1,* 28–42.

ROSENBERG, M.J. (1969). The conditions and consequences of evaluation apprehension. In R. Rosenthal, & R.L. Rosnow (Eds.), *Artifact in behavioral research* (pp. 279–349). New York: Academic Press.

ROSENHAN, D. (1970). The natural socialization of altruistic autonomy. In J. Macaulay, & L. Berkowitz (Eds.), *Altruism and helping behavior.* New York: Academic Press.

ROSENHAN, D. (1972). Learning theory and prosocial behavior. *Journal of Social Issues, 28,* 151–164.

ROSENMAN, R.H., BRAND, R.J., JENKINS, C.D., FRIEDMAN, M., STRAUS, R., & WURM, M. (1975). Coronary heart disease in the Western Collaborative Group Study: Final follow-up experience of 8 years. *Journal of the American Medical Association, 233,* 872–877.

ROSENTHAL, R. (1966). *Experimenter effects in behavioral research.* New York: Appleton-Century-Crofts.

ROSENZWEIG, J.M., & DALEY, D.M. (1989). Dyadic adjustment/sexual satisfaction in women and men as a function of psychological sex-role self-perception. *Journal of Sex and Marital Therapy, 15,* 42–56.

ROSKIES, E., SERAGANIAN, P., OSEASOHN, R., HANLEY, J.A., CALLU, R., MARTIN, N., & SMILGA, C. (1986). The Montreal Type A Intervention Project: Major findings. *Health Psychology, 5,* 45–70.

ROSKOS-EWOLDSEN, D.R., & FAZIO, R.H. (1992a). On the orienting value of attitudes: Attitude accessibility as a determinant of an object's attraction of visual attention. *Journal of Personality and Social Psychology, 63,* 198–211.

ROSKOS-EWOLDSEN, D.R., & FAZIO, R.H. (1992b). The accessibility of source likeability as a determinant of persuasion. *Personality and Social Psychology Bulletin, 18,* 19–25.

ROSNOW, R.L. (1980). Psychology of rumor reconsidered. *Psychological Bulletin, 87,* 578–591.

ROSNOW, R.L. (1991). Inside rumor. *American Psychologist, 46,* 484–496.

ROSNOW, R.L., & FINE, G.A. (1976). *Rumor and gossip: The social psychology of hearsay.* New York: Elsevier.

ROSNOW, R.L., YOST, J.H., & ESPOSITO, J.L. (1986). Belief in rumor and likelihood of rumor transmission. *Language and Communication, 6,* 189–194.

ROSS, A.S. (1978). *It's shorter in a crowd* [Film by W. Troyer]. Toronto: TAAW Productions.

ROSS, A.S., & BRABAND, J. (1973). Effect of increased responsibility on bystander intervention II: The cue value of a blind person. *Journal of Personality and Social Psychology, 25,* 254–258.

ROSS, L. (1977). The intuitive psychologist and his shortcomings: Distortions in the attribution process. In L. Berkowitz (Ed.), *Advances in experimental social psychology* (Vol. 10). New York: Academic Press.

ROSS, L. (1981). The "intuitive scientist": Formulation and its developmental implications. In J.H. Havell, & L. Ross (Eds.), *Social cognitive development: Frontiers and possible futures* (pp. 38–90). Cambridge: Cambridge University Press.

ROSS, L., GREENE, D., & HOUSE, P. (1977). The "false consensus effect": An egocentric bias in social perception and attribution processes. *Journal of Experimental Social Psychology, 13,* 279–301.

ROSS, M. (1989). Relation of implicit theories to the construction of personal histories. *Psychological Review, 96,* 341–357.

ROSS, M., & CONWAY, M. (1985). Remembering one's own past: The construction of personal histories. In R. Sorrentino, & E.T. Higgins (Eds.), *Handbook of motivation and cognition* (pp. 122–144). New York: Guilford.

ROSS, M., & SICOLY, F. (1979). Egocentric biases in availability and attribution. *Journal of Personality and Social Psychology, 37,* 322–336.

ROSS, M., MCFARLAND, C., CONWAY, M., & ZANNA, M.P. (1983). Reciprocal relation between attitude and behavior recall: Committing people to newly formed attitudes. *Journal of Personality and Social Psychology, 45,* 257–267.

ROSS, M., XUN, W.Q.E., & WILSON, A.E. (2002). Language and the bicultural self. *Personality and Social Psychology Bulletin, 28,* 1040–1050.

ROSS, W.H., & CONLON, D.E. (2000). Hybrid forms of third-party dispute resolution: Theoretical implications of combining mediation and arbitration. *Academy of Management Review, 25,* 416–427.

ROTER, D.L., & HALL, J.A. (1992). *Doctors talking with patients/Patients talking with doctors.* Westport, CT: Auburn House.

ROTER, D.L., HALL, J.A., MERISCA, R., & NORDSTROM, B. (1998). Effectiveness of interventions to improve patient compliance: A meta-analysis. *Medical Care, 36,* 1138–1161.

ROTH, D.L., WIEBE, D.J., FILLINGIM, R.B., & SHAY, K.A. (1989). Life events, hardiness and health: A simultaneous analysis of proposed stress-resistance effects. *Journal of Personality and Social Psychology, 57,* 136–142.

ROTHBART, M., & JOHN, O.P. (1985). Social categorization and behavioral episodes: A cognitive analysis of intergroup contact. *Journal of Social Issues, 41,* 81–104.

ROTHBART, M., FULERO, S., JENSEN, C., HOWARD, J., & BIRRELL, B. (1978). From individual to group impressions: Availability heuristics in stereotype formation. *Journal of Experimental Social Psychology, 14,* 237–255.

ROTTER, J.B. (1966). Generalized expectancies for internal versus external control of reinforcement. *Psychological Monographs, 80* (1, whole no. 609).

ROTTON, J., & COHN, E.G. (2000). Violence is a curvilinear function of temperature in Dallas. *JPSP, 78,* 1074–1081.

ROY, M.P., STEPTOE, A., & KIRSCHBAUM, C. (1998). Life events and social support as moderators of individual differences in cardiovascular and cortisol reactivity. *Journal of Personality and Social Psychology, 75,* 1273–1281.

RUBACK, R.B., & DABBS, J.M. (1988). Group vocal patterns and leadership in India: Effects of task, language, and sex of subjects. *Journal of Cross-Cultural Psychology, 19,* 446–464.

RUBEN, D.H. (1998). Social exchange theory: Dynamics of a system governing the dysfunctional family and guide to assessment. *Journal of Contemporary Psychotherapy, 28,* 307–325.

RUBENSTEIN, C.M., & SHAVER, P. (1982). The experience of loneliness. In L. Peplau, & D. Perlman (Eds.), *Loneliness: A sourcebook of current theory, research and therapy.* New York: Wiley.

RUBIN, J. (1976). How to tell when someone is saying no. *Topics in Culture Learning, 4,* 61–65.

RUBIN, J.Z. (1989). Some wise and mistaken assumptions about conflict and negotiation. *Journal of Social Sciences, 45,* 195–209.

RUBIN, Z. (1970a). Measurement of romantic love. *Journal of Personality and Social Psychology, 16,* 265–273.

RUBIN, Z. (1970b). *Liking and loving.* New York: Holt, Rinehart & Winston.

RUBIN, Z. (1973). *Liking and loving: An invitation to social psychology.* New York: Holt, Rinehart and Winston.

RUBIN, Z. (1974). Lovers and other strangers. The development of intimacy in encounters and relationships. *American Scientist, 62,* 182–190.

RUBIN, Z. (1975). Disclosing oneself to a stranger: Reciprocity and its limits. *Journal of Experimental Social Psychology, 11,* 233–260.

RUBY, C.L., & BRIGHAM, J.C. (1996). A criminal schema: Role of chronicity, race and SES in law enforcement officials' perception of others. *Journal of Applied Social Psychology, 26,* 95–111.

RUDMIN, F. (1985). William McDougall in the history of social psychology. *British Journal of Social Psychology, 24,* 75–76.

RUDMIN, F.W. (1989). The pleasure of serendipity in histological research: On finding "stereotype" in Morier's (1824) Hajji Baba. *Cross-Cultural Psychology Bulletin, 23,* 8–11.

RUGGIERO, K.M., & TAYLOR (1997). Why minority group members perceive or do not perceive the discrimination that confronts them. Role of self-esteem and perceived control.. *Journal of Personality and Social Psychology, 72,* 373–389.

RUGGIERO, K.M., & TAYLOR, D.M. (1995). Coping with discrimination. How disadvantaged group members perceive the discrimination that confronts them. *Journal of Personality and Social Psychology, 68,* 826–838.

RULE, B.G., & ADAIR, J. (1984). Contributions of psychology as a social science to Canadian society. *Canadian Psychology, 25,* 52–58.

RULE, B.G., & NESDALE, A.R. (1974). Differing functions of aggression. *Journal of Personality, 42,* 467–481.

RULE, B.G., & WELLS, G.L. (1981). Experimental social psychology in Canada: A look at the seventies. *Canadian Psychology, 22,* 69–84.

RUSBULT, C.E. (1983). A longitudinal test of the investment model: The development (and deterioration) of satisfaction and commitment in heterosexual involvement. *Journal of Personality and Social Psychology, 45,* 101–117.

RUSBULT, C.E., & MARTZ, J.M. (1995). Remaining in an abusive relationship: An investment model analysis of nonvoluntary dependence. *Personality and Social Psychology Bulletin, 21,* 558–571.

RUSH, M.C., & RUSSELL, J.E.A. (1988). Leader prototypes and prototype-contingent consensus in leader behavior descriptions. *Journal of Experimental Social Psychology, 24,* 88–104.

RUSHTON, J.P. (1977). *Television and prosocial behaviour. Report of the Royal Commission on Violence in the Communications Industry* (Vol. 5). (pp. 31–56). Toronto: Government of Ontario.

RUSHTON, J.P. (1978). Urban density: Helping strangers in a Canadian city, suburb, and small town. *Psychological Reports, 43,* 987–990.

RUSHTON, J.P. (1980). *Altruism, socialization, and society.* Englewood Cliffs, NJ: Prentice-Hall.

RUSHTON, J.P. (1984). The altruistic personality. In E. Staub, D. Bar-Tal, J. Karylowski, & J. Reykowski (Eds.), *Development and maintenance of prosocial behavior* (pp. 271–290). New York: Plenum Press.

RUSHTON, J.P. (1988a). Race differences in behaviour: A review and evolutionary analysis. *Personality and Individual Differences, 9,* 1009–1024.

RUSHTON, J.P. (1988b). The reality of racial differences: A rejoinder with new evidence. *Personality and Individual Differences, 9,* 1035–1040.

RUSHTON, J.P. (1989, January 19). Evolutionary biology and heritable traits (with reference to Oriental-White-Black differences). Annual Meeting of the American Association for the Advancement of Science, San Francisco.

RUSSELL, B. (1959). *Common sense and nuclear warfare.* London: Unwin Brothers.

RUSSELL, B. (1962). *Power.* New York: Barnes & Noble.

RUSSELL, D., PEPLAU, L.A., & CUTRONA, C.E. (1980). The revised UCLA loneliness scale: Concurrent and discriminant validity evidence. *Journal of Personality and Social Psychology, 39,* 472–480.

RUSSELL, J.A. (1994). Is there universal recognition of emotion from facial expression? A review of the cross-cultural studies. *Psychological Bulletin, 115,* 102–141.

RUSSELL, J.A., & MEHRABIAN, A. (1978). Approach-avoidance and affiliation as functions of the emotion-eliciting quality of an environment. *Environment and Behavior, 10,* 355–388.

RUTTER, M. (1987). Psychological resilience and protective mechanisms. *American Journal of Orthopsychiatry, 57,* 316–331.

RYAN, E.B., BARTOLUCCI, G., GILES, H., & HENWOOD, K. (1986). Psycholinguistics and social psychological components of communication by and with older adults. *Language and Communication, 6,* 1–22.

SABINI, J., SIEPMAN, M., & STEIN, J. (2001). The really fundamental attribution error in social psychological research. *Psychological Inquiry, 12,* 1–15.

SADAVA, S.W. (1978a). *From the outside looking in: The experience of the instructor and student of social psychology in Canada.* Annual Conference of the Canadian Psychological Association.

SADAVA, S.W. (1978b). Teaching social psychology: A Canadian dilemma. *Canadian Psychological Review, 19,* 145–151.

SADAVA, S.W. (1985). Problem behavior theory and consumption and consequences of alcohol use. *Journal of Studies on Alcohol, 46,* 392–397.

SADAVA, S.W. (1987). Interactional theories. In H.T. Blane, & K.E. Leonard (Eds.), *Psychological theories of drinking and alcoholism* (pp. 90–130). New York: Guilford.

SADAVA, S.W., & FORSYTH, R. (1977a). Person-environment interaction and college student drug use: A multivariate longitudinal study. *Genetic Psychology Monographs, 96,* 211–245.

SADAVA, S.W., & FORSYTH, R. (1977b). Turning on, turning off and relapse: Social psychological determinants of status change in cannabis use. *International Journal of the Addictions, 12,* 509–528.

SADAVA, S.W., & MATEJCIC, C. (1987). Generalized and specific loneliness in early marriage. *Canadian Journal of Behavioural Science, 19,* 56–66.

SADAVA, S.W., & MCCREARY, D. (1996, August). Adult attachment style and health: Mediating role of social support and health behaviours. International Congress of Psychology, Montréal.

SADAVA, S.W., & MOLNAR, D.S. (2003, June). Attachment style and health: Affective, social and behavioural mediation. Presented at the annual meeting of the Canadian Psychological Association, Hamilton, Ontario.

SADAVA, S.W., & THOMPSON, M.M. (1986). Loneliness, social drinking and vulnerability to alcohol problems. *Canadian Journal of Behavioural Science, 18,* 133–139.

SADAVA, S.W., ANGUS, L., & FORSYTH, R. (1980). Perceived mental illness and diminished responsibility: A study of attributions. *Social Behavior and Personality, 8,* 129–136.

SADAVA, S.W., DECOURVILLE, N., & MCCREARY, D. (1996). Depression and health: Linkages to health-protective behaviours. American Psychological Association, Toronto.

SAFER, M.A. (1980). Attributing evil to the subject, not the situation: Student reaction to Milgram's film on obedience. *Personality and Social Psychology Bulletin, 6,* 205–209.

SAGARIN, B.J., CIALDINI, R.B., RICE, W.E., & SERNA, S.B. (2002). Dispelling the illusion of invulnerability: The motivations and mechanisms of resistance to persuasion. *Journal of Personality and Social Psychology, 83,* 526–541.

SALOVEY, P., & RODIN, J. (1984). Some antecedents and consequences of social comparison jealousy. *Journal of Personality and Social Psychology, 47,* 780–792.

SAMPSON, E.E. (1975). On justice as equality. *Journal of Social Issues, 31,* 45–64.

SAMPSON, E.E. (1977). Psychology and the American ideal. *Journal of Personality and Social Psychology, 35,* 767–782.

SAMUELSON, C.D., & MESSICK, D.M. (1986). Inequities in access to and use of shared resources in social dilemmas. *Journal of Personality and Social Psychology, 51,* 960–967.

SAMUELSON, C.D., MESSICK, D.M., RUTTE, C.G., & WILKE, H. (1984). Individual and structural solutions to resource dilemmas in two cultures. *Journal of Personality and Social Psychology, 47,* 94–104.

SANDE, G.N. (1990). The multifaceted self. In J.M. Olson, & M.P. Zanna (Eds.), *Self-inference processes: The Ontario symposium* (Vol. 6). (pp. 1–16). Hillsdale, NJ: Erlbaum.

SANDERS, G.S. (1983). An attentional process model of social facilitation. In A. Hare, H. Blumberg, V. Kent, & M. Davies (Eds.), *Small Groups.* London: Wiley.

SANDERS, G.S., BARON, R.S., & MOORE, D.L. (1978). Distraction and social comparison as mediators of social facilitation effects. *Journal of Experimental Social Psychology, 14,* 291–303.

SANNER, M. (1994). Attitudes toward organ donation and transplantation: A model for understanding reactions to medical procedures after death. *Social Science and Medicine, 38,* 1141–1152.

SAPPINGTON, A.A., & BAKER, J. (1995). Refining religious belief–behavior relations. *International Journal for the Psychology of Religion, 5,* 38–48.

SARAT, A., & VIDMAR, N. (1976). Public opinion, the death penalty and the eighth amendment: Testing the Marshall hypothesis. *Wisconsin Law Review, 27,* 171–206.

SARLES, R.M. (1976). Child abuse. In D.S. Madden, & J.R. Lion (Eds.), *Rage, hate, assault and other forms of violence* (pp. 1–16). New York: Spectrum.

SASHKIN, M. (1977). The structure of charismatic leadership. In J.G. Hunt, & L.L. Larson (Eds.), *Leadership: The cutting edge* (pp. 212–218). Carbondale: Southern Illinois University Press.

SATOW, K.L. (1975). Social approval and helping. *Journal of Experimental Social Psychology, 11,* 501–509.

SAUL, E.V., & KASS, T.S. (1969). Study of anticipated anxiety in a medical school setting. *Journal of Medical Education, 44,* 526.

SAULNIER, K., & PERLMAN, D. (1981). The actor-observer bias is alive and well in prison: A sequel to Wells. *Personality and Social Psychology Bulletin, 7,* 559–564.

SAVAGE, S.A., & CLARKE, V.S. (1996). Factors associated with screening mammography and breast self-examination intentions. *Health Education Research, 11,* 409–421.

SAWADA, Y. (2003). Blood pressure and heart rate responses to an intrusion on personal space. *Japanese Psychological Research, 45,* 115–121.

SAWHNEY, M.M. (1967). Farm practice adoption and the use of information sources and media in a rural community in India. *Rural Sociology, 32,* 310–323.

SAWREY, J.M., & TELFORD, C.W. (1975). *Adjustment and personality* (5th ed.). Boston: Allyn & Bacon.

SCHACHTER, S. (1951). Deviation, rejection and communication. *Journal of Abnormal Social Psychology, 46*, 190–207.

SCHACHTER, S. (1959). *The psychology of affiliation.* Stanford, CA: Stanford University Press.

SCHACHTER, S. (1964). The interaction of cognitive and physiological determinants of emotional state. In L. Berkowitz (Ed.), *Advances in experimental social psychology* (Vol. 1). (pp. 48–81). New York: Academic Press.

SCHACHTER, S. (1982). Recidivism and self-cure of smoking and obesity. *American Psychologist, 37*, 436–444.

SCHACHTER, S., & BURDECK, H. (1955). A field experiment on rumour transmission and distortion. *Journal of Abnormal and Social Psychology, 50*, 363–371.

SCHACHTER, S., ELLERTSON, N., MCBRIDE, D., & GREGORY, D. (1951). An experimental study of cohesiveness and productivity. *Human Relations, 4*, 229–238.

SCHAIE, K.W. (1993). Ageist language in psychological research. *American Psychologist, 48*, 49–51.

SCHEIER, M.F., & BRIDGES, M.W. (1995). Person variables and health: Personality predispositions and acute psychological states as shared determinants for disease. *Psychosomatic Medicine, 57*, 255–268.

SCHELLING, T.C. (1960). *The strategy of conflict.* Cambridge: Harvard University Press.

SCHER, S.J., & COOPER, J. (1989). Motivational basis of dissonance: The singular role of behavioral consequences. *Journal of Personality and Social Psychology, 56*, 899–906.

SCHERER, K.R., & WALLBOTT, H.G. (1994). Evidence for universality and cultural variation of differential emotion response patterning. *Journal of Personality and Social Psychology, 66*, 310–328.

SCHLEGEL, R.P., D'AVERNAS, J.R., ZANNA, M.P., DE COURVILLE, N.H., & MANSKE, S.R. (1992). Problem drinking: A problem for the theory of reasoned action. *Journal of Applied Social Psychology, 22*, 358–385.

SCHLEGEL, R.P., MANSKE, S.R., & D'AVERNAS, J.R. (1985). Alcohol and drug use in young adults. Selected findings in a longitudinal study. *Bulletin of the Society of Psychologists in Addictive Behavior, 4*, 213–225.

SCHMIDT, D.E., & KEATING, J.P. (1979). Human crowding and personal control. *Psychological Bulletin, 86*, 680–700.

SCHMITT, B.H. (1988). Social comparison in romantic jealousy. *Personality and Social Psychology Bulletin, 14*, 374–387.

SCHMITT, B.H., GILOVICH, T., GOORE, N., & JOSEPH, L. (1986). Mere presence and socio-facilitation: One more time. *Journal of Experimental Social Psychology, 22*, 242–248.

SCHOENEMAN, T.J., & RUBANOWITX, D.E. (1985). Attributions in the advice columns: I. Actors, observers, causes and reasons. *Personality and Social Psychology Bulletin, 11*, 315–325.

SCHULLER, R.A. (1992). The impact of battered woman syndrome evidence on jury decision processes. *Law and Human Behavior, 16*, 597–620.

SCHULLER, R.A. (1994). Application of battered woman syndrome evidence in the courtroom. In M. Costanzo, & S. Oskamp (Eds.), *Violence and the law. The Claremont Symposium on Applied Social Psychology* (pp. 113–134). Thousand Oaks, CA: Sage.

SCHULLER, R.A., & HASTINGS, P.A. (1996). Trials of battered women who kill: The impact of alternative forms of expert evidence. *Law and Human Behavior, 20*, 167–187.

SCHULLER, R.A., & VIDMAR, N. (1992). Battered woman syndrome evidence in the courtroom: A review of the literature. *Law and Human Behavior, 16*, 273–291.

SCHULLER, R.A., SMITH, V.L., & OLSON, J.M. (1994). Jurors' decisions in trials of battered women who kill: The role of prior beliefs and expert testimony. *Journal of Applied Social Psychology, 24*, 316–337.

SCHULTZ, D.P. (1964). *Panic behavior.* New York: Random House.

SCHULTZ, T.R., & LEPPER, M.R. (1996). Cognitive dissonance as constraint satisfaction. *Psychological Review, 103*, 219–240.

SCHULTZ, T.R., LÉVEILLÉ, E., & LEPPTER, M.R. (1999). Free choice and cognitive dissonance revisited: Choosing the "lesser evils" versus "greater goods." *Personality & Social Psychology Bulletin 25*, 40–48.

SCHWARTZ, S. (1994). Heuristics and biases in medical judgement and decision making. In L. Heath, R.S. Tindale, J. Edwards, E.J. Posavac, F.B. Bryant, E. Henderson-King, Y. Suarez-Balcazar, & J. Myers (Eds.) *Applications of heuristics and biases to social issues* (pp. 45–72). New York: Plenum Press.

SCHWARTZ, S. (1996). Value priorities and behavior: Applying a theory of integrated value systems. In C. Seligman, J.M. Olson, & M.P. Zanna (Eds.), *The Psychology of values: The Ontario symposium* (Vol. 8). (pp. 1–24). Hillsdale, NJ: Lawrence Erlbaum Associates.

SCHWARTZ, S.H. (1992). Universals in the content and structure of values: theoretical advances and empirical tests in 20 countries. In M.P. Zanna (Ed.), *Advances in Experimental Social Psychology, 25*, 1–65. San Diego: Academic.

SCRIMSHAW, E.W. (2002). Social support, conflict and integration among women living with HIV/AIDS. *Journal of Applied Social Psychology, 32*, 2022–2042.

SCRIVNER, E., & SAFER, M.A. (1988). Eyewitnesses show hyperamnesia for details about a violent event. *Journal of Personality and Social Psychology, 73*, 371–377.

SEARLE, J.R. (1969). *Speech acts.* Cambridge: Cambridge University Press.

SEARLE, J.R. (1975). Indirect speech acts. In P. Cole, & J.L. Morgan (Eds.), *Syntax and semantics 3: Speech acts* (pp. 283–298). Hillsdale, NJ: Erlbaum.

SEARS, D.O. (1983). The person-positivity bias. *Journal of Personality and Social Psychology, 44*, 233–250.

SEDIKIDES, C., & ANDERSON, C.A. (1994). Causal perception of inter-trait relations: The glue that holds person types together. *Personality and Social Psychology Bulletin, 21*, 294–302.

SEEMAN, T.E., DUBIN, L.F.L., & SEEMAN, M. (2003). Religiosity/spirituality and health. A critical review of evidence for biological pathways. *American Psychologist, 58*, 53–63.

SEGALL, M.H., LONNER, W.J., & BERRY, J.W. (1998). Cross-cultural psychology as a scholarly discipline: On the flowering of culture in behavioral research. *American Psychologist, 53*, 1101–1110.

SEGALOWITZ, N. (1976). Communicative incompetence and the non-fluent bilingual. *Canadian Journal of Behavioural Science, 8*, 122–131.

SELIGMAN, C., FAZIO, R.H., & ZANNA, M.P. (1980). Effects of salience of extrinsic rewards on liking and loving. *Journal of Personality and Social Psychology, 38*, 453–460.

SELIGMAN, C., OLSON, J.M., & ZANNA, M.P. (Eds.). (1996). *The psychology of values: The Ontario symposium* (Vol. 8). Mahwah, NJ: Lawrence Erlbaum Associates.

SELIGMAN, C., TUCKER, G.R., & LAMBERT, W.E. (1972). The effects of speech style and other attributes on teachers' attitudes towards pupils. *Language in Society, 1*, 131–142.

SELIGMAN, M.E.P., & CSIKSZENTMIHALYI, M. (2000). Positive psychology: An introduction. *American Psychologist, 55*, 5–14.

SELYE, H. (1956). *The stress of life.* New York: McGraw-Hill.

SENSENIG, P.E., & CIALDINI, R.B. (1984). Social psychological influences on the compliance process: Implications for behavioral health. In J.D. Matarazzo, S.M. Weiss, J.A. Herd, N.E. Miller, & S.M. Weiss (Eds.), *Behavioral health* (pp. 384–392). Toronto: Wiley.

SERMAT, V. (1978). Sources of loneliness. *Essence, 2,* 271–276.

SEYDEL, E., TAAL, E., & WIEGMAN, O. (1990). Risk-appraisal, outcome and efficacy expectancies: Cognitive factors in preventive behavior related to cancer. *Psychology and Health, 4,* 99–109.

SHANTEAU, J., & NAGY, G.F. (1979). Probability of acceptance in dating choice. *Journal of Personality and Social Psychology, 37,* 522–533.

SHAPIRO, D.E., BOGGS, S.R., MELAMED, B.G., & GRAHAM-POLE, J. (1992). The effects of varied physician affect on recall anxiety and perceptions in women at risk for breast cancer: An analogue study. *Health Psychology, 11,* 61–66.

SHAPIRO, D.M., & STELCNER, M. (1987). Earning disparities among linguistic groups in Québec, 1970–1980. *Analyse de politique, 13,* 97–104.

SHAPIRO, P.N., & PENROD, S. (1986). Meta-analysis of facial identification studies. *Psychological Bulletin, 100,* 139–156.

SHARPSTEEN, D.J. (1995). The effects of relationship and self-esteem threats on the likelihood of romantic jealousy. *Journal of Social and Personal Relationships, 12,* 89–101.

SHARPSTEEN, D.J., & KIRKPATRICK, L.A. (1997). Romantic jealousy and adult attachment. *Journal of Personality and Social Psychology, 72,* 89–101.

SHAVER, K.G. (1970). Defensive attribution: Effects of severity and relevance on the responsibility assigned for an accident. *Journal of Personality and Social Psychology, 14,* 101–113.

SHAVER, P.R., & BRENNAN, K.A. (1992). Attachment styles and the "big five" personality traits: Their connection with each other and with romantic relationship outcomes. *Personality and Social Psychology Bulletin, 18,* 536–545.

SHAW, L.H., & GANT, L.M. (2002). In defence of the Internet. The relationship between Internet communication and depression, loneliness, self-esteem and perceived social support. *CyberPsychology and Behavior, 5,* 157–171.

SHAW, M.E. (1981). *Group dynamics: The psychology of small group behavior* (3rd ed.). New York: McGraw-Hill.

SHEPHERD, J.W., DEREGOWSKI, J.B., & ELLIS, H.D. (1974). A cross-cultural study of recognition memory for faces. *International Journal of Psychology, 9,* 205–211.

SHEPPARD, B.H., & VIDMAR, N. (1980). Adversary pretrial procedure and testimonial evidence: Effects of lawyer's role and Machiavellianism. *Journal of Personality and Social Psychology, 39,* 320–332.

SHERIF, M. (1936). *The psychology of social norms.* New York: Harper & Row.

SHERIF, M. (1937). An experimental approach to the study of attitudes. *Sociometry, 1,* 90–98.

SHERIF, M. (1958). Superordinate goals in the reduction of intergroup conflict. *American Journal of Sociology,* 349–356.

SHERIF, M., & CANTRIL, H. (1947). *The psychology of ego involvement: Social attitudes and identification.* New York: Wiley.

SHERIF, M., HARVEY, O.J., WHITE, B.J., HOOD, W.R., & SHERIF, C. (1961). *Intergroup conflict and cooperation: The Robber's Cave experiment.* Norman, OK: University of Oklahoma Press.

SHERMAN, D.K., & COHEN, G.L. (2002). Accepting threatening information: Self-affirmation and the decision of defensive biases. *Current Directions in Psychological Science, 11,* 119–123.

SHERMAN, S.J., CHASSIN, L., PRESSON, C.L., & AGNOSTINELLI, G. (1984). The role of evaluation and similarity principles in the false consensus effect. *Journal of Personality and Social Psychology, 47,* 1244–1262.

SHERROD, D.R. (1974). Crowding, perceived control and behavioral aftereffects. *Journal of Applied Social Psychology, 4,* 171–186.

SHESTOWSKI, D., WEGENER, D.T., & FABRIGAR, L.R. (1992). Need for cognition and interpersonal influence: Individual differences in dyadic decisions. *Journal of Personality and Social Psychology, 74,* 1317–1328.

SHETZ, J.N. (1974). An investigation of relationships among evaluative beliefs, affect, behavioral intentions, and behavior. In J.V. Farley, J.A. Howard, & L.W. Ring (Eds.), *Consumer behavior: Theory and applications* (pp. 89–114). Boston: Allyn & Bacon.

SHIBUTANI, T. (1966). *Improvised news: A sociological study of rumor.* Indianapolis, IL: Bobbs-Merrill.

SHILOH, S. (1994). Heuristics and biases in medical judgement and decision making. In L. Heath, R.S. Tindale, J. Edwards, E.J. Posavac, F.B. Bryant, E. Henderson-King, Y. Suarez-Balcazar, & J. Myers (Eds.), *Applications of heuristics and biases to social issues* (pp. 45–72). New York: Plenum Press.

SHOEMAKER, D.J., SOUTH, D.R., & LOWE, J. (1973). Facial stereotypes of deviants and judgements of guilt or innocence. *Social Forces, 51,* 427–433.

SHOTLAND, R.L., & GOODSTEIN, L. (1992). Sexual precedence reduces the perceived legitimacy of sexual refusal: An examination of attributions concerning date rape and consensual sex. *Personality and Social Psychology Bulletin, 18,* 756–764.

SIBICKY, M.E., SCHROEDER, D.A., & DOVIDIO, J.F. (1995). Empathy and helping: Considering the consequences of intervention. *Basic and Applied Social Psychology, 16,* 435–453.

SIEM, F.M., & SPENCE, J.T. (1986). Gender-related traits and helping behaviors. *Journal of Personality and Social Psychology, 51,* 615–621.

SIGALL, H., & OSTROVE, N. (1975). Beautiful but dangerous: Effects of offender attractiveness and nature of the crime on juridic judgement. *Journal of Personality and Social Psychology, 31,* 410–414.

SILVER, R.C., HOLMAN, E., MCINTOSH, D.N., POULIN, M., & GIL-RIVAS, V. (2002). Nationwide longitudinal study of psychological responses to September 11. *JAMA: Journal of the American Medical Association, 288,* 1235–1244.

SILVER, R.L., BOON, C., & STONES, M.H. (1983). Searching for meaning in misfortune: Making sense of incest. *Journal of Social Issues, 39,* 81–100.

SILVERMAN, I. (1971). On the resolution and tolerance of cognitive consistency in a natural occurring event: Attitudes and beliefs following the Senator Edward M. Kennedy incident. *Journal of Personality and Social Psychology, 17,* 171–178.

SILVERMAN, I. (1974). *Some hedonistic considerations regarding altruistic behavior.* Southeastern Psychological Association Annual Meeting, Miami.

SIMARD, L., TAYLOR, D.M., & GILES, H. (1977). Attribution processes and interpersonal accommodation in a bilingual setting. *Language and Speech, 19,* 374–387.

SIMMONS, R.G., SCHIMMEL, M., & BUTTERWORTH, V.A. (1993). The self-image of unrelated bone marrow donors. *Journal of Health and Social Behavior, 34,* 285–301.

SIMON, B., LOEWY, M., STÜRMER, S., WEBER, U., FREYTAG, P., HABIG, C., KAMPMEIER, C., & SPAHLINGER, P. (1998). Collective identification and social movement participation. *Journal of Personality and Social Psychology, 74,* 646–658.

SIMON, R.J., & MAHAN, L. (1971). Quantifying burdens of proof: A view from the bench, the jury and the classroom. *Law and Society Review, 5*, 319–330.

SIMPSON, J.A. (1987). The dissolution of romantic relationships: Factors involved in relationship stability and emotional distress. *Journal of Personality and Social Psychology, 53*, 683–692.

SIMPSON, J.A., RHOLES, W.S., & NELLIGAN, J.S. (1992). Support seeking and support giving within couples in an anxiety-provoking situation: The role of attachment styles. *Journal of Personality and Social Psychology, 62*, 434–446.

SIMPSON, S., MCCARRY, M., & EDWARDS, H.P. (1987). Relationship of supervisors' sex role stereotypes to performance evaluation of male and female subordinates in non-traditional jobs. *Canadian Journal of Administrative Science, 4*, 15–30.

SIMS, H.P., & MANZ, C.C. (1984). Observing leader verbal behavior: Toward reciprocal determinism in leadership theory. *Journal of Applied Psychology, 69*, 222–232.

SINCLAIR, C., POIZNER, S., GILMOUR-BARRETT, K., & RANDALL, D. (1987). The development of a code of ethics for Canadian psychologists. *Canadian Psychology, 28*, 1–8.

SINCLAIR, L., & KUNDA, Z. (2000). Motivated stereotyping of women. She's fine if she praised me but incompetent if she criticized me. *Personality & Social Psychology Bulletin, 26*, 1329–1342.

SINCLAIR, R.C., & MARK, M.M. (1992). The influence of mood state on judgement and action: Effects on persuasion, categorization, social justice, person perception and judgmental accuracy. In L.L. Martin, & A. Tesser (Eds.), *The construction of social judgements* (pp. 165–193). Hillsdale, NJ: Erlbaum.

SINCLAIR, R.C., LEE, T., & JOHNSON, T.E. (1995). The effect of social-comparison feedback on aggressive responses to erotic and aggressive films. *Journal of Applied Social Psychology, 25*, 818–837.

SINCLAIR, R.C., MARK, M.M., & CLORE, G.L. (1994). Mood-related persuasion depends on (mis)attributions. *Social Cognition, 12*, 309–326.

SINGER, J.E., BAUM, C.S., BAUM, A., & THEW, B.D. (1982). Mass psychogenic illness: The case for social comparison. In M.J. Colligan, J.W. Pennebaker, & L.R. Murphy (Eds.), *Mass psychogenic illness* (pp. 155–170). Hillsdale, NJ: Erlbaum.

SINGER, J.L., & SINGER, D.G. (1986). Family experiences and television viewing as predictors of children's imagination, restlessness and aggression. *Journal of Social Issues, 42*, 107–124.

SINGH, D., & YOUNG, R.K. (1995). Body weight, hip-to-waist ratio, breasts and hips: Role in judgments of female attractiveness and desirability for relationship. *Ethology and Sociobiology, 16*, 483–507.

SINGH, R., & HO, S.Y. (2000). Attitudes and attraction: A new test of the attraction, repulsion and similarity-dissimilarity asymmetry hypothesis. *British Journal of Social Psychology, 39*, 197–211.

SINGH, V.P., & PAREEK, U. (1970). Discriminant function in a profile pattern of key communicators in an Indian village. *International Journal of Psychology, 5*, 99–107.

SIROIS, F. (1982). Perspectives on epidemic hysteria. In M.J. Colligan, J.W. Pennebaker, & L.R. Murphy (Eds.), *Mass psychogenic illness: A social psychological analysis* (pp. 217–236). Hillsdale, NJ: Erlbaum.

SISTRUNK, F., & MCDAVID, V.W. (1971). Sex variable in conformity behavior. *Journal of Personality and Social Psychology, 17*, 200–207.

SIVACEK, J., & CRANO, W.D. (1982). Vested interest as a moderator of attitude-behavior consistency. *Journal of Personality and Social Psychology, 43*, 210–221.

SIX, U. (1989). The functions of sterotypes and prejudices in the process of cross-cultural understanding: A social psychologial approach. In P.

Funckle (Ed.), *Understanding the U.S.A.: A cross-cultural perspective.* Tubingen: Narr.

SKOWRONSKI, J.J., & CARLSTON, D.E. (1989). Negativity and extremity biases in impression formation: A review of explanations. *Psychological Bulletin, 105*, 131–142.

SLOAN, J.H., KELLERMANN, A.L., REAY, D.I., FENIS, J.A., KOEPSELL, T., RIVARA, F.P., RICE, C., GRAY, L., & LOGERFO, J. (1988). Handgun regulations, crime, assaults, and homicide: A tale of two cities. *New England Journal of Medicine, 319*, 1256–1262.

SMEATON, G., BYRNE, D., & MURNEN, S.K. (1989). The repulsion hypothesis revisited: Similarity irrelevance or dissimilarity bias? *Journal of Personality and Social Psychology, 56*, 54–59.

SMITH, C.P. (1983). Ethical issues: Research on deception, informed consent, and debriefing. In L. Wheeler, & P. Shaver (Eds.), *Review of personality and social psychology* (Vol. 4). (pp. 297–328). Beverly Hills, CA: Sage.

SMITH, P.M. (1985). *Language, the sexes and society.* Oxford: Basil Blackwell.

SMITH, R.H., TURNER, T.J., GARONZIK, R., LEACH, C.W., URCH-DRUSKAT, V., & WESTON, C.M. (1996). Envy and Schadenfreude. *Personality and Social Psychology Bulletin, 22*, 158–168.

SMITH, S.M., & PETTY, R.E. (1996). Message framing and persuasion: A message processing analysis. *Personality and Social Psychology Bulletin, 22*, 257–268.

SMITH, V.L., & ELLSWORTH, P.C. (1987). The social psychology of eyewitness accuracy: Misleading questions and communicator expertise. *Journal of Applied Psychology, 72*, 294–300.

SNAREY, J.R. (1985). Cross-cultural universality of social-moral development: A critical review of Kohlbergian research. *Psychological Bulletin, 97*, 202–232.

SNOW, C.P. (1961, February 24). Either-or. *Progressive.*

SNYDER, C.R. (1997). Control and the application of Occam's razor to terror management theory. *Psychological Inquiry, 8*, 48–49.

SNYDER, M. (1979). Self-monitoring processes. In L. Berkowitz (Ed.), *Advances in experimental social psychology* (Vol. 12). (pp. 85–128). New York: Academic Press.

SNYDER, M., & DEBONO, K.G. (1985). Appeals to image and claims about quality: Understanding the psychology of advertising. *Journal of Personality and Social Psychology, 49*, 586–597.

SOBAL, J., & STUNKARD, A.J. (1989). Socioeconomic status and obesity: A review of the literature. *Psychological Bulletin, 105*, 260–275.

SOIFER, E. (1996). Euthenasia and persistent vegetative state individuals: The role and moral status of autonomy. *Journal of Social Issues, 52* (2), 31–50.

SOLANO, C.H., & KOESTER, N.H. (1989). Loneliness and communication problems: Subjective anxiety or objective skills? *Personality and Social Psychology Bulletin, 15*, 126–133.

SOLANO, C.H., BATTEN, P.G., & PARISH, E.A. (1982). Loneliness and patterns of self-disclosure. *Journal of Personality and Social Psychology, 43*, 524–531.

SOLE, K., MARTON, J., & HORNSTEIN, H.A. (1975). Opinion similarity and helping: Three field experiments investigating the bases of promotive tension. *Journal of Experimental Social Psychology, 11*, 1–13.

SOLOMON, D., & YAEGER, J. (1969). Effect of content and intonation on perceptions of verbal reinforcers. *Perceptual and Motor Skills, 28*, 319–327.

SOLOMON, L. (1960). The influence of some types of power relationships and game strategies upon the development of interpersonal trust. *Journal of Abnormal and Social Psychology, 61*, 223–230.

SOLOMON, M.R. (1986). Dress for effect. *Psychology Today, 20* (4), 20–28.

SOMMER, B. (1992). Cognitive performance and the menstrual cycle. In J.T. Richardson (Ed.), *Cognition and the menstrual cycle: Research, theory and culture* (pp. 249–277). New York: Springer-Verlag.

SONTAG, S. (1978). *Illness as metaphor.* New York: Farrar, Straus & Giroux.

SOUSSIGNAN, R. (2002). Duchenne smile, emotional experience, and autonomic reactivity: A test of the facial feedback hypothesis. *Emotion, 2,* 52–54.

SPANOS, N.P. (1982). Hypnotic behavior: A cognitive, social psychological perspective. *Research Communications in Psychology, Psychiatry and Behavior, 3,* 199–213.

SPEER, A. (1970). *Inside the Third Reich.* Toronto: Macmillan.

SPELLMAN, B.A., & HOLYOAK, K.J. (1992). If Saddam is Hitler, then who is George Bush? Analogical mapping between systems of social roles. *Journal of Personality and Social Psychology, 62,* 913–933.

SPENCE, J.T. (1985). Gender identity and its implications for the concepts of masculinity and femininity. In T.B. Sonderegger (Ed.), *Nebraska symposium on motivation: Psychology and gender* (pp. 59–95). Lincoln, NE: University of Nebraska Press.

SPIEGEL, D., BLOOM, J.R., KRAEMER, H.C., & GOTTHEIL, E. (1989). Psychological support for cancer patients. *Lancet, 2,* 1447.

SPORER, S.L., PENROD, S., READ, D., & CUTLER, B. (1995). Choosing, confidence and accuracy: A meta-analysis of the confidence-accuracy relation in eyewitness identification studies. *Psychological Bulletin, 118,* 315–327.

SPRAFKIN, J.N., LIEBERT, R.M., & POULOS, R.W. (1975). Effects of a prosocial televised example on children's helping. *Journal of Experimental Child Psychology, 20,* 119–126.

SPRECHER, S. (2001). Equity and social exchange in dating couples; Associations with satisfaction, commitment and stability. *Journal of Marriage and the Family, 63,* 599–613.

SPRECHER, S. (2001). A comparison of emotional consequences of and changes in equity over time using global and domain-specific measures of equity. *Journal of Social and Personal Relationships, 18,* 477–501.

SPRECHER, S., FELMLEE, D., METTS, S., FEHR, B., & VANNI, D. (1998). Factors associated with distress following breakup of a close relationship. *Journal of Social and Personal Relationships, 15,* 791–809.

SPROULE, C.F., & KENNETT, D.J. (1988). The use of firearms in Canadian homicides 1972–1982: The need for gun control. *Canadian Journal of Criminology, 30,* 31–37.

SPROULE, L. & KEISLER, S. (1991). Computers, networks, and work. *Scientific American, 265,* 116–123.

SRULL, T.K., & WEYER, R.J. (1989). Person memory and judgement. *Psychological Review, 96,* 58–83.

SRULL, T.K., & WEYER, R.J., Jr. (1980). Category accessibility and social perception: Some implications for the study of personal memory and interpersonal judgements. *Journal of Personality and Social Psychology, 38,* 841–856.

STAFFIERI, J.R. (1972). Body build and behavioural expectancies in young females. *Developmental Psychology, 6,* 125–127.

STAHELSKI, A.J., & FROST, D.E. (1989). Use of socially dependent bases of power: French and Raven's theory applied to workgroup leadership. *Journal of Applied Social Psychology, 19,* 283–297.

STANG, D.J. (1972). Conformity, ability, and self-esteem. *Representative Research in Social Psychology, 3,* 97–103.

STARK-ADAMEC, C., & KIMBALL, M. (1984). Science free of sexism: A psychologist's guide to the conduct of non-sexist research. *Canadian Psychology, 25,* 23–34.

STATISTICS CANADA (1989). *Homicide in Canada 1988: A statistical perspective.* Ottawa: Ministry of Supply and Services.

STATISTICS CANADA (1992a). *Canadian Crime Statistics 1991.* Ottawa: Supplies and Services Canada.

STATISTICS CANADA (2002). http://www.statcan.ca/english/freepub/85–224–XIE/85–224–XIE00002.pdf *Family violence in Canada, 2002: A statistical profile.*

STATISTICS CANADA (2003). http://www12.statcan.ca/english/census01/Products/Analytic/companion/lang/bilingual.cfm

STATISTICS CANADA re sexual and physical assault http://www.statcan.ca/english/freepub/85–224–XIE/85–224–XIE00002.pdf

STAUB, E. (1974). Helping a distressed person: Social, personality and stimulus determinants. In L. Berkowitz (Ed.), *Advances in experimental social psychology* (Vol. 7). (pp. 294–341). New York: Academic Press.

STAUB, E. (1975). *The development of prosocial behavior in children.* Morristown, NJ: Silver Burdett/General Learning Press.

STAUB, E., & BAER, R.S. (1974). Stimulus characteristics of a sufferer and difficulty of escape as determinants of helping. *Journal of Personality and Social Psychology, 30,* 279–285.

STEBLAY, N.M. (1987). Helping behavior in rural and urban environmemts: A meta-analysis. *Psychological Bulletin, 102,* 346–356.

STEELE, C.M. (1997). A threat in the air. How stereotypes shape intellectual identity and performance. *American Psychologist, 52,* 613–629.

STEELE, C.M., & JOSEPHS, R.A. (1990). Alcohol myopia: Its prized and dangerous effects. *American Psychologist, 45,* 921–933.

STEELE, C.M., & LIU, T.J. (1983). Dissonance process as self-affirmation. *Journal of Personality and Social Psychology, 45,* 5–19.

STEELE, C.M., SOUTHWICK, L.C., & CRITCHLOW, B. (1981). Dissonance and alcohol: Drinking your troubles away. *Journal of Personality and Social Psychology, 41,* 831–846.

STEINER, I.D. (1972). *Group process and productivity.* New York: Academic Press.

STEPHAN, C.W., & STEPHAN, W.G. (1986). Habla ingles? The effects of language translation on simulated juror decisions. *Journal of Applied Social Psychology, 16,* 577–589.

STEPHAN, W.G., & STEPHAN, C.W. (1985). Intergroup anxiety. *Journal of Social Issues, 41,* 157–175.

STERNBERG, R.J. (1986). A triangular theory of love. *Psychological Review, 93,* 119–135.

STERNBERG, R.J., & GRAJEK, S. (1984). The nature of love. *Journal of Personality and Social Psychology, 47,* 312–329.

STIRLING, G., & REID, D.W. (1992). The application of participatory control to facilitate patient well-being. An experimental study of nursing impact on geriatric patients. *Canadian Journal of Behavioural Science, 24,* 204–219.

STOCKARD, J., VAN-DE-KRAGT, A.J., & DODGE, P.J. (1988). Gender roles and behaviour in social dilemmas: Are there sex differences in cooperation and its justification? *Social Psychology Quarterly, 51,* 154–163.

STOGDILL, R. (1974). *Handbook of leadership.* New York: Free Press.

STONE, A., & NEALE, J.M. (1982). Development of a methodology for assessing daily experiences. In A. Baum, & J.E. Singer (Eds.), *Advances in environmental psychology* (Vol. 4). (pp. 49–83). Hillsdale: Erlbaum.

STONE, A.A., HEDGES, S.M., NEALE, J.M., & SATIN, M.S. (1985). Prospective and cross-sectional mood reports offer no evidence of a "blue Monday"phenomenon. *Journal of Personality and Social Psychology 49*, 129–134.

STONE, G.C. (1979). Patient compliance and the role of the expert. *Journal of Social Issues, 35*, 34–59.

STONE, J., ARONSON, E., CRAIN, A.L., WINSLOW, M.P., & FRIED, C. (1994). Inducing hypocrisy as a means of encouraging young adults to use condoms. *Personality and Consumer Research, 28*, 636–649.

STORM, C., & STORM, T. (1987). A taxonomic study of the vocabulary of emotions. *Journal of Personality and Social Psychology, 53*, 805–816.

STORMS, M.D. (1973). Videotape and the attribution process: Reversing actor's and observer's points of view. *Journal of Personality and Social Psychology, 27*, 165–175.

STOVER, E., & NIGHTINGALE, E.O. (1985). *The breaking of bodies and minds. Torture, psychiatric abuse, and the health professions*. New York: W.H. Freeman.

STRAUMAN, T.J. (1996). Stability within the self: A longitudinal study of the structural implications of self-discrepancy theory. *Journal of Personality and Social Psychology, 71*, 1142–1153.

STRECHER, V.J., CHAMPION, V.L., & ROSENSTOCK, I.M. (1997). The health beliefs model and health behaviour. In D.S. Gochman et al. (Eds.), *Handbook of health behaviour research: 1. Personal and social determinants* (pp. 71–91). New York: Plenum Press.

STRICKLAND, B.R. (1978). Internal-external expectancies and health-related behaviors. *Journal of Consulting and Clinical Psychology, 46*, 1192–1211.

STRICKLAND, L.H. (1958). Surveillance and trust. *Journal of Personality, 26*, 200–215.

STRICKLAND, L.H. (1991). Russian and Soviet social psychology. *Canadian Psychology, 32*, 580–595.

STRODTBECK, F.L., & LIPINSKI, R.M. (1985). Becoming first among equals: Moral considerations in jury foreman selection. *Journal of Personality and Social Psychology, 49*, 927–936.

STROEBE, M.S., & STROEBE, W. (1983). Who suffers more? Sex differences in health risks of the widowed. *Psychological Bulletin, 93*, 279–301.

STROEBE, W., DIEHL, M., & ABAKOUMKIN, G. (1992). The illusion of group effectivity. *Personality and Social Psychology Bulletin, 18*, 643–650.

STROEBE, W.H., STROEBE, M., GERGEN, K.J., & GERGEN, M.M. (1982). The effects of bereavement on mortality: A social psychological analysis. In J.R. Eisere (Ed.), *Social psychology and behavioral medicine*. London: Wiley.

STRUBE, M.J., & GARCIA, J.E. (1981). A meta-analytic investigation of Fiedler's contingency model of leadership effectiveness. *Psychological Bulletin, 90*, 307–321.

STURGES, J.W., & ROGERS, R.W. (1996). Preventive health psychology from a developmental perspective: An extension of protection motivation theory. *Health Psychology, 15*, 158–166.

SUEDFELD, P. (2000). Reverberations of the Holocaust fifty years later: Psychology's contributions to understanding persecution and genocide. *Canadian Psychology, 41*, 1–9.

SUEDFELD, P. (2003). Canadian space psychology: The future may be almost here. *Canadian Psychology, 44, 85–92.*

SUEDFELD, P., & BLUCK, S. (1993). Changes in integrative complexity accompanying significant life events: Historical evidence. *Journal of Personality and Social Psychology, 64*, 124–130.

SUEDFELD, P., & LEIGHTON, D.C. (2002). Early communications in the war against terrorism: An integrative complexity analysis. *Political Psychology. 23*, 585–599.

SUEDFELD, P., & PIEDRAHITA, L.E. (1984). Intimations of mortality: Integrative simplification as a precursor of death. *Journal of Personality and Social Psychology, 47*, 848–852.

SUEDFELD, P., & RANK, A.D. (1976). Revolutionary leaders: Long-term success as a function of changes in conceptual complexity. *Journal of Personality and Social Psychology, 34*, 169–176.

SUEDFELD, P., RANK, A.D., & BORRIE, R. (1975). Frequency of exposure and evaluation of candidates and campaign speeches. *Journal of Applied Psychology, 5*, 118–126.

SULLIVAN, M.J.L., BISHOP, S.R., & PIVIK, J. (1995). The Pain Catastrophizing Scale: Development and validation. *Psychological Assessment. 7.* 524–532.

SULLIVAN, M.J.L., RODGERS, W.M., & KIRSCH, I. (2001). Catastrophizing, depression and expectancies for pain and emotional distress. *Pain, 91*, 147–154.

SULLIVAN, M.J.L., THORN, B., HAYTHORNTHWAITE, J.A., KEEFE, F., MARTIN, M., BRADLEY, L.A., & LEFEBVRE, J.C. (2001). Theoretical perspectives on the relation between catastrophizing and pain. *Clinical Journal of Pain, 17*, 52–64.

SULLIVAN, P.J., FELTZ, & FELTZ, D.L. (2001). The relationship between intrateam conflict and cohesion within hockey teams. *Small Group Research, 32*, 342–355.

SUPER, D.E. (1980). A life-span life-space approach to career development. *Journal of Vocational Behaviour, 16*, 282–298.

SUSSMAN, N.M., & ROSENFELD, H.M. (1982). Influence of culture, language and sex on conversational distance. *Journal of Personality and Social Psychology, 42*, 66–74.

SUTTON, S. (1998) Predicting and explaining intentions and behaviour. *Journal of Applied Social Psychology, 28*, 1317–1338.

SUTTON, S.R. (1982). Fear-arousing communications: A critical examination of theory and research. In J.R. Eiser (Ed.), *Social psychology and behavioral medicine* (pp. 303–338). New York: Wiley.

SWANN, W. (1992). Seeking "truth," finding despair: Some unhappy consequences of a negative self-concept. *Current Directions in Psychological Science, 1*, 15–18.

SWANN, W., & READ, S.J. (1981). Acquiring self-knowledge: The search for feedback that fits. *Journal of Personality and Social Psychology, 41*, 1119–1128.

SWANN, W., STEIN-SEROUSSI, A., & GIESLER, R. B. (1992). Why people self-verify. *Journal of Personality and Social Psychology, 62*, 392–401.

SWANN, W.B., Jr. (1990). To be adored or to be known? The interplay of self-enhancement and self-verification. In R.M. Sorrentino, & E.T. Higgins (Eds.), *Motivation and cognition* (pp. 414–448). New York: Guilford Press.

SWEENEY, P.D., ANDERSON, K., & BAILEY, S. (1986). Attribution style in depression: A meta-analytic review. *Journal of Personality and Social Psychology, 50*, 974–991.

SWIM, J., BORGIDA, E., & MARUYAMA, G. (1989). Joan McKay versus John McKay: Do gender stereotypes bias evaluation? *Psychological Bulletin, 105*, 409–429.

SWINGLE, P.G. (1968). Illusory power in a dangerous game. *Canadian Journal of Psychology, 22*, 176–185.

SWINGLE, P.G. (1970). Dangerous games. In P.G. Swingle (Ed.), *The structure of conflict* (pp. 235–276). New York: Academic Press.

SYKES, R.E., ROWLEY, R.D., & SCHAEFFER, J.M. (1993). The influence of time, gender and group size on heavy drinking in public bars. *Journal of Studies on Alcohol, 54,* 133–138.

SZYMANSKI, K., & HARKINS, S. (1987). Social loafing and self-evaluation with a social standard. *Journal of Personality and Social Psychology, 53,* 891–897.

TAJFEL, H. (1970). Experiments in intergroup discrimination. *Scientific American, 223* (5), 96–102.

TAJFEL, H. (1982). Social psychology of intergroup relations. *Annual Review of Psychology, 33,* 1–39.

TAJFEL, H. (Ed.) (1978). *Differentiation between social groups: Studies in the social psychology of inter-group relations.* London: Academic Press.

TAJFEL, H., & TURNER, J.C. (1979). An integrative theory of intergroup conflict. In W.G. Austin, & S. Worchel (Eds.), *The social psychology of intergroup relations* (pp. 33–47). Monterey, CA: Brooks/Cole.

TALLMAN, I., BURKE, P.J., & GECAS, V. (1998). Socialization into marital roles: Testing a contextual, developmental model of marital functioning. In T.N. Bradbury et al. (Eds.), *The developmental course of marital dysfunction* (pp. 312–342). New York, NY: Cambridge University Press.

TAM, B.K.Y., & BOND, M.H. (2002). Interpersonal behavior and friendship in a Chinese culture. *Asian Journal of Social Psychology, 5,* 63–74.

TAN, D.T.Y., & SINGH, R. (1995). Attitudes and attraction: A developmental study of the similarity-attraction and dissimilarity repulsion hypotheses. *Personality and Social Psychology Bulletin, 21,* 975–986.

TANFORD, J.A. (1990). The law and psychology of jury instructions. *Nebraska Law Review, 69* (1), 71–111.

TANFORD, S., & PENROD, S. (1984). Social influence processes in juror judgements of multiple offence trials. *Journal of Personality and Social Psychology, 95,* 189–225.

TANNEN, D. (1990). *You just don't understand: Women and men in conversation.* New York: Morrow.

TAYLOR, D.M. (1981). Stereotypes and intergroup relations. In R.C. Gardner, & R. Kalin (Eds.), *A Canadian social psychology of ethnic relations* (pp. 151–171). Toronto: Methuen.

TAYLOR, D.M., & LALONDE, R.N. (1987). Ethnic stereotypes: A psychological analysis. In L. Driedger (Ed.), *Ethnic Canada: Identities and inequalities.* Toronto: Copp Clark Pittman.

TAYLOR, D.M., & MCKIRNON, D.J. (1984). A five-stage model of intergroup relations. *British Journal of Social Psychology, 23,* 291–300.

TAYLOR, D.M., & MOGHADDAM, F.M. (1987). *Theories of intergroup relations: International social psychological perspective.* New York: Praeger.

TAYLOR, D.M., & SIMARD, L. (1975). Social interaction in a bilingual setting. *Canadian Psychological Review, 16,* 240–254.

TAYLOR, D.M., WRIGHT, S.C., & PORTER, L.E. (1994). Dimensions of perceived discrimination: The personal/group discrimination discrepancy. In M.P. Zanna, & J.M. Olson (Eds.), *The Ontario symposium. Vol. 7: The psychology of prejudice* (pp. 233–255). Hillsdale, NJ: Erlbaum.

TAYLOR, D.M., WRIGHT, S.C., MOGHADDAM, F.M., & LALONDE, R.N. (1990). The personal/group discrimination discrepancy: Perceiving my group but not myself to be a target of discrimination. *Personality and Social Psychology Bulletin, 16,* 254–262.

TAYLOR, J., & MACDONALD, J. (2002). The effects of asynchronous computer-mediated group interaction on group processes. *Social Science Computer Review, 20,* 260–274.

TAYLOR, J., & RIESS, M. (1989). Self-serving attributions to valenced causal factors. *Personality and Social Psychology Bulletin, 15,* 337–348.

TAYLOR, S.E. (1979). Hospital patient behavior: Reactance, helplessness or control? *Journal of Social Issues, 35,* 156–184.

TAYLOR, S.E., & BROWN, J.D. (1988). Illusion and well-being: A social-psychological perspective on mental health. *Psychological Bulletin, 103,* 193–210.

TAYLOR, S.E., FALKE, R.L., SHOPTAW, S.J., & LICHTMAN, R.R. (1986). Social support, support groups and the cancer patient. *Journal of Consulting and Clinical Psychology, 54,* 608–615.

TAYLOR, S.E., KEMENY, G.M., REED, G.M., BOWER, J.E., & GRUENWALD, T.L. (2000). Psychological resources, positive illusions and health. *American Psychologist, 55,* 99–109.

TAYLOR, S.E., KEMENY, M.E., ASPINWALL, L.G., SCHNEIDER, S.G., RODRIGUEZ, S.G., RODRIGUEZ, R., & HERBERT, M. (1992). Optimism, coping, psychological distress and high-risk sexual behavior among men at risk for acquired immunodeficiency syndrome (AIDS). *Journal of Personality and Social Psychology, 63,* 460–473.

TAYNOR, J., & DEAUX, K. (1973). Equity and perceived sex differences: Role behavior as defined by the task, the mode, and the actor. *Journal of Personality and Social Psychology, 32,* 381–390.

TEDESCHI, J.T. (1983). Social influence theory and aggression. In R.G. Geen, & E.I. Donnerstein (Eds.), *Aggression: Theoretical and empirical reviews* (Vol. 1). (pp. 135–162) New York: Academic Press.

TEDESCHI, J.T., SMITH, R.B., & BROWN, R.C. (1974). A reinterpretation of research on aggression. *Psychological Bulletin, 81,* 540–562.

TEMOSHOK, L., SWEET, D.M., & ZICH, J. (1987). A three-city comparison of the public's knowledge and attitudes about AIDS. *Psychology and Health, 1,* 43–60.

TENNEN, H., AFFLECK, G., URROWS, S., HIGGINS, P., & MENDOLA, R. (1992). Perceiving control, construing benefits and daily processes in rheumatoid arthritis. *Canadian Journal of Behavioural Science, 24,* 186–203.

TENNOV, D. (1979). *Love and limerance: The experience of being in love.* New York: Stein and Day.

TESSER, A. (1978). Self-generated attitude change. In L. Berkowitz (Ed.), *Advances in experimental social psychology* (Vol. 11). (pp. 288–338). New York: Academic Press.

TESSER, A. (1988). Toward a self-evaluation maintenance model of social behavior. In L. Berkowitz (Ed.), *Advances in experimental social psychology* (Vol. 21). (pp. 181–227). New York: Academic Press.

TESSER, A., & PAULHUS, D.L. (1976). Toward a causal model of love. *Journal of Personality and Social Psychology, 34,* 1095–1105.

TESSER, A., & ROSEN, S. (1975). *Why subjects say they would or would not communicate affectively-toned messages.* Annual Meeting of Southeastern Psychological Association, Atlanta, GA.

TESSER, A., MILLAR, M., & MOORE, J. (1988). Some affective consequences of social comparison and reflection processes: The pain and pleasure of being close. *Journal of Personality and Social Psychology, 54,* 49–61.

TETLOCK, P.E. (1979). Identifying victims of groupthink from public statements of decision makers. *Journal of Personality and Social Psychology, 37,* 1314–1324.

TETLOCK, P.E. (1983). Policymakers' images of international conflict. *Journal of Social Issues, 39,* 67–86.

TETLOCK, P.E. (1984). Cognitive style and political belief systems in the British House of Commons. *Journal of Personality and Social Psychology, 46,* 365–375.

TETLOCK, P.E. (1986). A value pluralism model of ideological reasoning. *Journal of Personality and Social Psychology, 50,* 819–827.

TETLOCK, P.E. (1987). Testing deterrence theory: Some conceptual and methodological issues. *Journal of Social Issues, 43,* 85–91.

TETLOCK, P.E., BERNZWEIG, J., & GALLANT, J.L. (1985). Supreme Court decision-making: Cognitive style as a predictor of ideological consistency of voting. *Journal of Personality and Social Psychology, 48,* 1227–1239.

TETLOCK, P.E., PETERSON, R.S., MCGUIRE, C., CHONG, S., & FIELD, P. (1992). Assessing political group dynamics: A test of the groupthink model. *Journal of Personality and Social Psychology, 63,* 403–425.

TETT, R.P., BOBOCEL, R., HAFER, C., LEES, M., SMITH, C.A., & JACKSON, D.N. (1992). The dimensionality of type A behavior within a stressful work simulation. *Journal of Personality, 60,* 534–551.

THAYER, S., & SAARNI, C. (1975). Demand characteristics are everywhere (anyway): A comment on the Stanford prison experiment. *American Psychologist, 30,* 1015–1016.

THIBAUT, J., & WALKER, L. (1975). *Procedural justice: A psychological analysis.* Hillsdale, NJ: Erlbaum.

THIBAUT, J.W., & KELLEY, H.H. (1959). *The social psychology of groups.* New York: Wiley.

THIBODEAU, R., & ARONSON, E. (1992). Taking a closer look: Reasserting the role of the self-concept in dissonance theory. *Personality and Social Psychology Bulletin, 18,* 591–602.

THOMPSON, B., & BORRELLO, G.M. (1992). Different views of love: Deductive and inductive lines of inquiry. *Current Directions in Psychological Science, 1,* 154–156.

THOMPSON, H.L., & RICHARDSON, D.R. (1983). The rooster effect: Same-sex rivalry and inequity as factors in retaliatory aggression. *Personality and Social Psychology Bulletin, 9,* 415–525.

THOMPSON, K.S., & OSKAMP, S. (1974). Difficulties in replicating the proselytizing effect in doomsday groups. *Psychological Reports, 35,* 971–978.

THOMPSON, S.C. (1999). Illusions of control: How we overestimate our personal influence. *Current Directions in Psychological Science, 8,* 187–190.

THOMPSON, S.C., ARMSTRONG, W., & THOMAS, C. (1998). Illusion of control, underestimations and accuracy: a control heuristic explanation. *Psychological Bulletin, 123,* 143–161.

THORESON, C.E., & POWELL, L.H. (1992). Type A behavior pattern: New perspectives on theory, assessment and intervention. *Journal of Consulting and Clinical Psychology, 60,* 595–604.

THORNHILL, R., & GANGESTAD, S.W. (1993). Human facial beauty: Averageness, symmetry and parasite resistance. *Human Nature 4,* 237–269.

TOCH, H. (1965). *The social psychology of social movements.* Indianapolis, IL: Bobbs-Merrill.

TOLSTEDT, B.E., & STOKES, J.P. (1984). Self-disclosure, intimacy and the depenetration process. *Journal of Personality and Social Psychology, 46,* 84–90.

TOMKINS, A.J., & PFEIFER, J.E. (1991). Modern social scientific theories and data concerning discrimination: Implications for using social science evidence in the courtroom. In D.K. Kagehiro, & W.S. Laufer (Eds.), *Handbook of psychology and law* (pp. 385–404). New York: Springer-Verlag.

TORMALA, Z.L., & PETTY, R.E. (2002). What doesn't kill me makes me stronger: The effects of resisting persuasion on attitude certainty. *Journal of Personality and Social Psychology, 83,* 1298–1313.

TOTTERDALL, P., KELLEEETT, S., TEUCHMANN, K., & BRINER, R.B. (1998). Evidence of mood linkage in work groups. *Journal of Personality and Social Psychology, 74,* 1504–1515.

TOUGAS, F., BROWN, R., BEATON, A.M., & JOLY, S. (1995). Neosexism: Plus ça change, plus c'est pareil. *Personality and Social Psychology Bulletin, 21,* 842–849.

TOUGAS, F., CROSBY, F., JOLY, S., & PELCHAT, D. (1995). Men's attitude toward affirmative action: Justice and Intergroup relations at the crossroads. *Social Justice Research, 8,* 57–70.

TOURANGEAU, R., & RASINSKI, K.A. (1988). Cognitive processes underlying context effects in attitude measurement. *Psychological Bulletin, 103,* 299–314.

TOWNSEND, P., & DAVIDSON, N. (1982). Inequalities in health. Harmondsworth, UK: Penguin.

TRAUPMANN, J., & HATFIELD, E. (1981). Love and its effect on mental and physical health. In R. Fogel, E. Hatfield, S. Kiesler, & E. Shanas (Eds.), *Aging: Stability and change in the family* (pp. 253–274). New York: Academic Press.

TRAVIS, L.E. (1925). The effect of a small audience upon eye-hand coordination. *Journal of Abnormal and Social Psychology, 20,* 142–146.

TREMBLAY, M. (1953). Orientations de la Pensée Sociale. In J.C. Falardeau (Ed.), *Essais sur le Québec contemporain.* Québec: Les Presses Universitaires Laval.

TRIANDIS, H.C. (1972). *The analysis of subjective culture.* New York: John Wiley & Sons.

TRIANDIS, H.C. (1989). The Self and Social Behavior in differing cultural contexts. *Psychological Review, 96,* 506–520.

TRIPLET, R.G., & SUGARMAN, D.B. (1987). Reactions to AIDS victims: Ambiguity breeds contempt. *Personality and Social Psychology Bulletin, 13,* 265–274.

TRIPLETT, N. (1897). The dynamogenic factors in pacemaking and competition. *American Journal of Psychology, 9,* 507–533.

TROCHIM, W.M.K. (1999). Research methods knowledge base (2nd ed.) [Online]. Retrieved from the World Wide Web: www.trochim.human.cornell.edu/kb/qual.htm

TRUMAN-SCHRAM, D.M., CANN, A., CALHOUN, L., & VANWALLENDAEL, L. (2000). Leaving an abusive dating relationship: An investment model comparison of women who stay versus women who leave. *Journal of Social & Clinical Psychology, 19,* 161–183.

TSENG, W., KAN-MING, M., HSU, J., LI-SHUEN, L., LI-WAH, O., GUO-QIAN, C., & DA-WEI, J. (1988). A sociocultural study of koro epidemics in Guangdong, China. *American Journal of Psychiatry, 145,* 1538–1543.

TUCKER, G.R. (1981). Social policy and second language teaching. In R.C. Gardner, & R. Kalin (Eds.), *A Canadian social psychology of ethnic relations* (pp. 77–92). Toronto: Metheun.

TURNER, J.C. (1982). Toward a cognitive redefinition of the social group. In H. Tajfel (Ed.), *Social identity and intergroup relations* (pp. 15–40). Cambridge: Cambridge University Press.

TURNER, J.C. (1985). Social categorization and the self-concept: A social-cognitive theory of group behaviour. In J.E. Lawler (Ed.), *Advances in group processes* (Vol. 2). (pp. 77–122). Greenwich: JAI Press.

TURNER, J.C., WETHERELL, M.S., & HOGG, M.A. (1989). Referent informational influence and group polarization. *British Journal of Social Psychology, 18,* 135–147.

TURNER, R.H. (1964). Collective behaviour. In R.E.L. Faris (Ed.), *Handbook of Modern Sociology* (pp. 382–425). Chicago: Rand McNally.

TURNER, R.H., & KILLIAN, L.M. (1972). *Collective behavior* (2nd ed.). Englewood Cliffs, NJ: Prentice-Hall.

TVERSKY, A., & KAHNEMAN, D. (1973). Availability: A heuristic for judging frequency and probability. *Cognitive Psychology, 5,* 207–232.

TVERSKY, A., & KAHNEMAN, D. (1974). Judgement under uncertainty: Heuristics and biases. *Science, 185,* 1124–1131.

TVERSKY, A., & KAHNEMAN, D. (1982). Judgment under uncertainty: Heuristics and biases. In D. Kahneman, P. Slovic, & A. Tversky (Eds.), *Judgment under uncertainty: Heuristics and biases* (pp. 3–20). Cambridge: Cambridge University Press.

TWENGE, J.M., & CAMPBELL, W.K. (2003). "Isn't it fun to get the respect that we're going to deserve?" Narcissism, social rejection and aggression. *PSPB, 29,* 261–272.

TYKOCINSKI, O.E., & PITTMAN, T.S. (1998). The consequences of doing nothing: Inaction inertia as avoidance of anticipated counterfactual regret. *Journal of Personality and Social Psychology 73,* 607–616.

TYLER, T.R., & CAINE, A. (1981). The influence of outcomes and procedures on satisfaction with formal leaders. *Journal of Personality and Social Psychology, 41,* 642–655.

TYLER, T.R., & DEGOEY, P. (1995). Collective restraint in social dilemmas: Procedural justice and social identification effects on support for authorities. *Journal of Personality and Social Psychology, 69,* 482–494.

TYLER, T.R., RASINSKI, K.A., & MCGRAW, K.M. (1985). The influence of perceived injustice on the endorsement of political leaders. *Journal of Applied Social Psychology, 15,* 700–725.

UBBINK, E.M., & SADAVA, S.W. (1974). Rotter's generalized expectancies as predictors of helping behavior. *Psychological Reports, 35,* 865–866.

UNDERWOOD, B., FROMING, W.J., & MOORE, B.S. (1977). Mood, attention, and altruism: A search for mediating variables. *Developmental Psychology, 13,* 541–542.

UNGER, D.G., & WANDERSMAN, L.P. (1985). Social support and adolescent mothers: Action research contributions to theory and applications. *Journal of Social Issues, 41,* 29–46.

VALENSTEIN, E.S. (1975). Brain stimulation and behavior control. *Nebraska Symposium on Motivation, 22,* 251–292.

VALINS, S. (1966). Cognitive effects of false heartrate feedback. *Journal of Personality and Social Psychology, 4,* 400–408.

VALLERAND, R.J., & REID, G. (1984). On the causal effects of perceived competence on intrinsic motivation: A test of cognitive evaluation theory. *Journal of Sports Psychology, 6,* 94–102.

VAN BAARSEN, B. (2002). Theories on coping with loss: The impact of social support and self-esteem on adjustment to emotional and social loneliness following a partner's death in later life. *Journal of Gerontology; Series B: Psychological Sciences and Social Sciences, 57B* (1), S33–S42.

VAN DEN BOS, G.R., & BULATAO, E.Q. (2000). Observations on entrepreneurial psychologists. *Psychologist-Manager Journal, 4,* 97–102.

VAN DEN BOS, K., BRUINS, J., WILKE, H.A.M., & DRONKERT, E. (1999). Sometimes unfair procedures have nice aspects: On the psychology of the fair process effect. *Journal of Personality and Social Psychology, 77,* 324–336.

VAN GELDER, L. (1985, October). The strange case of the electronic lover. *Ms., 94,* 99, 101–104, 117, 123–124.

VAN LANGE, P., OTTEN, W., DE BRUIN, E.M.N., & JOIREMAN, J.A. (1997). Development of prosocial, individualistic, and competitive orientations: Theory and preliminary evidence. *Journal of Personality and Social Psychology, 73,* 733–746.

VAN OVERWALLE, F. (1998). Causal explanation as constraint satisfaction: A critique and feedforward connectionist alternative. *Journal of Personality and Social Psychology, 74,* 312–328.

VANDER ZANDEN, J.W. (1977). *Social psychology.* New York: Random House.

VAN-LANGE, P.A.M., & VISSER, K. (1999). Locomotion in social dilemmas: How people adapt to cooperative, tit-for-tat, and non-cooperative partners. *Journal of Personality and Social Psychology, 77,* 762–773.

VANTRESS, F.E., & WILLIAMS, C.B. (1972). The effect of the presence of the provocator and the opportunity to counteraggress on systolic blood pressure. *Journal of General Psychology, 86,* 63–68.

VAUGHN, L.A. & WEARY, G. (2002). Roles of the availability of explanations, feelings of ease and dysphoria in judgments about the future. *Journal of Social & Clinical Psychology, 21,* 686–704.

VELICER, W.F., PROCHASKA, J.O., ROSSI, J.S., & SNOW, M.G. (1992). Assessing outcomes in smoking cessation studies. *Psychological Bulletin, 111,* 23–41.

VERPLANKEN, B. (1991). Persuasive communication of risk information: A test of cue versus message processing effects in a field experiment. *Personality and Social Psychology Bulletin, 17,* 188–193.

VESCIO, T.K., SECHRIST, G.B., & PAOLUCCI, M.P. (2003). Perspective taking and prejudice reduction: The mediational role of empathy arousal and situational attributions. *European Journal of Social Psychology, 33,* 455–472.

VICTOR, J.S. (1990). The spread of satanic-cult rumors. *Skeptical Inquirer, 14,* 287–291.

VIDMAR, N. (1974). Retributive and utilitarian motives of Canadian attitudes toward the death penalty. *Canadian Psychologist, 15,* 337–356.

VINACKE, W.E. (1969). Variables in experimental games: Toward a field theory. *Psychological Bulletin, 71,* 293–318.

VINACKE, W.E., & GULLICKSON, G.R. (1964). Age and sex differences in the formation of coalitions. *Child Development, 35,* 1217–1231.

VINAY, J.P., DAVIAULT, P., & ALEXANDER, H. (1962). *The Canadian dictionary.* Toronto: McClelland & Stewart.

VISSER, P.S., & KROSNICK, J.A. (1999). Development of attitude strength over the life cycle: Surge and decline. *Journal of Personality and Social Pyschology, 75,* 1389–1410.

VOISSEM, N.H., & SISTRUNK, F. (1971). Communication schedules and cooperative game behavior. *Journal of Personality and Social Psychology, 19,* 160–167.

VON NEUMANN, J., & MORGENSTERN, O. (1944). *Theory of games and economic behavior.* Princeton, NJ: Princeton University Press.

VORAUER, J., CAMERON, J.J., HOLMES, J.G., & PEARCE, D.G. (2003). Invisible overtures: Fear of rejection and the signal amplification bias. *Journal of Personality and Social Psychology, 84,* 793–812.

VROOM, V.H. (1964). *Work and motivation.* New York: Wiley.

VRUGT, A., & VAN EECHOUD, M. (2002). Smiling and self-presentation of men and women for job photographs. *European Journal of Social Psychology, 32,* 419–431.

WAGNER, H.L., MACDONALD, C.J., & MANSTEAD, A.S.R. (1986). Communication of individual emotions by spontaneous facial expression. *Journal of Personality and Social Psychology, 50,* 737–743.

WAGNER, U., HEWSTONE, M., & MACHLEIT, U. (1989). Contact and prejudice between Germans and Turks: A correlational study. *Human Relations, 42,* 561–574.

WAITZKIN, H. (1984). Doctor-patient communication: Clinical implications of social science research. *Journal of the American Medical Association, 252,* 2441–2446.

WALCHLI, S., & LANDMAN, J. (2003). Effects of counterfactual thought on postpurchase consumer affect. *Psychology & Marketing, 20,* 23–46.

WALKER, C.J., & BECKERLE, C.A. (1987). The effect of state anxiety on rumor transmission. *Journal of Social Behavior and Personality, 2,* 353–360.

WALKER, L.E. (1999). Psychology and domestic violence around the world. *American Psychologist, 54,* 21–29.

WALKER, M. (1992). *The psychology of gambling.* Oxford, UK: Butterworth-Heinemann Ltd.

WALKER, S.G. (1977). The interface between geliefs and behavior. *Journal of Conflict Resolution, 21,* 121–168.

WALLACH, M.A., & WALLACH, L. (1983). *Psychology's sanction for self-ishness.* San Francisco: WH Freeman.

WALLER, J. *Becoming evil. How ordinary people commit genocide and mass killing.* New York: Oxford University Press.

WALSTER, E. (1964). The temporal sequence of post-decision processes. In L. Festinger (Ed.), *Conflict, decision and dissonance* (pp. 112–128). Stanford, CA: Stanford University Press.

WALSTER, E. (1966). Assignment of responsibility for an accident. *Journal of Personality and Social Psychology, 3,* 73–79.

WALSTER, E., & WALSTER, G.W. (1978). *A new look at love.* Reading, MA: Addison-Wesley.

WALSTER, E., WALSTER, G.W., & BERSCHEID, E. (1978). *Equity theory and research.* Boston: Allyn & Bacon.

WALTERS, G.C., & GRUSEC, J.E. (1977). *Punishment.* San Francisco: W.H. Freeman.

WALTERS, V., LENTON, R., FRENCH, S., EYLES, J., MAYR, J., & NEWBOLD, B. (1996). Paid work, unpaid work and social support: a study of the health of male and female nurses. *Social Science Medical, 43,* 1627–1636.

WARE, J.E., & YOUNG, J. (1979). Issues in the conceptualization and measurements of the value placed on health. In S.J. Mushkin, & D.W. Dunlop (Eds.), *Health: What is it worth?* (pp. 141–156). New York: Pergamon.

WATKINS, D., ADAIR, J., AKANDE, A., GERONG, A., MCINERNEY, D., SUNAR, D., WATSON, S., WEN, Q., & WONDIMU, H. (1998). Individualism/collectivism, gender and the self-concept: A nine-culture investigation. *Psychologia: An International Journal of Psychology in the Orient, 41,* 259–271.

WATKINS, D., AKANDE, A., FLEMING, J., ISMAIL, M., LEFNER, K., REGMI, M., WATONS, S., YU, J., ADAIR, J., CHENG, C., GERONG, A., MCINERNEY, D., MPOFU, E., SINGH-SENGUPTA, S., & WONDIMU, H. (1998). Cultural dimensions, gender and the nature of self-concept: A fourteen country study. *International Journal of Psychology, 33,* 17–31.

WATSON, B., & GALLOIS, C. (2002). Patients' interactions with health providers: A linguistic category model approach. *Journal of Language and Social Psychology, 21,* 32–52.

WATSON, D. (1982). The actor and the observer: How are the perceptions of causality divergent? *Psychological Bulletin, 92,* 682–700.

WATSON, D., & PENNEBAKER, J.W. (1989). Health complaints, stress and distress: Exploring the central role of negative affectivity. *Psychological Review, 96,* 234–254.

WEBER, M. (1947). *The theory of social and economic organization.* Glencoe, IL: Free Press.

WEBSTER, C., DICKENS, B., & ADDARIO, S. (1985). *Constructing dangerousness: Scientific, legal and policy implications.* Toronto: Centre of Criminology, University of Toronto.

WEENIG, M.W.H., & MIDDEN, C.J.H. (1991). Communication network influences on information diffusion and persuasion. *Journal of Personality and Social Psychology, 61,* 734–742.

WEERMAN, F.M. (2003). Co-offending as social exchange. Explaining characteristics of co-offending. *British Journal of Criminology, 43,* 398–416.

WEGNER, D.M., & WHEATLEY, T. (1999). Apparent mental causation. Sources of the experience of will. *American Psychologist 54,* 480–492.

WEIDNER, G., ISTVAN, J., & MCKNIGHT, J.D. (1989). Clusters of behavioral coronary risk factors in employed men and women. *Journal of Applied Social Psychology, 19,* 468–480.

WEIGEL, R.H., & NEWMAN, L.S. (1976). Increasing attitude–behavior correspondence by broadening the scope of the behavioral measure. *Journal of Personality and Social Psychology, 33,* 793–802.

WEIGEL, R.H., WISER, P.L., & COOK, S.W. (1975). The impact of cooperative learning experience on cross-ethnic relations and attitudes. *Journal of Social Issues, 31,* 219–244.

WEIMANN, G., & WINN, C. (1986). *Hate on trial: The Zundel affair, the media, and public opinion in Canada.* Oakville: Mosaic Press.

WEINER, B. (1974). *Achievement motivation and attribution theory.* Morristown, NJ: General Learning Press.

WEINER, B. (1980). A cognitive (attribution)–emotion–action model of motivated behavior: An analysis of judgements of help giving. *Journal of Personality and Social Psychology, 39,* 186–200.

WEINER, B. (1985). "Spontaneous" causal thinking. *Psychological Bulletin, 97,* 74–84.

WEINER, B., & KUKLA, A. (1970). An attributional analysis of achievement motivation. *Journal of Personality and Social Psychology, 15,* 144–151.

WEINER, B., FIGUEROA-MUÑOZ, A., & KAKIHARA, C. (1991). The goals of excuses and communication strategies related to causal perceptions. *Personality and Social Psychology Bulletin, 17,* 4–13.

WEINSTEIN, E.A., DEVAUGHAN, W.L., & WILEY, M.G. (1969). Obligation and the flow of deference. *Sociometry, 32,* 1–12.

WEINSTEIN, M.D., SMITH, M.E., & WIESENTHAL. D.L. (1995). Masculinity and hockey violence. *Sex Roles, 33,* 831–847.

WEINSTEIN, N.D. (1984). Why it won't happen to me: Perceptions of risk factors and susceptibility. *Health Psychology, 3,* 431–457.

WEISS, R. (1973). *Loneliness: The experiences of emotional and social isolation.* Cambridge, MA: MIT Press.

WEISS, R.S. (1975). *Marital separation.* New York: Basic Books.

WEISS, W. (1971). Mass communication. *Annual Review of Psychology, 22,* 309–336.

WEISZ, A.E., & TAYLOR, R.L. (1969). American Presidential assassinations. *Diseases of the Nervous System, 30,* 659–668.

WEISZ, J.R., ROTHBAUM, F.M., & BLACKBURN, T.C. (1984). Swapping recipes for control. *American Psychologist, 39,* 974–975.

WEIZMANN, F., WIENER, N.I., WIESENTHAL, D.L., & ZIEGLER, M. (1990). Differential K theory and racial hierarchies. *Canadian Psychology, 31,* 1–13.

WEIZMANN, F., WIENER, N.I., WIESENTHAL, D.L., & ZIEGLER, M.E. (1996). Scientific racism in contemporary psychology. In M.G. Luther, E. Cole, & P.J. Gamlin (Eds.), *Dynamic assessment for instruction: From theory to application.* (pp. 7–14). North York, ON: Captus Press, Inc.

WELDON, E., & GARGANO, G.M. (1988). Cognitive loafing: The effects of accountability and shared responsibility on cognitive effort. *Personality and Social Psychology Bulletin, 14,* 159–171.

WELLMAN, B. (1992). Men in networks; Private communities, domestic friendships. In P.M. Nardi (Ed.), *Men's friendships* (pp. 74–114). Newbury Park: Sage.

WELLMAN, R.J., & SUGARMAN, D.B. (1996). Social perceptions of termination of medical treatment: Suicide or rational decision. *Journal of Social Psychology, 26,* 1378–1399.

WELLS, G.L. (1978). Applied eyewitness-testimony research: System variables and estimator variables. *Journal of Personality and Social Psychology, 36,* 1546–1557.

WELLS, G.L. (1984). The psychology of lineup identifications. *Journal of Applied Psychology, 14,* 89–103.

WELLS, G.L. (1992). Naked statistical evidence of liability: Is subjective probability enough? *Journal of Personality and Social Psychology, 62,* 739–752.

WELLS, G.L., & LINDSAY, R.C.L. (1980). On estimating the diagnosticity of eyewitness nonidentification. *Psychological Bulletin, 88,* 776–784.

WELLS, G.L., & LUUS, C.A.E. (1990). Police lineups as experiments: Social methodology as a framework for properly conducted lineups. *Personality and Social Psychology Bulletin, 16,* 106–117.

WELLS, G.L., & MURRAY, B.M. (1983). What can psychology say about the Neil vs. Biggers criteria for judging eyewitness accuracy? *Journal of Applied Psychology, 68,* 347–362.

WELLS, G.L., & TURTLE, J.W. (1986). Eye-witness identification: The importance of lineup models. *Psychological Bulletin, 29,* 320–329.

WERNER, E.E. (1989). High-risk children in young adulthood: A longitudinal study from birth to 32 years. *American Journal of Orthopsychiatry, 59,* 69–78.

WEST, C. (1984). *Routine complications.* Bloomington, IN: University of Indiana Press.

WHEELER, A., & PETTY, R. (2001). The effects of stereotype activation on behavior: A review of possible mechanisms, *127,* 792–826.

WHITE, G.L. (1981a). A model of romantic jealousy. *Motivation and Emotion, 5,* 295–310.

WHITE, G.L. (1981b). Some correlates of romantic jealousy. *Journal of Personality, 49,* 129–147.

WHITE, J.W. (1983). Sex and gender issues in aggression research. In R.G. Geen, & E.I. Donnerstein (Eds.), *Aggression: Theoretical and empirical reviews* (Vol. 2). (pp. 1–26). New York: Academic Press.

WHITE, R. (2002). Indigenous young Australians, criminal justice and offensive language. *Journal of Youth Studies, 5,* 21–34.

WHITE, S. (1989). Backchannels across cultures: A study of Americans and Japanese. *Language and Society, 18,* 59–76.

WHITING, B.B., & WHITING, J.W.M. (1975). *Children of six cultures: A psychocultural analysis.* Cambridge, MA: Harvard University Press.

WHITLET, B.E., & HERN, A.L. (1991). Perception of vulnerability to pregnancy and the use of effective contraception. *Personality and Social Psychology Bulletin, 17,* 104–110.

WHYTE, G. (1989). Group-think reconsidered. *Academy of Management Review, 14,* 40–56.

WHYTE, G. (1998). Recasting Janis's groupthink model: The key role of collective efficacy in decision fiascos. *Organizational Behavior and Human Decision Processes, 73,* 185–209.

WICKER, A.W. (1969). Attitudes versus actions: The relationship of verbal and overt behavioral responses to attitude objects. *Journal of Social Issues, 25,* 41–78.

WICKLUND, R.A., & BREHM, J.W. (1976). *Perspectives on cognitive dissonance.* New York: Wiley.

WIDOM, C.S. (1989). Does violence beget violence? A critical examination of the literature. *Psychological Bulletin, 106,* 3–28.

WIEGMAN, O. (1985). Two politicians in a realistic experiment: Attraction, discrepancy, intensity of delivery, and attitude change. *Journal of Applied Social Psychology, 15,* 673–686.

WIEMANN, J.M., & GILES, H. (1988). Interpersonal communication. In M. Hewstone, W. Stroebe, J-P. Codol, & G.M. Stephenson (Eds.), *Introduction to social psychology* (pp. 199–221). Oxford: Basil Blackwell.

WIENER, M., CARPENTER, J.T., & CARPENTER, B. (1957). Some determinants of conformity behavior. *Journal of Social Psychology, 45,* 289–297.

WIESENTHAL, D.L. (1974). Reweaving deception's tangled web. *Canadian Psychologist, 15,* 326–336.

WIESENTHAL, D.L. (1989). Recent developments in social psychology in response to ethical concerns. In D. MacNiven (Ed.), *Moral expertise: Studies in practical and professional ethics* (pp. 11–25). London: Routledge.

WILD, B., ERB, M., BARTELS, M. (2001). Are emotions contagious? Evoked emotions while viewing emotionally expressive faces: quality, quantity, time course and gender differences. *Psychiatry Research, 102,* 109–124.

WILDER, D.A. (1977). Perception of group size of opposition and social influence. *Journal of Experimental Social Psychology, 13,* 253–268.

WILDER, D.A. (1986). Social categorization: Implications for creation and reduction of intergroup bias. In L. Berkowitz (Ed.), *Advances in experimental social psychology, 19,* 291–355. New York: Academic Press.

WILDER, D.H., & SHAPIRO, P.N. (1989). Role of competition-induced anxiety in limiting the beneficial impact of positive behaviour by an out group member. *Journal of Personality and Social Psychology, 56,* 60–69.

WILDSCHUT, T., INSKO, C.A., & GAERTNER, L. (2002). Intragroup social influence and intergroup competition. *Journal of Personality and Social Psychology, 82,* 975–992.

WILLIAMS, E. (1975). Medium or message: Communications medium as a determinant of interpersonal evaluations. *Sociometry, 38,* 119–130.

WILLIAMS, P., & AAKER, J.L. (2002). Can mixed emotions peacefully coexist? *Journal of Consumer Research, 28,* 636–649.

WILLIAMS, S.S., KIMBLE, D.L., COVELL, N.H., WEISS, L.H., NEWTON, K.J., FISHER, J.D., & FISHER, W.A. (1992). College students' use of implicit personality theory instead of safer sex. *Journal of Applied Social Psychology, 22,* 921–933.

WILLIAMSON, S., HARE, R.D., & WONG, S. (1987). Violence: Criminal psychopaths and their victims. *Canadian Journal of Behavioural Science, 19,* 454–462.

WILLOUGHBY, T., CHALMERS, H., & BUSSERI, M. (2003). Where is the syndrome? Where is the risk? Examining co-occurrence among problem behaviors in adolescence. Submitted for publication.

WILLS, T.A. (1981). Downward comparison principles in social psychology. *Psychological Bulletin, 90,* 245–271.

WILLS, T.A. (1991). Social support and interpersonal relationships. In M.S. Clark (Ed.), *Prosocial behavior* (pp. 265–289). Newbury Park, CA: Sage.

WILSNACK, S. (1982). *Prevention of alcohol problems in women.* In N.I.A.A.A. alcohol and health monograph #4. Special population issues (77–110). D.H.H.S. Publication No. (ADM 82–1193. Washington: U.S. Government Printing Office.

WILSON, A. (1970). *War gaming.* Harmondsworth, UK: Penguin.

WILSON, D.W., & DONNERSTEIN, E. (1976). Legal and ethical aspects of nonreactive social research: An excursion into the public mind. *American Psychologist, 36,* 765–773.

WILSON, G.B.L. (1974). *A dictionary of ballet* (3rd ed.). London: Adam & Charles Black.

WILSON, G.T. (1984). Weight control treatments. In J.D. Mattarazzo, S.M. Weiss, J.A. Herd, N.E. Miller, & S.M. Weiss (Eds.), *Behavioral health* (pp. 657–670). New York: Wiley.

WILSON, T.D., & STONE, J.I. (1985). Limitations of self-knowledge: More on telling more than we can know. In P. Shaver (Ed.), *Review of personality and social psychology* (Vol. 6). (pp. 167–183). Beverly Hills, CA: Sage.

WILSON, W., & MILLER, H. (1968). Repetition, order of presentation, and timing of arguments and measures as determinants of opinion change. *Journal of Personality and Social Psychology, 9,* 184–188.

WINCH, R.F. (1954). The theory of complementary needs in mate selection: An analytic and descriptive study. *Annual Social Review, 19,* 241–249.

WINCH, R.F. (1958). *Mate selection: A study of complementary needs.* New York: Harper & Row.

WING-TUNG, & KOMORITA, S.S. (2002). Effects of initial choices in the prisoner's dilemma. *Journal of Behavioral Decision-Making, 15,* 343–359.

WINSLOW, R.W., RUMBAUT, R.G., & HWANG, J. (1989). AIDS, FRAIDS and quarantine: Student responses to pro-quarantine initiative in California. *Journal of Applied Social Psychology, 19,* 1453–1478.

WISHNER, J. (1960). Reanalysis of "impressions of personality." *Psychological Review, 67,* 96–112.

WISPÉ, L. (1986). The distinction between sympathy and empathy: To call forth a concept, a word is needed. *Journal of Personality and Social Psychology, 50,* 314–321.

WIT, A.P., & KERR, N.L. (2002). 'Me versus just us versus us all' categorization and cooperation in nested social dilemmas. *Journal of Personality and Social Psychology, 83,* 616–637.

WITT, L. (1989). Authoritarianism, knowledge of AIDS and affect toward persons with AIDS: Implications for health education. *Journal of Applied Social Psychology, 19,* 599–607.

WOLF, N. (1991). *The beauty myth.* Toronto: Vintage Books.

WOLF, S., & MONTGOMERY, D.A. (1977). Effects of inadmissible evidence and level of judicial admonishment to disregard on the judgements of mock jurors. *Journal of Applied Social Psychology, 7,* 205–219.

WOLLIN, D.D., & MONTAGNE, M. (1981). The college classroom environment. *Environment and Behavior, 13,* 707–716.

WOOD, J.V. (1989). Theory and research concerning social comparisons of personal attributes. *Psychological Bulletin, 106,* 231–248.

WOOD, W. (2000). Attitude change: Persuasion and social influence. *Annual Review of Psychology, 51,* 539–570.

WOOD, W., & VANDERZEE, K. (1997). Social comparisons among cancer patients: Under what conditions are comparisons upward and downward? In B.P. Buunk & F.X. Gibbons (Eds.), *Health, coping and well-being: Perspectives from social comparison theory.* Manwah, NJ: Erlbaum.

WORCHEL, S. (1984). The darker side of helping. In E. Staub, D. Bar-Tal, J. Karylowski, & J. Reykowski (Eds.), *Development and maintenance of prosocial behavior* (pp. 375–395). New York: Plenum Press.

WORCHEL, S., & TEDDLIE, C. (1976). The experience of crowding: A two-factor theory. *Journal of Personality and Social Psychology, 34,* 36–40.

WORCHEL, S., ANDREOLI, V., & EASON, J. (1975). Is the medium the message? A study of the effects of media, communicator and message characteristics on attitude change. *Journal of Applied Social Psychology, 5,* 157–172.

WORLD HEALTH ORGANIZATION (2002). World Report on Health and Violence. http://usinfo.state.gov/topical/global/02100401.htm.

WORMITH, J.S., & RUHL, M. (1986). *A survey of dangerous sexual offenders in Canada 1948–1977.* (Branch User Report No. 1986–6). Ottawa: Ministry of the Solicitor General of Canada.

WORTLEY, S. (1999, September 26). *The Toronto Star,* A17.

WORTMAN, C.B. (1975). Some determinants of perceived control. *Journal of Personality and Social Psychology, 31,* 282–294.

WRIGHT, E.F., RULE, B.G., FERGUSON, T.J., MCGUIRE, G.R., & WELLS, G.L. (1992). Misattribution of dissonance and behaviour-consistent attitude change. *Canadian Journal of Behavioural Science, 24,* 456–464.

WRIGHT, M.J. (1969). Canadian psychology comes of age. *Canadian Psychologist, 10,* 229–253.

WRIGHT, M.J. (1982). Psychology at Manitoba. In M.J. Wright, & C.R. Myers (Eds.), *History of academic psychology in Canada* (pp. 170–177). Toronto: Hogrefe.

WRIGHT, M.J. (1990). Personal communication.

WRIGHT, M.W. (1982). Psychology at Manitoba. In M.J. Wright, & C.R. Myers (Eds.), *History of academic psychology in Canada.* (pp. 170–177). Toronto: Hogrefe.

WRIGHT, S. (1978). *Crowds and riots.* Beverly Hills, CA: Sage.

WRIGHT, S.C., ARON, A., MCLAUGHLIN-VOLPE, T., & ROPP, S.A. (1997). He extended contact effect: Knowledge of cross-group friendships and prejudice. *Journal of Personality and Social Psychology, 73,* 73–90.

WULFERT, E., & WAN, C.K. (1993). Condom use: A self-efficacy model. *Health Psychology, 12,* 346–354.

YARMEY, A.D. (1979). *The psychology of eyewitness testimony.* New York: Free Press.

YARMEY, A.D. (1986a). Verbal, visual and voice identification of a rape suspect under different levels of illumination. *Journal of Applied Social Psychology, 71,* 363–370.

YARMEY, A.D. (1986b). Perceived expertness and credibility of police officers as eyewitnesses. *Canadian Police College Journal, 10,* 31–52.

YARMEY, A.D., & JONES, H.P. (1983b). Accuracy of memory of male and female eyewitnesses to a criminal assault and rape. *Bulletin of the Psychonomic Society, 21,* 89–92.

YASSI, A., WEEKS, J.L., SAMSON, K., & RABER, M.B. (1989). Epidemic of "shocks" in telephone operators: Lessons for the medical community. *Canadian Medical Association Journal, 140,* 816–820.

YOUNG, M.Y., & GARDNER, R.C. (1990). Modes of acculturation and second language proficiency. *Canadian Journal of Behavioural Science, 22,* 59–71.

YOUNGER, J.C., WALKER, L., & ARROWOOD, A.J. (1977). Post decision dissonance at the fair. *Personality and Social Psychology Bulletin, 3,* 284–287.

YOUNGS, G.A., Jr. (1986). Patterns of threat and punishment reciprocity in a conflict setting. *Journal of Personality and Social Psychology, 51,* 541–546.

YUILLE, J. (1980). A critical examination of the psychological and practical implications of eyewitness research. *Law and Behavior, 4,* 335–345.

YUILLE, J.C., & CUTSHALL, J.L. (1986). A case study of eyewitness memory of a crime. *Journal of Applied Psychology, 71,* 291–301.

YURCHESYN, K.A., KEITH, A., &. RENNER, K.E. (1992). Contrasting perspectives on the nature of sexual assault provided by a service for sexual assault victims and by the law courts. *Canadian Journal of Behavioural Science, 24,* 71–85.

ZAJONC, R.B. (1965). Social facilitation. *Science, 149,* 269–274.

ZAJONC, R.B. (1968). Attitudinal effects of mere exposure. *Journal of Personality and Social Psychology, Monograph Supplement, 9,* 1–27.

ZAJONC, R.B. (1969). *Animal social psychology.* New York: Wiley.

ZAJONC, R.B. (1970). Brainwashing: Familiarity breeds comfort. *Psychology Today (February),* 32–35, 60–62.

ZAJONC, R.B. (1980). Feeling and thinking: Preferences need no inferences. *American Psychologist, 35,* 151–175.

ZAJONC, R.B., & MARKUS, H. (1982). Affective and cognitive factors in preferences. *Journal of Consumer Research, 9,* 123–131.

ZARAGOZA, M.S., & MITCHELL, J.J. (1996). Repeated exposure to suggestion and the creation of false memories. *Psychological Science, 7,* 294–300.

ZBOROWSKI, M. (1969). *People in pain.* San Francisco: Jossey-Bass.

ZIEGLER, R., DIEHL, M., & RUTHER, A. (2002). Multiple source characteristics and persuasion: Source inconsistency as a determinant of message scrutiny. *Personality and Social Psychology Bulletin, 28,* 496–508.

ZIEGLER, S. (1981). The effectiveness of cooperative learning teams for increasing cross-ethnic friendship: additional evidence. *Human Organization, 40,* 264–267.

ZILLMANN, D. (1971). Excitation transfer in communication-mediated aggressive behavior. *Journal of Experimental Social Psychology, 7,* 419–434.

ZILLMANN, D. (1984). Transfer of excitation in emotional behavior. In J.T. Cacioppo, & R.E. Petty (Eds.), *Social psychophysiology: A sourcebook* (pp. 215–240). New York: Guilford Press.

ZILLMANN, D. (1989). Effects of prolonged consumption of pornography. In D. Zillmann, & J. Bryant (Eds.), *Pornography: Research advances and policy considerations* (pp. 127–157). Hillsdale, NJ: Erlbaum.

ZILLMANN, D., & BRYANT, J. (1984). Effects of massive exposure to pornography. In N.M. Malamuth, & E.M. Donnerstein (Eds.), *Pornography and sexual aggression* (pp. 115–138). New York: Academic Press.

ZILLMANN, D., & BRYANT, J. (1986). Shifting preferences in pornography consumption. *Communication Research, 13,* 560–578.

ZILLMER, E.A., HARROWER, M., RITZLER, B.A., & ARCHER, R.P. (1995). *The quest for the Nazi personality: A psychological investigation of Nazi was criminals.* Hillsdale: Erlbaum.

ZIMBARDO, P.G. (1970). The human choice: Individuation, reason, and order versus deindividuation, impulse, and chaos. In W.J. Arnold, & D. Levine (Eds.), *Nebraska symposium on motivation* (Vol. 17). (pp. 237–307). Lincoln: University of Nebraska Press.

ZIMBARDO, P.G. (1977). *Shyness: What it is and what to do about it.* Reading, MA: Addison-Wesley.

ZIMBARDO, P.G., EBBESEN, E.B., & MASLACH, C. (1977). *Influencing attitudes and changing behavior* (2nd ed.). Reading, MA: Addison-Wesley.

ZIMBARDO, P.G., HANEY, C., BANKS, W.C., & JAFFE, D. (1982). The psychology of imprisonment. In J.C. Brigham, & L. Wrightsman (Eds.), *Contemporary issues in social psychology* (4th ed.). (pp. 230–35). Monterey, CA: Brooks/Cole.

ZOPITO, M., FAIRBAIRN, L., & ZUBER, R. (2001). Peer harassment in individuals with developmental disabilities: Towards the development of a multidimensional bullying identification model. *Developmental Disabilities Bulletin, 29,* 170–195.

ZUCKERMAN, M., & BRODY, N. (1988). Oysters, rabbits and people: A critique of "race differences in behaviour" by J.P. Rushton. *Personality and Individual Differences, 9,* 1025–1033.

ZUCKERMAN, M., DEPAULO, B.M., & ROSENTHAL, R. (1981). Verbal and non-verbal communication of deception. In L. Berkowitz (Ed.), *Advances in Experimental Social Psychology* (pp. 1–59). New York: Academic Press.

ZUCKERMAN, M., KOESTNER, R., & ALTON, A.O. (1984). Learning to detect deception. *Journal of Personality and Social Psychology, 46,* 519–528.

ZUROFF, D.C. (1989). Judgements of the frequency of social stimuli: How schematic is personal memory? *Journal of Personality and Social Psychology, 56,* 890–898.

ZUWERINK, J.R., & DEVINE, P.G. (1996). Attitude importance and resistance to persuasion: It's not just the thought that counts. *Journal of Personality and Social Psychology, 70,* 931–944.

Name Index

Subject Index

Credits

Tables and Figures

Table 4-1, p. 96, Used by permission of Lawrence Erlbaum Associates Inc.; Figure 4-4, p. 100, From *Fire and Ice* by Michael Adams. Copyright © Michael Adams, 2003. Reprinted by permission of Penguin Group (Canada); Table 4-2, p. 101, Pew Global Attitudes Project; Figure 7-8, p. 202, Table compiled by authors from various data sources; Figure 11-2, p. 306, From Robert B. Cialdini, Douglas T. Kenrick, Steven L. Neuberg, *Social Psychology: Unravelling The Mystery*, 2e, Published by Allyn and Bacon, Boston, MA. Copyright © 2002 by Pearson Education. Adapted by permission of the publisher; Figure 11-3, p. 315, Evans, G.W., Lepore, S.J. & Allen, *K.M. Journal of Personality and Social Psychology Bulletin*, 29/2, p. 261–272, copyright © 2003. Reprinted by permission of Sage Publications; Figure 11-4, p. 315, Evans, G.W., Lepore, S.J. & Allen, *K.M. Journal of Personality and Social Psychology Bulletin*, 29/2. p. 261–272, copyright © 2003. Reprinted by permission of Sage Publications; Figure 14-1A, p. 398, Figure 1, p. 208, figure 2, p. 209, from *JPSP*, 2000, 79, 204–210. Copyright © 2000 by the American Psychological Association. Reprinted with permission; Figure 14-1B, p. 399, Figure 1, p. 208, figure 2, p. 209, from *JPSP*, 2000, 79, 204–210. Copyright © 2000 by the American Psychological Association. Reprinted with permission.

Cartoons

p. 132 (top), Reproduced by permission of EdgarArgo and *The Medical Post*; p. 285, Reproduced by permission of *Punch*; p. 317, As published in *The Calgary Herald*, Oct. 11, 1984. Reprinted with permission of the artist.

Photos

p. 3, PubliPhoto/Bossu-Sygma; p. 4, Alene McNeill; p. 8, Marko Shark; p. 16, www.hc-sc.gc/english/media/photos/tobacco-labelling/index.htm Health Canada 2004; p. 20, Jeff Greenberg © PhotoEdit; p. 31, Archive Photos/Reuters RR93165044; p. 33, Photodisc/Getty Images; p. 39, PH Archives; p. 42, CP/Fred Chartrand; p. 52, Getty Images/Mike Powell; p. 61, David Young Wolf © PhotoEdit; p. 71, CP/Tom Hanson; p. 73, PH Archives; p. 81, © Dorling Kindersley; p. 84, Japanese Consulate; p. 92, CP/Chuck Stoody; p. 100, © Tom Wagner/CORBIS SABA/MAGMA; p. 106, CP/*Toronto Sun*/Paul Henry; p. 111, Marko Sharp; p. 117, © Robert Harbison; p. 122, CP/Kevin Frayer; p. 132 (bottom), Sexuality Education Resource Centre., MB–Committee on Unplanned Pregnancy, "COUP"; p. 146, The Farmers' Museum, Inc., Cooperstown New York, USA; p. 148, Comstock; p. 163, Getty Images/Glislain and Marie David de Lossey; p. 166, From the film *OBEDIENCE* ©1965 by Stanley Milgram and distributed by Penn State Media Sales; p. 177, NASA & Paul Lieberhardt; p. 204, © Carl & Ann Purcell/CORBIS/MAGMA; p. 187, Roy Taylor; p. 194, French Connection Canada Ltd.; p. 209, Stone/Gary W. Nolton; p. 218, Kharen HillCourtesy of Nettwerk Management; p. 225, © Marc Roussel/Gamma/PONOPRESSE; p. 230, CP/Kevin Frayer; p. 242, Bethune Memorial House; p. 251, Marko Sharp; p. 266, Veterans Affairs Canada Web site: www.vac-acc.gc.ca 2001. Reproduced with the permission of the Minister of Public Works and Government Services, 2004; p. 267, CP/Richard Lam; p. 271, *Toronto Star*/Peter Power; p. 276, CP/Tom Hanson; p. 297, CP/Eyob Alemayeux; p. 301, CP/Richard Lam; p. 302, CP/Ali Fraidoon; p. 309, Stan Sadava; p. 335, NAC, PA-111213; p. 340, Famous People Players; p. 336, Tony Freeman © PhotoEdit; p. 348, CP/Fred Chartrand; p. 358, *The Globe and Mail*/Tibor Kolley; p. 368, Nikkio Internment Centre/photographer Trevor Harrop; p. 376, Edmonton Heritage Festival; p. 388, CITY-TV; p. 394, NAC, C-079586; p. 407, CP/Kevin Frayer; p. 409, CP/Kevin Frayer; p. 414, Getty Images/Tim Flach; p. 430, CP/J.P. Moczulski; p. 433, Composite drawing: *Toronto Sun*/Niagara Regional Police; Photo of Bernardo: *Toronto Sun*/Reekie; p. 438, *Toronto Sun*/Aoyagi; p. 440, Photofest; p. 459, Notman Photographic Archives, McCord Museum, Montreal; p. 462, © Dorling Kindersley; p. 463, Getty Images/Photodisc; p. 480, © Royalty-Free/CORBIS/MAGMA.